ALIENS™
VS.
PREDATOR™
OMNIBUS

ALIENS™ VS. PREDATOR™

OMNIBUS

VOLUME 1

DARK HORSE BOOKS®

CONTENTS

cover illustration **GLENN FABRY**

publisher **MIKE RICHARDSON**
designer **JOSHUA ELLIOTT**
technical assistance **DAN JACKSON**
art director **LIA RIBACCHI**
series editor **RANDY STRADLEY**
collection editor **CHRIS WARNER**

Special thanks to **DEBBIE OLSHAN** at Twentieth Century Fox Licensing.

ALIENS™ VS. PREDATOR™ OMNIBUS Volume 1

This volume collects material previously published as the Dark Horse graphic novels *Aliens vs. Predator, Aliens vs. Predator: War,* and *Aliens vs. Predator: Eternal*, stories from issues one hundred forty-six and one hundred forty-seven of the Dark Horse comic-book series *Dark Horse Presents*, and a story from the Dark Horse comic book *Aliens vs. Predator Annual.*

Dark Horse Books
a division of Dark Horse Comics, Inc.
10956 SE Main Street
Milwaukie, OR 97222

darkhorse.com | foxmovies.com

To find a comics shop in your area, call the Comic Shop Locator Service toll-free at 1-888-266-4226

First edition: May 2007
ISBN 978-1-59307-735-8

10 9 8 7 6 5 4 3
Printed in Hong Kong

ALIENS VS. PREDATOR

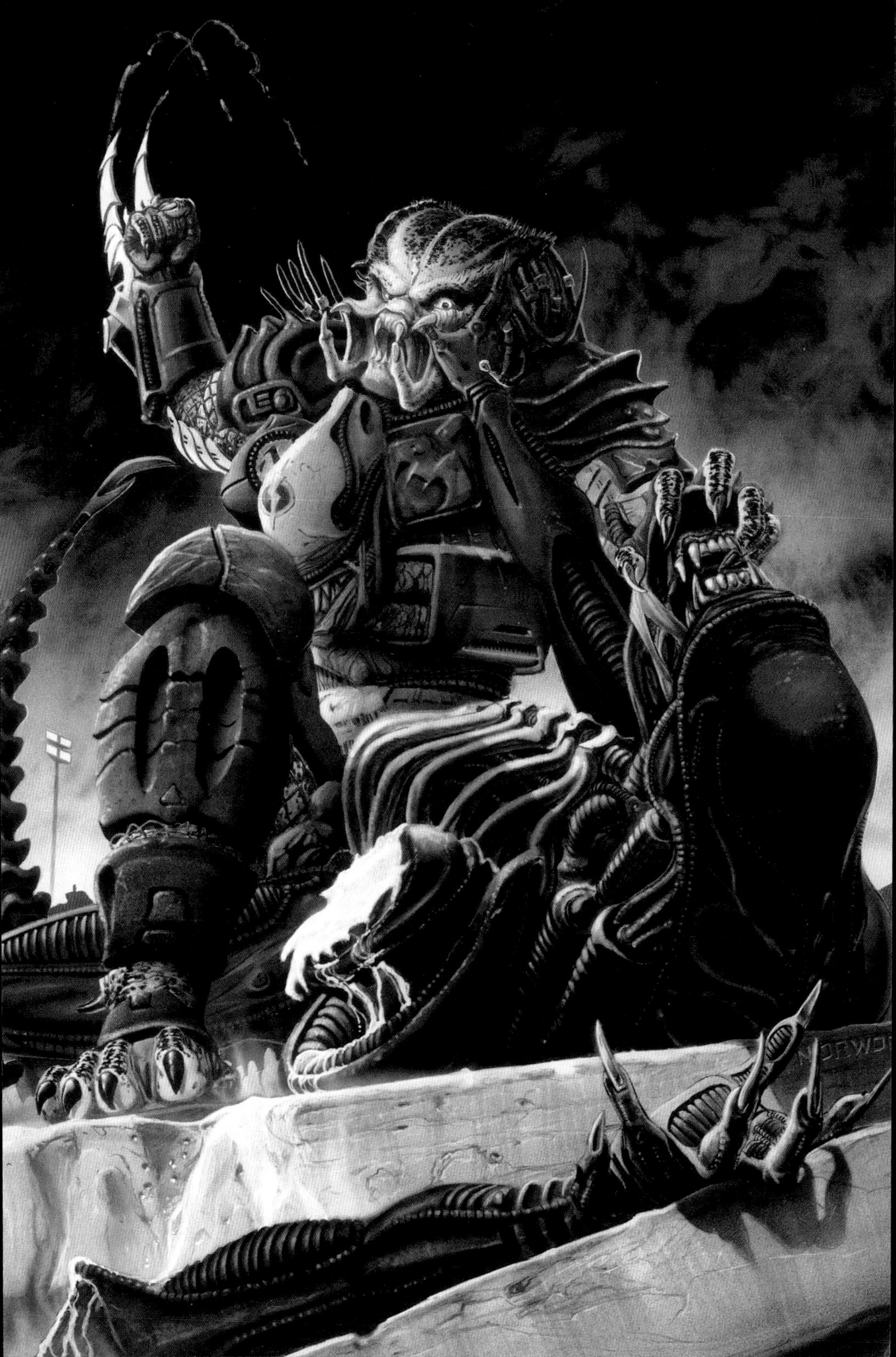

script
RANDY STRADLEY

pencils
PHILL NORWOOD (chapters 1–4, 6)
CHRIS WARNER (chapter 5)

inks
KARL STORY (chapters 1–3)
ROBERT CAMPANELLA (chapters 4, 5)
PHILL NORWOOD (chapter 6)

colors
INCOLOR

lettering
PAT BROSSEAU

title illustration
PHILL NORWOOD

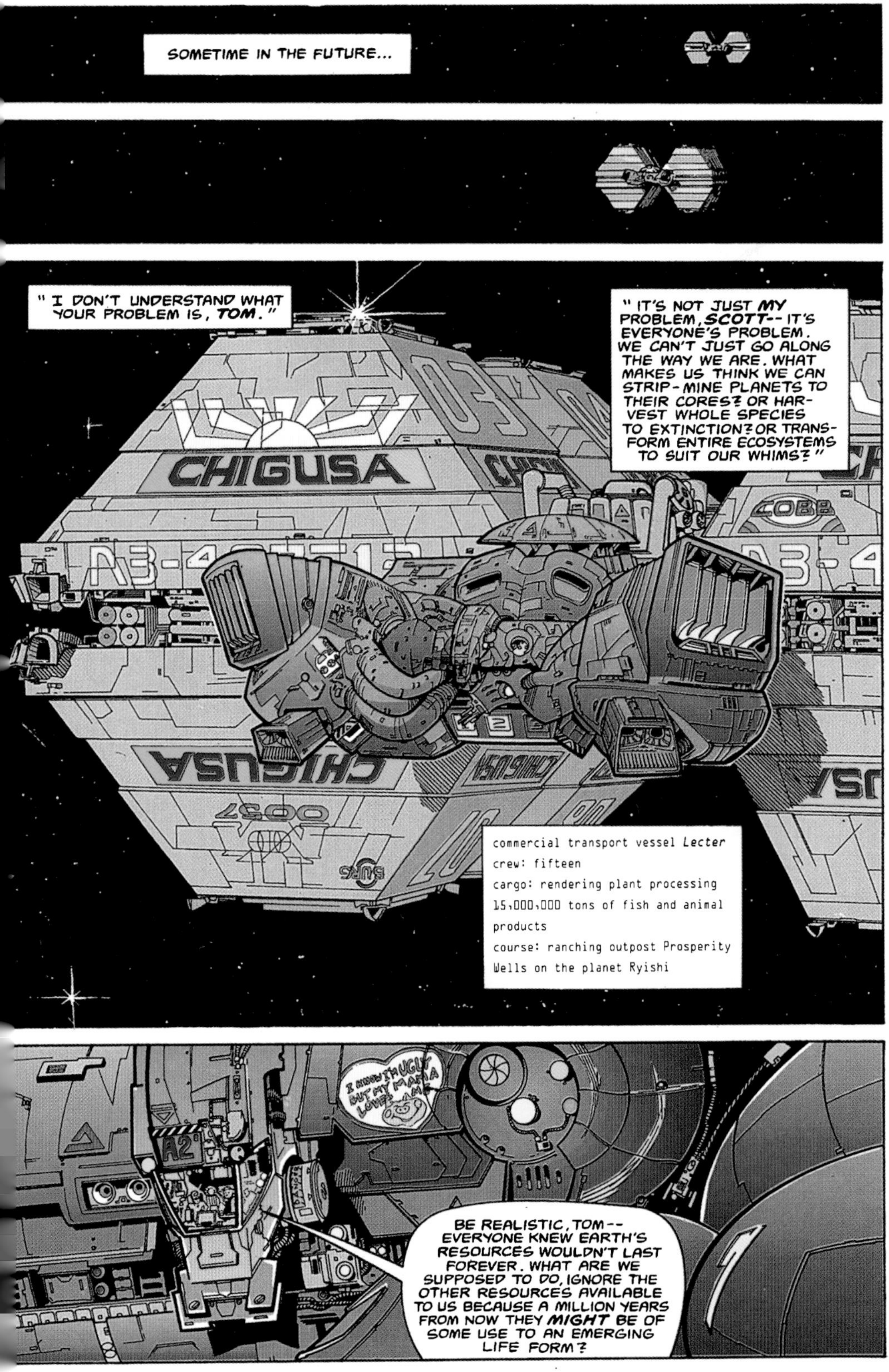
SOMETIME IN THE FUTURE...
"I DON'T UNDERSTAND WHAT YOUR PROBLEM IS, TOM."
"IT'S NOT JUST MY PROBLEM, SCOTT-- IT'S EVERYONE'S PROBLEM. WE CAN'T JUST GO ALONG THE WAY WE ARE. WHAT MAKES US THINK WE CAN STRIP-MINE PLANETS TO THEIR CORES? OR HARVEST WHOLE SPECIES TO EXTINCTION? OR TRANSFORM ENTIRE ECOSYSTEMS TO SUIT OUR WHIMS?"
CHIGUSA
COBB
commercial transport vessel Lecter
crew: fifteen
cargo: rendering plant processing
15,000,000 tons of fish and animal products
course: ranching outpost Prosperity Wells on the planet Ryishi
I KNOW I'M UGLY BUT MY MAMA LOVES ME
BE REALISTIC, TOM-- EVERYONE KNEW EARTH'S RESOURCES WOULDN'T LAST FOREVER. WHAT ARE WE SUPPOSED TO DO, IGNORE THE OTHER RESOURCES AVAILABLE TO US BECAUSE A MILLION YEARS FROM NOW THEY MIGHT BE OF SOME USE TO AN EMERGING LIFE FORM?

WHOA--!

THAT WAS CLOSE!

"WE'RE REGISTERING A *POWER SURGE!* WHAT THE HELL *WAS* THAT THING?"

"THE SCANNERS SAY IT'S MOSTLY METALLIC-- BUT WHATEVER IT IS, IT'S MOVING WAY *TOO FAST* TO BE ANYTHING MANMADE."

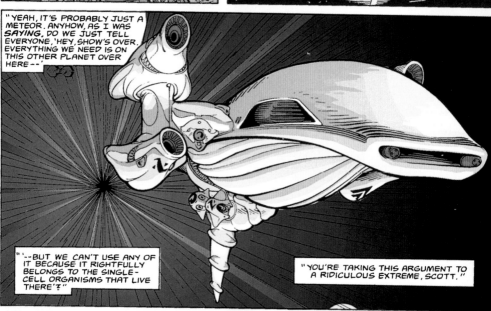

"YEAH, IT'S PROBABLY JUST A METEOR. ANYHOW, AS I WAS *SAYING,* DO WE JUST TELL EVERYONE, 'HEY, SHOW'S OVER. EVERYTHING WE NEED IS ON THIS OTHER PLANET OVER HERE--'

"--BUT WE CAN'T USE ANY OF IT BECAUSE IT RIGHTFULLY BELONGS TO THE SINGLE-CELL ORGANISMS THAT LIVE THERE'?"

"YOU'RE TAKING THIS ARGUMENT TO A RIDICULOUS EXTREME, SCOTT."

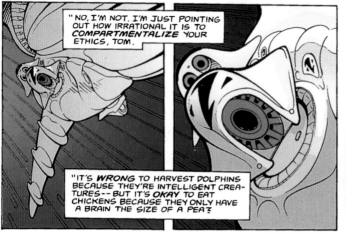

"NO, I'M NOT. I'M JUST POINTING OUT HOW IRRATIONAL IT IS TO *COMPARTMENTALIZE* YOUR ETHICS, TOM.

"IT'S *WRONG* TO HARVEST DOLPHINS BECAUSE THEY'RE INTELLIGENT CREA-TURES-- BUT IT'S *OKAY* TO EAT CHICKENS BECAUSE THEY ONLY HAVE A BRAIN THE SIZE OF A PEA?

"ULTIMATELY, EVERY DISTINCTION IS *SUBJECTIVE*, AND ANY LINE YOU DRAW IS *ARTIFICIAL*."

"WHO'S TO SAY WHAT *POTENTIAL* LIES WITHIN A CHICKEN -- OR EVEN ITS *EGG?*"

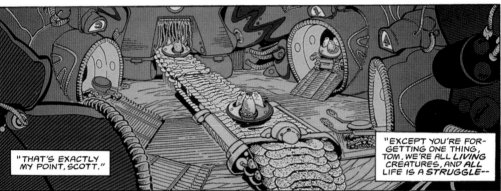

"THAT'S EXACTLY MY POINT, SCOTT."

"EXCEPT YOU'RE FORGETTING ONE THING, TOM. WE'RE ALL *LIVING* CREATURES, AND *ALL* LIFE IS A *STRUGGLE*--"

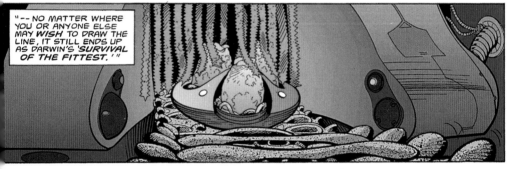

"-- NO MATTER WHERE YOU OR ANYONE ELSE MAY *WISH* TO DRAW THE LINE, IT STILL ENDS UP AS DARWIN'S *'SURVIVAL OF THE FITTEST.'* "

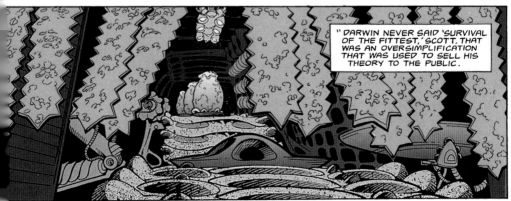

"DARWIN NEVER SAID 'SURVIVAL OF THE FITTEST,' SCOTT. THAT WAS AN OVERSIMPLIFICATION THAT WAS USED TO SELL HIS THEORY TO THE PUBLIC."

" WHAT YOU'RE TALKING ABOUT IS *MANIFEST DESTINY.* "

" YOU CAN CALL IT WHATEVER YOU WANT, TOM.

" THE FACT REMAINS THAT IF THE HUMAN RACE *NEEDS* TO DO SOMETHING TO SURVIVE --

"-AND THE LOWER ORDERS DON'T HAVE THE POWER TO *STOP* US --

"--WE'LL PREVAIL.

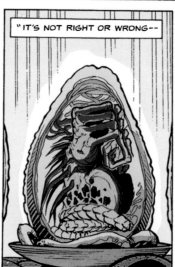

" IT'S NOT RIGHT OR WRONG--

"-- IT'S JUST THE WAY THINGS ARE.

"YOU'VE GOT TO STOP PROJECTING *HUMAN* MOTIVES AND EMOTIONS ONTO OTHER ORGANISMS.

"EVERYTHING IS MERELY WHAT IT IS.

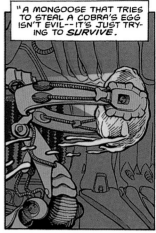

"A MONGOOSE THAT TRIES TO STEAL A COBRA'S EGG ISN'T EVIL-- IT'S JUST TRYING TO *SURVIVE.*

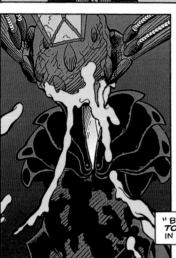

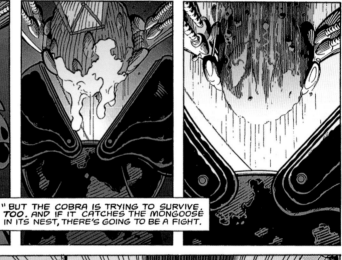

"BUT THE COBRA IS TRYING TO SURVIVE, *TOO.* AND IF IT CATCHES THE MONGOOSE IN ITS NEST, THERE'S GOING TO BE A FIGHT.

"FORTUNATELY FOR THE MONGOOSE, IT HAS *FASTER* REFLEXES AND A MORE *EFFICIENT* METABOLISM.

"WHETHER THAT'S *'FAIR'* OR NOT ISN'T EVEN PART OF THE EQUATION-- IT'S SIMPLY THE *WAY THINGS ARE.* "

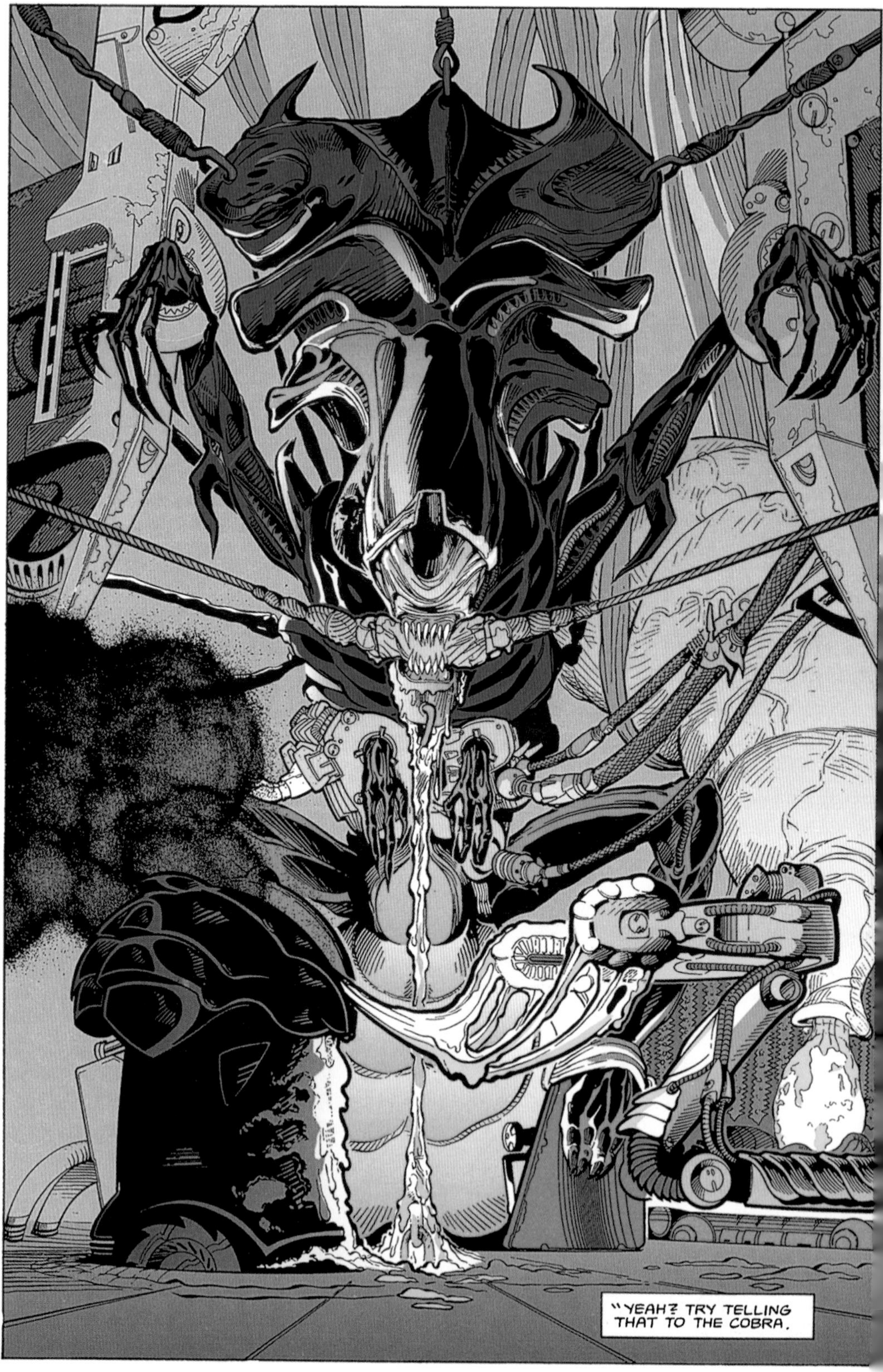
"YEAH? TRY TELLING THAT TO THE COBRA.

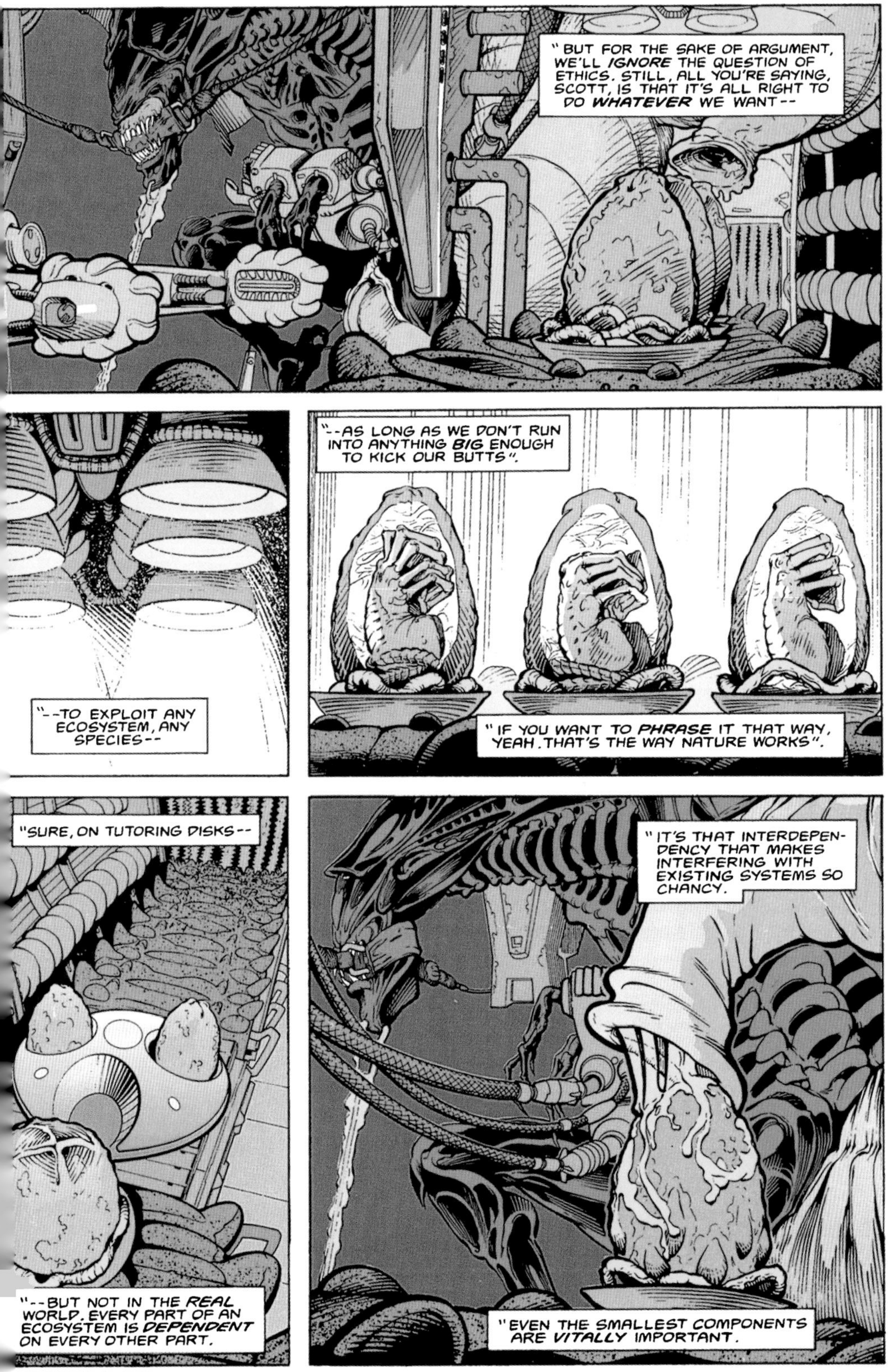
"BUT FOR THE SAKE OF ARGUMENT, WE'LL IGNORE THE QUESTION OF ETHICS. STILL, ALL YOU'RE SAYING, SCOTT, IS THAT IT'S ALL RIGHT TO DO WHATEVER WE WANT--
"--TO EXPLOIT ANY ECOSYSTEM, ANY SPECIES--
"--AS LONG AS WE DON'T RUN INTO ANYTHING BIG ENOUGH TO KICK OUR BUTTS".
"IF YOU WANT TO PHRASE IT THAT WAY, YEAH. THAT'S THE WAY NATURE WORKS".
"SURE, ON TUTORING DISKS--
"--BUT NOT IN THE REAL WORLD. EVERY PART OF AN ECOSYSTEM IS DEPENDENT ON EVERY OTHER PART.
"IT'S THAT INTERDEPENDENCY THAT MAKES INTERFERING WITH EXISTING SYSTEMS SO CHANCY.
"EVEN THE SMALLEST COMPONENTS ARE VITALLY IMPORTANT.

"WHO WOULD HAVE GUESSED THAT MILLIONS OF 'KILLER BEES' COULD SPRING FROM A *HANDFUL* OF ESCAPED AFRICAN BEES?"

"OR THAT A FEW BRAZILIAN FIRE ANTS COULD MAKE THE SOUTHEASTERN PORTION OF THE U.S. VIRTUALLY *UNINHABITABLE* IN JUST OVER SEVENTY YEARS?"

"AND WHAT ABOUT THE 'OIL-EATING' *BACTERIUM* THE GENE-SPLICERS AT THE PETROLEUM COMPANIES DEVELOPED TO CLEAN UP THEIR SPILLS?"

"REMEMBER HOW THEY THOUGHT THEY HAD IT *COMPLETELY* IN THEIR CONTROL?"

"COME ON, TOM, THE OIL WOULD'VE *DRIED UP* SOONER OR LATER ANYWAY, AND I HEAR THE NEW *REPRO-INHIBITORS* THEY'RE USING ARE MAKING A SUBSTANTIAL DENT IN THE FIRE ANT POPULATIONS--"

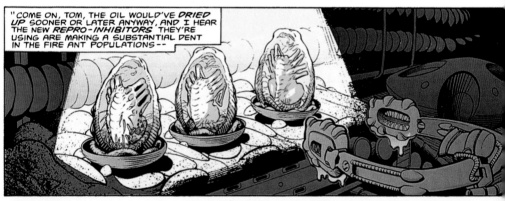

"--SURE, WE SUFFER SETBACKS, BUT WE'LL *ALWAYS* FIND WAYS *AROUND* THE PROBLEMS THAT NATURE THROWS AT US."

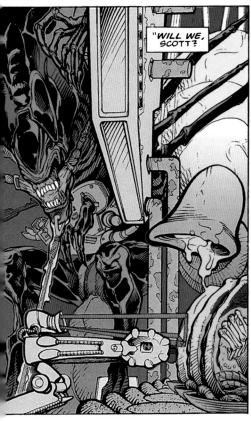

"WILL WE, SCOTT?"

"I'M NOT SO SURE. MANKIND NEVER SEEMS TO LEARN. WE GET OUR HANDS SLAPPED ON A REGULAR BASIS, BUT WE STILL CAN'T SEEM TO KEEP THEM TO OURSELVES.

"THE TIGHTER THE GRIP WE TRY TO GET ON NATURE, THE MORE NATURE PUSHES THROUGH THE CRACKS IN OUR TECHNOLOGY.

"AND WITH SOME OF THE THINGS WE'RE ENCOUNTERING IN THE *SETTLEMENTS*, WE HAVE NO IDEA OF *WHAT* KIND OF TROUBLE WE MAY BE LETTING OURSELVES IN FOR BY MESSING AROUND."

"WELL, SO FAR WE'VE DONE OKAY."

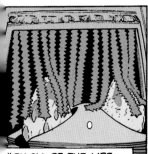

"ON ALL OF THE LIFE-SUPPORTING PLANETS WE'VE COME ACROSS, THE WORST THING WE'VE EVER ENCOUNTERED HAS BEEN THE 'BLOOD WILLIES' OF EPSILON INDI TWO.

"AND I HEAR THEY'VE GOT A *VACCINE* FOR THAT NOW.

"IF I WERE YOU, I'D PUT MY FAITH IN *SCIENCE* AND STOP WORRYING ABOUT THE BOGEY MAN. AND I'D WATCH WHAT I SAID AROUND THE CORPORATE TYPES, TOM--"

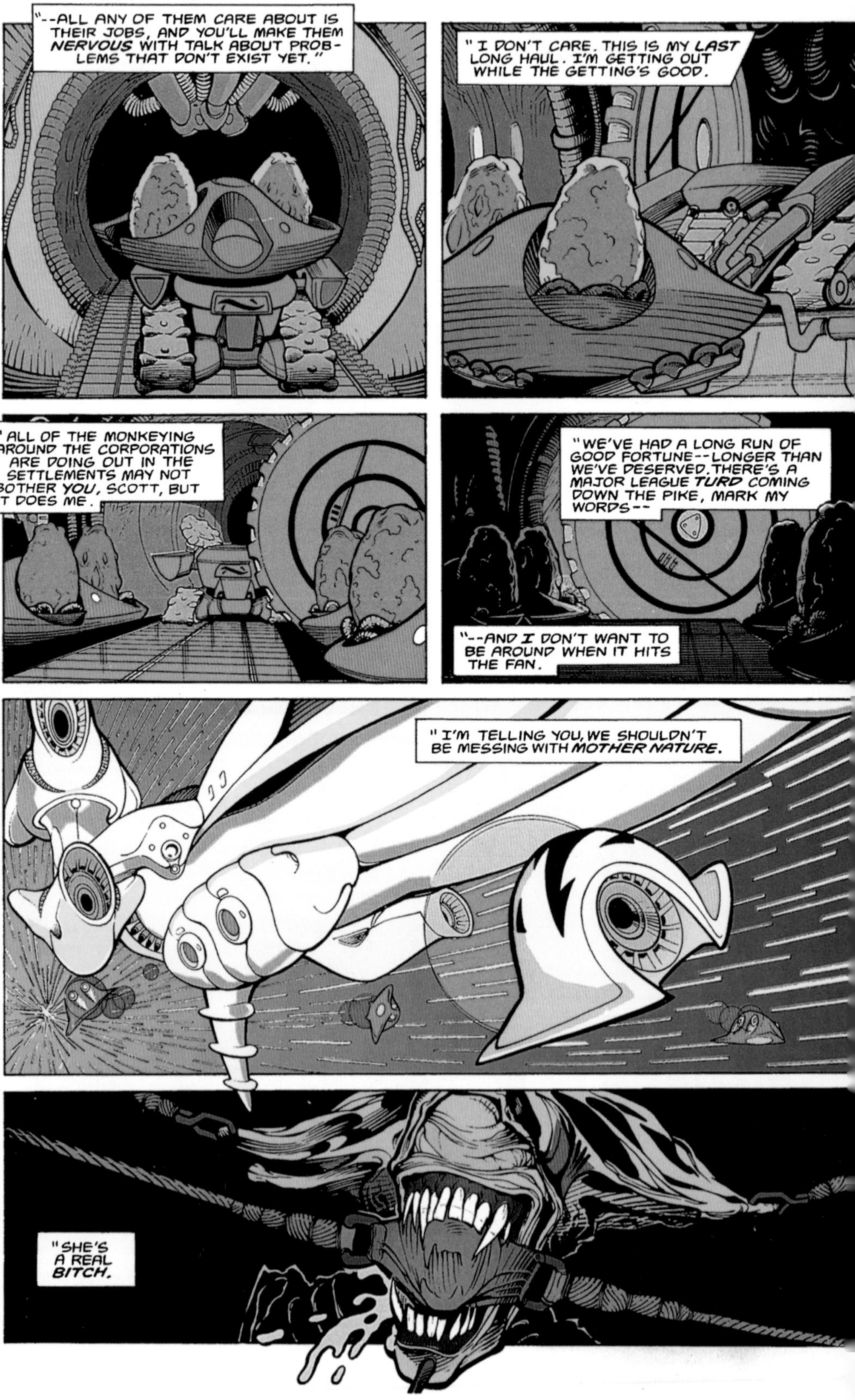
"--ALL ANY OF THEM CARE ABOUT IS THEIR JOBS, AND YOU'LL MAKE THEM NERVOUS WITH TALK ABOUT PROB-LEMS THAT DON'T EXIST YET."
"I DON'T CARE. THIS IS MY LAST LONG HAUL. I'M GETTING OUT WHILE THE GETTING'S GOOD.
"ALL OF THE MONKEYING AROUND THE CORPORATIONS ARE DOING OUT IN THE SETTLEMENTS MAY NOT BOTHER YOU, SCOTT, BUT IT DOES ME.
"WE'VE HAD A LONG RUN OF GOOD FORTUNE--LONGER THAN WE'VE DESERVED. THERE'S A MAJOR LEAGUE TURD COMING DOWN THE PIKE, MARK MY WORDS--
"--AND I DON'T WANT TO BE AROUND WHEN IT HITS THE FAN.
"I'M TELLING YOU, WE SHOULDN'T BE MESSING WITH MOTHER NATURE.
"SHE'S A REAL BITCH.

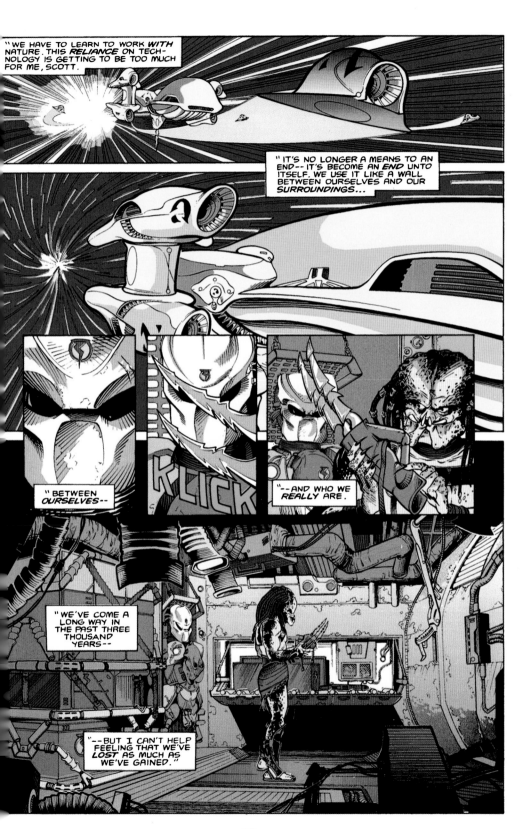

"WE HAVE TO LEARN TO WORK *WITH* NATURE. THIS *RELIANCE* ON TECHNOLOGY IS GETTING TO BE TOO MUCH FOR ME, SCOTT.

" IT'S NO LONGER A MEANS TO AN END-- IT'S BECOME AN *END* UNTO ITSELF. WE USE IT LIKE A WALL BETWEEN OURSELVES AND OUR *SURROUNDINGS*...

" BETWEEN *OURSELVES*--

KLICK

"--AND WHO WE *REALLY* ARE.

" WE'VE COME A LONG WAY IN THE PAST THREE THOUSAND YEARS--

"--BUT I CAN'T HELP FEELING THAT WE'VE *LOST* AS MUCH AS WE'VE GAINED."

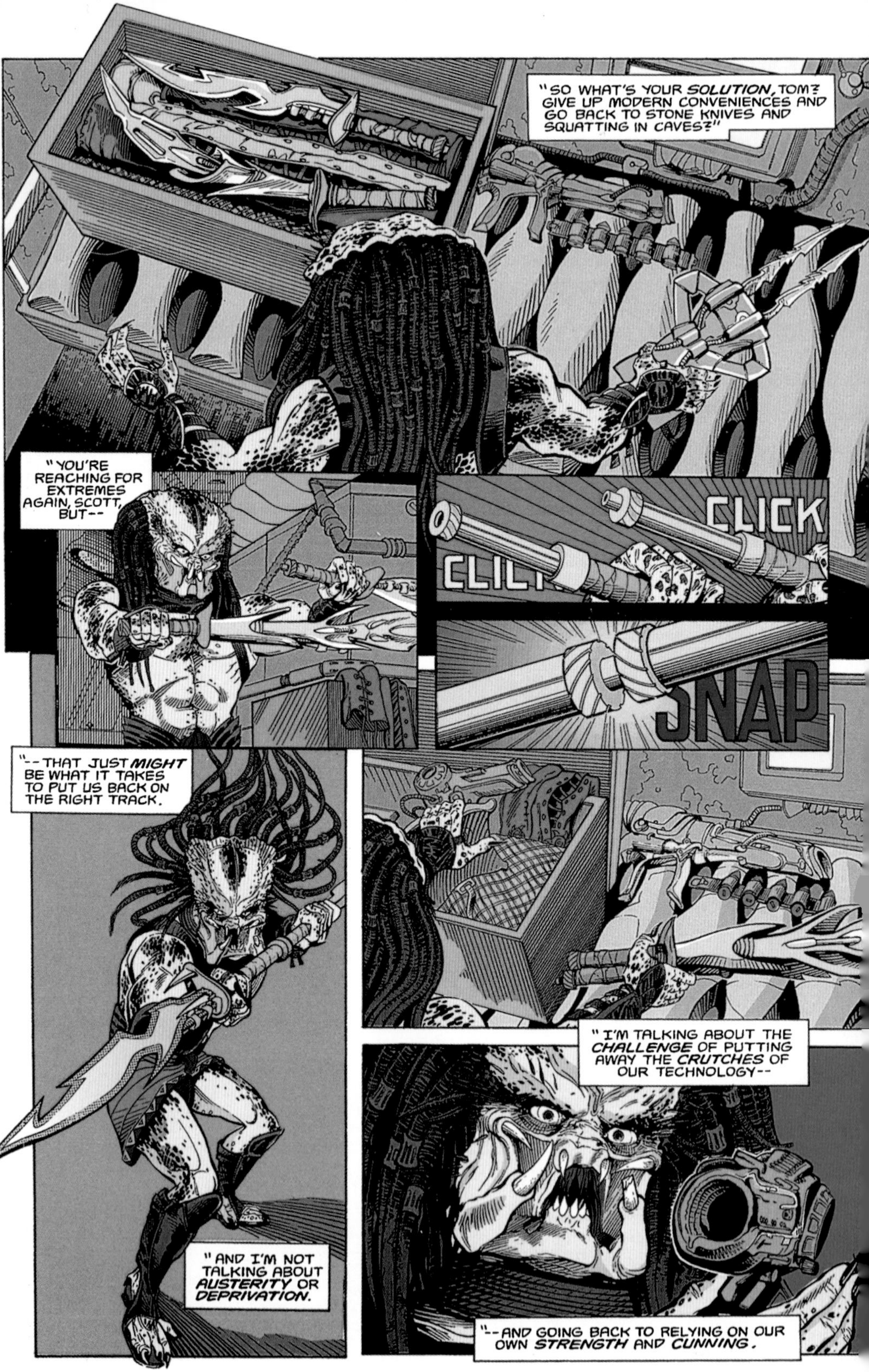
"SO WHAT'S YOUR SOLUTION, TOM? GIVE UP MODERN CONVENIENCES AND GO BACK TO STONE KNIVES AND SQUATTING IN CAVES?"
"YOU'RE REACHING FOR EXTREMES AGAIN, SCOTT, BUT--
CLICK
CLICK
SNAP
"--THAT JUST MIGHT BE WHAT IT TAKES TO PUT US BACK ON THE RIGHT TRACK.
"AND I'M NOT TALKING ABOUT AUSTERITY OR DEPRIVATION.
"I'M TALKING ABOUT THE CHALLENGE OF PUTTING AWAY THE CRUTCHES OF OUR TECHNOLOGY--
"--AND GOING BACK TO RELYING ON OUR OWN STRENGTH AND CUNNING.

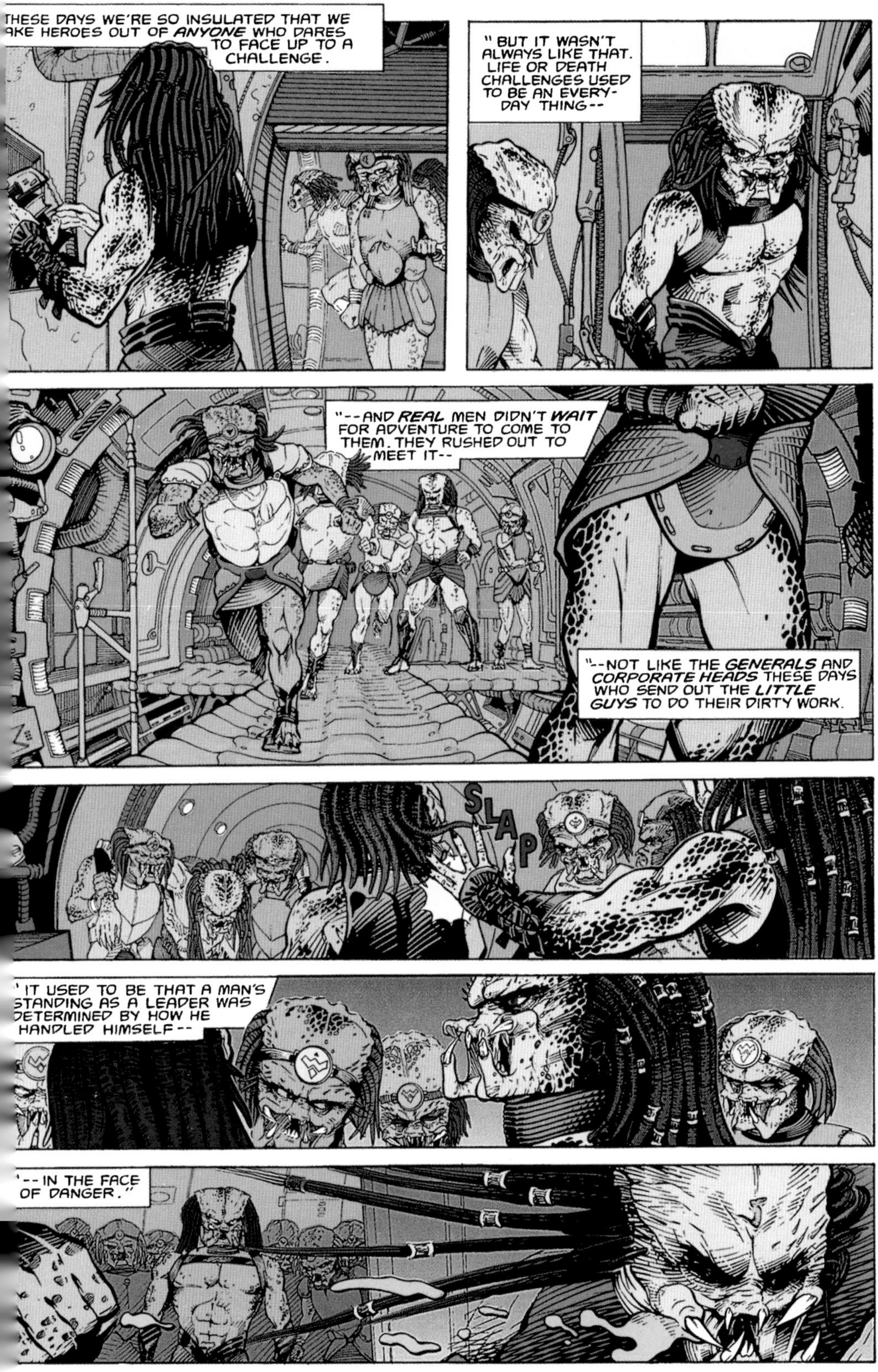
THESE DAYS WE'RE SO INSULATED THAT WE AKE HEROES OUT OF ANYONE WHO DARES TO FACE UP TO A CHALLENGE.
" BUT IT WASN'T ALWAYS LIKE THAT. LIFE OR DEATH CHALLENGES USED TO BE AN EVERY-DAY THING--
"--AND REAL MEN DIDN'T WAIT FOR ADVENTURE TO COME TO THEM. THEY RUSHED OUT TO MEET IT--
"--NOT LIKE THE GENERALS AND CORPORATE HEADS THESE DAYS WHO SEND OUT THE LITTLE GUYS TO DO THEIR DIRTY WORK.
SLAP
" IT USED TO BE THAT A MAN'S STANDING AS A LEADER WAS DETERMINED BY HOW HE HANDLED HIMSELF--
"--IN THE FACE OF DANGER."

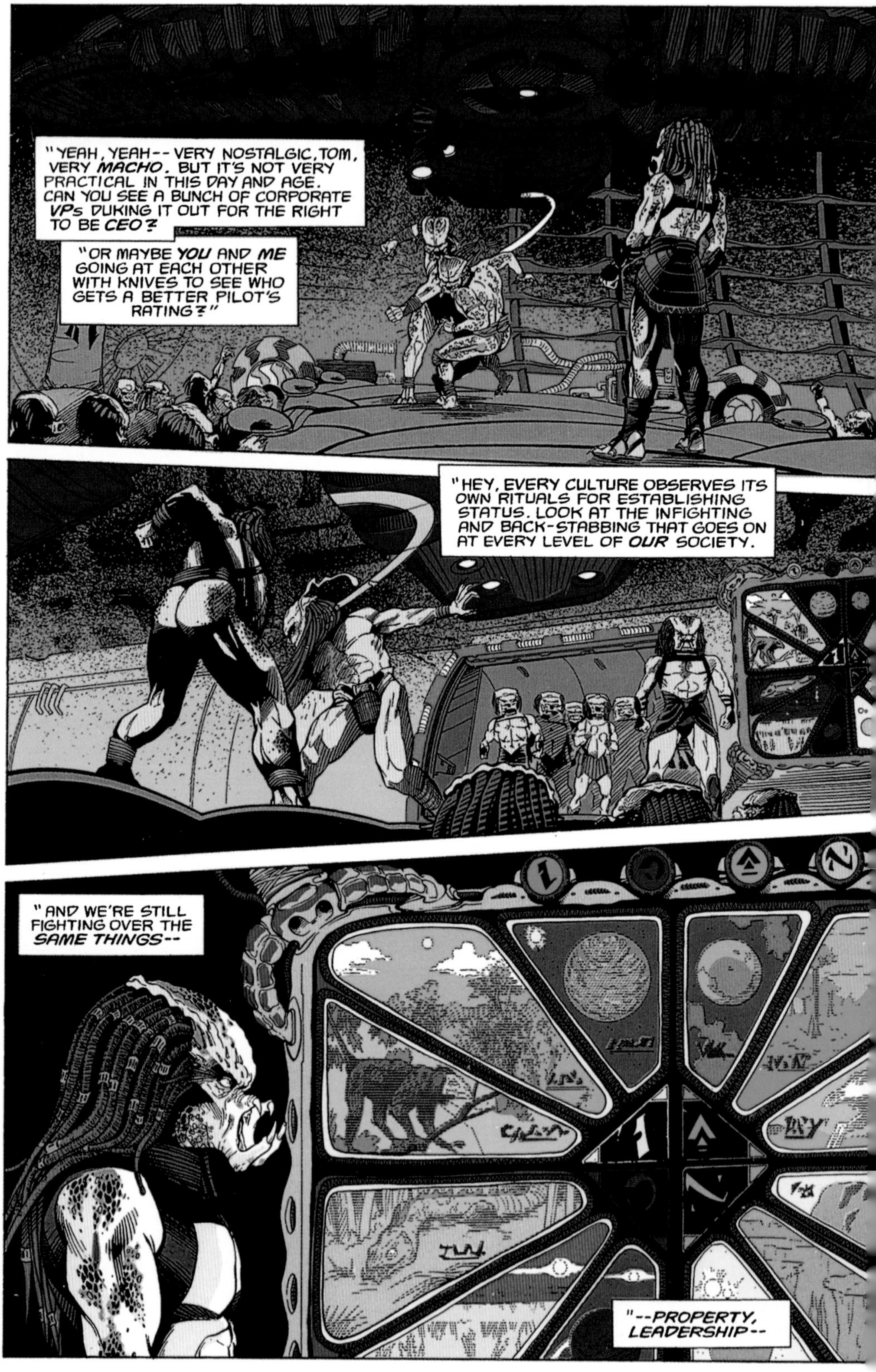
"YEAH, YEAH-- VERY NOSTALGIC, TOM, VERY MACHO. BUT IT'S NOT VERY PRACTICAL IN THIS DAY AND AGE. CAN YOU SEE A BUNCH OF CORPORATE VPs DUKING IT OUT FOR THE RIGHT TO BE CEO?
"OR MAYBE YOU AND ME GOING AT EACH OTHER WITH KNIVES TO SEE WHO GETS A BETTER PILOT'S RATING?"
"HEY, EVERY CULTURE OBSERVES ITS OWN RITUALS FOR ESTABLISHING STATUS. LOOK AT THE INFIGHTING AND BACK-STABBING THAT GOES ON AT EVERY LEVEL OF OUR SOCIETY.
"AND WE'RE STILL FIGHTING OVER THE SAME THINGS--
"--PROPERTY, LEADERSHIP--

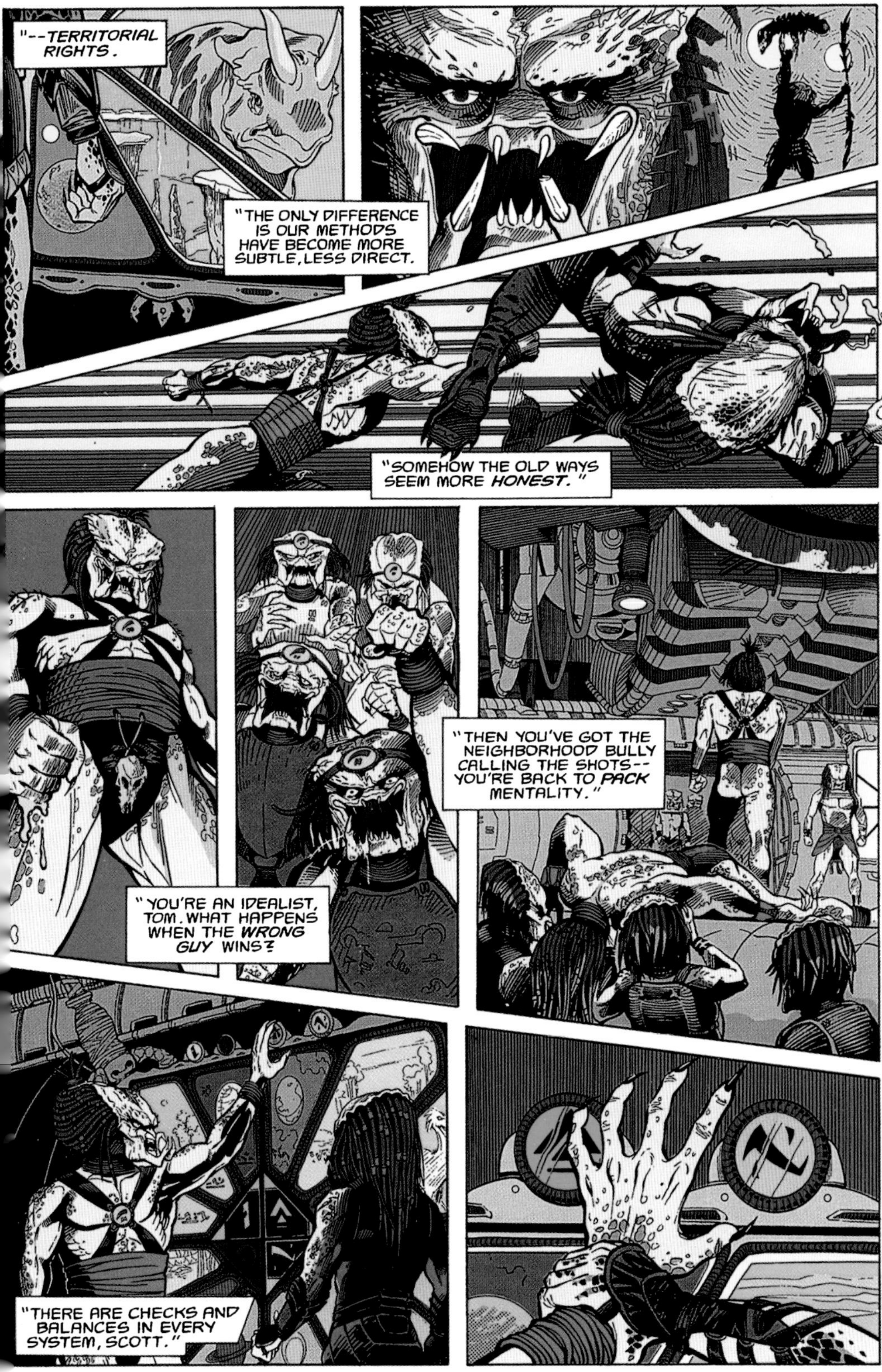
"--TERRITORIAL RIGHTS.
"THE ONLY DIFFERENCE IS OUR METHODS HAVE BECOME MORE SUBTLE, LESS DIRECT.
"SOMEHOW THE OLD WAYS SEEM MORE HONEST."
"YOU'RE AN IDEALIST, TOM. WHAT HAPPENS WHEN THE WRONG GUY WINS?
"THEN YOU'VE GOT THE NEIGHBORHOOD BULLY CALLING THE SHOTS-- YOU'RE BACK TO PACK MENTALITY."
"THERE ARE CHECKS AND BALANCES IN EVERY SYSTEM, SCOTT."

"YEAH, BUT YOUR WAY LEAVES THEM ALL UP TO *INDIVIDUAL* INITIATIVE!

"WITHOUT SOME KIND OF SANCTIONED AVENUE FOR DISSENT--

"--A GUY WOULD HAVE TO BE A *REAL HERO*--

"--OR A REAL *FOOL* TO BUTT HEADS WITH THE CHIEF."

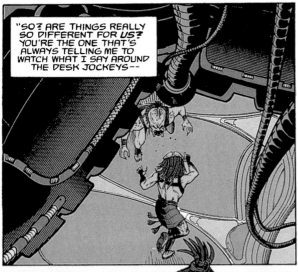

"SO? ARE THINGS REALLY SO DIFFERENT FOR *US?* YOU'RE THE ONE THAT'S ALWAYS TELLING ME TO WATCH WHAT I SAY AROUND THE DESK JOCKEYS--

"--WHERE'S *MY* 'SANCTIONED AVENUE FOR DISSENT'?

RRRRR REAR

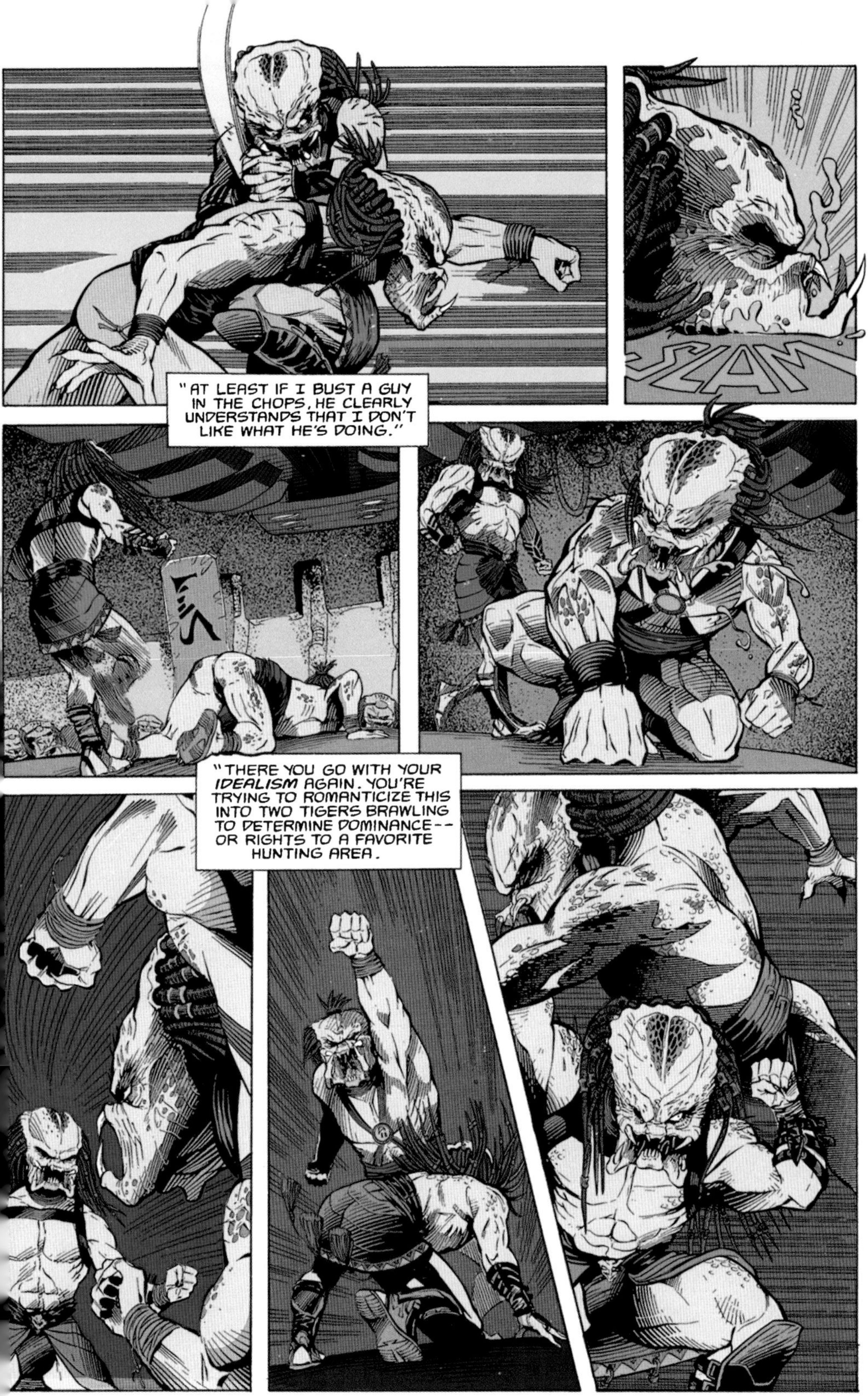
SLAM
"AT LEAST IF I BUST A GUY IN THE CHOPS, HE CLEARLY UNDERSTANDS THAT I DON'T LIKE WHAT HE'S DOING."
"THERE YOU GO WITH YOUR *IDEALISM* AGAIN. YOU'RE TRYING TO ROMANTICIZE THIS INTO TWO TIGERS BRAWLING TO DETERMINE DOMINANCE-- OR RIGHTS TO A FAVORITE HUNTING AREA.

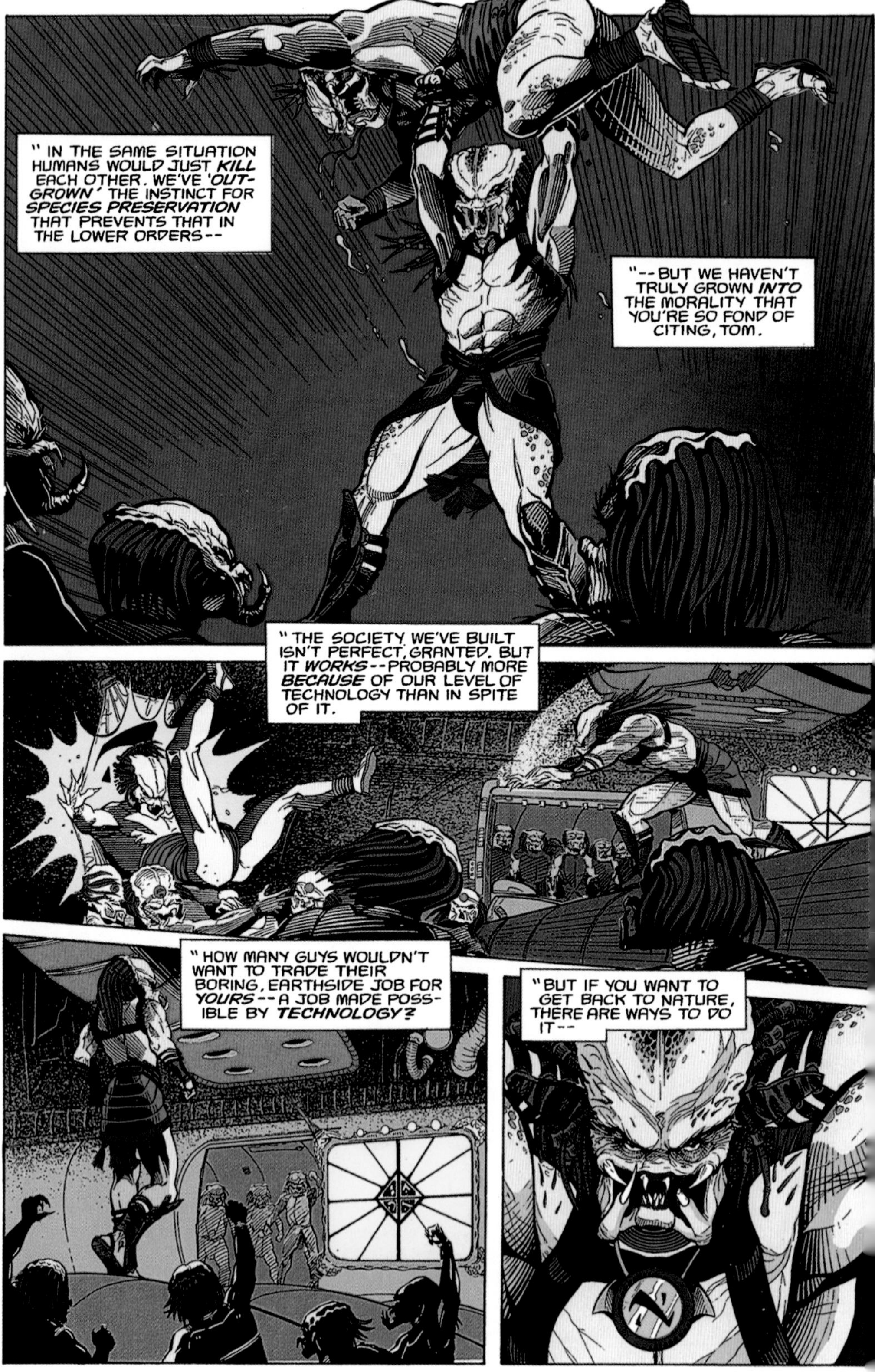

"IN THE SAME SITUATION HUMANS WOULD JUST KILL EACH OTHER. WE'VE 'OUT-GROWN' THE INSTINCT FOR SPECIES PRESERVATION THAT PREVENTS THAT IN THE LOWER ORDERS--
"--BUT WE HAVEN'T TRULY GROWN INTO THE MORALITY THAT YOU'RE SO FOND OF CITING, TOM.
"THE SOCIETY WE'VE BUILT ISN'T PERFECT, GRANTED. BUT IT WORKS--PROBABLY MORE BECAUSE OF OUR LEVEL OF TECHNOLOGY THAN IN SPITE OF IT.
"HOW MANY GUYS WOULDN'T WANT TO TRADE THEIR BORING, EARTHSIDE JOB FOR YOURS--A JOB MADE POSSIBLE BY TECHNOLOGY?
"BUT IF YOU WANT TO GET BACK TO NATURE, THERE ARE WAYS TO DO IT--

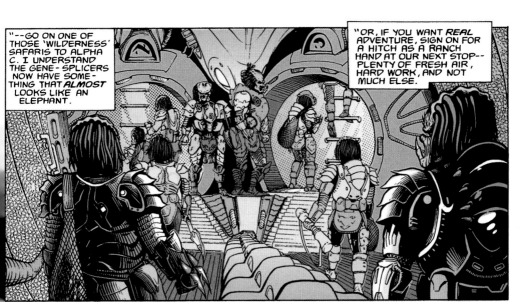

"--GO ON ONE OF THOSE 'WILDERNESS' SAFARIS TO ALPHA C. I UNDERSTAND THE GENE-SPLICERS NOW HAVE SOMETHING THAT *ALMOST* LOOKS LIKE AN ELEPHANT.

"OR, IF YOU WANT *REAL* ADVENTURE, SIGN ON FOR A HITCH AS A RANCH HAND AT OUR NEXT STOP-- PLENTY OF FRESH AIR, HARD WORK, AND NOT MUCH ELSE.

"MAYBE THAT'S *YOUR* IDEA OF FULFILLMENT--

"--THOUGH I CAN'T IMAGINE ANYONE ENVYING YOU THE JOB.

"ME, I CAN GET ENOUGH ADVENTURE FROM THE VIDS. GOD BLESS MODERN TECHNOLOGY!

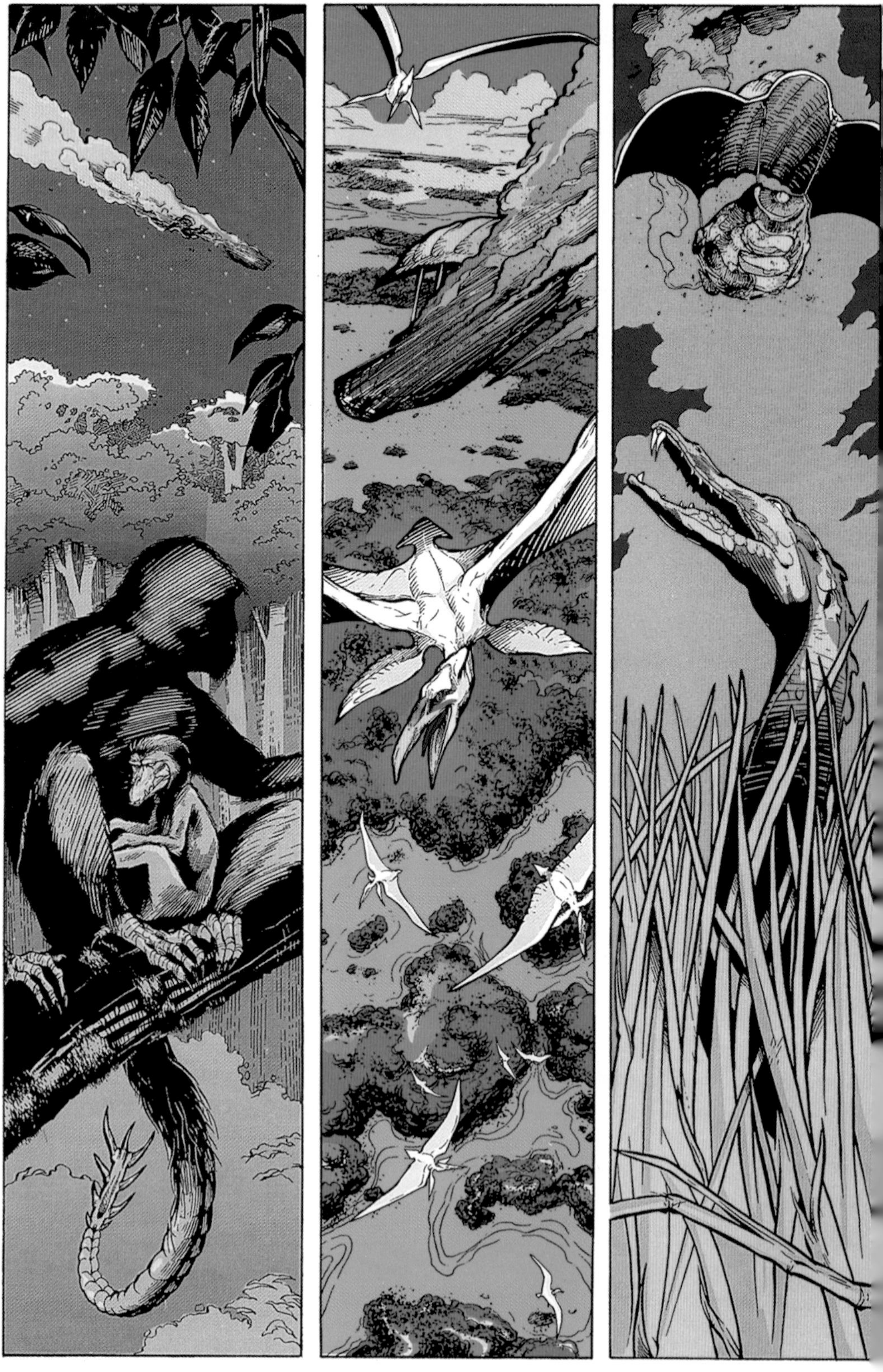

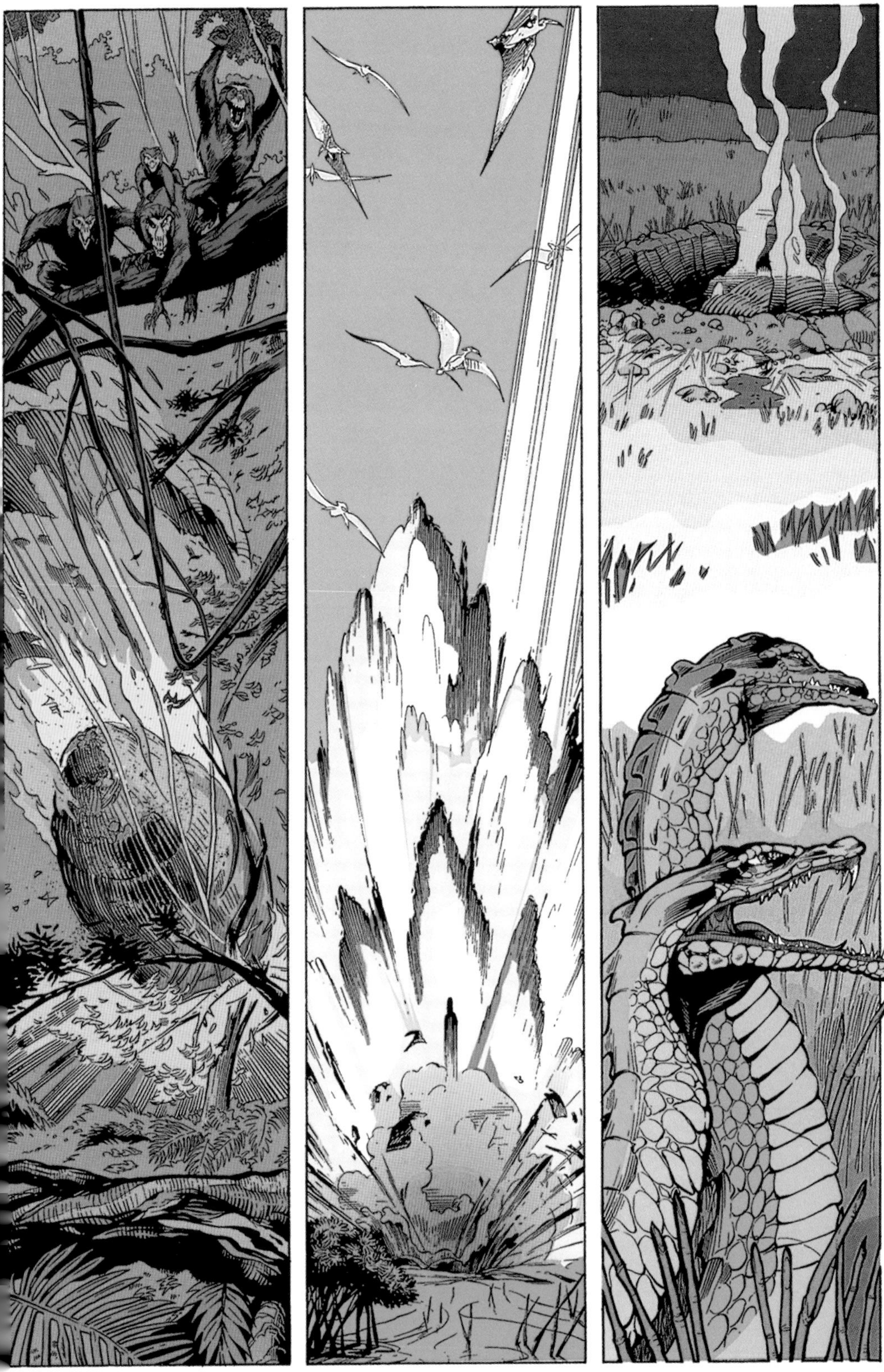

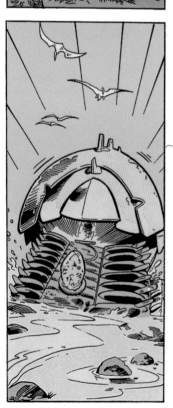

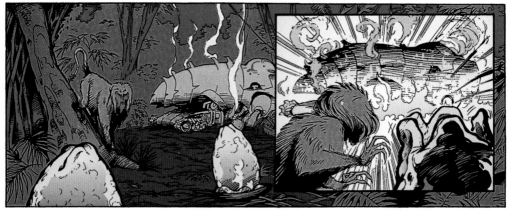

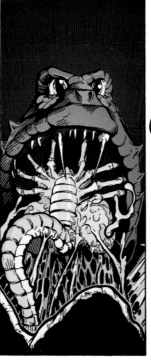

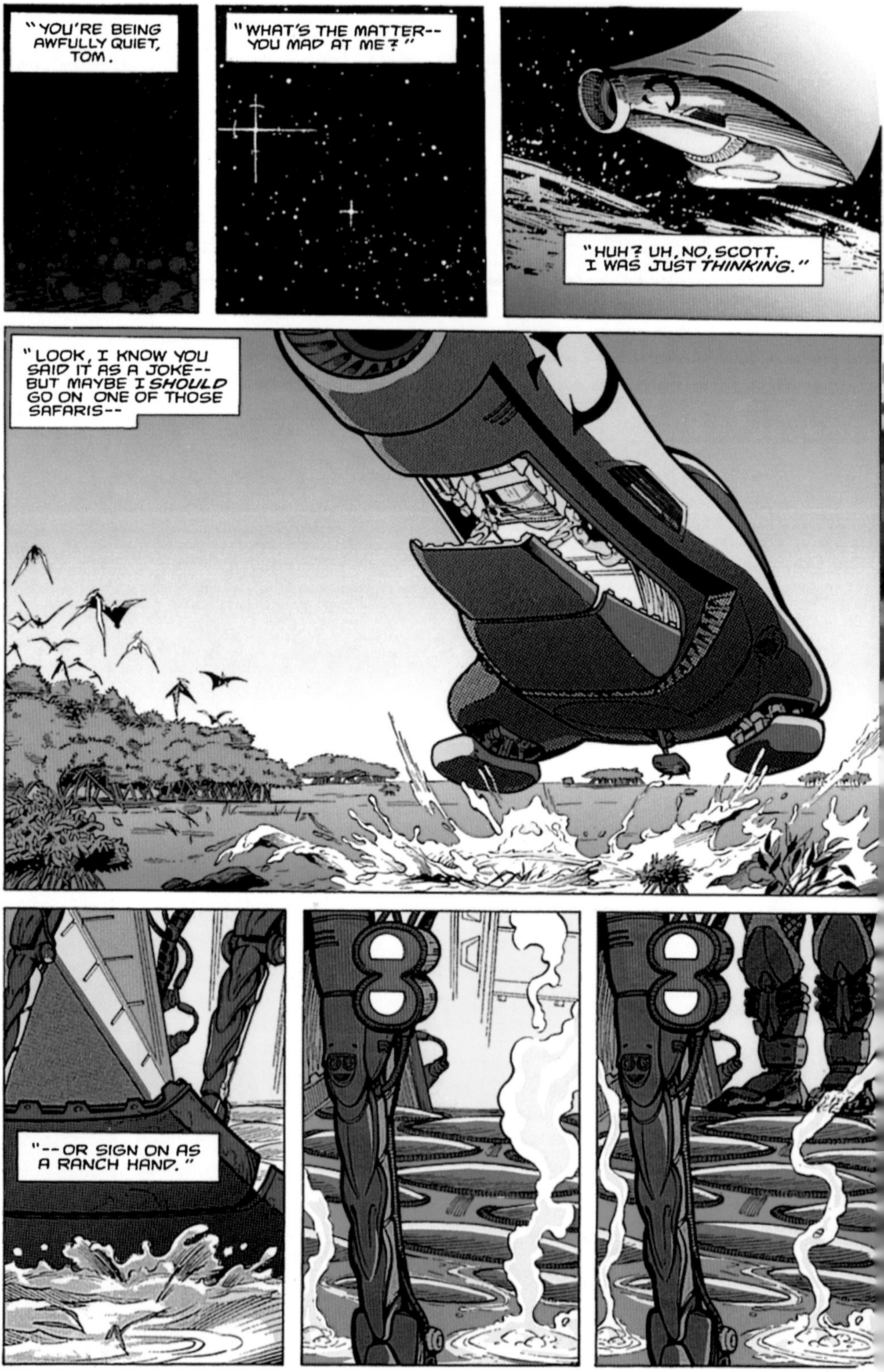
"YOU'RE BEING AWFULLY QUIET, TOM.
"WHAT'S THE MATTER-- YOU MAD AT ME?"
"HUH? UH, NO, SCOTT. I WAS JUST THINKING."
"LOOK, I KNOW YOU SAID IT AS A JOKE-- BUT MAYBE I SHOULD GO ON ONE OF THOSE SAFARIS--
"--OR SIGN ON AS A RANCH HAND."

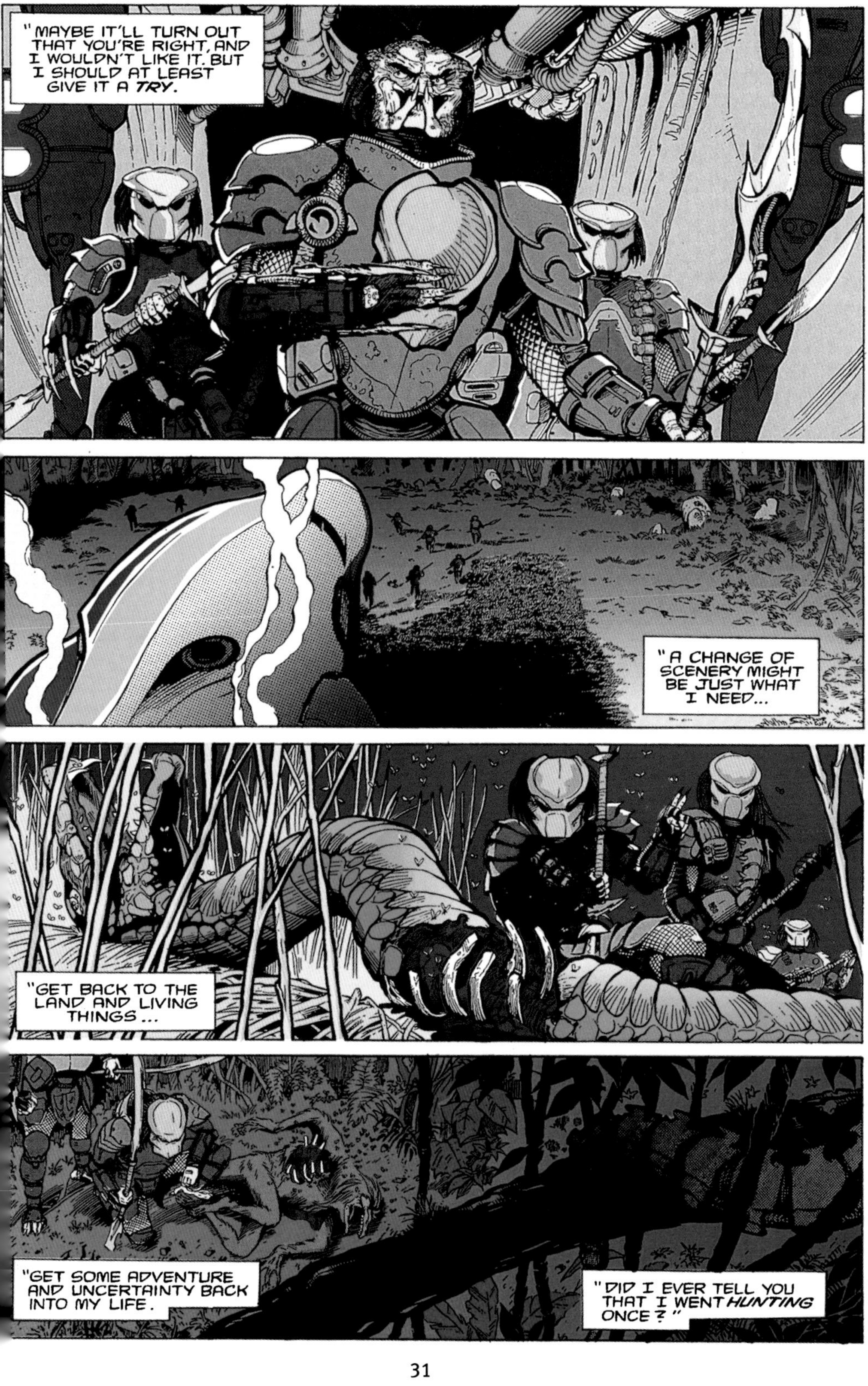
"MAYBE IT'LL TURN OUT THAT YOU'RE RIGHT, AND I WOULDN'T LIKE IT. BUT I SHOULD AT LEAST GIVE IT A *TRY*.
"A CHANGE OF SCENERY MIGHT BE JUST WHAT I NEED...
"GET BACK TO THE LAND AND LIVING THINGS ...
"GET SOME ADVENTURE AND UNCERTAINTY BACK INTO MY LIFE.
"DID I EVER TELL YOU THAT I WENT *HUNTING* ONCE?"

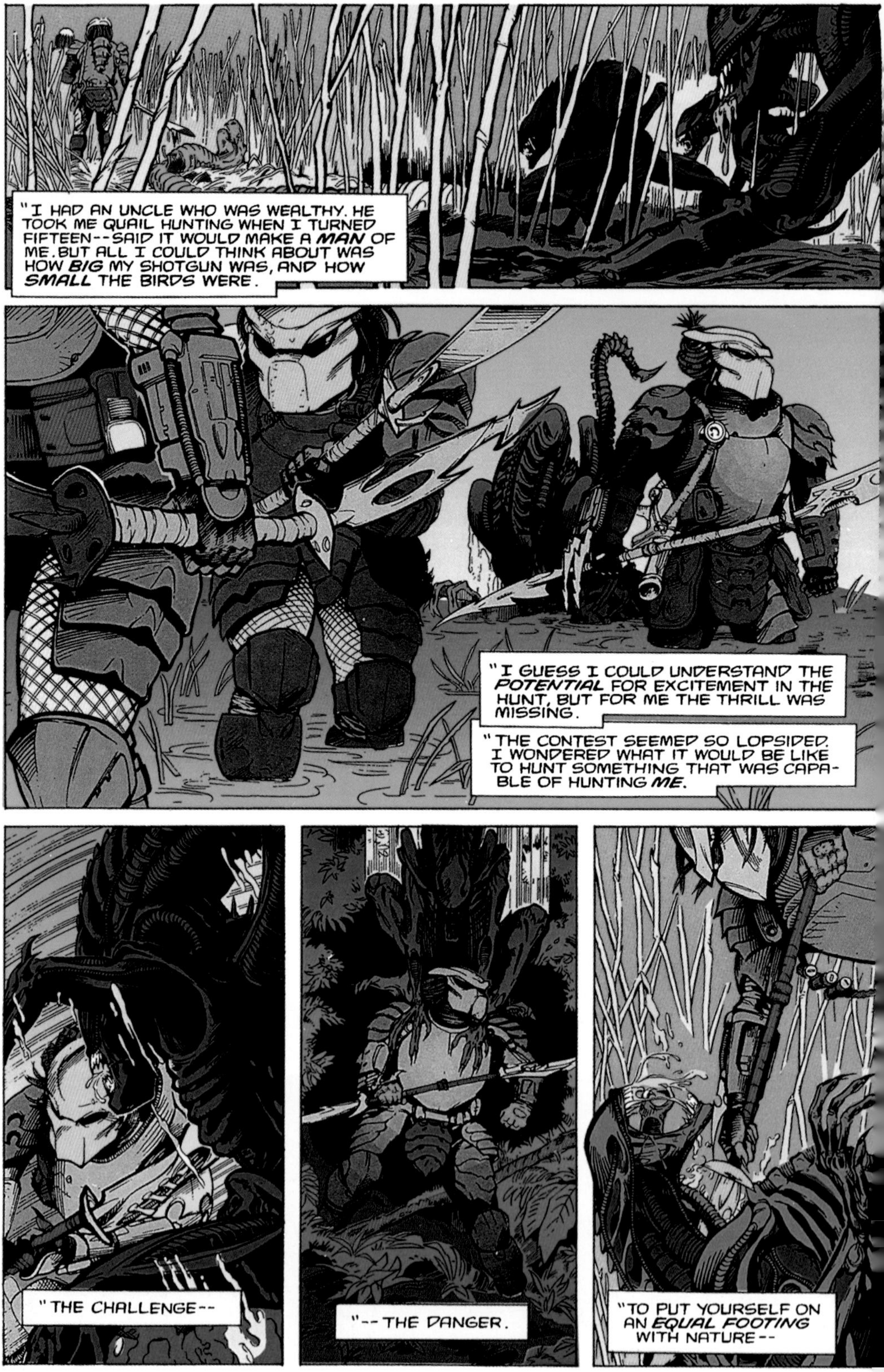
"I HAD AN UNCLE WHO WAS WEALTHY. HE TOOK ME QUAIL HUNTING WHEN I TURNED FIFTEEN--SAID IT WOULD MAKE A MAN OF ME. BUT ALL I COULD THINK ABOUT WAS HOW BIG MY SHOTGUN WAS, AND HOW SMALL THE BIRDS WERE.
"I GUESS I COULD UNDERSTAND THE POTENTIAL FOR EXCITEMENT IN THE HUNT, BUT FOR ME THE THRILL WAS MISSING.
"THE CONTEST SEEMED SO LOPSIDED. I WONDERED WHAT IT WOULD BE LIKE TO HUNT SOMETHING THAT WAS CAPABLE OF HUNTING ME.
"THE CHALLENGE--
"--THE DANGER.
"TO PUT YOURSELF ON AN EQUAL FOOTING WITH NATURE--

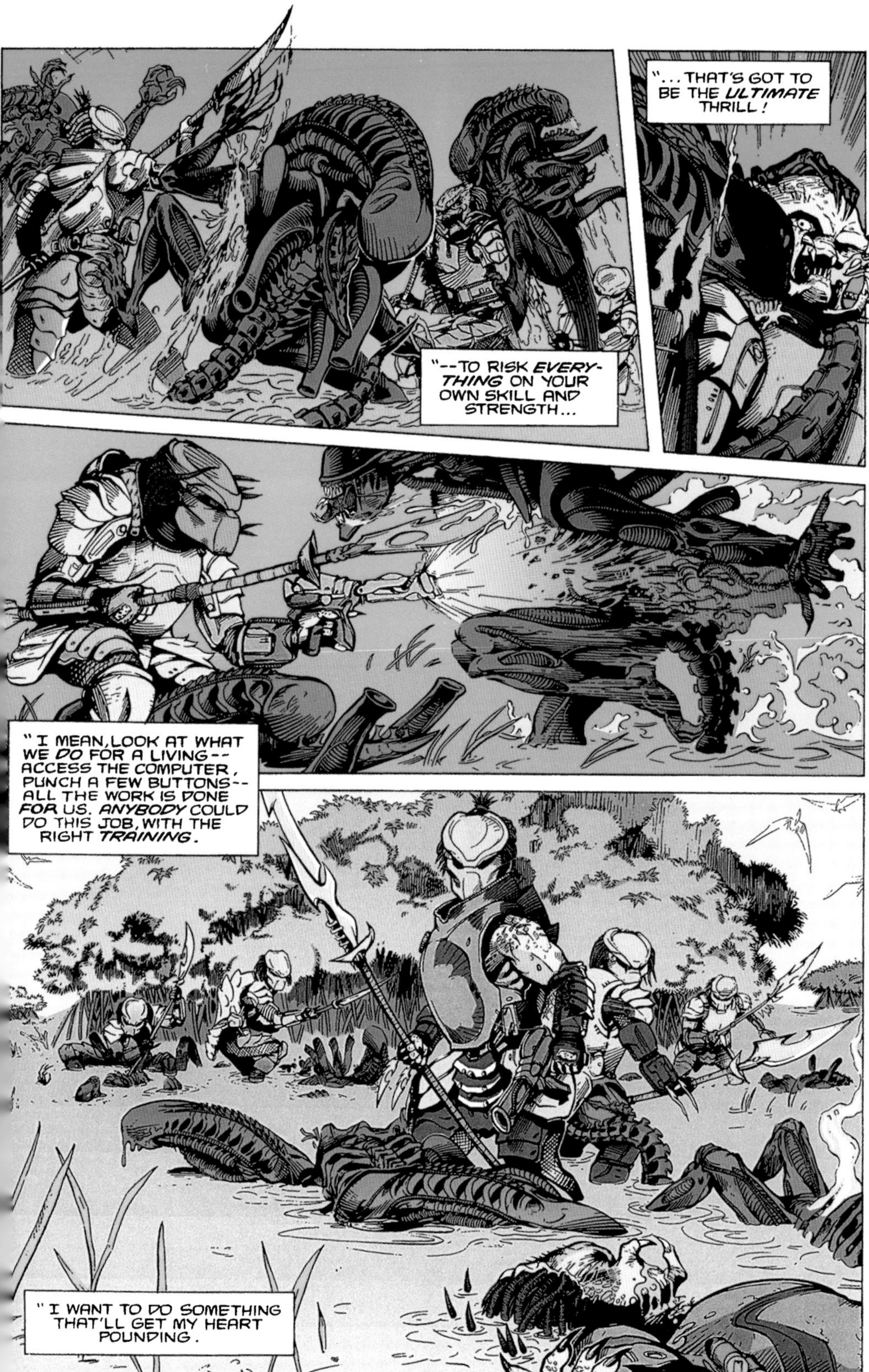
"--TO RISK *EVERYTHING* ON YOUR OWN SKILL AND STRENGTH...
"...THAT'S GOT TO BE THE *ULTIMATE* THRILL!
"I MEAN, LOOK AT WHAT WE *DO* FOR A LIVING--ACCESS THE COMPUTER, PUNCH A FEW BUTTONS--ALL THE WORK IS DONE *FOR* US. *ANYBODY* COULD DO THIS JOB, WITH THE RIGHT *TRAINING*.
"I WANT TO DO SOMETHING THAT'LL GET MY HEART POUNDING.

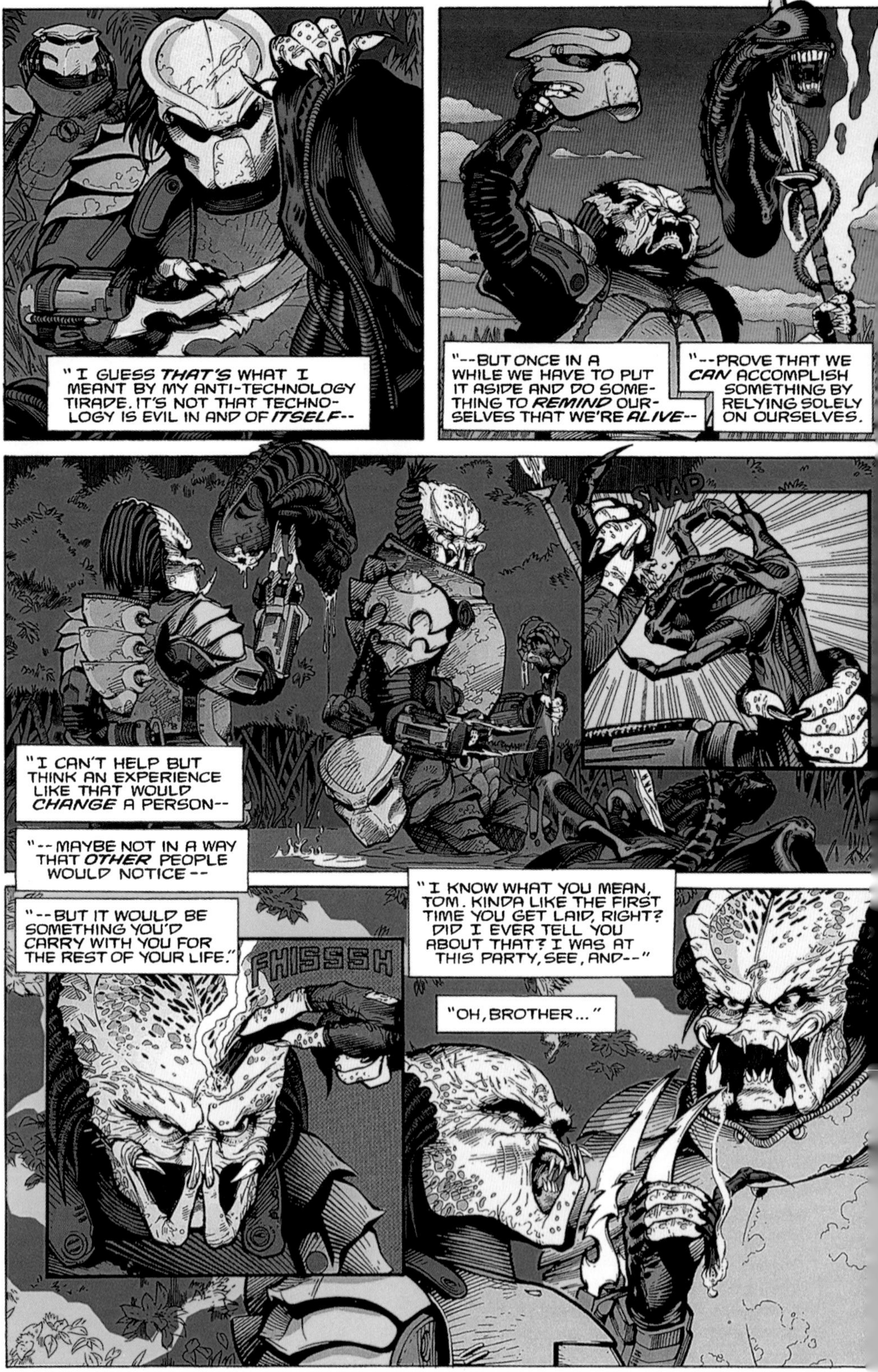
"I GUESS THAT'S WHAT I MEANT BY MY ANTI-TECHNOLOGY TIRADE. IT'S NOT THAT TECHNOLOGY IS EVIL IN AND OF ITSELF--
"--BUT ONCE IN A WHILE WE HAVE TO PUT IT ASIDE AND DO SOMETHING TO REMIND OURSELVES THAT WE'RE ALIVE--
"--PROVE THAT WE CAN ACCOMPLISH SOMETHING BY RELYING SOLELY ON OURSELVES.
SNAP
"I CAN'T HELP BUT THINK AN EXPERIENCE LIKE THAT WOULD CHANGE A PERSON--
"--MAYBE NOT IN A WAY THAT OTHER PEOPLE WOULD NOTICE--
"--BUT IT WOULD BE SOMETHING YOU'D CARRY WITH YOU FOR THE REST OF YOUR LIFE."
FHISSSH
"I KNOW WHAT YOU MEAN, TOM. KINDA LIKE THE FIRST TIME YOU GET LAID, RIGHT? DID I EVER TELL YOU ABOUT THAT? I WAS AT THIS PARTY, SEE, AND--"
"OH, BROTHER..."

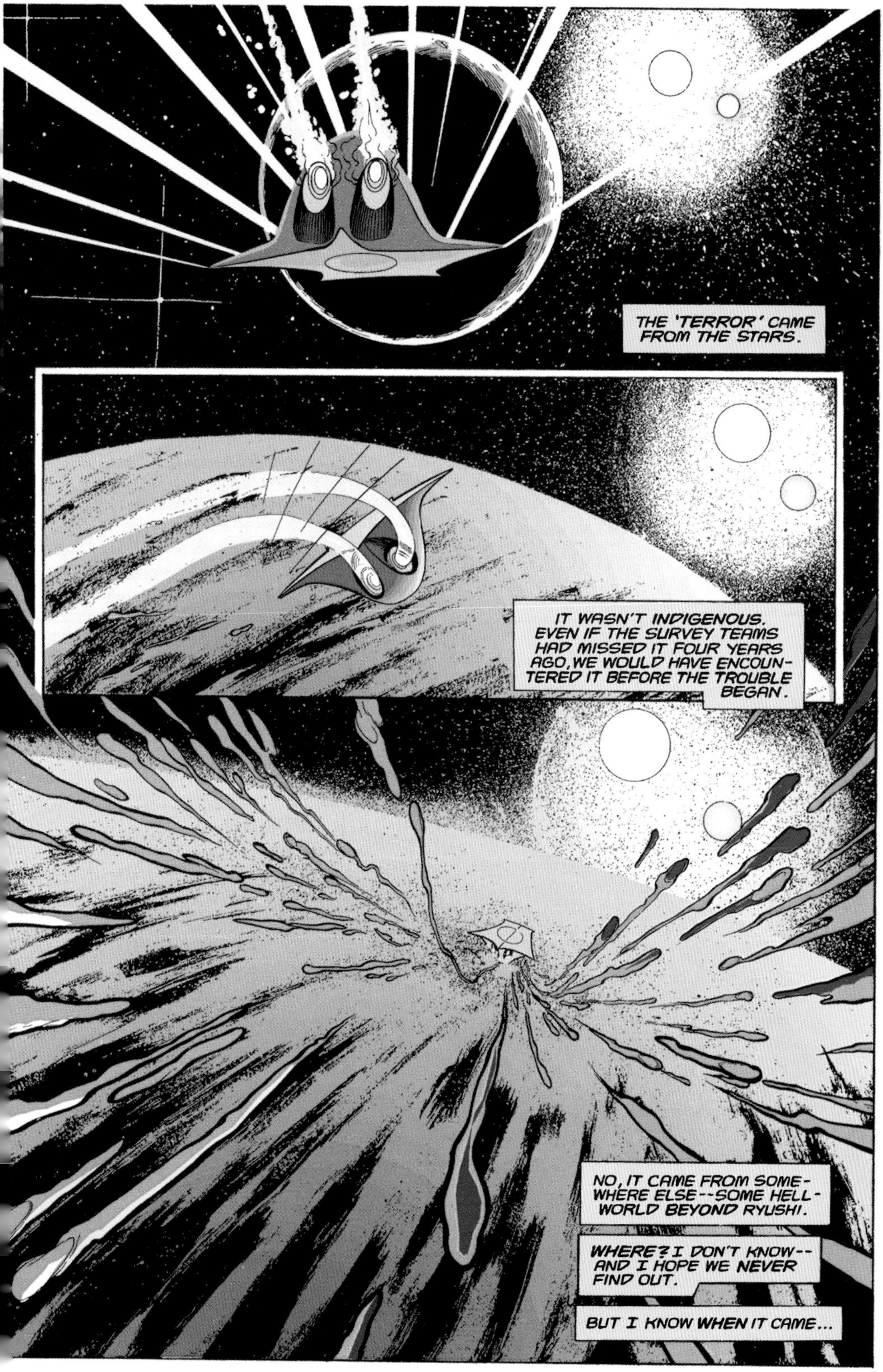
THE 'TERROR' CAME FROM THE STARS.
IT WASN'T INDIGENOUS. EVEN IF THE SURVEY TEAMS HAD MISSED IT FOUR YEARS AGO, WE WOULD HAVE ENCOUNTERED IT BEFORE THE TROUBLE BEGAN.
NO, IT CAME FROM SOMEWHERE ELSE--SOME HELL-WORLD BEYOND RYUSHI.
WHERE? I DON'T KNOW--AND I HOPE WE NEVER FIND OUT.
BUT I KNOW WHEN IT CAME...

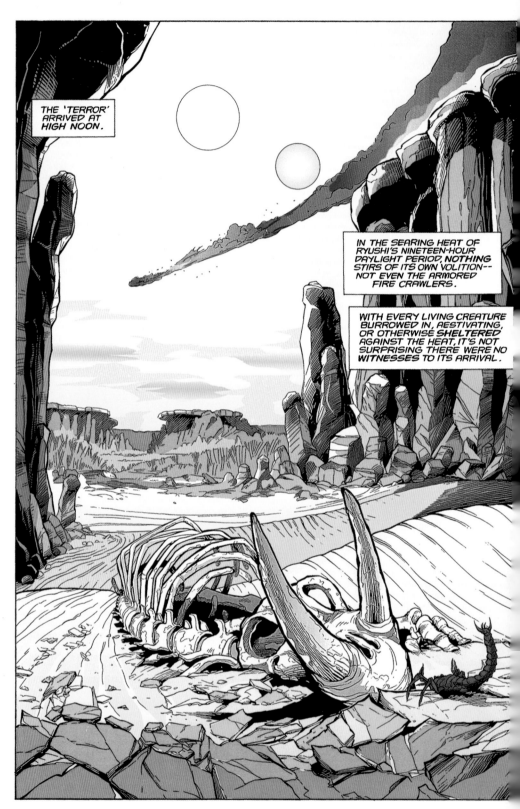

THE 'TERROR' ARRIVED AT HIGH NOON.

IN THE SEARING HEAT OF RYUSHI'S NINETEEN-HOUR DAYLIGHT PERIOD, NOTHING STIRS OF ITS OWN VOLITION-- NOT EVEN THE ARMORED FIRE CRAWLERS.

WITH EVERY LIVING CREATURE BURROWED IN, AESTIVATING, OR OTHERWISE SHELTERED AGAINST THE HEAT, IT'S NOT SURPRISING THERE WERE NO WITNESSES TO ITS ARRIVAL.

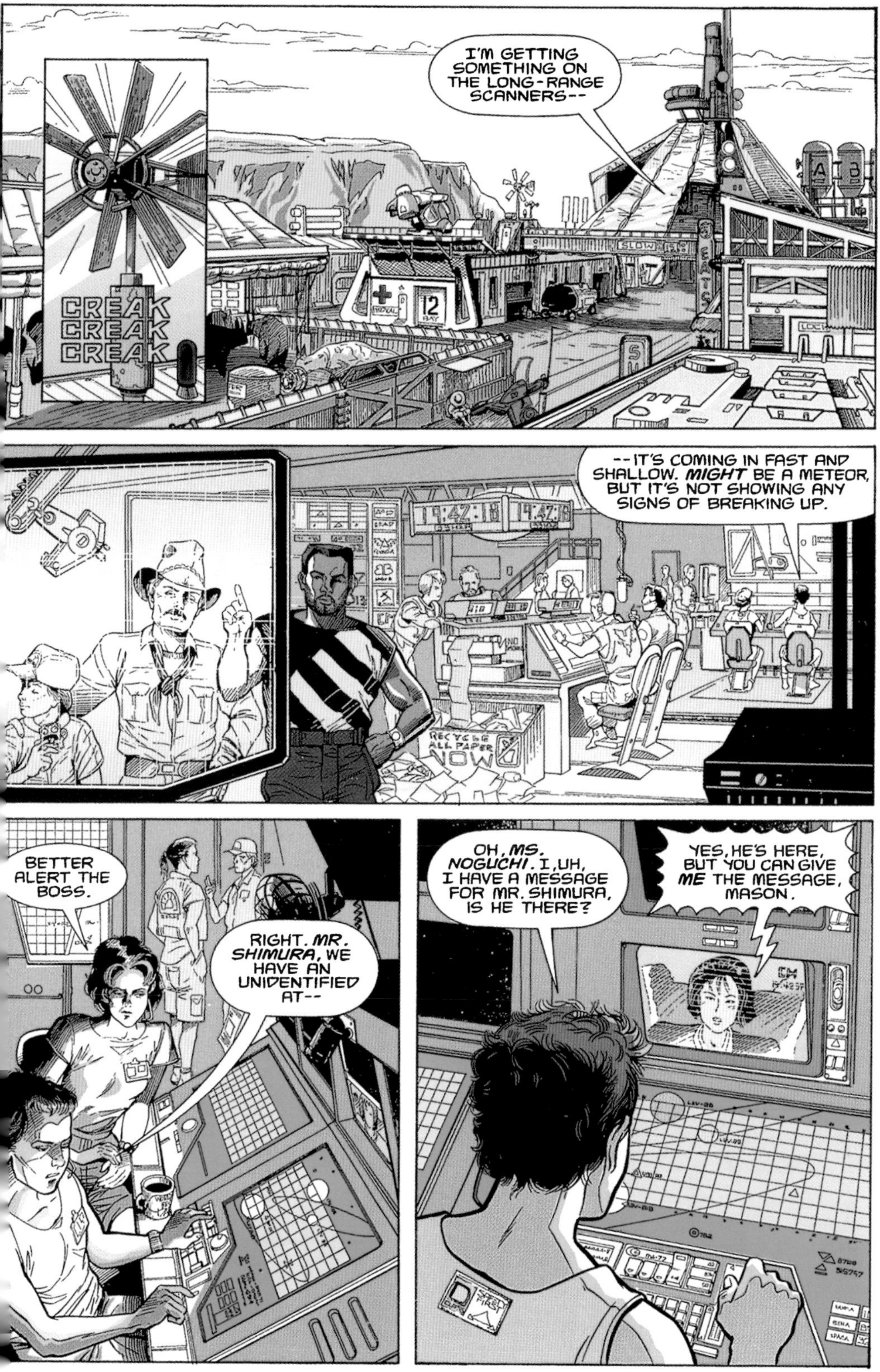
CREAK
CREAK
CREAK
I'M GETTING SOMETHING ON THE LONG-RANGE SCANNERS--
--IT'S COMING IN FAST AND SHALLOW. MIGHT BE A METEOR, BUT IT'S NOT SHOWING ANY SIGNS OF BREAKING UP.
RECYCLE ALL PAPER NOW
BETTER ALERT THE BOSS.
RIGHT. MR. SHIMURA, WE HAVE AN UNIDENTIFIED AT--
OH, MS. NOGUCHI. I, UH, I HAVE A MESSAGE FOR MR. SHIMURA, IS HE THERE?
YES, HE'S HERE, BUT YOU CAN GIVE ME THE MESSAGE, MASON.

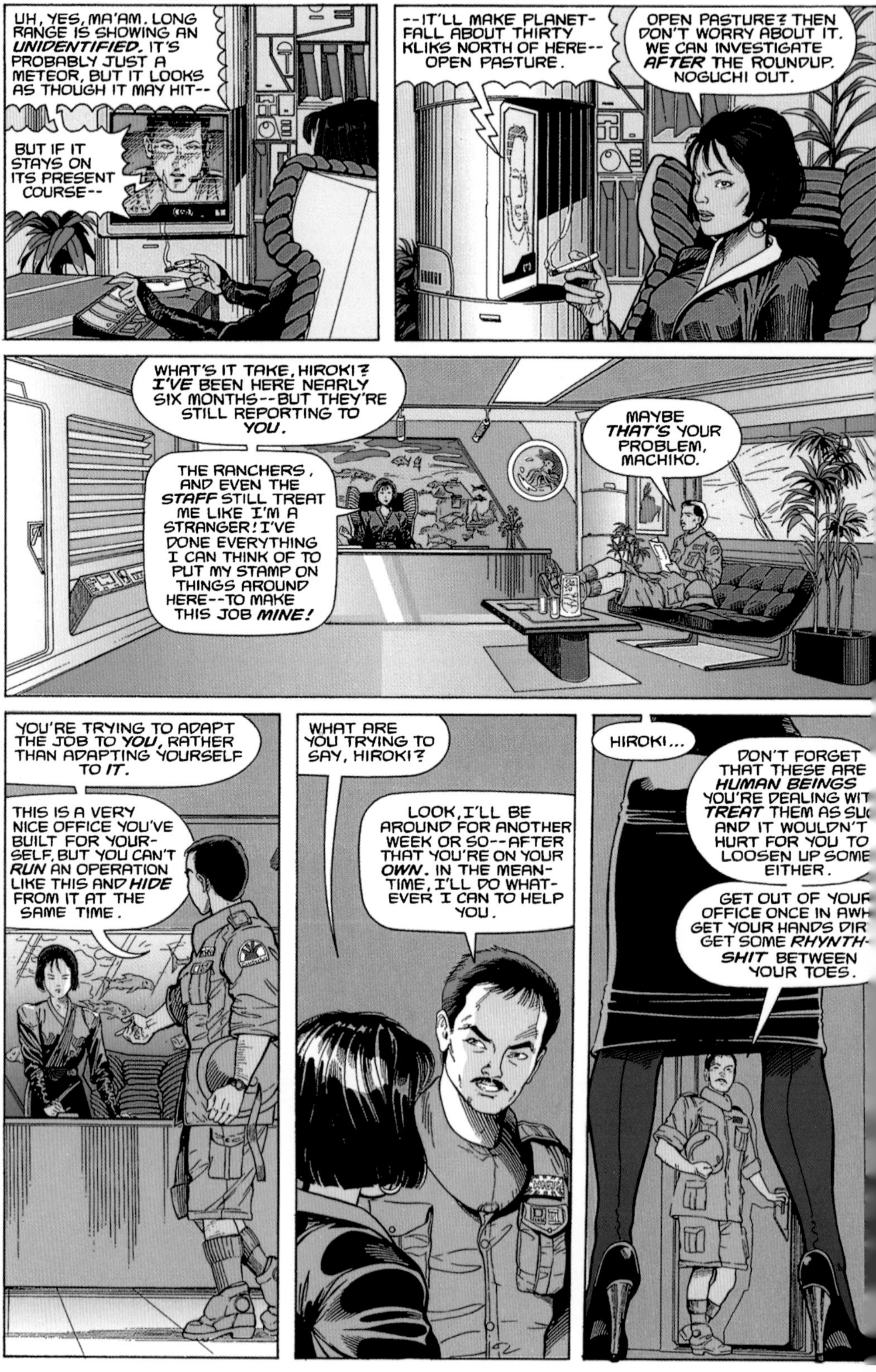

UH, YES, MA'AM. LONG RANGE IS SHOWING AN UNIDENTIFIED. IT'S PROBABLY JUST A METEOR, BUT IT LOOKS AS THOUGH IT MAY HIT--
BUT IF IT STAYS ON ITS PRESENT COURSE--
--IT'LL MAKE PLANET-FALL ABOUT THIRTY KLIKS NORTH OF HERE-- OPEN PASTURE.
OPEN PASTURE? THEN DON'T WORRY ABOUT IT. WE CAN INVESTIGATE AFTER THE ROUNDUP. NOGUCHI OUT.
WHAT'S IT TAKE, HIROKI? I'VE BEEN HERE NEARLY SIX MONTHS--BUT THEY'RE STILL REPORTING TO YOU.
THE RANCHERS, AND EVEN THE STAFF STILL TREAT ME LIKE I'M A STRANGER! I'VE DONE EVERYTHING I CAN THINK OF TO PUT MY STAMP ON THINGS AROUND HERE--TO MAKE THIS JOB MINE!
MAYBE THAT'S YOUR PROBLEM, MACHIKO.
YOU'RE TRYING TO ADAPT THE JOB TO YOU, RATHER THAN ADAPTING YOURSELF TO IT.
THIS IS A VERY NICE OFFICE YOU'VE BUILT FOR YOURSELF, BUT YOU CAN'T RUN AN OPERATION LIKE THIS AND HIDE FROM IT AT THE SAME TIME.
WHAT ARE YOU TRYING TO SAY, HIROKI?
LOOK, I'LL BE AROUND FOR ANOTHER WEEK OR SO--AFTER THAT YOU'RE ON YOUR OWN. IN THE MEANTIME, I'LL DO WHATEVER I CAN TO HELP YOU.
HIROKI...
DON'T FORGET THAT THESE ARE HUMAN BEINGS YOU'RE DEALING WIT TREAT THEM AS SU AND IT WOULDN'T HURT FOR YOU TO LOOSEN UP SOME EITHER.
GET OUT OF YOUR OFFICE ONCE IN AWH GET YOUR HANDS DIR GET SOME RHYNTH-SHIT BETWEEN YOUR TOES.

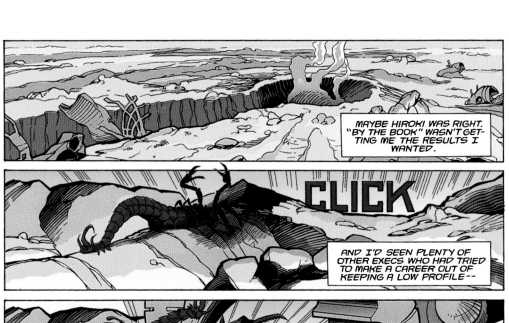

MAYBE HIROKI WAS RIGHT. "BY THE BOOK" WASN'T GETTING ME THE RESULTS I WANTED.

CLICK

AND I'D SEEN PLENTY OF OTHER EXECS WHO HAD TRIED TO MAKE A CAREER OUT OF KEEPING A LOW PROFILE--

--LEFT TWISTING IN THE WIND WHEN THE POLITICAL CLIMATE CHANGED.

THUNK

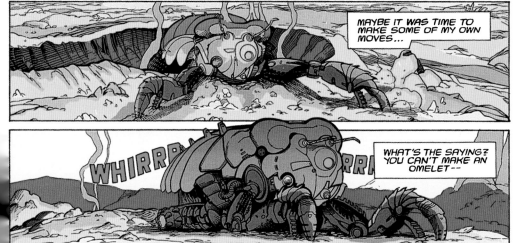

MAYBE IT WAS TIME TO MAKE SOME OF MY OWN MOVES...

WHAT'S THE SAYING? YOU CAN'T MAKE AN OMELET--

WHIRRR RRR

--WITHOUT BREAKING A FEW EGGS.

PLUT

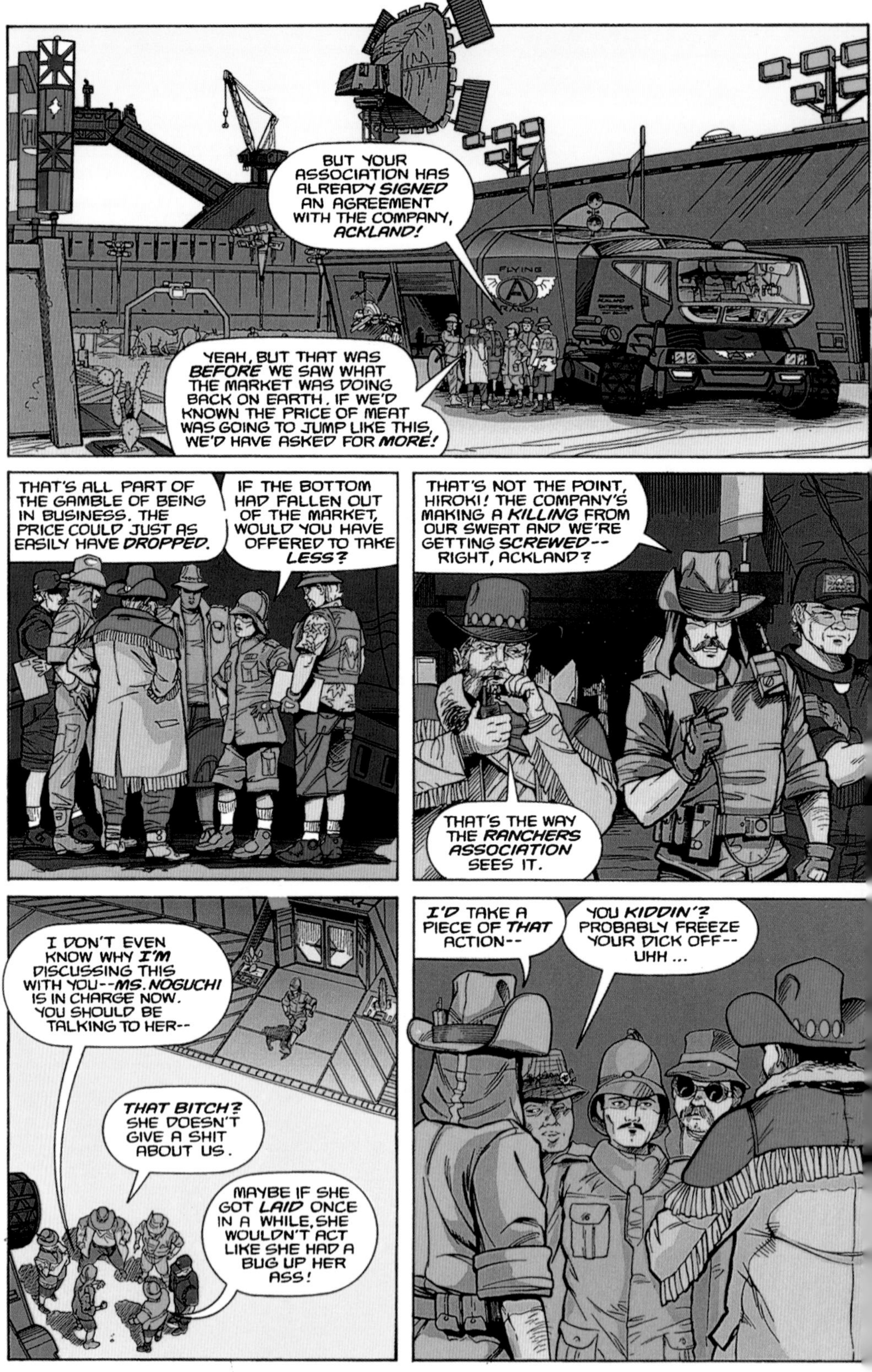
BUT YOUR ASSOCIATION HAS ALREADY SIGNED AN AGREEMENT WITH THE COMPANY, ACKLAND!
FLYING A RANCH
YEAH, BUT THAT WAS BEFORE WE SAW WHAT THE MARKET WAS DOING BACK ON EARTH. IF WE'D KNOWN THE PRICE OF MEAT WAS GOING TO JUMP LIKE THIS, WE'D HAVE ASKED FOR MORE!
THAT'S ALL PART OF THE GAMBLE OF BEING IN BUSINESS. THE PRICE COULD JUST AS EASILY HAVE DROPPED.
IF THE BOTTOM HAD FALLEN OUT OF THE MARKET, WOULD YOU HAVE OFFERED TO TAKE LESS?
THAT'S NOT THE POINT, HIROKI! THE COMPANY'S MAKING A KILLING FROM OUR SWEAT AND WE'RE GETTING SCREWED-- RIGHT, ACKLAND?
THAT'S THE WAY THE RANCHERS ASSOCIATION SEES IT.
I DON'T EVEN KNOW WHY I'M DISCUSSING THIS WITH YOU--MS. NOGUCHI IS IN CHARGE NOW. YOU SHOULD BE TALKING TO HER--
THAT BITCH? SHE DOESN'T GIVE A SHIT ABOUT US.
MAYBE IF SHE GOT LAID ONCE IN A WHILE, SHE WOULDN'T ACT LIKE SHE HAD A BUG UP HER ASS!
I'D TAKE A PIECE OF THAT ACTION--
YOU KIDDIN'? PROBABLY FREEZE YOUR DICK OFF-- UHH ...

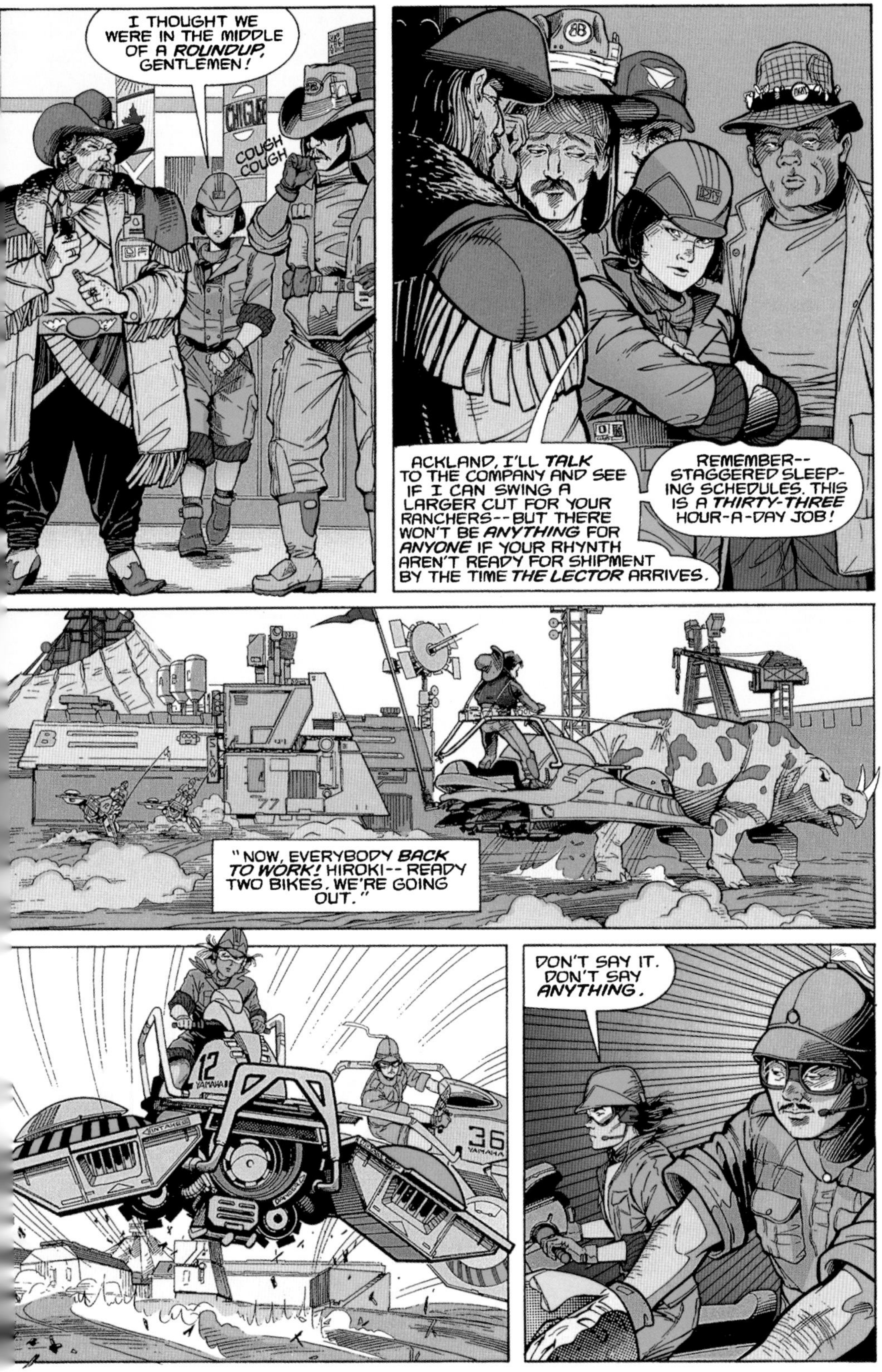
I THOUGHT WE WERE IN THE MIDDLE OF A ROUNDUP, GENTLEMEN!
COUGH COUGH
ACKLAND, I'LL TALK TO THE COMPANY AND SEE IF I CAN SWING A LARGER CUT FOR YOUR RANCHERS--BUT THERE WON'T BE ANYTHING FOR ANYONE IF YOUR RHYNTH AREN'T READY FOR SHIPMENT BY THE TIME THE LECTOR ARRIVES.
REMEMBER--STAGGERED SLEEPING SCHEDULES. THIS IS A THIRTY-THREE HOUR-A-DAY JOB!
"NOW, EVERYBODY BACK TO WORK! HIROKI--READY TWO BIKES. WE'RE GOING OUT."
DON'T SAY IT. DON'T SAY ANYTHING.

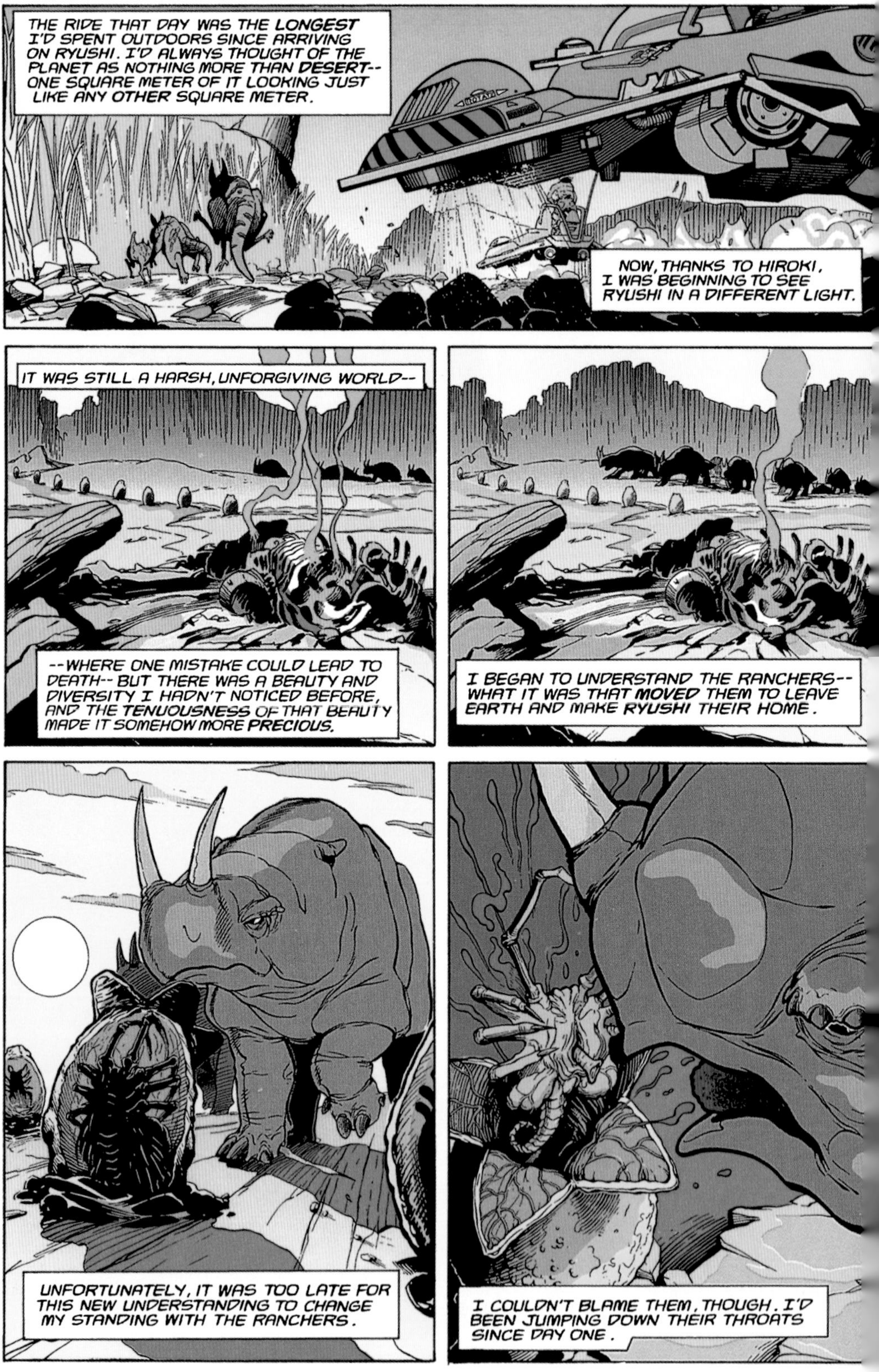
THE RIDE THAT DAY WAS THE LONGEST I'D SPENT OUTDOORS SINCE ARRIVING ON RYUSHI. I'D ALWAYS THOUGHT OF THE PLANET AS NOTHING MORE THAN DESERT-- ONE SQUARE METER OF IT LOOKING JUST LIKE ANY OTHER SQUARE METER.
NOW, THANKS TO HIROKI, I WAS BEGINNING TO SEE RYUSHI IN A DIFFERENT LIGHT.
IT WAS STILL A HARSH, UNFORGIVING WORLD--
--WHERE ONE MISTAKE COULD LEAD TO DEATH-- BUT THERE WAS A BEAUTY AND DIVERSITY I HADN'T NOTICED BEFORE, AND THE TENUOUSNESS OF THAT BEAUTY MADE IT SOMEHOW MORE PRECIOUS.
I BEGAN TO UNDERSTAND THE RANCHERS-- WHAT IT WAS THAT MOVED THEM TO LEAVE EARTH AND MAKE RYUSHI THEIR HOME.
UNFORTUNATELY, IT WAS TOO LATE FOR THIS NEW UNDERSTANDING TO CHANGE MY STANDING WITH THE RANCHERS.
I COULDN'T BLAME THEM, THOUGH. I'D BEEN JUMPING DOWN THEIR THROATS SINCE DAY ONE.

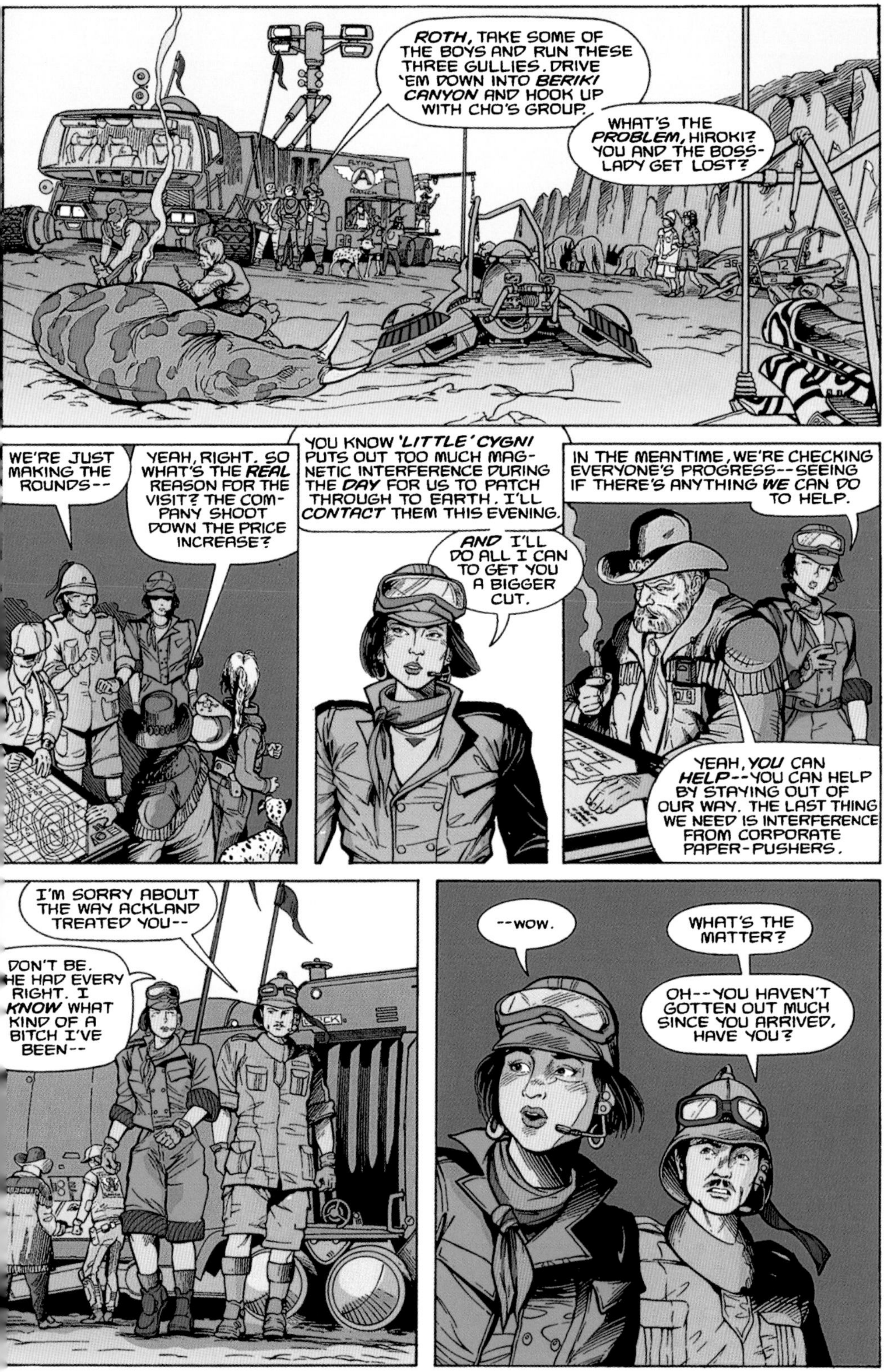

ROTH, TAKE SOME OF THE BOYS AND RUN THESE THREE GULLIES. DRIVE 'EM DOWN INTO BERIKI CANYON AND HOOK UP WITH CHO'S GROUP.
WHAT'S THE PROBLEM, HIROKI? YOU AND THE BOSS-LADY GET LOST?
WE'RE JUST MAKING THE ROUNDS--
YEAH, RIGHT. SO WHAT'S THE REAL REASON FOR THE VISIT? THE COMPANY SHOOT DOWN THE PRICE INCREASE?
YOU KNOW 'LITTLE' CYGNI PUTS OUT TOO MUCH MAGNETIC INTERFERENCE DURING THE DAY FOR US TO PATCH THROUGH TO EARTH. I'LL CONTACT THEM THIS EVENING.
AND I'LL DO ALL I CAN TO GET YOU A BIGGER CUT.
IN THE MEANTIME, WE'RE CHECKING EVERYONE'S PROGRESS--SEEING IF THERE'S ANYTHING WE CAN DO TO HELP.
YEAH, YOU CAN HELP--YOU CAN HELP BY STAYING OUT OF OUR WAY. THE LAST THING WE NEED IS INTERFERENCE FROM CORPORATE PAPER-PUSHERS.
I'M SORRY ABOUT THE WAY ACKLAND TREATED YOU--
DON'T BE. HE HAD EVERY RIGHT. I KNOW WHAT KIND OF A BITCH I'VE BEEN--
--WOW.
WHAT'S THE MATTER?
OH--YOU HAVEN'T GOTTEN OUT MUCH SINCE YOU ARRIVED, HAVE YOU?

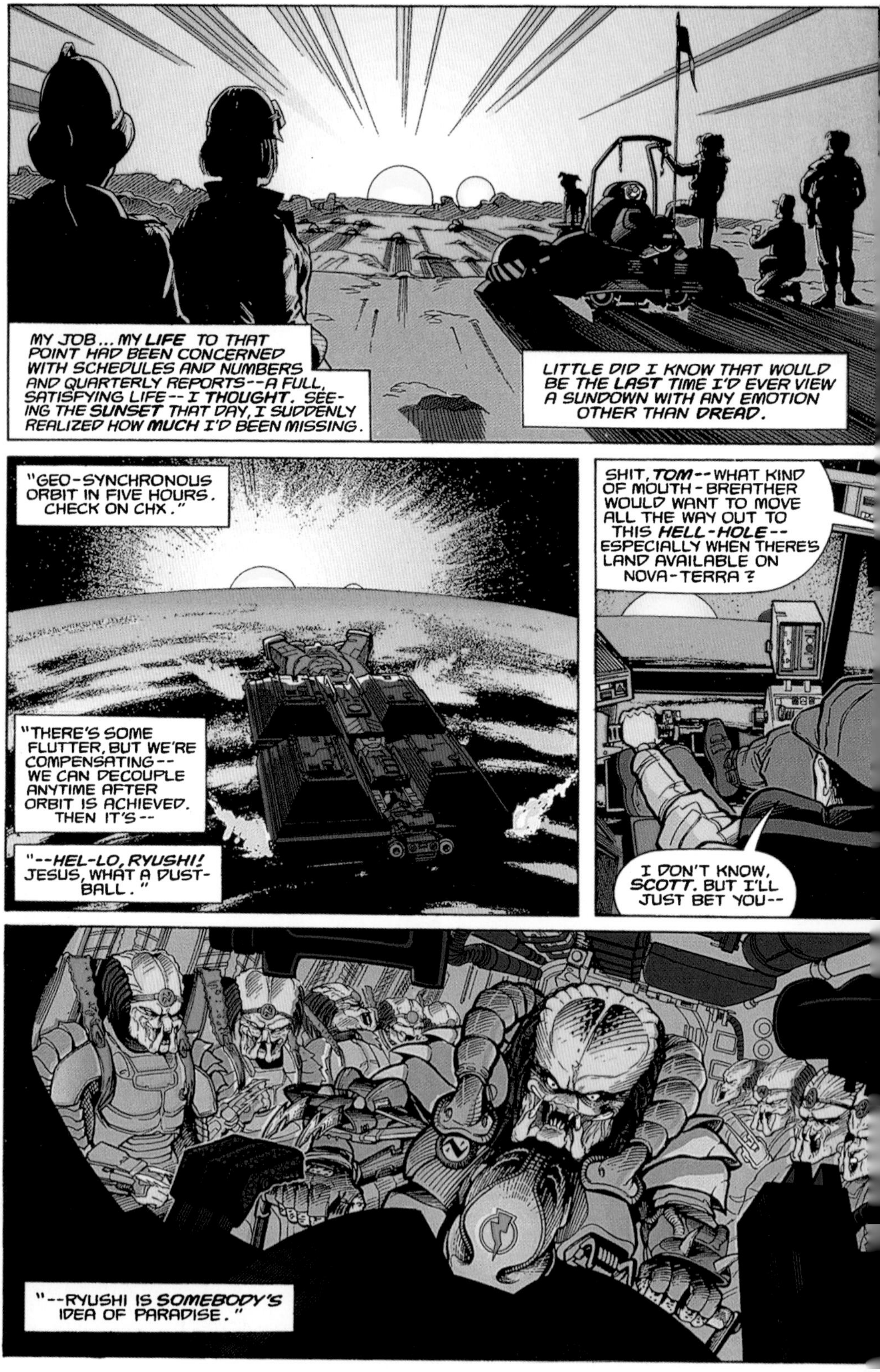
MY JOB... MY LIFE TO THAT POINT HAD BEEN CONCERNED WITH SCHEDULES AND NUMBERS AND QUARTERLY REPORTS--A FULL, SATISFYING LIFE--I THOUGHT. SEEING THE SUNSET THAT DAY, I SUDDENLY REALIZED HOW MUCH I'D BEEN MISSING.
LITTLE DID I KNOW THAT WOULD BE THE LAST TIME I'D EVER VIEW A SUNDOWN WITH ANY EMOTION OTHER THAN DREAD.
"GEO-SYNCHRONOUS ORBIT IN FIVE HOURS. CHECK ON CHX."
"THERE'S SOME FLUTTER, BUT WE'RE COMPENSATING--WE CAN DECOUPLE ANYTIME AFTER ORBIT IS ACHIEVED. THEN IT'S--
"--HEL-LO, RYUSHI! JESUS, WHAT A DUST-BALL."
SHIT, TOM--WHAT KIND OF MOUTH-BREATHER WOULD WANT TO MOVE ALL THE WAY OUT TO THIS HELL-HOLE--ESPECIALLY WHEN THERE'S LAND AVAILABLE ON NOVA-TERRA?
I DON'T KNOW, SCOTT. BUT I'LL JUST BET YOU--
"--RYUSHI IS SOMEBODY'S IDEA OF PARADISE."

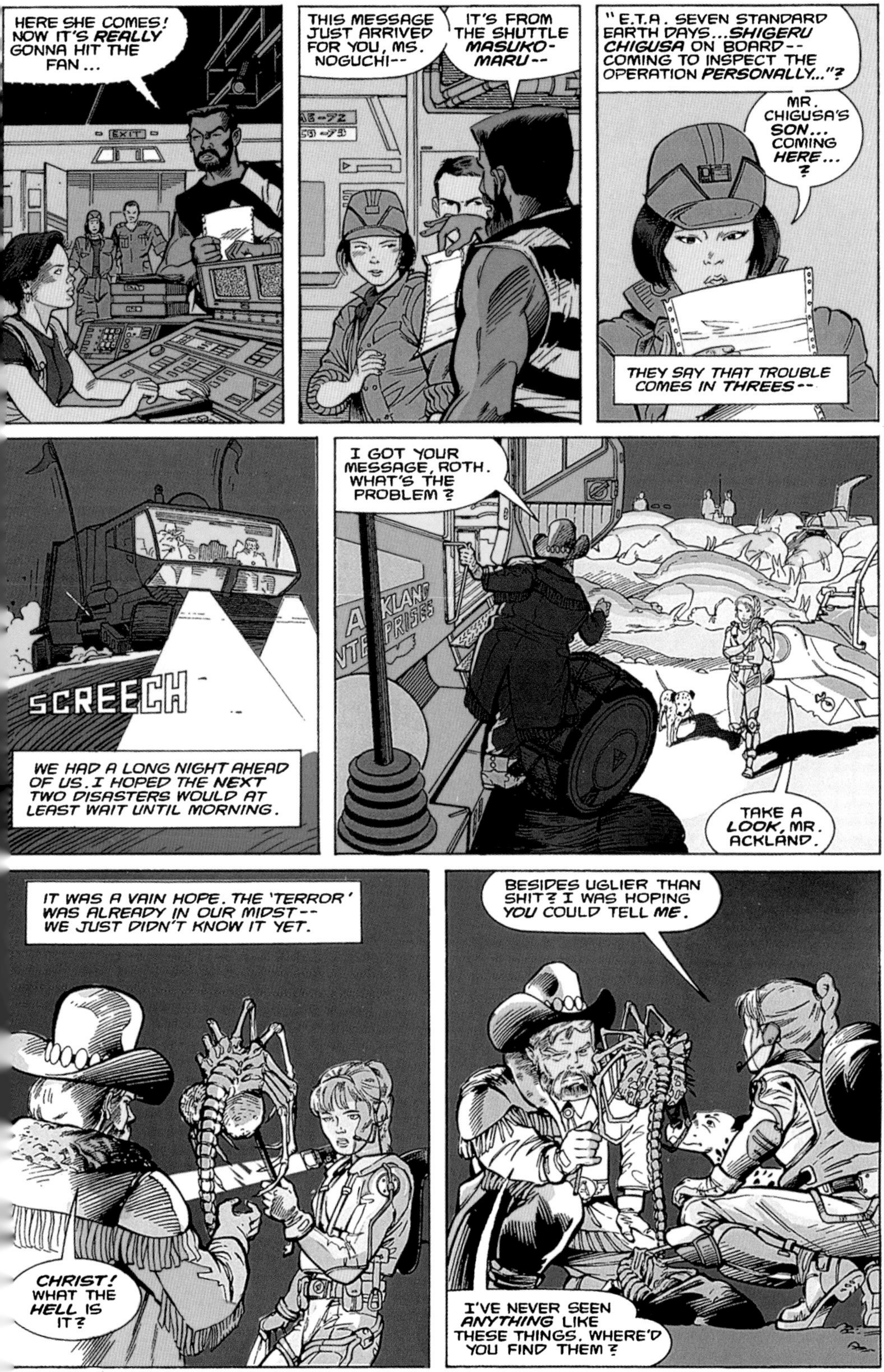
HERE SHE COMES! NOW IT'S REALLY GONNA HIT THE FAN...
EXIT
THIS MESSAGE JUST ARRIVED FOR YOU, MS. NOGUCHI--
IT'S FROM THE SHUTTLE MASUKO-MARU--
"E.T.A. SEVEN STANDARD EARTH DAYS...SHIGERU CHIGUSA ON BOARD--COMING TO INSPECT THE OPERATION PERSONALLY..."?
MR. CHIGUSA'S SON... COMING HERE...?
THEY SAY THAT TROUBLE COMES IN THREES--
SCREECH
WE HAD A LONG NIGHT AHEAD OF US. I HOPED THE NEXT TWO DISASTERS WOULD AT LEAST WAIT UNTIL MORNING.
I GOT YOUR MESSAGE, ROTH. WHAT'S THE PROBLEM?
TAKE A LOOK, MR. ACKLAND.
IT WAS A VAIN HOPE. THE 'TERROR' WAS ALREADY IN OUR MIDST--WE JUST DIDN'T KNOW IT YET.
CHRIST! WHAT THE HELL IS IT?
BESIDES UGLIER THAN SHIT? I WAS HOPING YOU COULD TELL ME.
I'VE NEVER SEEN ANYTHING LIKE THESE THINGS. WHERE'D YOU FIND THEM?

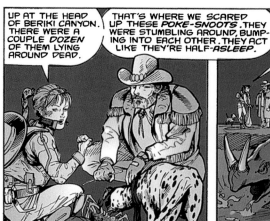

UP AT THE HEAD OF BERIKI CANYON, THERE WERE A COUPLE *DOZEN* OF THEM LYING AROUND DEAD.

THAT'S WHERE WE SCARED UP THESE *POKE-SNOOTS*. THEY WERE STUMBLING AROUND, BUMPING INTO EACH OTHER. THEY ACT LIKE THEY'RE HALF-*ASLEEP*.

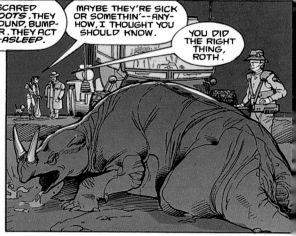

MAYBE THEY'RE SICK OR SOMETHIN'--ANYHOW, I THOUGHT YOU SHOULD KNOW.

YOU DID THE RIGHT THING, ROTH.

LOOK, LET'S NOT SPREAD THIS AROUND, OKAY? WE DON'T *KNOW* THAT THERE'S ANYTHING WRONG WITH THE RHYNTH, AND WE DON'T WANT SOME DICKHEAD FROM THE COMPANY TO PANIC AND *QUARANTINE* THE WHOLE HERD--

WE'VE GOT TOO MUCH RIDING ON THIS. YOU UNDERSTAND?

YEAH, I UNDERSTAND. WHAT SHOULD I DO WITH *THESE*?

"GIVE THEM TO *DR. REVNA*-- BUT TELL HIM YOU FOUND THEM IN *IWA GORGE*. YOU'RE DOING A GREAT JOB, ROTH. THERE'LL BE A *BONUS* FOR YOU WHEN THIS ROUNDUP'S OVER."

IWA GORGE, YOU SAY? I AM NOT FAMILIAR WITH THAT AREA--BUT IT APPEARS I WILL BECOME SO.

GIVE MR. ACKLAND MY THANKS!

WHAT DO YOU MAKE OF IT, KESAR?

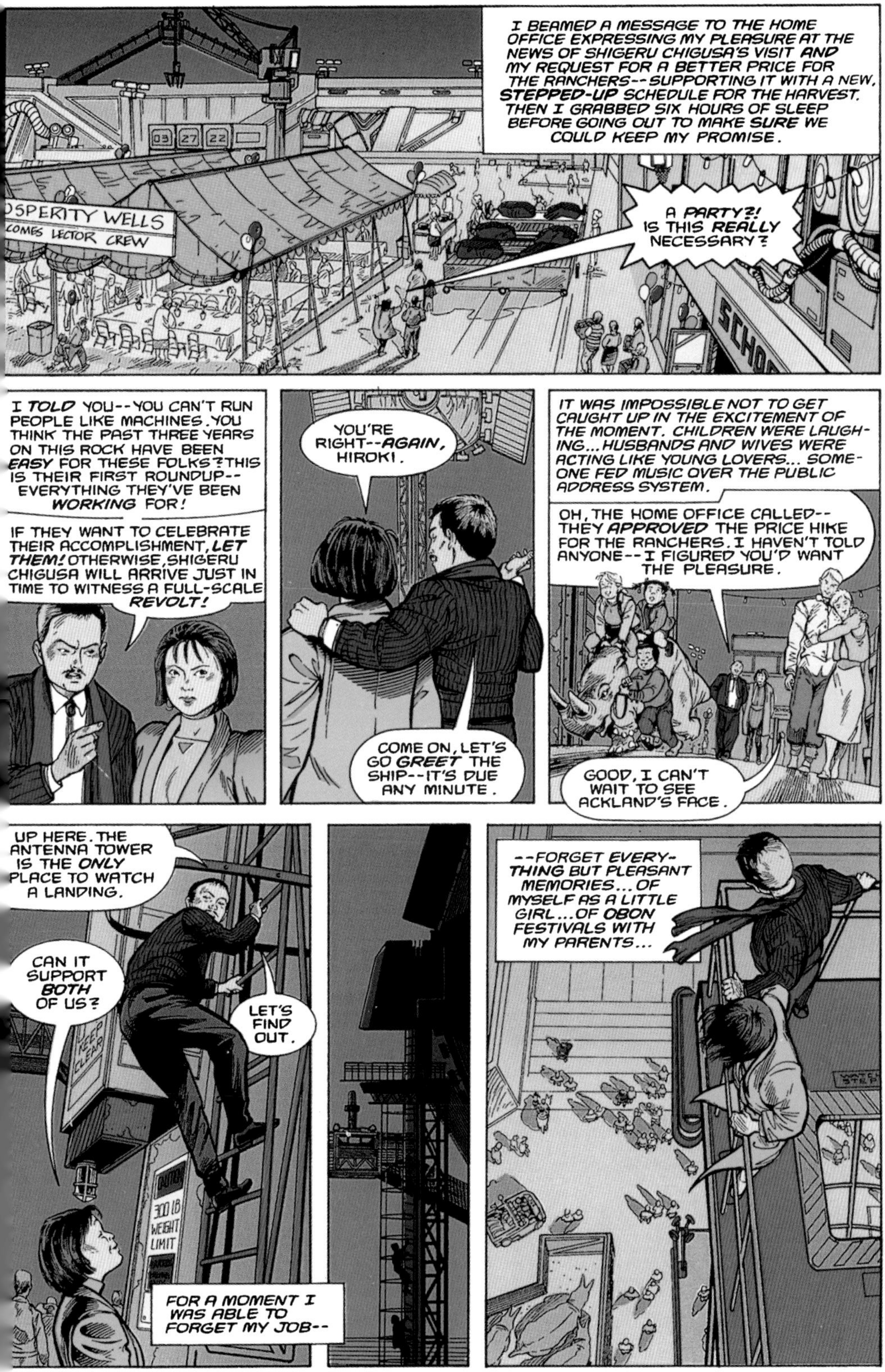
I BEAMED A MESSAGE TO THE HOME OFFICE EXPRESSING MY PLEASURE AT THE NEWS OF SHIGERU CHIGUSA'S VISIT AND MY REQUEST FOR A BETTER PRICE FOR THE RANCHERS--SUPPORTING IT WITH A NEW, STEPPED-UP SCHEDULE FOR THE HARVEST. THEN I GRABBED SIX HOURS OF SLEEP BEFORE GOING OUT TO MAKE SURE WE COULD KEEP MY PROMISE.
03 27 22
OSPERITY WELLS
COMES LECTOR CREW
A PARTY?! IS THIS REALLY NECESSARY?
I TOLD YOU--YOU CAN'T RUN PEOPLE LIKE MACHINES. YOU THINK THE PAST THREE YEARS ON THIS ROCK HAVE BEEN EASY FOR THESE FOLKS? THIS IS THEIR FIRST ROUNDUP-- EVERYTHING THEY'VE BEEN WORKING FOR!
IF THEY WANT TO CELEBRATE THEIR ACCOMPLISHMENT, LET THEM! OTHERWISE, SHIGERU CHIGUSA WILL ARRIVE JUST IN TIME TO WITNESS A FULL-SCALE REVOLT!
YOU'RE RIGHT--AGAIN, HIROKI.
COME ON, LET'S GO GREET THE SHIP--IT'S DUE ANY MINUTE.
IT WAS IMPOSSIBLE NOT TO GET CAUGHT UP IN THE EXCITEMENT OF THE MOMENT. CHILDREN WERE LAUGHING... HUSBANDS AND WIVES WERE ACTING LIKE YOUNG LOVERS... SOMEONE FED MUSIC OVER THE PUBLIC ADDRESS SYSTEM.
OH, THE HOME OFFICE CALLED-- THEY APPROVED THE PRICE HIKE FOR THE RANCHERS. I HAVEN'T TOLD ANYONE--I FIGURED YOU'D WANT THE PLEASURE.
GOOD, I CAN'T WAIT TO SEE ACKLAND'S FACE.
UP HERE. THE ANTENNA TOWER IS THE ONLY PLACE TO WATCH A LANDING.
CAN IT SUPPORT BOTH OF US?
LET'S FIND OUT.
KEEP CLEAR
300 LB WEIGHT LIMIT
FOR A MOMENT I WAS ABLE TO FORGET MY JOB--
--FORGET EVERYTHING BUT PLEASANT MEMORIES... OF MYSELF AS A LITTLE GIRL... OF OBON FESTIVALS WITH MY PARENTS...

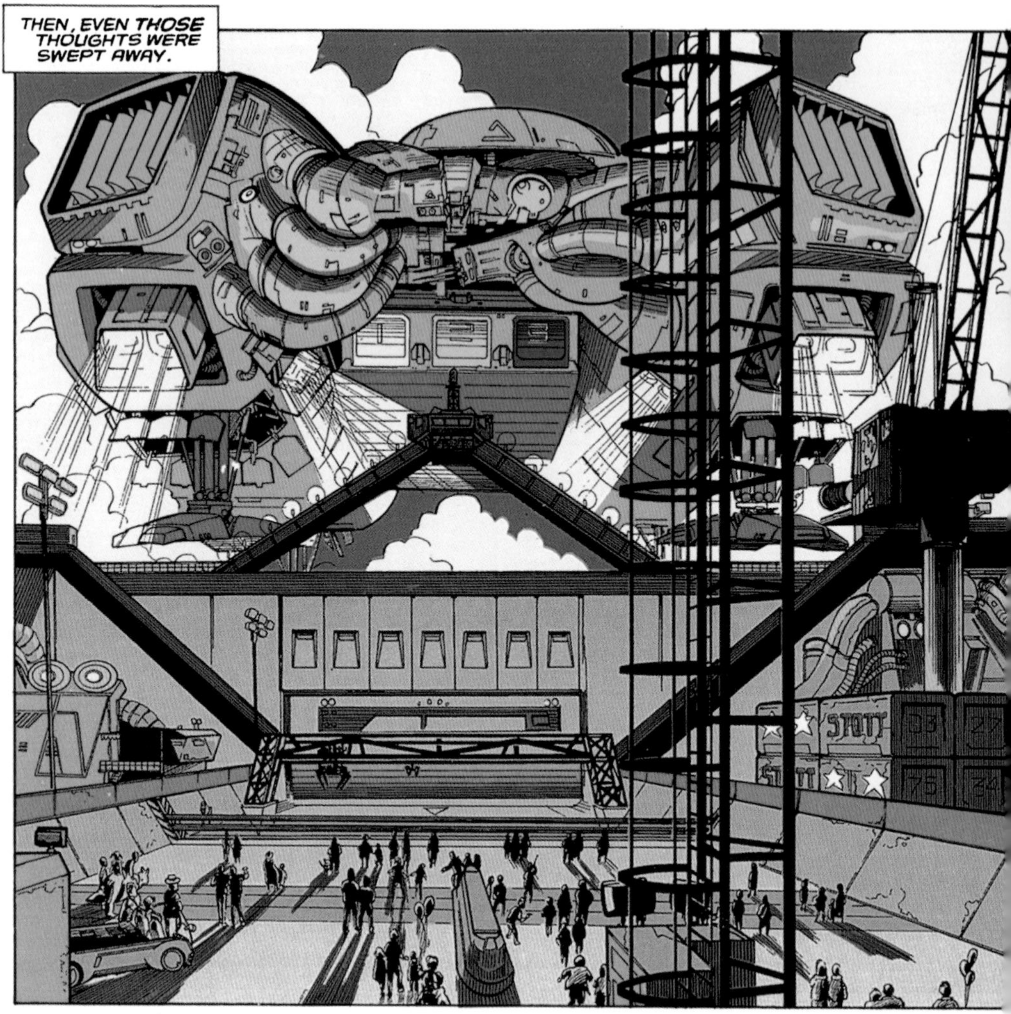
THEN, EVEN THOSE THOUGHTS WERE SWEPT AWAY.
STOTT
STOTT
33
27
75
34

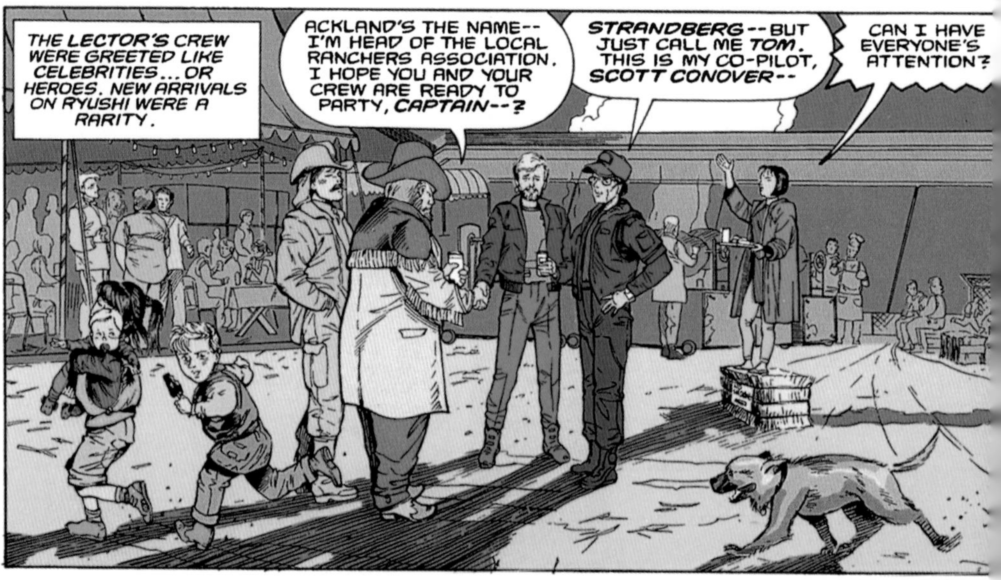
THE LECTOR'S CREW WERE GREETED LIKE CELEBRITIES... OR HEROES. NEW ARRIVALS ON RYUSHI WERE A RARITY.
ACKLAND'S THE NAME-- I'M HEAD OF THE LOCAL RANCHERS ASSOCIATION. I HOPE YOU AND YOUR CREW ARE READY TO PARTY, CAPTAIN--?
STRANDBERG--BUT JUST CALL ME TOM. THIS IS MY CO-PILOT, SCOTT CONOVER--
CAN I HAVE EVERYONE'S ATTENTION?

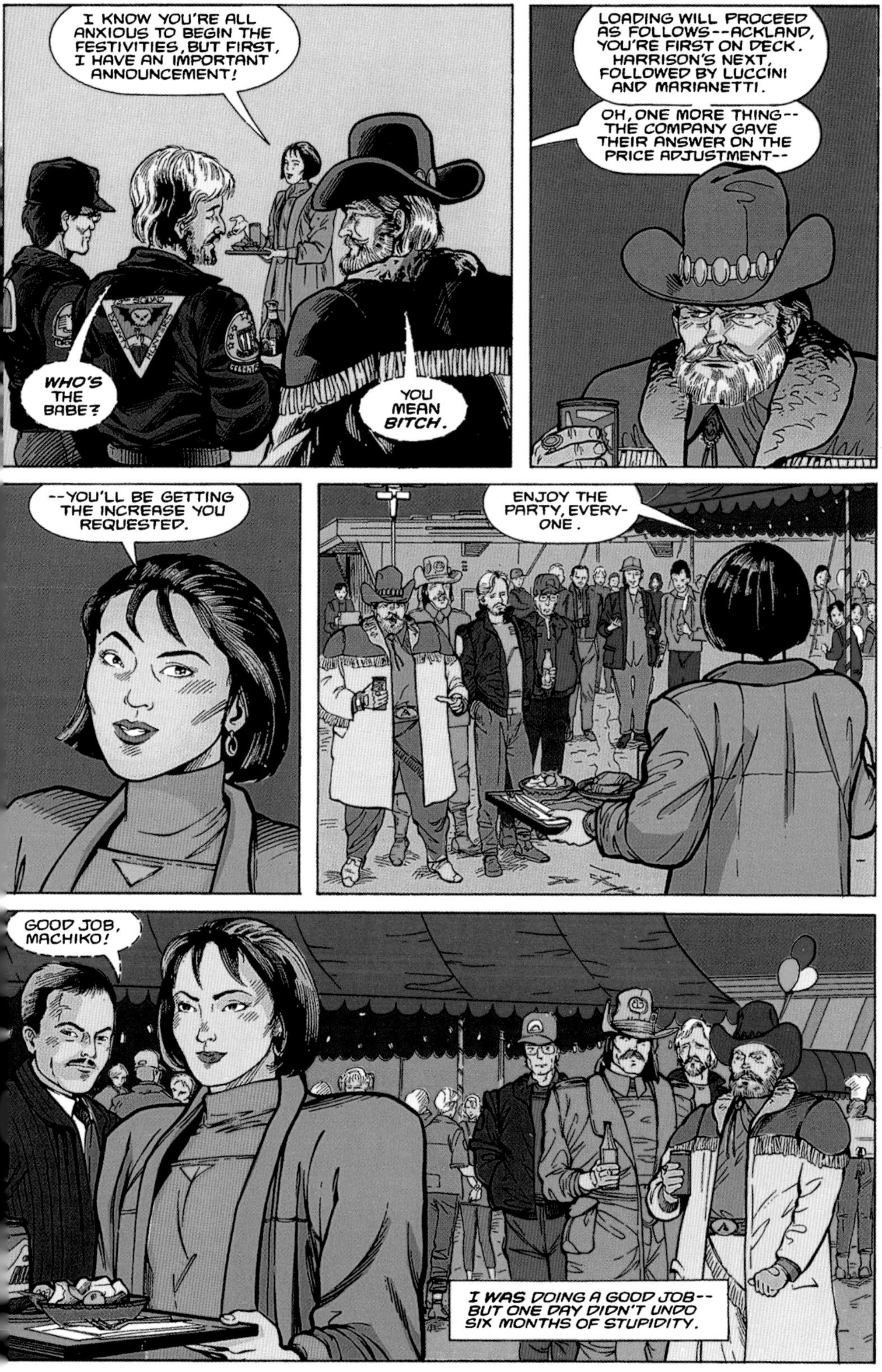

I KNOW YOU'RE ALL ANXIOUS TO BEGIN THE FESTIVITIES, BUT FIRST, I HAVE AN IMPORTANT ANNOUNCEMENT!
WHO'S THE BABE?
YOU MEAN BITCH.
LOADING WILL PROCEED AS FOLLOWS--ACKLAND, YOU'RE FIRST ON DECK. HARRISON'S NEXT, FOLLOWED BY LUCCINI AND MARIANETTI.
OH, ONE MORE THING--THE COMPANY GAVE THEIR ANSWER ON THE PRICE ADJUSTMENT--
--YOU'LL BE GETTING THE INCREASE YOU REQUESTED.
ENJOY THE PARTY, EVERY-ONE.
GOOD JOB, MACHIKO!
I WAS DOING A GOOD JOB--BUT ONE DAY DIDN'T UNDO SIX MONTHS OF STUPIDITY.

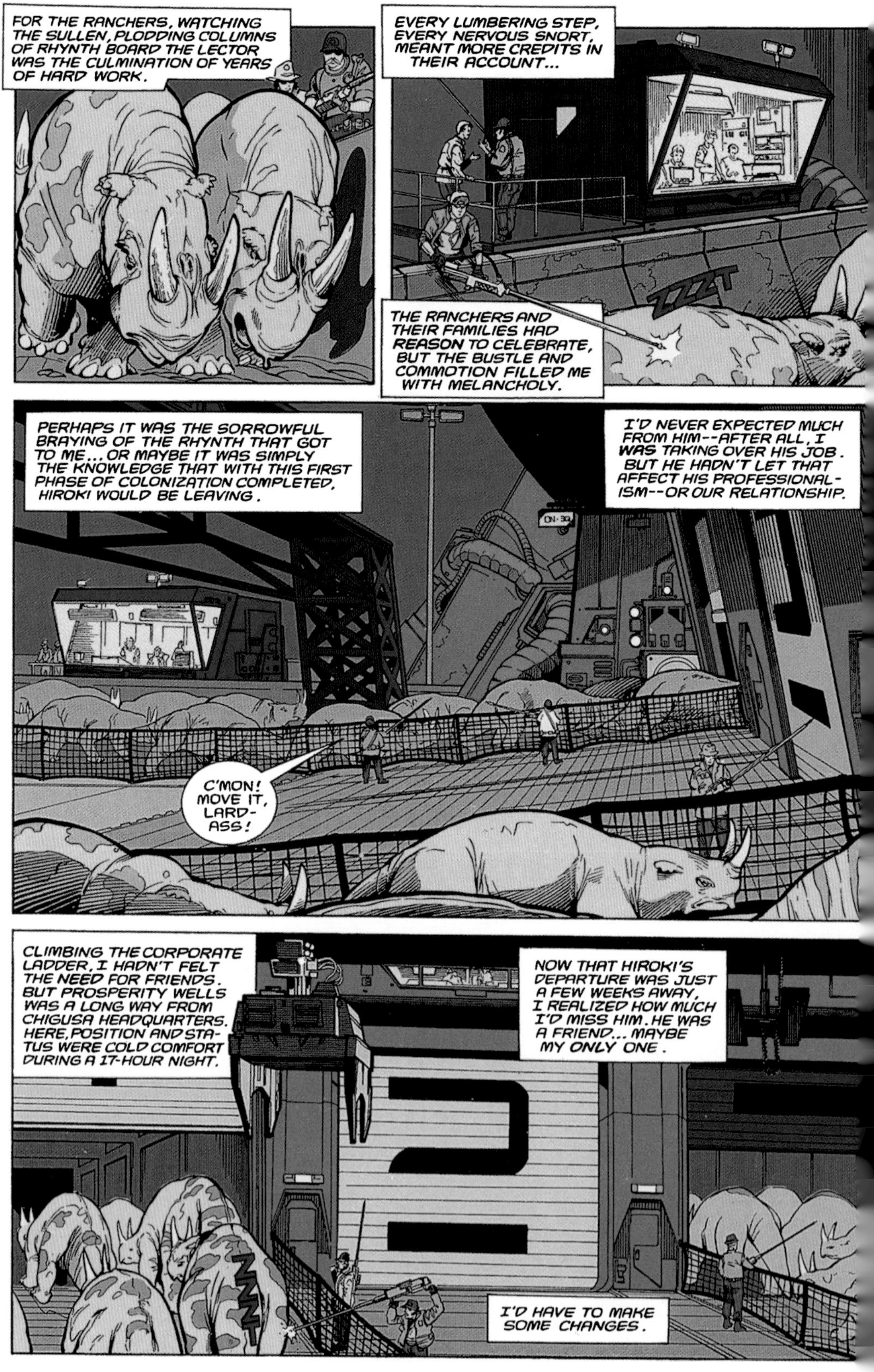
FOR THE RANCHERS, WATCHING THE SULLEN, PLODDING COLUMNS OF RHYNTH BOARD THE LECTOR WAS THE CULMINATION OF YEARS OF HARD WORK.
EVERY LUMBERING STEP, EVERY NERVOUS SNORT, MEANT MORE CREDITS IN THEIR ACCOUNT...
ZZZT
THE RANCHERS AND THEIR FAMILIES HAD REASON TO CELEBRATE, BUT THE BUSTLE AND COMMOTION FILLED ME WITH MELANCHOLY.
PERHAPS IT WAS THE SORROWFUL BRAYING OF THE RHYNTH THAT GOT TO ME... OR MAYBE IT WAS SIMPLY THE KNOWLEDGE THAT WITH THIS FIRST PHASE OF COLONIZATION COMPLETED, HIROKI WOULD BE LEAVING.
I'D NEVER EXPECTED MUCH FROM HIM--AFTER ALL, I WAS TAKING OVER HIS JOB. BUT HE HADN'T LET THAT AFFECT HIS PROFESSIONAL-ISM--OR OUR RELATIONSHIP.
C'MON! MOVE IT, LARD-ASS!
CLIMBING THE CORPORATE LADDER, I HADN'T FELT THE NEED FOR FRIENDS. BUT PROSPERITY WELLS WAS A LONG WAY FROM CHIGUSA HEADQUARTERS. HERE, POSITION AND STATUS WERE COLD COMFORT DURING A 17-HOUR NIGHT.
NOW THAT HIROKI'S DEPARTURE WAS JUST A FEW WEEKS AWAY, I REALIZED HOW MUCH I'D MISS HIM. HE WAS A FRIEND... MAYBE MY ONLY ONE.
NNNT
I'D HAVE TO MAKE SOME CHANGES.

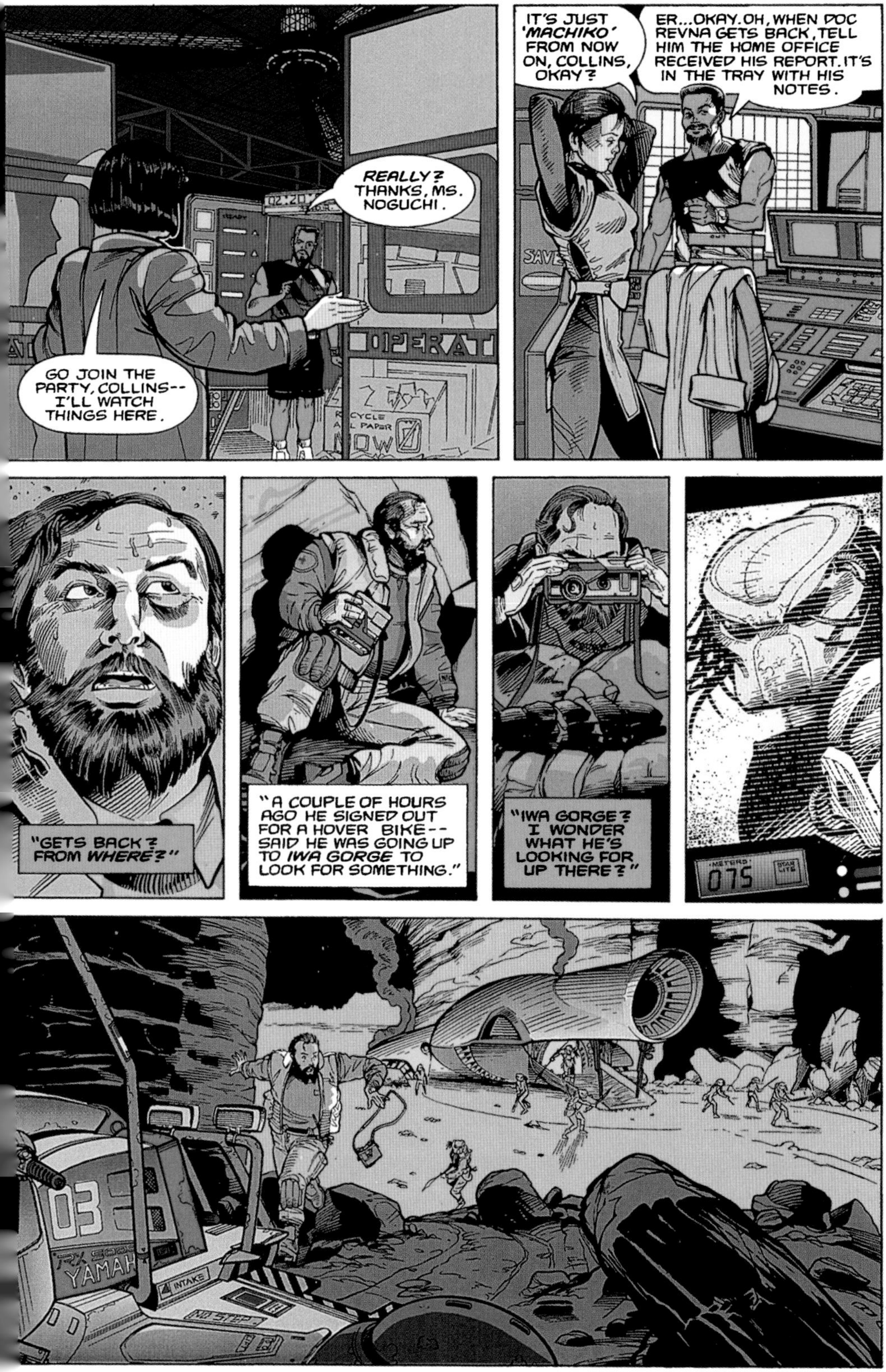

GO JOIN THE PARTY, COLLINS-- I'LL WATCH THINGS HERE.
REALLY? THANKS, MS. NOGUCHI.
OPERAT
RECYCLE ALL PAPER NOW
SAVE
IT'S JUST 'MACHIKO' FROM NOW ON, COLLINS, OKAY?
ER...OKAY. OH, WHEN DOC REVNA GETS BACK, TELL HIM THE HOME OFFICE RECEIVED HIS REPORT. IT'S IN THE TRAY WITH HIS NOTES.
"GETS BACK? FROM WHERE?"
"A COUPLE OF HOURS AGO HE SIGNED OUT FOR A HOVER BIKE-- SAID HE WAS GOING UP TO IWA GORGE TO LOOK FOR SOMETHING."
"IWA GORGE? I WONDER WHAT HE'S LOOKING FOR UP THERE?"
075
03
YAMAH
INTAKE
NO STEP

I SCANNED THE REPORT REVNA HAD BEAMED TO EARTH. MOST OF IT WENT BEYOND THE BASIC XT-BIOLOGY COURSES I HAD IN SCHOOL--

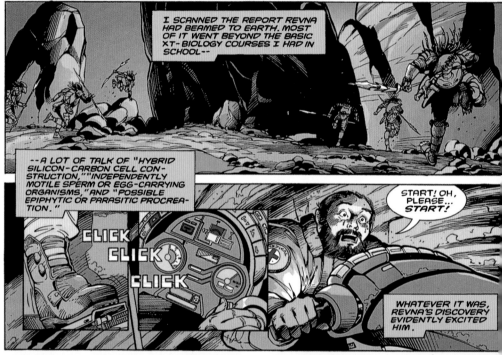

--A LOT OF TALK OF "HYBRID SILICON-CARBON CELL CONSTRUCTION," "INDEPENDENTLY MOTILE SPERM OR EGG-CARRYING ORGANISMS," AND "POSSIBLE EPIPHYTIC OR PARASITIC PROCREATION."

CLICK
CLICK
CLICK

START! OH, PLEASE... START!

WHATEVER IT WAS, REVNA'S DISCOVERY EVIDENTLY EXCITED HIM.

CLIC...

VA-ROOM

WHOOSH

52

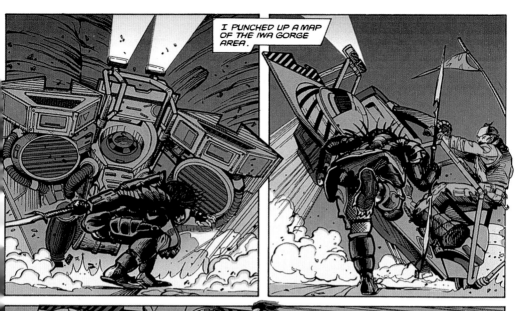

I PUNCHED UP A MAP OF THE IWA GORGE AREA.

SLAM

THUD

NOTHING BUT ROCKS AND SAND...

ROAR

...AND A MAZE OF NARROW GULLIES AND BOX CANYONS.

IT SEEMED AN UNLIKELY PLACE TO LOOK FOR ANYTHING--

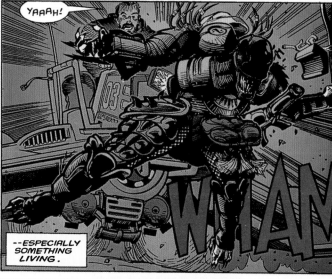

YAAAH!

--ESPECIALLY SOMETHING LIVING.

WHAM

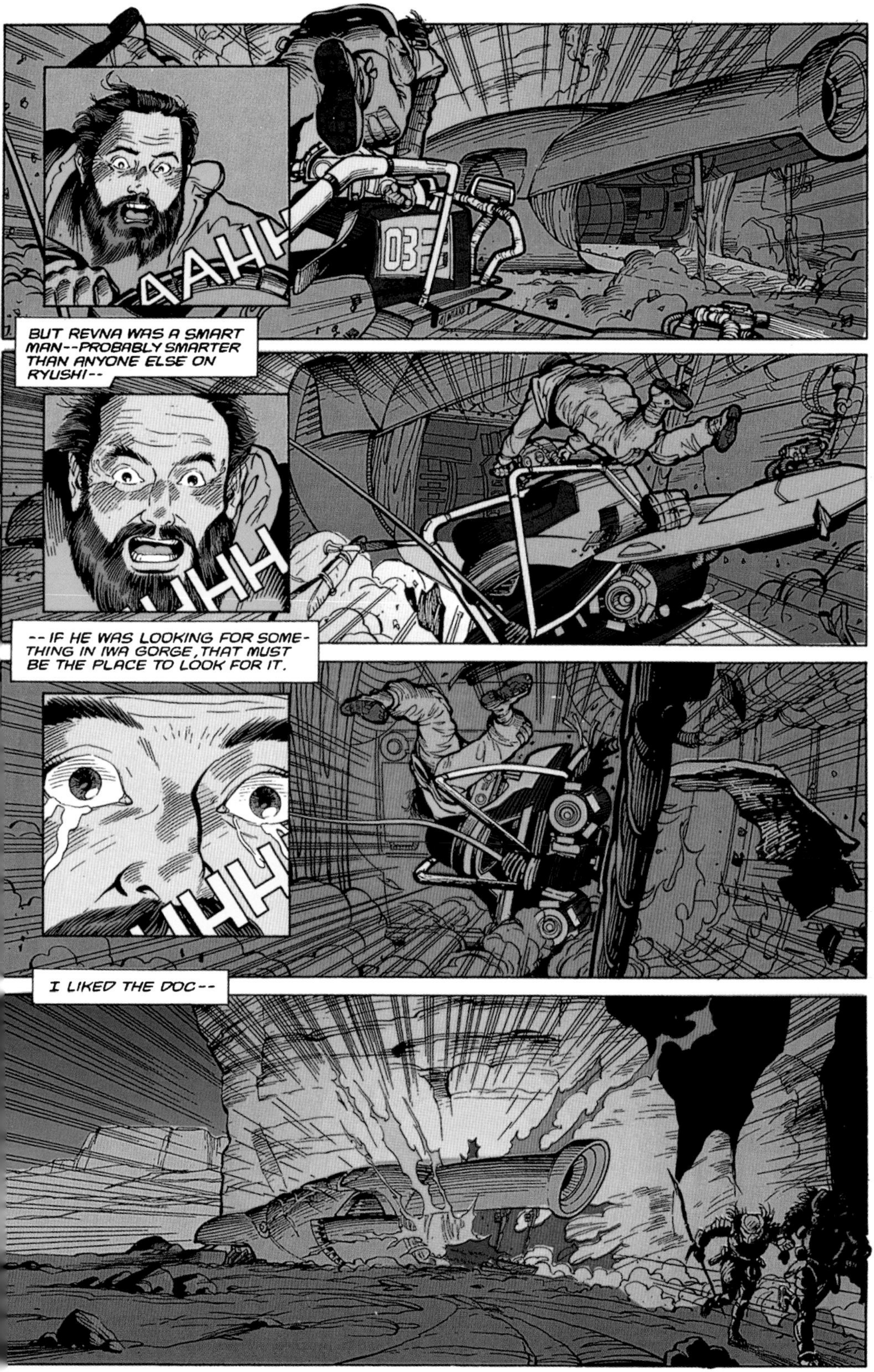
AAHH
BUT REVNA WAS A SMART MAN--PROBABLY SMARTER THAN ANYONE ELSE ON RYUSHI--
--IF HE WAS LOOKING FOR SOMETHING IN IWA GORGE, THAT MUST BE THE PLACE TO LOOK FOR IT.
I LIKED THE DOC--

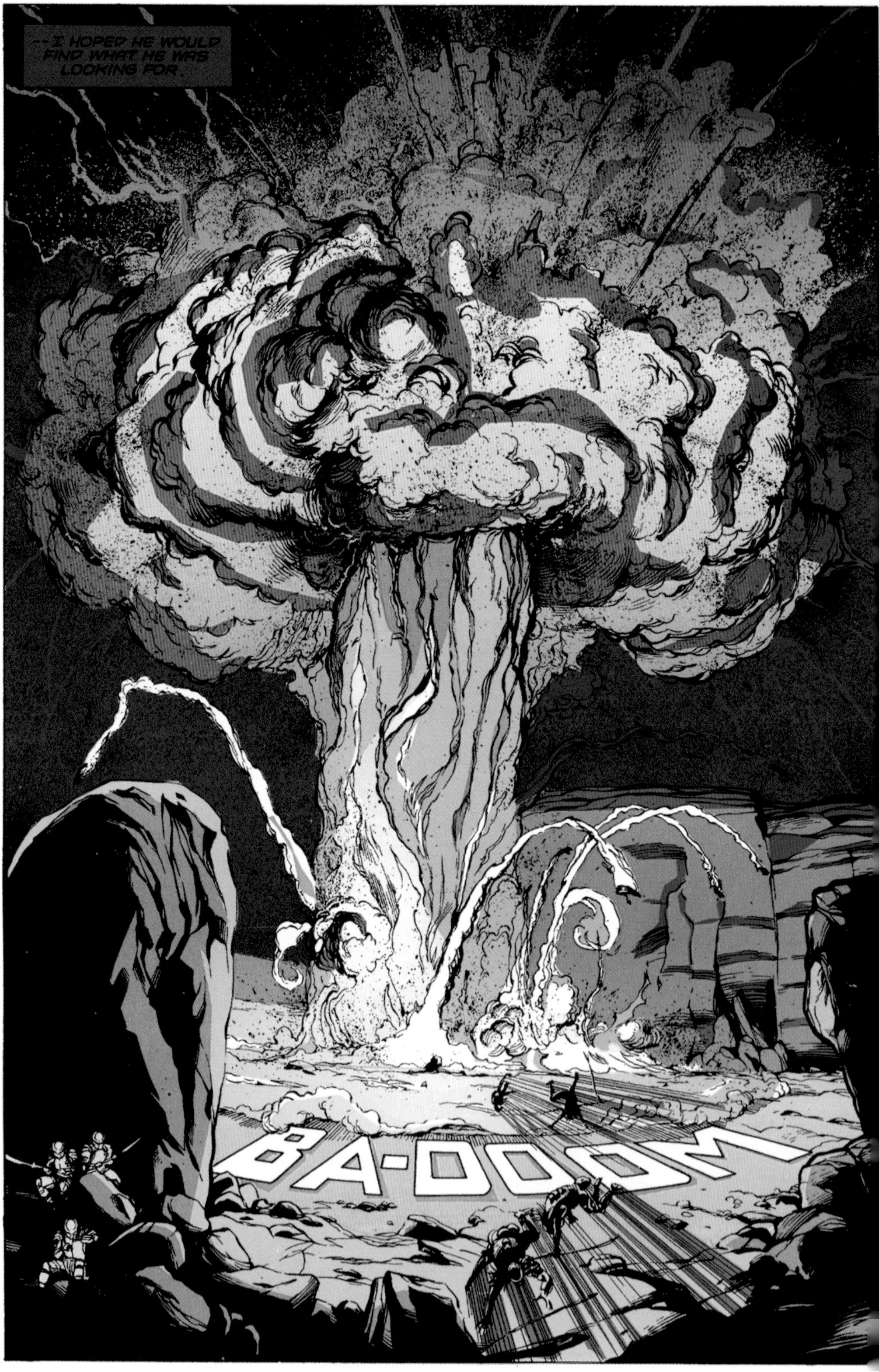
--I HOPED HE WOULD FIND WHAT HE WAS LOOKING FOR.
BA-DOOM

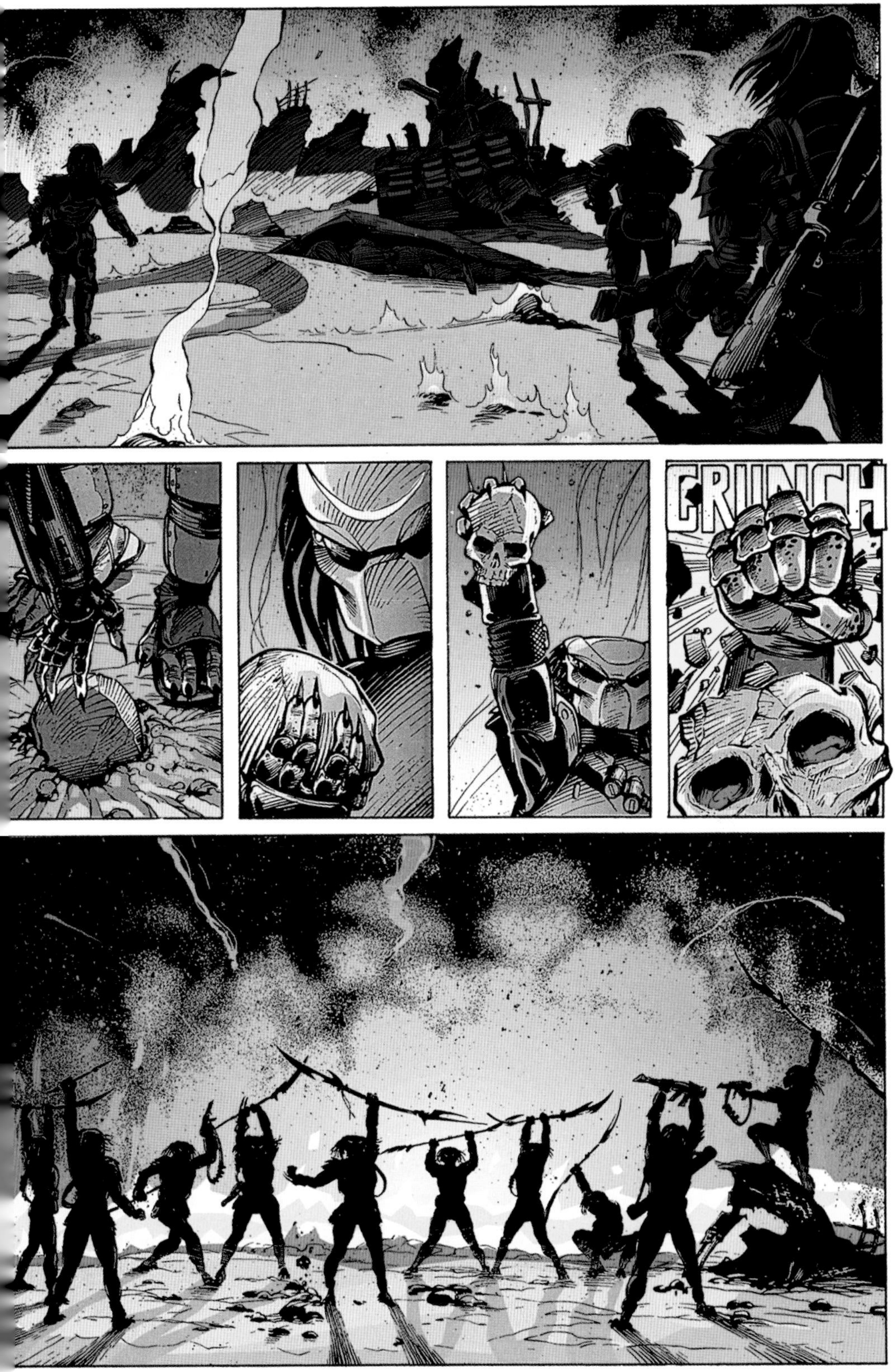
CRUNCH

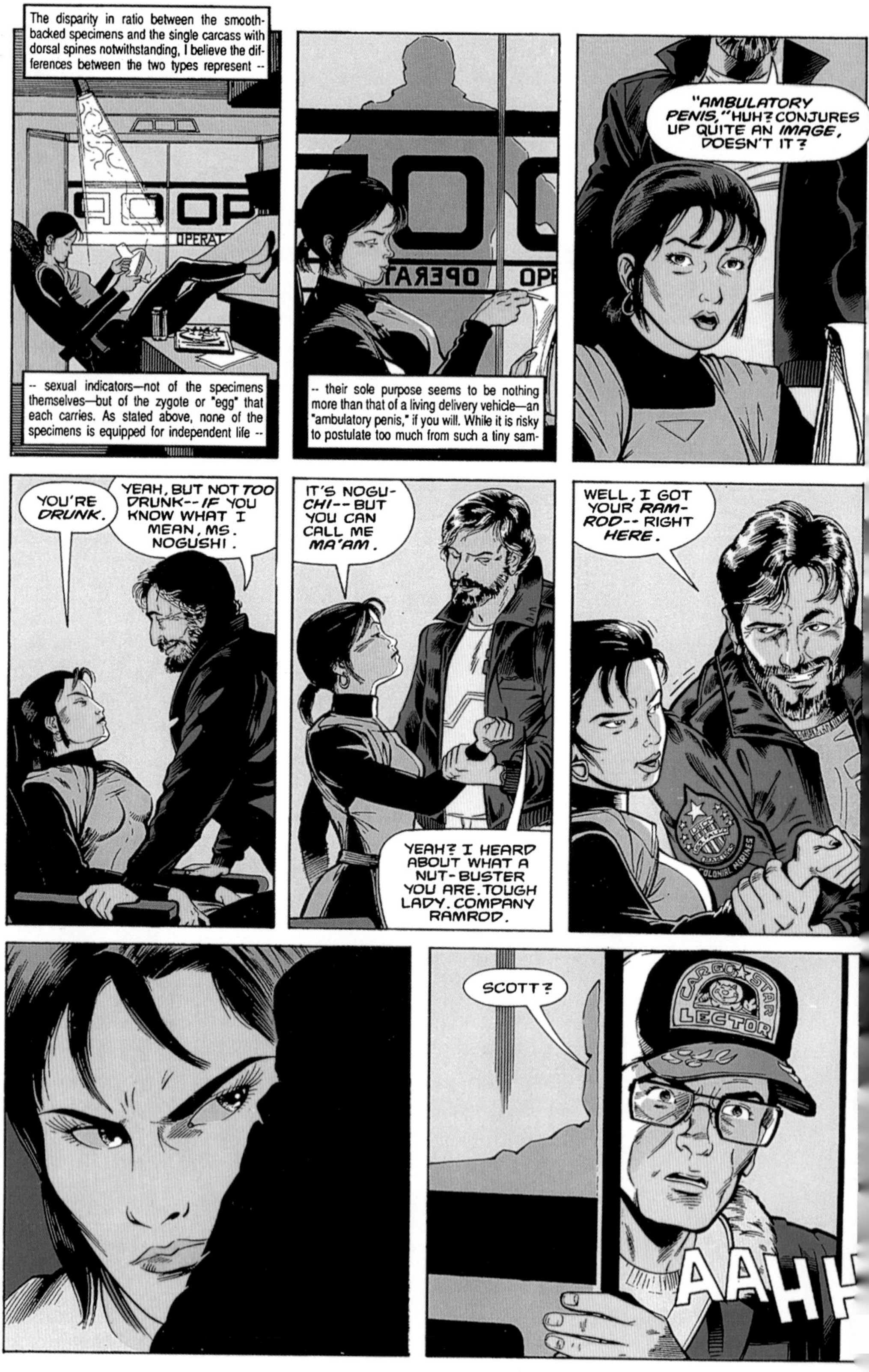
The disparity in ratio between the smooth-backed specimens and the single carcass with dorsal spines notwithstanding, I believe the differences between the two types represent --
-- sexual indicators—not of the specimens themselves—but of the zygote or "egg" that each carries. As stated above, none of the specimens is equipped for independent life --
-- their sole purpose seems to be nothing more than that of a living delivery vehicle—an "ambulatory penis," if you will. While it is risky to postulate too much from such a tiny sam-
"AMBULATORY PENIS," HUH? CONJURES UP QUITE AN IMAGE, DOESN'T IT?
YOU'RE DRUNK.
YEAH, BUT NOT TOO DRUNK-- IF YOU KNOW WHAT I MEAN, MS. NOGUSHI.
IT'S NOGU-CHI-- BUT YOU CAN CALL ME MA'AM.
YEAH? I HEARD ABOUT WHAT A NUT-BUSTER YOU ARE. TOUGH LADY. COMPANY RAMROD.
WELL, I GOT YOUR RAM-ROD-- RIGHT HERE.
COLONIAL MARINES
SCOTT?
CARGO STAR
LECTOR
AAHH

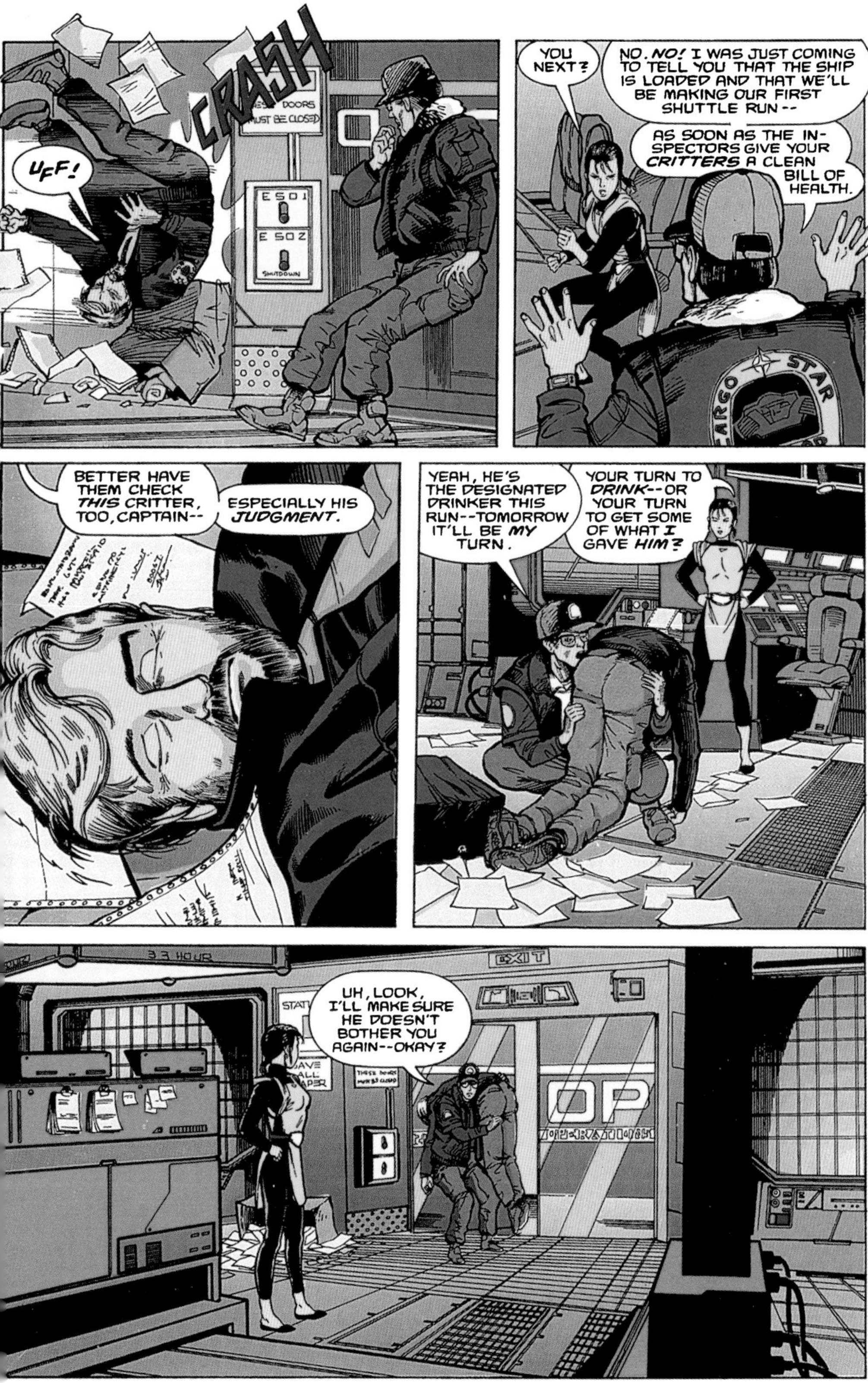
CRASH
THESE DOORS MUST BE CLOSED
UFF!
E S O 1
E S O 2
SHUTDOWN
YOU NEXT?
NO. NO! I WAS JUST COMING TO TELL YOU THAT THE SHIP IS LOADED AND THAT WE'LL BE MAKING OUR FIRST SHUTTLE RUN--
AS SOON AS THE INSPECTORS GIVE YOUR CRITTERS A CLEAN BILL OF HEALTH.
STAR
BETTER HAVE THEM CHECK THIS CRITTER, TOO, CAPTAIN--
ESPECIALLY HIS JUDGMENT.
YEAH, HE'S THE DESIGNATED DRINKER THIS RUN--TOMORROW IT'LL BE MY TURN.
YOUR TURN TO DRINK--OR YOUR TURN TO GET SOME OF WHAT I GAVE HIM?
EXIT
UH, LOOK, I'LL MAKE SURE HE DOESN'T BOTHER YOU AGAIN--OKAY?
THESE DOORS MUST BE CLOSED
OP

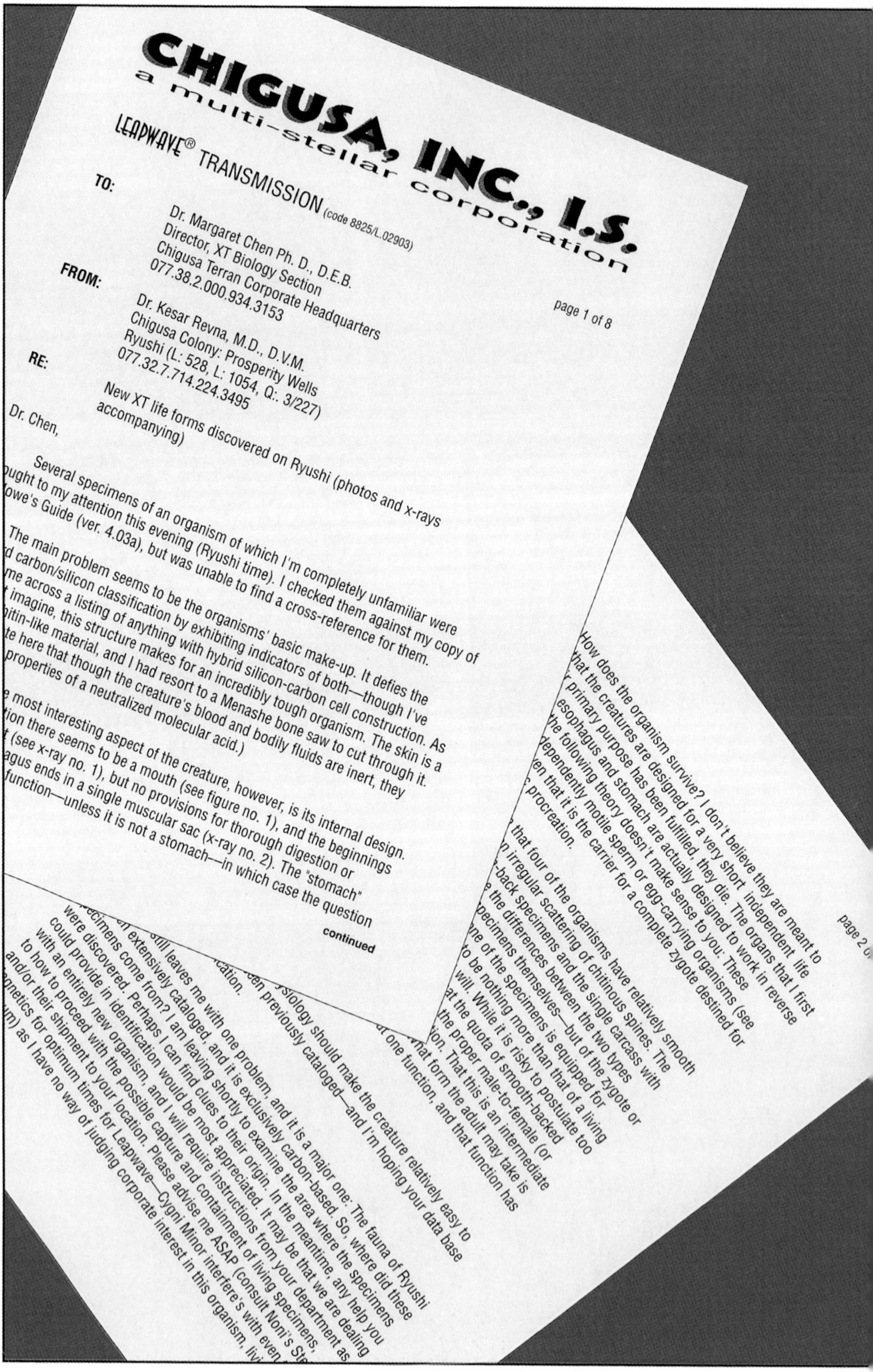

CHIGUSA, INC., I.S.
a multi-stellar corporation

LEAPWAVE® TRANSMISSION (code 8825/L.02903)

page 1 of 8

TO: Dr. Margaret Chen Ph. D., D.E.B.
Director, XT Biology Section
Chigusa Terran Corporate Headquarters
077.38.2.000.934.3153

FROM: Dr. Kesar Revna, M.D., D.V.M.
Chigusa Colony: Prosperity Wells
Ryushi (L: 528, L: 1054, Q:. 3/227)
077.32.7.714.224.3495

RE: New XT life forms discovered on Ryushi (photos and x-rays accompanying)

Dr. Chen,

Several specimens of an organism of which I'm completely unfamiliar were ought to my attention this evening (Ryushi time). I checked them against my copy of owe's Guide (ver. 4.03a), but was unable to find a cross-reference for them.

The main problem seems to be the organisms' basic make-up. It defies the d carbon/silicon classification by exhibiting indicators of both—though I've me across a listing of anything with hybrid silicon-carbon cell construction. As imagine, this structure makes for an incredibly tough organism. The skin is a itin-like material, and I had resort to a Menashe bone saw to cut through it. te here that though the creature's blood and bodily fluids are inert, they properties of a neutralized molecular acid.)

e most interesting aspect of the creature, however, is its internal design. tion there seems to be a mouth (see figure no. 1), and the beginnings t (see x-ray no. 1), but no provisions for thorough digestion or agus ends in a single muscular sac (x-ray no. 2). The "stomach" function—unless it is not a stomach—in which case the question

continued

How does the organism survive? I don't believe they are meant to
that the creatures are designed for a very short independent life
r primary purpose has been fulfilled, they die. The organs that I first
esophagus and stomach are actually designed to work in reverse
the following theory doesn't make sense to you: These
dependently motile sperm or egg-carrying organisms (see
en that it is the carrier for a complete zygote destined for
procreation.

that four of the organisms have relatively smooth
n irregular scattering of chitinous spines. The
-back specimens and the single carcass with
e the differences between the two types
e specimens themselves—but of the zygote or
ne of the specimens is equipped for
to be nothing more than that of a living
will. While it is risky to postulate too
at the quota of smooth-backed
the proper male-to-female (or
on. That this is an intermediate
hat form the adult may take is
t one function, and that function has

page 2 o

ysiology should make the creature relatively easy to
en previously cataloged—and I'm hoping your data base
ation.

still leaves me with one problem, and it is a major one: The fauna of Ryushi
n extensively cataloged, and it is exclusively carbon-based. So, where did these
ecimens come from? I am leaving shortly to examine the area where the specimens
were discovered. Perhaps I can find clues to their origin. In the meantime, any help you
could provide in identification would be most appreciated. It may be that we are dealing
with an entirely new organism, and I will require instructions from your department as
to how to proceed with the possible capture and containment of living specimens,
and/or their shipment to your location. Please advise me ASAP (consult Noni's Ste
netics for optimum times for Leapwave—Cygni Minor interfere's with even
m) as I have no way of judging corporate interest in this organism, livi

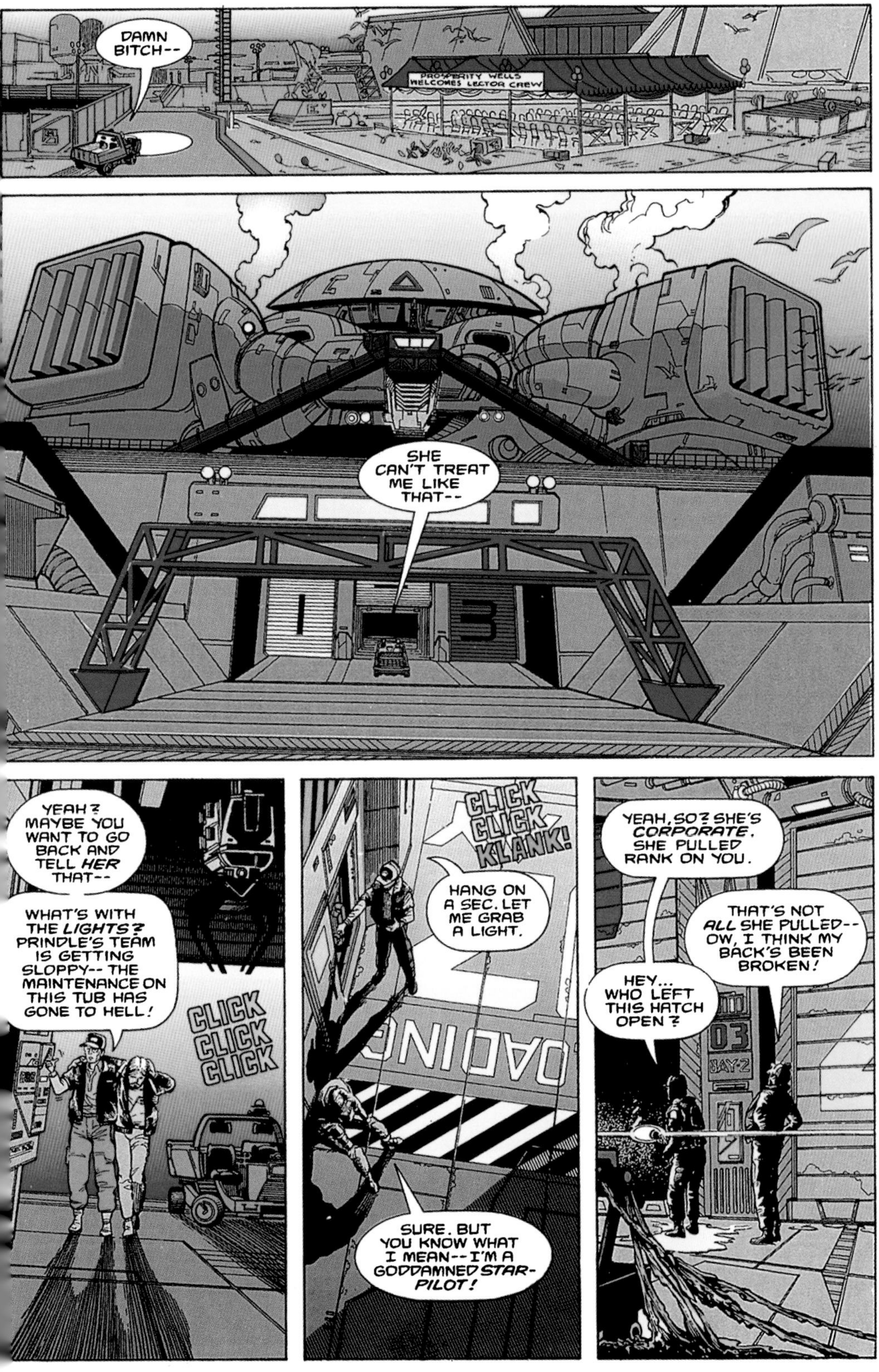
DAMN BITCH--
PROSPERITY WELLS WELCOMES LECTOR CREW
SHE CAN'T TREAT ME LIKE THAT--
YEAH? MAYBE YOU WANT TO GO BACK AND TELL *HER* THAT--
WHAT'S WITH THE *LIGHTS?* PRINDLE'S TEAM IS GETTING SLOPPY-- THE MAINTENANCE ON THIS TUB HAS GONE TO HELL!
CLICK CLICK CLICK
CLICK CLICK KLANK!
HANG ON A SEC. LET ME GRAB A LIGHT.
SURE. BUT YOU KNOW WHAT I MEAN--I'M A GODDAMNED *STAR-PILOT!*
YEAH, SO? SHE'S *CORPORATE.* SHE PULLED RANK ON YOU.
THAT'S NOT *ALL* SHE PULLED-- OW, I THINK MY BACK'S BEEN BROKEN!
HEY... WHO LEFT THIS HATCH OPEN?
03
BAY-2

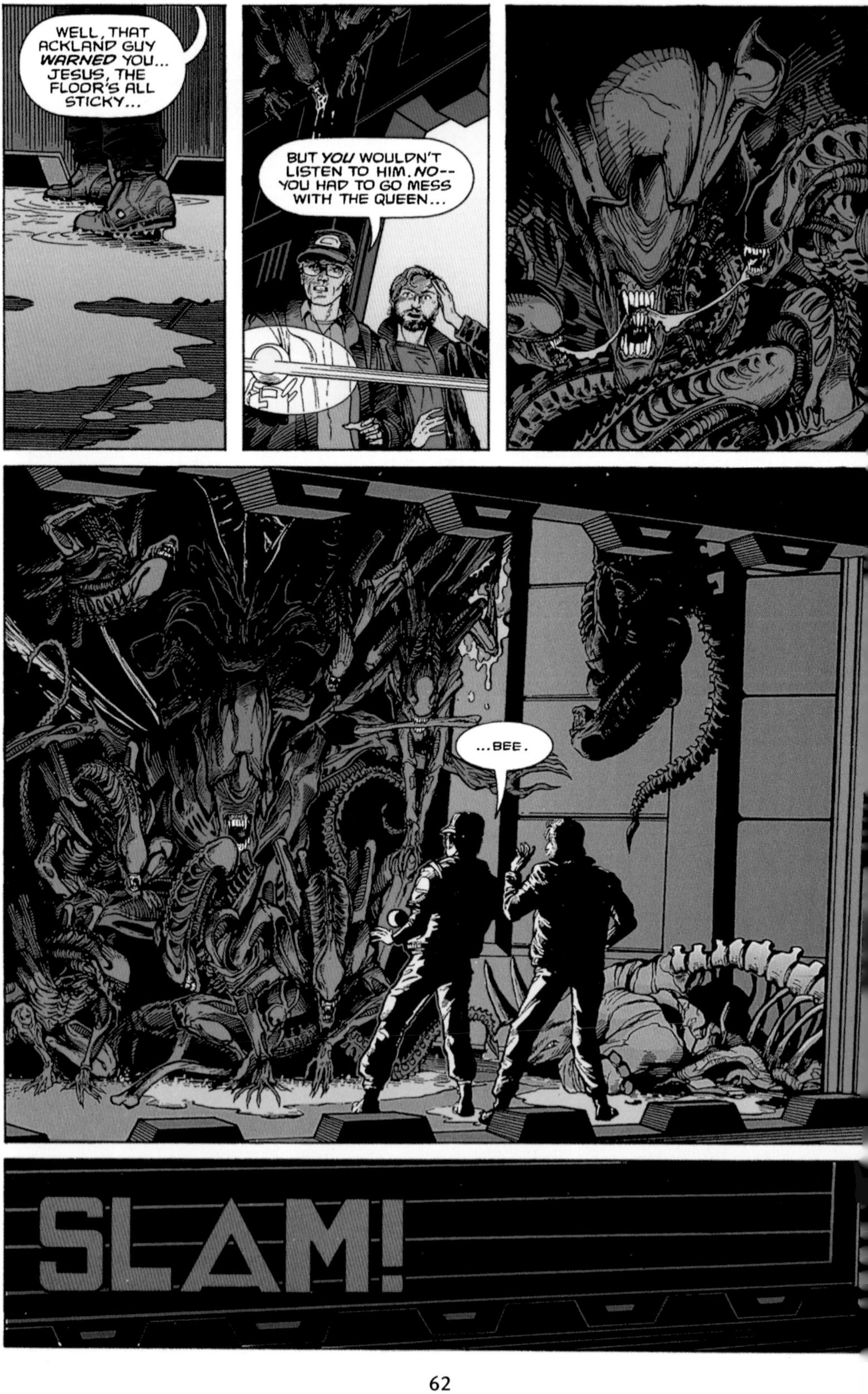
WELL, THAT ACKLAND GUY WARNED YOU... JESUS, THE FLOOR'S ALL STICKY...
BUT YOU WOULDN'T LISTEN TO HIM. NO-- YOU HAD TO GO MESS WITH THE QUEEN...
...BEE.
SLAM!

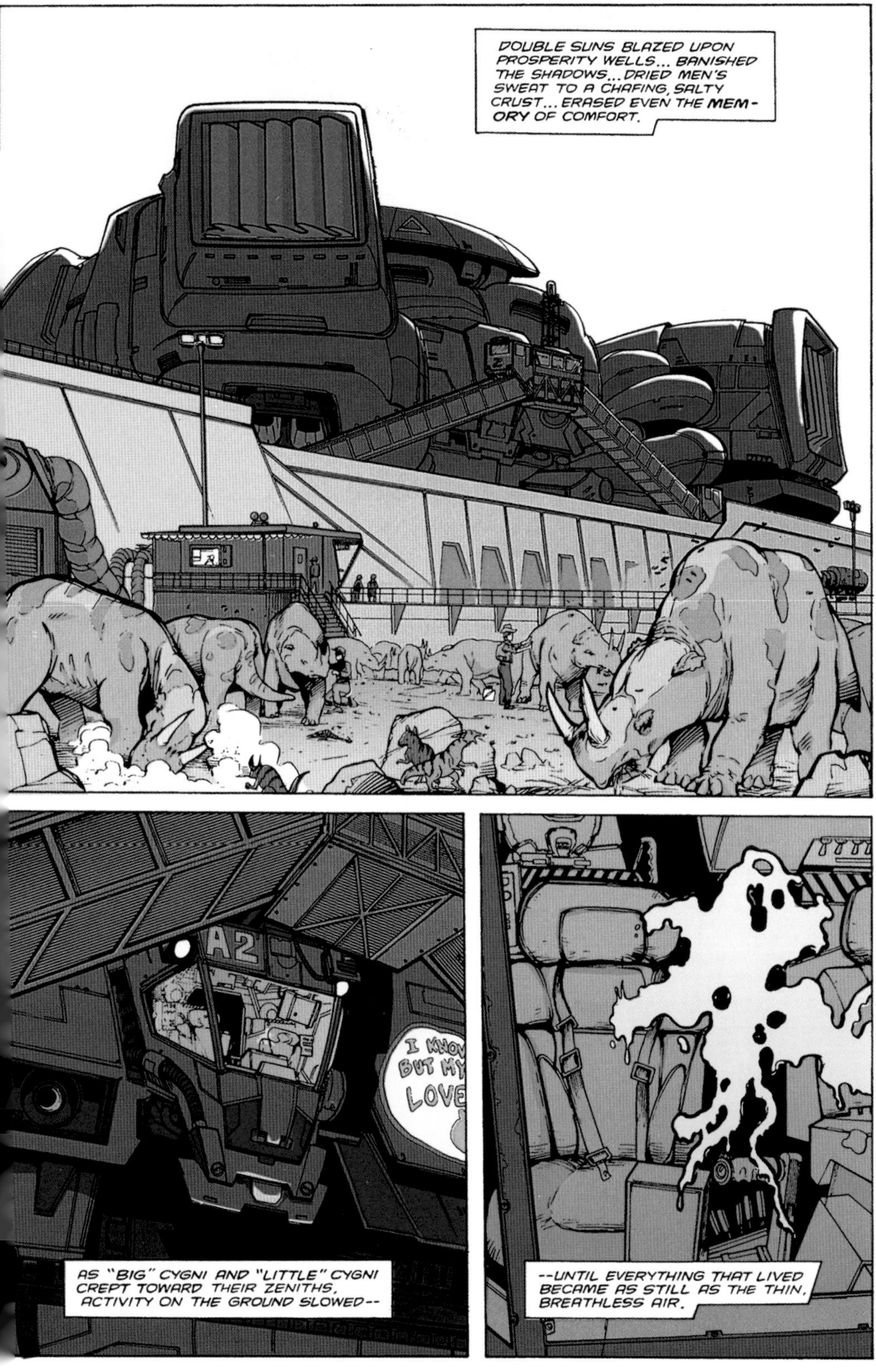
DOUBLE SUNS BLAZED UPON PROSPERITY WELLS... BANISHED THE SHADOWS... DRIED MEN'S SWEAT TO A CHAFING, SALTY CRUST... ERASED EVEN THE **MEMORY** OF COMFORT.
AS "BIG" CYGNI AND "LITTLE" CYGNI CREPT TOWARD THEIR ZENITHS, ACTIVITY ON THE GROUND SLOWED--
--UNTIL EVERYTHING THAT LIVED BECAME AS STILL AS THE THIN, BREATHLESS AIR.

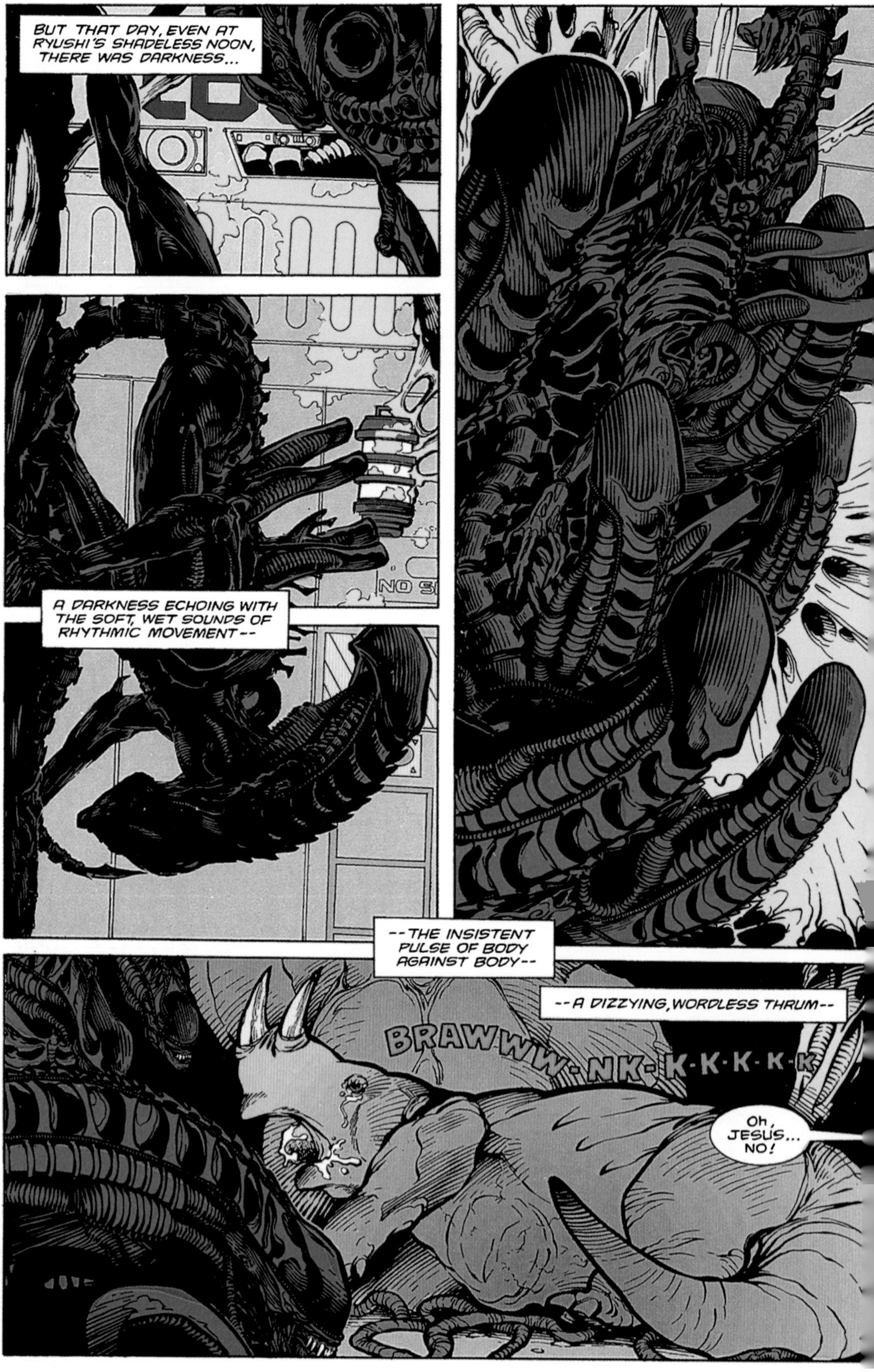
BUT THAT DAY, EVEN AT RYUSHI'S SHADELESS NOON, THERE WAS DARKNESS...
NO S
A DARKNESS ECHOING WITH THE SOFT, WET SOUNDS OF RHYTHMIC MOVEMENT--
--THE INSISTENT PULSE OF BODY AGAINST BODY--
--A DIZZYING, WORDLESS THRUM--
BRAWWWW-NK-K-K-K-K-K
Oh, JESUS... NO!

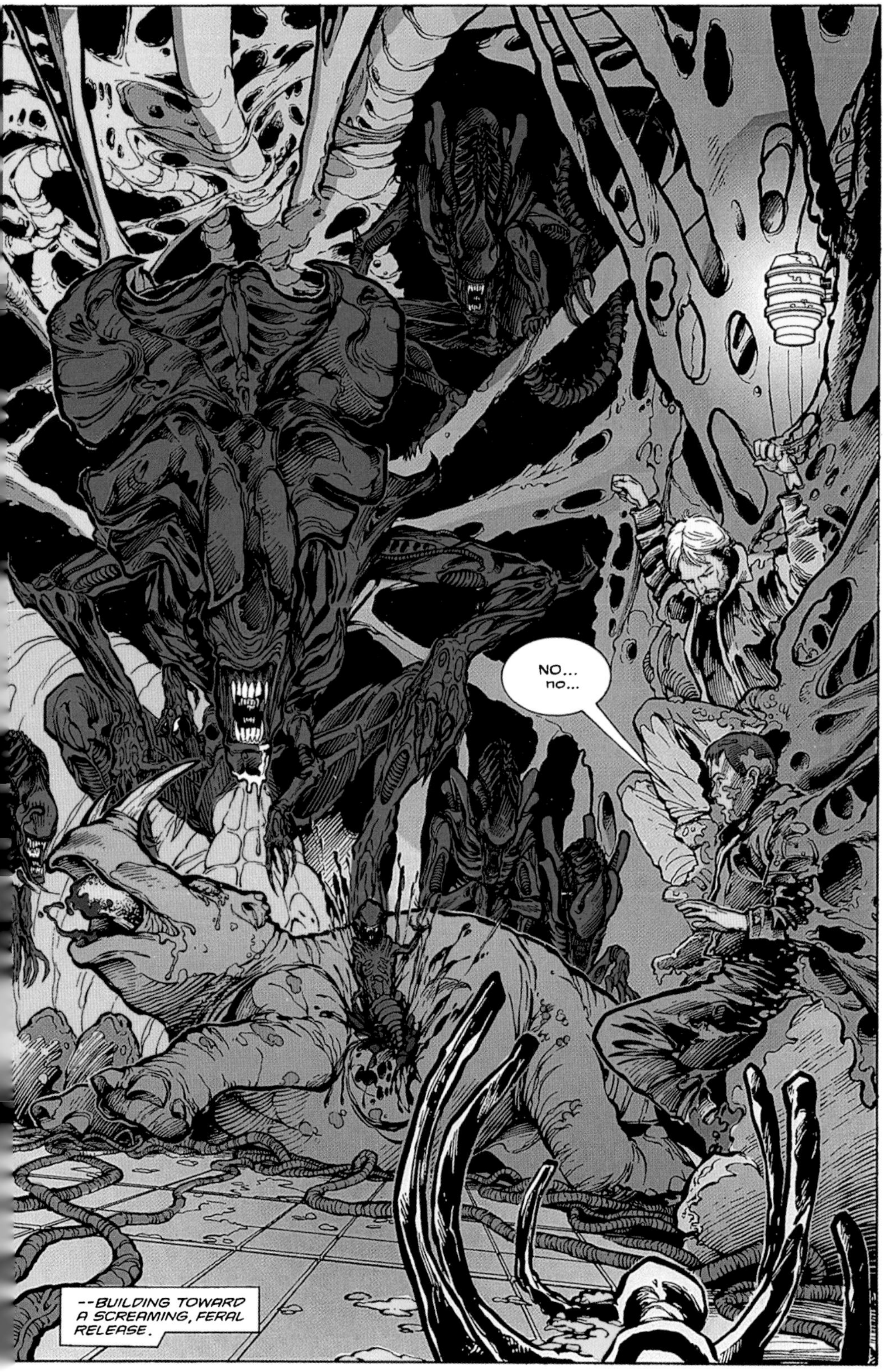
NO... no...
--BUILDING TOWARD A SCREAMING, FERAL RELEASE.

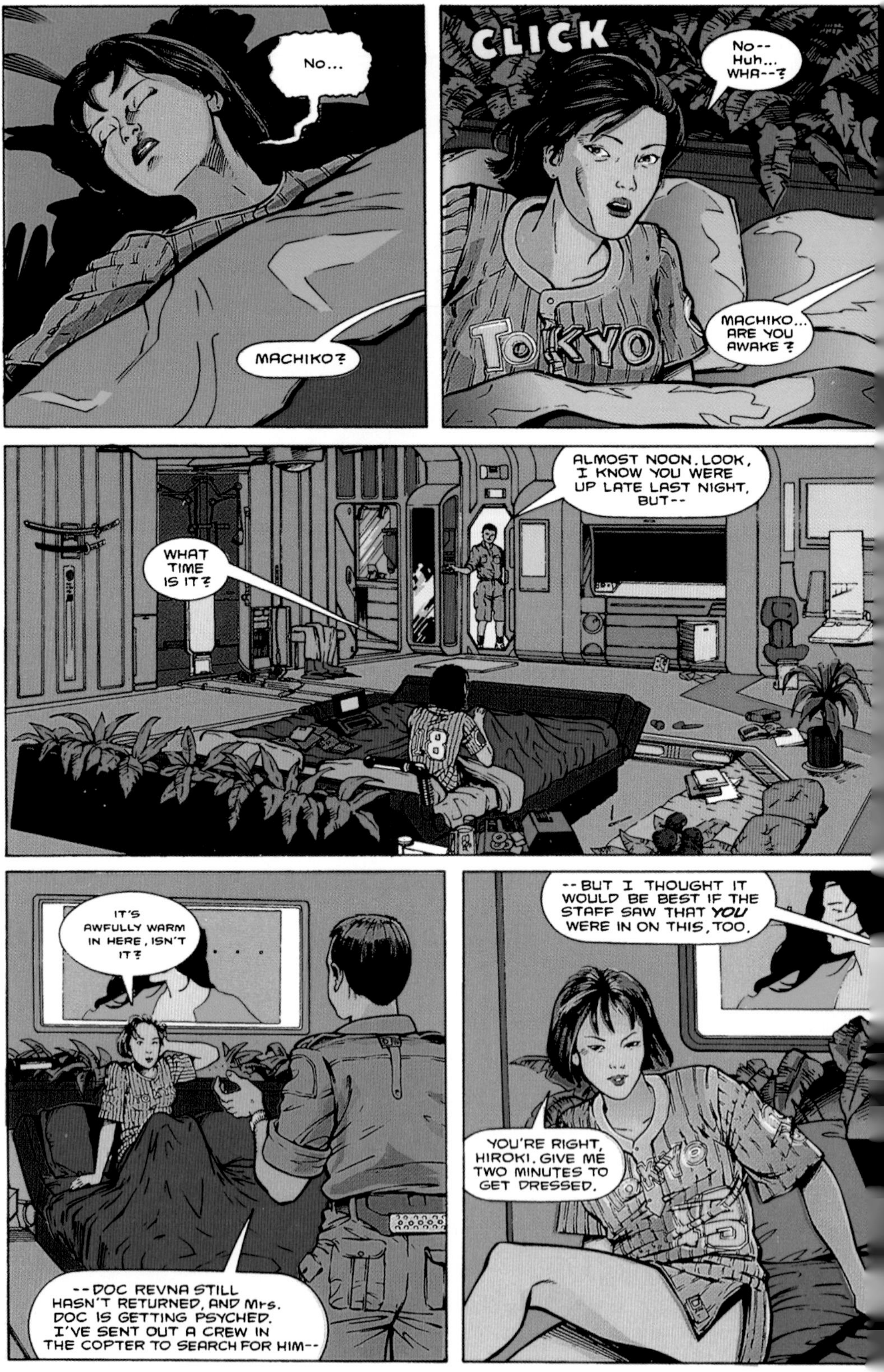
No...
MACHIKO?
CLICK
No-- Huh... WHA--?
MACHIKO... ARE YOU AWAKE?
WHAT TIME IS IT?
ALMOST NOON. LOOK, I KNOW YOU WERE UP LATE LAST NIGHT, BUT--
IT'S AWFULLY WARM IN HERE, ISN'T IT?
--DOC REVNA STILL HASN'T RETURNED, AND Mrs. DOC IS GETTING PSYCHED. I'VE SENT OUT A CREW IN THE COPTER TO SEARCH FOR HIM--
--BUT I THOUGHT IT WOULD BE BEST IF THE STAFF SAW THAT YOU WERE IN ON THIS, TOO.
YOU'RE RIGHT, HIROKI. GIVE ME TWO MINUTES TO GET DRESSED.

BAY **12**

DRS. KESAR & MIRIAM REVNA, MD, DVM, DE MEDICAL

OFFICE ENTRANCE

MrS. DOC WANTED TO CHECK OUT A HOVER BIKE AND GO LOOKING FOR HIM ON HER OWN, BUT I THOUGHT--

--WHY RISK HAVING *BOTH* OF THEM LOST OUT THERE?

RIGHT.

Oh, Ms. NOGUCHI-- DID THEY FIND MY KESAR?

NOT YET, Dr. REVNA, BUT WE'VE GOT OUR BEST PEOPLE OUT LOOKING FOR HIM.

IS THERE ANYTHING YOU CAN THINK OF THAT MIGHT HELP US LOCATE YOUR HUSBAND? SOMETHING YOU MIGHT NOT HAVE THOUGHT WAS IMPORTANT BEFORE?

NO--NO, I DON'T THINK SO. KESAR WAS ON HIS WAY UP TO IWA GORGE--

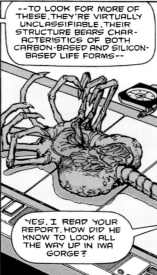

--TO LOOK FOR MORE OF THESE. THEY'RE VIRTUALLY UNCLASSIFIABLE. THEIR STRUCTURE BEARS CHARACTERISTICS OF BOTH CARBON-BASED AND SILICON-BASED LIFE FORMS--

YES. I READ YOUR REPORT. HOW DID HE KNOW TO LOOK ALL THE WAY UP IN IWA GORGE?

THAT'S WHERE SHE SAID SHE FOUND THEM.

"SHE"?

YES... WHAT'S HER NAME? THE YOUNG WOMAN WHO WORKS FOR *FLYING "A"*... ROTH.

WHAT WOULD ROTH BE DOING ALL THE WAY UP IN IWA GORGE? ACKLAND DOESN'T HAVE ANY HERDS WITHIN TWENTY KLIKS OF THERE.

THOSE THINGS *WEREN'T FOUND* IN IWA GORGE.

67

Huh?

THINK ABOUT IT. IF YOU WERE ACKLAND AND YOU DISCOVERED SOME NEW LIFE FORM THE NIGHT BEFORE YOUR RHYNTH WERE TO BE SHIPPED OFF-PLANET, WOULD *YOU* RISK HAVING YOUR ENTIRE YEAR'S PROFITS HELD UP IN QUARANTINE?

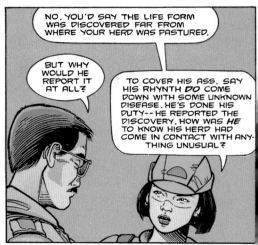

NO. YOU'D SAY THE LIFE FORM WAS DISCOVERED FAR FROM WHERE YOUR HERD WAS PASTURED.

BUT WHY WOULD HE REPORT IT AT ALL?

TO COVER HIS ASS. SAY HIS RHYNTH *DO* COME DOWN WITH SOME UNKNOWN DISEASE. HE'S DONE HIS DUTY-- HE REPORTED THE DISCOVERY. HOW WAS *HE* TO KNOW HIS HERD HAD COME IN CONTACT WITH ANYTHING UNUSUAL?

SO WHAT'S OUR NEXT MOVE?

WE TALK TO ROTH FIRST, THEN ACKLAND. IF ANYTHING HAS HAPPENED TO REVNA, HE'LL PAY.

HE SENT REVNA ON A WILD GOOSE CHASE--

"--THERE'S NOTHING UP AT IWA GORGE BUT ROCKS AND SAND."

I DON'T BELIEVE IT. I DON'T SHITTIN' BELIEVE IT!

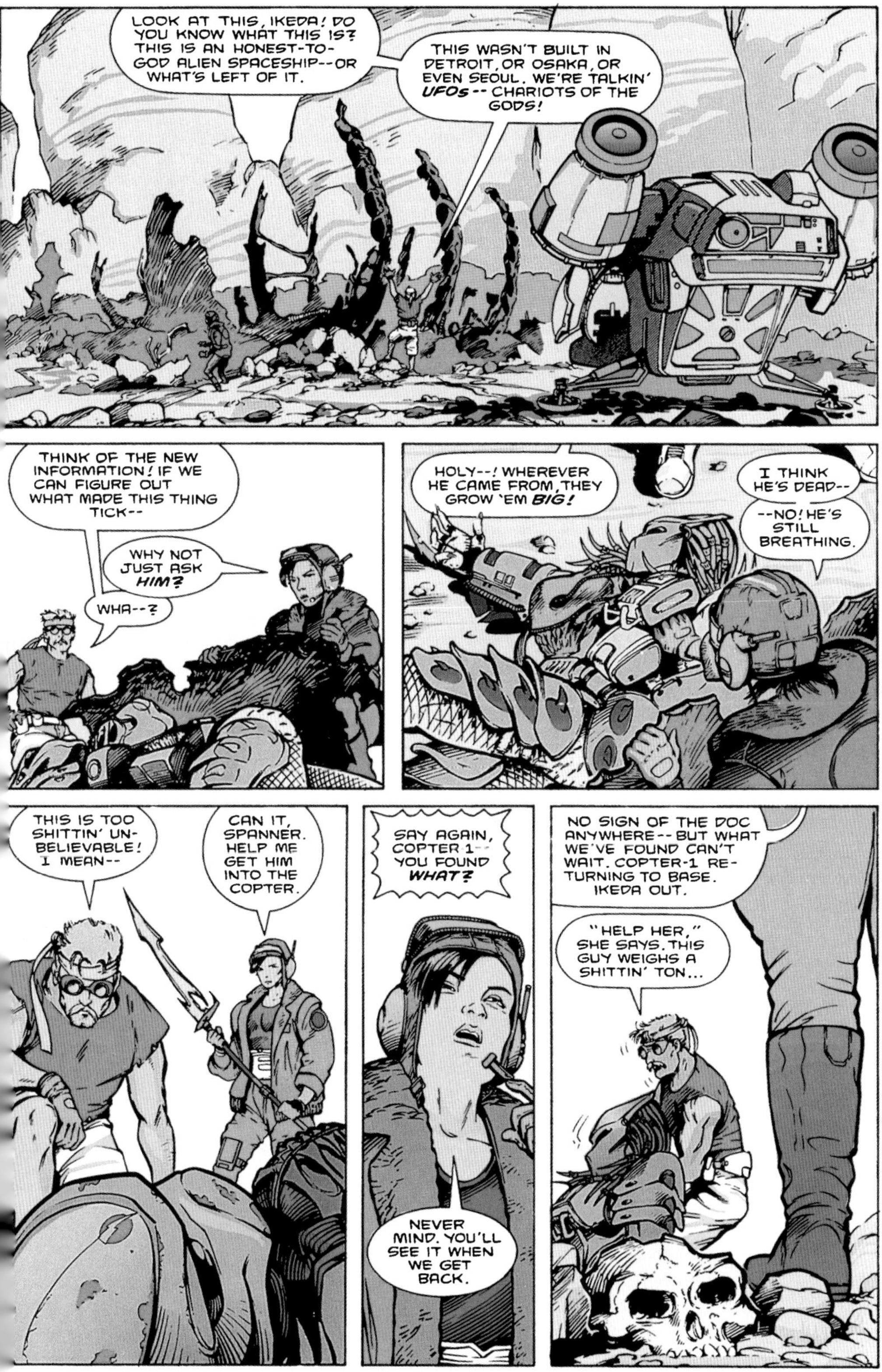
LOOK AT THIS, IKEDA! DO YOU KNOW WHAT THIS IS? THIS IS AN HONEST-TO-GOD ALIEN SPACESHIP--OR WHAT'S LEFT OF IT.
THIS WASN'T BUILT IN DETROIT, OR OSAKA, OR EVEN SEOUL. WE'RE TALKIN' UFOs -- CHARIOTS OF THE GODS!
THINK OF THE NEW INFORMATION! IF WE CAN FIGURE OUT WHAT MADE THIS THING TICK--
WHY NOT JUST ASK HIM?
WHA--?
HOLY--! WHEREVER HE CAME FROM, THEY GROW 'EM BIG!
I THINK HE'S DEAD--
--NO! HE'S STILL BREATHING.
THIS IS TOO SHITTIN' UN-BELIEVABLE! I MEAN--
CAN IT, SPANNER. HELP ME GET HIM INTO THE COPTER.
SAY AGAIN, COPTER 1-- YOU FOUND WHAT?
NEVER MIND. YOU'LL SEE IT WHEN WE GET BACK.
NO SIGN OF THE DOC ANYWHERE-- BUT WHAT WE'VE FOUND CAN'T WAIT. COPTER-1 RE-TURNING TO BASE. IKEDA OUT.
"HELP HER," SHE SAYS. THIS GUY WEIGHS A SHITTIN' TON...

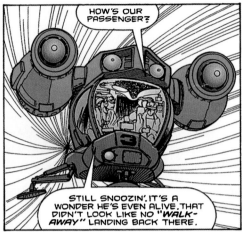

HOW'S OUR PASSENGER?

STILL SNOOZIN'. IT'S A WONDER HE'S EVEN ALIVE. THAT DIDN'T LOOK LIKE NO "WALK-AWAY" LANDING BACK THERE.

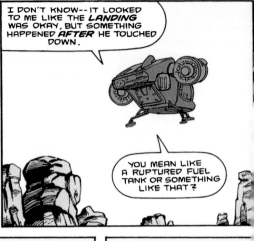

I DON'T KNOW-- IT LOOKED TO ME LIKE THE *LANDING* WAS OKAY, BUT SOMETHING HAPPENED *AFTER* HE TOUCHED DOWN.

YOU MEAN LIKE A RUPTURED FUEL TANK OR SOMETHING LIKE THAT?

Hmm... MAYBE WE DON'T WANT TO BORROW FROM THEIR TECHNOLOGY, AFTER ALL...

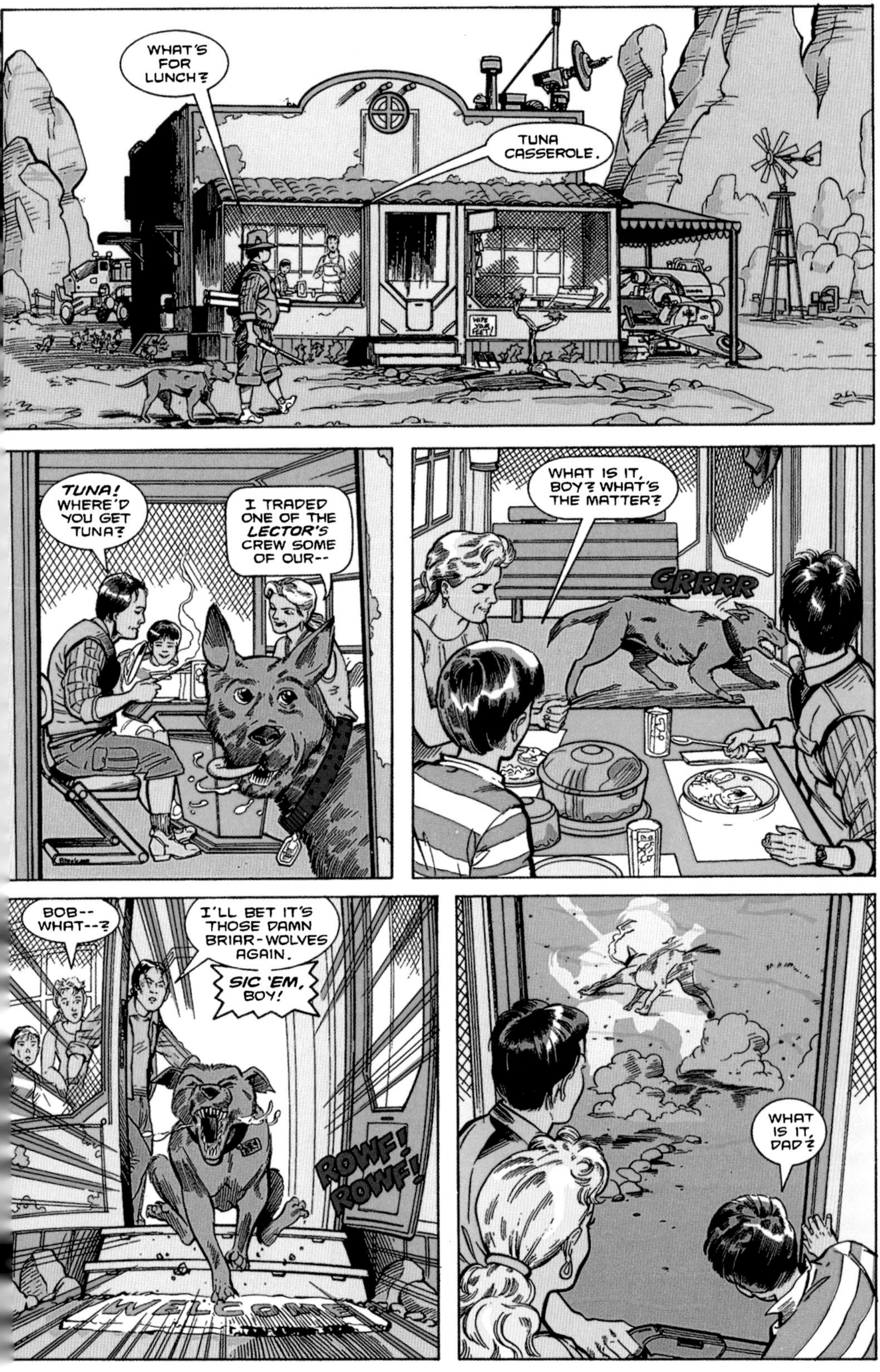
WHAT'S FOR LUNCH?
TUNA CASSEROLE.
TUNA! WHERE'D YOU GET TUNA?
I TRADED ONE OF THE LECTOR'S CREW SOME OF OUR--
WHAT IS IT, BOY? WHAT'S THE MATTER?
GRRRR
BOB-- WHAT--?
I'LL BET IT'S THOSE DAMN BRIAR-WOLVES AGAIN.
SIC 'EM, BOY!
ROWF! ROWF!
WELCOME
WHAT IS IT, DAD?

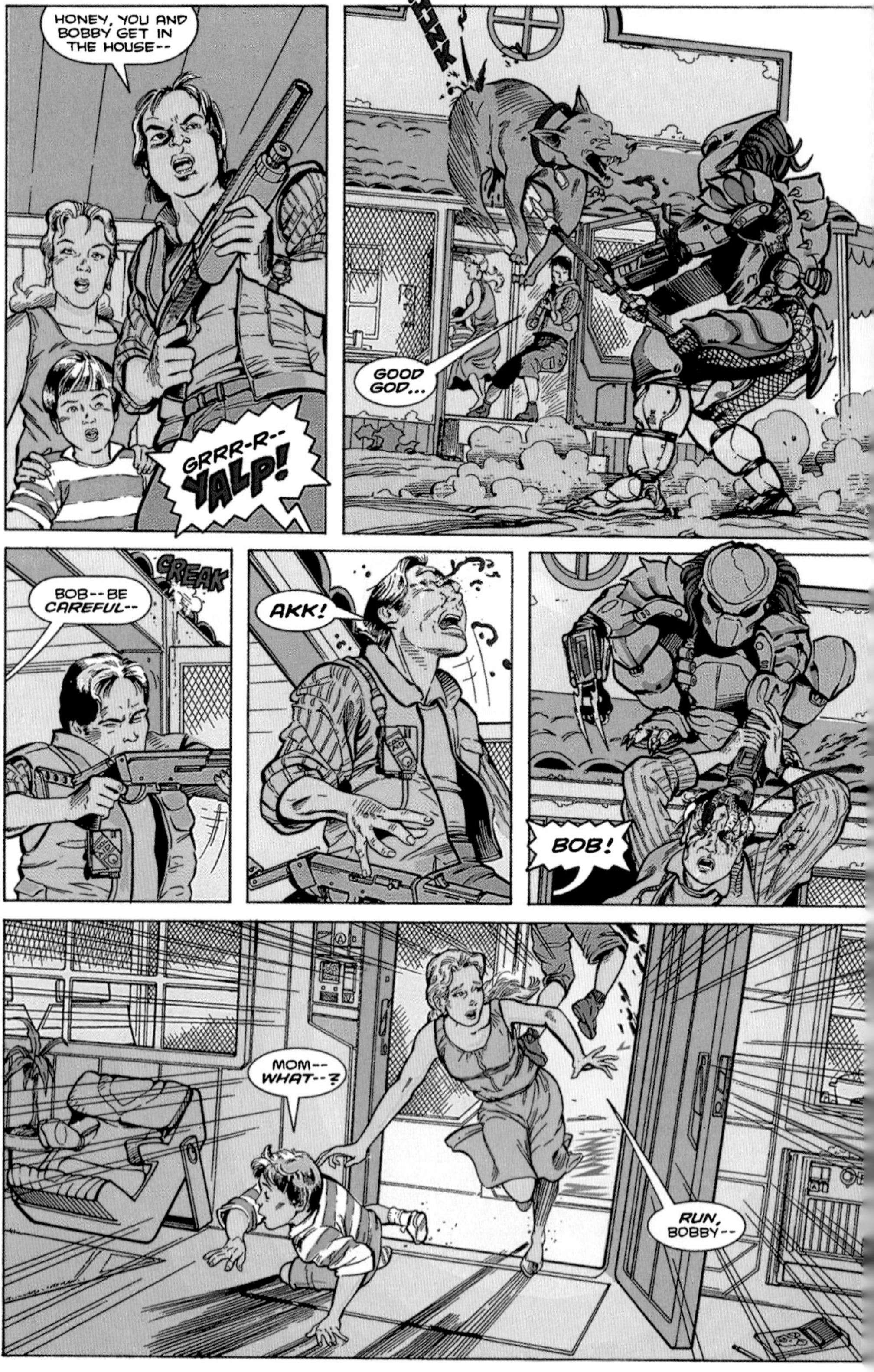
HONEY, YOU AND BOBBY GET IN THE HOUSE--
GRRR-R-- YALP!
CHUNK
GOOD GOD...
BOB--BE CAREFUL--
CREAK
AKK!
BOB!
MOM-- WHAT--?
RUN, BOBBY--

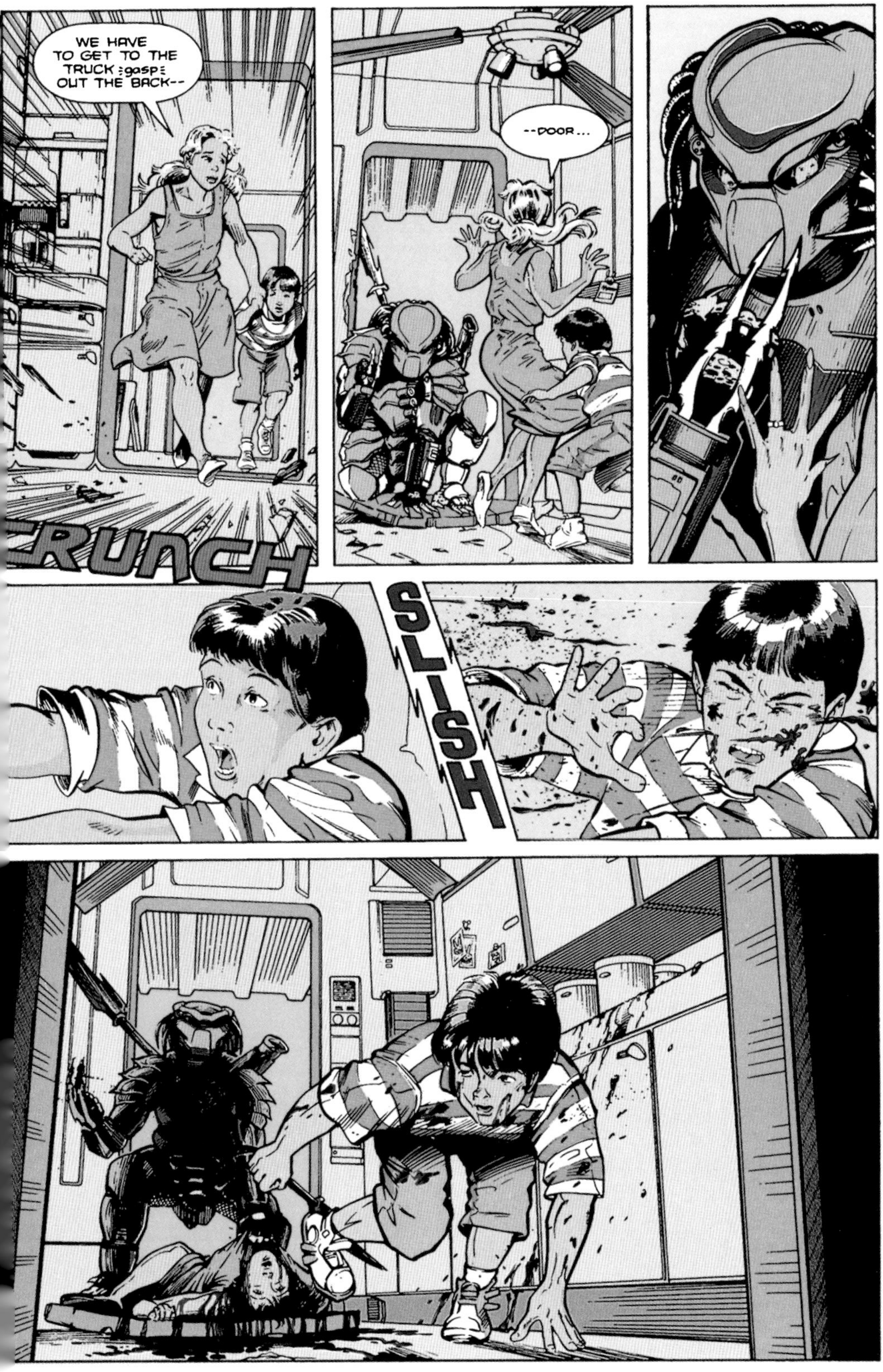

WE HAVE TO GET TO THE TRUCK :gasp: OUT THE BACK--
CRUNCH
--DOOR...
SLISH

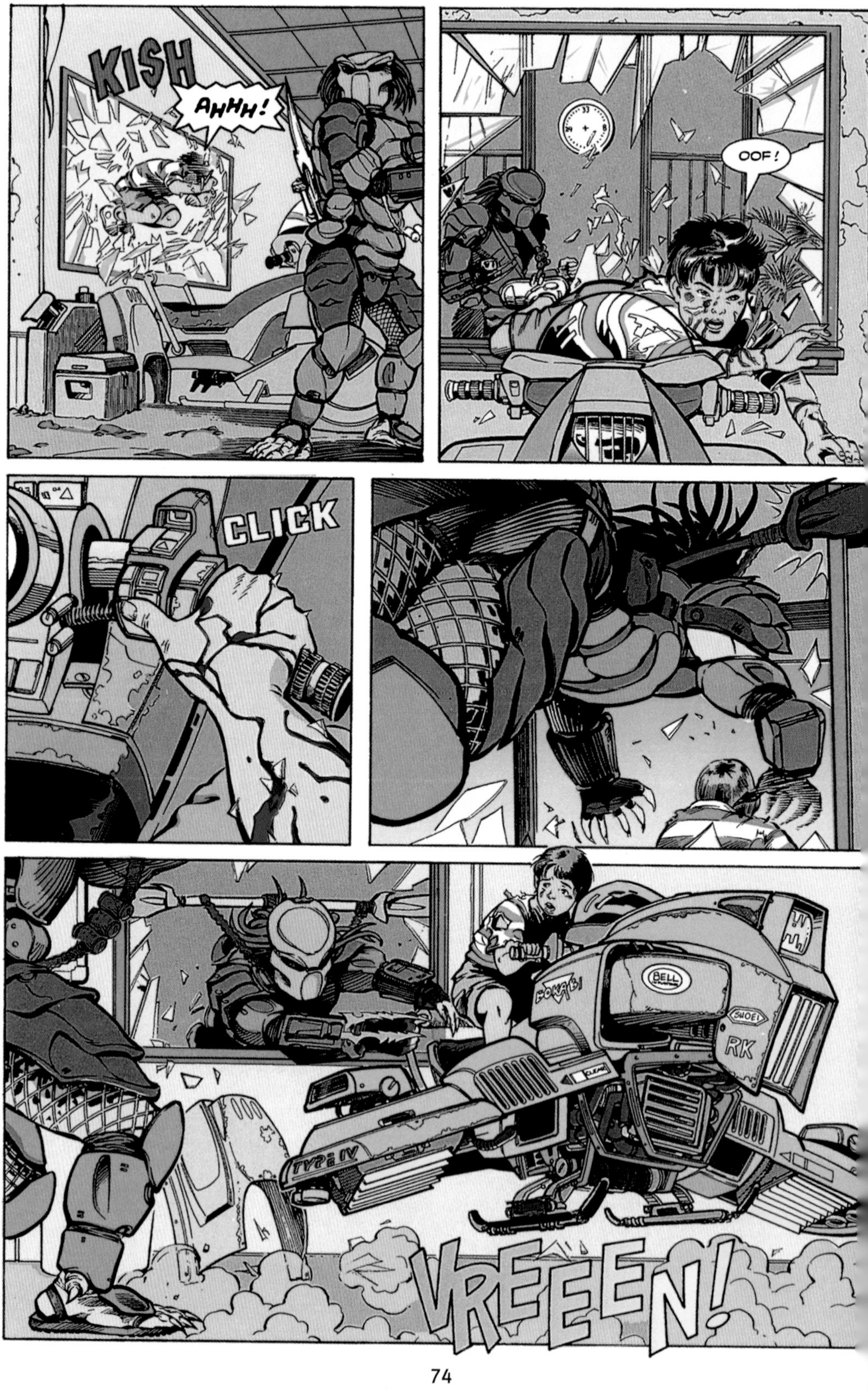
KISH
AHHH!
OOF!
CLICK
BELL
DOKABI
SHOEI
RK
TYPE IV
VREEEN!

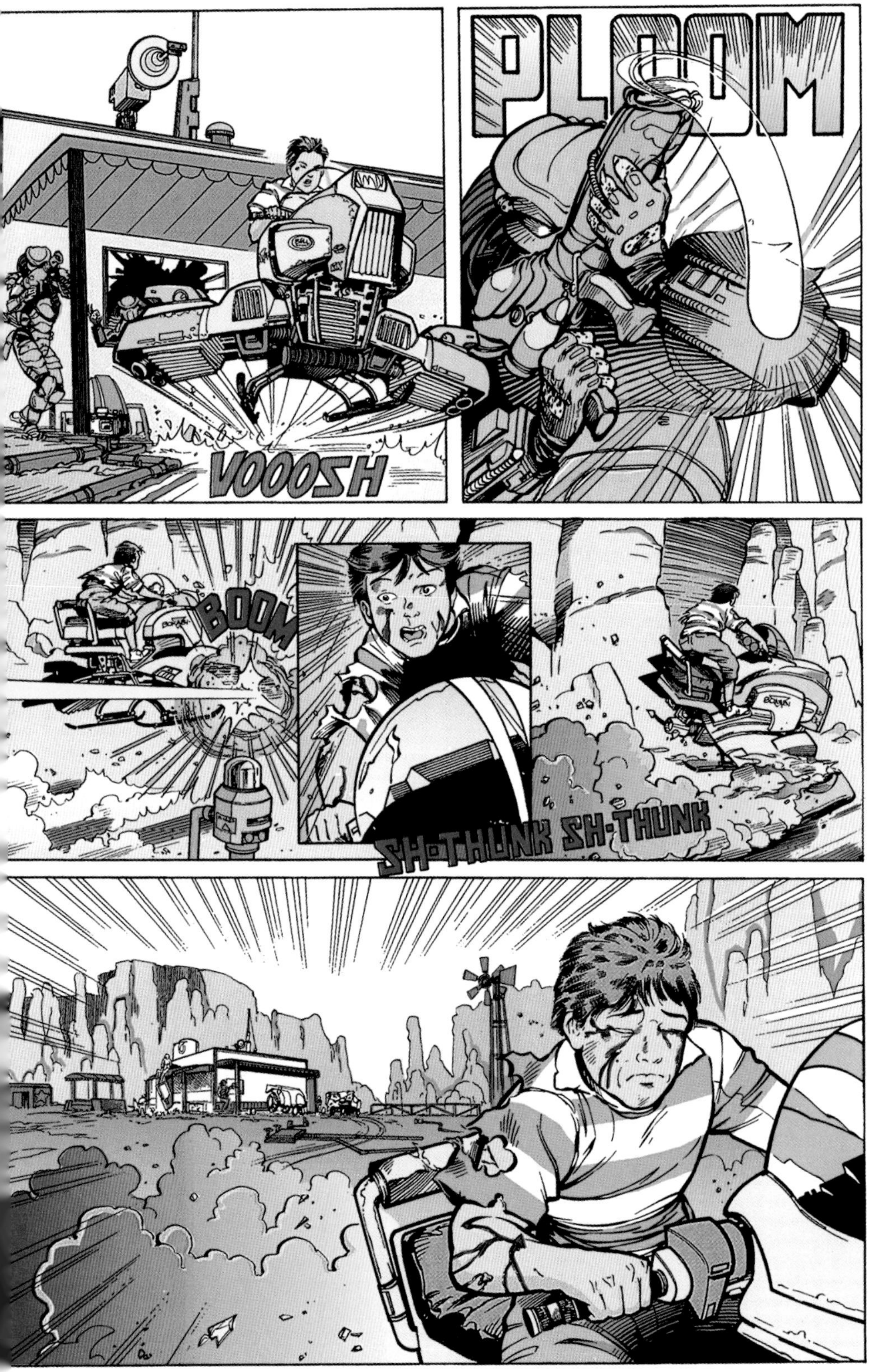
VOOOSH
PLOOM
BOOM
SH-THUNK SH-THUNK

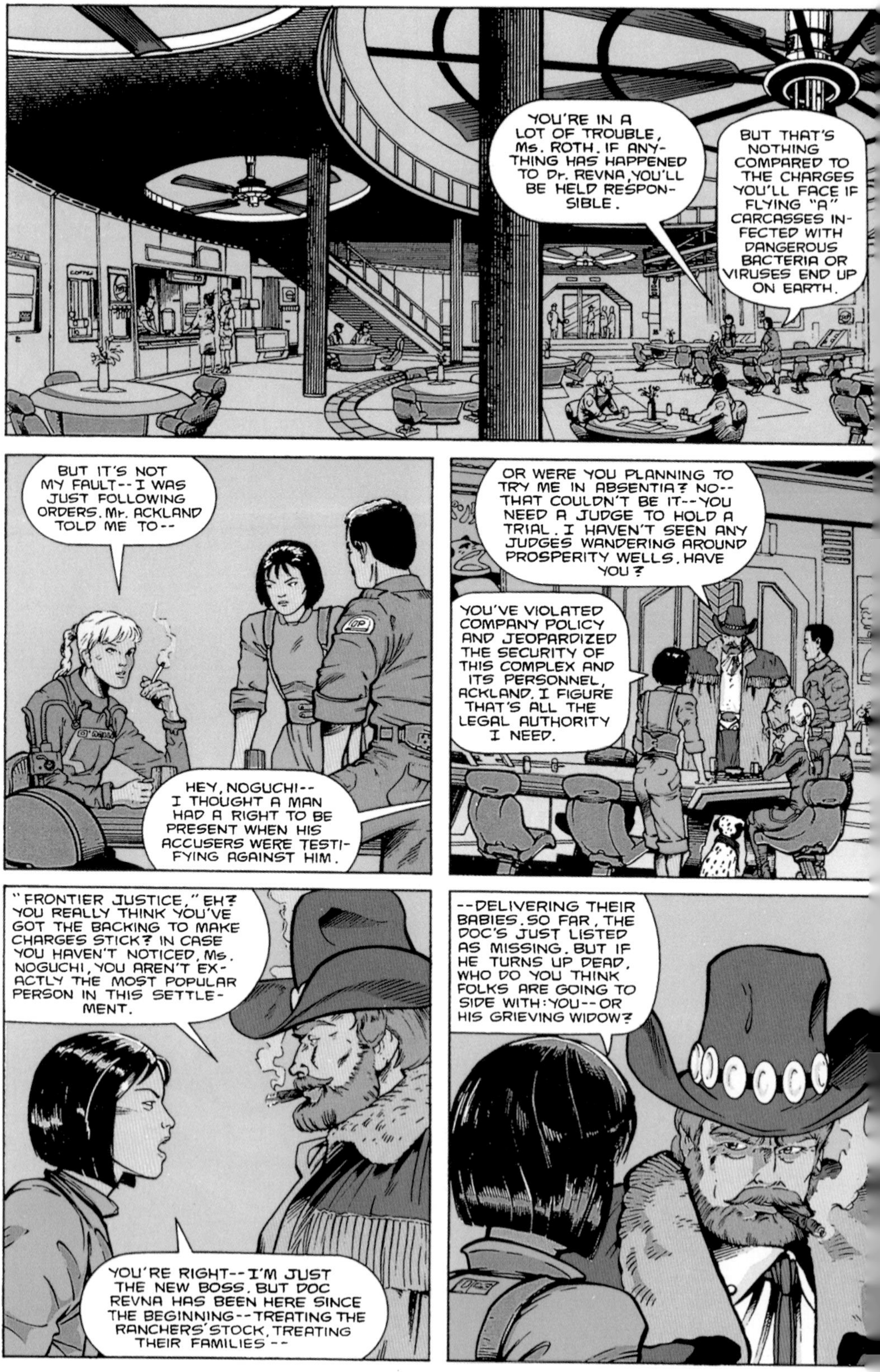
YOU'RE IN A LOT OF TROUBLE, Ms. ROTH. IF ANYTHING HAS HAPPENED TO Dr. REVNA, YOU'LL BE HELD RESPONSIBLE.
BUT THAT'S NOTHING COMPARED TO THE CHARGES YOU'LL FACE IF FLYING "A" CARCASSES INFECTED WITH DANGEROUS BACTERIA OR VIRUSES END UP ON EARTH.
BUT IT'S NOT MY FAULT-- I WAS JUST FOLLOWING ORDERS. Mr. ACKLAND TOLD ME TO--
HEY, NOGUCHI-- I THOUGHT A MAN HAD A RIGHT TO BE PRESENT WHEN HIS ACCUSERS WERE TESTIFYING AGAINST HIM.
OR WERE YOU PLANNING TO TRY ME IN ABSENTIA? NO-- THAT COULDN'T BE IT-- YOU NEED A JUDGE TO HOLD A TRIAL. I HAVEN'T SEEN ANY JUDGES WANDERING AROUND PROSPERITY WELLS. HAVE YOU?
YOU'VE VIOLATED COMPANY POLICY AND JEOPARDIZED THE SECURITY OF THIS COMPLEX AND ITS PERSONNEL, ACKLAND. I FIGURE THAT'S ALL THE LEGAL AUTHORITY I NEED.
"FRONTIER JUSTICE," EH? YOU REALLY THINK YOU'VE GOT THE BACKING TO MAKE CHARGES STICK? IN CASE YOU HAVEN'T NOTICED, Ms. NOGUCHI, YOU AREN'T EXACTLY THE MOST POPULAR PERSON IN THIS SETTLEMENT.
YOU'RE RIGHT-- I'M JUST THE NEW BOSS. BUT DOC REVNA HAS BEEN HERE SINCE THE BEGINNING-- TREATING THE RANCHERS' STOCK, TREATING THEIR FAMILIES--
--DELIVERING THEIR BABIES. SO FAR, THE DOC'S JUST LISTED AS MISSING. BUT IF HE TURNS UP DEAD, WHO DO YOU THINK FOLKS ARE GOING TO SIDE WITH: YOU-- OR HIS GRIEVING WIDOW?

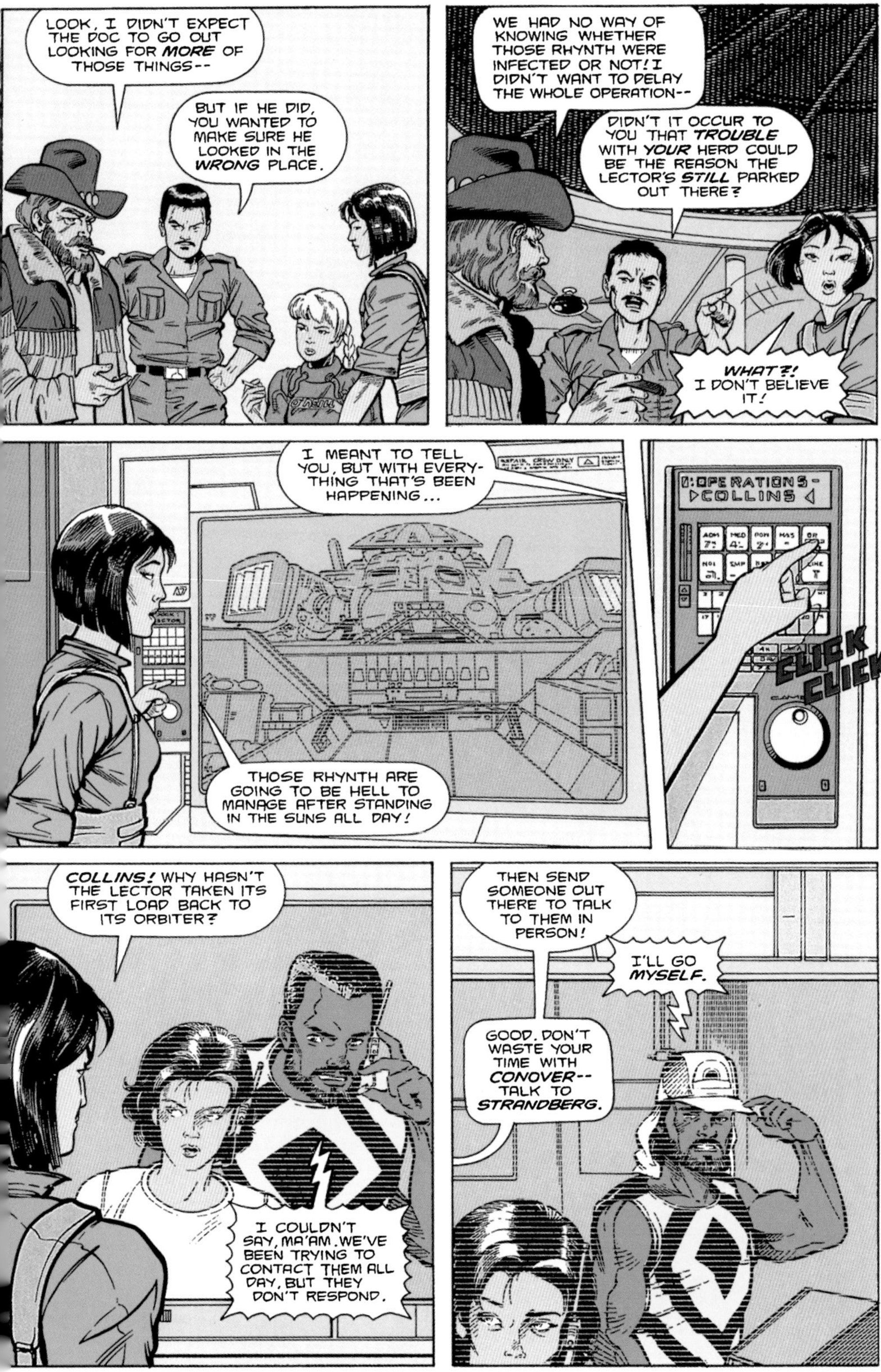

LOOK, I DIDN'T EXPECT THE DOC TO GO OUT LOOKING FOR MORE OF THOSE THINGS--
BUT IF HE DID, YOU WANTED TO MAKE SURE HE LOOKED IN THE WRONG PLACE.
WE HAD NO WAY OF KNOWING WHETHER THOSE RHYNTH WERE INFECTED OR NOT! I DIDN'T WANT TO DELAY THE WHOLE OPERATION--
DIDN'T IT OCCUR TO YOU THAT TROUBLE WITH YOUR HERD COULD BE THE REASON THE LECTOR'S STILL PARKED OUT THERE?
WHAT?! I DON'T BELIEVE IT!
I MEANT TO TELL YOU, BUT WITH EVERYTHING THAT'S BEEN HAPPENING...
THOSE RHYNTH ARE GOING TO BE HELL TO MANAGE AFTER STANDING IN THE SUNS ALL DAY!
OPERATIONS - COLLINS
CLICK CLICK
COLLINS! WHY HASN'T THE LECTOR TAKEN ITS FIRST LOAD BACK TO ITS ORBITER?
I COULDN'T SAY, MA'AM. WE'VE BEEN TRYING TO CONTACT THEM ALL DAY, BUT THEY DON'T RESPOND.
THEN SEND SOMEONE OUT THERE TO TALK TO THEM IN PERSON!
I'LL GO MYSELF.
GOOD. DON'T WASTE YOUR TIME WITH CONOVER-- TALK TO STRANDBERG.

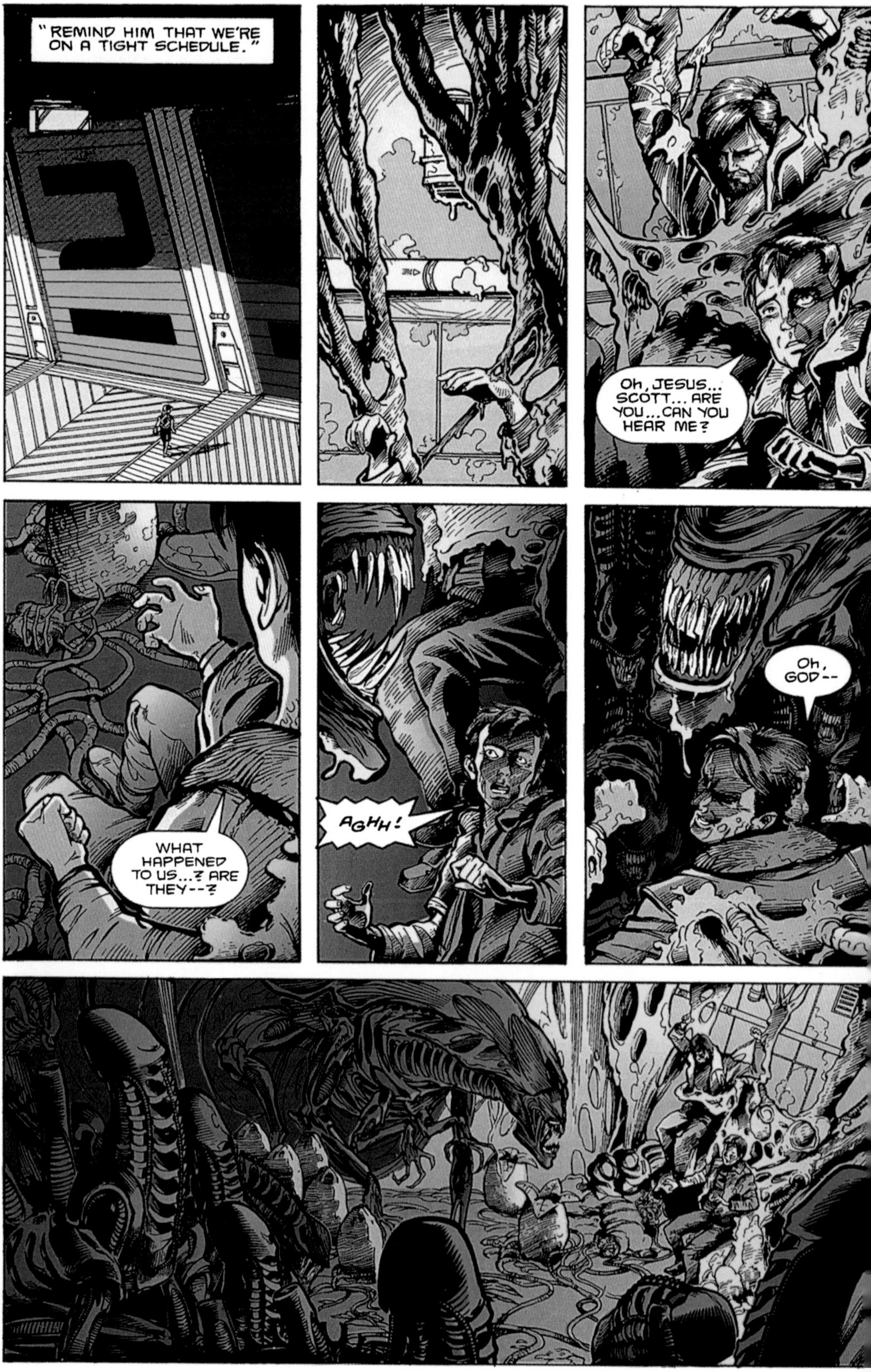
"REMIND HIM THAT WE'RE ON A TIGHT SCHEDULE."
Oh, JESUS... SCOTT... ARE YOU...CAN YOU HEAR ME?
WHAT HAPPENED TO US...? ARE THEY--?
AGHH!
Oh, GOD--

...THE COMPANY HAS BILLIONS INVESTED--

Ms. NOGUCHI, REPORT TO THE MED CENTER-- IMMEDIATELY! Ms. NOGUCHI TO THE MED CENTER!

:INCOMING MESSAGE ▼
NOGUCHI-MACHIKO

YOU'D BETTER PRAY THEY'VE FOUND REVNA, ACKLAND!

WEST

FOUR CRACKED RIBS AND EXTENSIVE CONTUSIONS IN THE DORSAL REGION.

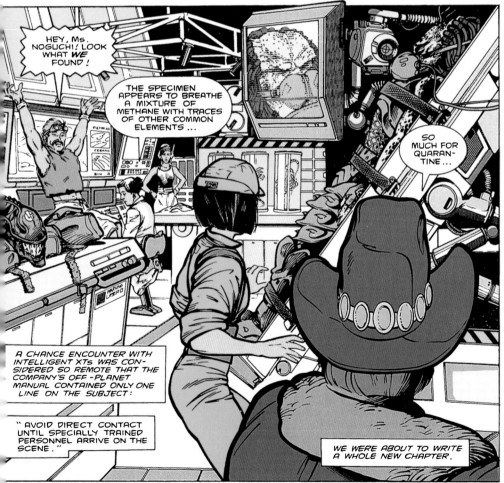

HEY, Ms. NOGUCHI! LOOK WHAT WE FOUND!

THE SPECIMEN APPEARS TO BREATHE A MIXTURE OF METHANE WITH TRACES OF OTHER COMMON ELEMENTS ...

SO MUCH FOR QUARAN- TINE ...

A CHANCE ENCOUNTER WITH INTELLIGENT XTs WAS CON- SIDERED SO REMOTE THAT THE COMPANY'S OFF-PLANET MANUAL CONTAINED ONLY ONE LINE ON THE SUBJECT:

"AVOID DIRECT CONTACT UNTIL SPECIALLY TRAINED PERSONNEL ARRIVE ON THE SCENE."

WE WERE ABOUT TO WRITE A WHOLE NEW CHAPTER.

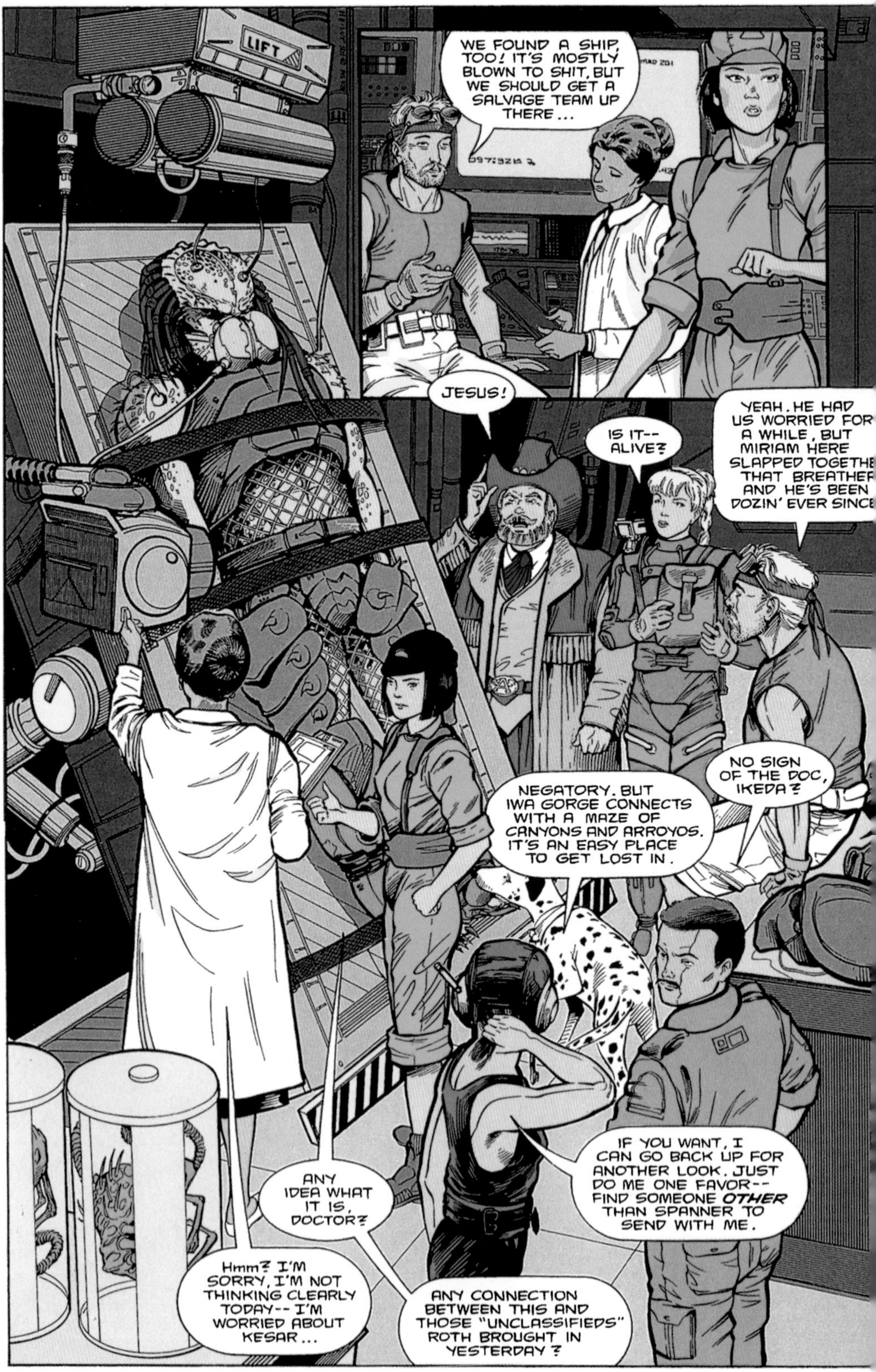
WE FOUND A SHIP, TOO! IT'S MOSTLY BLOWN TO SHIT, BUT WE SHOULD GET A SALVAGE TEAM UP THERE...
LIFT
JESUS!
IS IT-- ALIVE?
YEAH. HE HAD US WORRIED FOR A WHILE, BUT MIRIAM HERE SLAPPED TOGETHER THAT BREATHER AND HE'S BEEN DOZIN' EVER SINCE
NO SIGN OF THE DOC, IKEDA?
NEGATORY. BUT IWA GORGE CONNECTS WITH A MAZE OF CANYONS AND ARROYOS. IT'S AN EASY PLACE TO GET LOST IN.
IF YOU WANT, I CAN GO BACK UP FOR ANOTHER LOOK. JUST DO ME ONE FAVOR-- FIND SOMEONE *OTHER* THAN SPANNER TO SEND WITH ME.
ANY IDEA WHAT IT IS, DOCTOR?
Hmm? I'M SORRY, I'M NOT THINKING CLEARLY TODAY-- I'M WORRIED ABOUT KESAR...
ANY CONNECTION BETWEEN THIS AND THOSE "UNCLASSIFIEDS" ROTH BROUGHT IN YESTERDAY?

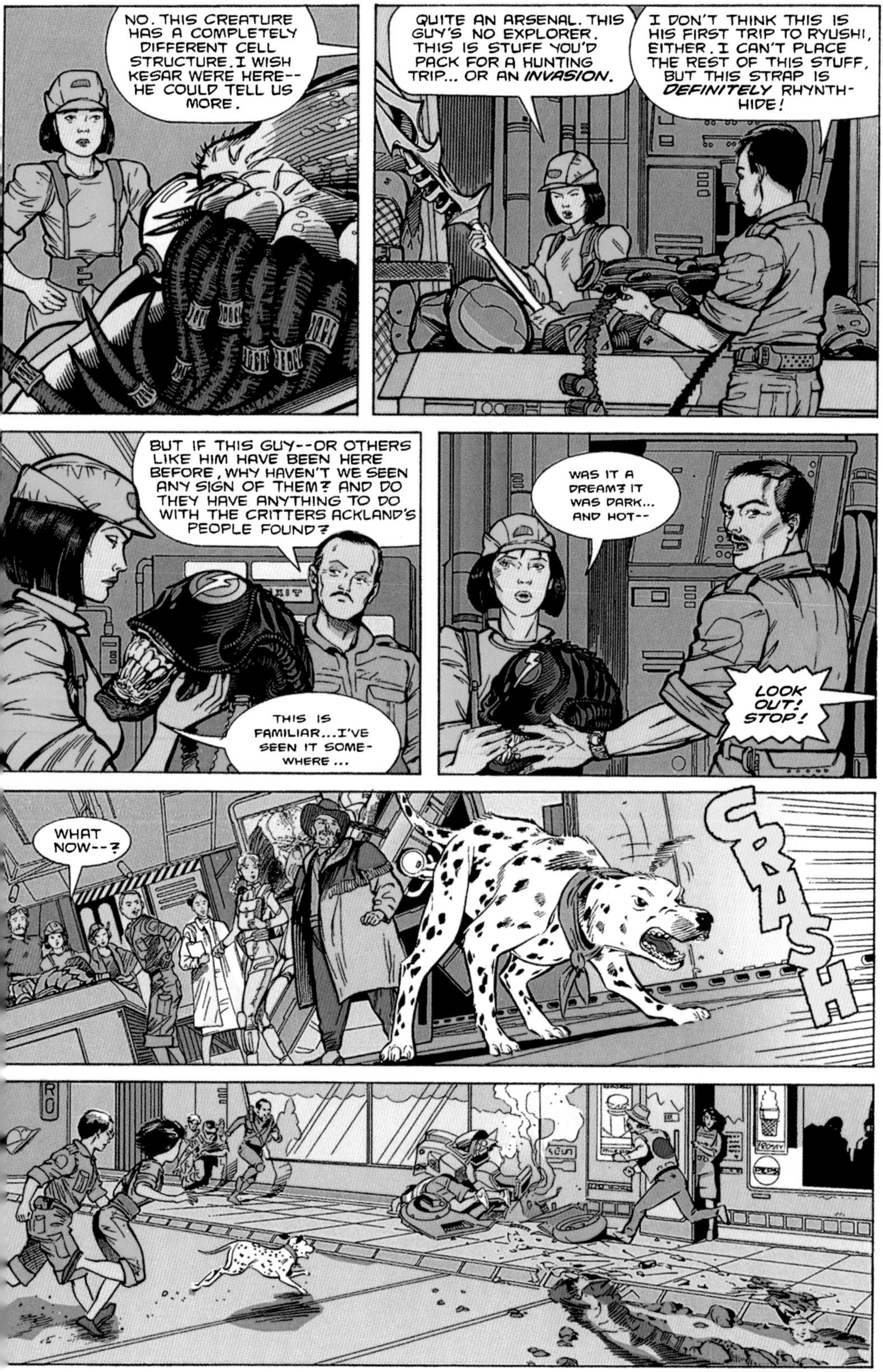
NO. THIS CREATURE HAS A COMPLETELY DIFFERENT CELL STRUCTURE. I WISH KESAR WERE HERE-- HE COULD TELL US MORE.
QUITE AN ARSENAL. THIS GUY'S NO EXPLORER. THIS IS STUFF YOU'D PACK FOR A HUNTING TRIP... OR AN *INVASION*.
I DON'T THINK THIS IS HIS FIRST TRIP TO RYUSHI, EITHER. I CAN'T PLACE THE REST OF THIS STUFF, BUT THIS STRAP IS *DEFINITELY* RHYNTH-HIDE!
BUT IF THIS GUY--OR OTHERS LIKE HIM HAVE BEEN HERE BEFORE, WHY HAVEN'T WE SEEN ANY SIGN OF THEM? AND DO THEY HAVE ANYTHING TO DO WITH THE CRITTERS ACKLAND'S PEOPLE FOUND?
EXIT
THIS IS FAMILIAR...I'VE SEEN IT SOME-WHERE...
WAS IT A DREAM? IT WAS DARK... AND HOT--
LOOK OUT! STOP!
WHAT NOW--?
CRASH
RO
FROSTY

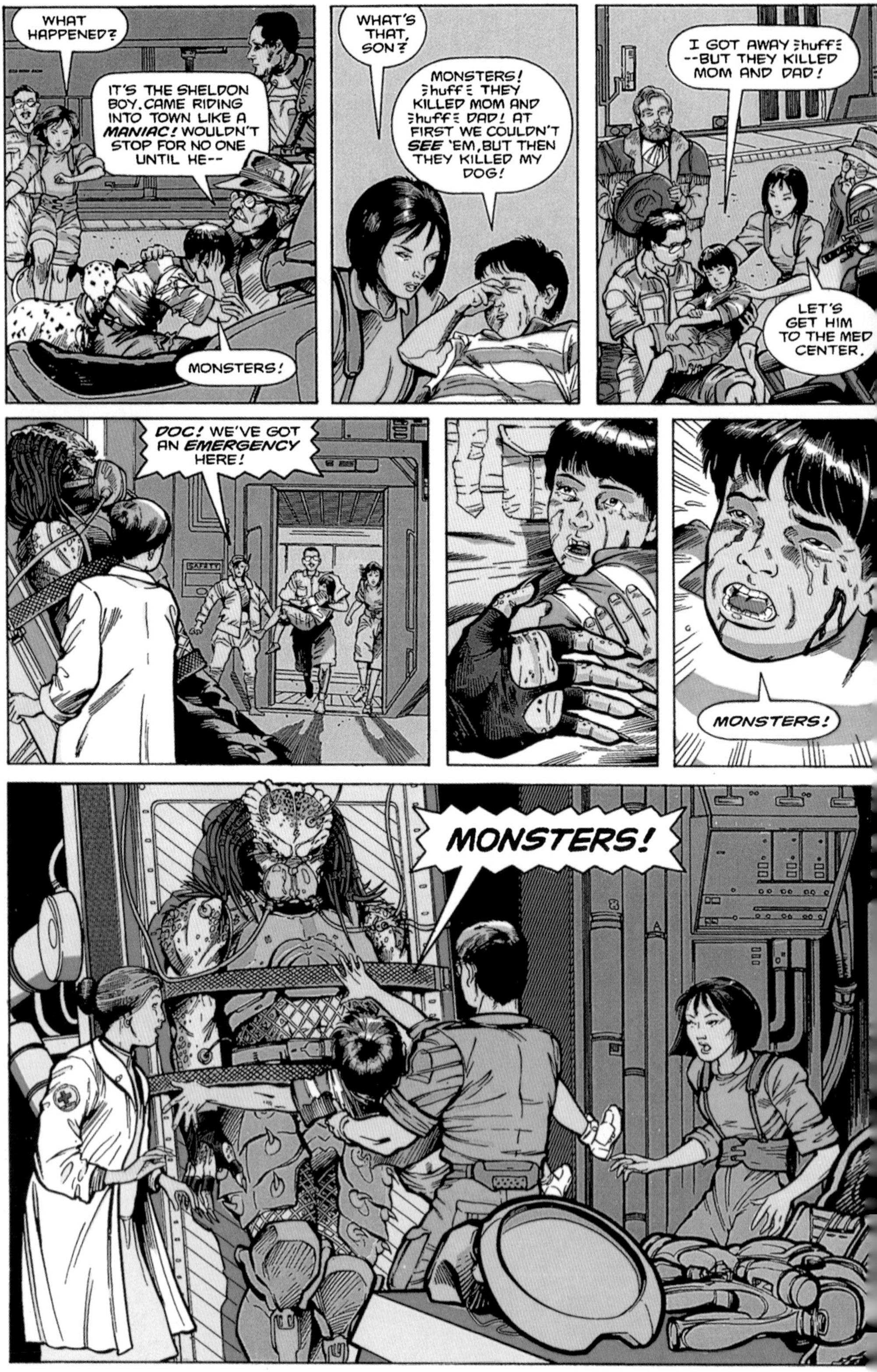
WHAT HAPPENED?
IT'S THE SHELDON BOY. CAME RIDING INTO TOWN LIKE A MANIAC! WOULDN'T STOP FOR NO ONE UNTIL HE--
MONSTERS!
WHAT'S THAT, SON?
MONSTERS! huff THEY KILLED MOM AND huff DAD! AT FIRST WE COULDN'T SEE 'EM, BUT THEN THEY KILLED MY DOG!
I GOT AWAY huff --BUT THEY KILLED MOM AND DAD!
LET'S GET HIM TO THE MED CENTER.
DOC! WE'VE GOT AN EMERGENCY HERE!
MONSTERS!
MONSTERS!

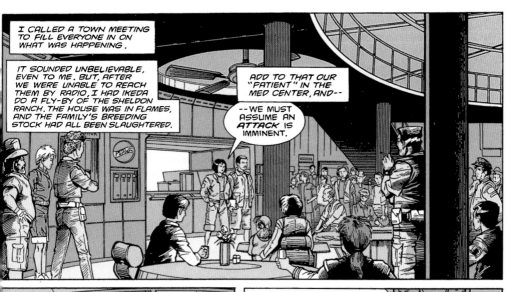

I CALLED A TOWN MEETING TO FILL EVERYONE IN ON WHAT WAS HAPPENING.
IT SOUNDED UNBELIEVABLE, EVEN TO ME. BUT, AFTER WE WERE UNABLE TO REACH THEM BY RADIO, I HAD IKEDA DO A FLY-BY OF THE SHELDON RANCH. THE HOUSE WAS IN FLAMES, AND THE FAMILY'S BREEDING STOCK HAD ALL BEEN SLAUGHTERED.
ADD TO THAT OUR "PATIENT" IN THE MED CENTER, AND--
--WE MUST ASSUME AN ATTACK IS IMMINENT.
PHONE
Mr. SHIMURA IS IN CHARGE OF SECURITY. ALL ABLE-BODIED PERSONNEL WILL BE EXPECTED TO TAKE A SHIFT ON WATCH. ANYONE NOT ON DUTY WILL REMAIN WITHIN THE MAIN COMPLEX.
THERE IS A THIRTY-THREE-HOUR CURFEW IN EFFECT AS OF NOW.
THE FOLLOWING PERSONNEL WILL REPORT TO ME AT THE END OF THIS MEETING FOR FIRST WATCH...
FEW OF THE RANCHERS HAD WEAPONS OF THEIR OWN, AND THE CORPORATE ARMORY CONSISTED OF FIFTEEN SCATTER-GUNS--PRIMARILY FOR USE AGAINST FIRE-CRAWLERS AND BRIAR-WOLVES--AND TEN PISTOLS EAR-MARKED FOR A POLICE FORCE THE TOWN HAD NEVER NEEDED.
CARGO COLD
STOTT
NC-13702
NICCOLI CARGO
ST
STAR LINES
PROSPERITY WELLS WAS NEVER INTENDED TO BE A FORTRESS, BUT THE RANCHERS, UNDER HIROKI'S DIRECTION, SET UP AN ADMIRABLE LINE OF DEFENSE.

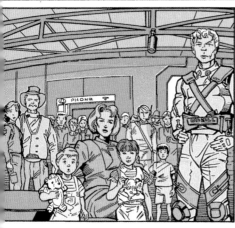

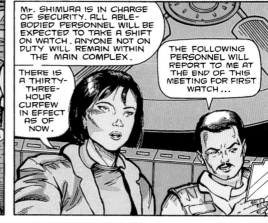

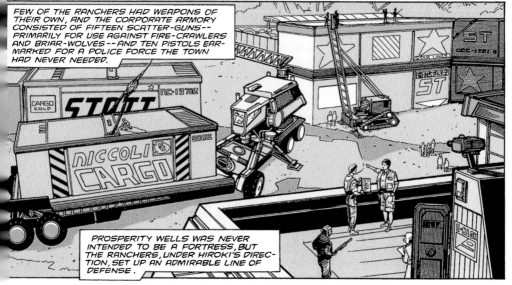

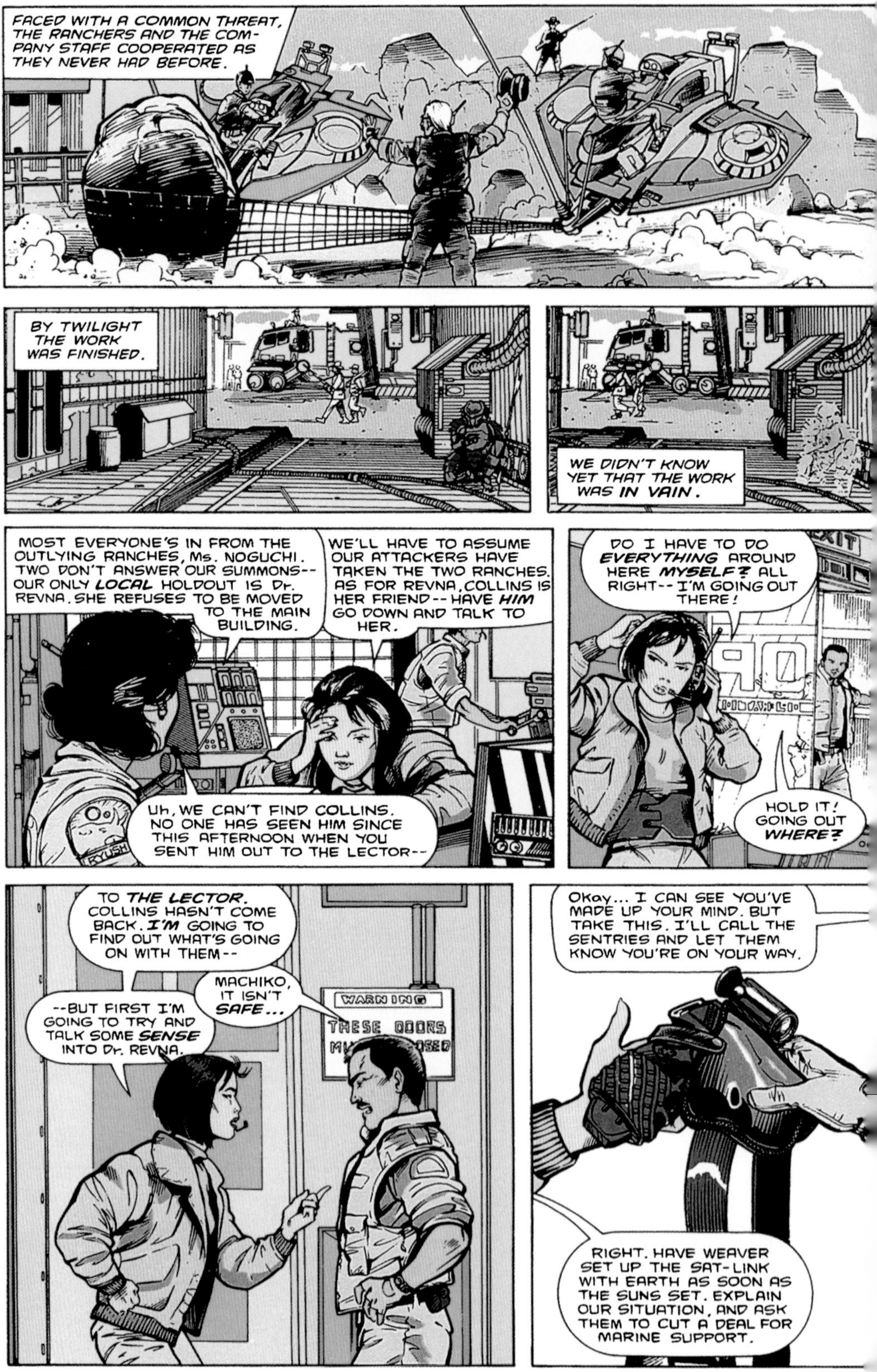

FACED WITH A COMMON THREAT, THE RANCHERS AND THE COMPANY STAFF COOPERATED AS THEY NEVER HAD BEFORE.
BY TWILIGHT THE WORK WAS FINISHED.
WE DIDN'T KNOW YET THAT THE WORK WAS IN VAIN.
MOST EVERYONE'S IN FROM THE OUTLYING RANCHES, Ms. NOGUCHI. TWO DON'T ANSWER OUR SUMMONS-- OUR ONLY LOCAL HOLDOUT IS Dr. REVNA. SHE REFUSES TO BE MOVED TO THE MAIN BUILDING.
WE'LL HAVE TO ASSUME OUR ATTACKERS HAVE TAKEN THE TWO RANCHES. AS FOR REVNA, COLLINS IS HER FRIEND-- HAVE HIM GO DOWN AND TALK TO HER.
Uh, WE CAN'T FIND COLLINS. NO ONE HAS SEEN HIM SINCE THIS AFTERNOON WHEN YOU SENT HIM OUT TO THE LECTOR--
RYUSH
DO I HAVE TO DO EVERYTHING AROUND HERE MYSELF? ALL RIGHT-- I'M GOING OUT THERE!
EXIT
HOLD IT! GOING OUT WHERE?
TO THE LECTOR. COLLINS HASN'T COME BACK. I'M GOING TO FIND OUT WHAT'S GOING ON WITH THEM--
--BUT FIRST I'M GOING TO TRY AND TALK SOME SENSE INTO Dr. REVNA.
MACHIKO, IT ISN'T SAFE...
WARNING
THESE DOORS
Okay... I CAN SEE YOU'VE MADE UP YOUR MIND. BUT TAKE THIS. I'LL CALL THE SENTRIES AND LET THEM KNOW YOU'RE ON YOUR WAY.
RIGHT. HAVE WEAVER SET UP THE SAT-LINK WITH EARTH AS SOON AS THE SUNS SET. EXPLAIN OUR SITUATION, AND ASK THEM TO CUT A DEAL FOR MARINE SUPPORT.

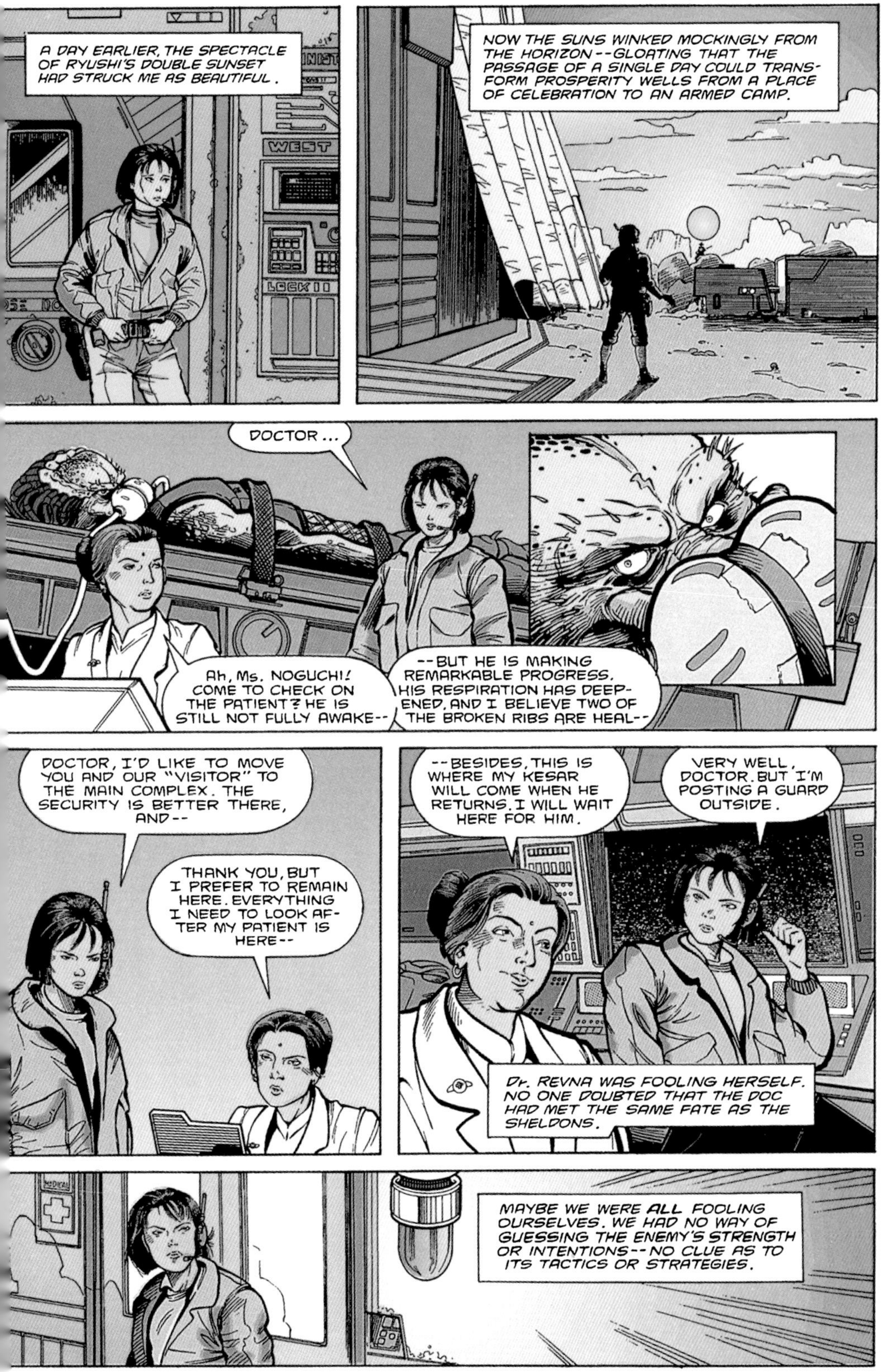
A DAY EARLIER, THE SPECTACLE OF RYUSHI'S DOUBLE SUNSET HAD STRUCK ME AS BEAUTIFUL.
NOW THE SUNS WINKED MOCKINGLY FROM THE HORIZON--GLOATING THAT THE PASSAGE OF A SINGLE DAY COULD TRANSFORM PROSPERITY WELLS FROM A PLACE OF CELEBRATION TO AN ARMED CAMP.
DOCTOR...
Ah, Ms. NOGUCHI! COME TO CHECK ON THE PATIENT? HE IS STILL NOT FULLY AWAKE--
--BUT HE IS MAKING REMARKABLE PROGRESS. HIS RESPIRATION HAS DEEPENED, AND I BELIEVE TWO OF THE BROKEN RIBS ARE HEAL--
DOCTOR, I'D LIKE TO MOVE YOU AND OUR "VISITOR" TO THE MAIN COMPLEX. THE SECURITY IS BETTER THERE, AND--
THANK YOU, BUT I PREFER TO REMAIN HERE. EVERYTHING I NEED TO LOOK AFTER MY PATIENT IS HERE--
--BESIDES, THIS IS WHERE MY KESAR WILL COME WHEN HE RETURNS. I WILL WAIT HERE FOR HIM.
VERY WELL, DOCTOR. BUT I'M POSTING A GUARD OUTSIDE.
Dr. REVNA WAS FOOLING HERSELF. NO ONE DOUBTED THAT THE DOC HAD MET THE SAME FATE AS THE SHELDONS.
MAYBE WE WERE ALL FOOLING OURSELVES. WE HAD NO WAY OF GUESSING THE ENEMY'S STRENGTH OR INTENTIONS--NO CLUE AS TO ITS TACTICS OR STRATEGIES.

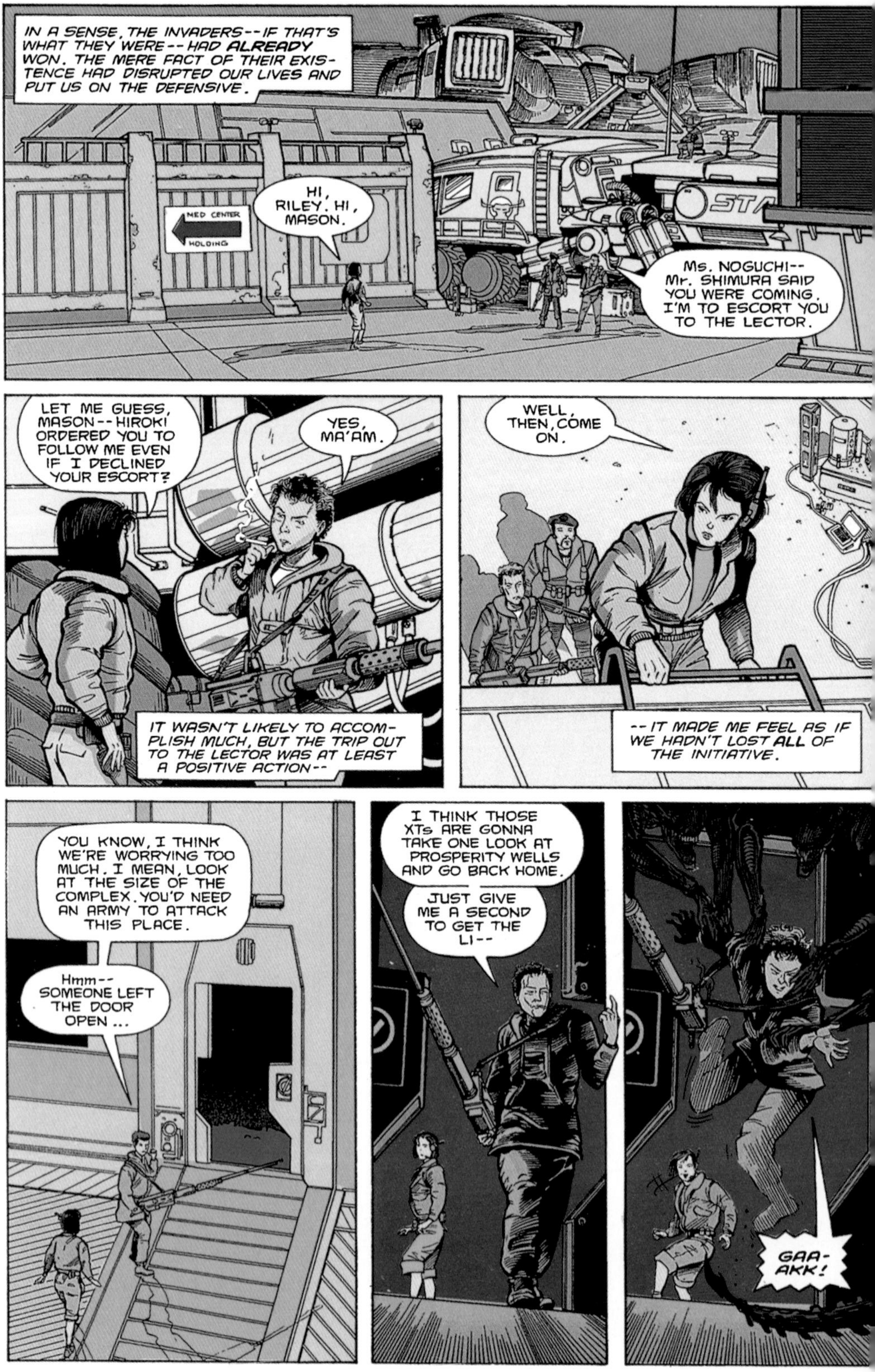
IN A SENSE, THE INVADERS--IF THAT'S WHAT THEY WERE--HAD ALREADY WON. THE MERE FACT OF THEIR EXISTENCE HAD DISRUPTED OUR LIVES AND PUT US ON THE DEFENSIVE.
MED CENTER
HOLDING
HI, RILEY. HI, MASON.
Ms. NOGUCHI-- Mr. SHIMURA SAID YOU WERE COMING. I'M TO ESCORT YOU TO THE LECTOR.
LET ME GUESS, MASON--HIROKI ORDERED YOU TO FOLLOW ME EVEN IF I DECLINED YOUR ESCORT?
YES, MA'AM.
IT WASN'T LIKELY TO ACCOMPLISH MUCH, BUT THE TRIP OUT TO THE LECTOR WAS AT LEAST A POSITIVE ACTION--
WELL, THEN, COME ON.
--IT MADE ME FEEL AS IF WE HADN'T LOST ALL OF THE INITIATIVE.
YOU KNOW, I THINK WE'RE WORRYING TOO MUCH. I MEAN, LOOK AT THE SIZE OF THE COMPLEX. YOU'D NEED AN ARMY TO ATTACK THIS PLACE.
Hmm-- SOMEONE LEFT THE DOOR OPEN...
I THINK THOSE XTs ARE GONNA TAKE ONE LOOK AT PROSPERITY WELLS AND GO BACK HOME.
JUST GIVE ME A SECOND TO GET THE LI--
GAA-AKK!

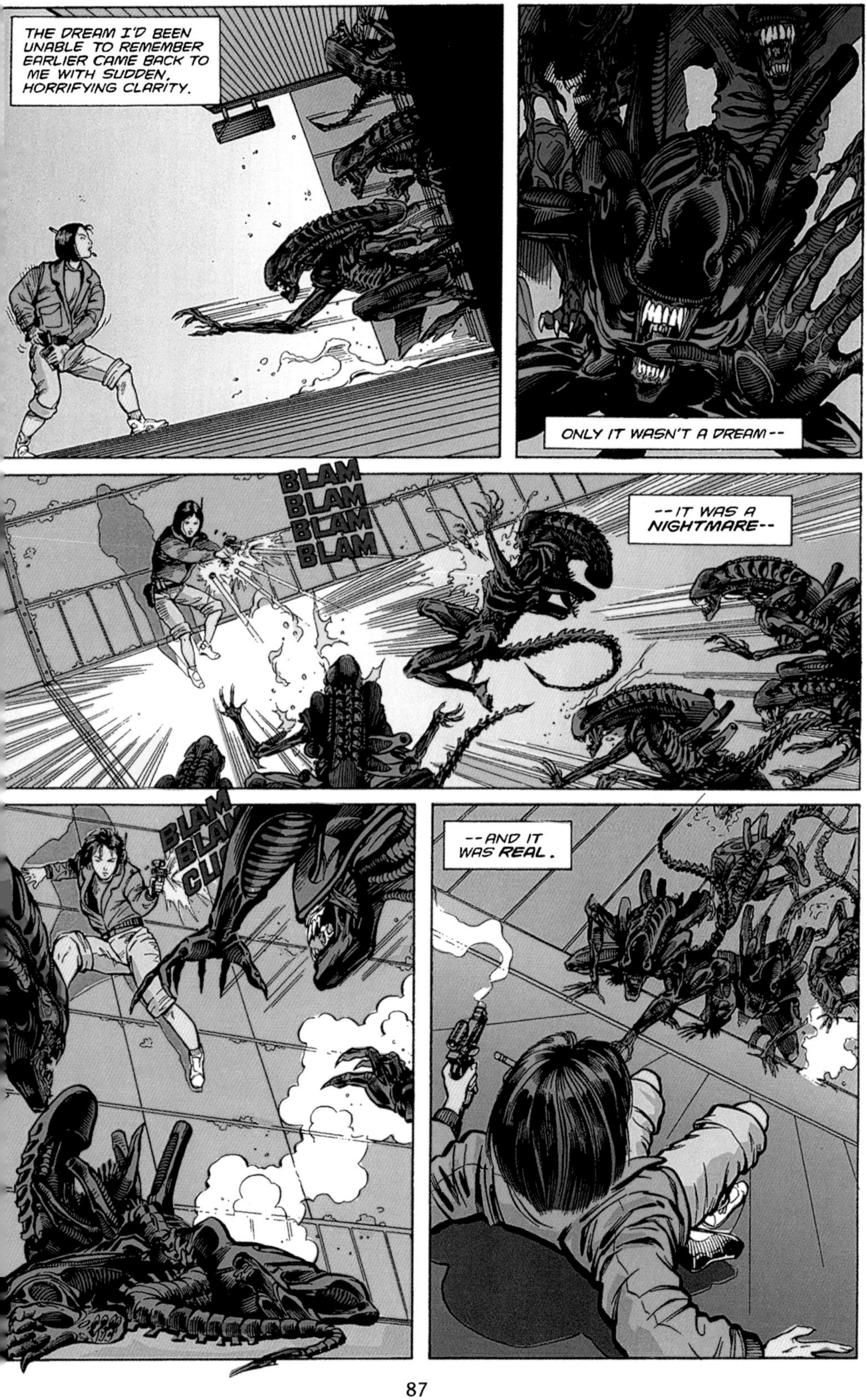
THE DREAM I'D BEEN UNABLE TO REMEMBER EARLIER CAME BACK TO ME WITH SUDDEN, HORRIFYING CLARITY.
ONLY IT WASN'T A DREAM--
BLAM BLAM BLAM BLAM
--IT WAS A NIGHTMARE--
BLAM
--AND IT WAS REAL.

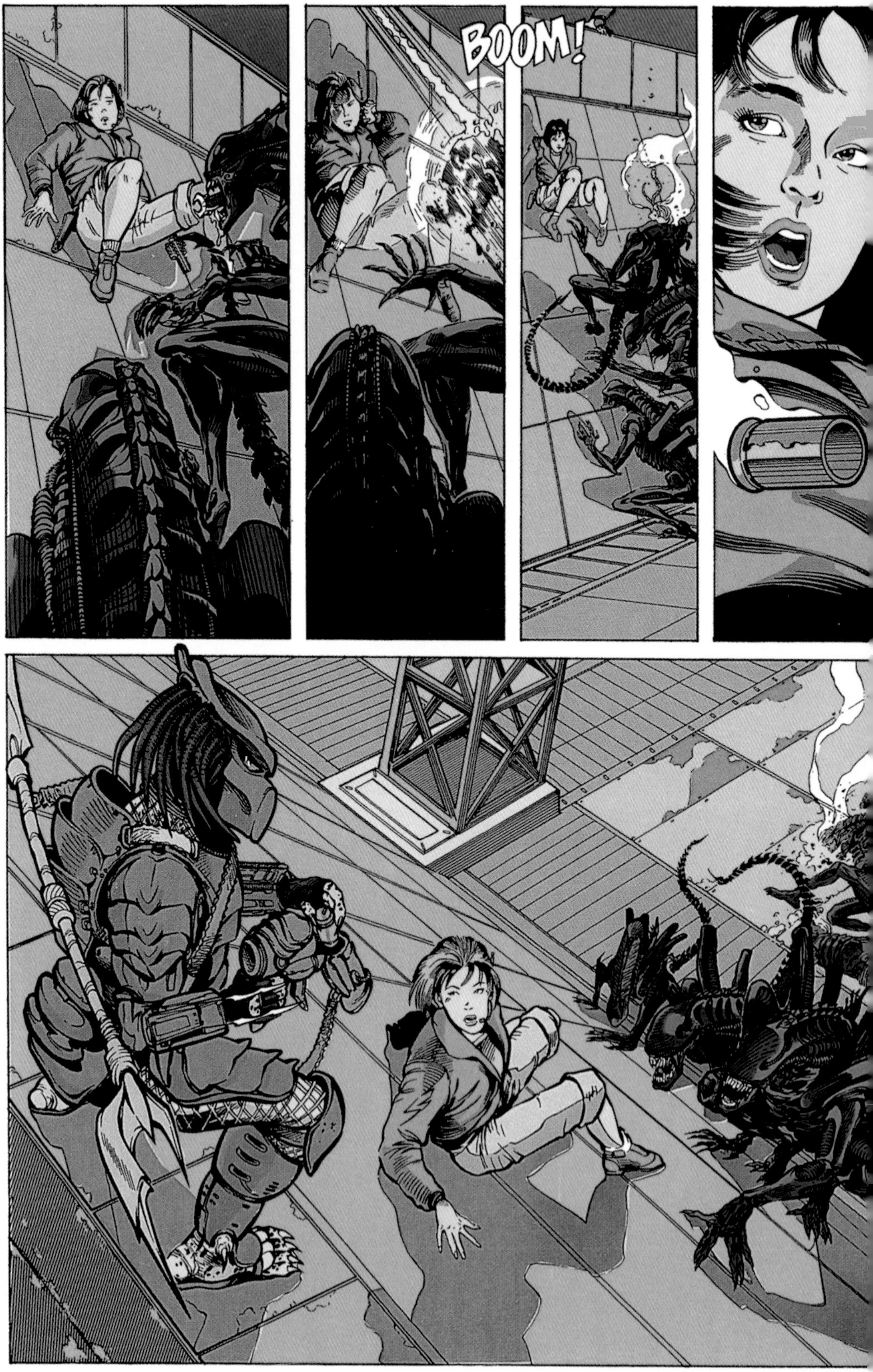
BOOM!

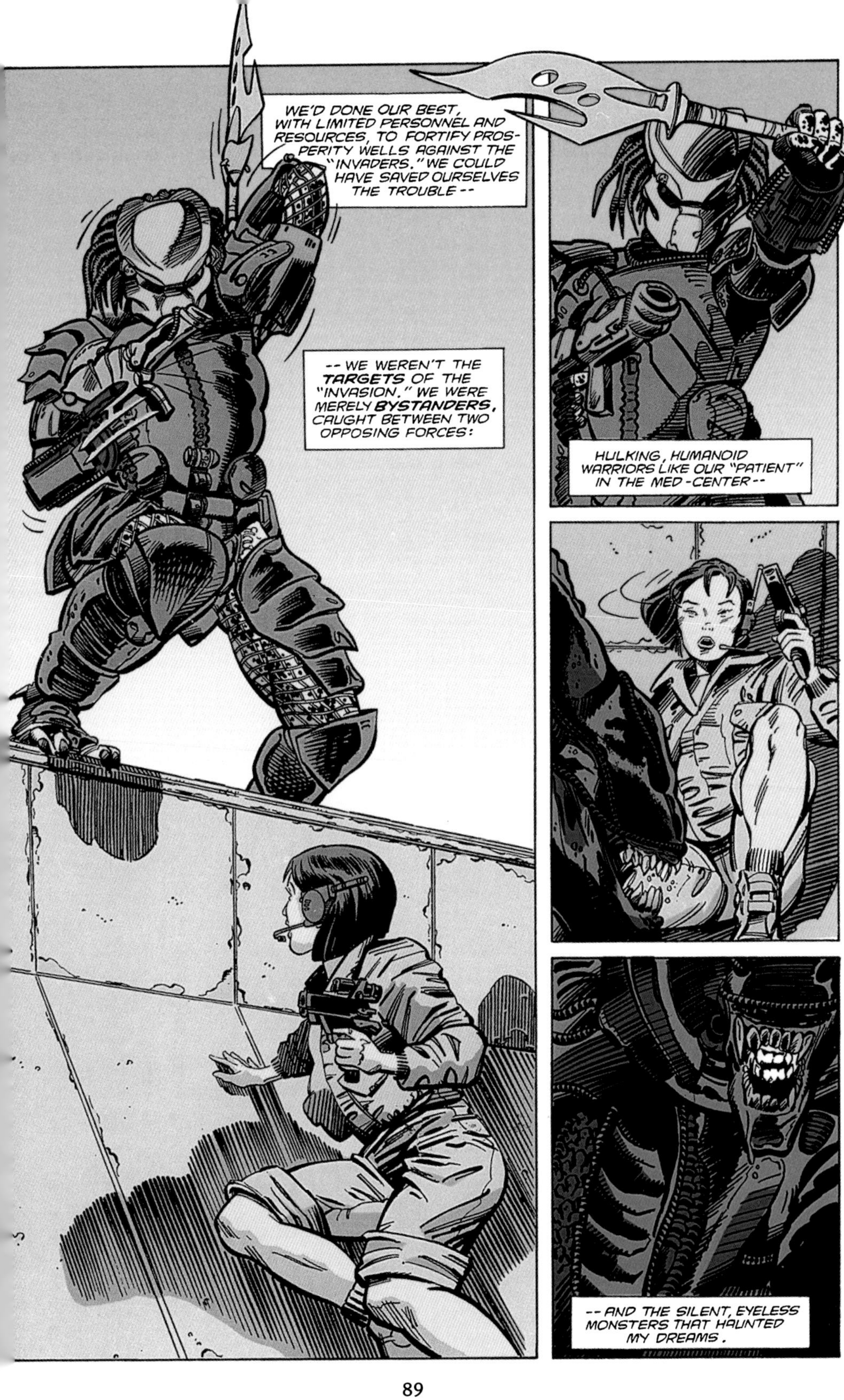
WE'D DONE OUR BEST, WITH LIMITED PERSONNEL AND RESOURCES, TO FORTIFY PROSPERITY WELLS AGAINST THE "INVADERS." WE COULD HAVE SAVED OURSELVES THE TROUBLE --
-- WE WEREN'T THE TARGETS OF THE "INVASION." WE WERE MERELY BYSTANDERS, CAUGHT BETWEEN TWO OPPOSING FORCES:
HULKING, HUMANOID WARRIORS LIKE OUR "PATIENT" IN THE MED-CENTER --
-- AND THE SILENT, EYELESS MONSTERS THAT HAUNTED MY DREAMS.

PERHAPS IT WAS THIS CONNECTION TO MY NIGHTMARES--AS WELL AS THE FACT THAT THE MONSTERS HAD KILLED MASON--THAT PREDISPOSED ME AGAINST THEM...

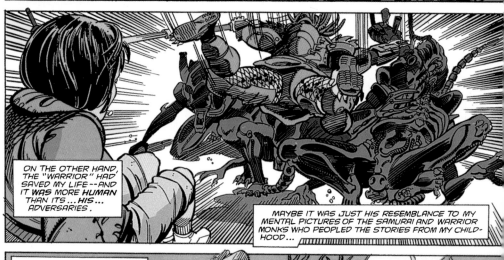

ON THE OTHER HAND, THE "WARRIOR" HAD SAVED MY LIFE--AND IT *WAS* MORE *HUMAN* THAN ITS...*HIS*... ADVERSARIES.

MAYBE IT WAS JUST HIS RESEMBLANCE TO MY MENTAL PICTURES OF THE SAMURAI AND WARRIOR MONKS WHO PEOPLED THE STORIES FROM MY CHILD-HOOD...

...OR IT COULD HAVE BEEN THAT IT'S SIMPLY HUMAN NATURE TO CHEER FOR THE UNDERDOG.

WHATEVER THE REASON, I CAUGHT MY BREATH AS THE "WARRIOR" LEAPT--HEROICALLY, IT SEEMED--INTO BATTLE.

90

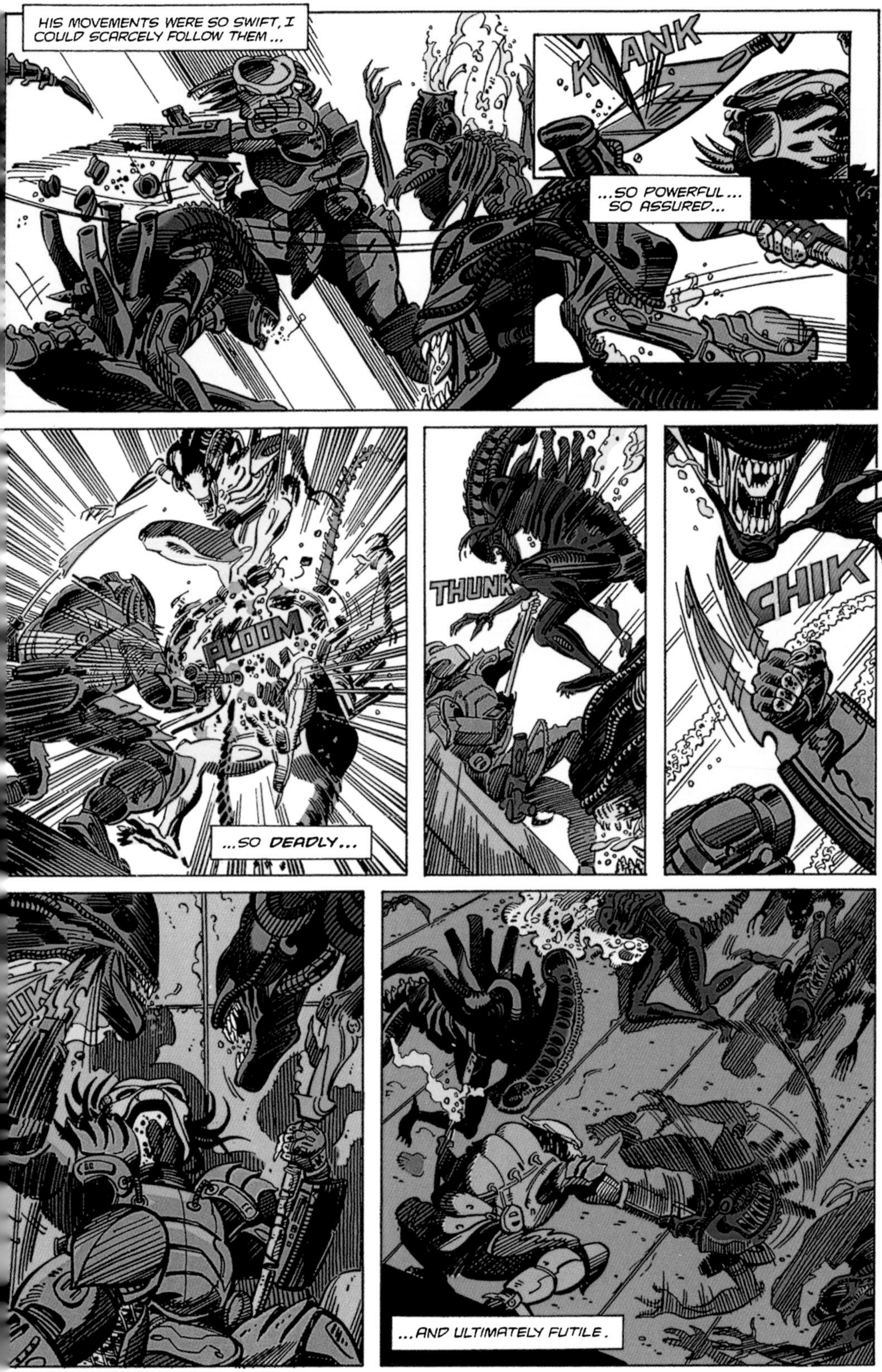
HIS MOVEMENTS WERE SO SWIFT, I COULD SCARCELY FOLLOW THEM ...
KLANK
...SO POWERFUL... SO ASSURED...
BLOOM
...SO DEADLY...
THUNK
CHIK
...AND ULTIMATELY FUTILE.

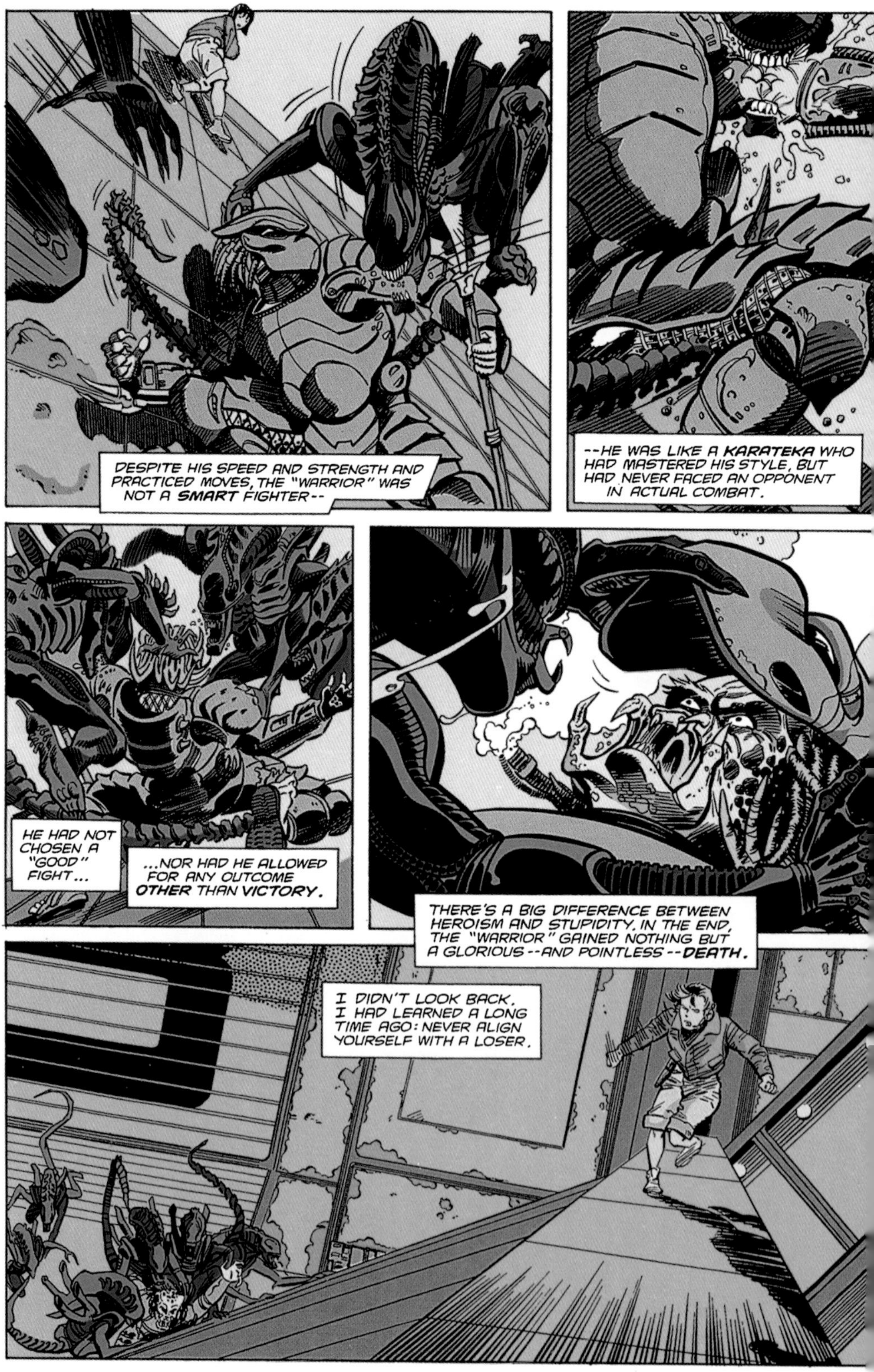
DESPITE HIS SPEED AND STRENGTH AND PRACTICED MOVES, THE "WARRIOR" WAS NOT A SMART FIGHTER--
--HE WAS LIKE A KARATEKA WHO HAD MASTERED HIS STYLE, BUT HAD NEVER FACED AN OPPONENT IN ACTUAL COMBAT.
HE HAD NOT CHOSEN A "GOOD" FIGHT...
...NOR HAD HE ALLOWED FOR ANY OUTCOME OTHER THAN VICTORY.
THERE'S A BIG DIFFERENCE BETWEEN HEROISM AND STUPIDITY. IN THE END, THE "WARRIOR" GAINED NOTHING BUT A GLORIOUS--AND POINTLESS--DEATH.
I DIDN'T LOOK BACK. I HAD LEARNED A LONG TIME AGO: NEVER ALIGN YOURSELF WITH A LOSER.

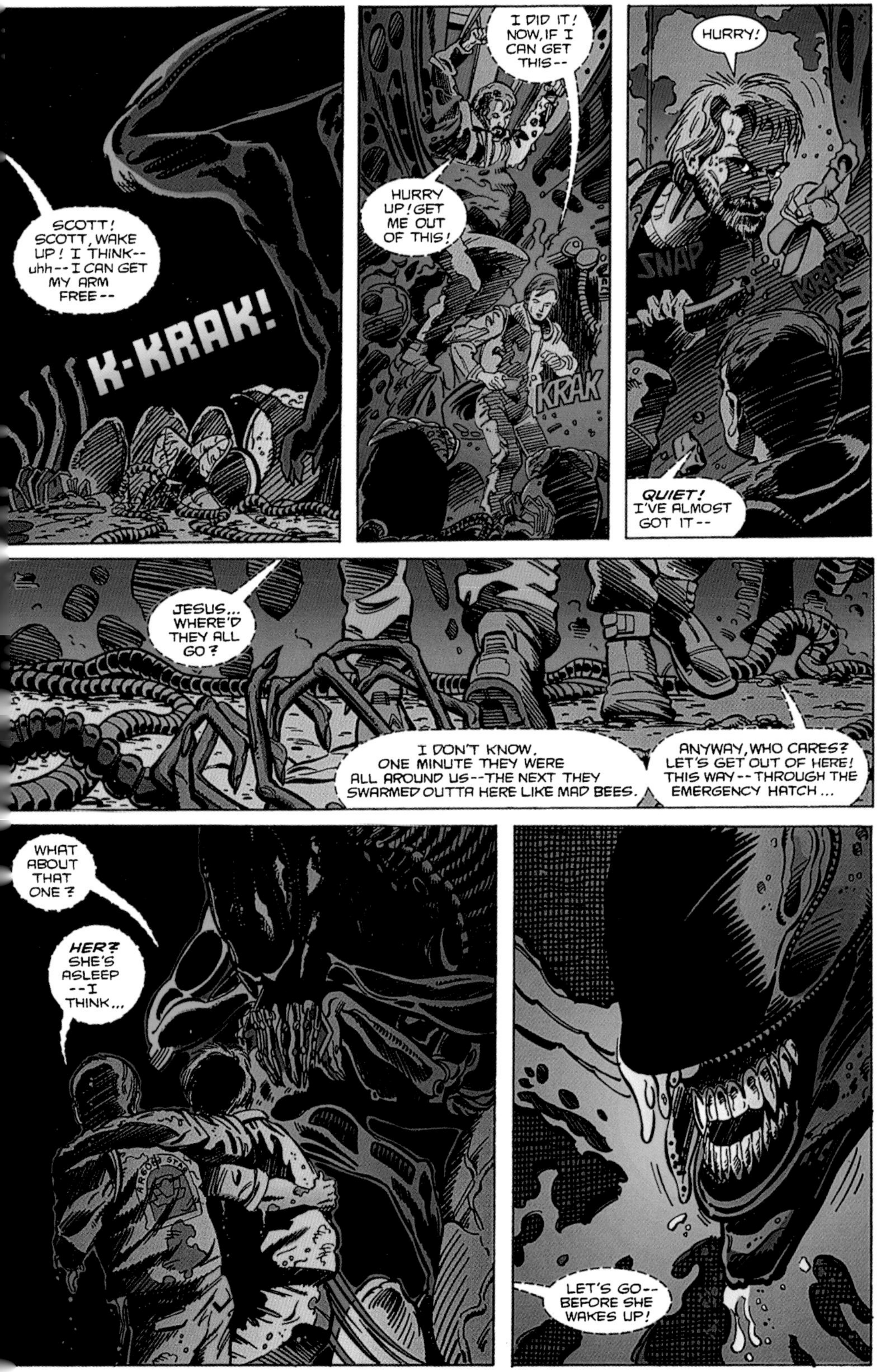
SCOTT! SCOTT, WAKE UP! I THINK-- uhh--I CAN GET MY ARM FREE--
K-KRAK!
I DID IT! NOW, IF I CAN GET THIS--
HURRY UP! GET ME OUT OF THIS!
KRAK
HURRY!
SNAP
KRAK
QUIET! I'VE ALMOST GOT IT--
JESUS... WHERE'D THEY ALL GO?
I DON'T KNOW. ONE MINUTE THEY WERE ALL AROUND US--THE NEXT THEY SWARMED OUTTA HERE LIKE MAD BEES.
ANYWAY, WHO CARES? LET'S GET OUT OF HERE! THIS WAY--THROUGH THE EMERGENCY HATCH...
WHAT ABOUT THAT ONE?
HER? SHE'S ASLEEP --I THINK...
LET'S GO-- BEFORE SHE WAKES UP!

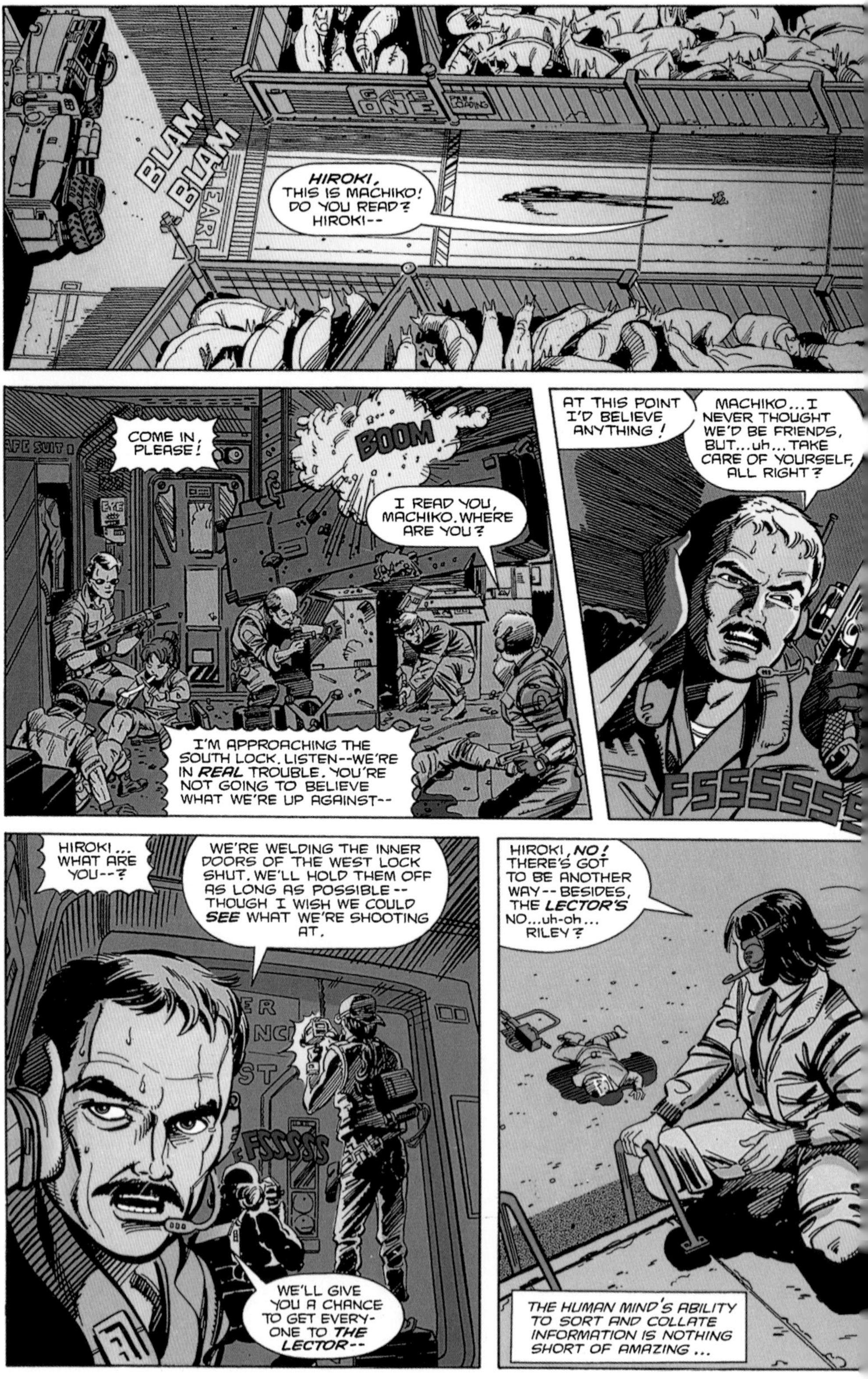
BLAM
BLAM
GATE ONE
HIROKI, THIS IS MACHIKO! DO YOU READ? HIROKI--
COME IN, PLEASE!
BOOM
I READ YOU, MACHIKO. WHERE ARE YOU?
I'M APPROACHING THE SOUTH LOCK. LISTEN--WE'RE IN REAL TROUBLE. YOU'RE NOT GOING TO BELIEVE WHAT WE'RE UP AGAINST--
AT THIS POINT I'D BELIEVE ANYTHING!
MACHIKO...I NEVER THOUGHT WE'D BE FRIENDS, BUT...uh...TAKE CARE OF YOURSELF, ALL RIGHT?
FSSSSSS
HIROKI... WHAT ARE YOU--?
WE'RE WELDING THE INNER DOORS OF THE WEST LOCK SHUT. WE'LL HOLD THEM OFF AS LONG AS POSSIBLE -- THOUGH I WISH WE COULD SEE WHAT WE'RE SHOOTING AT.
FSSSSS
WE'LL GIVE YOU A CHANCE TO GET EVERY-ONE TO THE LECTOR--
HIROKI, NO! THERE'S GOT TO BE ANOTHER WAY-- BESIDES, THE LECTOR'S NO...uh-oh... RILEY?
THE HUMAN MIND'S ABILITY TO SORT AND COLLATE INFORMATION IS NOTHING SHORT OF AMAZING...

...I WAS LISTENING TO HIROKI'S VOICE ON THE COM, THE SOUND OF GUNFIRE ECHOED THROUGH THE STREETS OF THE COMPLEX, MY HEART WAS POUNDING LIKE THUNDER IN MY CHEST--

--AND, SOMEHOW, I HEARD ANOTHER SOUND...OR A HINT OF A SOUND. NOTHING MORE THAN AN INTAKE OF BREATH.

IT WASN'T MINE-- AND IT CERTAINLY WASN'T RILEY'S.

FAINT THOUGH IT WAS, IT WAS ENOUGH.

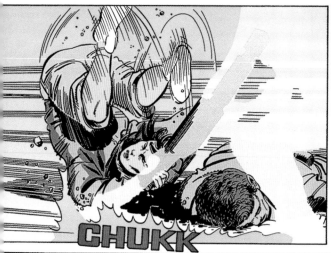

CHUKK

INVISIBILITY. THAT'S HOW THE "WARRIORS" HAD GOTTEN PAST OUR DEFENSES.

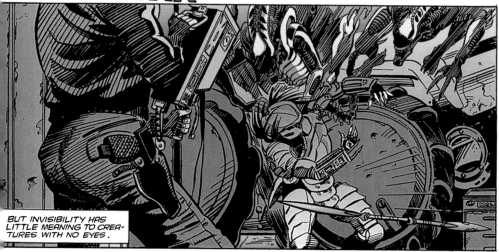

BUT INVISIBILITY HAS LITTLE MEANING TO CREATURES WITH NO EYES.

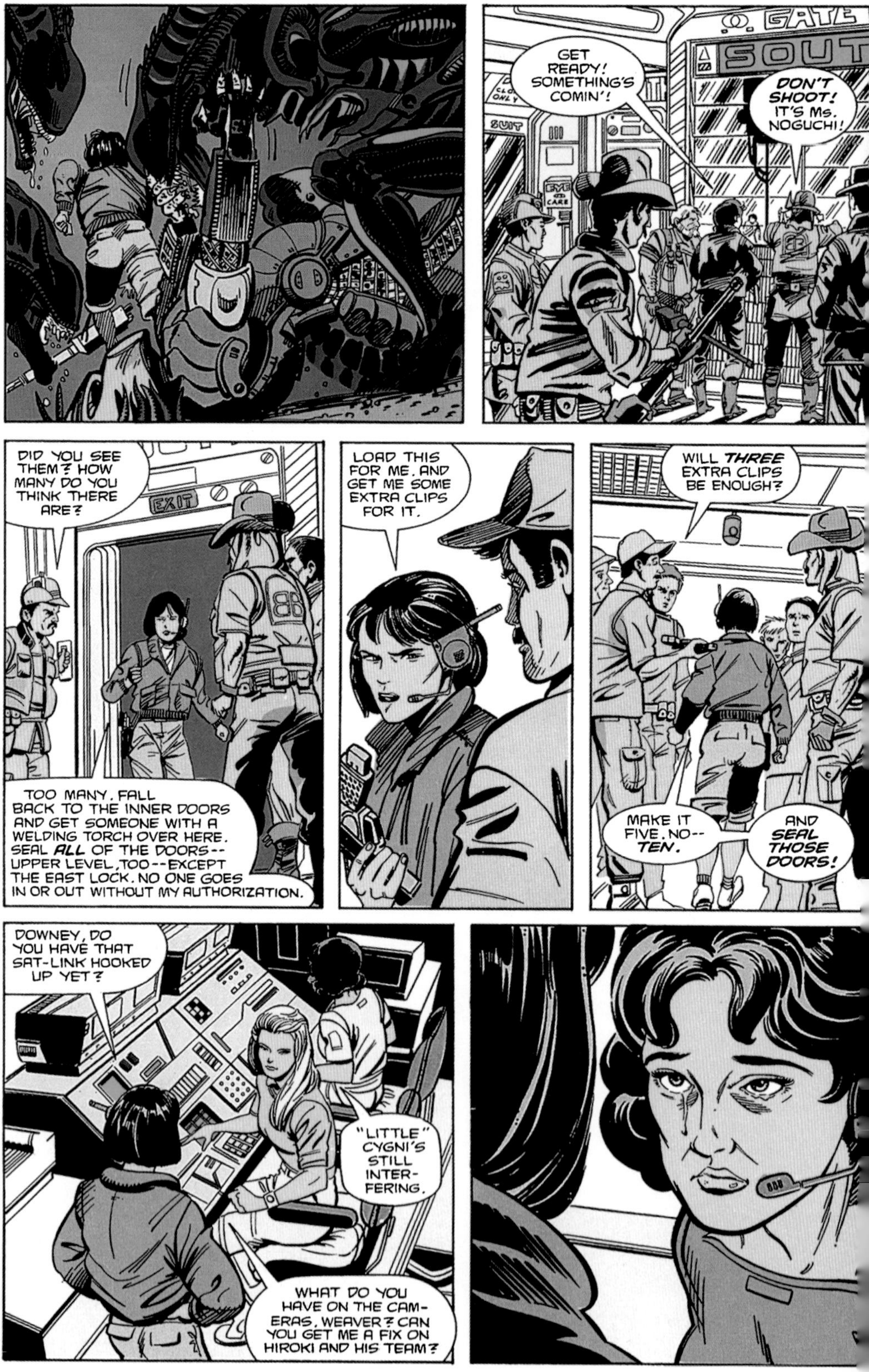
GET READY! SOMETHING'S COMIN'!
DON'T SHOOT! IT'S Ms. NOGUCHI!
DID YOU SEE THEM? HOW MANY DO YOU THINK THERE ARE?
TOO MANY. FALL BACK TO THE INNER DOORS AND GET SOMEONE WITH A WELDING TORCH OVER HERE. SEAL ALL OF THE DOORS--UPPER LEVEL, TOO--EXCEPT THE EAST LOCK. NO ONE GOES IN OR OUT WITHOUT MY AUTHORIZATION.
LOAD THIS FOR ME. AND GET ME SOME EXTRA CLIPS FOR IT.
WILL THREE EXTRA CLIPS BE ENOUGH?
MAKE IT FIVE. NO-- TEN.
AND SEAL THOSE DOORS!
DOWNEY, DO YOU HAVE THAT SAT-LINK HOOKED UP YET?
"LITTLE" CYGNI'S STILL INTERFERING.
WHAT DO YOU HAVE ON THE CAMERAS, WEAVER? CAN YOU GET ME A FIX ON HIROKI AND HIS TEAM?

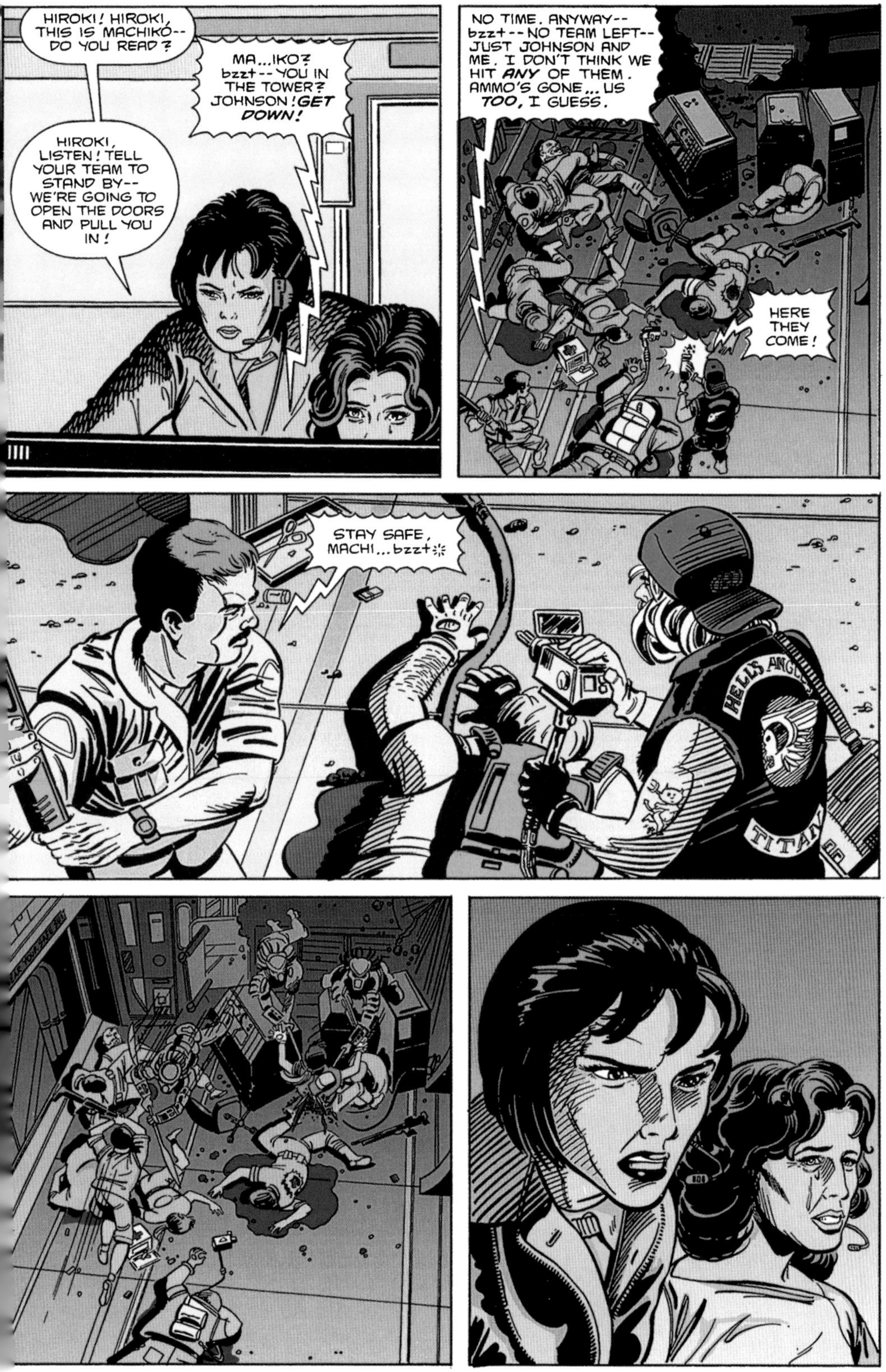
HIROKI! HIROKI, THIS IS MACHIKO-- DO YOU READ?
MA...IKO? bzzt--YOU IN THE TOWER? JOHNSON! **GET DOWN!**
HIROKI, LISTEN! TELL YOUR TEAM TO STAND BY-- WE'RE GOING TO OPEN THE DOORS AND PULL YOU IN!
NO TIME. ANYWAY-- bzzt--NO TEAM LEFT-- JUST JOHNSON AND ME. I DON'T THINK WE HIT **ANY** OF THEM. AMMO'S GONE... US **TOO**, I GUESS.
HERE THEY COME!
STAY SAFE, MACHI...bzzt

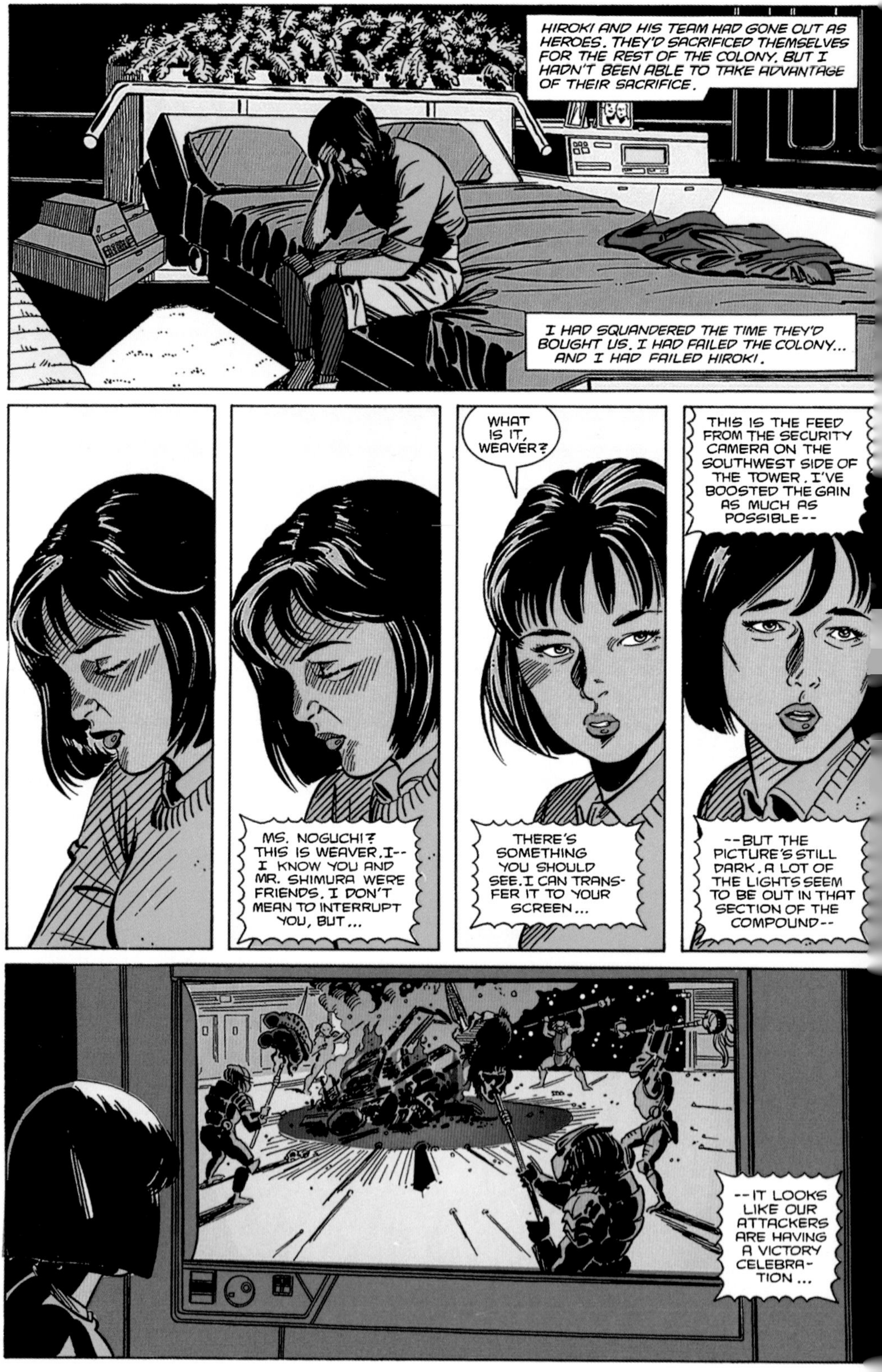
HIROKI AND HIS TEAM HAD GONE OUT AS HEROES. THEY'D SACRIFICED THEMSELVES FOR THE REST OF THE COLONY. BUT I HADN'T BEEN ABLE TO TAKE ADVANTAGE OF THEIR SACRIFICE.
I HAD SQUANDERED THE TIME THEY'D BOUGHT US. I HAD FAILED THE COLONY... AND I HAD FAILED HIROKI.
MS. NOGUCHI? THIS IS WEAVER. I-- I KNOW YOU AND MR. SHIMURA WERE FRIENDS. I DON'T MEAN TO INTERRUPT YOU, BUT...
WHAT IS IT, WEAVER?
THERE'S SOMETHING YOU SHOULD SEE. I CAN TRANSFER IT TO YOUR SCREEN...
THIS IS THE FEED FROM THE SECURITY CAMERA ON THE SOUTHWEST SIDE OF THE TOWER. I'VE BOOSTED THE GAIN AS MUCH AS POSSIBLE--
--BUT THE PICTURE'S STILL DARK. A LOT OF THE LIGHTS SEEM TO BE OUT IN THAT SECTION OF THE COMPOUND--
--IT LOOKS LIKE OUR ATTACKERS ARE HAVING A VICTORY CELEBRATION...

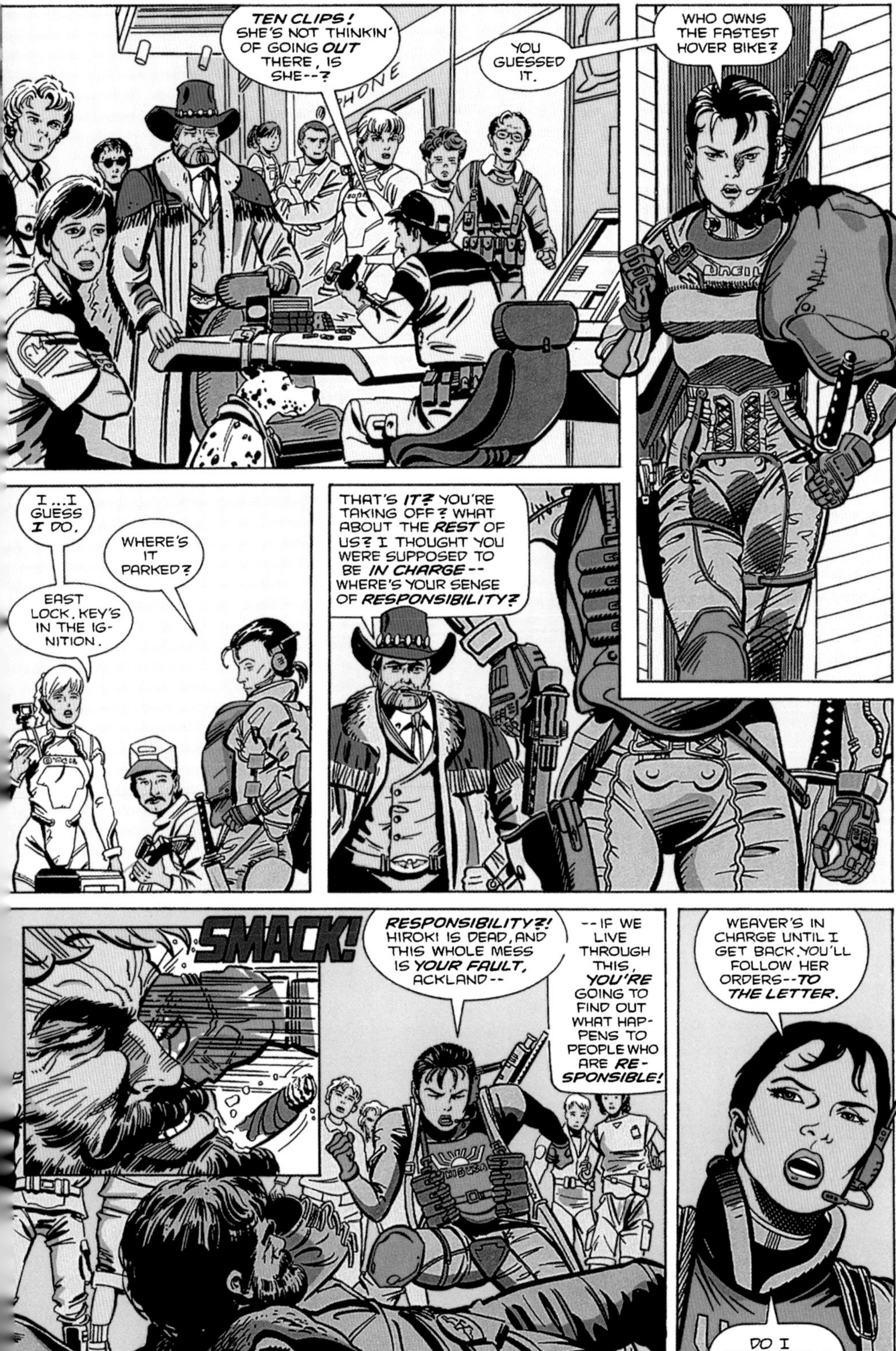

TEN CLIPS! SHE'S NOT THINKIN' OF GOING OUT THERE, IS SHE--?
YOU GUESSED IT.
WHO OWNS THE FASTEST HOVER BIKE?
I...I GUESS I DO.
WHERE'S IT PARKED?
EAST LOCK. KEY'S IN THE IG-NITION.
THAT'S IT? YOU'RE TAKING OFF? WHAT ABOUT THE REST OF US? I THOUGHT YOU WERE SUPPOSED TO BE IN CHARGE -- WHERE'S YOUR SENSE OF RESPONSIBILITY?
SMACK!
RESPONSIBILITY?! HIROKI IS DEAD, AND THIS WHOLE MESS IS YOUR FAULT, ACKLAND--
--IF WE LIVE THROUGH THIS, YOU'RE GOING TO FIND OUT WHAT HAP-PENS TO PEOPLE WHO ARE RE-SPONSIBLE!
WEAVER'S IN CHARGE UNTIL I GET BACK. YOU'LL FOLLOW HER ORDERS--TO THE LETTER.
DO I MAKE MYSELF CLEAR?

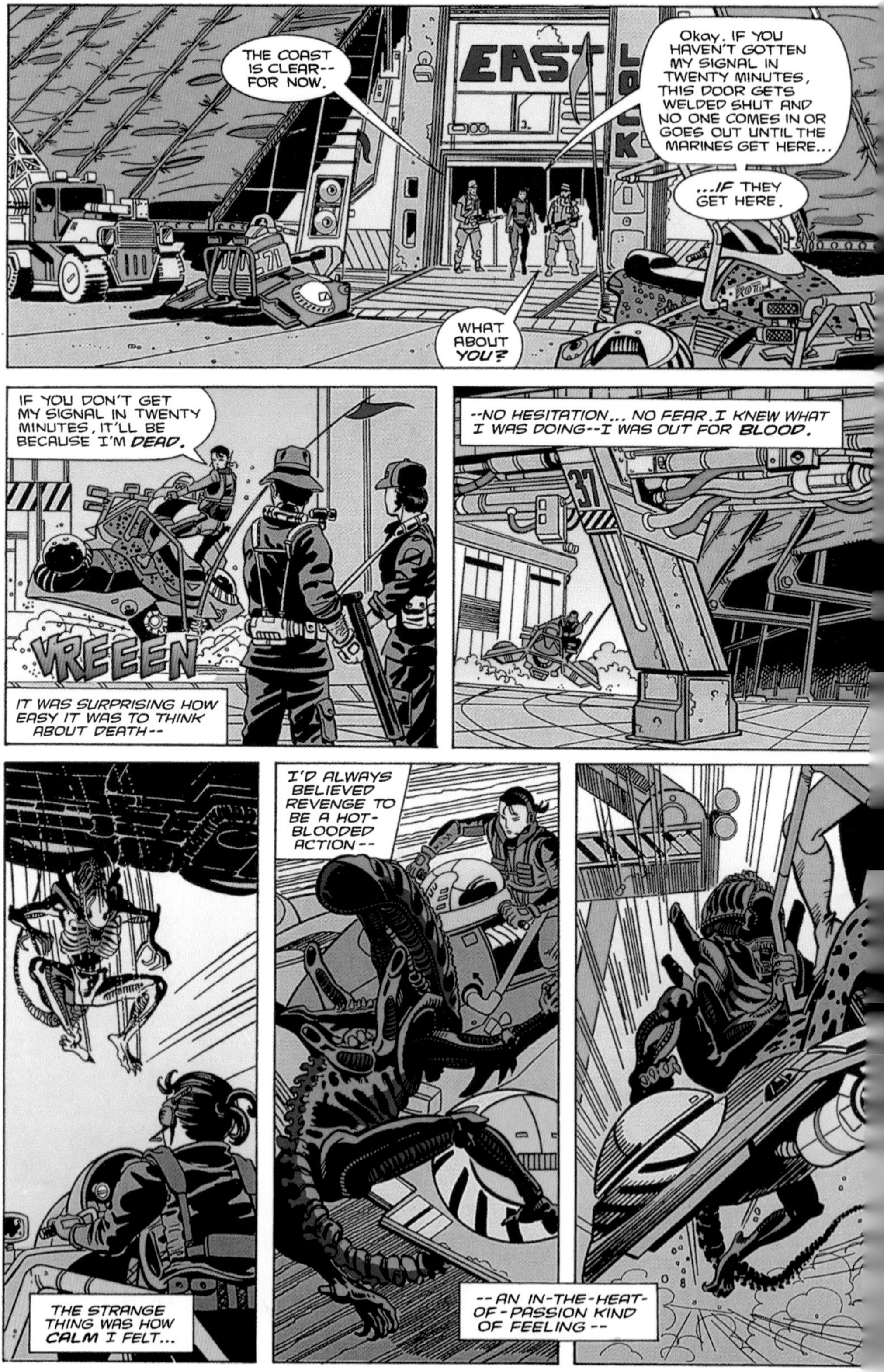
THE COAST IS CLEAR-- FOR NOW.
EAST
LOCK
Okay. IF YOU HAVEN'T GOTTEN MY SIGNAL IN TWENTY MINUTES, THIS DOOR GETS WELDED SHUT AND NO ONE COMES IN OR GOES OUT UNTIL THE MARINES GET HERE...
...IF THEY GET HERE.
WHAT ABOUT YOU?
IF YOU DON'T GET MY SIGNAL IN TWENTY MINUTES, IT'LL BE BECAUSE I'M DEAD.
VREEEN
IT WAS SURPRISING HOW EASY IT WAS TO THINK ABOUT DEATH--
--NO HESITATION... NO FEAR. I KNEW WHAT I WAS DOING--I WAS OUT FOR BLOOD.
37
THE STRANGE THING WAS HOW CALM I FELT...
I'D ALWAYS BELIEVED REVENGE TO BE A HOT-BLOODED ACTION--
--AN IN-THE-HEAT-OF-PASSION KIND OF FEELING--

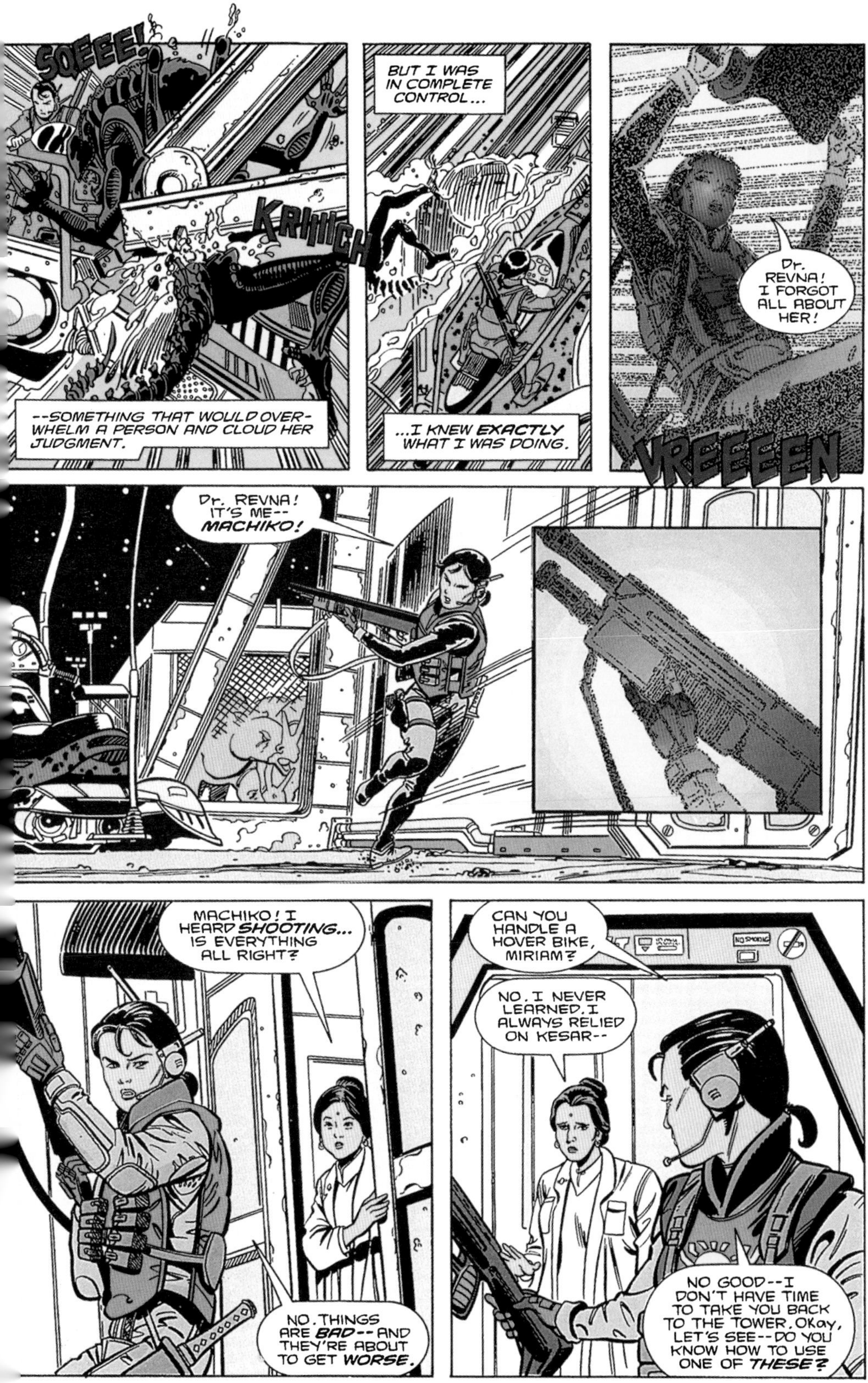

SQEEEE!
KRIIIICH
--SOMETHING THAT WOULD OVER-WHELM A PERSON AND CLOUD HER JUDGMENT.
BUT I WAS IN COMPLETE CONTROL...
...I KNEW EXACTLY WHAT I WAS DOING.
Dr. REVNA! I FORGOT ALL ABOUT HER!
VREEEEN
Dr. REVNA! IT'S ME-- MACHIKO!
MACHIKO! I HEARD SHOOTING... IS EVERYTHING ALL RIGHT?
NO. THINGS ARE BAD-- AND THEY'RE ABOUT TO GET WORSE.
CAN YOU HANDLE A HOVER BIKE, MIRIAM?
NO. I NEVER LEARNED. I ALWAYS RELIED ON KESAR--
NO GOOD--I DON'T HAVE TIME TO TAKE YOU BACK TO THE TOWER. OKay, LET'S SEE--DO YOU KNOW HOW TO USE ONE OF THESE?

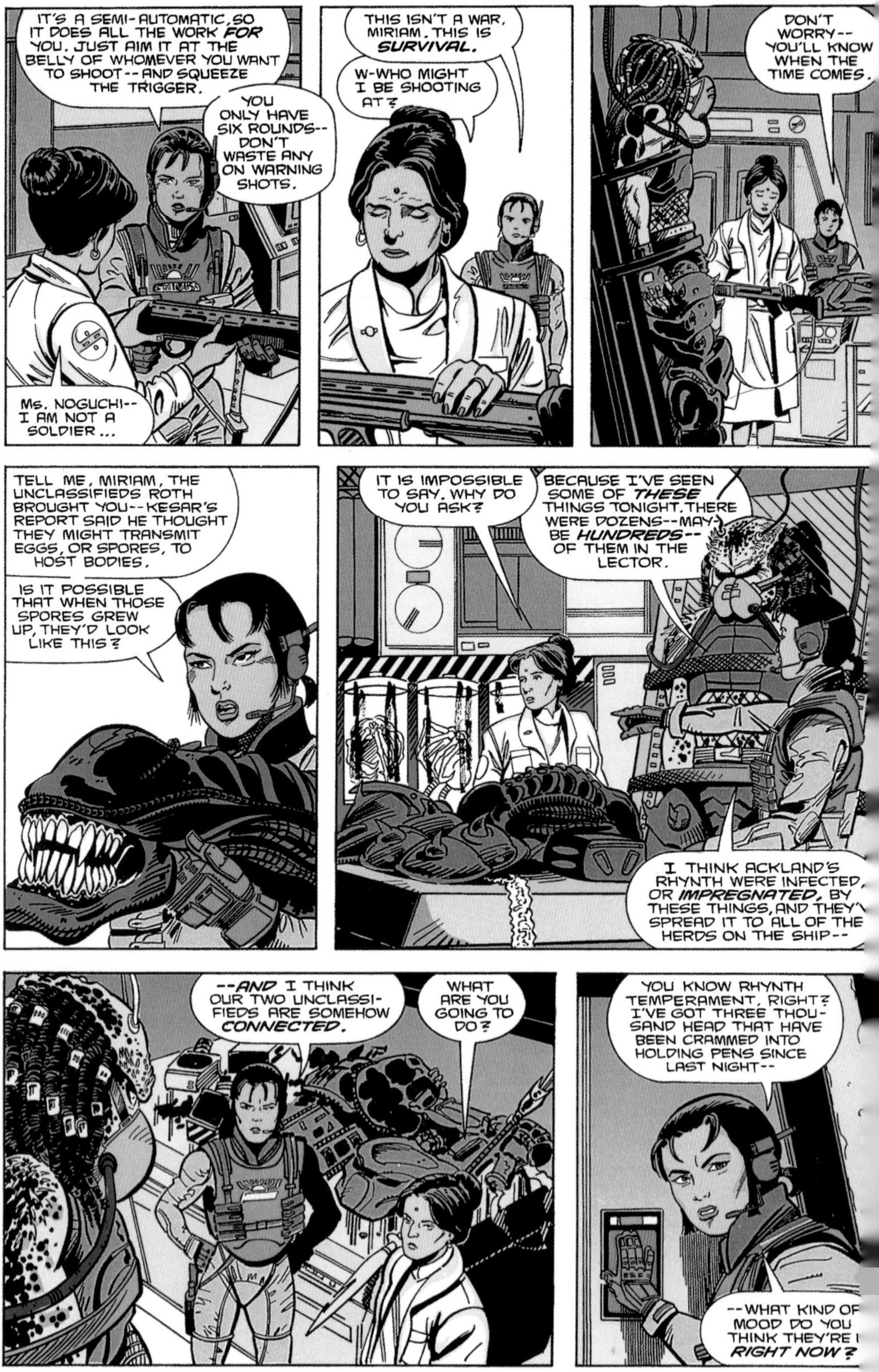
IT'S A SEMI-AUTOMATIC, SO IT DOES ALL THE WORK FOR YOU. JUST AIM IT AT THE BELLY OF WHOMEVER YOU WANT TO SHOOT--AND SQUEEZE THE TRIGGER.
YOU ONLY HAVE SIX ROUNDS--DON'T WASTE ANY ON WARNING SHOTS.
Ms. NOGUCHI--I AM NOT A SOLDIER...
THIS ISN'T A WAR, MIRIAM. THIS IS SURVIVAL.
W-WHO MIGHT I BE SHOOTING AT?
DON'T WORRY--YOU'LL KNOW WHEN THE TIME COMES.
TELL ME, MIRIAM, THE UNCLASSIFIEDS ROTH BROUGHT YOU--KESAR'S REPORT SAID HE THOUGHT THEY MIGHT TRANSMIT EGGS, OR SPORES, TO HOST BODIES.
IS IT POSSIBLE THAT WHEN THOSE SPORES GREW UP, THEY'D LOOK LIKE THIS?
IT IS IMPOSSIBLE TO SAY. WHY DO YOU ASK?
BECAUSE I'VE SEEN SOME OF THESE THINGS TONIGHT. THERE WERE DOZENS--MAYBE HUNDREDS--OF THEM IN THE LECTOR.
I THINK ACKLAND'S RHYNTH WERE INFECTED, OR IMPREGNATED, BY THESE THINGS, AND THEY'VE SPREAD IT TO ALL OF THE HERDS ON THE SHIP--
--AND I THINK OUR TWO UNCLASSIFIEDS ARE SOMEHOW CONNECTED.
WHAT ARE YOU GOING TO DO?
YOU KNOW RHYNTH TEMPERAMENT, RIGHT? I'VE GOT THREE THOUSAND HEAD THAT HAVE BEEN CRAMMED INTO HOLDING PENS SINCE LAST NIGHT--
--WHAT KIND OF MOOD DO YOU THINK THEY'RE IN RIGHT NOW?

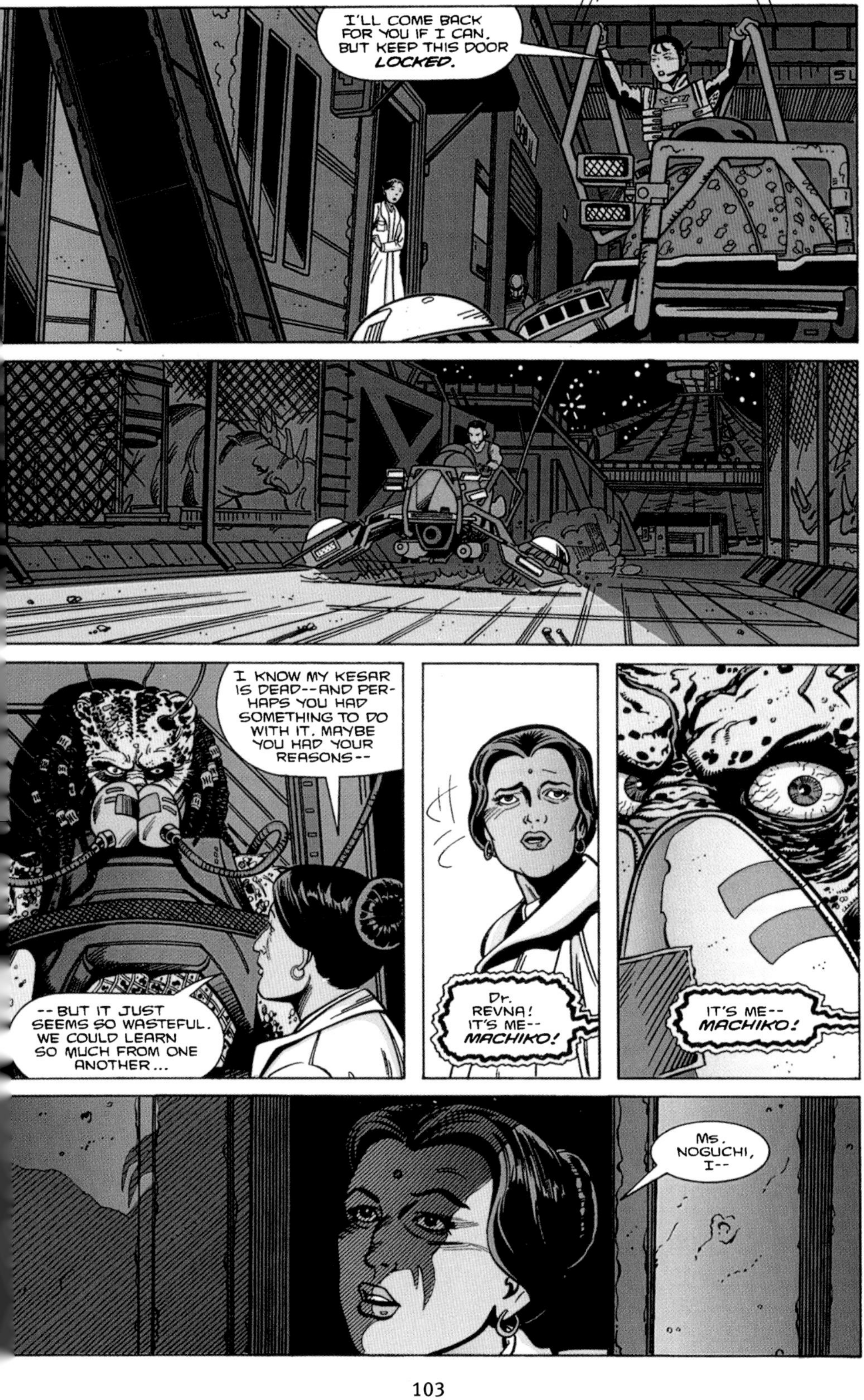
I'LL COME BACK FOR YOU IF I CAN. BUT KEEP THIS DOOR LOCKED.
I KNOW MY KESAR IS DEAD--AND PERHAPS YOU HAD SOMETHING TO DO WITH IT. MAYBE YOU HAD YOUR REASONS--
--BUT IT JUST SEEMS SO WASTEFUL. WE COULD LEARN SO MUCH FROM ONE ANOTHER...
Dr. REVNA! IT'S ME-- MACHIKO!
IT'S ME-- MACHIKO!
Ms. NOGUCHI, I--

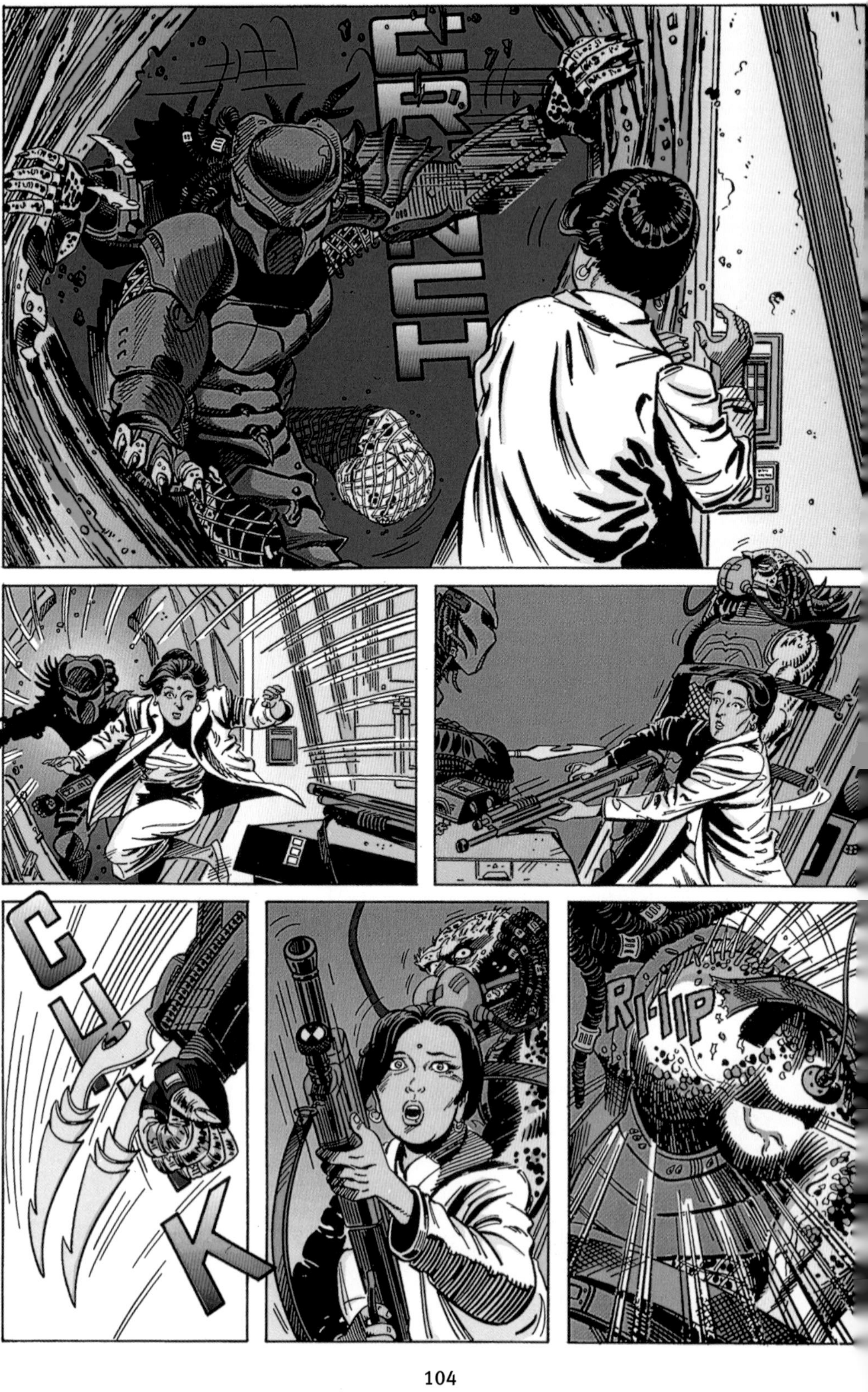
RIIP

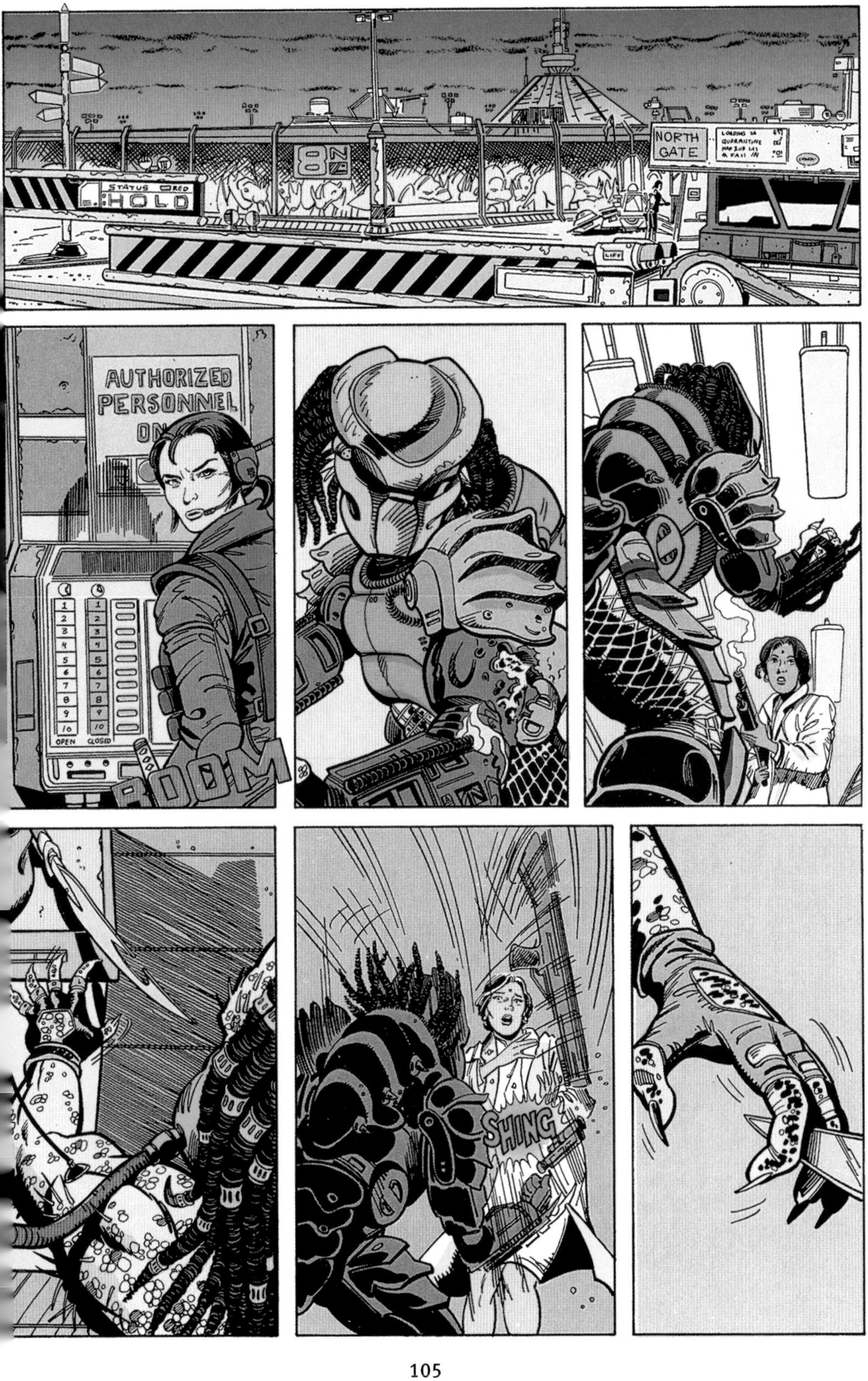
STATUS RED
HOLD
8N
NORTH GATE
AUTHORIZED
PERSONNEL
ON
OPEN
CLOSED
BOOM
SHING

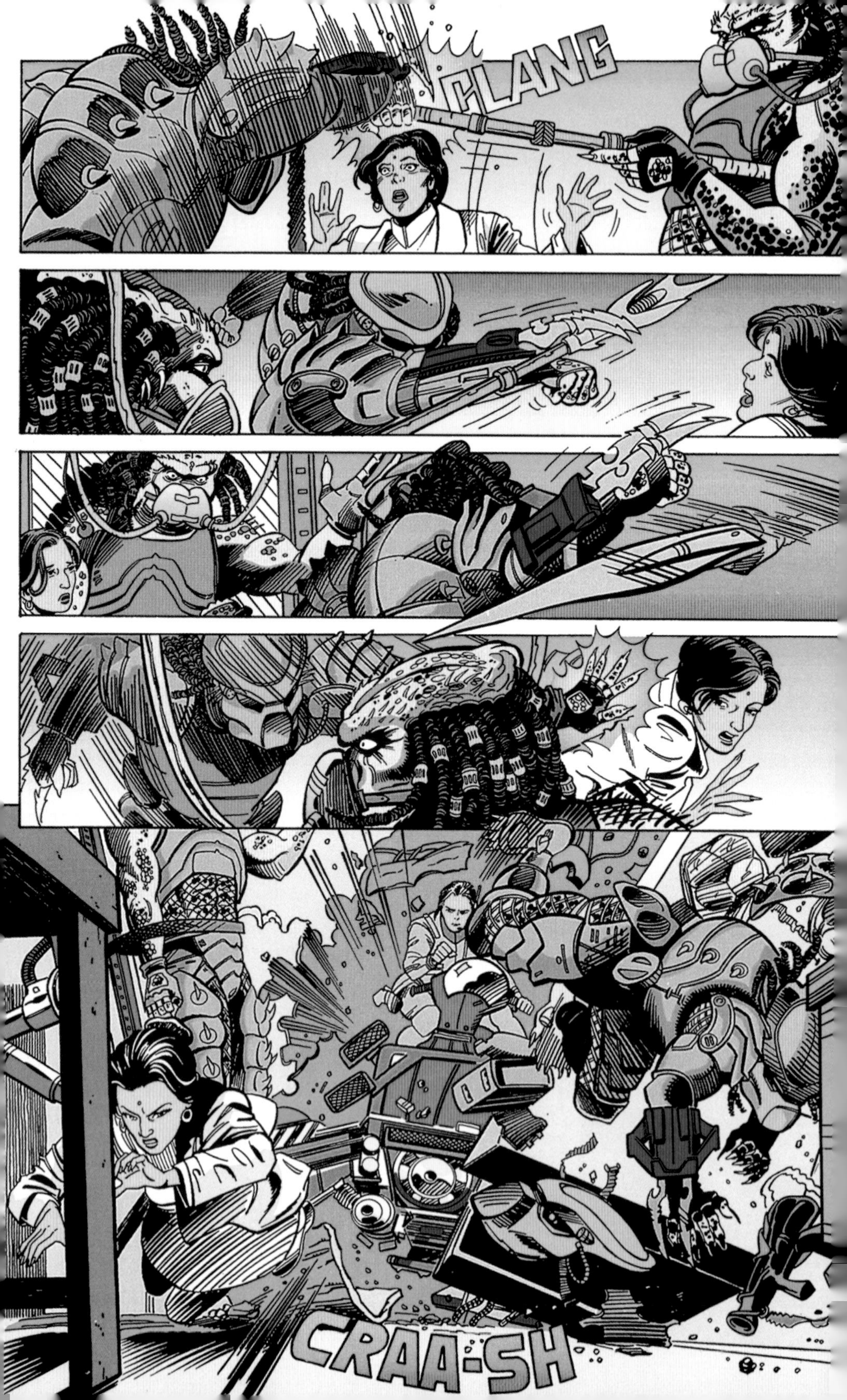
CLANG
CRAA-SH

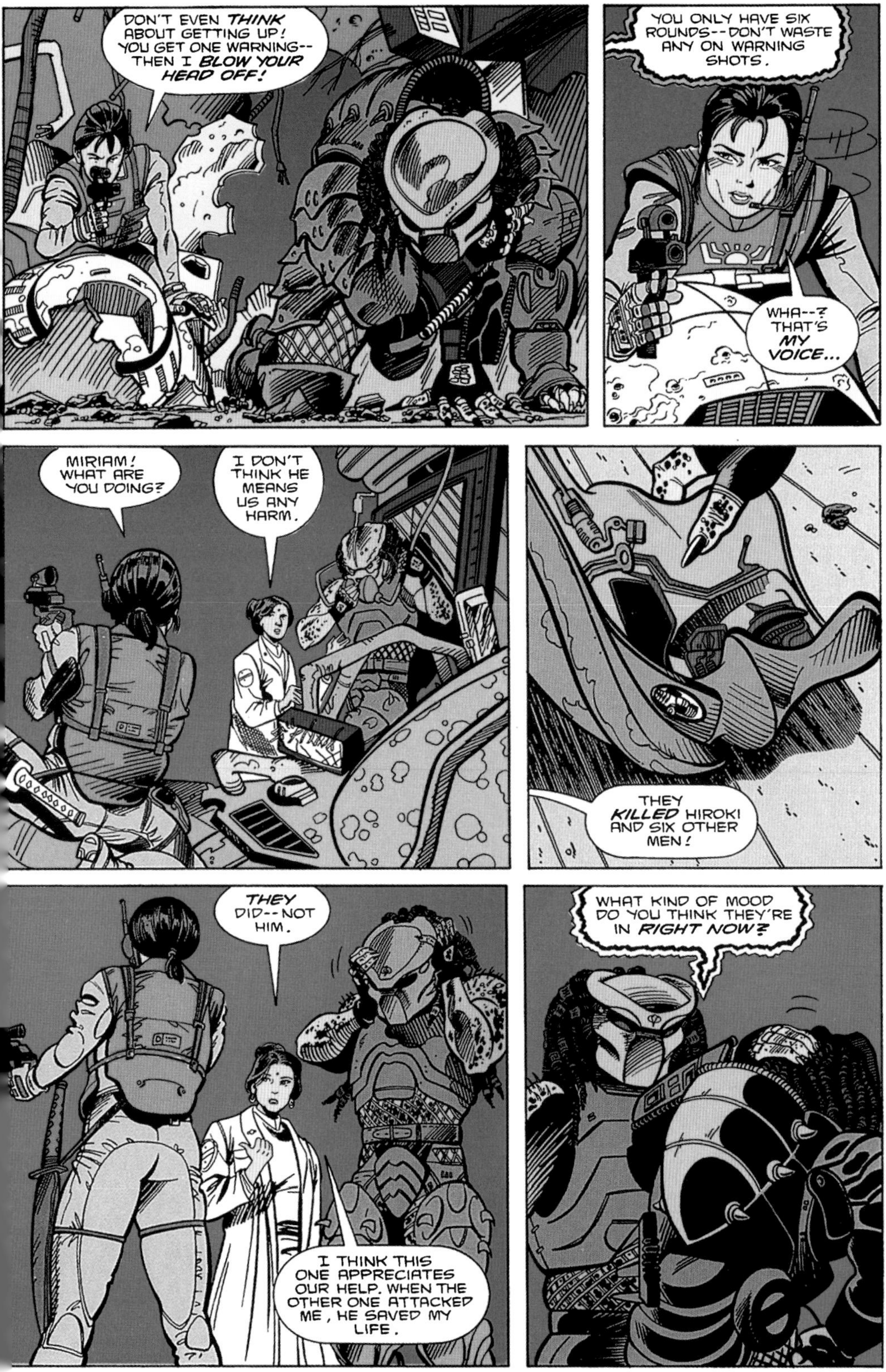
DON'T EVEN THINK ABOUT GETTING UP! YOU GET ONE WARNING-- THEN I BLOW YOUR HEAD OFF!
YOU ONLY HAVE SIX ROUNDS--DON'T WASTE ANY ON WARNING SHOTS.
WHA--? THAT'S MY VOICE...
MIRIAM! WHAT ARE YOU DOING?
I DON'T THINK HE MEANS US ANY HARM.
THEY KILLED HIROKI AND SIX OTHER MEN!
THEY DID--NOT HIM.
I THINK THIS ONE APPRECIATES OUR HELP. WHEN THE OTHER ONE ATTACKED ME, HE SAVED MY LIFE.
WHAT KIND OF MOOD DO YOU THINK THEY'RE IN RIGHT NOW?

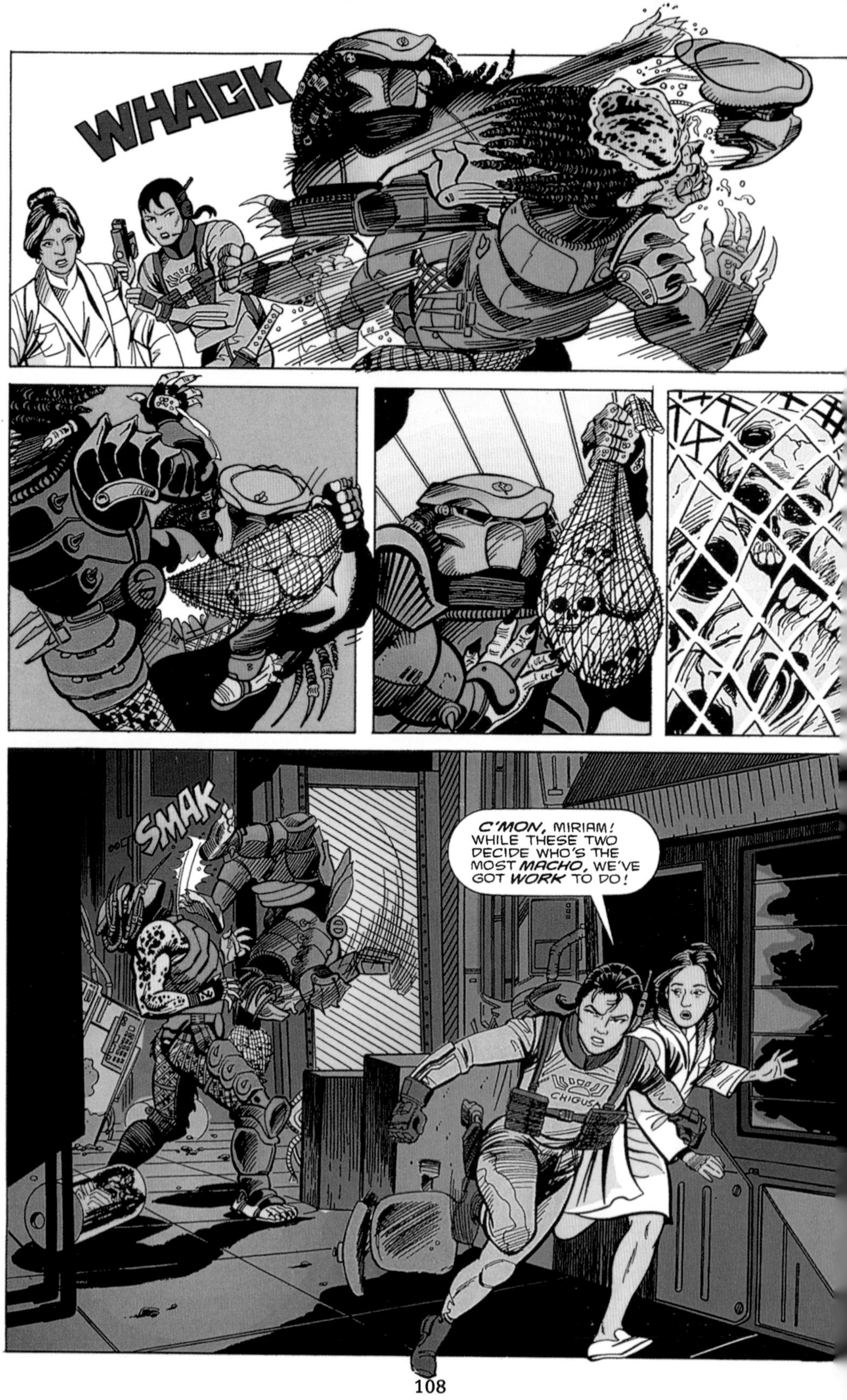
WHACK
SMAK
C'MON, MIRIAM! WHILE THESE TWO DECIDE WHO'S THE MOST MACHO, WE'VE GOT WORK TO DO!
CHIGUSA

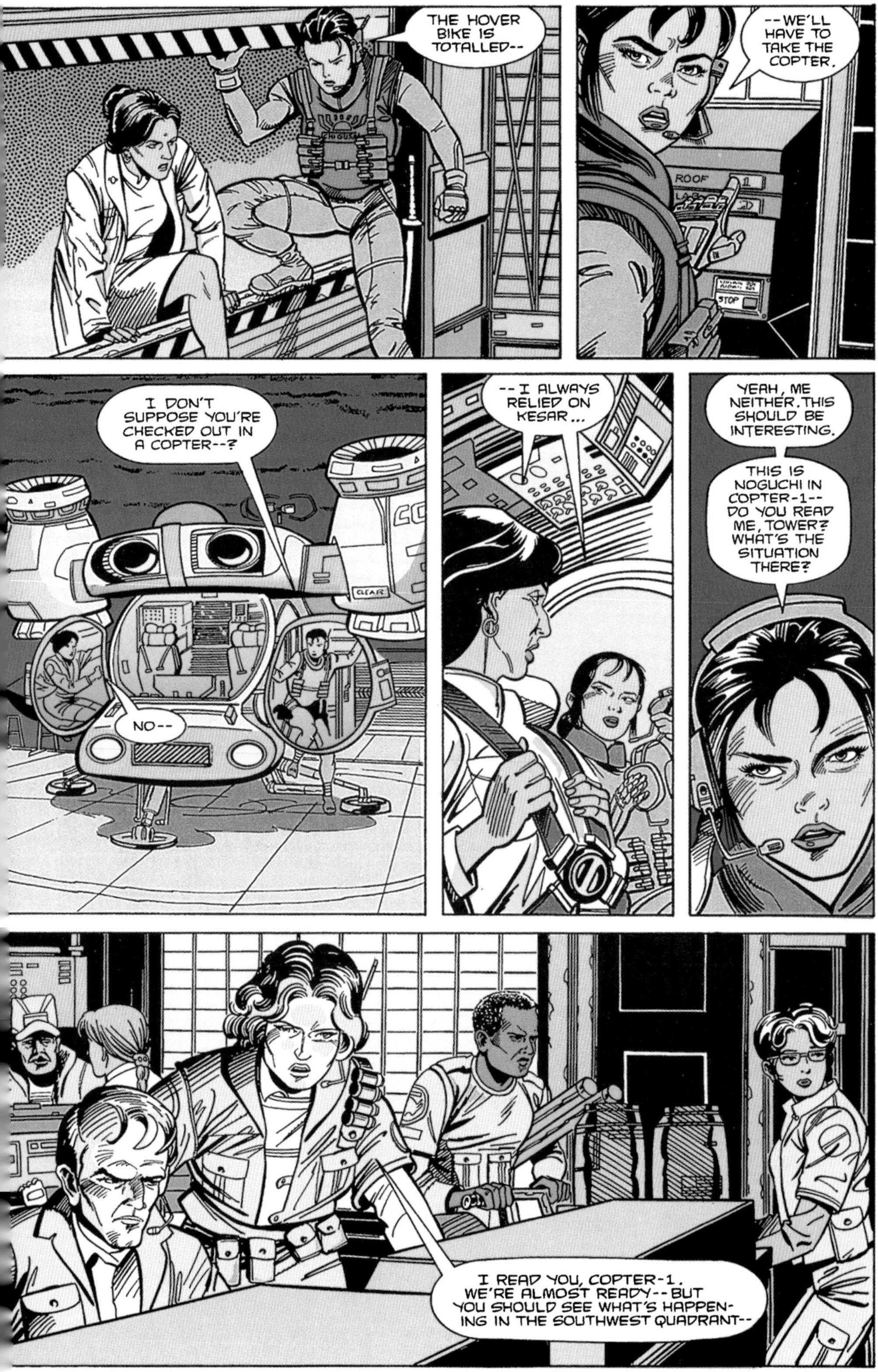

THE HOVER BIKE IS TOTALLED--
--WE'LL HAVE TO TAKE THE COPTER.
ROOF
STOP
I DON'T SUPPOSE YOU'RE CHECKED OUT IN A COPTER--?
NO--
--I ALWAYS RELIED ON KESAR...
YEAH, ME NEITHER. THIS SHOULD BE INTERESTING.
THIS IS NOGUCHI IN COPTER-1-- DO YOU READ ME, TOWER? WHAT'S THE SITUATION THERE?
I READ YOU, COPTER-1. WE'RE ALMOST READY-- BUT YOU SHOULD SEE WHAT'S HAPPENING IN THE SOUTHWEST QUADRANT--

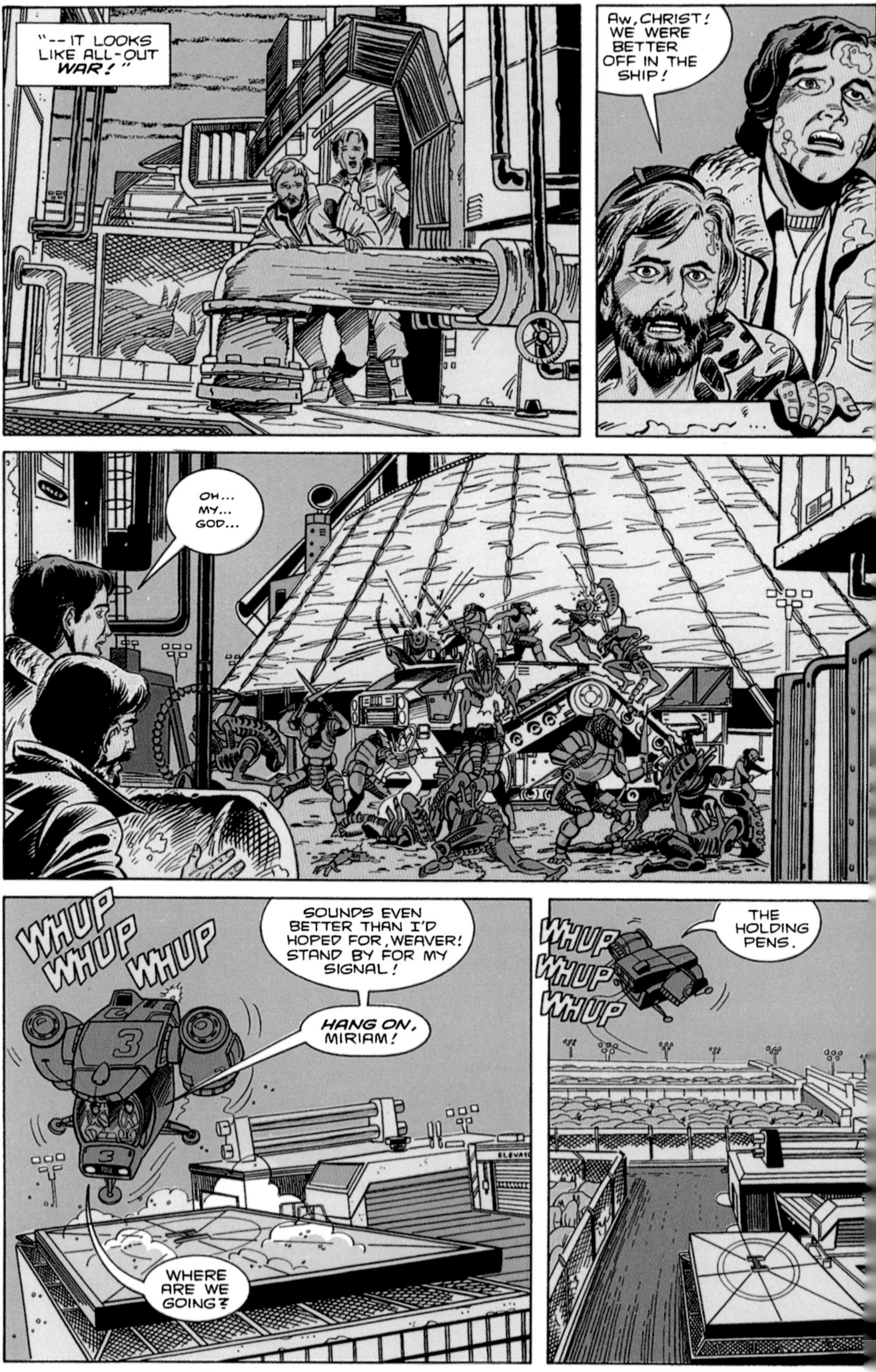
"-- IT LOOKS LIKE ALL-OUT WAR!"
AW, CHRIST! WE WERE BETTER OFF IN THE SHIP!
OH... MY... GOD...
WHUP WHUP WHUP
SOUNDS EVEN BETTER THAN I'D HOPED FOR, WEAVER! STAND BY FOR MY SIGNAL!
HANG ON, MIRIAM!
WHERE ARE WE GOING?
WHUP WHUP WHUP
THE HOLDING PENS.

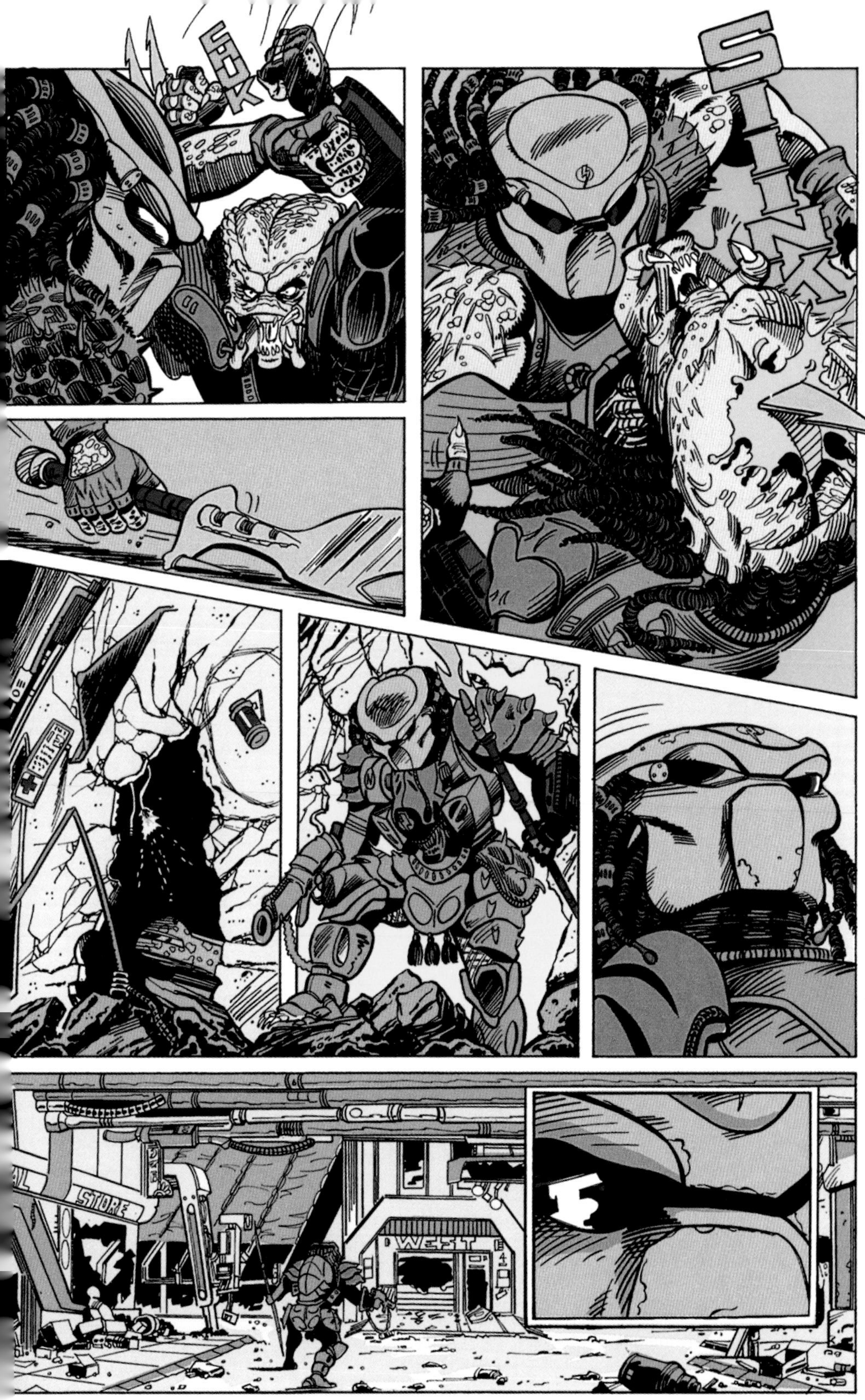
GOK
STORE
WEST

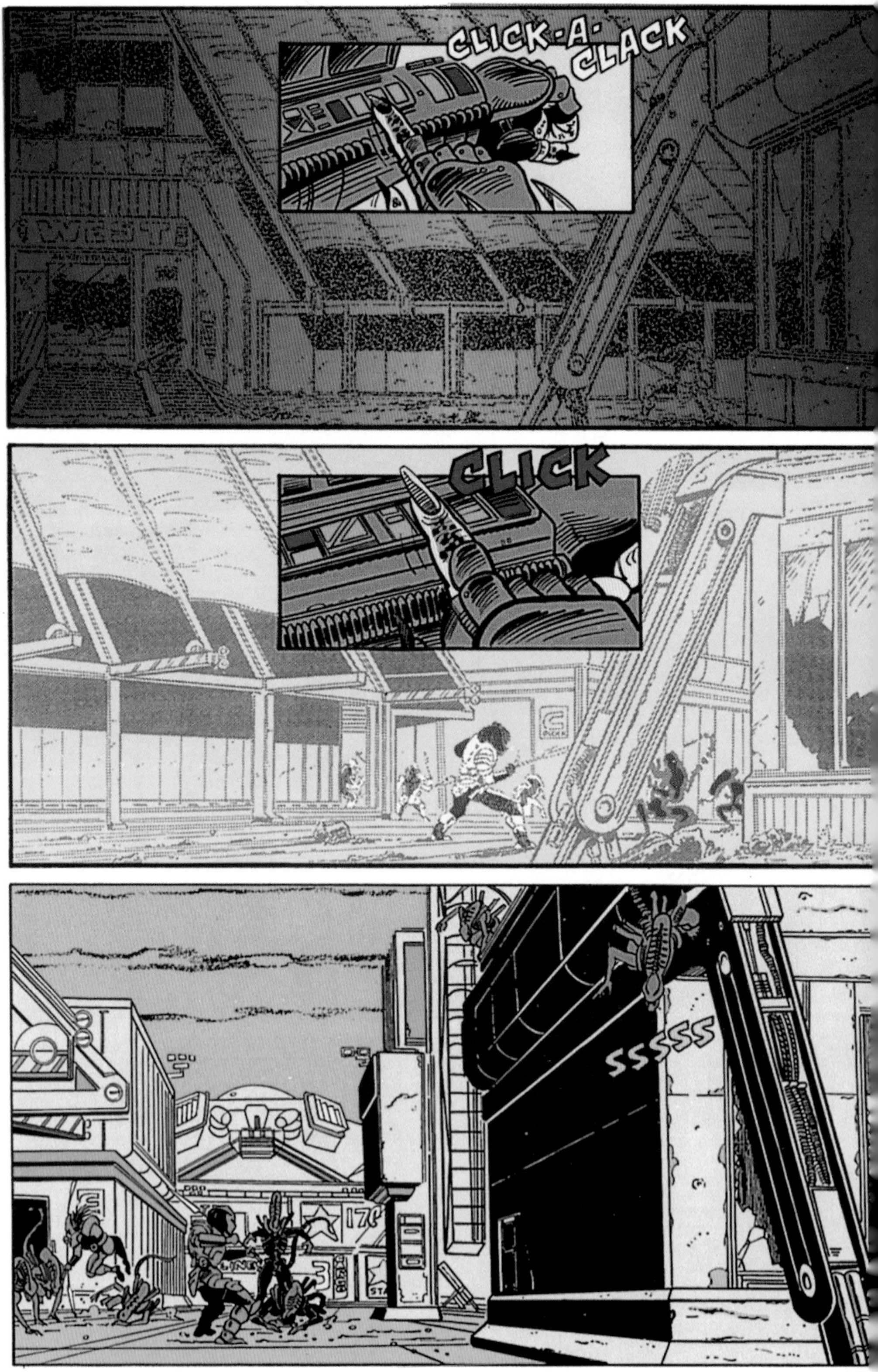
CLICK-A-CLACK
CLICK
SSSSS

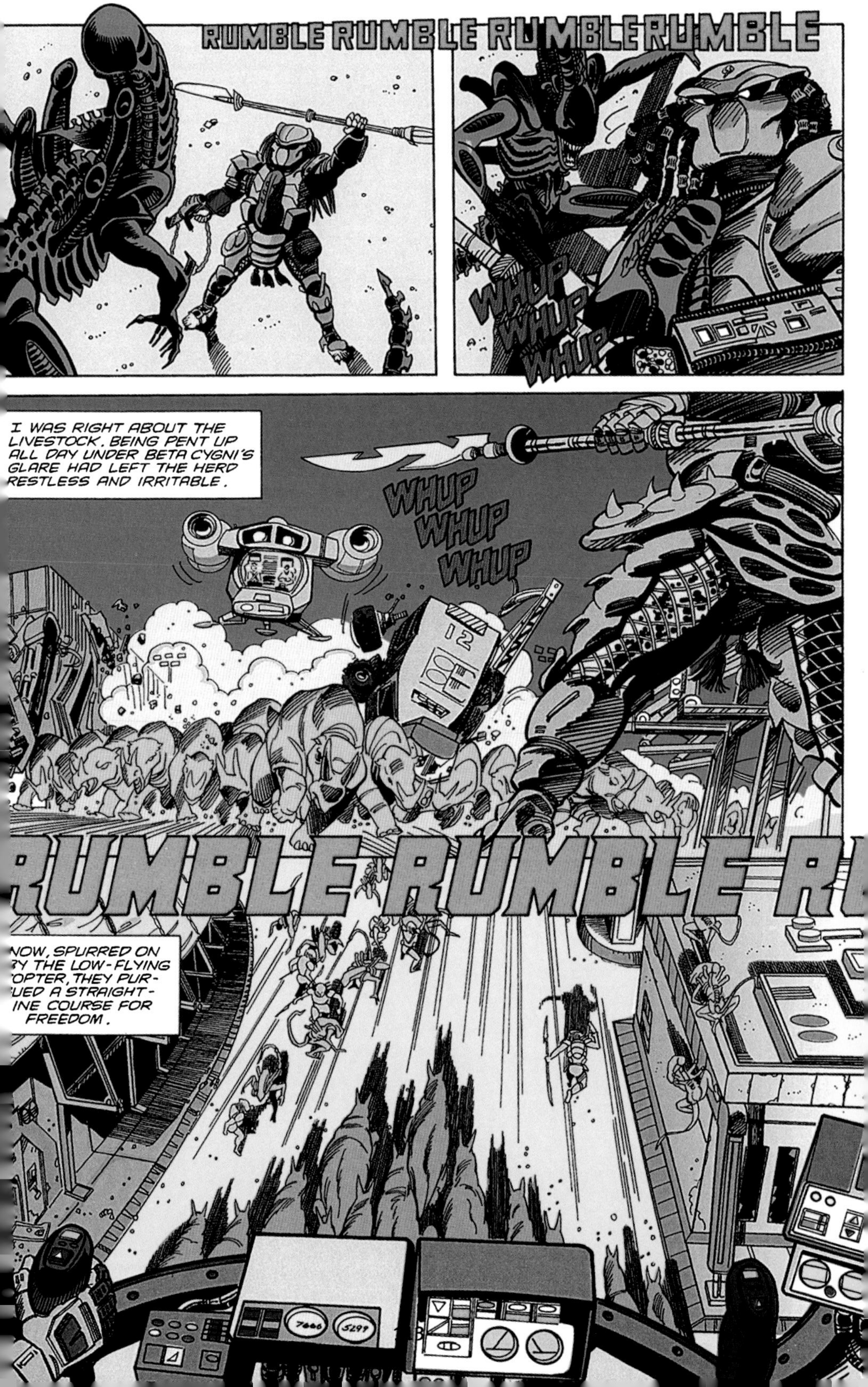

RUMBLE RUMBLE RUMBLE RUMBLE
WHUP WHUP WHUP
I WAS RIGHT ABOUT THE LIVESTOCK. BEING PENT UP ALL DAY UNDER BETA CYGNI'S GLARE HAD LEFT THE HERD RESTLESS AND IRRITABLE.
WHUP WHUP WHUP
12
RUMBLE RUMBLE
NOW, SPURRED ON BY THE LOW-FLYING 'COPTER, THEY PURSUED A STRAIGHT-LINE COURSE FOR FREEDOM.

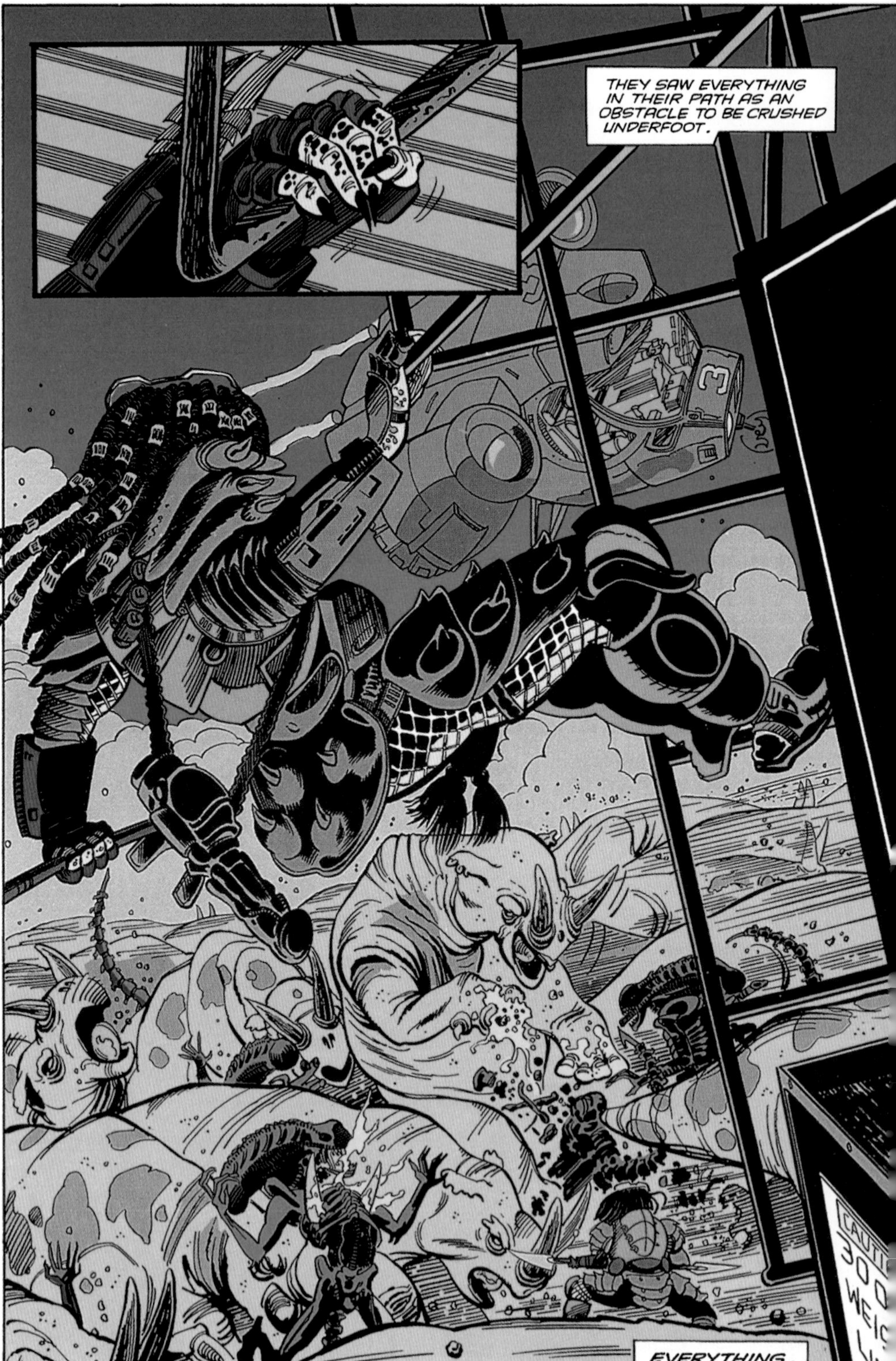
THEY SAW EVERYTHING IN THEIR PATH AS AN OBSTACLE TO BE CRUSHED UNDERFOOT.
EVERYTHING.

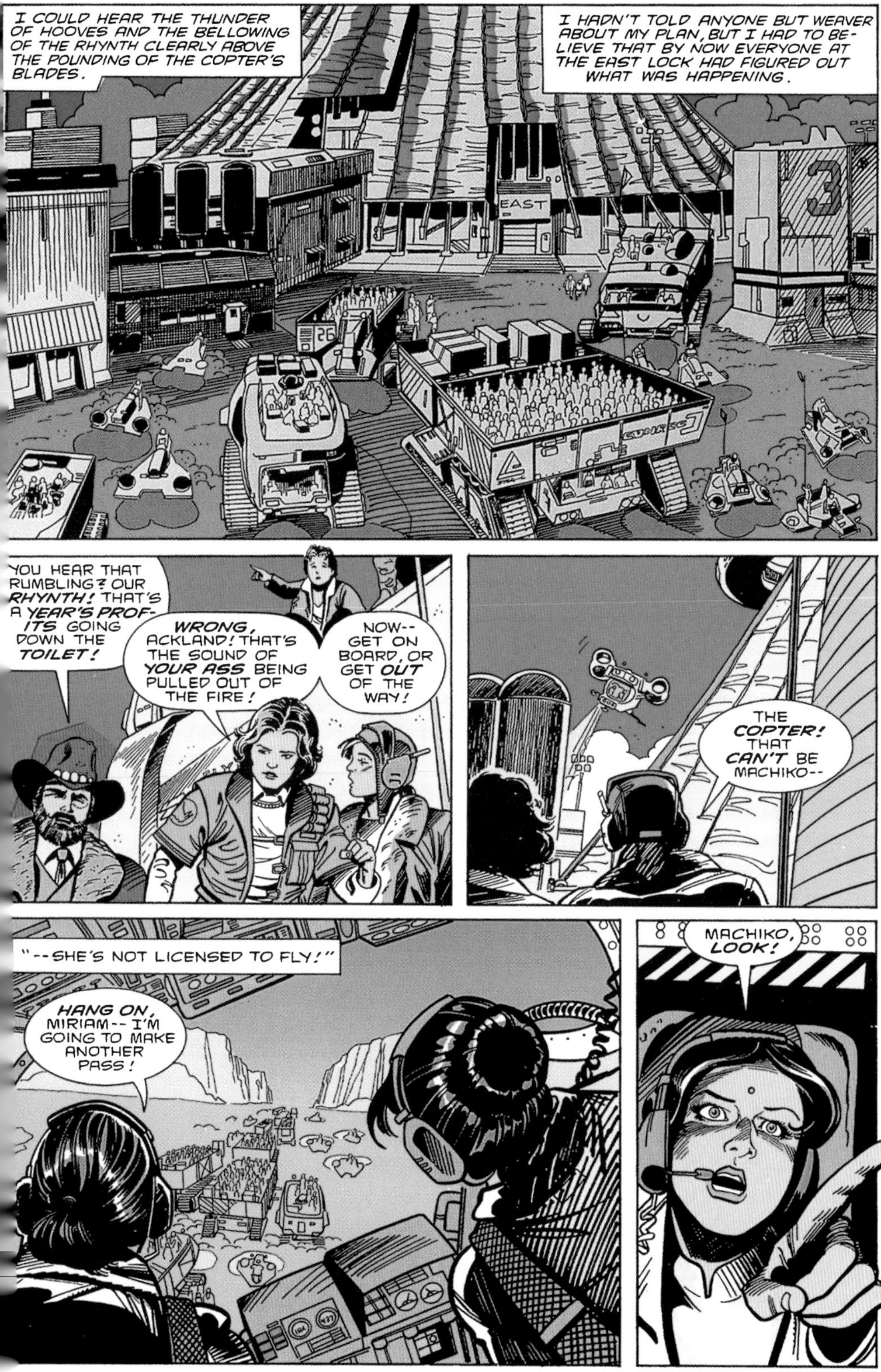

I COULD HEAR THE THUNDER OF HOOVES AND THE BELLOWING OF THE RHYNTH CLEARLY ABOVE THE POUNDING OF THE COPTER'S BLADES.
I HADN'T TOLD ANYONE BUT WEAVER ABOUT MY PLAN, BUT I HAD TO BELIEVE THAT BY NOW EVERYONE AT THE EAST LOCK HAD FIGURED OUT WHAT WAS HAPPENING.
EAST
YOU HEAR THAT RUMBLING? OUR RHYNTH! THAT'S A YEAR'S PROFITS GOING DOWN THE TOILET!
WRONG, ACKLAND! THAT'S THE SOUND OF YOUR ASS BEING PULLED OUT OF THE FIRE!
NOW-- GET ON BOARD, OR GET OUT OF THE WAY!
THE COPTER! THAT CAN'T BE MACHIKO--
"--SHE'S NOT LICENSED TO FLY!"
HANG ON, MIRIAM-- I'M GOING TO MAKE ANOTHER PASS!
MACHIKO, LOOK!

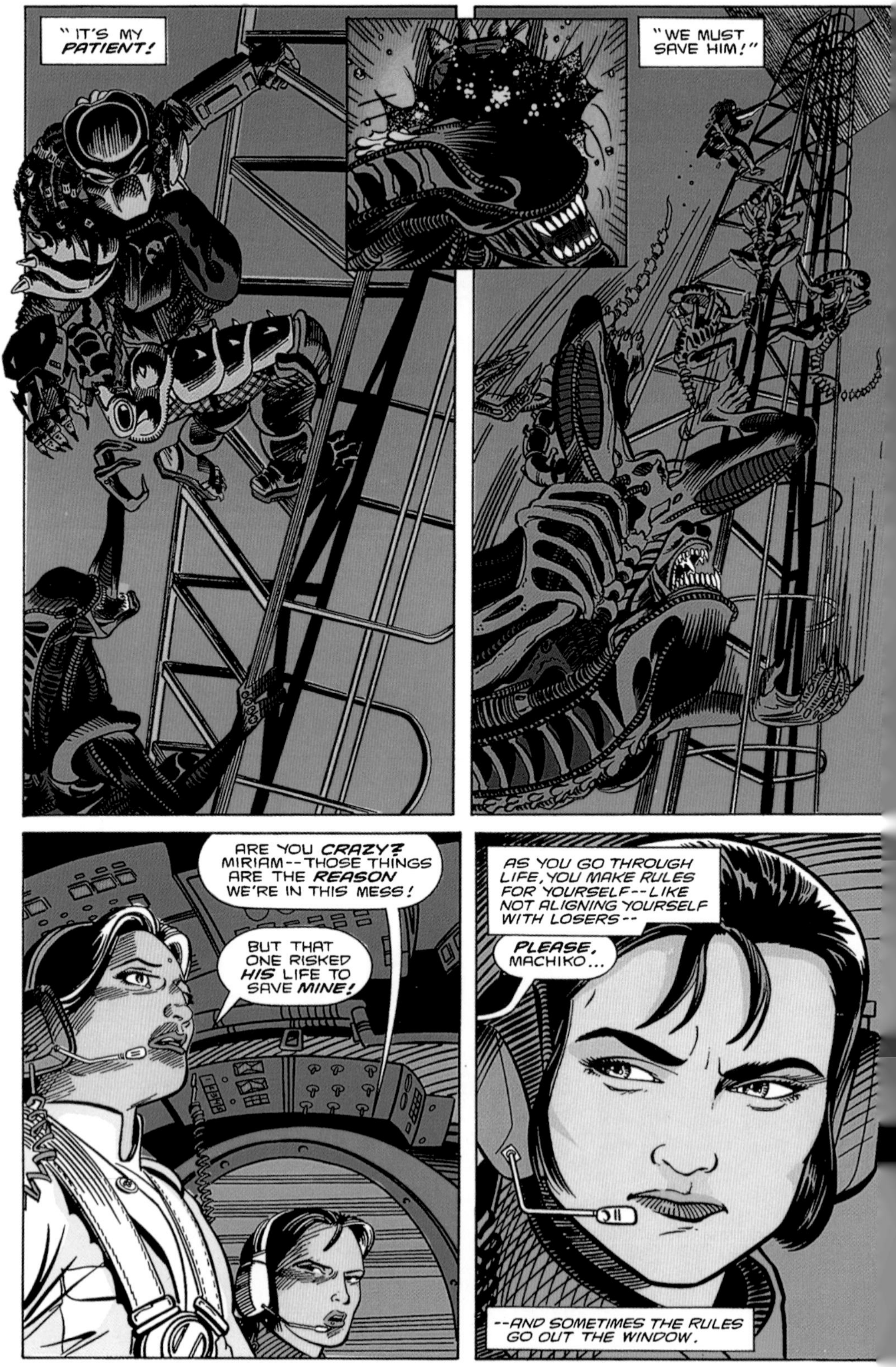
"IT'S MY PATIENT!
"WE MUST SAVE HIM!"
ARE YOU CRAZY? MIRIAM--THOSE THINGS ARE THE REASON WE'RE IN THIS MESS!
BUT THAT ONE RISKED HIS LIFE TO SAVE MINE!
AS YOU GO THROUGH LIFE, YOU MAKE RULES FOR YOURSELF--LIKE NOT ALIGNING YOURSELF WITH LOSERS--
PLEASE, MACHIKO...
--AND SOMETIMES THE RULES GO OUT THE WINDOW.

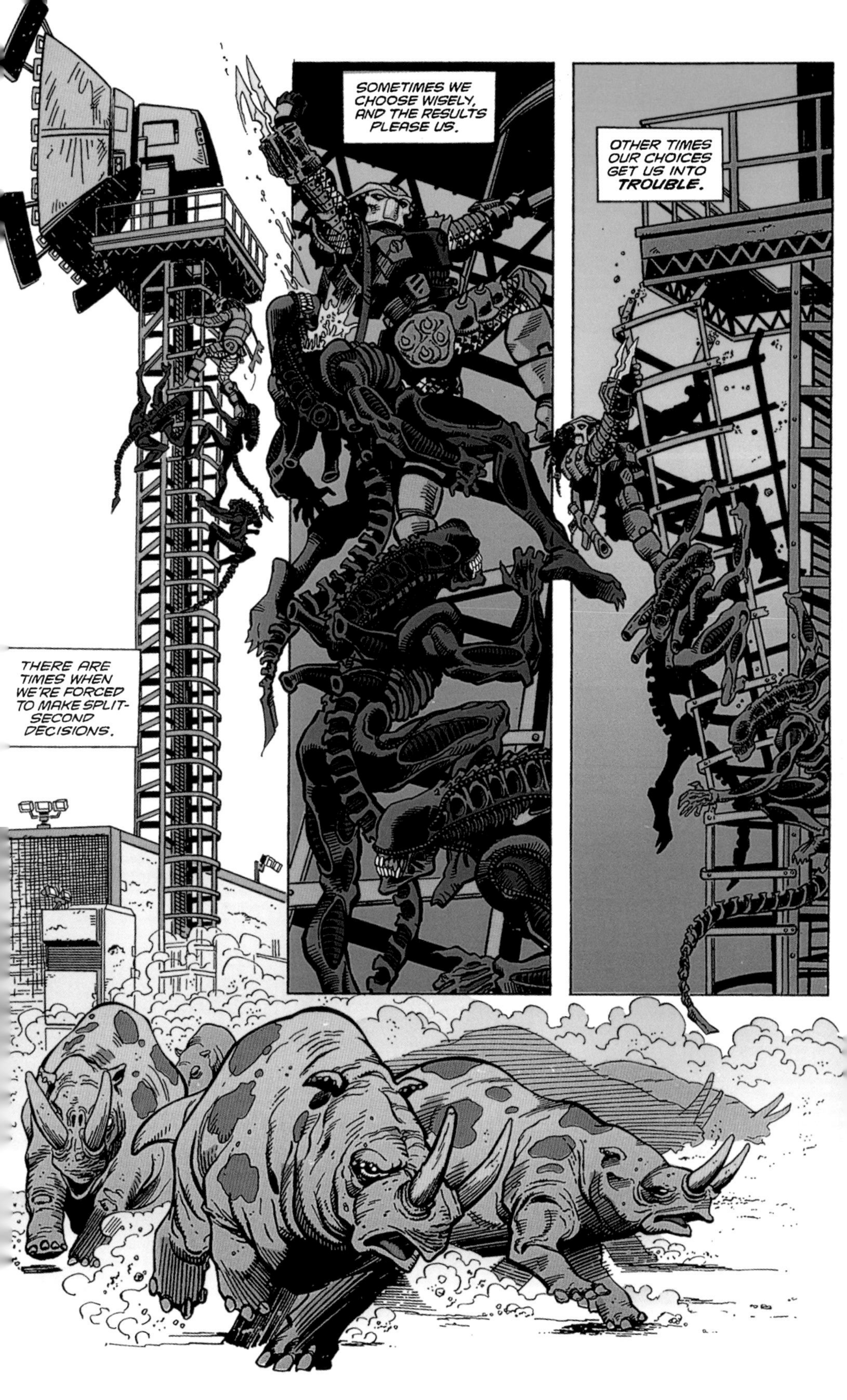
THERE ARE TIMES WHEN WE'RE FORCED TO MAKE SPLIT-SECOND DECISIONS.
SOMETIMES WE CHOOSE WISELY, AND THE RESULTS PLEASE US.
OTHER TIMES OUR CHOICES GET US INTO TROUBLE.

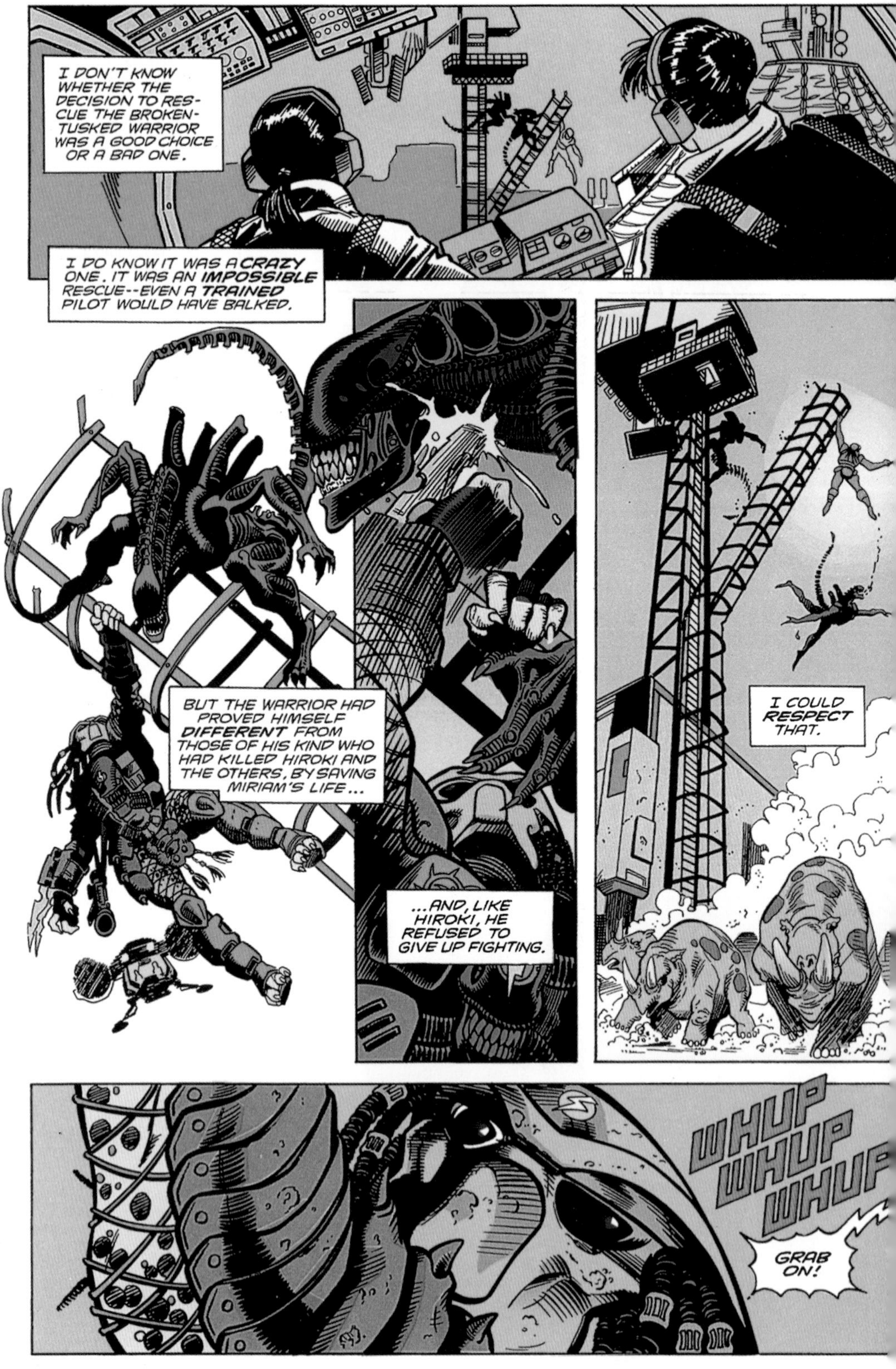
I DON'T KNOW WHETHER THE DECISION TO RESCUE THE BROKEN-TUSKED WARRIOR WAS A GOOD CHOICE OR A BAD ONE.
I DO KNOW IT WAS A CRAZY ONE. IT WAS AN IMPOSSIBLE RESCUE--EVEN A TRAINED PILOT WOULD HAVE BALKED.
BUT THE WARRIOR HAD PROVED HIMSELF DIFFERENT FROM THOSE OF HIS KIND WHO HAD KILLED HIROKI AND THE OTHERS, BY SAVING MIRIAM'S LIFE...
...AND, LIKE HIROKI, HE REFUSED TO GIVE UP FIGHTING.
I COULD RESPECT THAT.
WHUP WHUP WHUP
GRAB ON!

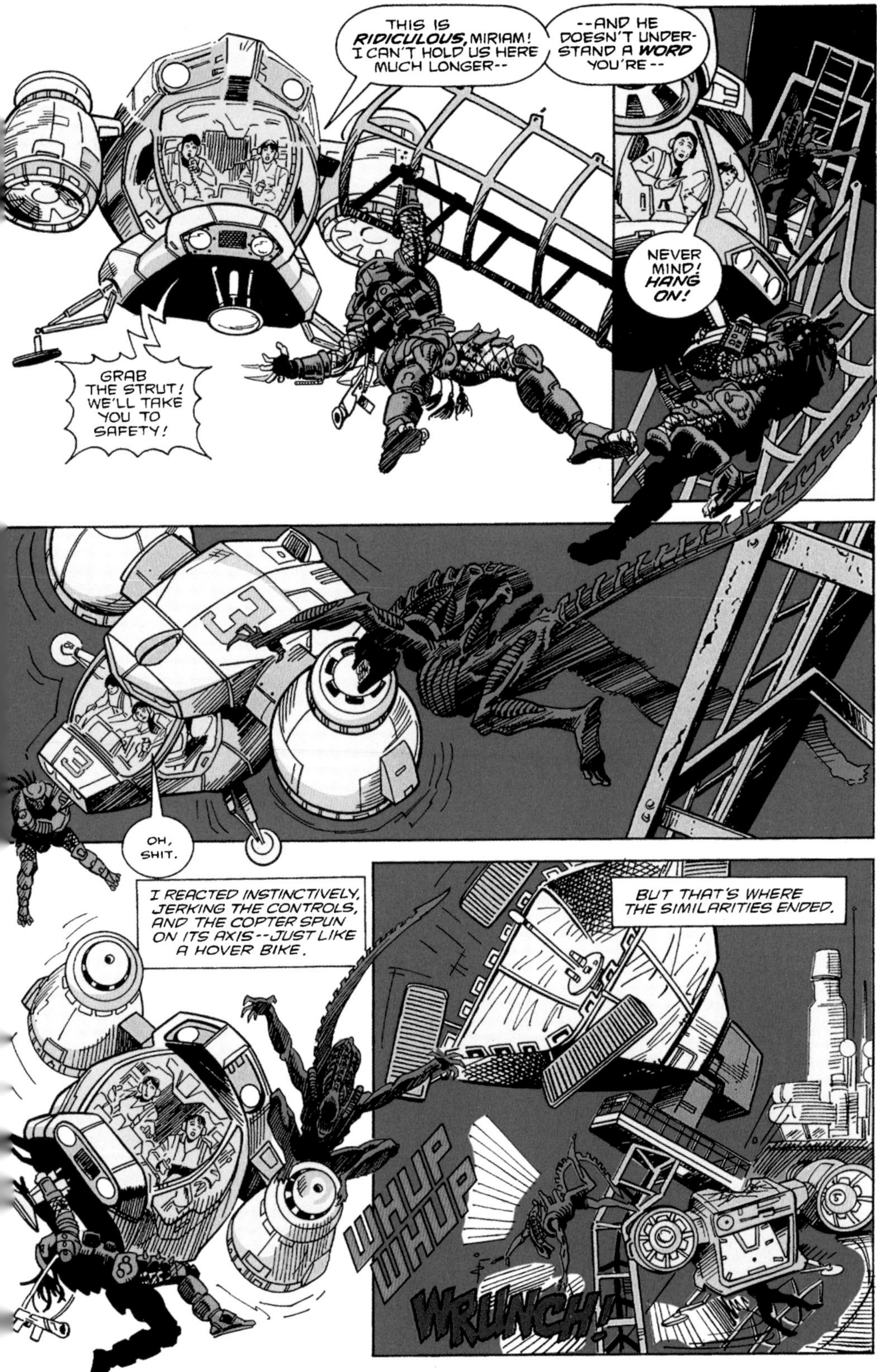
THIS IS RIDICULOUS, MIRIAM! I CAN'T HOLD US HERE MUCH LONGER--
--AND HE DOESN'T UNDERSTAND A WORD YOU'RE--
GRAB THE STRUT! WE'LL TAKE YOU TO SAFETY!
NEVER MIND! HANG ON!
OH, SHIT.
I REACTED INSTINCTIVELY, JERKING THE CONTROLS, AND THE COPTER SPUN ON ITS AXIS--JUST LIKE A HOVER BIKE.
BUT THAT'S WHERE THE SIMILARITIES ENDED.
WHUP WHUP
WRUNCH!

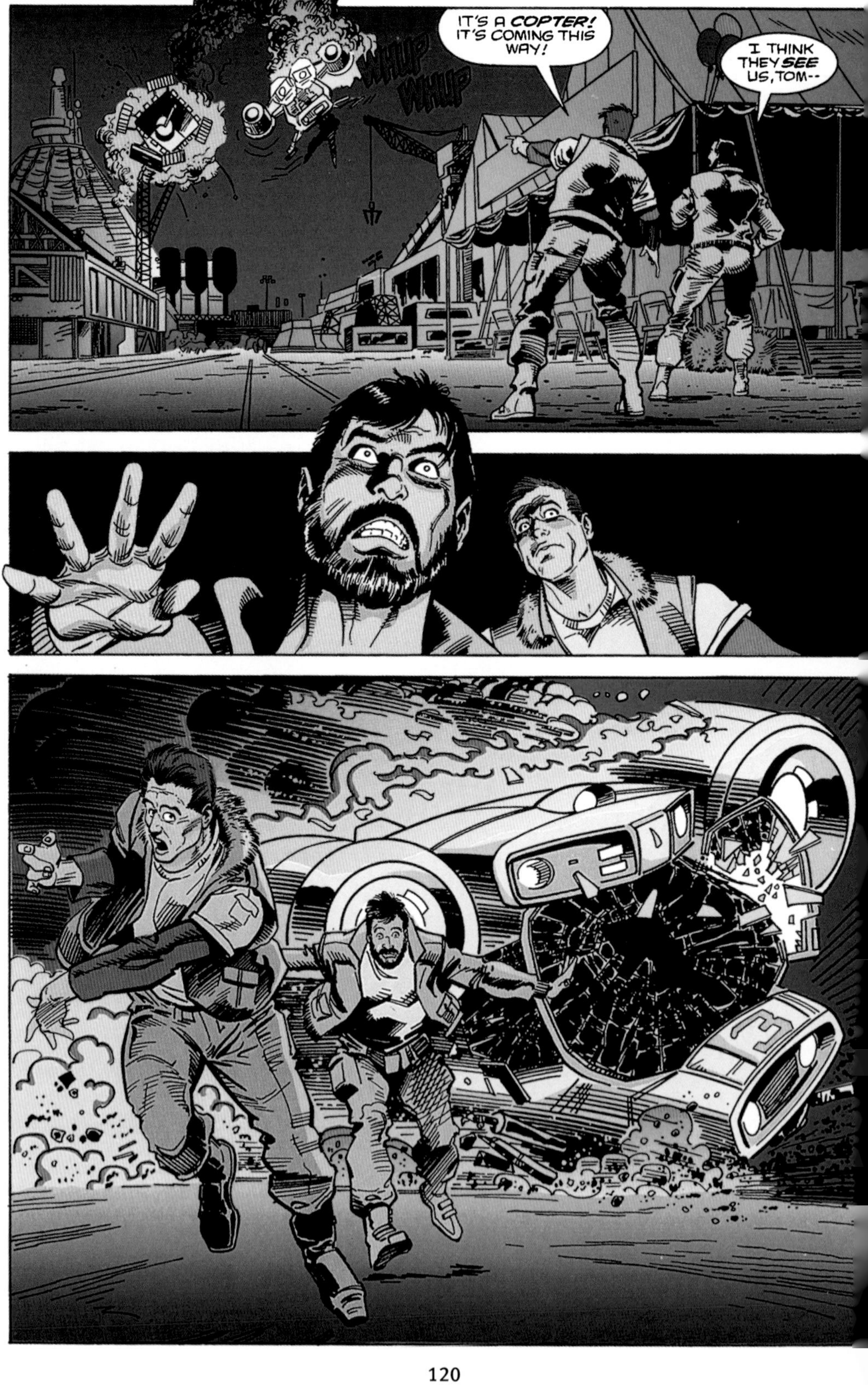
WHUP WHUP
IT'S A COPTER! IT'S COMING THIS WAY!
I THINK THEY SEE US, TOM--

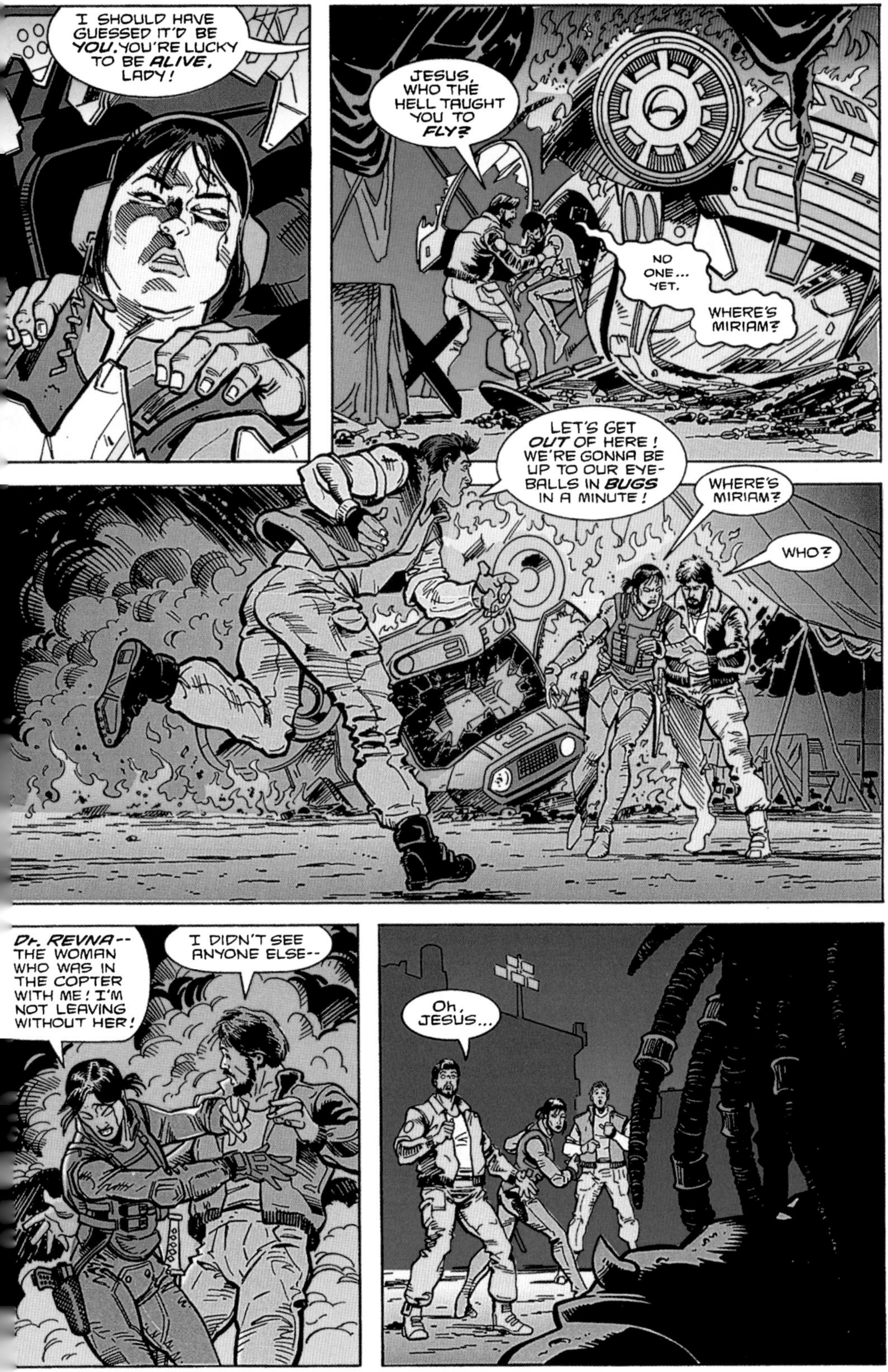
I SHOULD HAVE GUESSED IT'D BE YOU. YOU'RE LUCKY TO BE ALIVE, LADY!
JESUS, WHO THE HELL TAUGHT YOU TO FLY?
NO ONE... YET.
WHERE'S MIRIAM?
LET'S GET OUT OF HERE! WE'RE GONNA BE UP TO OUR EYE-BALLS IN BUGS IN A MINUTE!
WHERE'S MIRIAM?
WHO?
Dr. REVNA-- THE WOMAN WHO WAS IN THE COPTER WITH ME! I'M NOT LEAVING WITHOUT HER!
I DIDN'T SEE ANYONE ELSE--
Oh, JESUS...

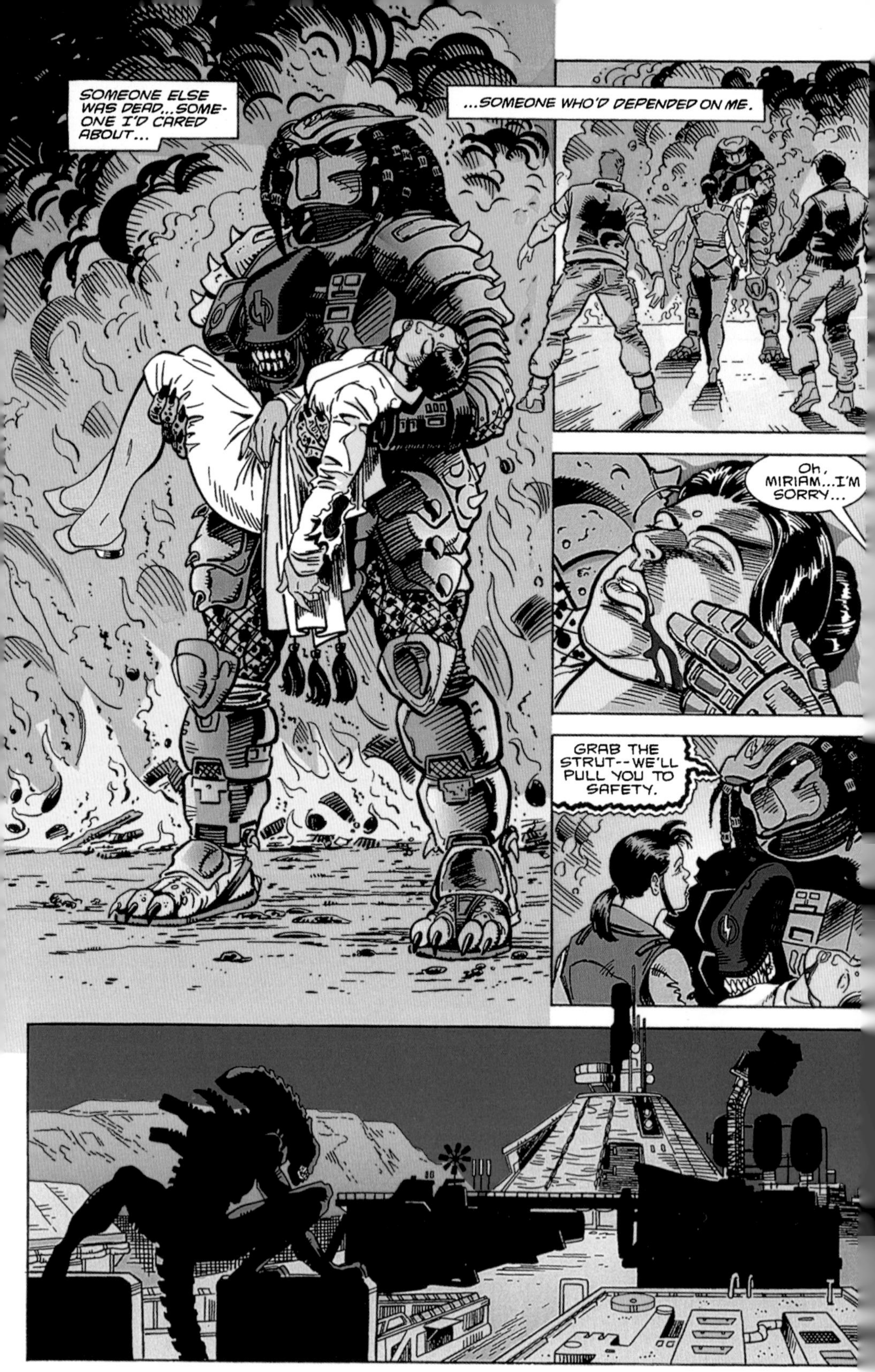
SOMEONE ELSE WAS DEAD...SOME-ONE I'D CARED ABOUT...
...SOMEONE WHO'D DEPENDED ON ME.
Oh, MIRIAM...I'M SORRY...
GRAB THE STRUT--WE'LL PULL YOU TO SAFETY.

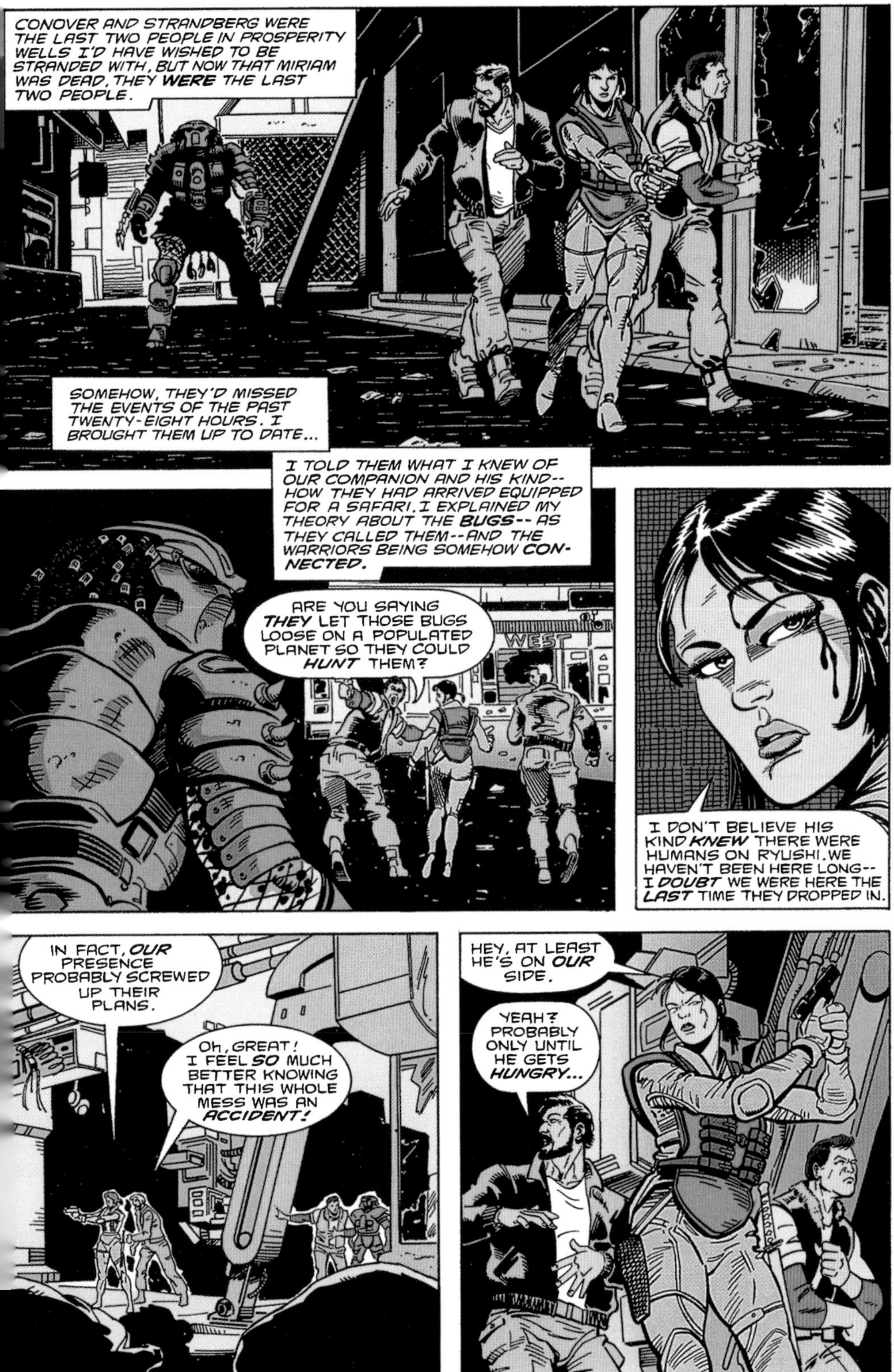
CONOVER AND STRANDBERG WERE THE LAST TWO PEOPLE IN PROSPERITY WELLS I'D HAVE WISHED TO BE STRANDED WITH, BUT NOW THAT MIRIAM WAS DEAD, THEY WERE THE LAST TWO PEOPLE.
SOMEHOW, THEY'D MISSED THE EVENTS OF THE PAST TWENTY-EIGHT HOURS. I BROUGHT THEM UP TO DATE...
I TOLD THEM WHAT I KNEW OF OUR COMPANION AND HIS KIND-- HOW THEY HAD ARRIVED EQUIPPED FOR A SAFARI. I EXPLAINED MY THEORY ABOUT THE BUGS-- AS THEY CALLED THEM-- AND THE WARRIORS BEING SOMEHOW CON-NECTED.
ARE YOU SAYING THEY LET THOSE BUGS LOOSE ON A POPULATED PLANET SO THEY COULD HUNT THEM?
WEST
I DON'T BELIEVE HIS KIND KNEW THERE WERE HUMANS ON RYUSHI. WE HAVEN'T BEEN HERE LONG-- I DOUBT WE WERE HERE THE LAST TIME THEY DROPPED IN.
IN FACT, OUR PRESENCE PROBABLY SCREWED UP THEIR PLANS.
Oh, GREAT! I FEEL SO MUCH BETTER KNOWING THAT THIS WHOLE MESS WAS AN ACCIDENT!
HEY, AT LEAST HE'S ON OUR SIDE.
YEAH? PROBABLY ONLY UNTIL HE GETS HUNGRY...

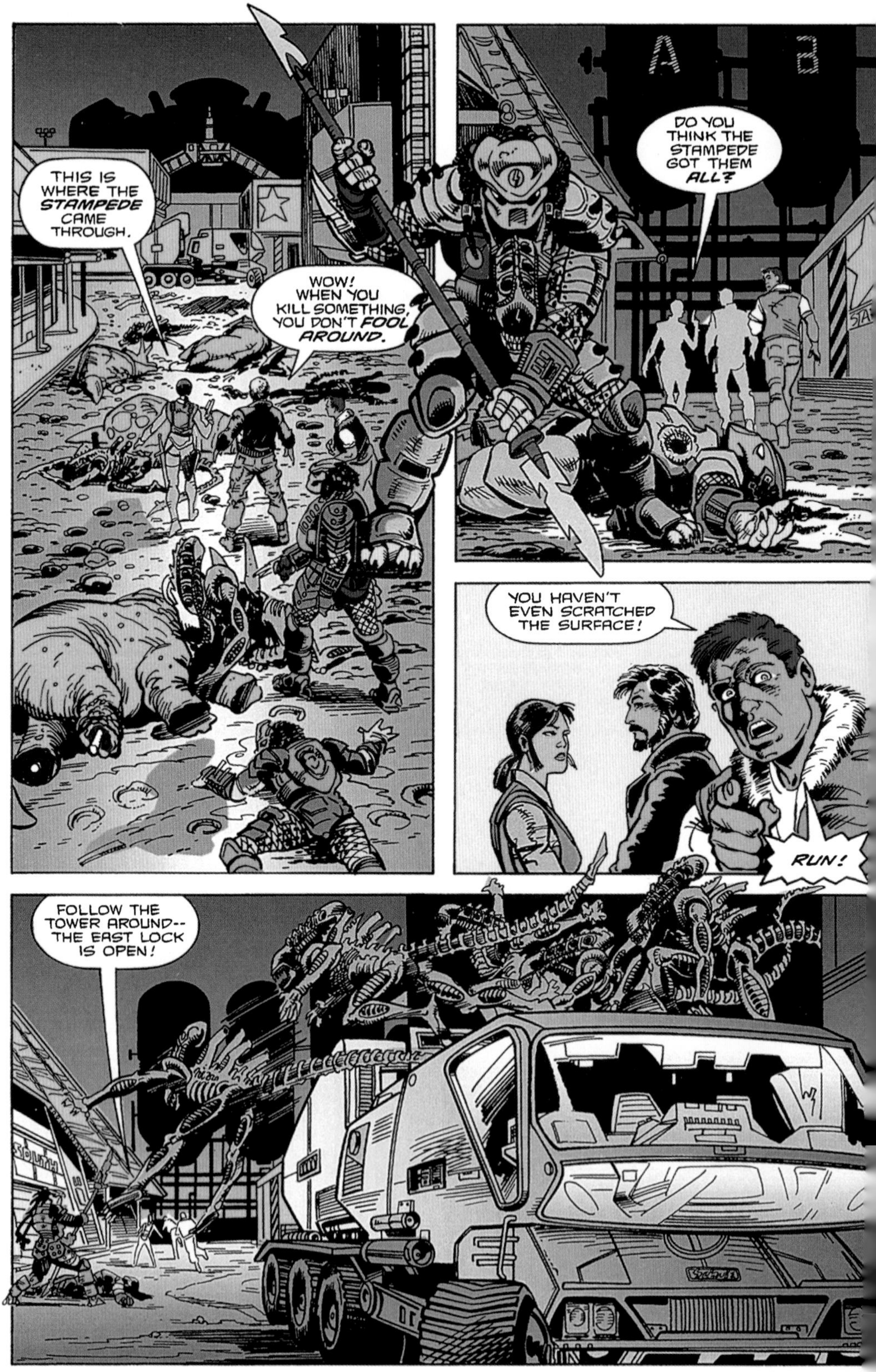
THIS IS WHERE THE STAMPEDE CAME THROUGH.
WOW! WHEN YOU KILL SOMETHING, YOU DON'T FOOL AROUND.
DO YOU THINK THE STAMPEDE GOT THEM ALL?
YOU HAVEN'T EVEN SCRATCHED THE SURFACE!
RUN!
FOLLOW THE TOWER AROUND-- THE EAST LOCK IS OPEN!

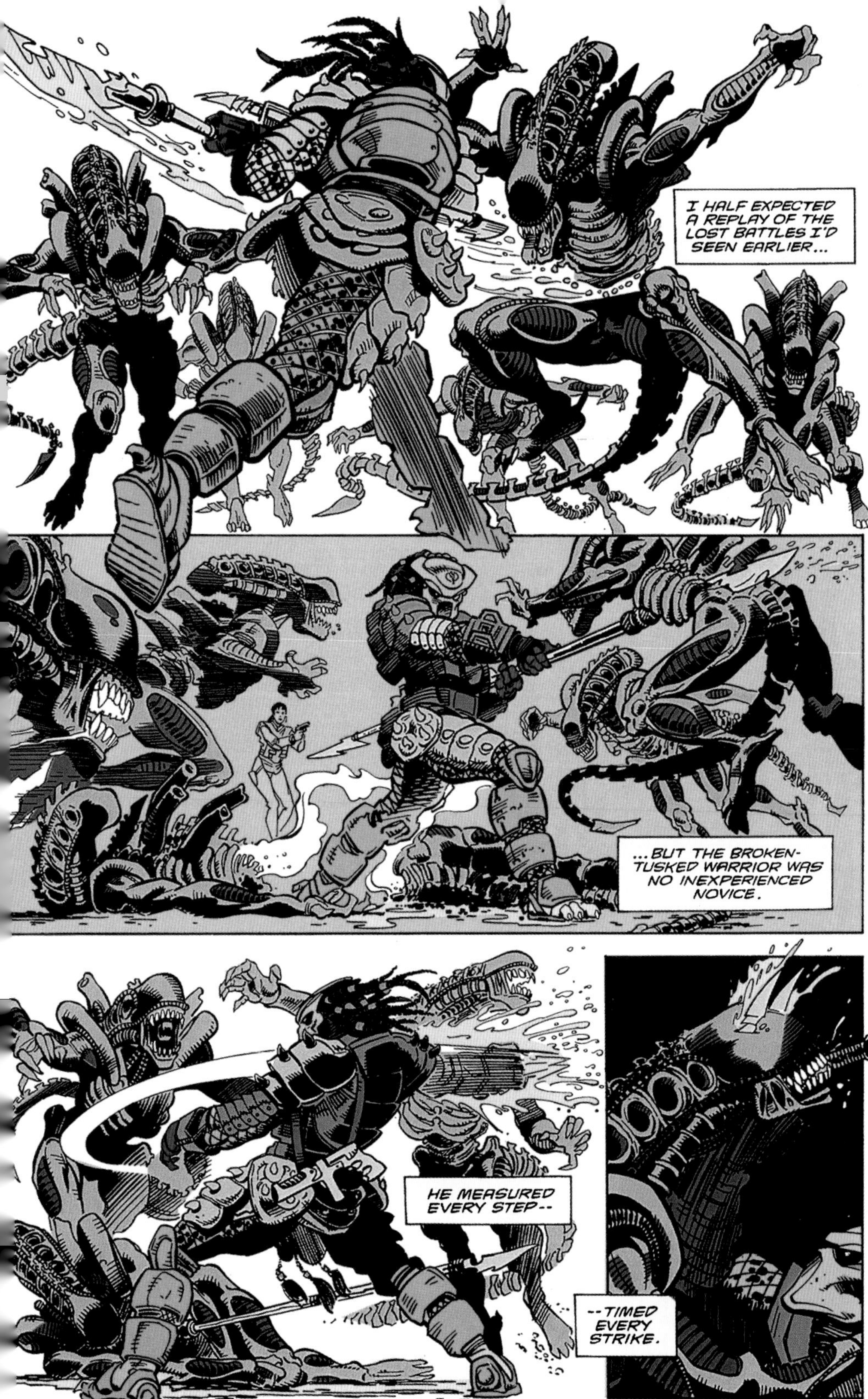
I HALF EXPECTED A REPLAY OF THE LOST BATTLES I'D SEEN EARLIER...
...BUT THE BROKEN-TUSKED WARRIOR WAS NO INEXPERIENCED NOVICE.
HE MEASURED EVERY STEP--
--TIMED EVERY STRIKE.

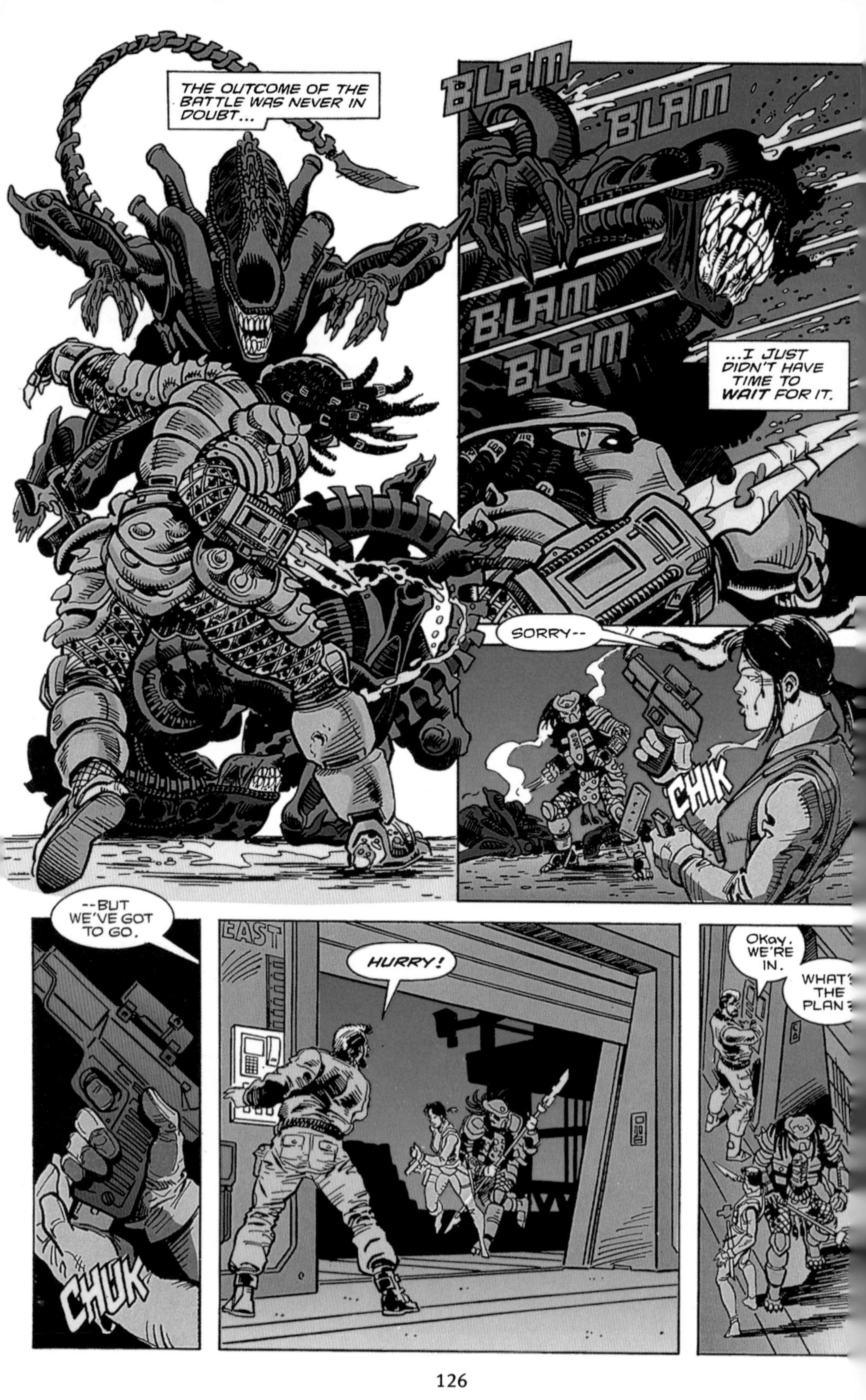

THE OUTCOME OF THE BATTLE WAS NEVER IN DOUBT...
BLAM
BLAM
BLAM
BLAM
...I JUST DIDN'T HAVE TIME TO WAIT FOR IT.
SORRY--
CHIK
--BUT WE'VE GOT TO GO.
CHUK
EAST
HURRY!
OKay. WE'RE IN.
WHAT'S THE PLAN?

WELL, THE COLONISTS MADE IT OUT SAFELY-- THAT'S THE MAIN THING. WE'VE GOT POWER HERE, WATER, AND FOOD.

I GUESS *WE'LL* JUST SEAL OUR-SELVES IN AND WAIT FOR THE MARINES.

WRONG. THE MARINES AREN'T COMING. SEEMS YOUR BOSS WANTS THE BUGS *ALIVE--*

LET ME *SEE* THAT!

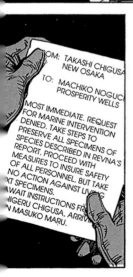

OM: TAKASHI CHIGUSA
NEW OSAKA

TO: MACHIKO NOGUC
PROSPERITY WELLS

MOST IMMEDIATE. REQUEST
FOR MARINE INTERVENTION
DENIED. TAKE STEPS TO
PRESERVE ALL SPECIMENS OF
SPECIES DESCRIBED IN REVNA'S
REPORT. PROCEED WITH
MEASURES TO INSURE SAFETY
OF ALL PERSONNEL, BUT TAKE
NO ACTION AGAINST LIVING
XT SPECIMENS.
WAIT INSTRUCTIONS FR
IIGERU CHIGUSA, ARRIVI
N MASUKO MARU.

SCREW *THAT* SHIT! I SAY WE SCRAM OUT OF HERE AND *JOIN* THE COLONISTS!

YEAH? AND HOW LONG BEFORE THE BUGS SPREAD INTO THE DESERT?

LOOK, I DON'T KNOW ABOUT YOU TWO, BUT I'M *TIRED* OF BEING *PUSHED AROUND.*

I WANT TO START PUSHING *BACK.*

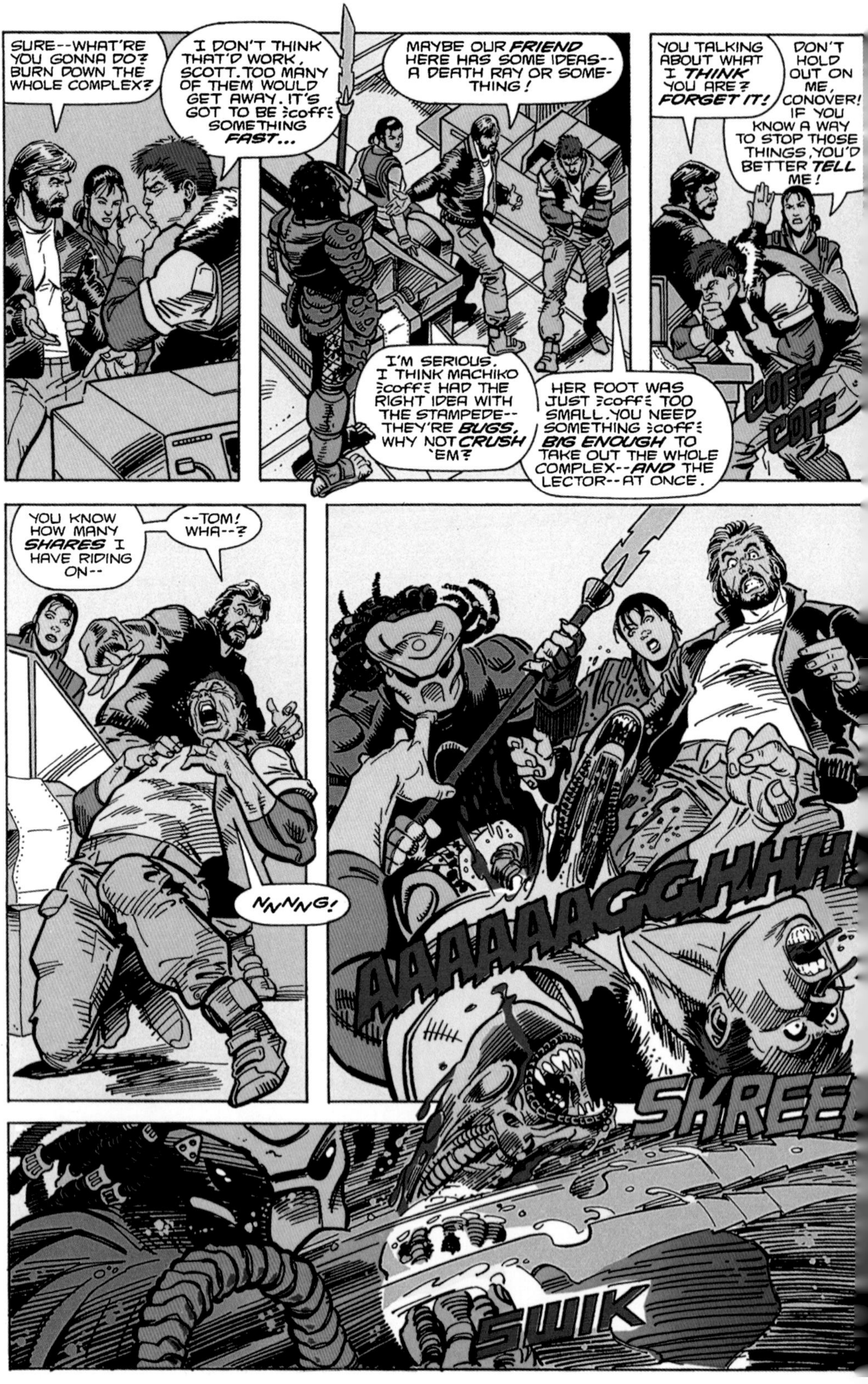
SURE--WHAT'RE YOU GONNA DO? BURN DOWN THE WHOLE COMPLEX?
I DON'T THINK THAT'D WORK, SCOTT. TOO MANY OF THEM WOULD GET AWAY. IT'S GOT TO BE :coff: SOMETHING FAST...
MAYBE OUR FRIEND HERE HAS SOME IDEAS-- A DEATH RAY OR SOME-THING!
I'M SERIOUS. I THINK MACHIKO :coff: HAD THE RIGHT IDEA WITH THE STAMPEDE-- THEY'RE BUGS. WHY NOT CRUSH 'EM?
HER FOOT WAS JUST :coff: TOO SMALL. YOU NEED SOMETHING :coff: BIG ENOUGH TO TAKE OUT THE WHOLE COMPLEX--AND THE LECTOR--AT ONCE.
YOU TALKING ABOUT WHAT I THINK YOU ARE? FORGET IT!
DON'T HOLD OUT ON ME, CONOVER! IF YOU KNOW A WAY TO STOP THOSE THINGS, YOU'D BETTER TELL ME!
COFF COFF
YOU KNOW HOW MANY SHARES I HAVE RIDING ON--
--TOM! WHA--?
NNNNG!
AAAAAAGGHHHH!
SKREE
SWIK

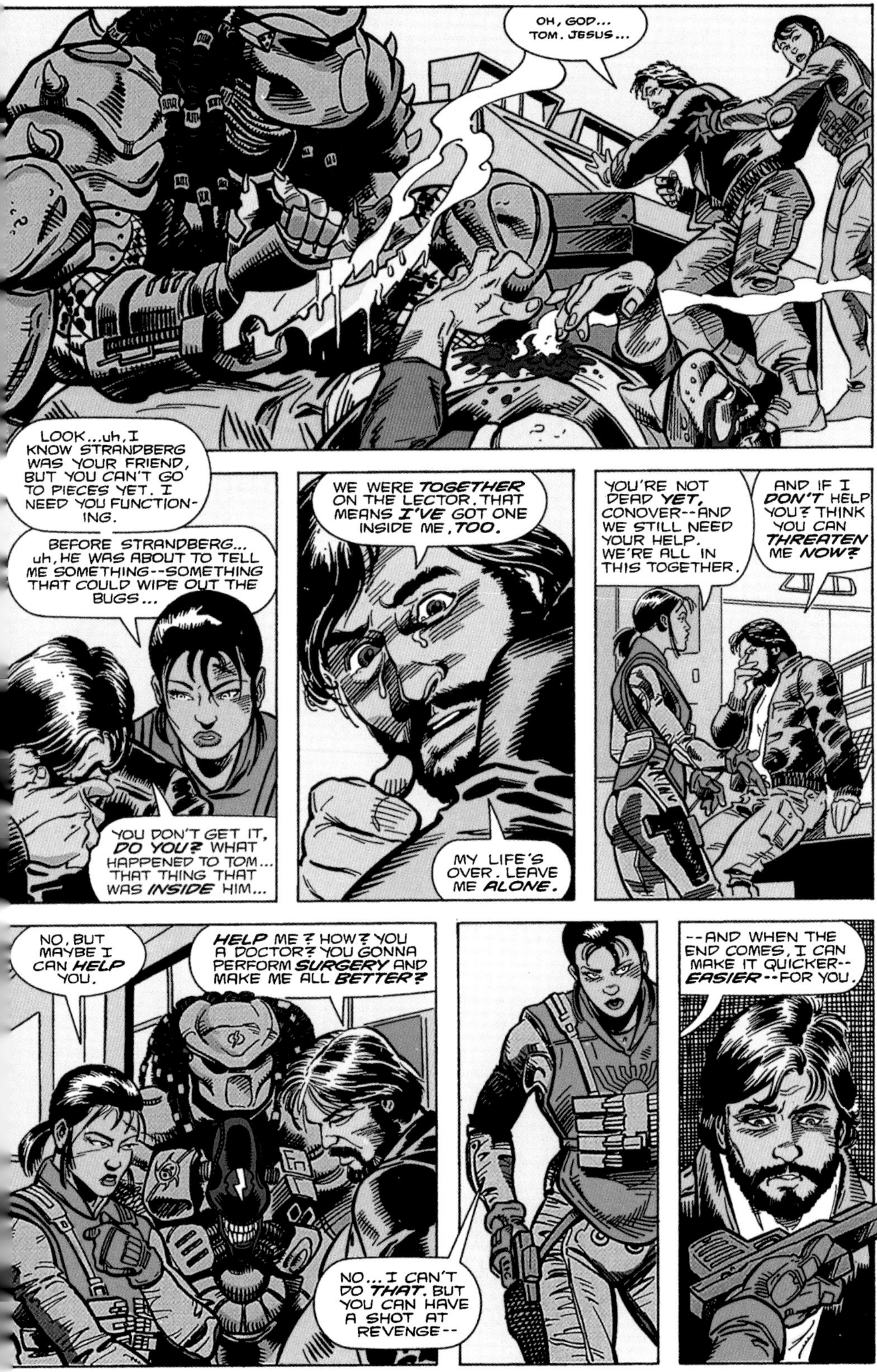
OH, GOD... TOM. JESUS...
LOOK...uh, I KNOW STRANDBERG WAS YOUR FRIEND, BUT YOU CAN'T GO TO PIECES YET. I NEED YOU FUNCTIONING.
BEFORE STRANDBERG... uh, HE WAS ABOUT TO TELL ME SOMETHING--SOMETHING THAT COULD WIPE OUT THE BUGS...
YOU DON'T GET IT, DO YOU? WHAT HAPPENED TO TOM... THAT THING THAT WAS INSIDE HIM...
WE WERE TOGETHER ON THE LECTOR. THAT MEANS I'VE GOT ONE INSIDE ME, TOO.
MY LIFE'S OVER. LEAVE ME ALONE.
YOU'RE NOT DEAD YET, CONOVER--AND WE STILL NEED YOUR HELP. WE'RE ALL IN THIS TOGETHER.
AND IF I DON'T HELP YOU? THINK YOU CAN THREATEN ME NOW?
NO, BUT MAYBE I CAN HELP YOU.
HELP ME? HOW? YOU A DOCTOR? YOU GONNA PERFORM SURGERY AND MAKE ME ALL BETTER?
NO... I CAN'T DO THAT. BUT YOU CAN HAVE A SHOT AT REVENGE--
--AND WHEN THE END COMES, I CAN MAKE IT QUICKER--EASIER--FOR YOU.

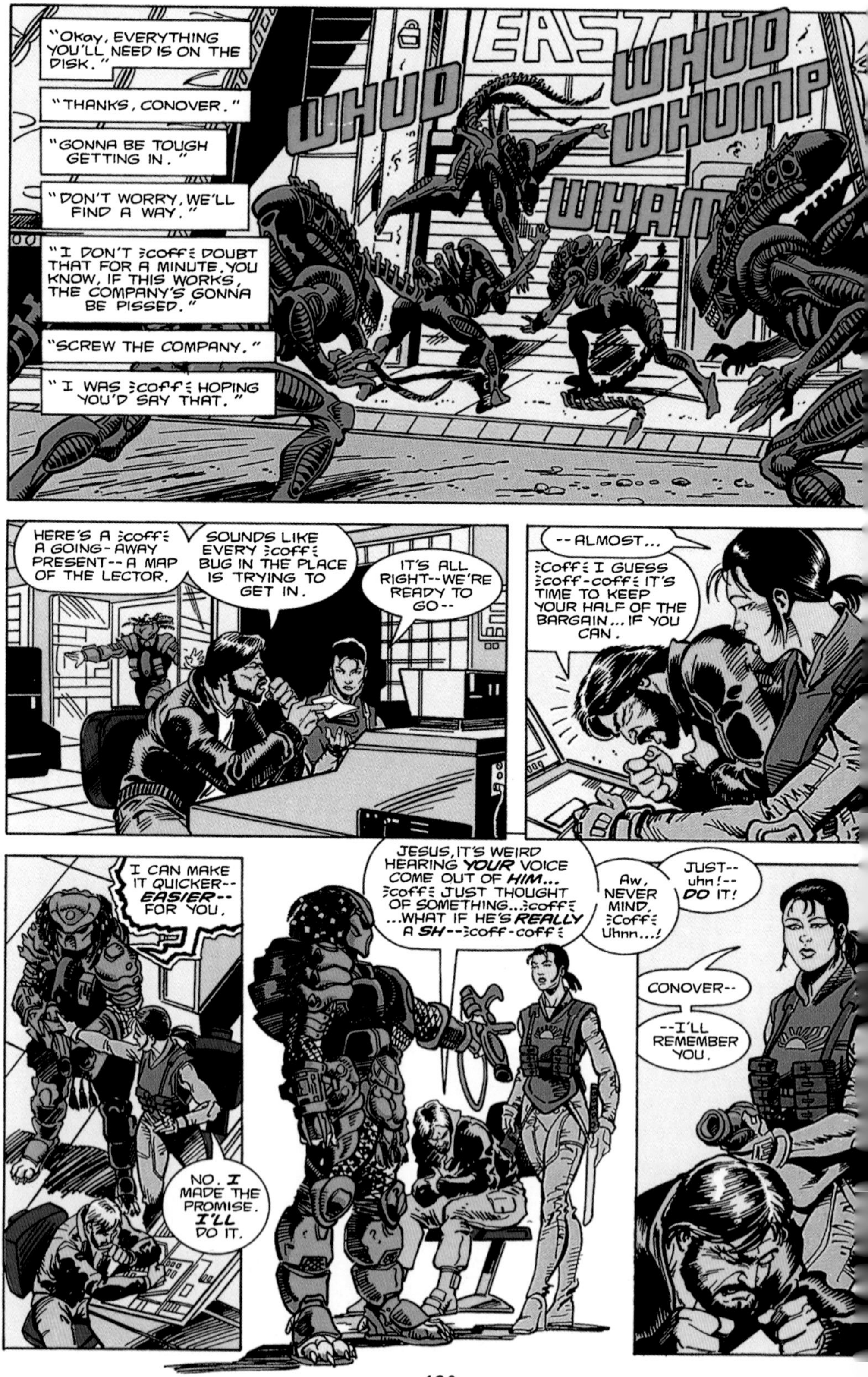
"Okay, EVERYTHING YOU'LL NEED IS ON THE DISK."
"THANKS, CONOVER."
"GONNA BE TOUGH GETTING IN."
"DON'T WORRY, WE'LL FIND A WAY."
"I DON'T :coff: DOUBT THAT FOR A MINUTE. YOU KNOW, IF THIS WORKS, THE COMPANY'S GONNA BE PISSED."
"SCREW THE COMPANY."
"I WAS :coff: HOPING YOU'D SAY THAT."
EAST
WHUD
WHUD
WHUMP
WHAM
HERE'S A :coff: A GOING-AWAY PRESENT--A MAP OF THE LECTOR.
SOUNDS LIKE EVERY :coff: BUG IN THE PLACE IS TRYING TO GET IN.
IT'S ALL RIGHT--WE'RE READY TO GO--
--ALMOST...
:Coff: I GUESS :coff-coff: IT'S TIME TO KEEP YOUR HALF OF THE BARGAIN... IF YOU CAN.
I CAN MAKE IT QUICKER--EASIER--FOR YOU.
NO. I MADE THE PROMISE. I'LL DO IT.
JESUS, IT'S WEIRD HEARING YOUR VOICE COME OUT OF HIM... :coff: JUST THOUGHT OF SOMETHING... :coff: ...WHAT IF HE'S REALLY A SH-- :coff-coff:
Aw, NEVER MIND. :Coff: Uhnn...!
JUST-- uhn!-- DO IT!
CONOVER--
--I'LL REMEMBER YOU.

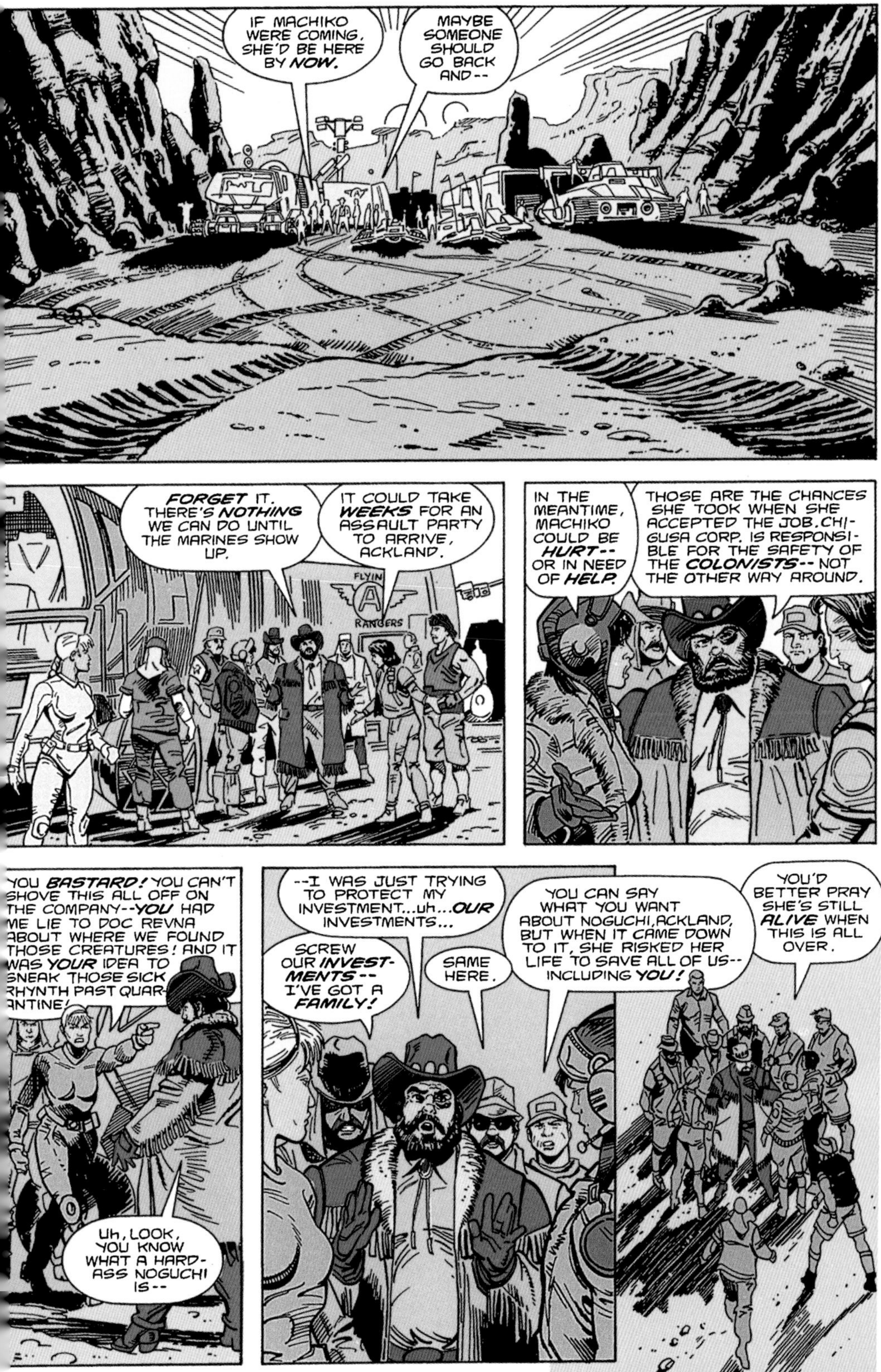
IF MACHIKO WERE COMING, SHE'D BE HERE BY NOW.
MAYBE SOMEONE SHOULD GO BACK AND--
FORGET IT. THERE'S NOTHING WE CAN DO UNTIL THE MARINES SHOW UP.
IT COULD TAKE WEEKS FOR AN ASSAULT PARTY TO ARRIVE, ACKLAND.
FLYIN A RANGERS
IN THE MEANTIME, MACHIKO COULD BE HURT-- OR IN NEED OF HELP.
THOSE ARE THE CHANCES SHE TOOK WHEN SHE ACCEPTED THE JOB. CHIGUSA CORP. IS RESPONSIBLE FOR THE SAFETY OF THE COLONISTS-- NOT THE OTHER WAY AROUND.
YOU BASTARD! YOU CAN'T SHOVE THIS ALL OFF ON THE COMPANY--YOU HAD ME LIE TO DOC REVNA ABOUT WHERE WE FOUND THOSE CREATURES! AND IT WAS YOUR IDEA TO SNEAK THOSE SICK RHYNTH PAST QUARANTINE!
Uh, LOOK, YOU KNOW WHAT A HARD-ASS NOGUCHI IS--
--I WAS JUST TRYING TO PROTECT MY INVESTMENT...uh...OUR INVESTMENTS...
SCREW OUR INVESTMENTS-- I'VE GOT A FAMILY!
SAME HERE.
YOU CAN SAY WHAT YOU WANT ABOUT NOGUCHI, ACKLAND, BUT WHEN IT CAME DOWN TO IT, SHE RISKED HER LIFE TO SAVE ALL OF US-- INCLUDING YOU!
YOU'D BETTER PRAY SHE'S STILL ALIVE WHEN THIS IS ALL OVER.

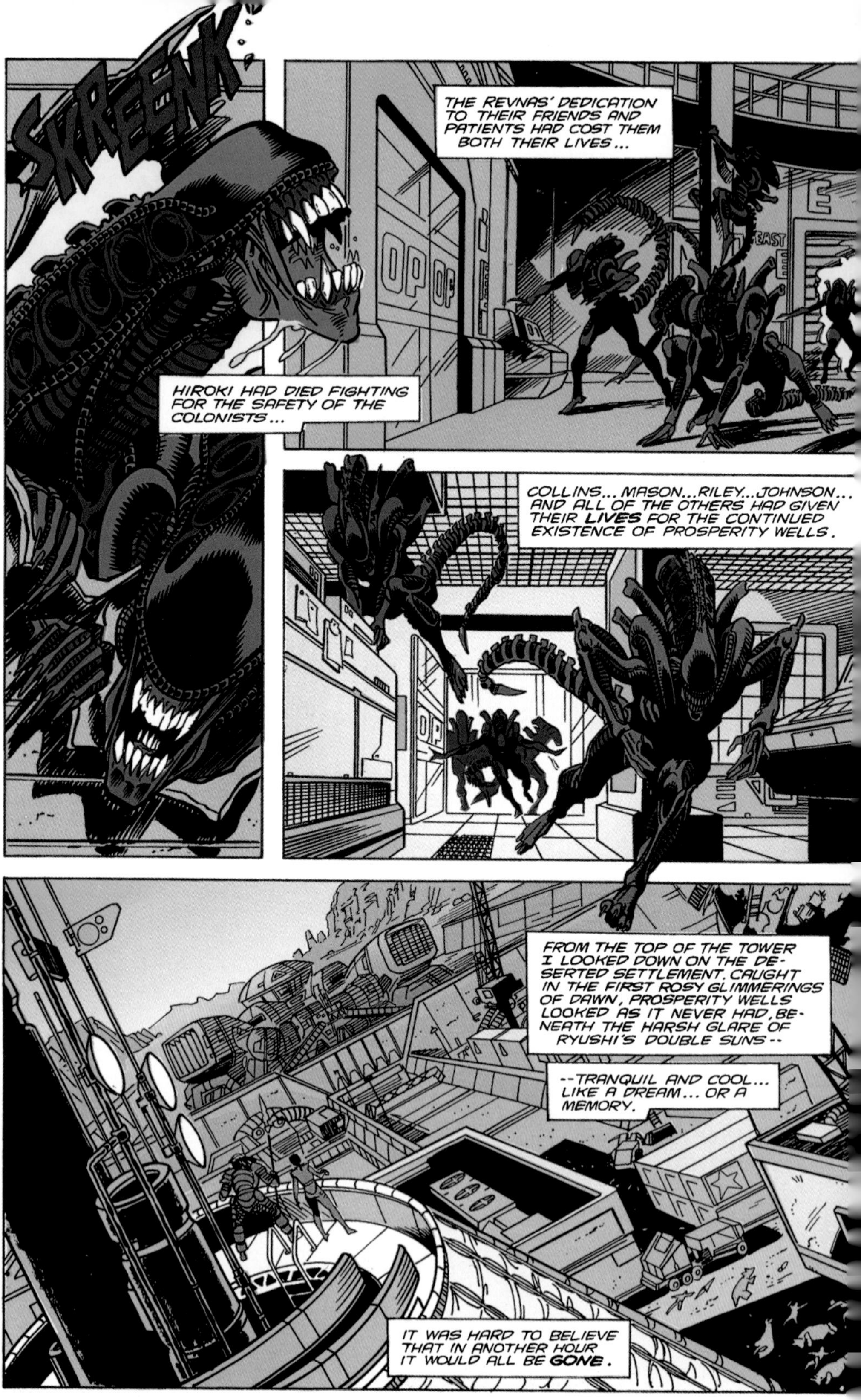
SKREENK
THE REVNAS' DEDICATION TO THEIR FRIENDS AND PATIENTS HAD COST THEM BOTH THEIR LIVES...
HIROKI HAD DIED FIGHTING FOR THE SAFETY OF THE COLONISTS...
COLLINS... MASON... RILEY... JOHNSON... AND ALL OF THE OTHERS HAD GIVEN THEIR LIVES FOR THE CONTINUED EXISTENCE OF PROSPERITY WELLS.
FROM THE TOP OF THE TOWER I LOOKED DOWN ON THE DESERTED SETTLEMENT. CAUGHT IN THE FIRST ROSY GLIMMERINGS OF DAWN, PROSPERITY WELLS LOOKED AS IT NEVER HAD, BENEATH THE HARSH GLARE OF RYUSHI'S DOUBLE SUNS--
--TRANQUIL AND COOL... LIKE A DREAM... OR A MEMORY.
IT WAS HARD TO BELIEVE THAT IN ANOTHER HOUR IT WOULD ALL BE GONE.

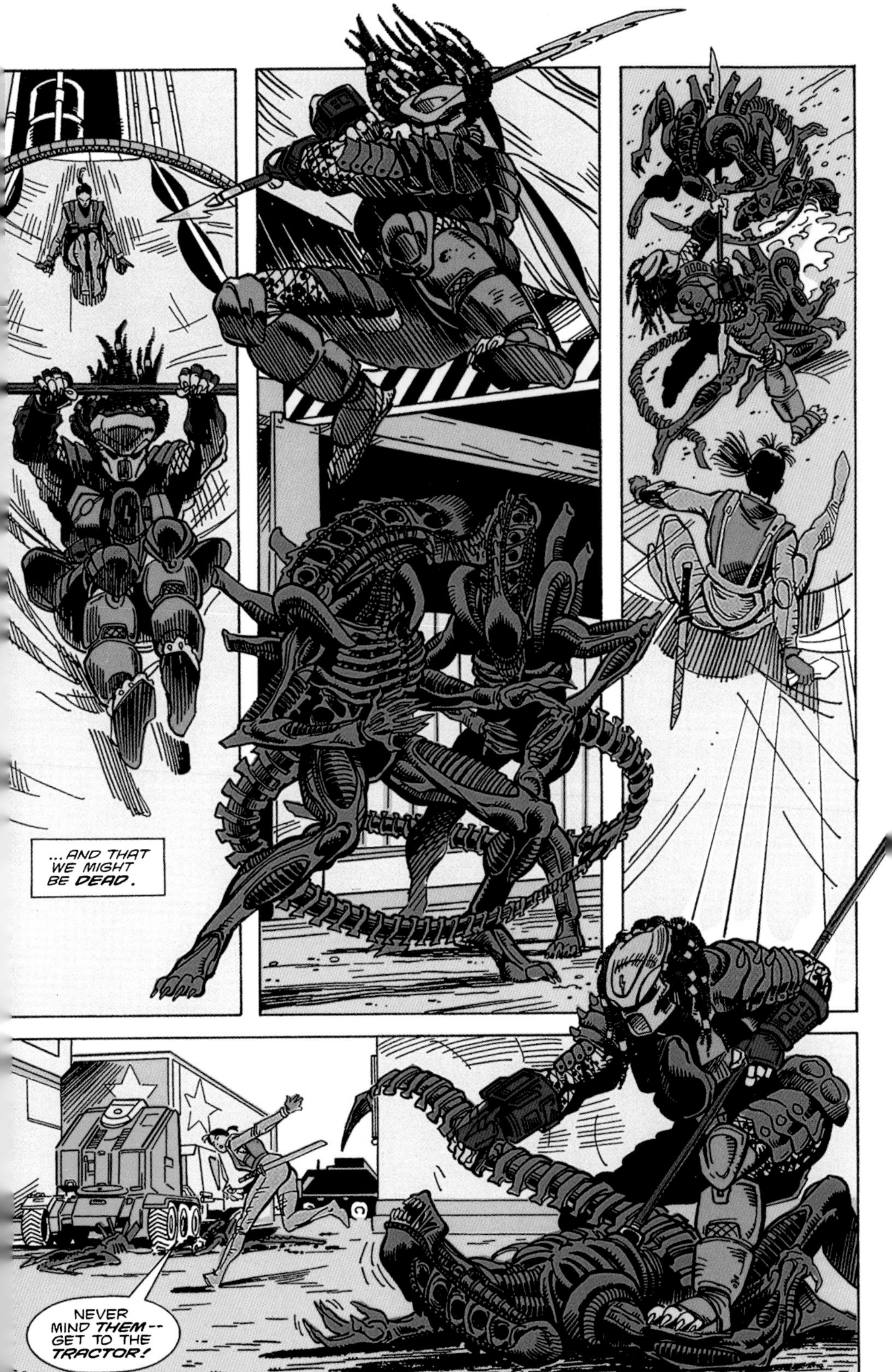
...AND THAT WE MIGHT BE DEAD.
NEVER MIND THEM -- GET TO THE TRACTOR!

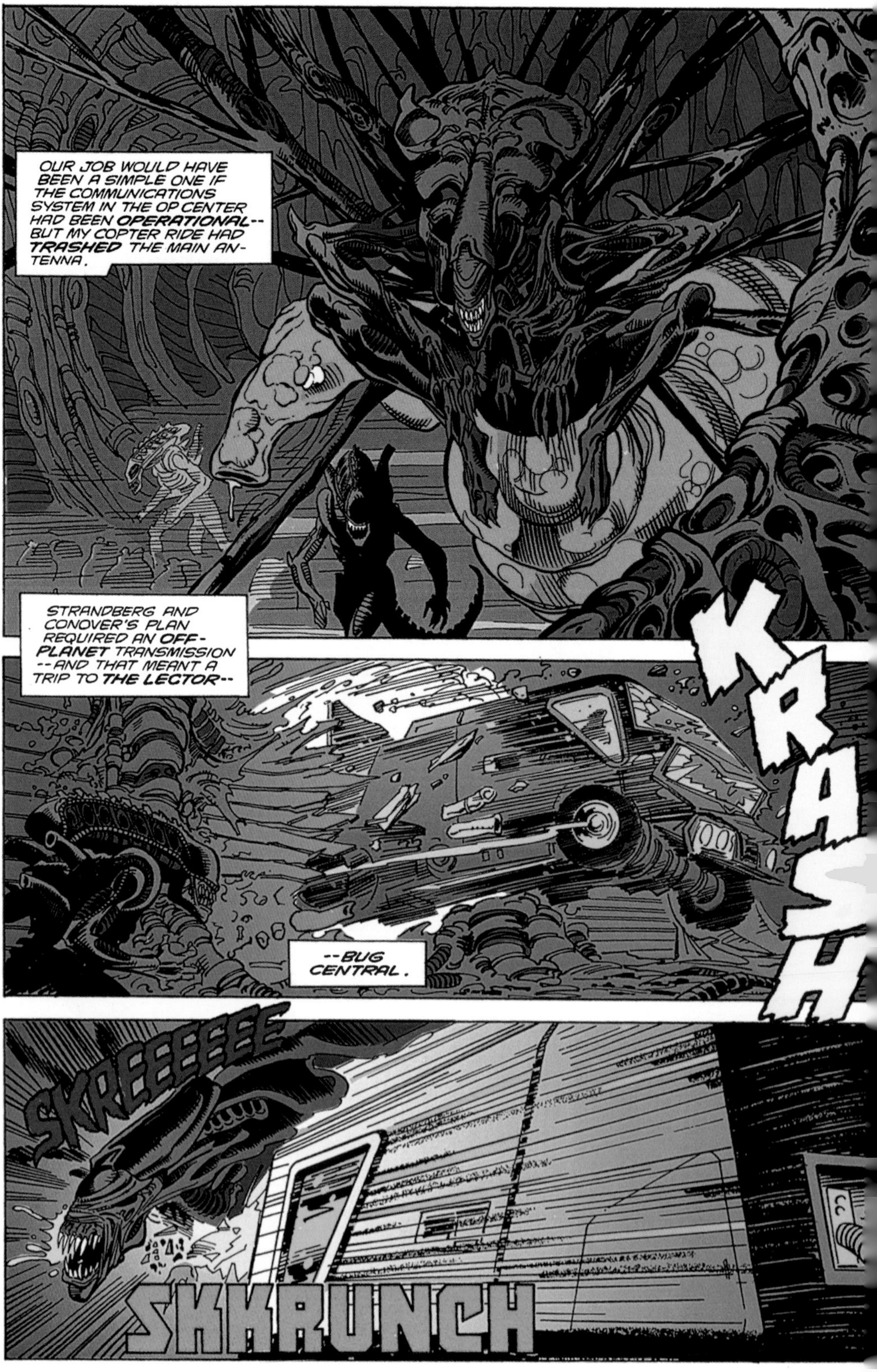
OUR JOB WOULD HAVE BEEN A SIMPLE ONE IF THE COMMUNICATIONS SYSTEM IN THE OP CENTER HAD BEEN OPERATIONAL-- BUT MY COPTER RIDE HAD TRASHED THE MAIN ANTENNA.
STRANDBERG AND CONOVER'S PLAN REQUIRED AN OFF-PLANET TRANSMISSION --AND THAT MEANT A TRIP TO THE LECTOR--
KRASH
--BUG CENTRAL.
SKREEEEEEE
SKKRUNCH

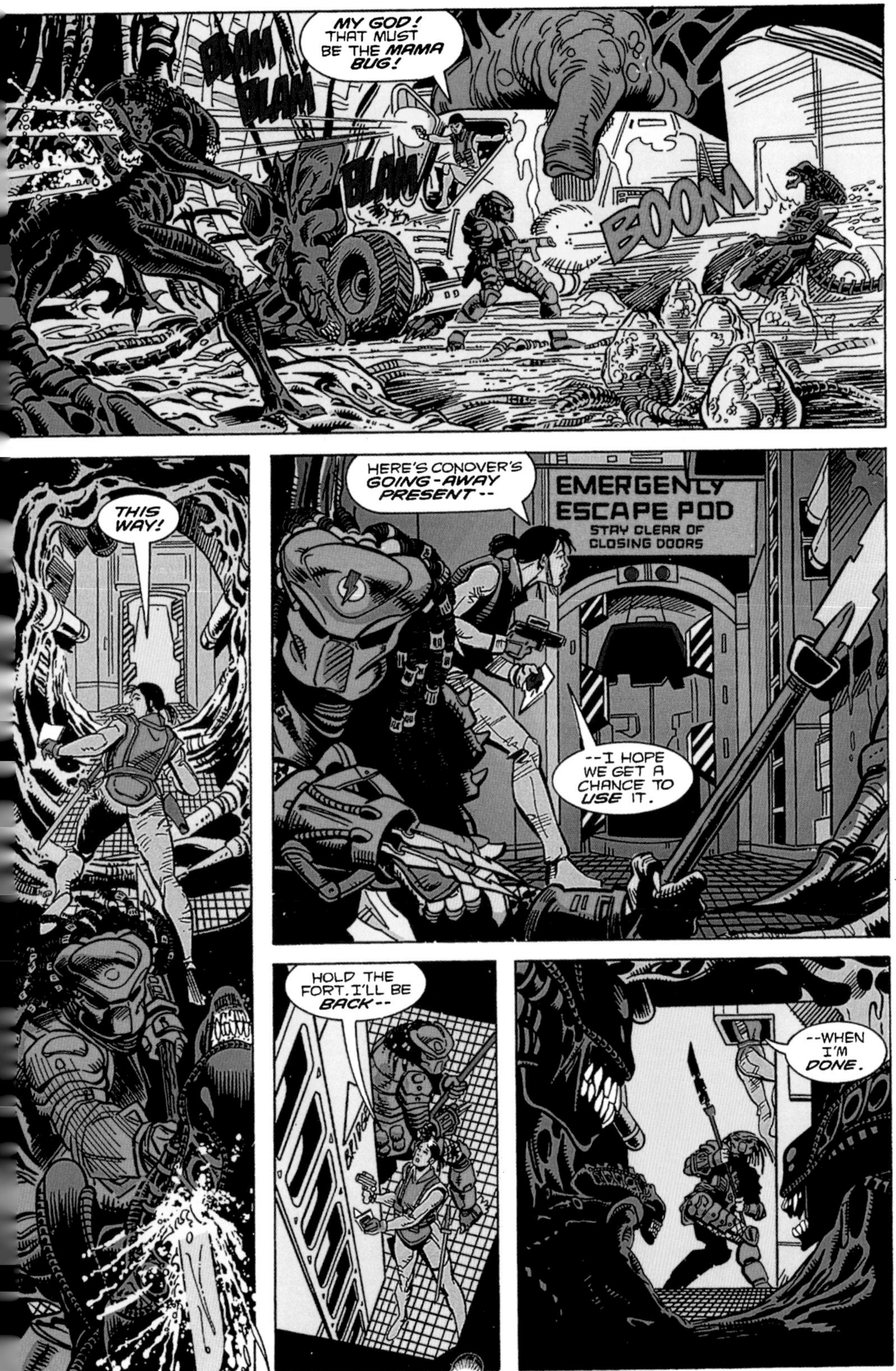
BLAM
BLAM
BLAM
MY GOD! THAT MUST BE THE MAMA BUG!
BOOM
THIS WAY!
HERE'S CONOVER'S GOING-AWAY PRESENT--
EMERGENCY ESCAPE POD
STAY CLEAR OF CLOSING DOORS
--I HOPE WE GET A CHANCE TO USE IT.
HOLD THE FORT. I'LL BE BACK--
--WHEN I'M DONE.

BIG SHIP...

FOR ALL HER SIZE, THE LECTOR WAS ONLY A *TUG*--

--*TINY* COMPARED TO THE MASSIVE REFRIGERATED *BARGE* SHE TOWED ACROSS THE HEAVENS.

SSSSS

THE BUGS HAD TAKEN *CONTROL* OF THE LECTOR-- TURNING IT INTO A VIRTUAL "BUG FORTRESS."

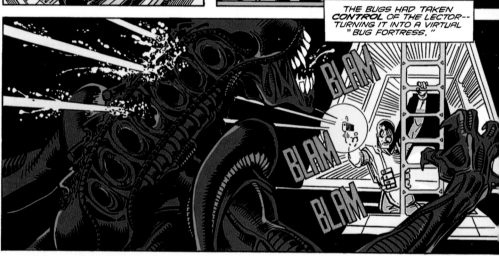

BLAM

BLAM

BLAM

BUT IF THE PLAN WORKED...

...WE'D SHOW THE BUGS *JUST* HOW *SMALL* AND *EXPOSED* THEIR FORTRESS WAS.

KLIK

DO YOUR STUFF, COMPUTER.

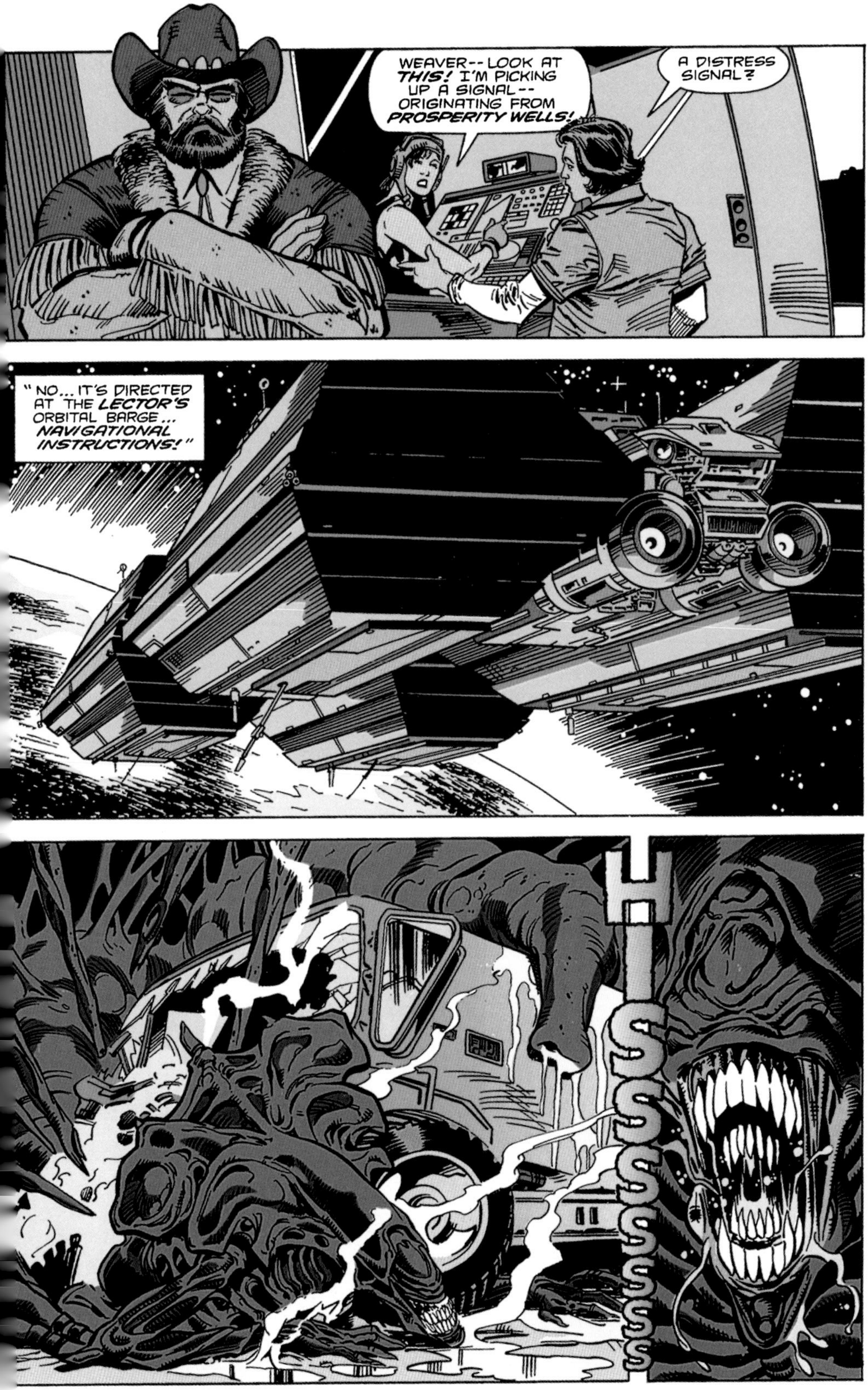
WEAVER--LOOK AT THIS! I'M PICKING UP A SIGNAL--ORIGINATING FROM PROSPERITY WELLS!
A DISTRESS SIGNAL?
"NO... IT'S DIRECTED AT THE LECTOR'S ORBITAL BARGE... NAVIGATIONAL INSTRUCTIONS!"
HISSSSSSS

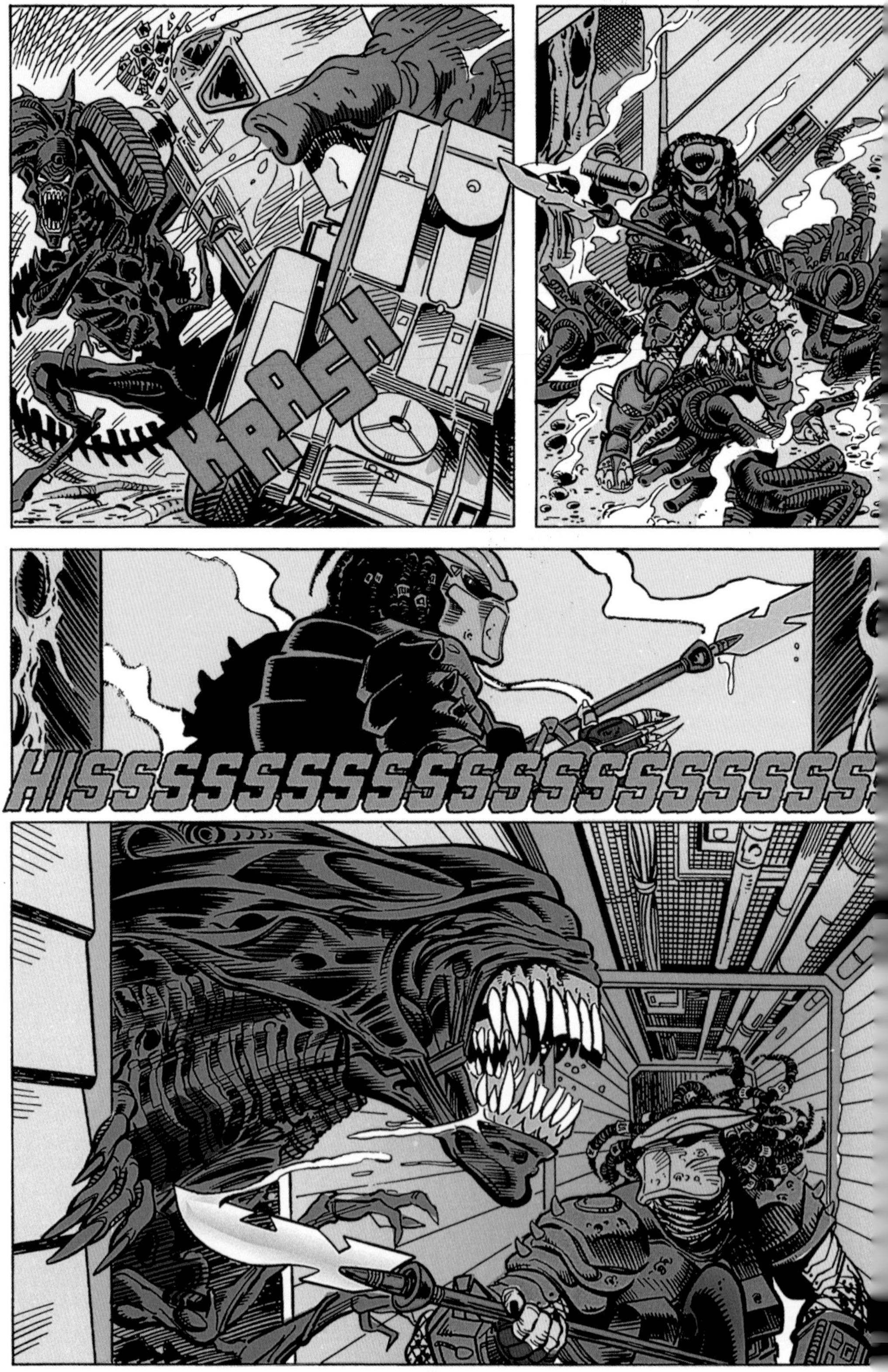
KRASH
HISSSSSSSSSSSSSSSSSSS

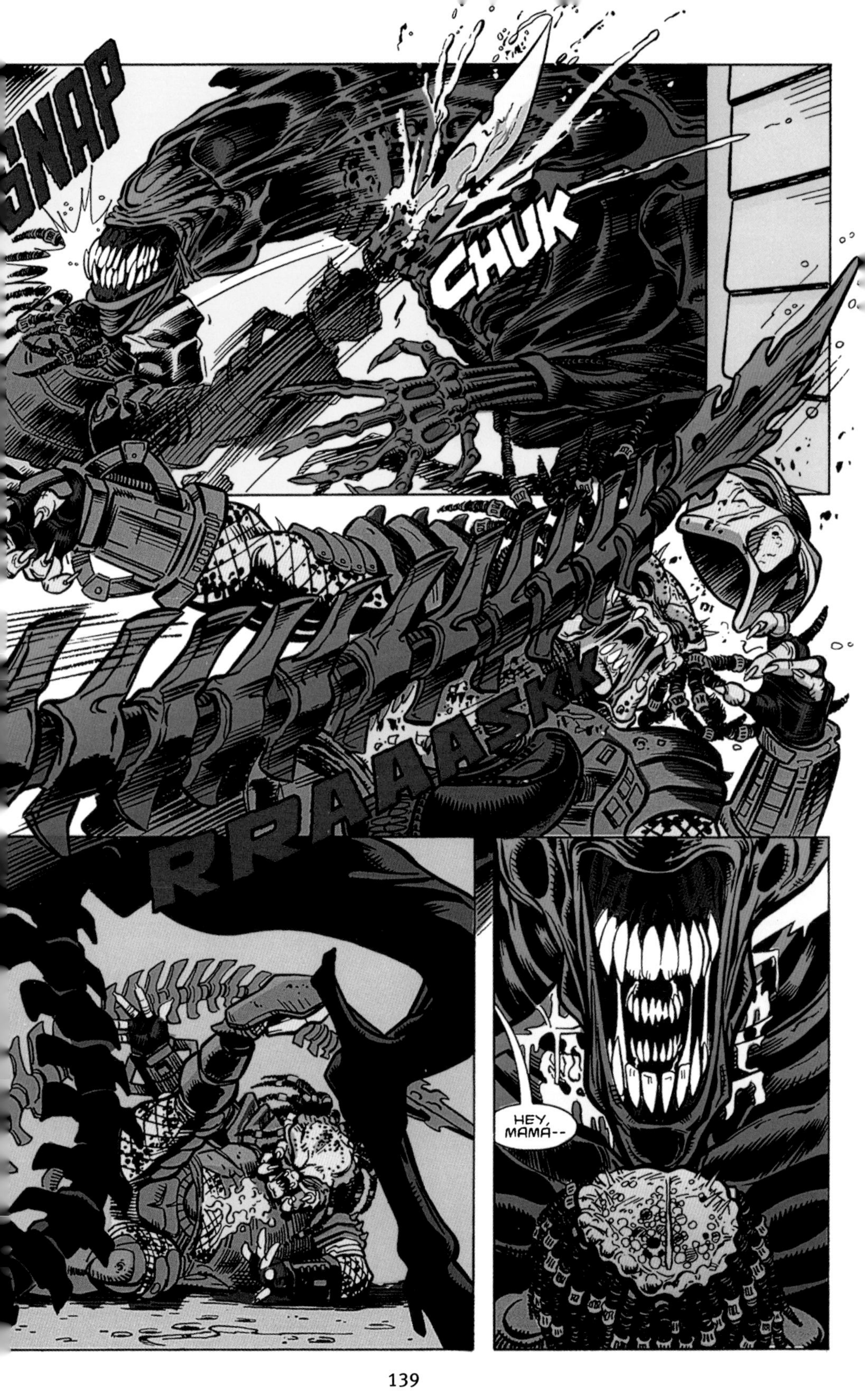
SNAP
CHUK
RRAAASKK
HEY, MAMÁ--

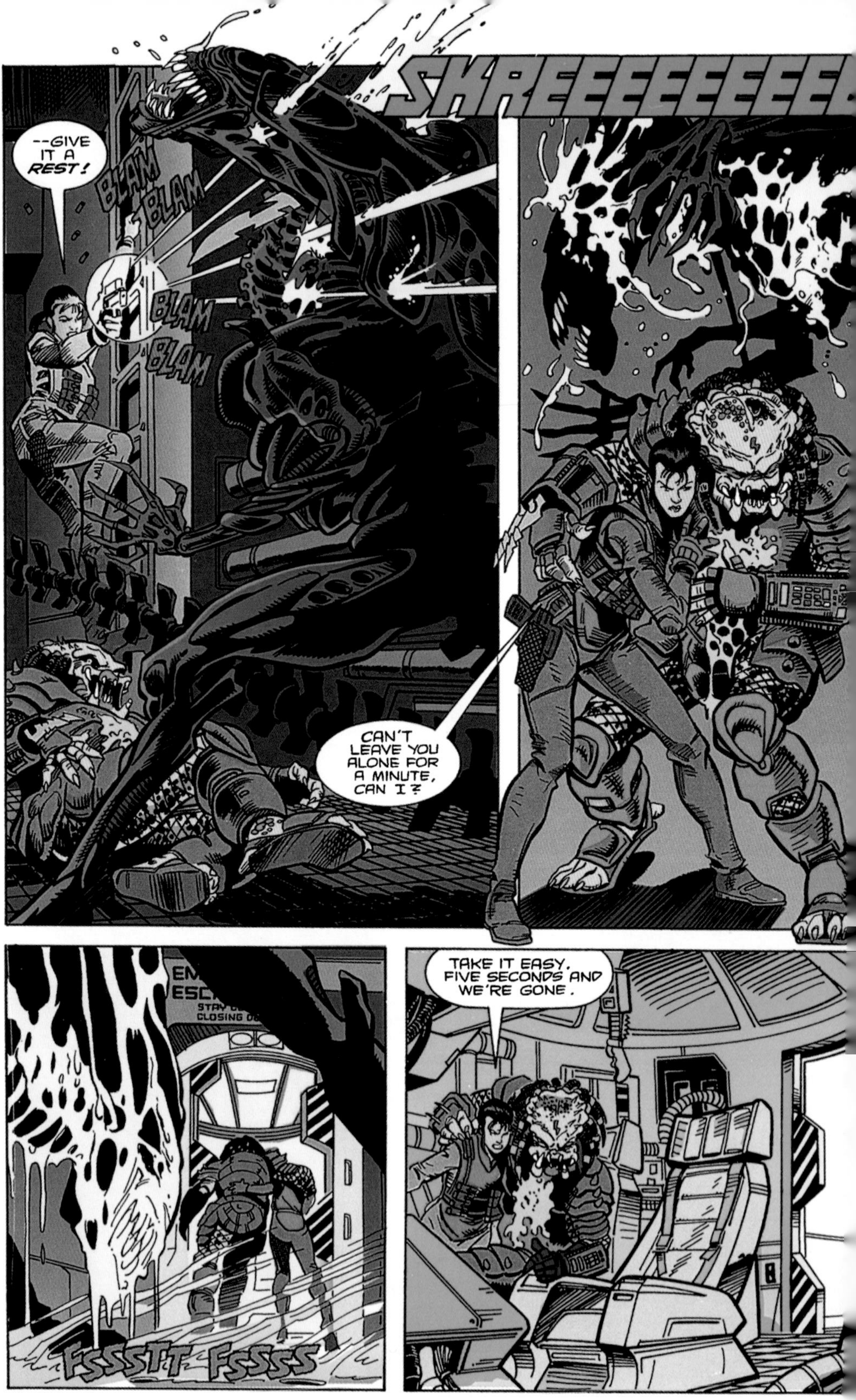
SKREEEEEEEEE
--GIVE IT A REST!
BLAM BLAM
BLAM BLAM
CAN'T LEAVE YOU ALONE FOR A MINUTE, CAN I?
CLOSING
FSSSTT FSSSS
TAKE IT EASY. FIVE SECONDS AND WE'RE GONE.

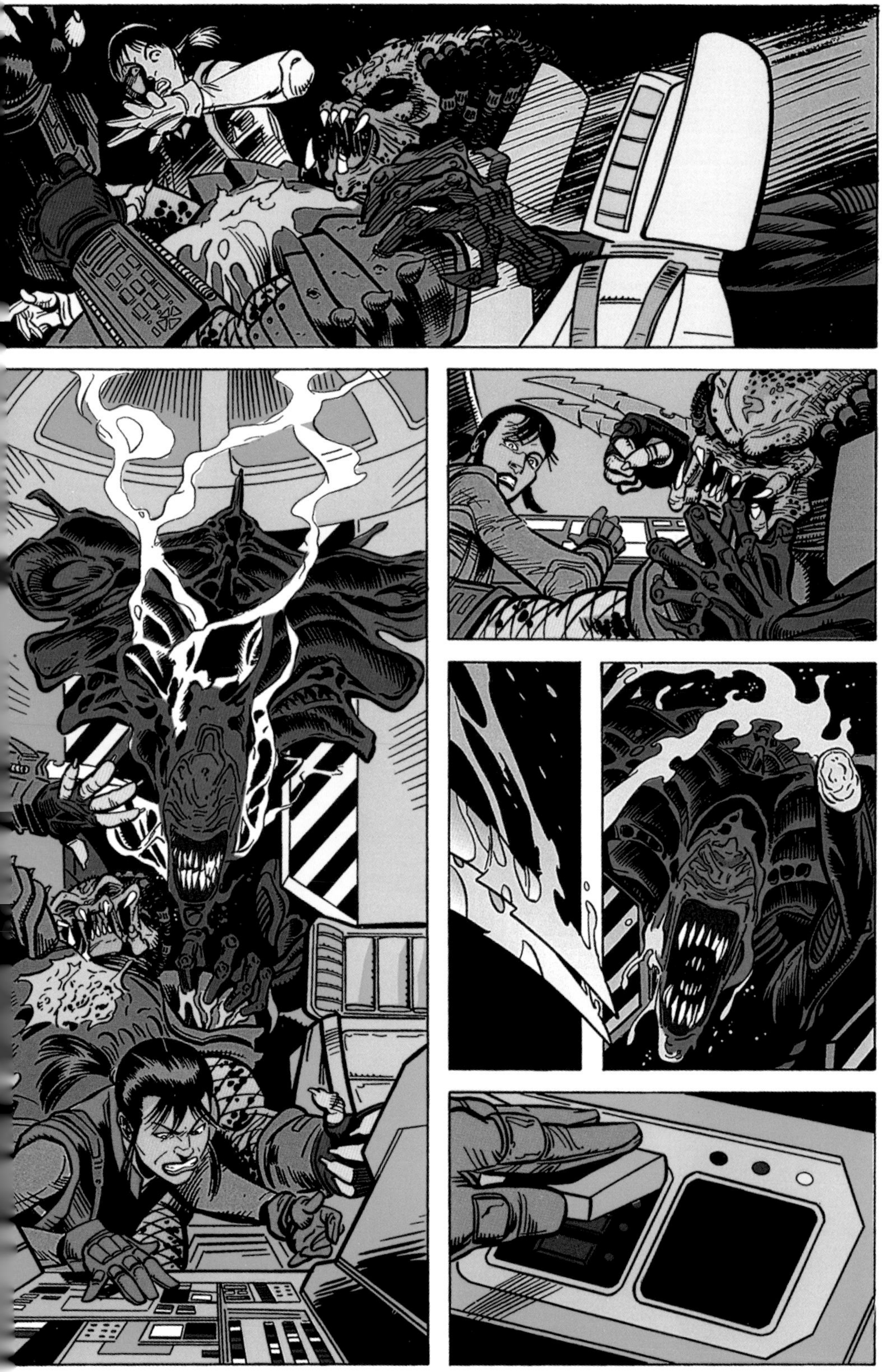

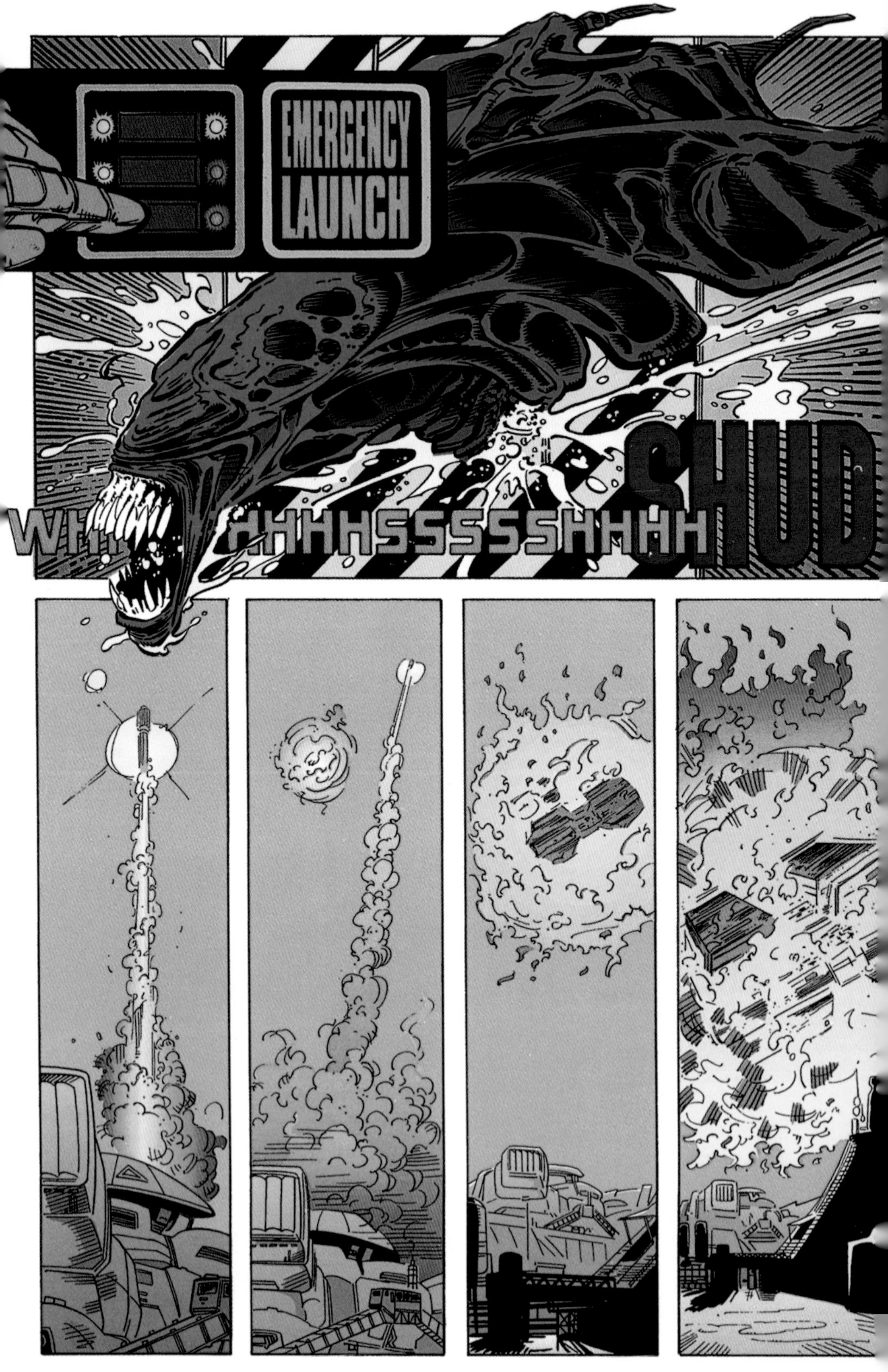
EMERGENCY
LAUNCH
WHH HHHHSSSSSSHHHH
SHUD

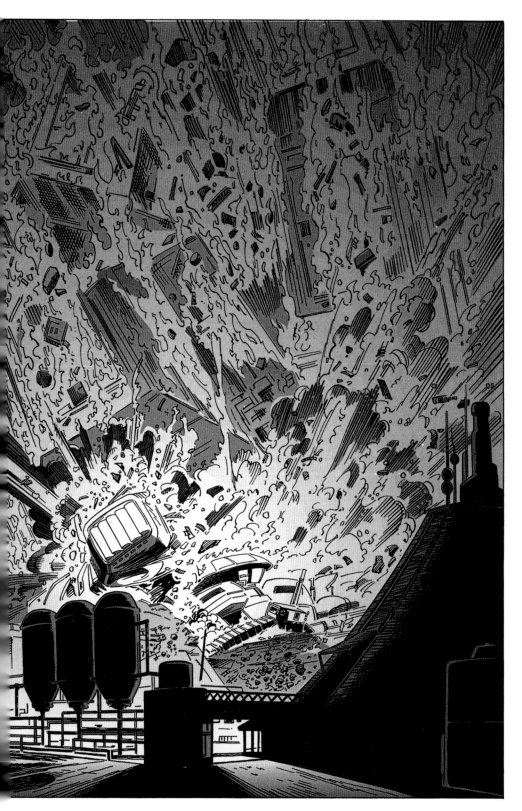

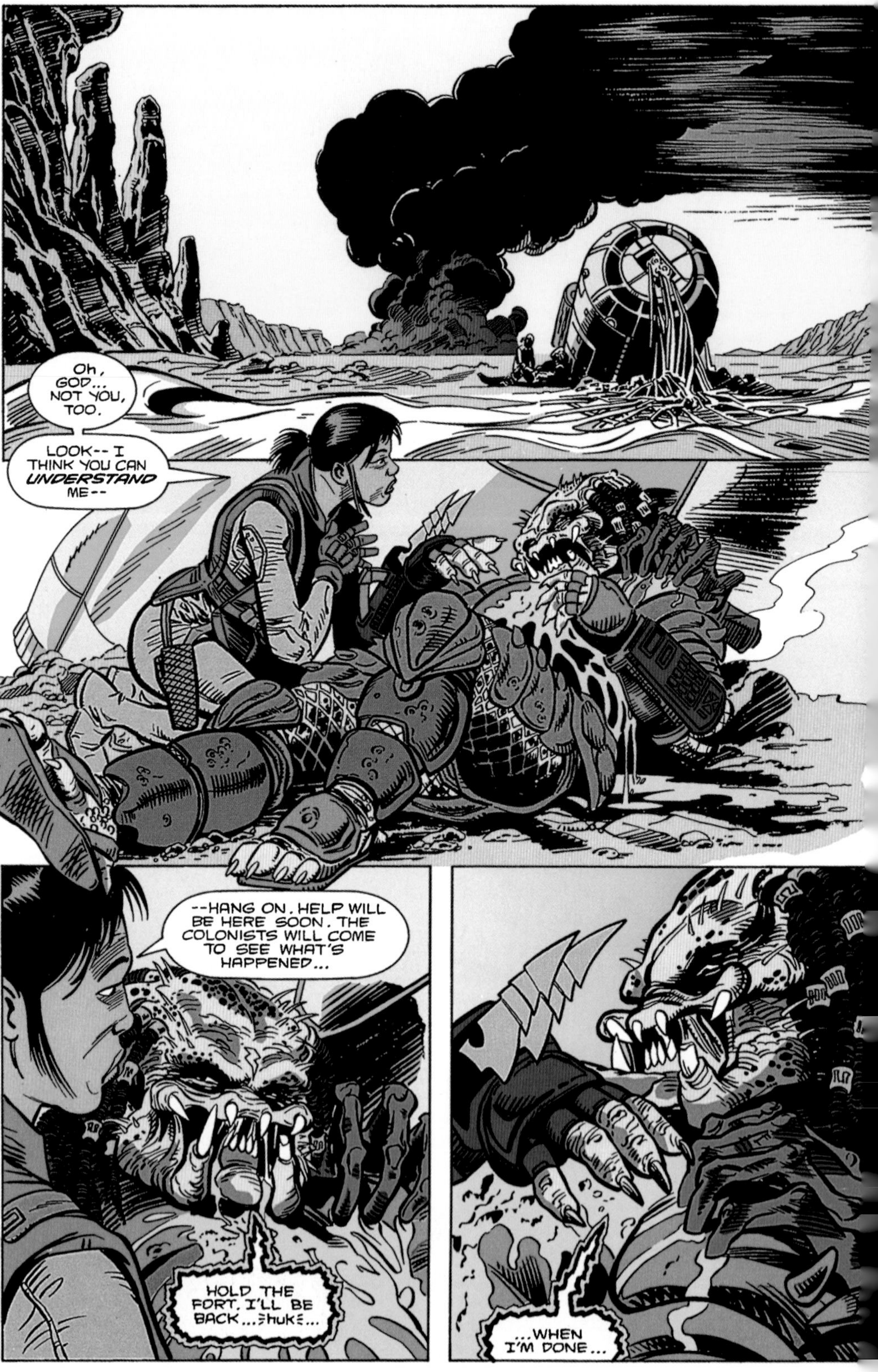

OH, GOD... NOT YOU, TOO.
LOOK-- I THINK YOU CAN *UNDERSTAND* ME--
--HANG ON. HELP WILL BE HERE SOON. THE COLONISTS WILL COME TO SEE WHAT'S HAPPENED...
HOLD THE FORT. I'LL BE BACK... ≡huk≡...
...WHEN I'M DONE...

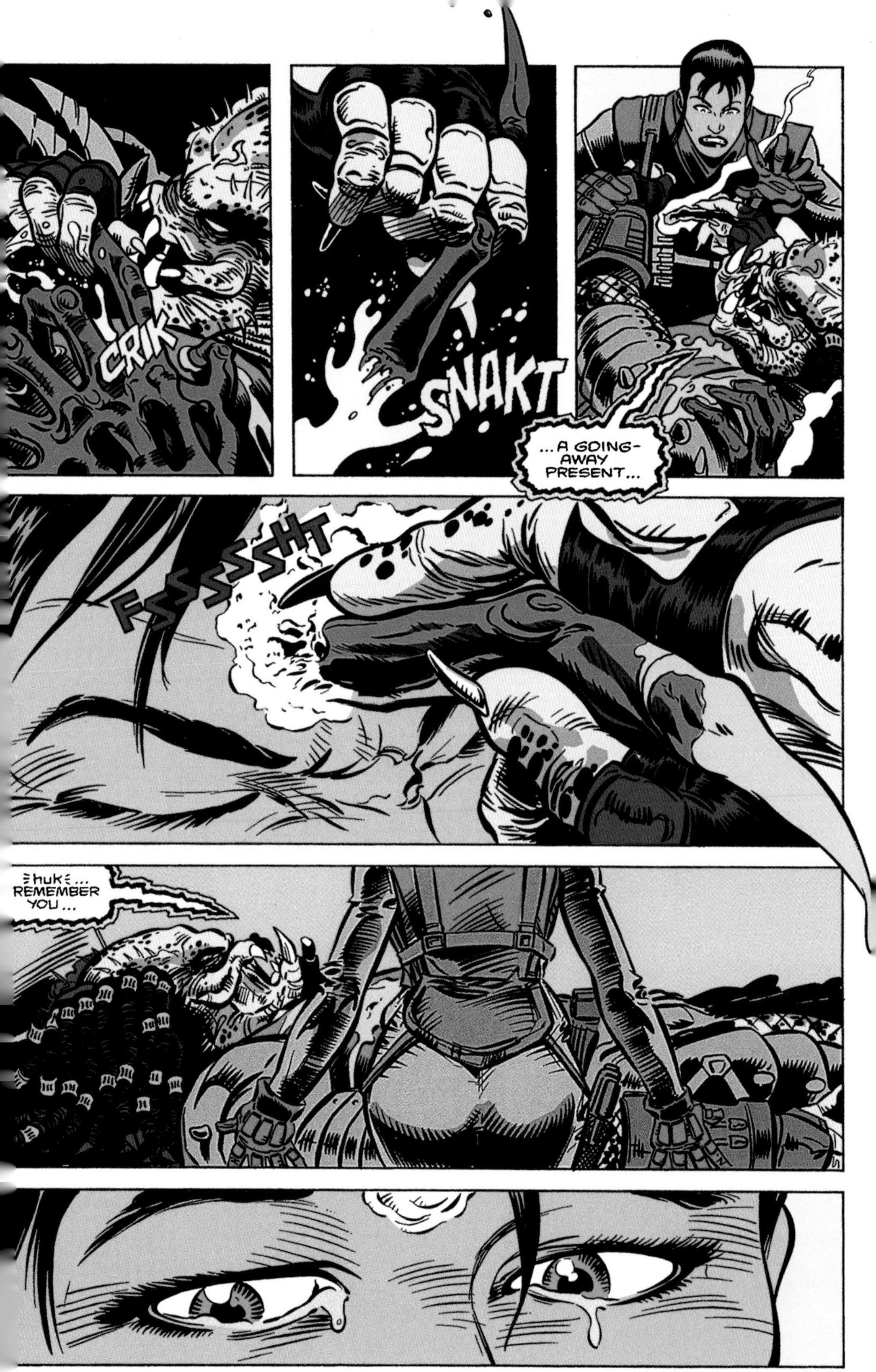

CRIK
SNAKT
...A GOING-AWAY PRESENT...
FSSSSSHT
≡huk≡... REMEMBER YOU...

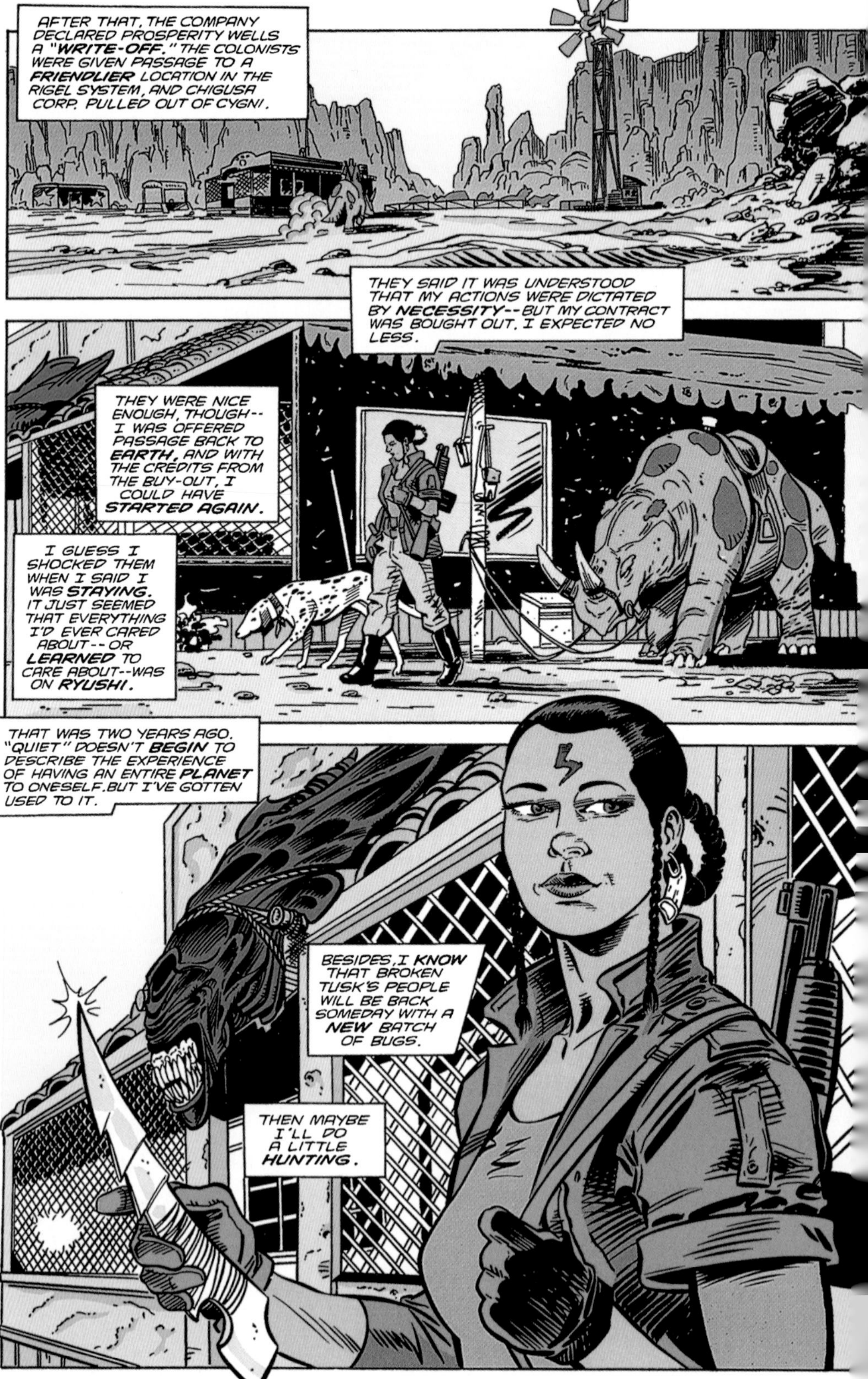
AFTER THAT, THE COMPANY DECLARED PROSPERITY WELLS A "WRITE-OFF." THE COLONISTS WERE GIVEN PASSAGE TO A FRIENDLIER LOCATION IN THE RIGEL SYSTEM, AND CHIGUSA CORP. PULLED OUT OF CYGNI.
THEY SAID IT WAS UNDERSTOOD THAT MY ACTIONS WERE DICTATED BY NECESSITY--BUT MY CONTRACT WAS BOUGHT OUT. I EXPECTED NO LESS.
THEY WERE NICE ENOUGH, THOUGH--I WAS OFFERED PASSAGE BACK TO EARTH, AND WITH THE CREDITS FROM THE BUY-OUT, I COULD HAVE STARTED AGAIN.
I GUESS I SHOCKED THEM WHEN I SAID I WAS STAYING. IT JUST SEEMED THAT EVERYTHING I'D EVER CARED ABOUT--OR LEARNED TO CARE ABOUT--WAS ON RYUSHI.
THAT WAS TWO YEARS AGO. "QUIET" DOESN'T BEGIN TO DESCRIBE THE EXPERIENCE OF HAVING AN ENTIRE PLANET TO ONESELF. BUT I'VE GOTTEN USED TO IT.
BESIDES, I KNOW THAT BROKEN TUSK'S PEOPLE WILL BE BACK SOMEDAY WITH A NEW BATCH OF BUGS.
THEN MAYBE I'LL DO A LITTLE HUNTING.

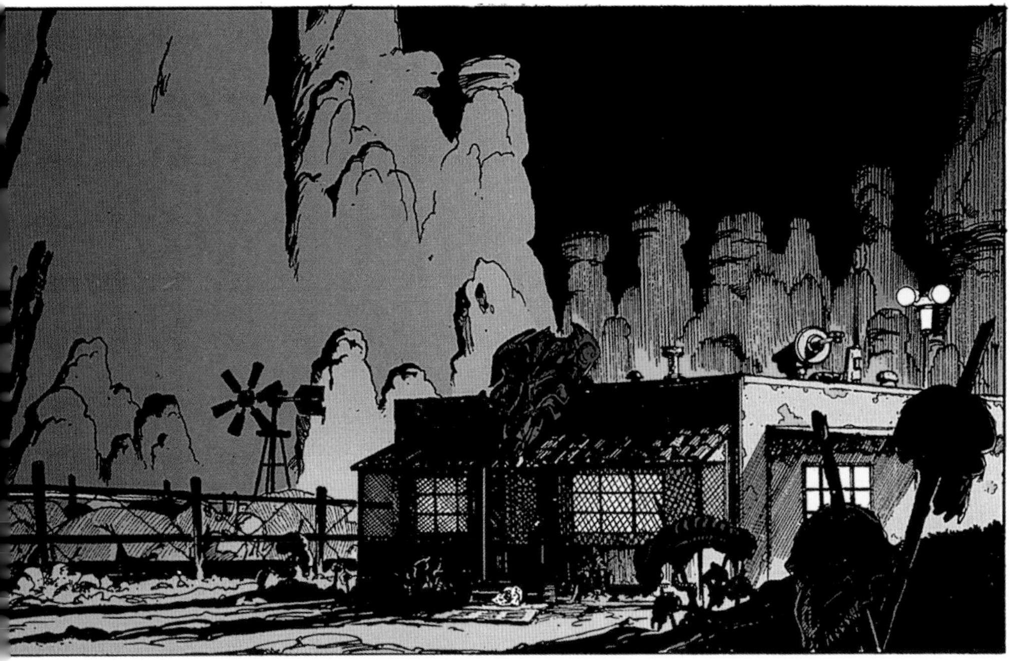

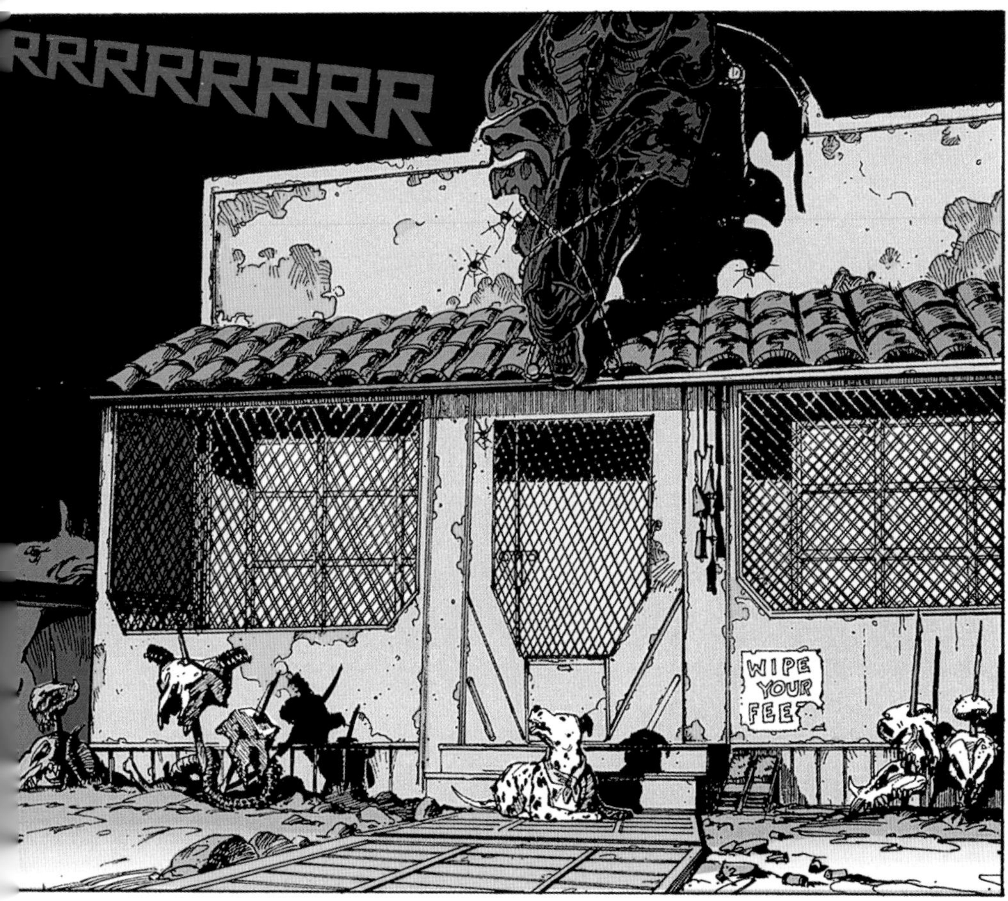
RRRRRRRRR
WIPE YOUR FEET

RRRRRRRRRRRRRRRRRRRRRRRRRRRRRR

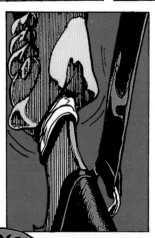

THEY'VE RETURNED.

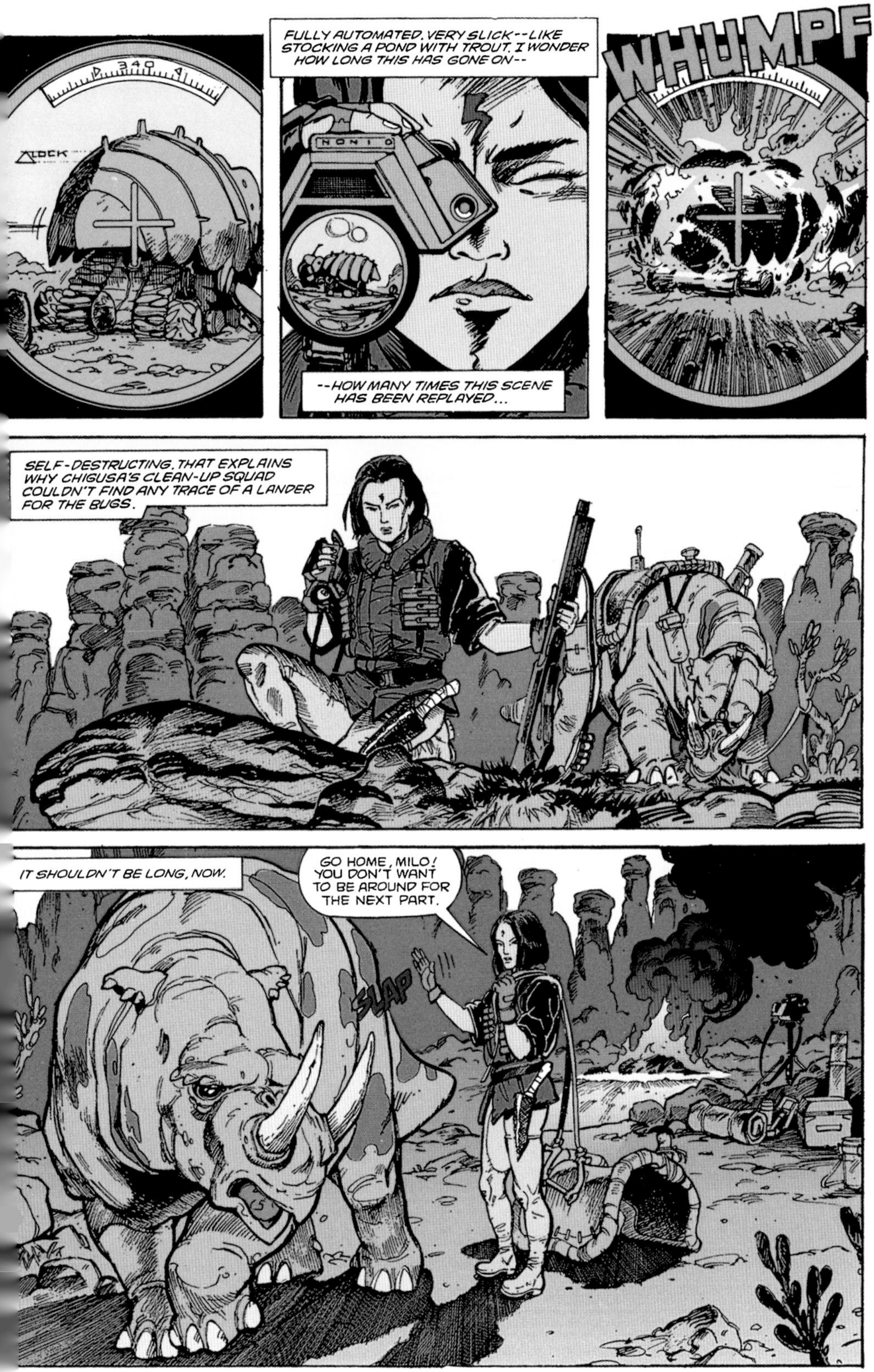

FULLY AUTOMATED. VERY SLICK--LIKE STOCKING A POND WITH TROUT. I WONDER HOW LONG THIS HAS GONE ON--
--HOW MANY TIMES THIS SCENE HAS BEEN REPLAYED...
WHUMPF
SELF-DESTRUCTING. THAT EXPLAINS WHY CHIGUSA'S CLEAN-UP SQUAD COULDN'T FIND ANY TRACE OF A LANDER FOR THE BUGS.
IT SHOULDN'T BE LONG, NOW.
GO HOME, MILO! YOU DON'T WANT TO BE AROUND FOR THE NEXT PART.
SLAP

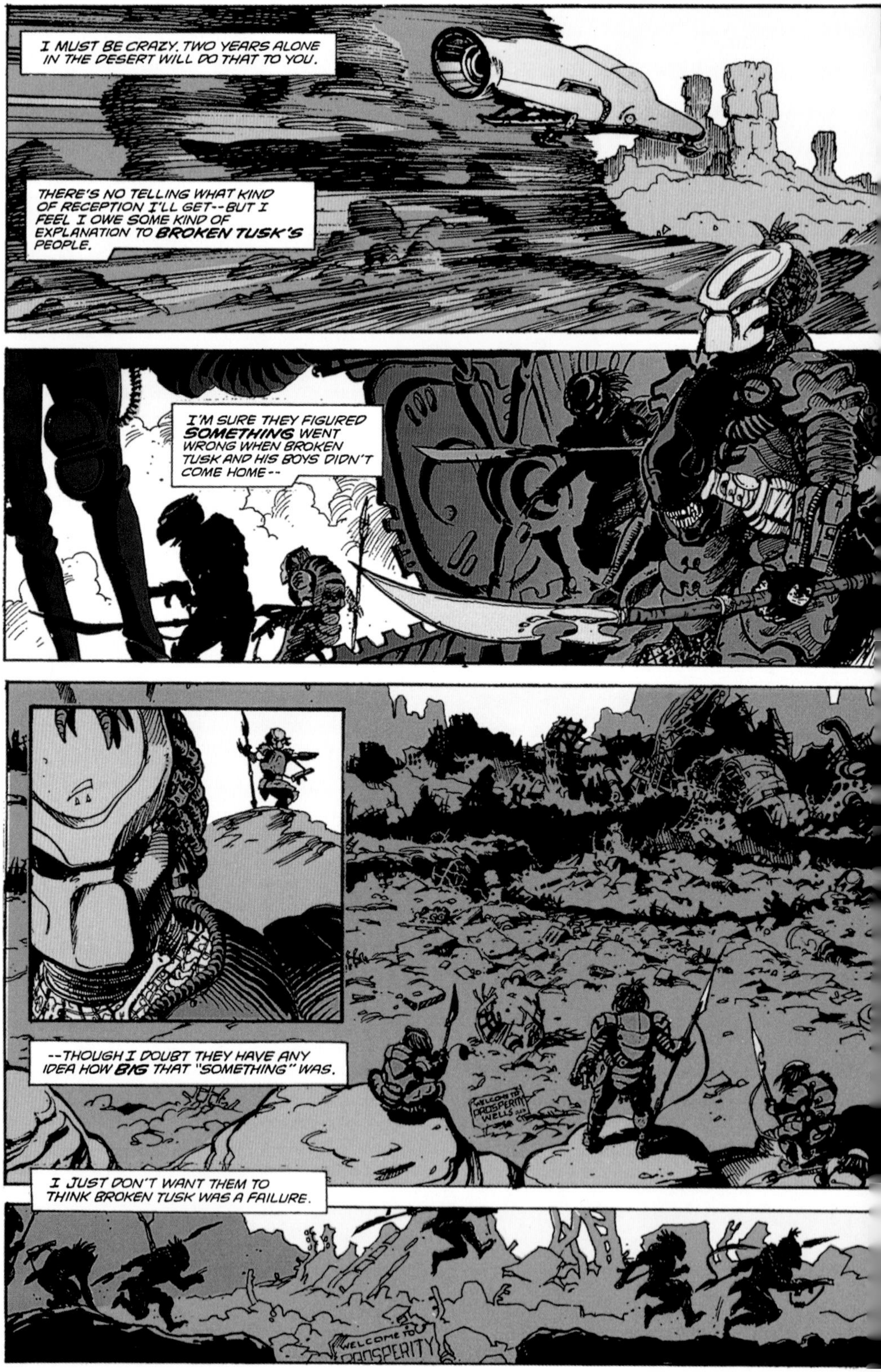

I MUST BE CRAZY. TWO YEARS ALONE IN THE DESERT WILL DO THAT TO YOU.
THERE'S NO TELLING WHAT KIND OF RECEPTION I'LL GET--BUT I FEEL I OWE SOME KIND OF EXPLANATION TO BROKEN TUSK'S PEOPLE.
I'M SURE THEY FIGURED SOMETHING WENT WRONG WHEN BROKEN TUSK AND HIS BOYS DIDN'T COME HOME--
--THOUGH I DOUBT THEY HAVE ANY IDEA HOW BIG THAT "SOMETHING" WAS.
I JUST DON'T WANT THEM TO THINK BROKEN TUSK WAS A FAILURE.
WELCOME TO PROSPERITY

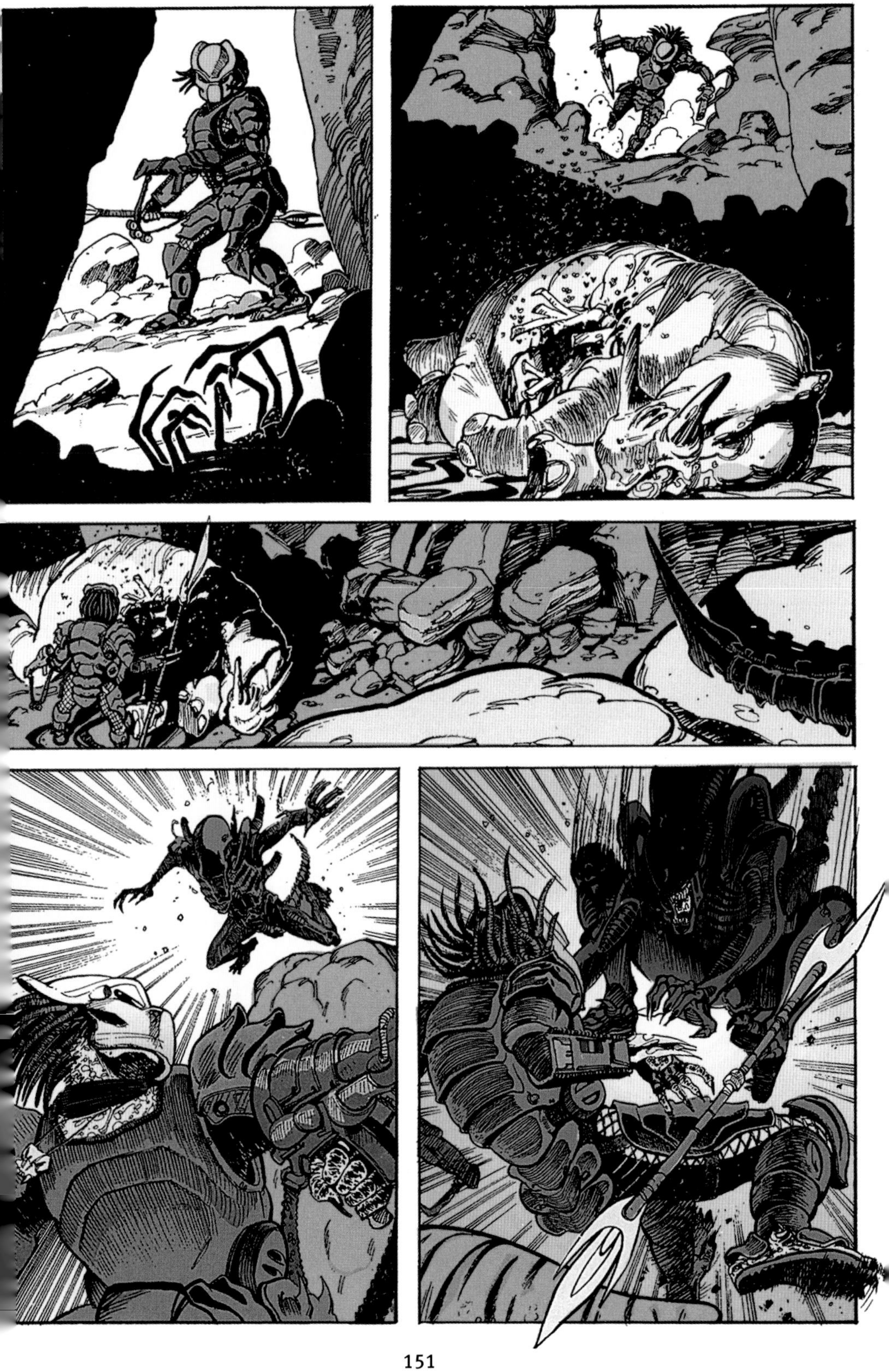

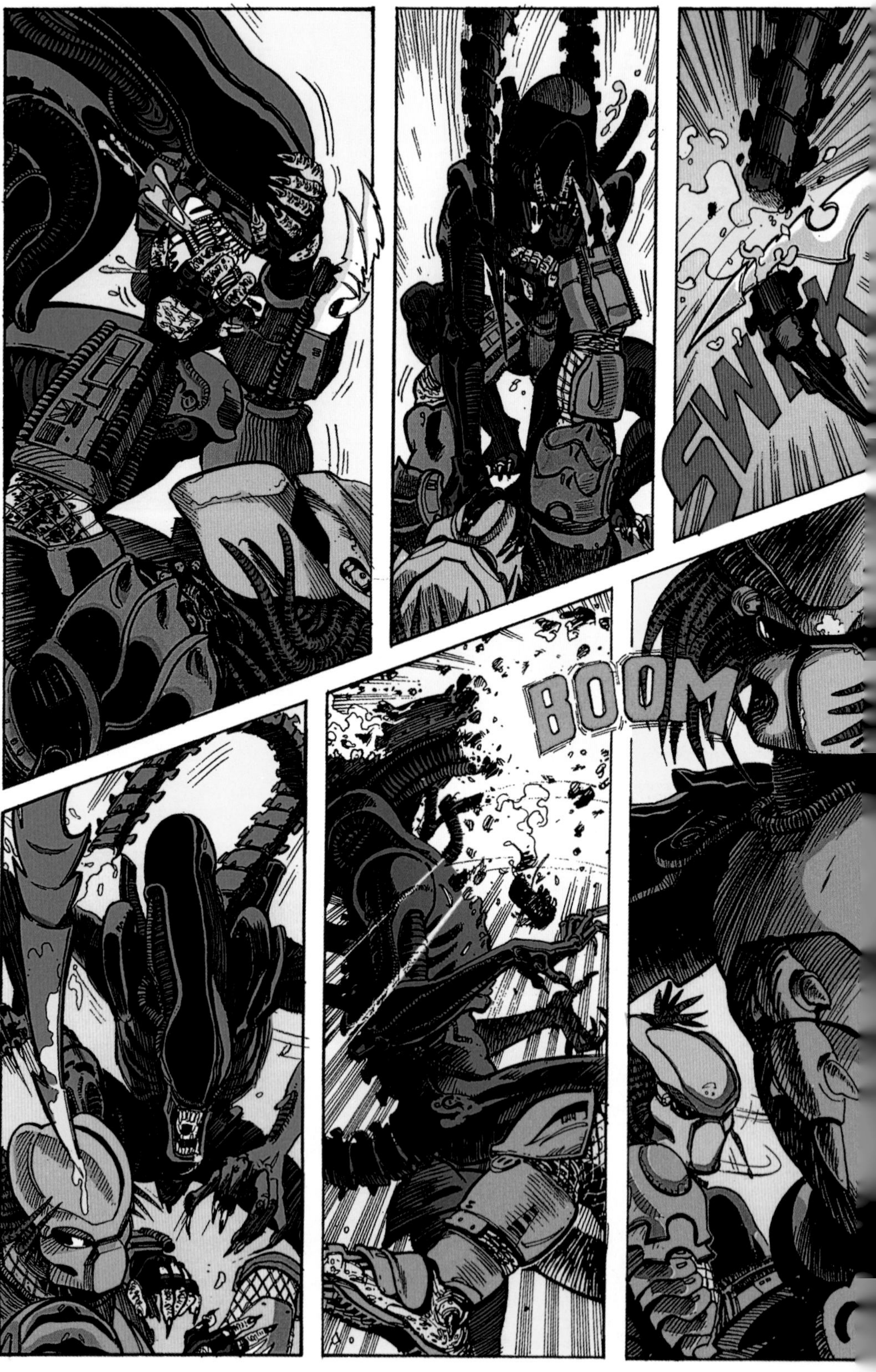
BOOM

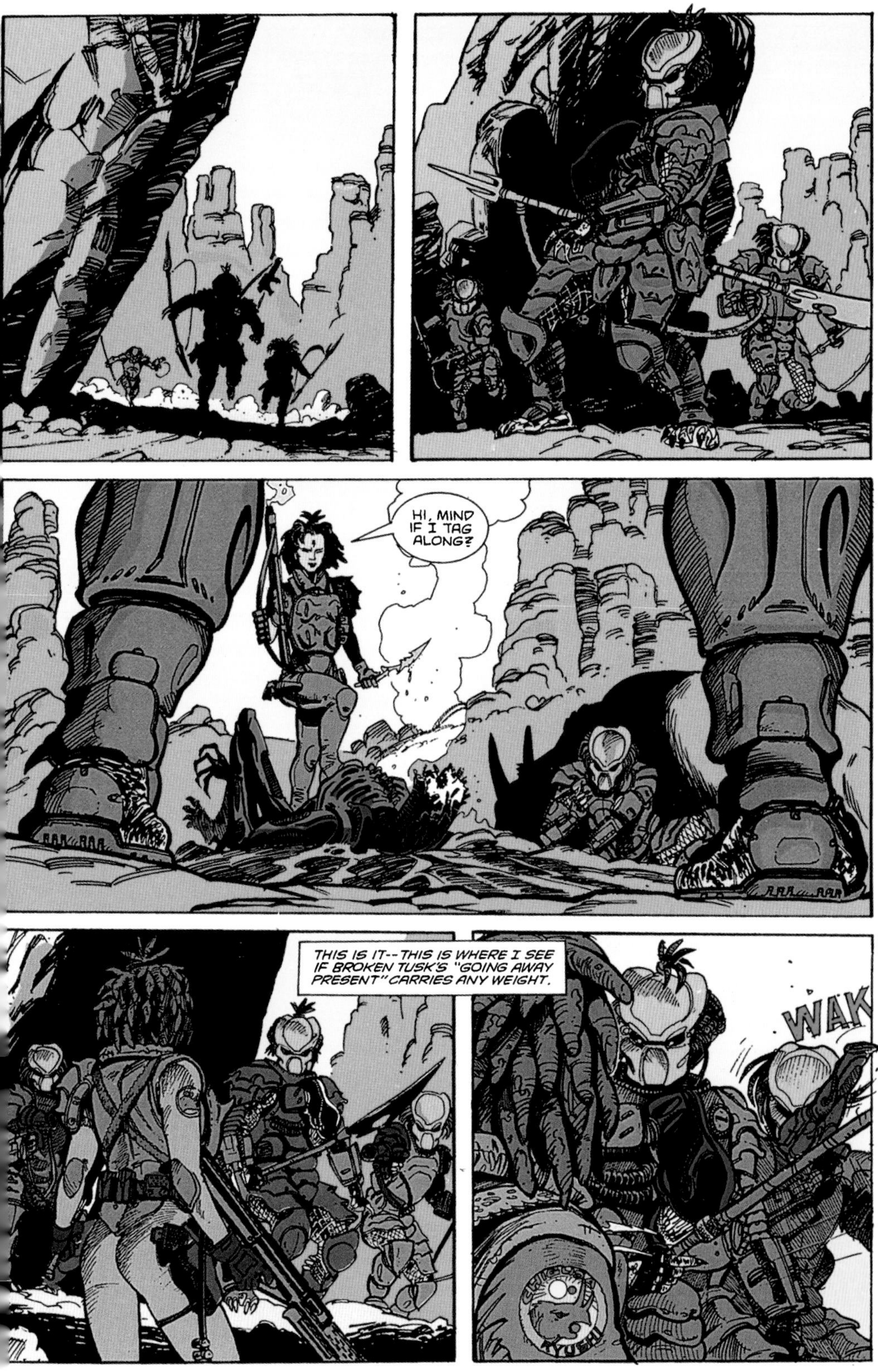
HI, MIND IF I TAG ALONG?
THIS IS IT--THIS IS WHERE I SEE IF BROKEN TUSK'S "GOING AWAY PRESENT" CARRIES ANY WEIGHT.
WAK

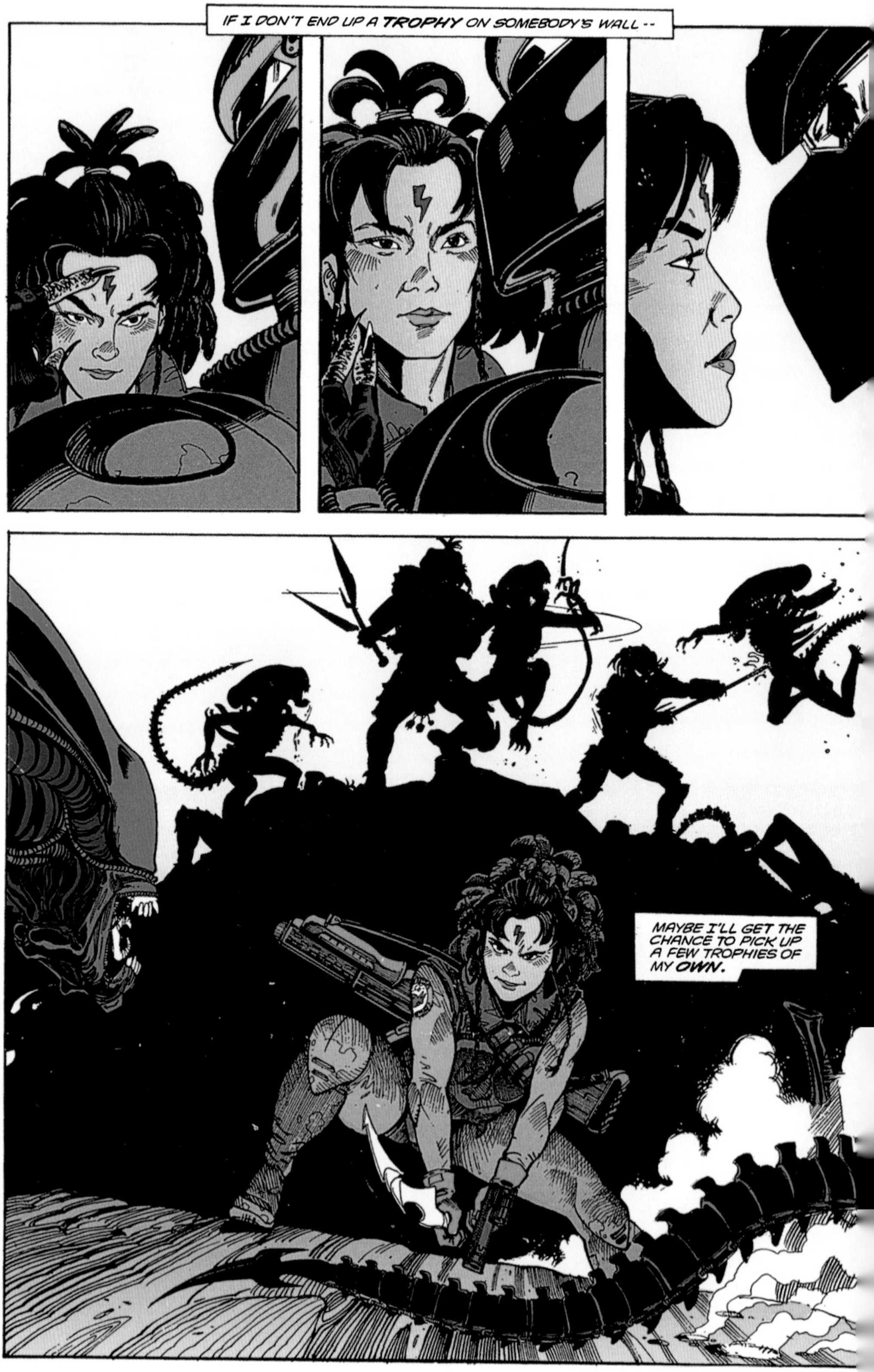
IF I DON'T END UP A TROPHY ON SOMEBODY'S WALL --
MAYBE I'LL GET THE CHANCE TO PICK UP A FEW TROPHIES OF MY OWN.

BLOOD TIME

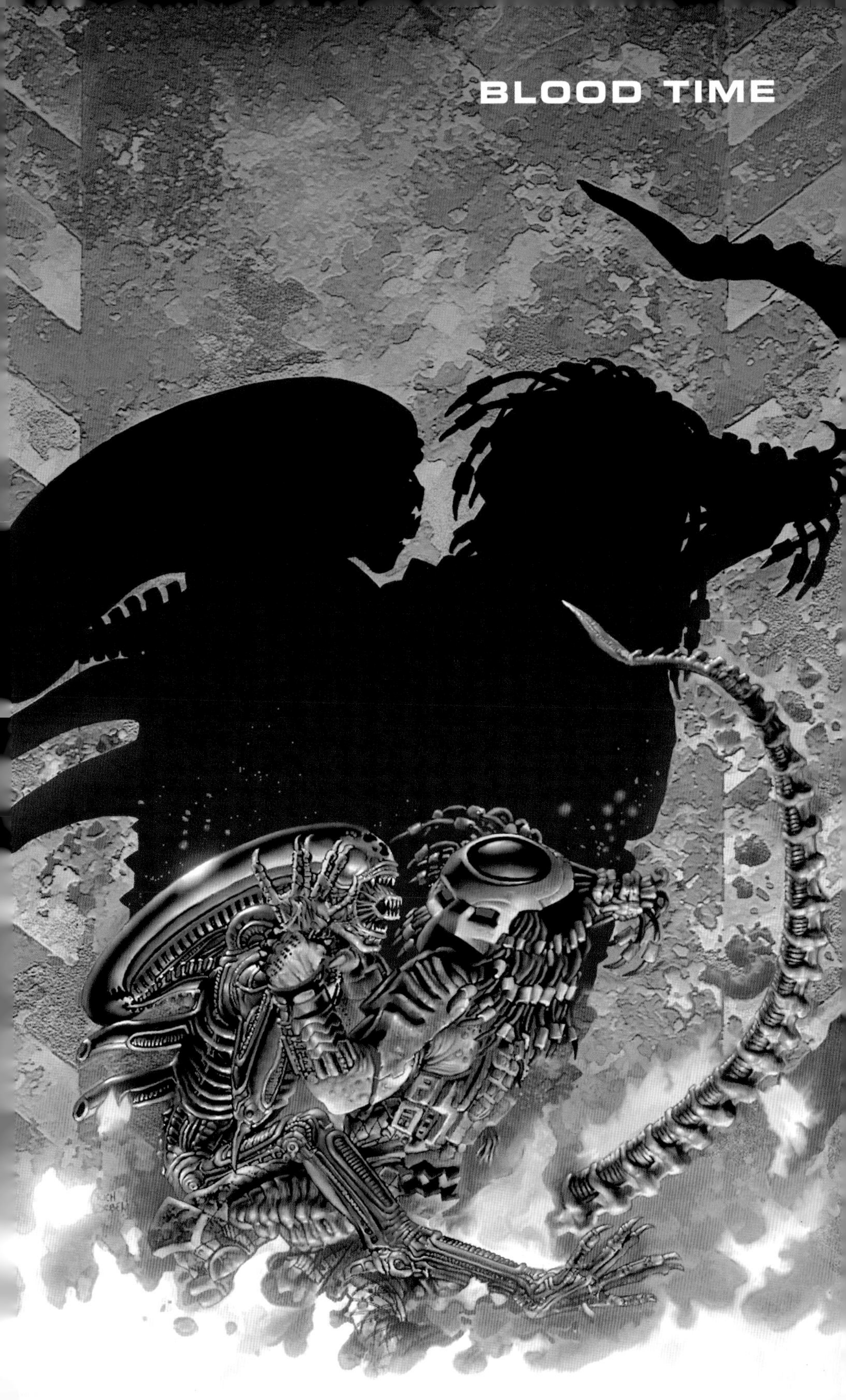

script
RANDY STRADLEY

art
PHILL NORWOOD

colors
FRANK LOPEZ

lettering
VICKIE WILLIAMS

title illustration
RICHARD CORBEN

IT IS TWO-STRIPES' TIME.

ALONG WITH NINE OTHER YOUNG HUNTERS, TWO-STRIPES HAS BEEN CHOSEN TO STALK THE MOST DANGEROUS PREY THE TRIBE WORLDS HAVE EVER ENCOUNTERED.

A SUCCESSFUL HUNT HERE WILL RAISE TWO-STRIPES' STANDING IN THE TRIBE MORE THAN ANY TWENTY LESSER TROPHIES--

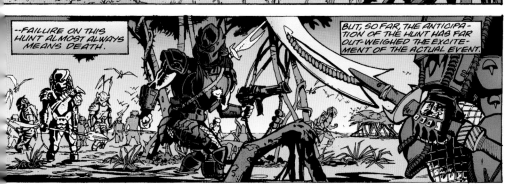

--FAILURE ON THIS HUNT ALMOST ALWAYS MEANS DEATH.

BUT, SO FAR, THE ANTICIPATION OF THE HUNT HAS FAR OUT-WEIGHED THE EXCITEMENT OF THE ACTUAL EVENT.

FOR TWO PLANET-DAYS, THE HUNTING PARTY HAS SLOGGED THROUGH THE SWAMPS, AND TWO-STRIPES SUSPECTS THAT THEIR GUIDE, OLD TOP-KNOT, HAS LOST THE TRAIL.

THEN LIGHT-STEPPER PROVES TWO-STRIPES WRONG.

K-KT-KT-T-T-T.

157

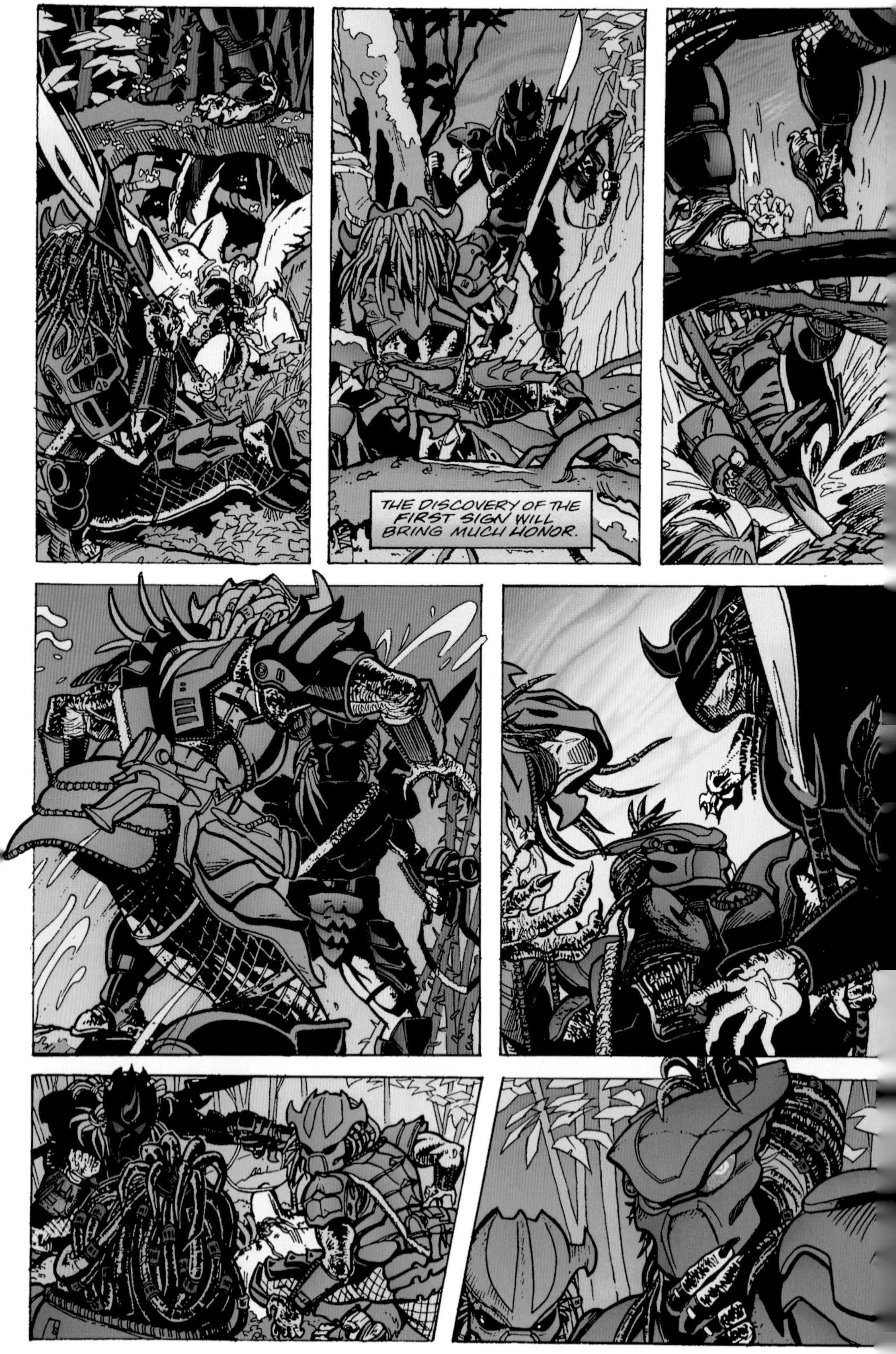
THE DISCOVERY OF THE FIRST SIGN WILL BRING MUCH HONOR.

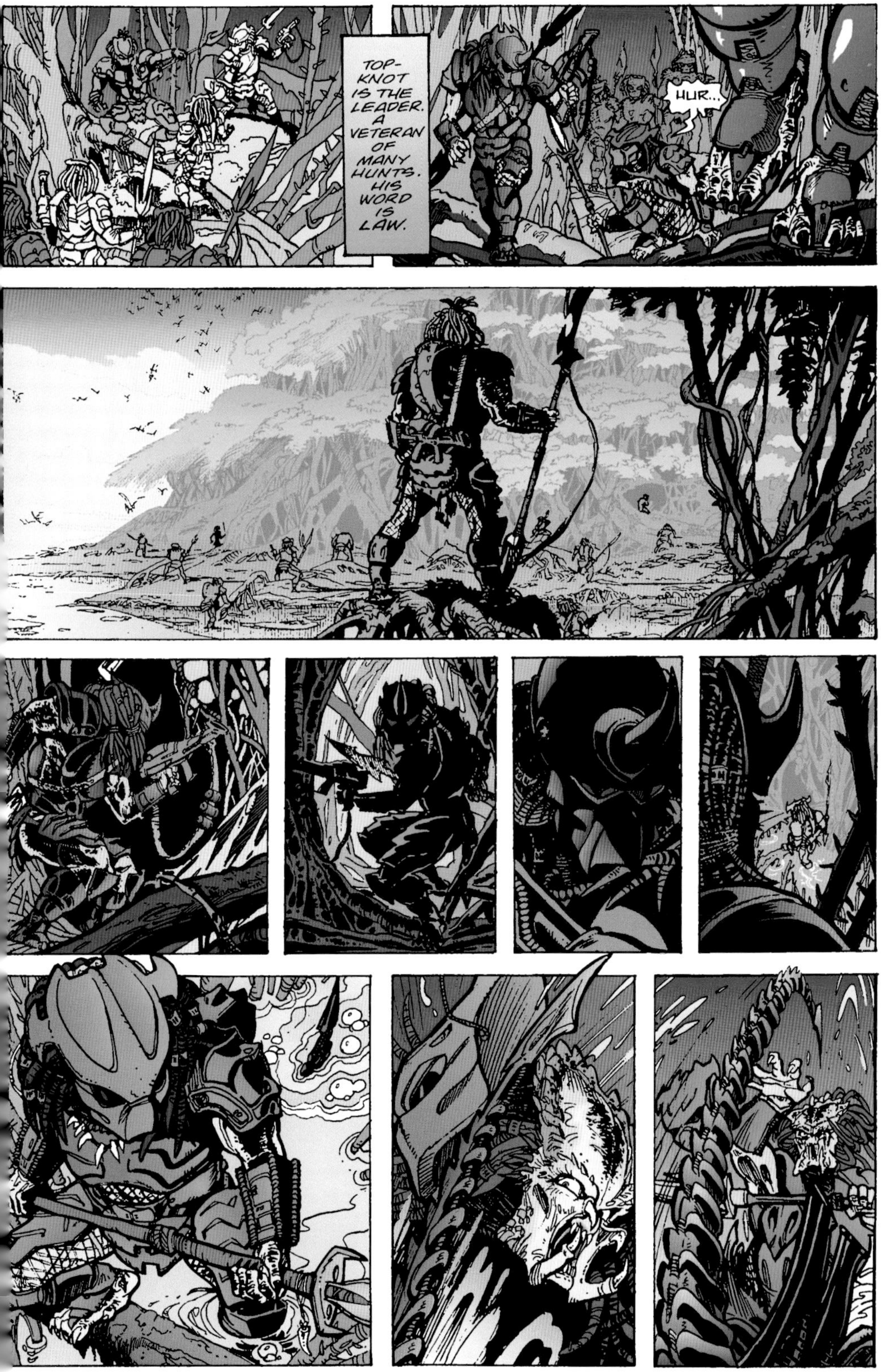
TOP-KNOT IS THE LEADER. A VETERAN OF MANY HUNTS. HIS WORD IS LAW.
HUR...

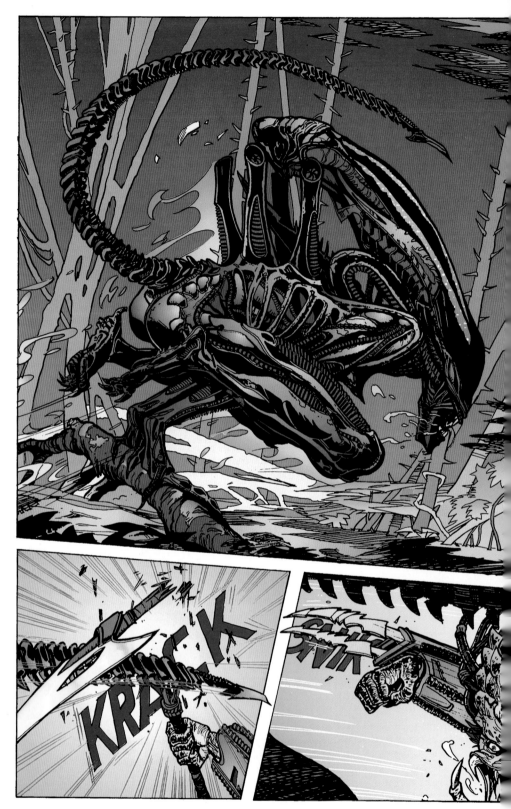

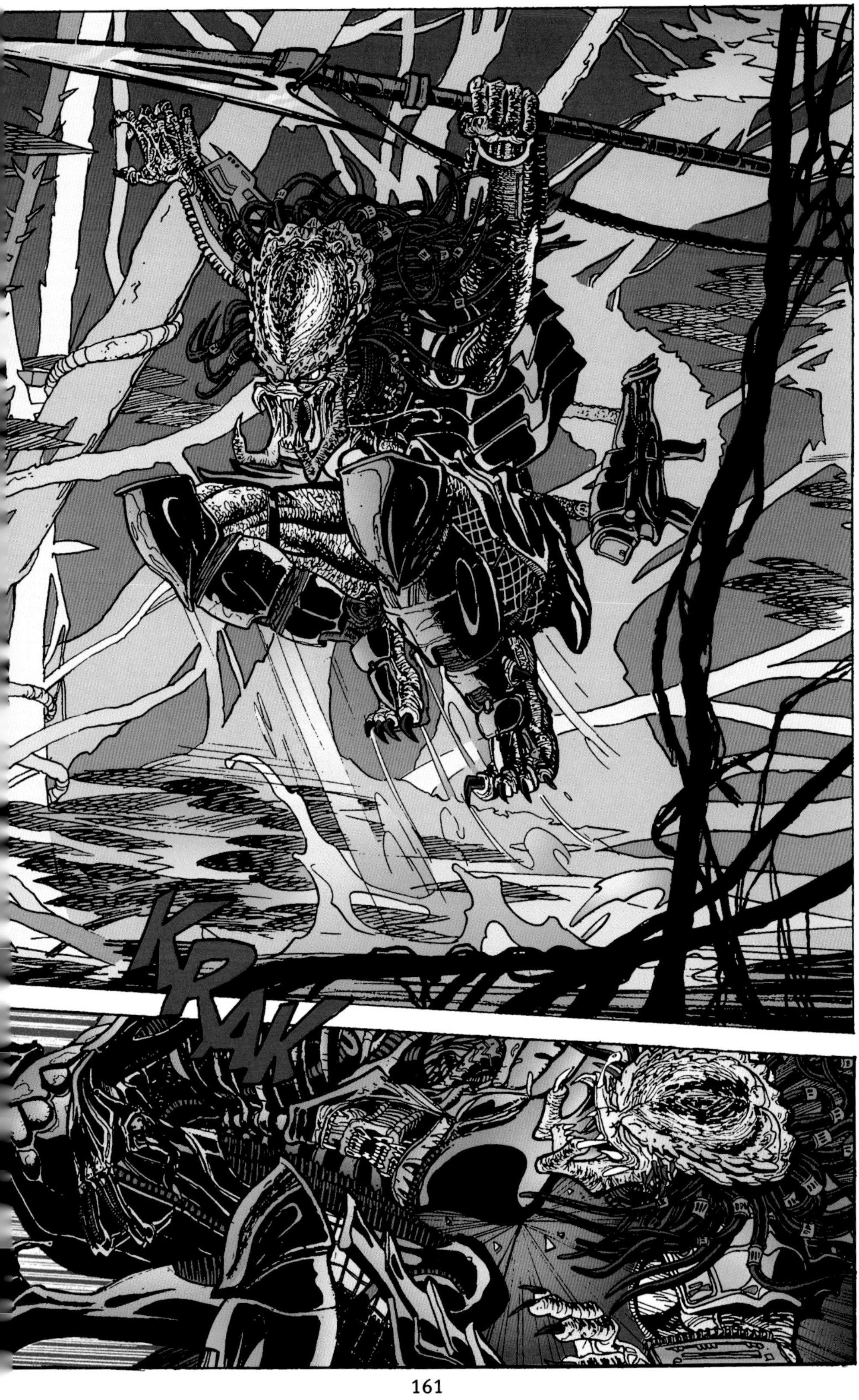
KRAK

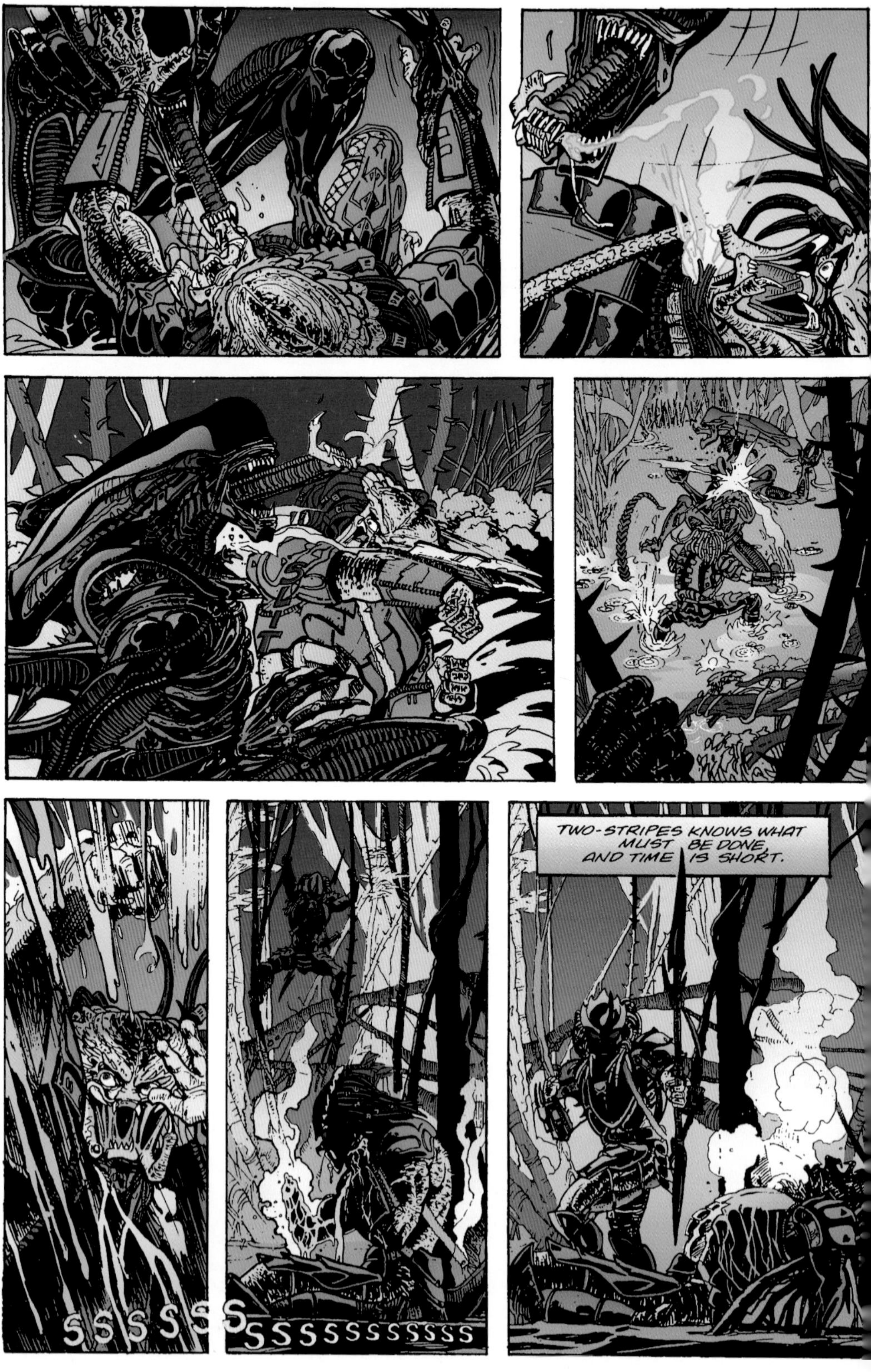
SSSSSSSSSSSSSSSSS
TWO-STRIPES KNOWS WHAT MUST BE DONE, AND TIME IS SHORT.

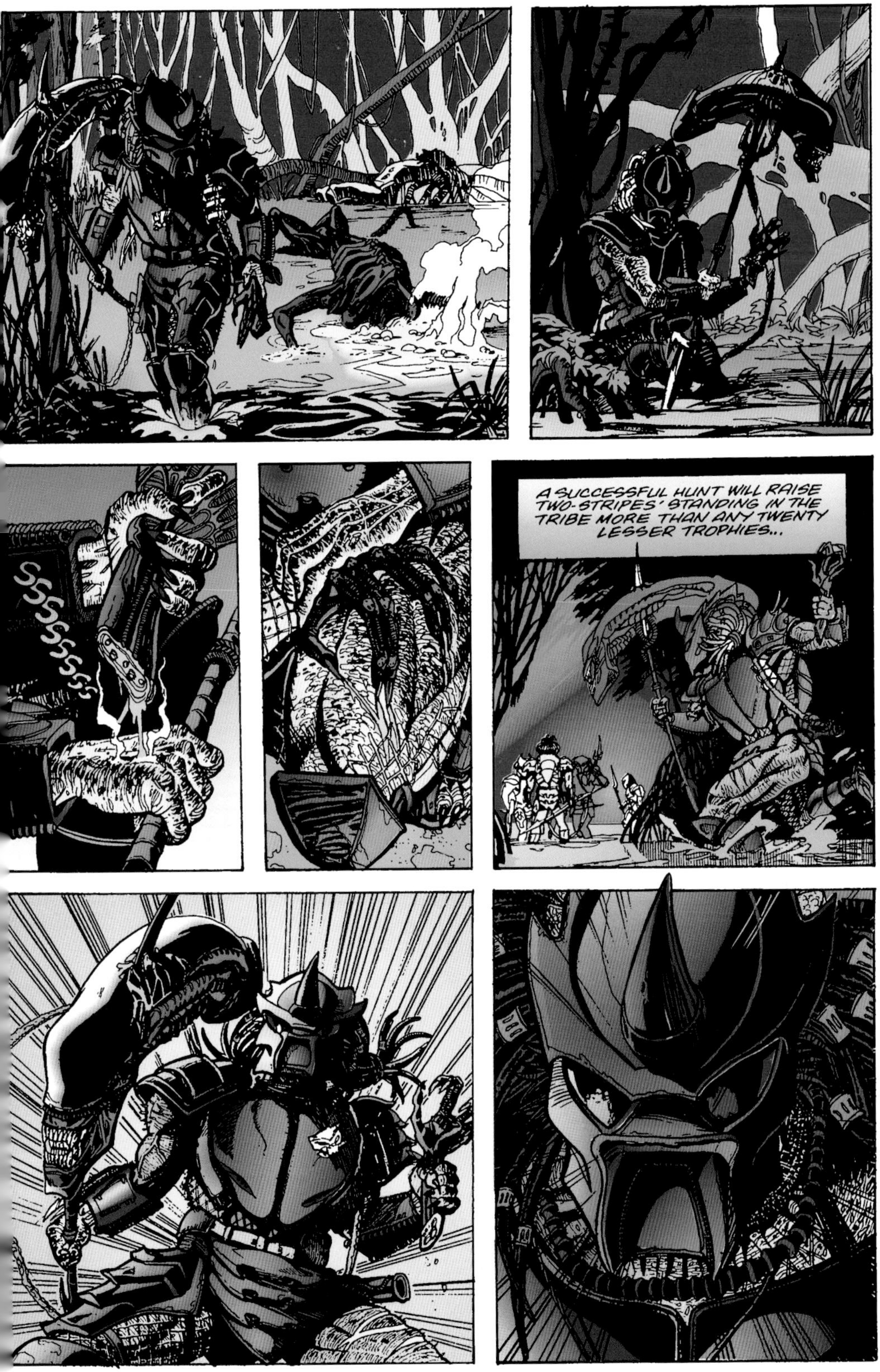

A SUCCESSFUL HUNT WILL RAISE TWO-STRIPES' STANDING IN THE TRIBE MORE THAN ANY TWENTY LESSER TROPHIES...
SSSSSSSSS

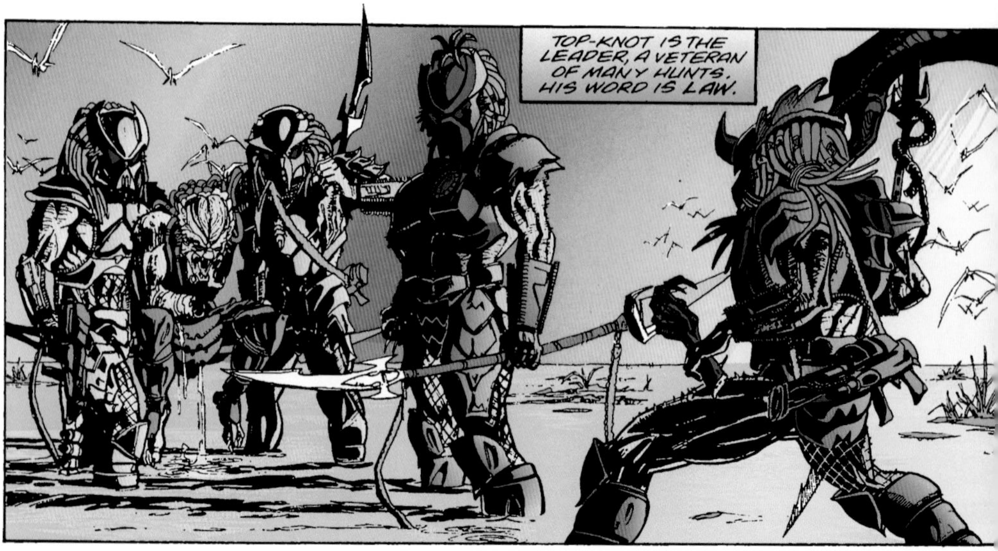
TOP-KNOT IS THE LEADER, A VETERAN OF MANY HUNTS. HIS WORD IS LAW.

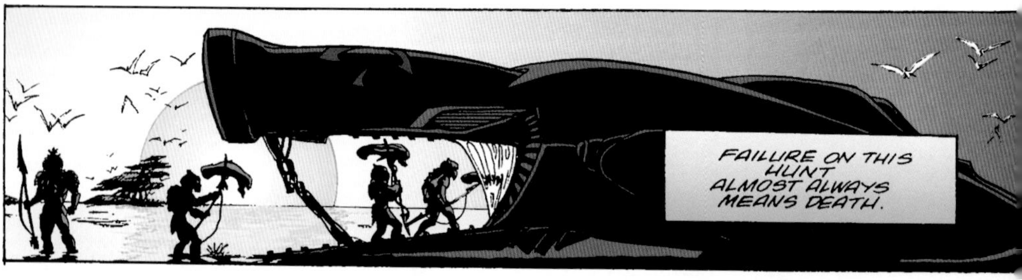
FAILURE ON THIS HUNT ALMOST ALWAYS MEANS DEATH.

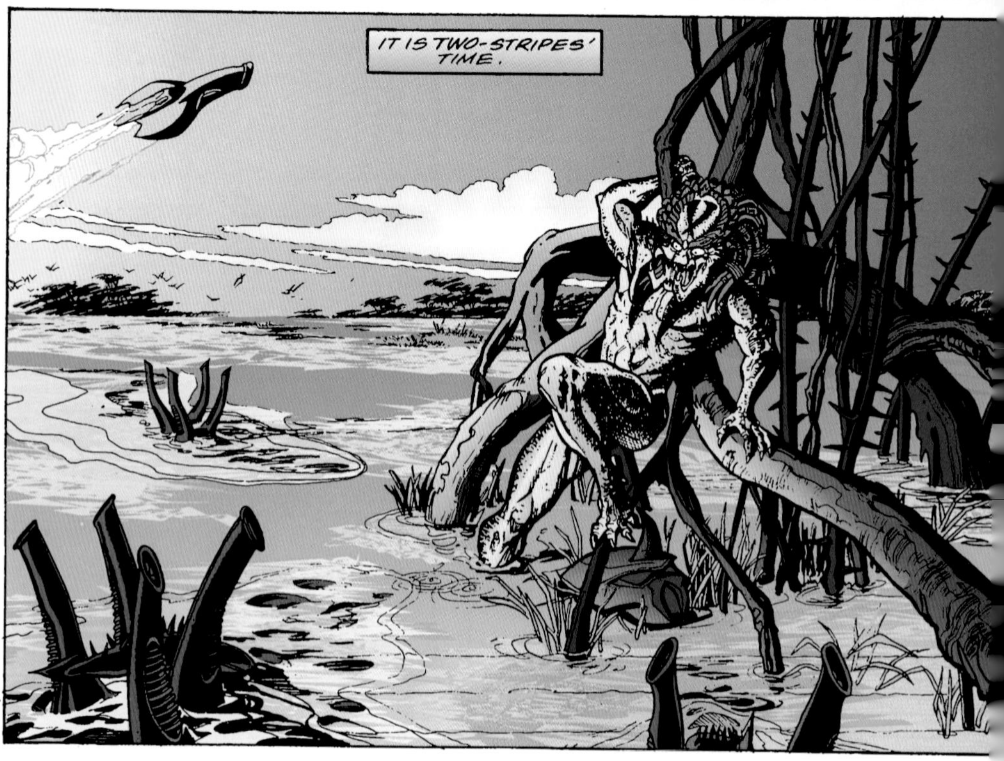
IT IS TWO-STRIPES' TIME.

DUEL

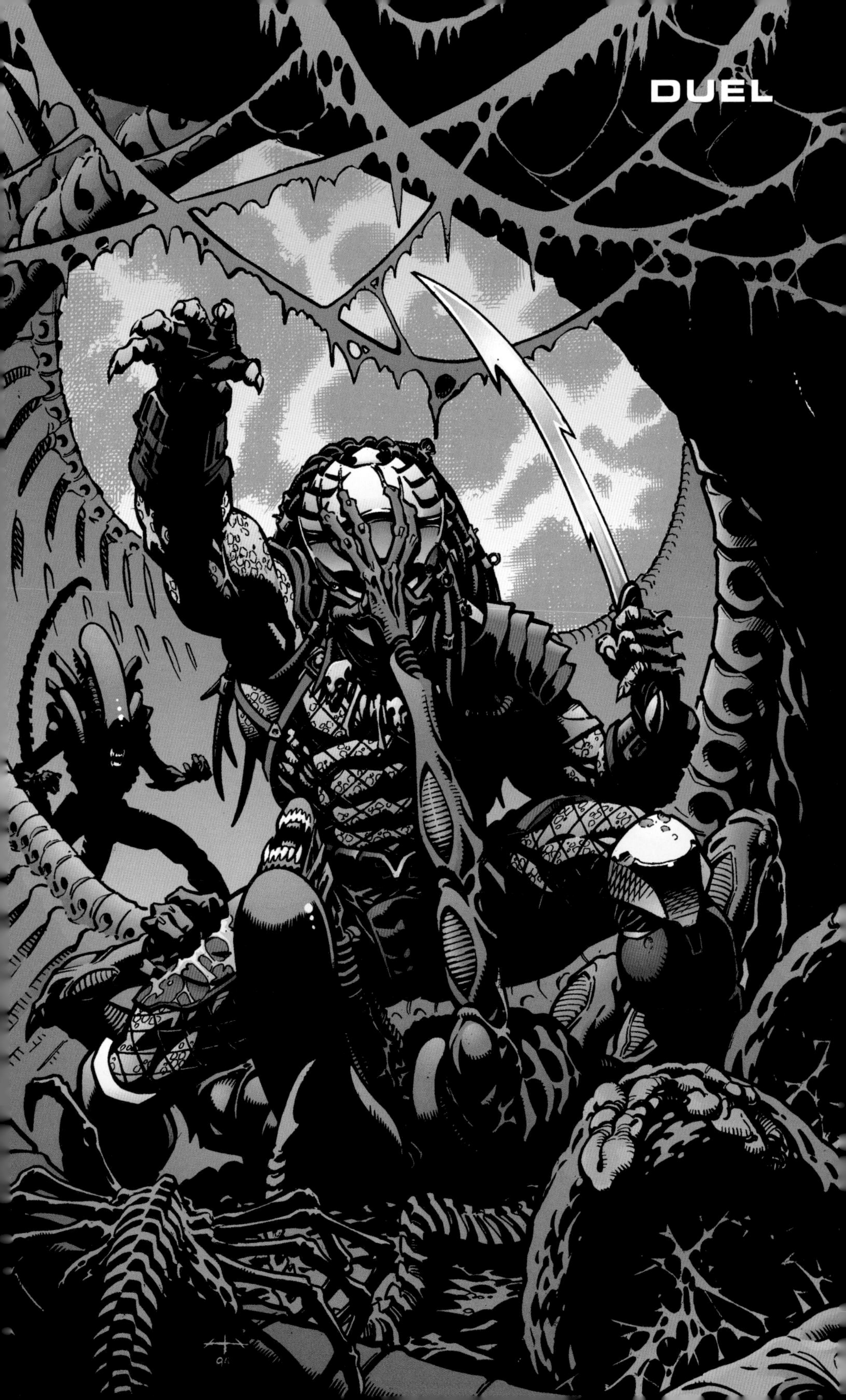

script
RANDY STRADLEY

pencils
JAVIER SALTARES

inks
JIMMY PALMIOTTI

colors
JAMES SINCLAIR

lettering
STEVE DUTRO

title illustration
CHRIS WARNER

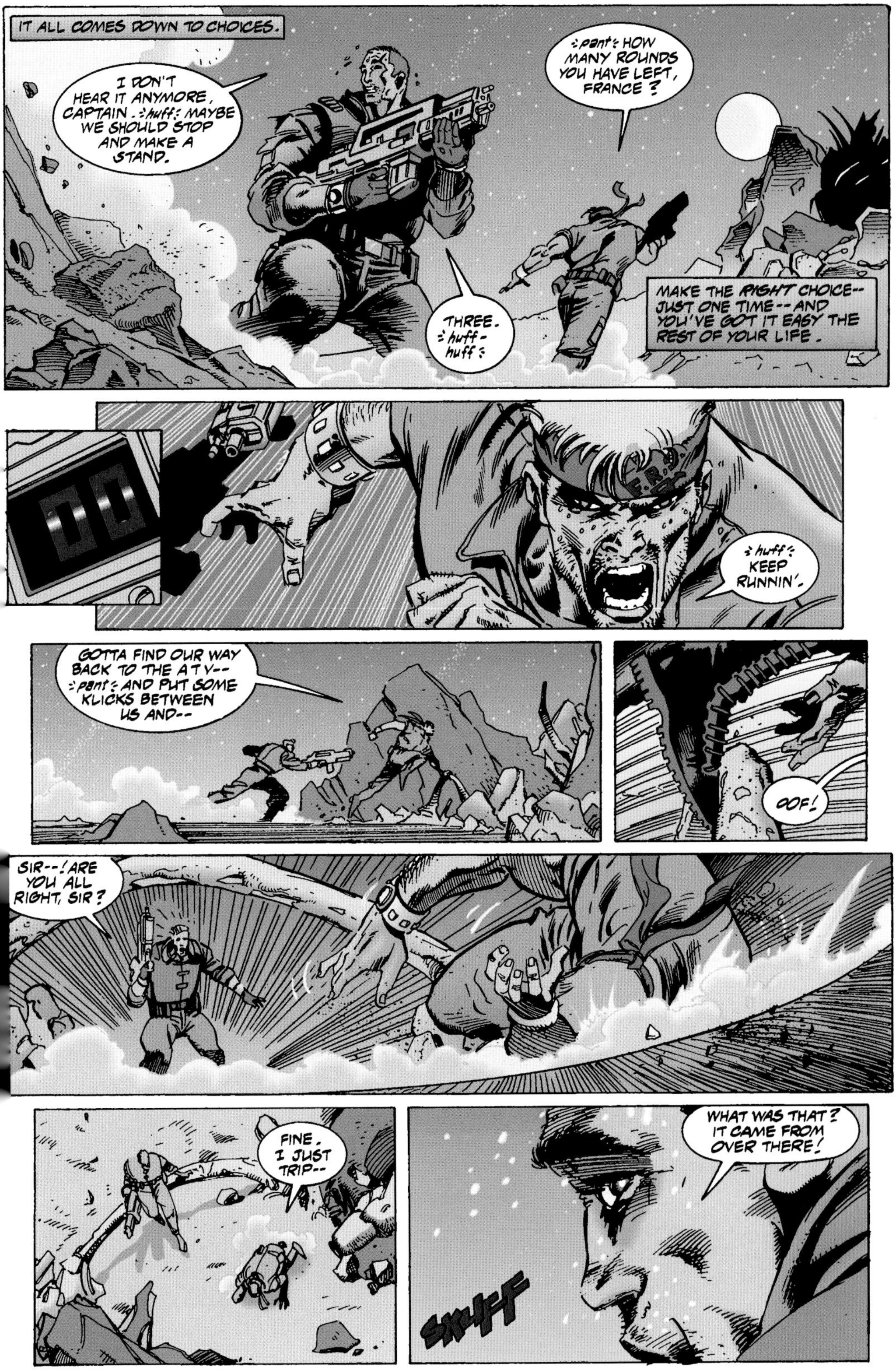
IT ALL COMES DOWN TO CHOICES.
I DON'T HEAR IT ANYMORE, CAPTAIN. :huff: MAYBE WE SHOULD STOP AND MAKE A STAND.
:pant: HOW MANY ROUNDS YOU HAVE LEFT, FRANCE?
THREE. :huff-huff:
MAKE THE RIGHT CHOICE-- JUST ONE TIME--AND YOU'VE GOT IT EASY THE REST OF YOUR LIFE.
:huff: KEEP RUNNIN'.
GOTTA FIND OUR WAY BACK TO THE ATV-- :pant: AND PUT SOME KLICKS BETWEEN US AND--
OOF!
SIR--! ARE YOU ALL RIGHT, SIR?
FINE. I JUST TRIP--
WHAT WAS THAT? IT CAME FROM OVER THERE!
SKUFF

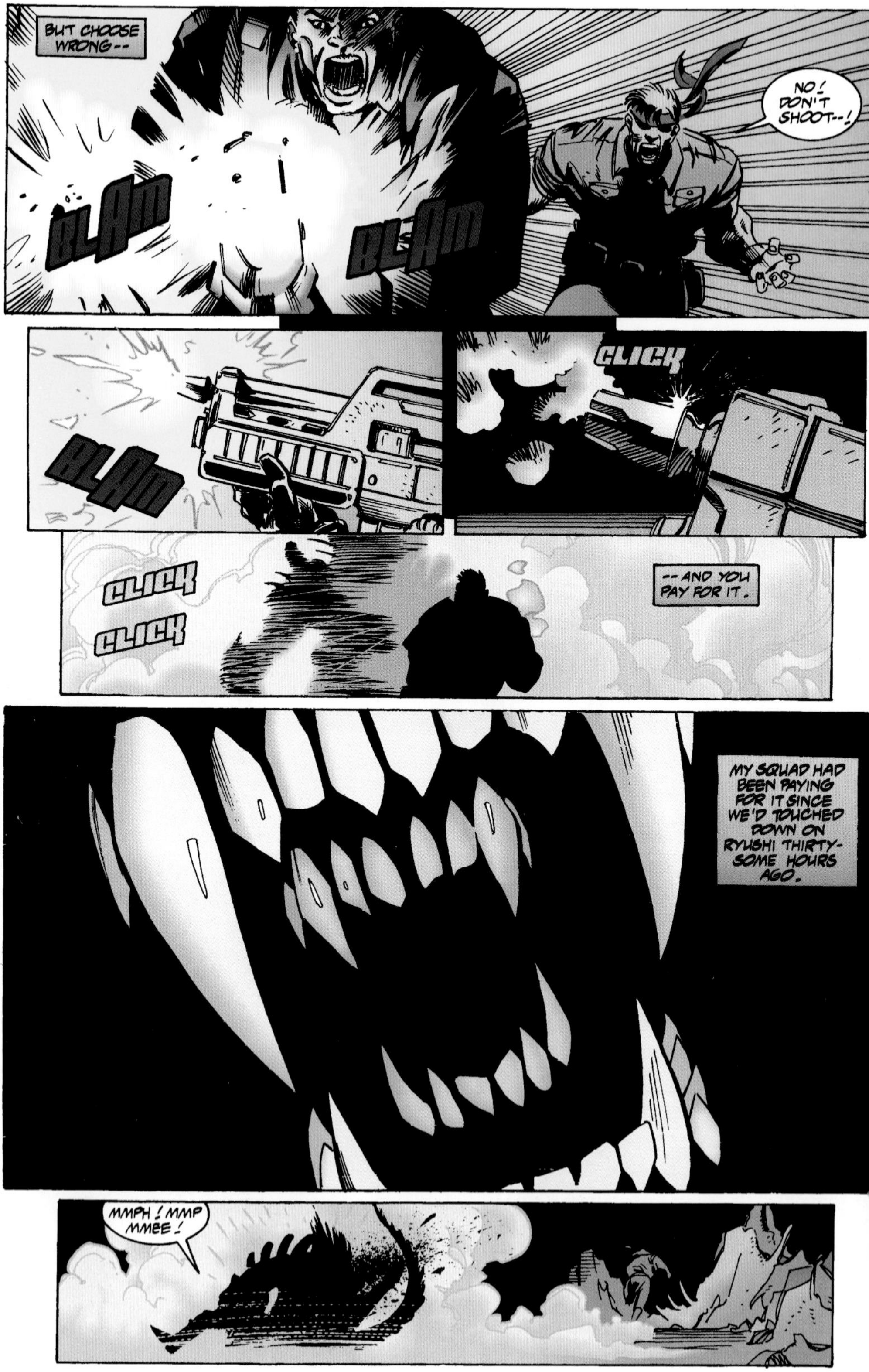
BUT CHOOSE WRONG --
NO! DON'T SHOOT--!
BLAM
BLAM
BLAM
CLICK
CLICK
CLICK
-- AND YOU PAY FOR IT.
MY SQUAD HAD BEEN PAYING FOR IT SINCE WE'D TOUCHED DOWN ON RYUSHI THIRTY-SOME HOURS AGO.
MMPH! MMP MMEE!

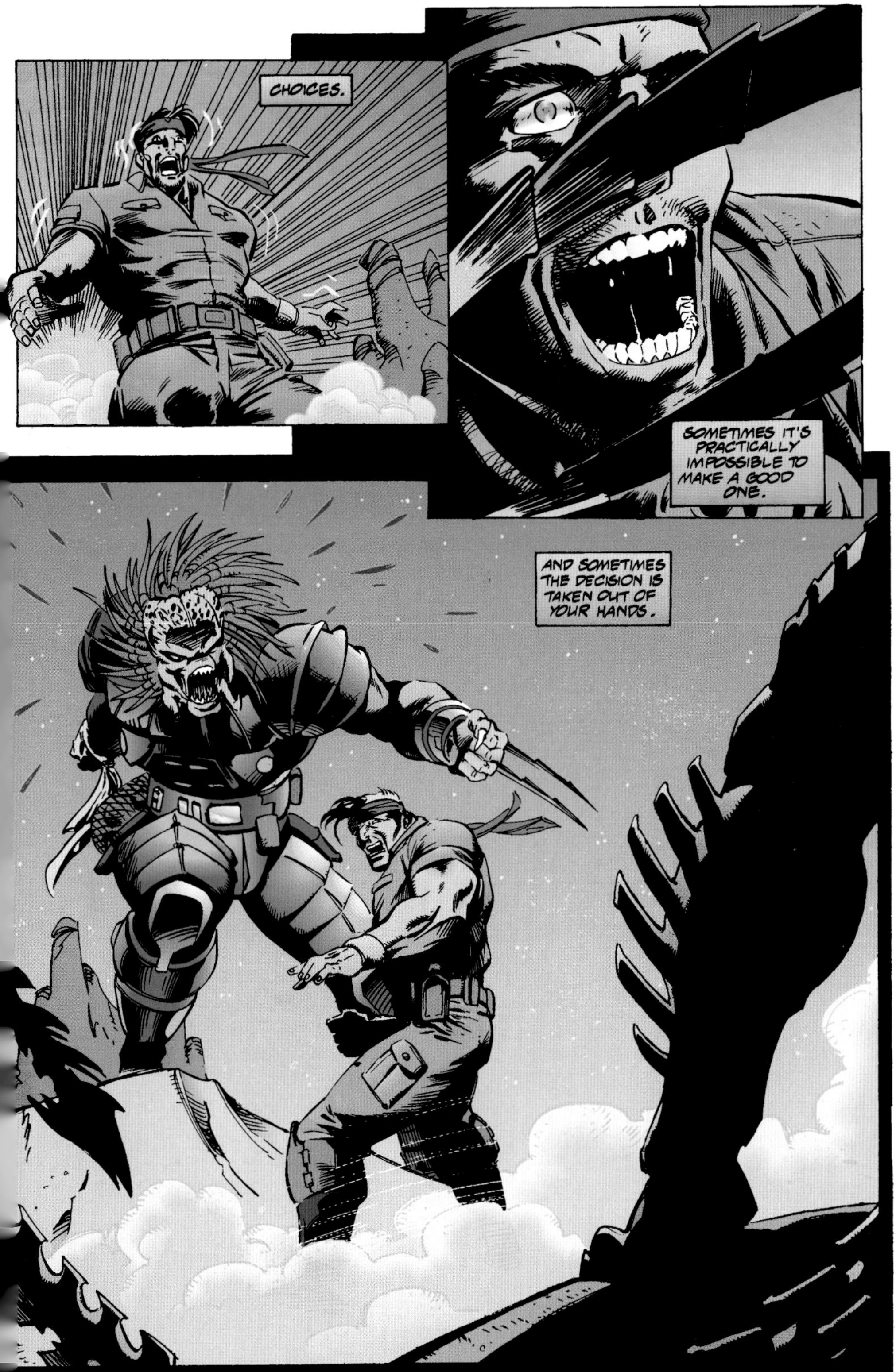
CHOICES.
SOMETIMES IT'S PRACTICALLY IMPOSSIBLE TO MAKE A GOOD ONE.
AND SOMETIMES THE DECISION IS TAKEN OUT OF YOUR HANDS.

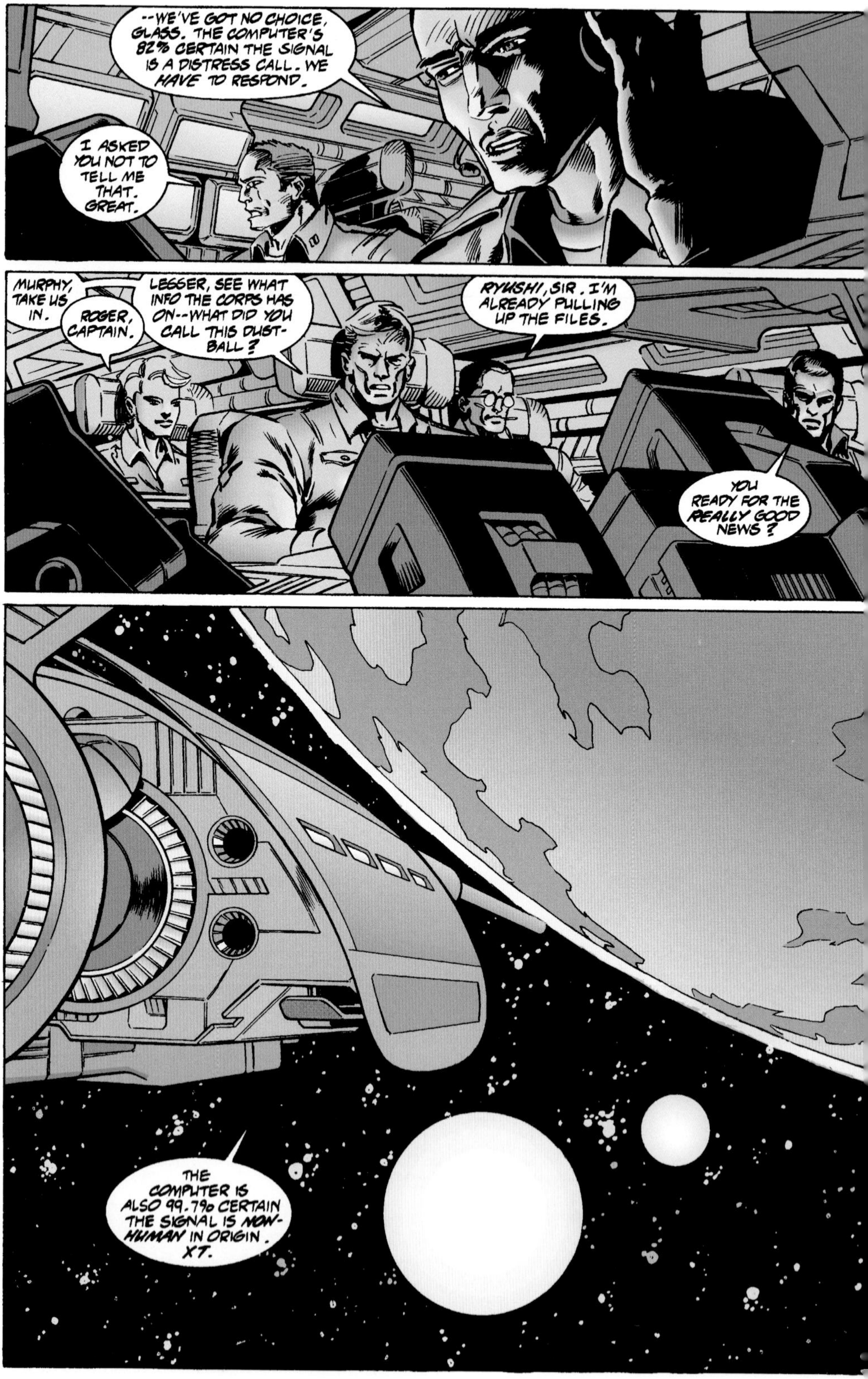
--WE'VE GOT NO CHOICE, GLASS. THE COMPUTER'S 82% CERTAIN THE SIGNAL IS A DISTRESS CALL. WE HAVE TO RESPOND.
I ASKED YOU NOT TO TELL ME THAT. GREAT.
MURPHY, TAKE US IN.
ROGER, CAPTAIN.
LESSER, SEE WHAT INFO THE CORPS HAS ON--WHAT DID YOU CALL THIS DUST-BALL?
RYUSHI, SIR. I'M ALREADY PULLING UP THE FILES.
YOU READY FOR THE REALLY GOOD NEWS?
THE COMPUTER IS ALSO 99.7% CERTAIN THE SIGNAL IS NON-HUMAN IN ORIGIN. XT.

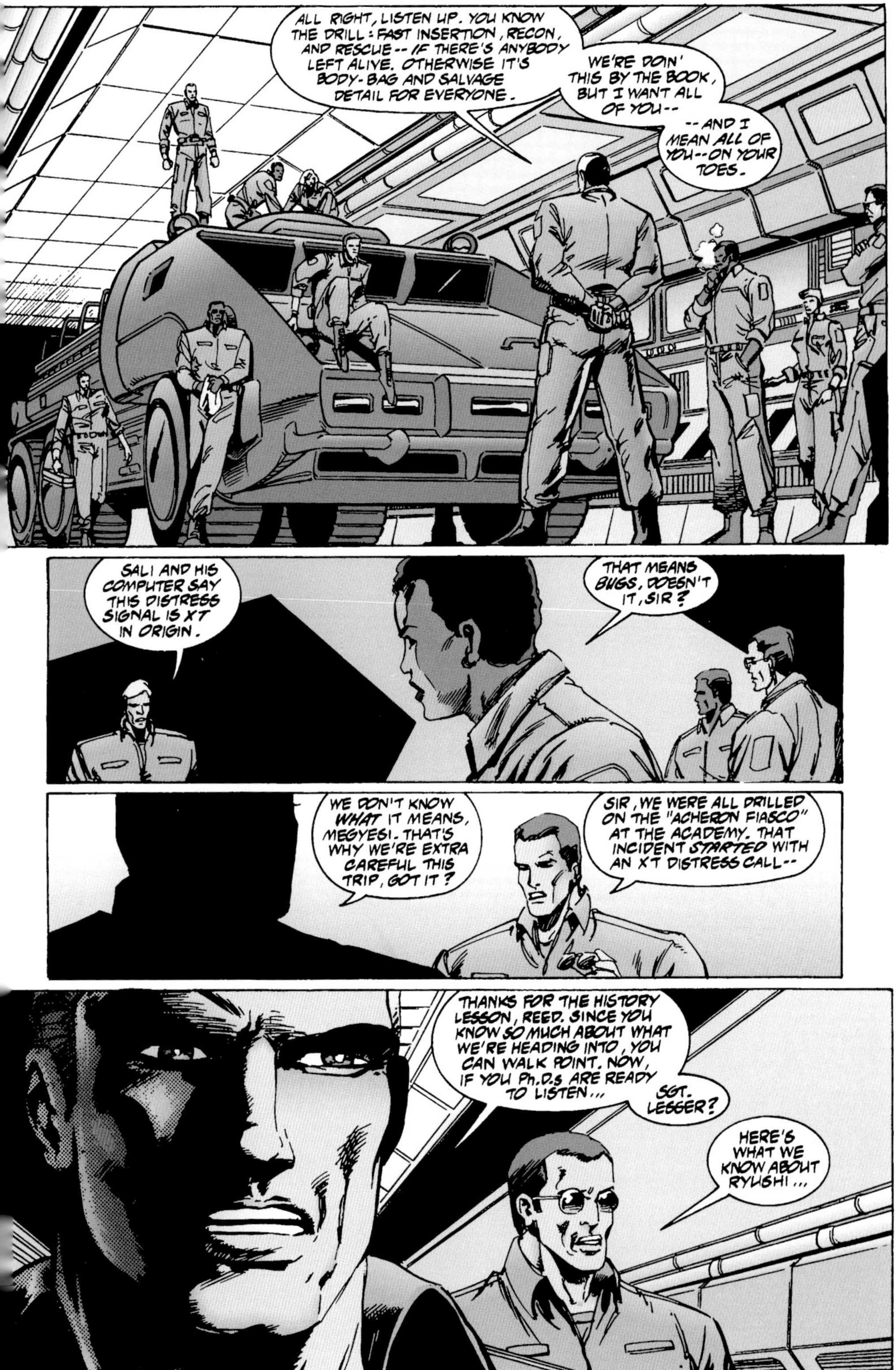
ALL RIGHT, LISTEN UP. YOU KNOW THE DRILL: FAST INSERTION, RECON, AND RESCUE -- IF THERE'S ANYBODY LEFT ALIVE. OTHERWISE IT'S BODY-BAG AND SALVAGE DETAIL FOR EVERYONE.
WE'RE DOIN' THIS BY THE BOOK, BUT I WANT ALL OF YOU--
-- AND I MEAN ALL OF YOU--ON YOUR TOES.
SALI AND HIS COMPUTER SAY THIS DISTRESS SIGNAL IS XT IN ORIGIN.
THAT MEANS BUGS, DOESN'T IT, SIR?
WE DON'T KNOW WHAT IT MEANS, MEGYESI. THAT'S WHY WE'RE EXTRA CAREFUL THIS TRIP, GOT IT?
SIR, WE WERE ALL DRILLED ON THE "ACHERON FIASCO" AT THE ACADEMY. THAT INCIDENT STARTED WITH AN XT DISTRESS CALL--
THANKS FOR THE HISTORY LESSON, REED. SINCE YOU KNOW SO MUCH ABOUT WHAT WE'RE HEADING INTO, YOU CAN WALK POINT. NOW, IF YOU Ph.D.s ARE READY TO LISTEN...
SGT. LESSER?
HERE'S WHAT WE KNOW ABOUT RYUSHI...

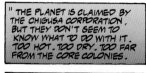

" THE PLANET IS CLAIMED BY THE CHIGUSA CORPORATION, BUT THEY DON'T SEEM TO KNOW WHAT TO DO WITH IT. TOO HOT. TOO DRY. TOO FAR FROM THE CORE COLONIES.

" THEY TRIED SETTLING IT, BUT GAVE UP ON IT FOR SOME REASON. NOW THERE'S ONLY ONE HUMAN INHABITANT LISTED--

" --A MACHIKO NOGUCHI-- AND WE'VE BEEN UNABLE TO CONTACT HER.

" WE'LL CHECK OUT HER PLACE FIRST. THE SOURCE OF THE DISTRESS SIGNAL IS AN EASY DRIVE FROM THERE.

" LT. MURPHY WILL TAKE THE SHIP BACK TO SAFE ORBIT, AND RENDEZVOUS WITH US WHEN SHE GETS OUR SIGNAL, OR IN ONE PLANET DAY, WHICHEVER COMES FIRST.

" THAT'S THIRTY-THREE HOURS, LADIES AND GENTLEMEN-- NINETEEN OF IT DOUBLE-SUN DAYLIGHT. I HOPE YOU BROUGHT YOUR SUNBLOCK. "

LET'S ROLL!

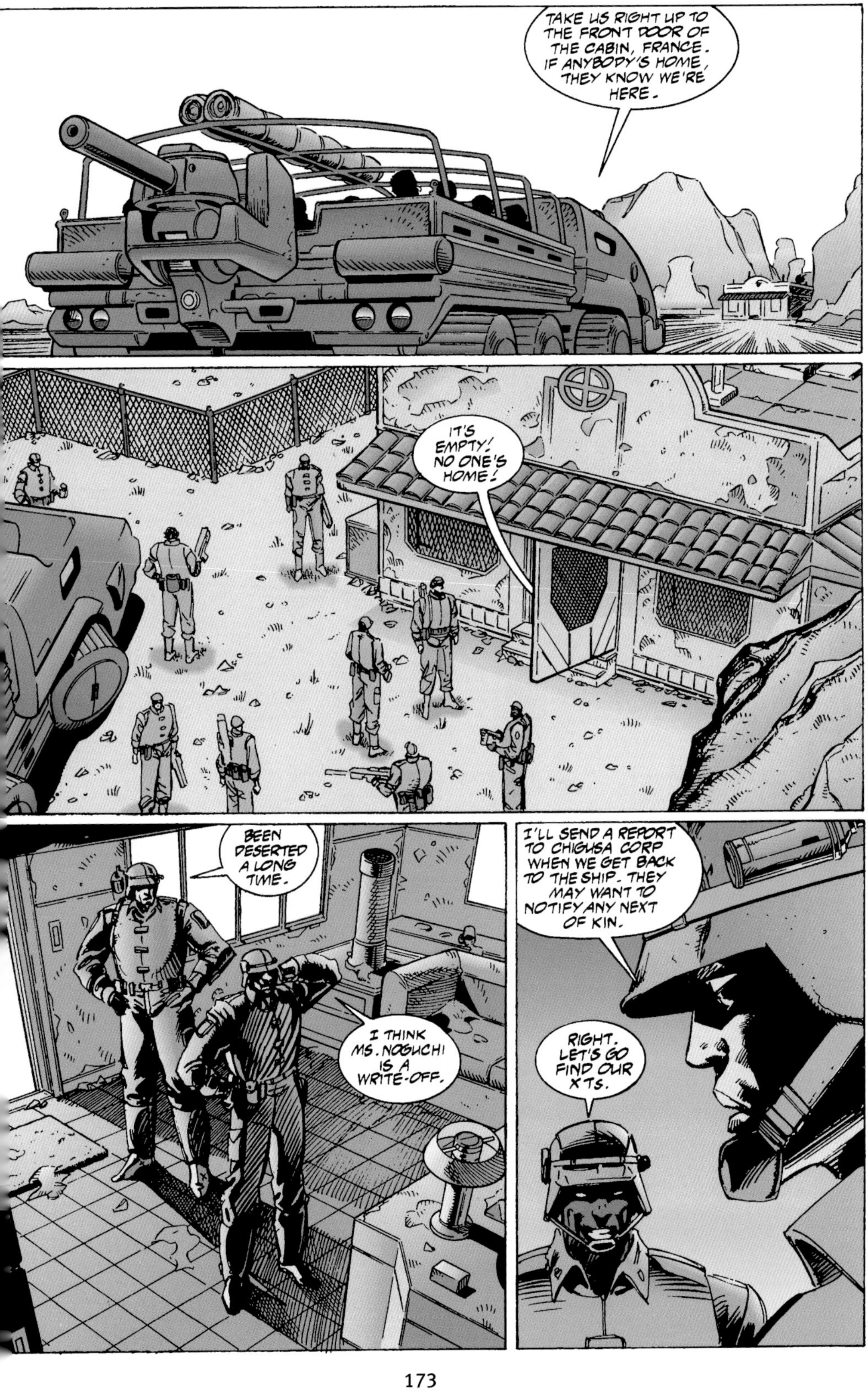
TAKE US RIGHT UP TO THE FRONT DOOR OF THE CABIN, FRANCE. IF ANYBODY'S HOME, THEY KNOW WE'RE HERE.
IT'S EMPTY! NO ONE'S HOME!
BEEN DESERTED A LONG TIME.
I THINK MS. NOGUCHI IS A WRITE-OFF.
I'LL SEND A REPORT TO CHIGUSA CORP WHEN WE GET BACK TO THE SHIP. THEY MAY WANT TO NOTIFY ANY NEXT OF KIN.
RIGHT. LET'S GO FIND OUR XTS.

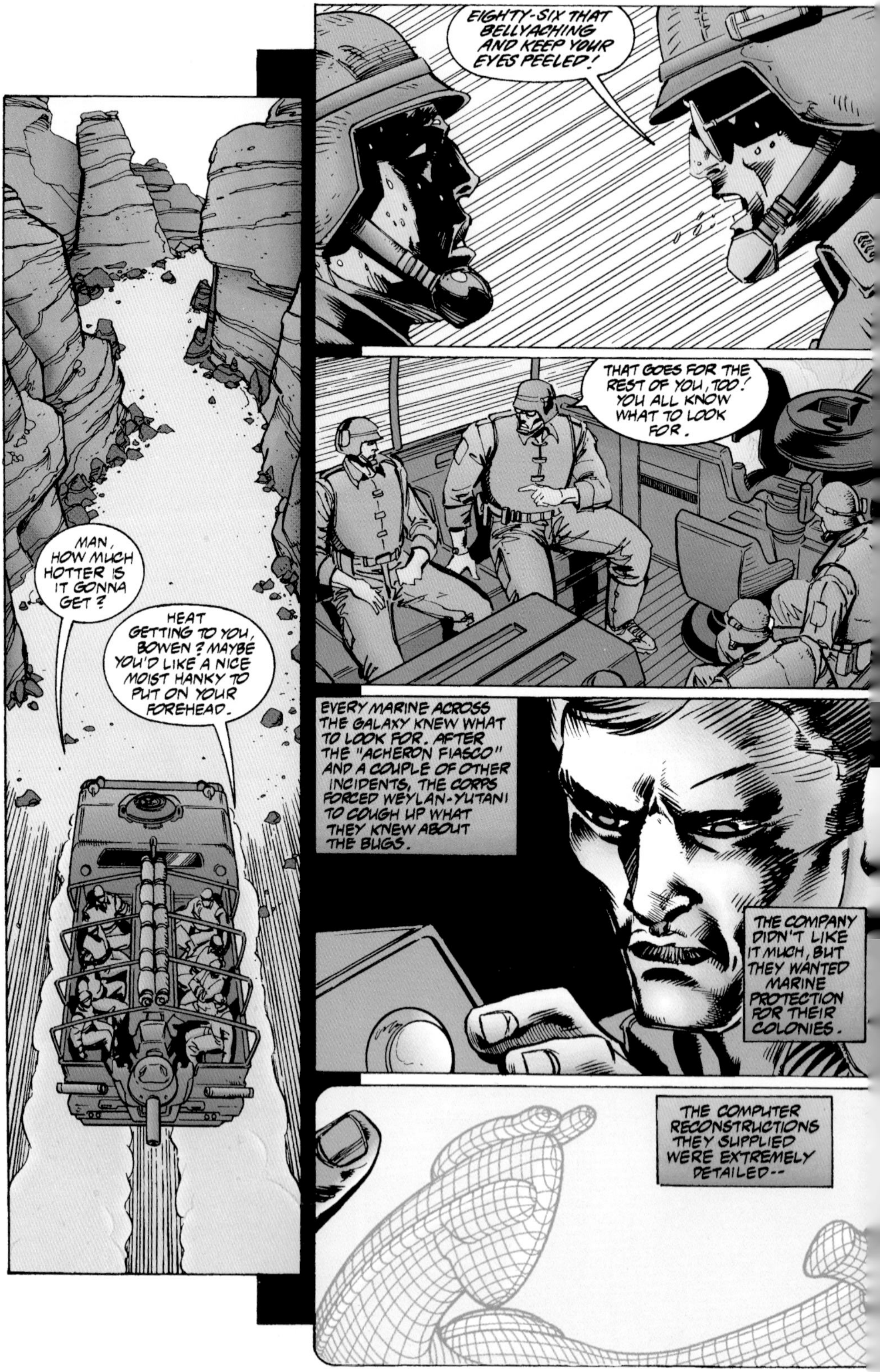
MAN, HOW MUCH HOTTER IS IT GONNA GET?
HEAT GETTING TO YOU, BOWEN? MAYBE YOU'D LIKE A NICE MOIST HANKY TO PUT ON YOUR FOREHEAD.
EIGHTY-SIX THAT BELLYACHING AND KEEP YOUR EYES PEELED!
THAT GOES FOR THE REST OF YOU, TOO! YOU ALL KNOW WHAT TO LOOK FOR.
EVERY MARINE ACROSS THE GALAXY KNEW WHAT TO LOOK FOR. AFTER THE "ACHERON FIASCO" AND A COUPLE OF OTHER INCIDENTS, THE CORPS FORCED WEYLAN-YUTANI TO COUGH UP WHAT THEY KNEW ABOUT THE BUGS.
THE COMPANY DIDN'T LIKE IT MUCH, BUT THEY WANTED MARINE PROTECTION FOR THEIR COLONIES.
THE COMPUTER RECONSTRUCTIONS THEY SUPPLIED WERE EXTREMELY DETAILED--

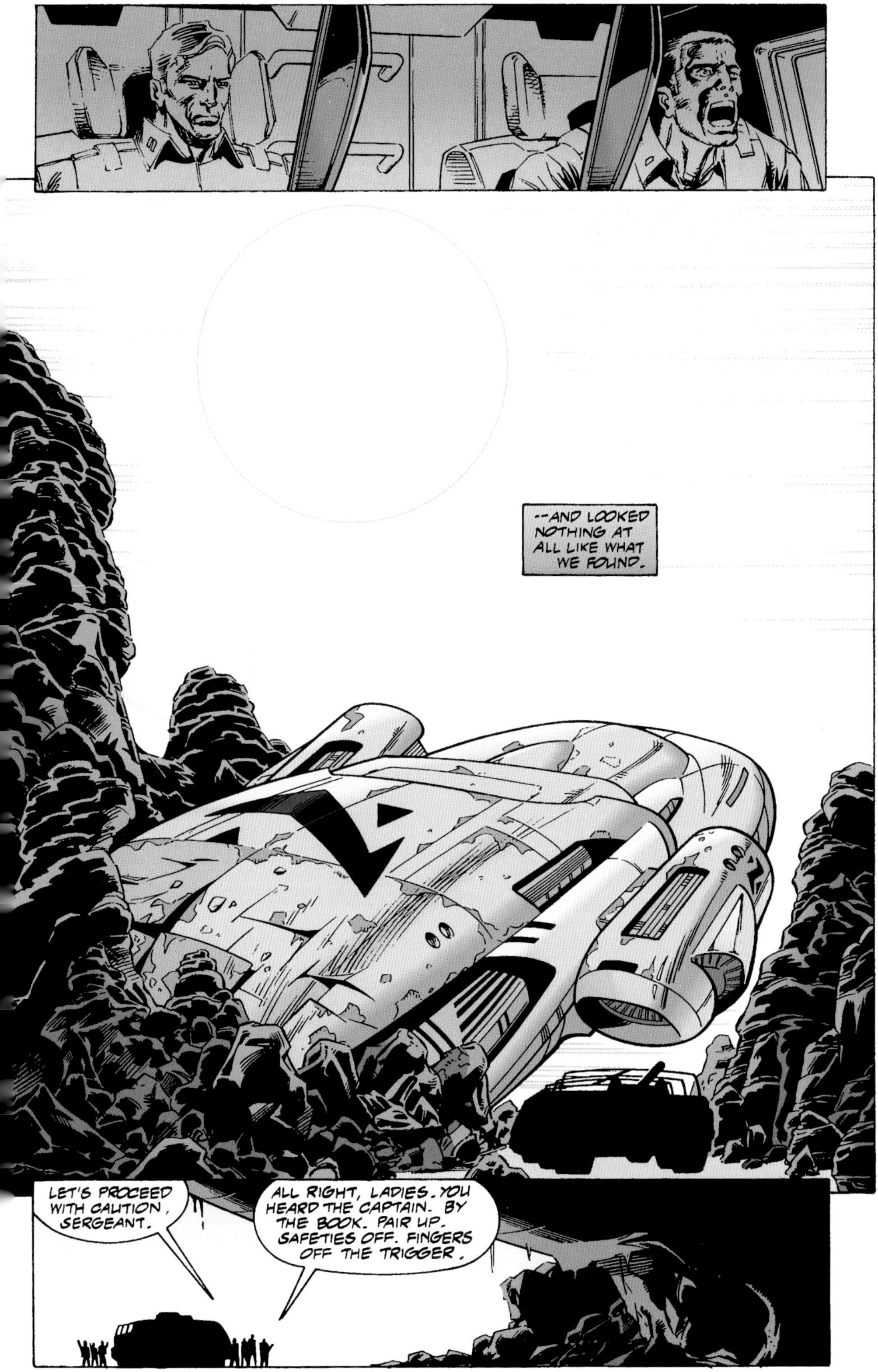
--AND LOOKED NOTHING AT ALL LIKE WHAT WE FOUND.
LET'S PROCEED WITH CAUTION, SERGEANT.
ALL RIGHT, LADIES. YOU HEARD THE CAPTAIN. BY THE BOOK. PAIR UP. SAFETIES OFF. FINGERS OFF THE TRIGGER.

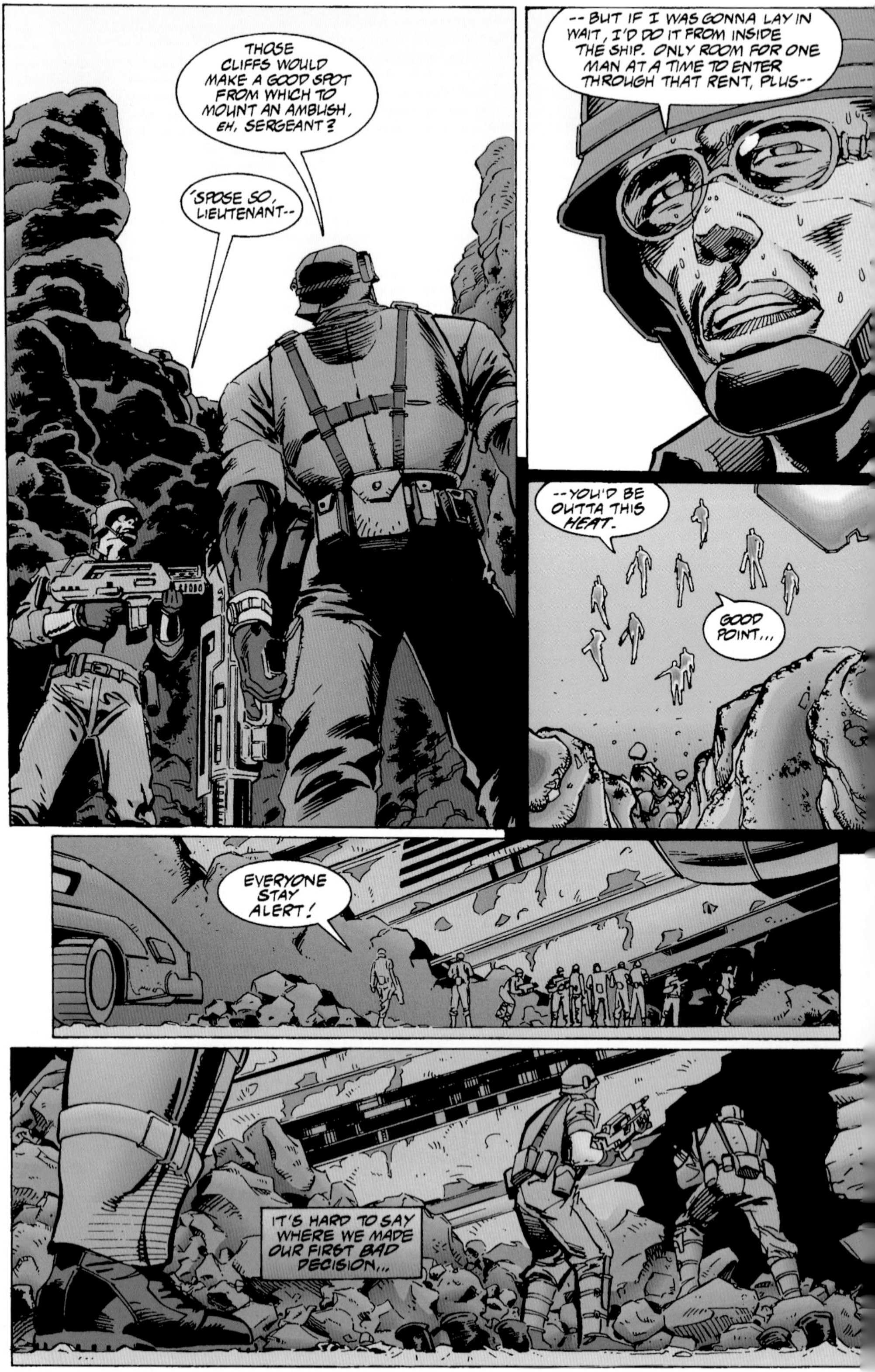
THOSE CLIFFS WOULD MAKE A GOOD SPOT FROM WHICH TO MOUNT AN AMBUSH, EH, SERGEANT?
'SPOSE SO, LIEUTENANT--
-- BUT IF I WAS GONNA LAY IN WAIT, I'D DO IT FROM INSIDE THE SHIP. ONLY ROOM FOR ONE MAN AT A TIME TO ENTER THROUGH THAT RENT, PLUS--
--YOU'D BE OUTTA THIS HEAT.
GOOD POINT...
EVERYONE STAY ALERT!
IT'S HARD TO SAY WHERE WE MADE OUR FIRST BAD DECISION...

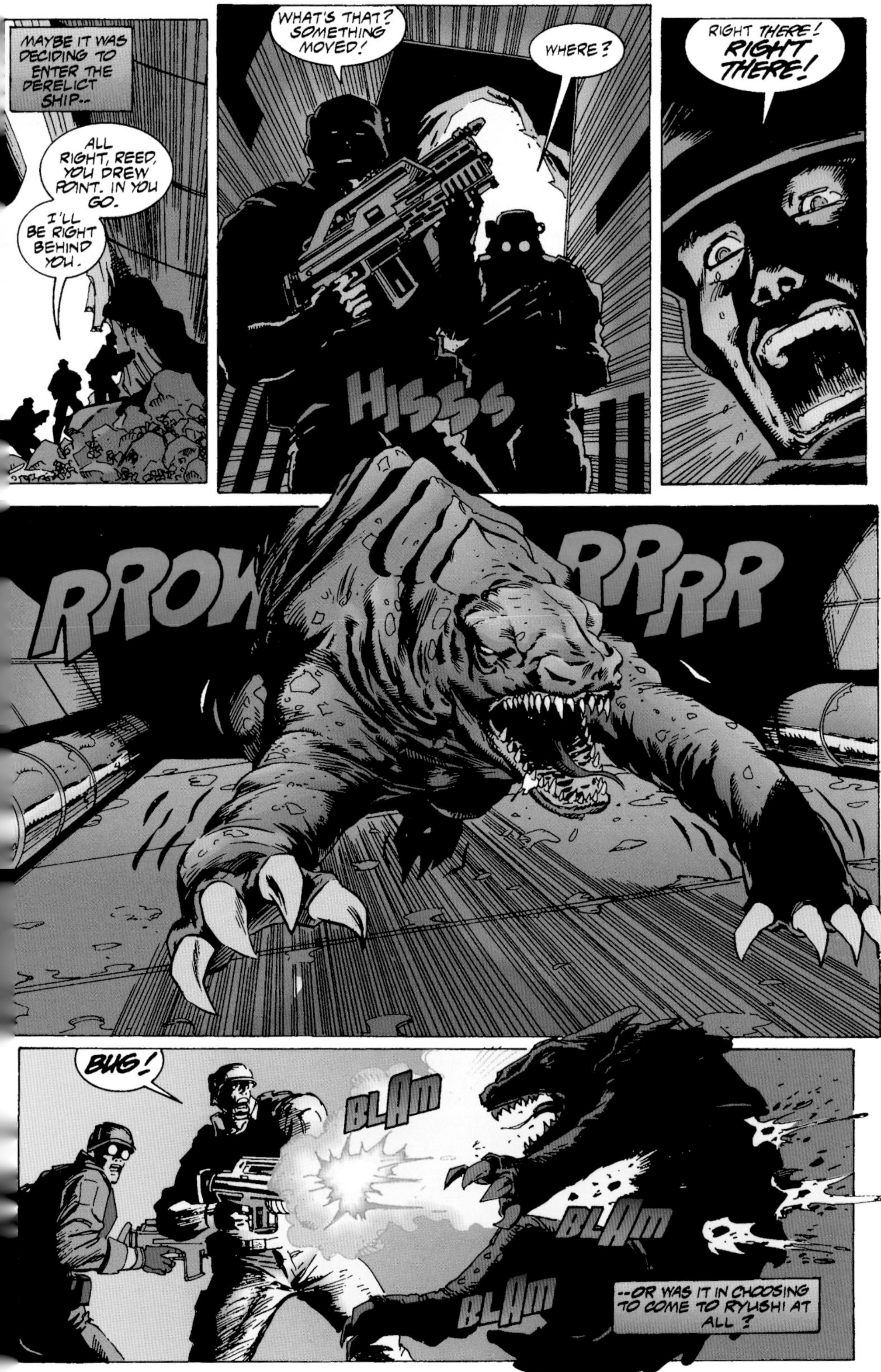
MAYBE IT WAS DECIDING TO ENTER THE DERELICT SHIP--
ALL RIGHT, REED, YOU DREW POINT. IN YOU GO.
I'LL BE RIGHT BEHIND YOU.
WHAT'S THAT? SOMETHING MOVED!
WHERE?
HISSS
RIGHT THERE! RIGHT THERE!
RROWRRRR
BUG!
BLAM
BLAM
BLAM
--OR WAS IT IN CHOOSING TO COME TO RYUSHI AT ALL?

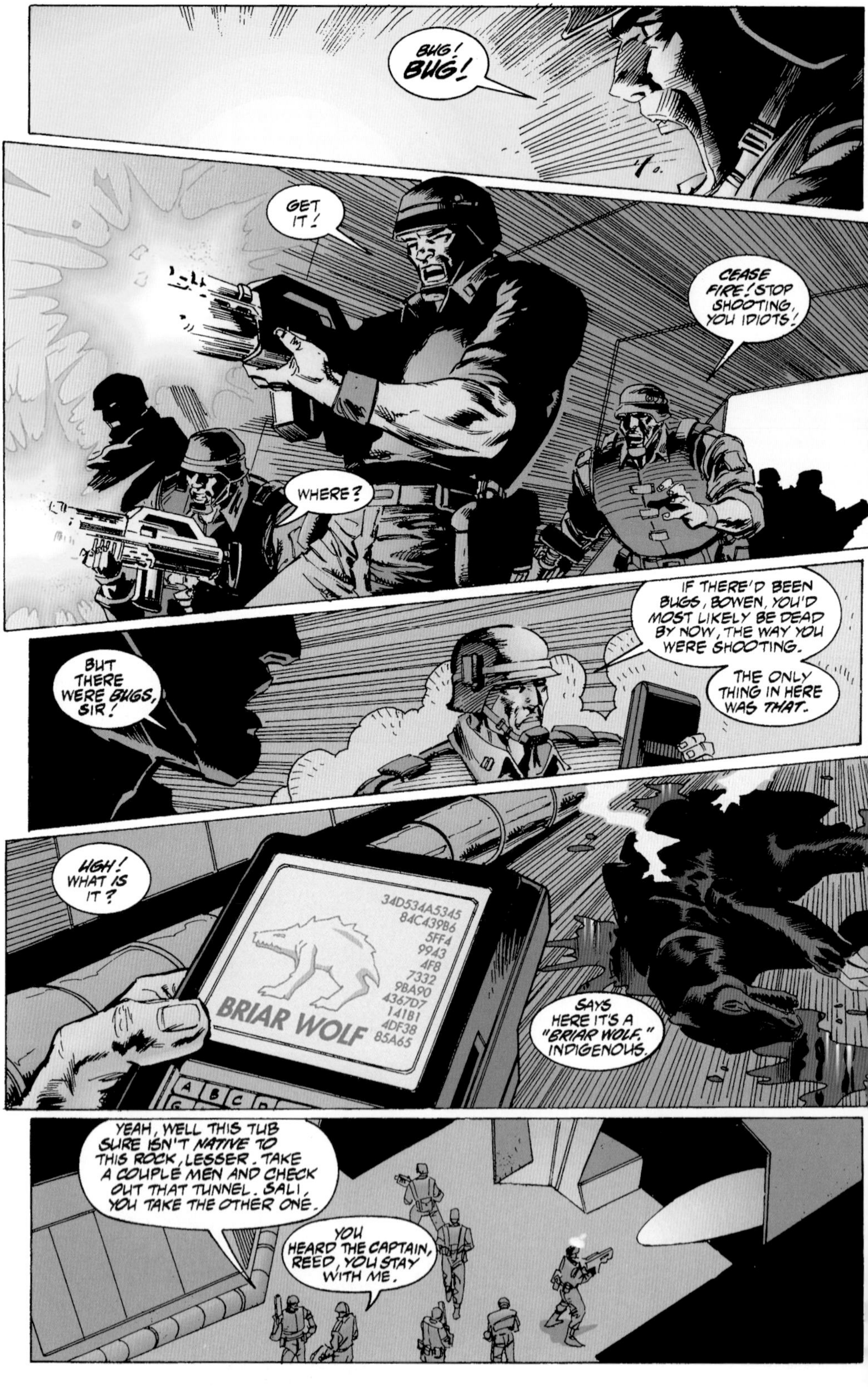
BUG! BUG!
GET IT!
CEASE FIRE! STOP SHOOTING, YOU IDIOTS!
WHERE?
BUT THERE WERE BUGS, SIR!
IF THERE'D BEEN BUGS, BOWEN, YOU'D MOST LIKELY BE DEAD BY NOW, THE WAY YOU WERE SHOOTING.
THE ONLY THING IN HERE WAS THAT.
UGH! WHAT IS IT?
34D534A5345
84C439B6
5FF4
9943
4F8
7332
9BA90
4367D7
141B1
4DF38
85A65
BRIAR WOLF
SAYS HERE IT'S A "BRIAR WOLF." INDIGENOUS.
YEAH, WELL THIS TUB SURE ISN'T NATIVE TO THIS ROCK, LESSER. TAKE A COUPLE MEN AND CHECK OUT THAT TUNNEL. SALI, YOU TAKE THE OTHER ONE.
YOU HEARD THE CAPTAIN, REED, YOU STAY WITH ME.

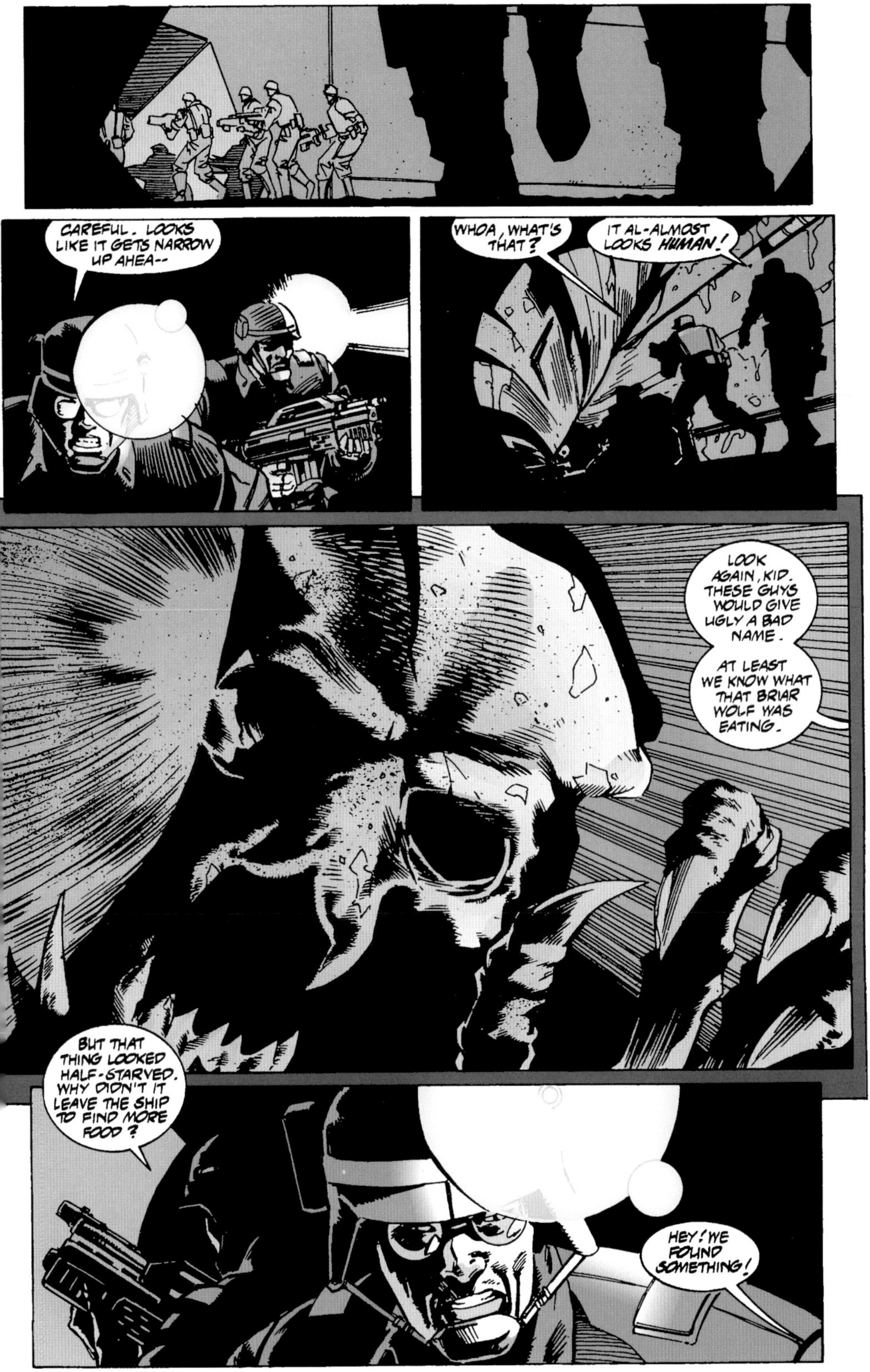
CAREFUL. LOOKS LIKE IT GETS NARROW UP AHEA--
WHOA, WHAT'S THAT?
IT AL-ALMOST LOOKS HUMAN!
LOOK AGAIN, KID. THESE GUYS WOULD GIVE UGLY A BAD NAME.
AT LEAST WE KNOW WHAT THAT BRIAR WOLF WAS EATING.
BUT THAT THING LOOKED HALF-STARVED. WHY DIDN'T IT LEAVE THE SHIP TO FIND MORE FOOD?
HEY! WE FOUND SOMETHING!

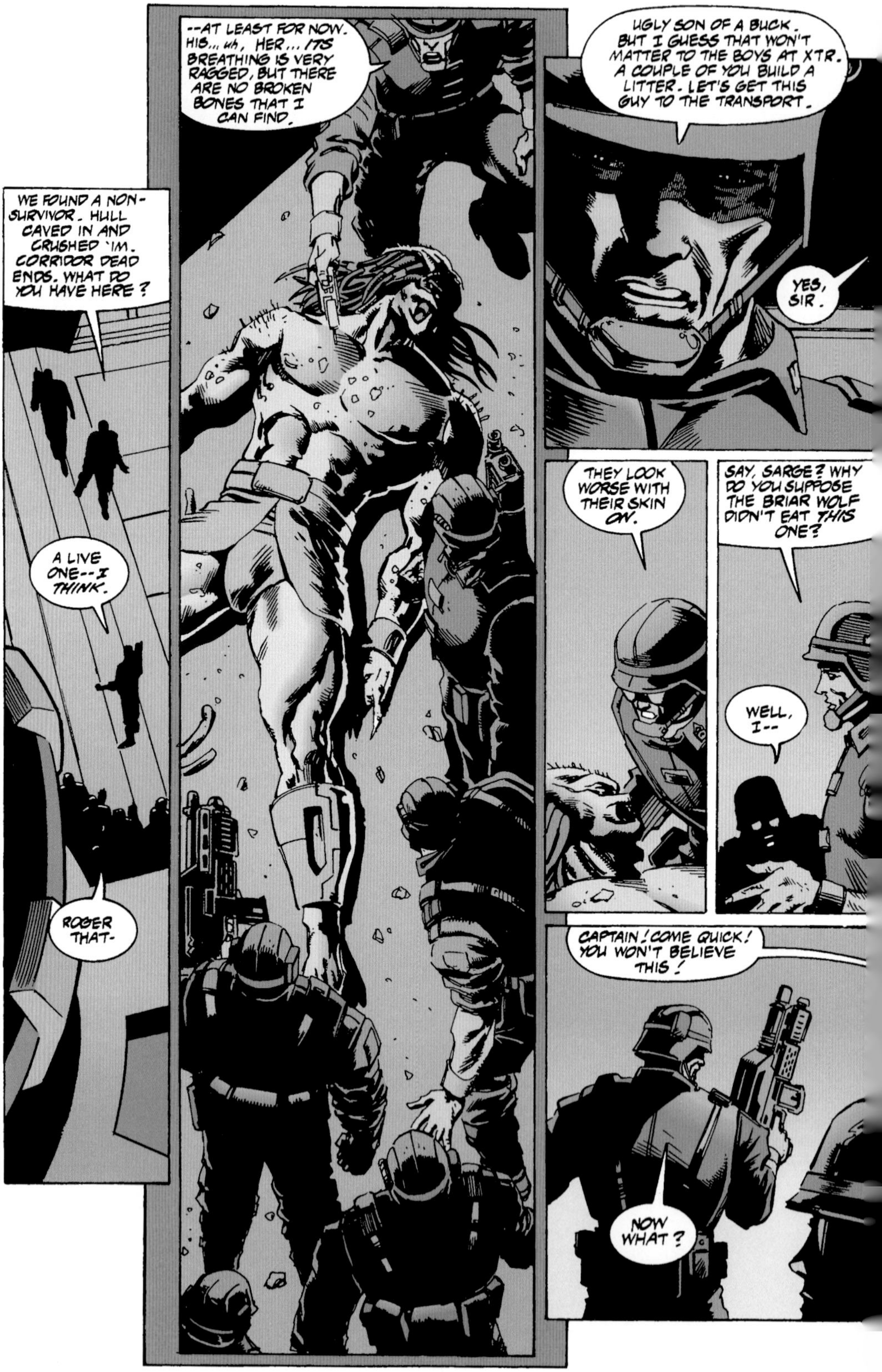
WE FOUND A NON-SURVIVOR. HULL CAVED IN AND CRUSHED 'IM. CORRIDOR DEAD ENDS. WHAT DO YOU HAVE HERE?
A LIVE ONE--I THINK.
ROGER THAT-
--AT LEAST FOR NOW. HIS... uh, HER... ITS BREATHING IS VERY RAGGED, BUT THERE ARE NO BROKEN BONES THAT I CAN FIND.
UGLY SON OF A BUCK. BUT I GUESS THAT WON'T MATTER TO THE BOYS AT XTR. A COUPLE OF YOU BUILD A LITTER. LET'S GET THIS GUY TO THE TRANSPORT.
YES, SIR.
THEY LOOK WORSE WITH THEIR SKIN ON.
SAY, SARGE? WHY DO YOU SUPPOSE THE BRIAR WOLF DIDN'T EAT THIS ONE?
WELL, I--
CAPTAIN! COME QUICK! YOU WON'T BELIEVE THIS!
NOW WHAT?

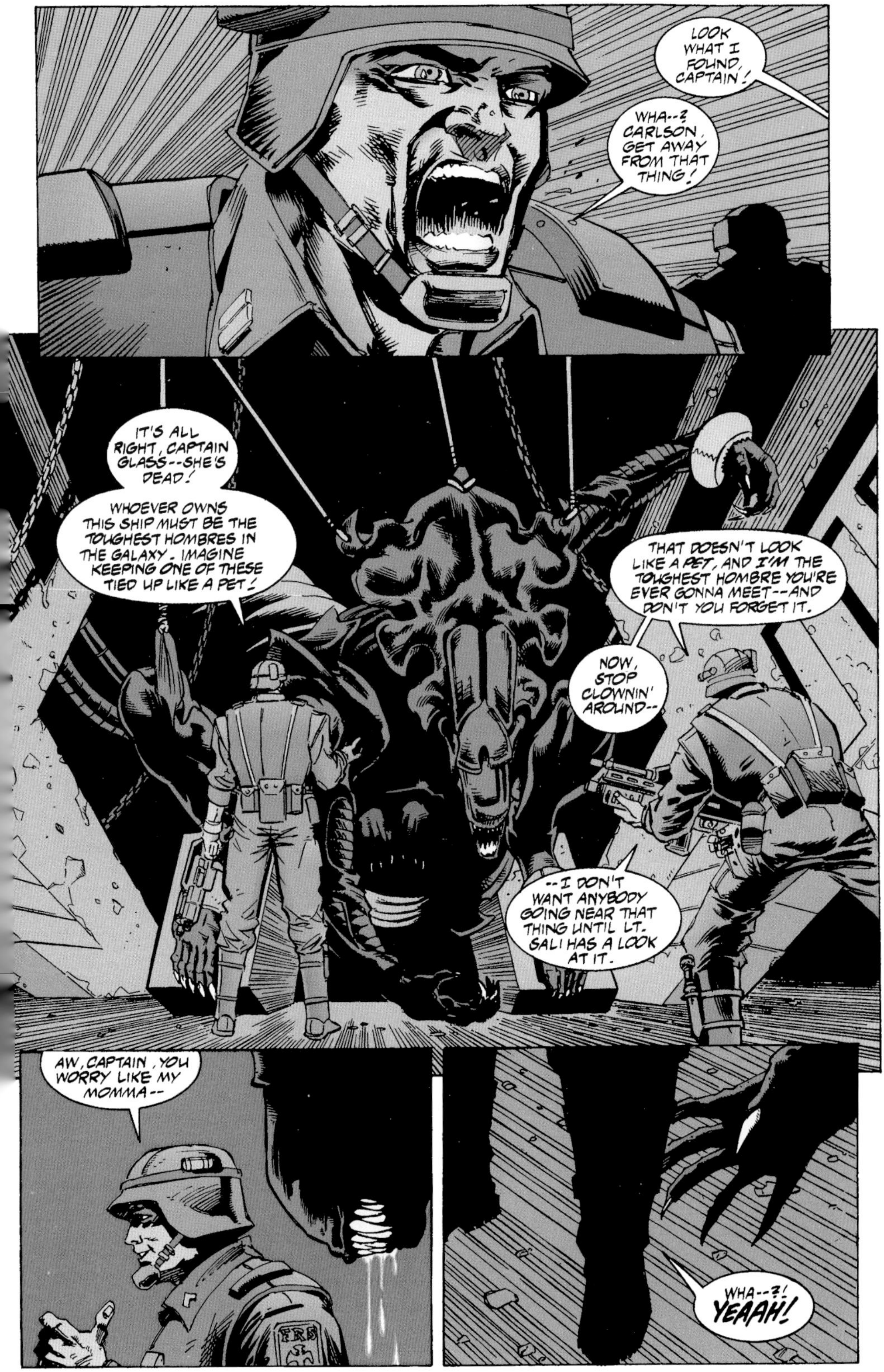
LOOK WHAT I FOUND, CAPTAIN!
WHA--? CARLSON, GET AWAY FROM THAT THING!
IT'S ALL RIGHT, CAPTAIN GLASS--SHE'S DEAD!
WHOEVER OWNS THIS SHIP MUST BE THE TOUGHEST HOMBRES IN THE GALAXY. IMAGINE KEEPING ONE OF THESE TIED UP LIKE A PET!
THAT DOESN'T LOOK LIKE A PET, AND I'M THE TOUGHEST HOMBRE YOU'RE EVER GONNA MEET--AND DON'T YOU FORGET IT.
NOW, STOP CLOWNIN' AROUND--
--I DON'T WANT ANYBODY GOING NEAR THAT THING UNTIL LT. GALI HAS A LOOK AT IT.
AW, CAPTAIN, YOU WORRY LIKE MY MOMMA--
WHA--?! YEAAH!

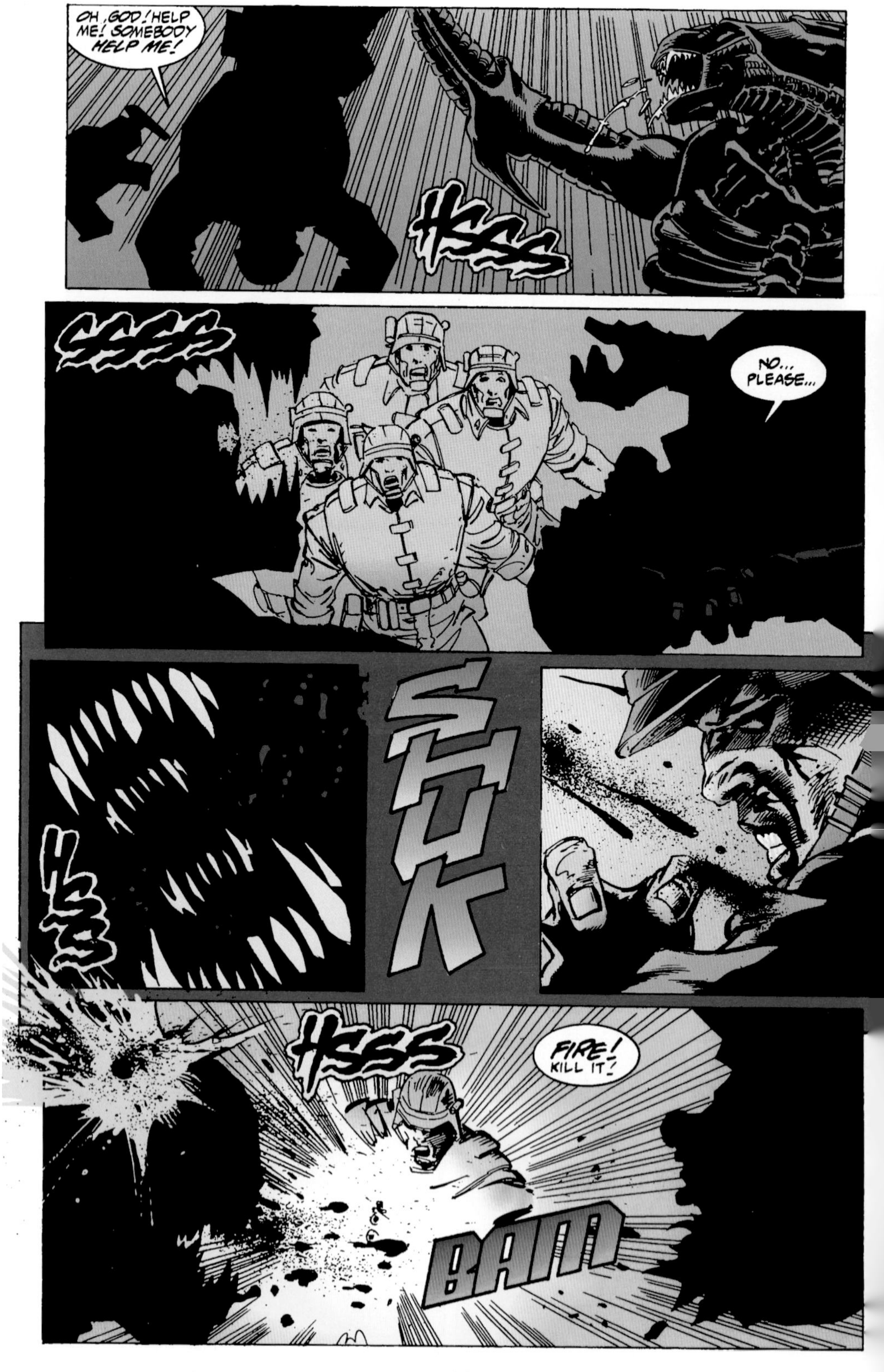
OH, GOD! HELP ME! SOMEBODY HELP ME!
HSSS
SSSS
NO... PLEASE...
HSSS
SHUK
HSSS
FIRE! KILL IT!
BAM

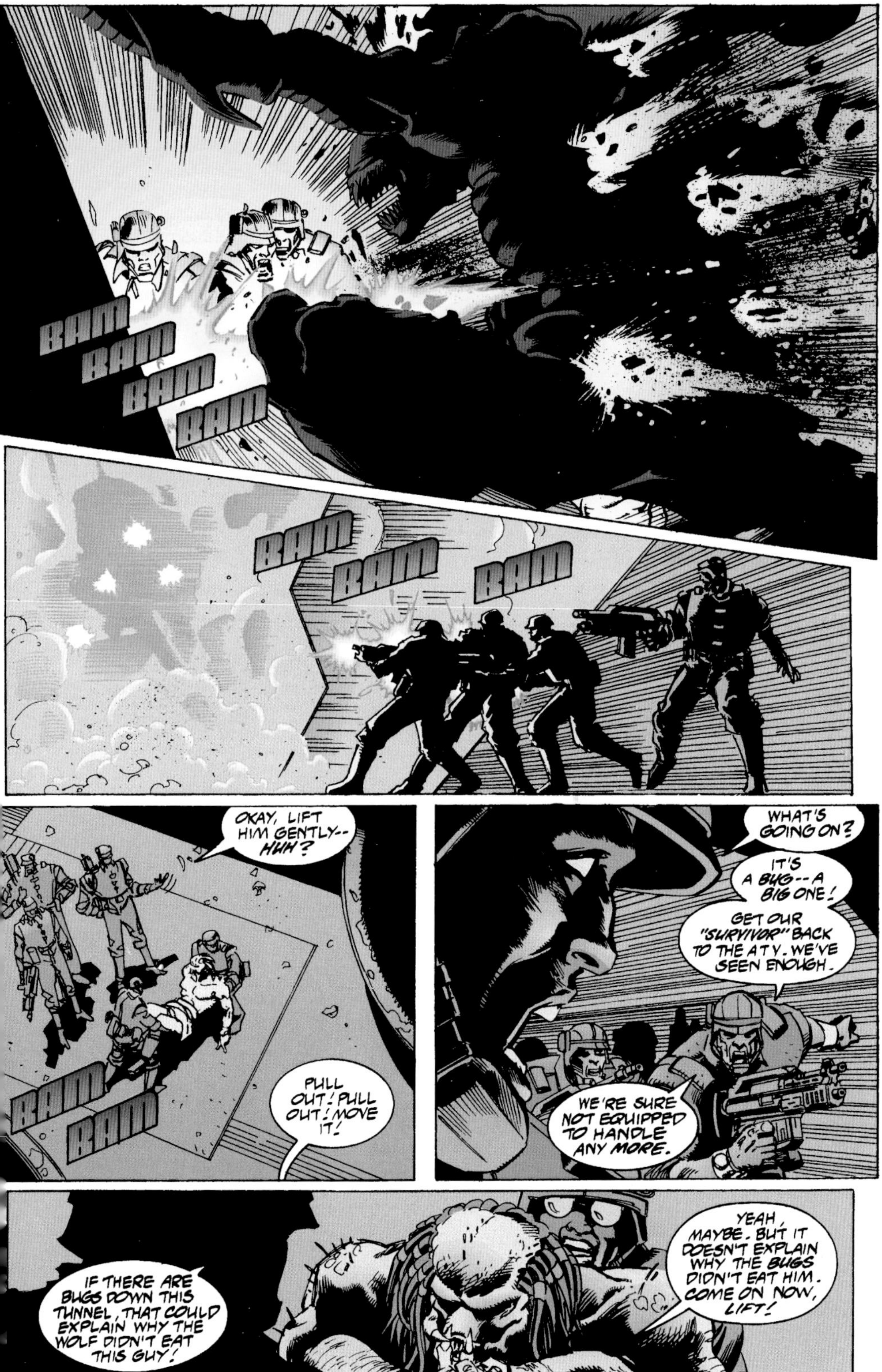
BAM BAM BAM BAM
BAM BAM BAM
OKAY, LIFT HIM GENTLY-- HUH?
PULL OUT! PULL OUT! MOVE IT!
BAM BAM
WHAT'S GOING ON?
IT'S A BUG-- A BIG ONE!
GET OUR "SURVIVOR" BACK TO THE ATV. WE'VE SEEN ENOUGH.
WE'RE SURE NOT EQUIPPED TO HANDLE ANY MORE.
IF THERE ARE BUGS DOWN THIS TUNNEL, THAT COULD EXPLAIN WHY THE WOLF DIDN'T EAT THIS GUY!
YEAH, MAYBE. BUT IT DOESN'T EXPLAIN WHY THE BUGS DIDN'T EAT HIM. COME ON NOW, LIFT!

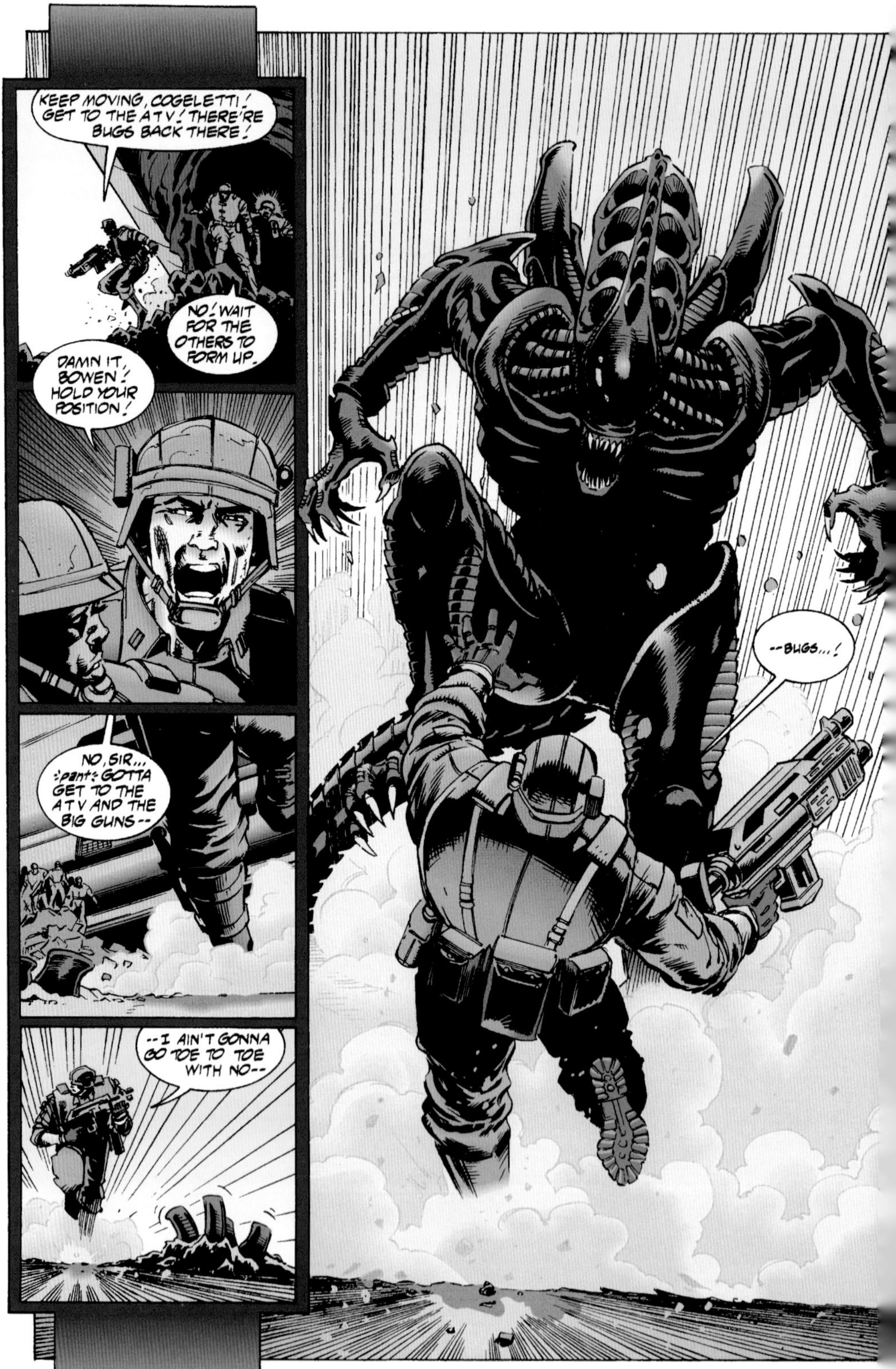
KEEP MOVING, COGELETTI! GET TO THE ATV! THERE'RE BUGS BACK THERE!
NO! WAIT FOR THE OTHERS TO FORM UP.
DAMN IT, BOWEN! HOLD YOUR POSITION!
NO, SIR... :pant: GOTTA GET TO THE ATV AND THE BIG GUNS--
--I AIN'T GONNA GO TOE TO TOE WITH NO--
--BUGS...!

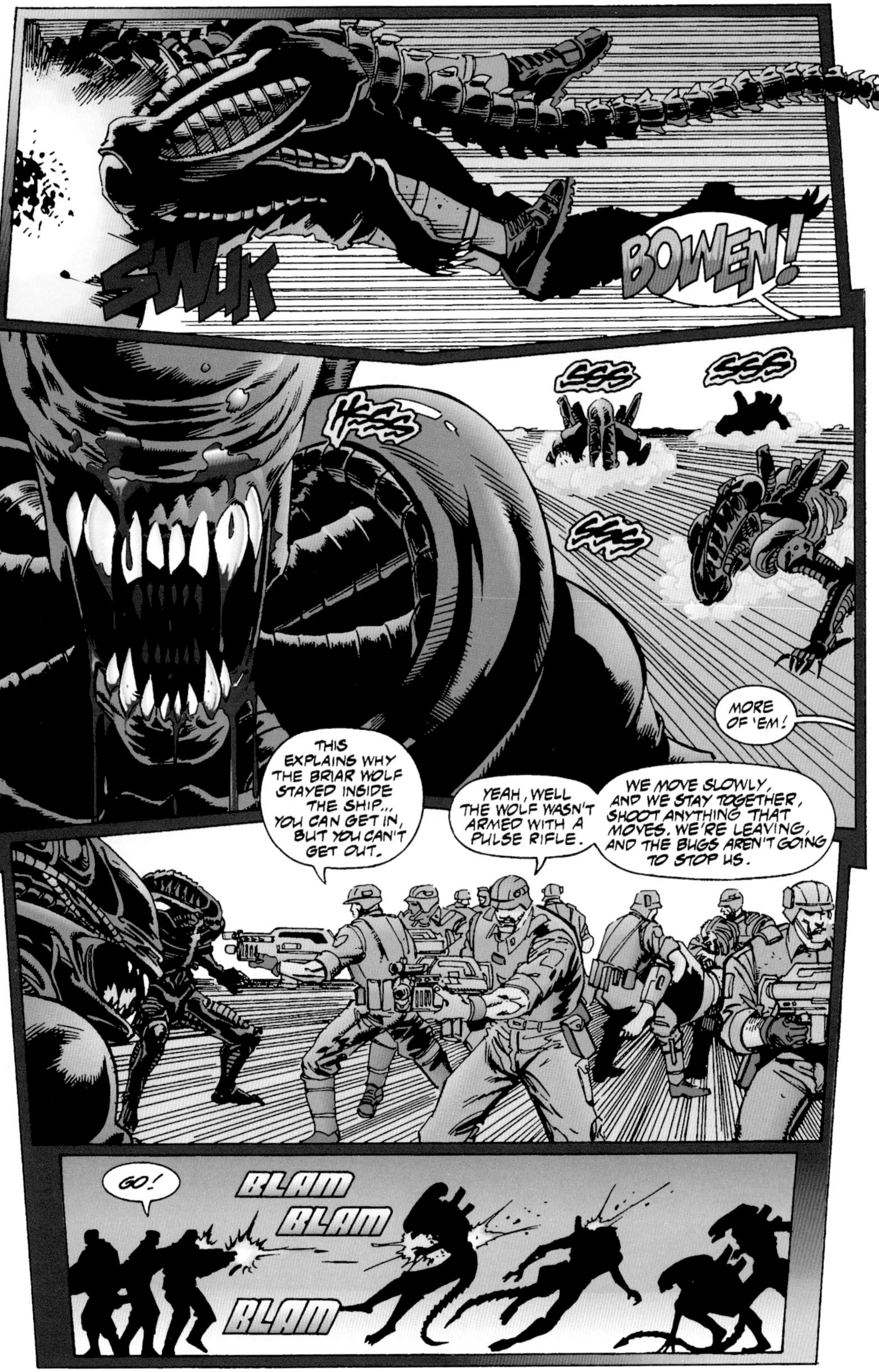
SWUK
BOWEN!
HSSS
SSS
SSS
SSS
MORE OF 'EM!
THIS EXPLAINS WHY THE BRIAR WOLF STAYED INSIDE THE SHIP... YOU CAN GET IN, BUT YOU CAN'T GET OUT.
YEAH, WELL THE WOLF WASN'T ARMED WITH A PULSE RIFLE.
WE MOVE SLOWLY, AND WE STAY TOGETHER, SHOOT ANYTHING THAT MOVES. WE'RE LEAVING, AND THE BUGS AREN'T GOING TO STOP US.
GO!
BLAM
BLAM
BLAM

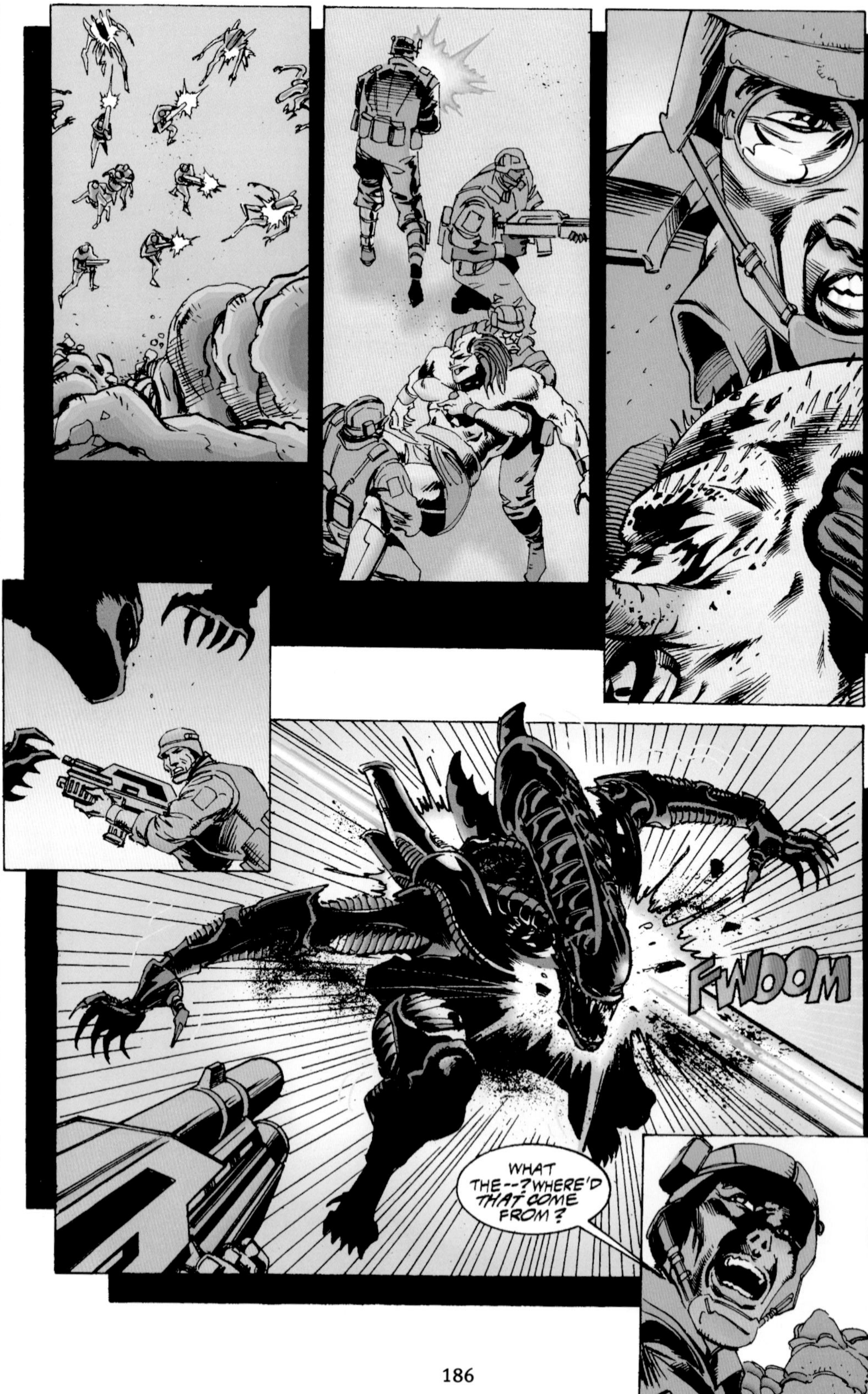
FWOOM
WHAT THE--? WHERE'D THAT COME FROM?

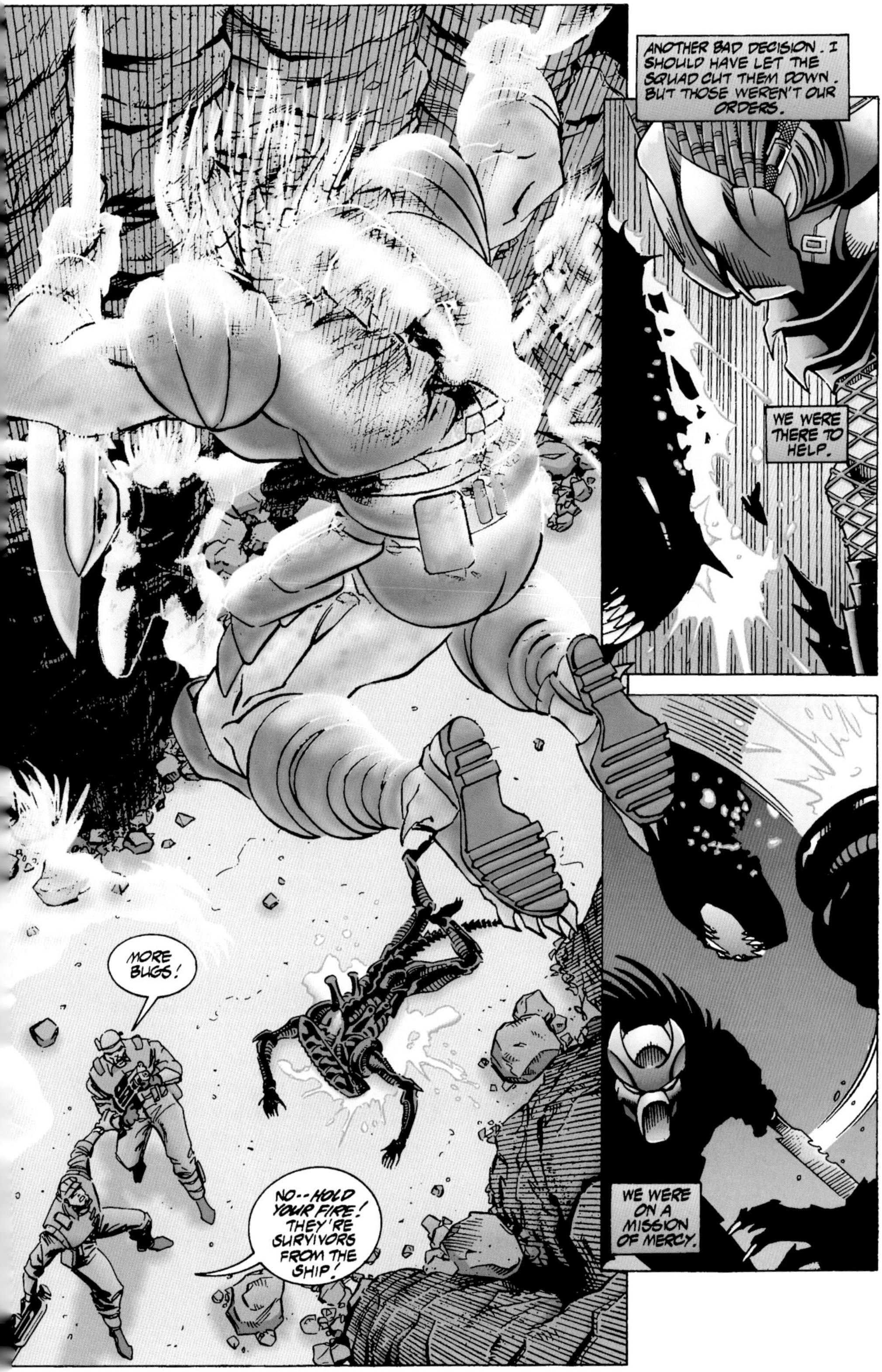
ANOTHER BAD DECISION. I SHOULD HAVE LET THE SQUAD CUT THEM DOWN. BUT THOSE WEREN'T OUR ORDERS.
WE WERE THERE TO HELP.
MORE BUGS!
NO--HOLD YOUR FIRE! THEY'RE SURVIVORS FROM THE SHIP!
WE WERE ON A MISSION OF MERCY.

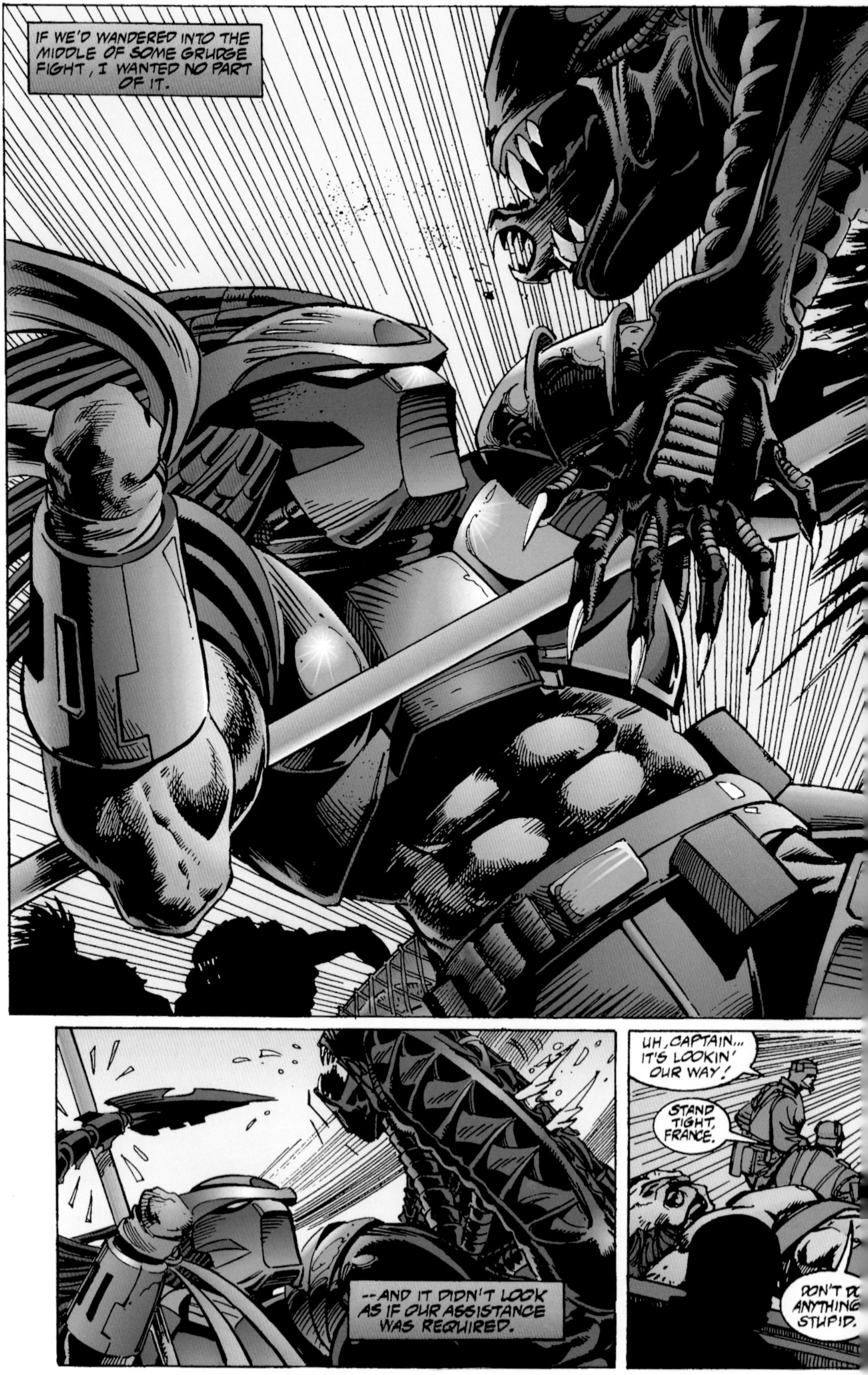
IF WE'D WANDERED INTO THE MIDDLE OF SOME GRUDGE FIGHT, I WANTED NO PART OF IT.
--AND IT DIDN'T LOOK AS IF OUR ASSISTANCE WAS REQUIRED.
UH, CAPTAIN... IT'S LOOKIN' OUR WAY!
STAND TIGHT, FRANCE.
DON'T DO ANYTHING STUPID.

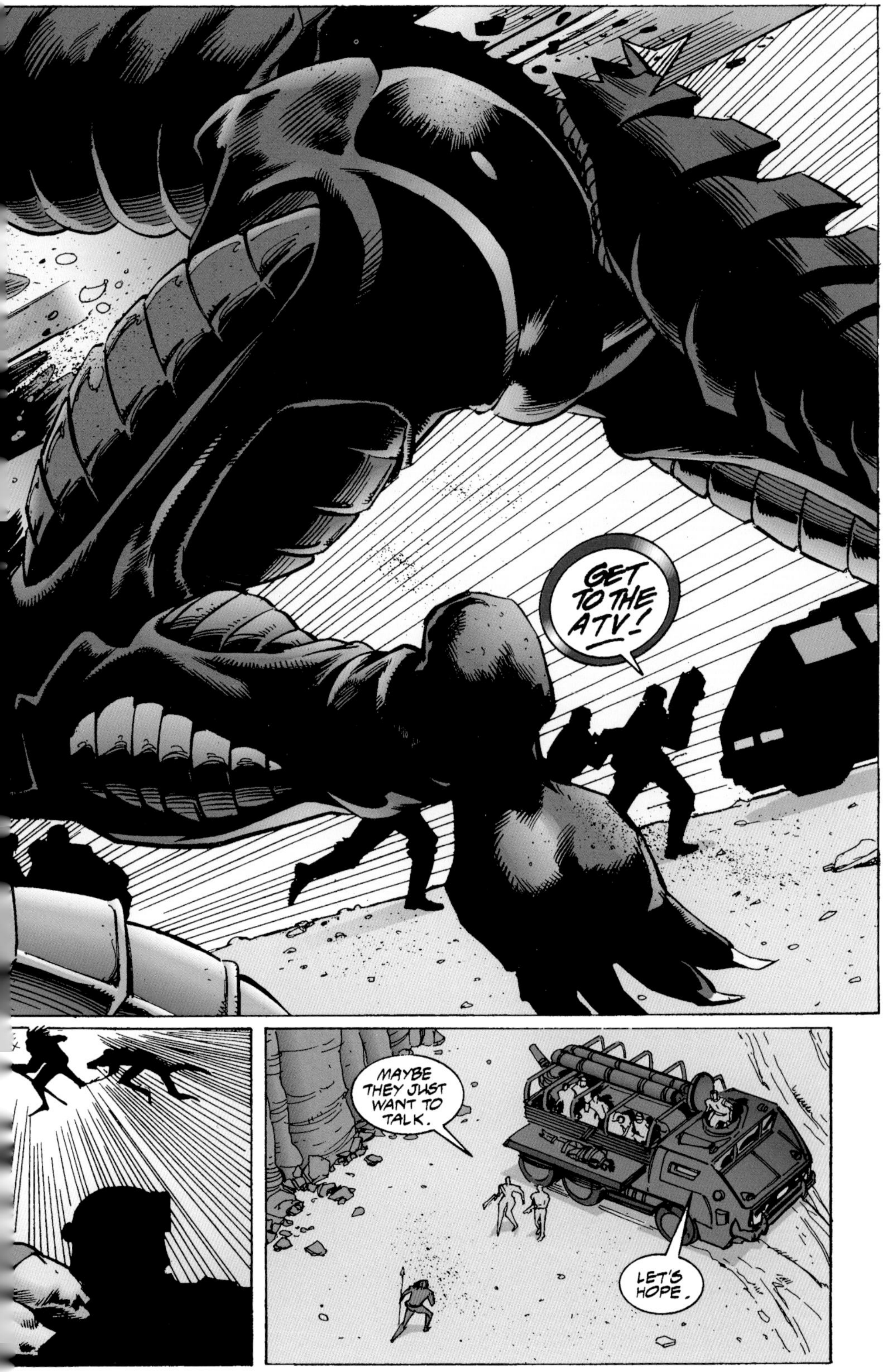
GET TO THE ATV!
MAYBE THEY JUST WANT TO TALK.
LET'S HOPE.

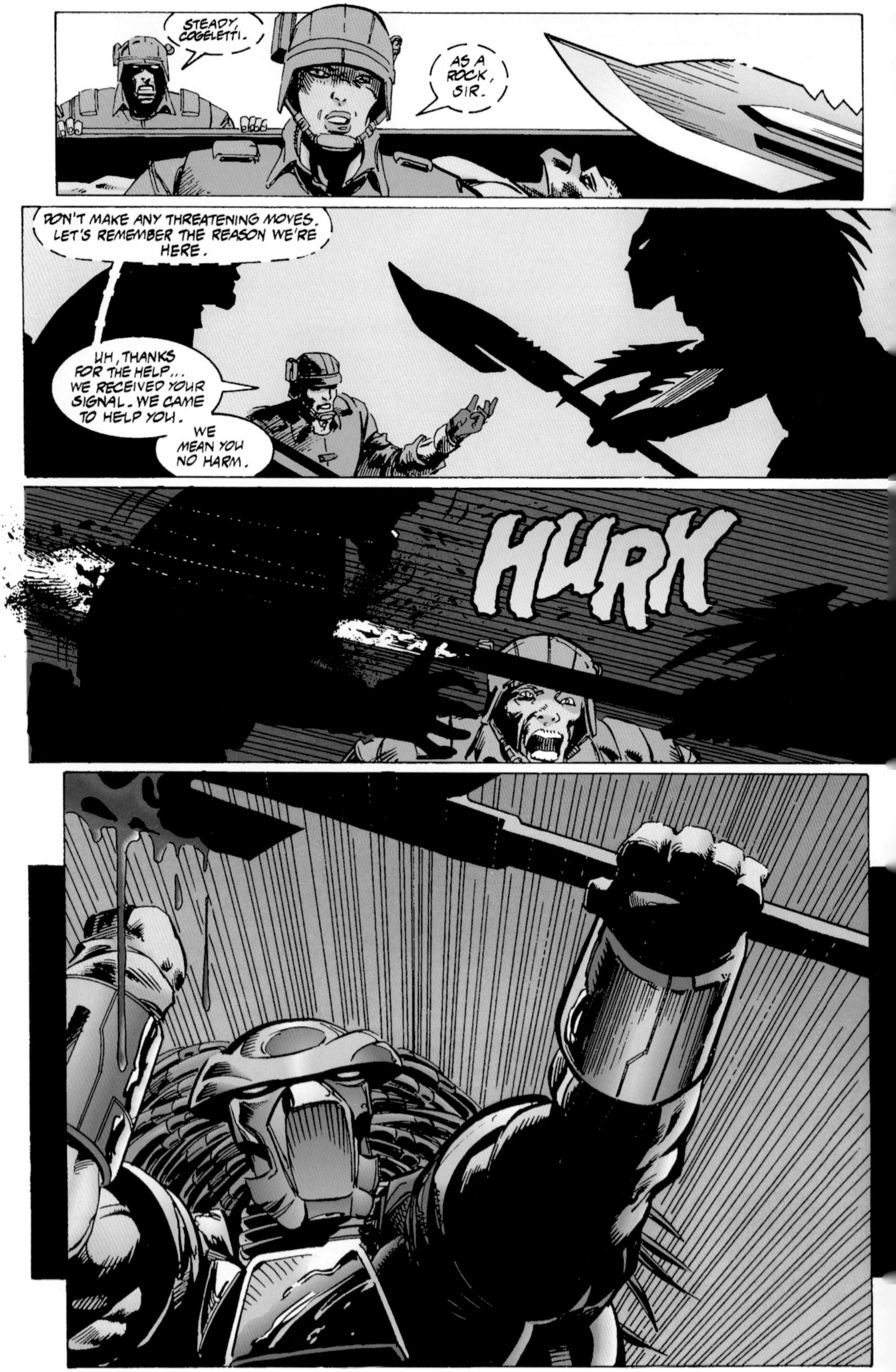

STEADY, COGELETTI.
AS A ROCK, SIR.
DON'T MAKE ANY THREATENING MOVES. LET'S REMEMBER THE REASON WE'RE HERE.
UH, THANKS FOR THE HELP... WE RECEIVED YOUR SIGNAL. WE CAME TO HELP YOU.
WE MEAN YOU NO HARM.
HURK

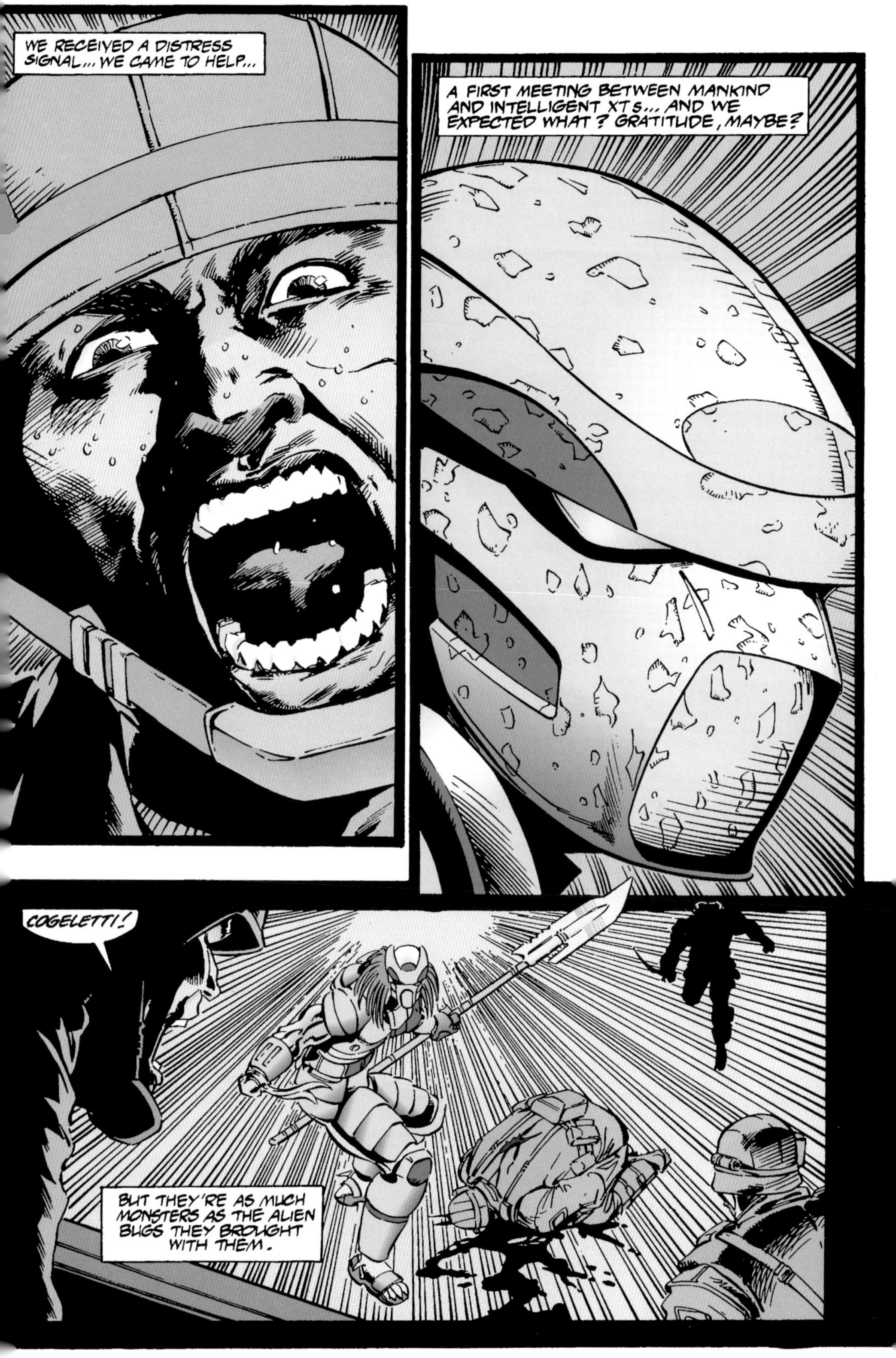
WE RECEIVED A DISTRESS SIGNAL... WE CAME TO HELP...
A FIRST MEETING BETWEEN MANKIND AND INTELLIGENT XT'S... AND WE EXPECTED WHAT? GRATITUDE, MAYBE?
COGELETTI!
BUT THEY'RE AS MUCH MONSTERS AS THE ALIEN BUGS THEY BROUGHT WITH THEM.

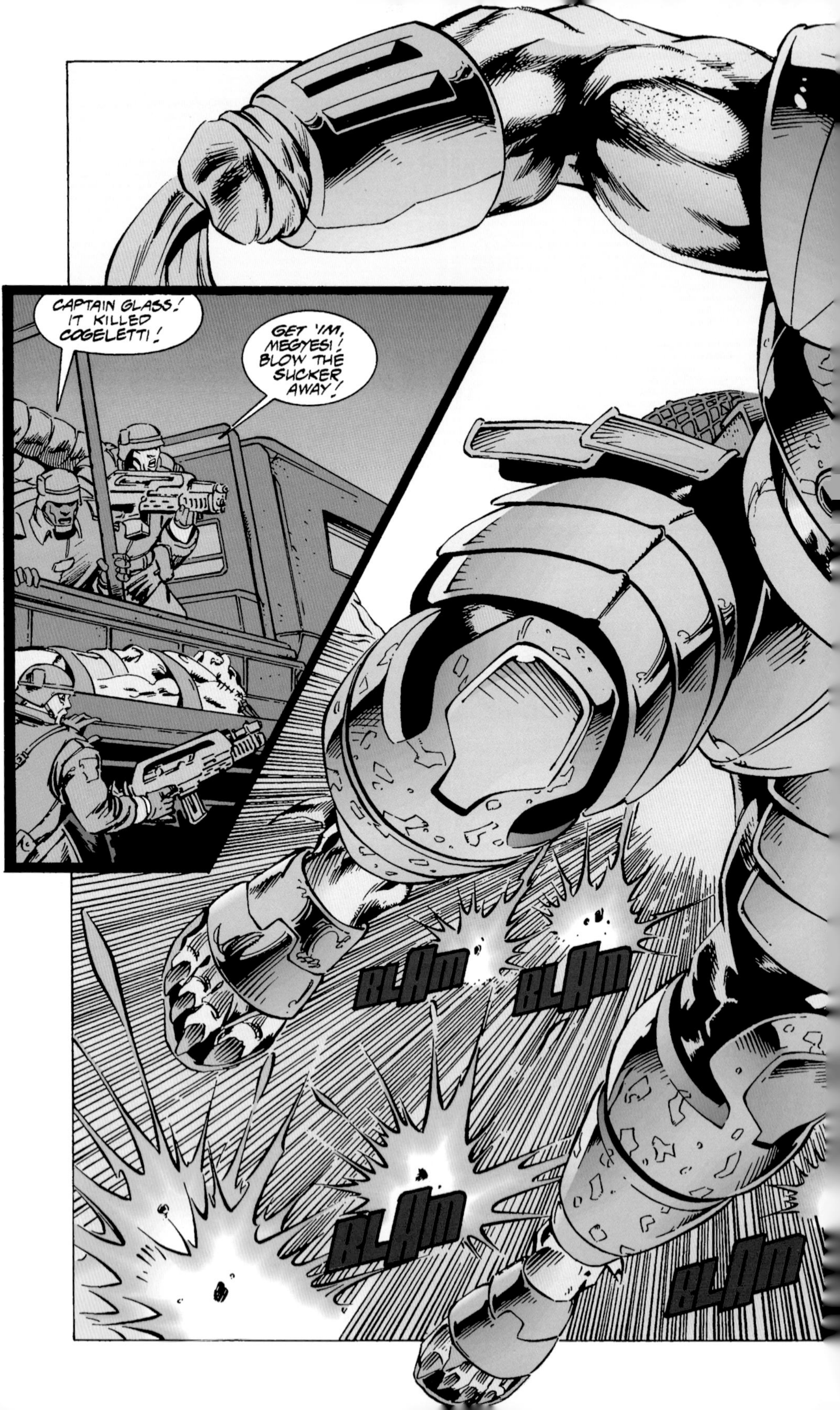
CAPTAIN GLASS! IT KILLED COGELETTI!
GET 'IM, MEGYESI! BLOW THE SUCKER AWAY!
BLAM
BLAM
BLAM
BLAM

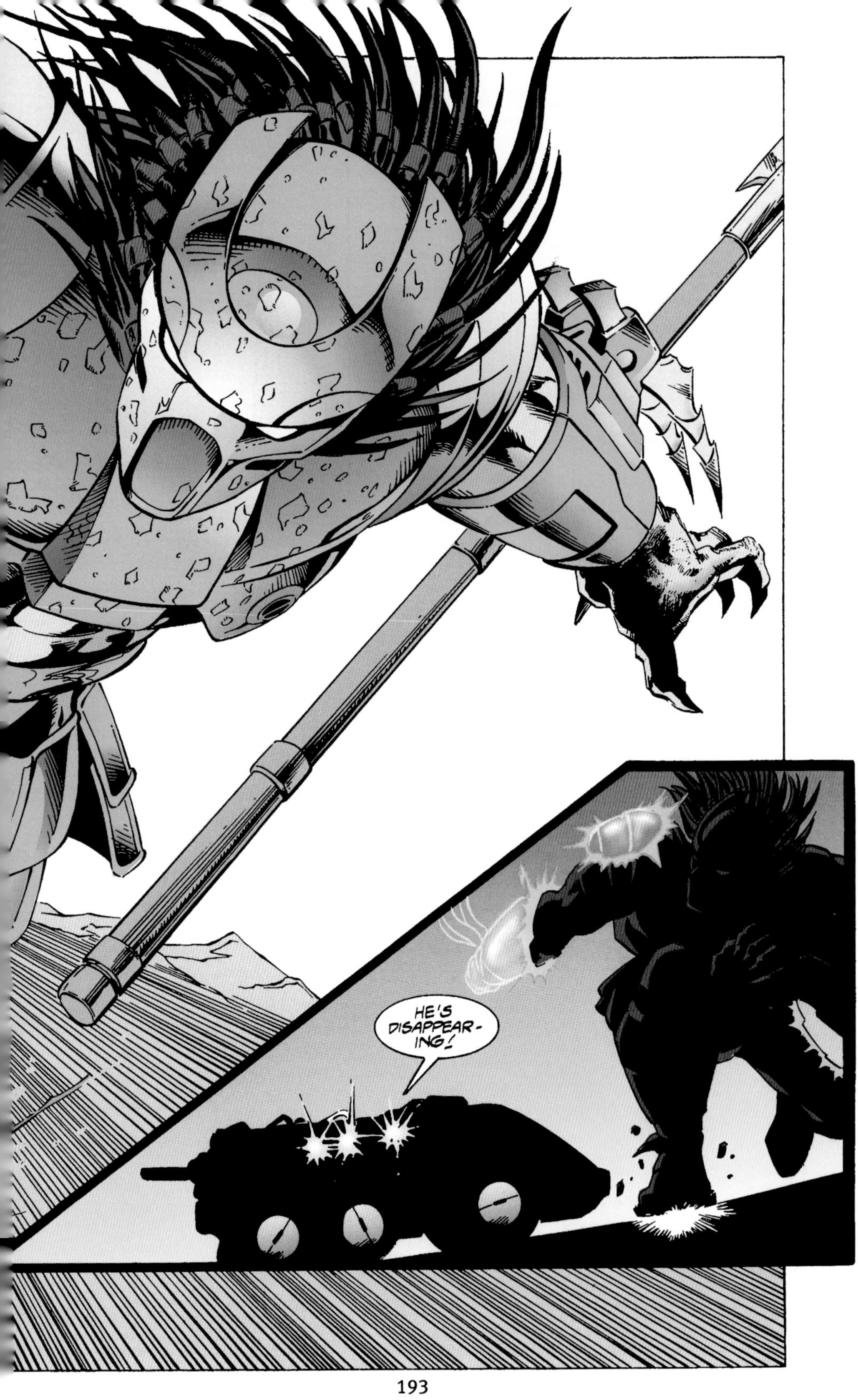
HE'S DISAPPEAR-ING!

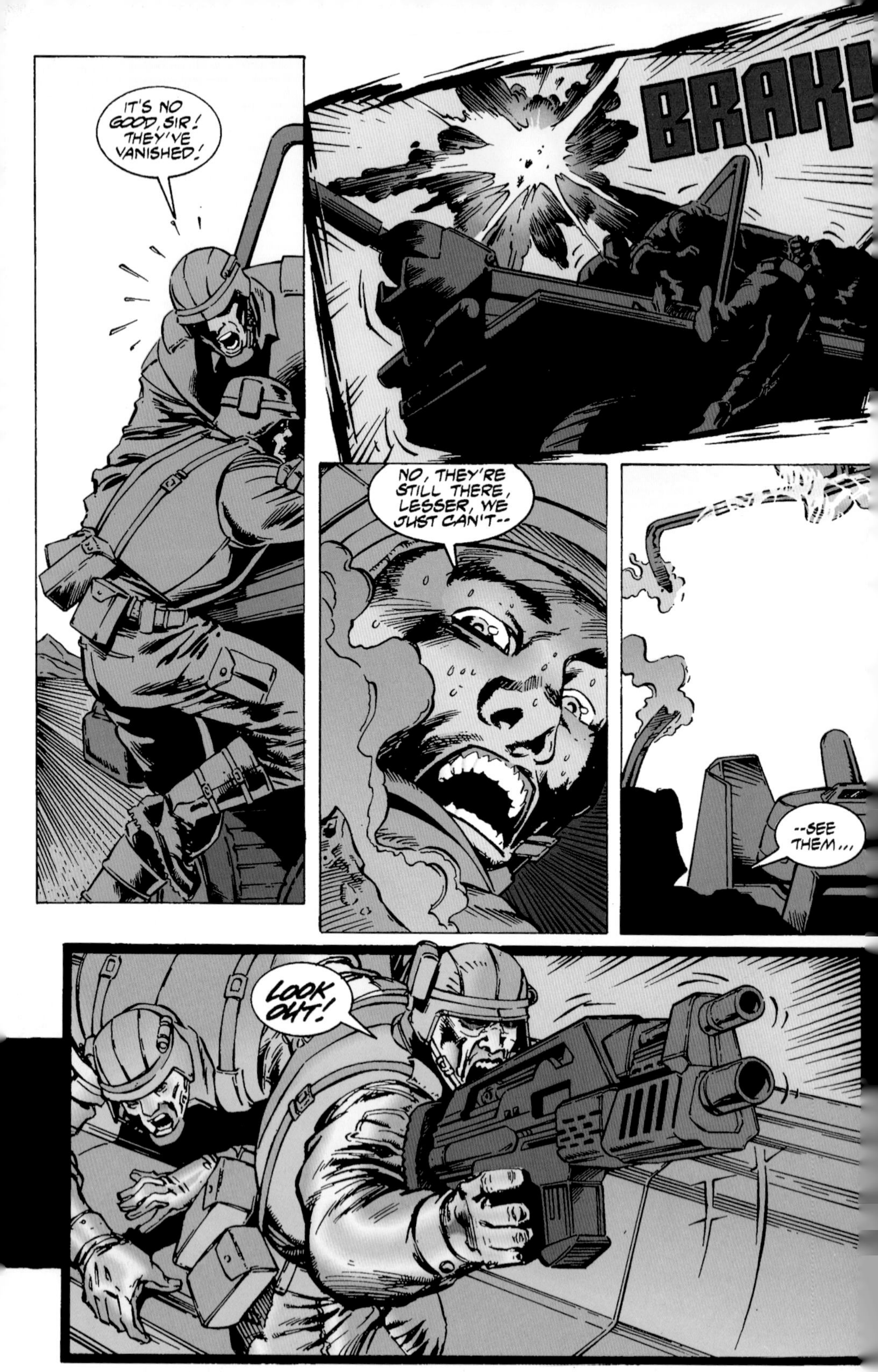

IT'S NO GOOD, SIR! THEY'VE VANISHED!
BRAK!
NO, THEY'RE STILL THERE, LESSER, WE JUST CAN'T--
--SEE THEM...
LOOK OUT!

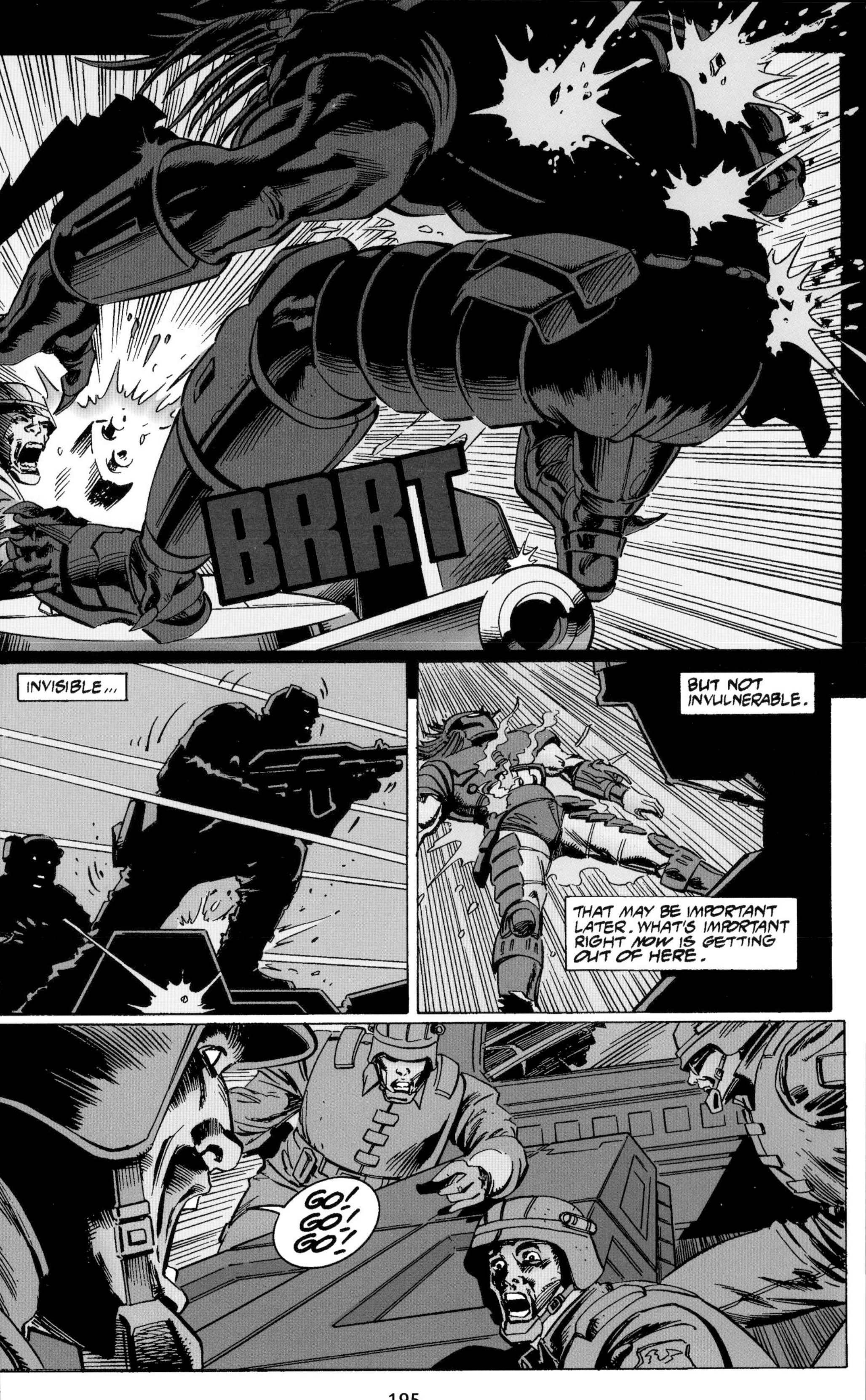
BRRT
INVISIBLE...
BUT NOT INVULNERABLE.
THAT MAY BE IMPORTANT LATER. WHAT'S IMPORTANT RIGHT NOW IS GETTING OUT OF HERE.
GO! GO! GO!

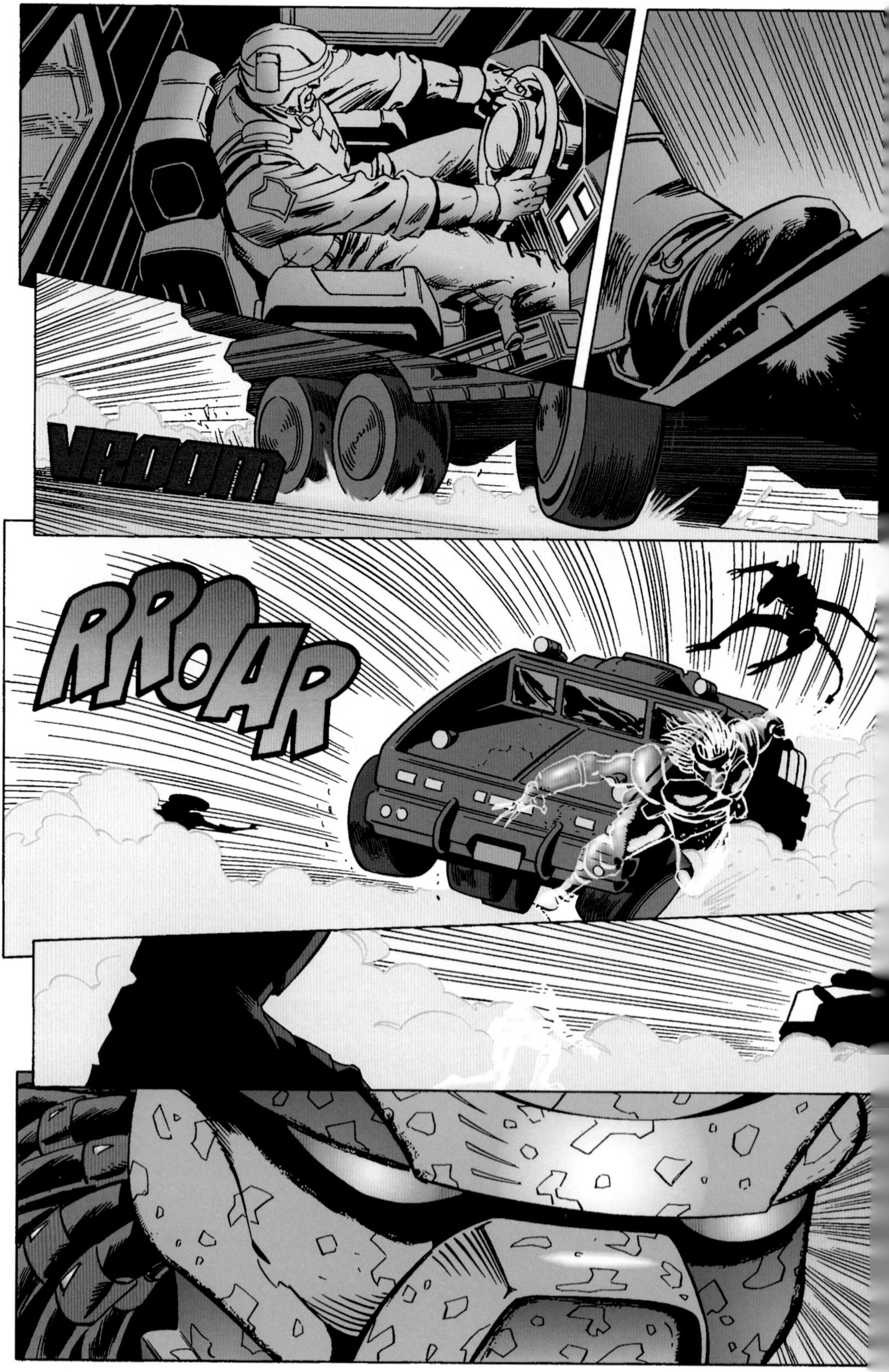
VROOM
RROAR

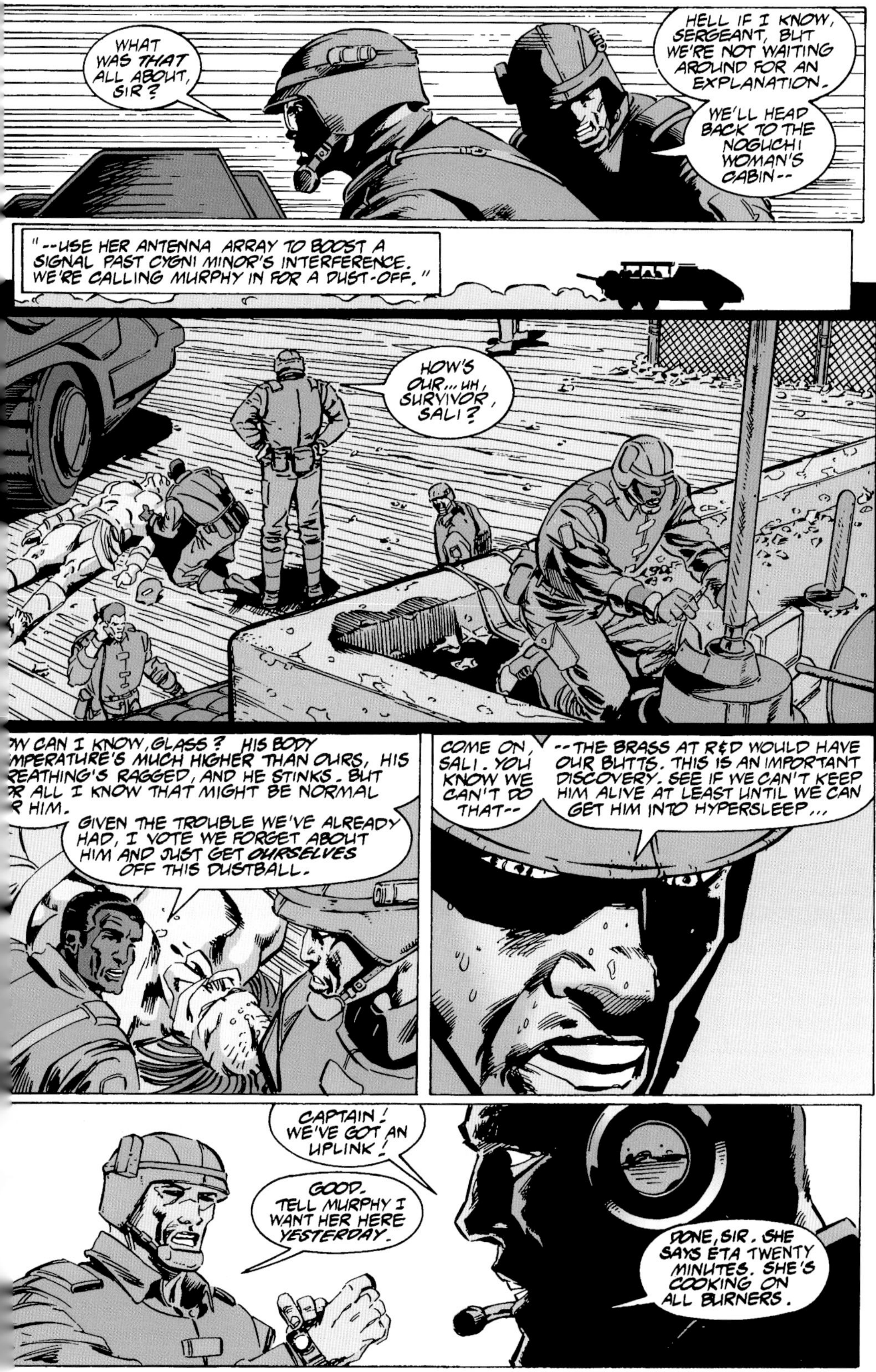
WHAT WAS THAT ALL ABOUT, SIR?
HELL IF I KNOW, SERGEANT, BUT WE'RE NOT WAITING AROUND FOR AN EXPLANATION.
WE'LL HEAD BACK TO THE NOGUCHI WOMAN'S CABIN--
"--USE HER ANTENNA ARRAY TO BOOST A SIGNAL PAST CYGNI MINOR'S INTERFERENCE. WE'RE CALLING MURPHY IN FOR A DUST-OFF."
HOW'S OUR... UH, SURVIVOR, SALI?
W CAN I KNOW, GLASS? HIS BODY MPERATURE'S MUCH HIGHER THAN OURS, HIS REATHING'S RAGGED, AND HE STINKS. BUT R ALL I KNOW THAT MIGHT BE NORMAL R HIM.
GIVEN THE TROUBLE WE'VE ALREADY HAD, I VOTE WE FORGET ABOUT HIM AND JUST GET OURSELVES OFF THIS DUSTBALL.
COME ON, SALI. YOU KNOW WE CAN'T DO THAT--
--THE BRASS AT R&D WOULD HAVE OUR BUTTS. THIS IS AN IMPORTANT DISCOVERY. SEE IF WE CAN'T KEEP HIM ALIVE AT LEAST UNTIL WE CAN GET HIM INTO HYPERSLEEP...
CAPTAIN! WE'VE GOT AN UPLINK!
GOOD. TELL MURPHY I WANT HER HERE YESTERDAY.
DONE, SIR. SHE SAYS ETA TWENTY MINUTES. SHE'S COOKING ON ALL BURNERS.

ALL RIGHT, PACK UP. LET'S HIT THE L.Z.

KEEP YOUR EYES OPEN. THIS IS NO TIME TO GET SLOPPY.

HEY, REED-- GIVE ME A HAND STOWING THIS CABLE.

LEAVE IT MEGYESI--

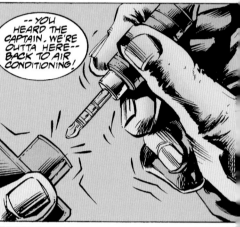

-- YOU HEARD THE CAPTAIN. WE'RE OUTTA HERE-- BACK TO AIR CONDITIONING!

SIR, YOU THINK MURPHY WILL GET HERE BEFORE THIS GUY'S BUDDIES DO?

WHAT'RE YOU TALKING ABOUT, FRANCE? WHY WOULD THEY FOLLOW US?

BESIDES, WE PUT TEN KLIKS BETWEEN US AND THAT SHIP.

THE KID'S GOT A POINT, SIR. WE STUCK OUR NOSES IN THE MIDDLE OF SOMETHING WE DON'T UNDERSTAND, THAT'S FOR SURE.

TRYING TO GUESS WHAT THE XTS WILL OR WON'T DO IS A SUCKER'S BET.

AND YOU SAW HOW FAST THEY WERE. NO TELLING HOW QUICKLY THEY CAN COVER OPEN GROUND.

AND DON'T FORGET-- WE'D NEVER SEE THEM COMING.

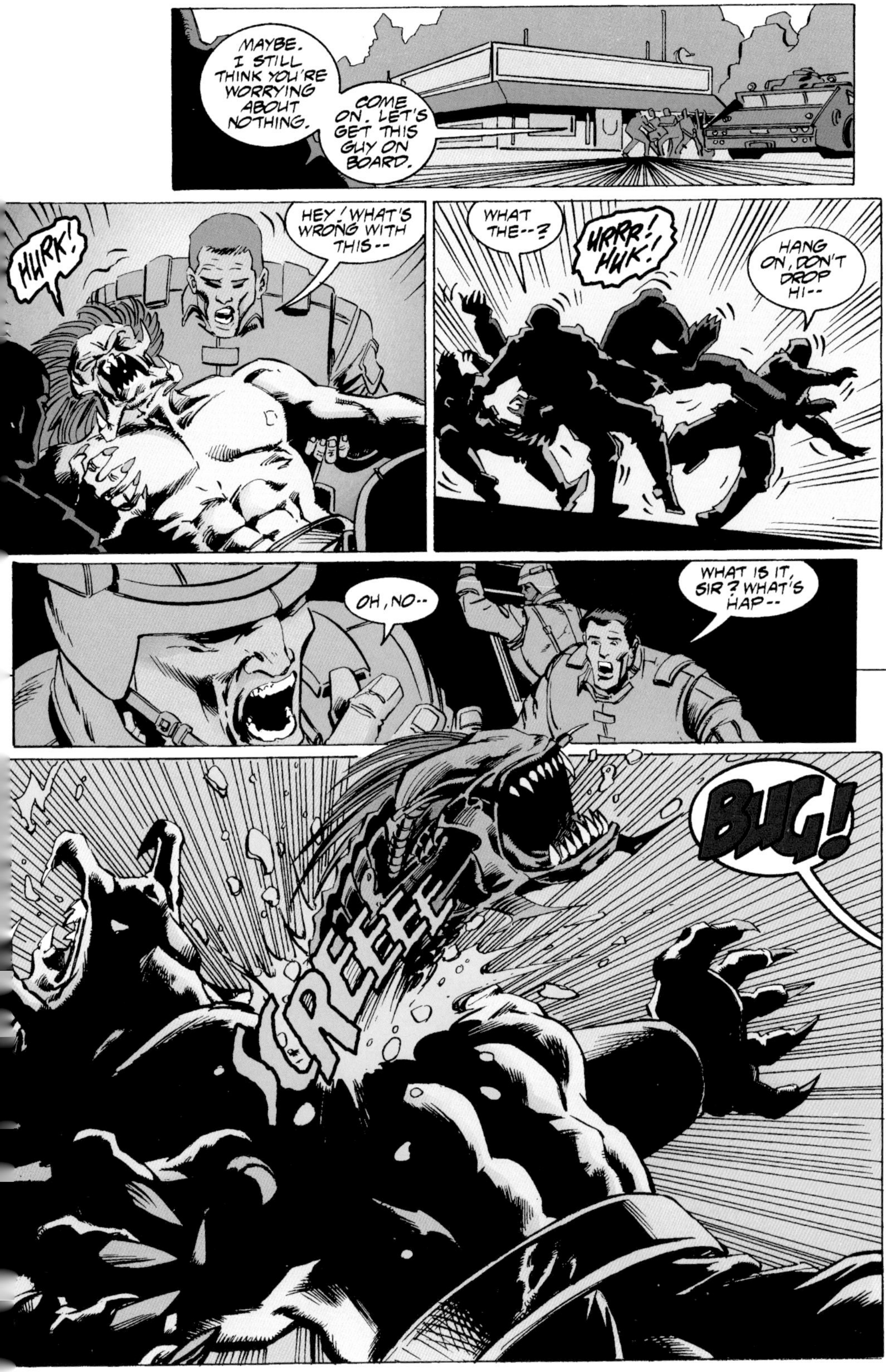
MAYBE. I STILL THINK YOU'RE WORRYING ABOUT NOTHING.
COME ON. LET'S GET THIS GUY ON BOARD.
HURK!
HEY! WHAT'S WRONG WITH THIS--
WHAT THE--?
URRR! HUK!
HANG ON, DON'T DROP HI--
OH, NO--
WHAT IS IT, SIR? WHAT'S HAP--
BUG!

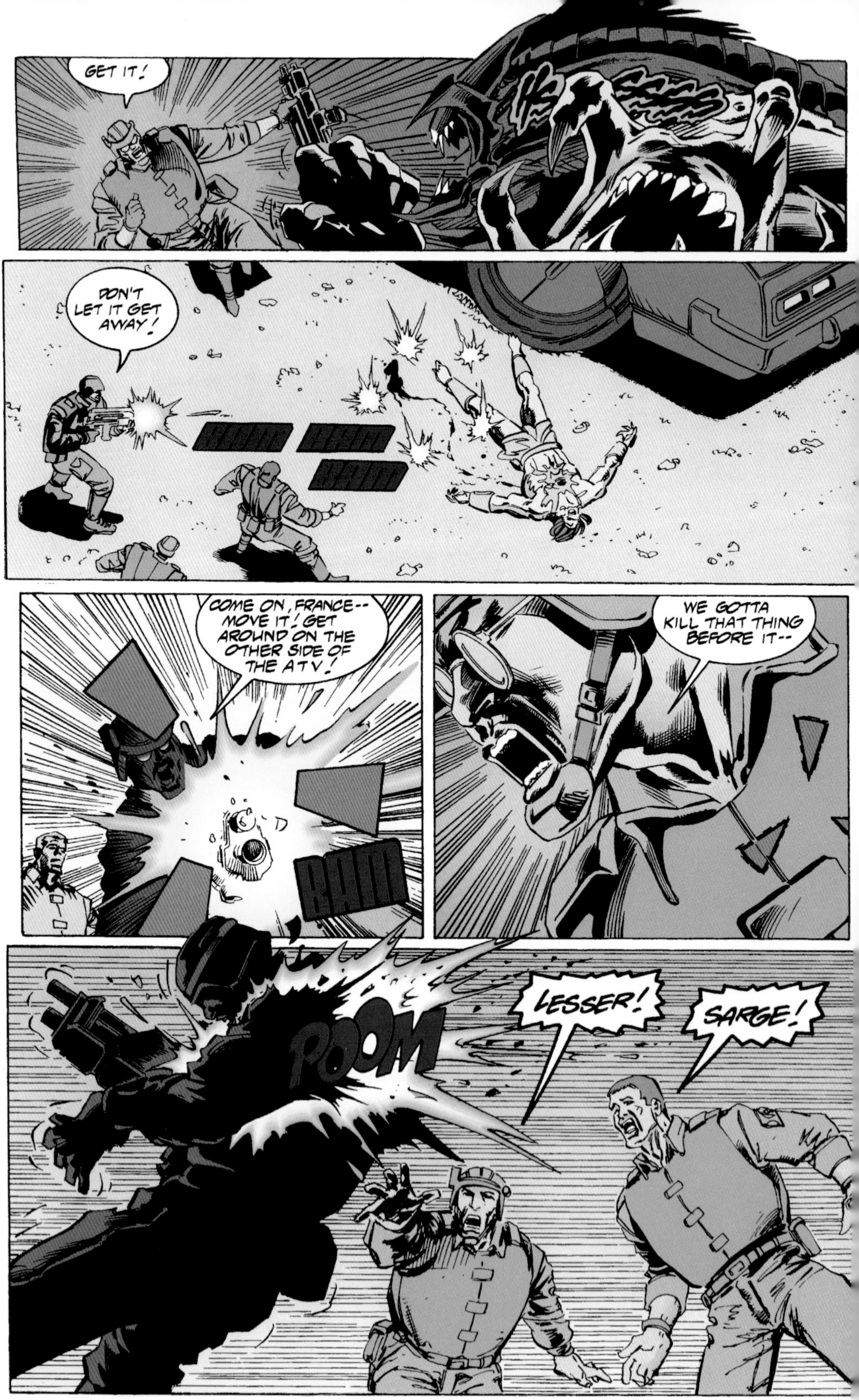
GET IT!
DON'T LET IT GET AWAY!
COME ON, FRANCE-- MOVE IT! GET AROUND ON THE OTHER SIDE OF THE ATV!
WE GOTTA KILL THAT THING BEFORE IT--
POOM
LESSER!
SARGE!

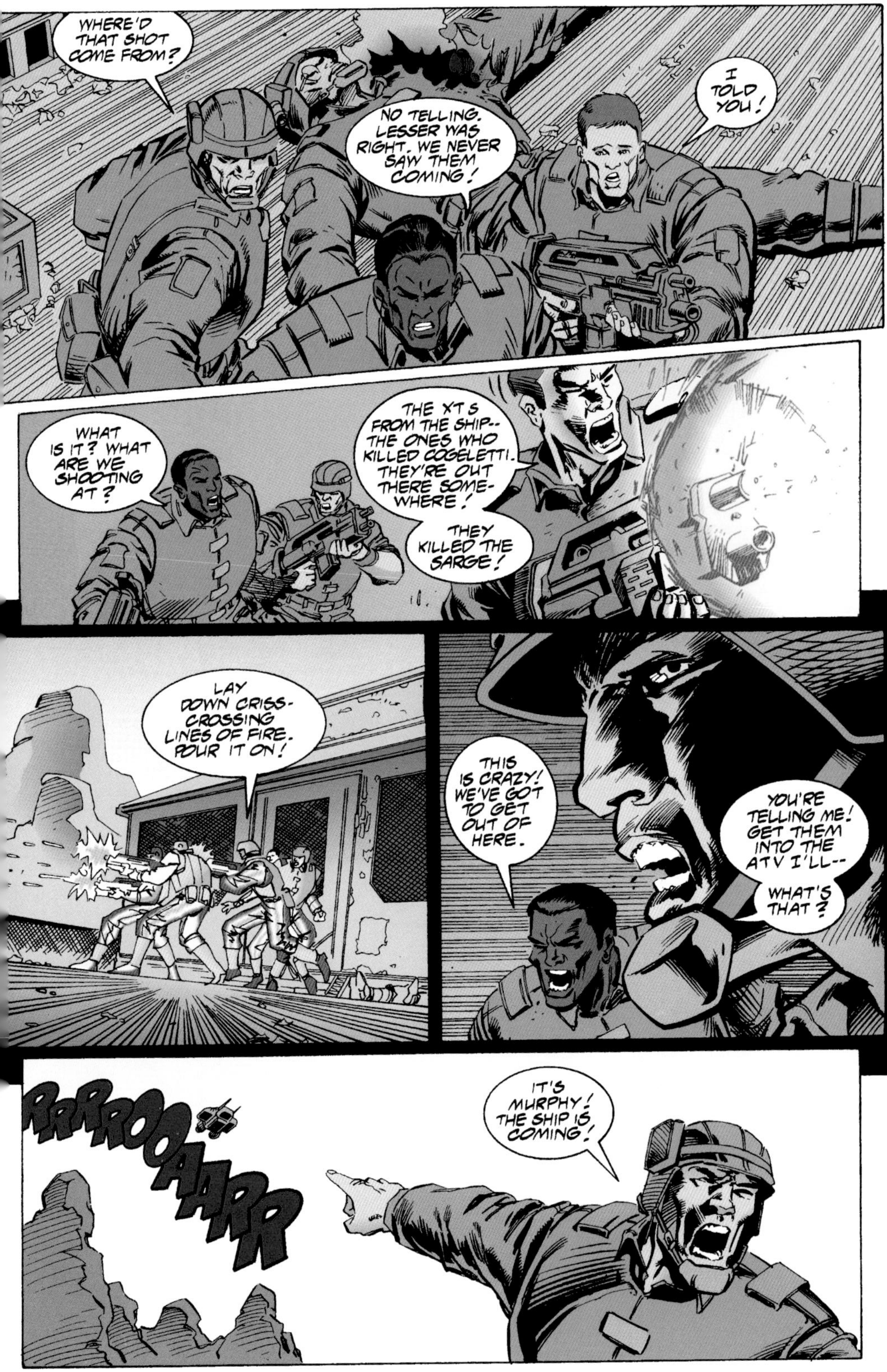
WHERE'D THAT SHOT COME FROM?
NO TELLING. LESSER WAS RIGHT. WE NEVER SAW THEM COMING!
I TOLD YOU!
WHAT IS IT? WHAT ARE WE SHOOTING AT?
THE XT S FROM THE SHIP-- THE ONES WHO KILLED COGELETTI. THEY'RE OUT THERE SOME-WHERE!
THEY KILLED THE SARGE!
LAY DOWN CRISS-CROSSING LINES OF FIRE. POUR IT ON!
THIS IS CRAZY! WE'VE GOT TO GET OUT OF HERE.
YOU'RE TELLING ME! GET THEM INTO THE ATV I'LL--
WHAT'S THAT?
RRRROOAARRR
IT'S MURPHY! THE SHIP IS COMING!

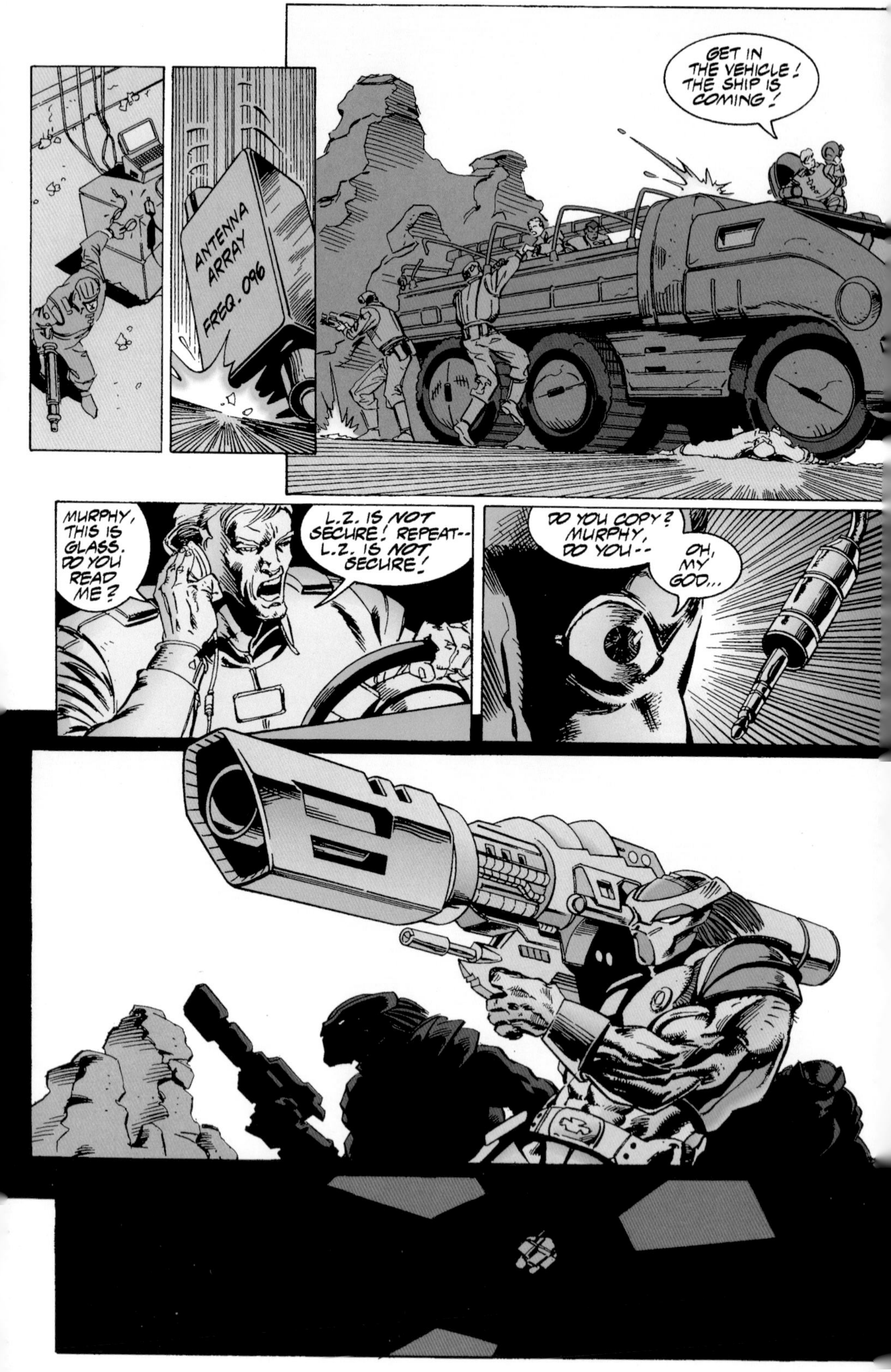
ANTENNA ARRAY FREQ. 096
GET IN THE VEHICLE! THE SHIP IS COMING!
MURPHY, THIS IS GLASS. DO YOU READ ME?
L.Z. IS NOT SECURE! REPEAT-- L.Z. IS NOT SECURE!
DO YOU COPY? MURPHY, DO YOU--
OH, MY GOD...

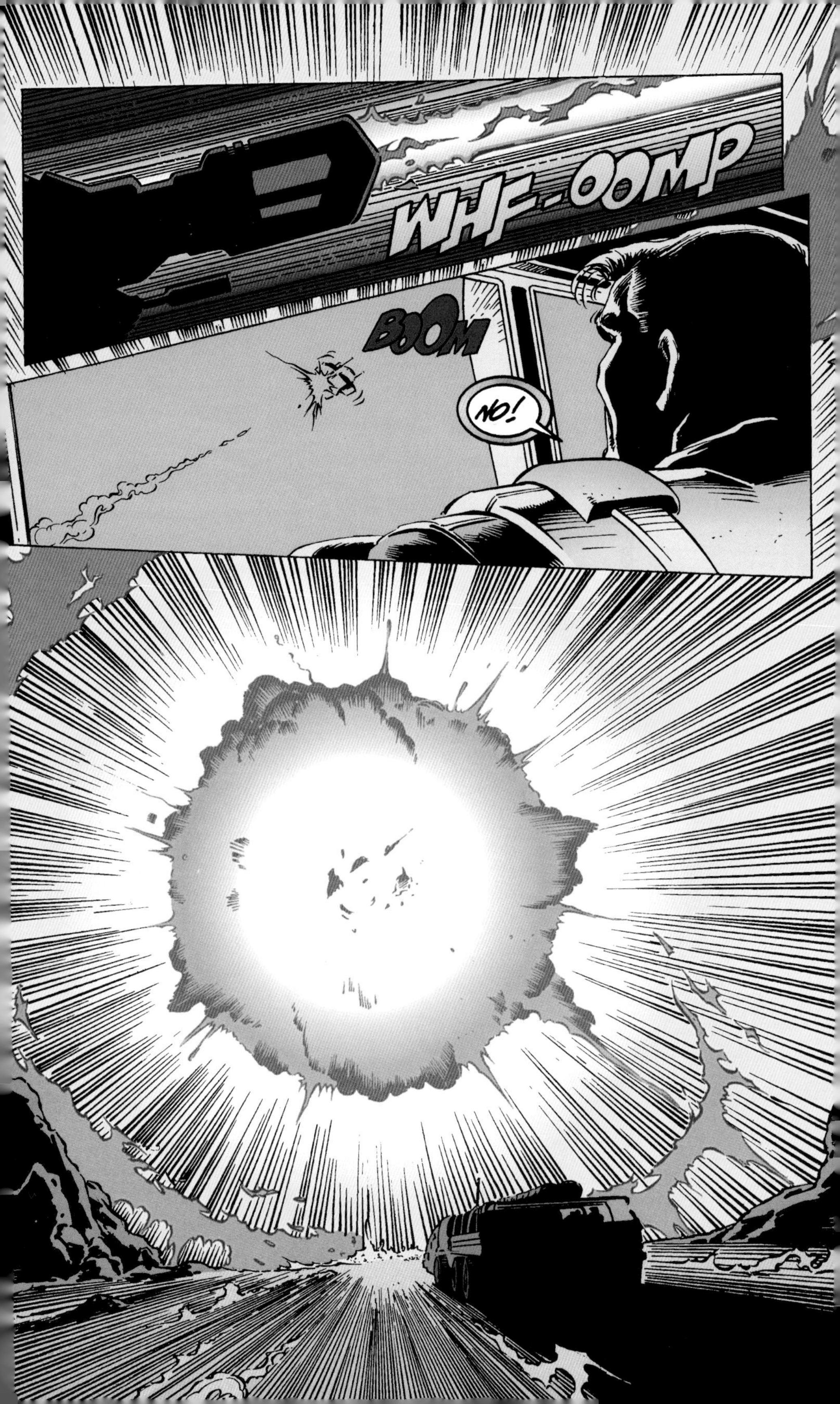
WHF-OOMP
BOOM
NO!

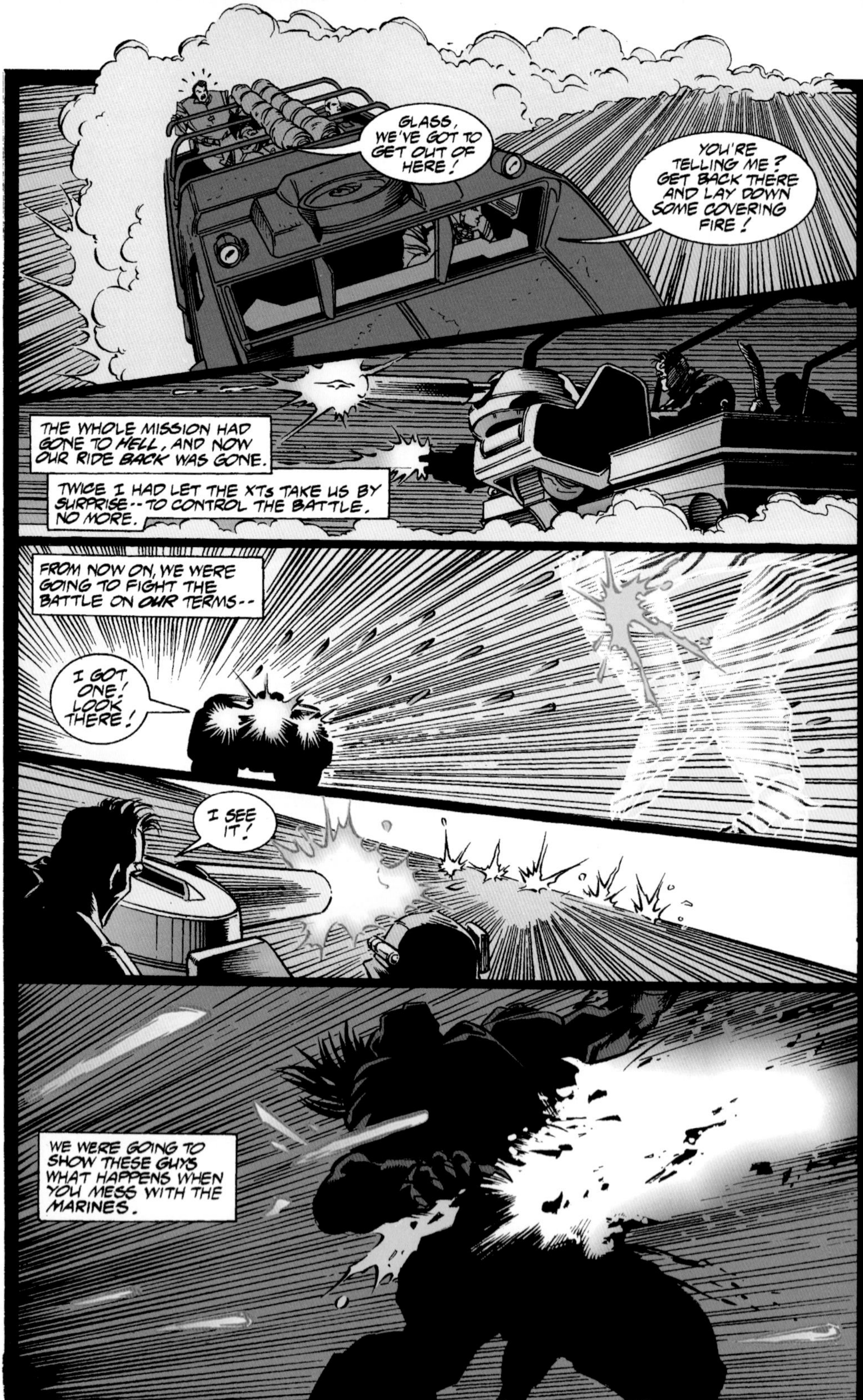
GLASS, WE'VE GOT TO GET OUT OF HERE!
YOU'RE TELLING ME? GET BACK THERE AND LAY DOWN SOME COVERING FIRE!
THE WHOLE MISSION HAD GONE TO HELL, AND NOW OUR RIDE BACK WAS GONE.
TWICE I HAD LET THE XTs TAKE US BY SURPRISE--TO CONTROL THE BATTLE. NO MORE.
FROM NOW ON, WE WERE GOING TO FIGHT THE BATTLE ON OUR TERMS--
I GOT ONE! LOOK THERE!
I SEE IT!
WE WERE GOING TO SHOW THESE GUYS WHAT HAPPENS WHEN YOU MESS WITH THE MARINES.

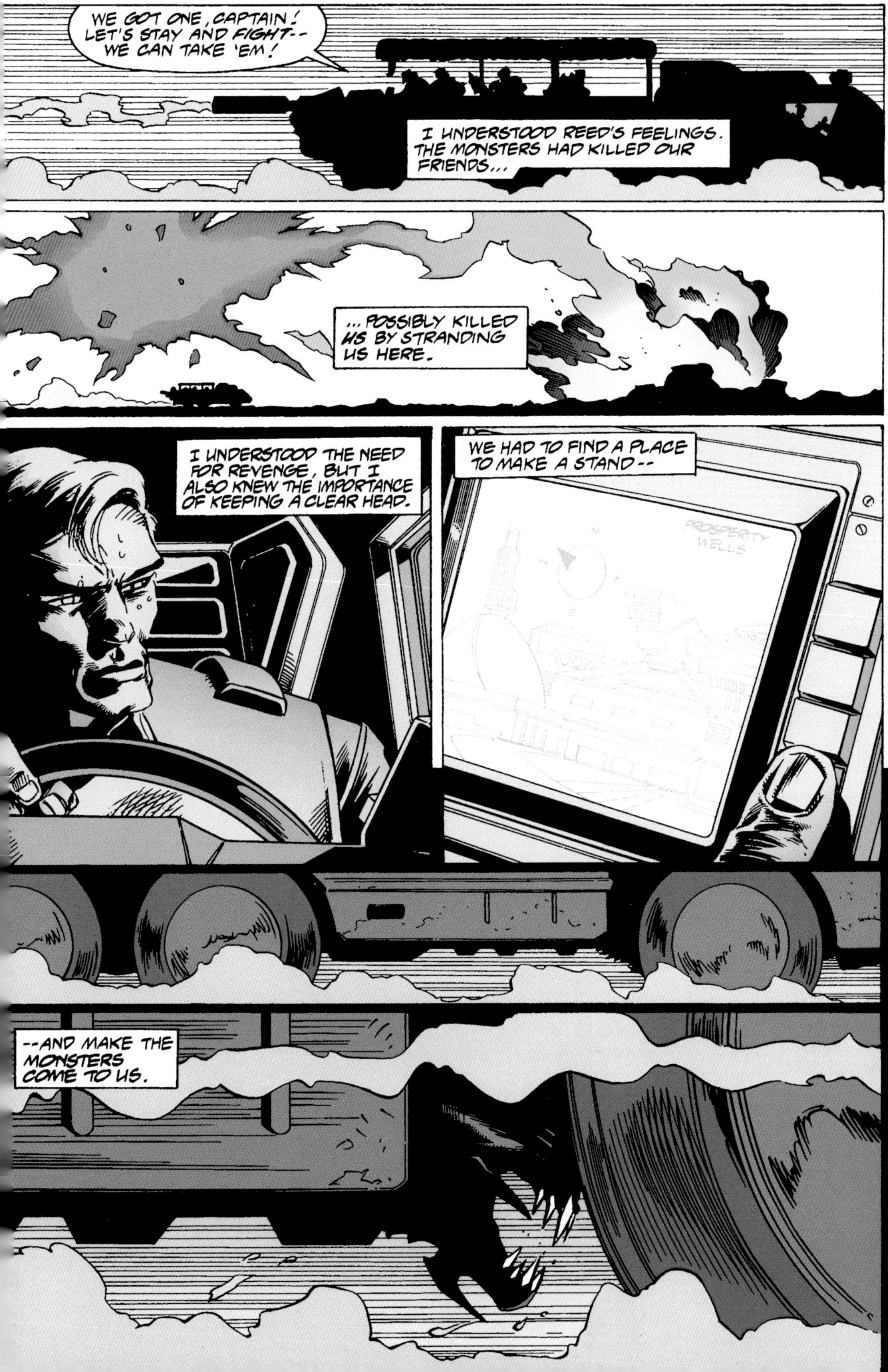
WE GOT ONE, CAPTAIN! LET'S STAY AND FIGHT-- WE CAN TAKE 'EM!
I UNDERSTOOD REED'S FEELINGS. THE MONSTERS HAD KILLED OUR FRIENDS...
...POSSIBLY KILLED US BY STRANDING US HERE.
I UNDERSTOOD THE NEED FOR REVENGE, BUT I ALSO KNEW THE IMPORTANCE OF KEEPING A CLEAR HEAD.
WE HAD TO FIND A PLACE TO MAKE A STAND--
PROSPERITY WELLS
--AND MAKE THE MONSTERS COME TO US.

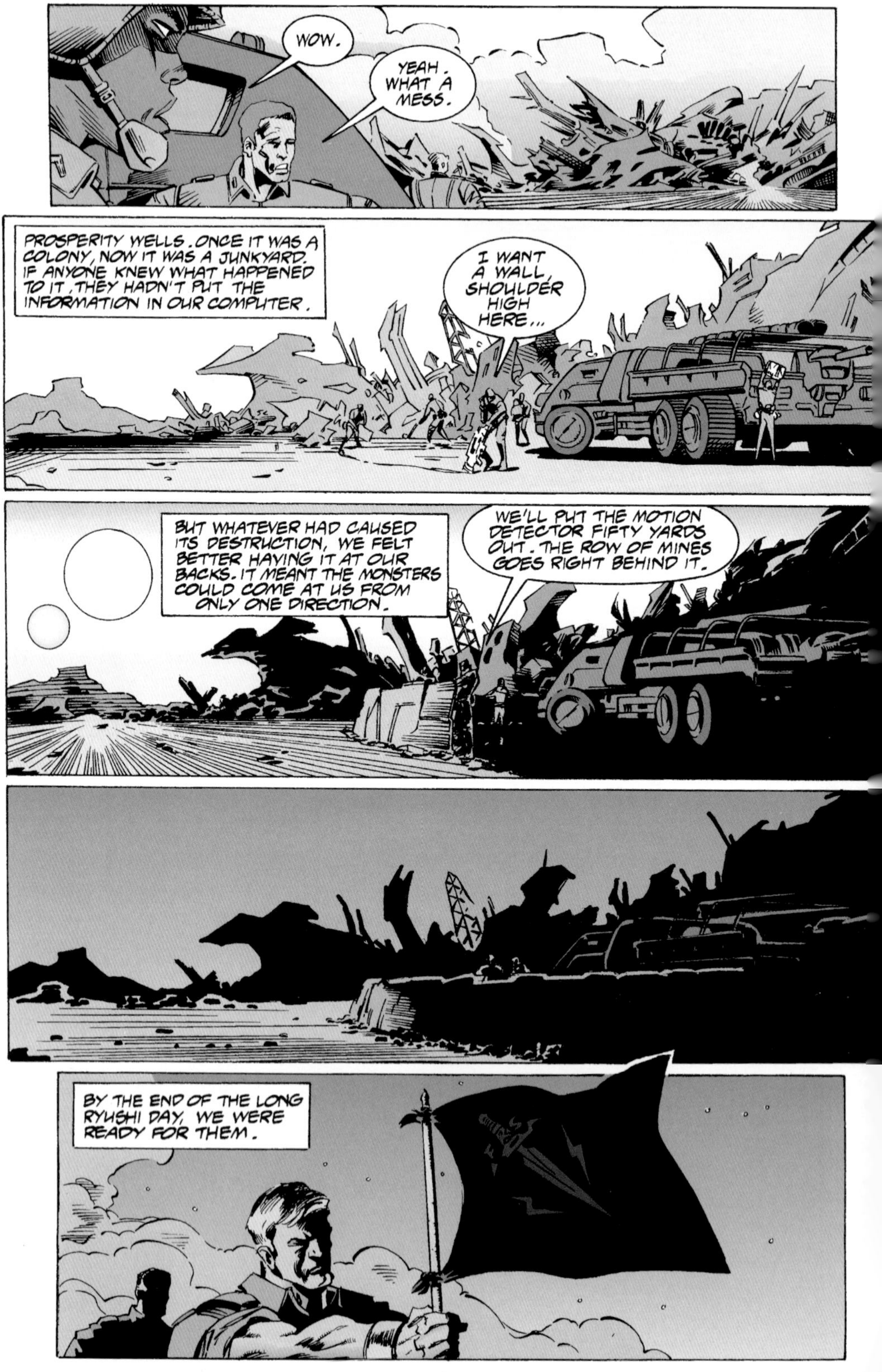
WOW.
YEAH. WHAT A MESS.
PROSPERITY WELLS. ONCE IT WAS A COLONY, NOW IT WAS A JUNKYARD. IF ANYONE KNEW WHAT HAPPENED TO IT, THEY HADN'T PUT THE INFORMATION IN OUR COMPUTER.
I WANT A WALL, SHOULDER HIGH HERE...
BUT WHATEVER HAD CAUSED ITS DESTRUCTION, WE FELT BETTER HAVING IT AT OUR BACKS. IT MEANT THE MONSTERS COULD COME AT US FROM ONLY ONE DIRECTION.
WE'LL PUT THE MOTION DETECTOR FIFTY YARDS OUT. THE ROW OF MINES GOES RIGHT BEHIND IT.
BY THE END OF THE LONG RYUSHI DAY, WE WERE READY FOR THEM.

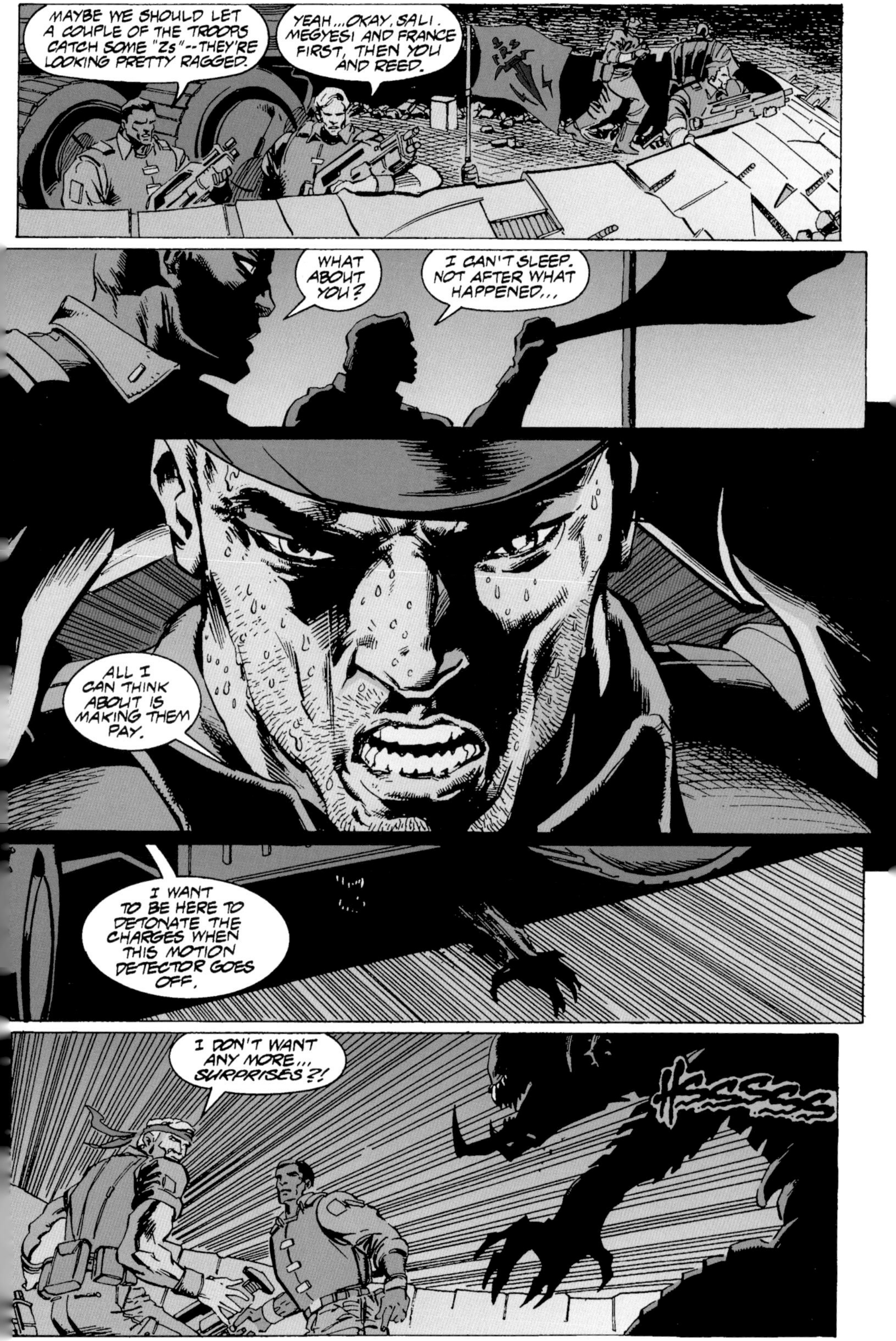
MAYBE WE SHOULD LET A COUPLE OF THE TROOPS CATCH SOME "Zs"--THEY'RE LOOKING PRETTY RAGGED.
YEAH...OKAY, SALI. MEGYESI AND FRANCE FIRST, THEN YOU AND REED.
WHAT ABOUT YOU?
I CAN'T SLEEP. NOT AFTER WHAT HAPPENED...
ALL I CAN THINK ABOUT IS MAKING THEM PAY.
I WANT TO BE HERE TO DETONATE THE CHARGES WHEN THIS MOTION DETECTOR GOES OFF.
I DON'T WANT ANY MORE... SURPRISES?!
HSSSSS

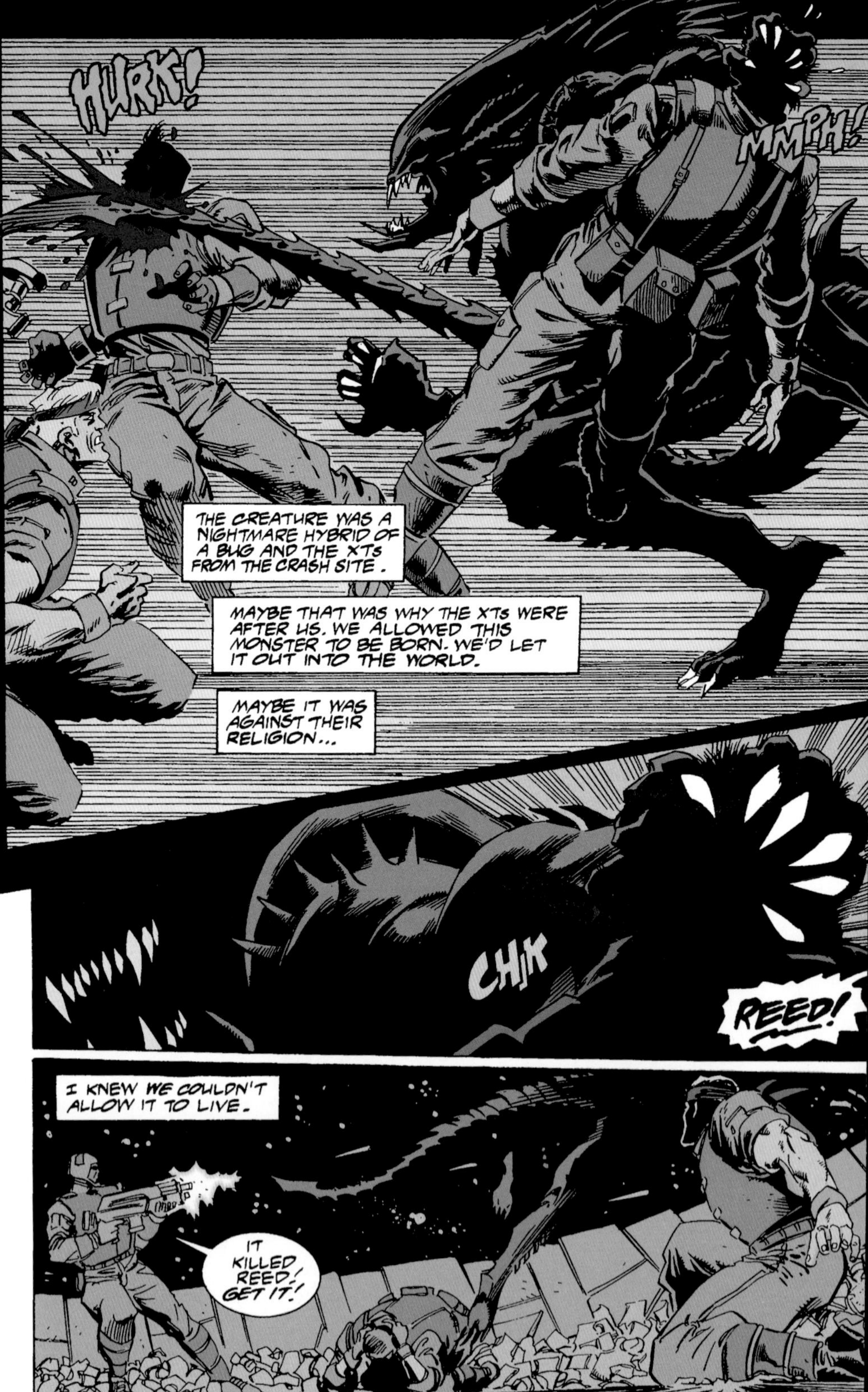
HURK!
MMPH!
THE CREATURE WAS A NIGHTMARE HYBRID OF A BUG AND THE XTs FROM THE CRASH SITE.
MAYBE THAT WAS WHY THE XTs WERE AFTER US. WE ALLOWED THIS MONSTER TO BE BORN. WE'D LET IT OUT INTO THE WORLD.
MAYBE IT WAS AGAINST THEIR RELIGION...
CHK
REED!
I KNEW WE COULDN'T ALLOW IT TO LIVE.
IT KILLED REED! GET IT!

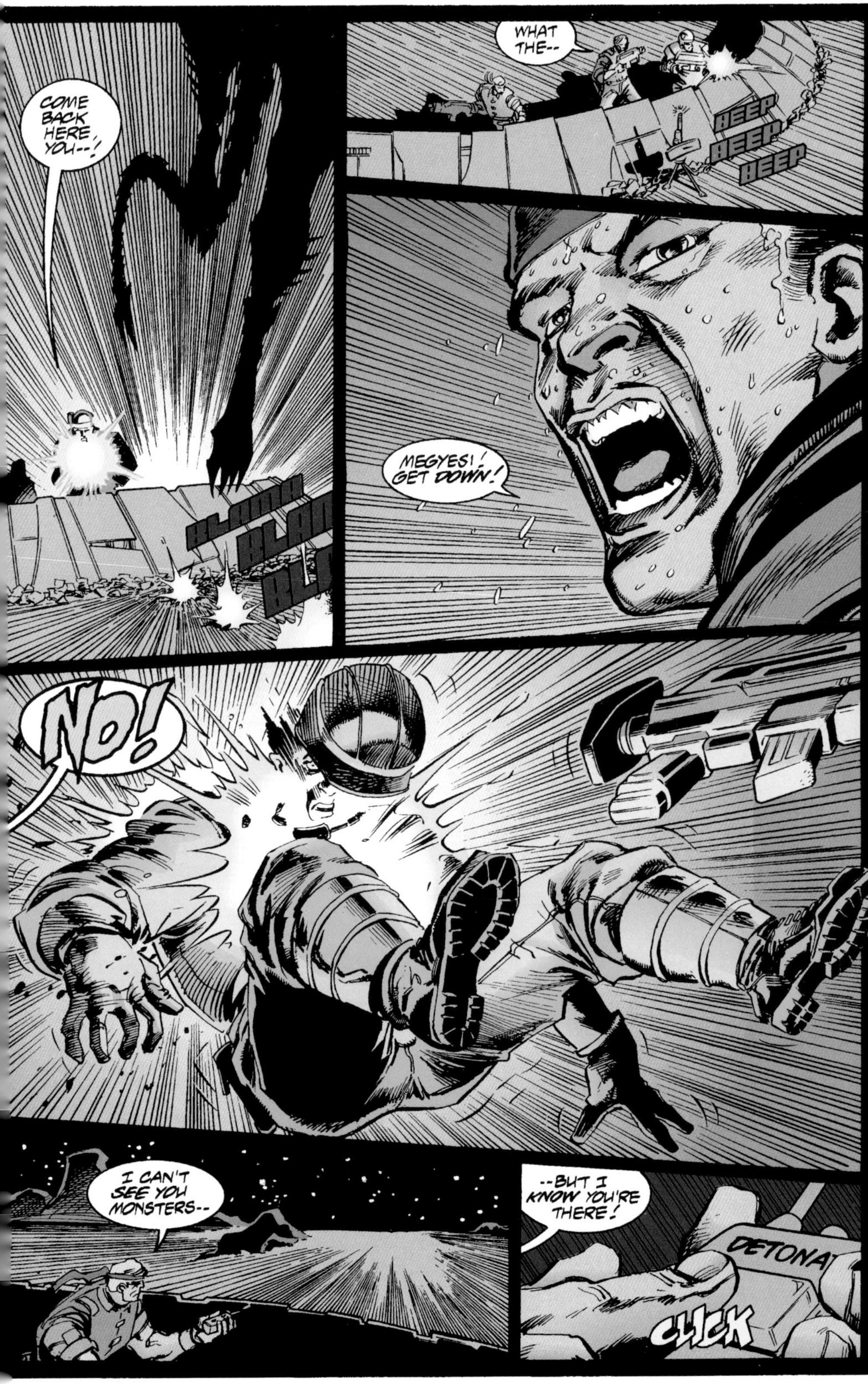
COME BACK HERE, YOU--!
WHAT THE--
BEEP BEEP BEEP
MEGYES! GET DOWN!
NO!
I CAN'T SEE YOU MONSTERS--
--BUT I KNOW YOU'RE THERE!
DETONA
CLICK

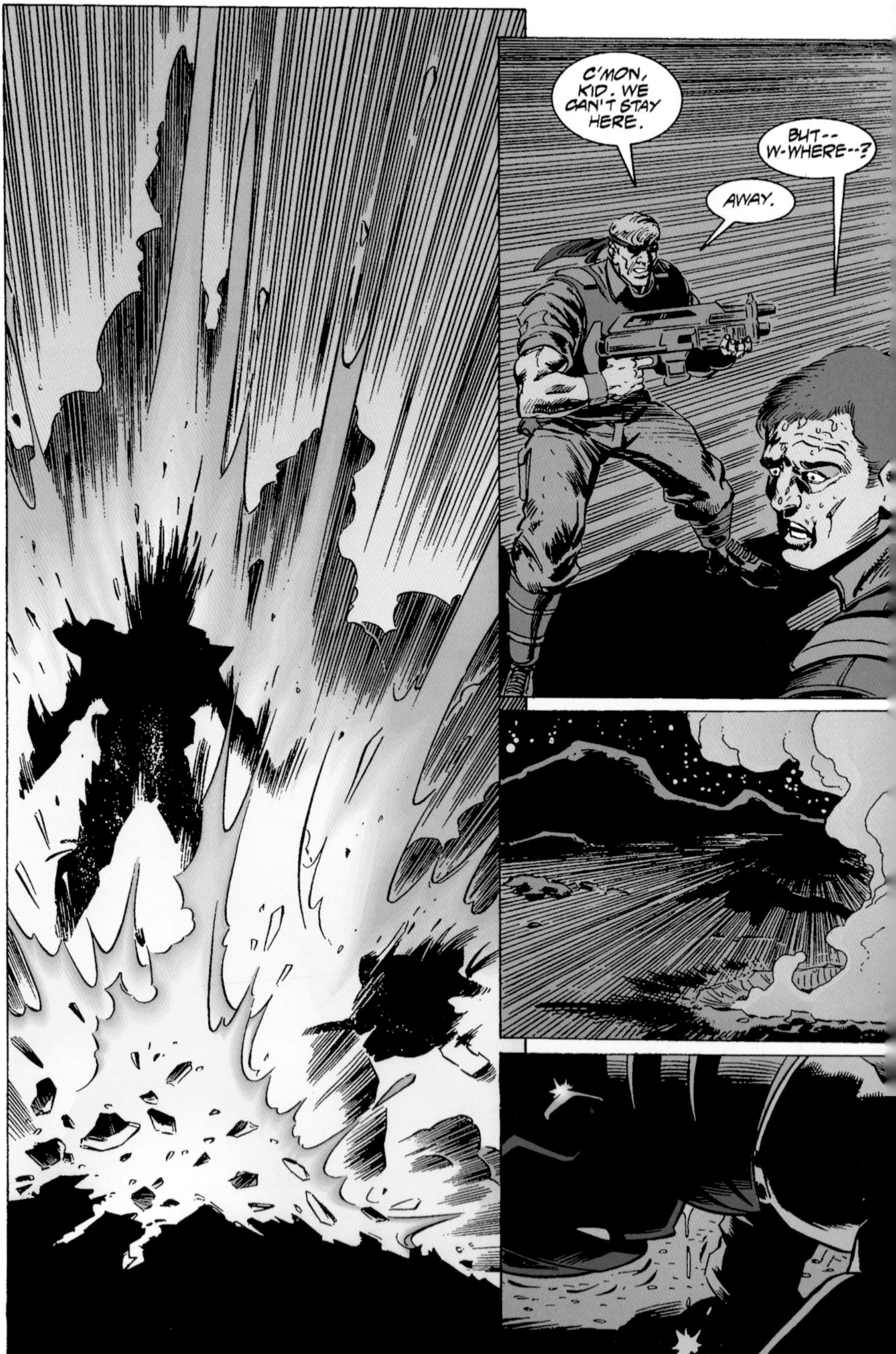
C'MON, KID. WE CAN'T STAY HERE.
BUT-- W-WHERE--?
AWAY.

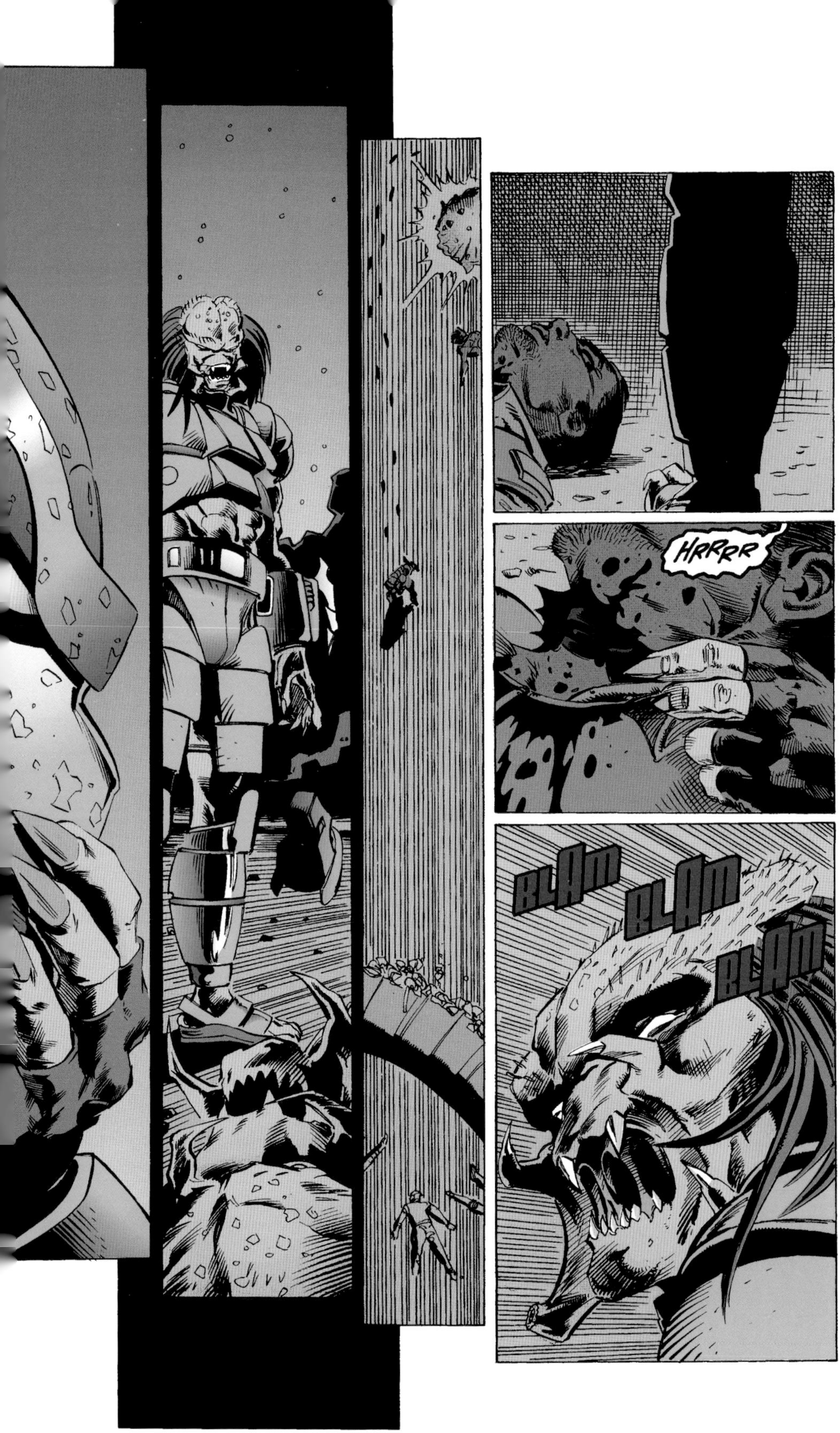
HRRRR
BLAM
BLAM
BLAM

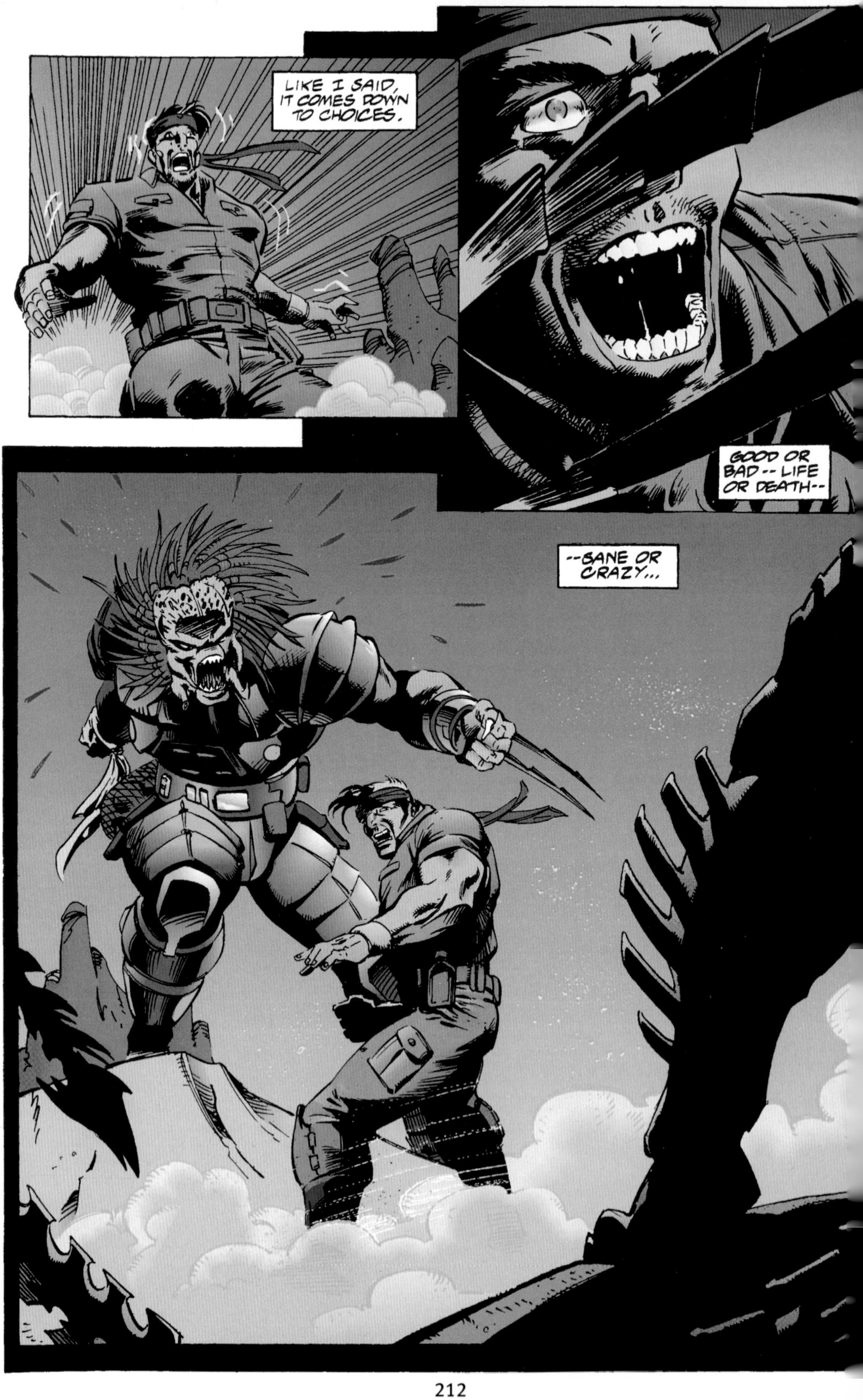
LIKE I SAID, IT COMES DOWN TO CHOICES.
GOOD OR BAD -- LIFE OR DEATH --
-- SANE OR CRAZY...

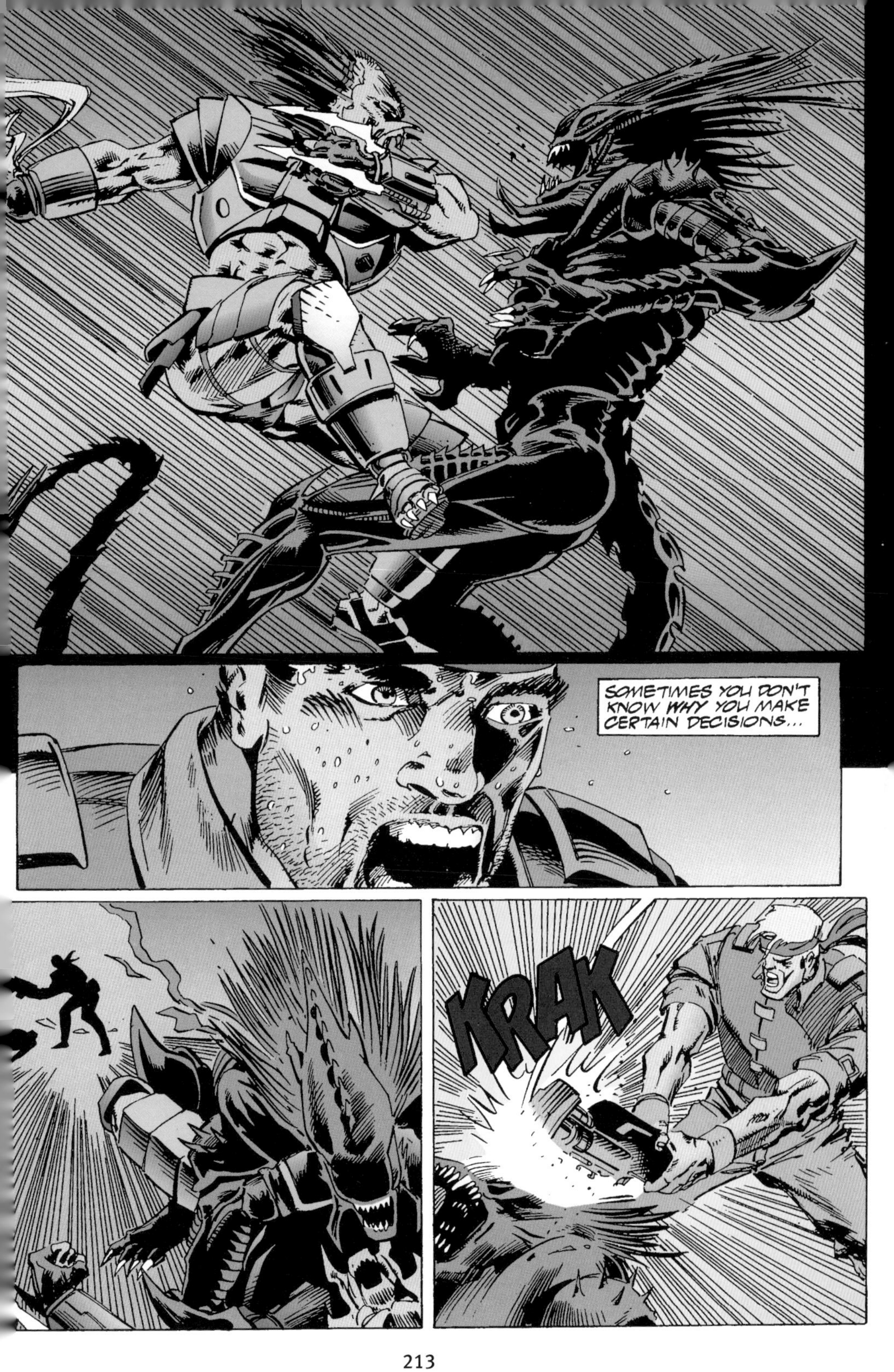
SOMETIMES YOU DON'T KNOW WHY YOU MAKE CERTAIN DECISIONS...
KRAK

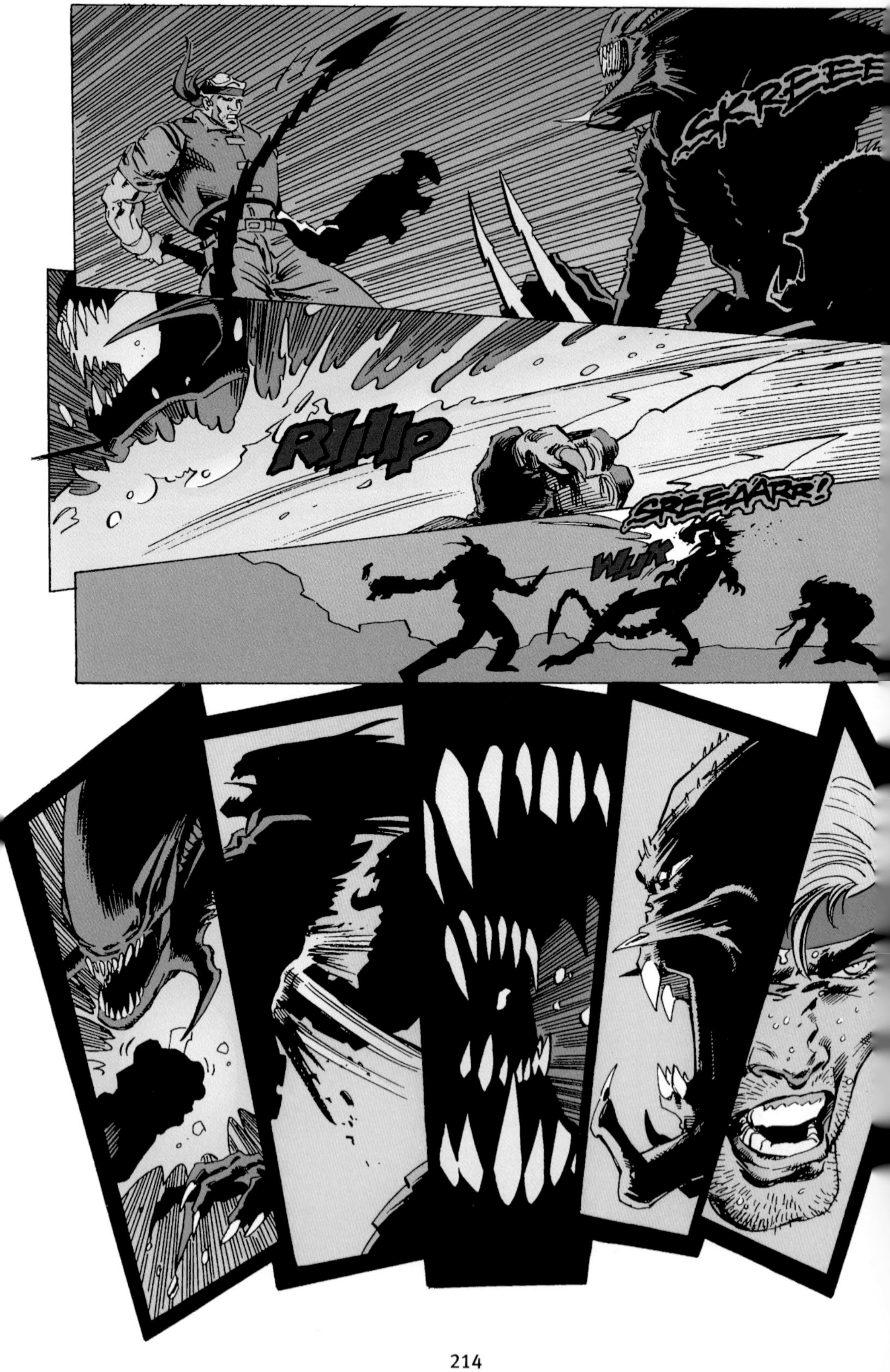
SKREEE
RIIIP
SREEAARR!
WUK

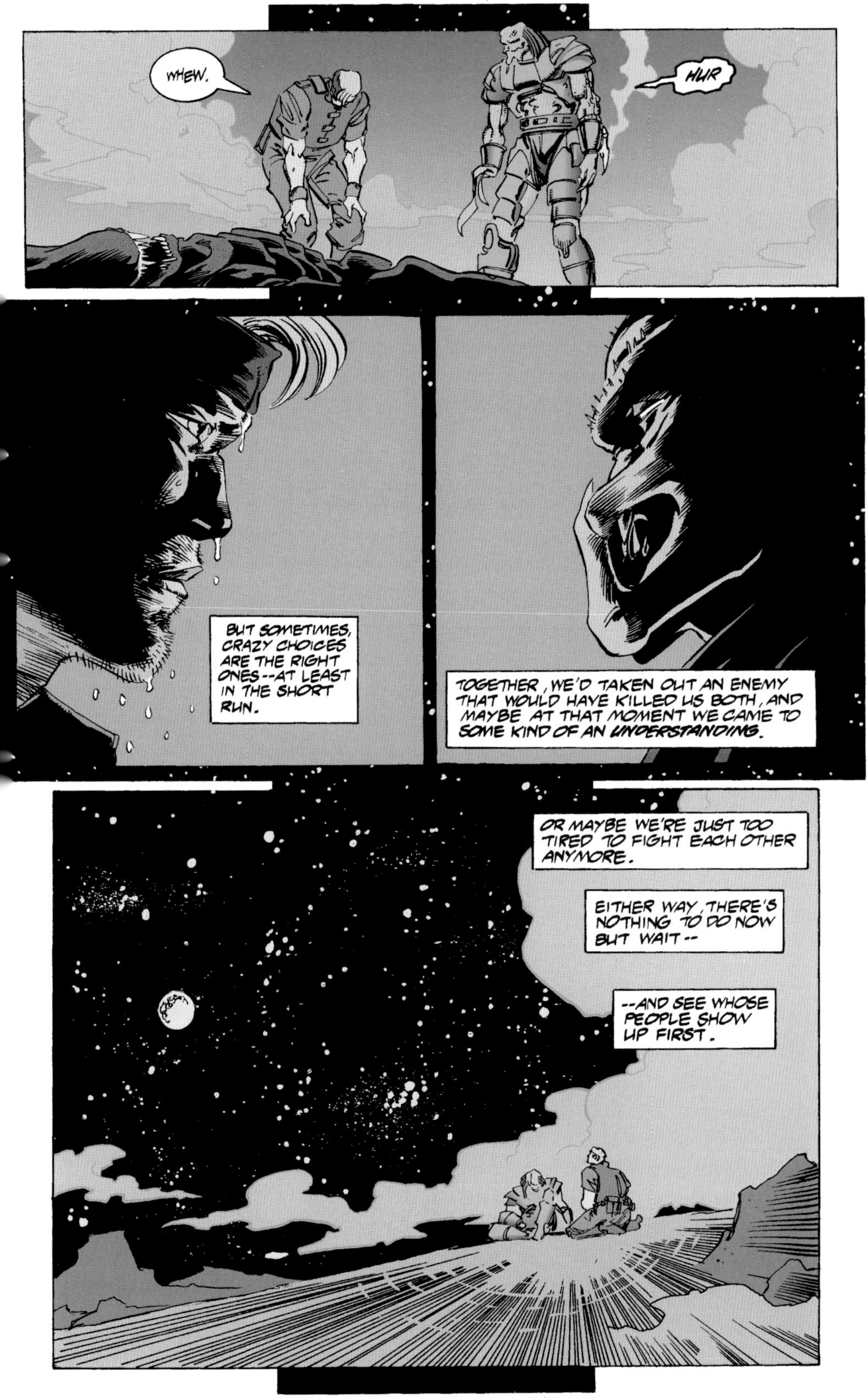
WHEW.
HUR
BUT SOMETIMES, CRAZY CHOICES ARE THE RIGHT ONES--AT LEAST IN THE SHORT RUN.
TOGETHER, WE'D TAKEN OUT AN ENEMY THAT WOULD HAVE KILLED US BOTH, AND MAYBE AT THAT MOMENT WE CAME TO SOME KIND OF AN UNDERSTANDING.
OR MAYBE WE'RE JUST TOO TIRED TO FIGHT EACH OTHER ANYMORE.
EITHER WAY, THERE'S NOTHING TO DO NOW BUT WAIT--
--AND SEE WHOSE PEOPLE SHOW UP FIRST.

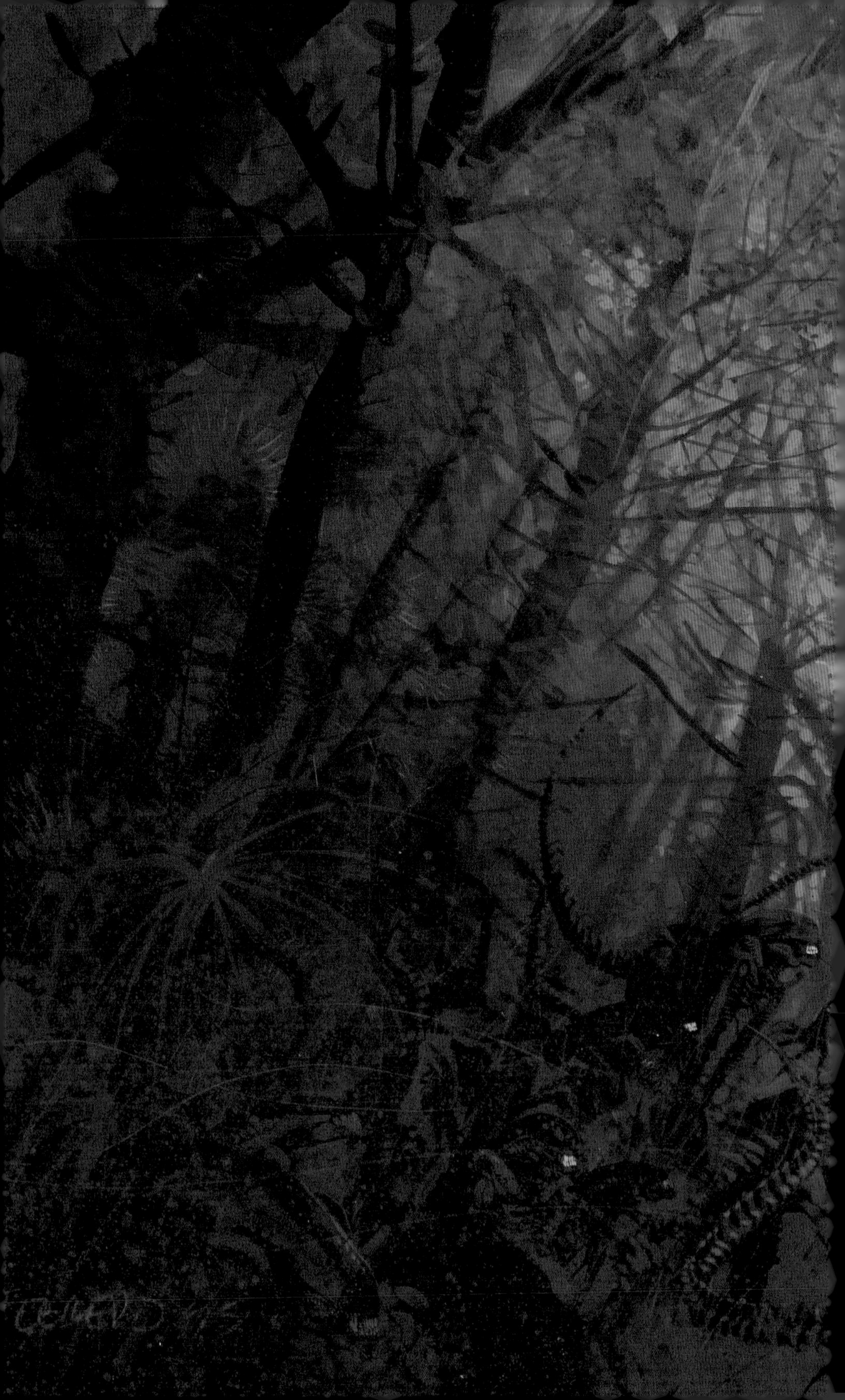

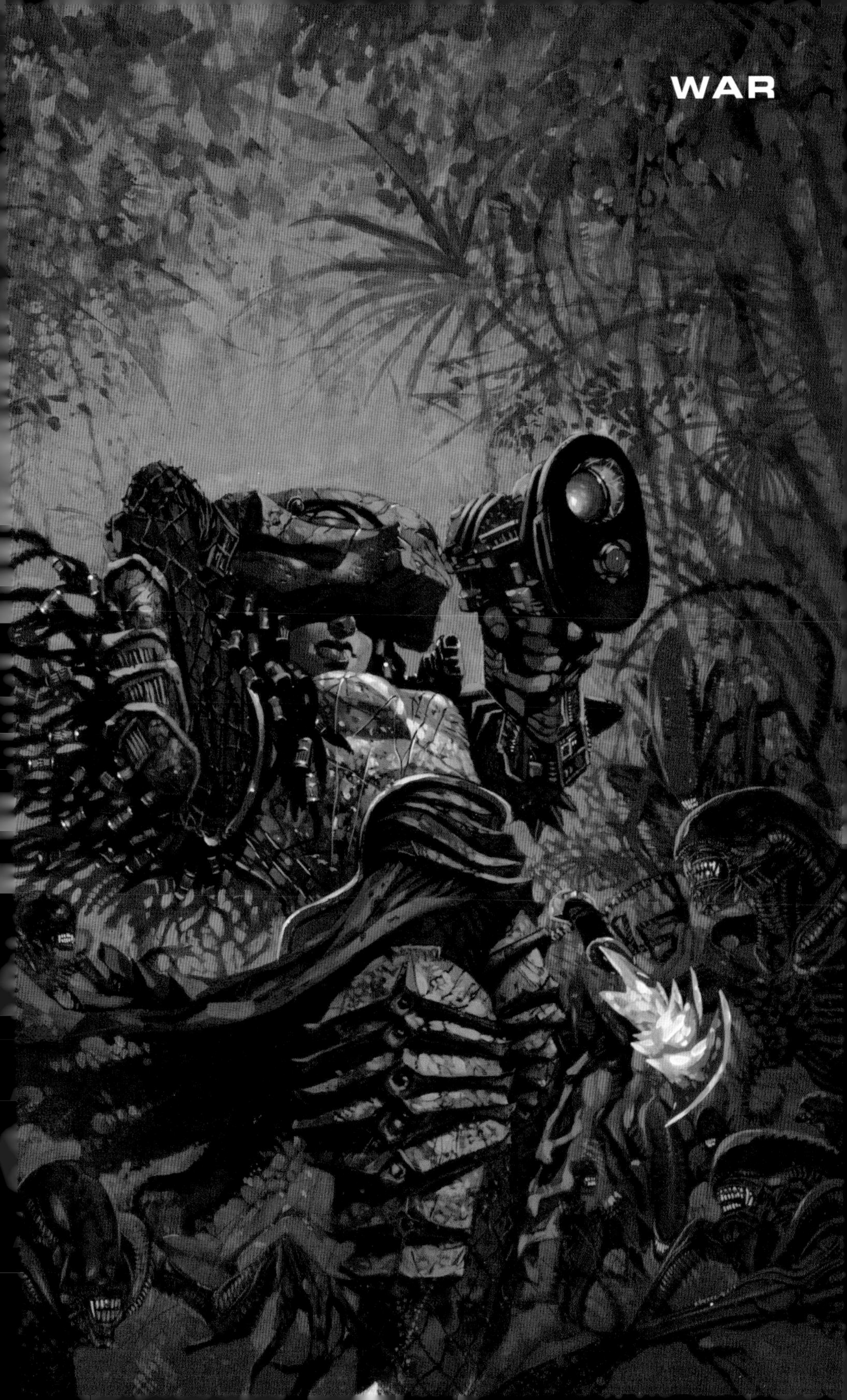
WAR

PART 1

script
RANDY STRADLEY

art
CHRIS WARNER

colors
JAMES SINCLAIR

lettering
STEVE DUTRO

title illustration
DUNCAN FEGREDO

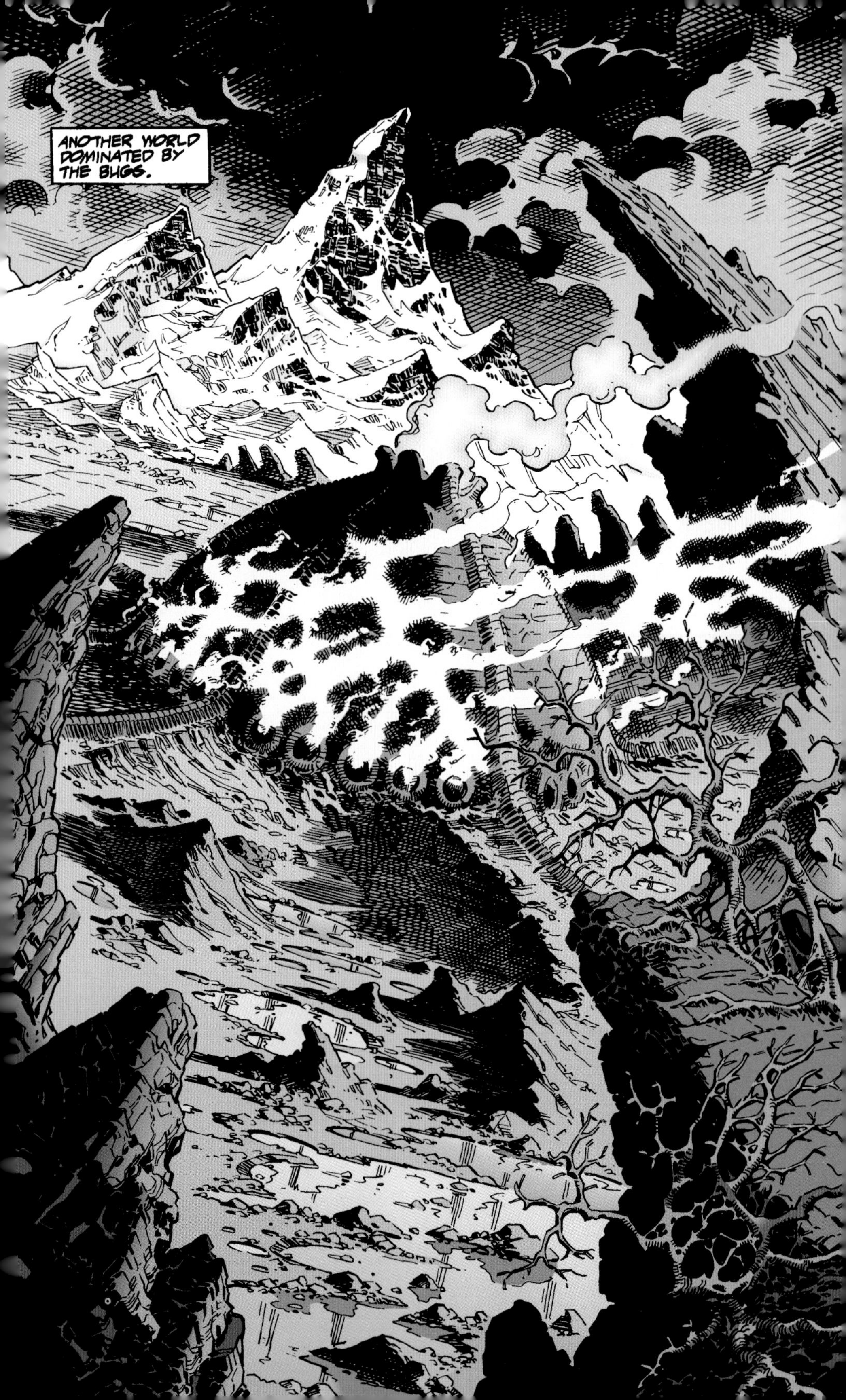
ANOTHER WORLD DOMINATED BY THE BUGS.

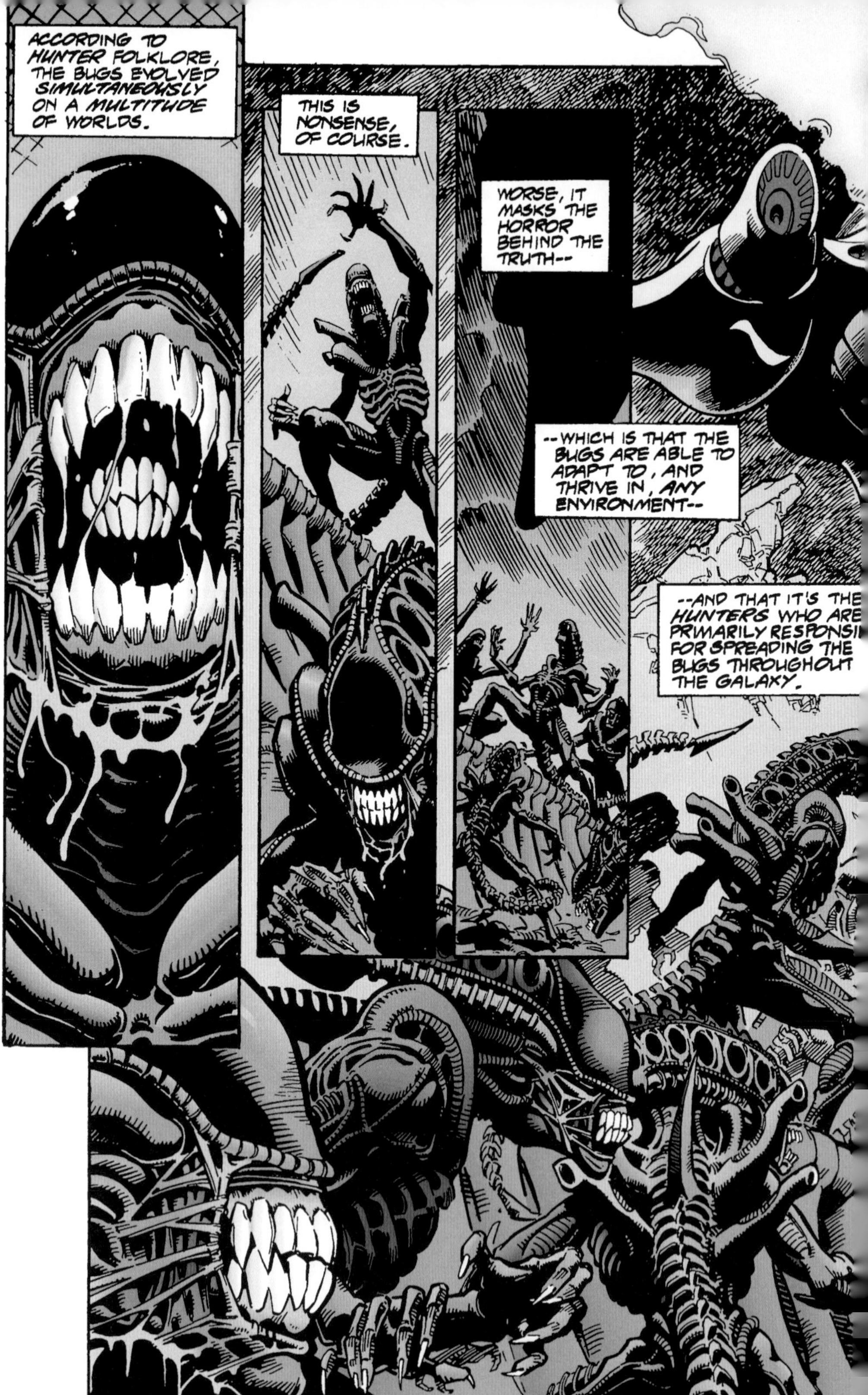
ACCORDING TO HUNTER FOLKLORE, THE BUGS EVOLVED SIMULTANEOUSLY ON A MULTITUDE OF WORLDS.
THIS IS NONSENSE, OF COURSE.
WORSE, IT MASKS THE HORROR BEHIND THE TRUTH--
--WHICH IS THAT THE BUGS ARE ABLE TO ADAPT TO, AND THRIVE IN, ANY ENVIRONMENT--
--AND THAT IT'S THE HUNTERS WHO ARE PRIMARILY RESPONSI FOR SPREADING THE BUGS THROUGHOUT THE GALAXY.

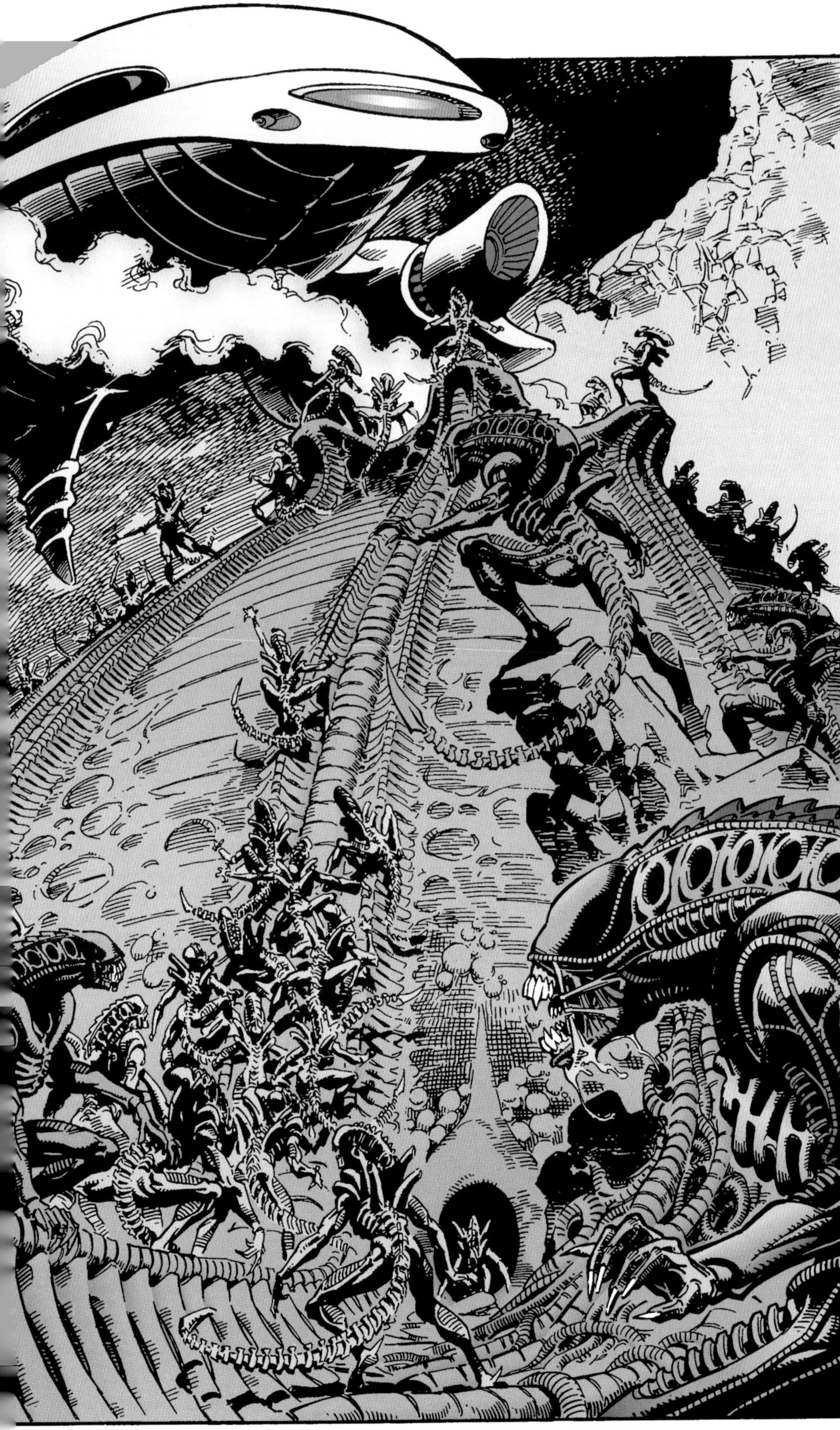

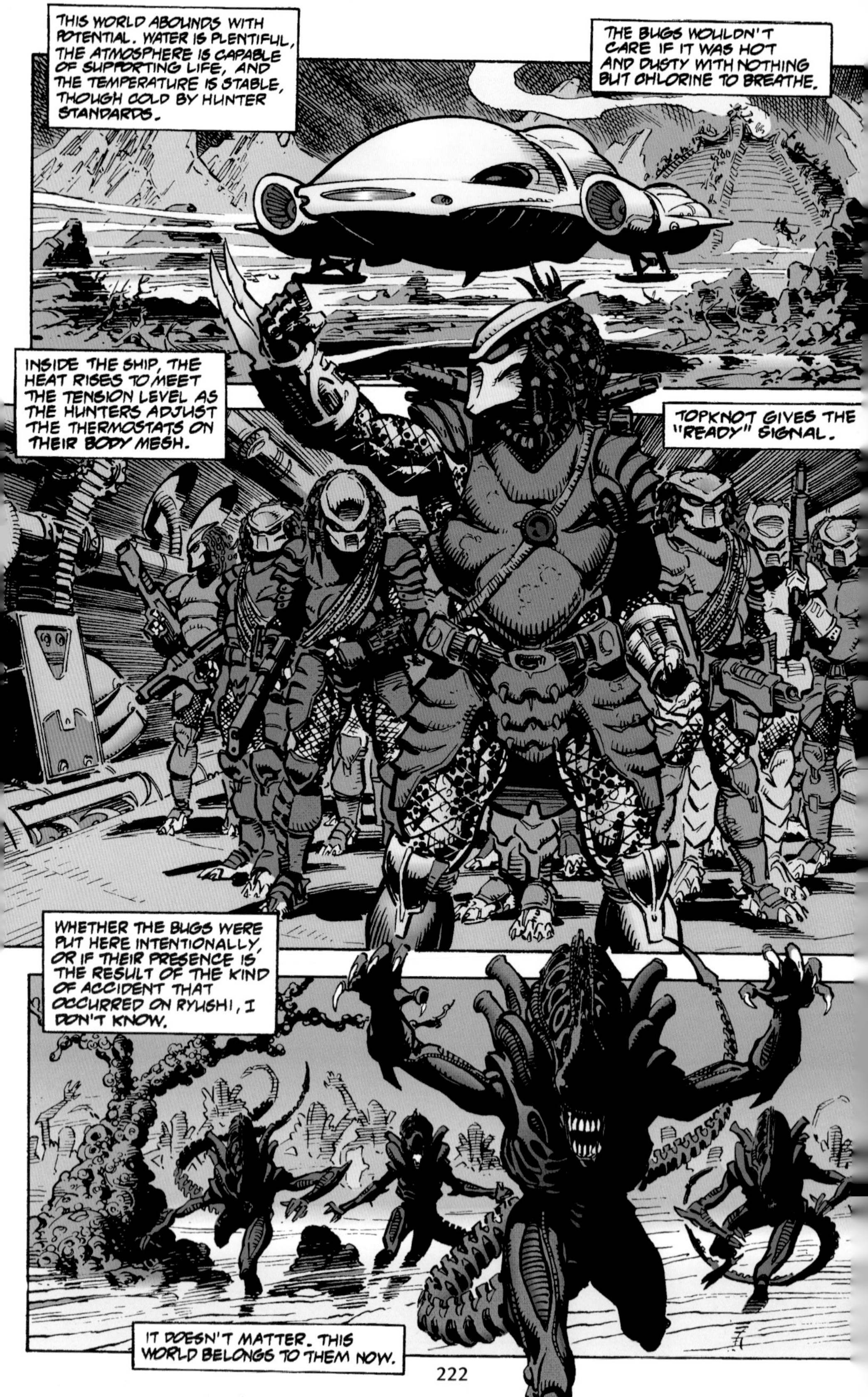
THIS WORLD ABOUNDS WITH POTENTIAL. WATER IS PLENTIFUL, THE ATMOSPHERE IS CAPABLE OF SUPPORTING LIFE, AND THE TEMPERATURE IS STABLE, THOUGH COLD BY HUNTER STANDARDS.
THE BUGS WOULDN'T CARE IF IT WAS HOT AND DUSTY WITH NOTHING BUT CHLORINE TO BREATHE.
INSIDE THE SHIP, THE HEAT RISES TO MEET THE TENSION LEVEL AS THE HUNTERS ADJUST THE THERMOSTATS ON THEIR BODY MESH.
TOPKNOT GIVES THE "READY" SIGNAL.
WHETHER THE BUGS WERE PUT HERE INTENTIONALLY, OR IF THEIR PRESENCE IS THE RESULT OF THE KIND OF ACCIDENT THAT OCCURRED ON RYUSHI, I DON'T KNOW.
IT DOESN'T MATTER. THIS WORLD BELONGS TO THEM NOW.

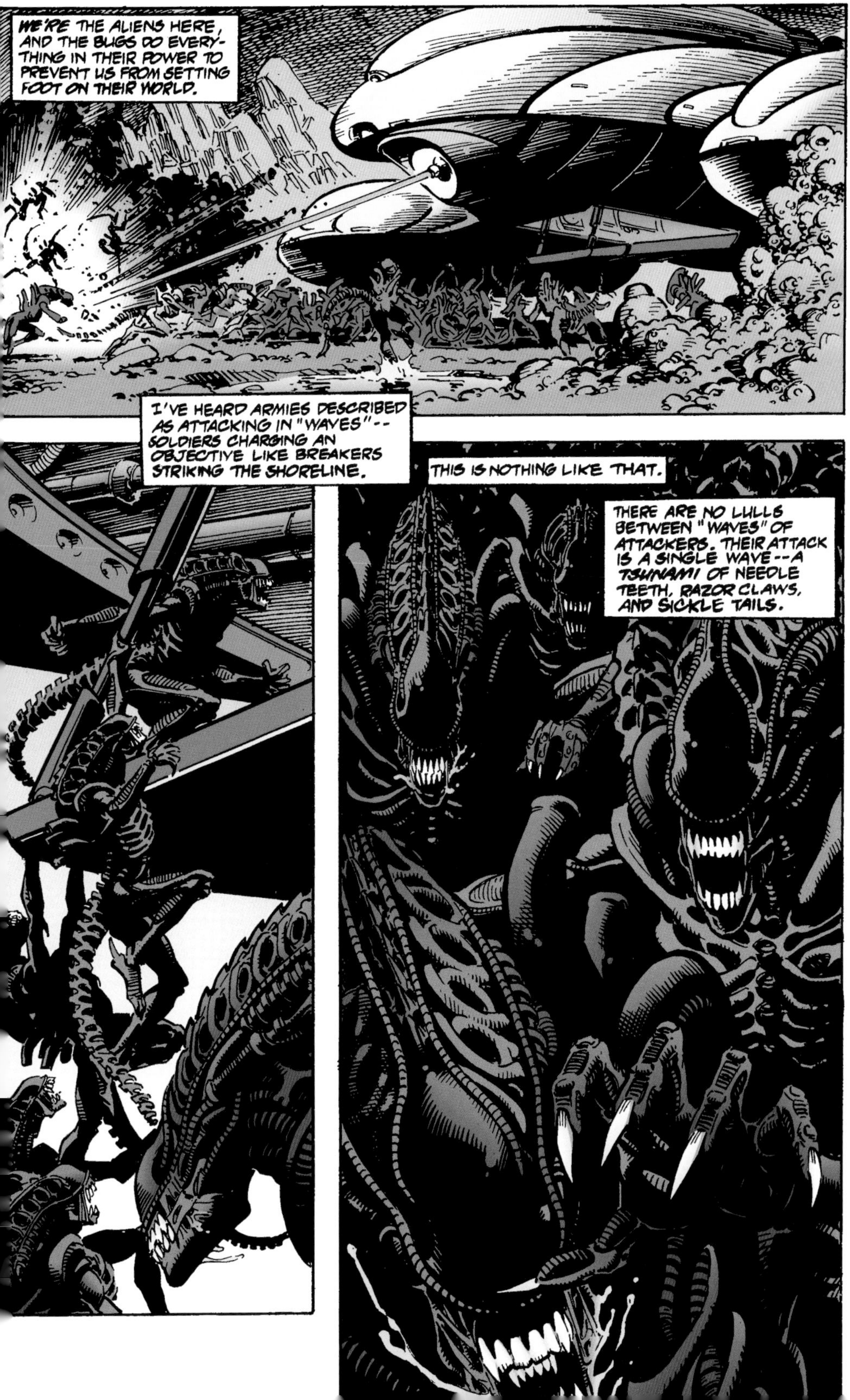
WE'RE THE ALIENS HERE, AND THE BUGS DO EVERYTHING IN THEIR POWER TO PREVENT US FROM SETTING FOOT ON THEIR WORLD.
I'VE HEARD ARMIES DESCRIBED AS ATTACKING IN "WAVES"-- SOLDIERS CHARGING AN OBJECTIVE LIKE BREAKERS STRIKING THE SHORELINE.
THIS IS NOTHING LIKE THAT.
THERE ARE NO LULLS BETWEEN "WAVES" OF ATTACKERS. THEIR ATTACK IS A SINGLE WAVE--A TSUNAMI OF NEEDLE TEETH, RAZOR CLAWS, AND SICKLE TAILS.

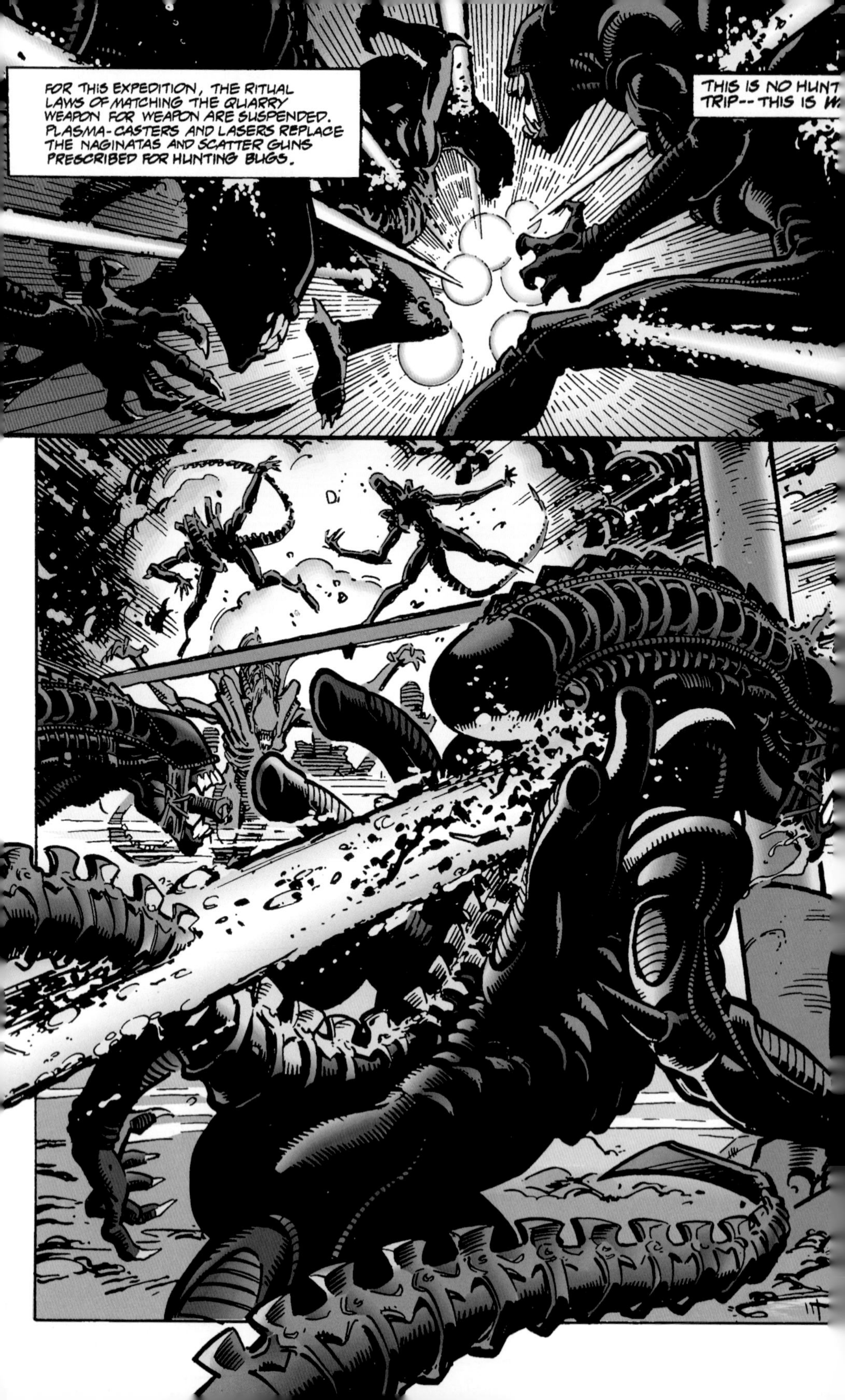
FOR THIS EXPEDITION, THE RITUAL LAWS OF MATCHING THE QUARRY WEAPON FOR WEAPON ARE SUSPENDED. PLASMA-CASTERS AND LASERS REPLACE THE NAGINATAS AND SCATTER GUNS PRESCRIBED FOR HUNTING BUGS.
THIS IS NO HUNT
TRIP-- THIS IS

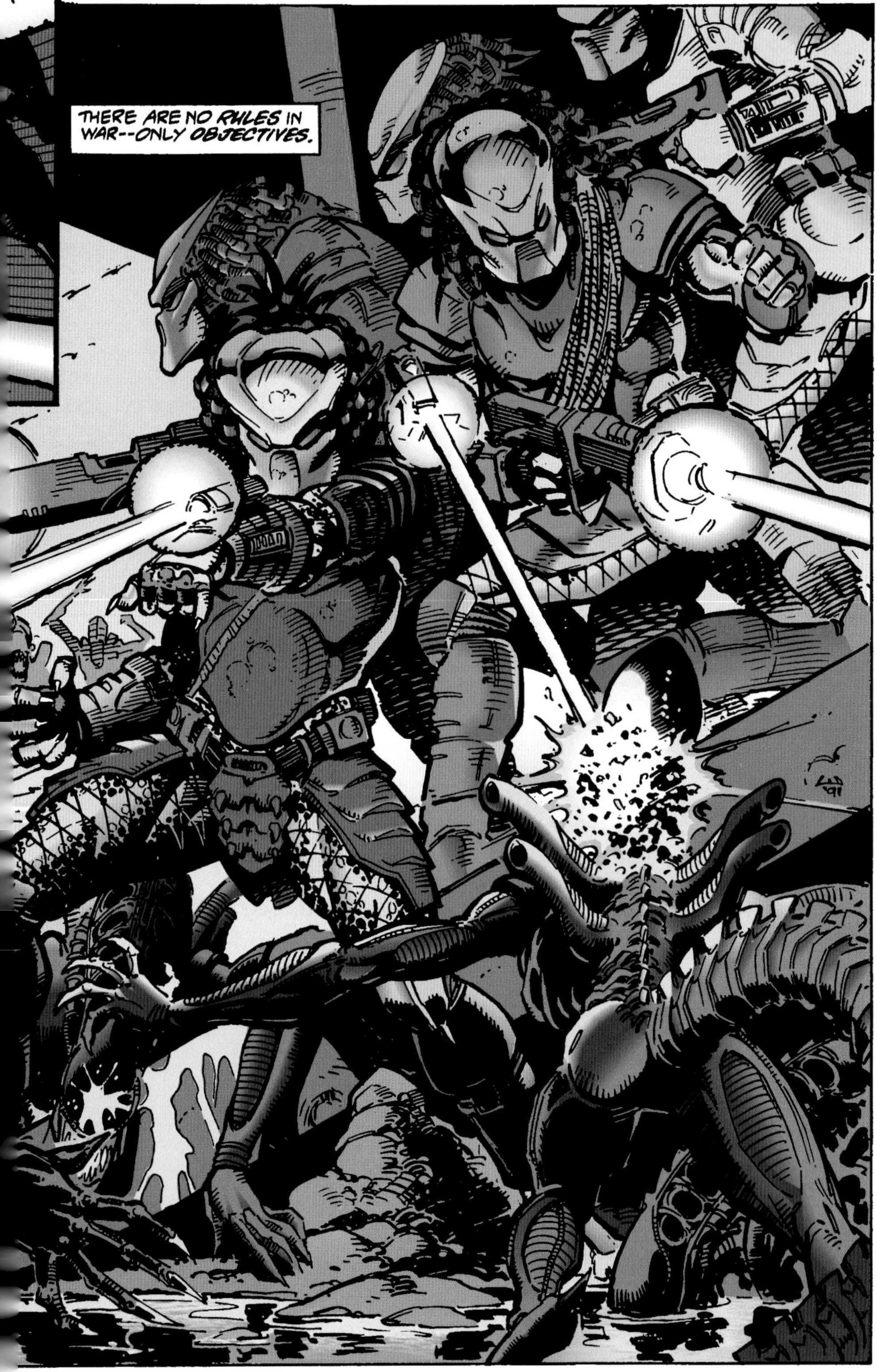
THERE ARE NO RULES IN WAR--ONLY OBJECTIVES.

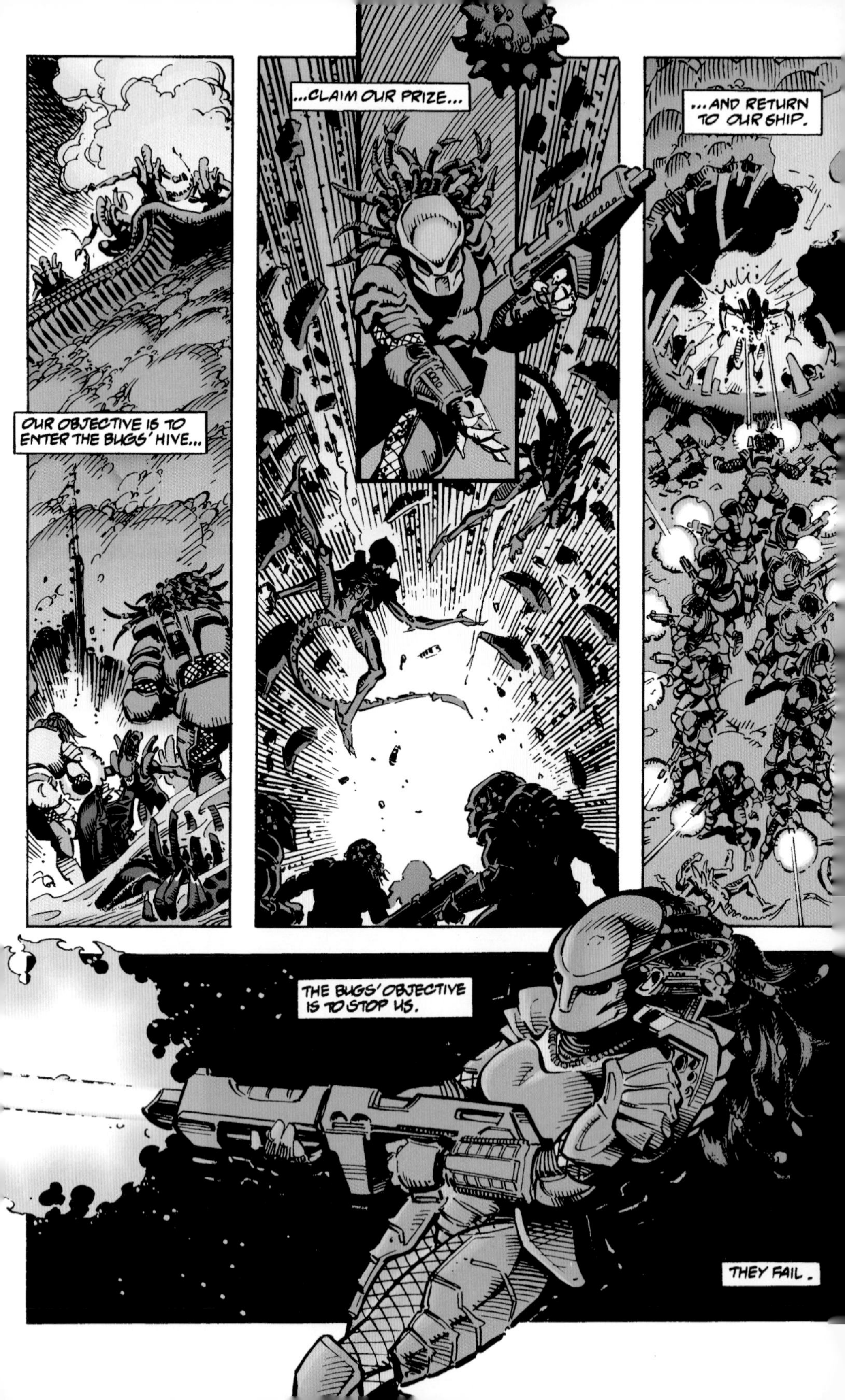
OUR OBJECTIVE IS TO ENTER THE BUGS' HIVE...
...CLAIM OUR PRIZE...
...AND RETURN TO OUR SHIP.
THE BUGS' OBJECTIVE IS TO STOP US.
THEY FAIL.

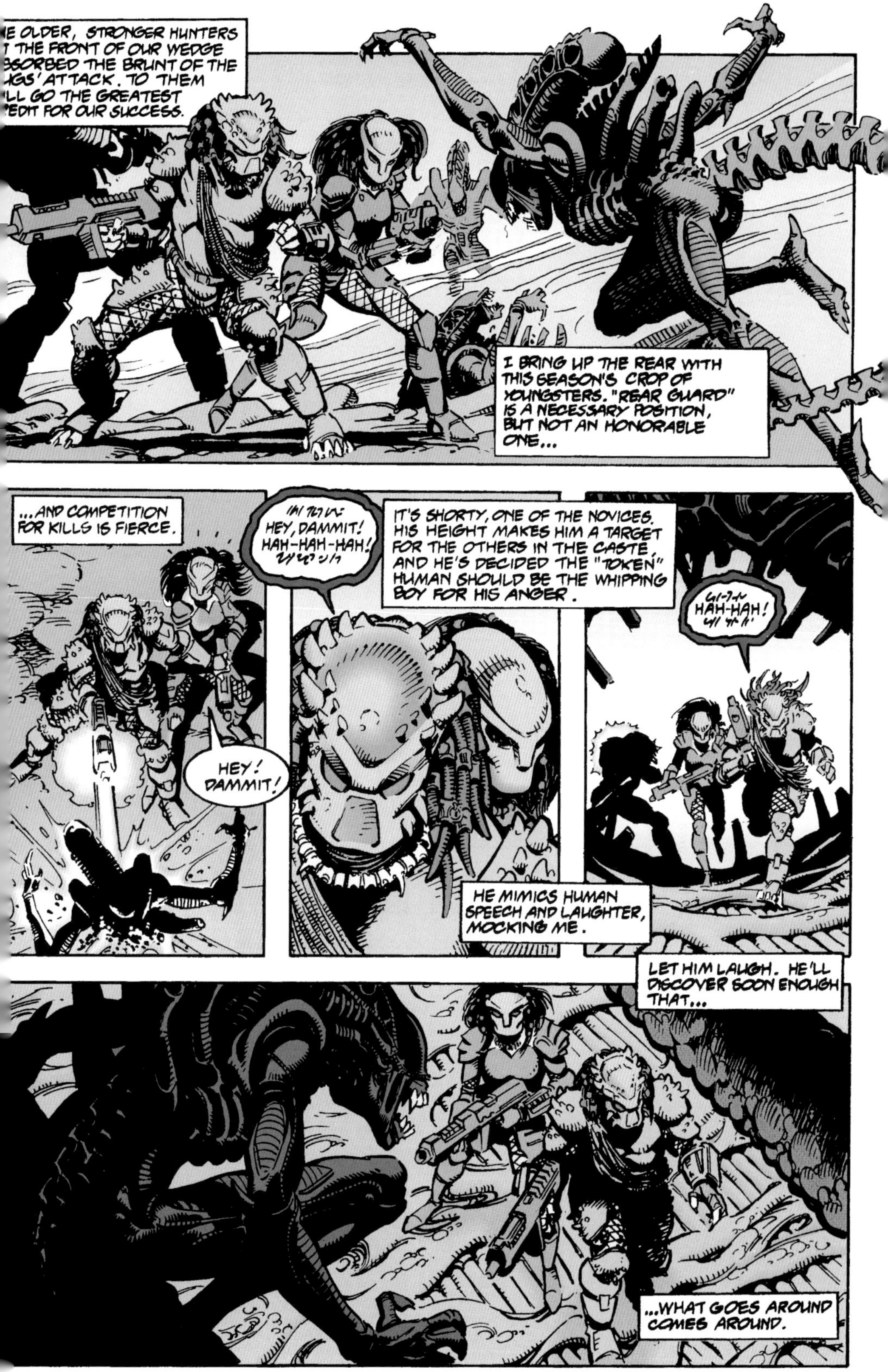

E OLDER, STRONGER HUNTERS T THE FRONT OF OUR WEDGE BSORBED THE BRUNT OF THE UGS' ATTACK. TO THEM LL GO THE GREATEST EDIT FOR OUR SUCCESS.
I BRING UP THE REAR WITH THIS SEASON'S CROP OF YOUNGSTERS. "REAR GUARD" IS A NECESSARY POSITION, BUT NOT AN HONORABLE ONE...
...AND COMPETITION FOR KILLS IS FIERCE.
HEY! DAMMIT!
HEY, DAMMIT! HAH-HAH-HAH!
IT'S SHORTY, ONE OF THE NOVICES. HIS HEIGHT MAKES HIM A TARGET FOR THE OTHERS IN THE CASTE, AND HE'S DECIDED THE "TOKEN" HUMAN SHOULD BE THE WHIPPING BOY FOR HIS ANGER.
HAH-HAH!
HE MIMICS HUMAN SPEECH AND LAUGHTER, MOCKING ME.
LET HIM LAUGH. HE'LL DISCOVER SOON ENOUGH THAT...
...WHAT GOES AROUND COMES AROUND.

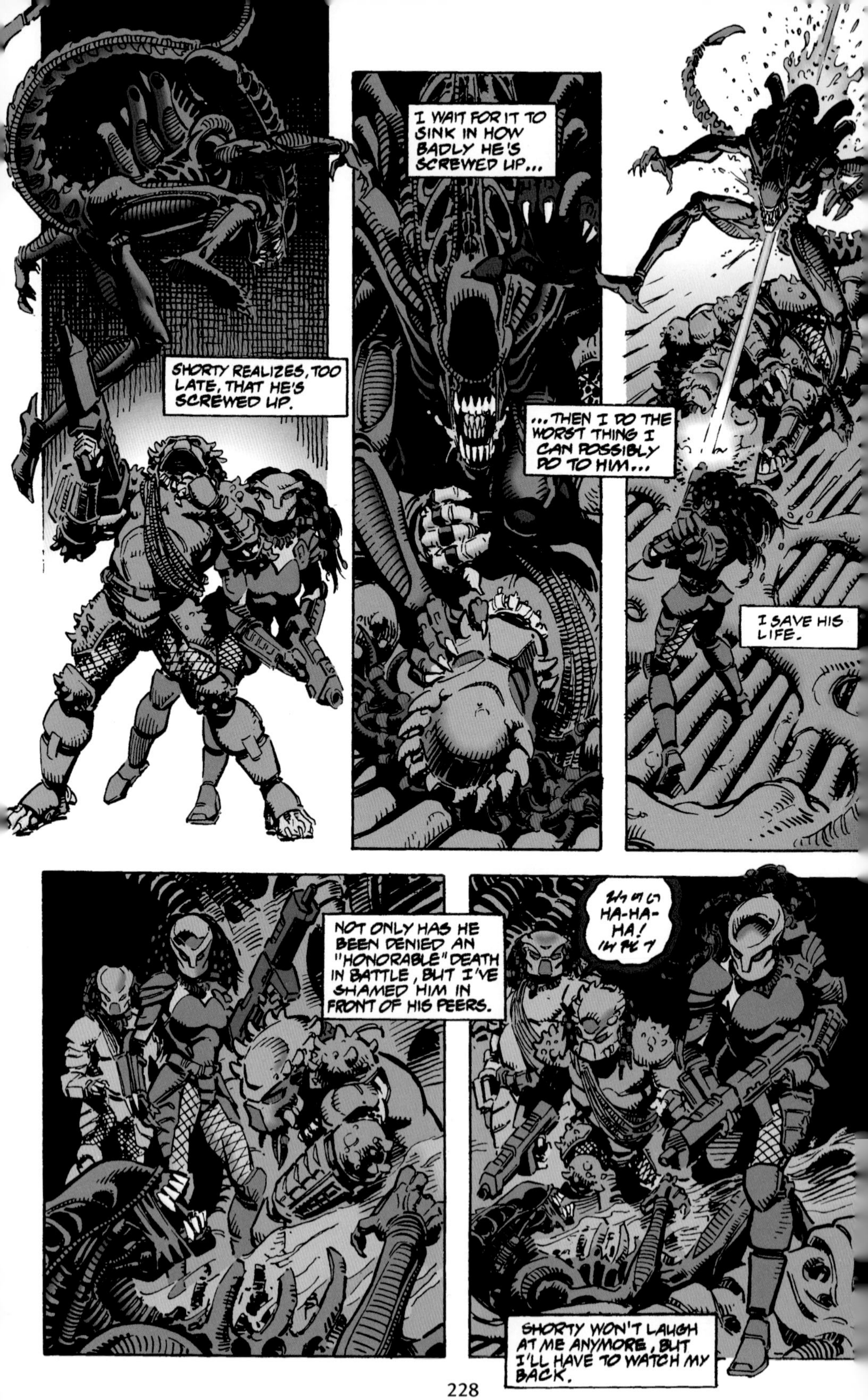
SHORTY REALIZES, TOO LATE, THAT HE'S SCREWED UP.
I WAIT FOR IT TO SINK IN HOW BADLY HE'S SCREWED UP...
...THEN I DO THE WORST THING I CAN POSSIBLY DO TO HIM...
I SAVE HIS LIFE.
NOT ONLY HAS HE BEEN DENIED AN "HONORABLE" DEATH IN BATTLE, BUT I'VE SHAMED HIM IN FRONT OF HIS PEERS.
HA-HA-HA!
SHORTY WON'T LAUGH AT ME ANYMORE, BUT I'LL HAVE TO WATCH MY BACK.

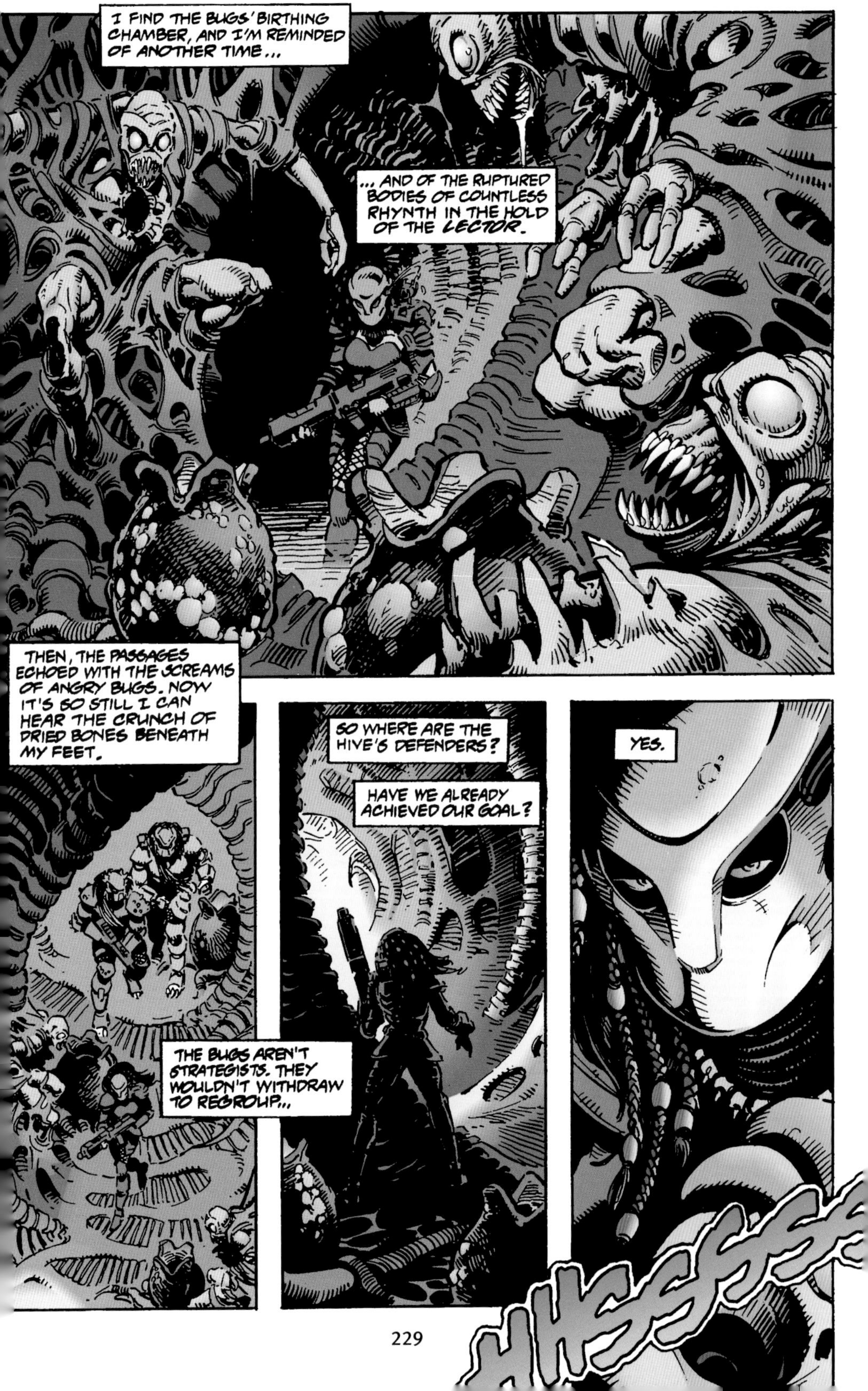
I FIND THE BUGS' BIRTHING CHAMBER, AND I'M REMINDED OF ANOTHER TIME...
...AND OF THE RUPTURED BODIES OF COUNTLESS RHYNTH IN THE HOLD OF THE LECTOR.
THEN, THE PASSAGES ECHOED WITH THE SCREAMS OF ANGRY BUGS. NOW IT'S SO STILL I CAN HEAR THE CRUNCH OF DRIED BONES BENEATH MY FEET.
THE BUGS AREN'T STRATEGISTS. THEY WOULDN'T WITHDRAW TO REGROUP...
SO WHERE ARE THE HIVE'S DEFENDERS?
HAVE WE ALREADY ACHIEVED OUR GOAL?
YES.
HISSSSS

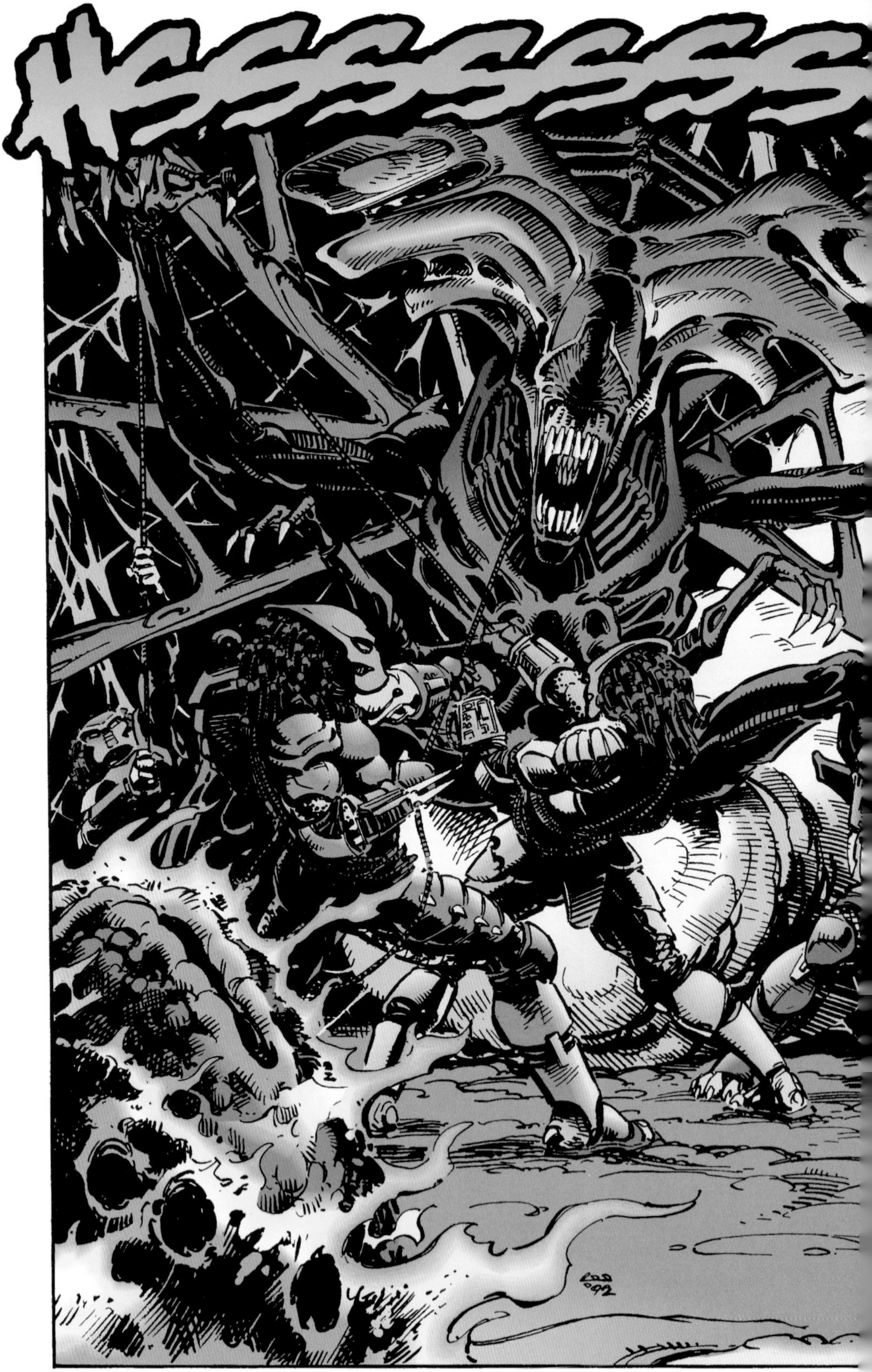
HSSSSSS

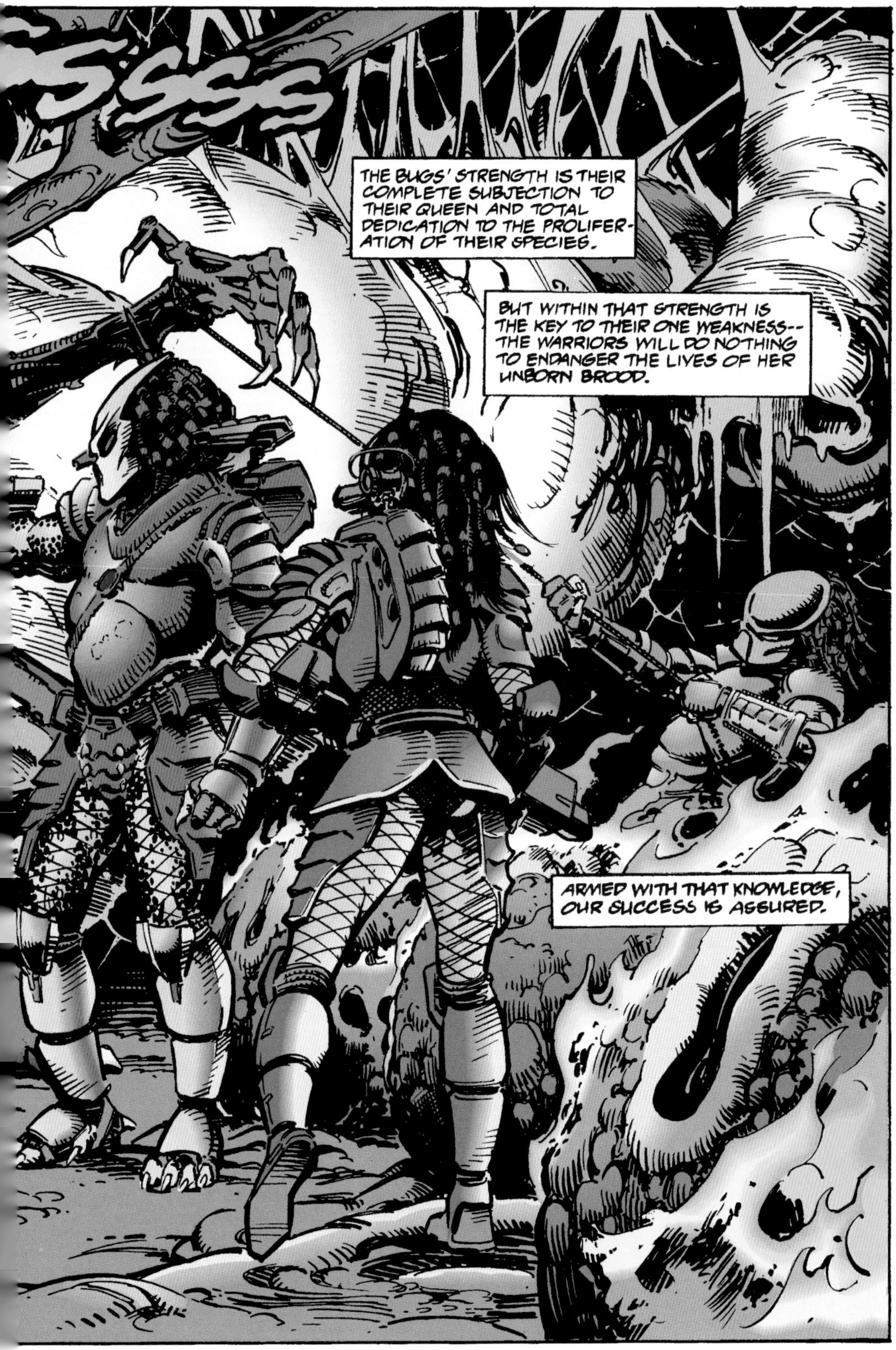
SSSS
THE BUGS' STRENGTH IS THEIR COMPLETE SUBJECTION TO THEIR QUEEN AND TOTAL DEDICATION TO THE PROLIFER-ATION OF THEIR SPECIES.
BUT WITHIN THAT STRENGTH IS THE KEY TO THEIR ONE WEAKNESS-- THE WARRIORS WILL DO NOTHING TO ENDANGER THE LIVES OF HER UNBORN BROOD.
ARMED WITH THAT KNOWLEDGE, OUR SUCCESS IS ASSURED.

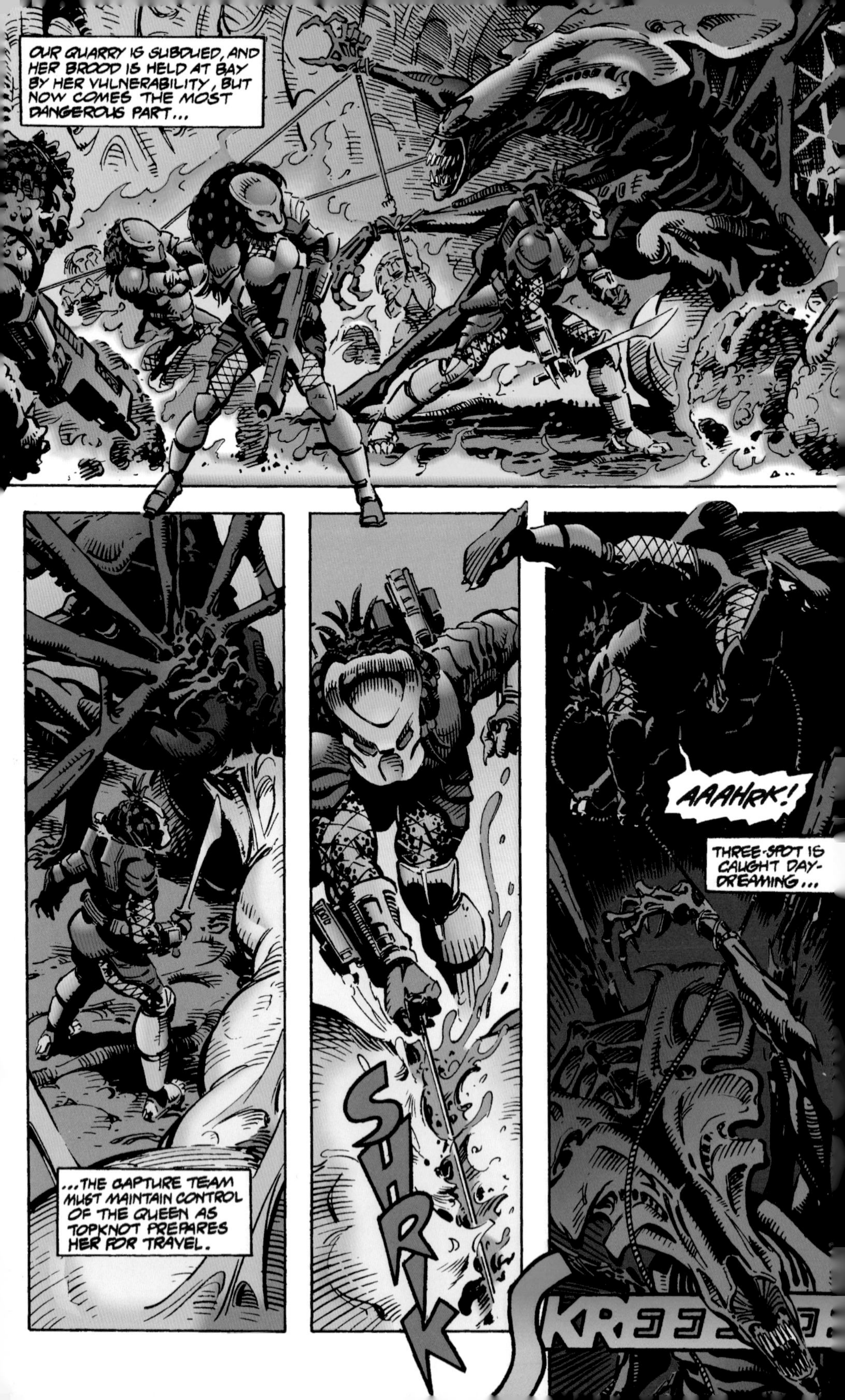
OUR QUARRY IS SUBDUED, AND HER BROOD IS HELD AT BAY BY HER VULNERABILITY, BUT NOW COMES THE MOST DANGEROUS PART...
...THE CAPTURE TEAM MUST MAINTAIN CONTROL OF THE QUEEN AS TOPKNOT PREPARES HER FOR TRAVEL.
SHRK
AAAHRK!
THREE-SPOT IS CAUGHT DAY-DREAMING...
KREEE

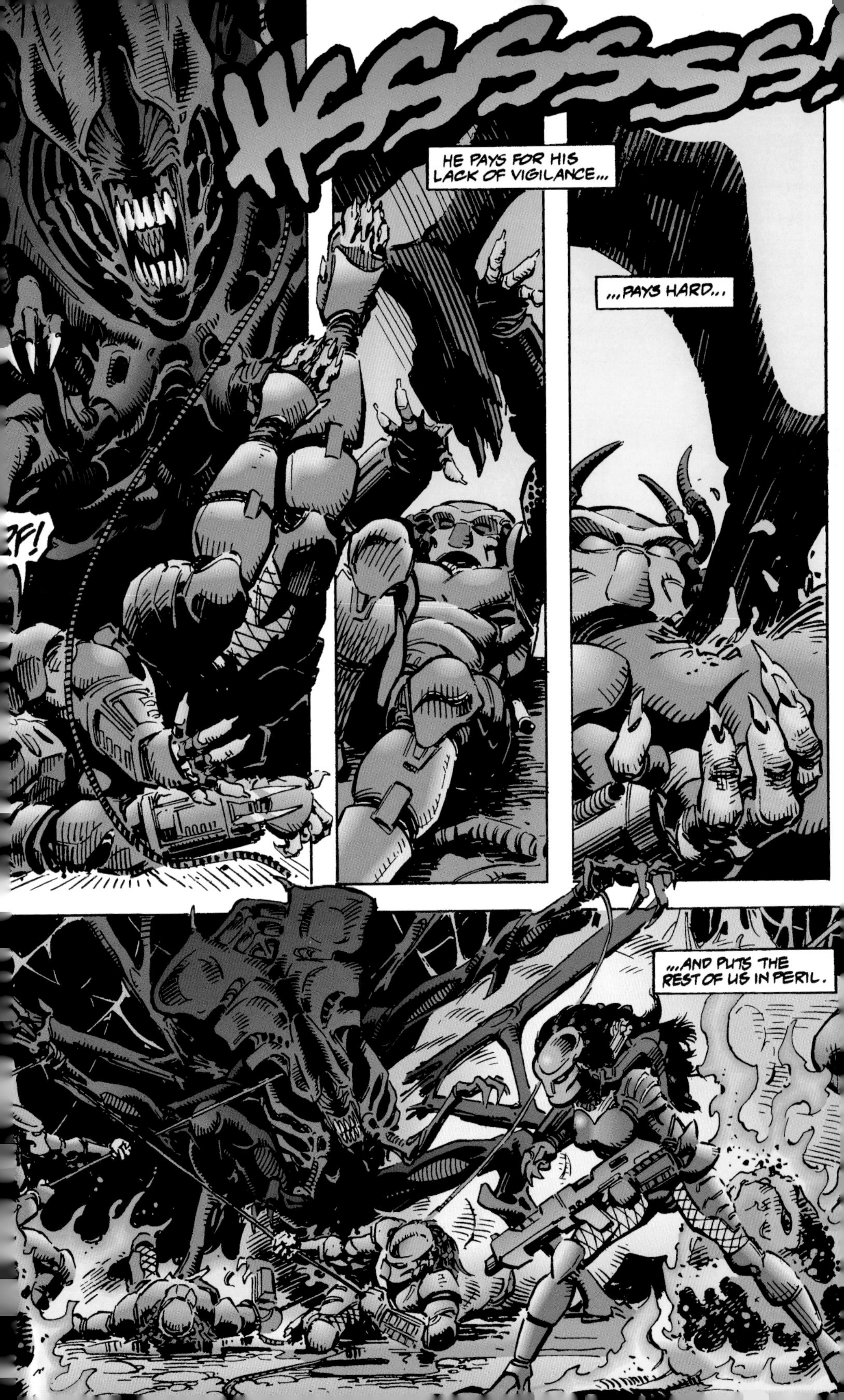
HE PAYS FOR HIS LACK OF VIGILANCE...
...PAYS HARD...
...AND PUTS THE REST OF US IN PERIL.

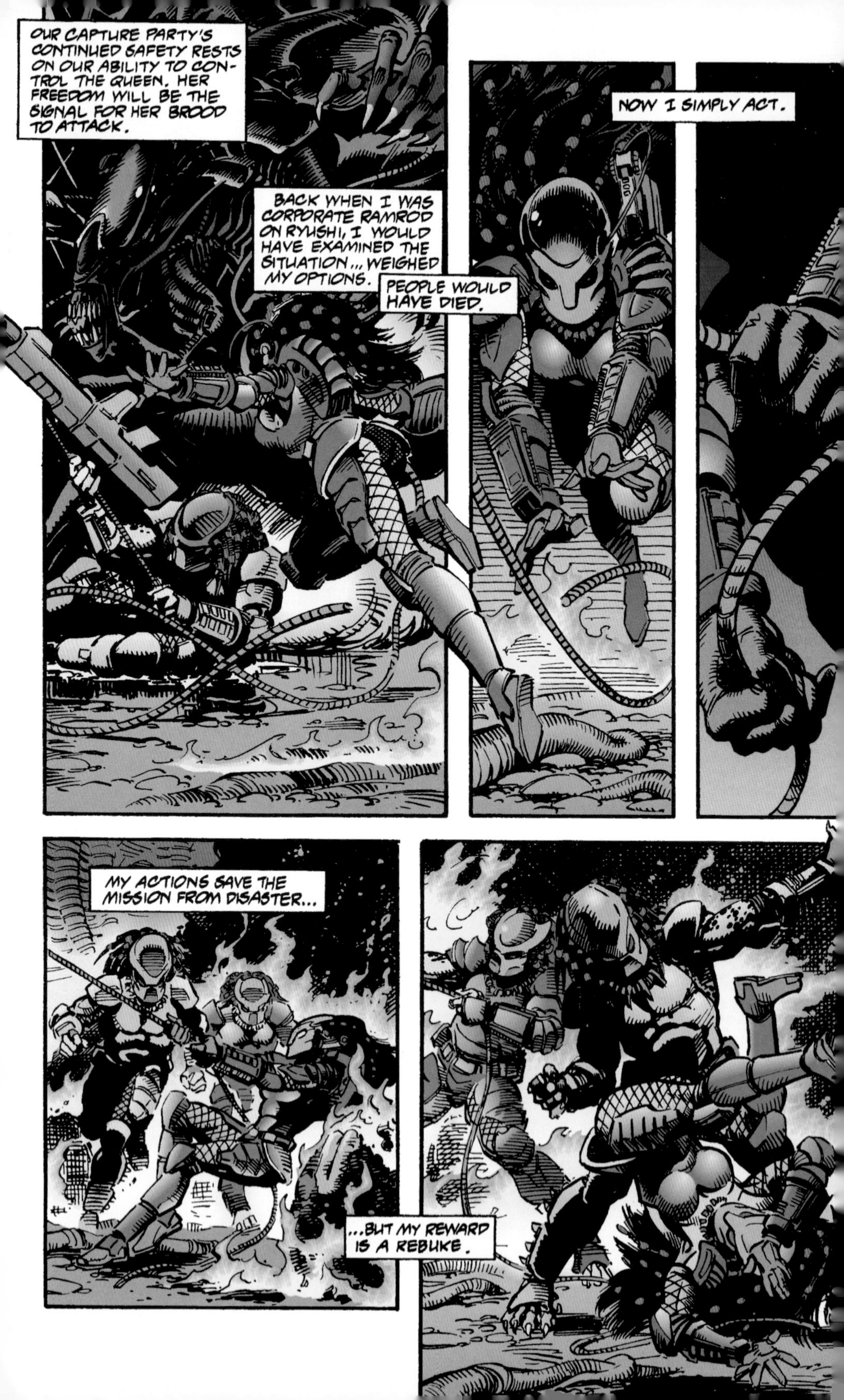
OUR CAPTURE PARTY'S CONTINUED SAFETY RESTS ON OUR ABILITY TO CONTROL THE QUEEN. HER FREEDOM WILL BE THE SIGNAL FOR HER BROOD TO ATTACK.
BACK WHEN I WAS CORPORATE RAMROD ON RYUSHI, I WOULD HAVE EXAMINED THE SITUATION... WEIGHED MY OPTIONS.
PEOPLE WOULD HAVE DIED.
NOW I SIMPLY ACT.
MY ACTIONS SAVE THE MISSION FROM DISASTER...
...BUT MY REWARD IS A REBUKE.

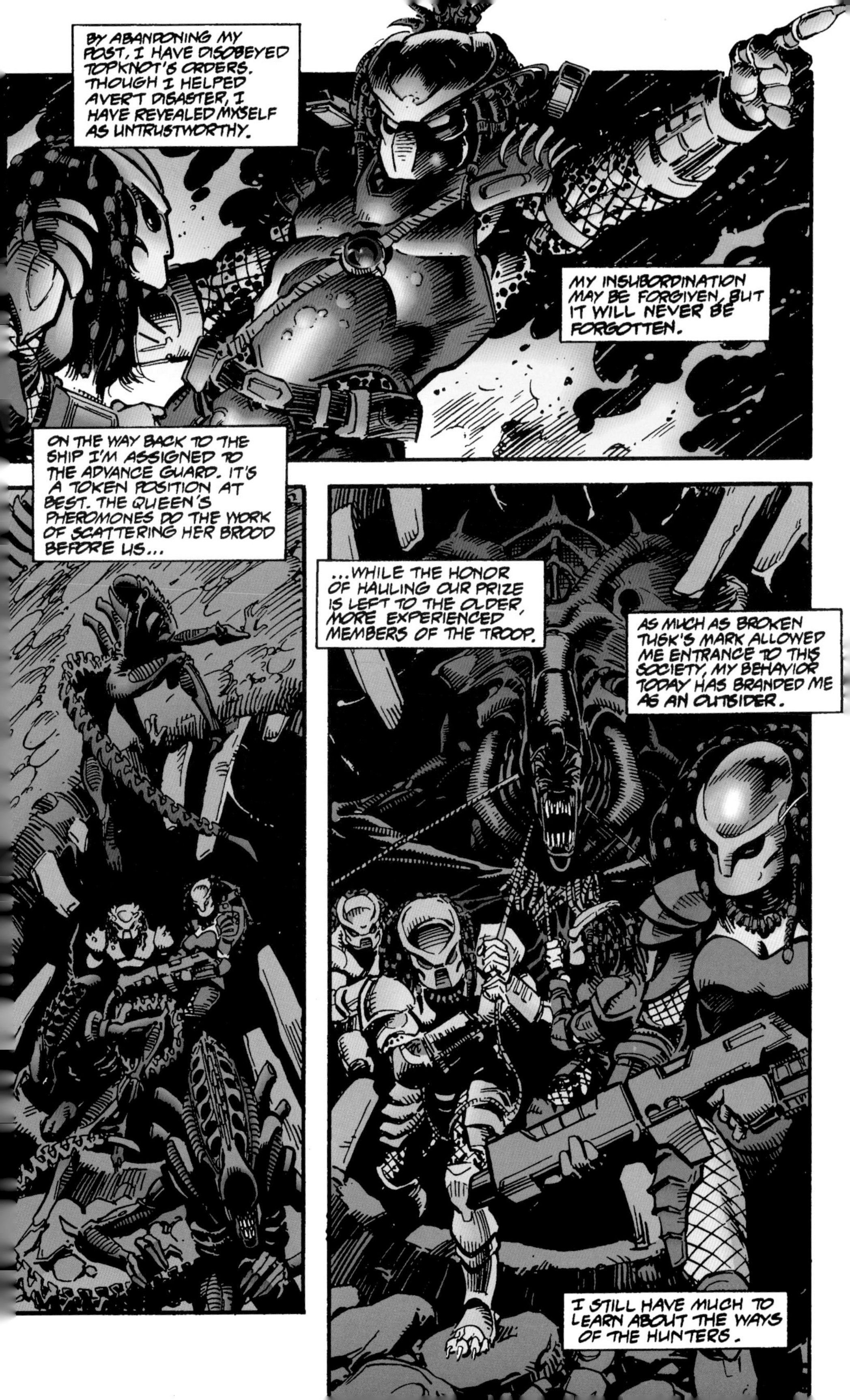
BY ABANDONING MY POST, I HAVE DISOBEYED TOPKNOT'S ORDERS. THOUGH I HELPED AVERT DISASTER, I HAVE REVEALED MYSELF AS UNTRUSTWORTHY.
MY INSUBORDINATION MAY BE FORGIVEN, BUT IT WILL NEVER BE FORGOTTEN.
ON THE WAY BACK TO THE SHIP I'M ASSIGNED TO THE ADVANCE GUARD. IT'S A TOKEN POSITION AT BEST. THE QUEEN'S PHEROMONES DO THE WORK OF SCATTERING HER BROOD BEFORE US...
...WHILE THE HONOR OF HAULING OUR PRIZE IS LEFT TO THE OLDER, MORE EXPERIENCED MEMBERS OF THE TROOP.
AS MUCH AS BROKEN TUSK'S MARK ALLOWED ME ENTRANCE TO THIS SOCIETY, MY BEHAVIOR TODAY HAS BRANDED ME AS AN OUTSIDER.
I STILL HAVE MUCH TO LEARN ABOUT THE WAYS OF THE HUNTERS.

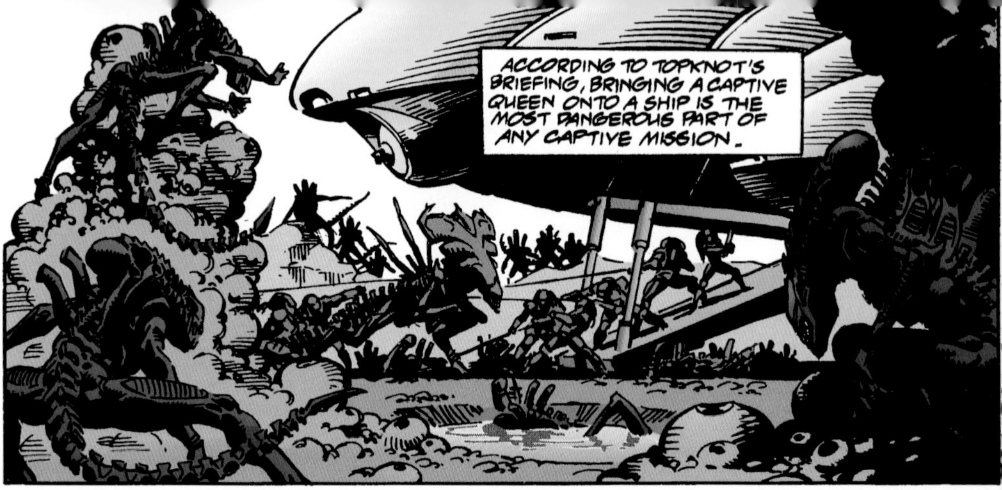
ACCORDING TO TOPKNOT'S BRIEFING, BRINGING A CAPTIVE QUEEN ONTO A SHIP IS THE MOST DANGEROUS PART OF ANY CAPTIVE MISSION.

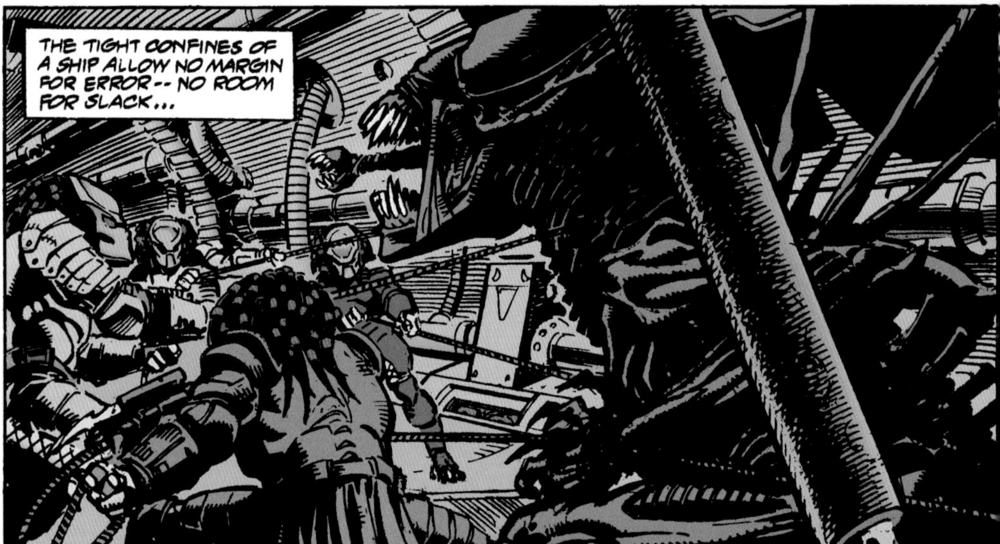
THE TIGHT CONFINES OF A SHIP ALLOW NO MARGIN FOR ERROR -- NO ROOM FOR SLACK...

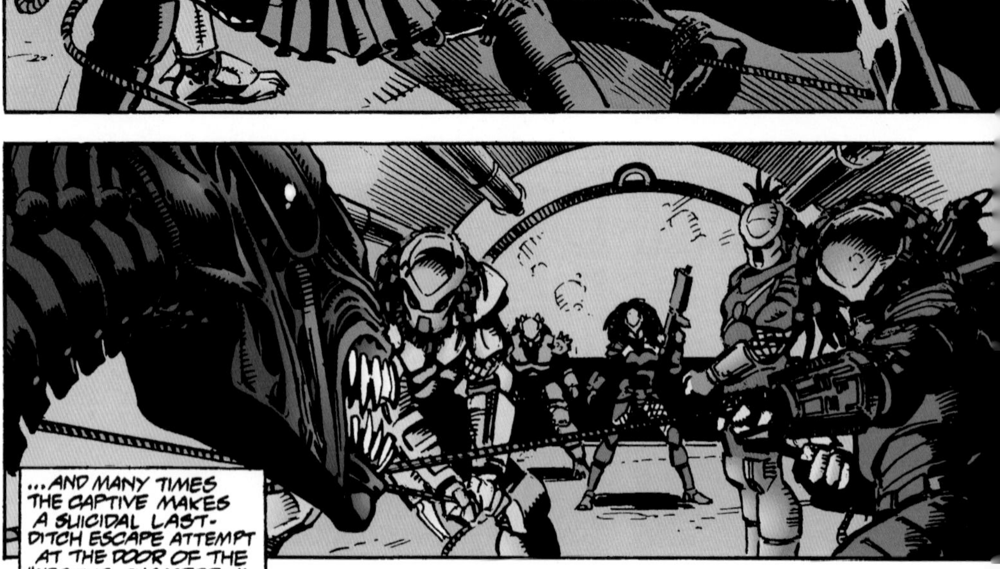
...AND MANY TIMES THE CAPTIVE MAKES A SUICIDAL LAST-DITCH ESCAPE ATTEMPT AT THE DOOR OF THE "NESTING CHAMBER."

WHAT CATCHES US BY SURPRISE IS THAT THE ATTEMPT IS MADE NOT BY THE QUEEN, BUT BY HER CHILDREN.

AN UNSEEN SIGNAL--OR A SILENT CALL--SPURS HER OFFSPRING INTO ACTION.

IT'S A CALCULATED RISK ON HER PART...

THE SACRIFICE OF HER CURRENT BROOD FOR THE SAKE OF HER OWN SURVIVAL AND THAT OF FUTURE GENERATIONS.

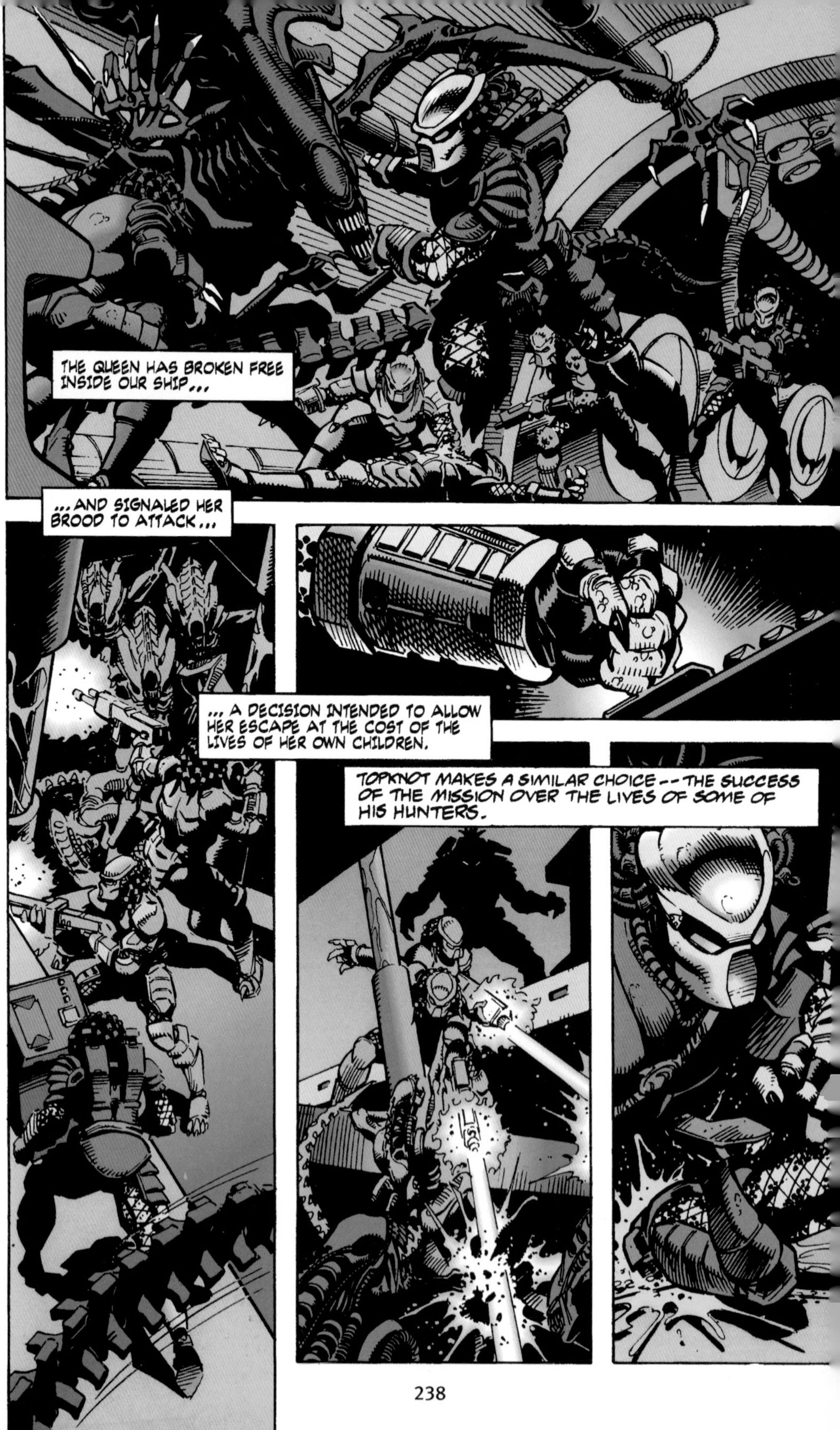
THE QUEEN HAS BROKEN FREE INSIDE OUR SHIP...
...AND SIGNALED HER BROOD TO ATTACK...
... A DECISION INTENDED TO ALLOW HER ESCAPE AT THE COST OF THE LIVES OF HER OWN CHILDREN.
TOPKNOT MAKES A SIMILAR CHOICE -- THE SUCCESS OF THE MISSION OVER THE LIVES OF SOME OF HIS HUNTERS.

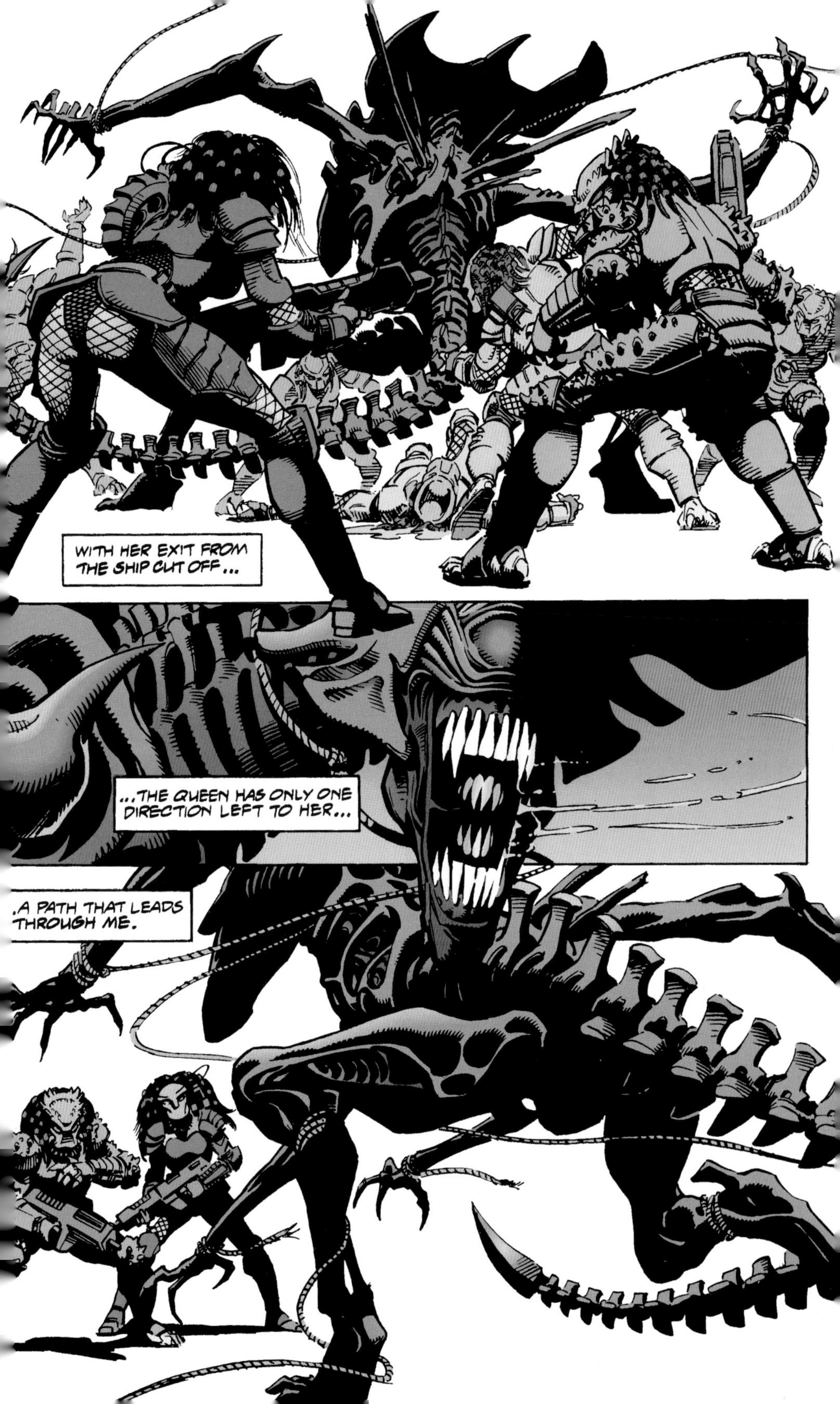
WITH HER EXIT FROM THE SHIP CUT OFF...
...THE QUEEN HAS ONLY ONE DIRECTION LEFT TO HER...
.A PATH THAT LEADS THROUGH ME.

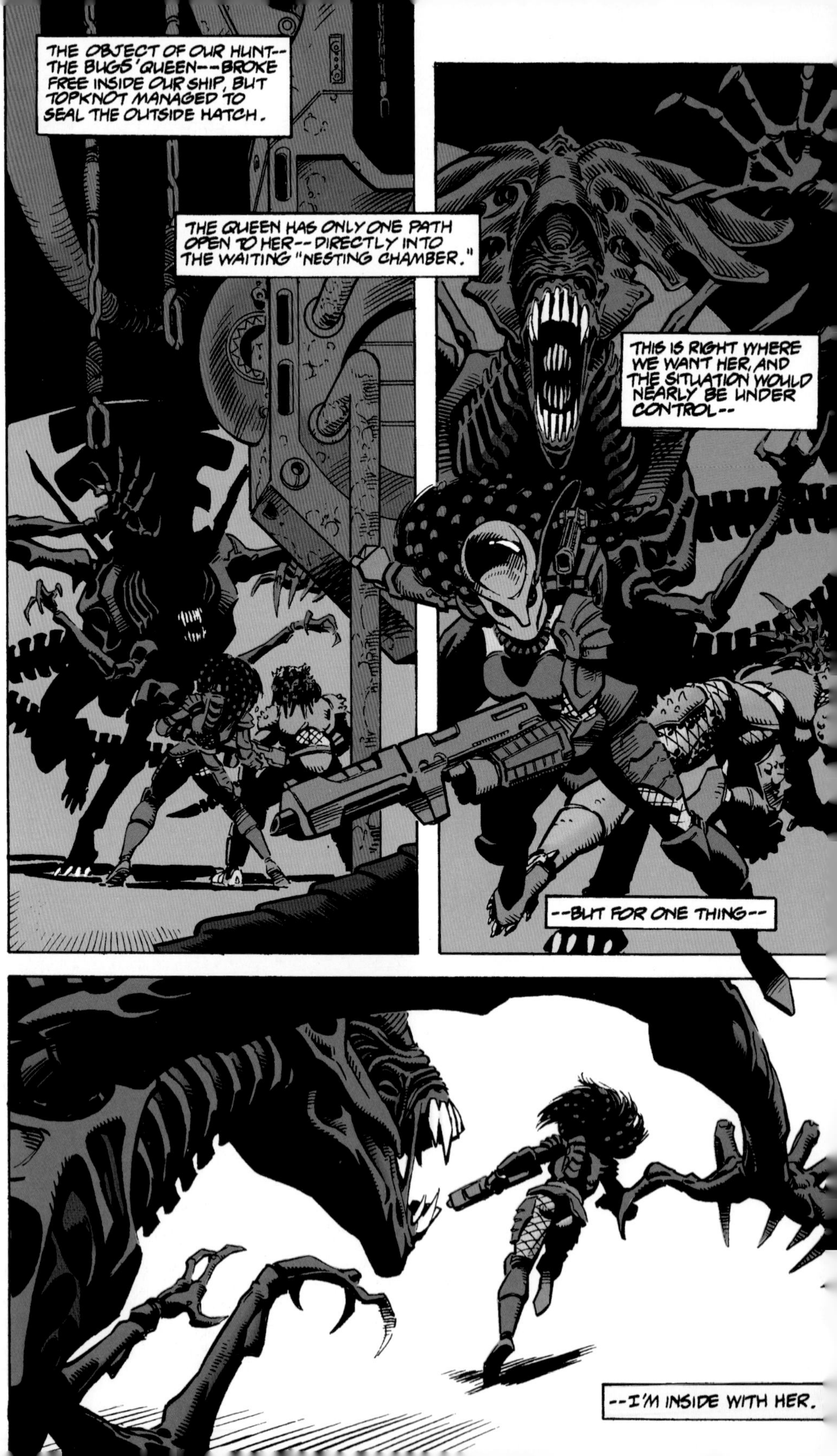
THE OBJECT OF OUR HUNT-- THE BUGS' QUEEN--BROKE FREE INSIDE OUR SHIP, BUT TOPKNOT MANAGED TO SEAL THE OUTSIDE HATCH.
THE QUEEN HAS ONLY ONE PATH OPEN TO HER--DIRECTLY INTO THE WAITING "NESTING CHAMBER."
THIS IS RIGHT WHERE WE WANT HER, AND THE SITUATION WOULD NEARLY BE UNDER CONTROL--
--BUT FOR ONE THING--
--I'M INSIDE WITH HER.

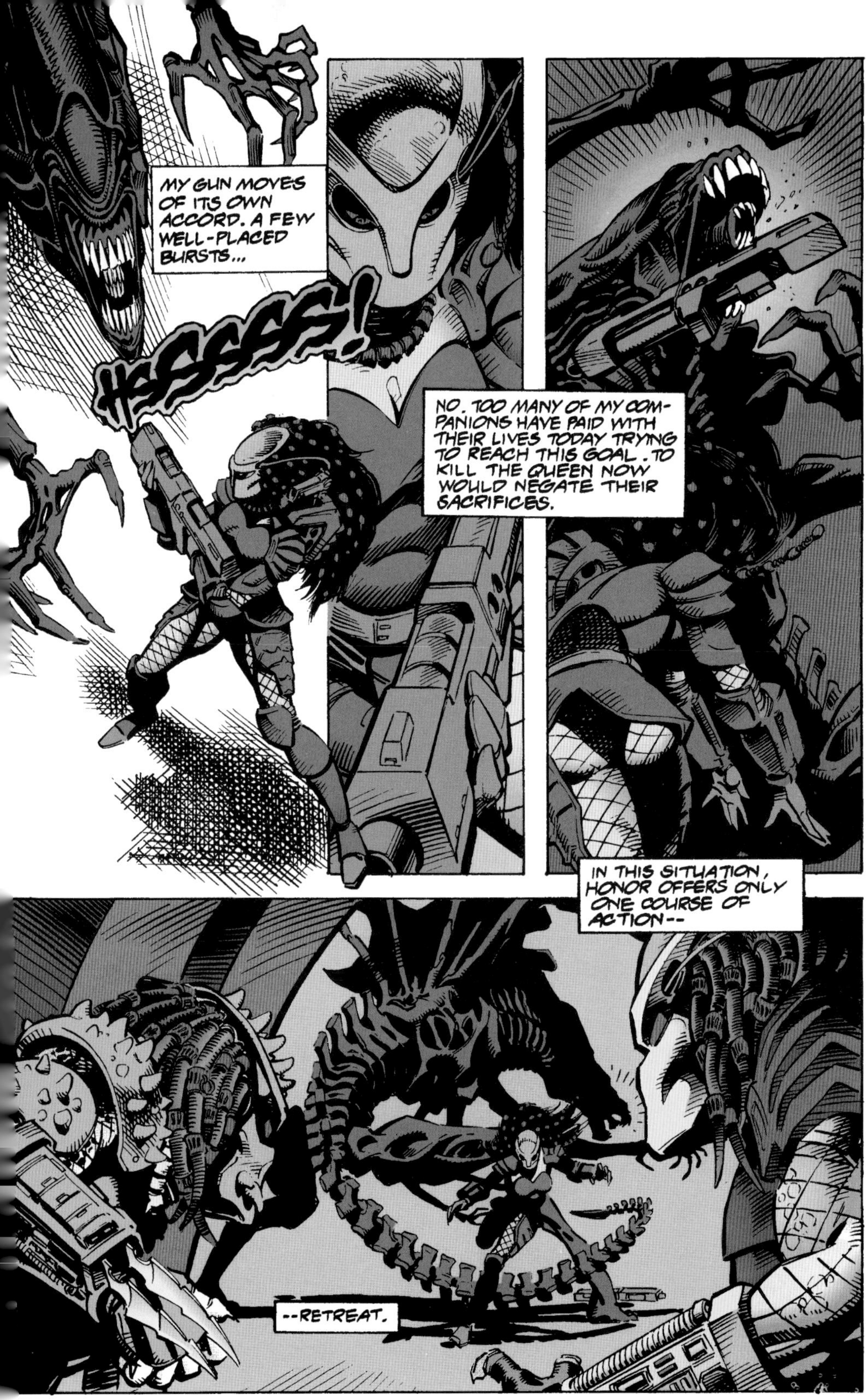
MY GUN MOVES OF ITS OWN ACCORD. A FEW WELL-PLACED BURSTS...
HSSSSS!
NO. TOO MANY OF MY COMPANIONS HAVE PAID WITH THEIR LIVES TODAY TRYING TO REACH THIS GOAL. TO KILL THE QUEEN NOW WOULD NEGATE THEIR SACRIFICES.
IN THIS SITUATION, HONOR OFFERS ONLY ONE COURSE OF ACTION--
--RETREAT.

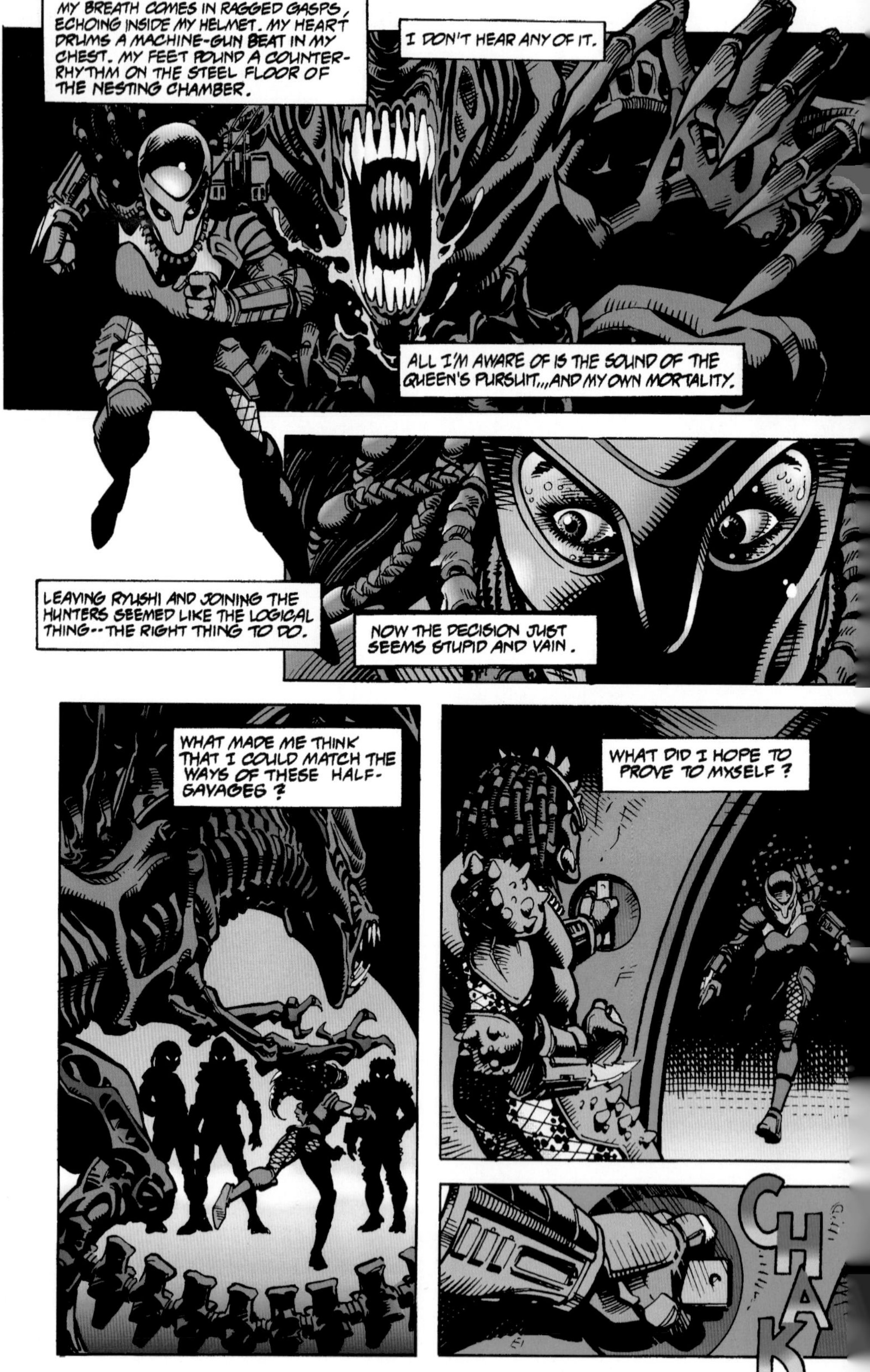
MY BREATH COMES IN RAGGED GASPS, ECHOING INSIDE MY HELMET. MY HEART DRUMS A MACHINE-GUN BEAT IN MY CHEST. MY FEET POUND A COUNTER-RHYTHM ON THE STEEL FLOOR OF THE NESTING CHAMBER.
I DON'T HEAR ANY OF IT.
ALL I'M AWARE OF IS THE SOUND OF THE QUEEN'S PURSUIT,,,AND MY OWN MORTALITY.
LEAVING RYUSHI AND JOINING THE HUNTERS SEEMED LIKE THE LOGICAL THING--THE RIGHT THING TO DO.
NOW THE DECISION JUST SEEMS STUPID AND VAIN.
WHAT MADE ME THINK THAT I COULD MATCH THE WAYS OF THESE HALF-SAVAGES?
WHAT DID I HOPE TO PROVE TO MYSELF?
CHAK

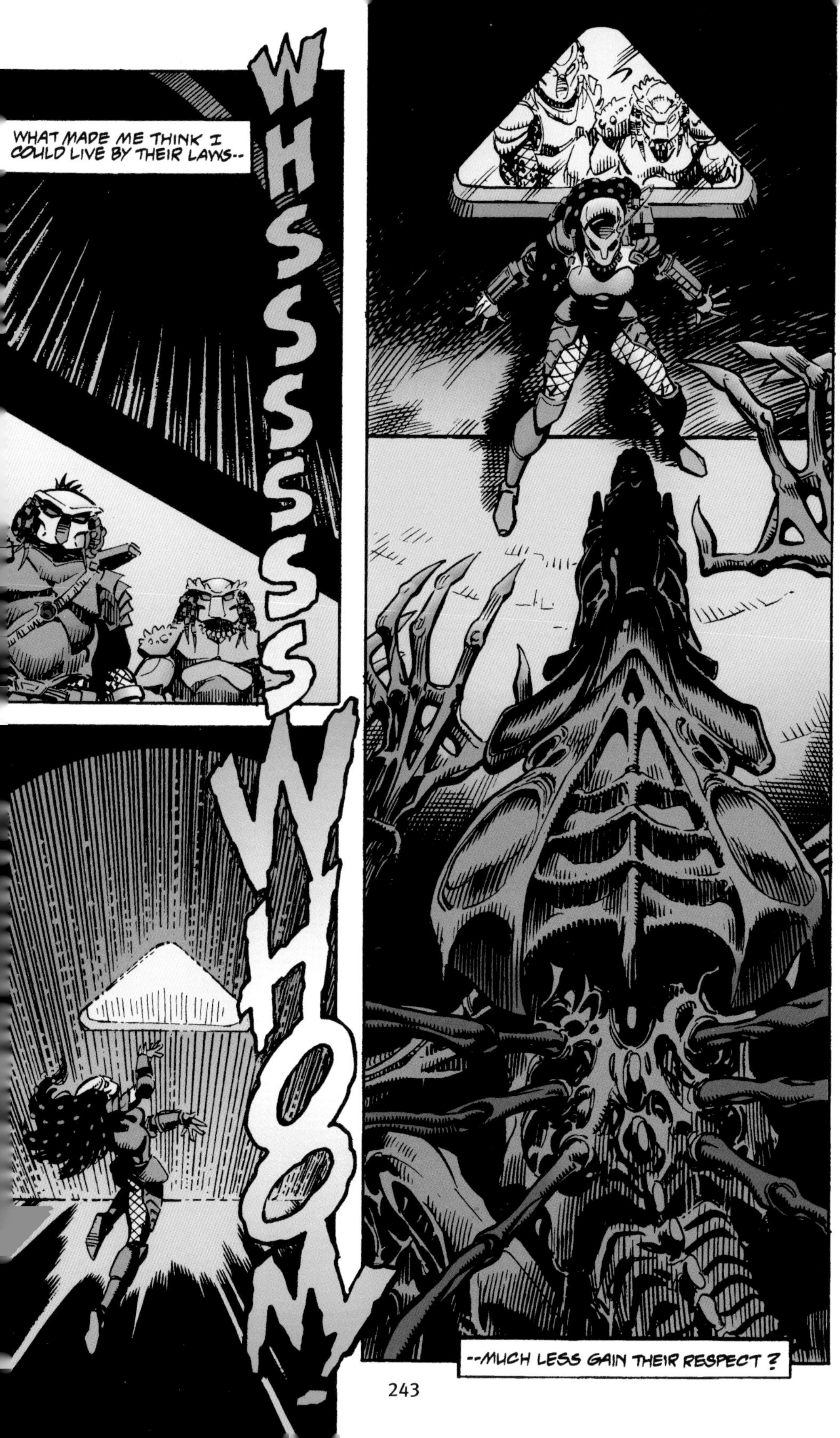
WHAT MADE ME THINK I COULD LIVE BY THEIR LAWS--
WHSSSSSS
WHOOOM
--MUCH LESS GAIN THEIR RESPECT?

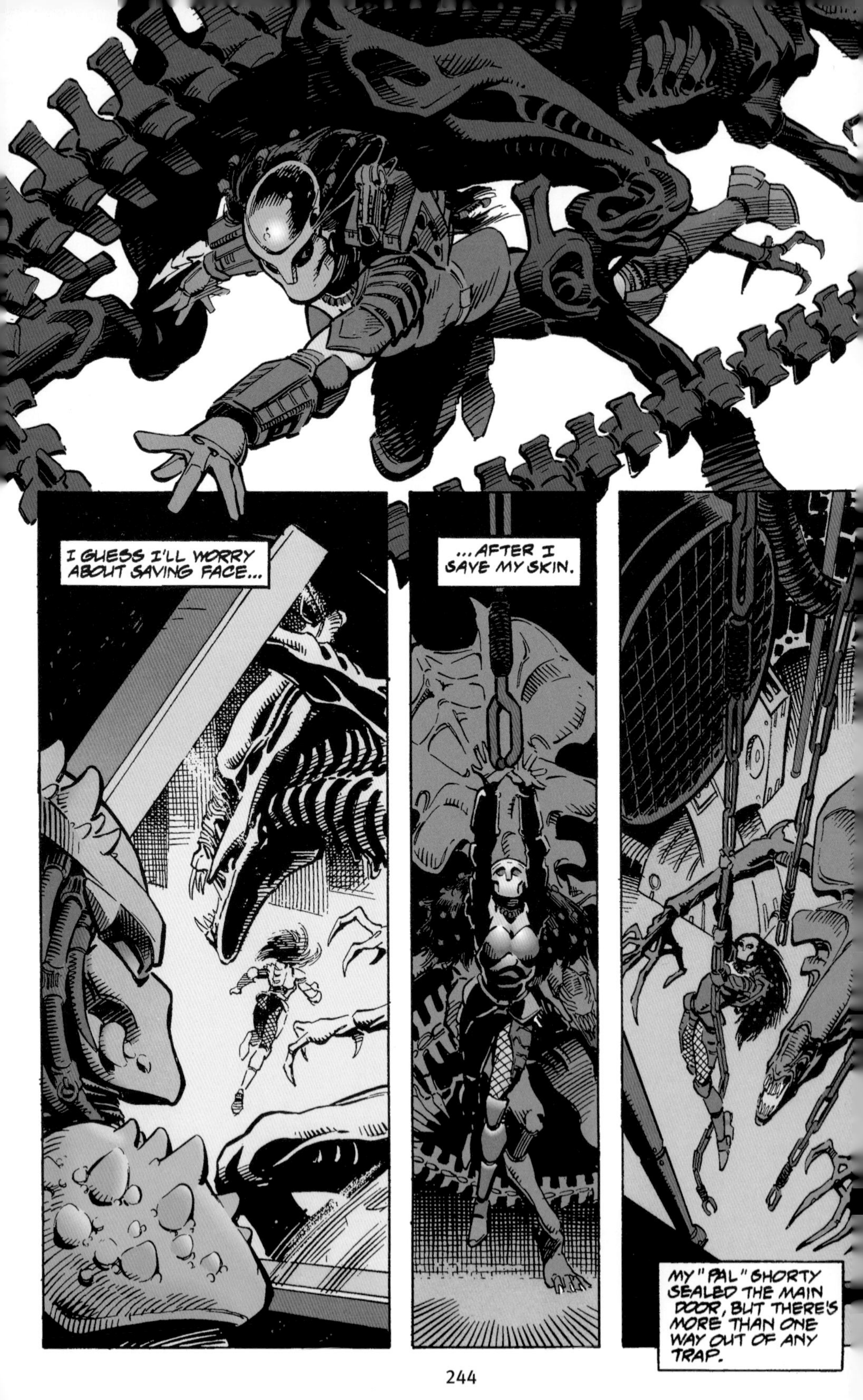
I GUESS I'LL WORRY ABOUT SAVING FACE...
...AFTER I SAVE MY SKIN.
MY "PAL" SHORTY SEALED THE MAIN DOOR, BUT THERE'S MORE THAN ONE WAY OUT OF ANY TRAP.

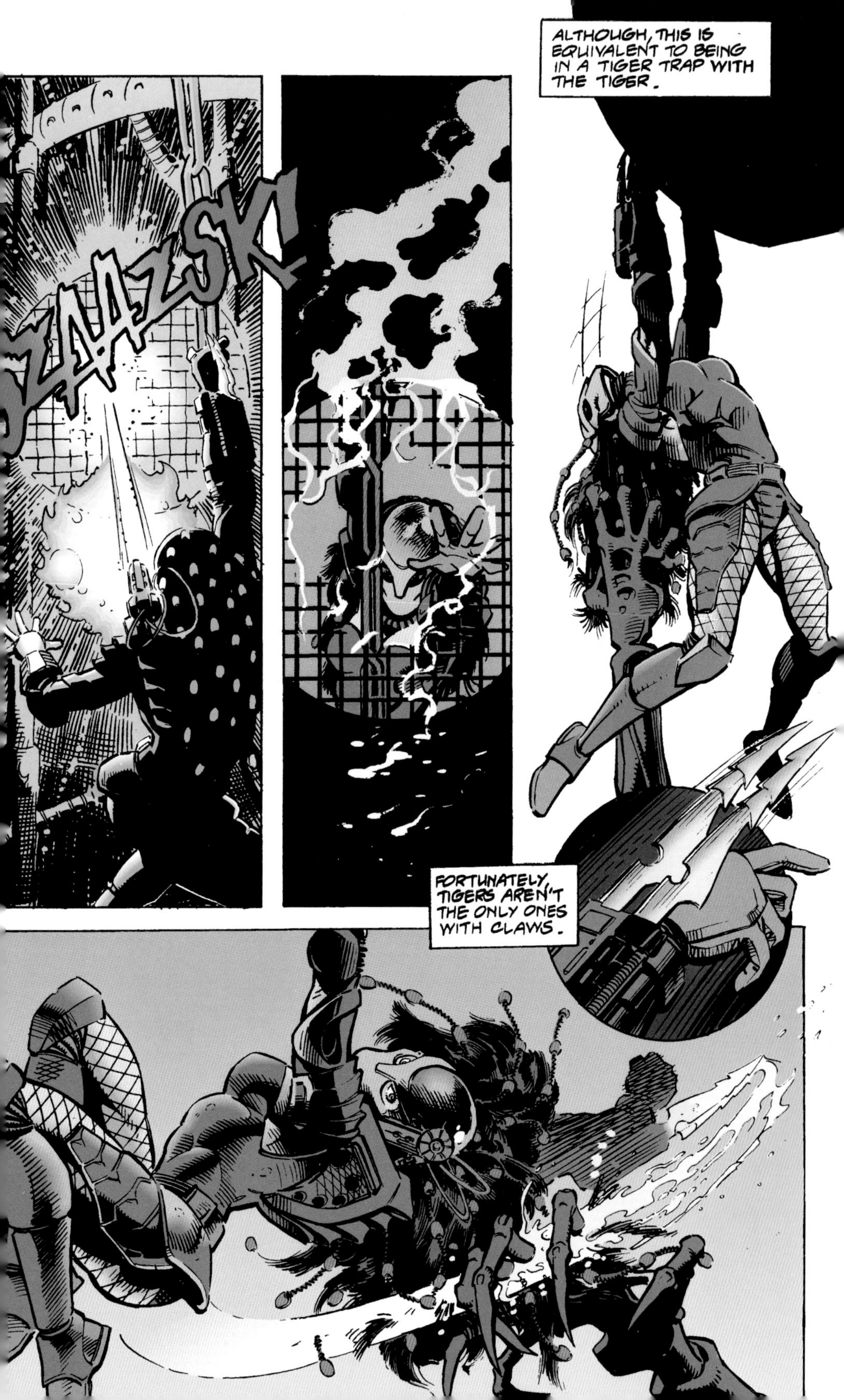
ALTHOUGH, THIS IS EQUIVALENT TO BEING IN A TIGER TRAP WITH THE TIGER.
ZAAZSK!
FORTUNATELY, TIGERS AREN'T THE ONLY ONES WITH CLAWS.

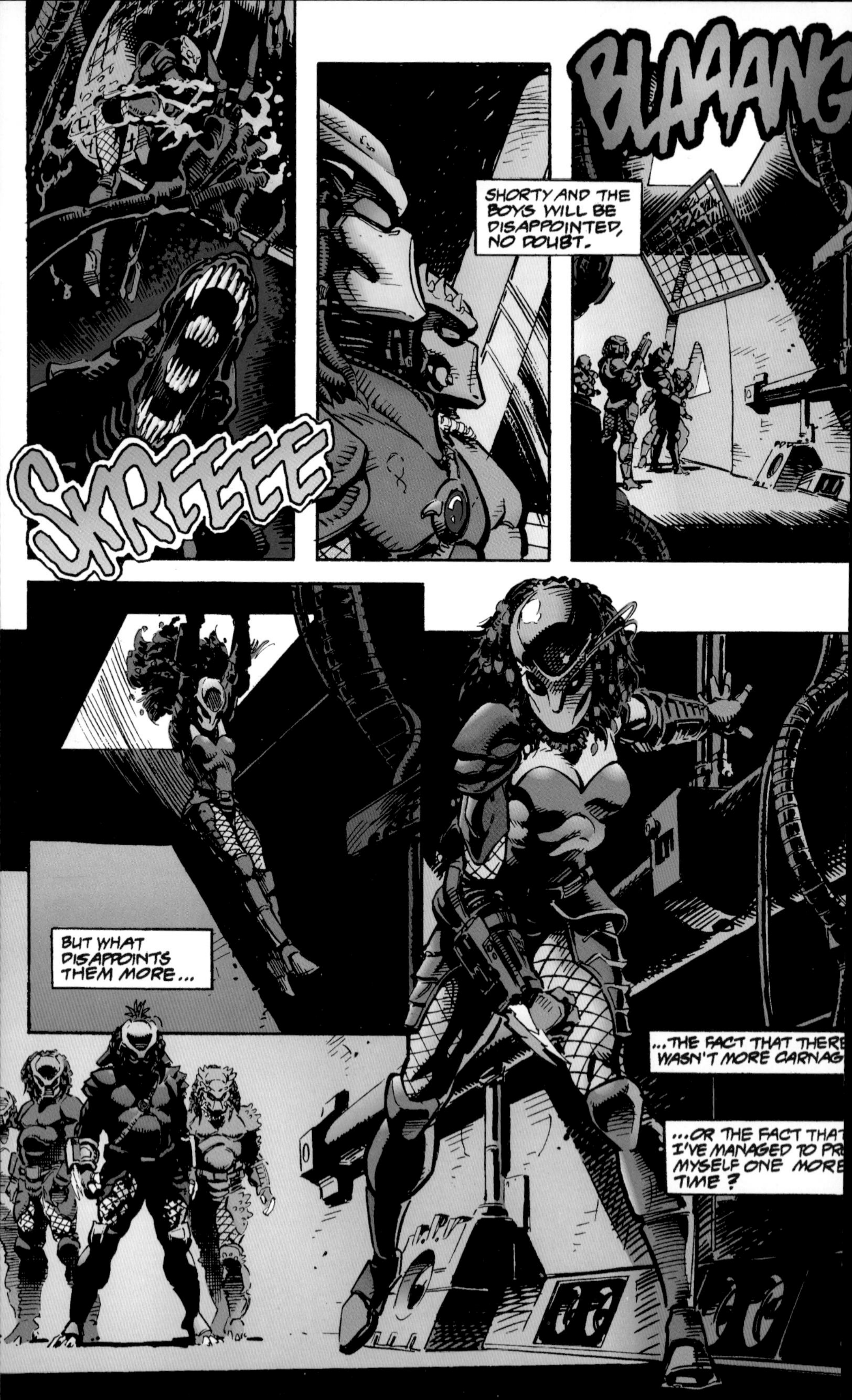
SKREEEE
SHORTY AND THE BOYS WILL BE DISAPPOINTED, NO DOUBT.
BLAAANG
BUT WHAT DISAPPOINTS THEM MORE...
...THE FACT THAT THERE WASN'T MORE CARNAG
...OR THE FACT THAT I'VE MANAGED TO PR MYSELF ONE MORE TIME?

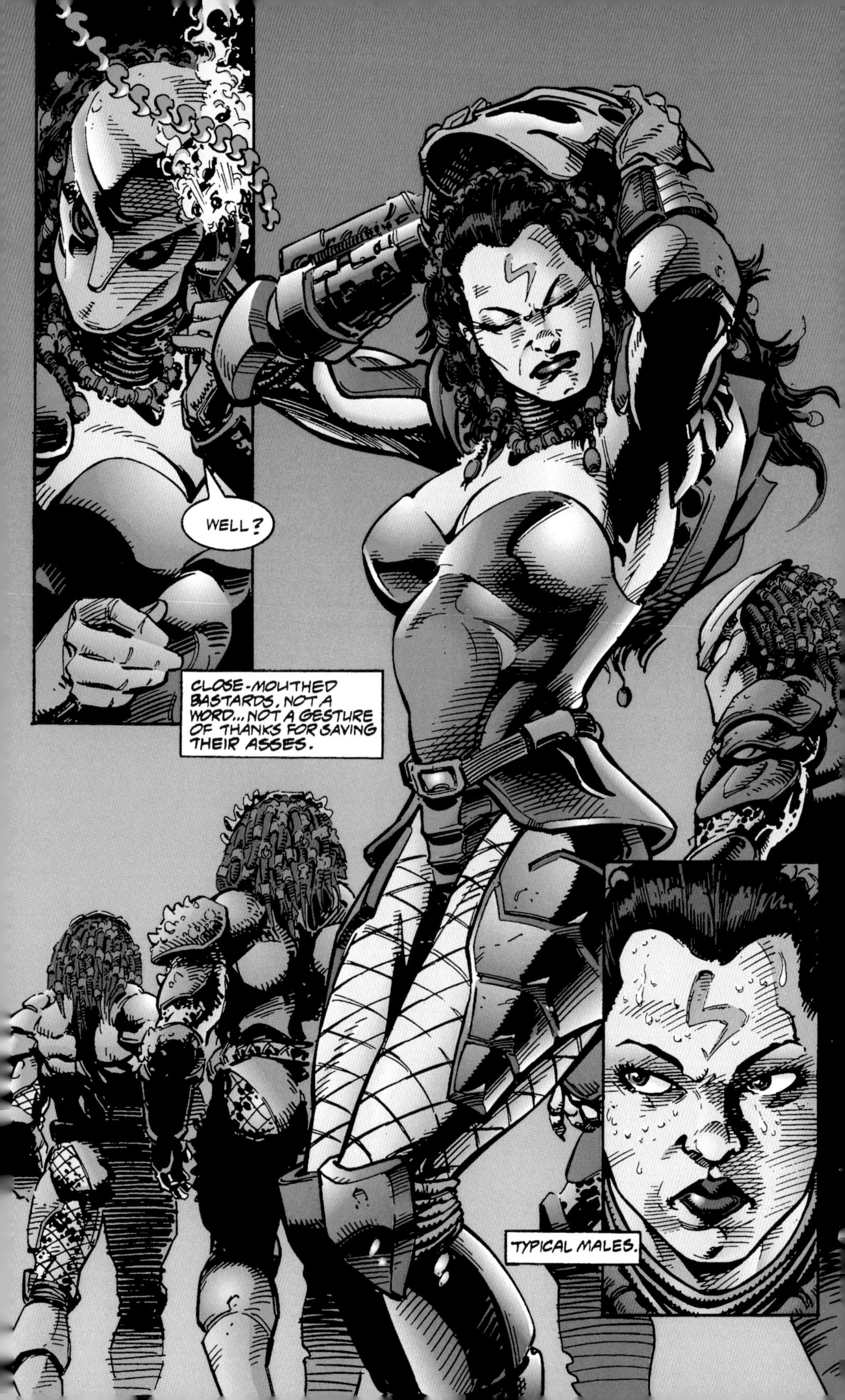
WELL?
CLOSE-MOUTHED BASTARDS, NOT A WORD... NOT A GESTURE OF THANKS FOR SAVING THEIR ASSES.
TYPICAL MALES.

PART 2

script
RANDY STRADLEY

pencils
MIKE MANLEY
JIM HALL
MARK HEIKE

inks
RICARDO VILLAGRÁN

colors
CHRIS CHALENOR

lettering
STEVE DUTRO

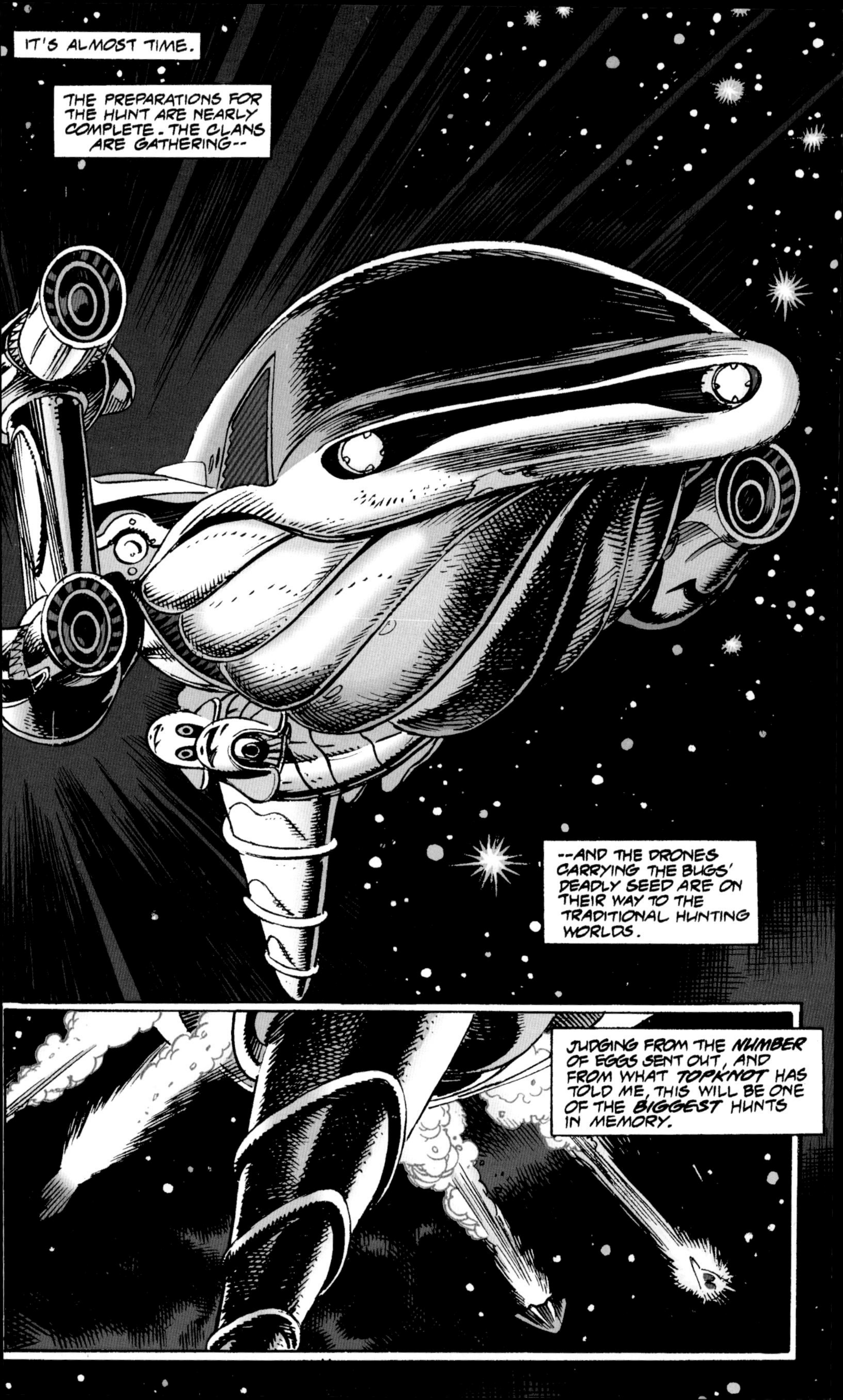
IT'S ALMOST TIME.
THE PREPARATIONS FOR THE HUNT ARE NEARLY COMPLETE. THE CLANS ARE GATHERING--
--AND THE DRONES CARRYING THE BUGS' DEADLY SEED ARE ON THEIR WAY TO THE TRADITIONAL HUNTING WORLDS.
JUDGING FROM THE NUMBER OF EGGS SENT OUT, AND FROM WHAT TOPKNOT HAS TOLD ME, THIS WILL BE ONE OF THE BIGGEST HUNTS IN MEMORY.

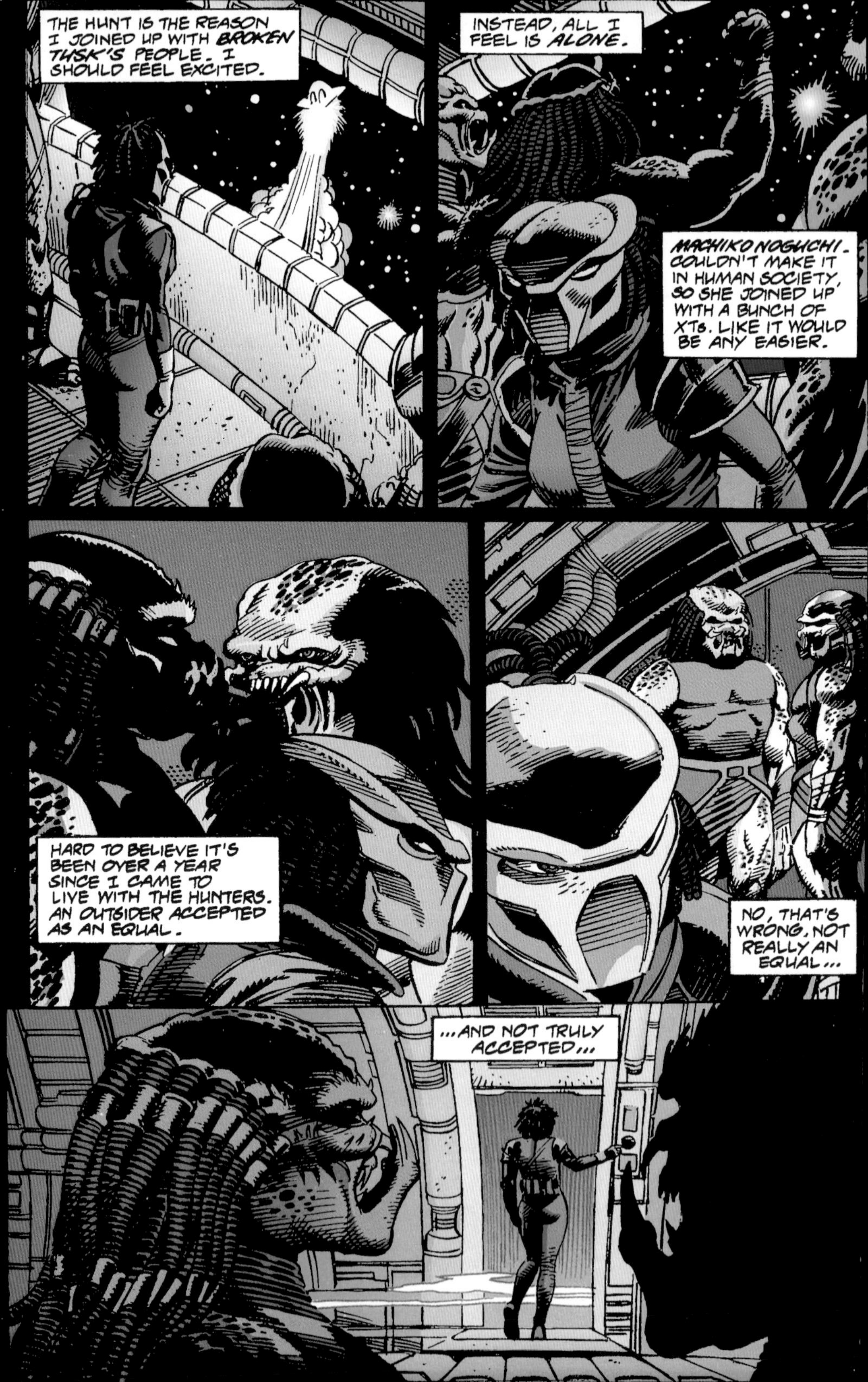
THE HUNT IS THE REASON I JOINED UP WITH BROKEN TUSK'S PEOPLE. I SHOULD FEEL EXCITED.
INSTEAD, ALL I FEEL IS ALONE.
MACHIKO NOGUCHI - COULDN'T MAKE IT IN HUMAN SOCIETY, SO SHE JOINED UP WITH A BUNCH OF XTs. LIKE IT WOULD BE ANY EASIER.
HARD TO BELIEVE IT'S BEEN OVER A YEAR SINCE I CAME TO LIVE WITH THE HUNTERS. AN OUTSIDER ACCEPTED AS AN EQUAL.
NO, THAT'S WRONG. NOT REALLY AN EQUAL...
...AND NOT TRULY ACCEPTED...

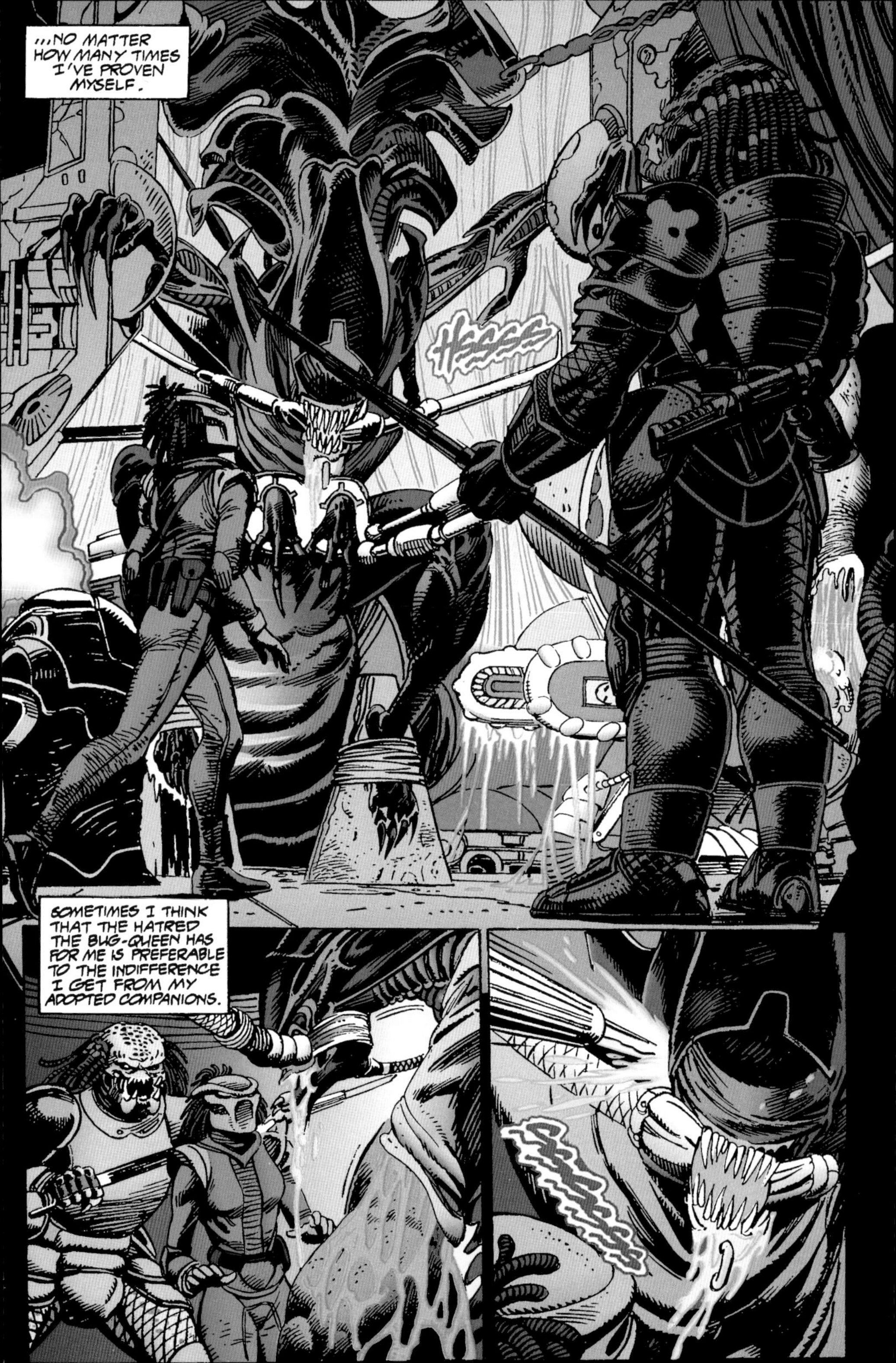

...NO MATTER HOW MANY TIMES I'VE PROVEN MYSELF.
HSSSS
SOMETIMES I THINK THAT THE HATRED THE BUG-QUEEN HAS FOR ME IS PREFERABLE TO THE INDIFFERENCE I GET FROM MY ADOPTED COMPANIONS.

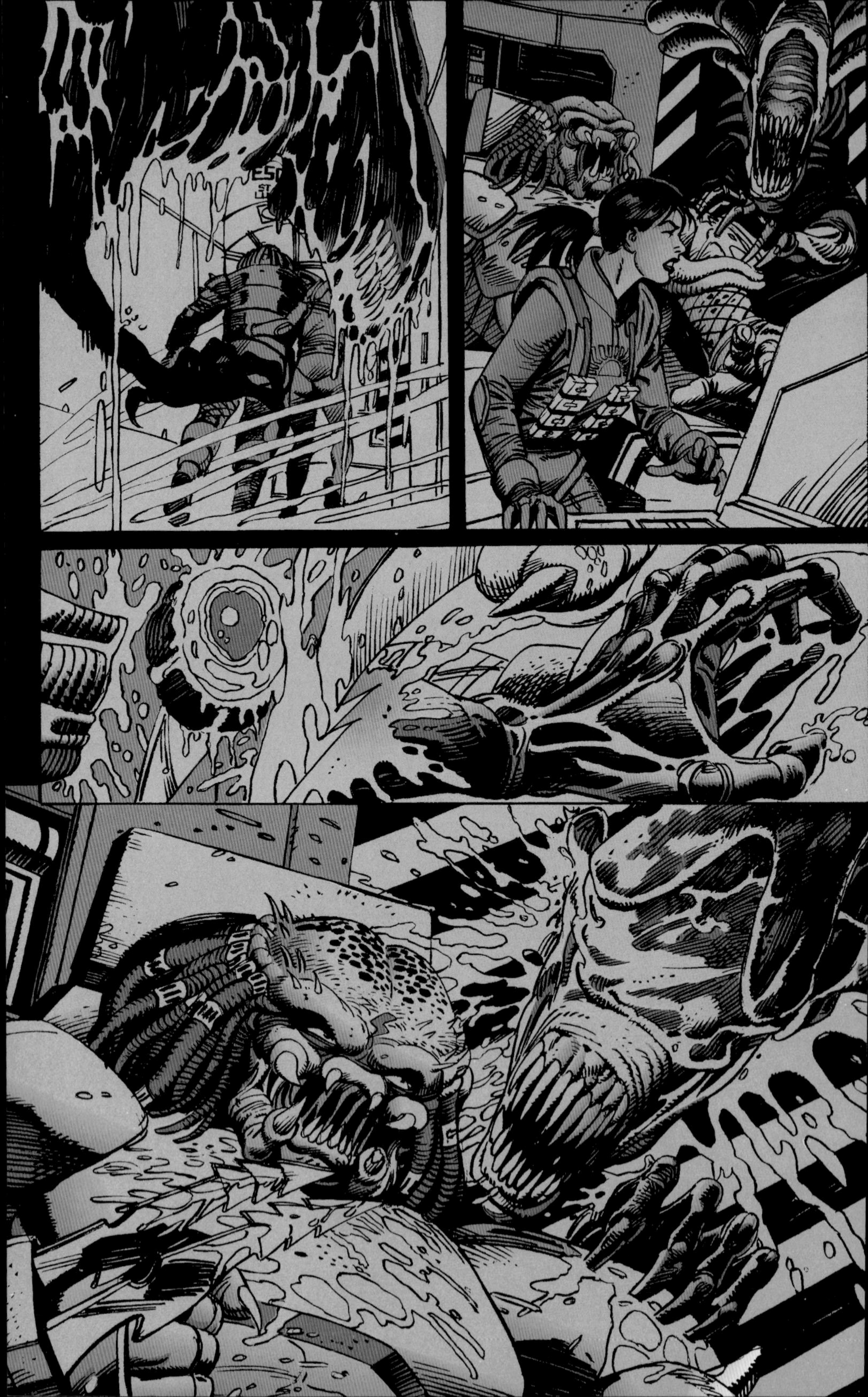

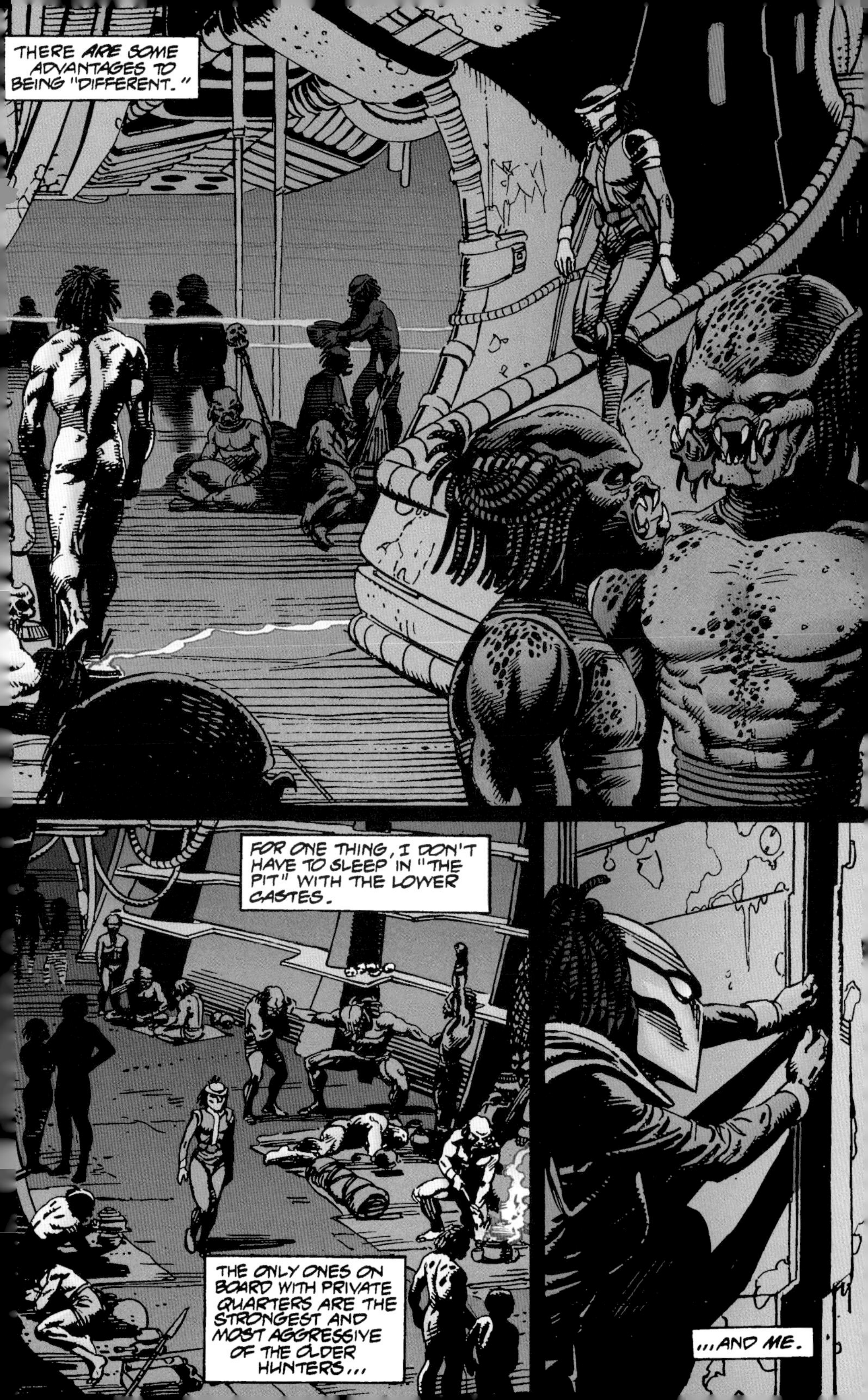
THERE ARE SOME ADVANTAGES TO BEING "DIFFERENT."
FOR ONE THING, I DON'T HAVE TO SLEEP IN "THE PIT" WITH THE LOWER CASTES.
THE ONLY ONES ON BOARD WITH PRIVATE QUARTERS ARE THE STRONGEST AND MOST AGGRESSIVE OF THE OLDER HUNTERS...
...AND ME.

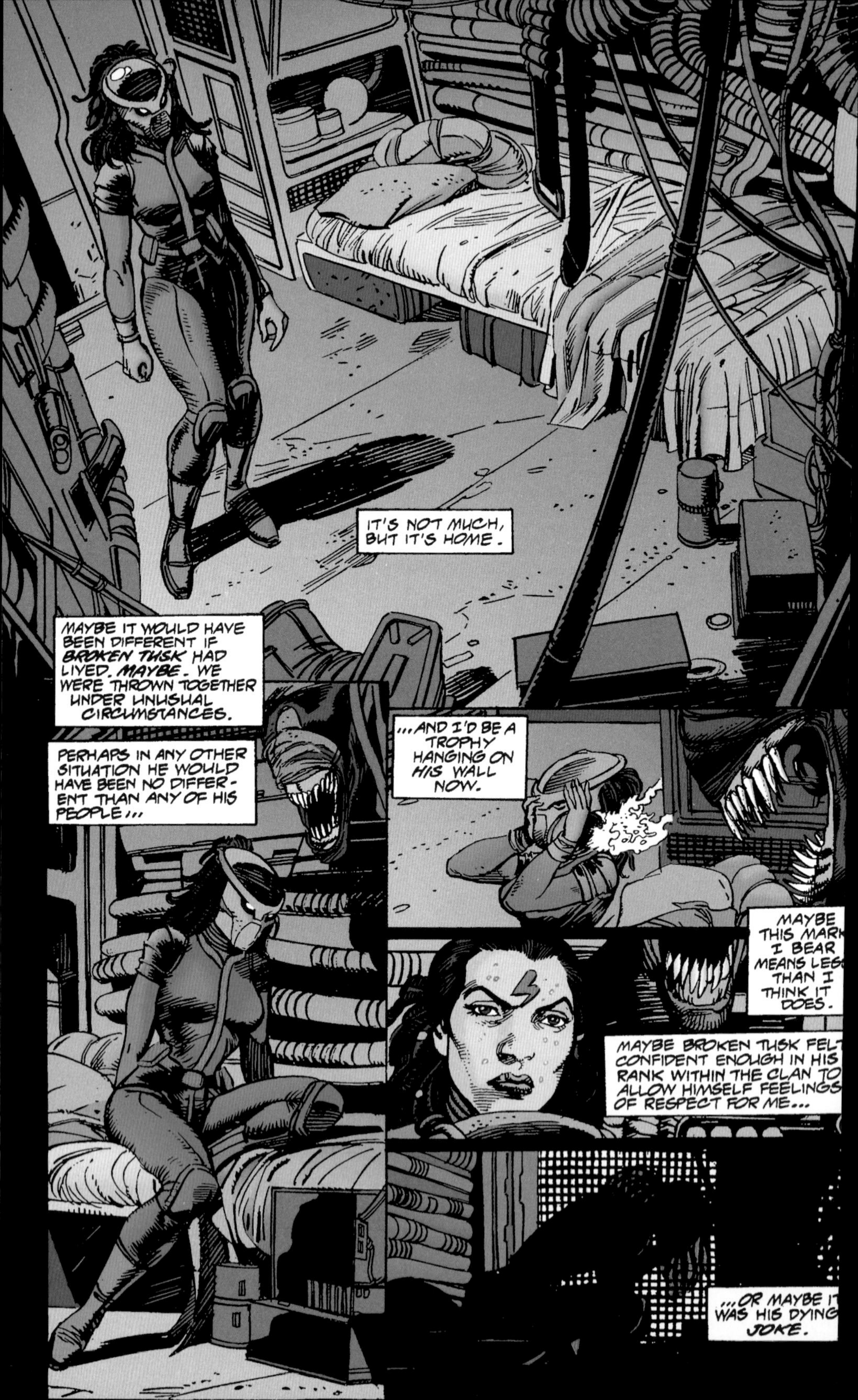
IT'S NOT MUCH, BUT IT'S HOME.
MAYBE IT WOULD HAVE BEEN DIFFERENT IF BROKEN TUSK HAD LIVED. MAYBE. WE WERE THROWN TOGETHER UNDER UNUSUAL CIRCUMSTANCES.
PERHAPS IN ANY OTHER SITUATION HE WOULD HAVE BEEN NO DIFFERENT THAN ANY OF HIS PEOPLE...
...AND I'D BE A TROPHY HANGING ON HIS WALL NOW.
MAYBE THIS MARK I BEAR MEANS LESS THAN I THINK IT DOES.
MAYBE BROKEN TUSK FELT CONFIDENT ENOUGH IN HIS RANK WITHIN THE CLAN TO ALLOW HIMSELF FEELINGS OF RESPECT FOR ME...
...OR MAYBE IT WAS HIS DYING JOKE.

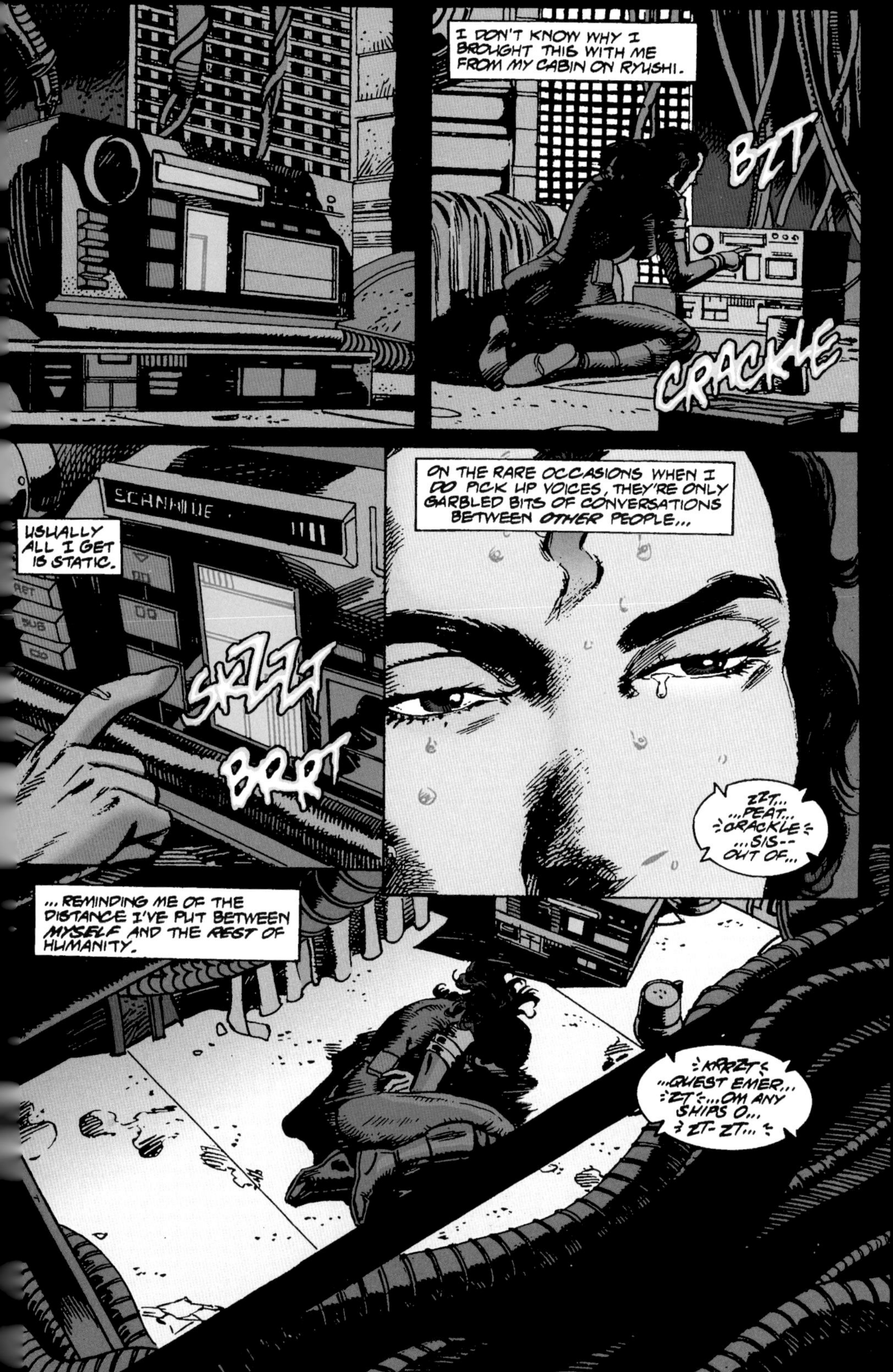
I DON'T KNOW WHY I BROUGHT THIS WITH ME FROM MY CABIN ON RYUSHI.
BZZT
CRACKLE
SCANHIIDE
USUALLY ALL I GET IS STATIC.
SKZZZT
BRRT
ON THE RARE OCCASIONS WHEN I *DO* PICK UP VOICES, THEY'RE ONLY GARBLED BITS OF CONVERSATIONS BETWEEN *OTHER* PEOPLE...
ZZT... ...PEAT... CRACKLE ...SIS-- OUT OF...
... REMINDING ME OF THE DISTANCE I'VE PUT BETWEEN *MYSELF* AND THE *REST* OF HUMANITY.
KRRZZT ...QUEST EMER... ZZT ...OM ANY SHIPS O... ZZT- ZZT...

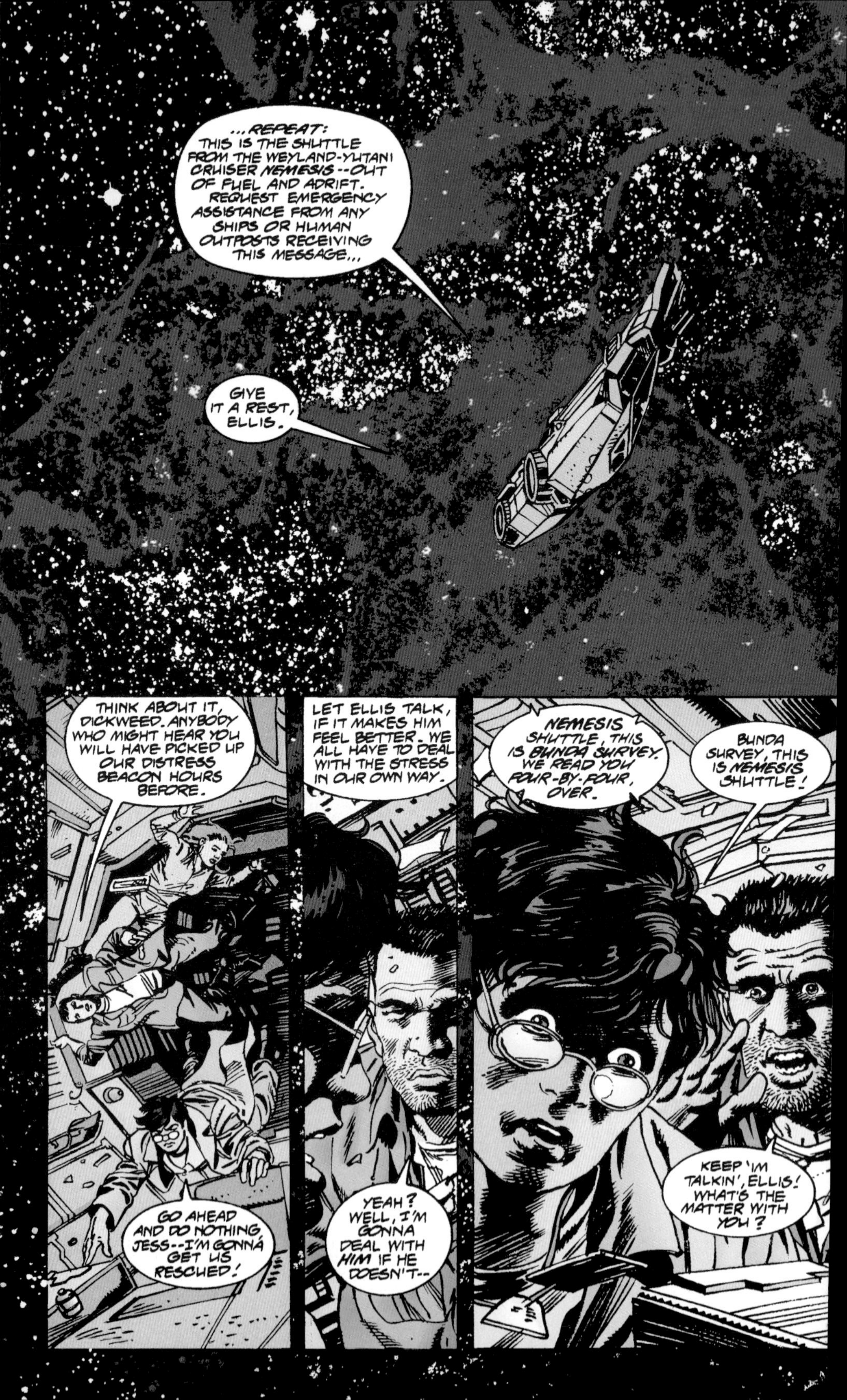
...REPEAT: THIS IS THE SHUTTLE FROM THE WEYLAND-YUTANI CRUISER NEMESIS--OUT OF FUEL AND ADRIFT. REQUEST EMERGENCY ASSISTANCE FROM ANY SHIPS OR HUMAN OUTPOSTS RECEIVING THIS MESSAGE...
GIVE IT A REST, ELLIS.
THINK ABOUT IT, DICKWEED. ANYBODY WHO MIGHT HEAR YOU WILL HAVE PICKED UP OUR DISTRESS BEACON HOURS BEFORE.
GO AHEAD AND DO NOTHING, JESS--I'M GONNA GET US RESCUED!
LET ELLIS TALK, IF IT MAKES HIM FEEL BETTER. WE ALL HAVE TO DEAL WITH THE STRESS IN OUR OWN WAY.
YEAH? WELL, I'M GONNA DEAL WITH HIM IF HE DOESN'T--
NEMESIS SHUTTLE, THIS IS BUNDA SURVEY. WE READ YOU FOUR-BY-FOUR, OVER.
BUNDA SURVEY, THIS IS NEMESIS SHUTTLE!
KEEP 'IM TALKIN', ELLIS! WHAT'S THE MATTER WITH YOU?

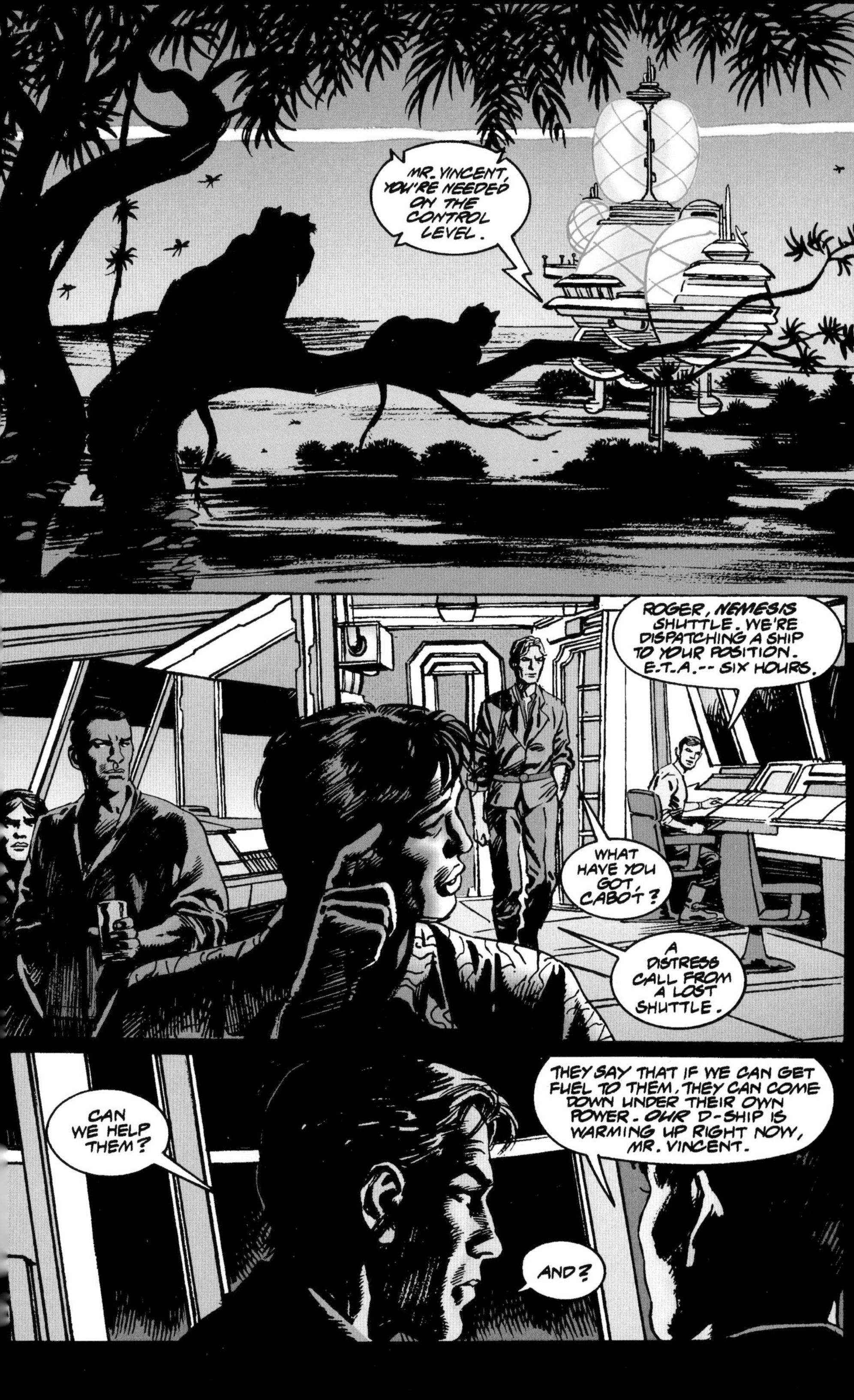
MR. VINCENT, YOU'RE NEEDED ON THE CONTROL LEVEL.
ROGER, NEMESIS SHUTTLE. WE'RE DISPATCHING A SHIP TO YOUR POSITION. E.T.A.-- SIX HOURS.
WHAT HAVE YOU GOT, CABOT?
A DISTRESS CALL FROM A LOST SHUTTLE.
CAN WE HELP THEM?
THEY SAY THAT IF WE CAN GET FUEL TO THEM, THEY CAN COME DOWN UNDER THEIR OWN POWER. OUR D-SHIP IS WARMING UP RIGHT NOW, MR. VINCENT.
AND?

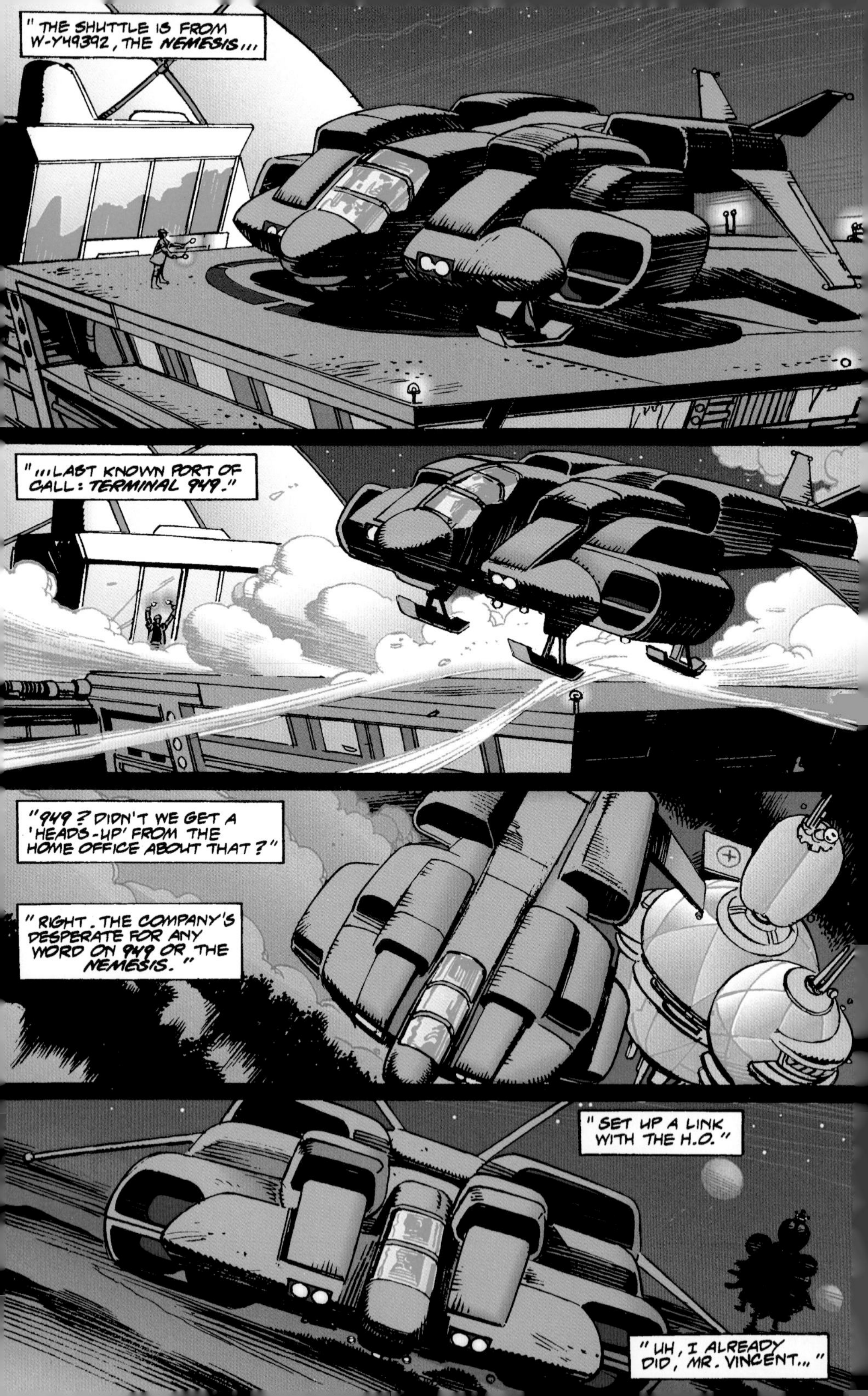
"THE SHUTTLE IS FROM W-Y49392, THE NEMESIS...
"...LAST KNOWN PORT OF CALL: TERMINAL 949."
"949? DIDN'T WE GET A 'HEADS-UP' FROM THE HOME OFFICE ABOUT THAT?"
"RIGHT. THE COMPANY'S DESPERATE FOR ANY WORD ON 949 OR THE NEMESIS."
"SET UP A LINK WITH THE H.O."
"UH, I ALREADY DID, MR. VINCENT..."

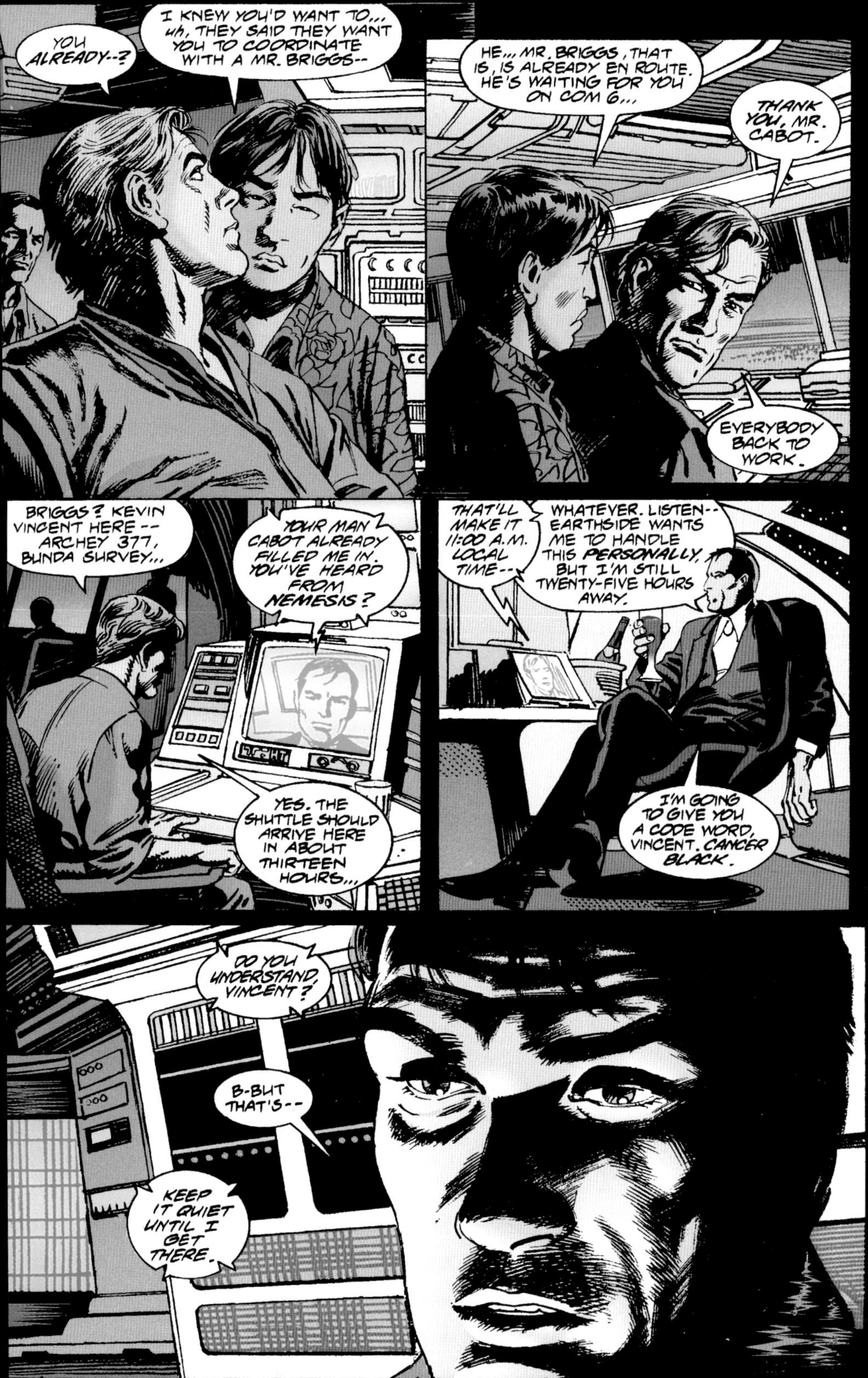
YOU ALREADY--?
I KNEW YOU'D WANT TO... uh, THEY SAID THEY WANT YOU TO COORDINATE WITH A MR. BRIGGS--
HE... MR. BRIGGS, THAT IS, IS ALREADY EN ROUTE. HE'S WAITING FOR YOU ON COM 6...
THANK YOU, MR. CABOT.
EVERYBODY BACK TO WORK.
BRIGGS? KEVIN VINCENT HERE -- ARCHEY 377, BUNDA SURVEY...
YOUR MAN CABOT ALREADY FILLED ME IN. YOU'VE HEARD FROM NEMESIS?
YES. THE SHUTTLE SHOULD ARRIVE HERE IN ABOUT THIRTEEN HOURS...
THAT'LL MAKE IT 11:00 A.M. LOCAL TIME--
WHATEVER. LISTEN-- EARTHSIDE WANTS ME TO HANDLE THIS PERSONALLY, BUT I'M STILL TWENTY-FIVE HOURS AWAY.
I'M GOING TO GIVE YOU A CODE WORD, VINCENT. CANCER BLACK.
DO YOU UNDERSTAND, VINCENT?
B-BUT THAT'S--
KEEP IT QUIET UNTIL I GET THERE.

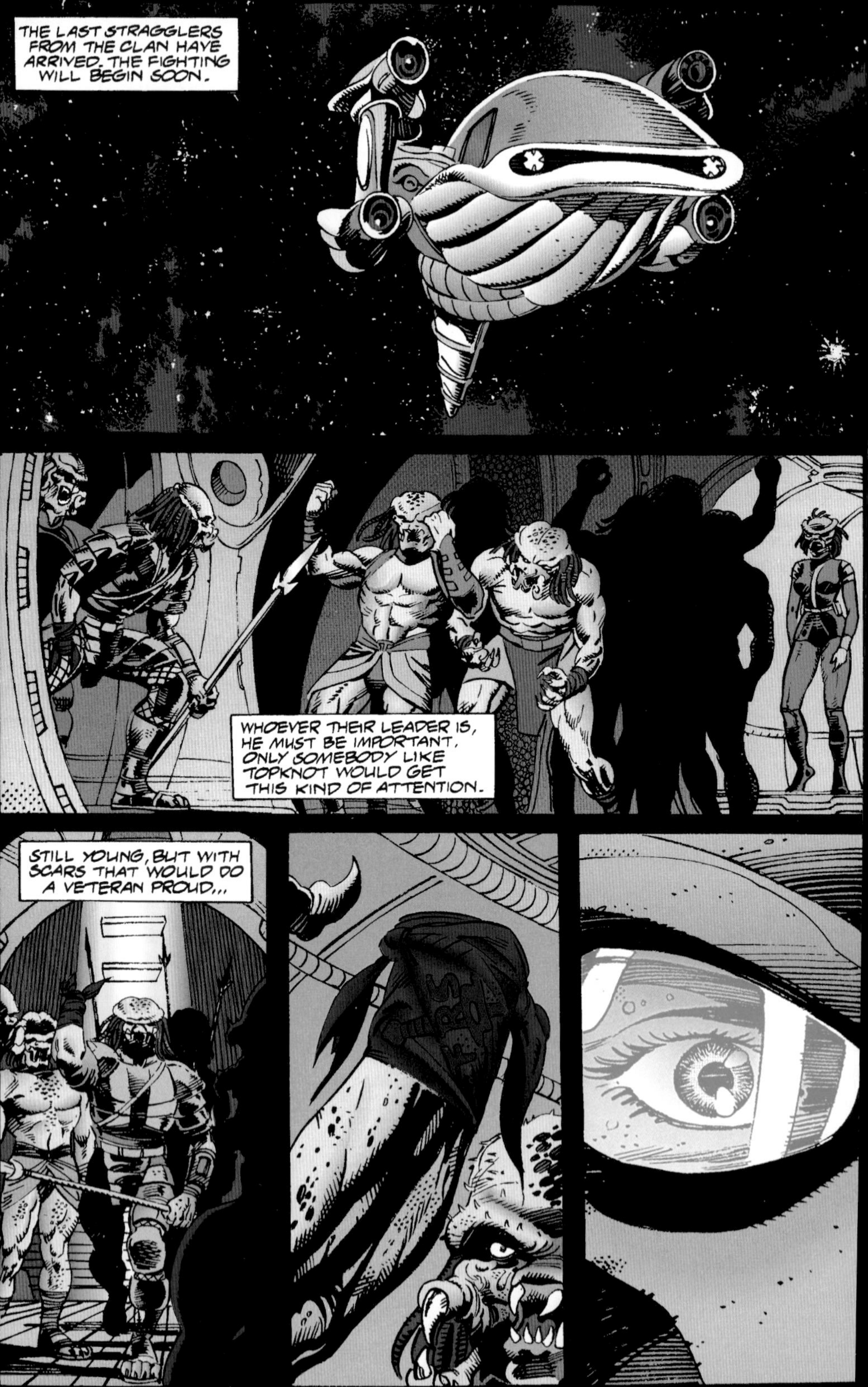
THE LAST STRAGGLERS FROM THE CLAN HAVE ARRIVED. THE FIGHTING WILL BEGIN SOON.
WHOEVER THEIR LEADER IS, HE MUST BE IMPORTANT. ONLY SOMEBODY LIKE TOPKNOT WOULD GET THIS KIND OF ATTENTION.
STILL YOUNG, BUT WITH SCARS THAT WOULD DO A VETERAN PROUD...

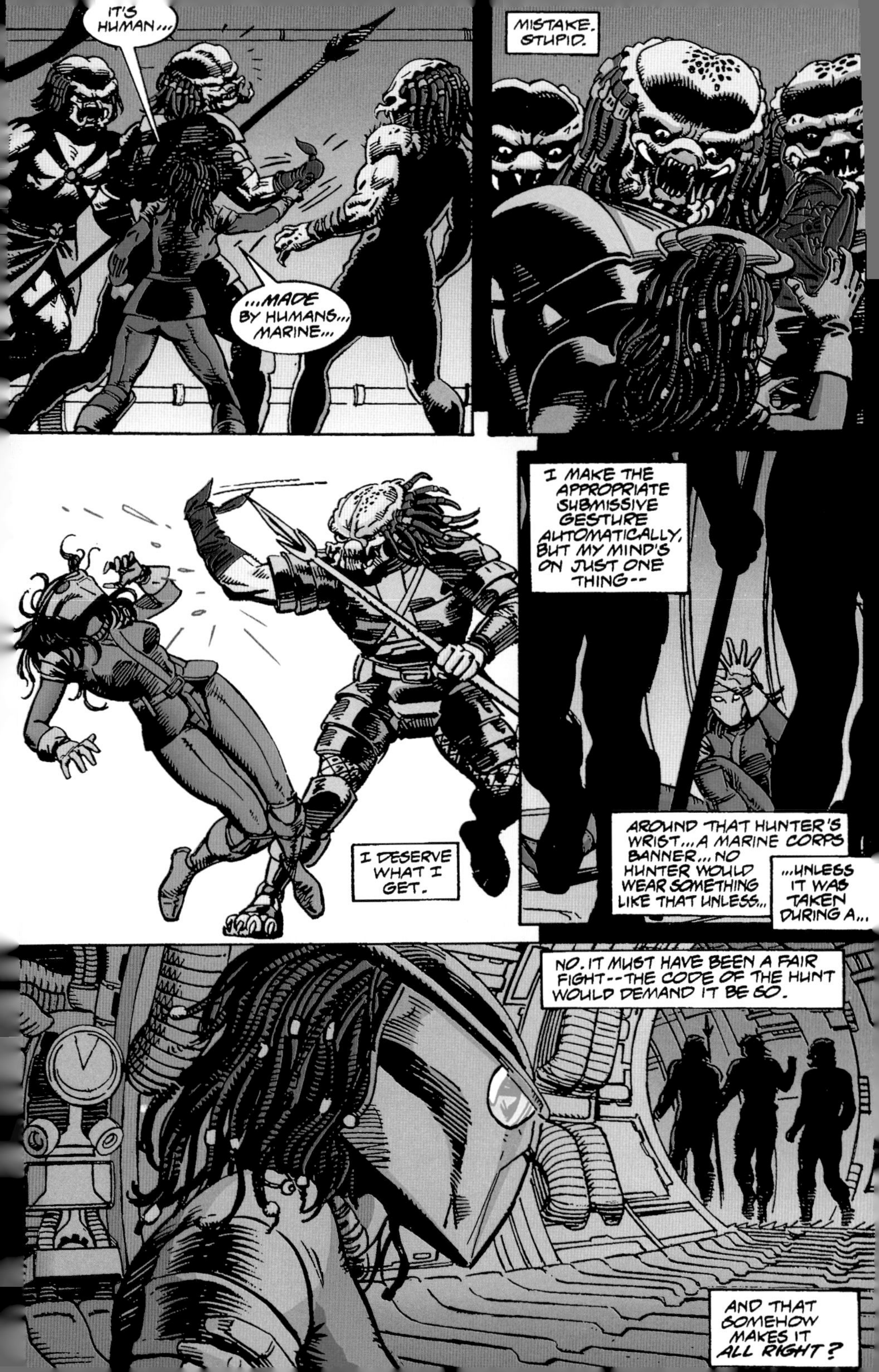
IT'S HUMAN...
...MADE BY HUMANS... MARINE...
MISTAKE. STUPID.
I DESERVE WHAT I GET.
I MAKE THE APPROPRIATE SUBMISSIVE GESTURE AUTOMATICALLY, BUT MY MIND'S ON JUST ONE THING--
AROUND THAT HUNTER'S WRIST... A MARINE CORPS BANNER... NO HUNTER WOULD WEAR SOMETHING LIKE THAT UNLESS...
...UNLESS IT WAS TAKEN DURING A...
NO. IT MUST HAVE BEEN A FAIR FIGHT--THE CODE OF THE HUNT WOULD DEMAND IT BE SO.
AND THAT SOMEHOW MAKES IT ALL RIGHT?

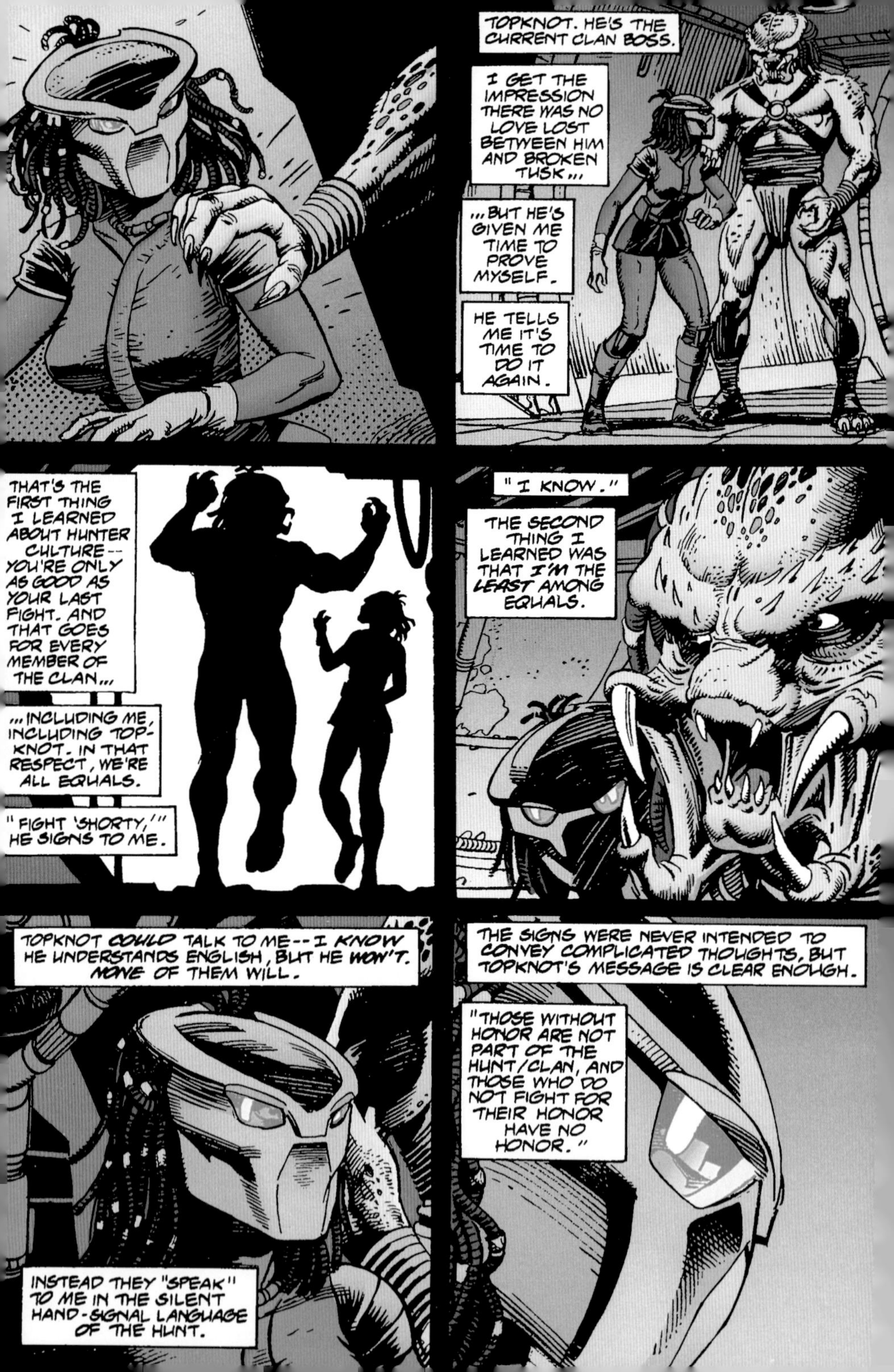
TOPKNOT. HE'S THE CURRENT CLAN BOSS.
I GET THE IMPRESSION THERE WAS NO LOVE LOST BETWEEN HIM AND BROKEN TUSK...
...BUT HE'S GIVEN ME TIME TO PROVE MYSELF.
HE TELLS ME IT'S TIME TO DO IT AGAIN.
THAT'S THE FIRST THING I LEARNED ABOUT HUNTER CULTURE-- YOU'RE ONLY AS GOOD AS YOUR LAST FIGHT. AND THAT GOES FOR EVERY MEMBER OF THE CLAN...
...INCLUDING ME, INCLUDING TOP-KNOT. IN THAT RESPECT, WE'RE ALL EQUALS.
"FIGHT 'SHORTY,'" HE SIGNS TO ME.
"I KNOW."
THE SECOND THING I LEARNED WAS THAT I'M THE LEAST AMONG EQUALS.
TOPKNOT COULD TALK TO ME--I KNOW HE UNDERSTANDS ENGLISH, BUT HE WON'T. NONE OF THEM WILL.
INSTEAD THEY "SPEAK" TO ME IN THE SILENT HAND-SIGNAL LANGUAGE OF THE HUNT.
THE SIGNS WERE NEVER INTENDED TO CONVEY COMPLICATED THOUGHTS, BUT TOPKNOT'S MESSAGE IS CLEAR ENOUGH.
"THOSE WITHOUT HONOR ARE NOT PART OF THE HUNT/CLAN, AND THOSE WHO DO NOT FIGHT FOR THEIR HONOR HAVE NO HONOR."

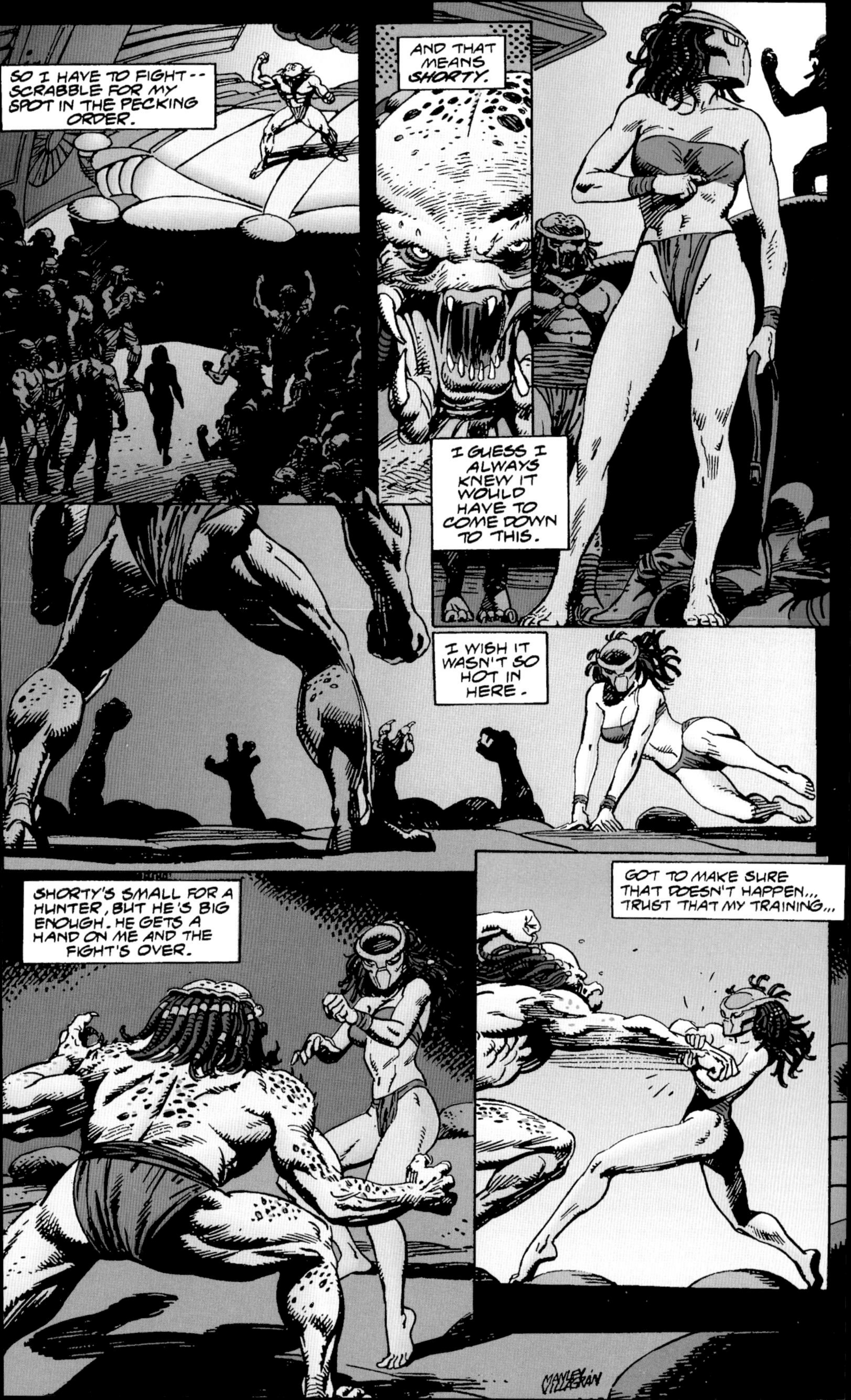
SO I HAVE TO FIGHT--SCRABBLE FOR MY SPOT IN THE PECKING ORDER.
AND THAT MEANS SHORTY.
I GUESS I ALWAYS KNEW IT WOULD HAVE TO COME DOWN TO THIS.
I WISH IT WASN'T SO HOT IN HERE.
SHORTY'S SMALL FOR A HUNTER, BUT HE'S BIG ENOUGH. HE GETS A HAND ON ME AND THE FIGHT'S OVER.
GOT TO MAKE SURE THAT DOESN'T HAPPEN... TRUST THAT MY TRAINING...
MANLEY VILLAGRAN

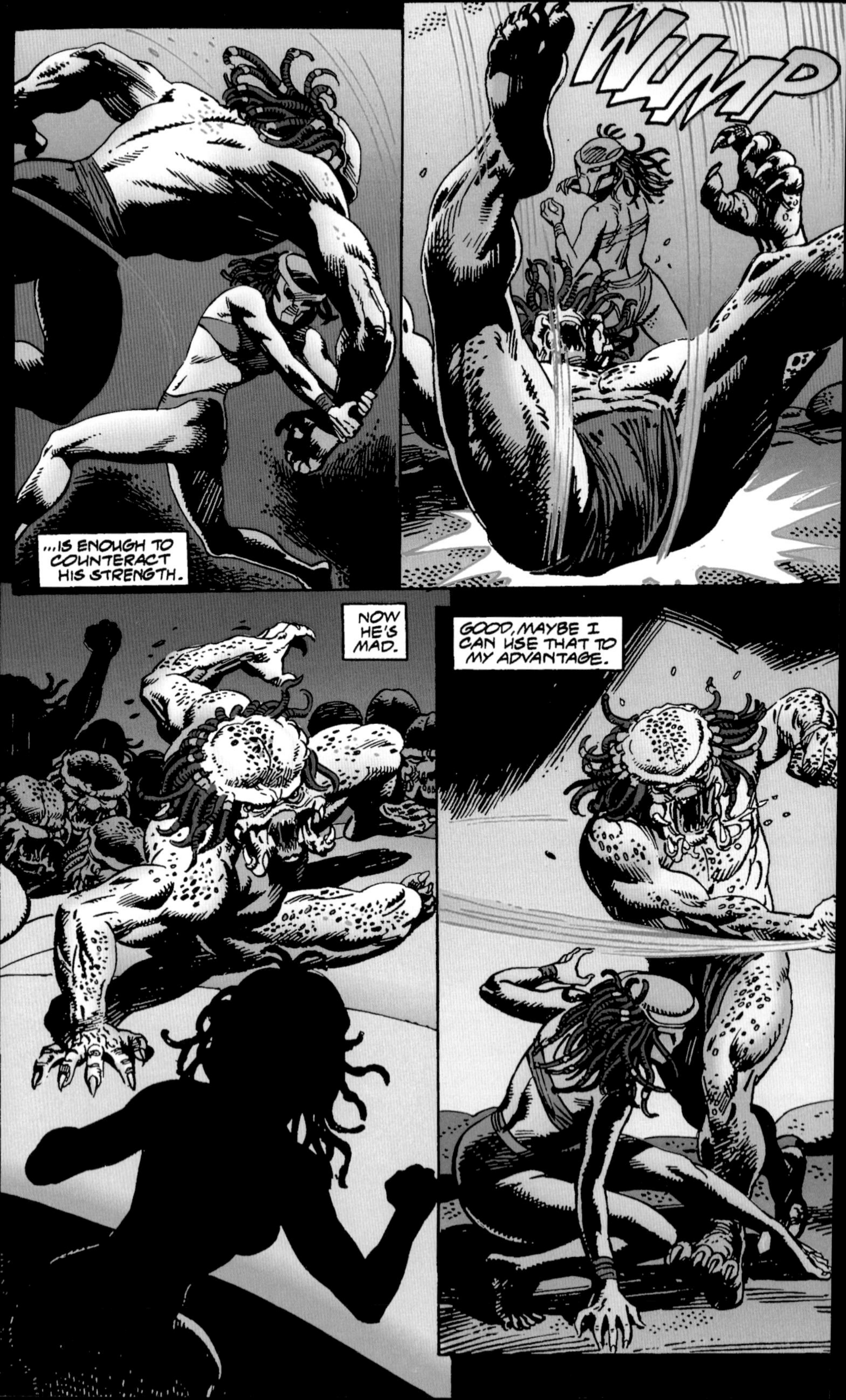
...IS ENOUGH TO COUNTERACT HIS STRENGTH.
WUMP
NOW HE'S MAD.
GOOD, MAYBE I CAN USE THAT TO MY ADVANTAGE.

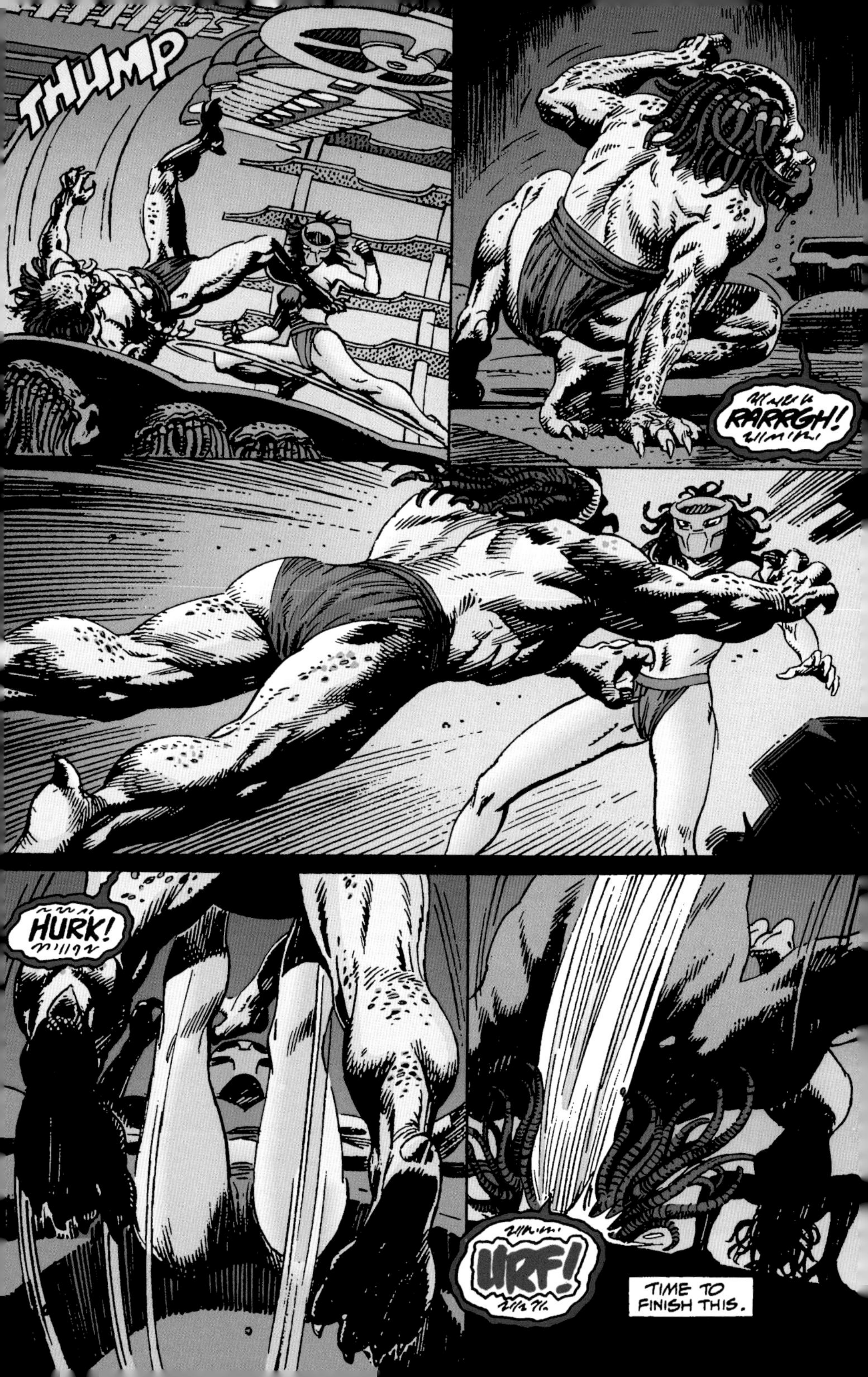
THUMP
RARRGH!
HURK!
URF!
TIME TO FINISH THIS.

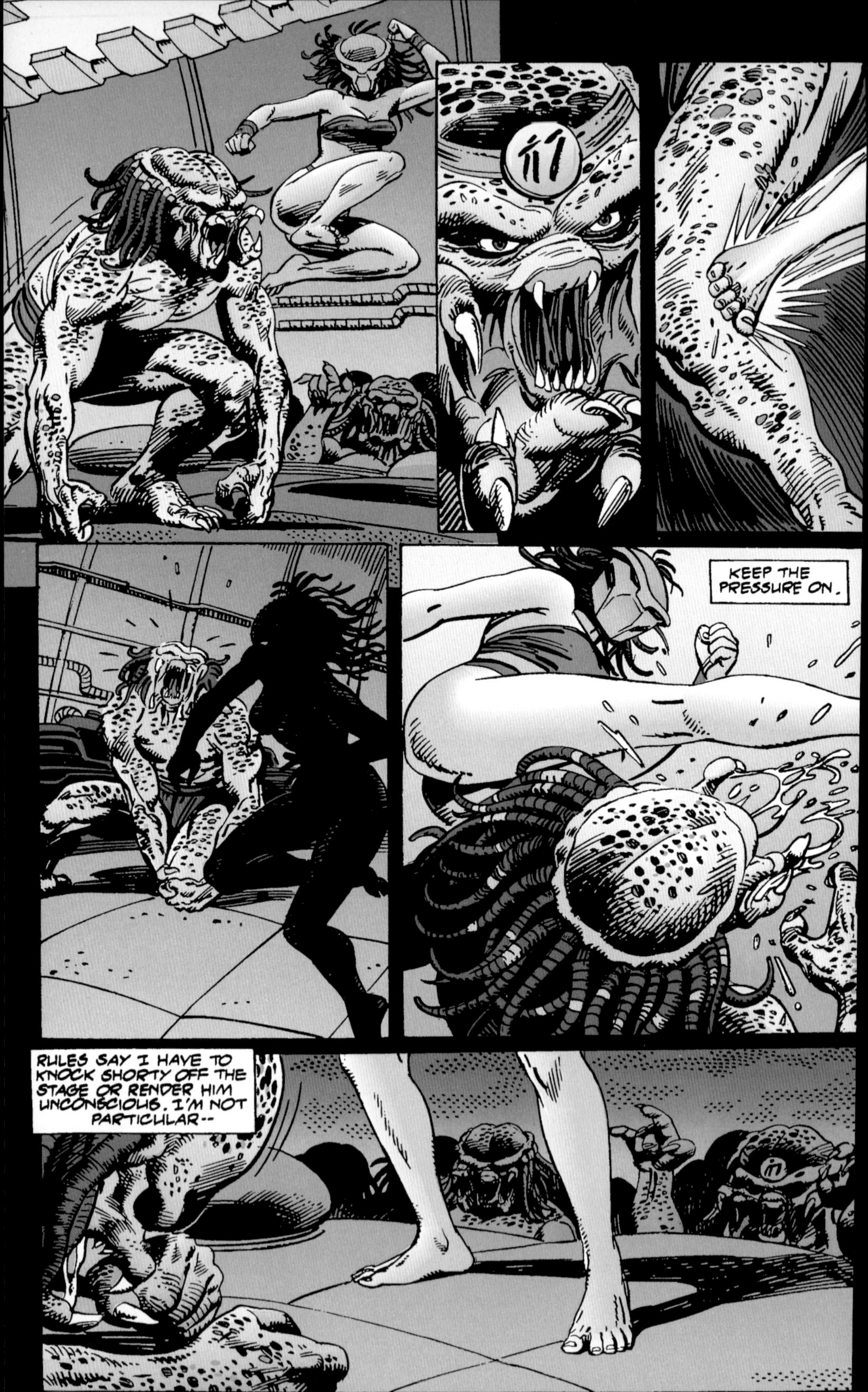
KEEP THE PRESSURE ON.
RULES SAY I HAVE TO KNOCK SHORTY OFF THE STAGE OR RENDER HIM UNCONSCIOUS. I'M NOT PARTICULAR--

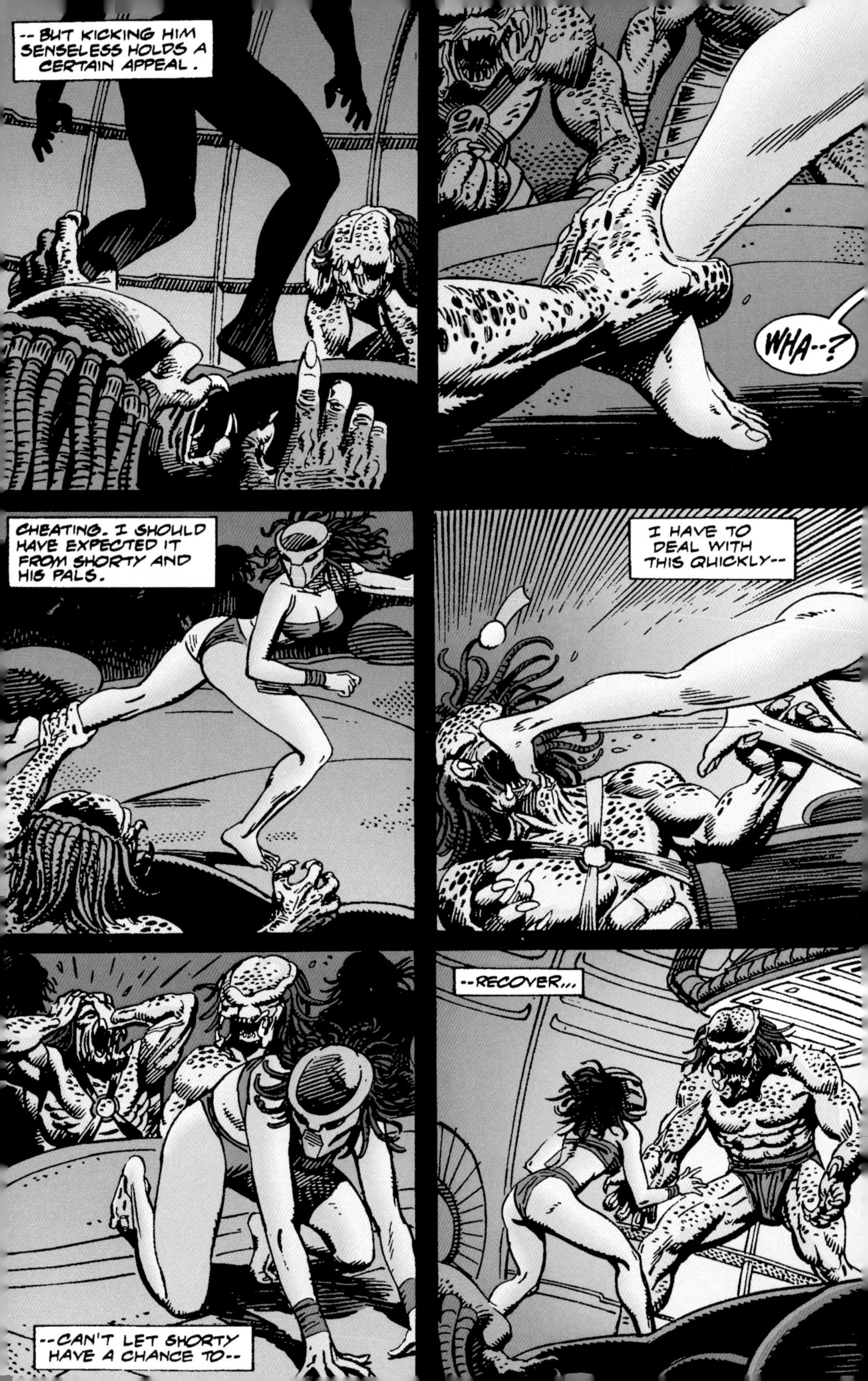

-- BUT KICKING HIM SENSELESS HOLDS A CERTAIN APPEAL.
WHA--?
CHEATING. I SHOULD HAVE EXPECTED IT FROM SHORTY AND HIS PALS.
I HAVE TO DEAL WITH THIS QUICKLY--
--CAN'T LET SHORTY HAVE A CHANCE TO--
--RECOVER...

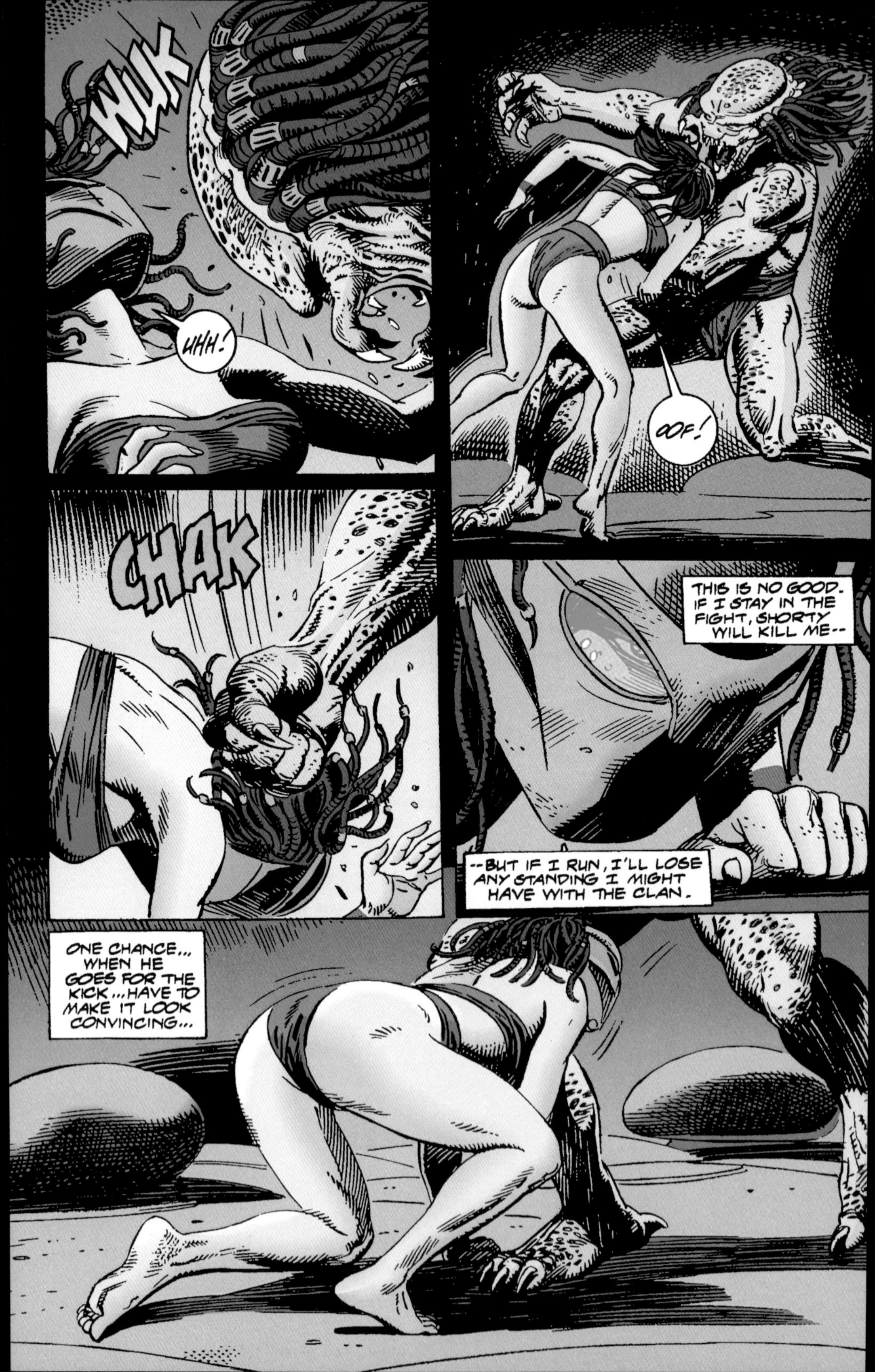
WUK
UHH!
OOF!
CHAK
THIS IS NO GOOD. IF I STAY IN THE FIGHT, SHORTY WILL KILL ME--
--BUT IF I RUN, I'LL LOSE ANY STANDING I MIGHT HAVE WITH THE CLAN.
ONE CHANCE... WHEN HE GOES FOR THE KICK... HAVE TO MAKE IT LOOK CONVINCING...

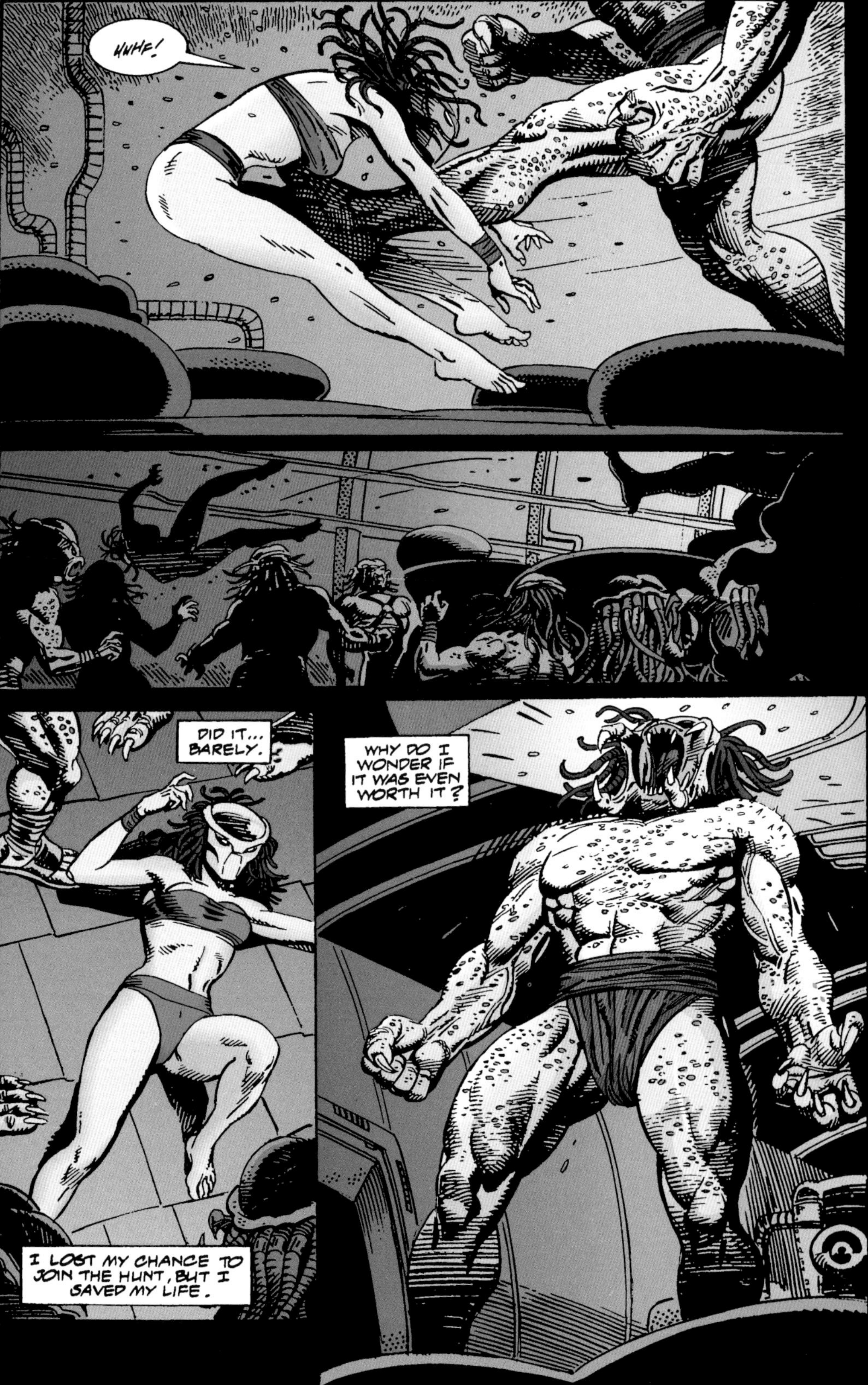
UNHF!
DID IT... BARELY.
I LOST MY CHANCE TO JOIN THE HUNT, BUT I SAVED MY LIFE.
WHY DO I WONDER IF IT WAS EVEN WORTH IT?

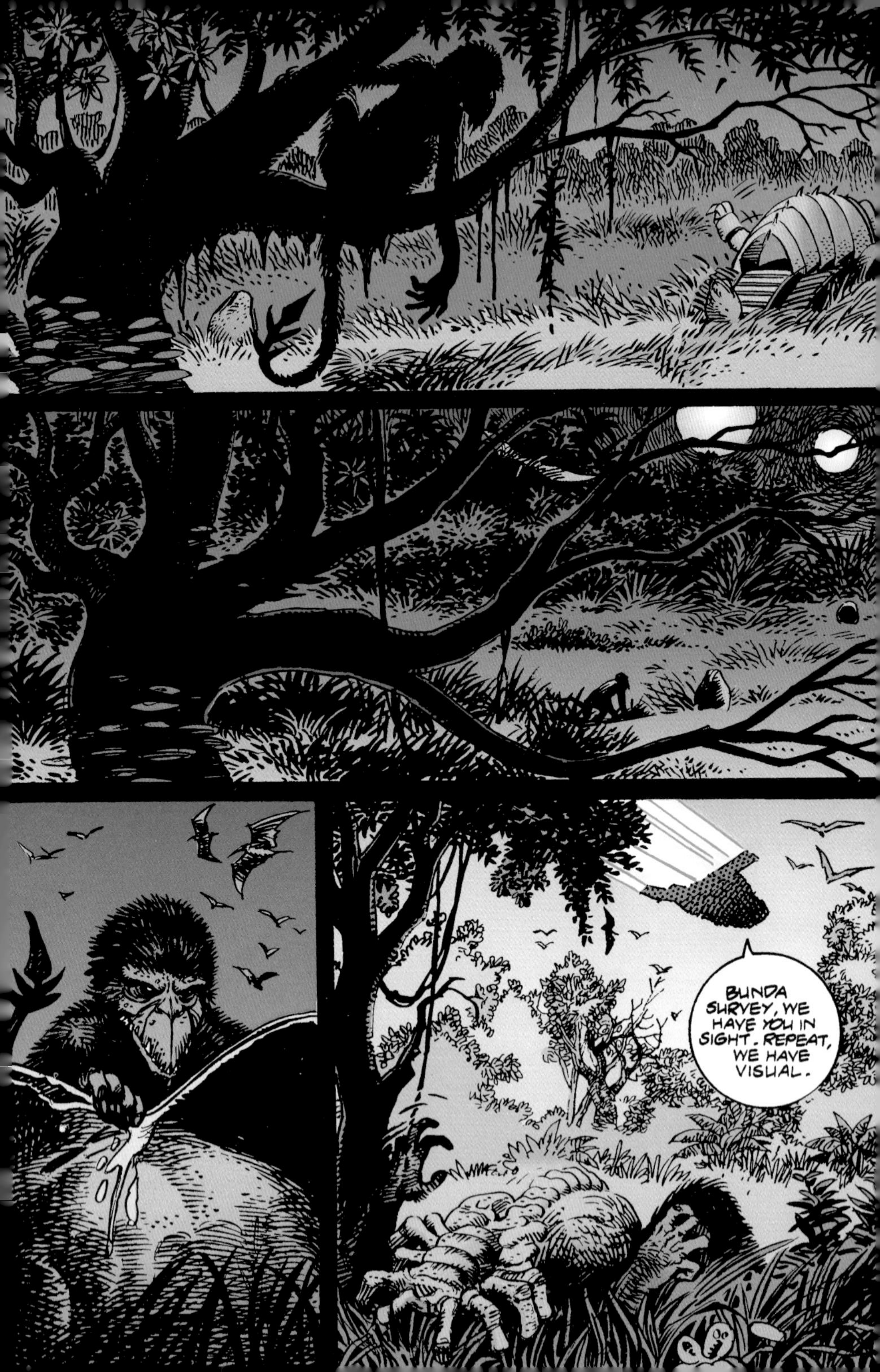
BUNDA SURVEY, WE HAVE YOU IN SIGHT. REPEAT, WE HAVE VISUAL.

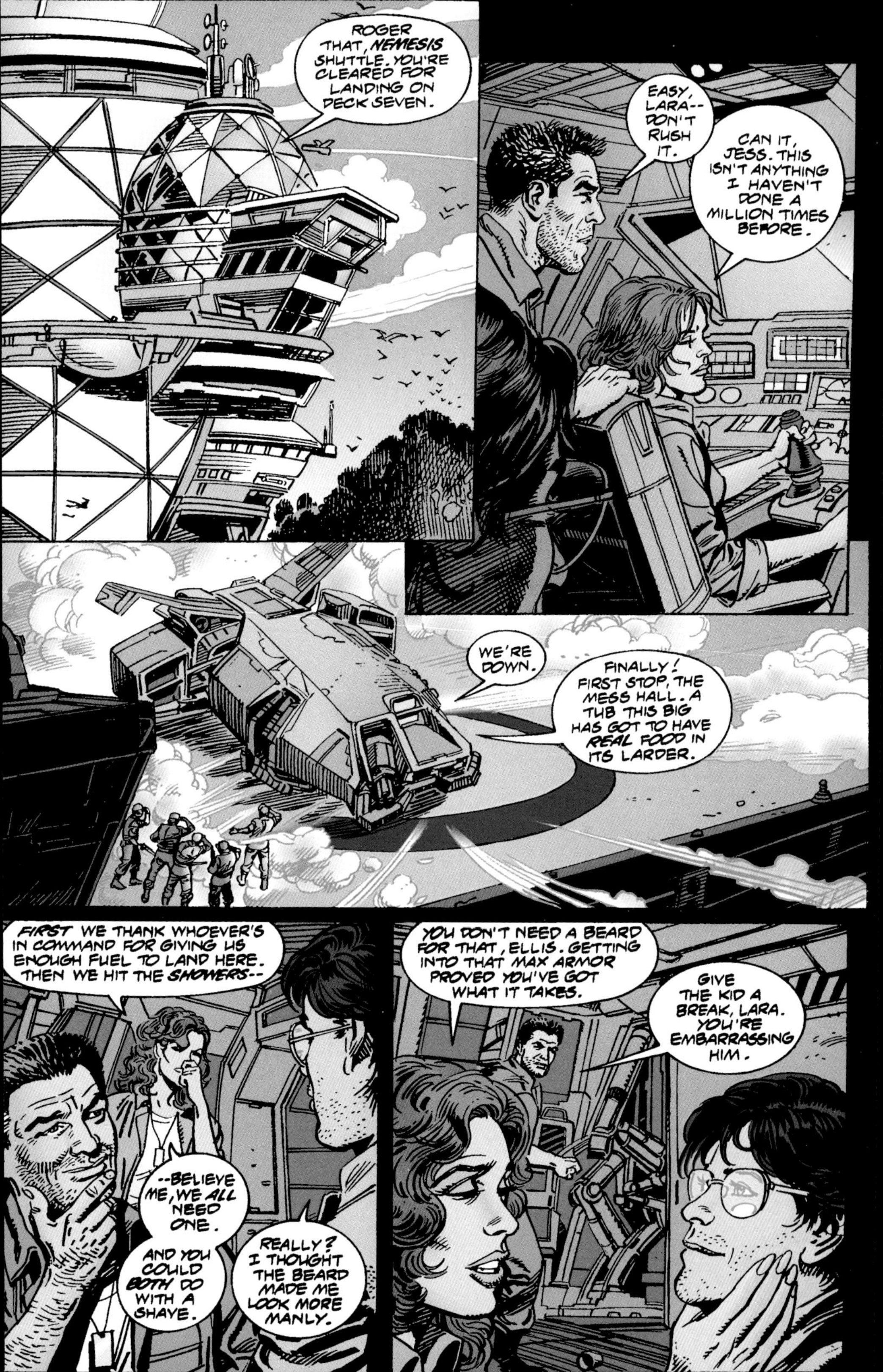
ROGER THAT, NEMESIS SHUTTLE. YOU'RE CLEARED FOR LANDING ON DECK SEVEN.
EASY, LARA-- DON'T RUSH IT.
CAN IT, JESS. THIS ISN'T ANYTHING I HAVEN'T DONE A MILLION TIMES BEFORE.
WE'RE DOWN.
FINALLY! FIRST STOP, THE MESS HALL. A TUB THIS BIG HAS GOT TO HAVE REAL FOOD IN ITS LARDER.
FIRST WE THANK WHOEVER'S IN COMMAND FOR GIVING US ENOUGH FUEL TO LAND HERE. THEN WE HIT THE SHOWERS--
--BELIEVE ME, WE ALL NEED ONE.
AND YOU COULD BOTH DO WITH A SHAVE.
REALLY? I THOUGHT THE BEARD MADE ME LOOK MORE MANLY.
YOU DON'T NEED A BEARD FOR THAT, ELLIS. GETTING INTO THAT MAX ARMOR PROVED YOU'VE GOT WHAT IT TAKES.
GIVE THE KID A BREAK, LARA. YOU'RE EMBARRASSING HIM.

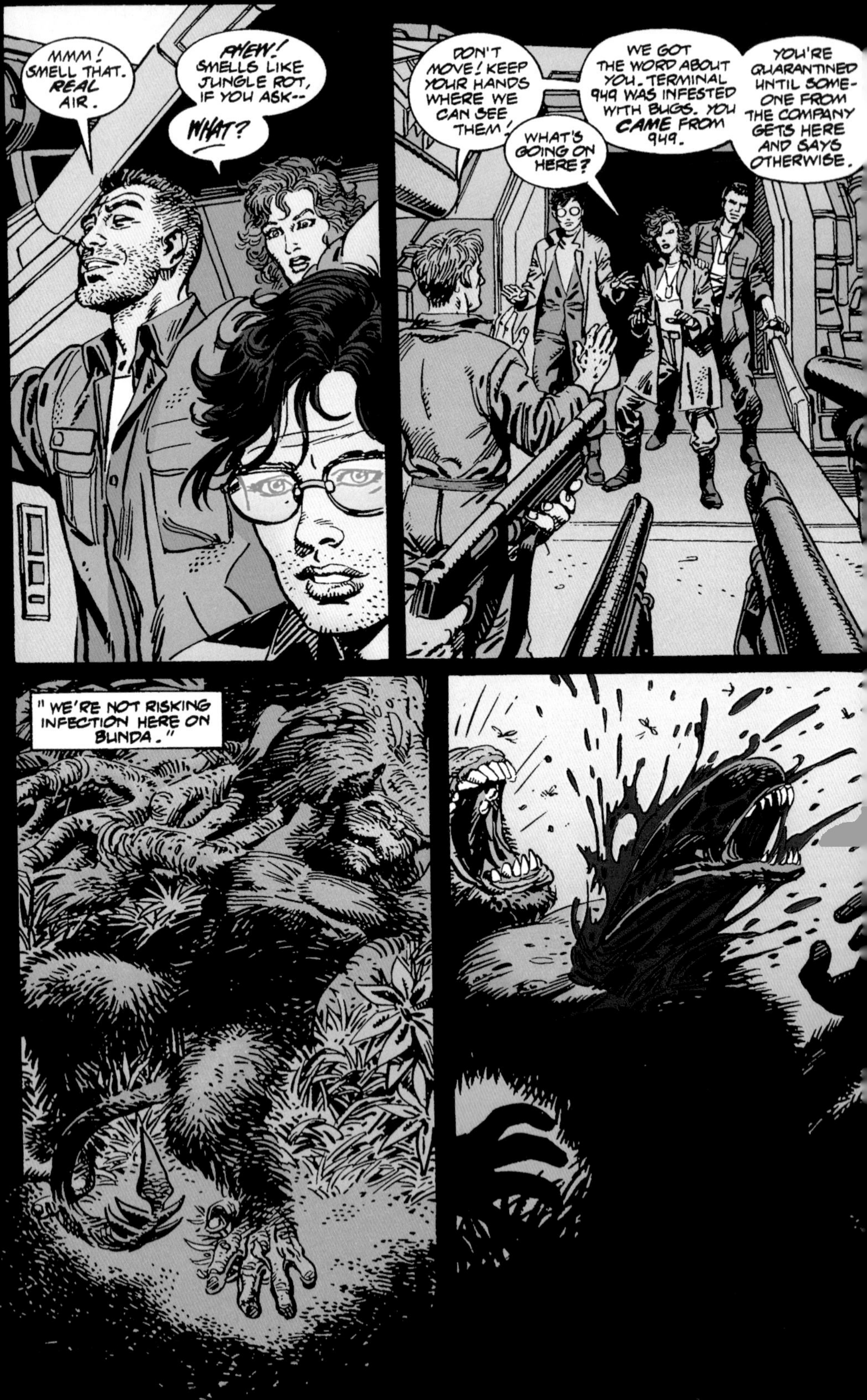

MMM! SMELL THAT. REAL AIR.
PHEW! SMELLS LIKE JUNGLE ROT, IF YOU ASK--
WHAT?
DON'T MOVE! KEEP YOUR HANDS WHERE WE CAN SEE THEM!
WHAT'S GOING ON HERE?
WE GOT THE WORD ABOUT YOU. TERMINAL 949 WAS INFESTED WITH BUGS. YOU CAME FROM 949.
YOU'RE QUARANTINED UNTIL SOMEONE FROM THE COMPANY GETS HERE AND SAYS OTHERWISE.
"WE'RE NOT RISKING INFECTION HERE ON BUNDA."

ALL OF THE BEST HUNTING SITES HAVE BEEN FOUGHT OVER, ALL OF THE RANKINGS HAVE BEEN DECIDED.

THE FIRST SHUTTLE IS AWAY.

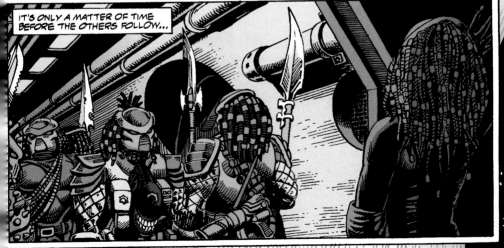

IT'S ONLY A MATTER OF TIME BEFORE THE OTHERS FOLLOW...

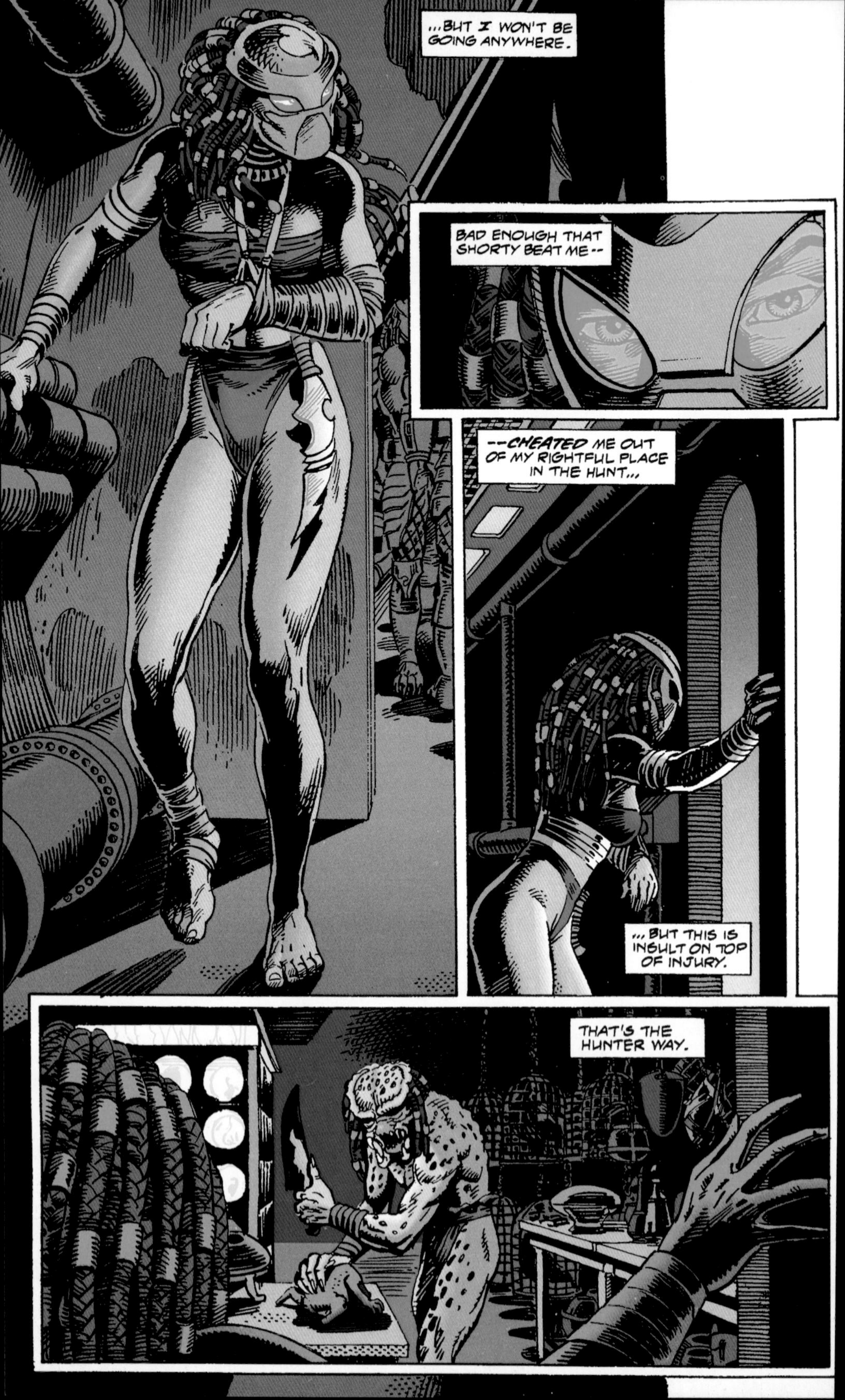

...BUT I WON'T BE GOING ANYWHERE.
BAD ENOUGH THAT SHORTY BEAT ME--
--CHEATED ME OUT OF MY RIGHTFUL PLACE IN THE HUNT...
...BUT THIS IS INSULT ON TOP OF INJURY.
THAT'S THE HUNTER WAY.

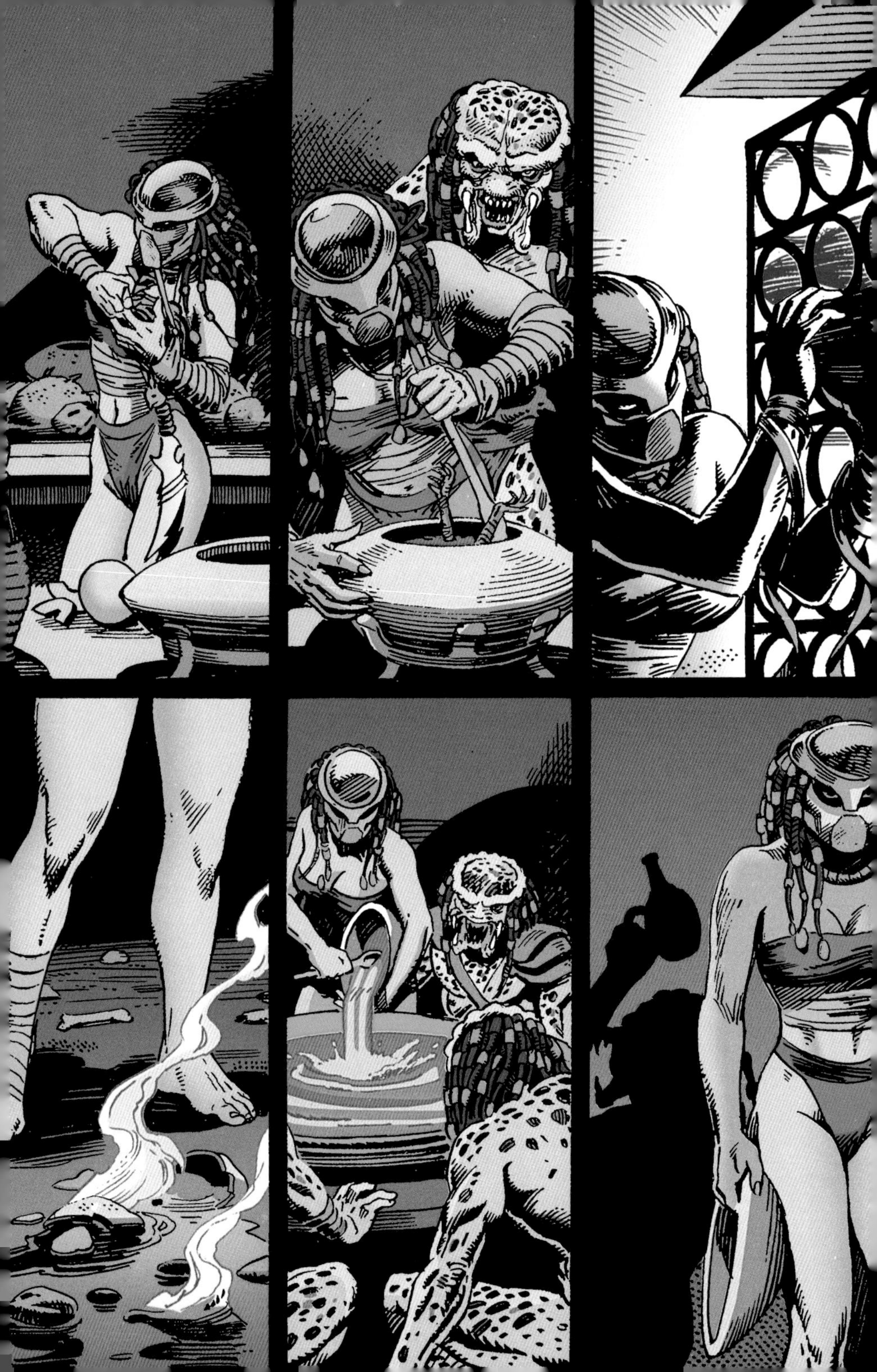

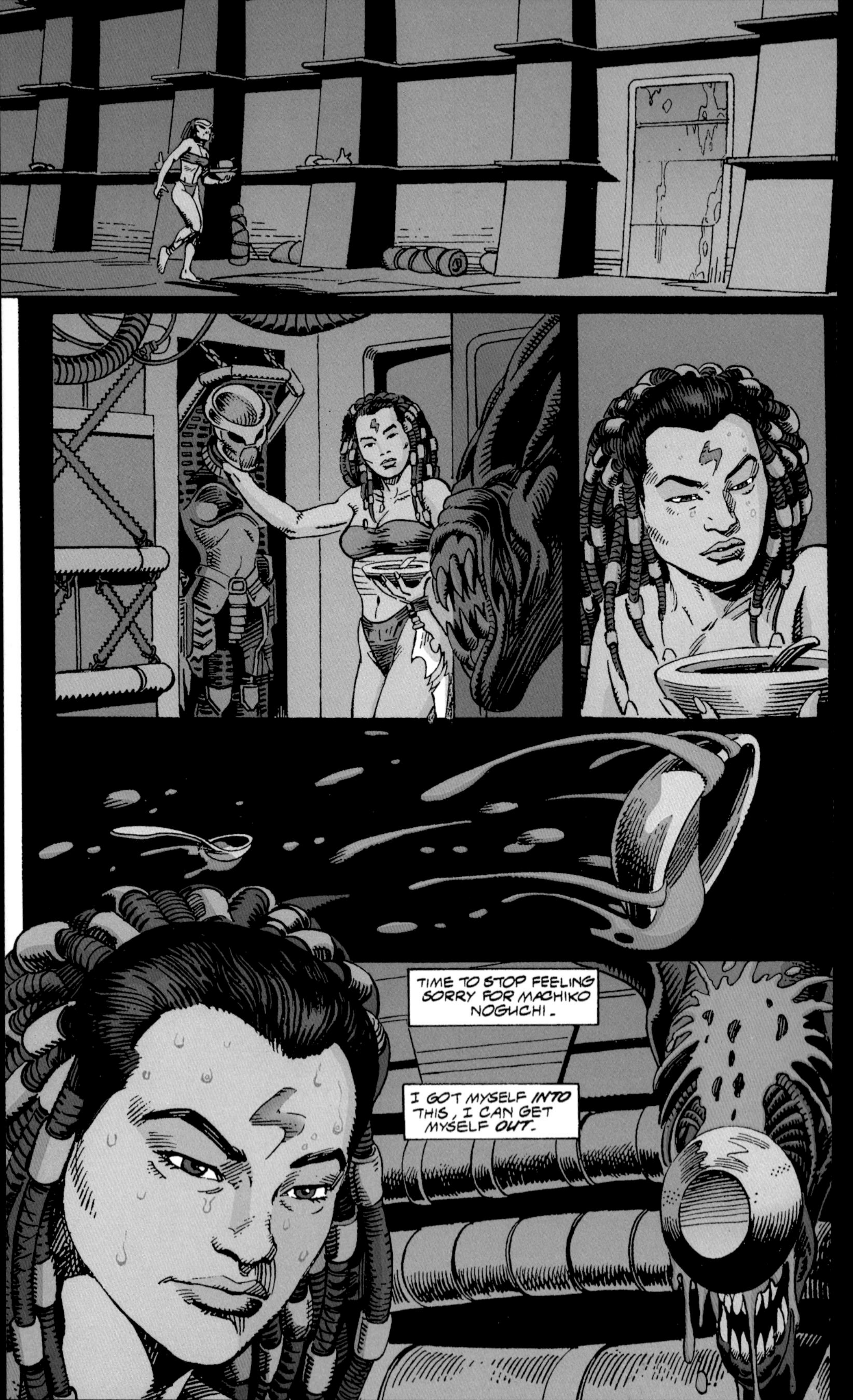
TIME TO STOP FEELING SORRY FOR MACHIKO NOGUCHI.
I GOT MYSELF INTO THIS, I CAN GET MYSELF OUT.

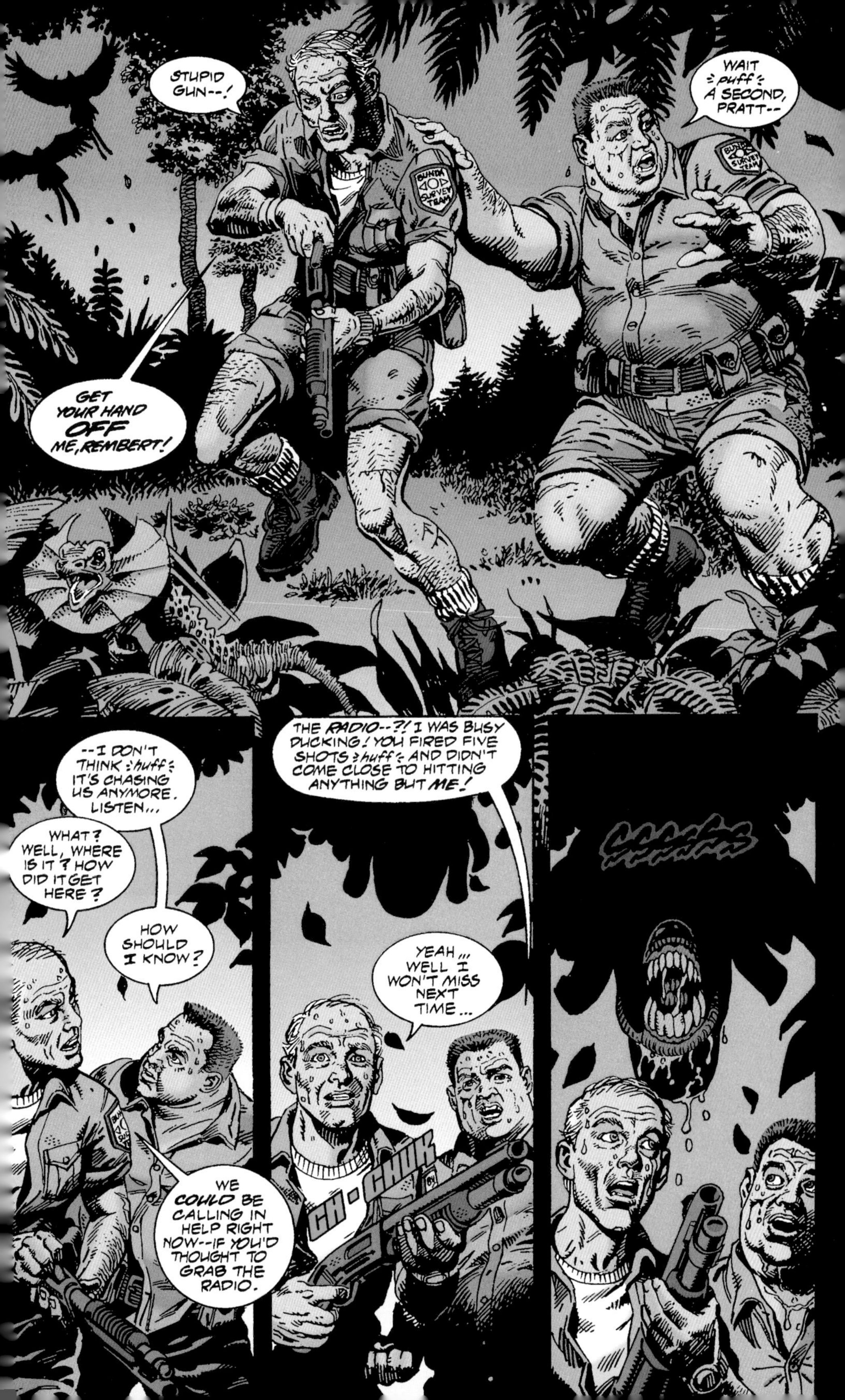
STUPID GUN--!
WAIT *puff* A SECOND, PRATT--
GET YOUR HAND **OFF** ME, REMBERT!
--I DON'T THINK *huff* IT'S CHASING US ANYMORE. LISTEN...
WHAT? WELL, WHERE IS IT? HOW DID IT GET HERE?
HOW SHOULD I KNOW?
WE **COULD** BE CALLING IN HELP RIGHT NOW--IF **YOU'D** THOUGHT TO GRAB THE RADIO.
THE *RADIO*--?! I WAS BUSY DUCKING! YOU FIRED FIVE SHOTS *huff* AND DIDN'T COME CLOSE TO HITTING ANYTHING BUT **ME**!
YEAH... WELL I WON'T MISS NEXT TIME...
CH-CHUK

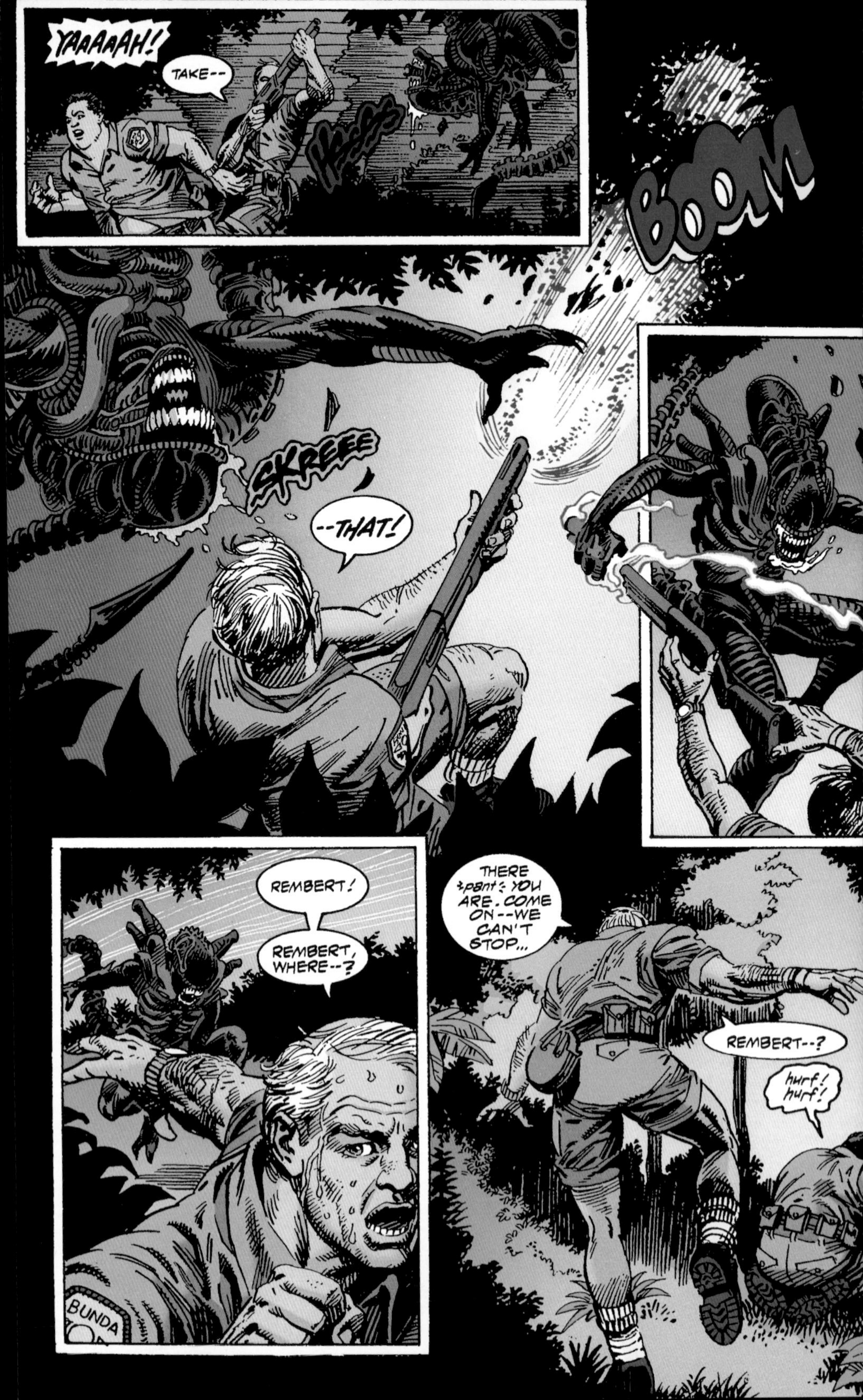
YAAAAAH!
TAKE--
BOOM
SKREEE
--THAT!
REMBERT!
REMBERT, WHERE--?
BUNDA
THERE *pant* YOU ARE. COME ON--WE CAN'T STOP...
REMBERT--?
hurf! hurf!

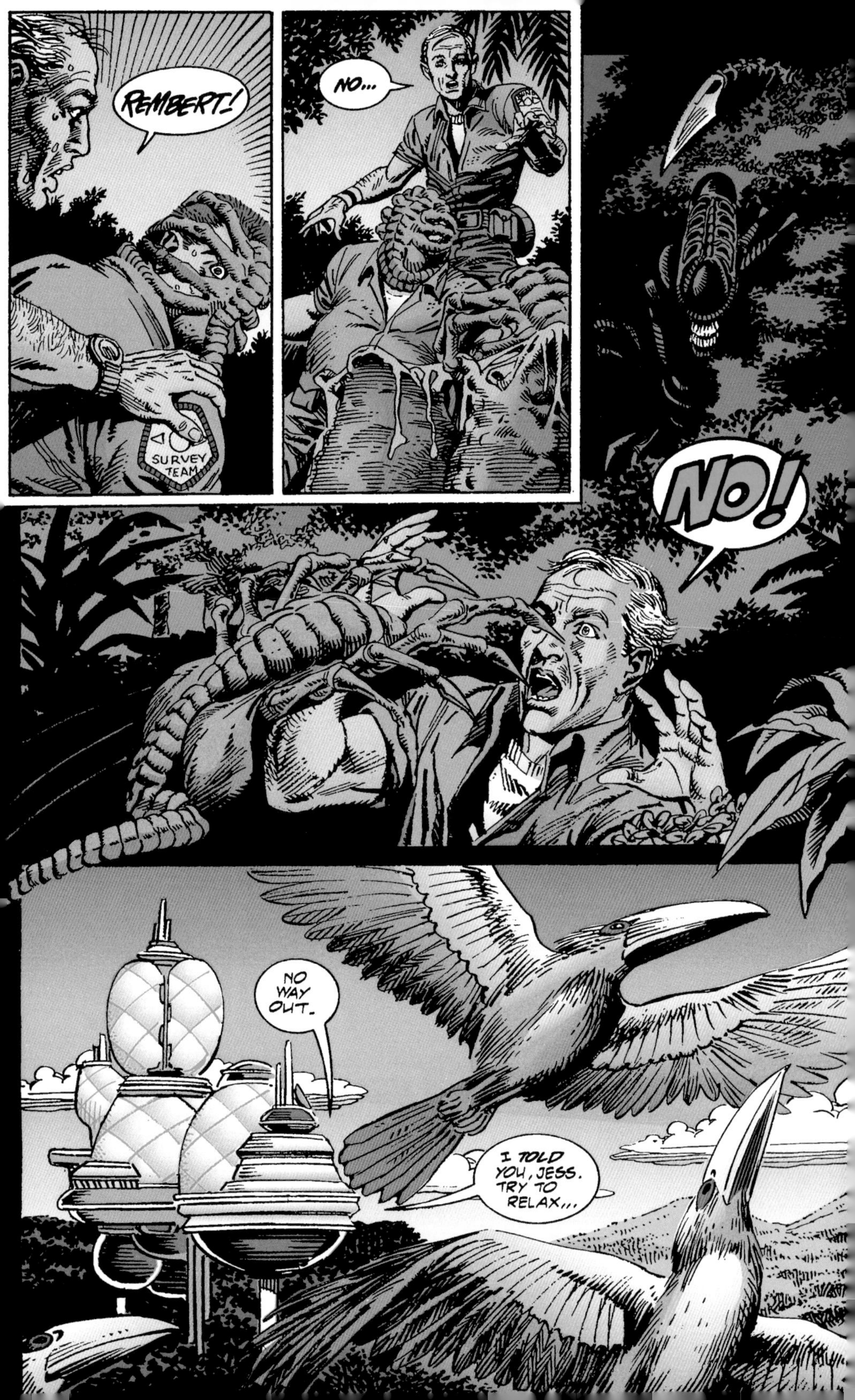
REMBERT!
SURVEY TEAM
NO...
NO!
NO WAY OUT.
I TOLD YOU, JESS. TRY TO RELAX...

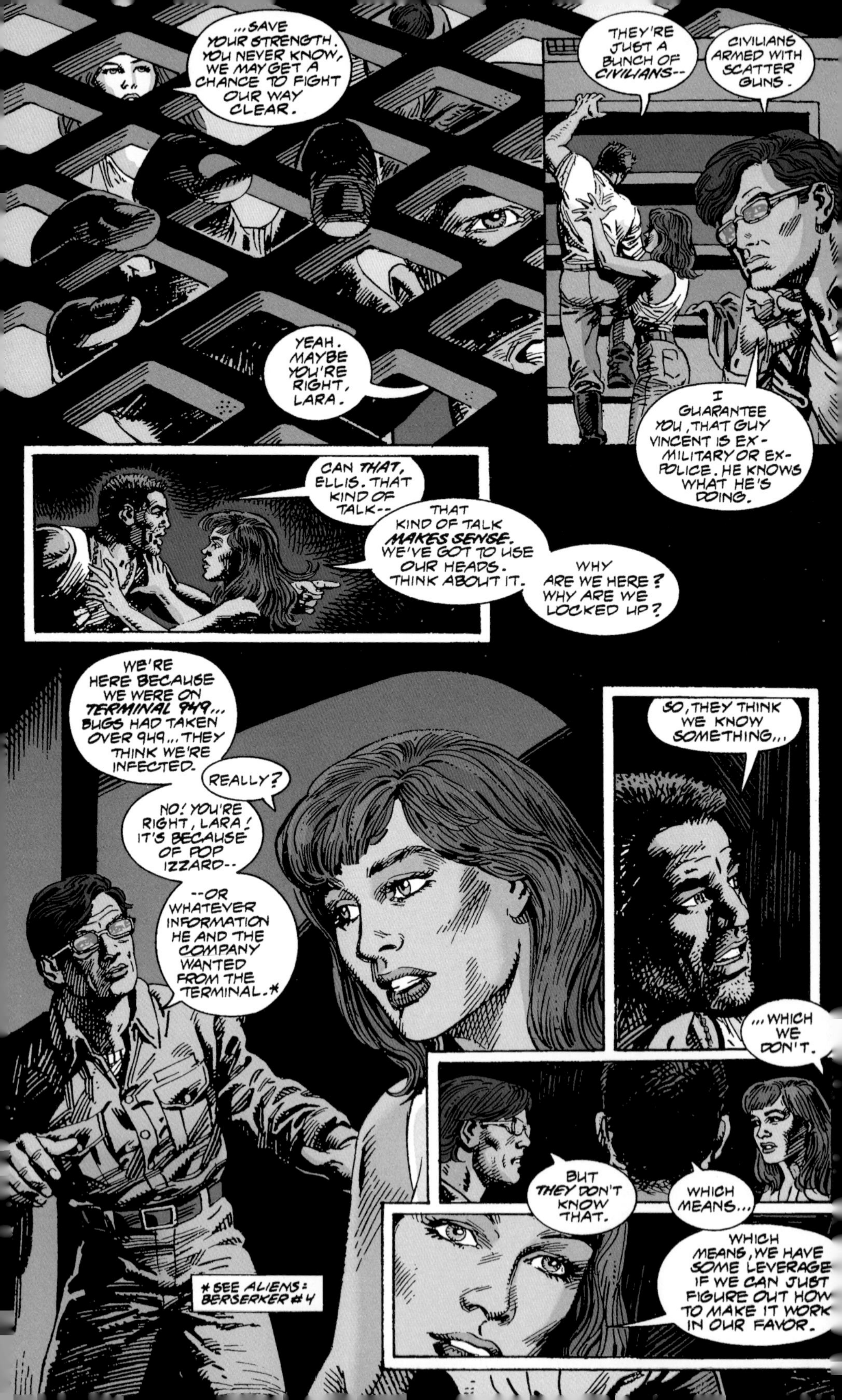
...SAVE YOUR STRENGTH. YOU NEVER KNOW, WE MAY GET A CHANCE TO FIGHT OUR WAY CLEAR.
YEAH. MAYBE YOU'RE RIGHT, LARA.
THEY'RE JUST A BUNCH OF CIVILIANS--
CIVILIANS ARMED WITH SCATTER GUNS.
I GUARANTEE YOU, THAT GUY VINCENT IS EX-MILITARY OR EX-POLICE. HE KNOWS WHAT HE'S DOING.
CAN THAT, ELLIS. THAT KIND OF TALK--
THAT KIND OF TALK MAKES SENSE. WE'VE GOT TO USE OUR HEADS. THINK ABOUT IT.
WHY ARE WE HERE? WHY ARE WE LOCKED UP?
WE'RE HERE BECAUSE WE WERE ON TERMINAL 949... BUGS HAD TAKEN OVER 949... THEY THINK WE'RE INFECTED.
REALLY?
NO! YOU'RE RIGHT, LARA! IT'S BECAUSE OF POP IZZARD--
--OR WHATEVER INFORMATION HE AND THE COMPANY WANTED FROM THE TERMINAL.*
*SEE ALIENS: BERSERKER #4
SO, THEY THINK WE KNOW SOMETHING...
...WHICH WE DON'T.
BUT THEY DON'T KNOW THAT.
WHICH MEANS...
WHICH MEANS, WE HAVE SOME LEVERAGE IF WE CAN JUST FIGURE OUT HOW TO MAKE IT WORK IN OUR FAVOR.

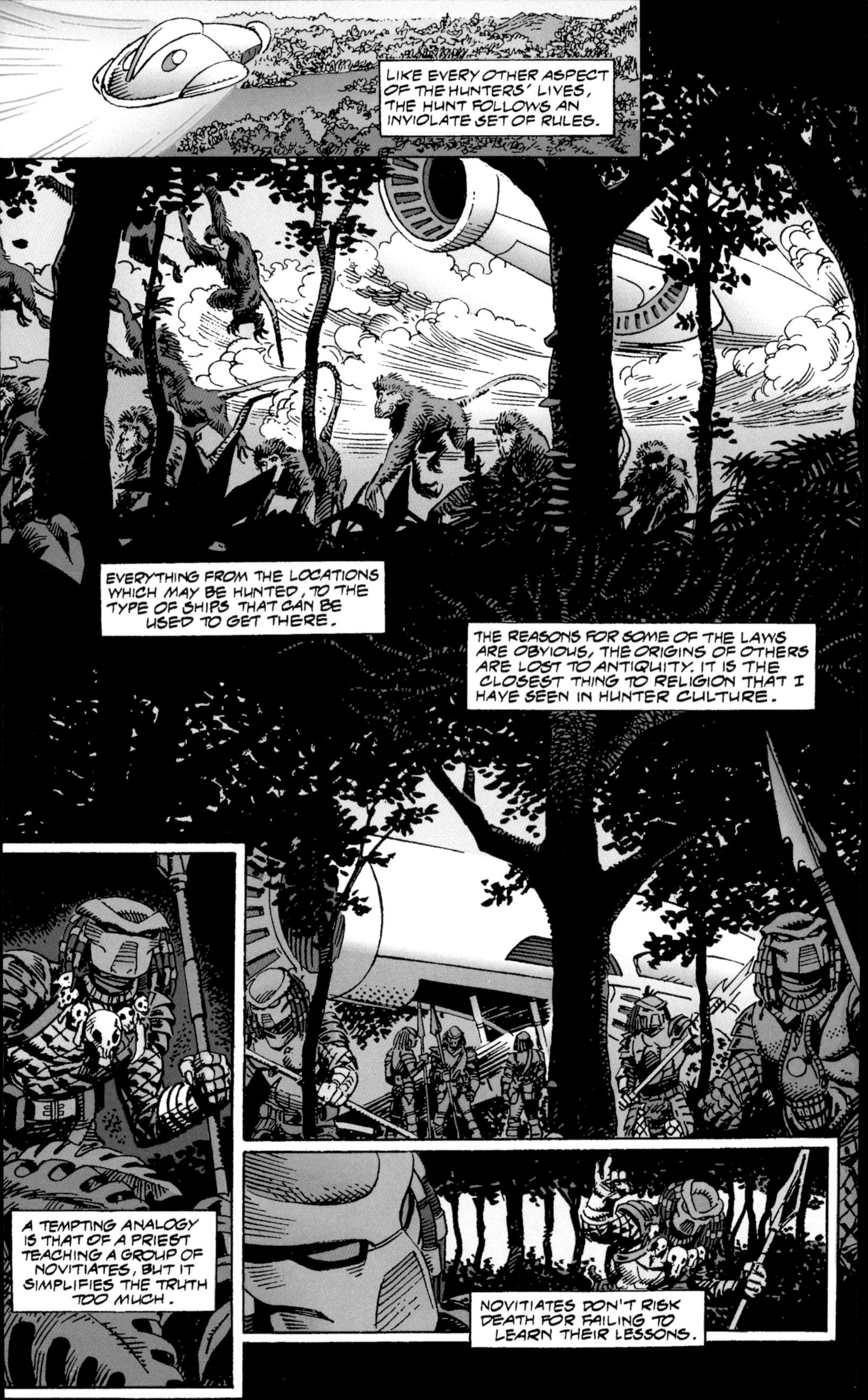
LIKE EVERY OTHER ASPECT OF THE HUNTERS' LIVES, THE HUNT FOLLOWS AN INVIOLATE SET OF RULES.
EVERYTHING FROM THE LOCATIONS WHICH MAY BE HUNTED, TO THE TYPE OF SHIPS THAT CAN BE USED TO GET THERE.
THE REASONS FOR SOME OF THE LAWS ARE OBVIOUS, THE ORIGINS OF OTHERS ARE LOST TO ANTIQUITY. IT IS THE CLOSEST THING TO RELIGION THAT I HAVE SEEN IN HUNTER CULTURE.
A TEMPTING ANALOGY IS THAT OF A PRIEST TEACHING A GROUP OF NOVITIATES, BUT IT SIMPLIFIES THE TRUTH TOO MUCH.
NOVITIATES DON'T RISK DEATH FOR FAILING TO LEARN THEIR LESSONS.

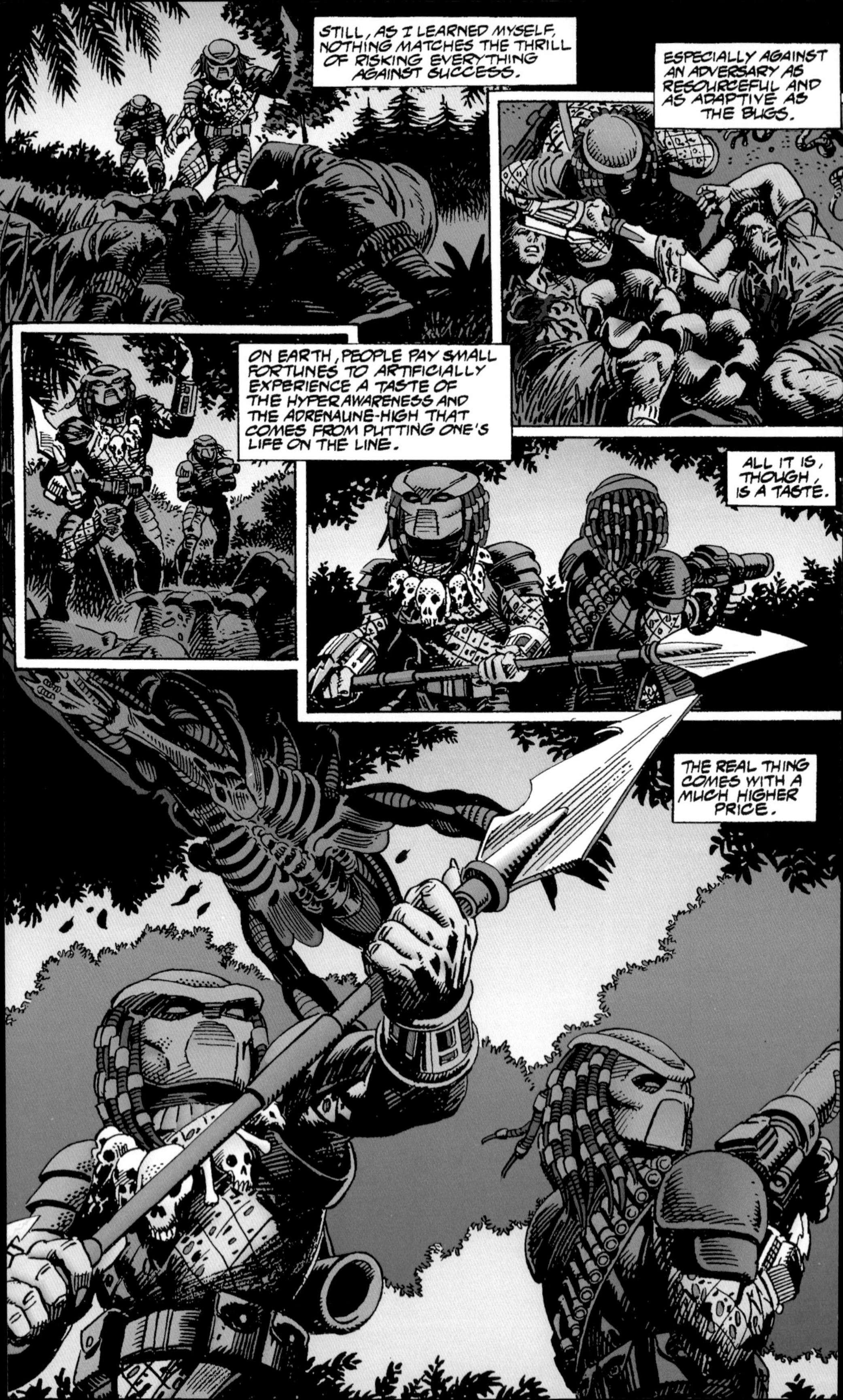
STILL, AS I LEARNED MYSELF, NOTHING MATCHES THE THRILL OF RISKING EVERYTHING AGAINST SUCCESS.
ESPECIALLY AGAINST AN ADVERSARY AS RESOURCEFUL AND AS ADAPTIVE AS THE BUGS.
ON EARTH, PEOPLE PAY SMALL FORTUNES TO ARTIFICIALLY EXPERIENCE A TASTE OF THE HYPERAWARENESS AND THE ADRENALINE-HIGH THAT COMES FROM PUTTING ONE'S LIFE ON THE LINE.
ALL IT IS, THOUGH, IS A TASTE.
THE REAL THING COMES WITH A MUCH HIGHER PRICE.

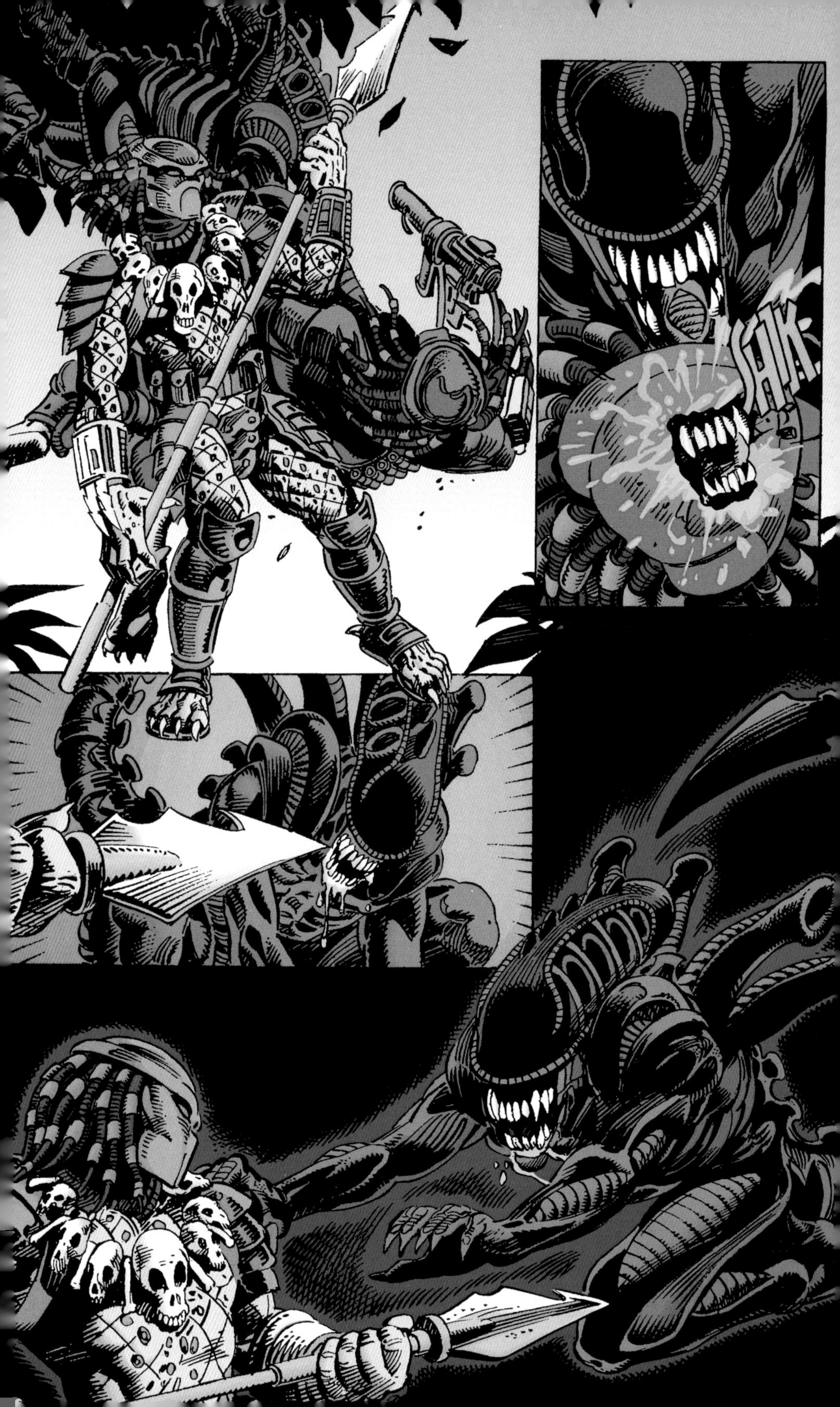
SHK!

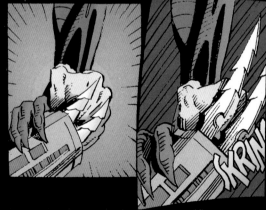

SKRIN

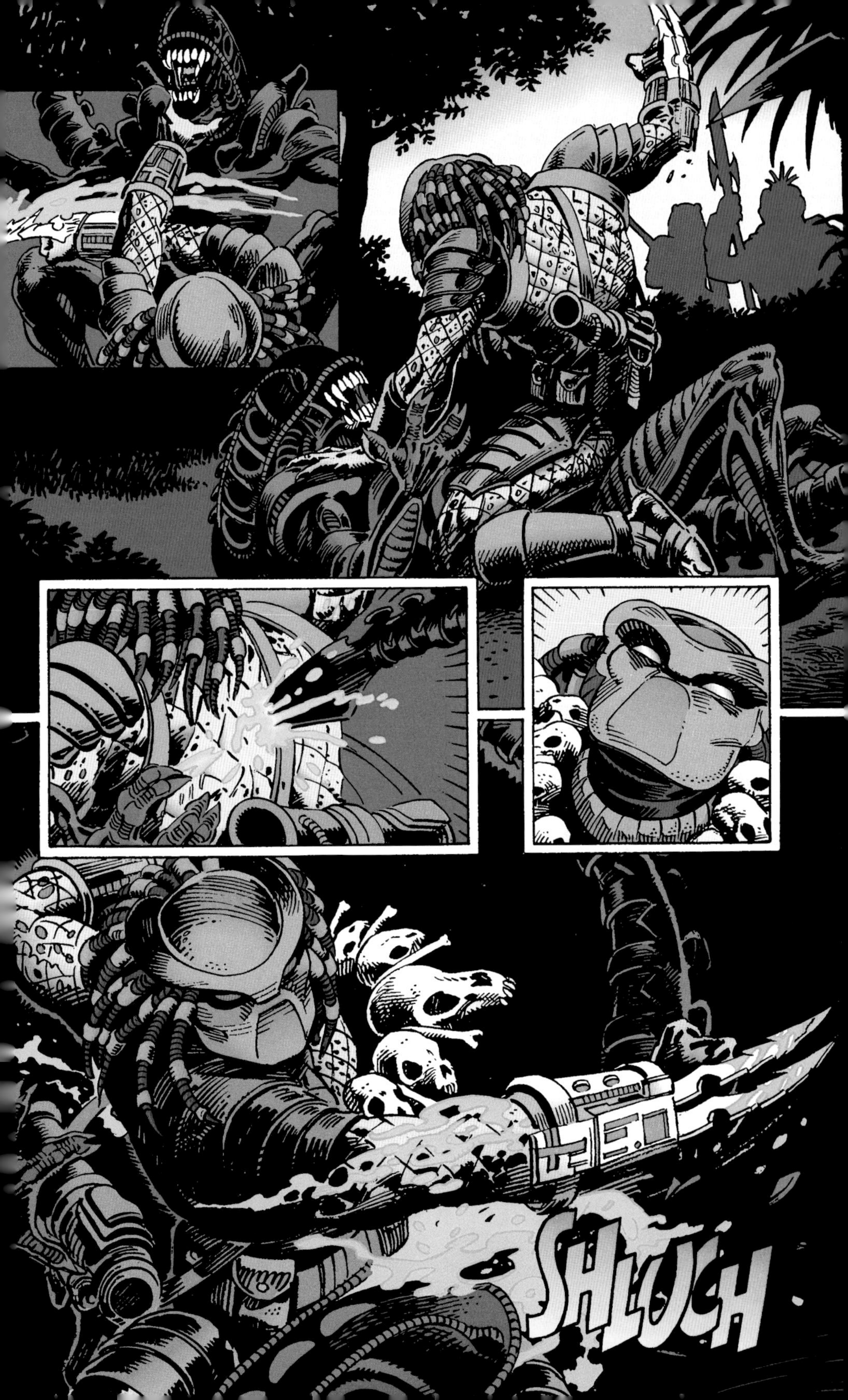
SHLUCH

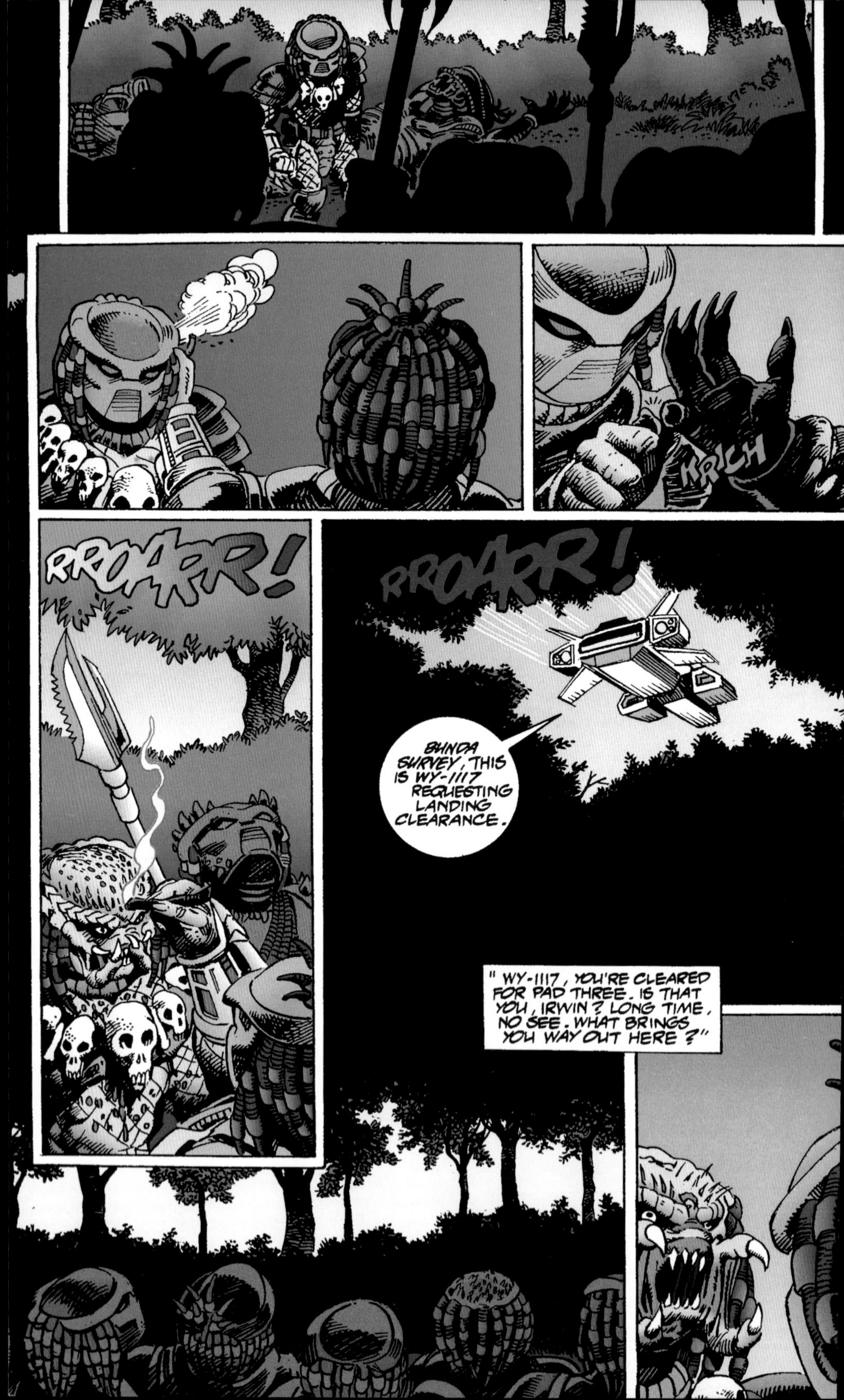
KRICH
RROARR!
RROARR!
BUNDA SURVEY, THIS IS WY-1117 REQUESTING LANDING CLEARANCE.
" WY-1117, YOU'RE CLEARED FOR PAD THREE. IS THAT YOU, IRWIN? LONG TIME, NO SEE. WHAT BRINGS YOU WAY OUT HERE?"

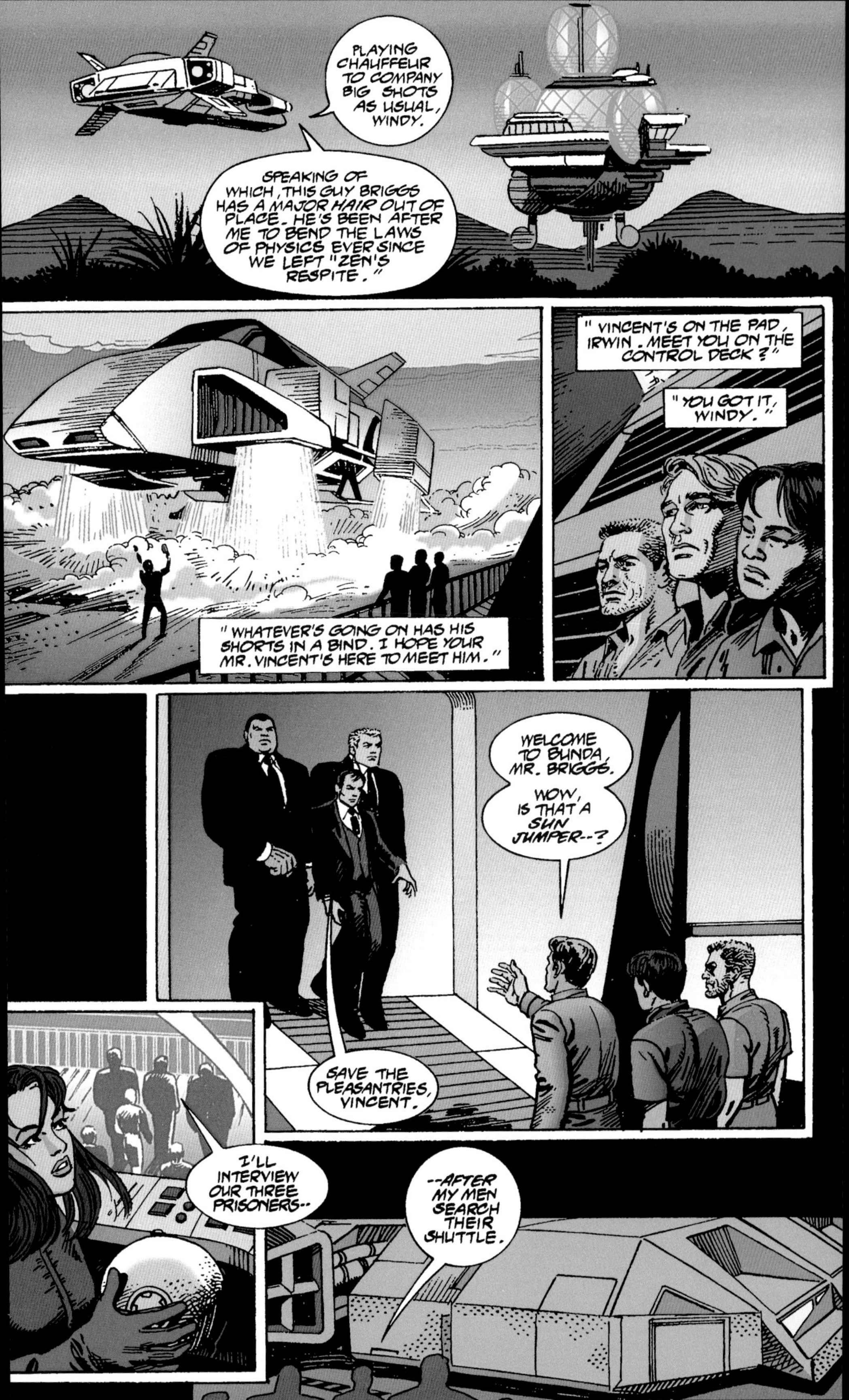
PLAYING CHAUFFEUR TO COMPANY BIG SHOTS AS USUAL, WINDY.
SPEAKING OF WHICH, THIS GUY BRIGGS HAS A MAJOR HAIR OUT OF PLACE. HE'S BEEN AFTER ME TO BEND THE LAWS OF PHYSICS EVER SINCE WE LEFT "ZEN'S RESPITE."
"WHATEVER'S GOING ON HAS HIS SHORTS IN A BIND. I HOPE YOUR MR. VINCENT'S HERE TO MEET HIM."
"VINCENT'S ON THE PAD, IRWIN. MEET YOU ON THE CONTROL DECK?"
"YOU GOT IT, WINDY."
WELCOME TO BUNDA, MR. BRIGGS.
WOW, IS THAT A SUN JUMPER--?
SAVE THE PLEASANTRIES, VINCENT.
I'LL INTERVIEW OUR THREE PRISONERS--
--AFTER MY MEN SEARCH THEIR SHUTTLE.

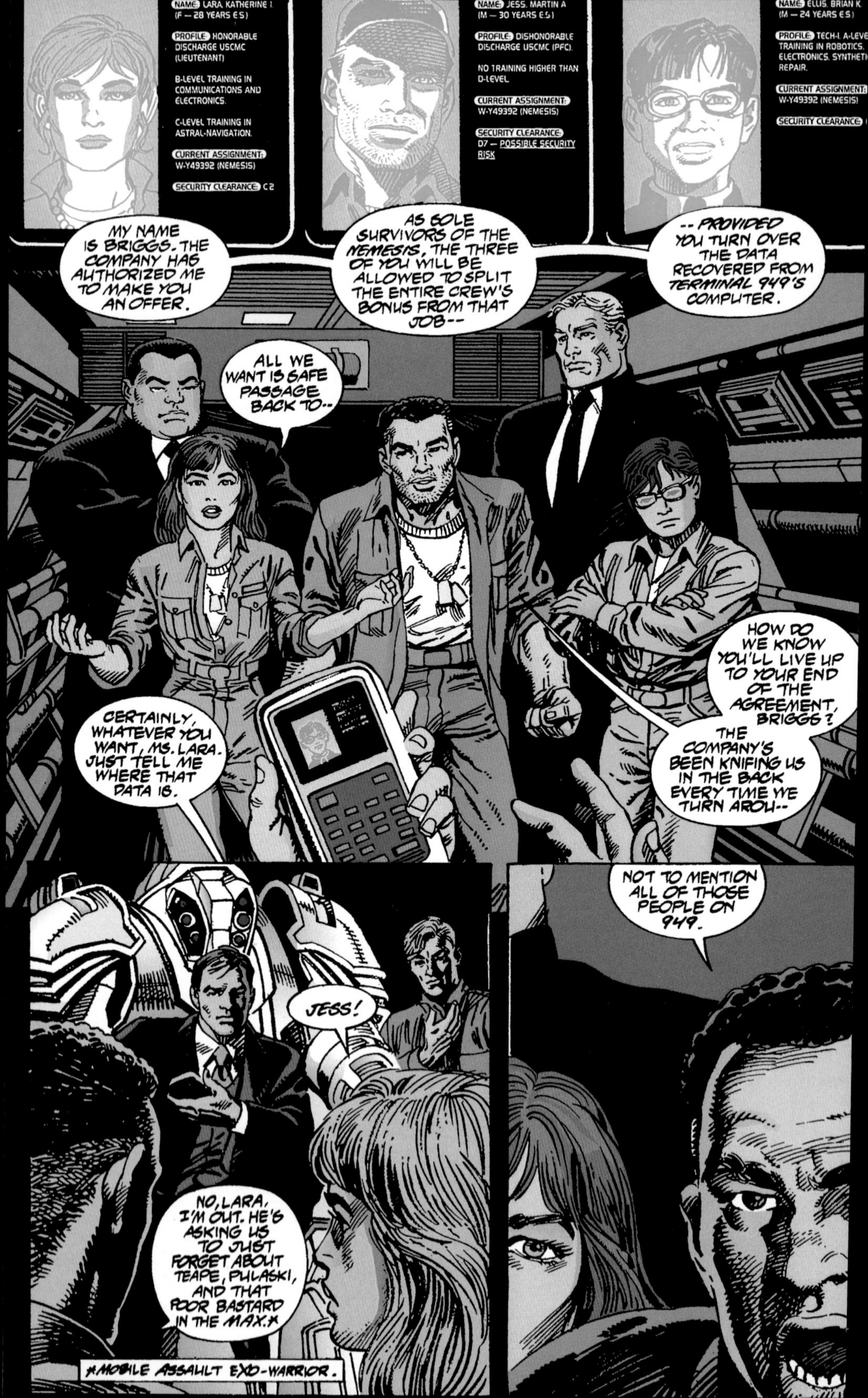

NAME: LARA, KATHERINE I.
(F — 28 YEARS E.S.)
PROFILE: HONORABLE DISCHARGE USCMC (LIEUTENANT)
B-LEVEL TRAINING IN COMMUNICATIONS AND ELECTRONICS.
C-LEVEL TRAINING IN ASTRAL-NAVIGATION.
CURRENT ASSIGNMENT: W-Y49392 (NEMESIS)
SECURITY CLEARANCE: C2
NAME: JESS, MARTIN A.
(M — 30 YEARS E.S.)
PROFILE: DISHONORABLE DISCHARGE USCMC (PFC).
NO TRAINING HIGHER THAN D-LEVEL.
CURRENT ASSIGNMENT: W-Y49392 (NEMESIS)
SECURITY CLEARANCE: D7 — POSSIBLE SECURITY RISK
NAME: ELLIS, BRIAN K.
(M — 24 YEARS E.S.)
PROFILE: TECH-I, A-LEVE
TRAINING IN ROBOTICS,
ELECTRONICS, SYNTHETI
REPAIR.
CURRENT ASSIGNMENT: W-Y49392 (NEMESIS)
SECURITY CLEARANCE:
MY NAME IS BRIGGS. THE COMPANY HAS AUTHORIZED ME TO MAKE YOU AN OFFER.
AS SOLE SURVIVORS OF THE NEMESIS, THE THREE OF YOU WILL BE ALLOWED TO SPLIT THE ENTIRE CREW'S BONUS FROM THAT JOB--
-- PROVIDED YOU TURN OVER THE DATA RECOVERED FROM TERMINAL 949'S COMPUTER.
ALL WE WANT IS SAFE PASSAGE BACK TO--
HOW DO WE KNOW YOU'LL LIVE UP TO YOUR END OF THE AGREEMENT, BRIGGS?
THE COMPANY'S BEEN KNIFING US IN THE BACK EVERY TIME WE TURN AROU--
CERTAINLY, WHATEVER YOU WANT, MS. LARA. JUST TELL ME WHERE THAT DATA IS.
JESS!
NO, LARA, I'M OUT. HE'S ASKING US TO JUST FORGET ABOUT TEAPE, PULASKI, AND THAT POOR BASTARD IN THE MAX.*
*MOBILE ASSAULT EXO-WARRIOR.
NOT TO MENTION ALL OF THOSE PEOPLE ON 949.

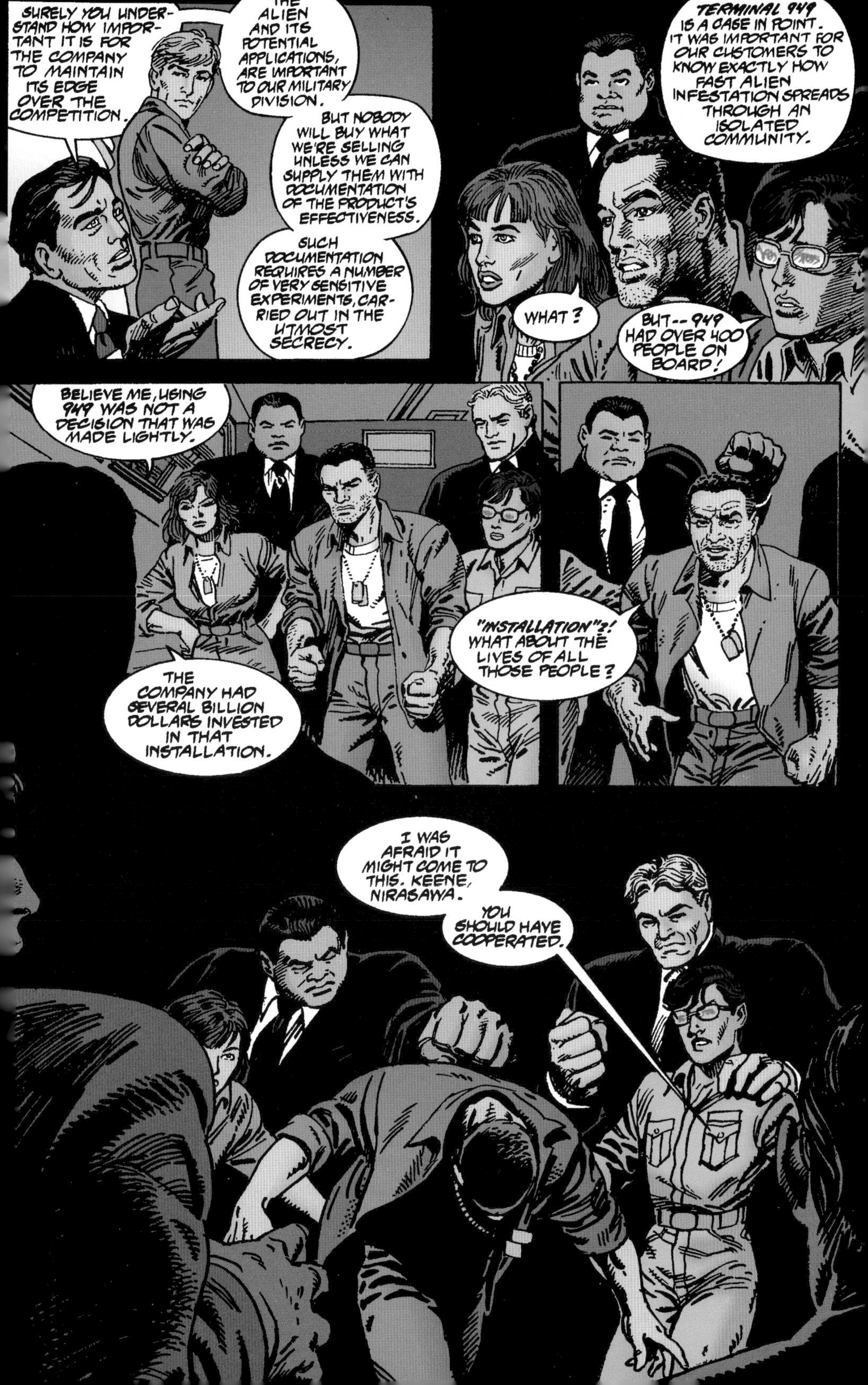

SURELY YOU UNDERSTAND HOW IMPORTANT IT IS FOR THE COMPANY TO MAINTAIN ITS EDGE OVER THE COMPETITION.
THE ALIEN AND ITS POTENTIAL APPLICATIONS, ARE IMPORTANT TO OUR MILITARY DIVISION.
BUT NOBODY WILL BUY WHAT WE'RE SELLING UNLESS WE CAN SUPPLY THEM WITH DOCUMENTATION OF THE PRODUCT'S EFFECTIVENESS.
SUCH DOCUMENTATION REQUIRES A NUMBER OF VERY SENSITIVE EXPERIMENTS, CARRIED OUT IN THE UTMOST SECRECY.
TERMINAL 949 IS A CASE IN POINT. IT WAS IMPORTANT FOR OUR CUSTOMERS TO KNOW EXACTLY HOW FAST ALIEN INFESTATION SPREADS THROUGH AN ISOLATED COMMUNITY.
WHAT?
BUT-- 949 HAD OVER 400 PEOPLE ON BOARD!
BELIEVE ME, USING 949 WAS NOT A DECISION THAT WAS MADE LIGHTLY.
THE COMPANY HAD SEVERAL BILLION DOLLARS INVESTED IN THAT INSTALLATION.
"INSTALLATION"?! WHAT ABOUT THE LIVES OF ALL THOSE PEOPLE?
I WAS AFRAID IT MIGHT COME TO THIS. KEENE, NIRASAWA.
YOU SHOULD HAVE COOPERATED.

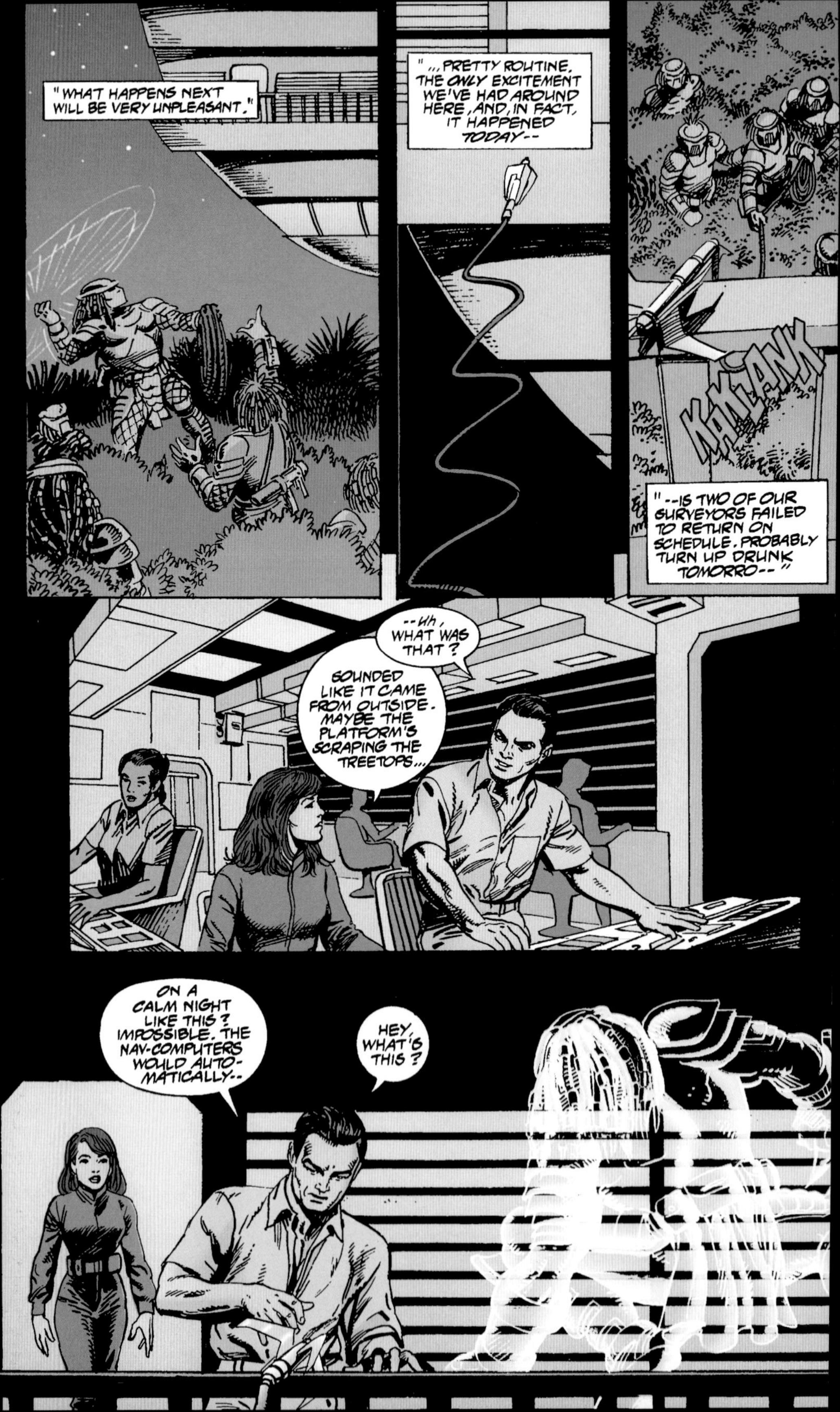
"WHAT HAPPENS NEXT WILL BE VERY UNPLEASANT."
"...PRETTY ROUTINE. THE ONLY EXCITEMENT WE'VE HAD AROUND HERE, AND, IN FACT, IT HAPPENED TODAY--
KA-LANK
"--IS TWO OF OUR SURVEYORS FAILED TO RETURN ON SCHEDULE. PROBABLY TURN UP DRUNK TOMORRO--"
--UH, WHAT WAS THAT?
SOUNDED LIKE IT CAME FROM OUTSIDE. MAYBE THE PLATFORM'S SCRAPING THE TREETOPS...
ON A CALM NIGHT LIKE THIS? IMPOSSIBLE. THE NAV-COMPUTERS WOULD AUTO-MATICALLY--
HEY, WHAT'S THIS?

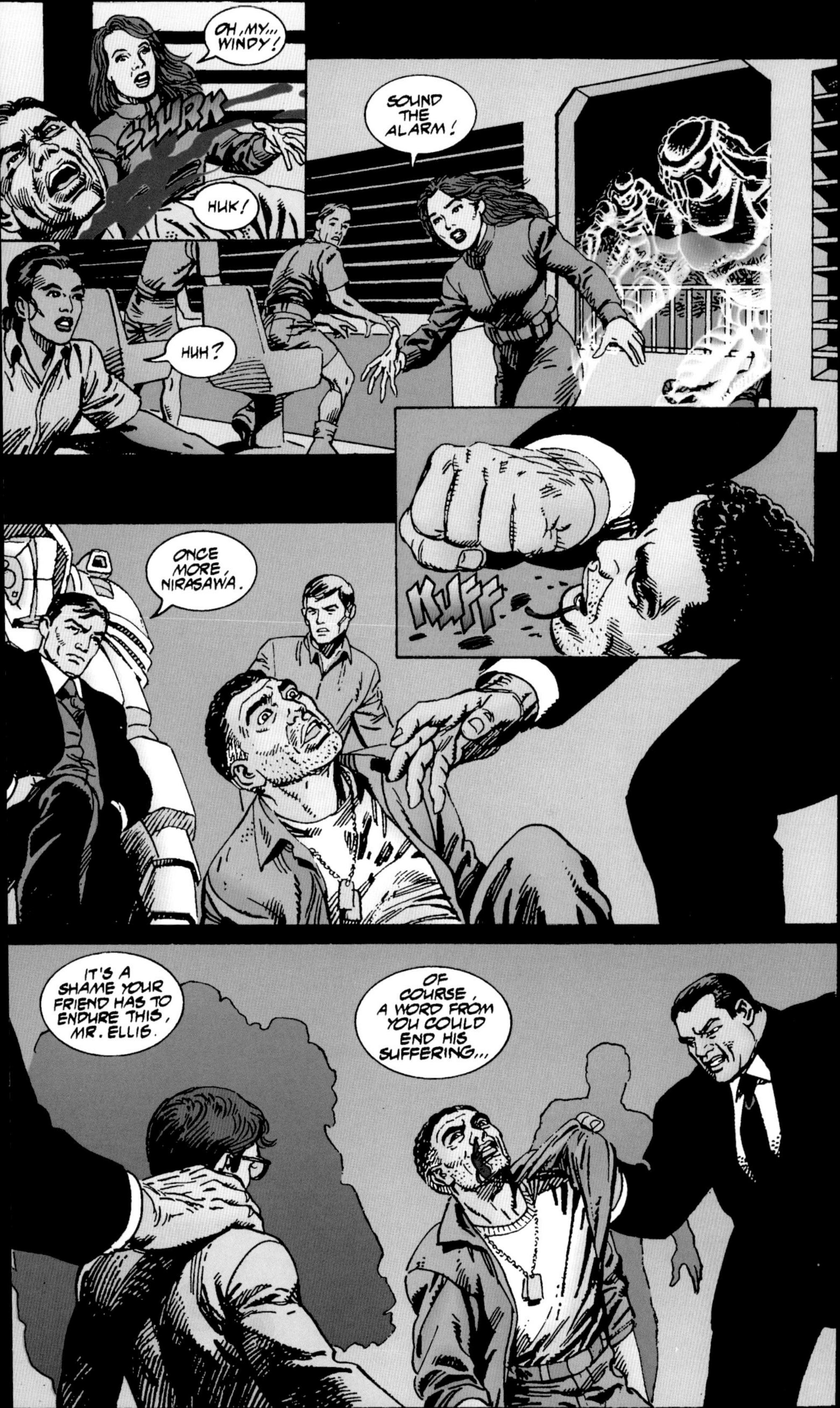
OH, MY... WINDY!
SLURK
HUK!
SOUND THE ALARM!
HUH?
KUFF
ONCE MORE, NIRASAWA.
IT'S A SHAME YOUR FRIEND HAS TO ENDURE THIS, MR. ELLIS.
OF COURSE, A WORD FROM YOU COULD END HIS SUFFERING...

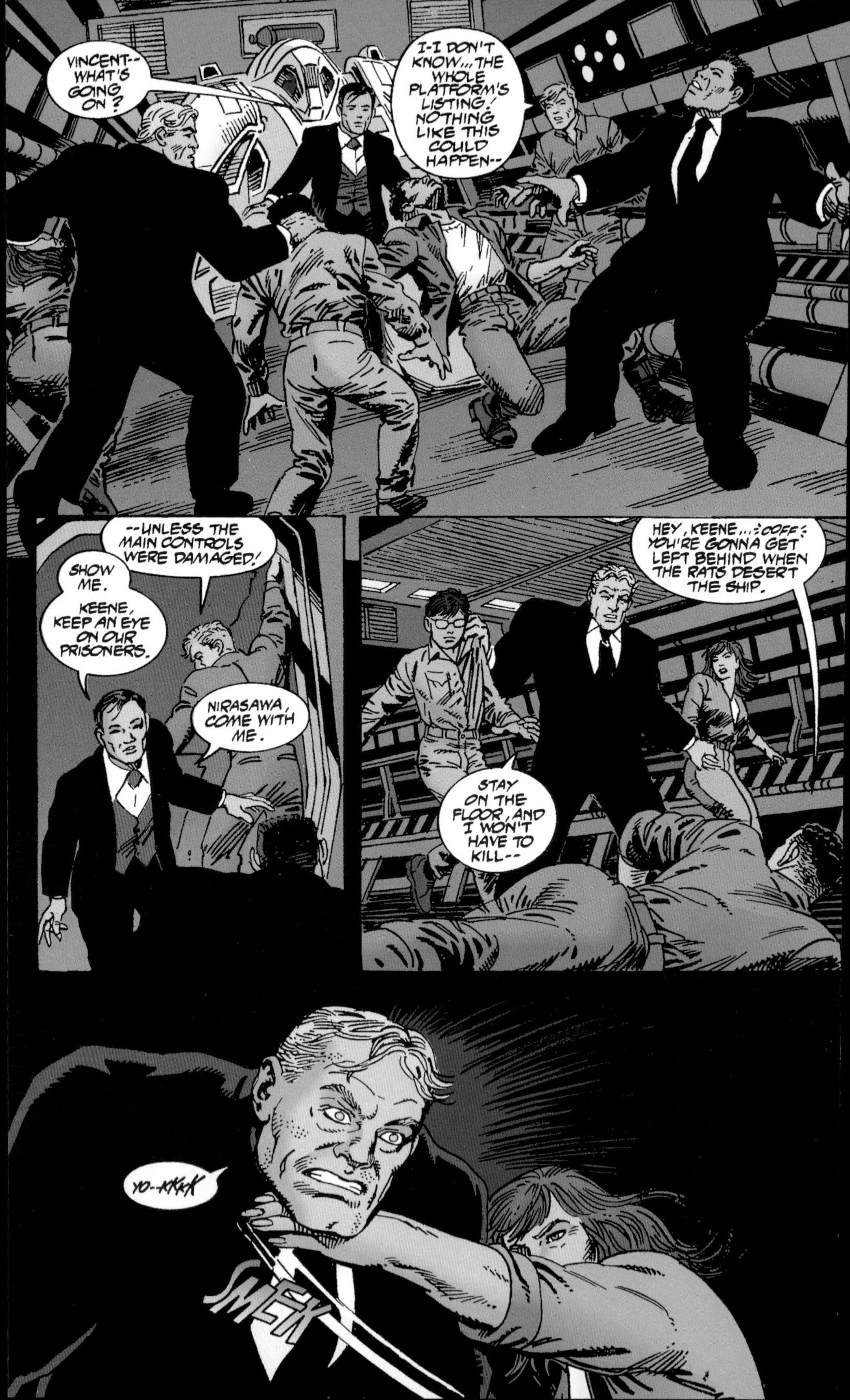
VINCENT-- WHAT'S GOING ON?
I-I DON'T KNOW... THE WHOLE PLATFORM'S LISTING! NOTHING LIKE THIS COULD HAPPEN--
--UNLESS THE MAIN CONTROLS WERE DAMAGED!
SHOW ME.
KEENE, KEEP AN EYE ON OUR PRISONERS.
NIRASAWA, COME WITH ME.
HEY, KEENE... COFF YOU'RE GONNA GET LEFT BEHIND WHEN THE RATS DESERT THE SHIP.
STAY ON THE FLOOR, AND I WON'T HAVE TO KILL--
YO--KKKK
SMEK

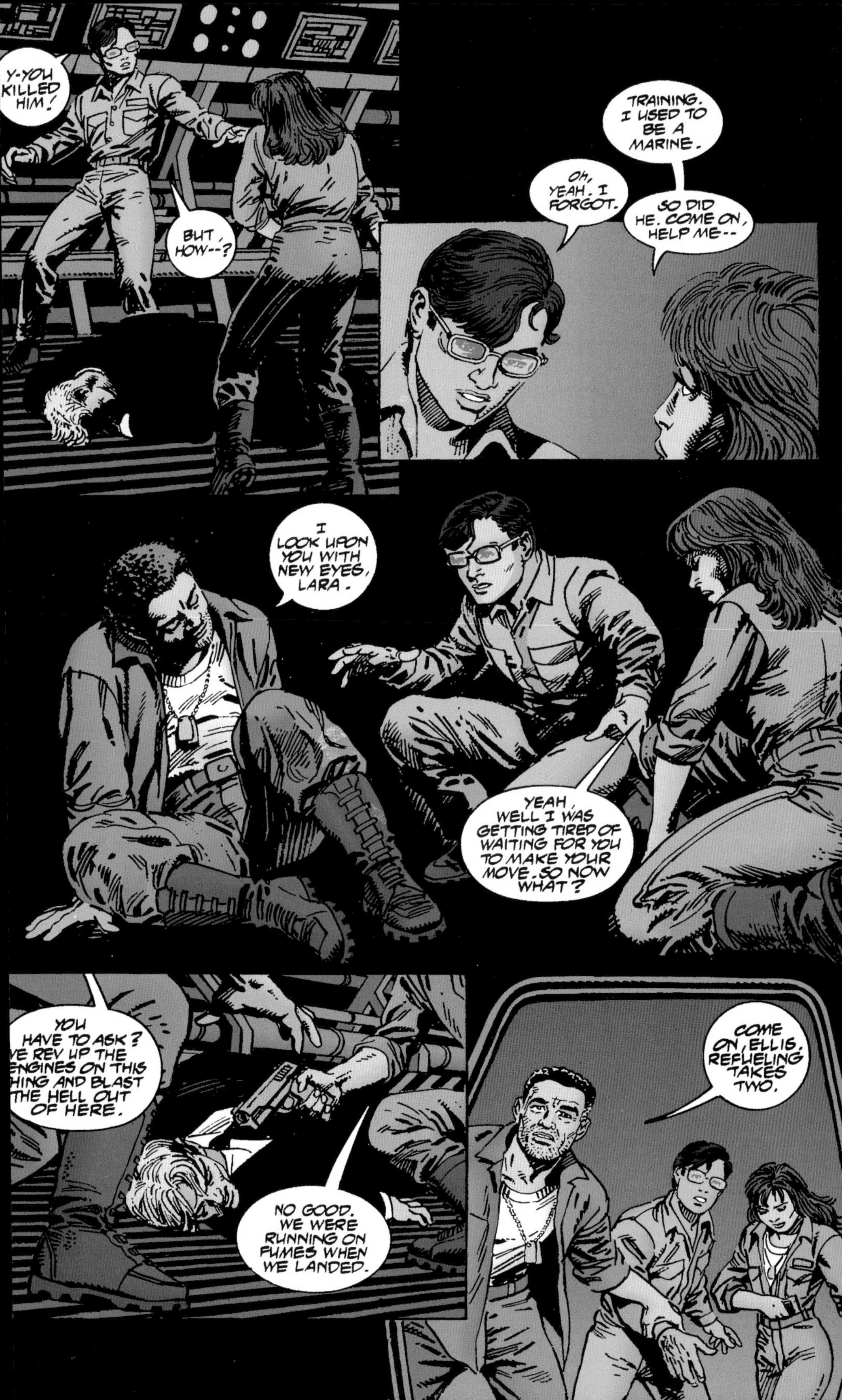
Y-YOU KILLED HIM!
BUT, HOW--?
TRAINING. I USED TO BE A MARINE.
OH, YEAH. I FORGOT.
SO DID HE. COME ON, HELP ME--
I LOOK UPON YOU WITH NEW EYES, LARA.
YEAH, WELL I WAS GETTING TIRED OF WAITING FOR YOU TO MAKE YOUR MOVE. SO NOW WHAT?
YOU HAVE TO ASK? WE REV UP THE ENGINES ON THIS THING AND BLAST THE HELL OUT OF HERE.
NO GOOD. WE WERE RUNNING ON FUMES WHEN WE LANDED.
COME ON, ELLIS. REFUELING TAKES TWO.

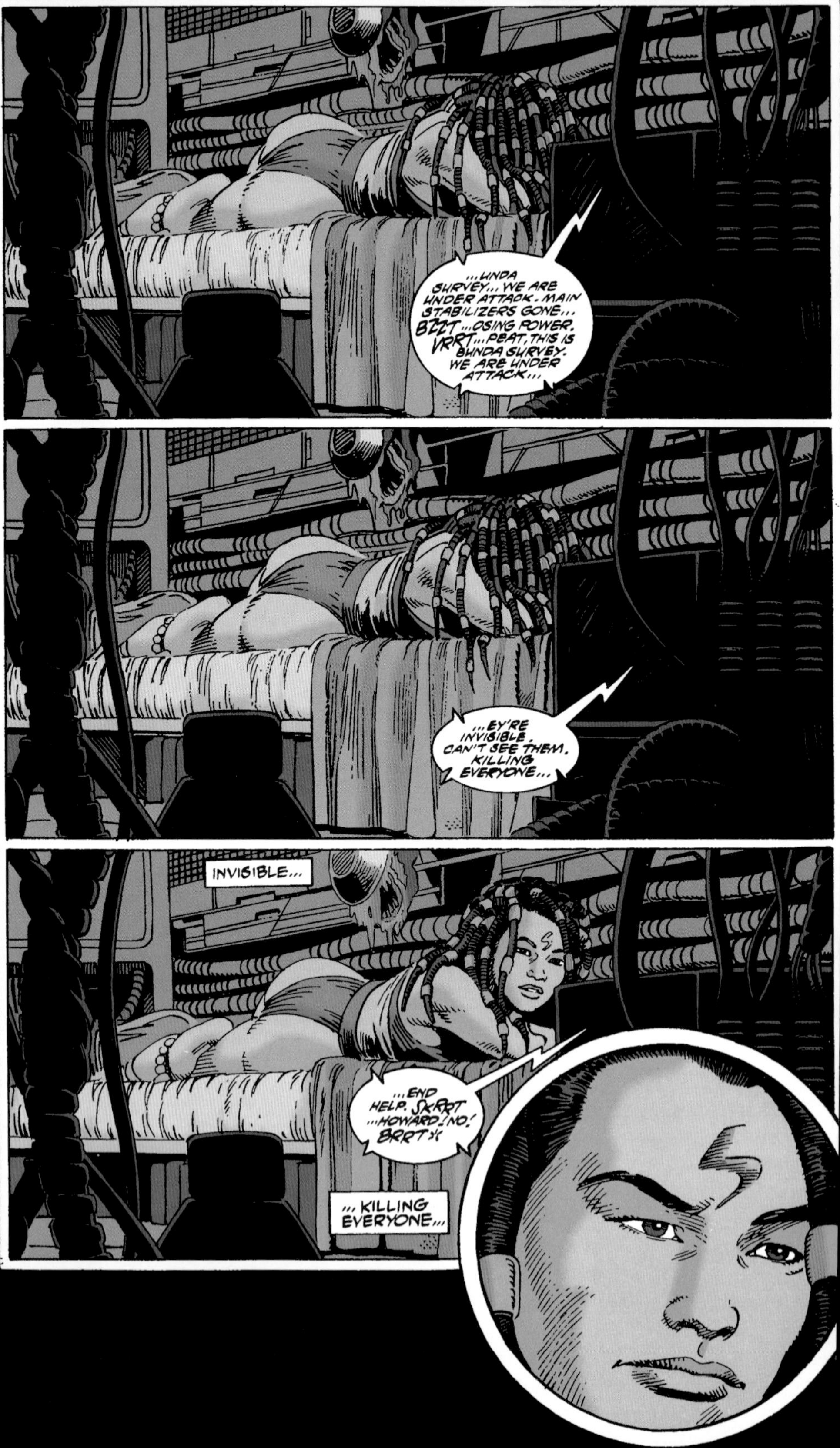
...UNDA SURVEY... WE ARE UNDER ATTACK. MAIN STABILIZERS GONE... BZZT...OSING POWER. VRRT...PEAT, THIS IS BUNDA SURVEY. WE ARE UNDER ATTACK...
...EY'RE INVISIBLE. CAN'T SEE THEM. KILLING EVERYONE...
INVISIBLE...
...END HELP. SKRRT ...HOWARD! NO! BRRT*
...KILLING EVERYONE...

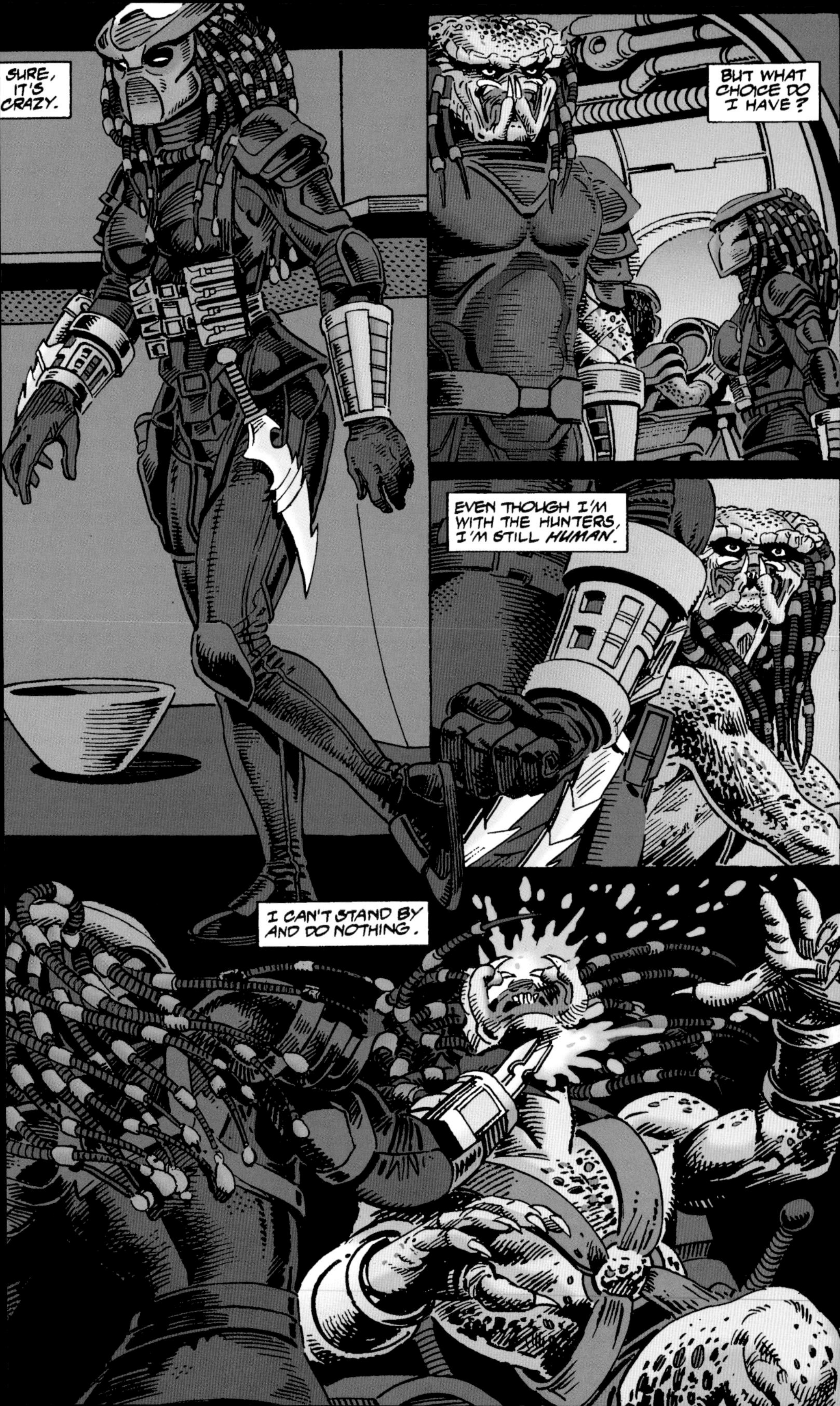
SURE, IT'S CRAZY.
BUT WHAT CHOICE DO I HAVE?
EVEN THOUGH I'M WITH THE HUNTERS, I'M STILL *HUMAN*.
I CAN'T STAND BY AND DO NOTHING.

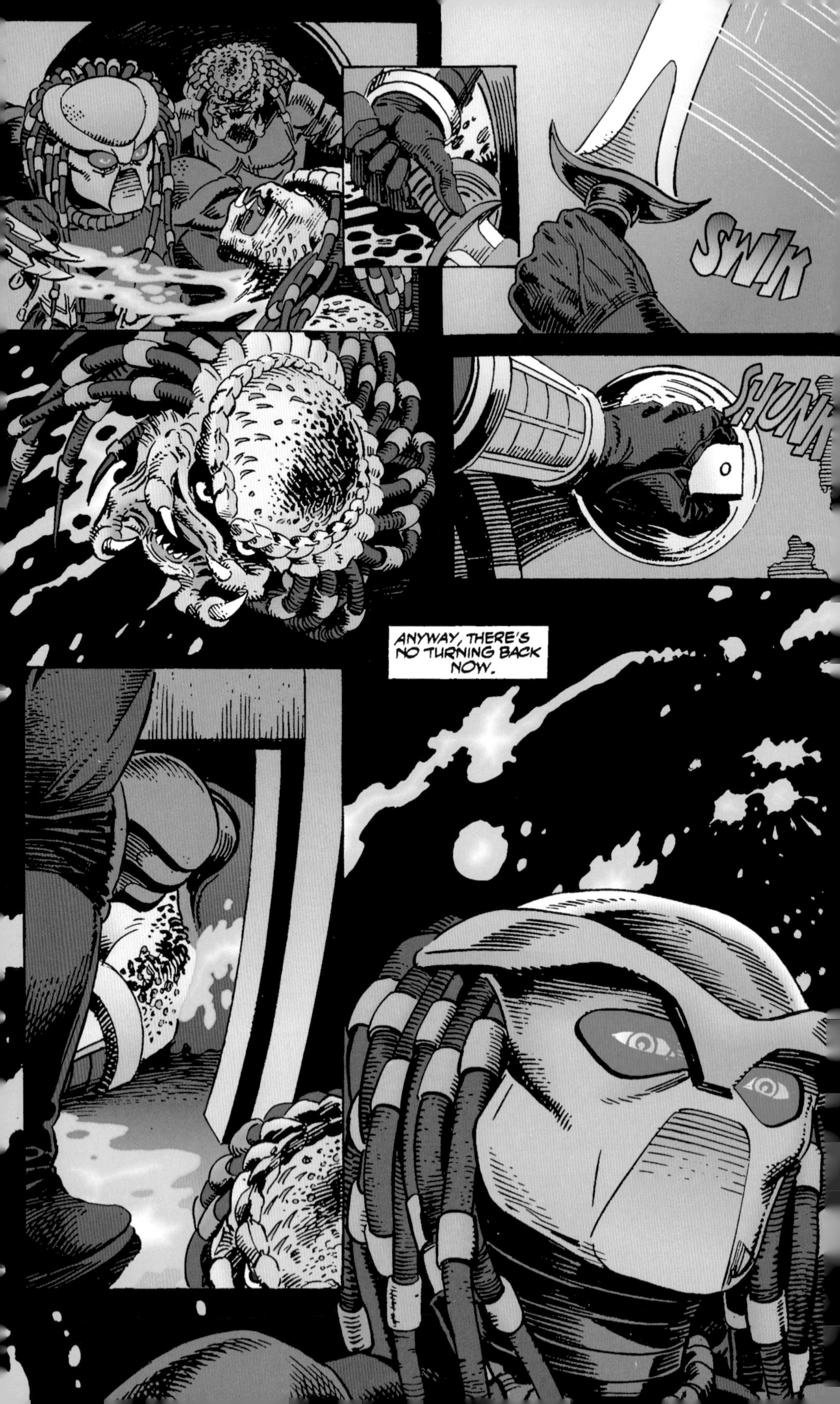
SWIK
SHUNK
ANYWAY, THERE'S NO TURNING BACK NOW.

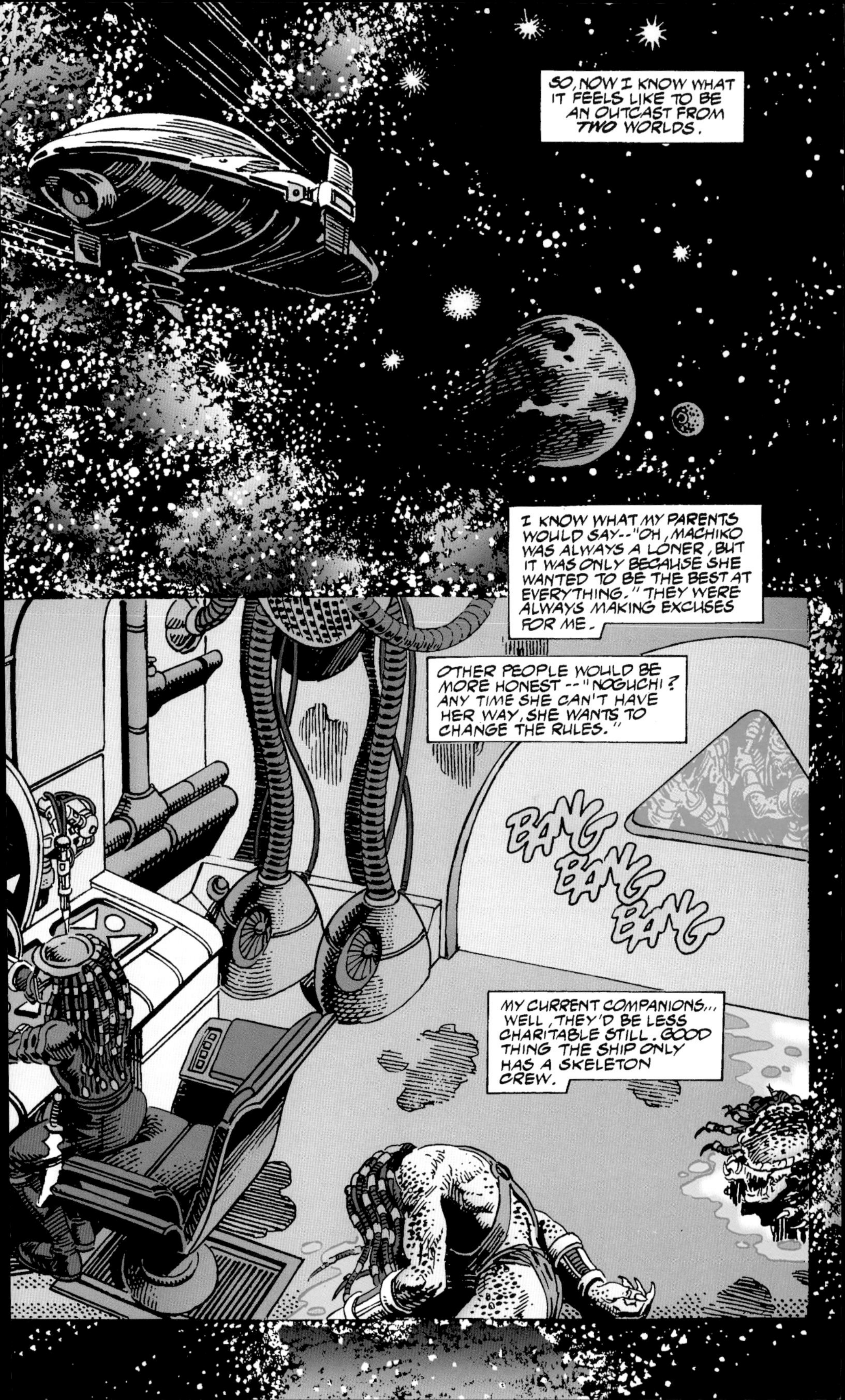
SO, NOW I KNOW WHAT IT FEELS LIKE TO BE AN OUTCAST FROM TWO WORLDS.
I KNOW WHAT MY PARENTS WOULD SAY--"OH, MACHIKO WAS ALWAYS A LONER, BUT IT WAS ONLY BECAUSE SHE WANTED TO BE THE BEST AT EVERYTHING." THEY WERE ALWAYS MAKING EXCUSES FOR ME.
OTHER PEOPLE WOULD BE MORE HONEST --"NOGUCHI? ANY TIME SHE CAN'T HAVE HER WAY, SHE WANTS TO CHANGE THE RULES."
BANG BANG BANG
MY CURRENT COMPANIONS... WELL, THEY'D BE LESS CHARITABLE STILL. GOOD THING THE SHIP ONLY HAS A SKELETON CREW.

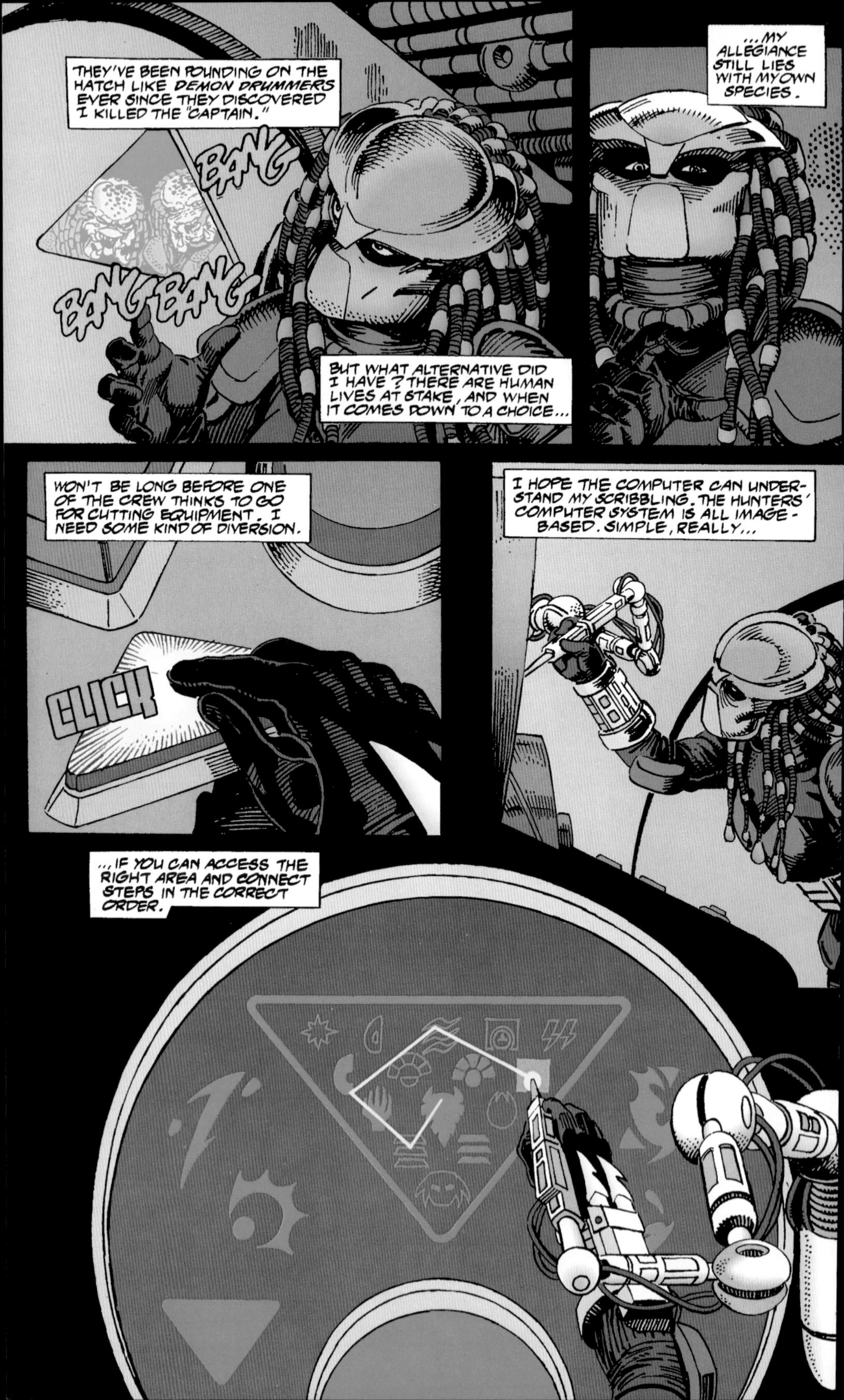
THEY'VE BEEN POUNDING ON THE HATCH LIKE DEMON DRUMMERS EVER SINCE THEY DISCOVERED I KILLED THE "CAPTAIN."
BANG
BANG BANG
BUT WHAT ALTERNATIVE DID I HAVE? THERE ARE HUMAN LIVES AT STAKE, AND WHEN IT COMES DOWN TO A CHOICE...
...MY ALLEGIANCE STILL LIES WITH MY OWN SPECIES.
WON'T BE LONG BEFORE ONE OF THE CREW THINKS TO GO FOR CUTTING EQUIPMENT. I NEED SOME KIND OF DIVERSION.
CLICK
I HOPE THE COMPUTER CAN UNDERSTAND MY SCRIBBLING. THE HUNTERS' COMPUTER SYSTEM IS ALL IMAGE-BASED. SIMPLE, REALLY...
...IF YOU CAN ACCESS THE RIGHT AREA AND CONNECT STEPS IN THE CORRECT ORDER.

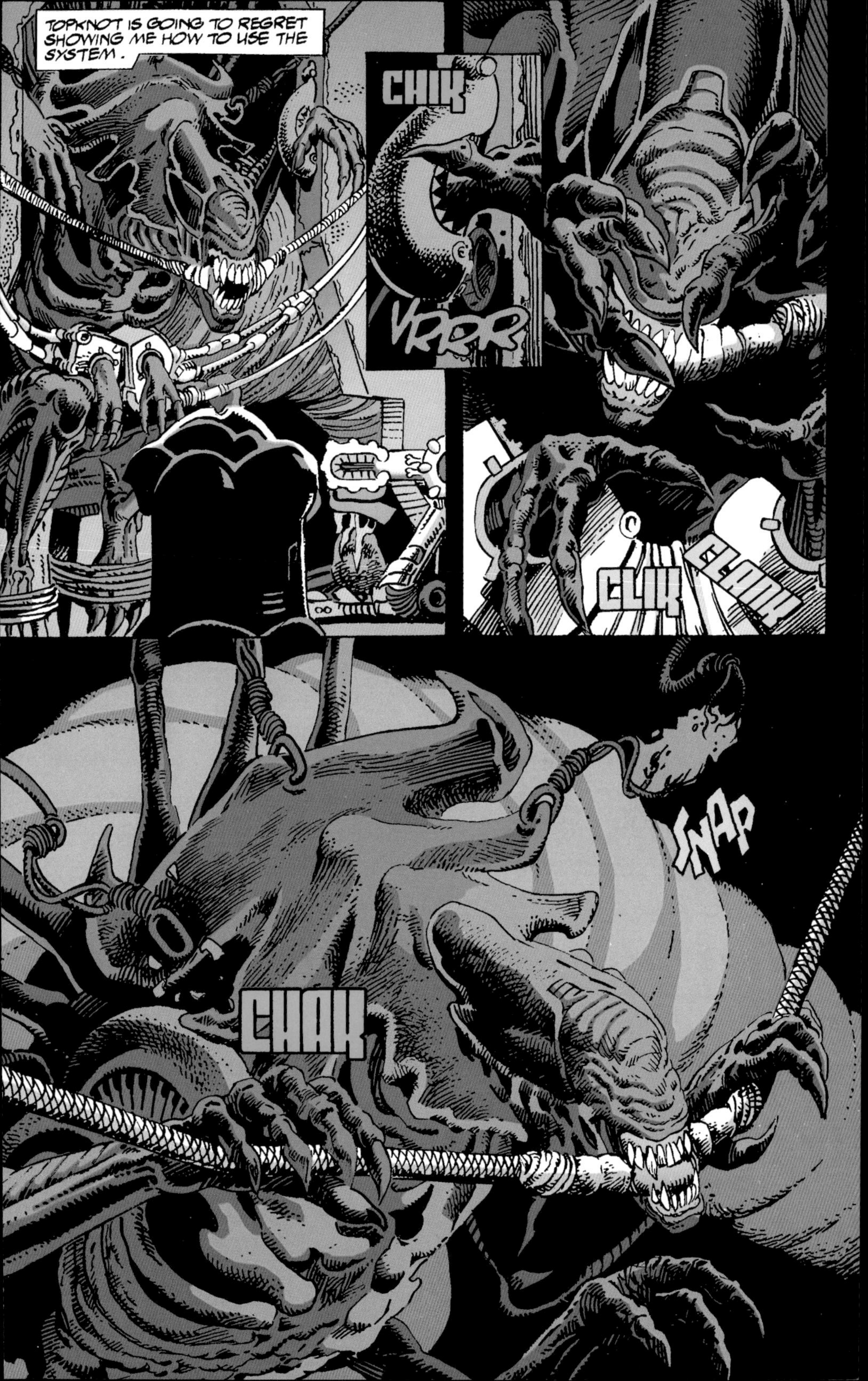
TOPKNOT IS GOING TO REGRET SHOWING ME HOW TO USE THE SYSTEM.
CHIK
VRRR
CLIK
CLANK
SNAP
CHAK

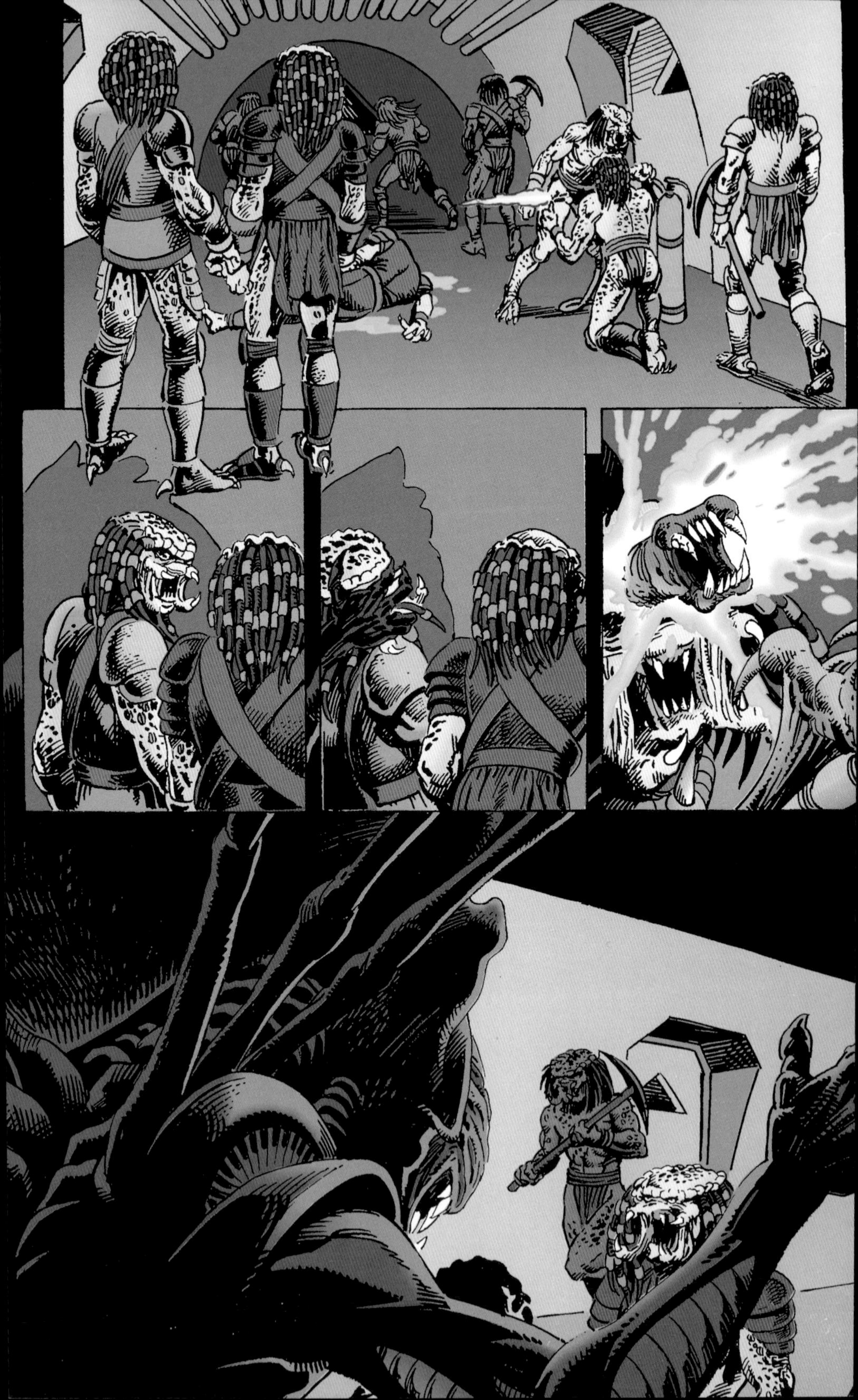

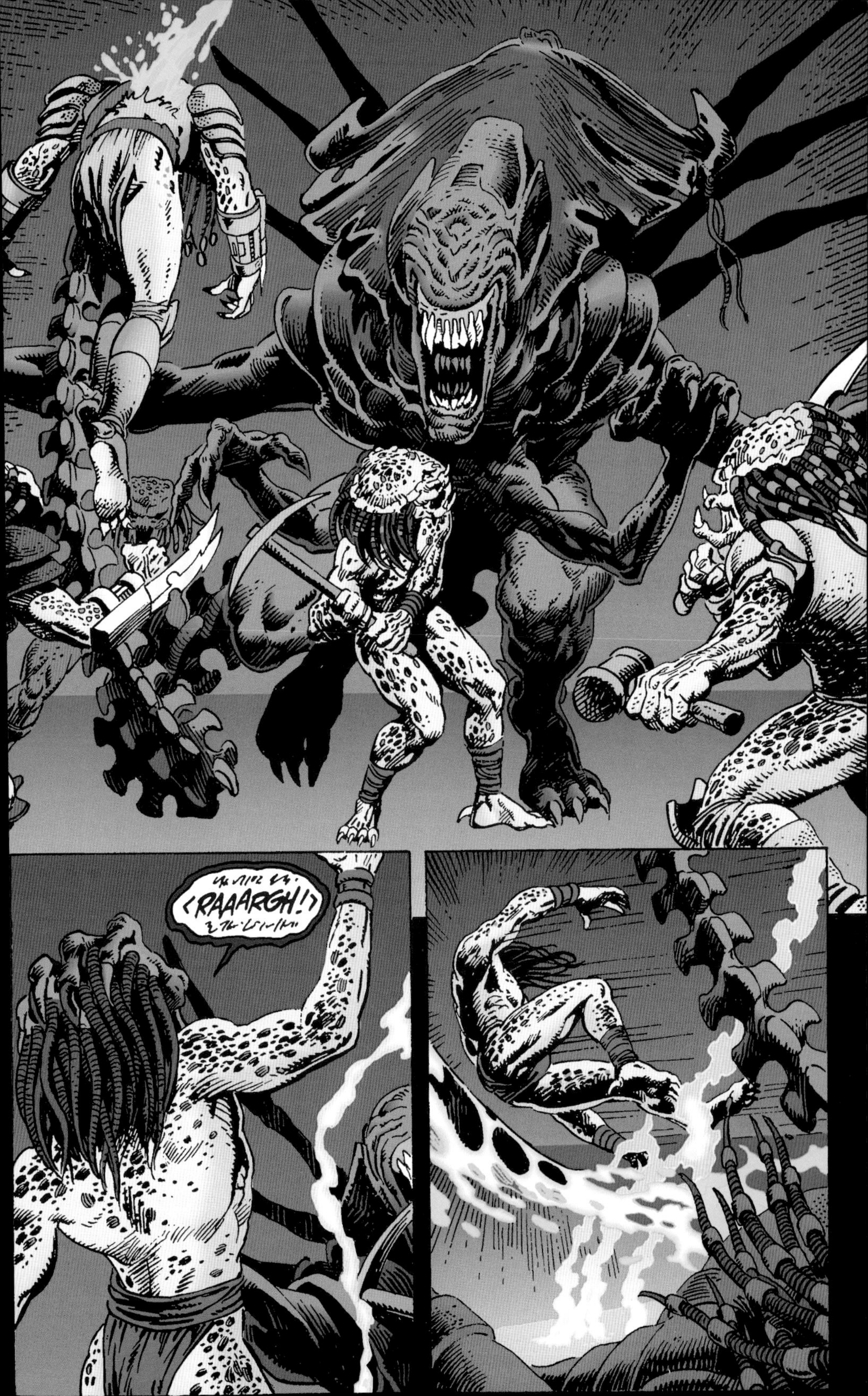
<RAAARGH!>

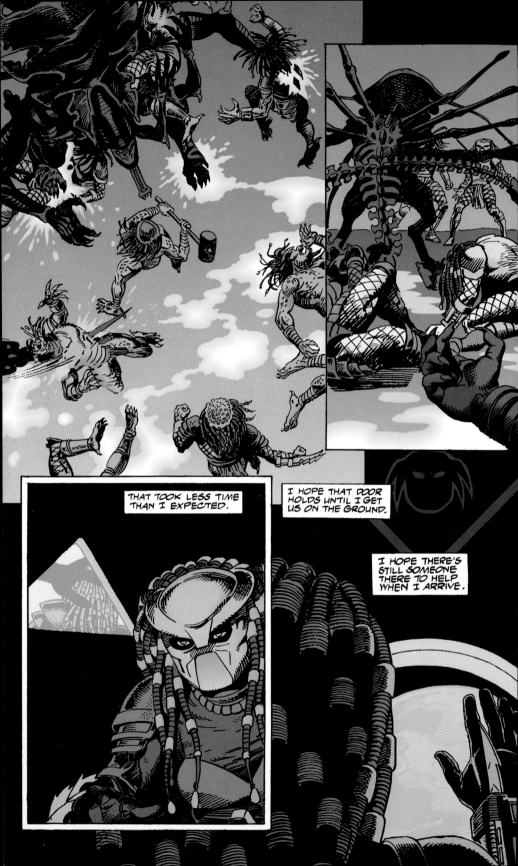

THAT TOOK LESS TIME THAN I EXPECTED.

I HOPE THAT DOOR HOLDS UNTIL I GET US ON THE GROUND.

I HOPE THERE'S STILL *SOMEONE* THERE TO HELP WHEN I ARRIVE.

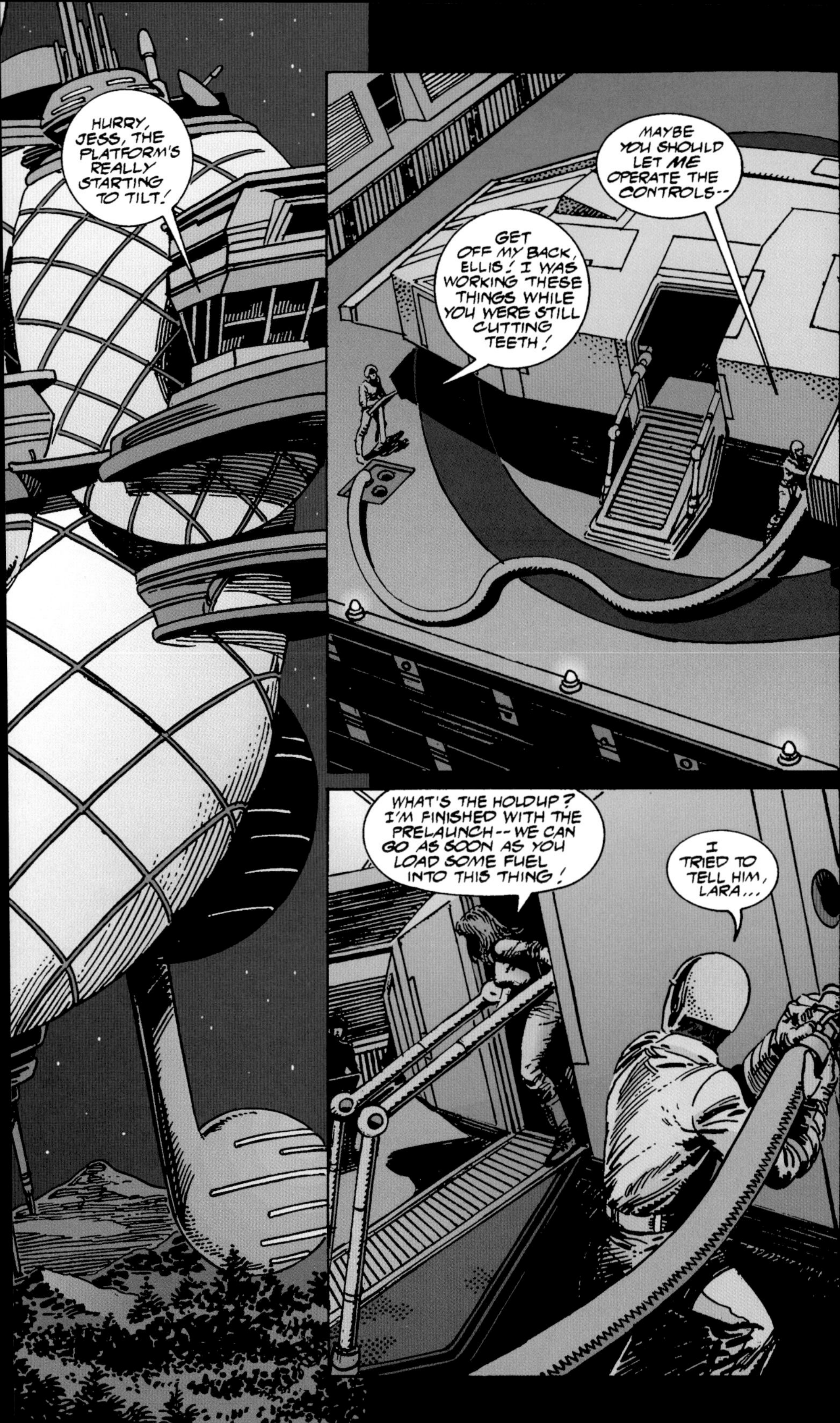
HURRY, JESS, THE PLATFORM'S REALLY STARTING TO TILT!
MAYBE YOU SHOULD LET ME OPERATE THE CONTROLS--
GET OFF MY BACK, ELLIS! I WAS WORKING THESE THINGS WHILE YOU WERE STILL CUTTING TEETH!
WHAT'S THE HOLDUP? I'M FINISHED WITH THE PRELAUNCH -- WE CAN GO AS SOON AS YOU LOAD SOME FUEL INTO THIS THING!
I TRIED TO TELL HIM, LARA...

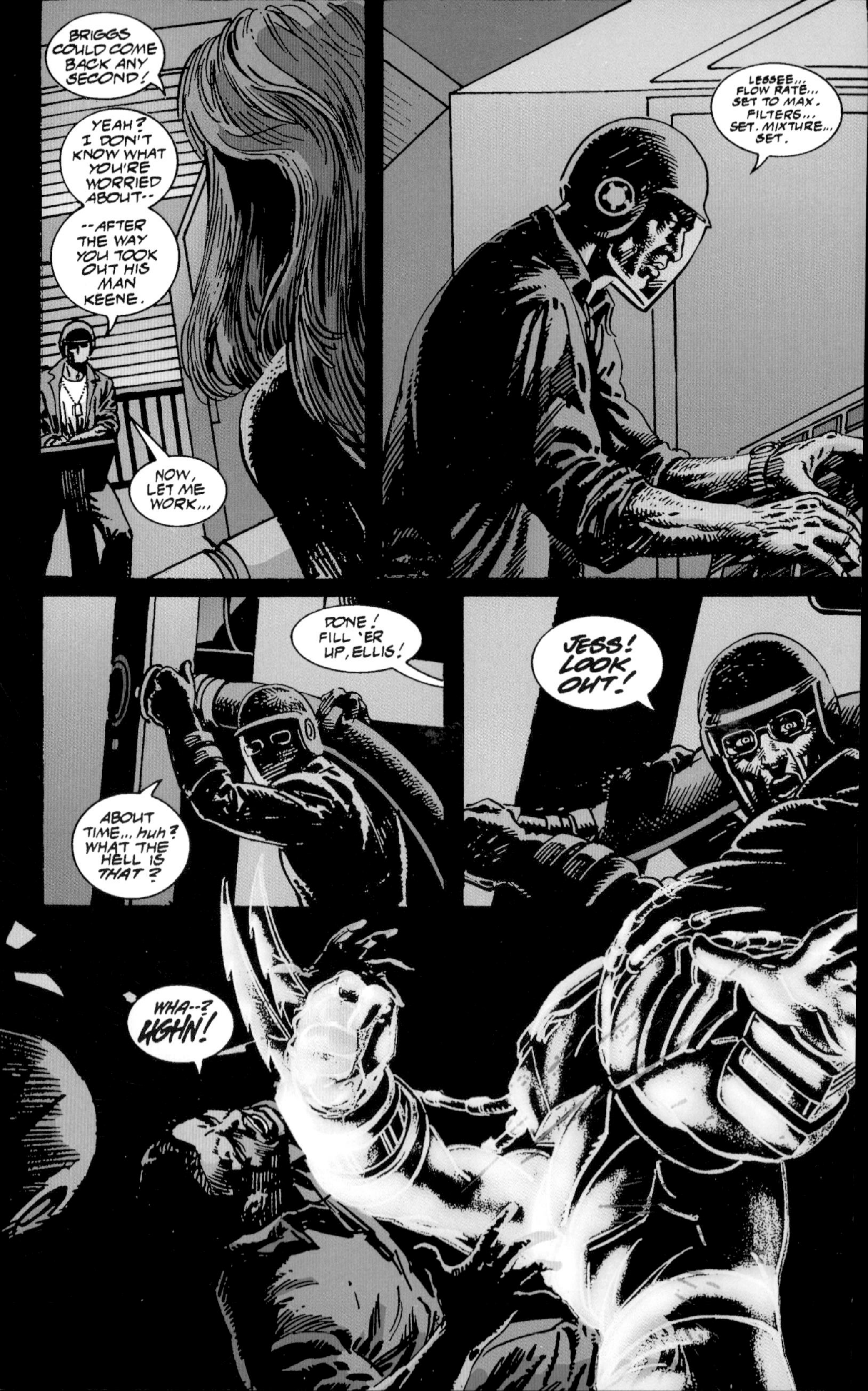
BRIGGS COULD COME BACK ANY SECOND!
YEAH? I DON'T KNOW WHAT YOU'RE WORRIED ABOUT--
--AFTER THE WAY YOU TOOK OUT HIS MAN KEENE.
NOW, LET ME WORK...
LESSEE... FLOW RATE... SET TO MAX. FILTERS... SET. MIXTURE... SET.
DONE! FILL 'ER UP, ELLIS!
ABOUT TIME... huh? WHAT THE HELL IS THAT?
JESS! LOOK OUT!
WHA--? UGHN!

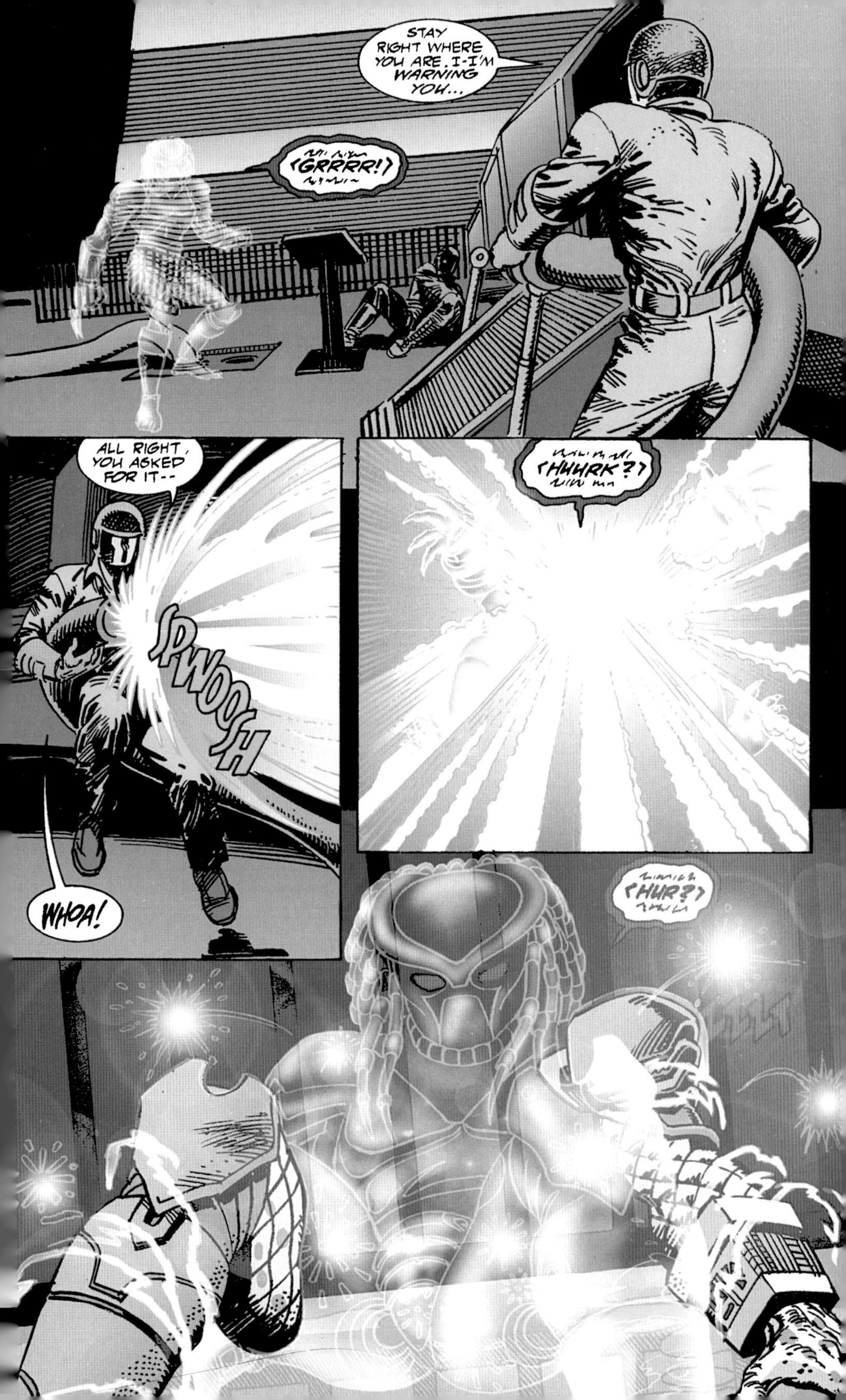
STAY RIGHT WHERE YOU ARE. I-I'M WARNING YOU...
<GRRRR!>
ALL RIGHT, YOU ASKED FOR IT--
SPWOOSH
WHOA!
<HUURK?>
<HUR?>

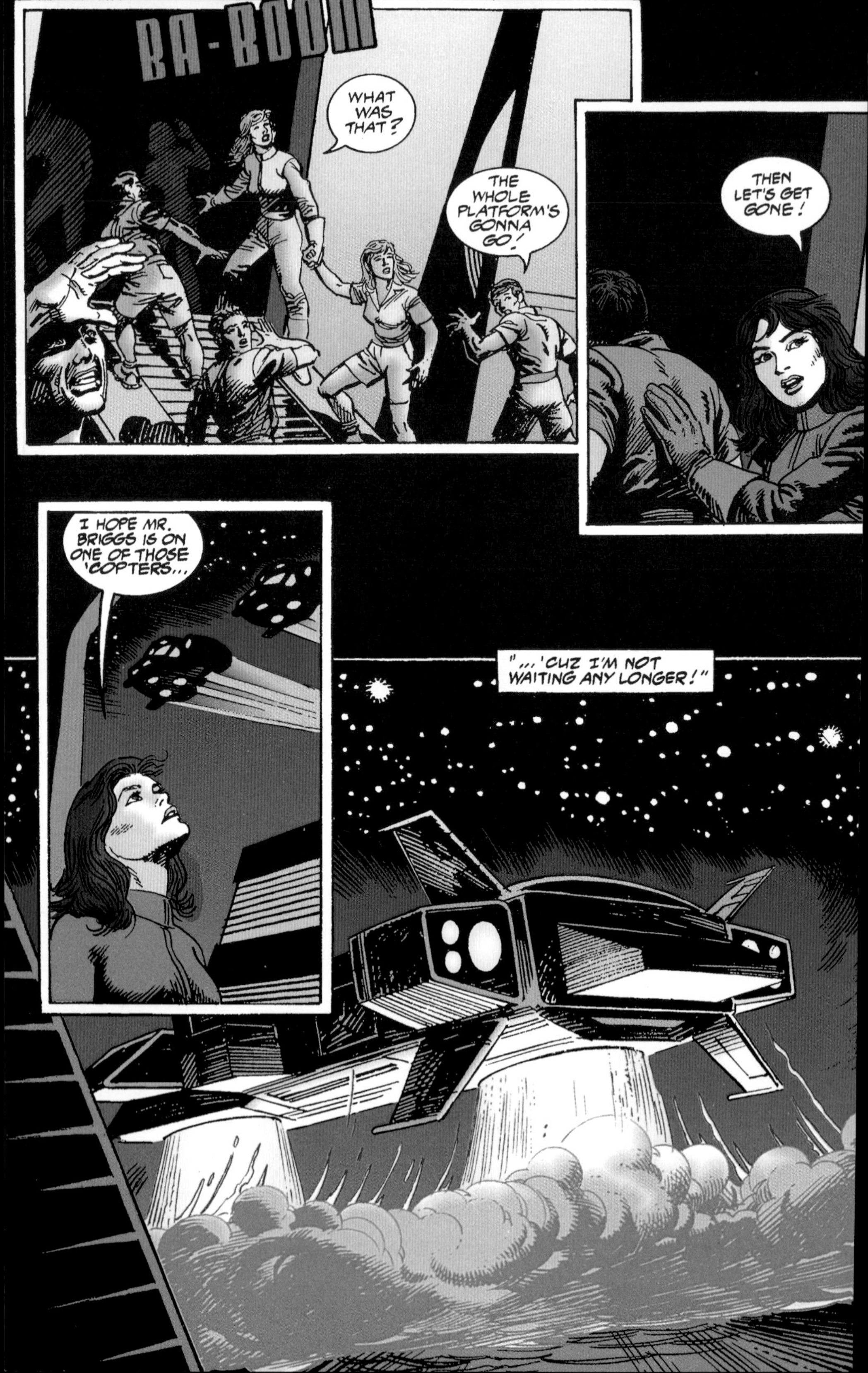
BA-BOOM
WHAT WAS THAT?
THE WHOLE PLATFORM'S GONNA GO!
THEN LET'S GET GONE!
I HOPE MR. BRIGGS IS ON ONE OF THOSE 'COPTERS...
"...'CUZ I'M NOT WAITING ANY LONGER!"

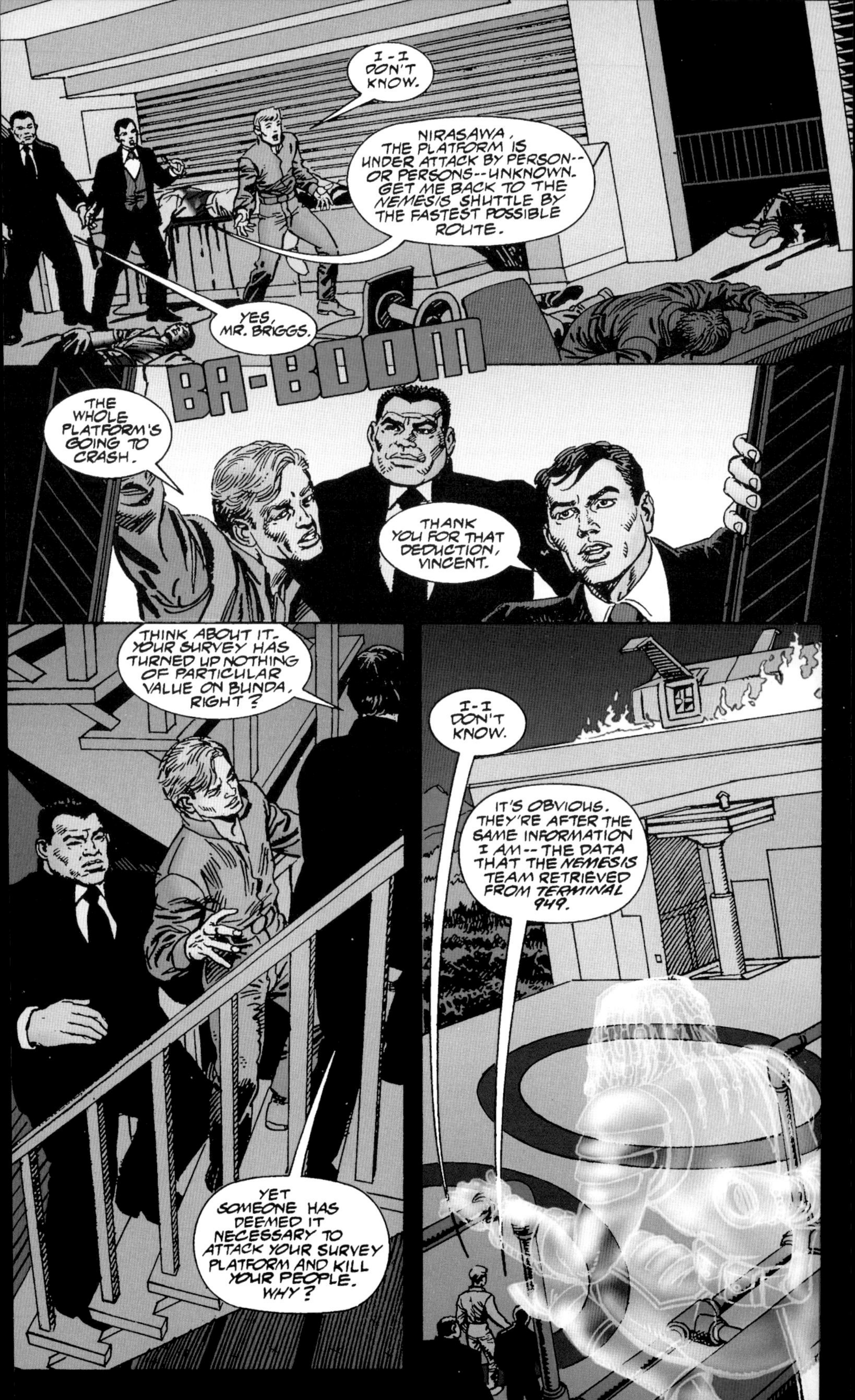
I-I DON'T KNOW.
NIRASAWA, THE PLATFORM IS UNDER ATTACK BY PERSON-- OR PERSONS--UNKNOWN. GET ME BACK TO THE NEMESIS SHUTTLE BY THE FASTEST POSSIBLE ROUTE.
YES, MR. BRIGGS.
BA-BOOM
THE WHOLE PLATFORM'S GOING TO CRASH.
THANK YOU FOR THAT DEDUCTION, VINCENT.
THINK ABOUT IT. YOUR SURVEY HAS TURNED UP NOTHING OF PARTICULAR VALUE ON BUNDA, RIGHT?
YET SOMEONE HAS DEEMED IT NECESSARY TO ATTACK YOUR SURVEY PLATFORM AND KILL YOUR PEOPLE. WHY?
I-I DON'T KNOW.
IT'S OBVIOUS. THEY'RE AFTER THE SAME INFORMATION I AM -- THE DATA THAT THE NEMESIS TEAM RETRIEVED FROM TERMINAL 949.

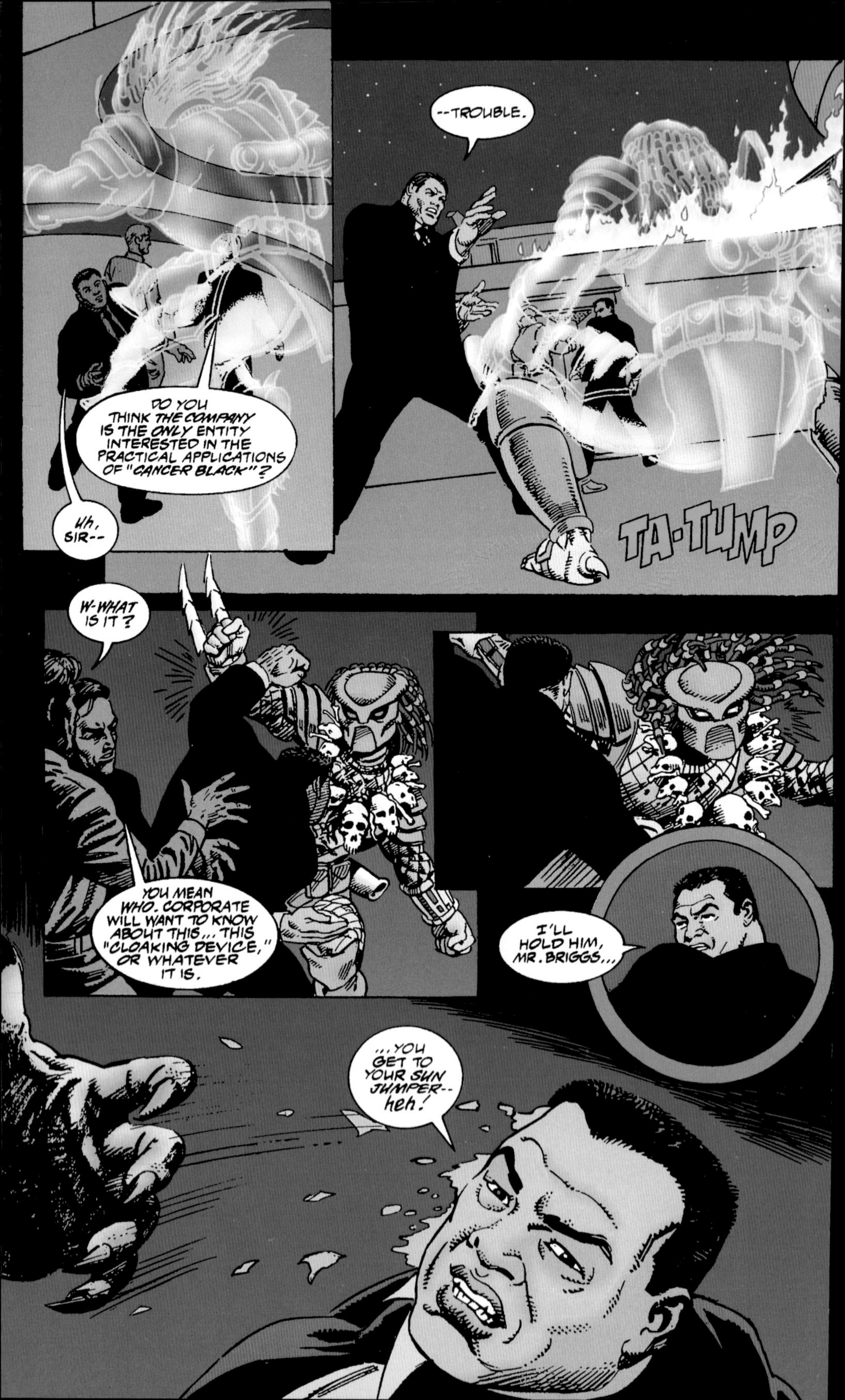

--TROUBLE.
DO YOU THINK THE COMPANY IS THE ONLY ENTITY INTERESTED IN THE PRACTICAL APPLICATIONS OF "CANCER BLACK"?
UH, SIR--
TA-TUMP
W-WHAT IS IT?
YOU MEAN WHO. CORPORATE WILL WANT TO KNOW ABOUT THIS... THIS "CLOAKING DEVICE," OR WHATEVER IT IS.
I'LL HOLD HIM, MR. BRIGGS...
...YOU GET TO YOUR SUN JUMPER-- heh!

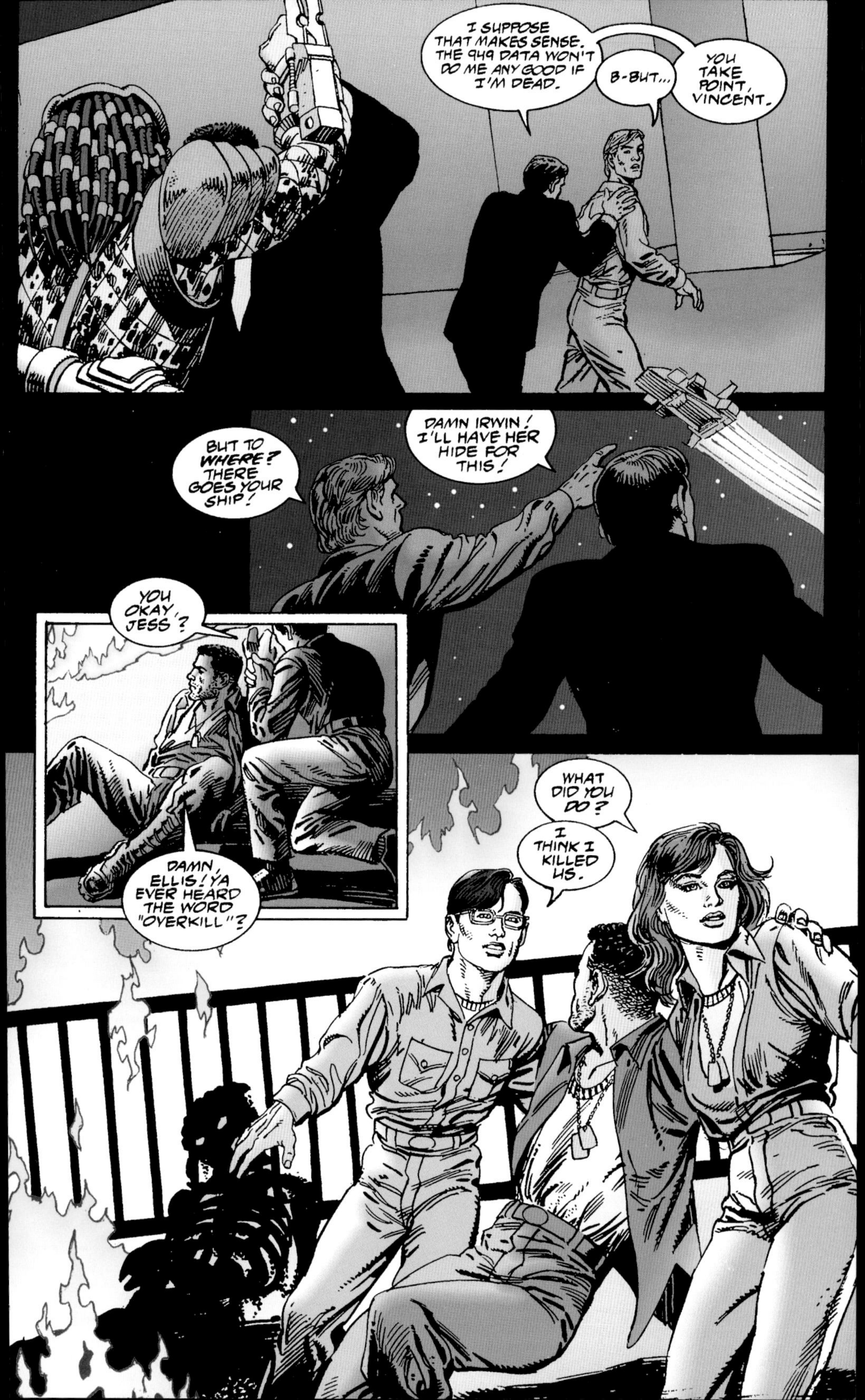
I SUPPOSE THAT MAKES SENSE. THE 949 DATA WON'T DO ME ANY GOOD IF I'M DEAD.
B-BUT...
YOU TAKE POINT, VINCENT.
BUT TO WHERE? THERE GOES YOUR SHIP!
DAMN IRWIN! I'LL HAVE HER HIDE FOR THIS!
YOU OKAY JESS?
DAMN, ELLIS! YA EVER HEARD THE WORD "OVERKILL"?
WHAT DID YOU DO?
I THINK I KILLED US.

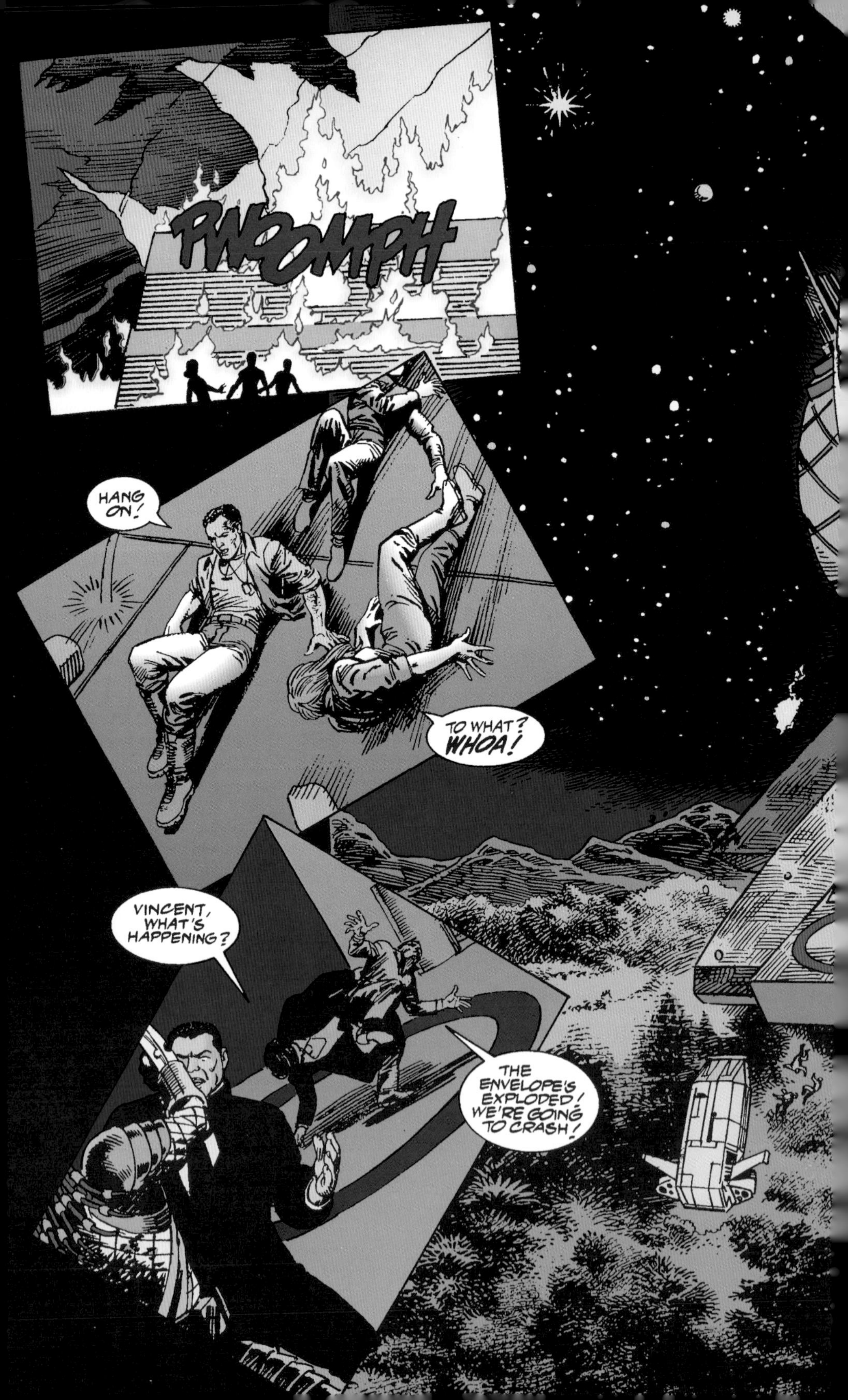
PWOOMPH
HANG ON!
TO WHAT? WHOA!
VINCENT, WHAT'S HAPPENING?
THE ENVELOPE'S EXPLODED! WE'RE GOING TO CRASH!

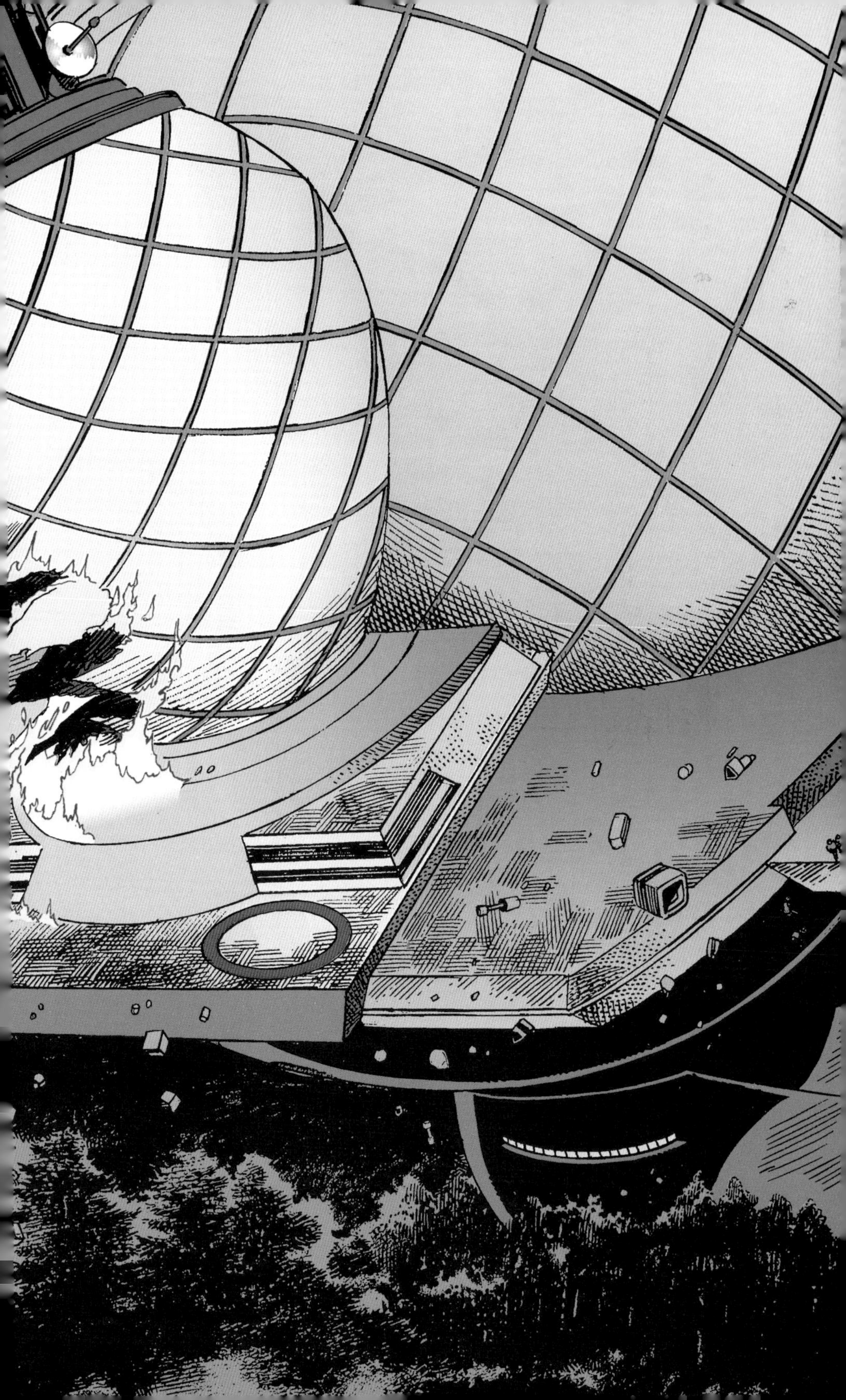

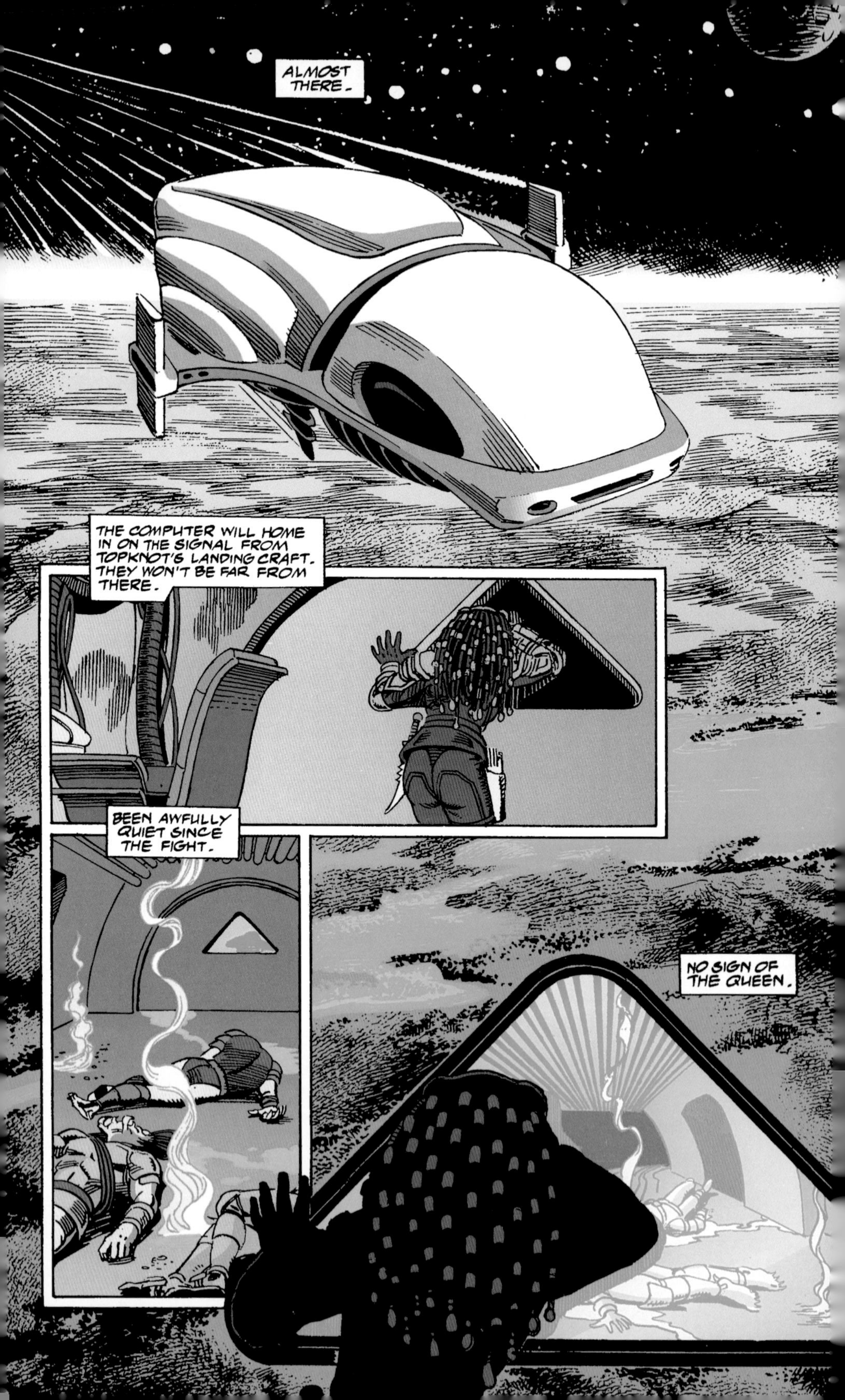
ALMOST THERE-
THE COMPUTER WILL HOME IN ON THE SIGNAL FROM TOPKNOT'S LANDING CRAFT. THEY WON'T BE FAR FROM THERE.
BEEN AWFULLY QUIET SINCE THE FIGHT.
NO SIGN OF THE QUEEN.

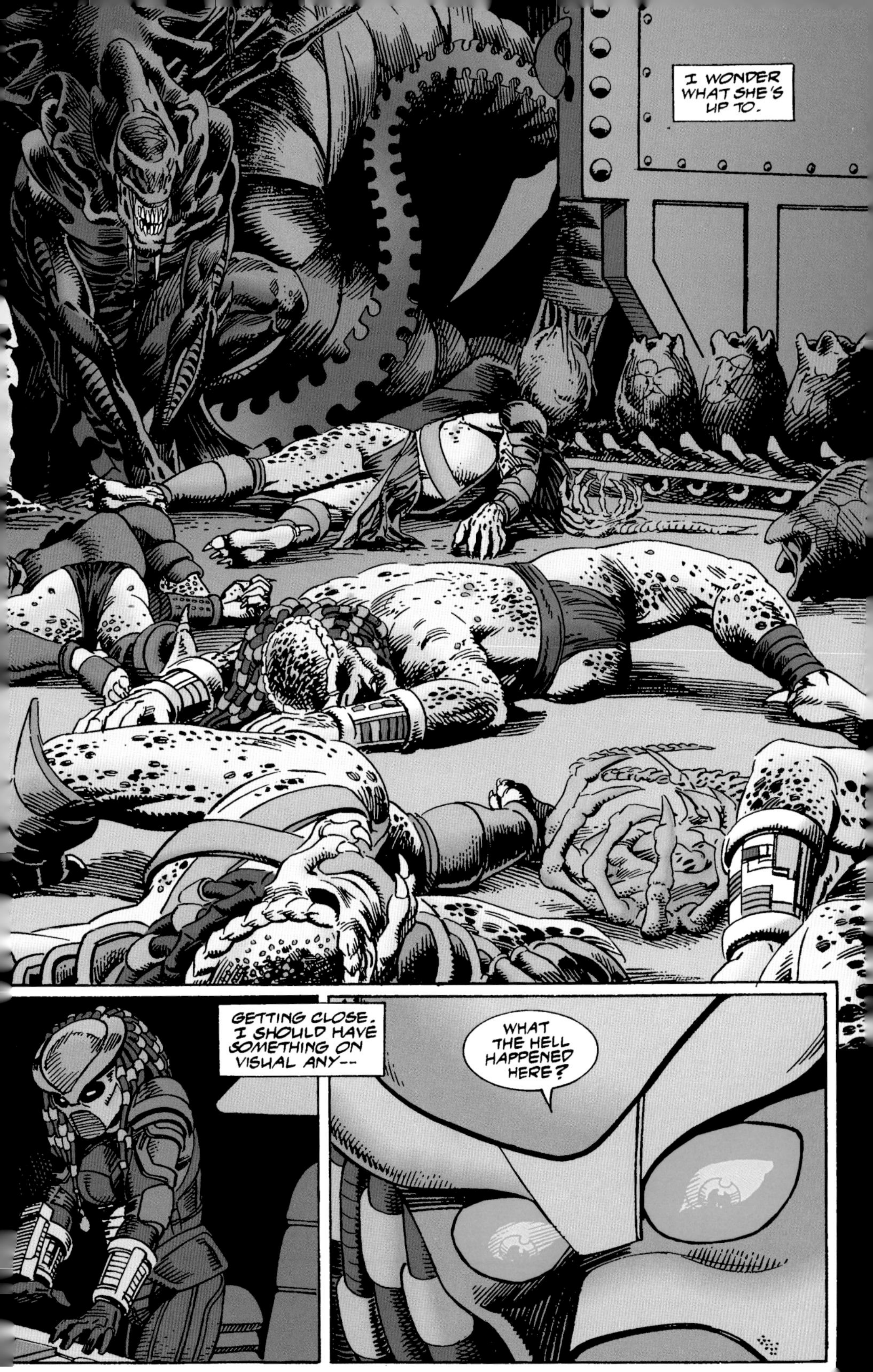
I WONDER WHAT SHE'S UP TO.
GETTING CLOSE. I SHOULD HAVE SOMETHING ON VISUAL ANY--
WHAT THE HELL HAPPENED HERE?

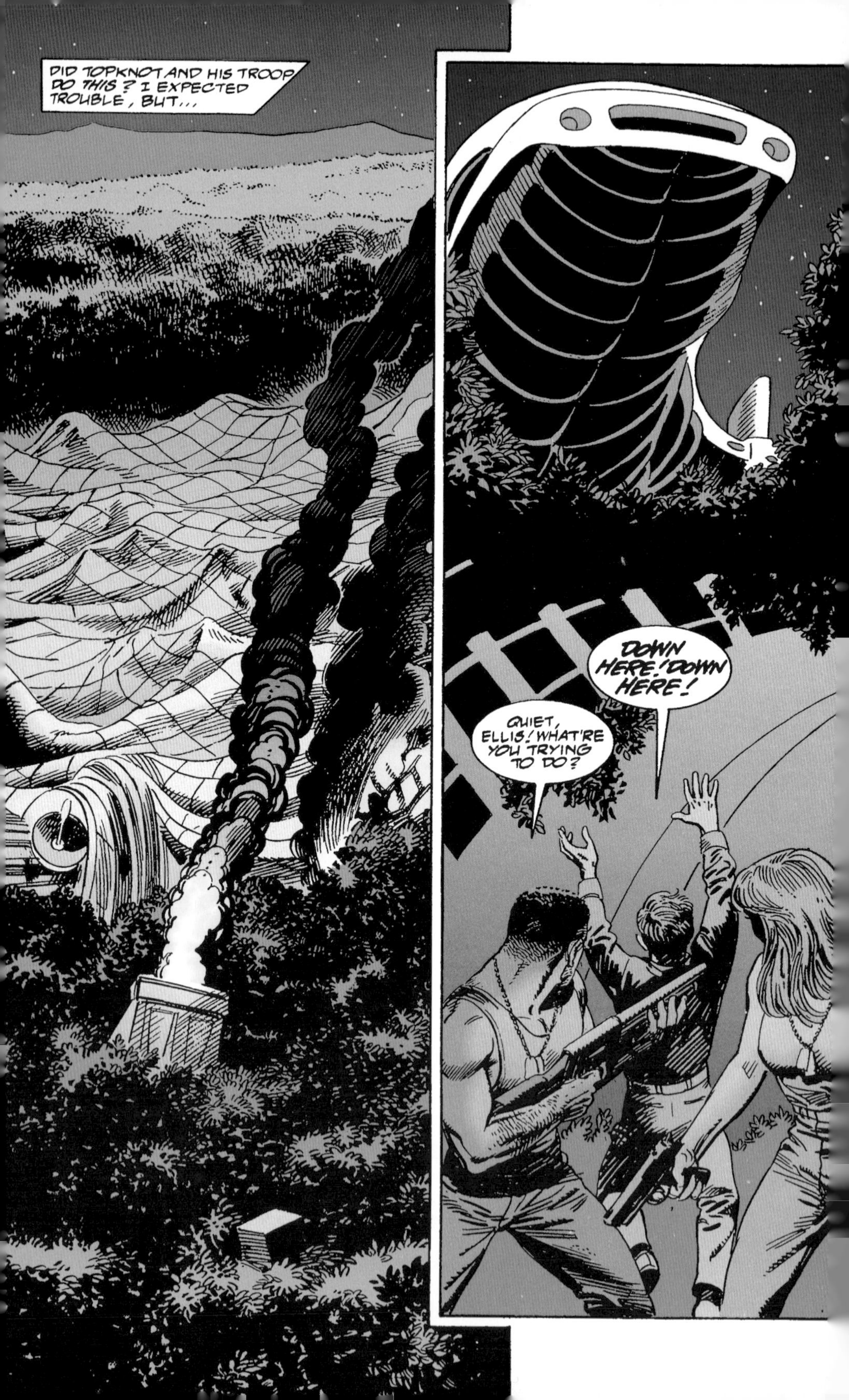
DID TOPKNOT AND HIS TROOP DO THIS? I EXPECTED TROUBLE, BUT...
DOWN HERE! DOWN HERE!
QUIET, ELLIS! WHAT'RE YOU TRYING TO DO?

"DOES THAT LOOK LIKE A RESCUE SHIP?"

"WE'RE IN DEEP, KID, AND IT LOOKS LIKE MORE TROUBLE'S ON THE WAY."

IT'S OBVIOUS WHERE THE ACTION IS. I'D BETTER FORGET ABOUT TOPKNOT'S LANDING CRAFT AND GET THE SHIP DOWN NEAR THAT WRECK.

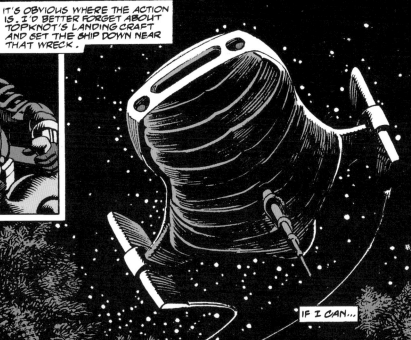

IF I CAN...

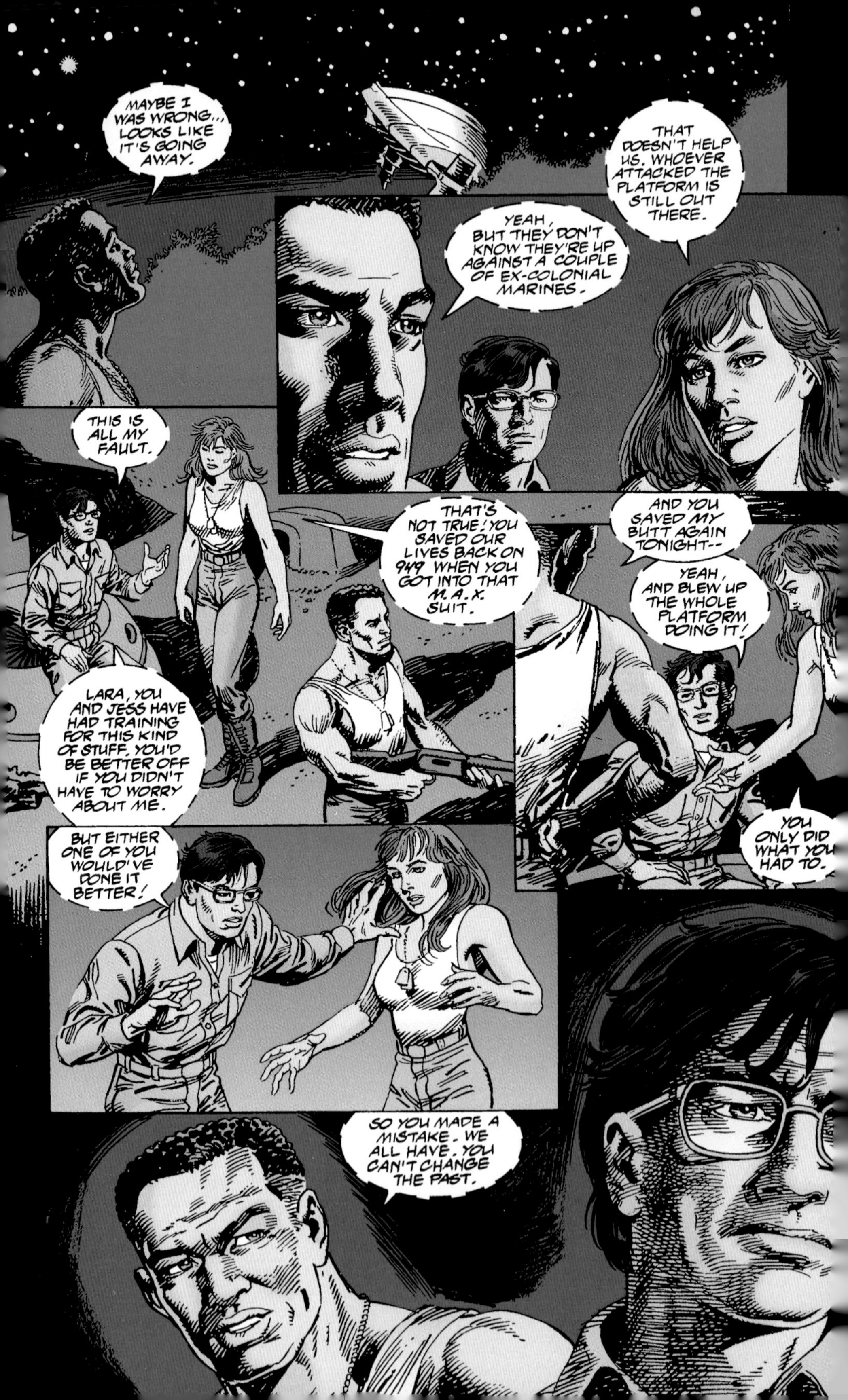
MAYBE I WAS WRONG... LOOKS LIKE IT'S GOING AWAY.
THAT DOESN'T HELP US. WHOEVER ATTACKED THE PLATFORM IS STILL OUT THERE.
YEAH, BUT THEY DON'T KNOW THEY'RE UP AGAINST A COUPLE OF EX-COLONIAL MARINES.
THIS IS ALL MY FAULT.
THAT'S NOT TRUE! YOU SAVED OUR LIVES BACK ON 949 WHEN YOU GOT INTO THAT M.A.X. SUIT.
AND YOU SAVED MY BUTT AGAIN TONIGHT--
YEAH, AND BLEW UP THE WHOLE PLATFORM DOING IT!
LARA, YOU AND JESS HAVE HAD TRAINING FOR THIS KIND OF STUFF. YOU'D BE BETTER OFF IF YOU DIDN'T HAVE TO WORRY ABOUT ME.
YOU ONLY DID WHAT YOU HAD TO.
BUT EITHER ONE OF YOU WOULD'VE DONE IT BETTER!
SO YOU MADE A MISTAKE. WE ALL HAVE. YOU CAN'T CHANGE THE PAST.

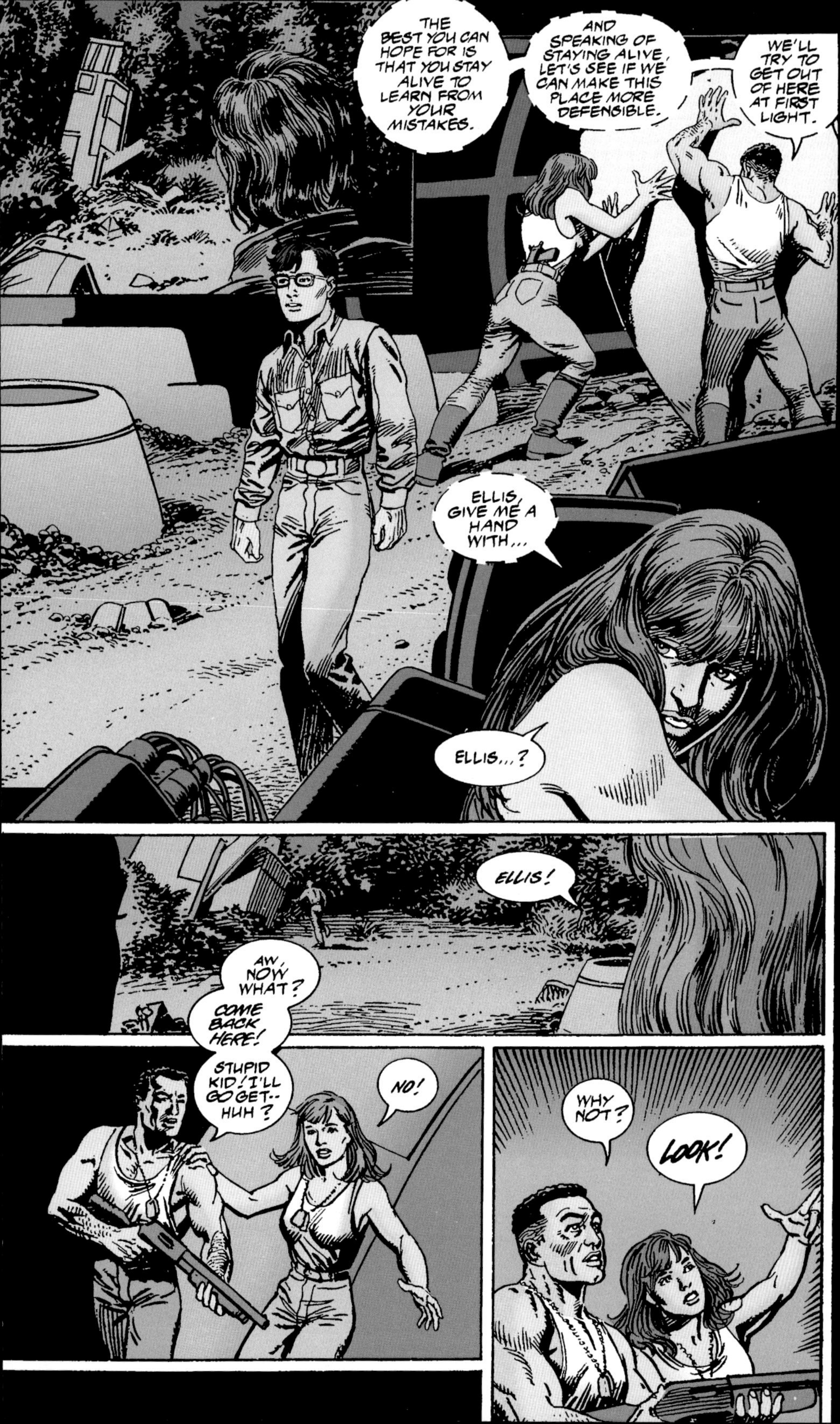
THE BEST YOU CAN HOPE FOR IS THAT YOU STAY ALIVE TO LEARN FROM YOUR MISTAKES.
AND SPEAKING OF STAYING ALIVE, LET'S SEE IF WE CAN MAKE THIS PLACE MORE DEFENSIBLE.
WE'LL TRY TO GET OUT OF HERE AT FIRST LIGHT.
ELLIS, GIVE ME A HAND WITH...
ELLIS...?
ELLIS!
AW, NOW WHAT?
COME BACK HERE!
STUPID KID! I'LL GO GET-- HUH?
NO!
WHY NOT?
LOOK!

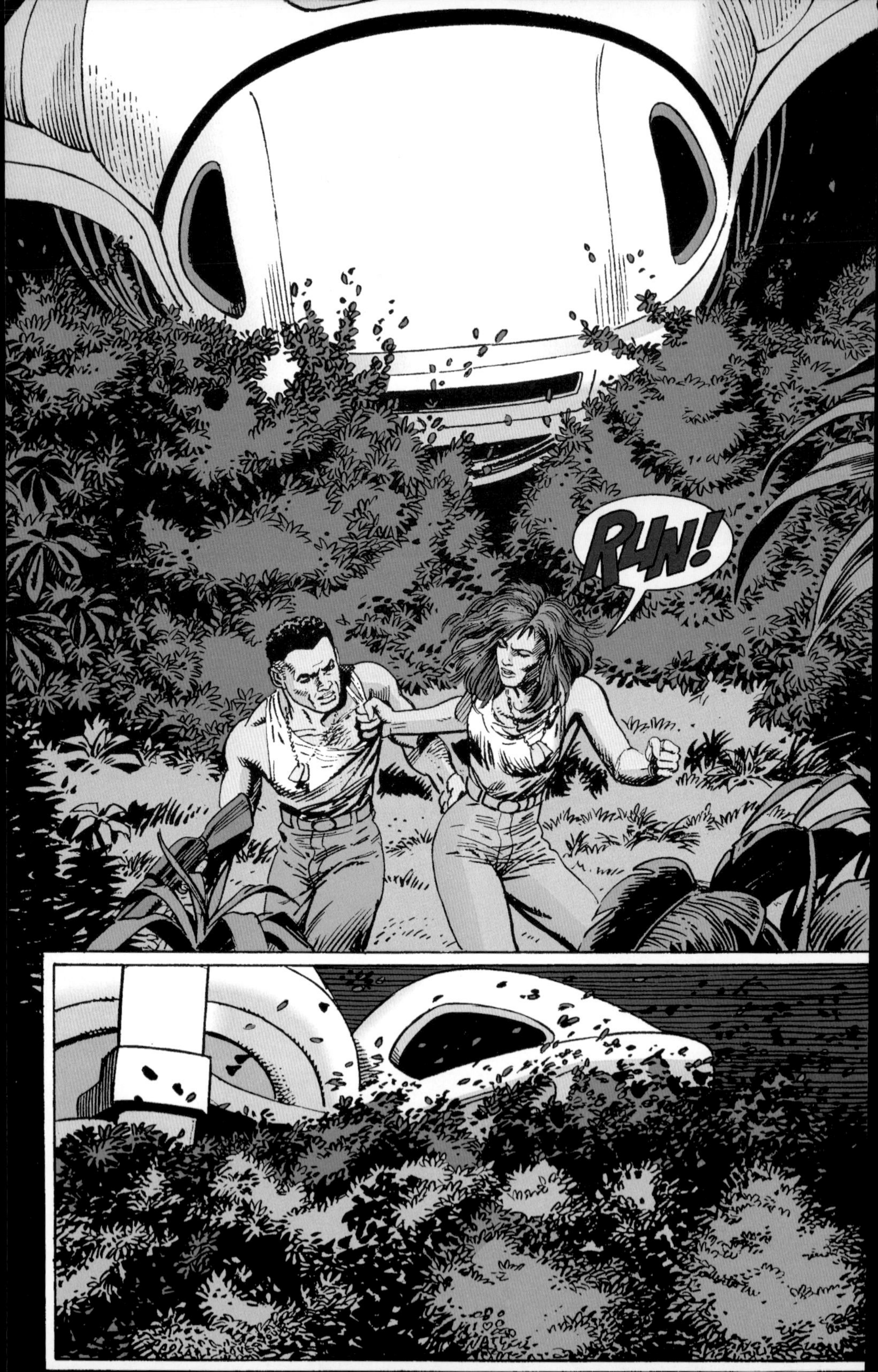
RUN!

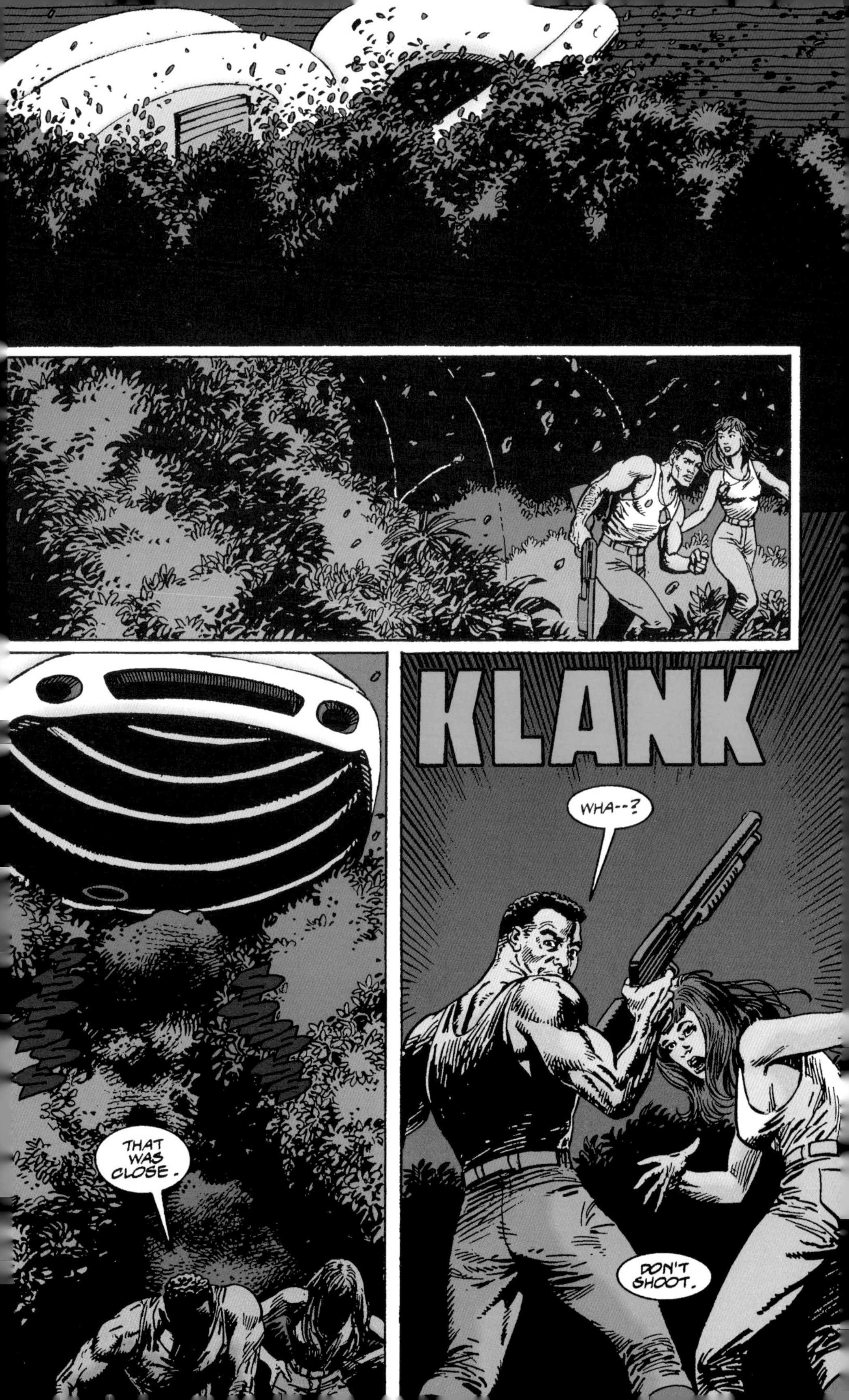
THAT WAS CLOSE.
KLANK
WHA--?
DON'T SHOOT.

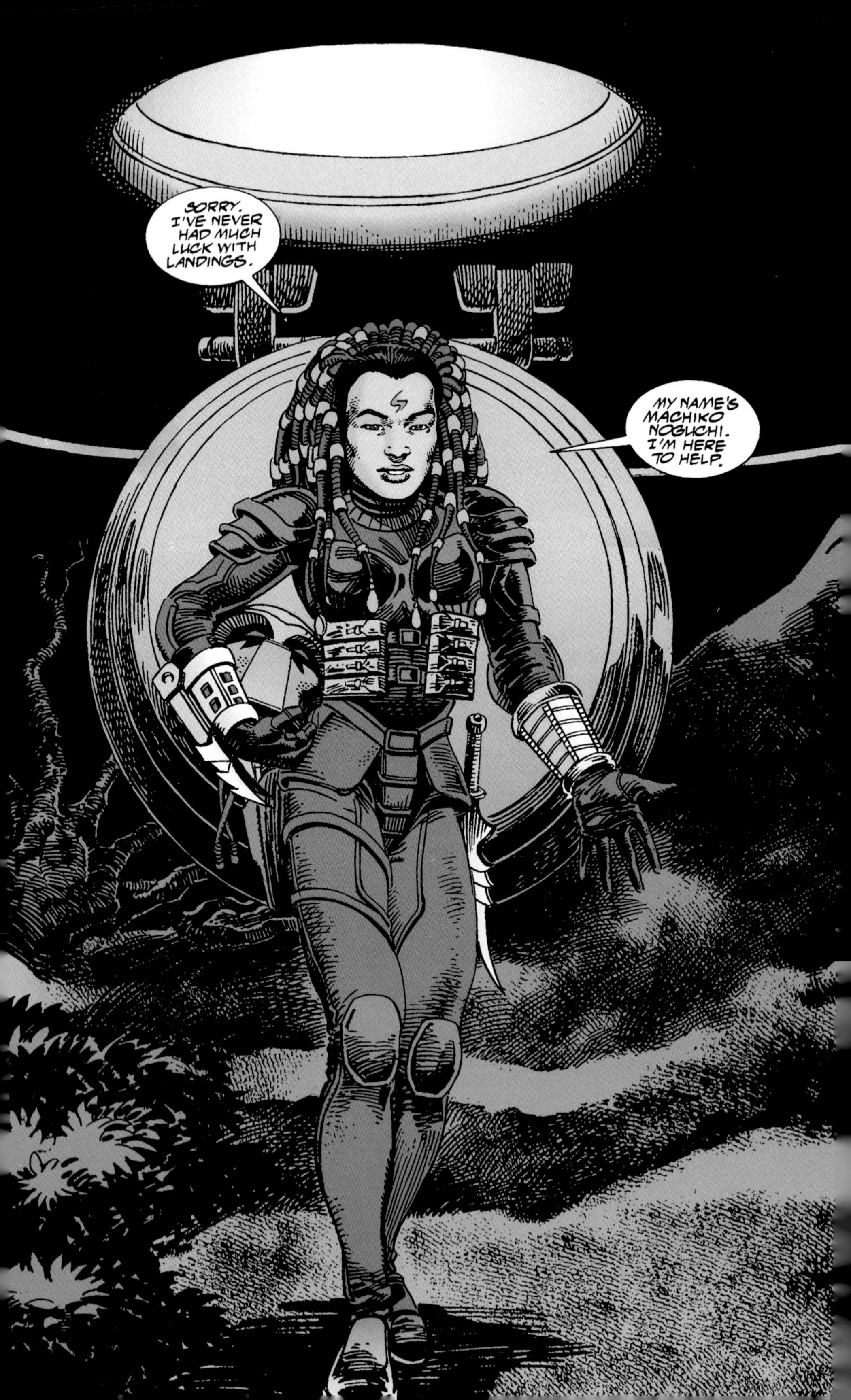
SORRY. I'VE NEVER HAD MUCH LUCK WITH LANDINGS.
MY NAME'S MACHIKO NOGUCHI. I'M HERE TO HELP.

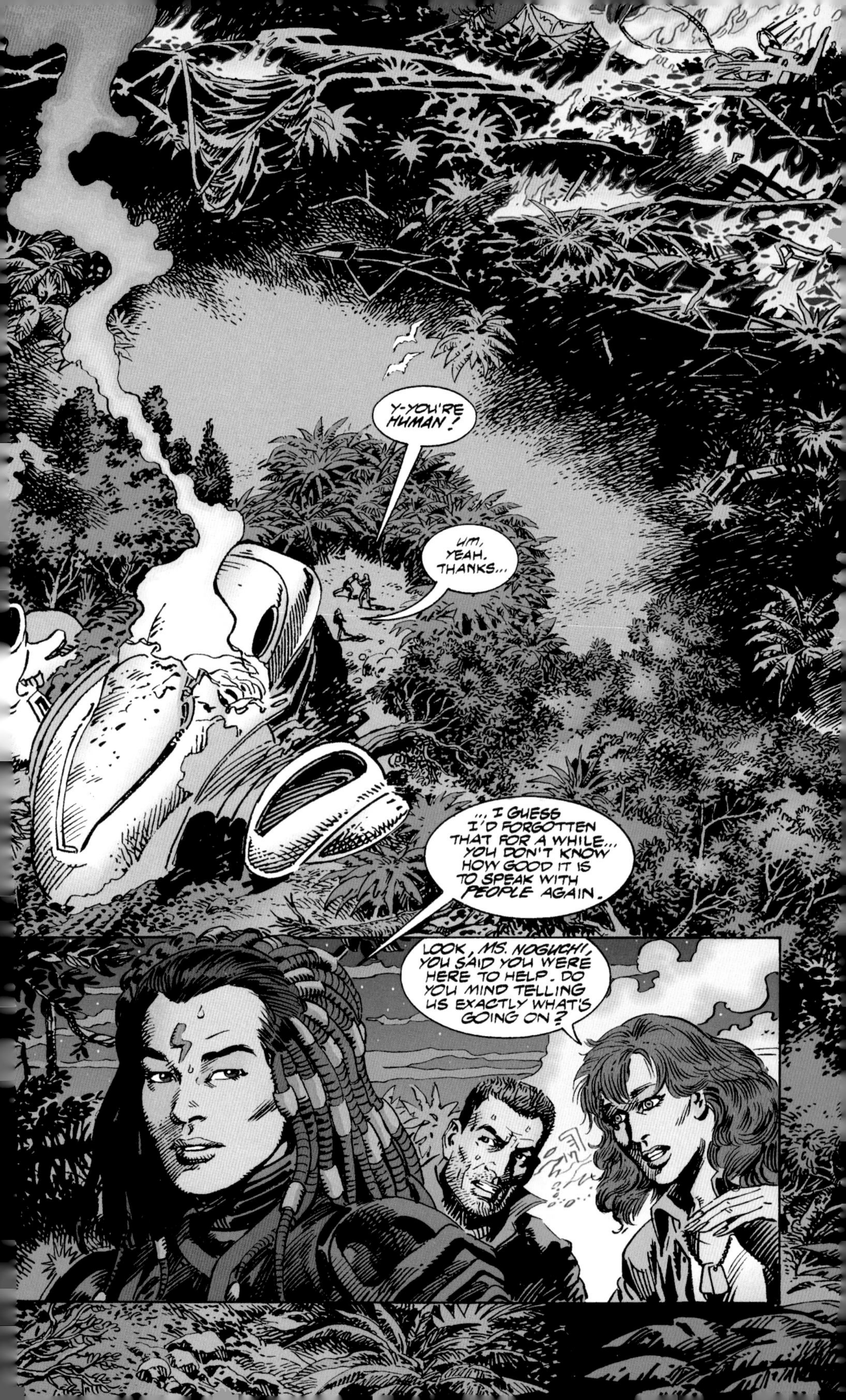
Y-YOU'RE HUMAN!
UM, YEAH. THANKS...
... I GUESS I'D FORGOTTEN THAT FOR A WHILE... YOU DON'T KNOW HOW GOOD IT IS TO SPEAK WITH PEOPLE AGAIN.
LOOK, MS. NOGUCHI, YOU SAID YOU WERE HERE TO HELP. DO YOU MIND TELLING US EXACTLY WHAT'S GOING ON?

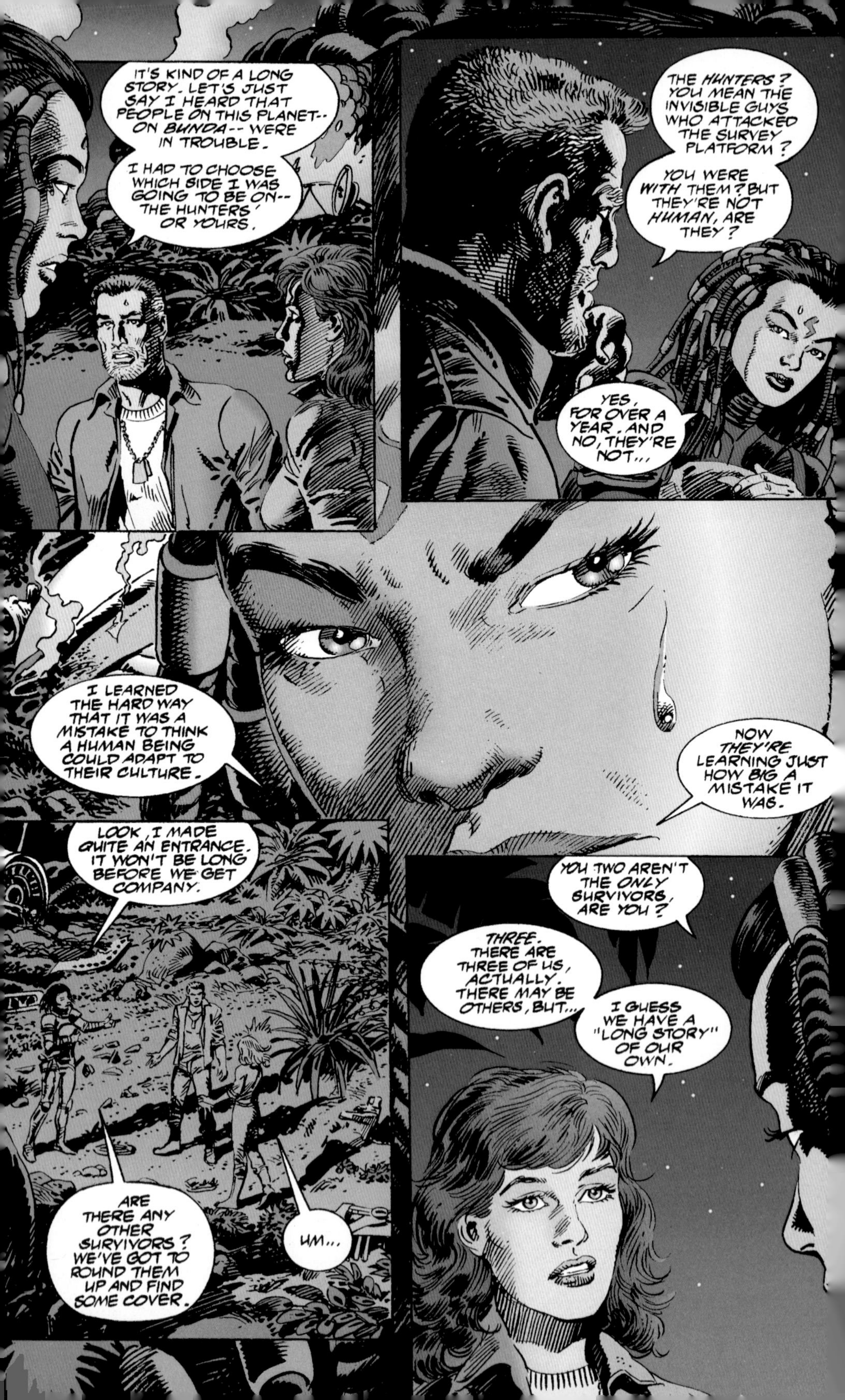

IT'S KIND OF A LONG STORY. LET'S JUST SAY I HEARD THAT PEOPLE ON THIS PLANET-- ON BUNDA-- WERE IN TROUBLE.
I HAD TO CHOOSE WHICH SIDE I WAS GOING TO BE ON-- THE HUNTERS' OR YOURS.
THE HUNTERS? YOU MEAN THE INVISIBLE GUYS WHO ATTACKED THE SURVEY PLATFORM?
YOU WERE WITH THEM? BUT THEY'RE NOT HUMAN, ARE THEY?
YES, FOR OVER A YEAR. AND NO, THEY'RE NOT...
I LEARNED THE HARD WAY THAT IT WAS A MISTAKE TO THINK A HUMAN BEING COULD ADAPT TO THEIR CULTURE.
NOW THEY'RE LEARNING JUST HOW BIG A MISTAKE IT WAS.
LOOK, I MADE QUITE AN ENTRANCE. IT WON'T BE LONG BEFORE WE GET COMPANY.
ARE THERE ANY OTHER SURVIVORS? WE'VE GOT TO ROUND THEM UP AND FIND SOME COVER.
UM...
YOU TWO AREN'T THE ONLY SURVIVORS, ARE YOU?
THREE. THERE ARE THREE OF US, ACTUALLY. THERE MAY BE OTHERS, BUT...
I GUESS WE HAVE A "LONG STORY" OF OUR OWN.

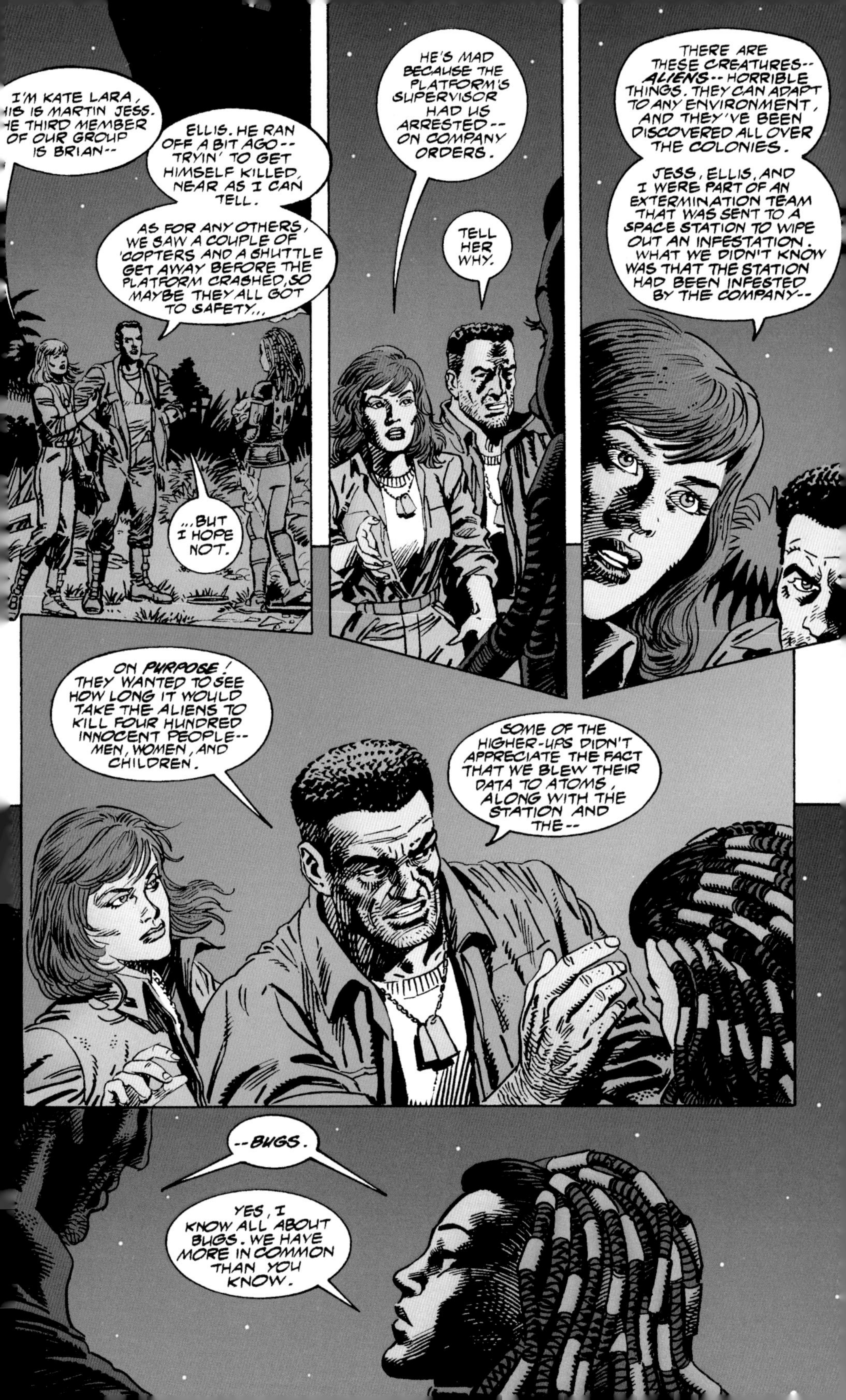
I'M KATE LARA, THIS IS MARTIN JESS. THE THIRD MEMBER OF OUR GROUP IS BRIAN--
ELLIS. HE RAN OFF A BIT AGO--TRYIN' TO GET HIMSELF KILLED, NEAR AS I CAN TELL.
AS FOR ANY OTHERS, WE SAW A COUPLE OF 'COPTERS AND A SHUTTLE GET AWAY BEFORE THE PLATFORM CRASHED, SO MAYBE THEY ALL GOT TO SAFETY...
...BUT I HOPE NOT.
HE'S MAD BECAUSE THE PLATFORM'S SUPERVISOR HAD US ARRESTED--ON COMPANY ORDERS.
TELL HER WHY.
THERE ARE THESE CREATURES--ALIENS--HORRIBLE THINGS. THEY CAN ADAPT TO ANY ENVIRONMENT, AND THEY'VE BEEN DISCOVERED ALL OVER THE COLONIES.
JESS, ELLIS, AND I WERE PART OF AN EXTERMINATION TEAM THAT WAS SENT TO A SPACE STATION TO WIPE OUT AN INFESTATION. WHAT WE DIDN'T KNOW WAS THAT THE STATION HAD BEEN INFESTED BY THE COMPANY--
ON PURPOSE! THEY WANTED TO SEE HOW LONG IT WOULD TAKE THE ALIENS TO KILL FOUR HUNDRED INNOCENT PEOPLE--MEN, WOMEN, AND CHILDREN.
SOME OF THE HIGHER-UPS DIDN'T APPRECIATE THE FACT THAT WE BLEW THEIR DATA TO ATOMS, ALONG WITH THE STATION AND THE--
--BUGS.
YES, I KNOW ALL ABOUT BUGS. WE HAVE MORE IN COMMON THAN YOU KNOW.

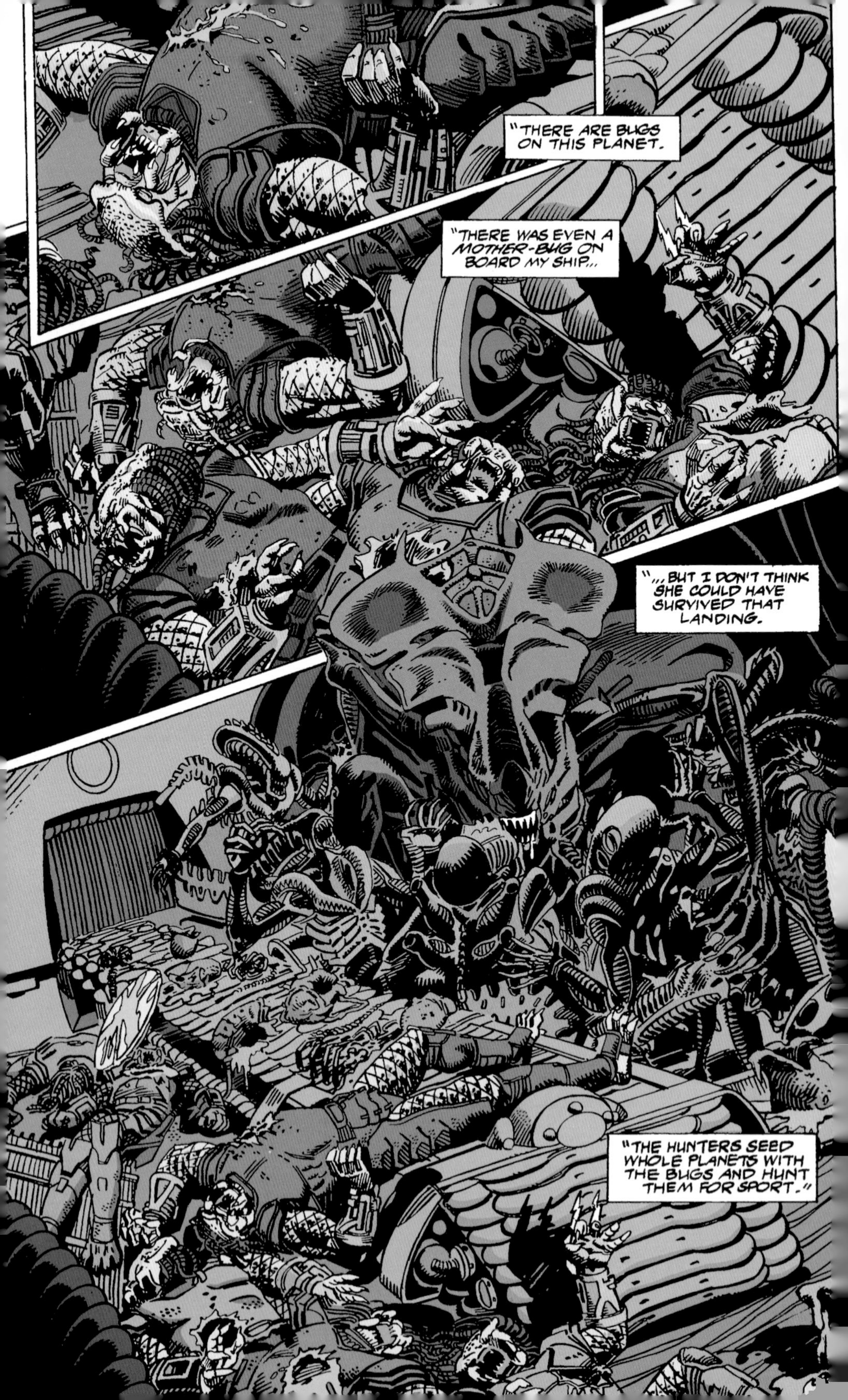
"THERE ARE BUGS ON THIS PLANET.
"THERE WAS EVEN A MOTHER-BUG ON BOARD MY SHIP...
"... BUT I DON'T THINK SHE COULD HAVE SURVIVED THAT LANDING.
"THE HUNTERS SEED WHOLE PLANETS WITH THE BUGS AND HUNT THEM FOR SPORT."

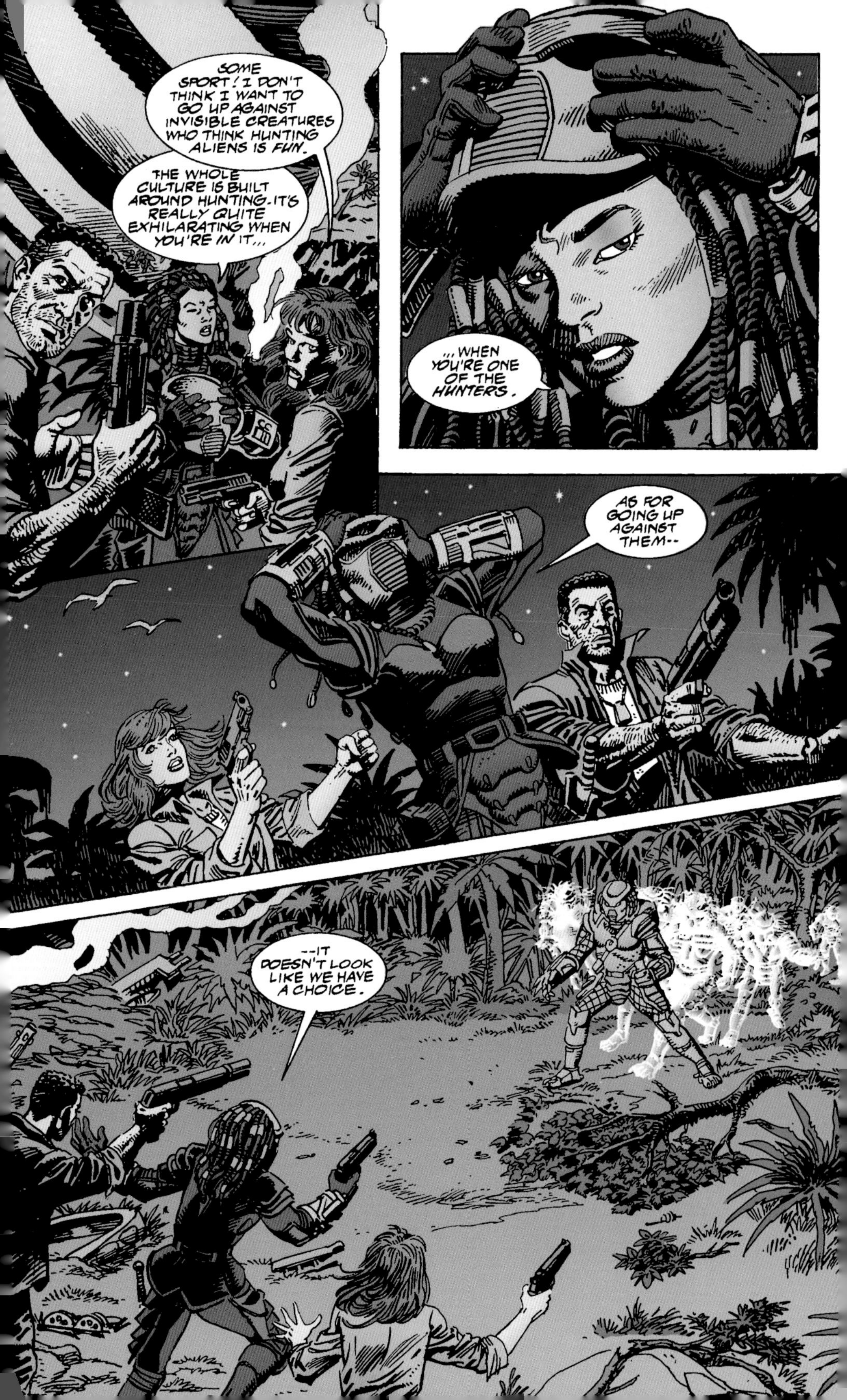
SOME SPORT! I DON'T THINK I WANT TO GO UP AGAINST INVISIBLE CREATURES WHO THINK HUNTING ALIENS IS FUN.
THE WHOLE CULTURE IS BUILT AROUND HUNTING. IT'S REALLY QUITE EXHILARATING WHEN YOU'RE IN IT...
...WHEN YOU'RE ONE OF THE HUNTERS.
AS FOR GOING UP AGAINST THEM--
--IT DOESN'T LOOK LIKE WE HAVE A CHOICE.

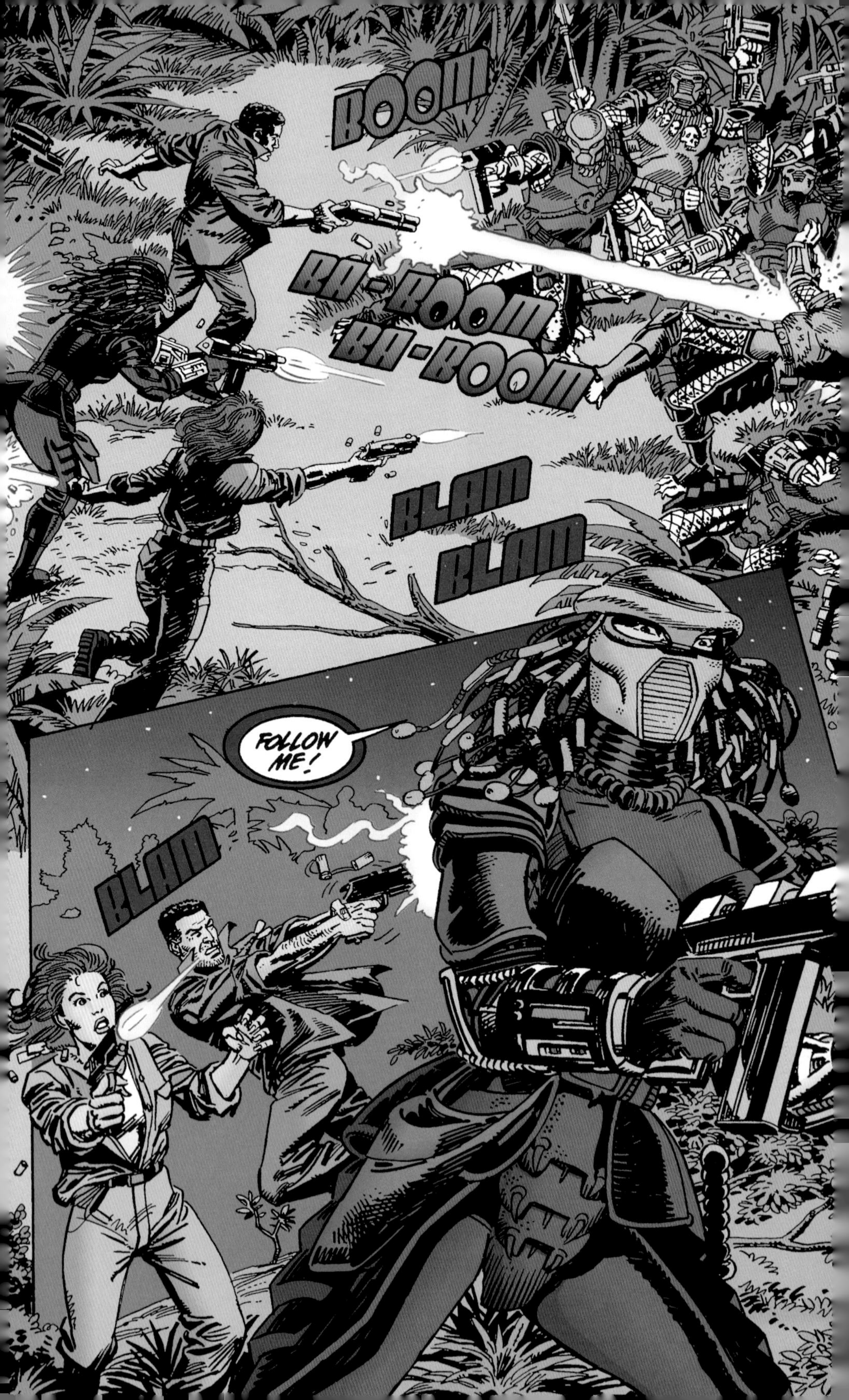
BOOM
BA-BOOM
BA-BOOM
BLAM
BLAM
FOLLOW ME!
BLAM

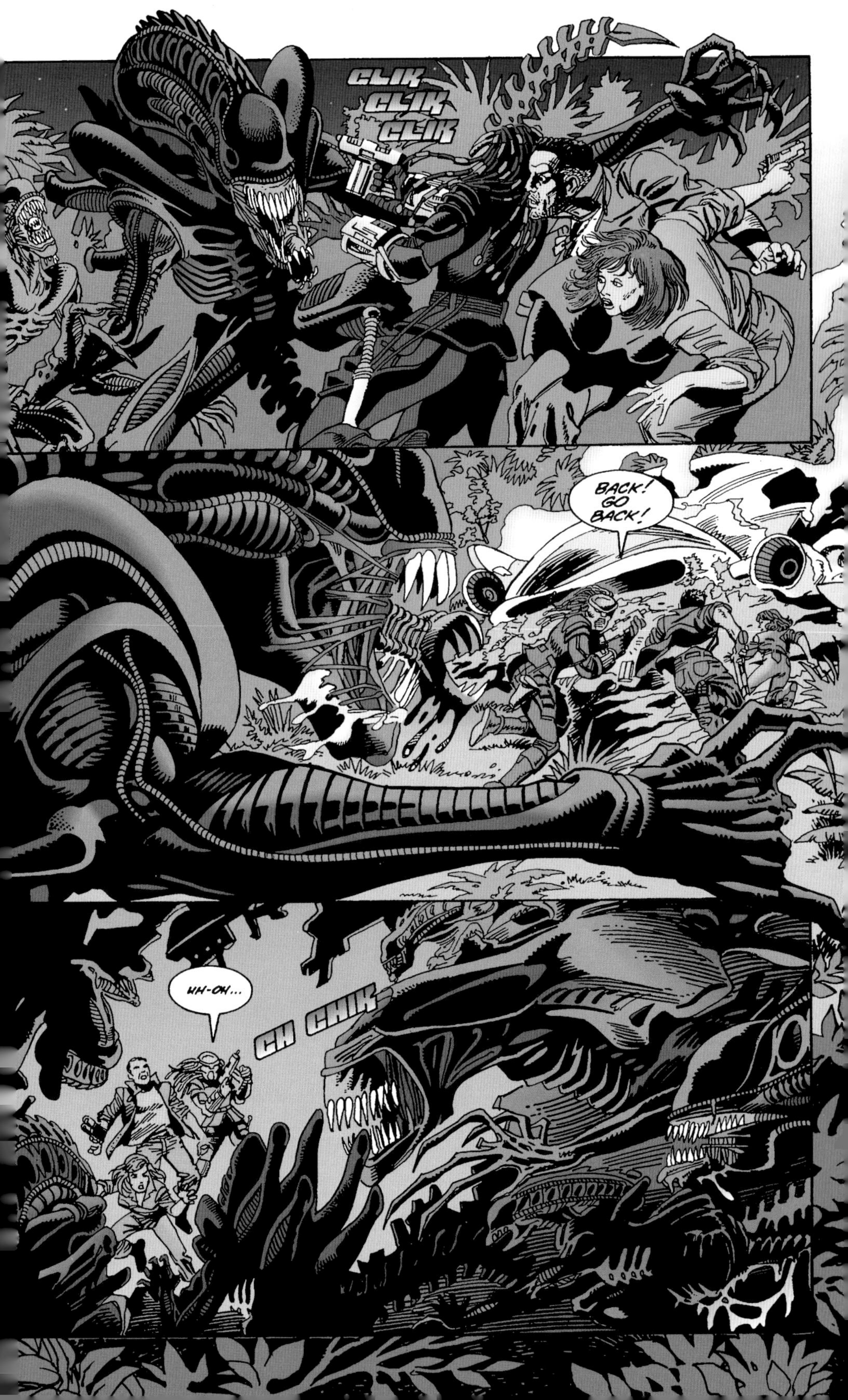
CLIK
CLIK
CLIK
BACK! GO BACK!
UH-OH...
CH CHIK

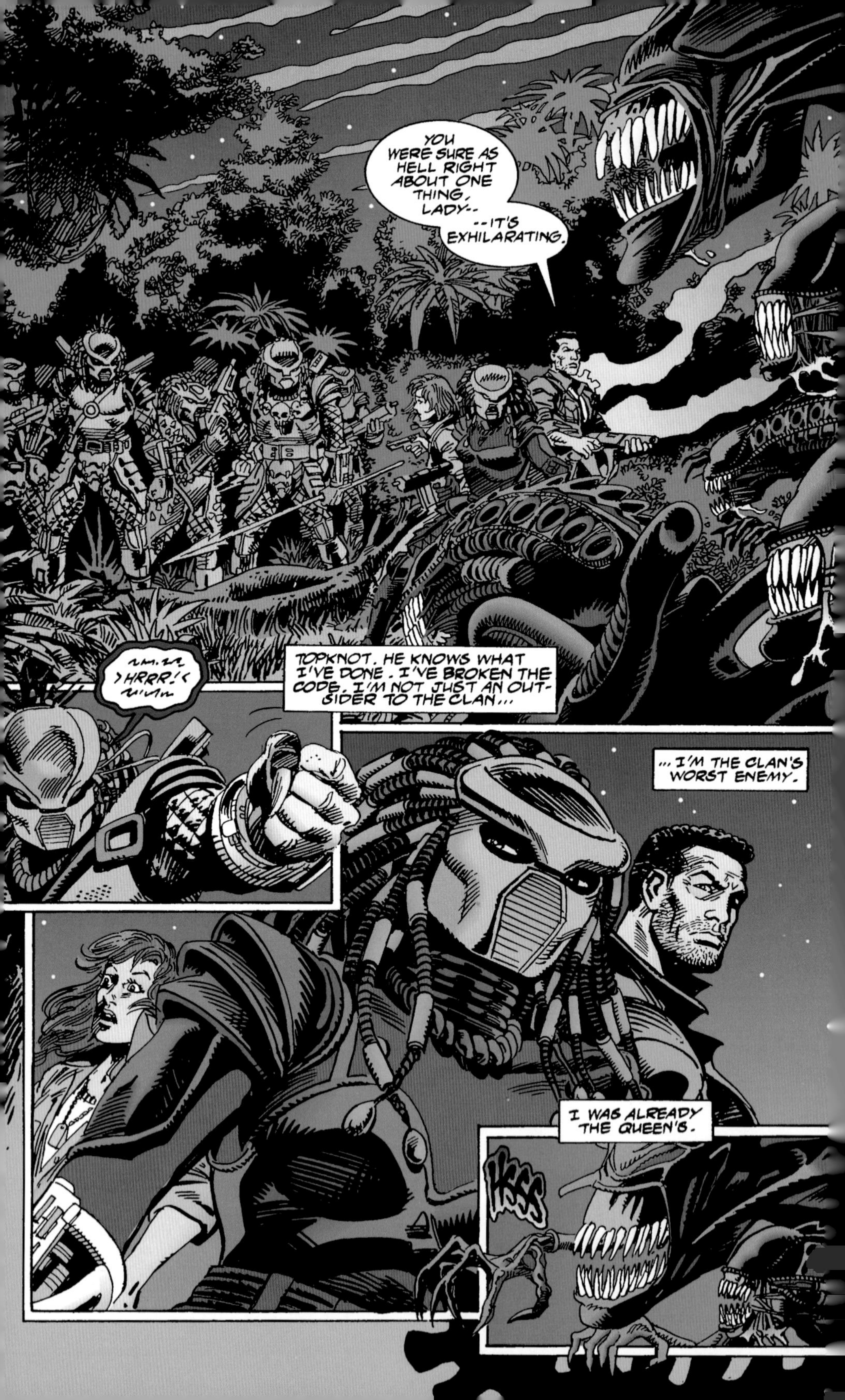
YOU WERE SURE AS HELL RIGHT ABOUT ONE THING, LADY--
--IT'S EXHILARATING.
HRRR!
TOPKNOT. HE KNOWS WHAT I'VE DONE. I'VE BROKEN THE CODE. I'M NOT JUST AN OUT-SIDER TO THE CLAN...
...I'M THE CLAN'S WORST ENEMY.
I WAS ALREADY THE QUEEN'S.
HSSS

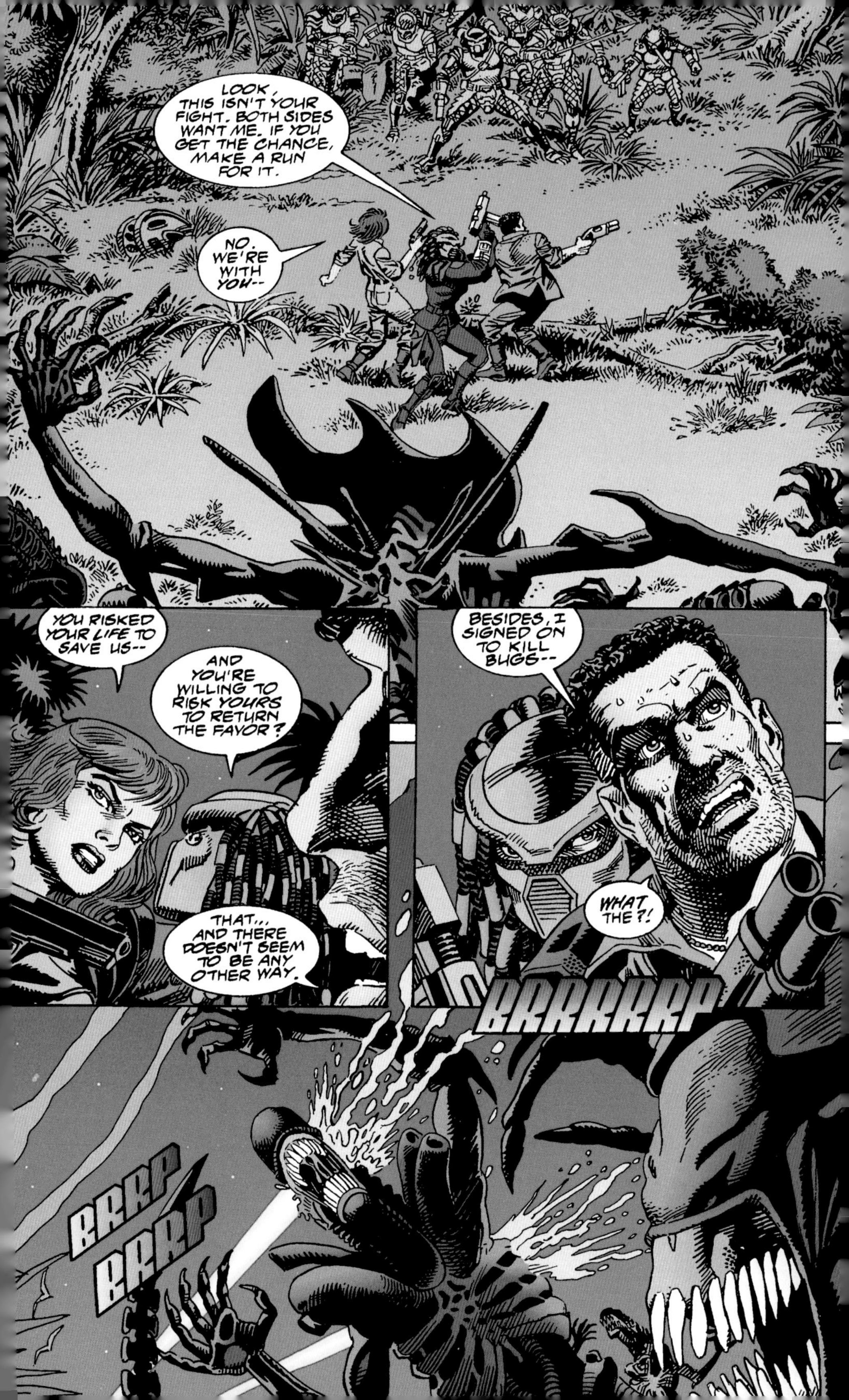

LOOK, THIS ISN'T YOUR FIGHT. BOTH SIDES WANT ME. IF YOU GET THE CHANCE, MAKE A RUN FOR IT.
NO. WE'RE WITH YOU--
YOU RISKED YOUR LIFE TO SAVE US--
AND YOU'RE WILLING TO RISK YOURS TO RETURN THE FAVOR?
THAT... AND THERE DOESN'T SEEM TO BE ANY OTHER WAY.
BESIDES, I SIGNED ON TO KILL BUGS--
WHAT THE ?!
BRRRRRRP
BRRP
BRRP

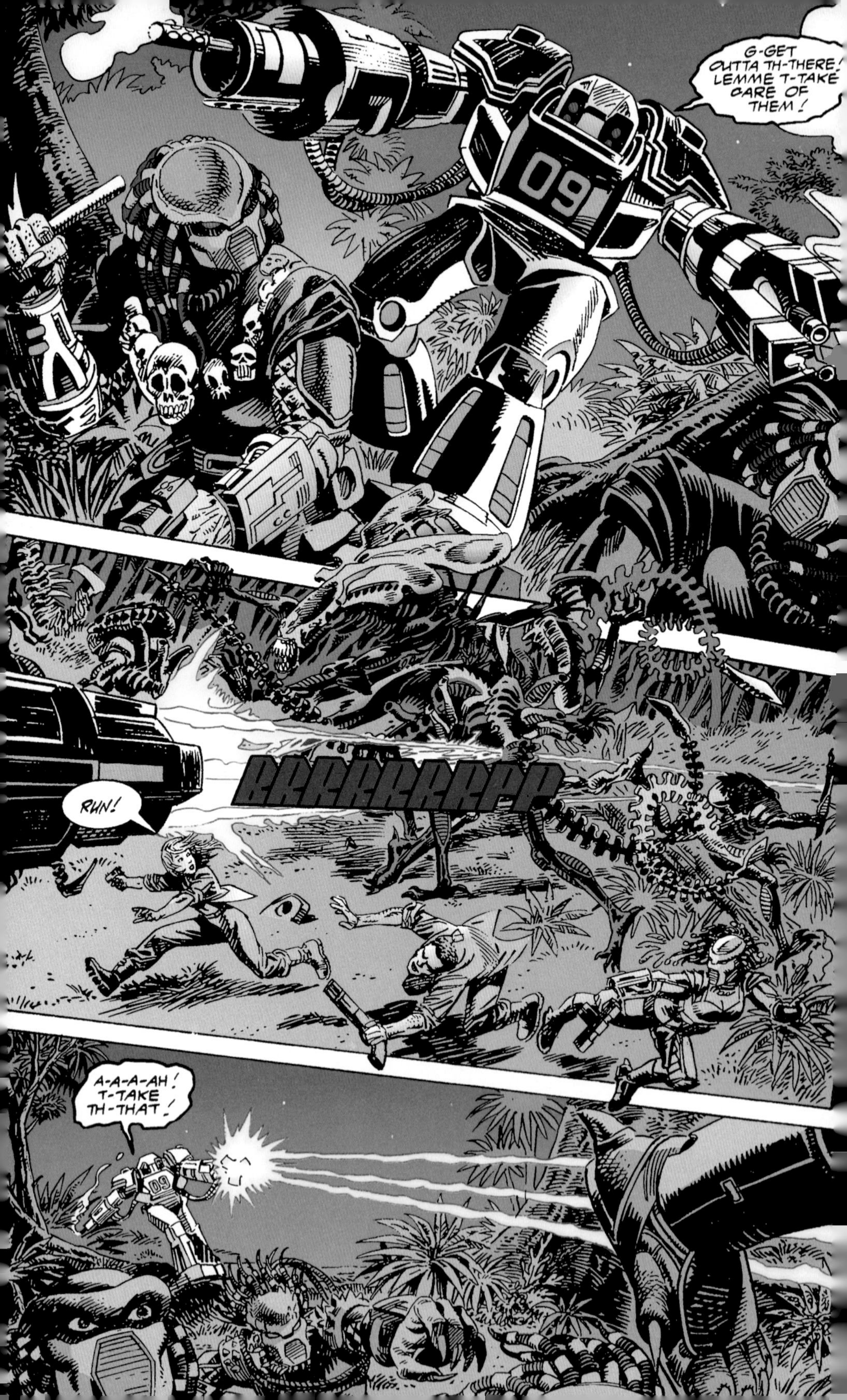
G-GET OUTTA TH-THERE! LEMME T-TAKE CARE OF THEM!
BRRRRRRRRPP
RUN!
A-A-A-AH! T-TAKE TH-THAT!

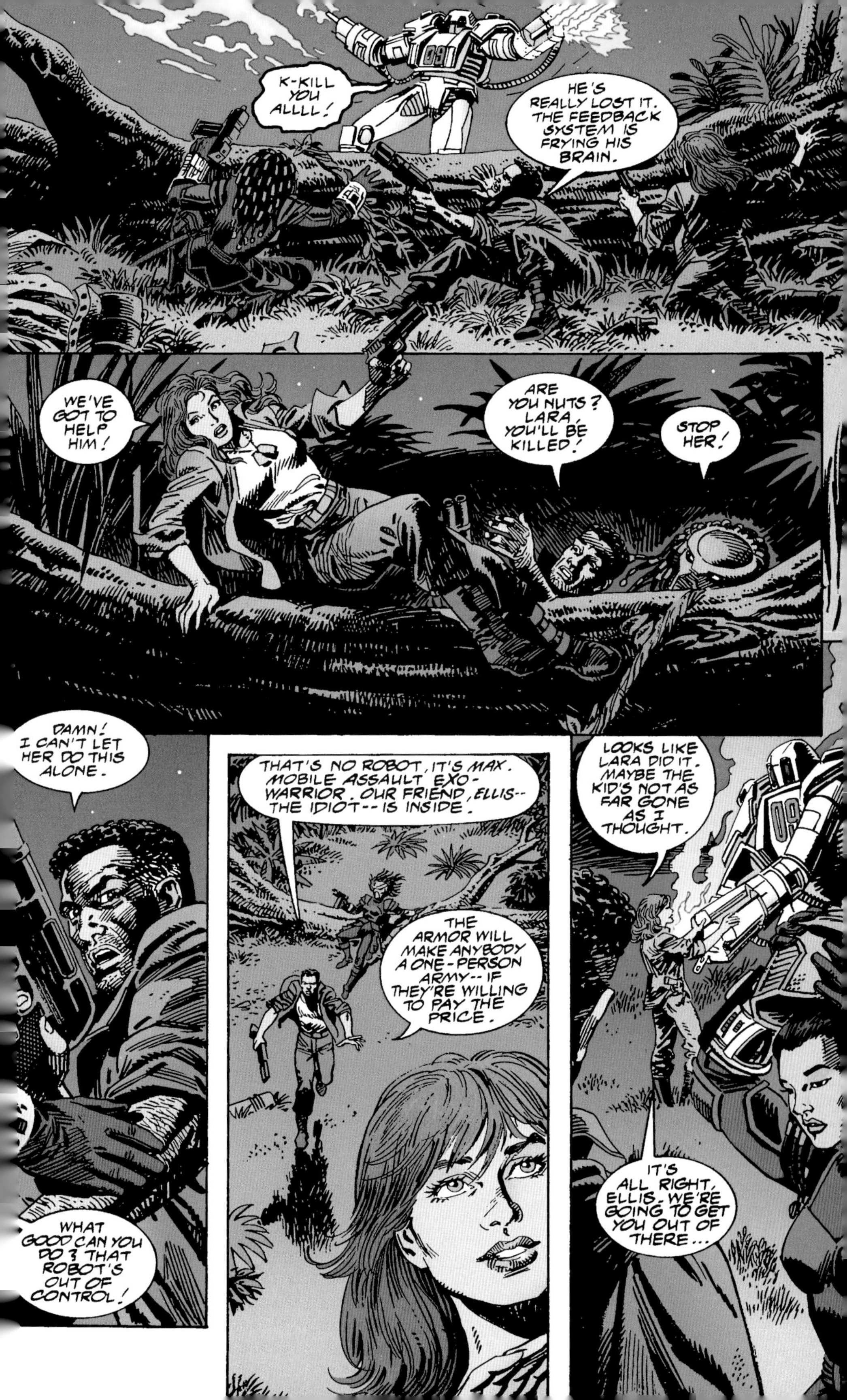
K-KILL YOU ALLLL!
HE'S REALLY LOST IT. THE FEEDBACK SYSTEM IS FRYING HIS BRAIN.
WE'VE GOT TO HELP HIM!
ARE YOU NUTS? LARA, YOU'LL BE KILLED!
STOP HER!
DAMN! I CAN'T LET HER DO THIS ALONE.
WHAT GOOD CAN YOU DO? THAT ROBOT'S OUT OF CONTROL!
THAT'S NO ROBOT, IT'S MAX. MOBILE ASSAULT EXO-WARRIOR. OUR FRIEND, ELLIS-- THE IDIOT--IS INSIDE.
THE ARMOR WILL MAKE ANYBODY A ONE-PERSON ARMY--IF THEY'RE WILLING TO PAY THE PRICE.
LOOKS LIKE LARA DID IT. MAYBE THE KID'S NOT AS FAR GONE AS I THOUGHT.
IT'S ALL RIGHT, ELLIS. WE'RE GOING TO GET YOU OUT OF THERE...

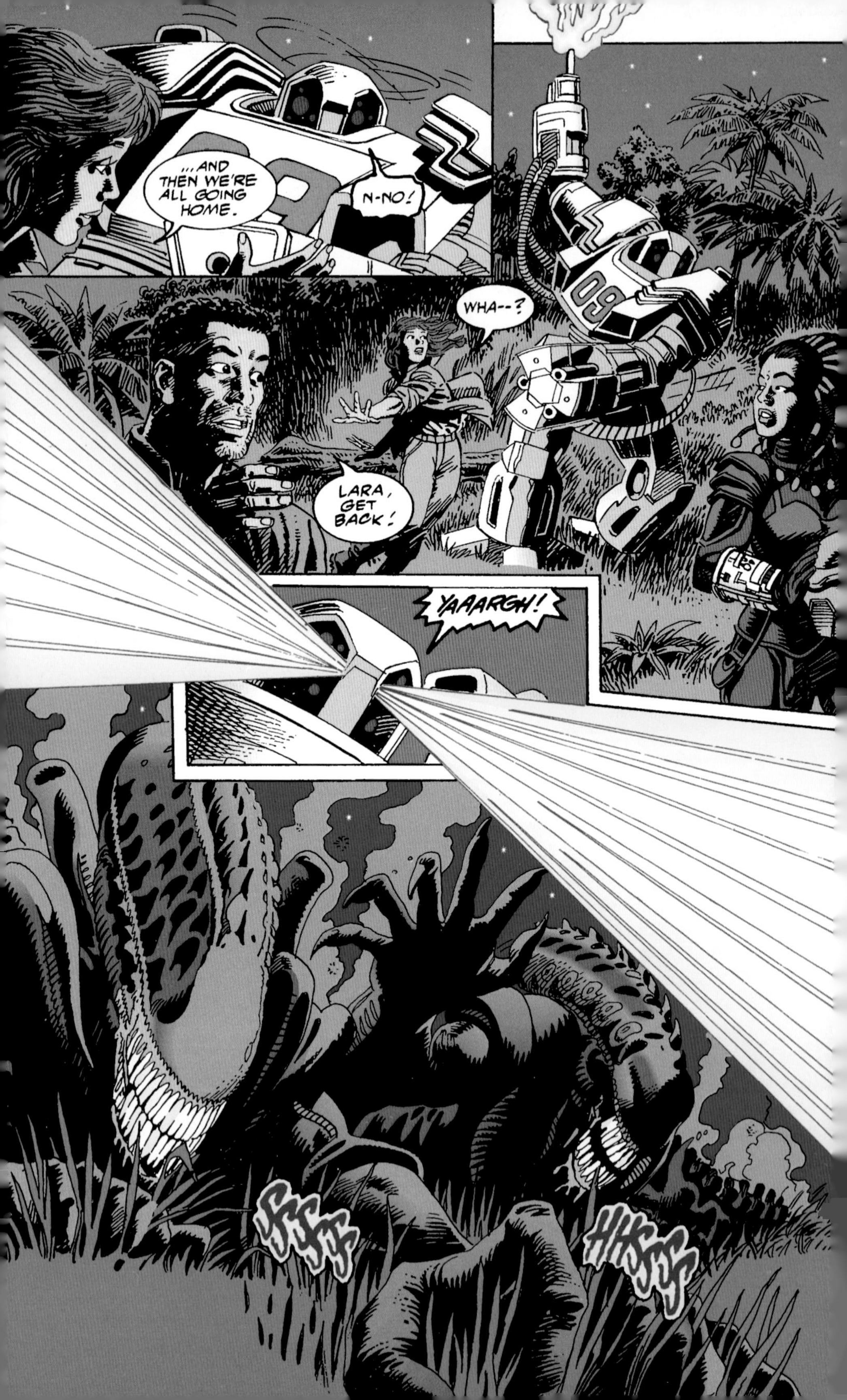
...AND THEN WE'RE ALL GOING HOME.
N-NO!
WHA--?
LARA, GET BACK!
YAAARGH!
SSSSS
HHSSSS

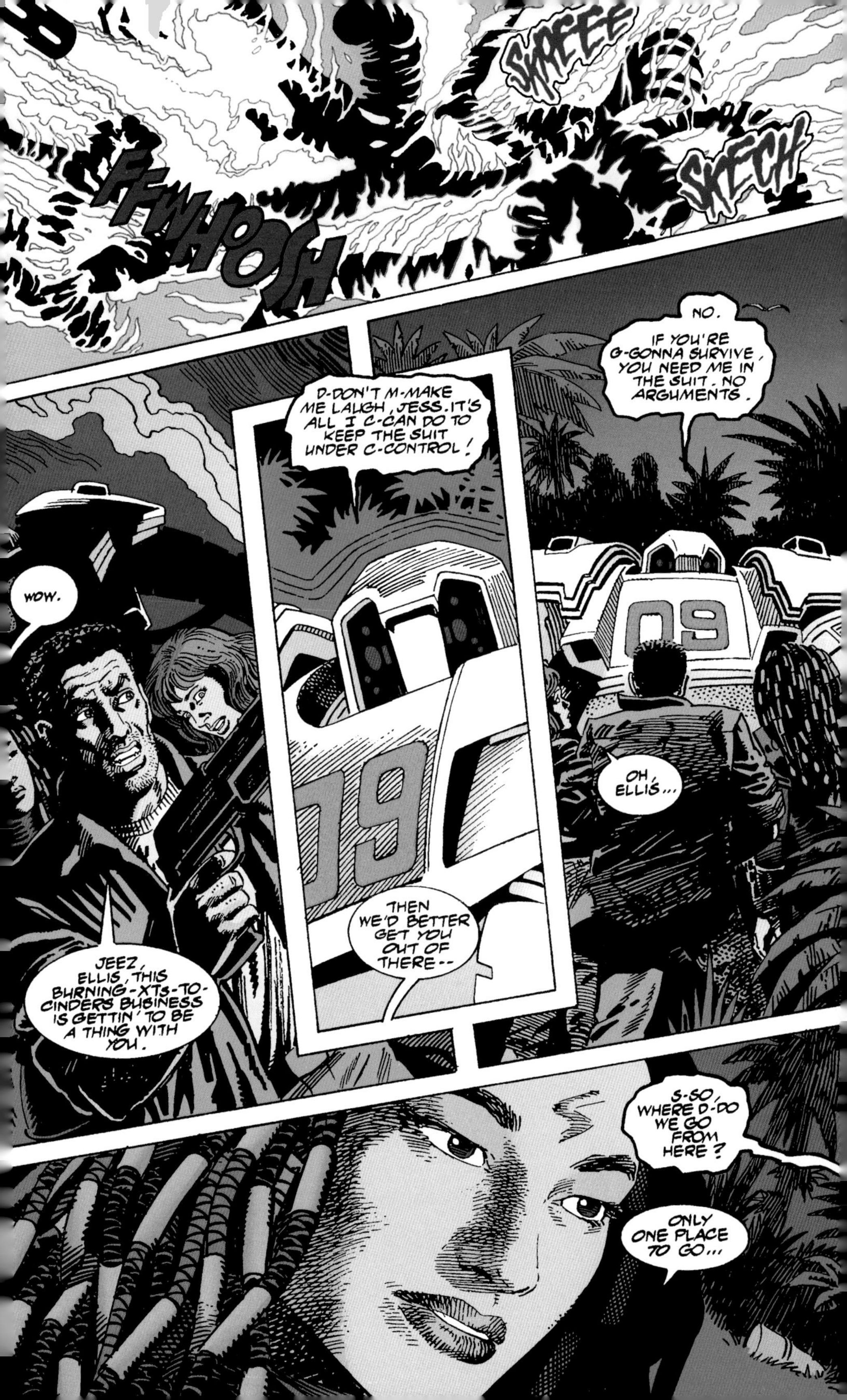
SKREEE
SKECH
PFFWHOOSH
D-DON'T M-MAKE ME LAUGH, JESS. IT'S ALL I C-CAN DO TO KEEP THE SUIT UNDER C-CONTROL!
NO.
IF YOU'RE G-GONNA SURVIVE, YOU NEED ME IN THE SUIT. NO ARGUMENTS.
WOW.
OH, ELLIS...
THEN WE'D BETTER GET YOU OUT OF THERE--
JEEZ, ELLIS, THIS BURNING-XTS-TO-CINDERS BUSINESS IS GETTIN' TO BE A THING WITH YOU.
S-SO, WHERE D-DO WE GO FROM HERE?
ONLY ONE PLACE TO GO...

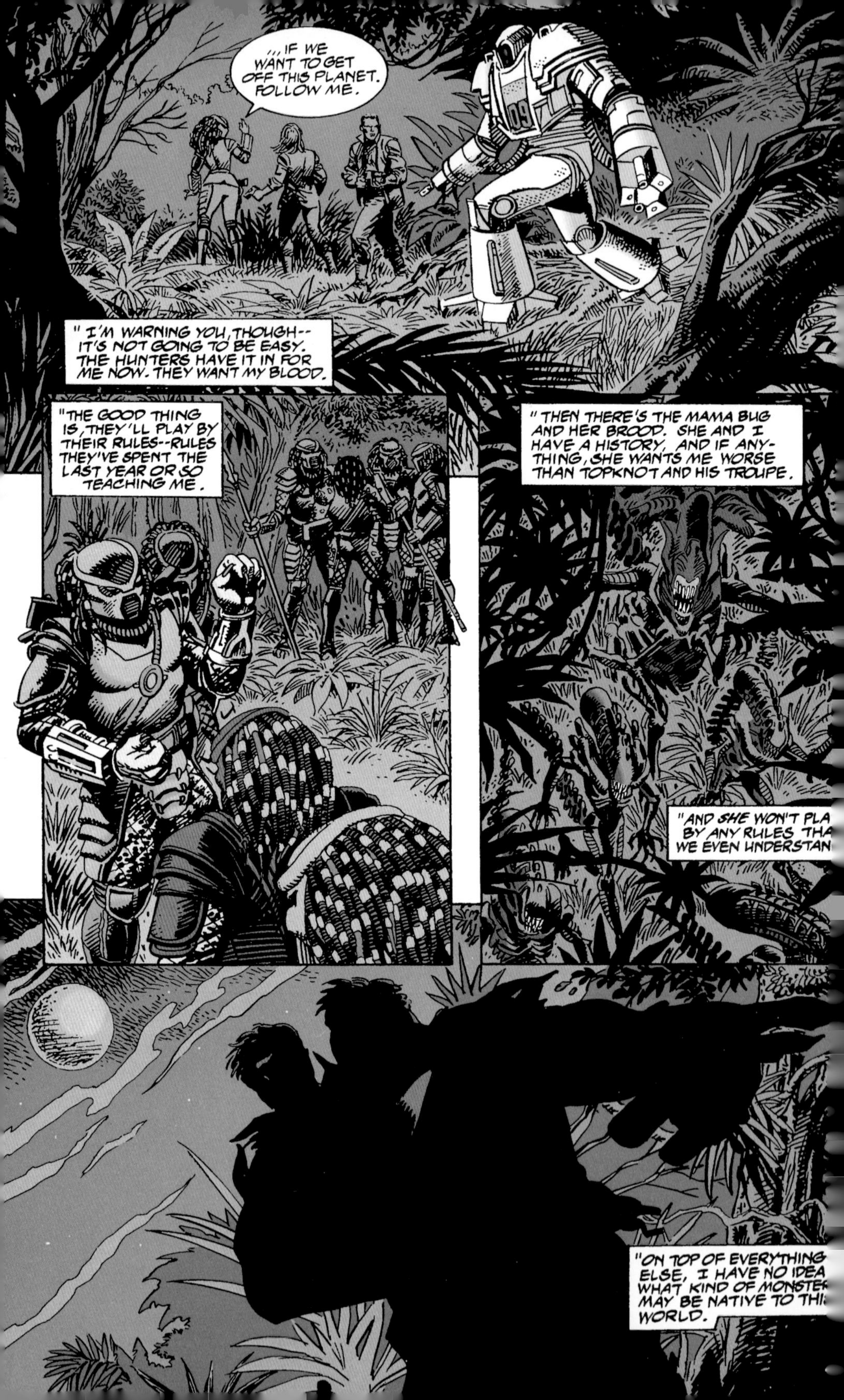

...IF WE WANT TO GET OFF THIS PLANET. FOLLOW ME.
"I'M WARNING YOU, THOUGH-- IT'S NOT GOING TO BE EASY. THE HUNTERS HAVE IT IN FOR ME NOW. THEY WANT MY BLOOD.
"THE GOOD THING IS, THEY'LL PLAY BY THEIR RULES--RULES THEY'VE SPENT THE LAST YEAR OR SO TEACHING ME.
"THEN THERE'S THE MAMA BUG AND HER BROOD. SHE AND I HAVE A HISTORY, AND IF ANYTHING, SHE WANTS ME WORSE THAN TOPKNOT AND HIS TROUPE.
"AND SHE WON'T PLA BY ANY RULES THA WE EVEN UNDERSTAN
"ON TOP OF EVERYTHING ELSE, I HAVE NO IDEA WHAT KIND OF MONSTER MAY BE NATIVE TO THI WORLD.

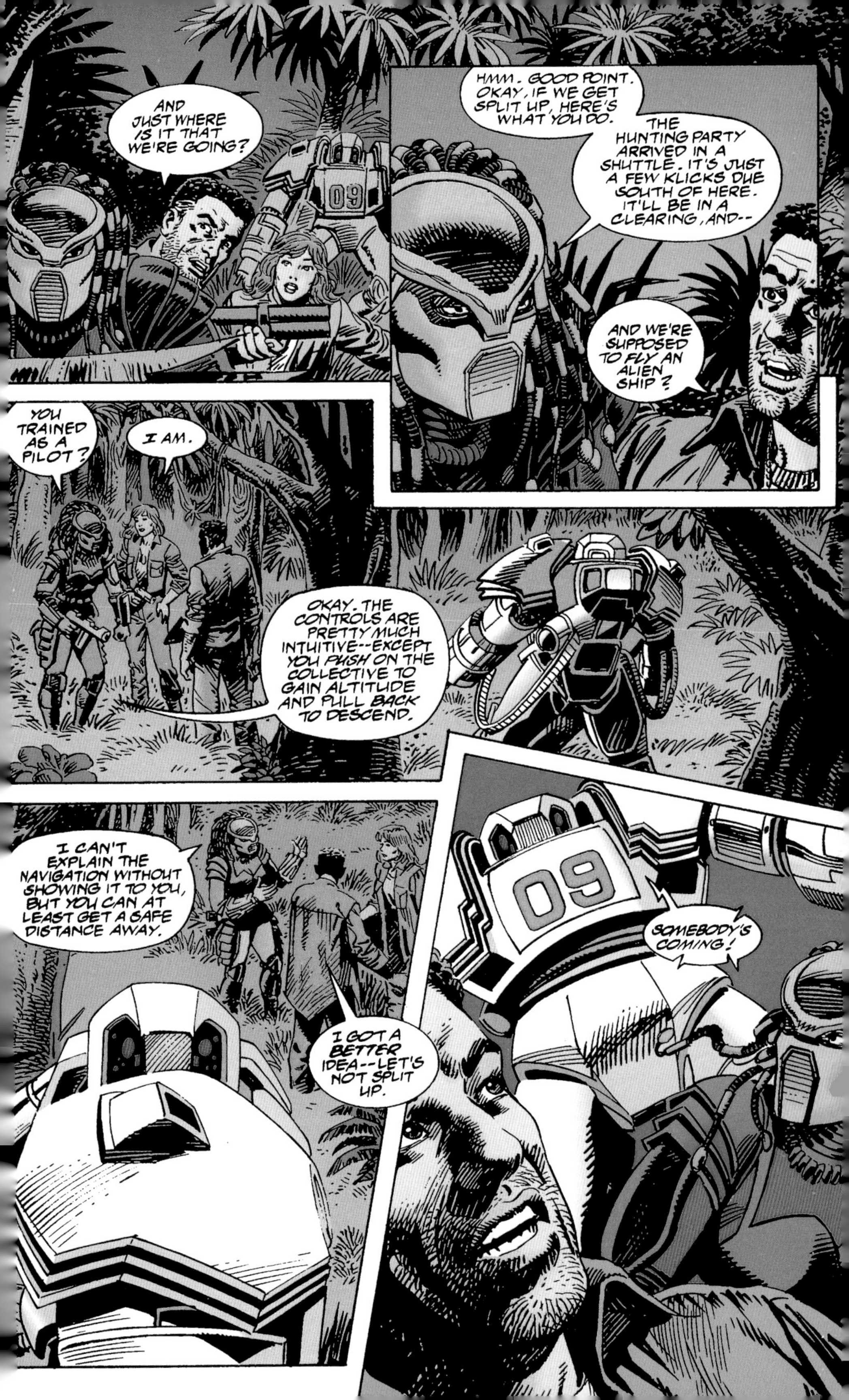
AND JUST WHERE IS IT THAT WE'RE GOING?
HMM. GOOD POINT. OKAY, IF WE GET SPLIT UP, HERE'S WHAT YOU DO.
THE HUNTING PARTY ARRIVED IN A SHUTTLE. IT'S JUST A FEW KLICKS DUE SOUTH OF HERE. IT'LL BE IN A CLEARING, AND--
AND WE'RE SUPPOSED TO FLY AN ALIEN SHIP?
YOU TRAINED AS A PILOT?
I AM.
OKAY. THE CONTROLS ARE PRETTY MUCH INTUITIVE--EXCEPT YOU PUSH ON THE COLLECTIVE TO GAIN ALTITUDE AND PULL BACK TO DESCEND.
I CAN'T EXPLAIN THE NAVIGATION WITHOUT SHOWING IT TO YOU, BUT YOU CAN AT LEAST GET A SAFE DISTANCE AWAY.
I GOT A BETTER IDEA--LET'S NOT SPLIT UP.
SOMEBODY'S COMING!

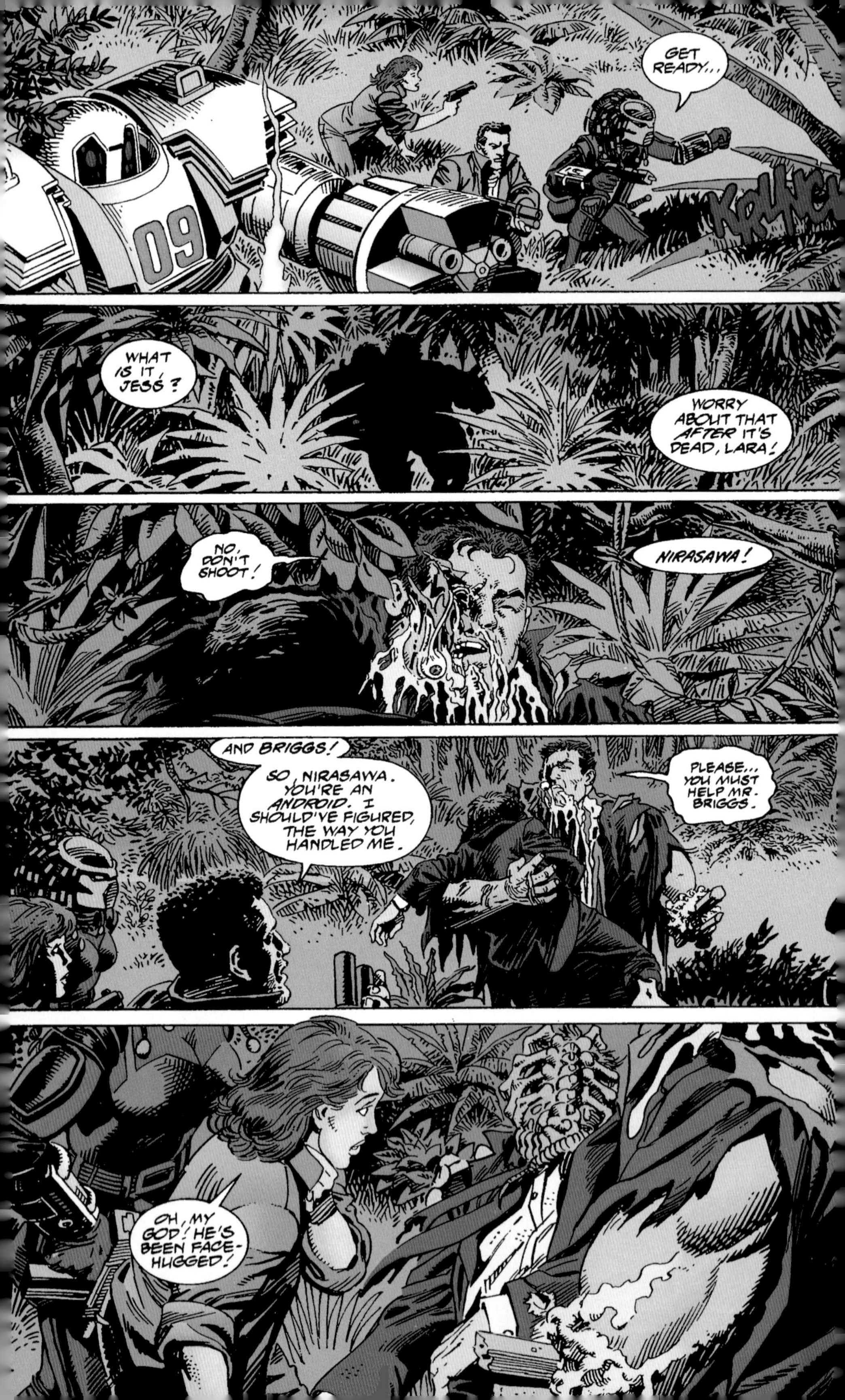
GET READY...
KRUNCH
WHAT IS IT, JESS?
WORRY ABOUT THAT AFTER IT'S DEAD, LARA!
NO, DON'T SHOOT!
NIRASAWA!
AND BRIGGS!
SO, NIRASAWA. YOU'RE AN ANDROID. I SHOULD'VE FIGURED, THE WAY YOU HANDLED ME.
PLEASE... YOU MUST HELP MR. BRIGGS.
OH, MY GOD! HE'S BEEN FACE-HUGGED!

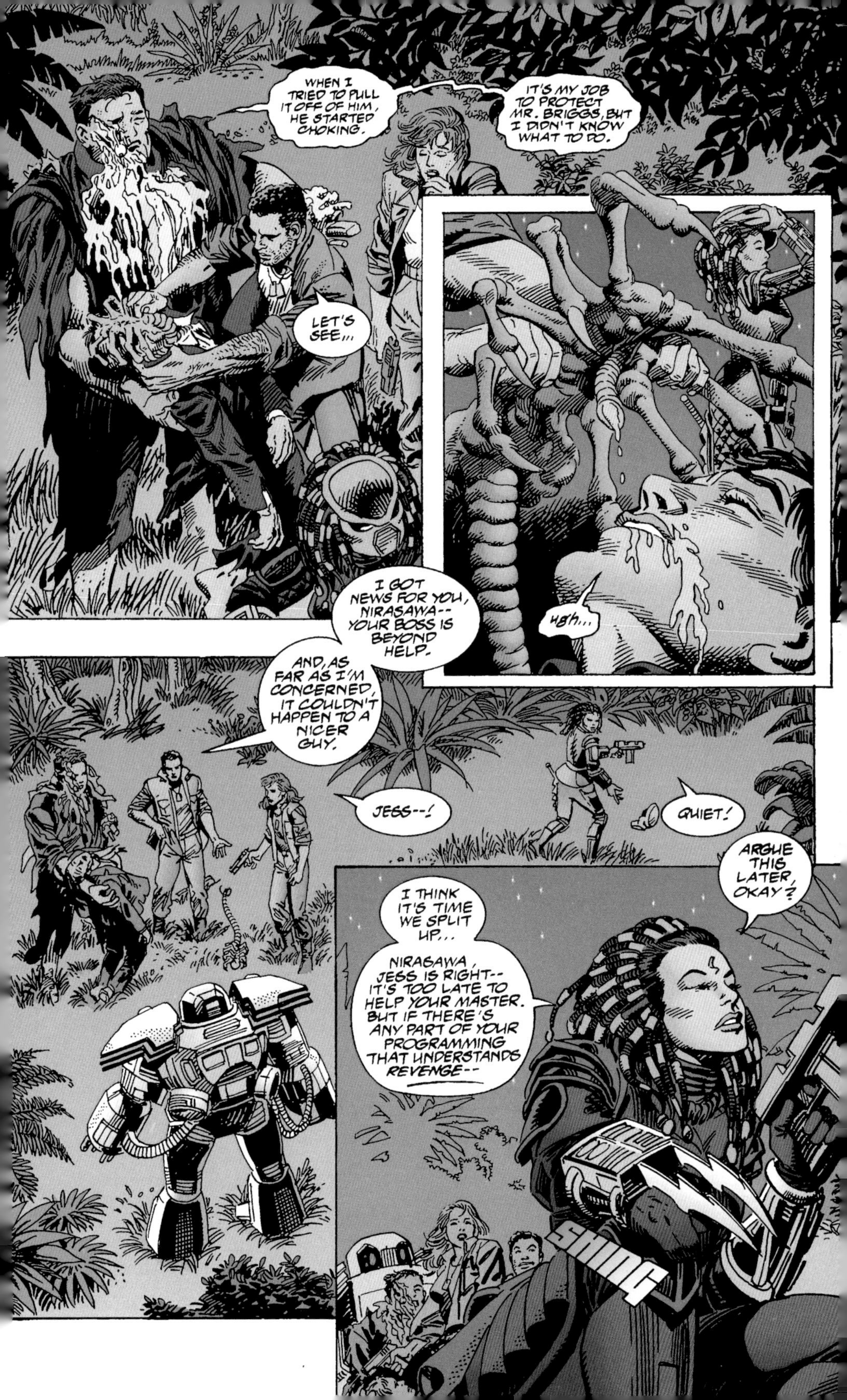
WHEN I TRIED TO PULL IT OFF OF HIM, HE STARTED CHOKING.
IT'S MY JOB TO PROTECT MR. BRIGGS, BUT I DIDN'T KNOW WHAT TO DO.
LET'S SEE...
I GOT NEWS FOR YOU, NIRASAWA-- YOUR BOSS IS BEYOND HELP.
UGH...
AND, AS FAR AS I'M CONCERNED, IT COULDN'T HAPPEN TO A NICER GUY.
JESS--!
QUIET!
ARGUE THIS LATER, OKAY?
I THINK IT'S TIME WE SPLIT UP...
NIRASAWA, JESS IS RIGHT-- IT'S TOO LATE TO HELP YOUR MASTER. BUT IF THERE'S ANY PART OF YOUR PROGRAMMING THAT UNDERSTANDS REVENGE--
SHING

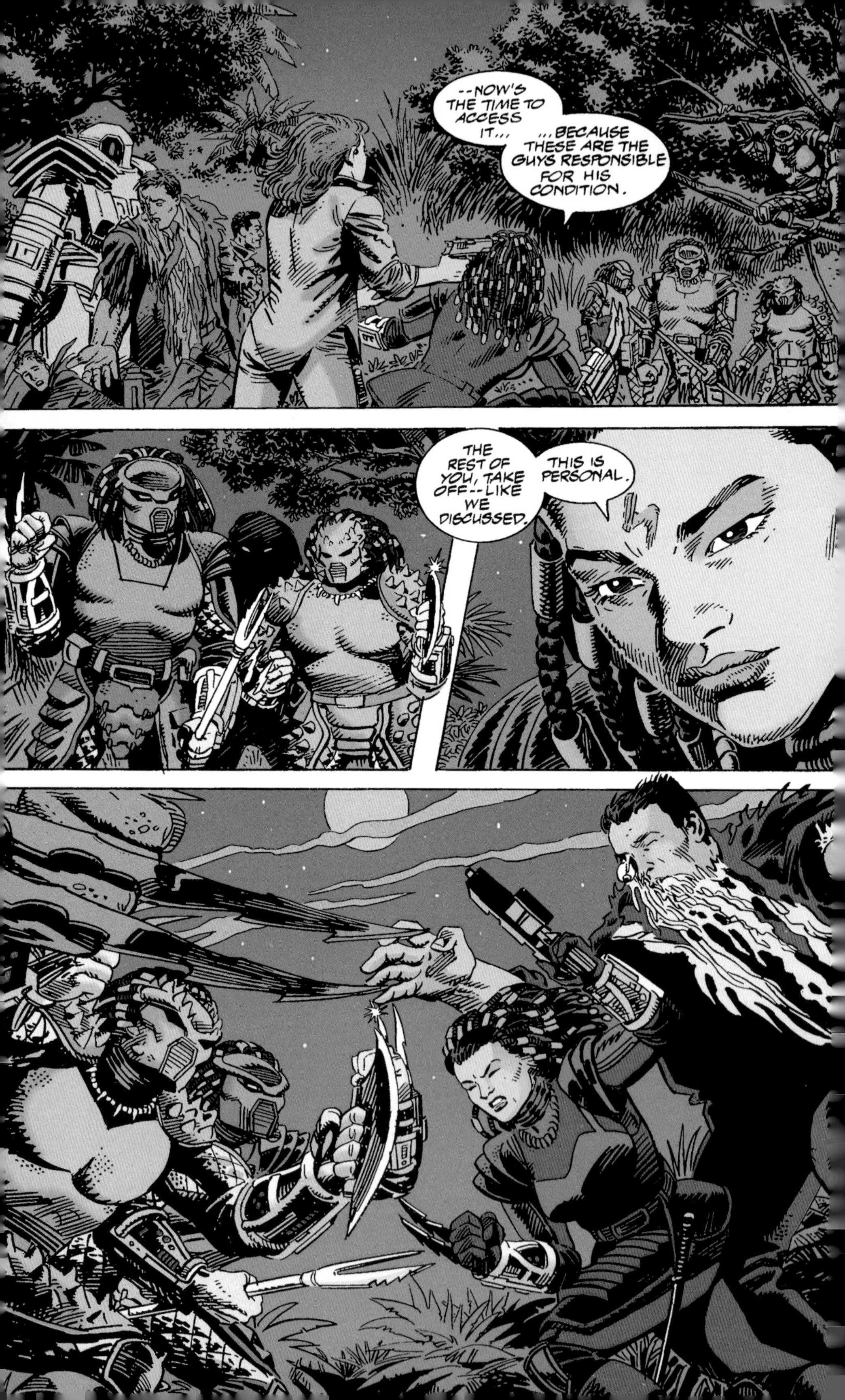
--NOW'S THE TIME TO ACCESS IT...
...BECAUSE THESE ARE THE GUYS RESPONSIBLE FOR HIS CONDITION.
THE REST OF YOU, TAKE OFF--LIKE WE DISCUSSED.
THIS IS PERSONAL.

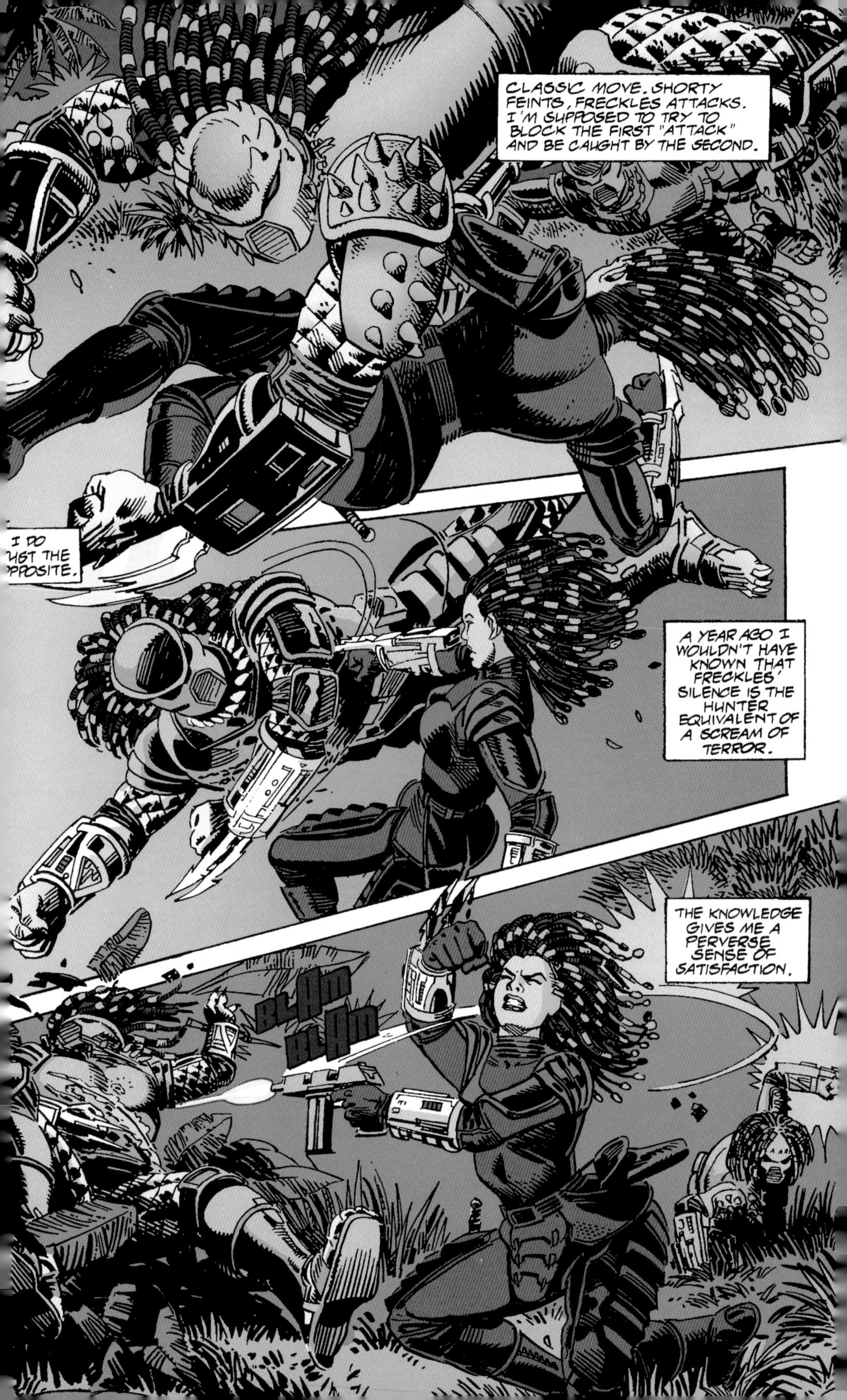
CLASSIC MOVE. SHORTY FEINTS, FRECKLES ATTACKS. I'M SUPPOSED TO TRY TO BLOCK THE FIRST "ATTACK" AND BE CAUGHT BY THE SECOND.
I DO JUST THE OPPOSITE.
A YEAR AGO I WOULDN'T HAVE KNOWN THAT FRECKLES' SILENCE IS THE HUNTER EQUIVALENT OF A SCREAM OF TERROR.
THE KNOWLEDGE GIVES ME A PERVERSE SENSE OF SATISFACTION.
BLAM
BLAM

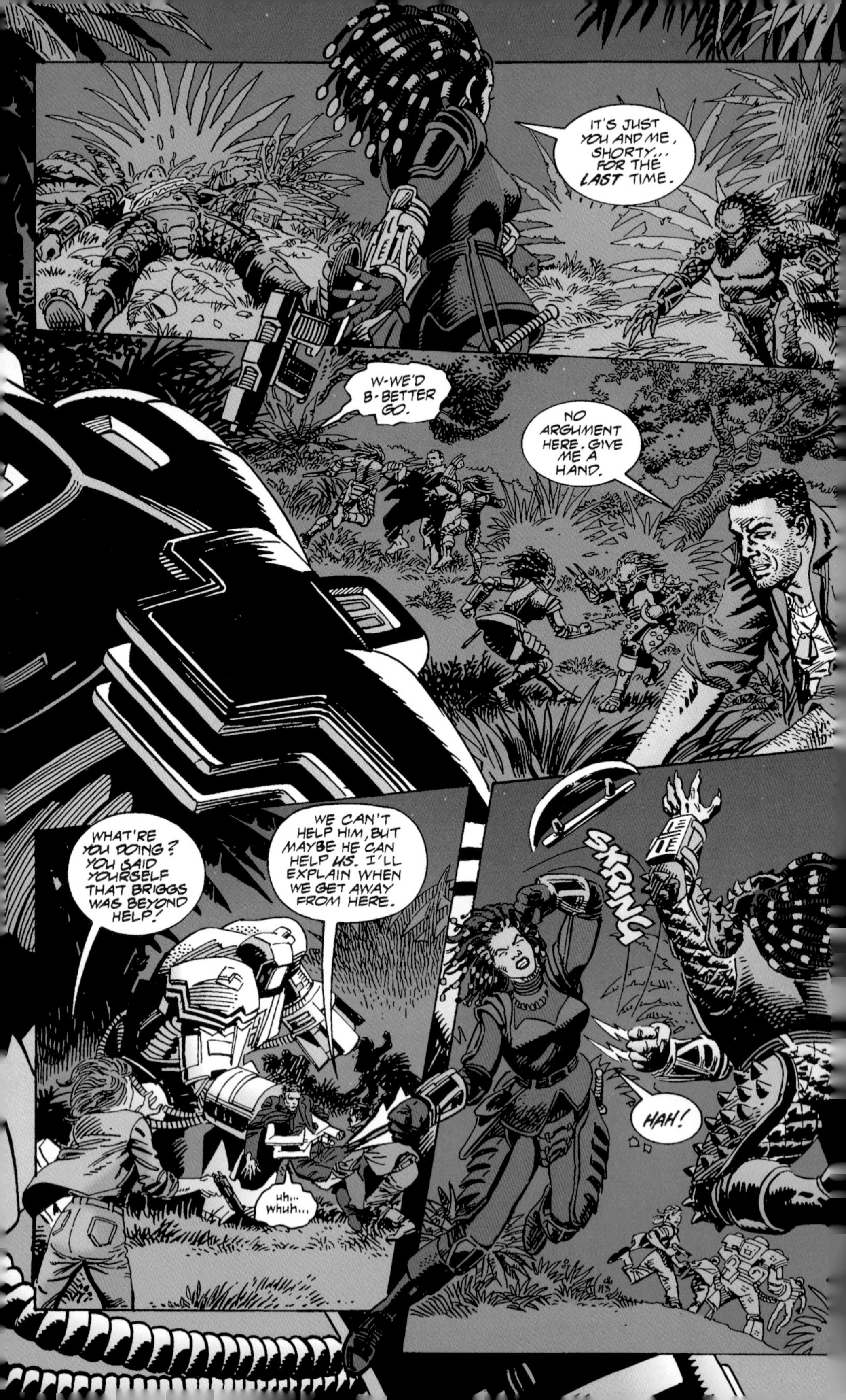
IT'S JUST YOU AND ME, SHORTY... FOR THE LAST TIME.
W-WE'D B-BETTER GO.
NO ARGUMENT HERE. GIVE ME A HAND.
WHAT'RE YOU DOING? YOU SAID YOURSELF THAT BRIGGS WAS BEYOND HELP!
WE CAN'T HELP HIM, BUT MAYBE HE CAN HELP US. I'LL EXPLAIN WHEN WE GET AWAY FROM HERE.
uh... whuh...
SKRING
HAH!

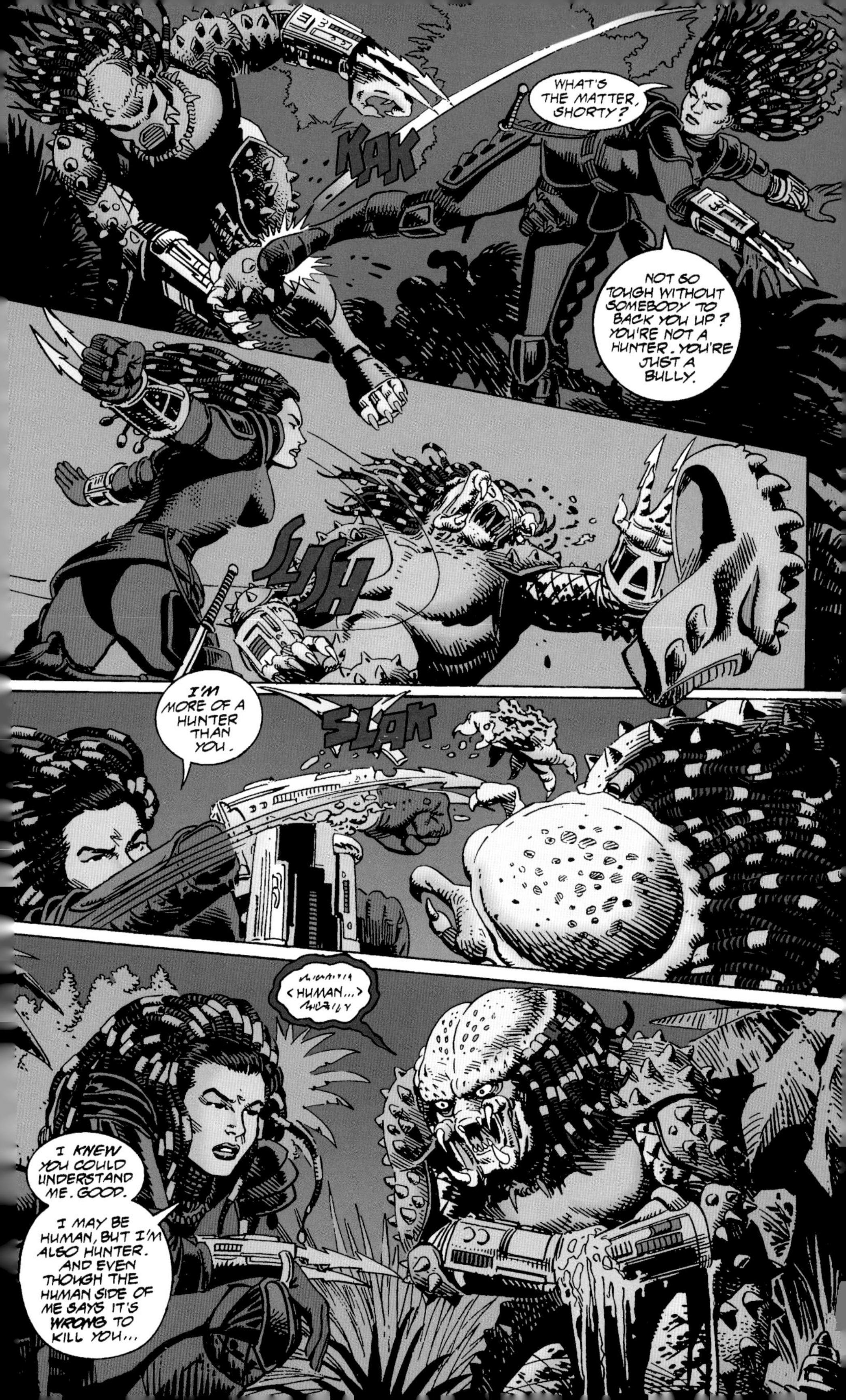

WHAT'S THE MATTER, SHORTY?
KAK
NOT SO TOUGH WITHOUT SOMEBODY TO BACK YOU UP? YOU'RE NOT A HUNTER. YOU'RE JUST A BULLY.
LISH
I'M MORE OF A HUNTER THAN YOU.
SLAK
<HUMAN...>
I KNEW YOU COULD UNDERSTAND ME. GOOD.
I MAY BE HUMAN, BUT I'M ALSO HUNTER. AND EVEN THOUGH THE HUMAN SIDE OF ME SAYS IT'S WRONG TO KILL YOU...

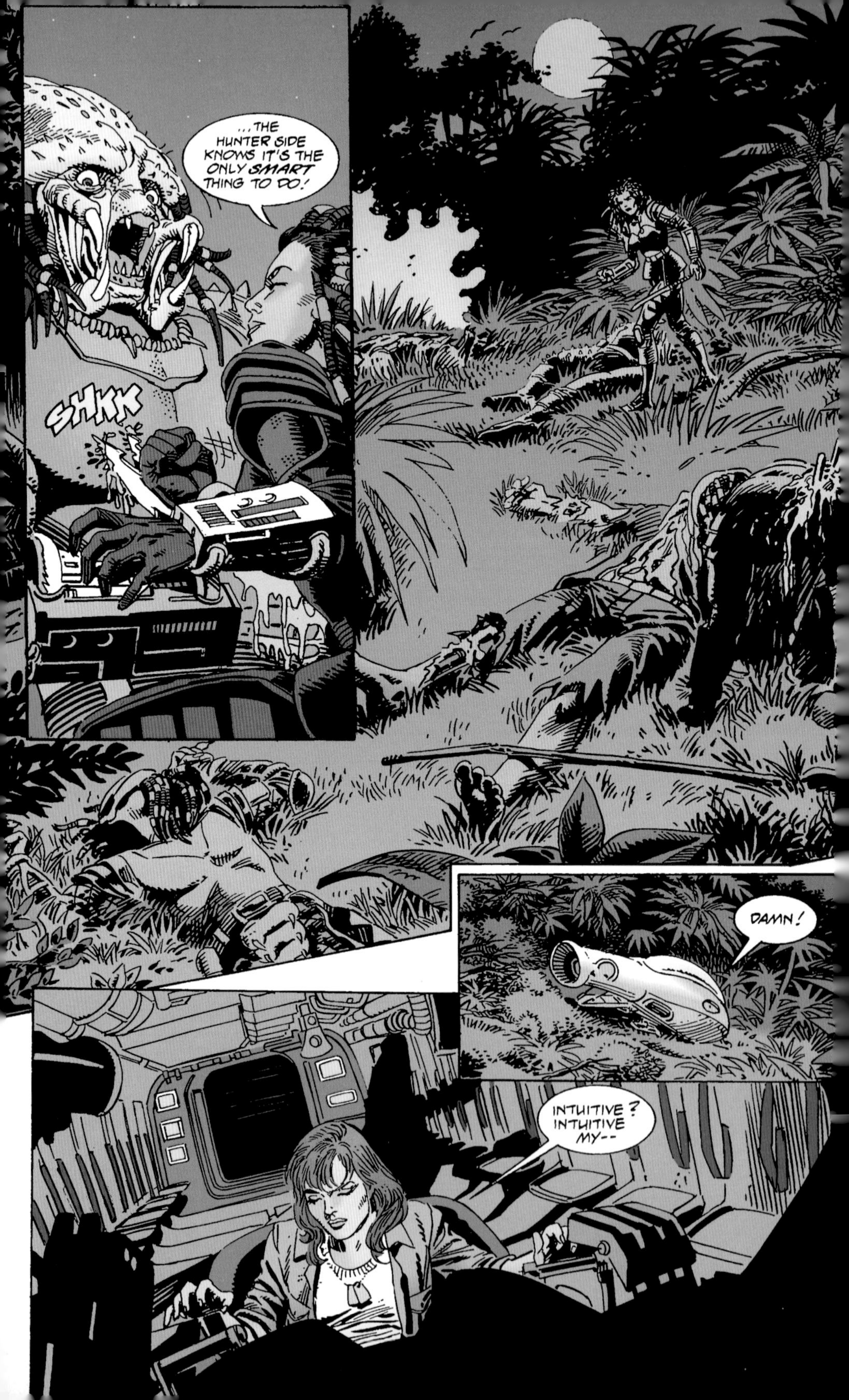
...THE HUNTER SIDE KNOWS IT'S THE ONLY SMART THING TO DO!
SHKK
DAMN!
INTUITIVE? INTUITIVE MY--

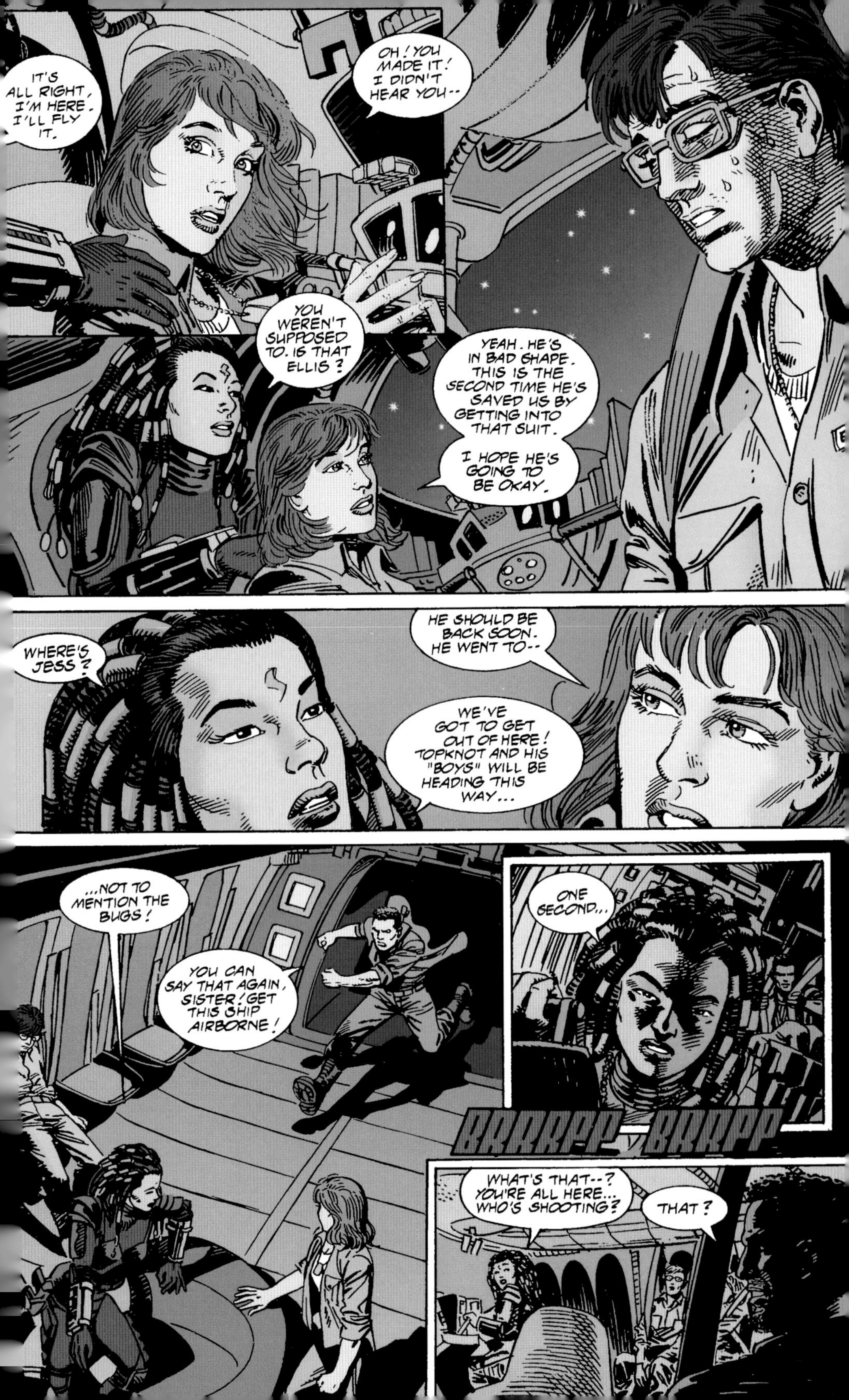
IT'S ALL RIGHT, I'M HERE. I'LL FLY IT.
OH! YOU MADE IT! I DIDN'T HEAR YOU--
YOU WEREN'T SUPPOSED TO. IS THAT ELLIS?
YEAH. HE'S IN BAD SHAPE. THIS IS THE SECOND TIME HE'S SAVED US BY GETTING INTO THAT SUIT.
I HOPE HE'S GOING TO BE OKAY.
WHERE'S JESS?
HE SHOULD BE BACK SOON. HE WENT TO--
WE'VE GOT TO GET OUT OF HERE! TOPKNOT AND HIS "BOYS" WILL BE HEADING THIS WAY...
...NOT TO MENTION THE BUGS!
YOU CAN SAY THAT AGAIN, SISTER! GET THIS SHIP AIRBORNE!
ONE SECOND...
BRRRPP BRRAPP
WHAT'S THAT--? YOU'RE ALL HERE... WHO'S SHOOTING?
THAT?

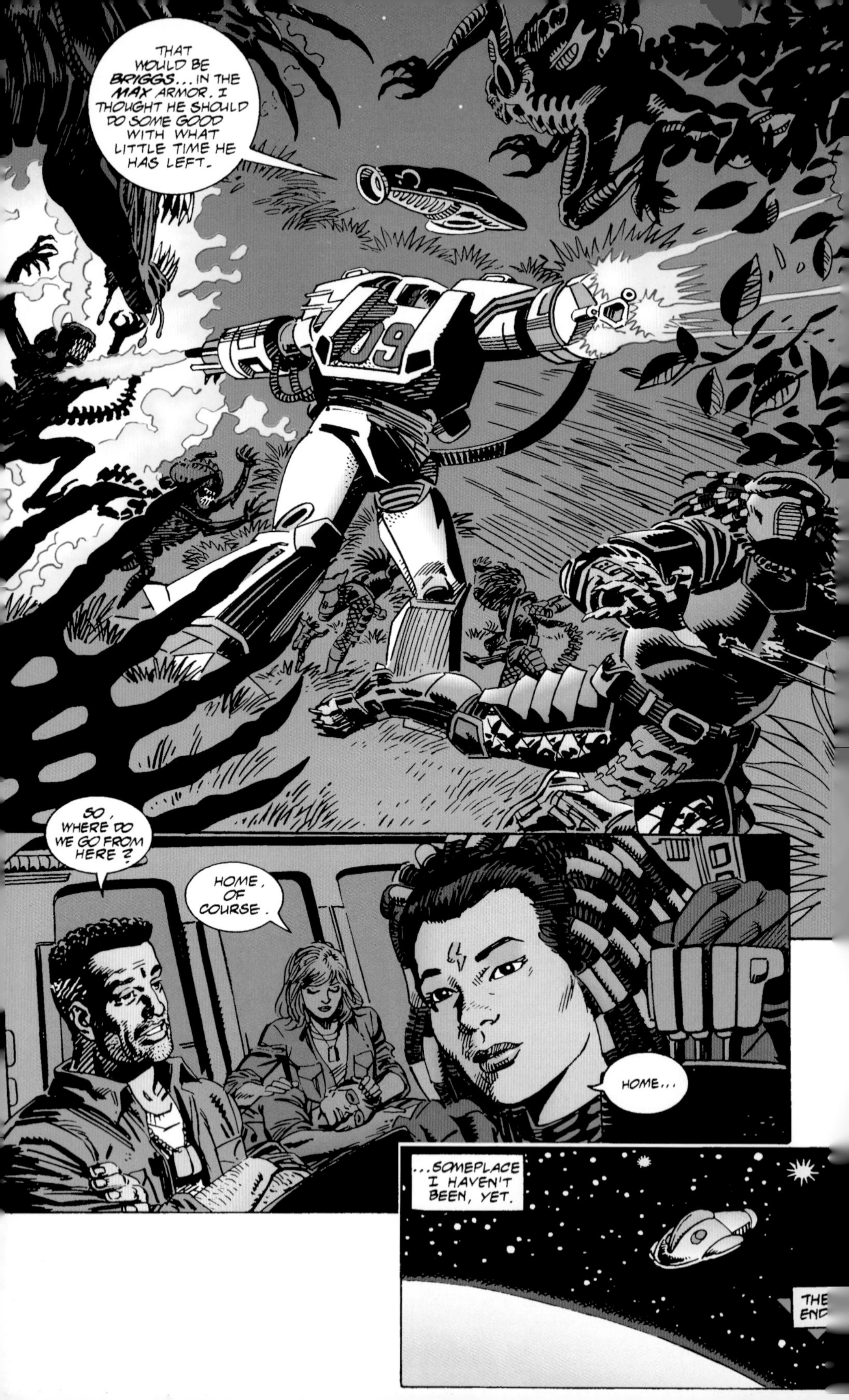
THAT WOULD BE BRIGGS... IN THE MAX ARMOR. I THOUGHT HE SHOULD DO SOME GOOD WITH WHAT LITTLE TIME HE HAS LEFT.
SO, WHERE DO WE GO FROM HERE?
HOME, OF COURSE.
HOME...
...SOMEPLACE I HAVEN'T BEEN, YET.
THE END

ETERNAL

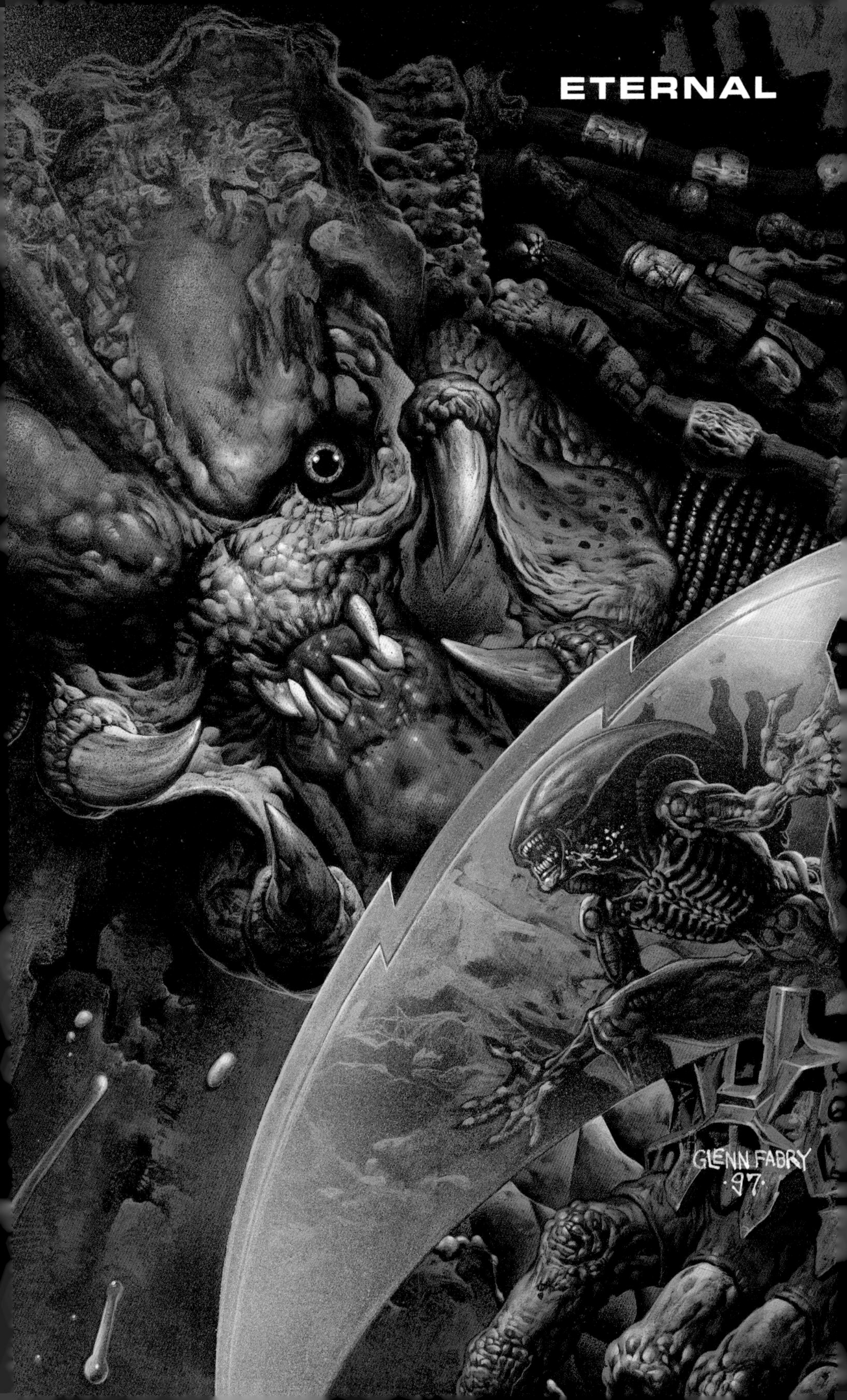
GLENN FABRY
·97·

script
IAN EDGINTON

art
ALEX MALEEV

colors
PERRY McNAMEE / DARK HORSE DIGITAL

lettering
CLEM ROBINS

title illustration
GLENN FABRY

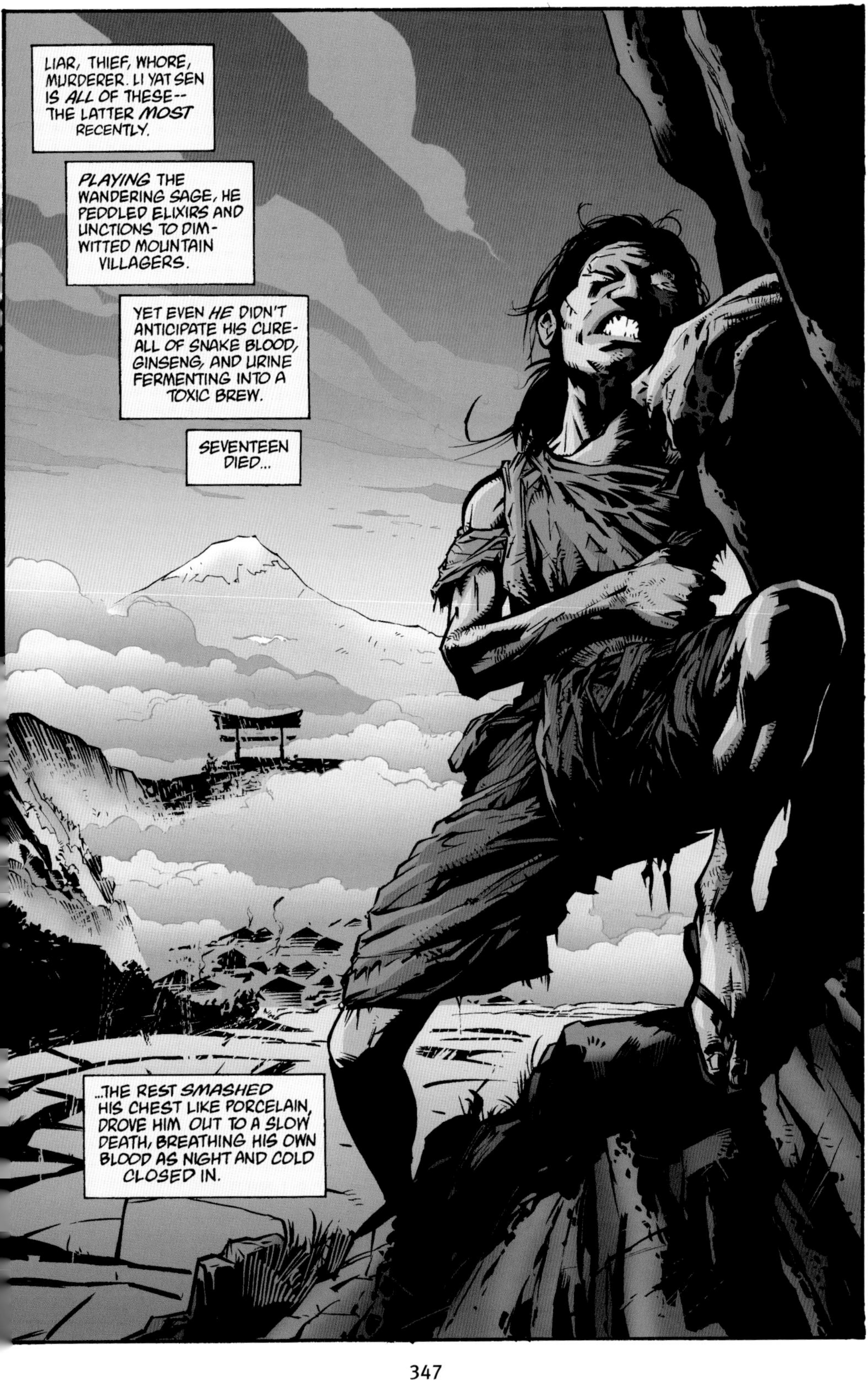
LIAR, THIEF, WHORE, MURDERER. LI YAT SEN IS *ALL* OF THESE-- THE LATTER *MOST* RECENTLY.
PLAYING THE WANDERING SAGE, HE PEDDLED ELIXIRS AND UNCTIONS TO DIM-WITTED MOUNTAIN VILLAGERS.
YET EVEN *HE* DIDN'T ANTICIPATE HIS CURE-ALL OF SNAKE BLOOD, GINSENG, AND URINE FERMENTING INTO A TOXIC BREW.
SEVENTEEN DIED...
...THE REST *SMASHED* HIS CHEST LIKE PORCELAIN, DROVE HIM OUT TO A SLOW DEATH, BREATHING HIS OWN BLOOD AS NIGHT AND COLD CLOSED IN.

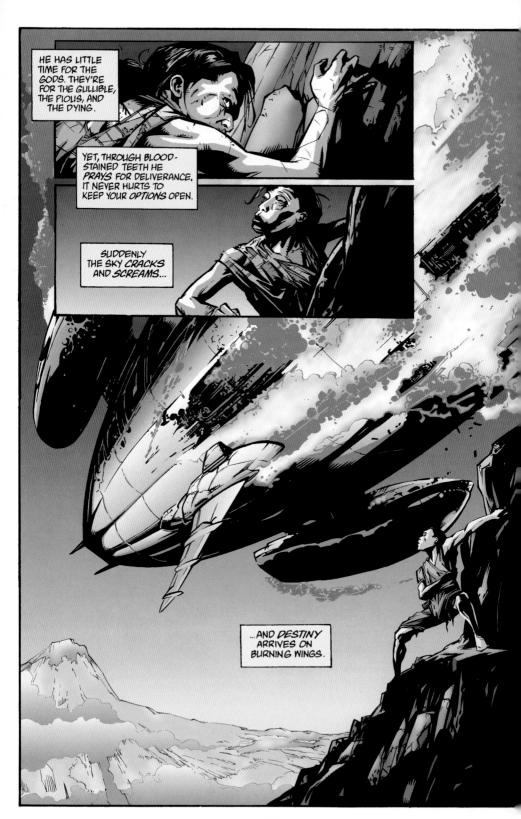

HE HAS LITTLE TIME FOR THE GODS. THEY'RE FOR THE GULLIBLE, THE PIOUS, AND THE DYING.

YET, THROUGH BLOOD-STAINED TEETH HE *PRAYS* FOR DELIVERANCE. IT NEVER HURTS TO KEEP YOUR *OPTIONS* OPEN.

SUDDENLY THE SKY *CRACKS* AND *SCREAMS*...

...AND *DESTINY* ARRIVES ON BURNING WINGS.

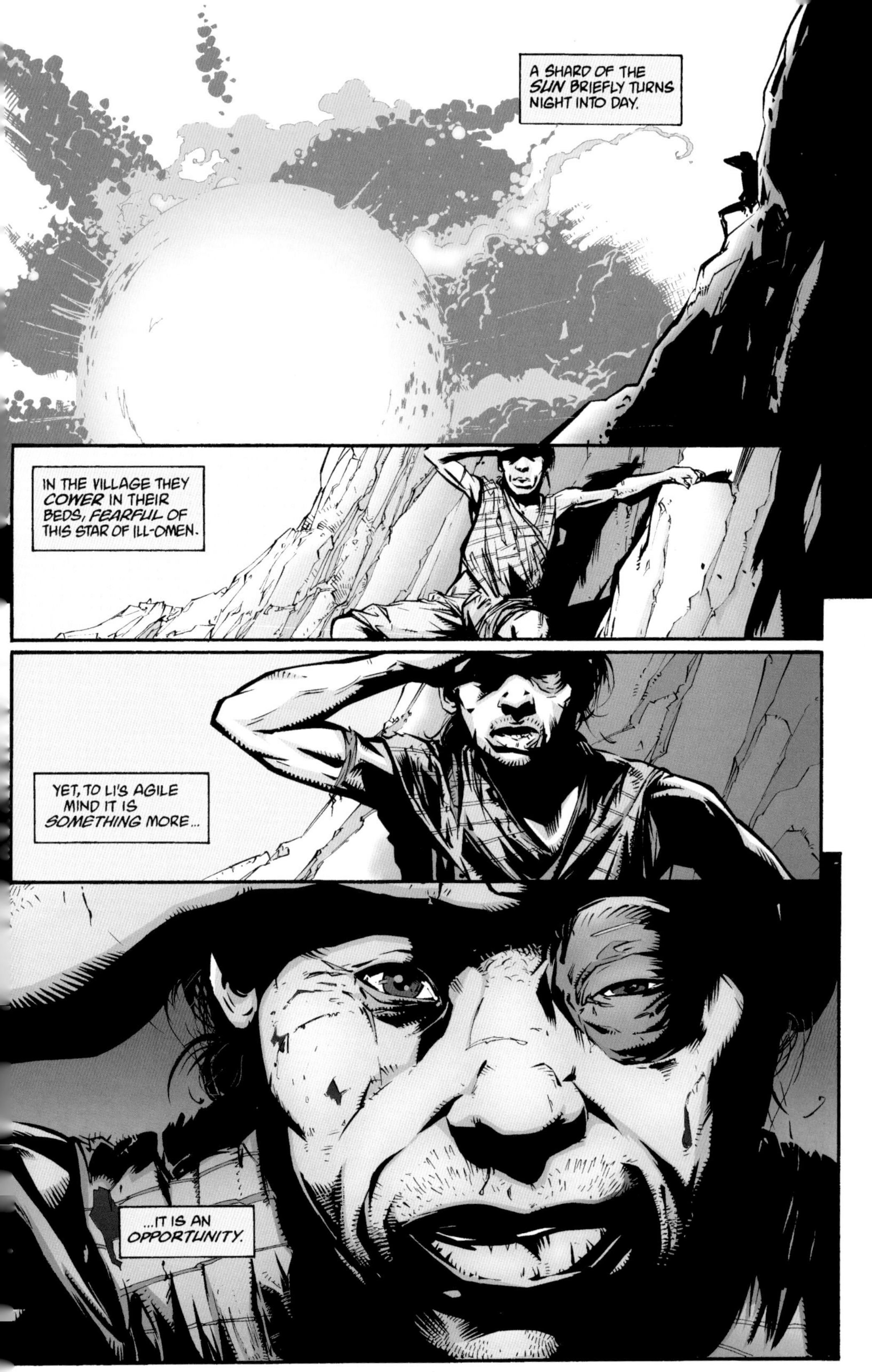
A SHARD OF THE SUN BRIEFLY TURNS NIGHT INTO DAY.
IN THE VILLAGE THEY COWER IN THEIR BEDS, FEARFUL OF THIS STAR OF ILL-OMEN.
YET, TO LI'S AGILE MIND IT IS SOMETHING MORE...
...IT IS AN OPPORTUNITY.

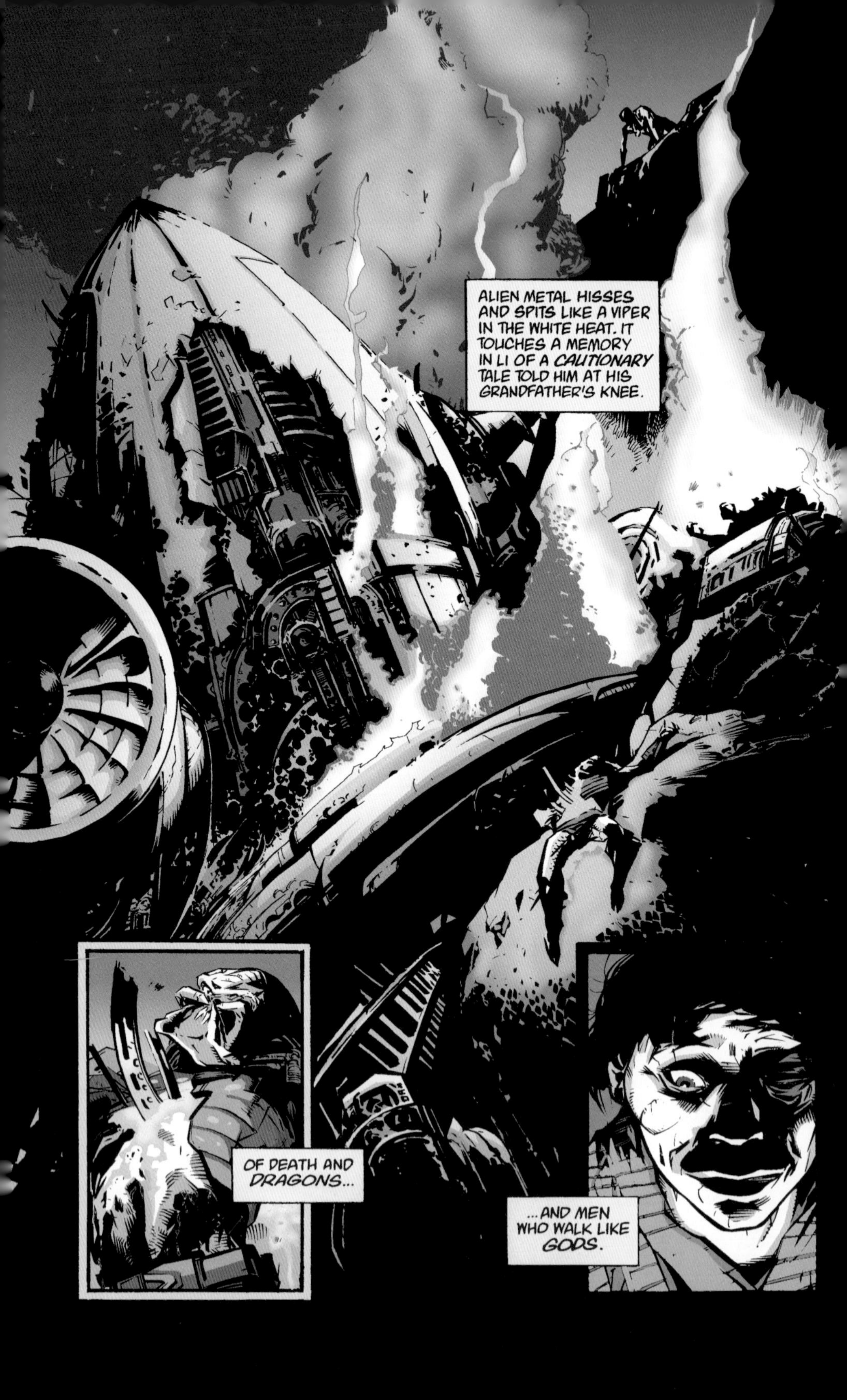
ALIEN METAL HISSES AND SPITS LIKE A VIPER IN THE WHITE HEAT. IT TOUCHES A MEMORY IN LI OF A CAUTIONARY TALE TOLD HIM AT HIS GRANDFATHER'S KNEE.
OF DEATH AND DRAGONS...
...AND MEN WHO WALK LIKE GODS.

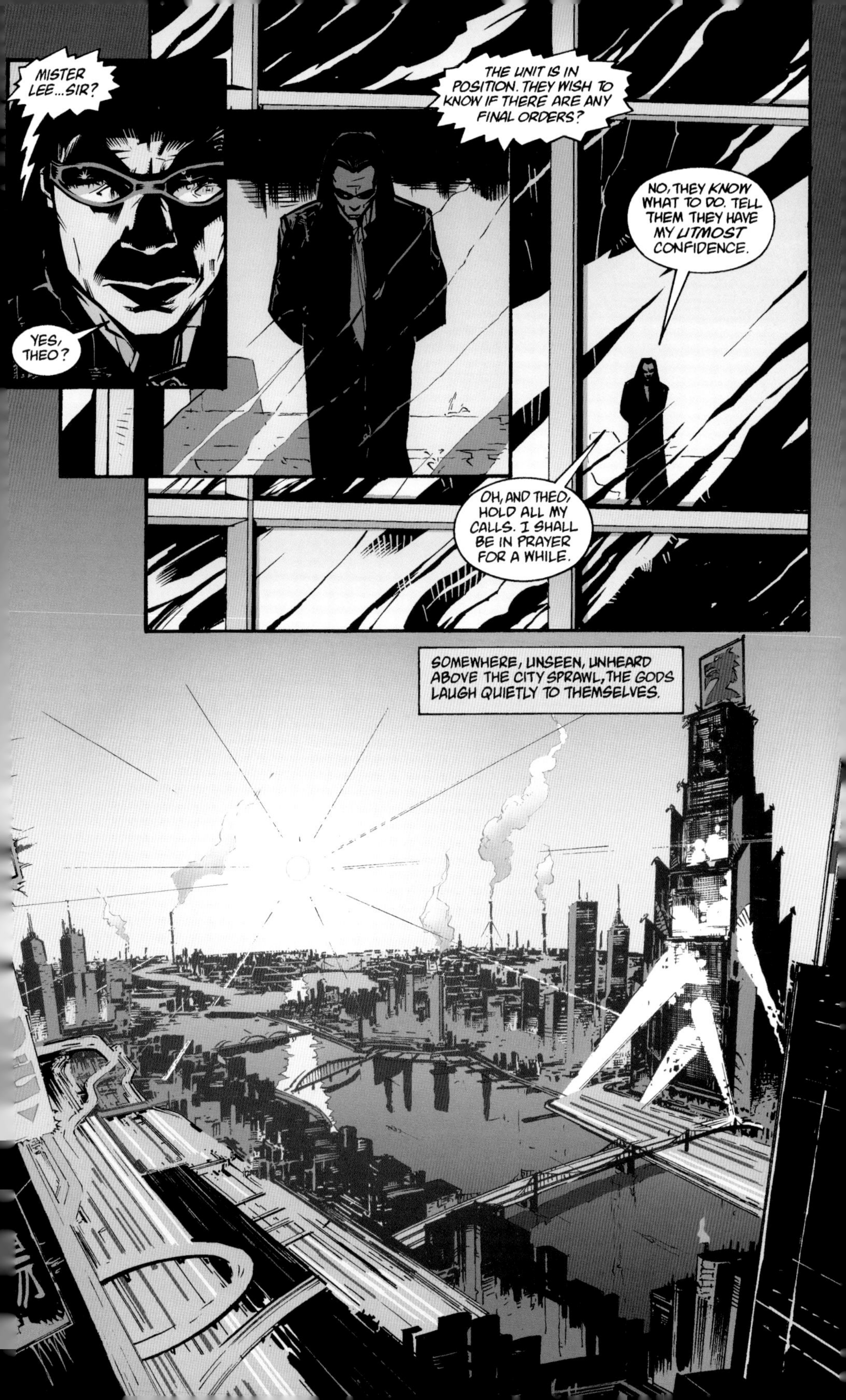
MISTER LEE...SIR?
YES, THEO?
THE UNIT IS IN POSITION. THEY WISH TO KNOW IF THERE ARE ANY FINAL ORDERS?
NO, THEY KNOW WHAT TO DO. TELL THEM THEY HAVE MY UTMOST CONFIDENCE.
OH, AND THEO, HOLD ALL MY CALLS. I SHALL BE IN PRAYER FOR A WHILE.
SOMEWHERE, UNSEEN, UNHEARD ABOVE THE CITY SPRAWL, THE GODS LAUGH QUIETLY TO THEMSELVES.

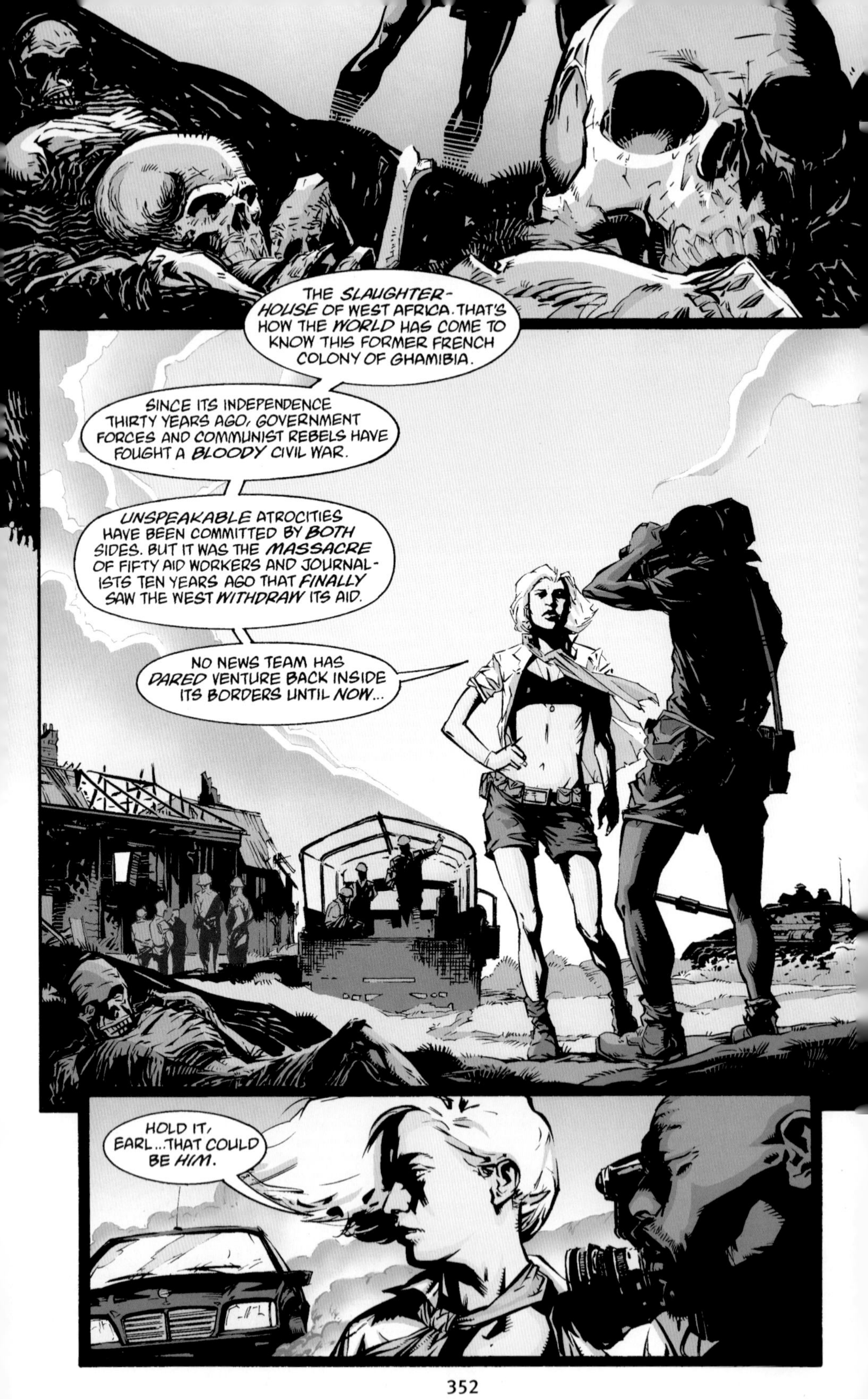
THE SLAUGHTER-HOUSE OF WEST AFRICA. THAT'S HOW THE WORLD HAS COME TO KNOW THIS FORMER FRENCH COLONY OF GHAMIBIA.
SINCE ITS INDEPENDENCE THIRTY YEARS AGO, GOVERNMENT FORCES AND COMMUNIST REBELS HAVE FOUGHT A BLOODY CIVIL WAR.
UNSPEAKABLE ATROCITIES HAVE BEEN COMMITTED BY BOTH SIDES. BUT IT WAS THE MASSACRE OF FIFTY AID WORKERS AND JOURNAL-ISTS TEN YEARS AGO THAT FINALLY SAW THE WEST WITHDRAW ITS AID.
NO NEWS TEAM HAS DARED VENTURE BACK INSIDE ITS BORDERS UNTIL NOW...
HOLD IT, EARL...THAT COULD BE HIM.

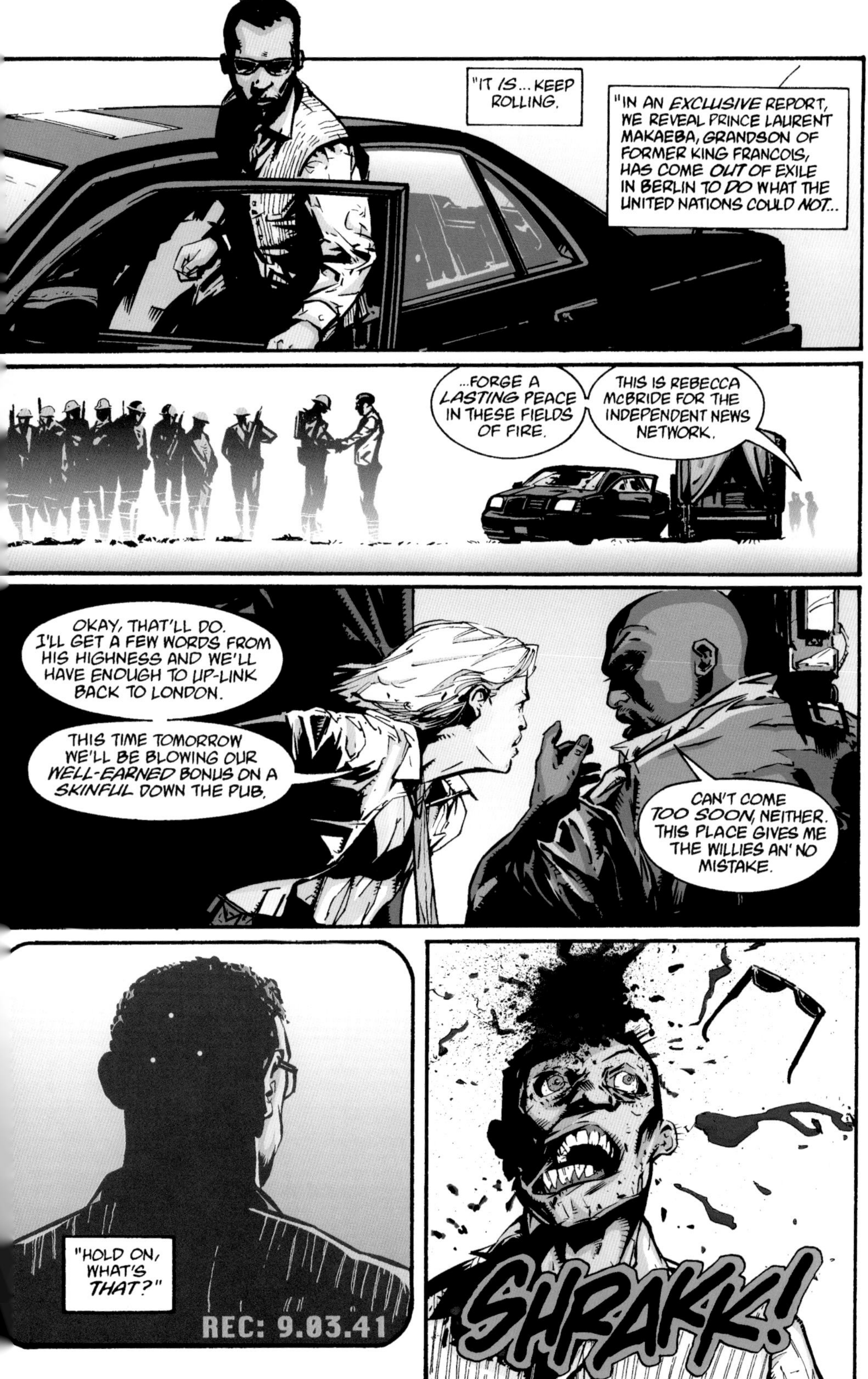

"IT *IS*... KEEP ROLLING.
"IN AN *EXCLUSIVE* REPORT, WE REVEAL PRINCE LAURENT MAKAEBA, GRANDSON OF FORMER KING FRANCOIS, HAS COME *OUT* OF EXILE IN BERLIN TO *DO* WHAT THE UNITED NATIONS COULD *NOT*...
...FORGE A *LASTING* PEACE IN THESE FIELDS OF FIRE.
THIS IS REBECCA McBRIDE FOR THE INDEPENDENT NEWS NETWORK.
OKAY, THAT'LL DO. I'LL GET A FEW WORDS FROM HIS HIGHNESS AND WE'LL HAVE ENOUGH TO UP-LINK BACK TO LONDON.
THIS TIME TOMORROW WE'LL BE BLOWING OUR *WELL-EARNED* BONUS ON A *SKINFUL* DOWN THE PUB.
CAN'T COME *TOO SOON*, NEITHER. THIS PLACE GIVES ME THE WILLIES AN' NO MISTAKE.
"HOLD ON, WHAT'S *THAT*?"
REC: 9.03.41
SHRAKK!

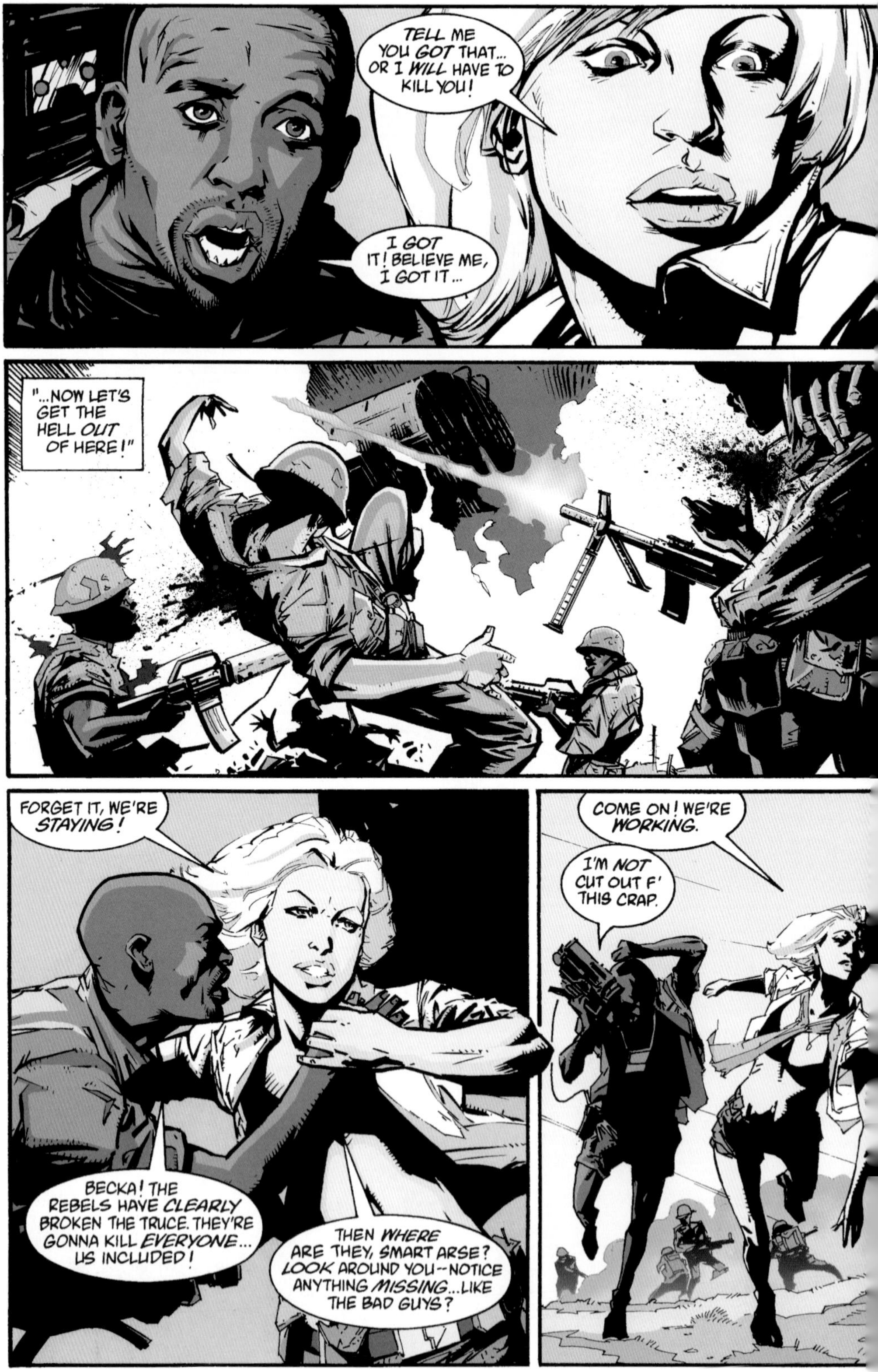

TELL ME YOU GOT THAT... OR I WILL HAVE TO KILL YOU!
I GOT IT! BELIEVE ME, I GOT IT...
"...NOW LET'S GET THE HELL OUT OF HERE!"
FORGET IT, WE'RE STAYING!
BECKA! THE REBELS HAVE CLEARLY BROKEN THE TRUCE. THEY'RE GONNA KILL EVERYONE... US INCLUDED!
THEN WHERE ARE THEY, SMART ARSE? LOOK AROUND YOU--NOTICE ANYTHING MISSING...LIKE THE BAD GUYS?
COME ON! WE'RE WORKING.
I'M NOT CUT OUT F' THIS CRAP.

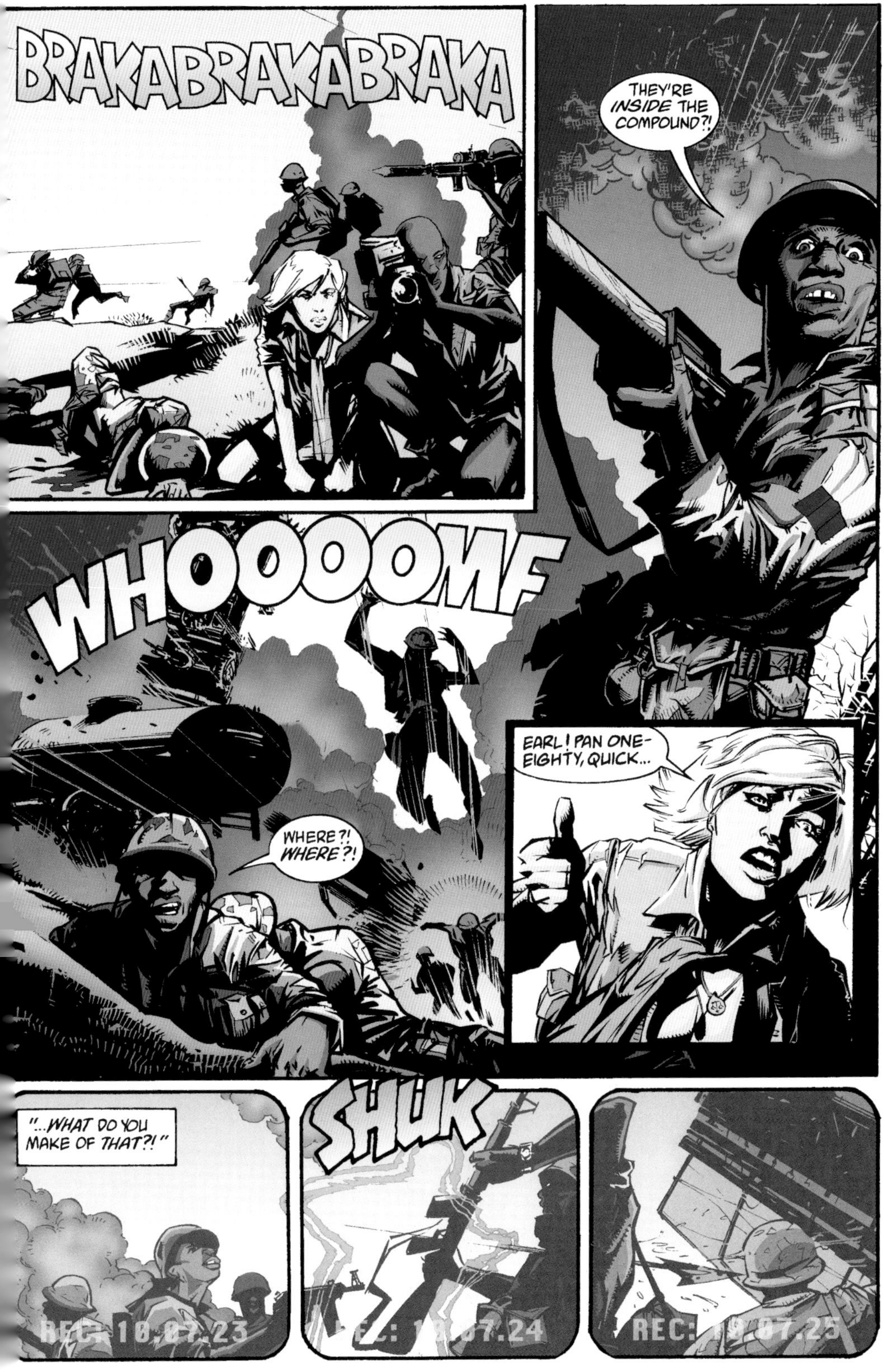
BRAKABRAKABRAKA
THEY'RE INSIDE THE COMPOUND?!
WHOOOOMF
WHERE?! WHERE?!
EARL! PAN ONE-EIGHTY, QUICK...
"...WHAT DO YOU MAKE OF THAT?!"
REC: 10.07.23
SHUK
REC: 10.07.24
REC: 10.07.25

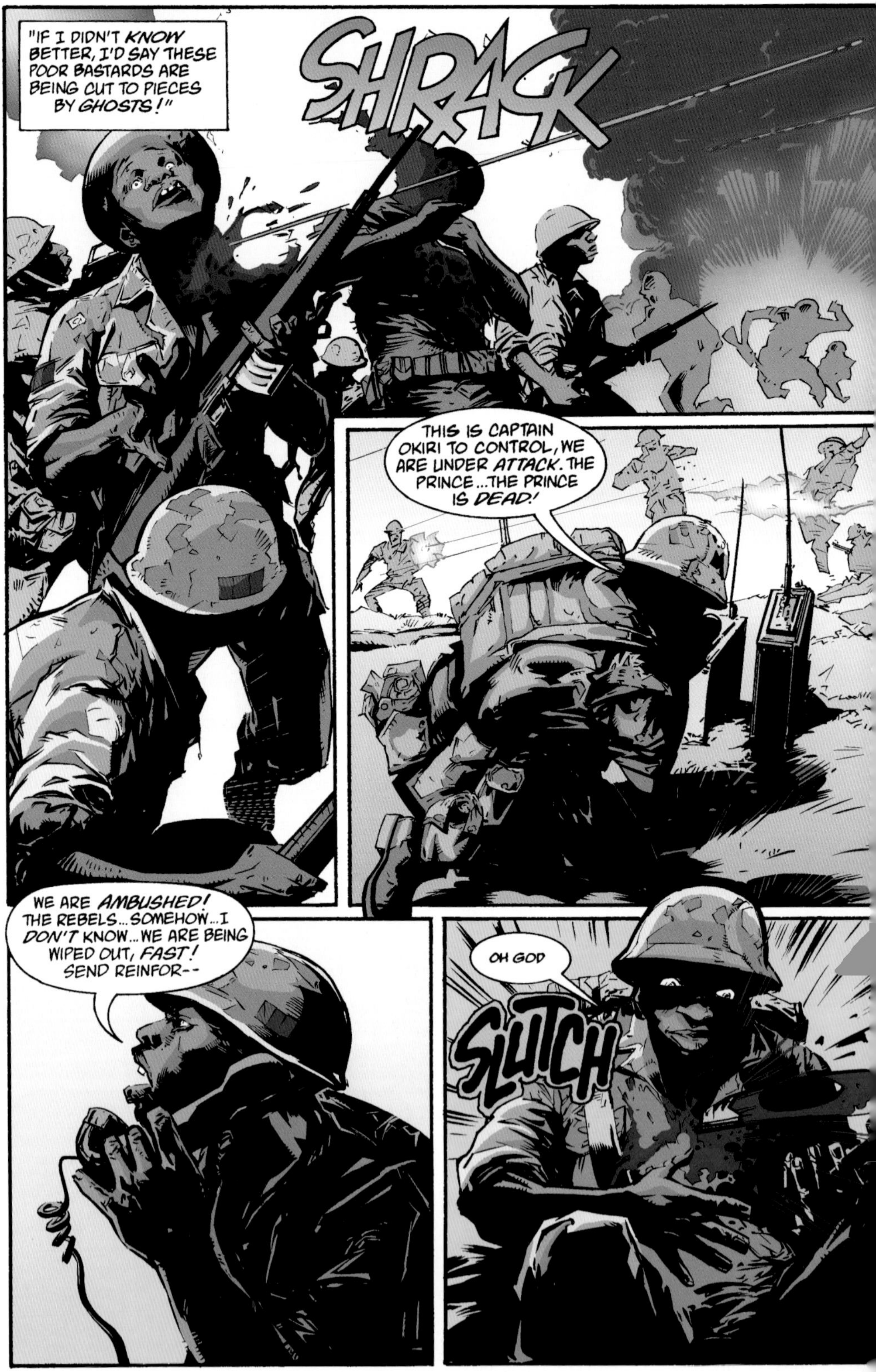
"IF I DIDN'T KNOW BETTER, I'D SAY THESE POOR BASTARDS ARE BEING CUT TO PIECES BY GHOSTS!"
SHRACK
THIS IS CAPTAIN OKIRI TO CONTROL, WE ARE UNDER ATTACK. THE PRINCE...THE PRINCE IS DEAD!
WE ARE AMBUSHED! THE REBELS...SOMEHOW...I DON'T KNOW...WE ARE BEING WIPED OUT, FAST! SEND REINFOR--
OH GOD
SLUTCH

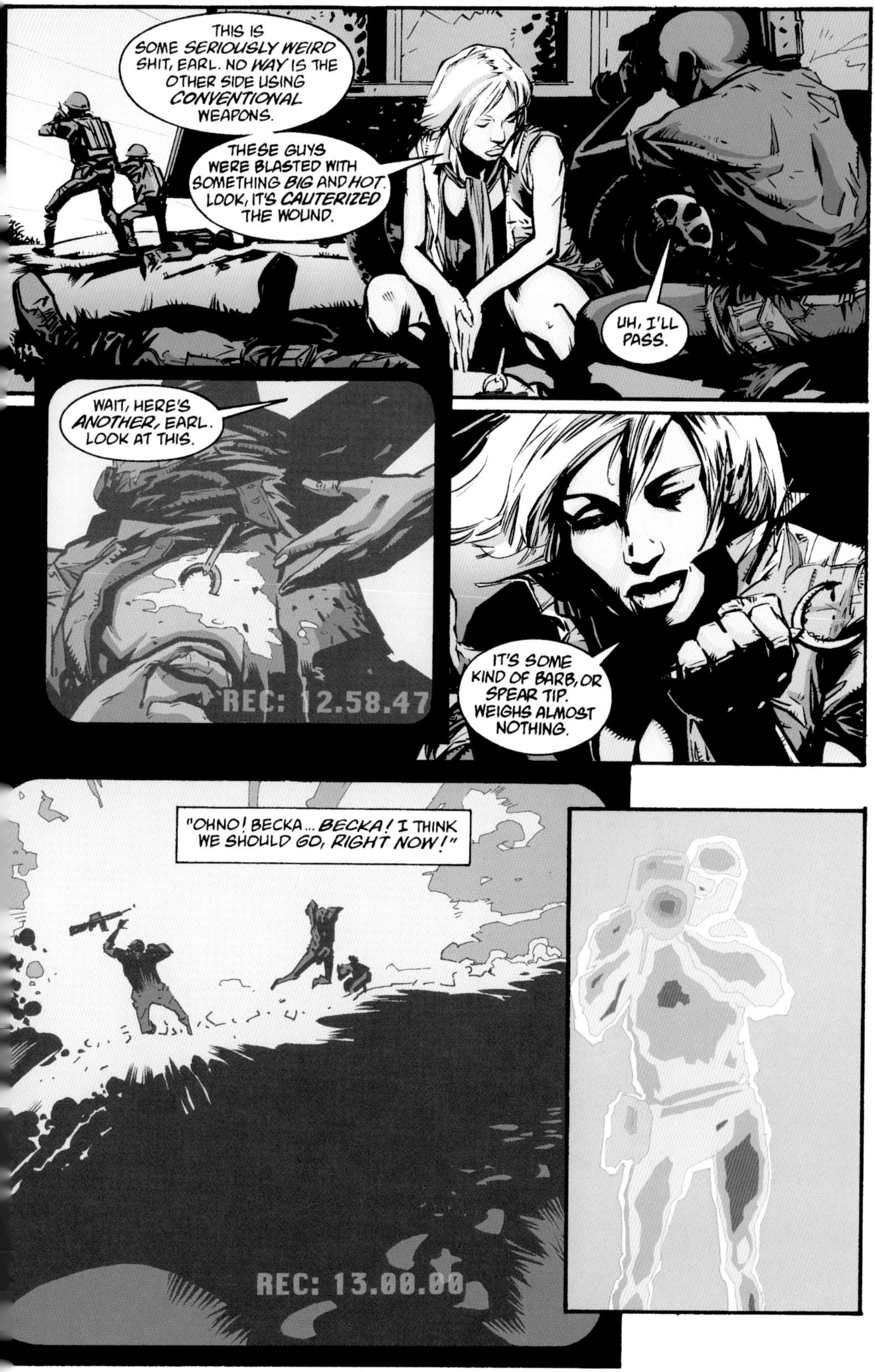
THIS IS SOME SERIOUSLY WEIRD SHIT, EARL. NO WAY IS THE OTHER SIDE USING CONVENTIONAL WEAPONS.
THESE GUYS WERE BLASTED WITH SOMETHING BIG AND HOT. LOOK, IT'S CAUTERIZED THE WOUND.
UH, I'LL PASS.
WAIT, HERE'S ANOTHER, EARL. LOOK AT THIS.
REC: 12.58.47
IT'S SOME KIND OF BARB, OR SPEAR TIP. WEIGHS ALMOST NOTHING.
"OHNO! BECKA... BECKA! I THINK WE SHOULD GO, RIGHT NOW!"
REC: 13.00.00

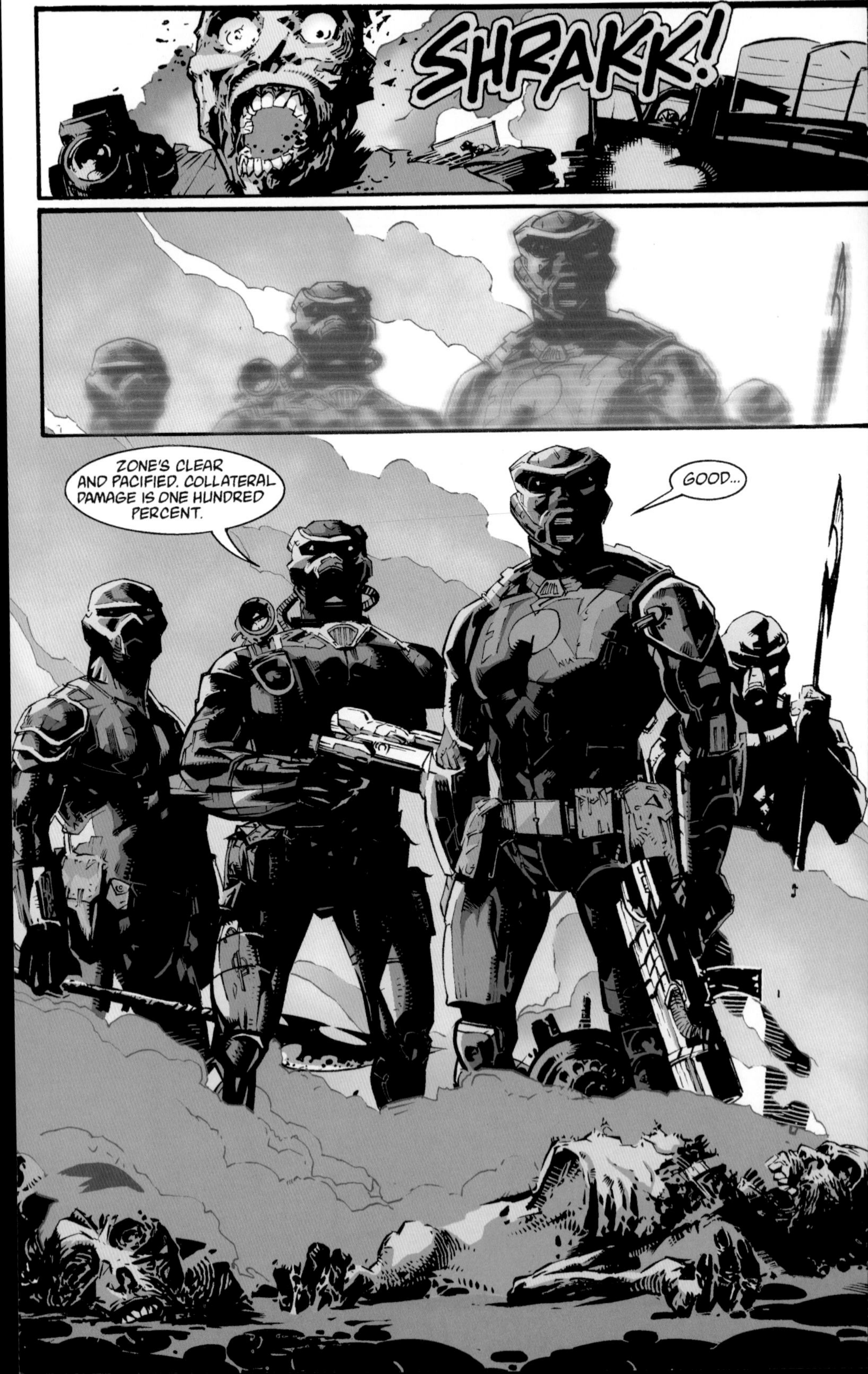
SHRAKK!
ZONE'S CLEAR AND PACIFIED. COLLATERAL DAMAGE IS ONE HUNDRED PERCENT.
GOOD...

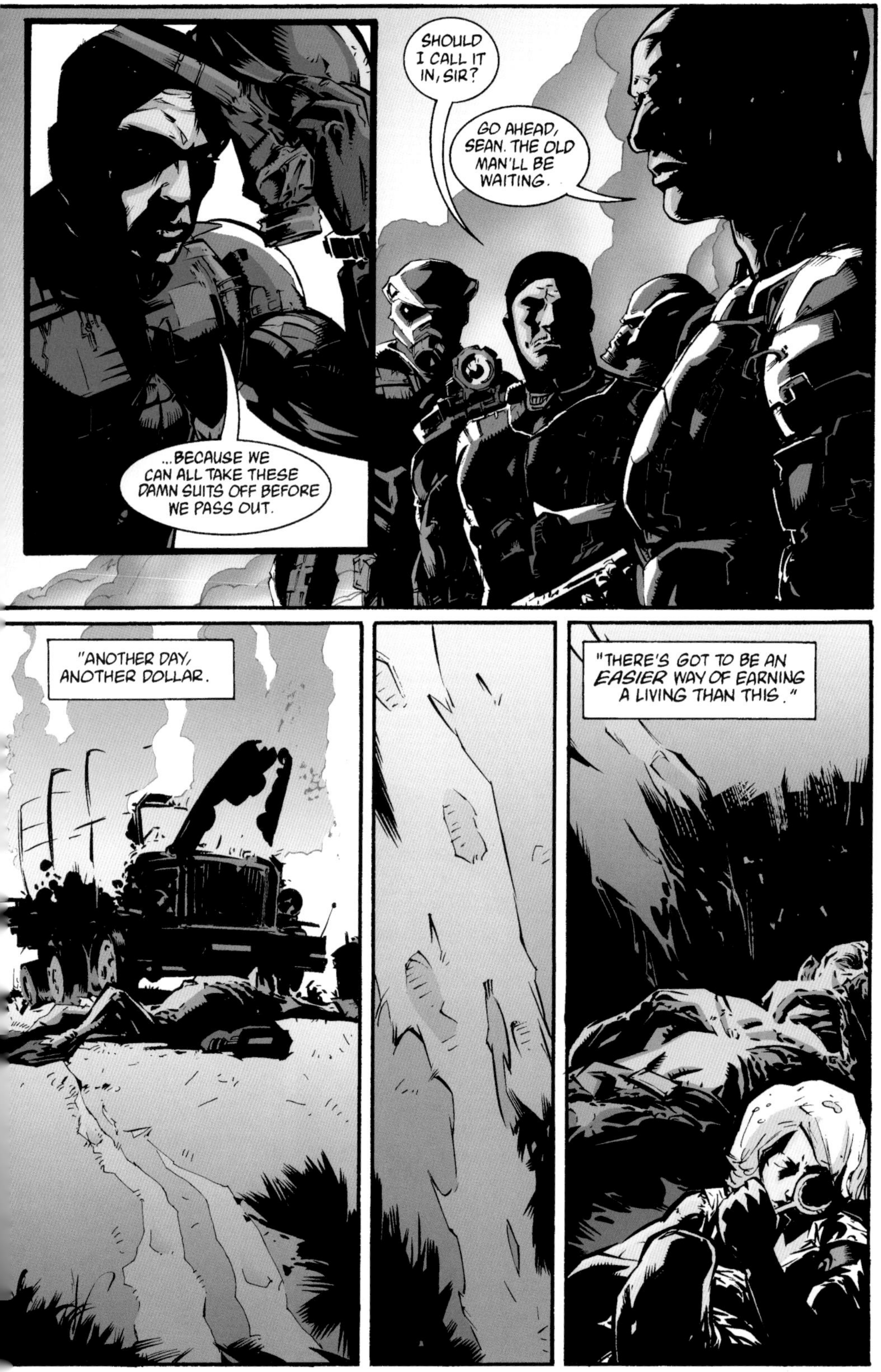
...BECAUSE WE CAN ALL TAKE THESE DAMN SUITS OFF BEFORE WE PASS OUT.
SHOULD I CALL IT IN, SIR?
GO AHEAD, SEAN. THE OLD MAN'LL BE WAITING.
"ANOTHER DAY, ANOTHER DOLLAR.
"THERE'S GOT TO BE AN EASIER WAY OF EARNING A LIVING THAN THIS."

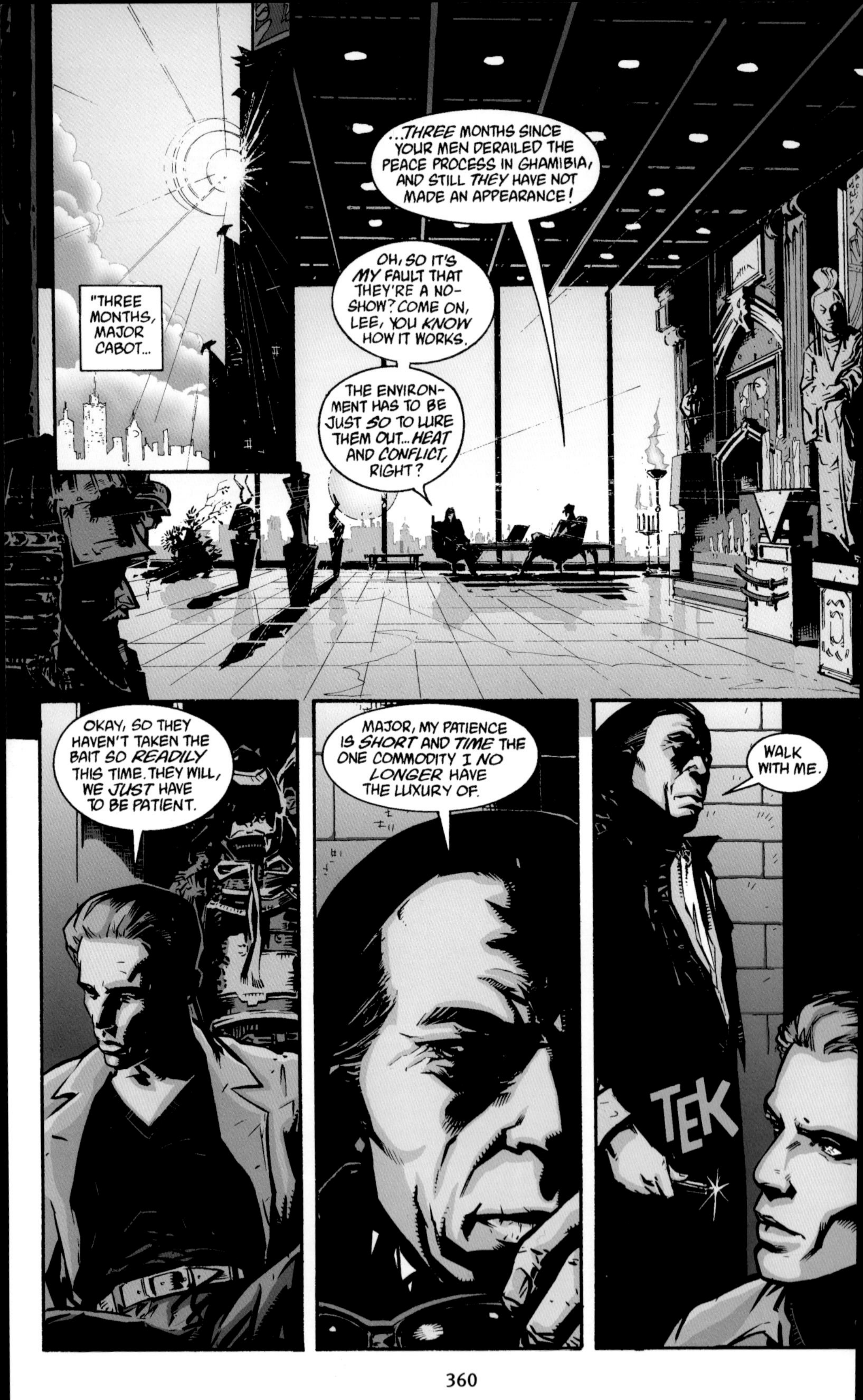
"THREE MONTHS, MAJOR CABOT...
...THREE MONTHS SINCE YOUR MEN DERAILED THE PEACE PROCESS IN GHAMIBIA, AND STILL THEY HAVE NOT MADE AN APPEARANCE!
OH, SO IT'S MY FAULT THAT THEY'RE A NO-SHOW? COME ON, LEE, YOU KNOW HOW IT WORKS.
THE ENVIRONMENT HAS TO BE JUST SO TO LURE THEM OUT... HEAT AND CONFLICT, RIGHT?
OKAY, SO THEY HAVEN'T TAKEN THE BAIT SO READILY THIS TIME. THEY WILL, WE JUST HAVE TO BE PATIENT.
MAJOR, MY PATIENCE IS SHORT AND TIME THE ONE COMMODITY I NO LONGER HAVE THE LUXURY OF.
WALK WITH ME.
TEK

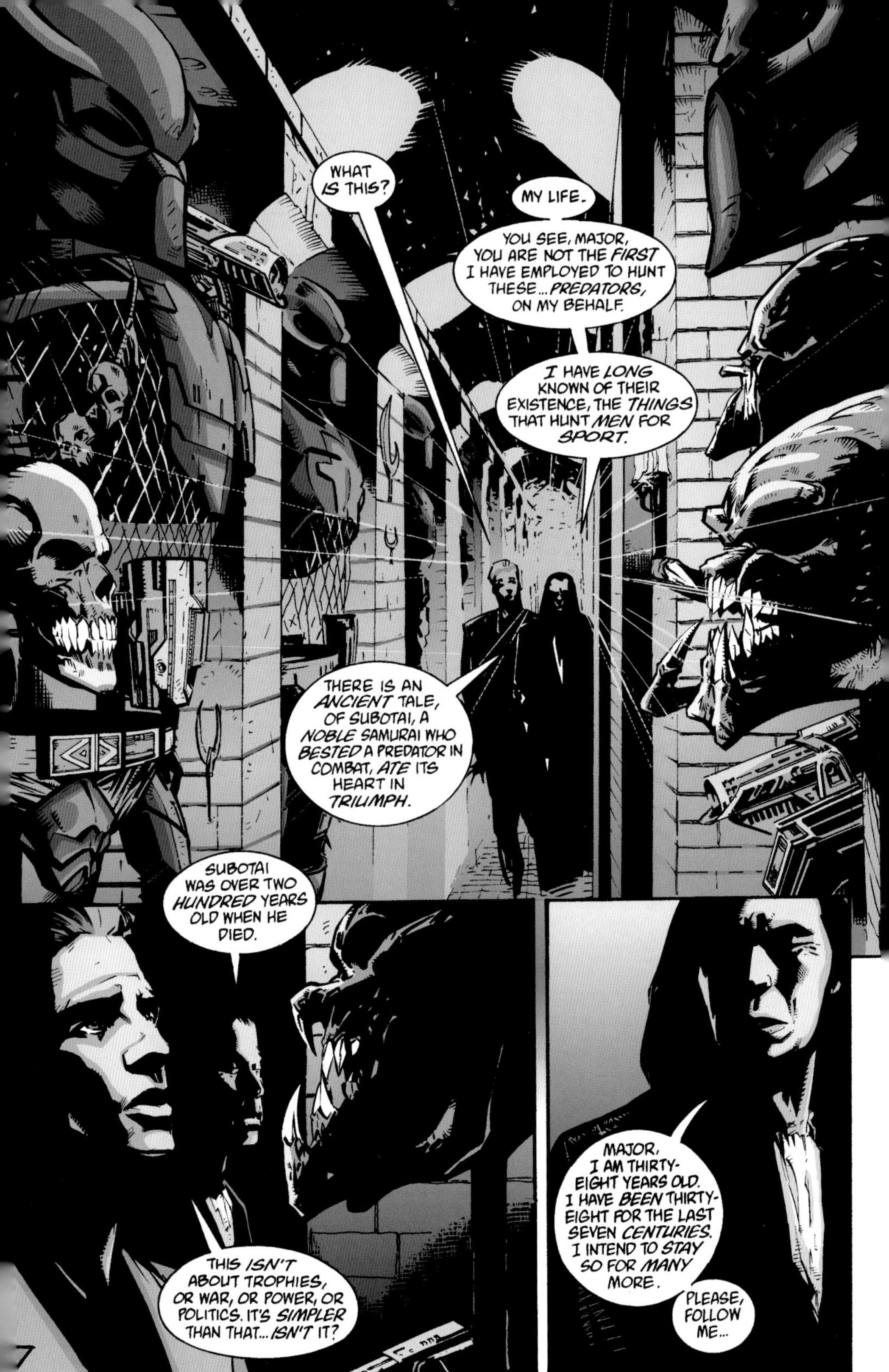
WHAT IS THIS?
MY LIFE.
YOU SEE, MAJOR, YOU ARE NOT THE FIRST I HAVE EMPLOYED TO HUNT THESE... PREDATORS, ON MY BEHALF.
I HAVE LONG KNOWN OF THEIR EXISTENCE, THE THINGS THAT HUNT MEN FOR SPORT.
THERE IS AN ANCIENT TALE, OF SUBOTAI, A NOBLE SAMURAI WHO BESTED A PREDATOR IN COMBAT, ATE ITS HEART IN TRIUMPH.
SUBOTAI WAS OVER TWO HUNDRED YEARS OLD WHEN HE DIED.
THIS ISN'T ABOUT TROPHIES, OR WAR, OR POWER, OR POLITICS. IT'S SIMPLER THAN THAT... ISN'T IT?
MAJOR, I AM THIRTY-EIGHT YEARS OLD. I HAVE BEEN THIRTY-EIGHT FOR THE LAST SEVEN CENTURIES. I INTEND TO STAY SO FOR MANY MORE.
PLEASE, FOLLOW ME...
7

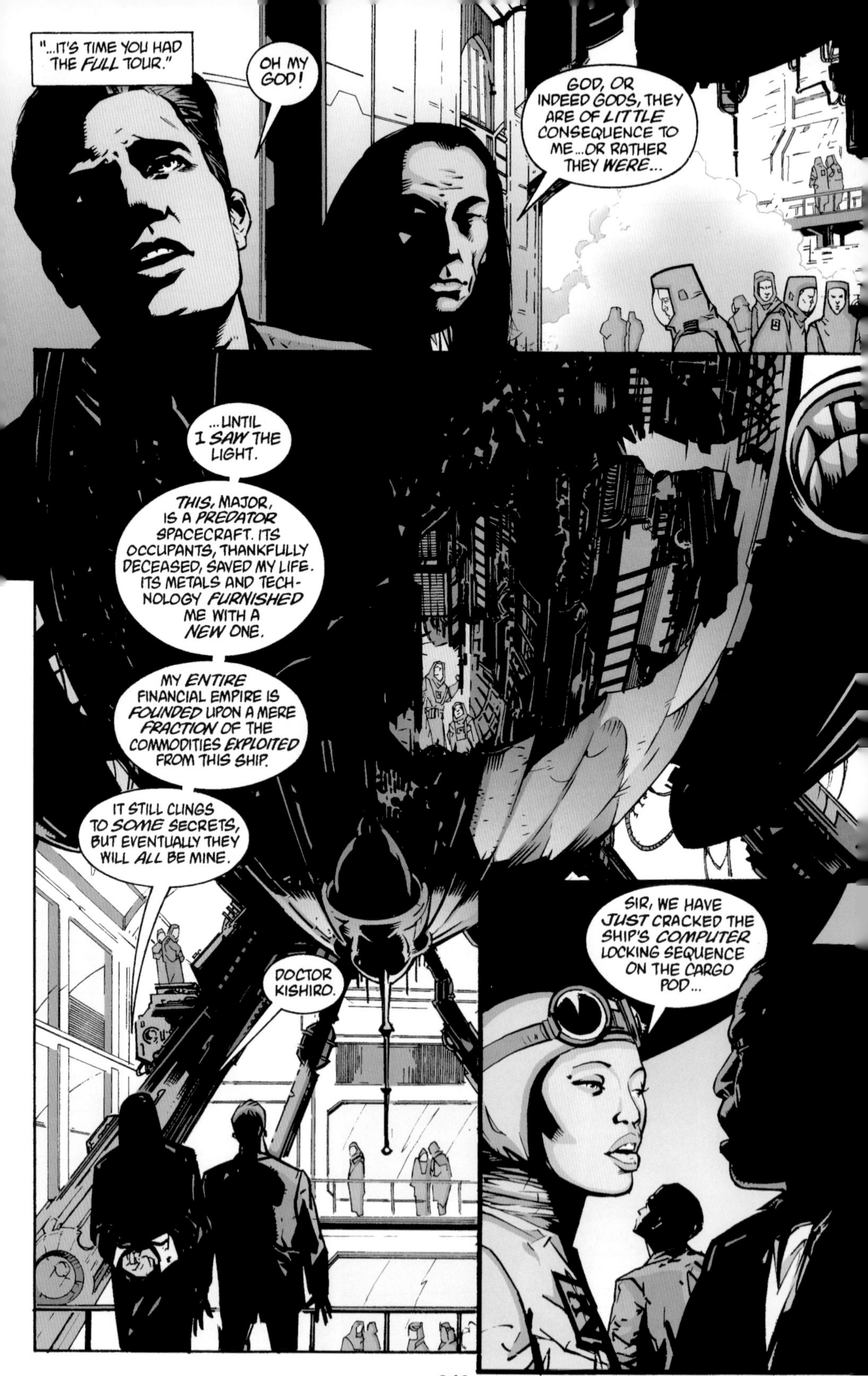
"...IT'S TIME YOU HAD THE FULL TOUR."
OH MY GOD!
GOD, OR INDEED GODS, THEY ARE OF LITTLE CONSEQUENCE TO ME...OR RATHER THEY WERE...
...UNTIL I SAW THE LIGHT.
THIS, MAJOR, IS A PREDATOR SPACECRAFT. ITS OCCUPANTS, THANKFULLY DECEASED, SAVED MY LIFE. ITS METALS AND TECHNOLOGY FURNISHED ME WITH A NEW ONE.
MY ENTIRE FINANCIAL EMPIRE IS FOUNDED UPON A MERE FRACTION OF THE COMMODITIES EXPLOITED FROM THIS SHIP.
IT STILL CLINGS TO SOME SECRETS, BUT EVENTUALLY THEY WILL ALL BE MINE.
DOCTOR KISHIRO.
SIR, WE HAVE JUST CRACKED THE SHIP'S COMPUTER LOCKING SEQUENCE ON THE CARGO POD...

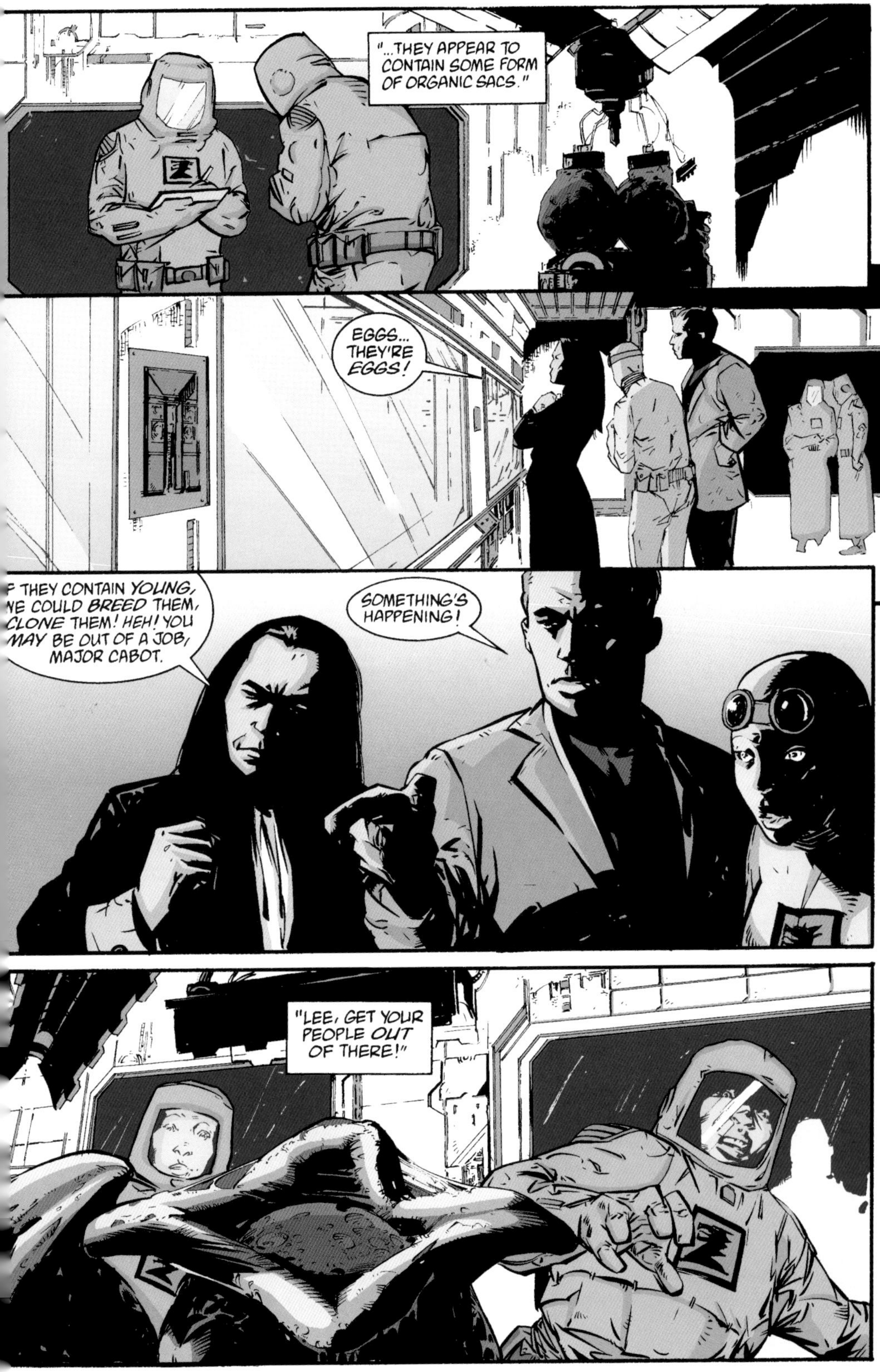
"...THEY APPEAR TO CONTAIN SOME FORM OF ORGANIC SACS."
EGGS... THEY'RE EGGS!
F THEY CONTAIN YOUNG, NE COULD BREED THEM, CLONE THEM! HEH! YOU MAY BE OUT OF A JOB, MAJOR CABOT.
SOMETHING'S HAPPENING!
"LEE, GET YOUR PEOPLE OUT OF THERE!"

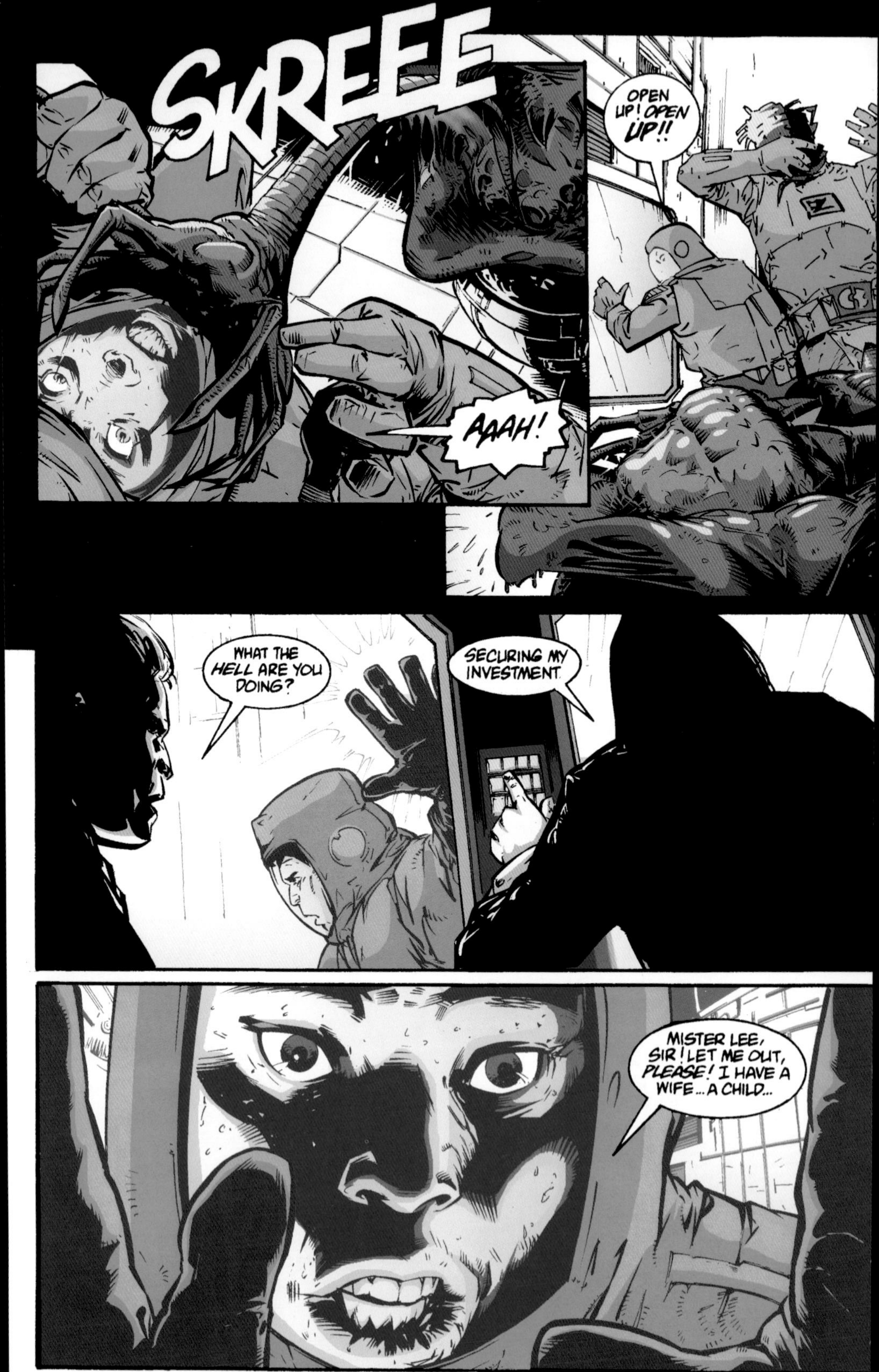
SKREEE
OPEN UP! OPEN UP!!
AAAH!
WHAT THE HELL ARE YOU DOING?
SECURING MY INVESTMENT.
MISTER LEE, SIR! LET ME OUT, PLEASE! I HAVE A WIFE... A CHILD...

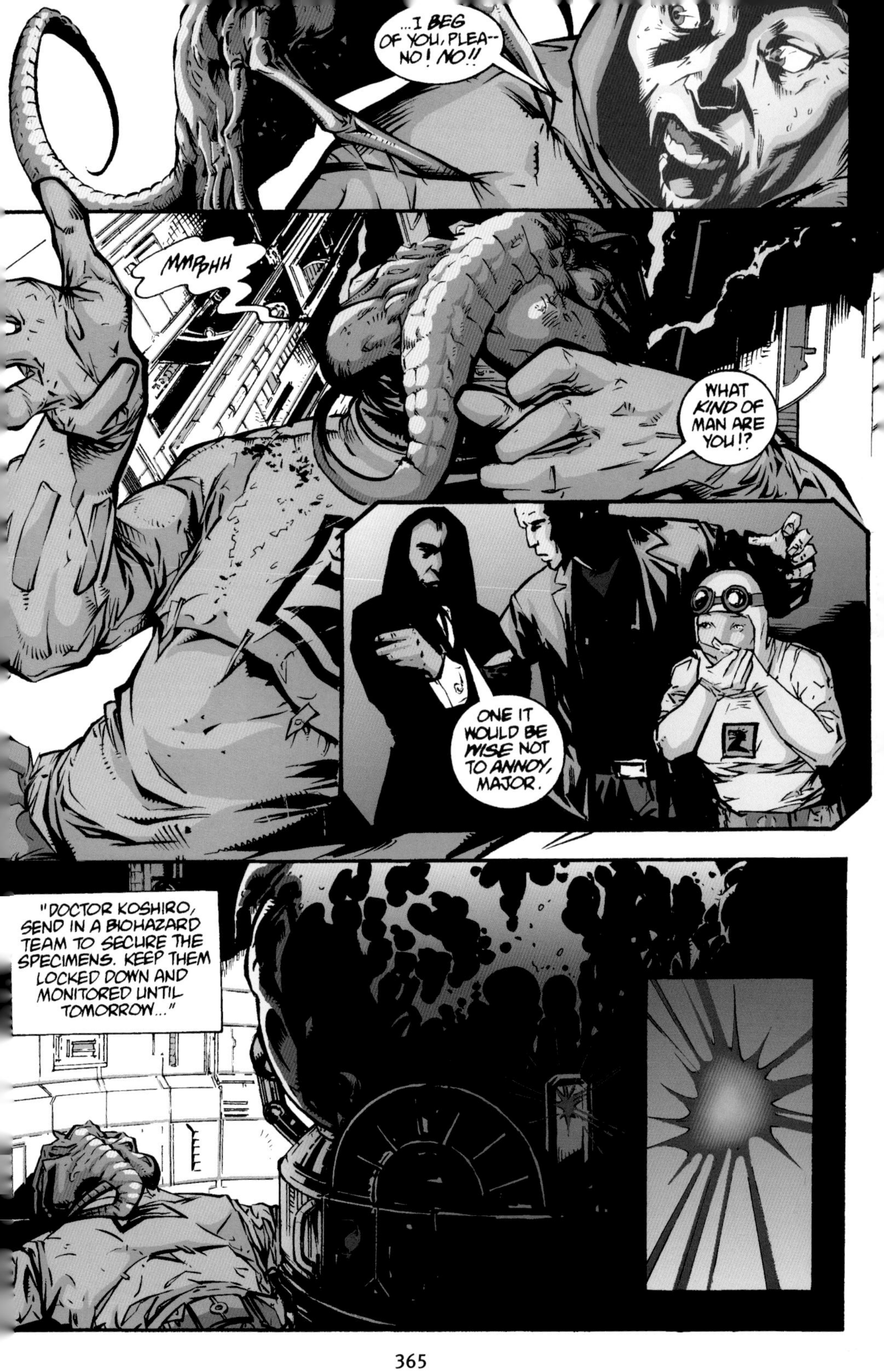
...I BEG OF YOU, PLEA-- NO! NO!!
MMPHH
WHAT KIND OF MAN ARE YOU!?
ONE IT WOULD BE WISE NOT TO ANNOY, MAJOR.
"DOCTOR KOSHIRO, SEND IN A BIOHAZARD TEAM TO SECURE THE SPECIMENS. KEEP THEM LOCKED DOWN AND MONITORED UNTIL TOMORROW..."

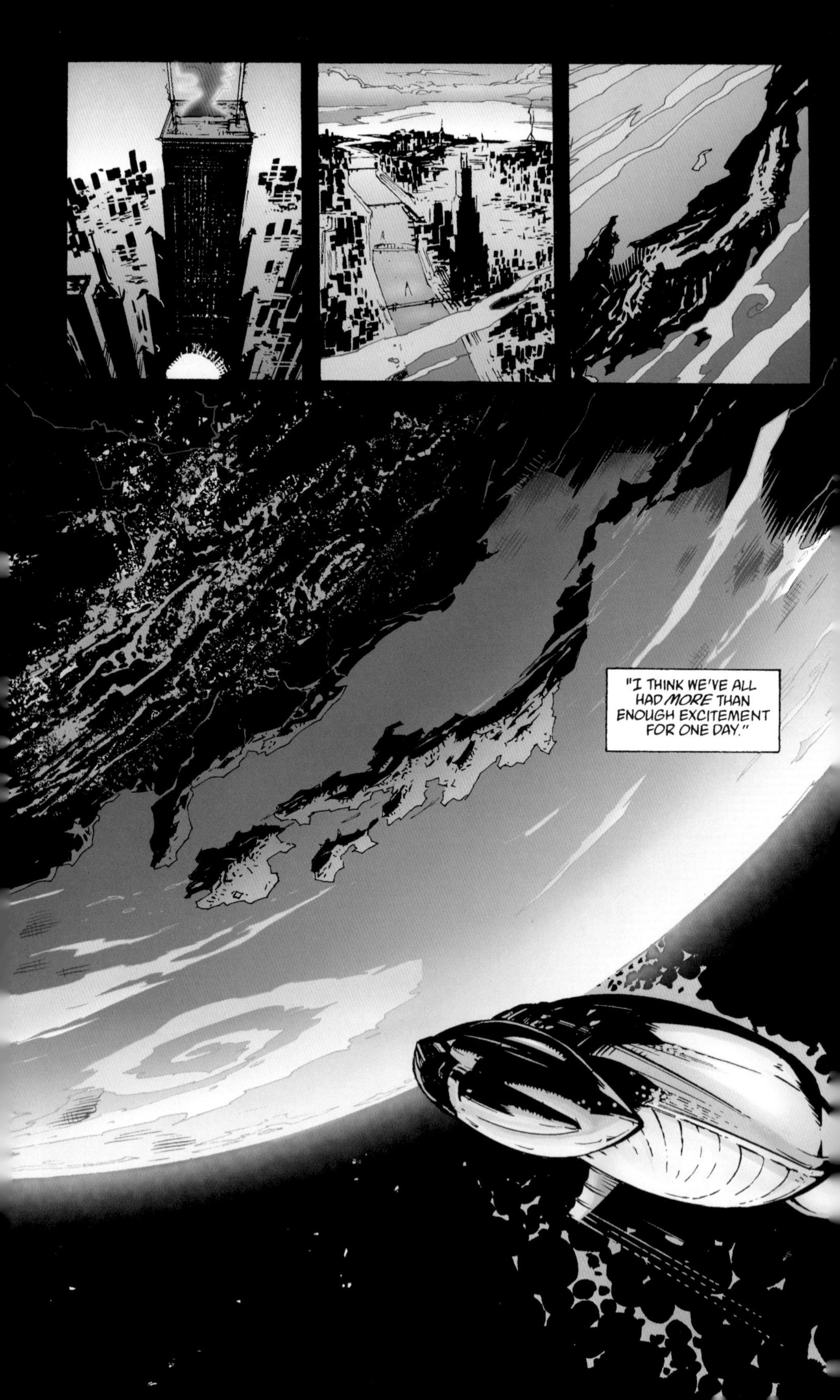
"I THINK WE'VE ALL HAD MORE THAN ENOUGH EXCITEMENT FOR ONE DAY."

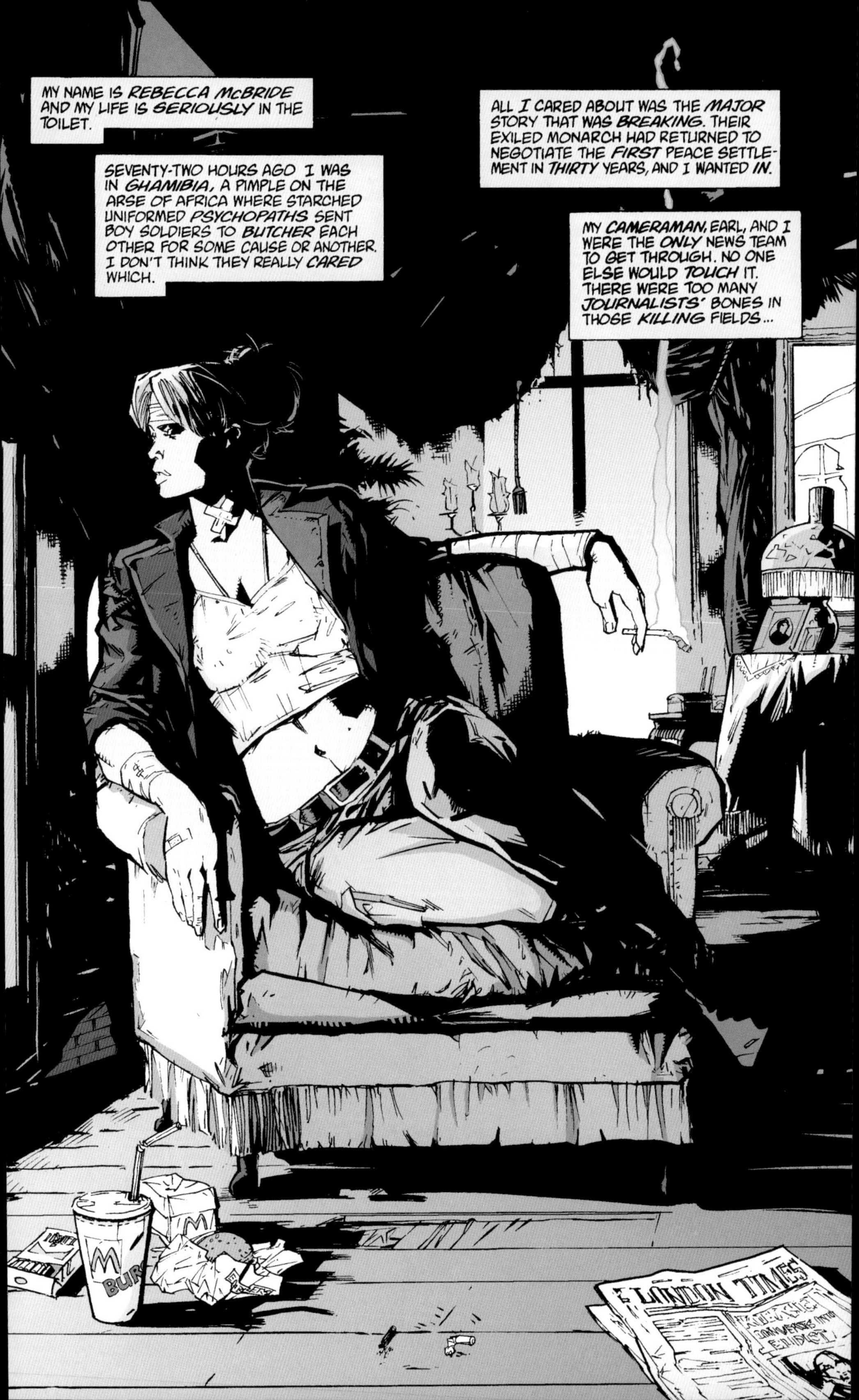
MY NAME IS REBECCA McBRIDE AND MY LIFE IS SERIOUSLY IN THE TOILET.
SEVENTY-TWO HOURS AGO I WAS IN GHAMIBIA, A PIMPLE ON THE ARSE OF AFRICA WHERE STARCHED UNIFORMED PSYCHOPATHS SENT BOY SOLDIERS TO BUTCHER EACH OTHER FOR SOME CAUSE OR ANOTHER. I DON'T THINK THEY REALLY CARED WHICH.
ALL I CARED ABOUT WAS THE MAJOR STORY THAT WAS BREAKING. THEIR EXILED MONARCH HAD RETURNED TO NEGOTIATE THE FIRST PEACE SETTLEMENT IN THIRTY YEARS, AND I WANTED IN.
MY CAMERAMAN, EARL, AND I WERE THE ONLY NEWS TEAM TO GET THROUGH. NO ONE ELSE WOULD TOUCH IT. THERE WERE TOO MANY JOURNALISTS' BONES IN THOSE KILLING FIELDS...
LONDON TIMES

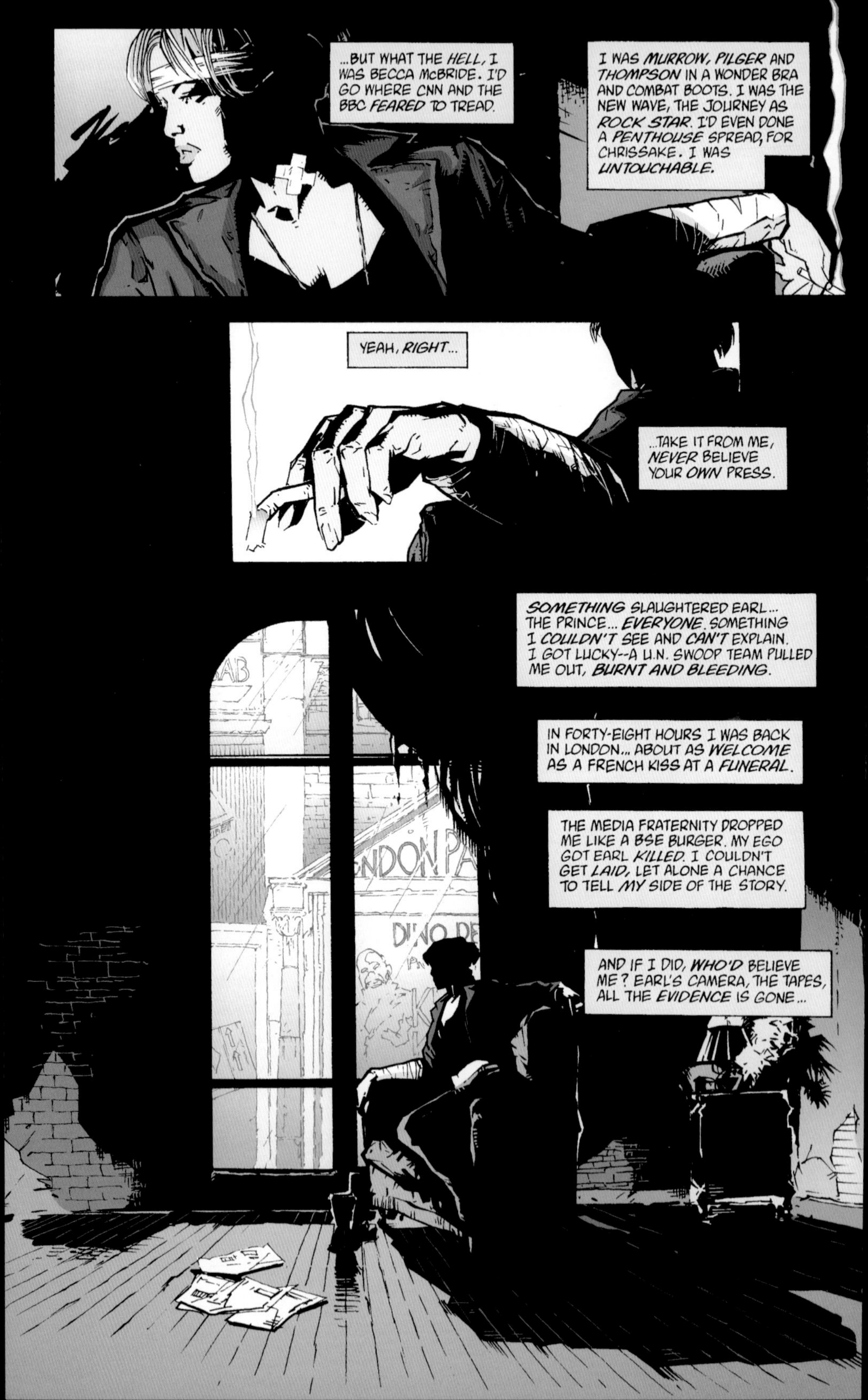
...BUT WHAT THE HELL, I WAS BECCA McBRIDE. I'D GO WHERE CNN AND THE BBC FEARED TO TREAD.
I WAS MURROW, PILGER AND THOMPSON IN A WONDER BRA AND COMBAT BOOTS. I WAS THE NEW WAVE, THE JOURNEY AS ROCK STAR. I'D EVEN DONE A PENTHOUSE SPREAD, FOR CHRISSAKE. I WAS UNTOUCHABLE.
YEAH, RIGHT...
...TAKE IT FROM ME, NEVER BELIEVE YOUR OWN PRESS.
SOMETHING SLAUGHTERED EARL... THE PRINCE... EVERYONE. SOMETHING I COULDN'T SEE AND CAN'T EXPLAIN. I GOT LUCKY--A U.N. SWOOP TEAM PULLED ME OUT, BURNT AND BLEEDING.
IN FORTY-EIGHT HOURS I WAS BACK IN LONDON... ABOUT AS WELCOME AS A FRENCH KISS AT A FUNERAL.
THE MEDIA FRATERNITY DROPPED ME LIKE A BSE BURGER. MY EGO GOT EARL KILLED. I COULDN'T GET LAID, LET ALONE A CHANCE TO TELL MY SIDE OF THE STORY.
AND IF I DID, WHO'D BELIEVE ME? EARL'S CAMERA, THE TAPES, ALL THE EVIDENCE IS GONE...

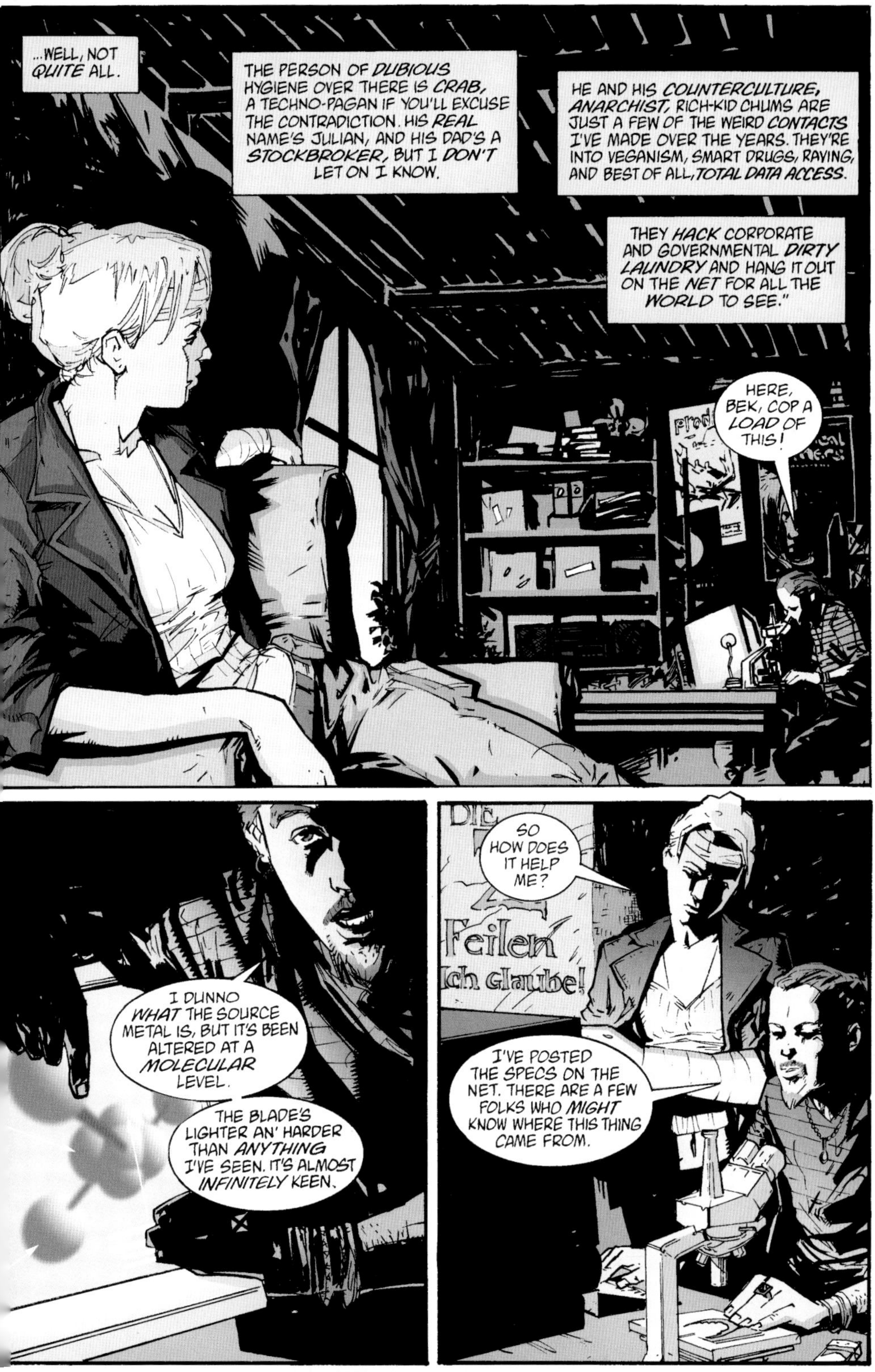
...WELL, NOT QUITE ALL.
THE PERSON OF DUBIOUS HYGIENE OVER THERE IS CRAB, A TECHNO-PAGAN IF YOU'LL EXCUSE THE CONTRADICTION. HIS REAL NAME'S JULIAN, AND HIS DAD'S A STOCKBROKER, BUT I DON'T LET ON I KNOW.
HE AND HIS COUNTERCULTURE, ANARCHIST, RICH-KID CHUMS ARE JUST A FEW OF THE WEIRD CONTACTS I'VE MADE OVER THE YEARS. THEY'RE INTO VEGANISM, SMART DRUGS, RAVING, AND BEST OF ALL, TOTAL DATA ACCESS.
THEY HACK CORPORATE AND GOVERNMENTAL DIRTY LAUNDRY AND HANG IT OUT ON THE NET FOR ALL THE WORLD TO SEE."
HERE, BEK, COP A LOAD OF THIS!
I DUNNO WHAT THE SOURCE METAL IS, BUT IT'S BEEN ALTERED AT A MOLECULAR LEVEL.
THE BLADE'S LIGHTER AN' HARDER THAN ANYTHING I'VE SEEN. IT'S ALMOST INFINITELY KEEN.
SO HOW DOES IT HELP ME?
Feilen
Ich glaube!
I'VE POSTED THE SPECS ON THE NET. THERE ARE A FEW FOLKS WHO MIGHT KNOW WHERE THIS THING CAME FROM.

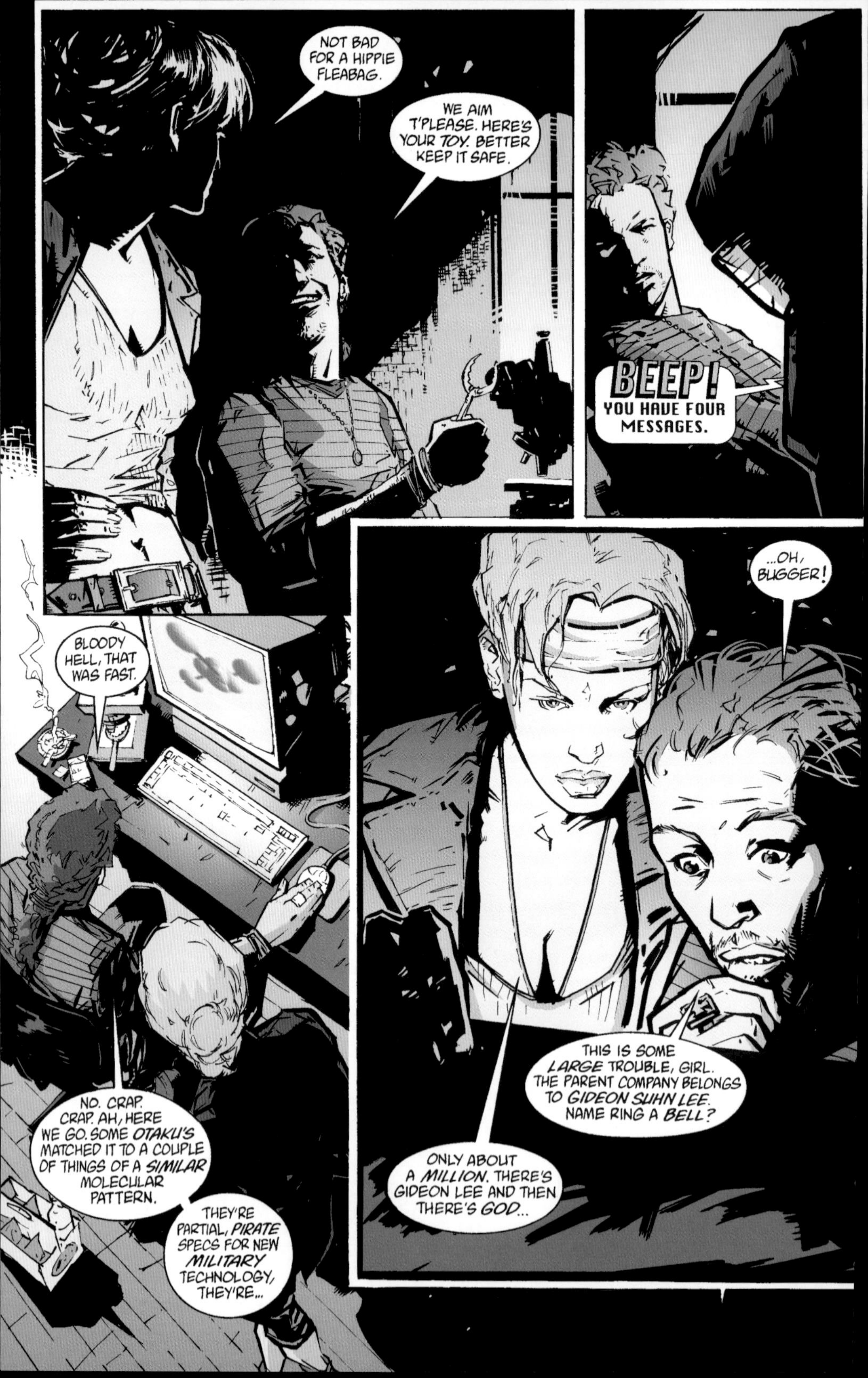
NOT BAD FOR A HIPPIE FLEABAG.
WE AIM T'PLEASE. HERE'S YOUR TOY. BETTER KEEP IT SAFE.
BEEP! YOU HAVE FOUR MESSAGES.
BLOODY HELL, THAT WAS FAST.
NO. CRAP. CRAP. AH, HERE WE GO. SOME OTAKU'S MATCHED IT TO A COUPLE OF THINGS OF A SIMILAR MOLECULAR PATTERN.
THEY'RE PARTIAL, PIRATE SPECS FOR NEW MILITARY TECHNOLOGY, THEY'RE...
...OH, BUGGER!
THIS IS SOME LARGE TROUBLE, GIRL. THE PARENT COMPANY BELONGS TO GIDEON SUHN LEE. NAME RING A BELL?
ONLY ABOUT A MILLION. THERE'S GIDEON LEE AND THEN THERE'S GOD...

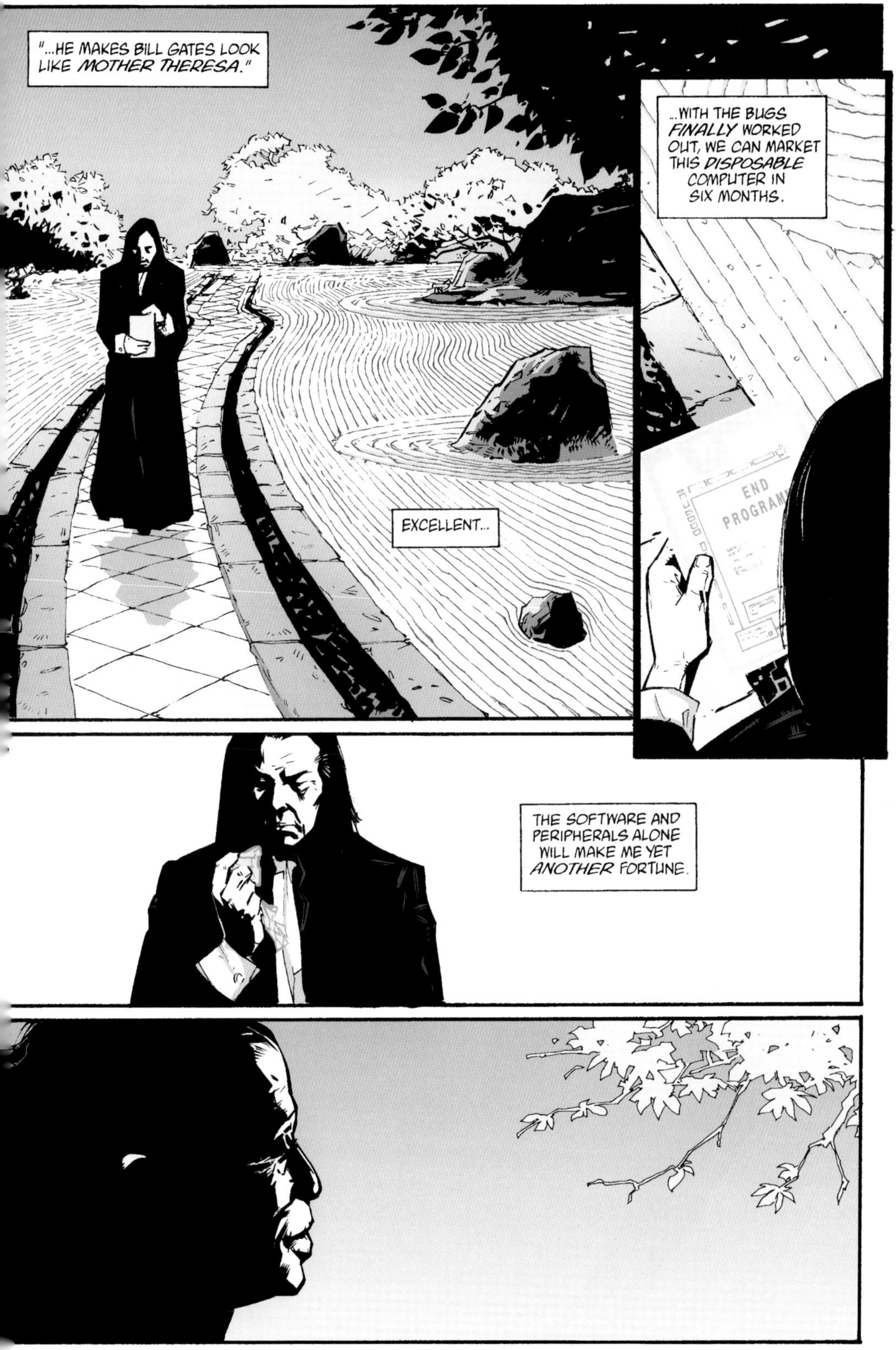
"...HE MAKES BILL GATES LOOK LIKE MOTHER THERESA."
...WITH THE BUGS FINALLY WORKED OUT, WE CAN MARKET THIS DISPOSABLE COMPUTER IN SIX MONTHS.
EXCELLENT...
END PROGRAM
THE SOFTWARE AND PERIPHERALS ALONE WILL MAKE ME YET ANOTHER FORTUNE.

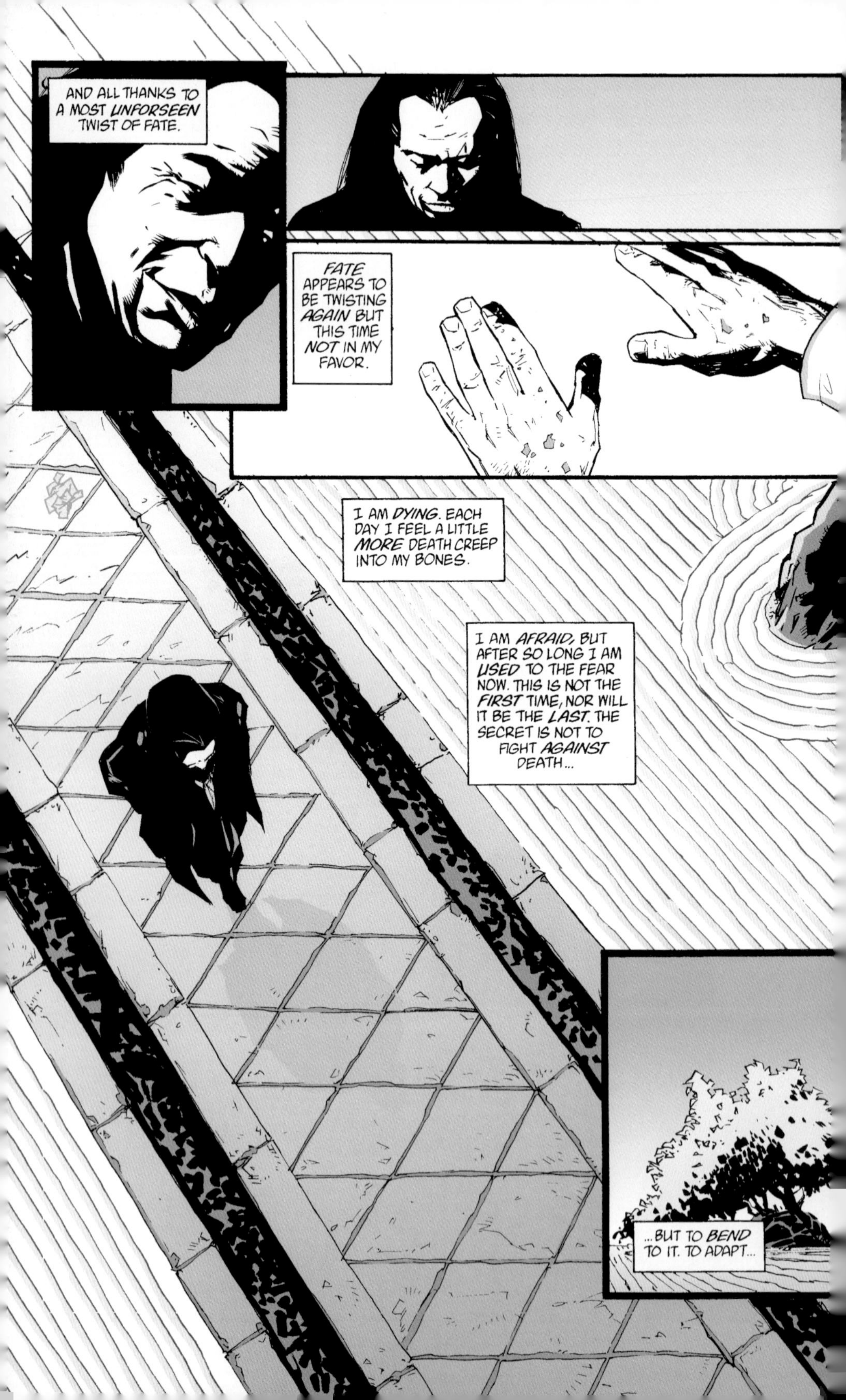
AND ALL THANKS TO A MOST UNFORSEEN TWIST OF FATE.
FATE APPEARS TO BE TWISTING AGAIN BUT THIS TIME NOT IN MY FAVOR.
I AM DYING. EACH DAY I FEEL A LITTLE MORE DEATH CREEP INTO MY BONES.
I AM AFRAID, BUT AFTER SO LONG I AM USED TO THE FEAR NOW. THIS IS NOT THE FIRST TIME, NOR WILL IT BE THE LAST. THE SECRET IS NOT TO FIGHT AGAINST DEATH...
...BUT TO BEND TO IT. TO ADAPT...

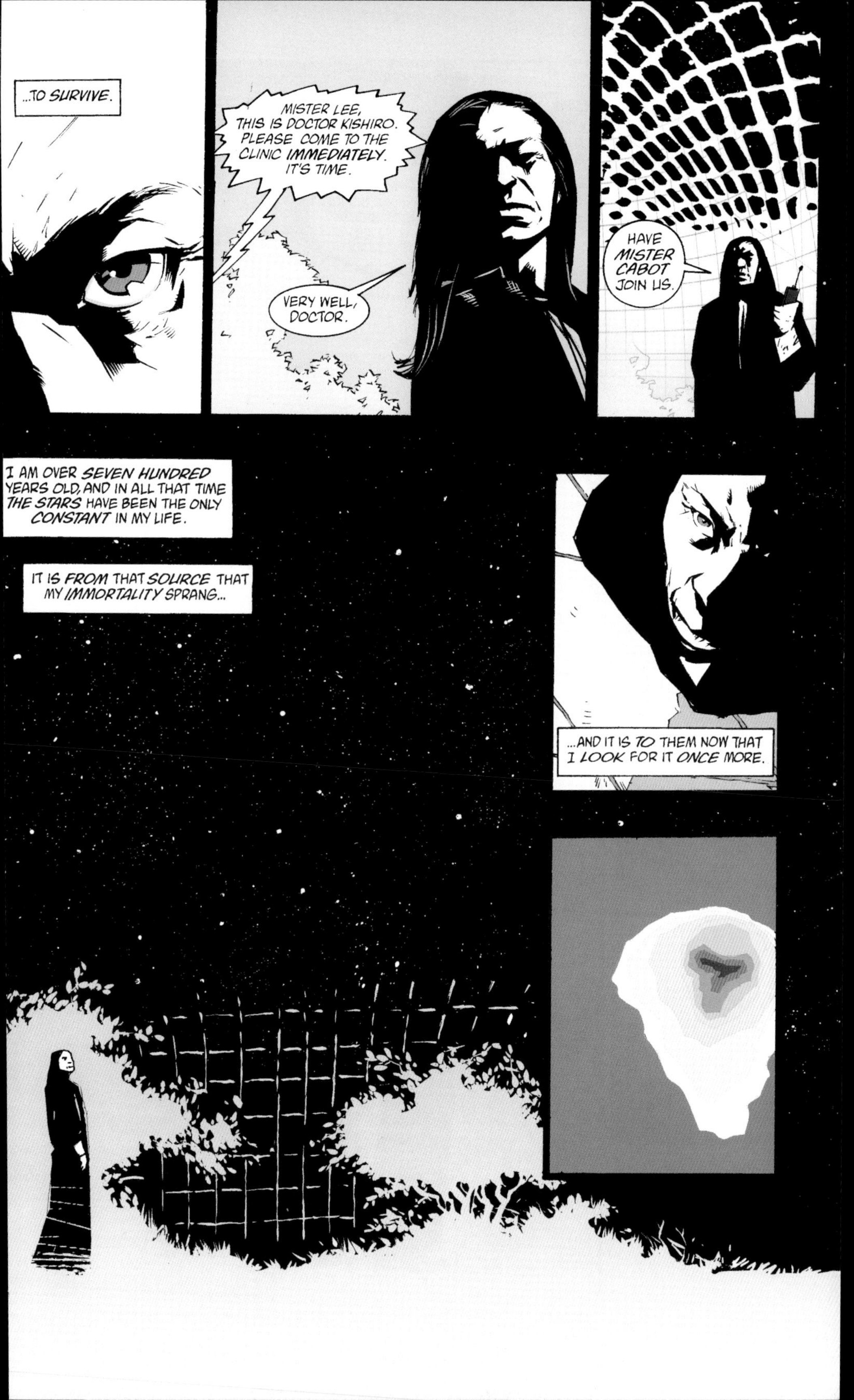
...TO SURVIVE.
MISTER LEE, THIS IS DOCTOR KISHIRO. PLEASE COME TO THE CLINIC IMMEDIATELY. IT'S TIME.
VERY WELL, DOCTOR.
HAVE MISTER CABOT JOIN US.
I AM OVER SEVEN HUNDRED YEARS OLD, AND IN ALL THAT TIME THE STARS HAVE BEEN THE ONLY CONSTANT IN MY LIFE.
IT IS FROM THAT SOURCE THAT MY IMMORTALITY SPRANG...
...AND IT IS TO THEM NOW THAT I LOOK FOR IT ONCE MORE.

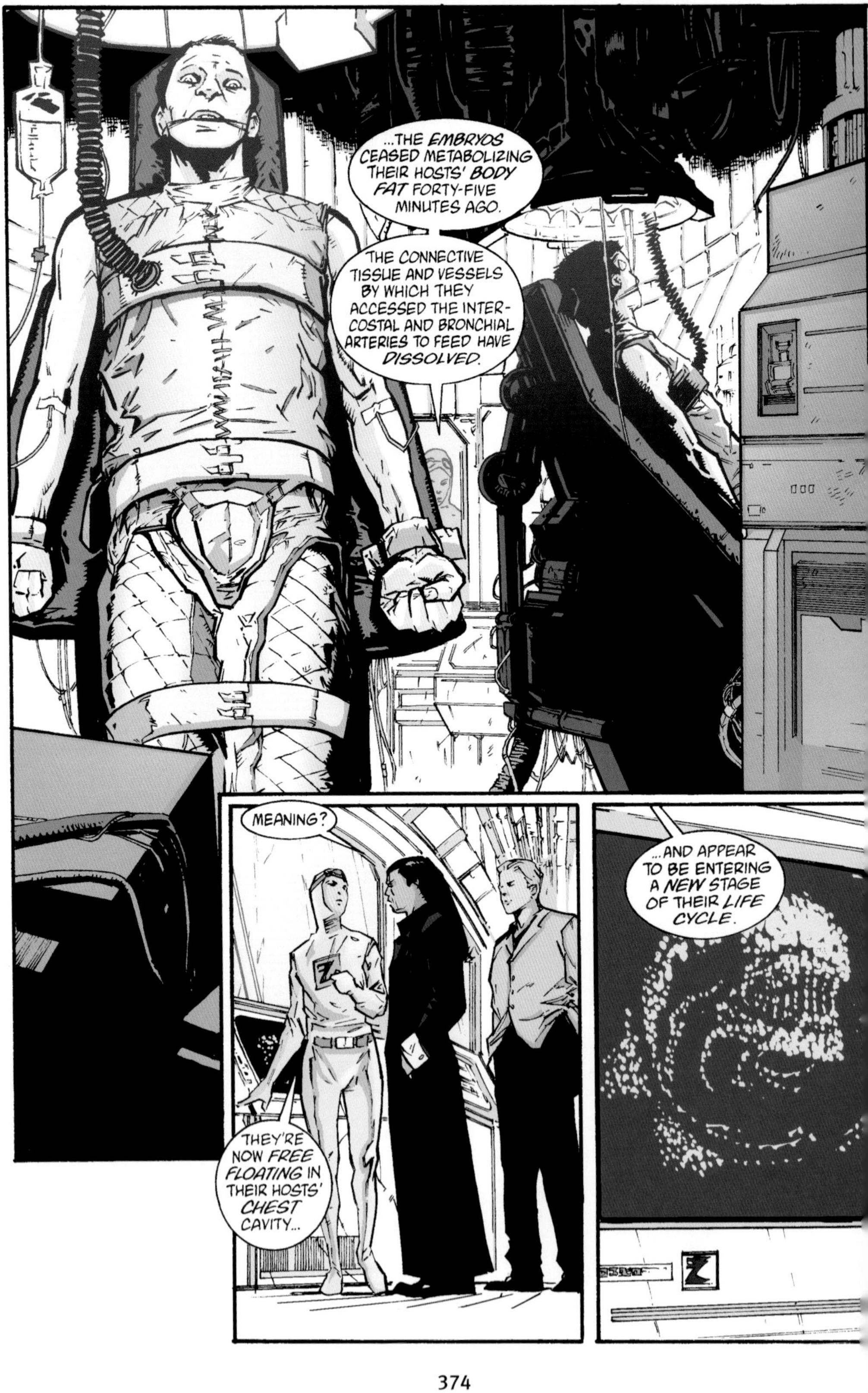
...THE EMBRYOS CEASED METABOLIZING THEIR HOSTS' BODY FAT FORTY-FIVE MINUTES AGO.
THE CONNECTIVE TISSUE AND VESSELS BY WHICH THEY ACCESSED THE INTER-COSTAL AND BRONCHIAL ARTERIES TO FEED HAVE DISSOLVED.
MEANING?
THEY'RE NOW FREE FLOATING IN THEIR HOSTS' CHEST CAVITY...
...AND APPEAR TO BE ENTERING A NEW STAGE OF THEIR LIFE CYCLE.

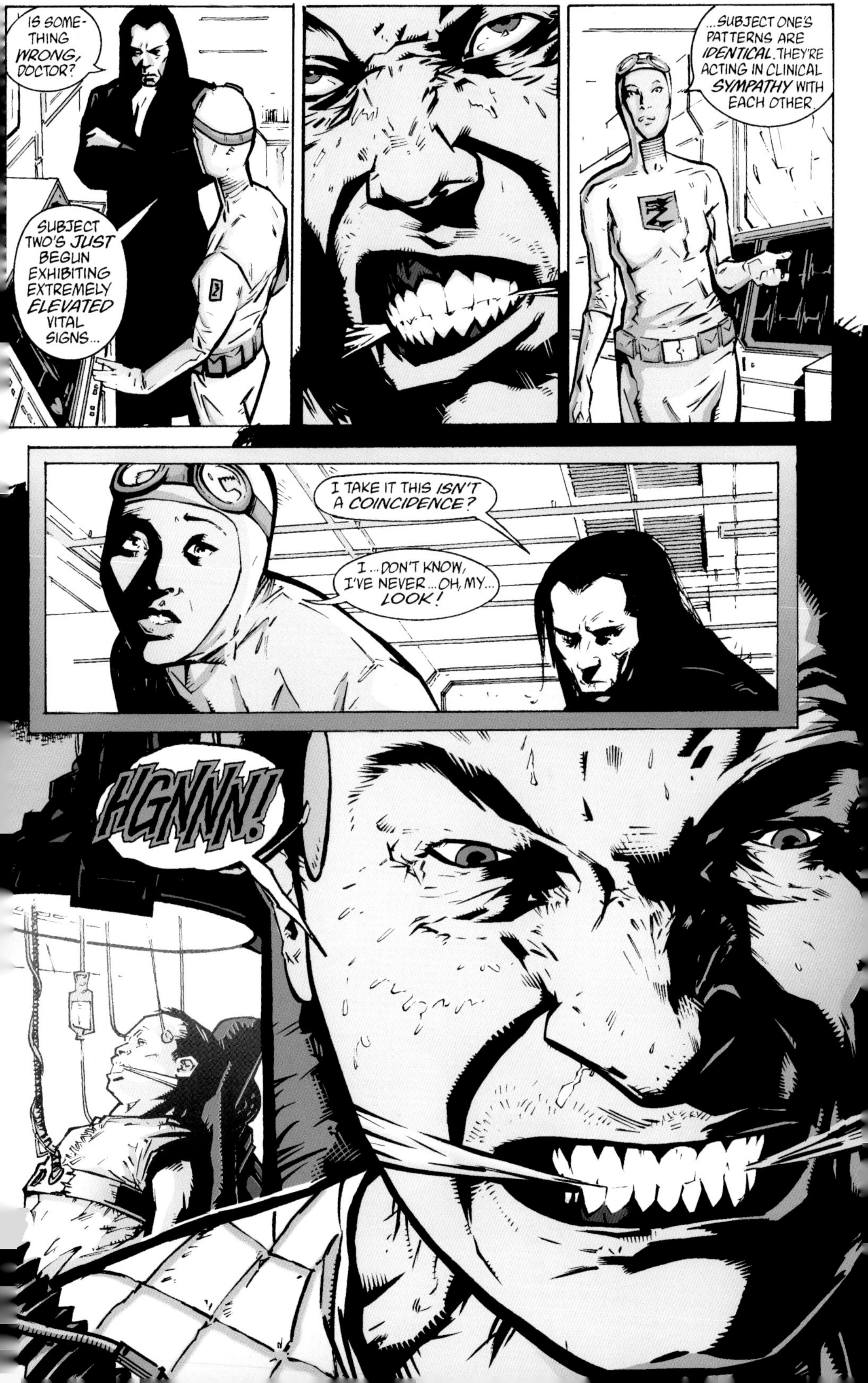
IS SOMETHING WRONG, DOCTOR?
SUBJECT TWO'S JUST BEGUN EXHIBITING EXTREMELY ELEVATED VITAL SIGNS...
...SUBJECT ONE'S PATTERNS ARE IDENTICAL. THEY'RE ACTING IN CLINICAL SYMPATHY WITH EACH OTHER.
I TAKE IT THIS ISN'T A COINCIDENCE?
I...DON'T KNOW, I'VE NEVER...OH, MY... LOOK!
HGNNN!

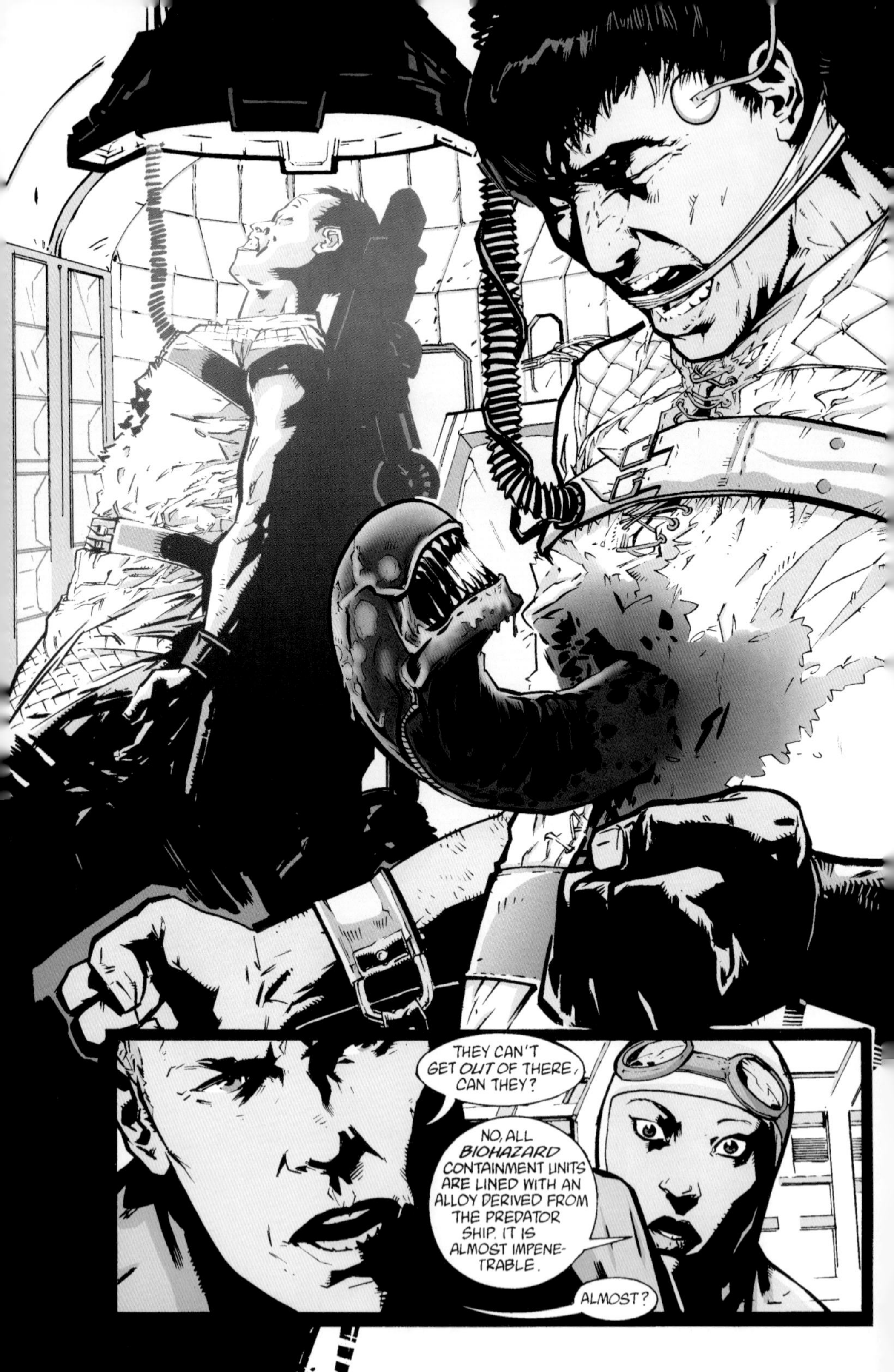
THEY CAN'T GET OUT OF THERE, CAN THEY?
NO, ALL BIOHAZARD CONTAINMENT UNITS ARE LINED WITH AN ALLOY DERIVED FROM THE PREDATOR SHIP. IT IS ALMOST IMPENETRABLE.
ALMOST?

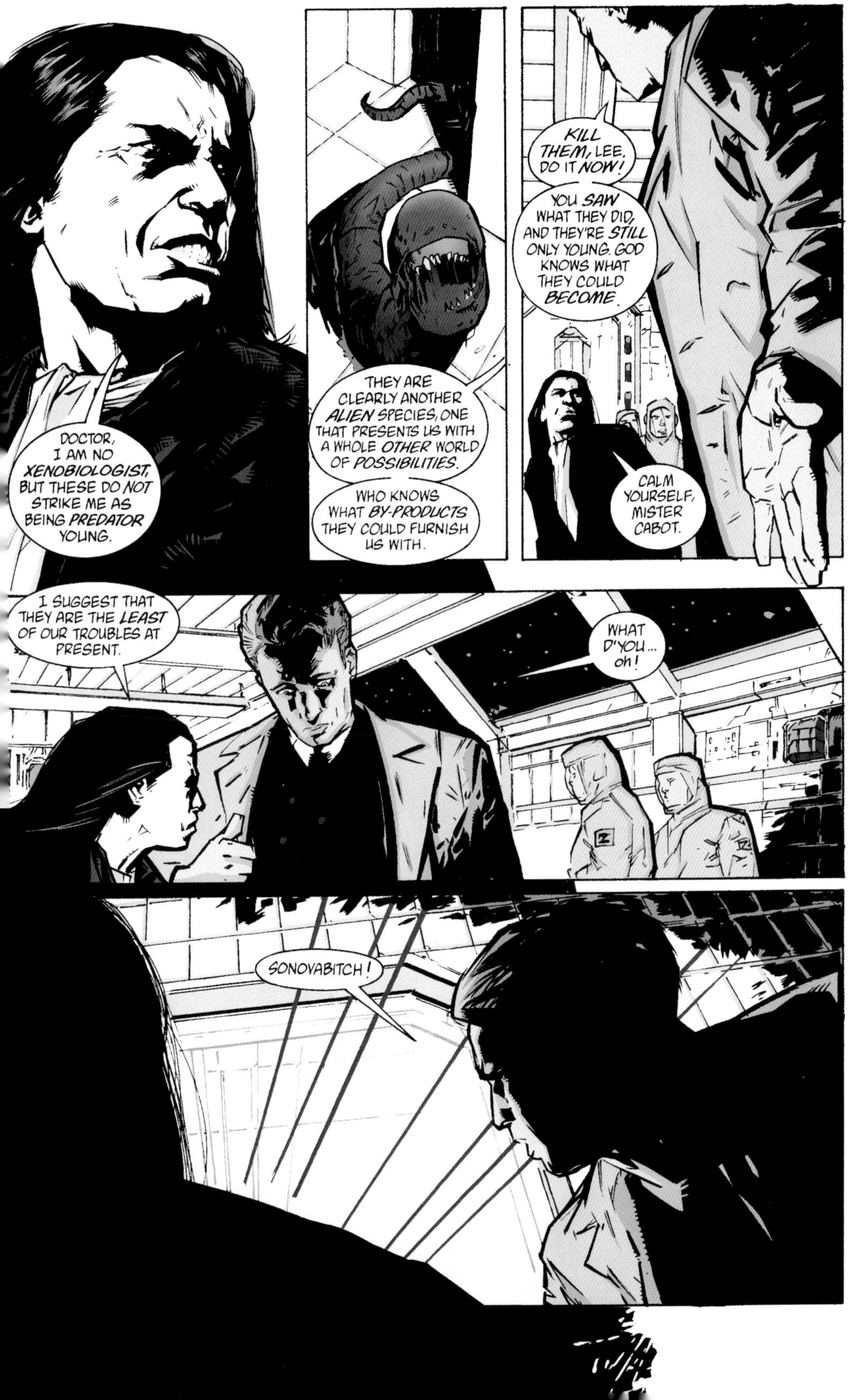

DOCTOR, I AM NO XENOBIOLOGIST, BUT THESE DO NOT STRIKE ME AS BEING PREDATOR YOUNG.
THEY ARE CLEARLY ANOTHER ALIEN SPECIES, ONE THAT PRESENTS US WITH A WHOLE OTHER WORLD OF POSSIBILITIES.
WHO KNOWS WHAT BY-PRODUCTS THEY COULD FURNISH US WITH.
KILL THEM, LEE. DO IT NOW!
YOU SAW WHAT THEY DID, AND THEY'RE STILL ONLY YOUNG. GOD KNOWS WHAT THEY COULD BECOME.
CALM YOURSELF, MISTER CABOT.
I SUGGEST THAT THEY ARE THE LEAST OF OUR TROUBLES AT PRESENT.
WHAT D'YOU... oh!
SONOVABITCH!

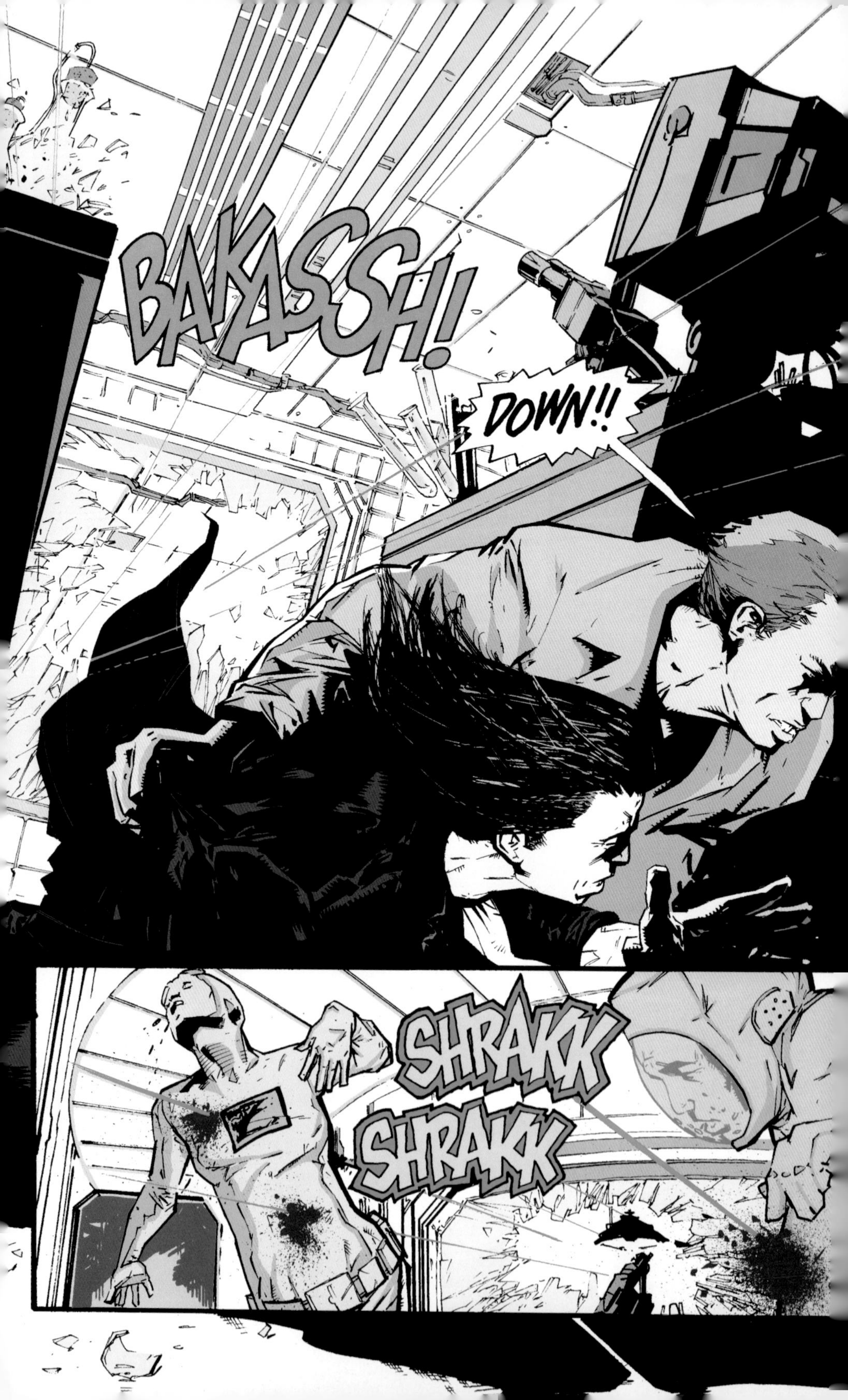
BAKASSH!
DOWN!!
SHRAKK
SHRAKK

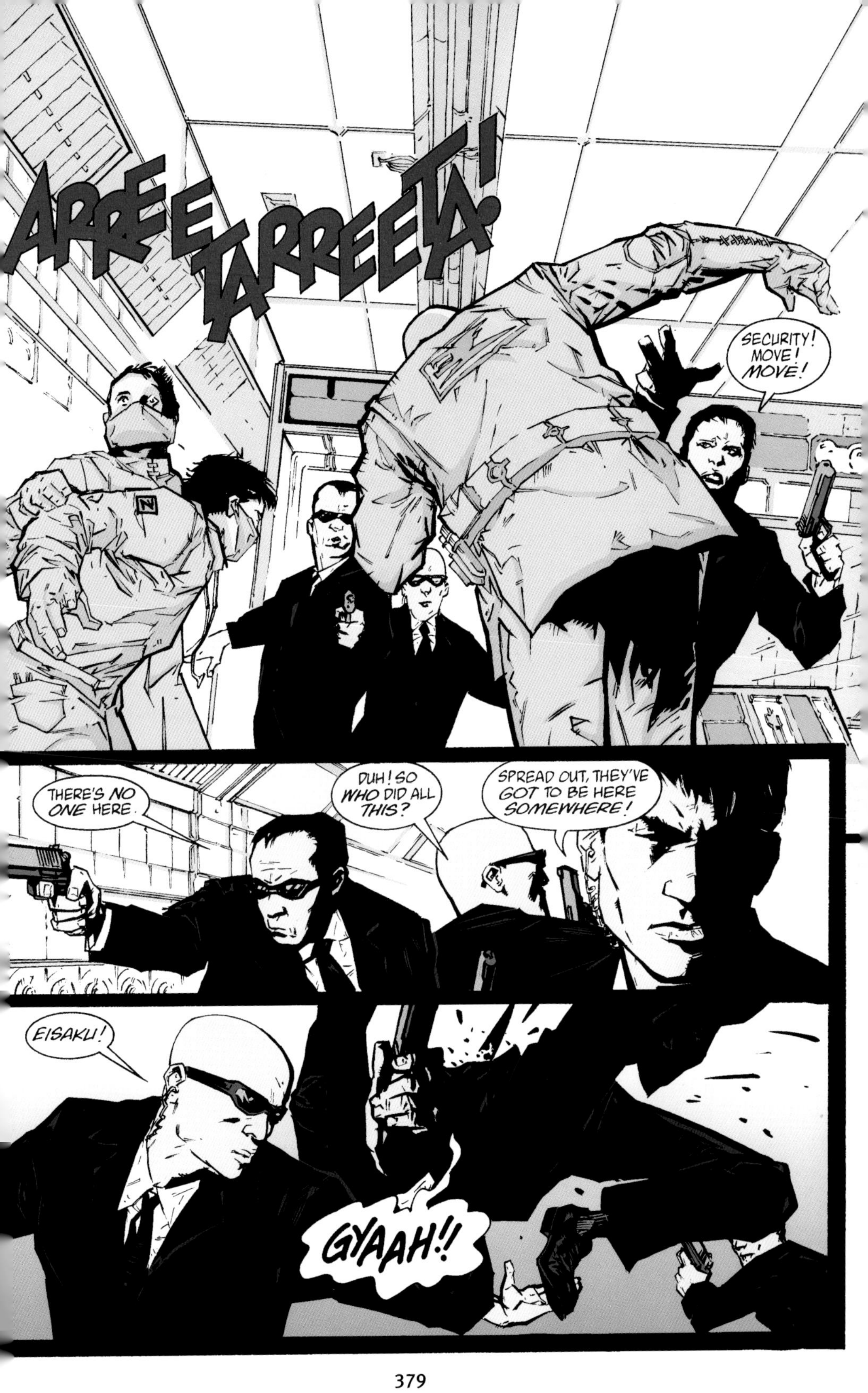
ARREE TARREETA!
SECURITY! MOVE! MOVE!
THERE'S NO ONE HERE.
DUH! SO WHO DID ALL THIS?
SPREAD OUT, THEY'VE GOT TO BE HERE SOMEWHERE!
EISAKU!
GYAAH!!

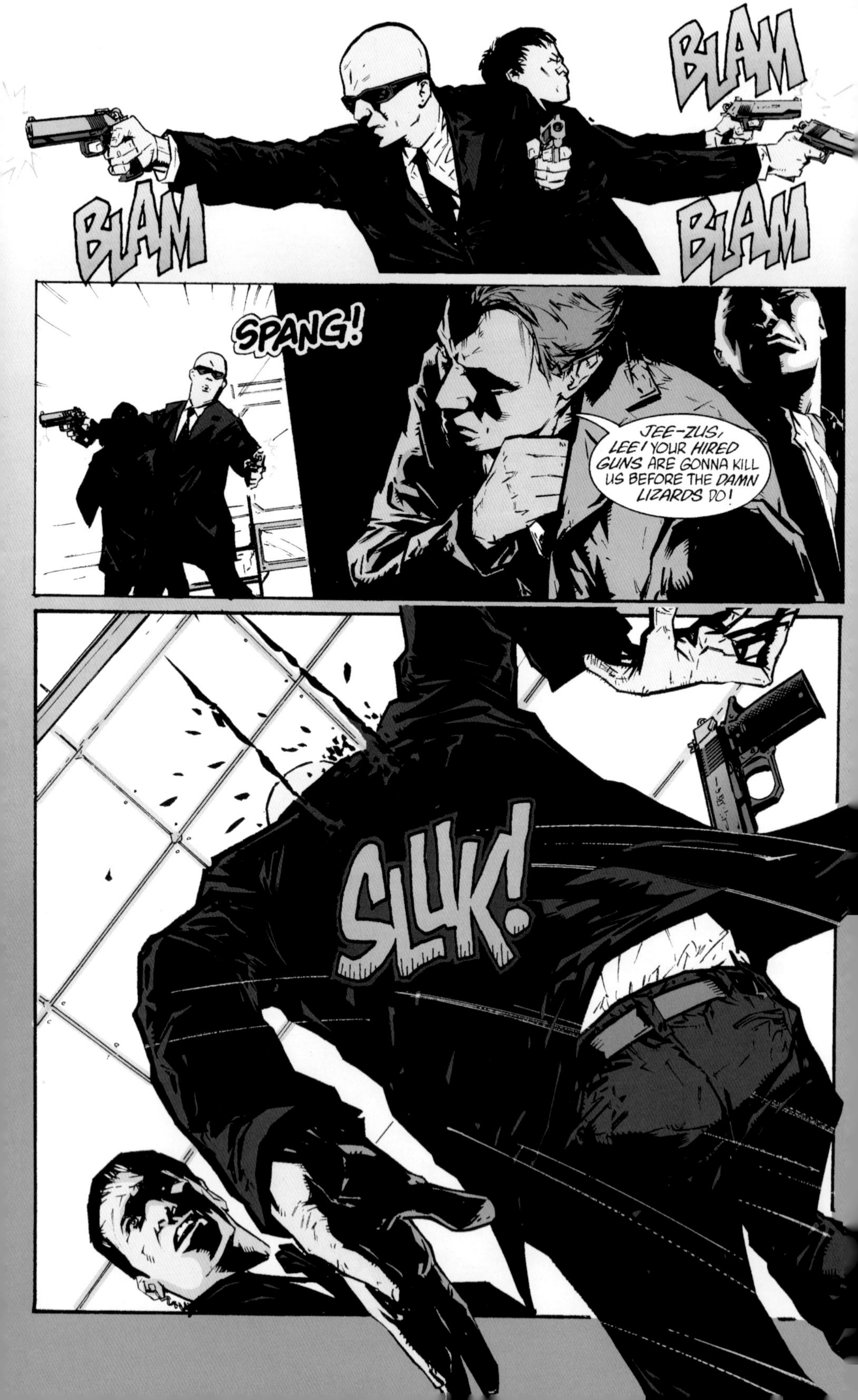
BLAM
BLAM
BLAM
SPANG!
JEE-ZUS, LEE! YOUR HIRED GUNS ARE GONNA KILL US BEFORE THE DAMN LIZARDS DO!
SLUK!

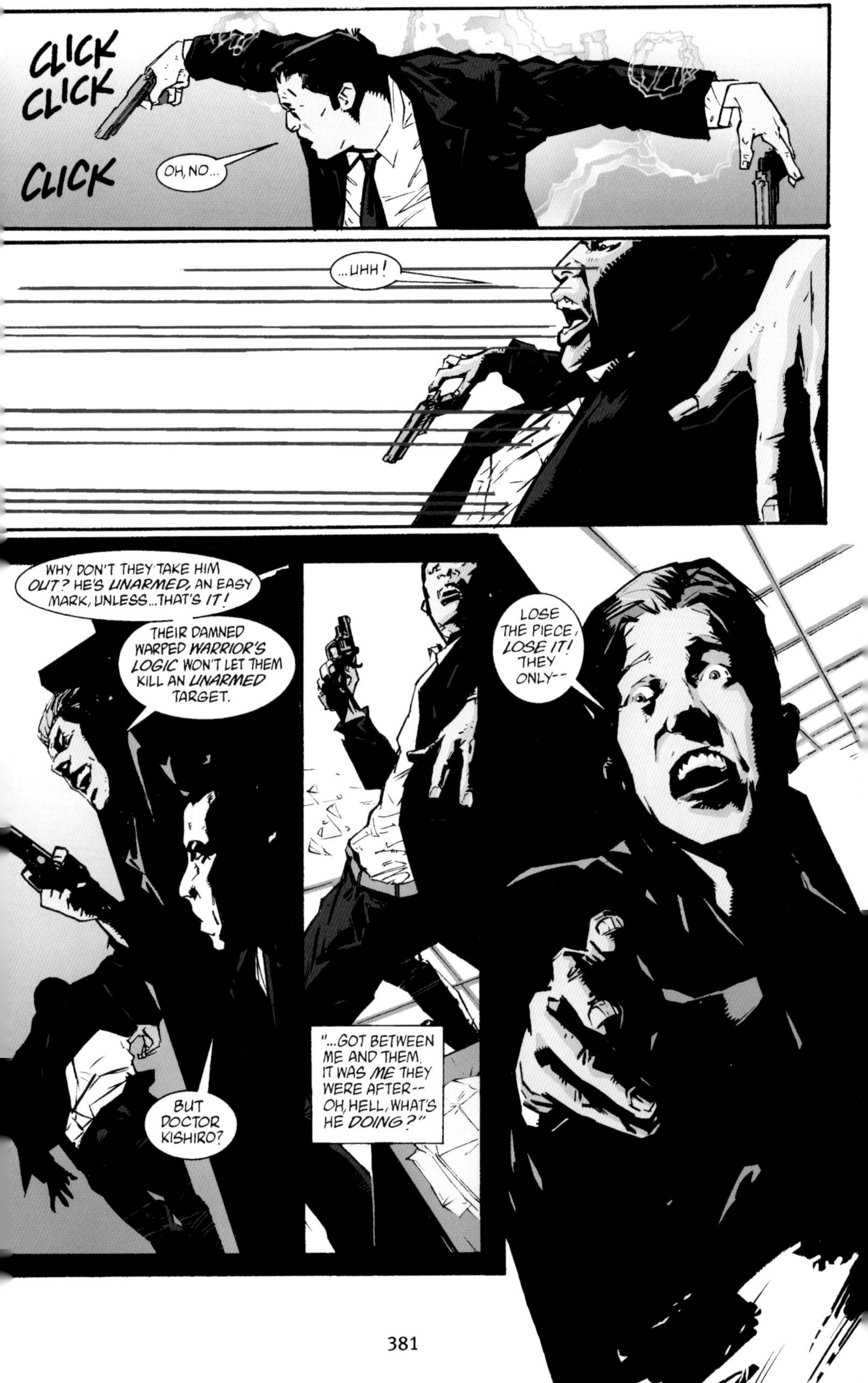
CLICK CLICK
CLICK
OH, NO...
...UHH!
WHY DON'T THEY TAKE HIM OUT? HE'S UNARMED, AN EASY MARK, UNLESS...THAT'S IT!
THEIR DAMNED WARPED WARRIOR'S LOGIC WON'T LET THEM KILL AN UNARMED TARGET.
BUT DOCTOR KISHIRO?
LOSE THE PIECE, LOSE IT! THEY ONLY--
"...GOT BETWEEN ME AND THEM. IT WAS ME THEY WERE AFTER-- OH, HELL, WHAT'S HE DOING?"

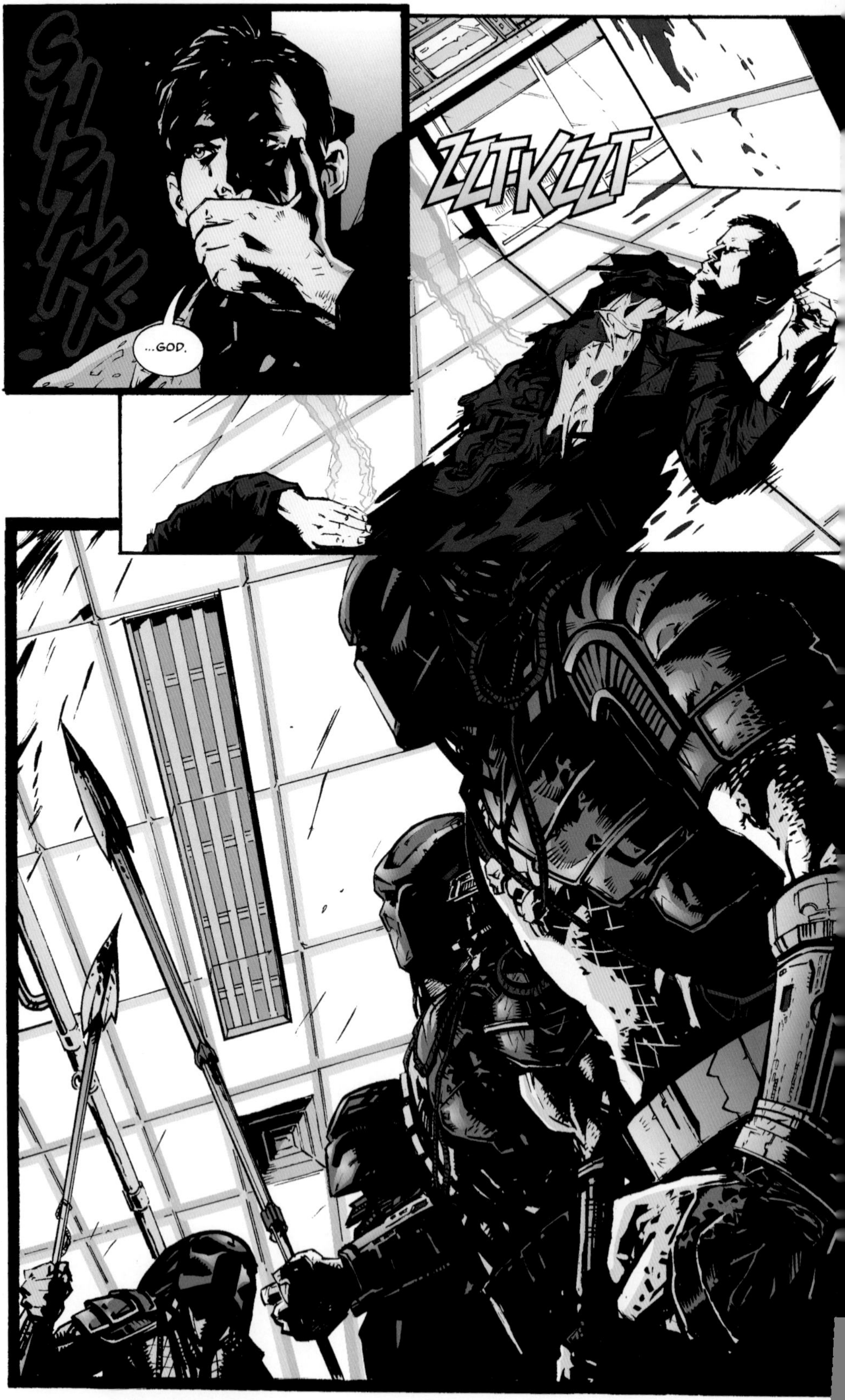
SHRAKK
...GOD.
ZZT-KZZT

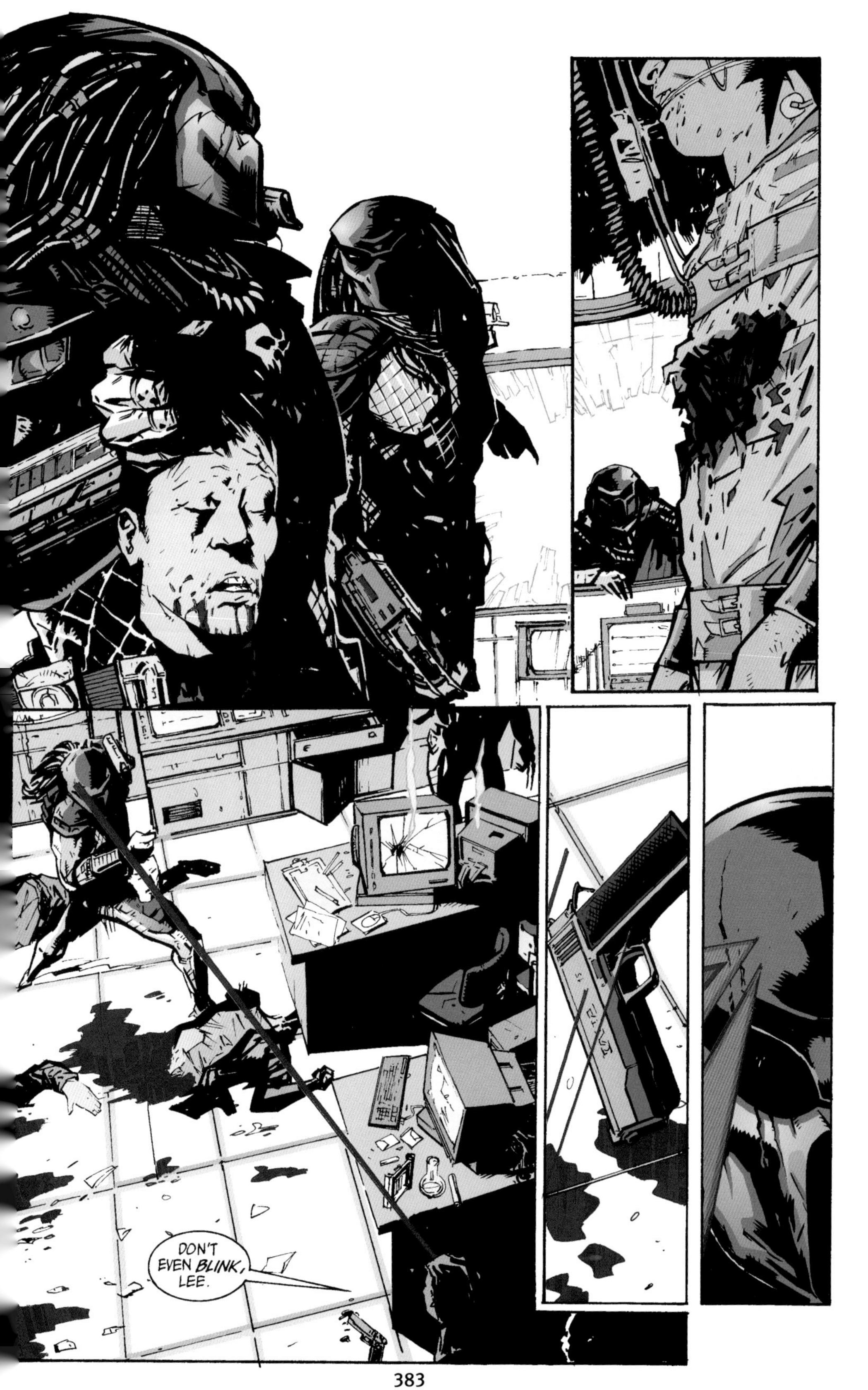
DON'T EVEN BLINK, LEE.

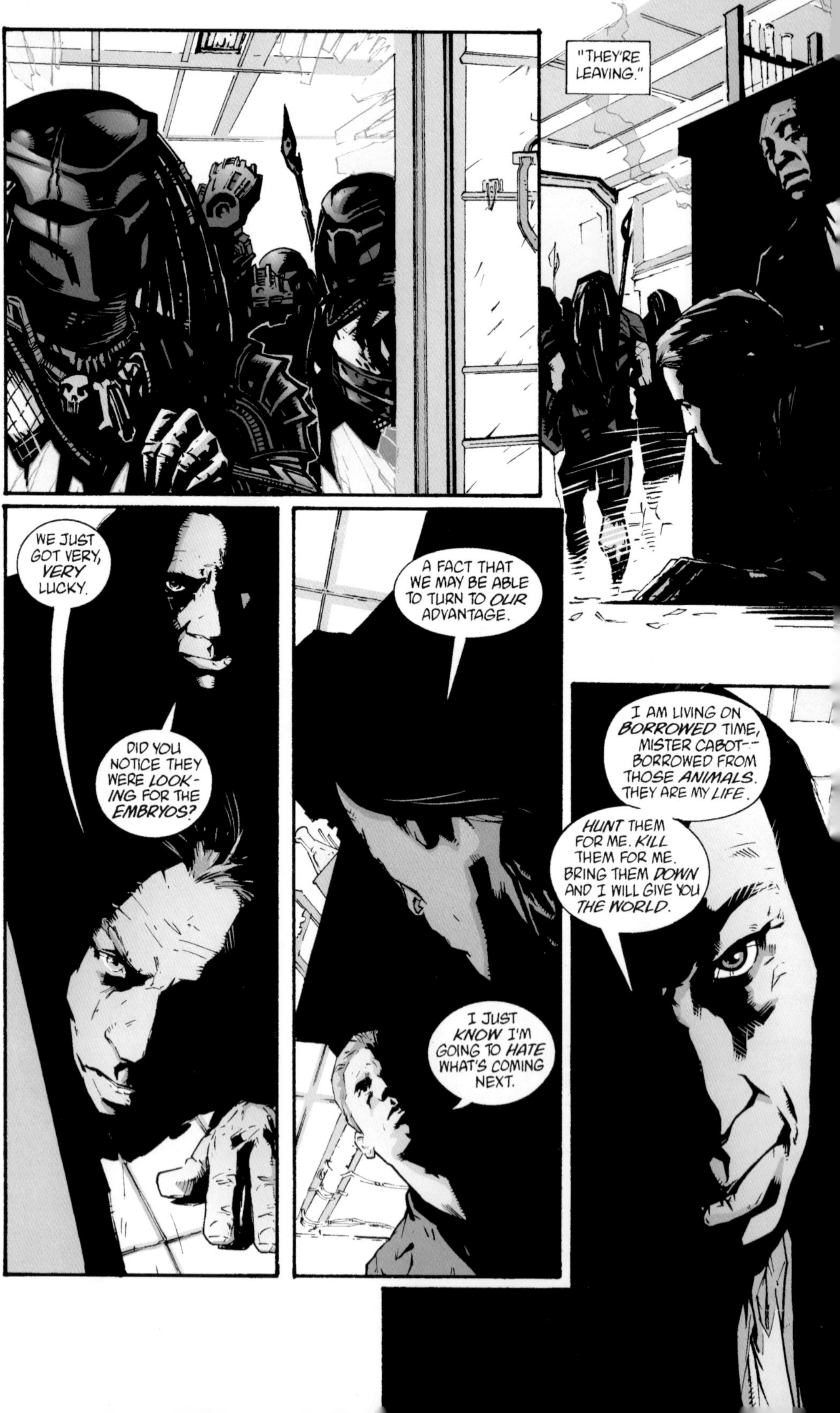
"THEY'RE LEAVING."
WE JUST GOT VERY, VERY LUCKY.
DID YOU NOTICE THEY WERE LOOKING FOR THE EMBRYOS?
A FACT THAT WE MAY BE ABLE TO TURN TO OUR ADVANTAGE.
I JUST KNOW I'M GOING TO HATE WHAT'S COMING NEXT.
I AM LIVING ON BORROWED TIME, MISTER CABOT-- BORROWED FROM THOSE ANIMALS. THEY ARE MY LIFE.
HUNT THEM FOR ME. KILL THEM FOR ME. BRING THEM DOWN AND I WILL GIVE YOU THE WORLD.

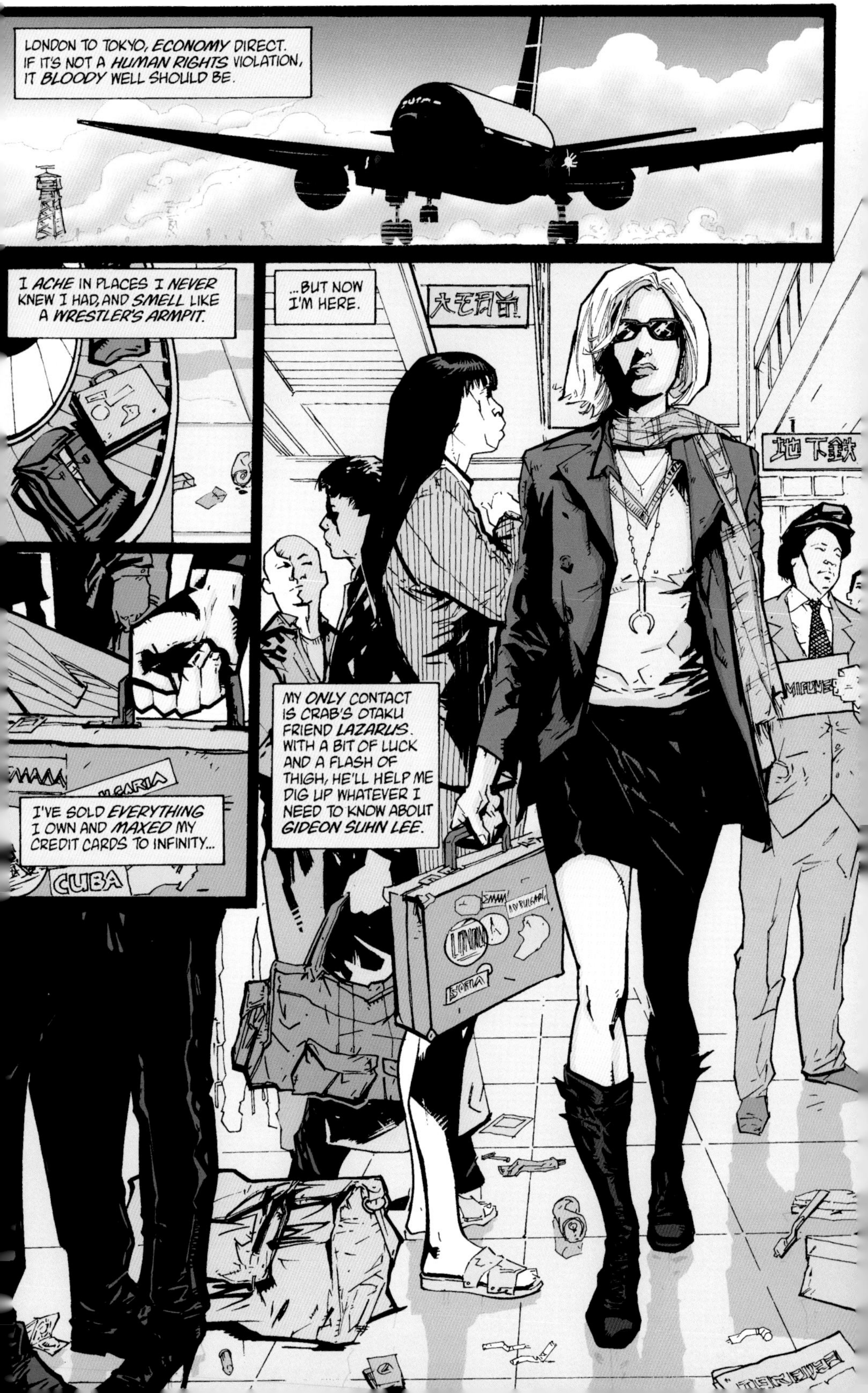
LONDON TO TOKYO, ECONOMY DIRECT. IF IT'S NOT A HUMAN RIGHTS VIOLATION, IT BLOODY WELL SHOULD BE.
I ACHE IN PLACES I NEVER KNEW I HAD, AND SMELL LIKE A WRESTLER'S ARMPIT.
I'VE SOLD EVERYTHING I OWN AND MAXED MY CREDIT CARDS TO INFINITY...
...BUT NOW I'M HERE.
MY ONLY CONTACT IS CRAB'S OTAKU FRIEND LAZARUS. WITH A BIT OF LUCK AND A FLASH OF THIGH, HE'LL HELP ME DIG UP WHATEVER I NEED TO KNOW ABOUT GIDEON SUHN LEE.
地下鉄
CUBA

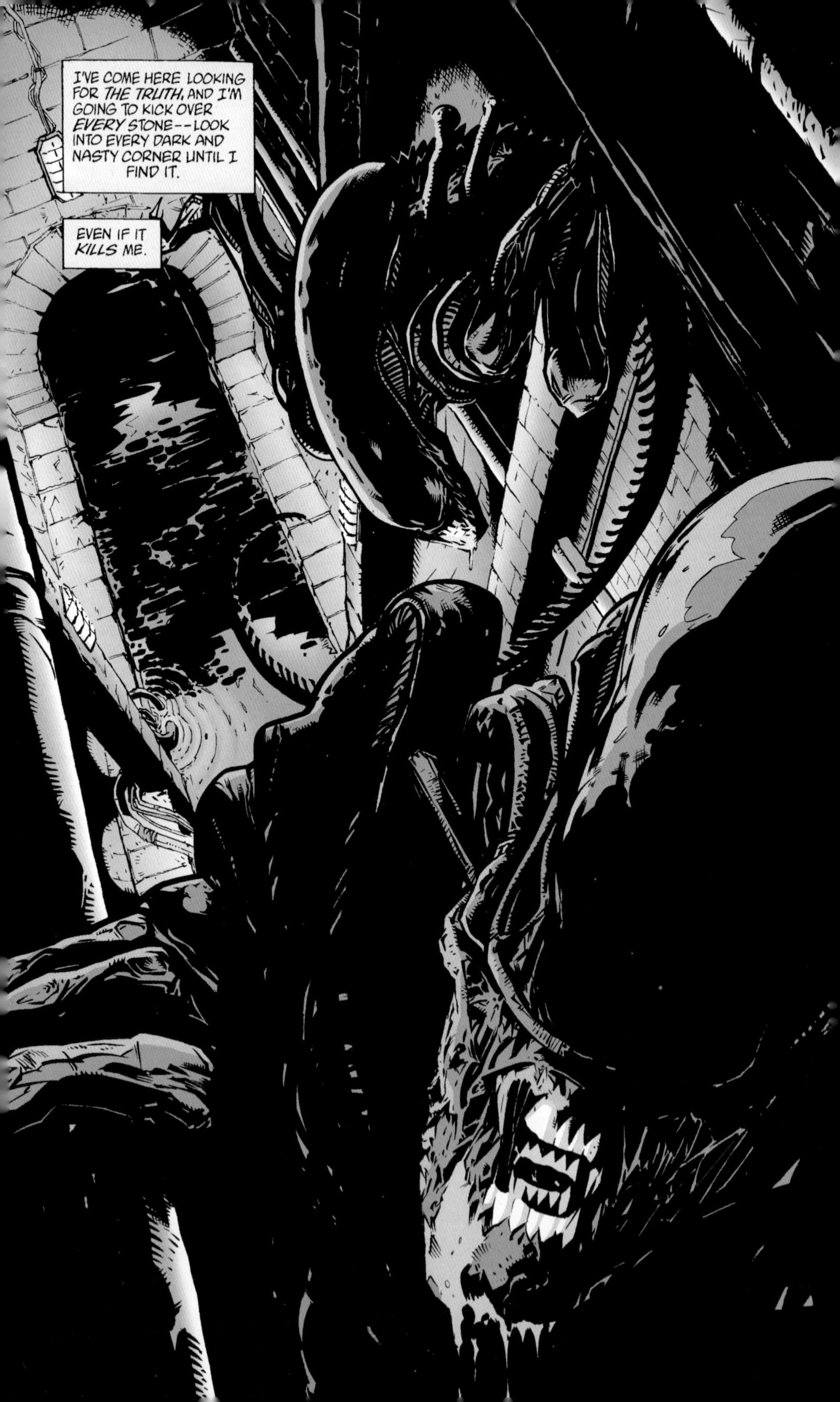
I'VE COME HERE LOOKING FOR *THE TRUTH*, AND I'M GOING TO KICK OVER *EVERY* STONE--LOOK INTO EVERY DARK AND NASTY CORNER UNTIL I FIND IT.
EVEN IF IT *KILLS* ME.

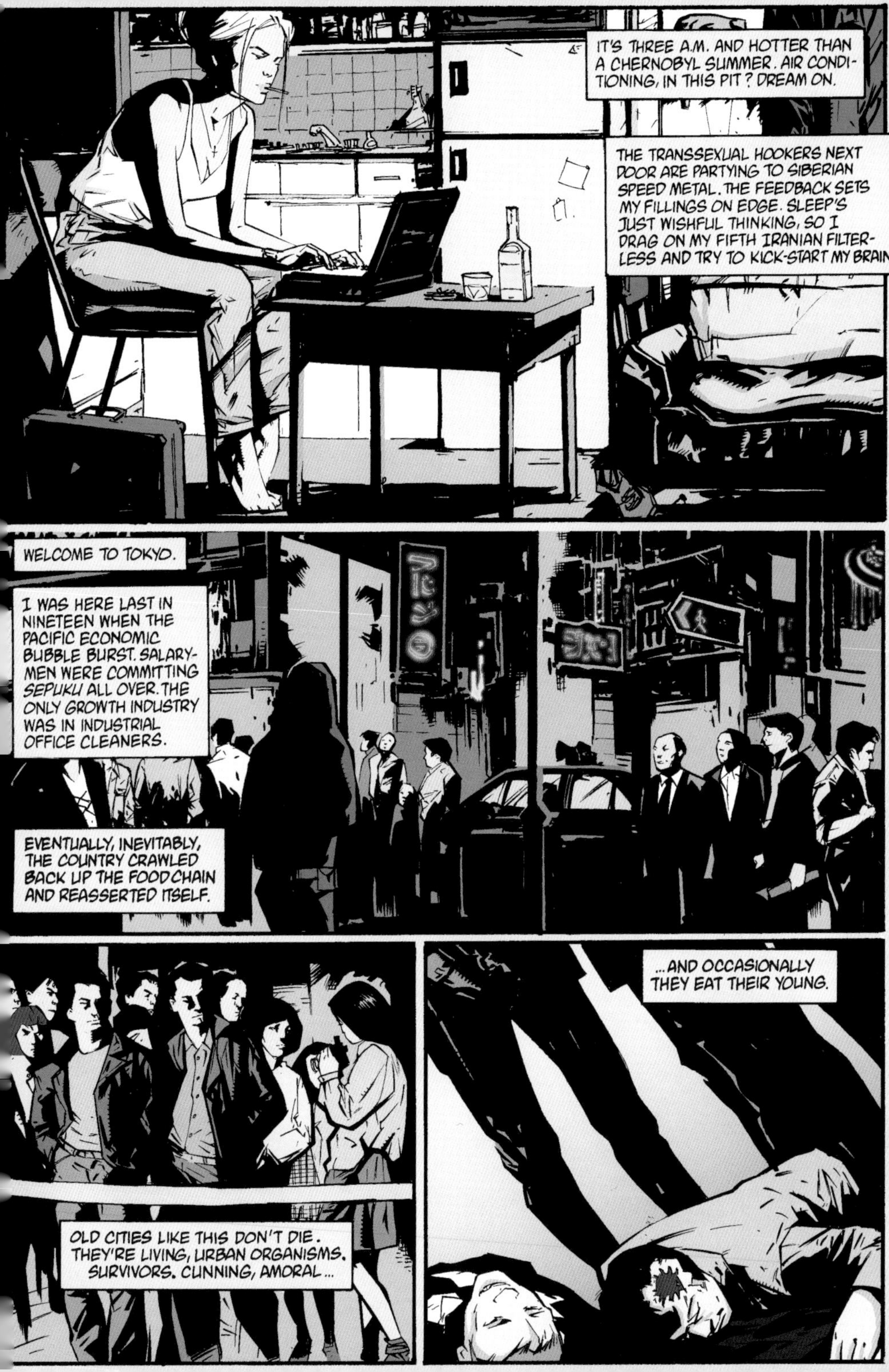
IT'S THREE A.M. AND HOTTER THAN A CHERNOBYL SUMMER. AIR CONDITIONING, IN THIS PIT? DREAM ON.
THE TRANSSEXUAL HOOKERS NEXT DOOR ARE PARTYING TO SIBERIAN SPEED METAL. THE FEEDBACK SETS MY FILLINGS ON EDGE. SLEEP'S JUST WISHFUL THINKING, SO I DRAG ON MY FIFTH IRANIAN FILTERLESS AND TRY TO KICK-START MY BRAIN
WELCOME TO TOKYO.
I WAS HERE LAST IN NINETEEN WHEN THE PACIFIC ECONOMIC BUBBLE BURST. SALARYMEN WERE COMMITTING SEPUKU ALL OVER. THE ONLY GROWTH INDUSTRY WAS IN INDUSTRIAL OFFICE CLEANERS.
EVENTUALLY, INEVITABLY, THE COUNTRY CRAWLED BACK UP THE FOOD CHAIN AND REASSERTED ITSELF.
OLD CITIES LIKE THIS DON'T DIE. THEY'RE LIVING, URBAN ORGANISMS. SURVIVORS. CUNNING, AMORAL...
...AND OCCASIONALLY THEY EAT THEIR YOUNG.

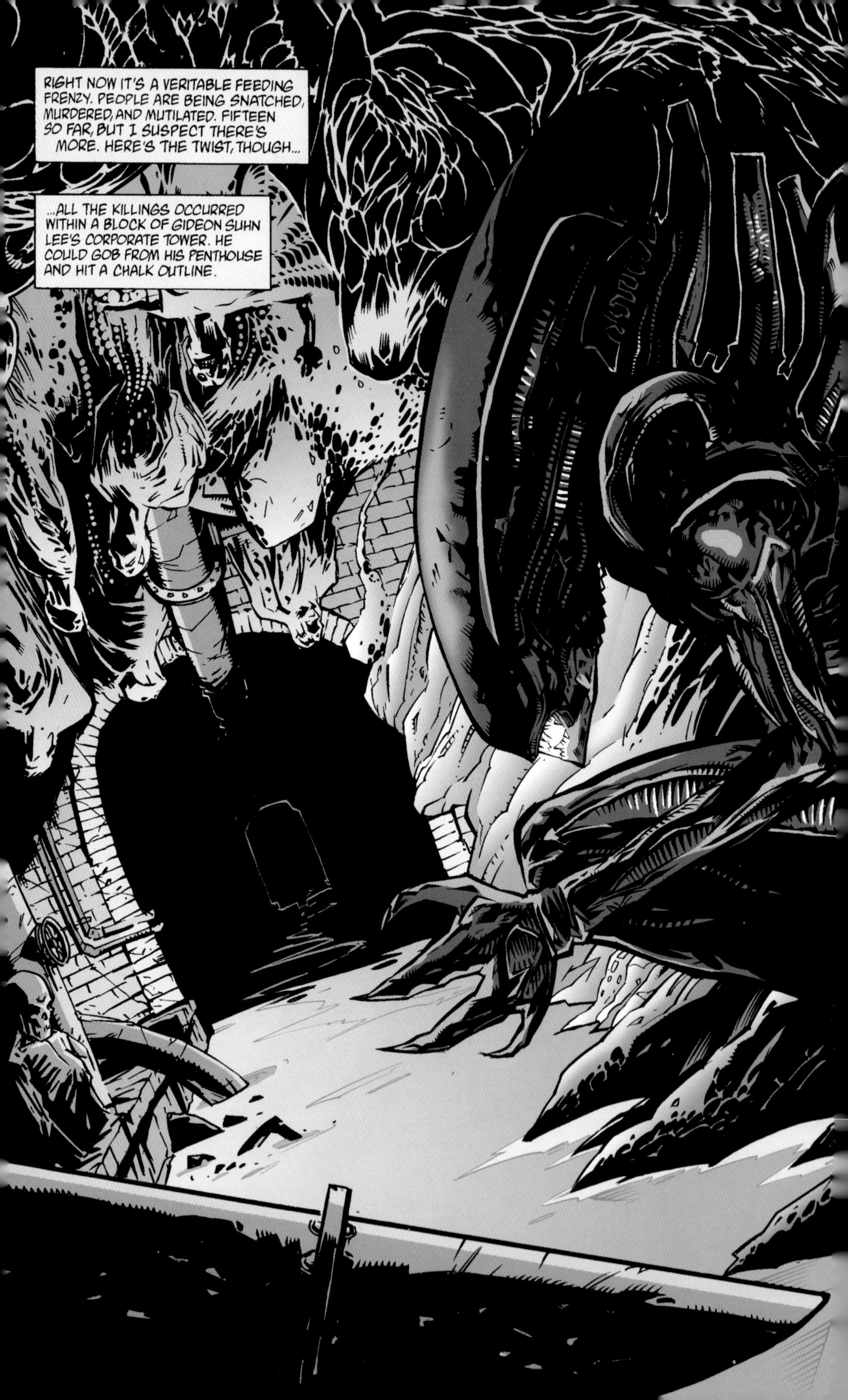
RIGHT NOW IT'S A VERITABLE FEEDING FRENZY. PEOPLE ARE BEING SNATCHED, MURDERED, AND MUTILATED. FIFTEEN SO FAR, BUT I SUSPECT THERE'S MORE. HERE'S THE TWIST, THOUGH...
...ALL THE KILLINGS OCCURRED WITHIN A BLOCK OF GIDEON SUHN LEE'S CORPORATE TOWER. HE COULD GOB FROM HIS PENTHOUSE AND HIT A CHALK OUTLINE.

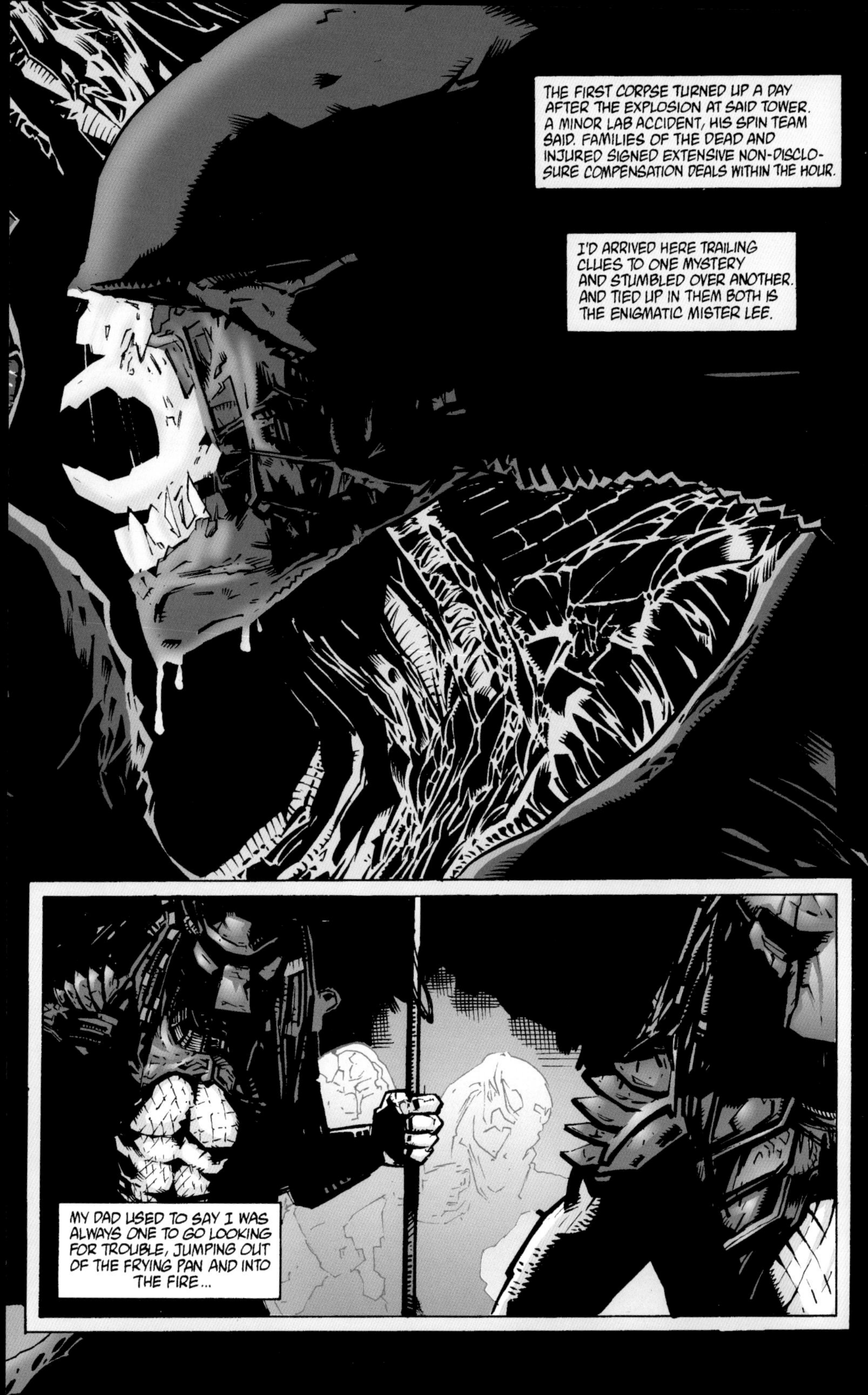
THE FIRST CORPSE TURNED UP A DAY AFTER THE EXPLOSION AT SAID TOWER. A MINOR LAB ACCIDENT, HIS SPIN TEAM SAID. FAMILIES OF THE DEAD AND INJURED SIGNED EXTENSIVE NON-DISCLOSURE COMPENSATION DEALS WITHIN THE HOUR.
I'D ARRIVED HERE TRAILING CLUES TO ONE MYSTERY AND STUMBLED OVER ANOTHER. AND TIED UP IN THEM BOTH IS THE ENIGMATIC MISTER LEE.
MY DAD USED TO SAY I WAS ALWAYS ONE TO GO LOOKING FOR TROUBLE, JUMPING OUT OF THE FRYING PAN AND INTO THE FIRE...

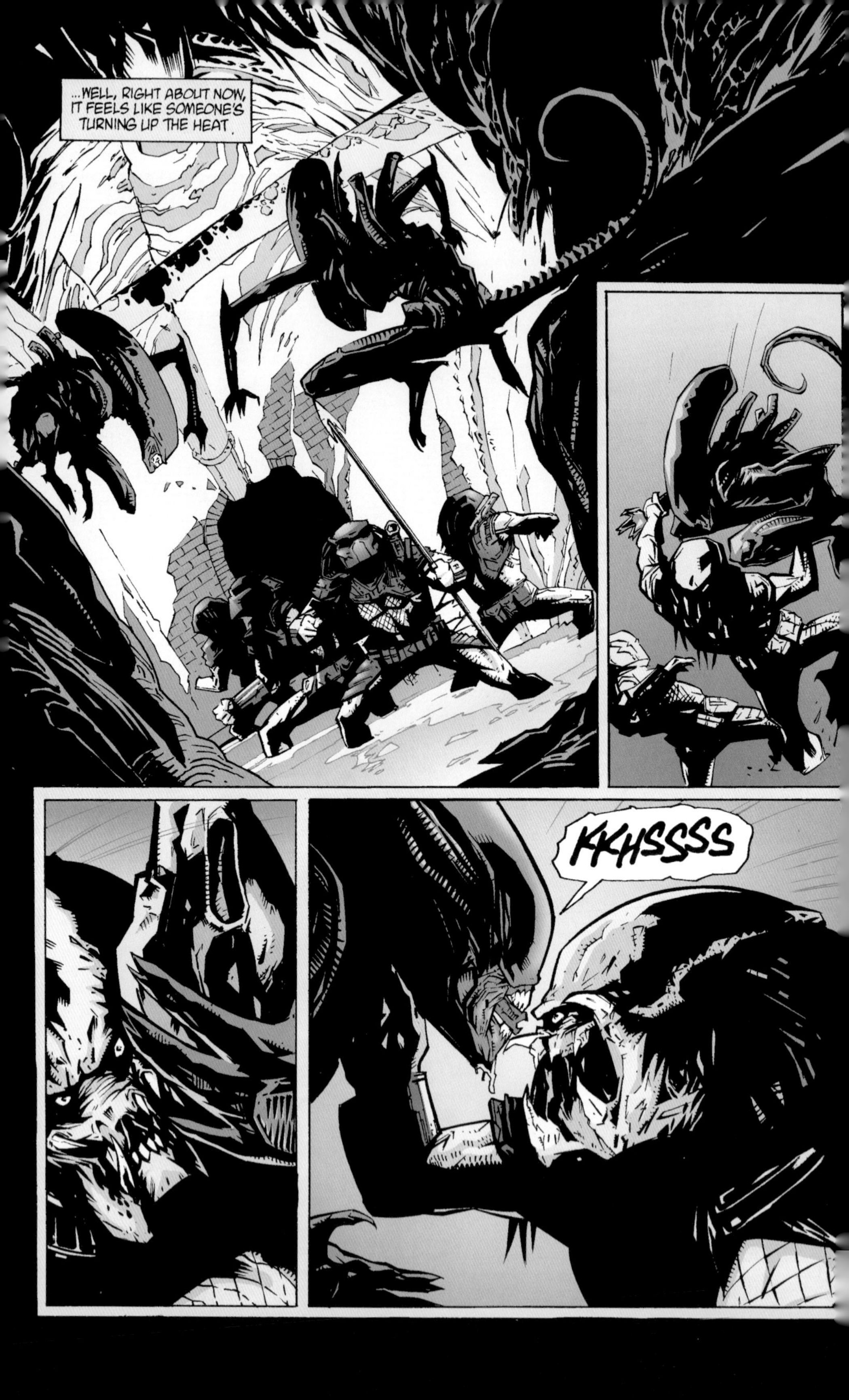
...WELL, RIGHT ABOUT NOW, IT FEELS LIKE SOMEONE'S TURNING UP THE HEAT.
KKHSSSS

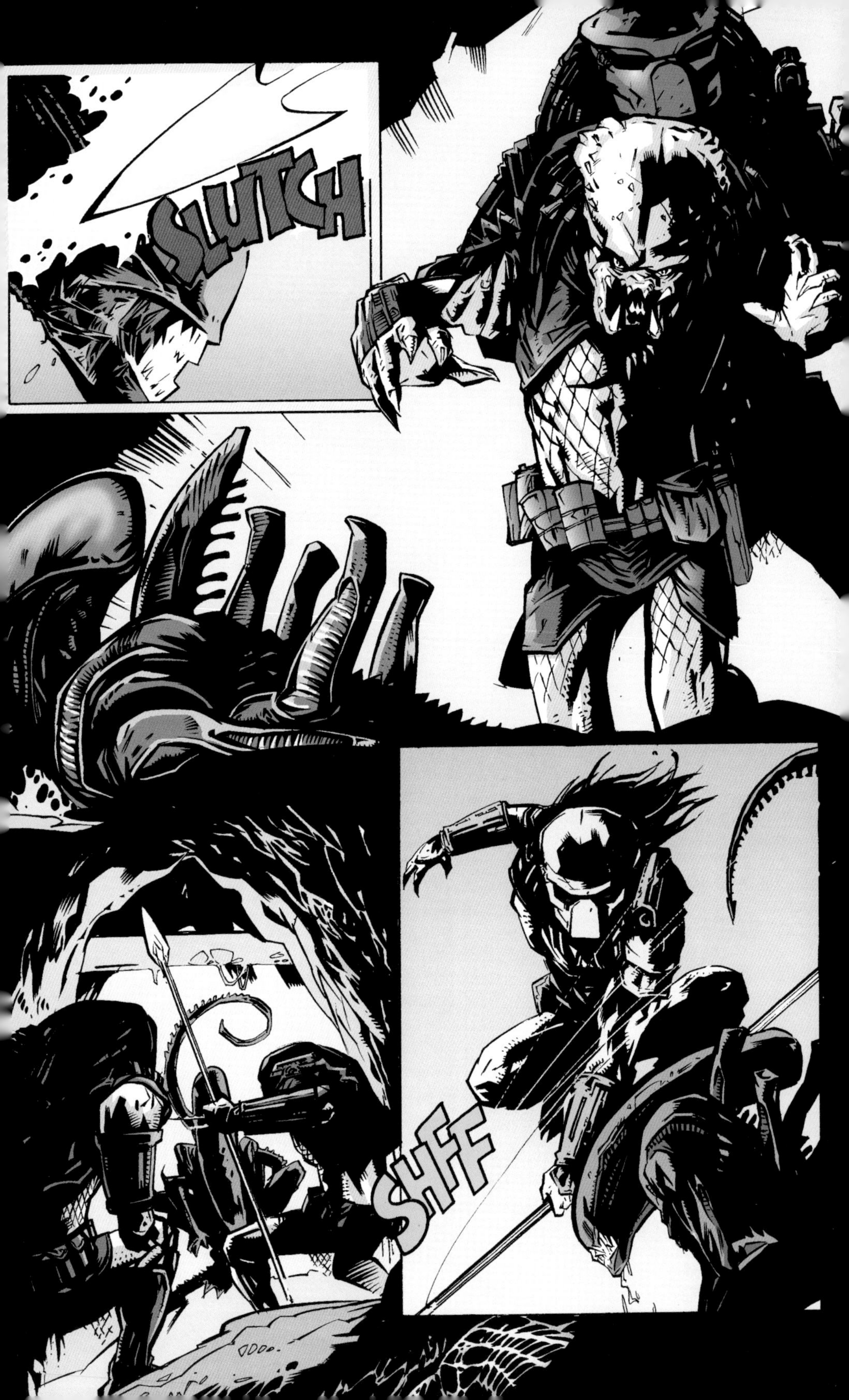
SLUTCH
SHFF

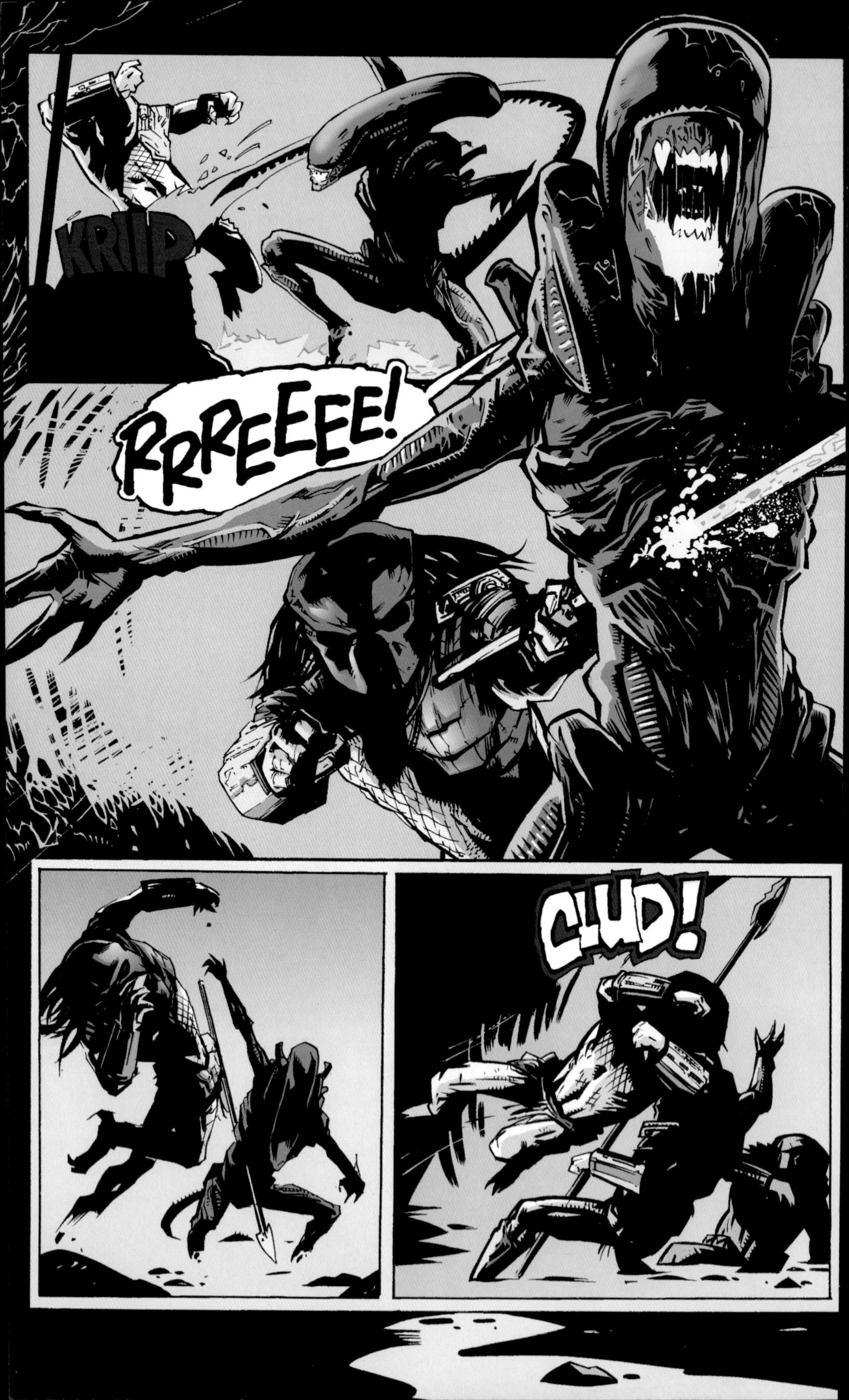
KRIIP
RRREEEEE!
CLUD!

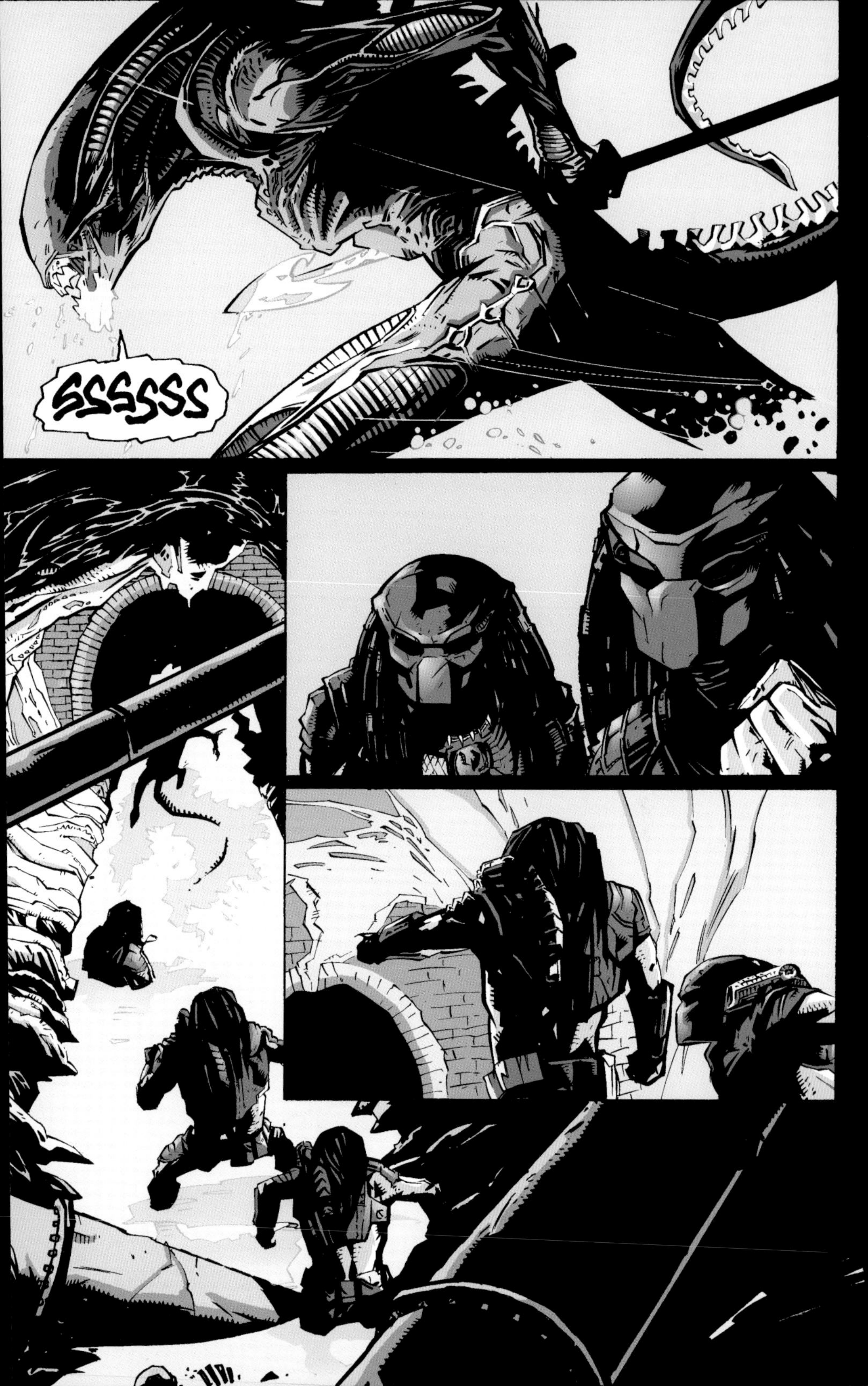
SSSSSS

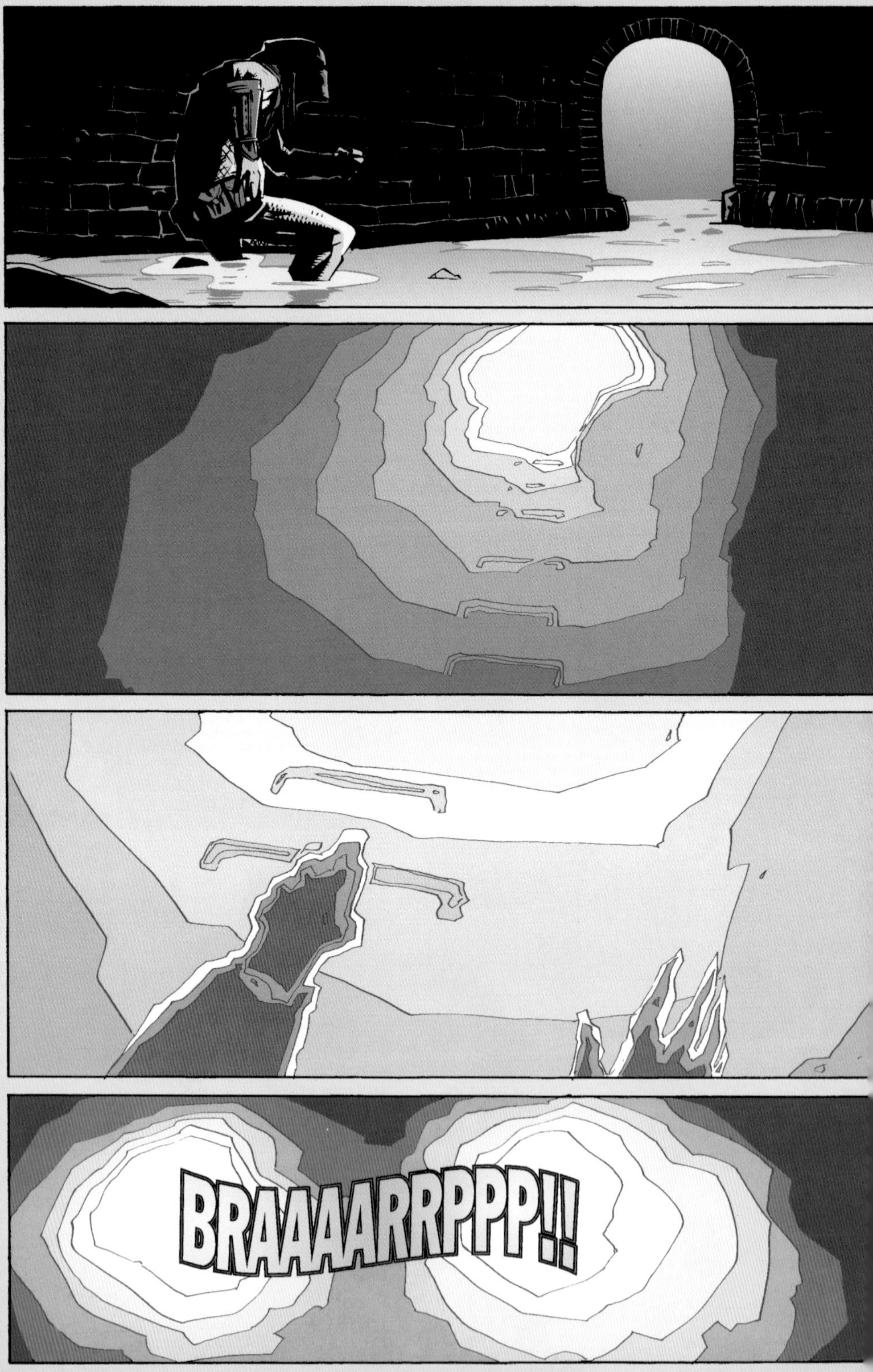
BRAAAARRPPP!!!

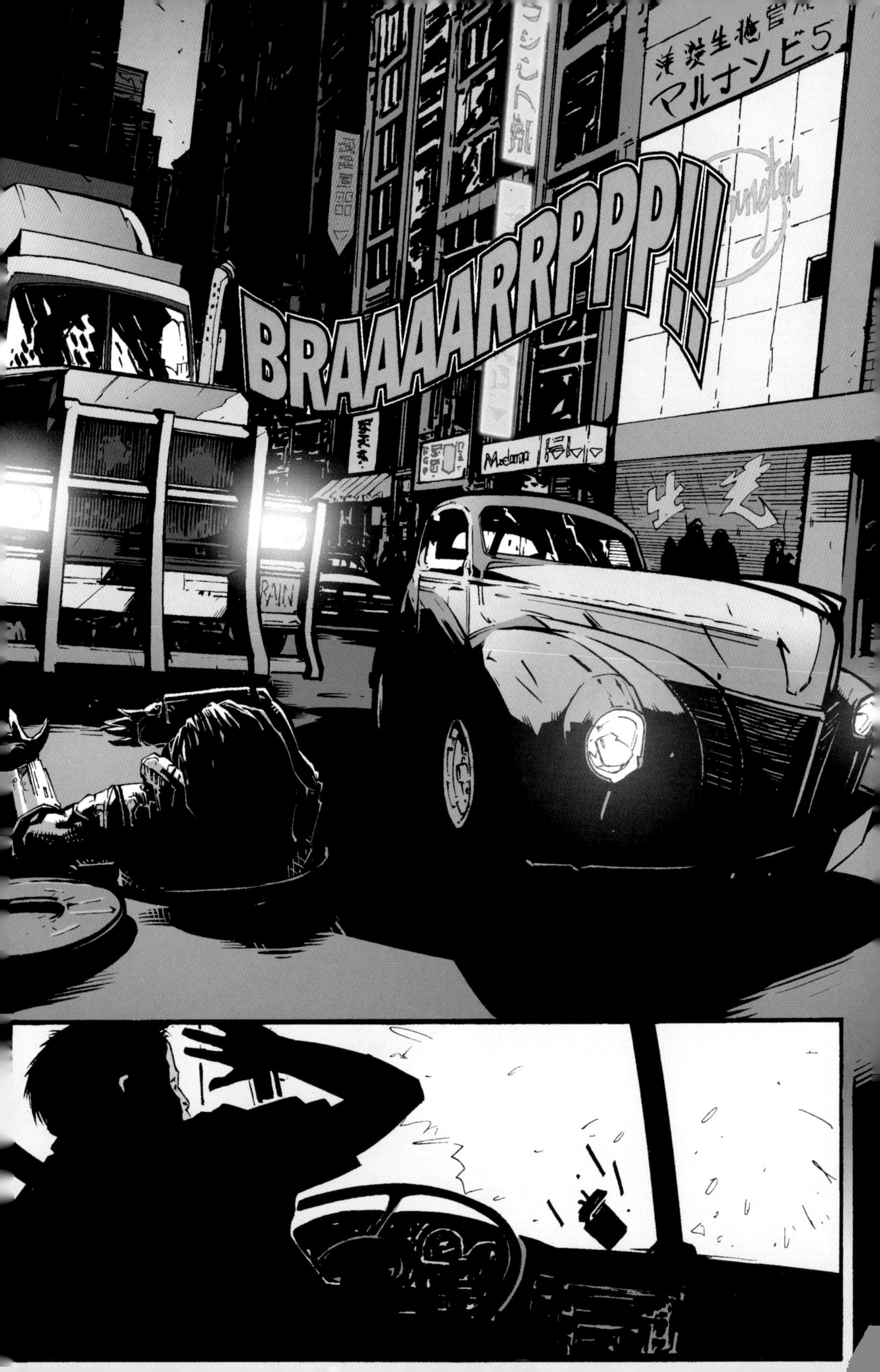
BRAAAARRRPPP!!
RAIN

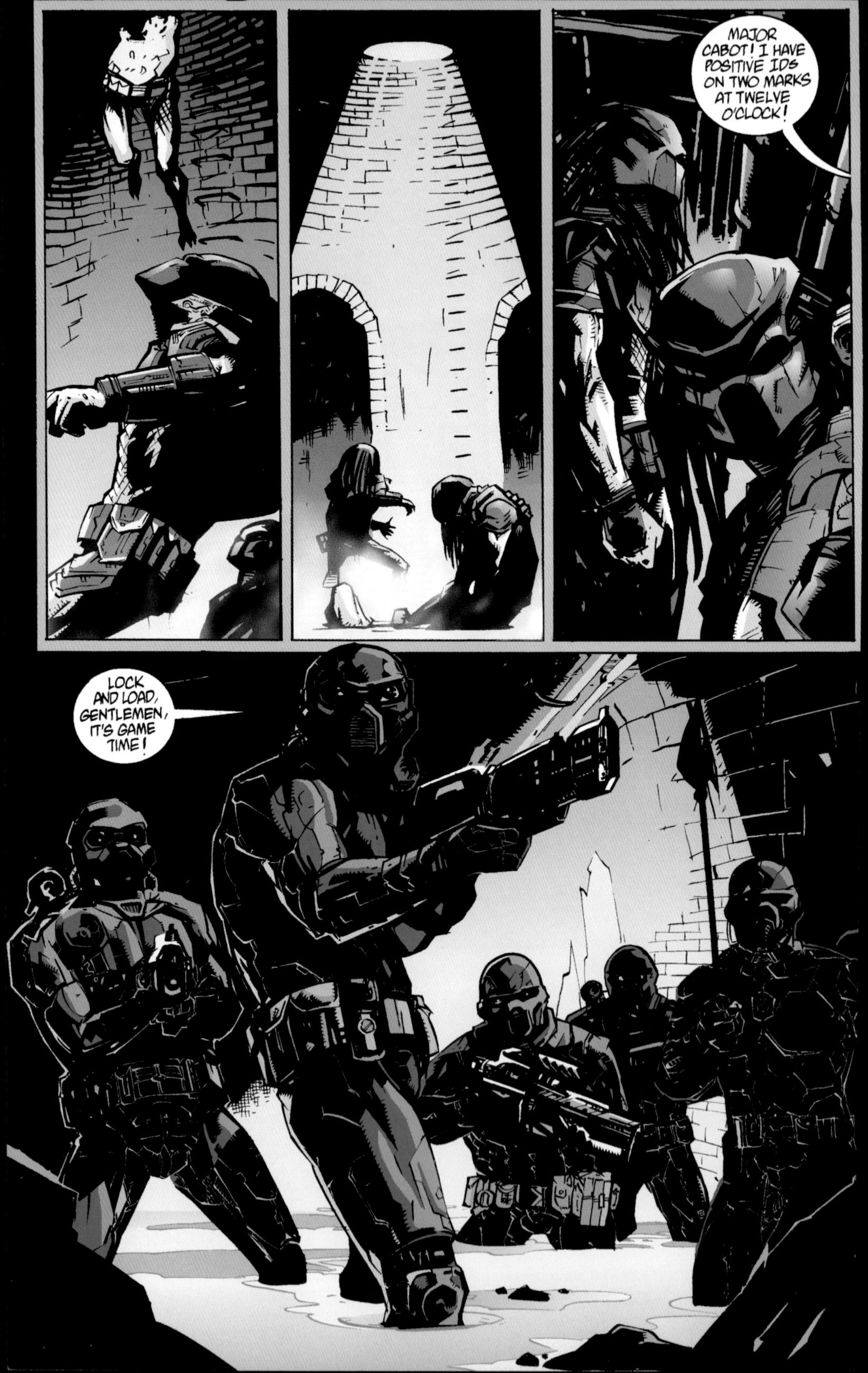
MAJOR CABOT! I HAVE POSITIVE IDS ON TWO MARKS AT TWELVE O'CLOCK!
LOCK AND LOAD, GENTLEMEN, IT'S GAME TIME!

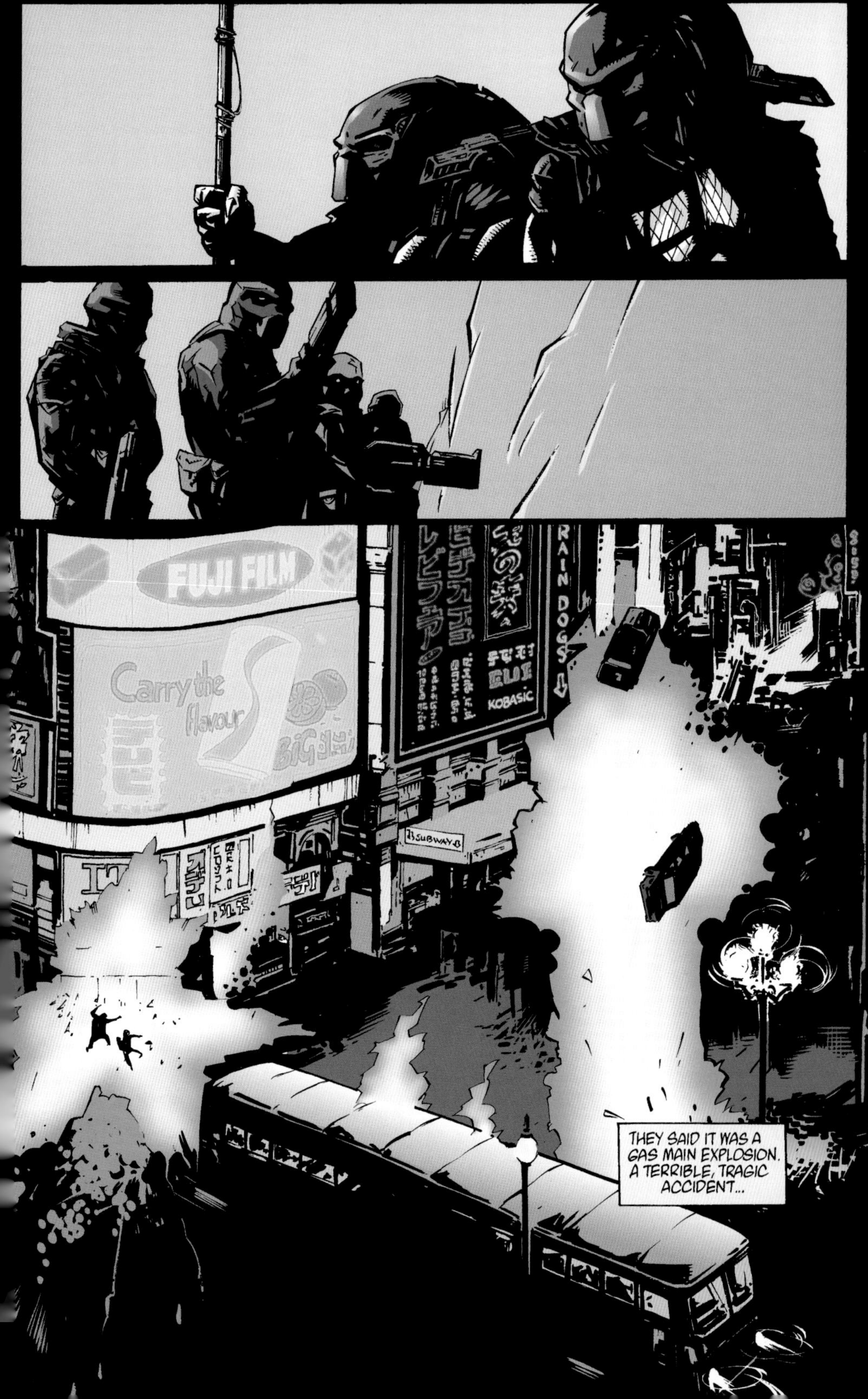
FUJI FILM
Carry the flavour
RAIN DOGS
KOBASIC
SUBWAY
THEY SAID IT WAS A GAS MAIN EXPLOSION. A TERRIBLE, TRAGIC ACCIDENT...

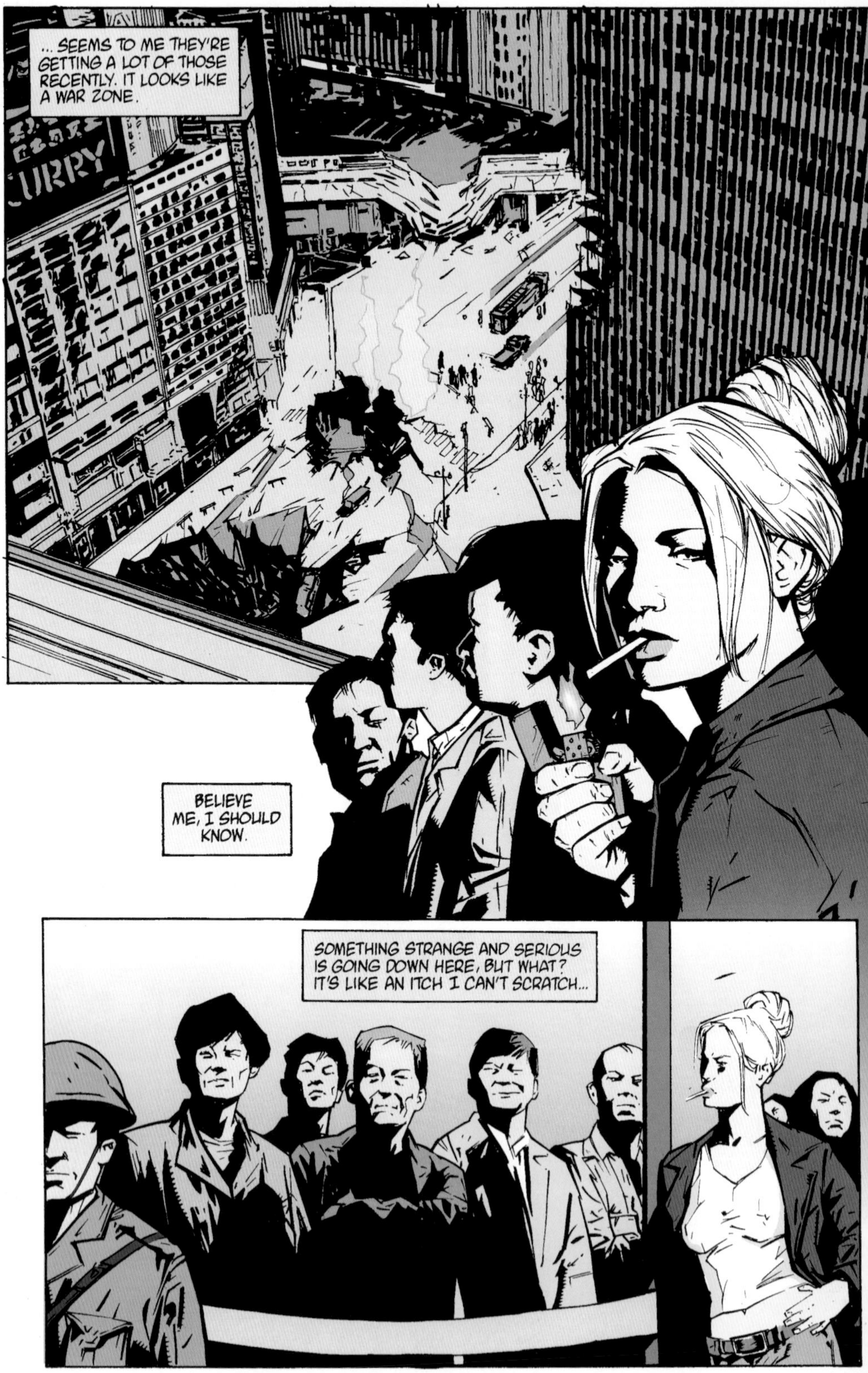
... SEEMS TO ME THEY'RE GETTING A LOT OF THOSE RECENTLY. IT LOOKS LIKE A WAR ZONE.
CURRY
BELIEVE ME, I SHOULD KNOW.
SOMETHING STRANGE AND SERIOUS IS GOING DOWN HERE, BUT WHAT? IT'S LIKE AN ITCH I CAN'T SCRATCH...

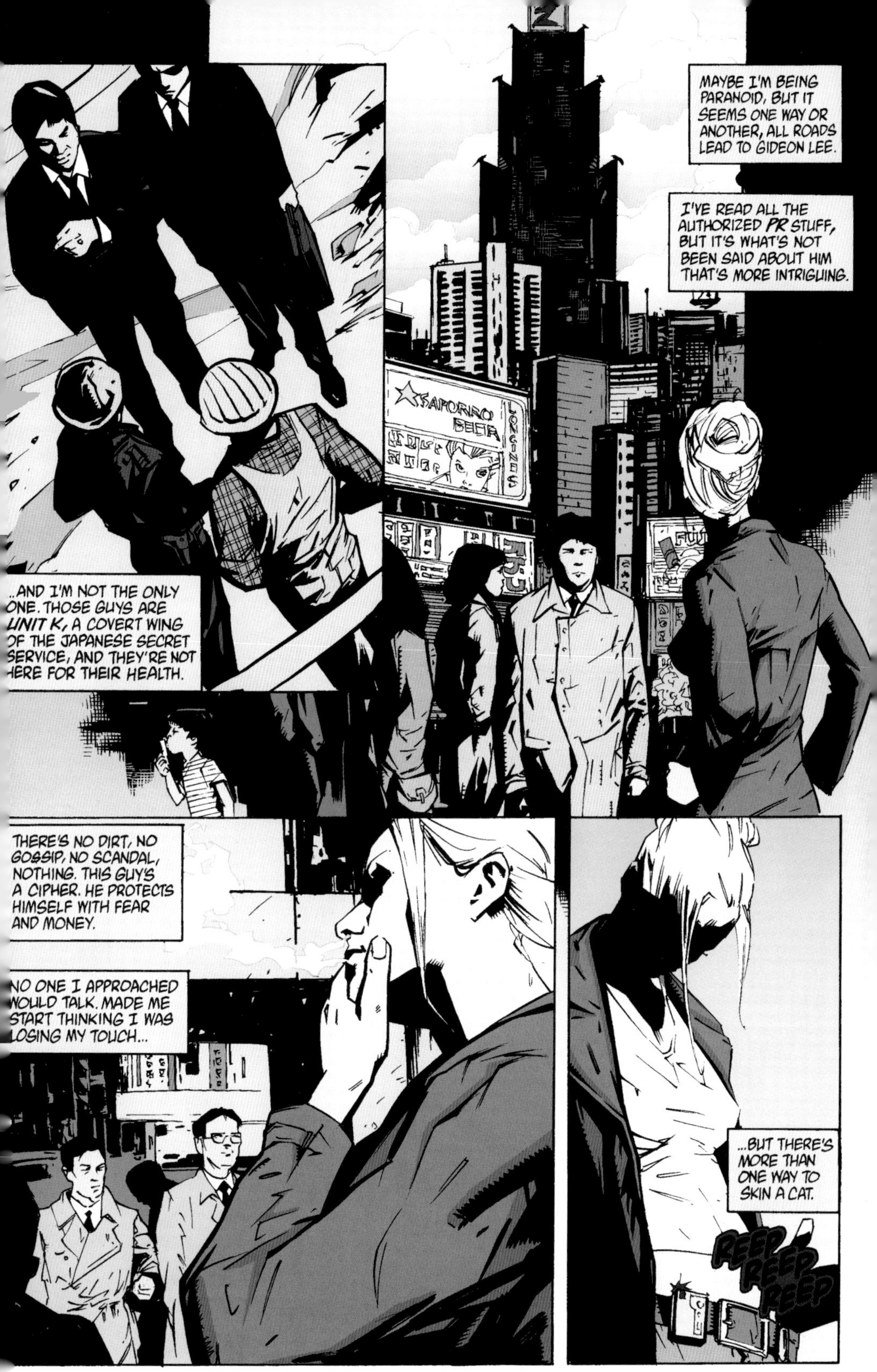
MAYBE I'M BEING PARANOID, BUT IT SEEMS ONE WAY OR ANOTHER, ALL ROADS LEAD TO GIDEON LEE.
I'VE READ ALL THE AUTHORIZED PR STUFF, BUT IT'S WHAT'S NOT BEEN SAID ABOUT HIM THAT'S MORE INTRIGUING.
..AND I'M NOT THE ONLY ONE. THOSE GUYS ARE UNIT K, A COVERT WING OF THE JAPANESE SECRET SERVICE, AND THEY'RE NOT HERE FOR THEIR HEALTH.
THERE'S NO DIRT, NO GOSSIP, NO SCANDAL, NOTHING. THIS GUY'S A CIPHER. HE PROTECTS HIMSELF WITH FEAR AND MONEY.
NO ONE I APPROACHED WOULD TALK. MADE ME START THINKING I WAS LOSING MY TOUCH...
...BUT THERE'S MORE THAN ONE WAY TO SKIN A CAT.
REEP REEP REEP

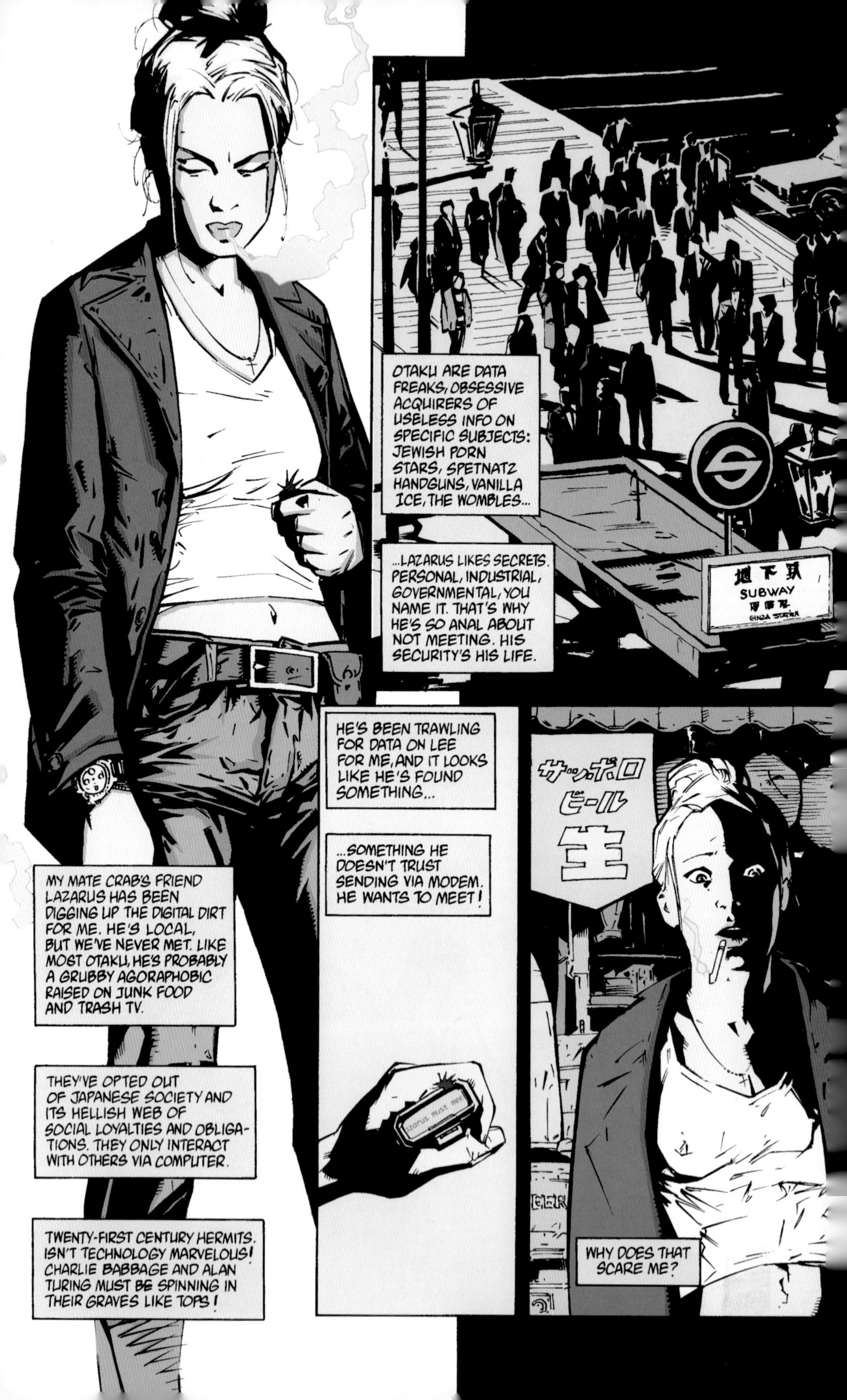
MY MATE CRAB'S FRIEND LAZARUS HAS BEEN DIGGING UP THE DIGITAL DIRT FOR ME. HE'S LOCAL, BUT WE'VE NEVER MET. LIKE MOST OTAKU, HE'S PROBABLY A GRUBBY AGORAPHOBIC RAISED ON JUNK FOOD AND TRASH TV.
THEY'VE OPTED OUT OF JAPANESE SOCIETY AND ITS HELLISH WEB OF SOCIAL LOYALTIES AND OBLIGATIONS. THEY ONLY INTERACT WITH OTHERS VIA COMPUTER.
TWENTY-FIRST CENTURY HERMITS. ISN'T TECHNOLOGY MARVELOUS! CHARLIE BABBAGE AND ALAN TURING MUST BE SPINNING IN THEIR GRAVES LIKE TOPS!
OTAKU ARE DATA FREAKS, OBSESSIVE ACQUIRERS OF USELESS INFO ON SPECIFIC SUBJECTS: JEWISH PORN STARS, SPETNATZ HANDGUNS, VANILLA ICE, THE WOMBLES...
...LAZARUS LIKES SECRETS. PERSONAL, INDUSTRIAL, GOVERNMENTAL, YOU NAME IT. THAT'S WHY HE'S SO ANAL ABOUT NOT MEETING. HIS SECURITY'S HIS LIFE.
SUBWAY
GINZA STATION
HE'S BEEN TRAWLING FOR DATA ON LEE FOR ME, AND IT LOOKS LIKE HE'S FOUND SOMETHING...
...SOMETHING HE DOESN'T TRUST SENDING VIA MODEM. HE WANTS TO MEET!
サッポロ
ビール
生
WHY DOES THAT SCARE ME?

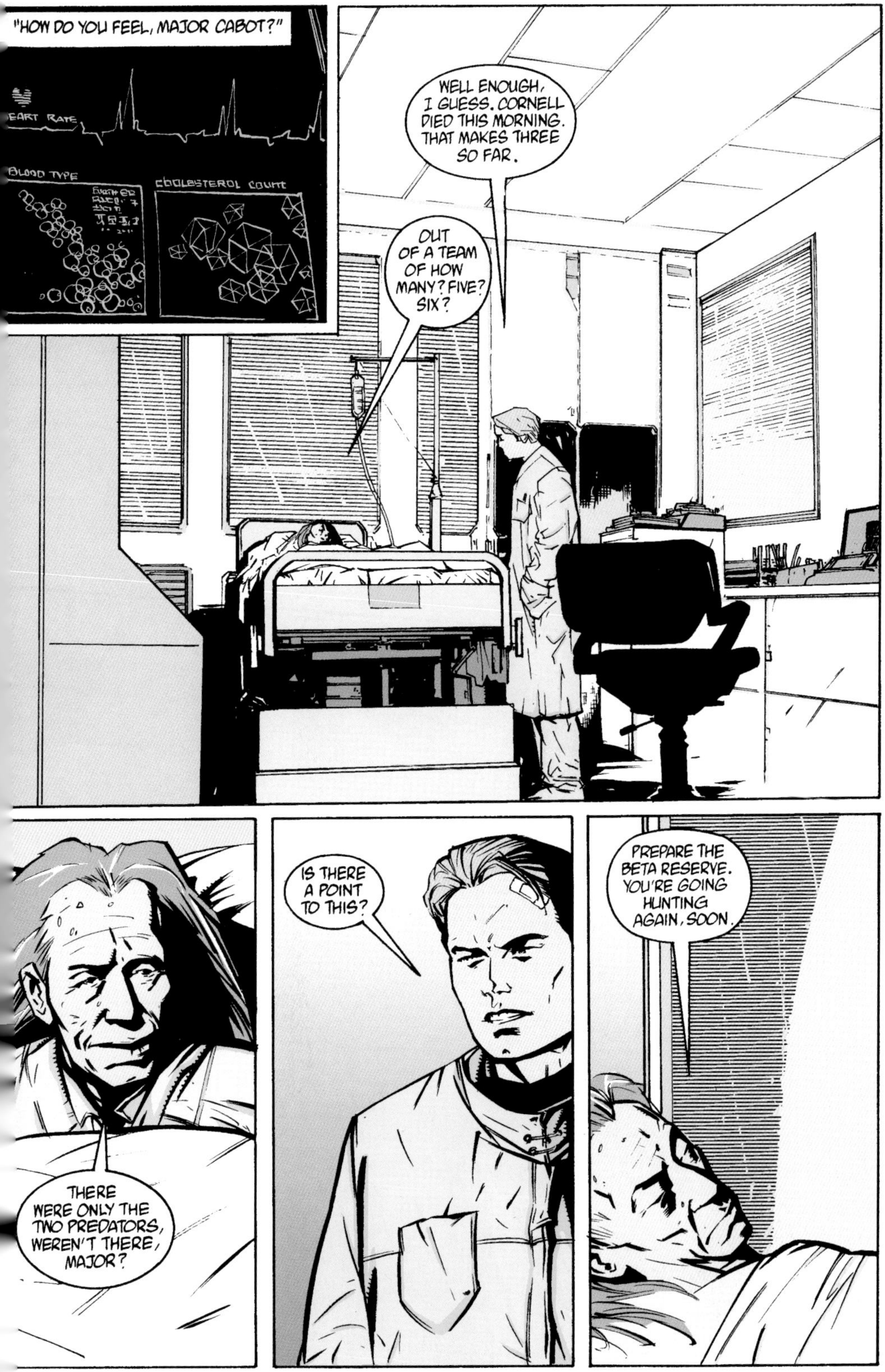
"HOW DO YOU FEEL, MAJOR CABOT?"
BLOOD TYPE
CHOLESTEROL COUNT
WELL ENOUGH, I GUESS. CORNELL DIED THIS MORNING. THAT MAKES THREE SO FAR.
OUT OF A TEAM OF HOW MANY? FIVE? SIX?
THERE WERE ONLY THE TWO PREDATORS, WEREN'T THERE, MAJOR?
IS THERE A POINT TO THIS?
PREPARE THE BETA RESERVE. YOU'RE GOING HUNTING AGAIN, SOON.

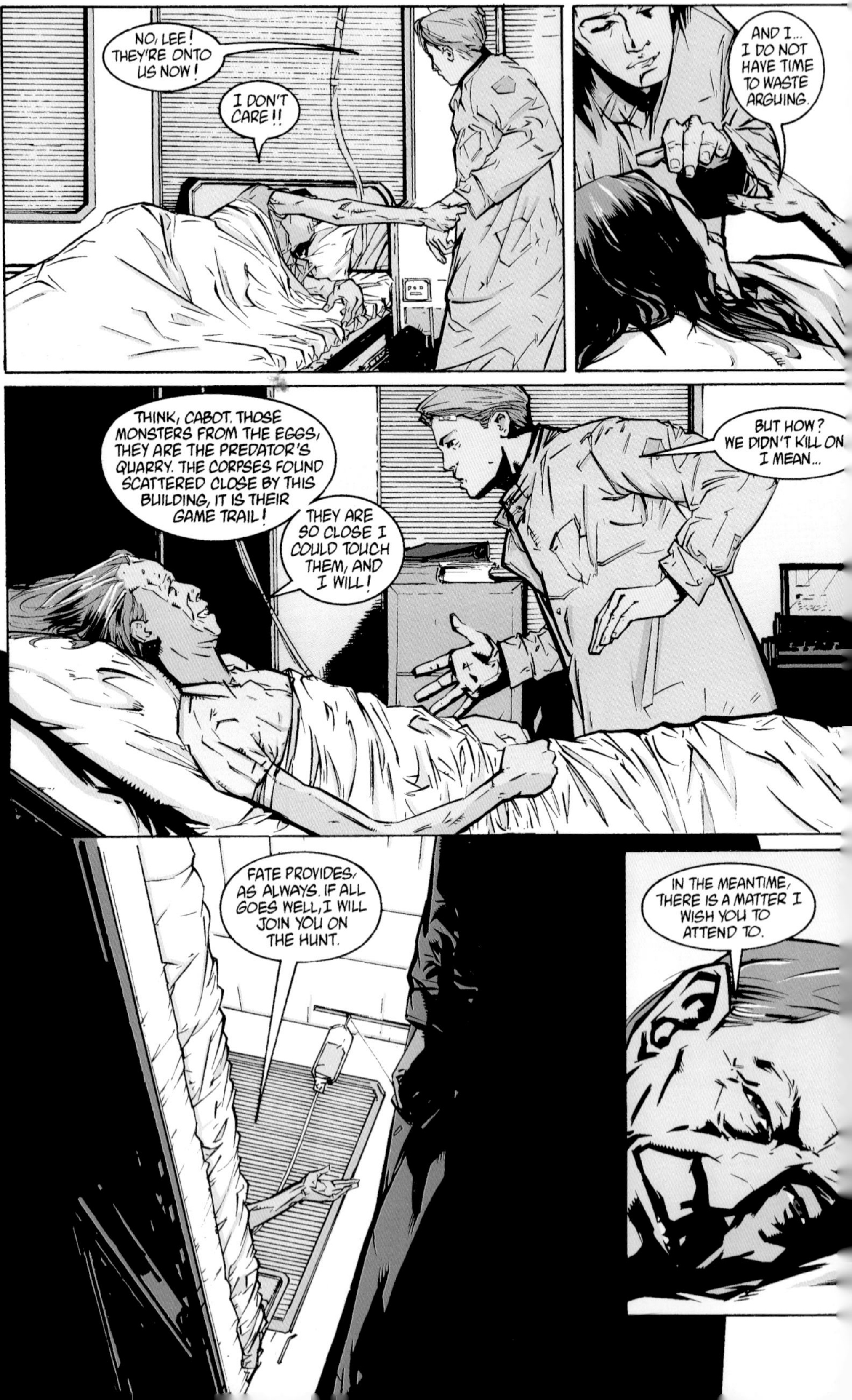
NO, LEE! THEY'RE ONTO US NOW!
I DON'T CARE!!
AND I... I DO NOT HAVE TIME TO WASTE ARGUING.
THINK, CABOT. THOSE MONSTERS FROM THE EGGS, THEY ARE THE PREDATOR'S QUARRY. THE CORPSES FOUND SCATTERED CLOSE BY THIS BUILDING, IT IS THEIR GAME TRAIL!
THEY ARE SO CLOSE I COULD TOUCH THEM, AND I WILL!
BUT HOW? WE DIDN'T KILL ON I MEAN...
FATE PROVIDES, AS ALWAYS. IF ALL GOES WELL, I WILL JOIN YOU ON THE HUNT.
IN THE MEANTIME, THERE IS A MATTER I WISH YOU TO ATTEND TO.

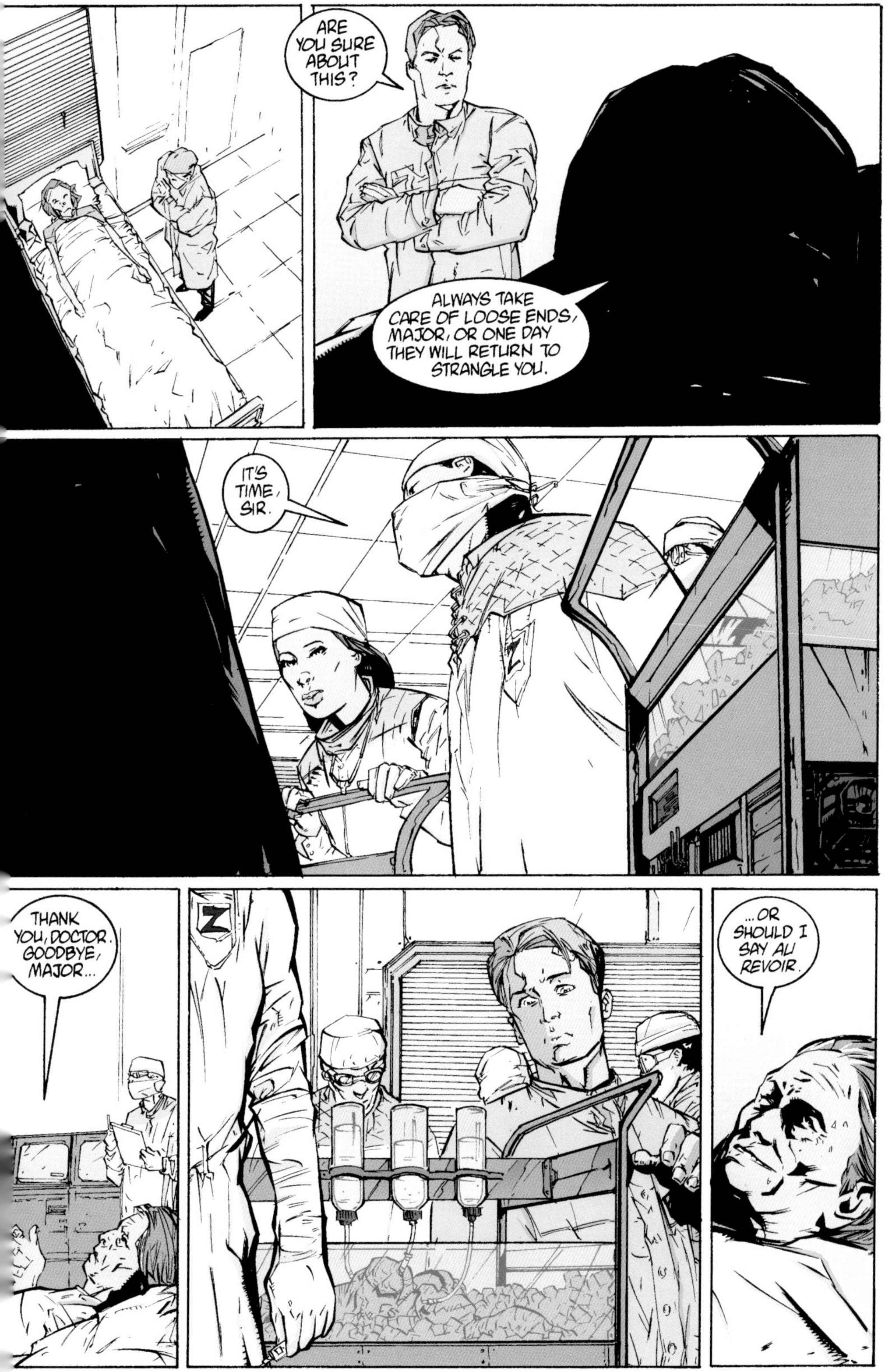
ARE YOU SURE ABOUT THIS?
ALWAYS TAKE CARE OF LOOSE ENDS, MAJOR, OR ONE DAY THEY WILL RETURN TO STRANGLE YOU.
IT'S TIME, SIR.
THANK YOU, DOCTOR. GOODBYE, MAJOR...
...OR SHOULD I SAY AU REVOIR.

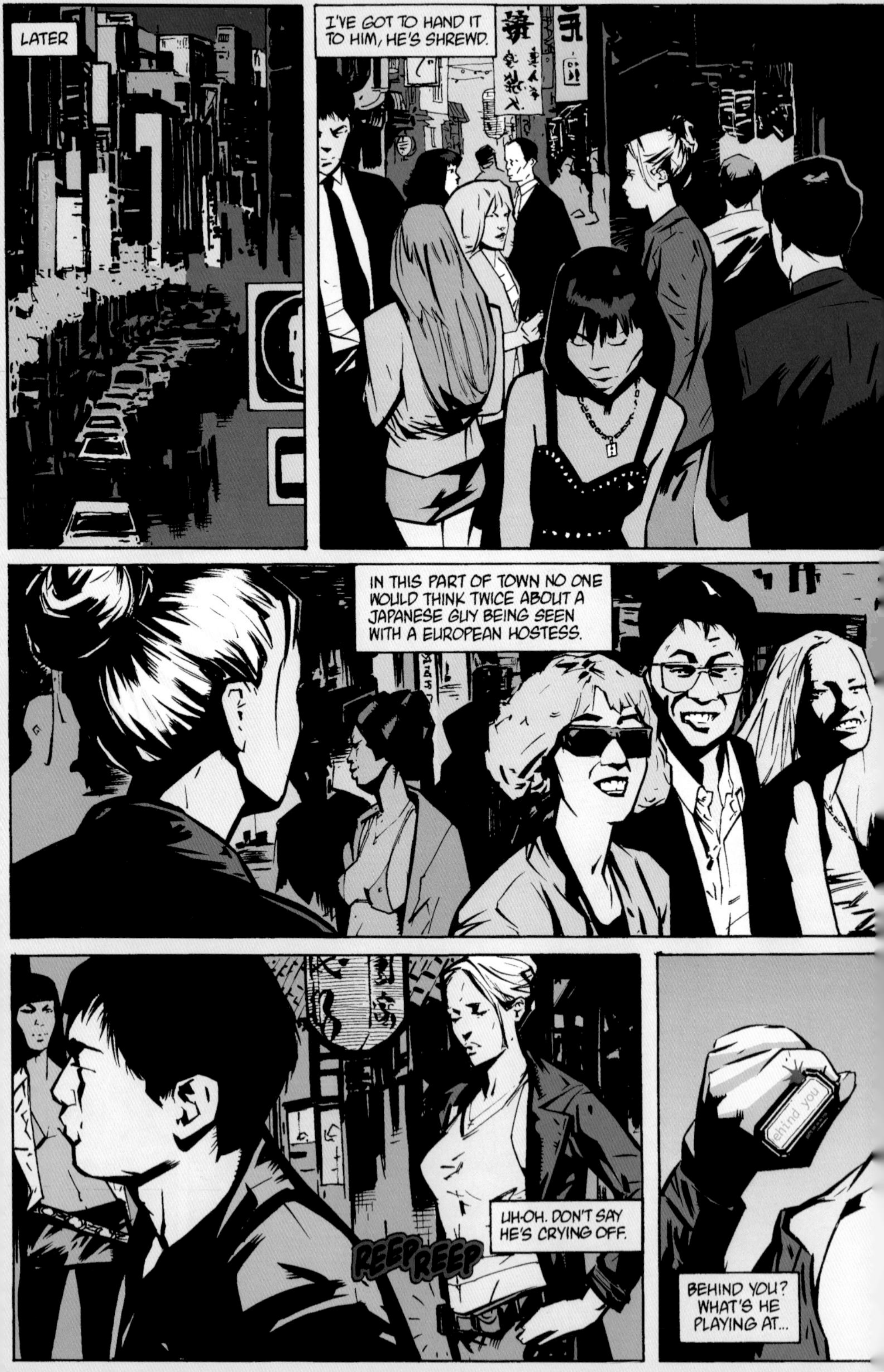
LATER
I'VE GOT TO HAND IT TO HIM, HE'S SHREWD.
IN THIS PART OF TOWN NO ONE WOULD THINK TWICE ABOUT A JAPANESE GUY BEING SEEN WITH A EUROPEAN HOSTESS.
REEP REEP
UH-OH. DON'T SAY HE'S CRYING OFF.
BEHIND YOU? WHAT'S HE PLAYING AT...

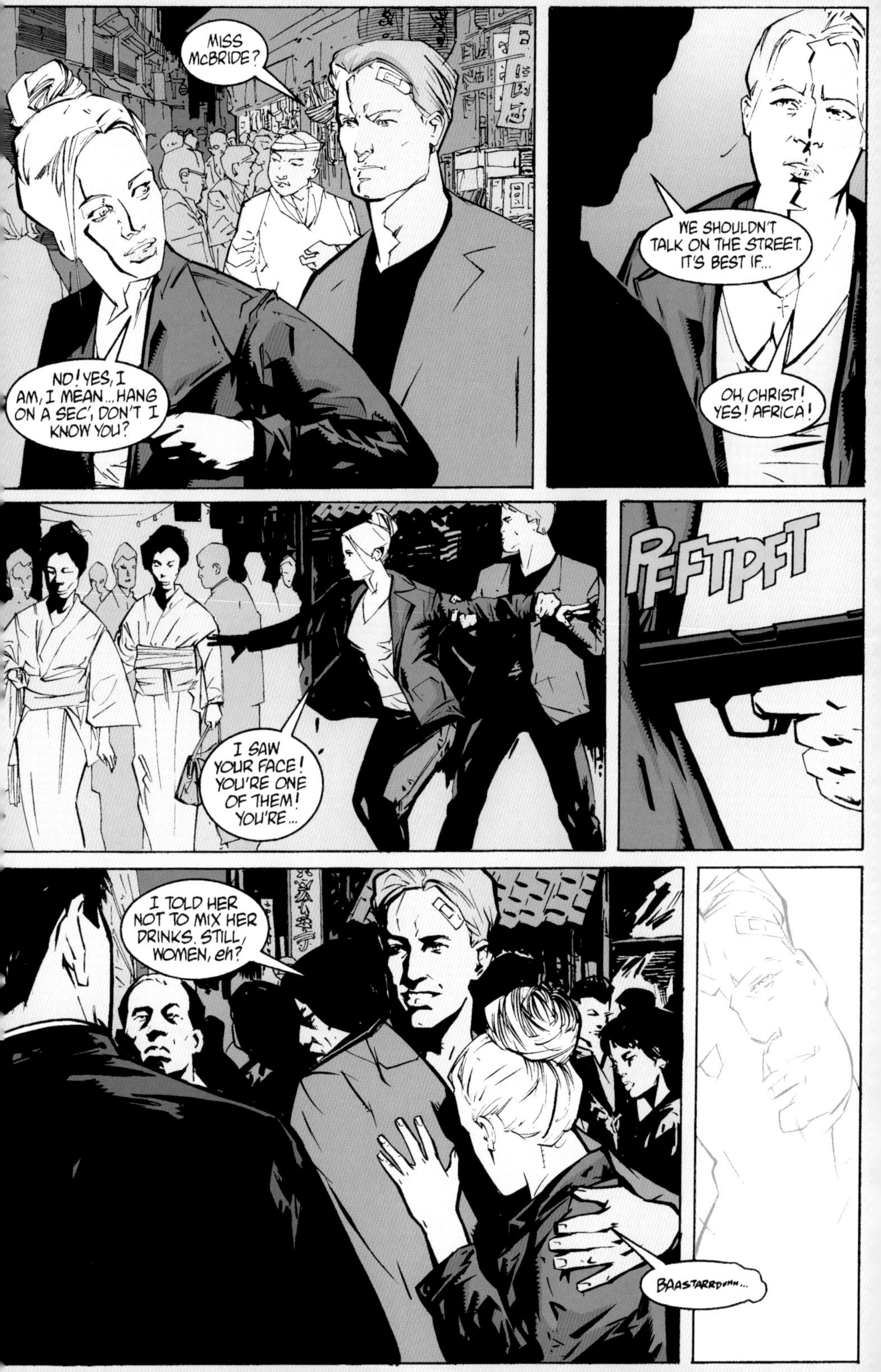
MISS McBRIDE?
NO! YES, I AM, I MEAN... HANG ON A SEC', DON'T I KNOW YOU?
WE SHOULDN'T TALK ON THE STREET. IT'S BEST IF...
OH, CHRIST! YES! AFRICA!
I SAW YOUR FACE! YOU'RE ONE OF THEM! YOU'RE...
PFFTPFT
I TOLD HER NOT TO MIX HER DRINKS. STILL, WOMEN, eh?
BAASTARRDUHH...

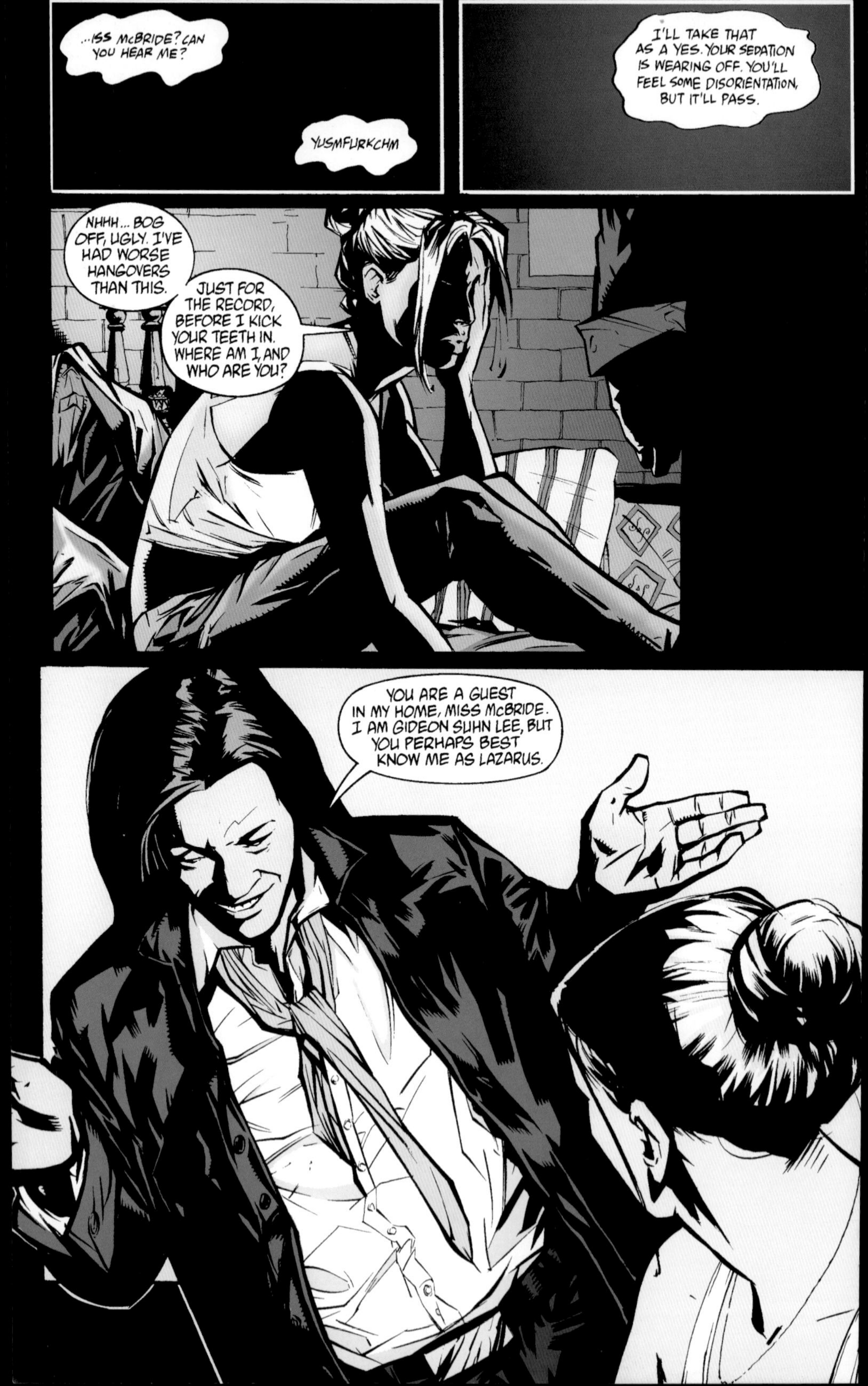
...ISS McBRIDE? CAN YOU HEAR ME?
YUSMFURKCHM
I'LL TAKE THAT AS A YES. YOUR SEDATION IS WEARING OFF. YOU'LL FEEL SOME DISORIENTATION, BUT IT'LL PASS.
NHHH... BOG OFF, UGLY. I'VE HAD WORSE HANGOVERS THAN THIS.
JUST FOR THE RECORD, BEFORE I KICK YOUR TEETH IN. WHERE AM I, AND WHO ARE YOU?
YOU ARE A GUEST IN MY HOME, MISS McBRIDE. I AM GIDEON SUHN LEE, BUT YOU PERHAPS BEST KNOW ME AS LAZARUS.

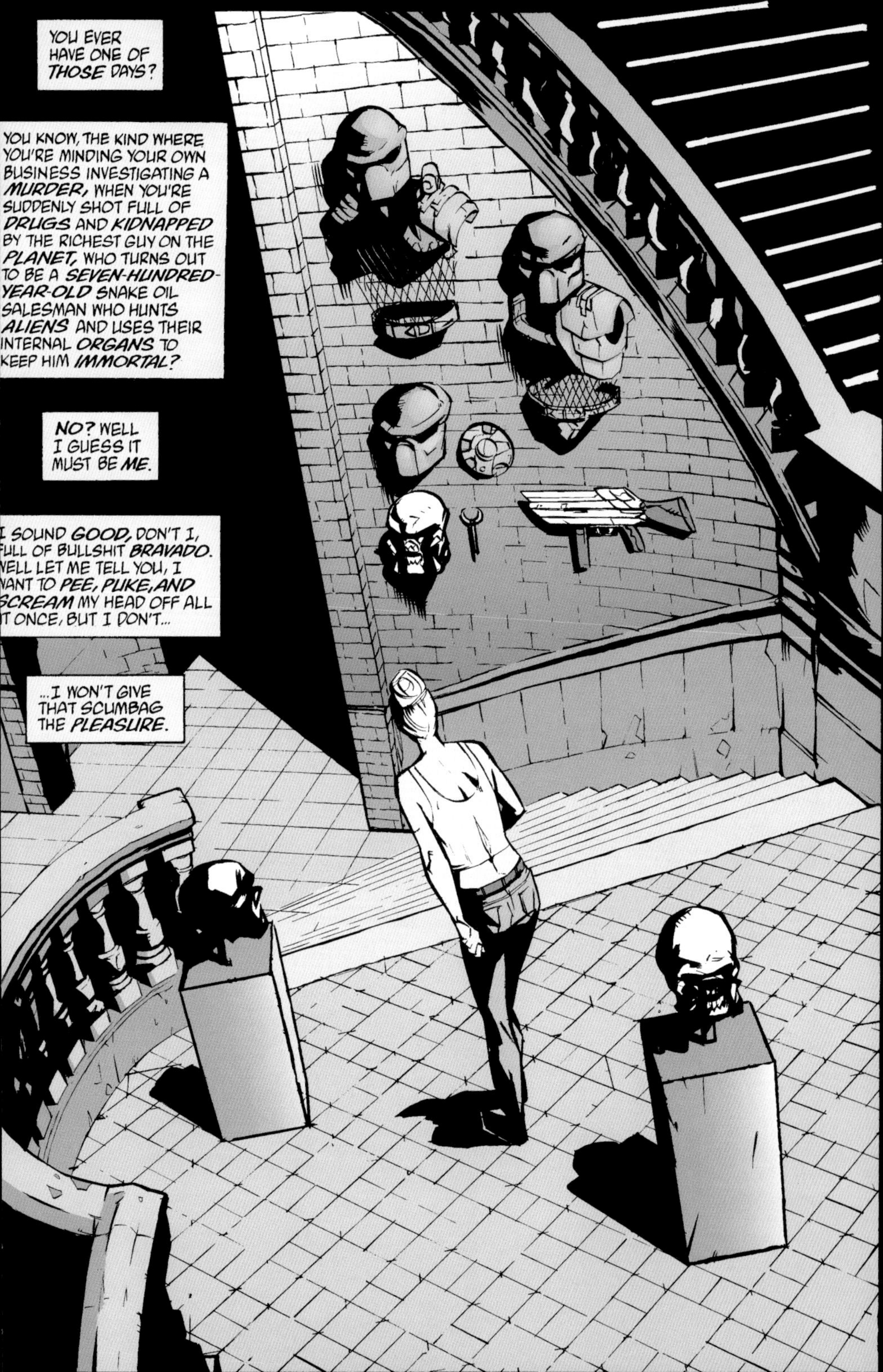
YOU EVER HAVE ONE OF THOSE DAYS?
YOU KNOW, THE KIND WHERE YOU'RE MINDING YOUR OWN BUSINESS INVESTIGATING A MURDER, WHEN YOU'RE SUDDENLY SHOT FULL OF DRUGS AND KIDNAPPED BY THE RICHEST GUY ON THE PLANET, WHO TURNS OUT TO BE A SEVEN-HUNDRED-YEAR-OLD SNAKE OIL SALESMAN WHO HUNTS ALIENS AND USES THEIR INTERNAL ORGANS TO KEEP HIM IMMORTAL?
NO? WELL I GUESS IT MUST BE ME.
I SOUND GOOD, DON'T I, FULL OF BULLSHIT BRAVADO. WELL LET ME TELL YOU, I WANT TO PEE, PUKE, AND SCREAM MY HEAD OFF ALL AT ONCE, BUT I DON'T...
...I WON'T GIVE THAT SCUMBAG THE PLEASURE.

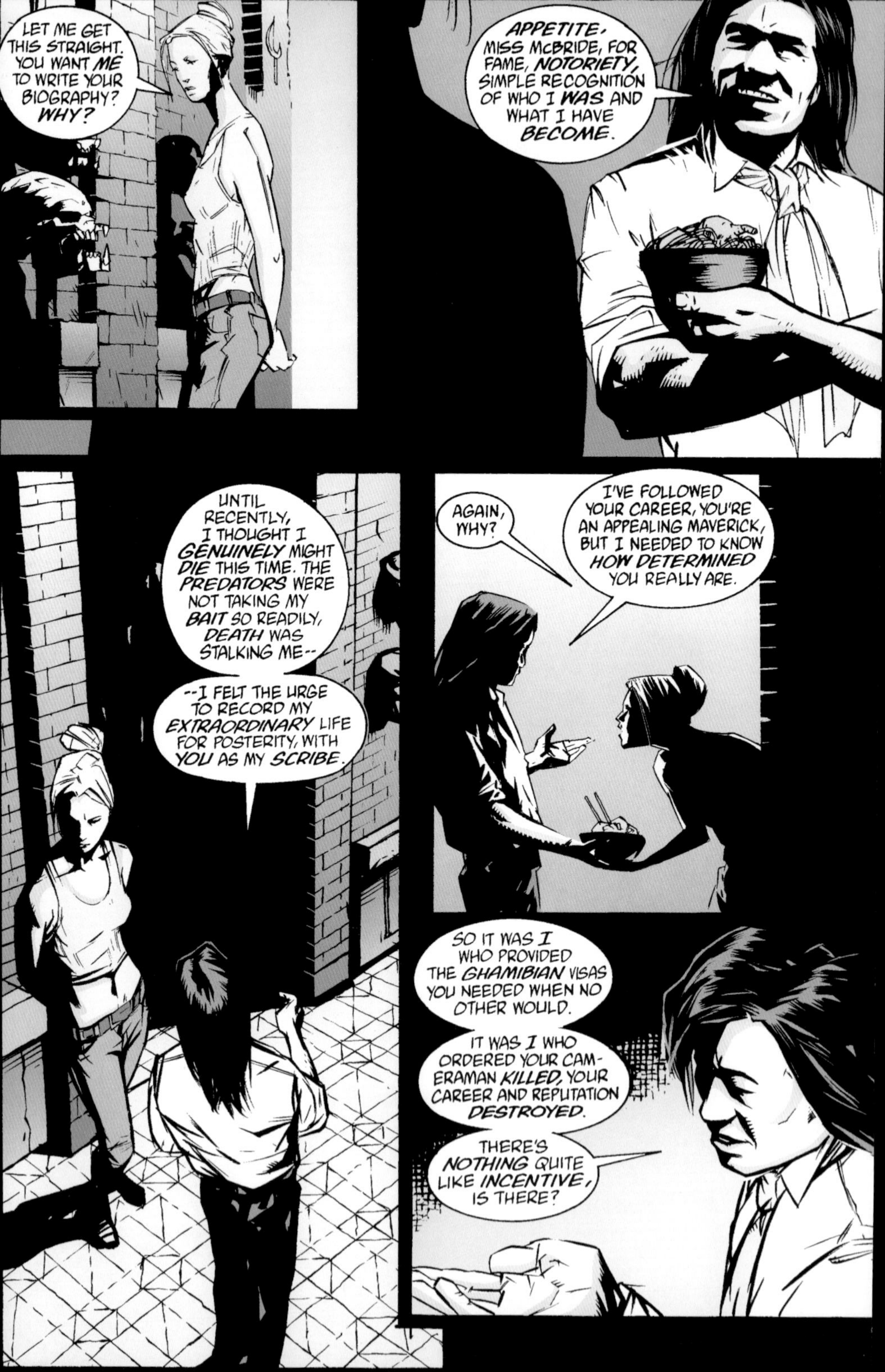
LET ME GET THIS STRAIGHT. YOU WANT ME TO WRITE YOUR BIOGRAPHY? WHY?
APPETITE, MISS McBRIDE, FOR FAME, NOTORIETY, SIMPLE RECOGNITION OF WHO I WAS AND WHAT I HAVE BECOME.
UNTIL RECENTLY, I THOUGHT I GENUINELY MIGHT DIE THIS TIME. THE PREDATORS WERE NOT TAKING MY BAIT SO READILY, DEATH WAS STALKING ME--
--I FELT THE URGE TO RECORD MY EXTRAORDINARY LIFE FOR POSTERITY, WITH YOU AS MY SCRIBE.
AGAIN, WHY?
I'VE FOLLOWED YOUR CAREER, YOU'RE AN APPEALING MAVERICK, BUT I NEEDED TO KNOW HOW DETERMINED YOU REALLY ARE.
SO IT WAS I WHO PROVIDED THE GHAMIBIAN VISAS YOU NEEDED WHEN NO OTHER WOULD.
IT WAS I WHO ORDERED YOUR CAMERAMAN KILLED, YOUR CAREER AND REPUTATION DESTROYED.
THERE'S NOTHING QUITE LIKE INCENTIVE, IS THERE?

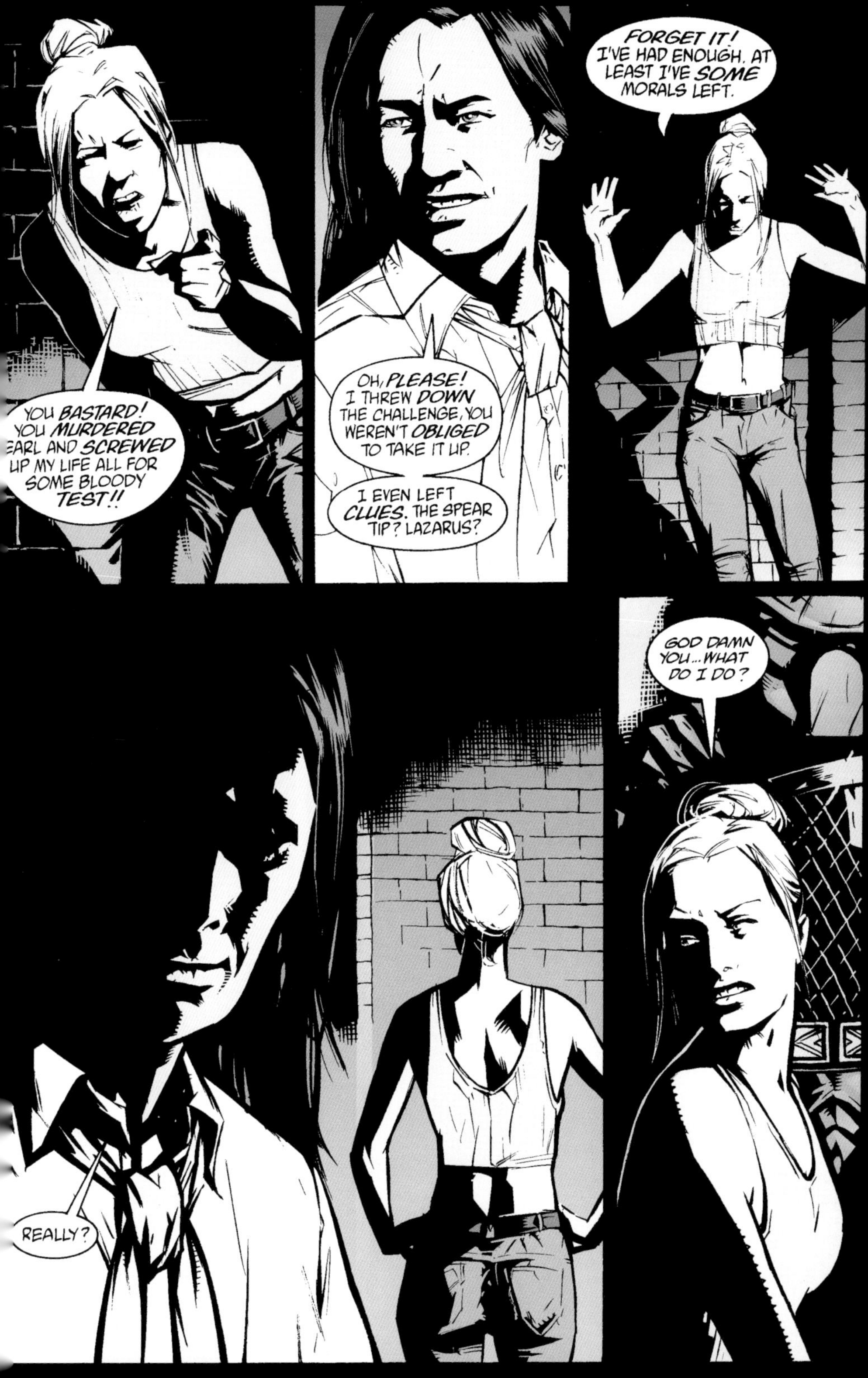
YOU BASTARD! YOU MURDERED EARL AND SCREWED UP MY LIFE ALL FOR SOME BLOODY TEST!!
OH, PLEASE! I THREW DOWN THE CHALLENGE, YOU WEREN'T OBLIGED TO TAKE IT UP.
I EVEN LEFT CLUES. THE SPEAR TIP? LAZARUS?
FORGET IT! I'VE HAD ENOUGH. AT LEAST I'VE SOME MORALS LEFT.
REALLY?
GOD DAMN YOU... WHAT DO I DO?

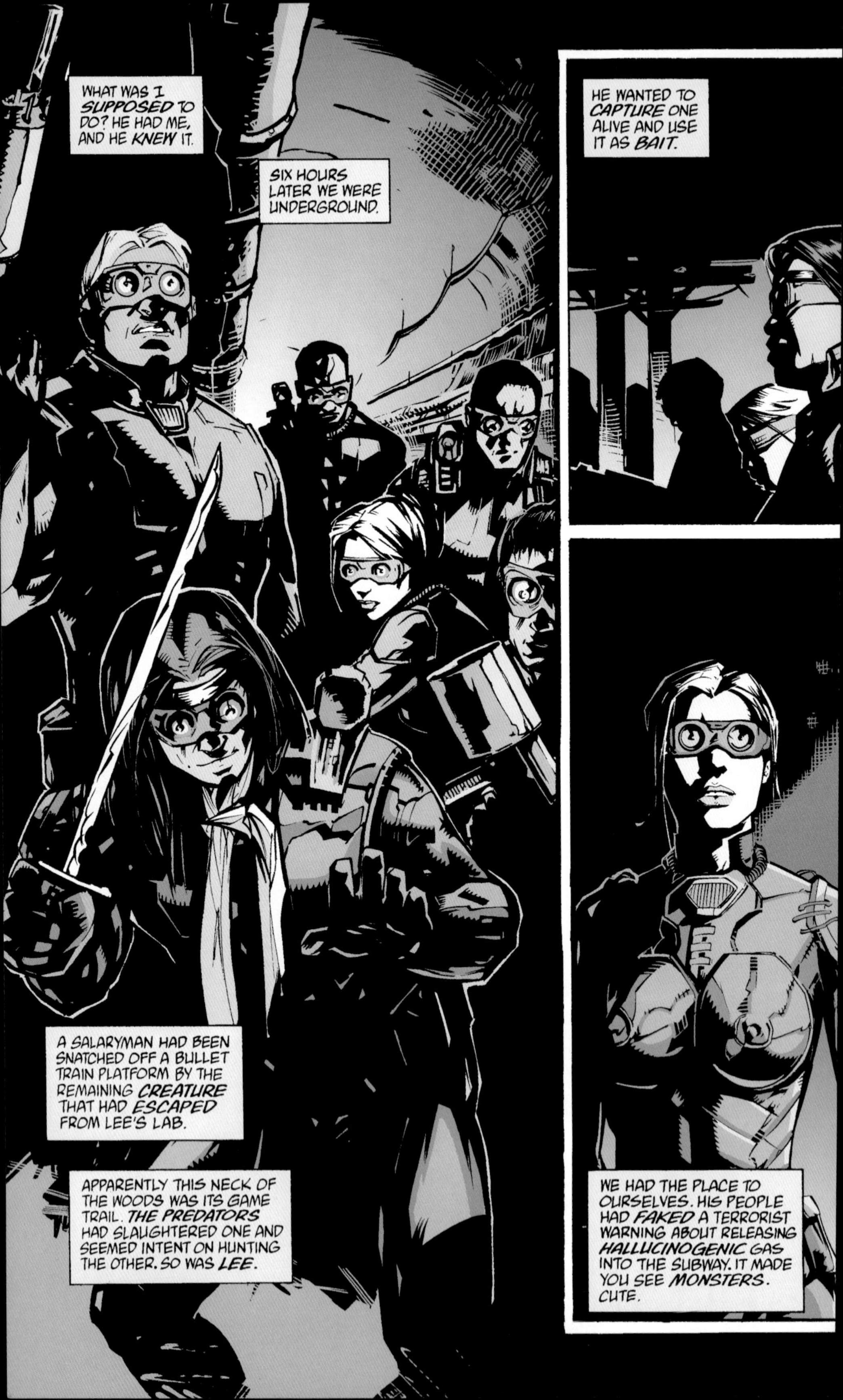
WHAT WAS I SUPPOSED TO DO? HE HAD ME, AND HE KNEW IT.
SIX HOURS LATER WE WERE UNDERGROUND.
A SALARYMAN HAD BEEN SNATCHED OFF A BULLET TRAIN PLATFORM BY THE REMAINING CREATURE THAT HAD ESCAPED FROM LEE'S LAB.
APPARENTLY THIS NECK OF THE WOODS WAS ITS GAME TRAIL. THE PREDATORS HAD SLAUGHTERED ONE AND SEEMED INTENT ON HUNTING THE OTHER. SO WAS LEE.
HE WANTED TO CAPTURE ONE ALIVE AND USE IT AS BAIT.
WE HAD THE PLACE TO OURSELVES. HIS PEOPLE HAD FAKED A TERRORIST WARNING ABOUT RELEASING HALLUCINOGENIC GAS INTO THE SUBWAY. IT MADE YOU SEE MONSTERS. CUTE.

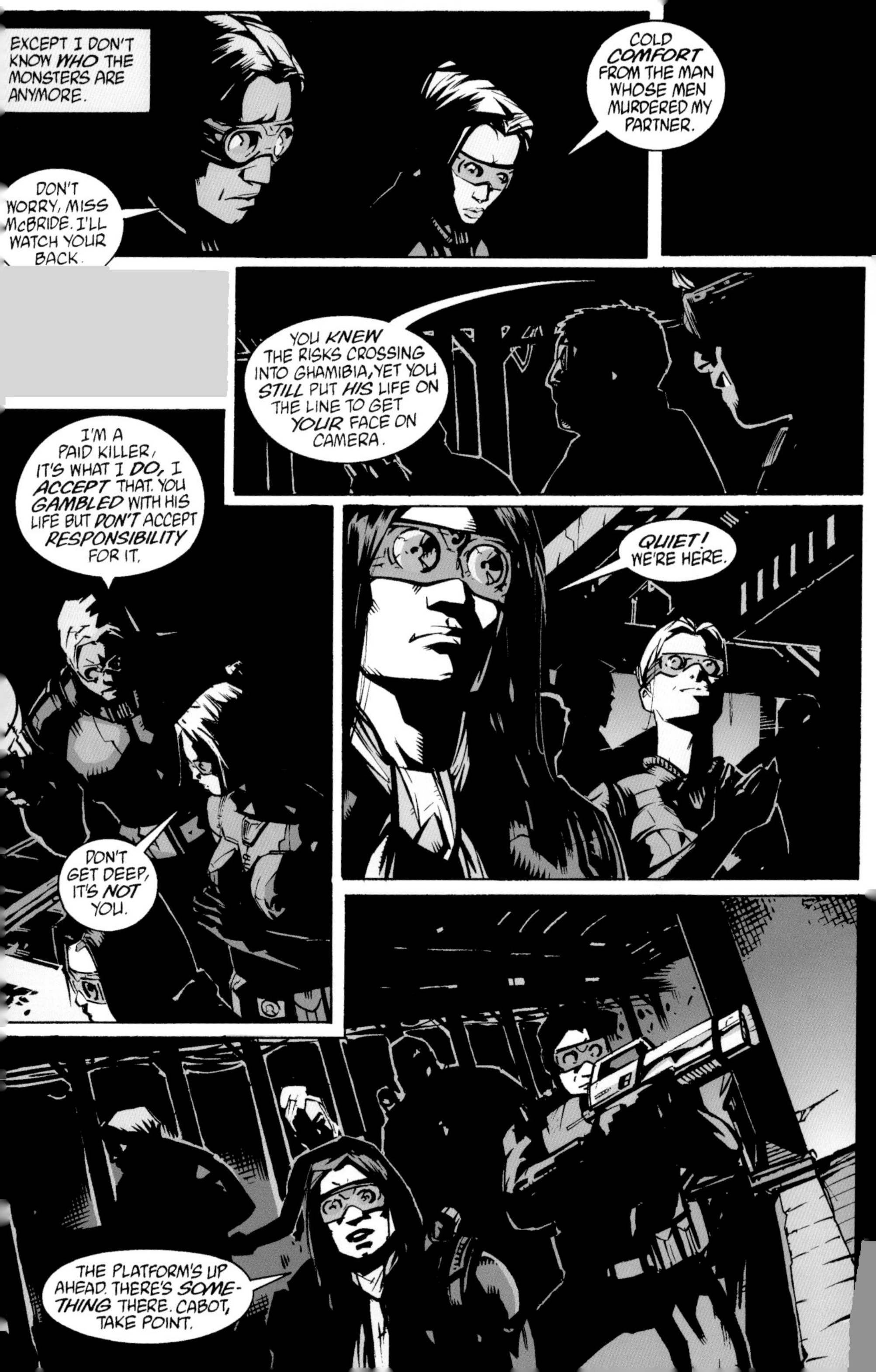
EXCEPT I DON'T KNOW WHO THE MONSTERS ARE ANYMORE.
DON'T WORRY, MISS McBRIDE. I'LL WATCH YOUR BACK.
COLD COMFORT FROM THE MAN WHOSE MEN MURDERED MY PARTNER.
YOU KNEW THE RISKS CROSSING INTO GHAMIBIA, YET YOU STILL PUT HIS LIFE ON THE LINE TO GET YOUR FACE ON CAMERA.
I'M A PAID KILLER, IT'S WHAT I DO, I ACCEPT THAT. YOU GAMBLED WITH HIS LIFE BUT DON'T ACCEPT RESPONSIBILITY FOR IT.
DON'T GET DEEP, IT'S NOT YOU.
QUIET! WE'RE HERE.
THE PLATFORM'S UP AHEAD. THERE'S SOME-THING THERE. CABOT, TAKE POINT.

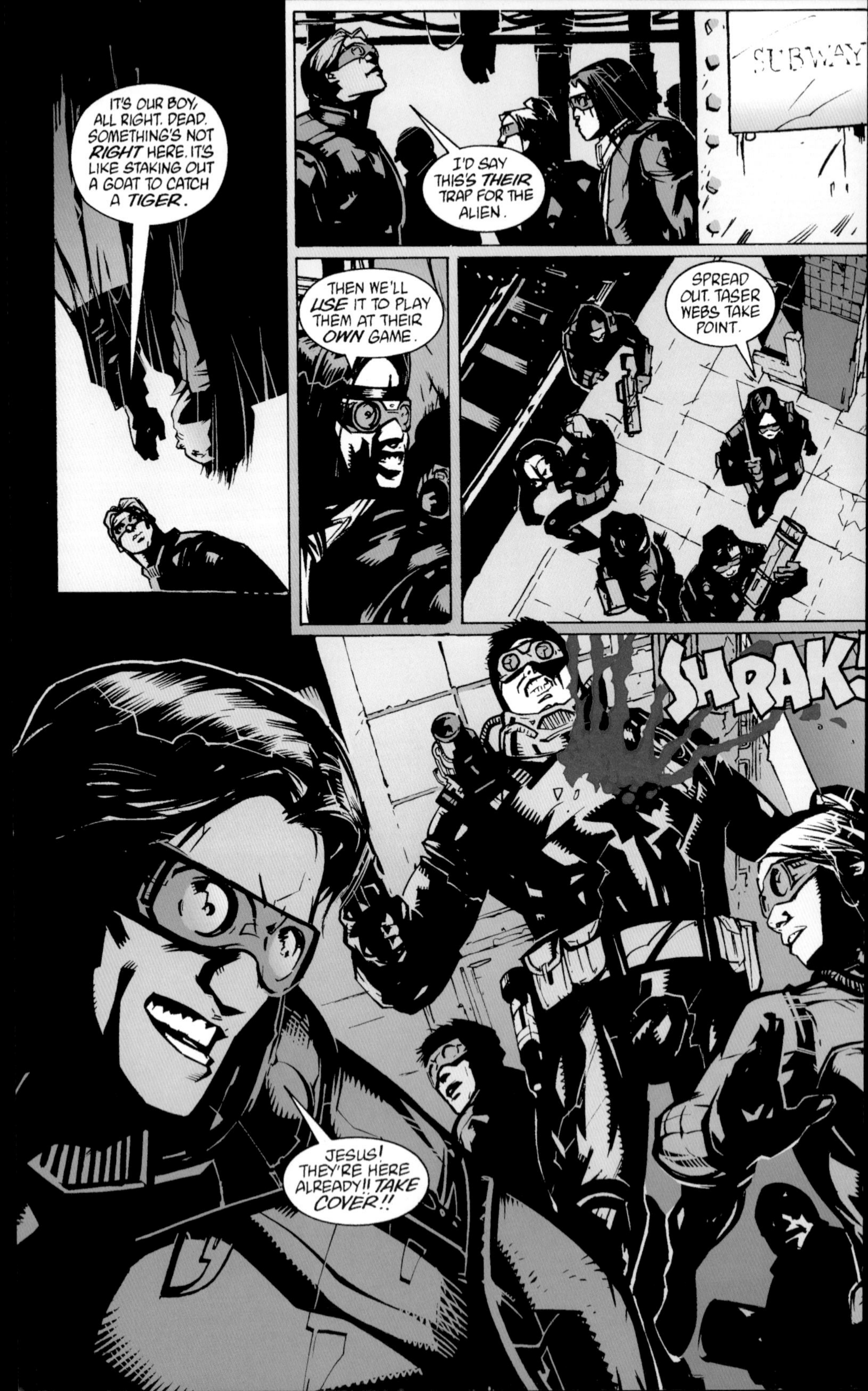
IT'S OUR BOY, ALL RIGHT. DEAD. SOMETHING'S NOT RIGHT HERE. IT'S LIKE STAKING OUT A GOAT TO CATCH A TIGER.
SUBWAY
I'D SAY THIS'S THEIR TRAP FOR THE ALIEN.
THEN WE'LL USE IT TO PLAY THEM AT THEIR OWN GAME.
SPREAD OUT. TASER WEBS TAKE POINT.
SHRAK!
JESUS! THEY'RE HERE ALREADY!! TAKE COVER!!

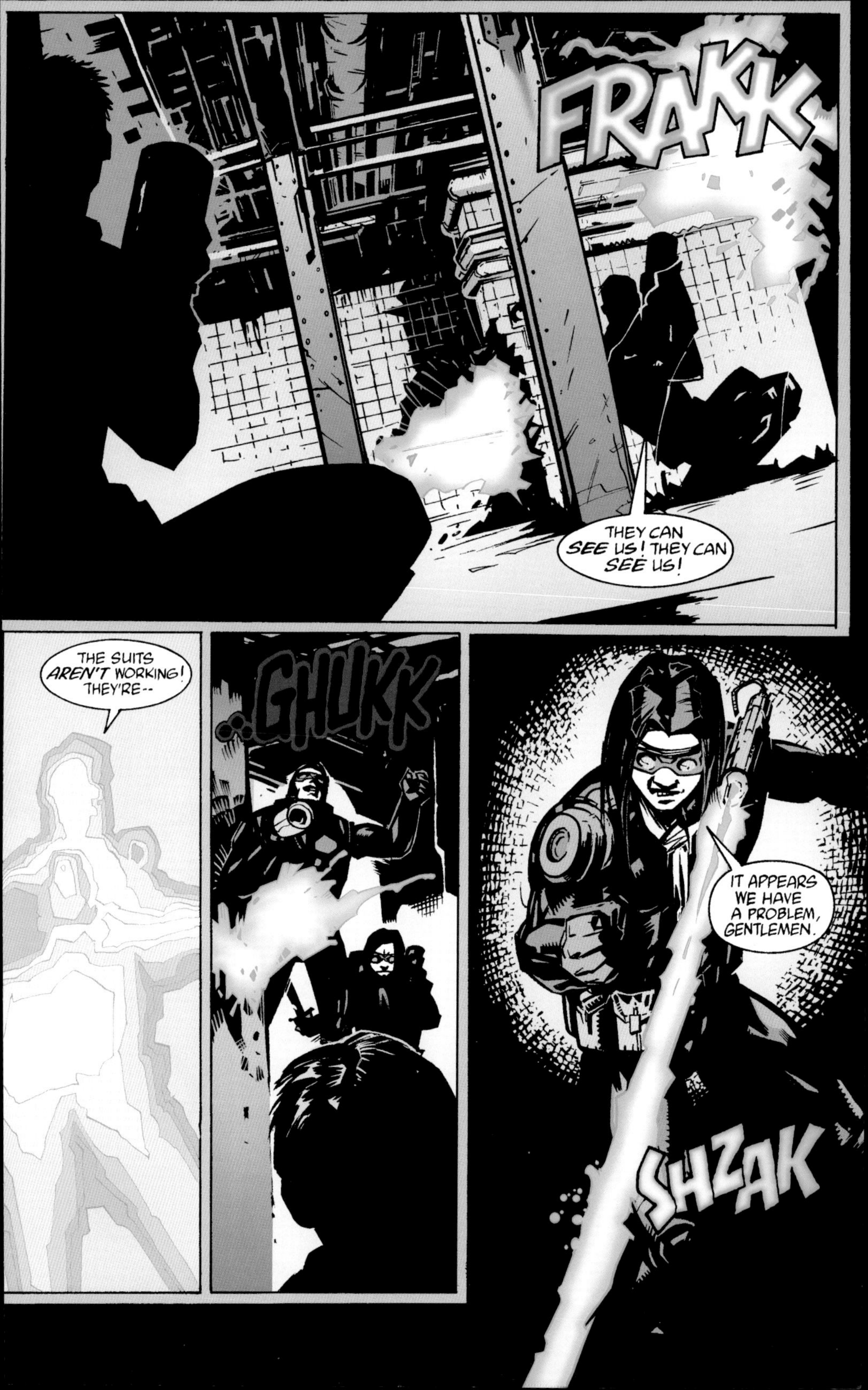
FRAKK
THEY CAN SEE US! THEY CAN SEE US!
THE SUITS AREN'T WORKING! THEY'RE--
..GHUKK
IT APPEARS WE HAVE A PROBLEM, GENTLEMEN.
SHZAK

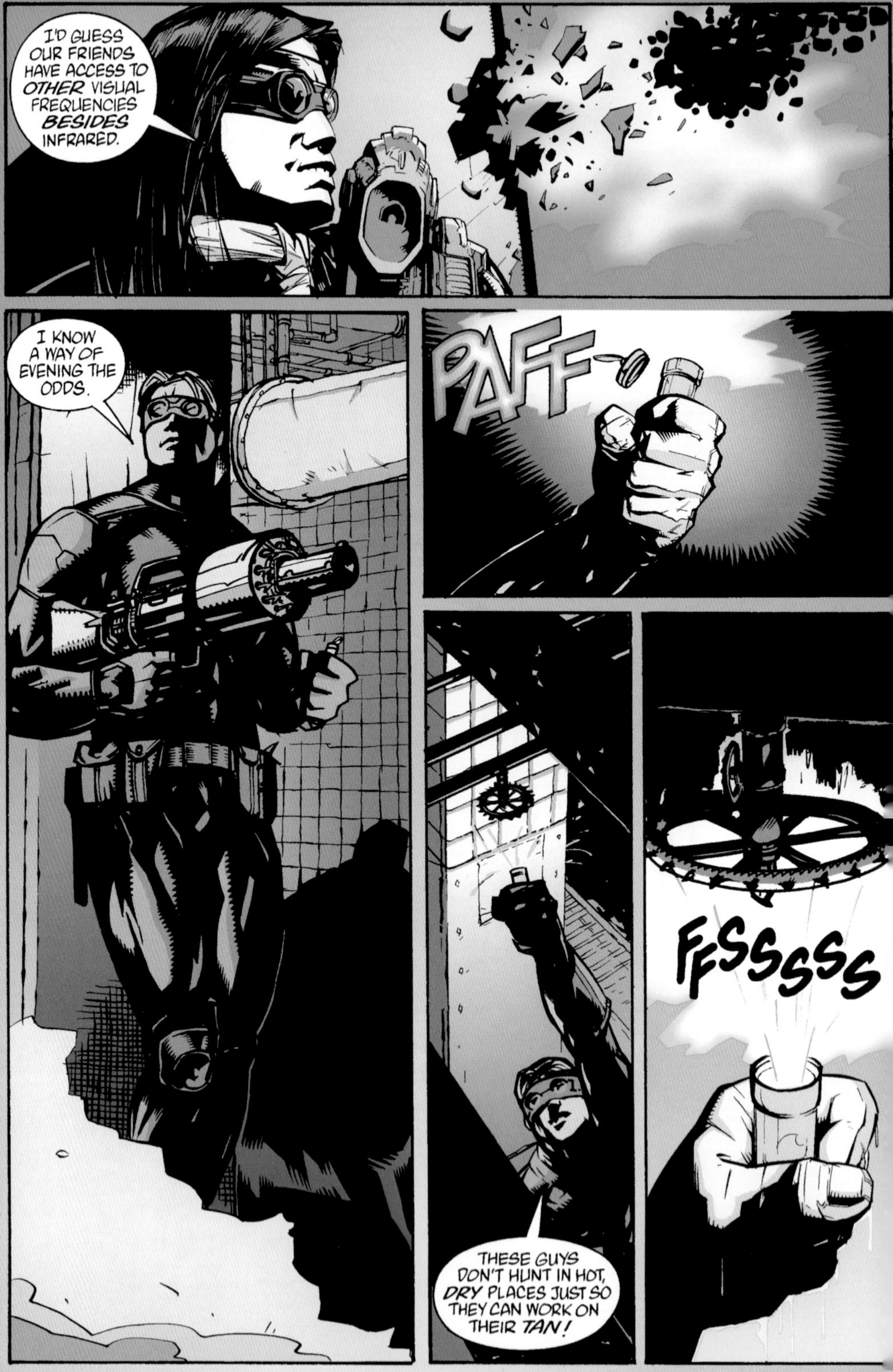

I'D GUESS OUR FRIENDS HAVE ACCESS TO OTHER VISUAL FREQUENCIES BESIDES INFRARED.
I KNOW A WAY OF EVENING THE ODDS.
PAFF
THESE GUYS DON'T HUNT IN HOT, DRY PLACES JUST SO THEY CAN WORK ON THEIR TAN!
FFSSSSSS

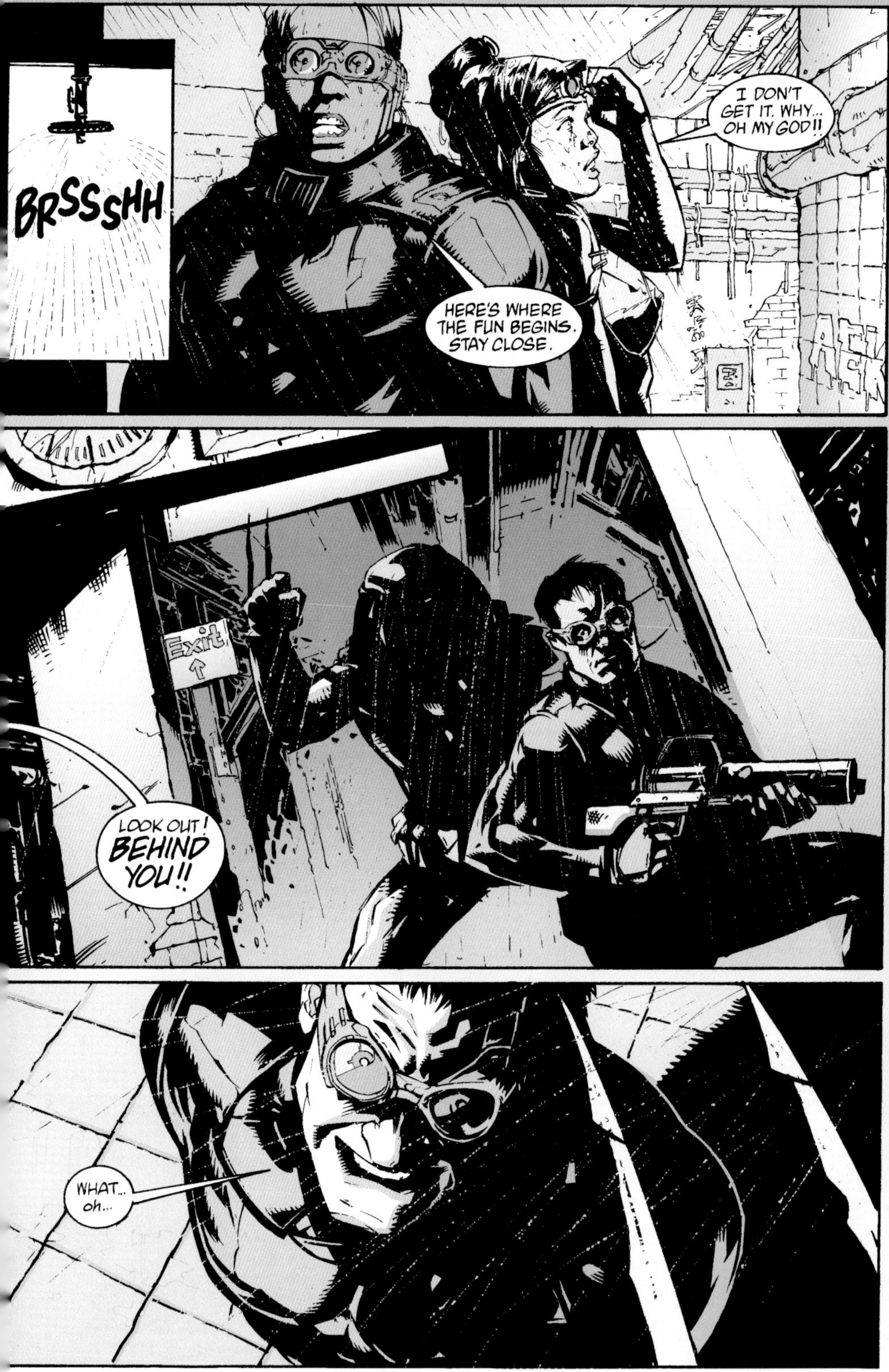
BRSSSHH
I DON'T GET IT. WHY... OH MY GOD!!
HERE'S WHERE THE FUN BEGINS. STAY CLOSE.
Exit
LOOK OUT! BEHIND YOU!!
WHAT... oh...

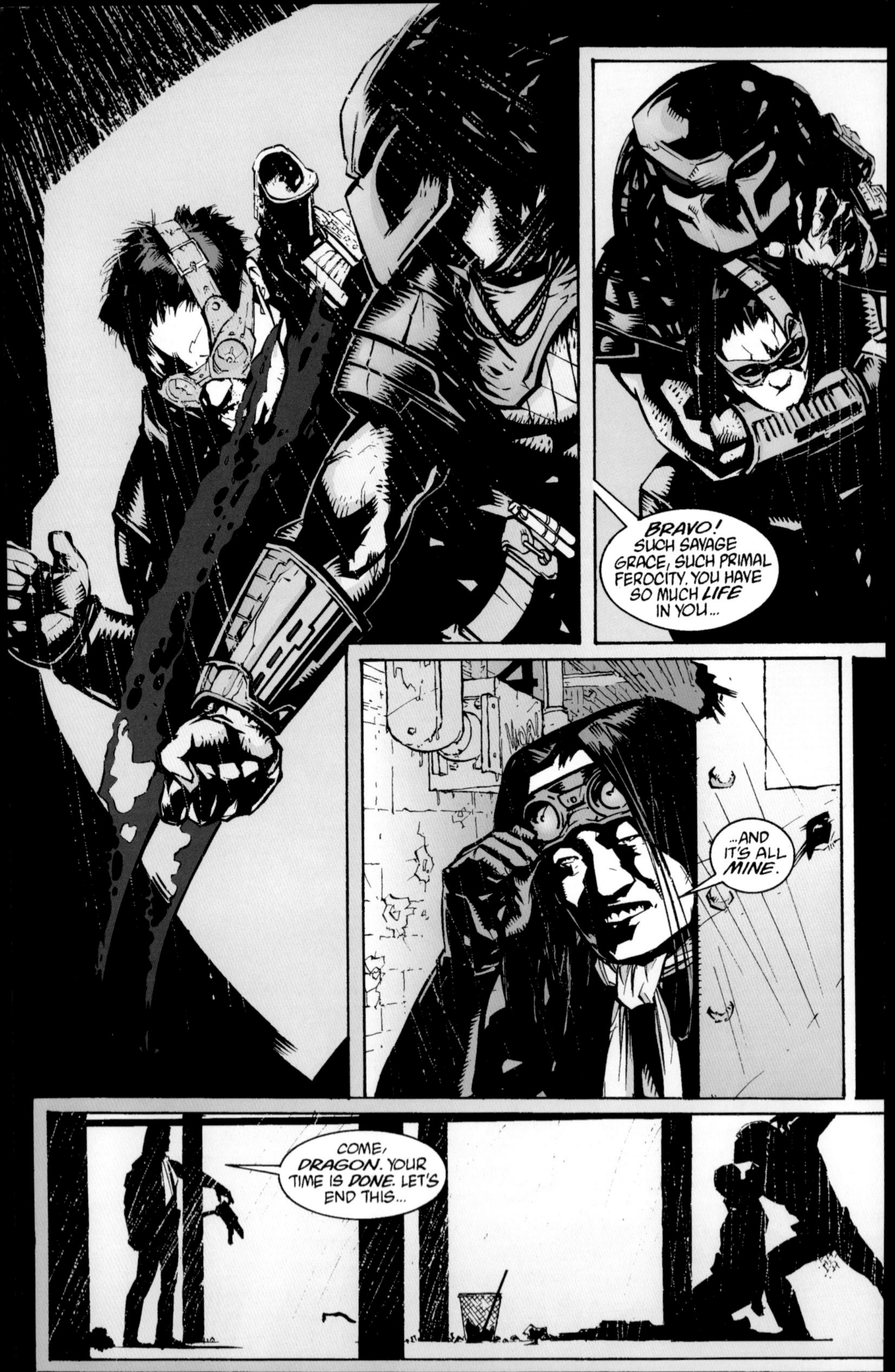
BRAVO! SUCH SAVAGE GRACE, SUCH PRIMAL FEROCITY. YOU HAVE SO MUCH LIFE IN YOU...
...AND IT'S ALL MINE.
COME, DRAGON. YOUR TIME IS DONE. LET'S END THIS...

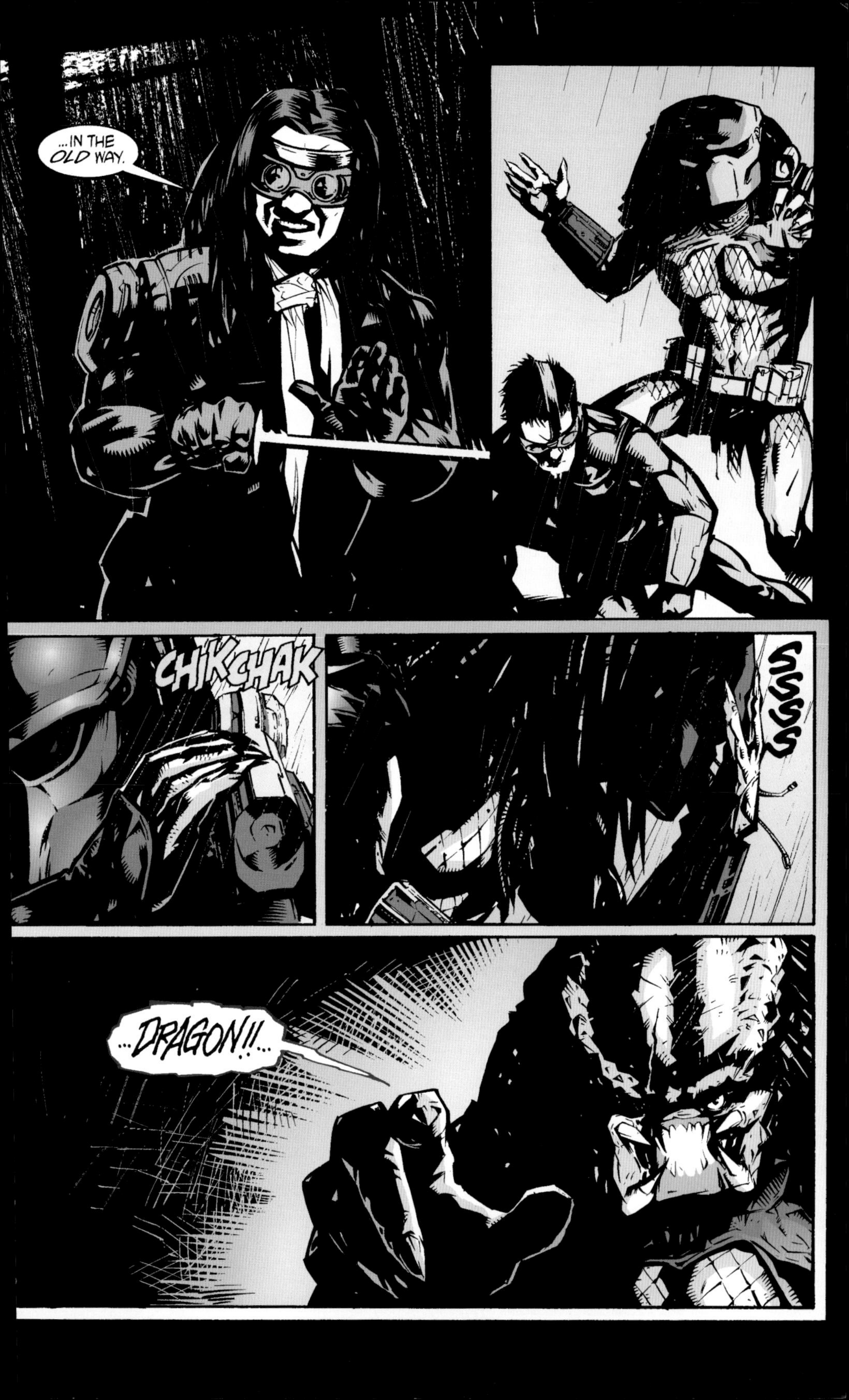
...IN THE OLD WAY.
CHIKCHAK
SSSSS
...DRAGON!!...

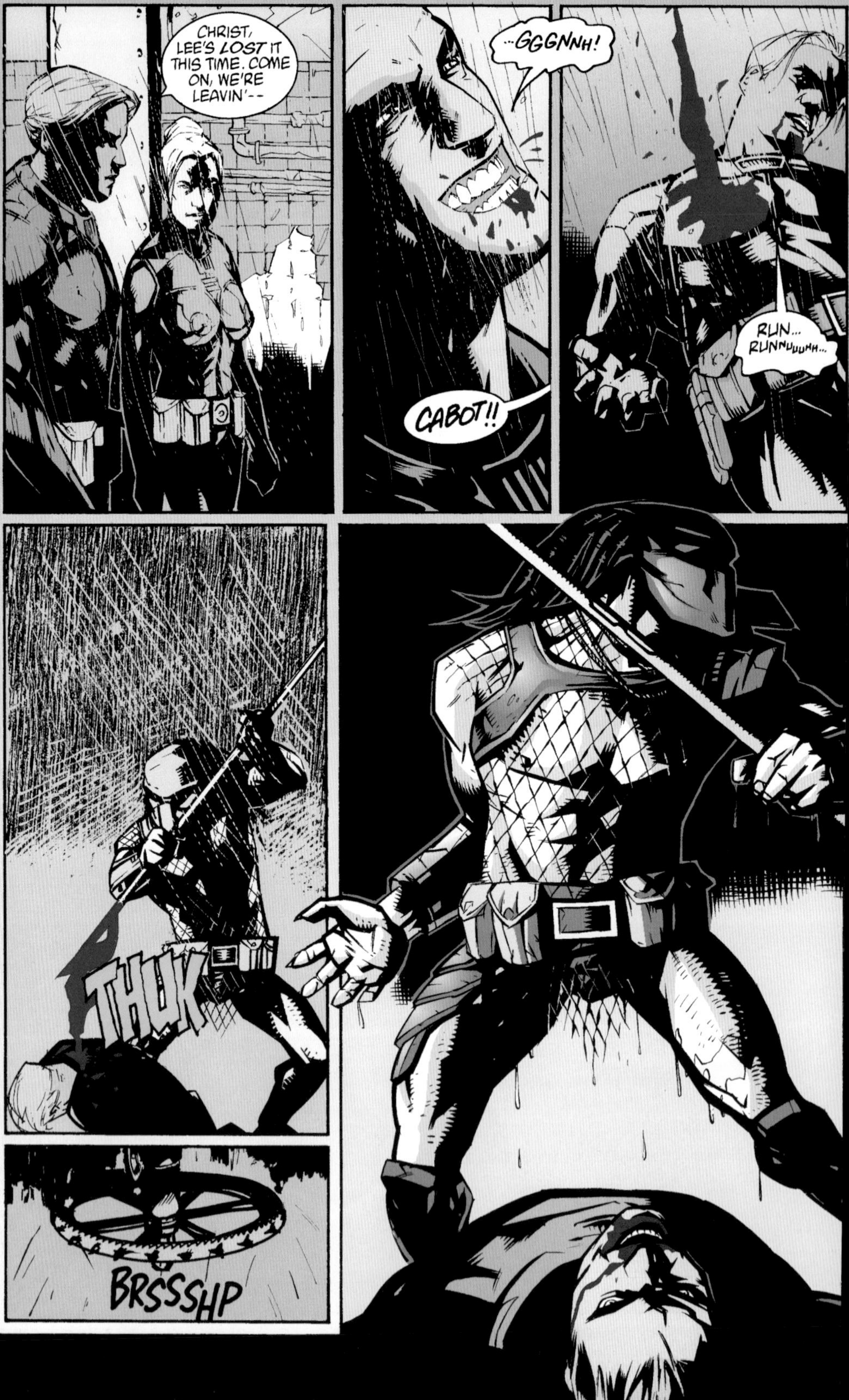

CHRIST, LEE'S LOST IT THIS TIME. COME ON, WE'RE LEAVIN'--
...GGGNNH!
CABOT!!
RUN... RUNNuuuhh...
THUK
BRSSSHP

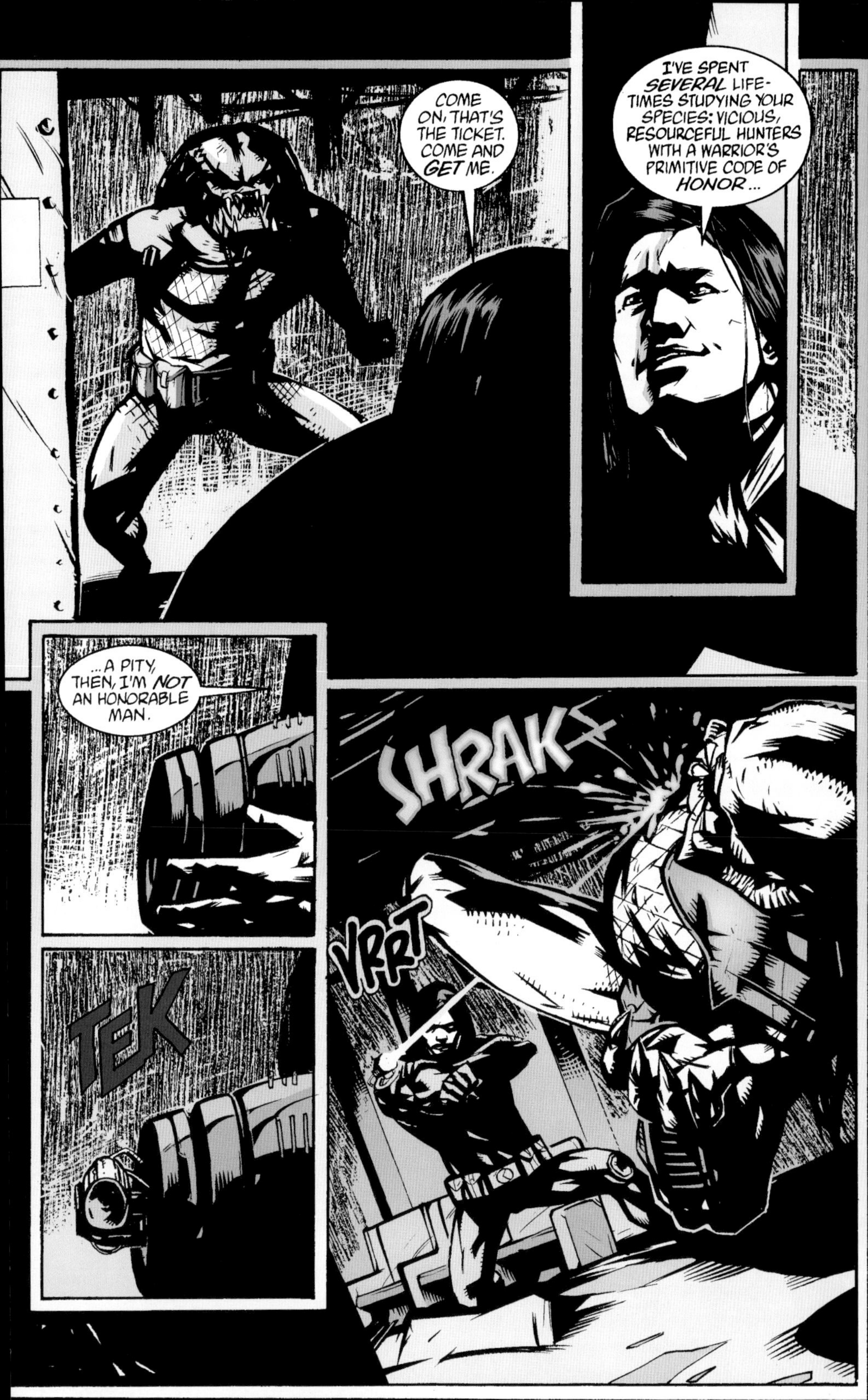
COME ON, THAT'S THE TICKET. COME AND GET ME.
I'VE SPENT SEVERAL LIFE-TIMES STUDYING YOUR SPECIES: VICIOUS, RESOURCEFUL HUNTERS WITH A WARRIOR'S PRIMITIVE CODE OF HONOR...
...A PITY, THEN, I'M NOT AN HONORABLE MAN.
TEK
SHRAK
VRRT

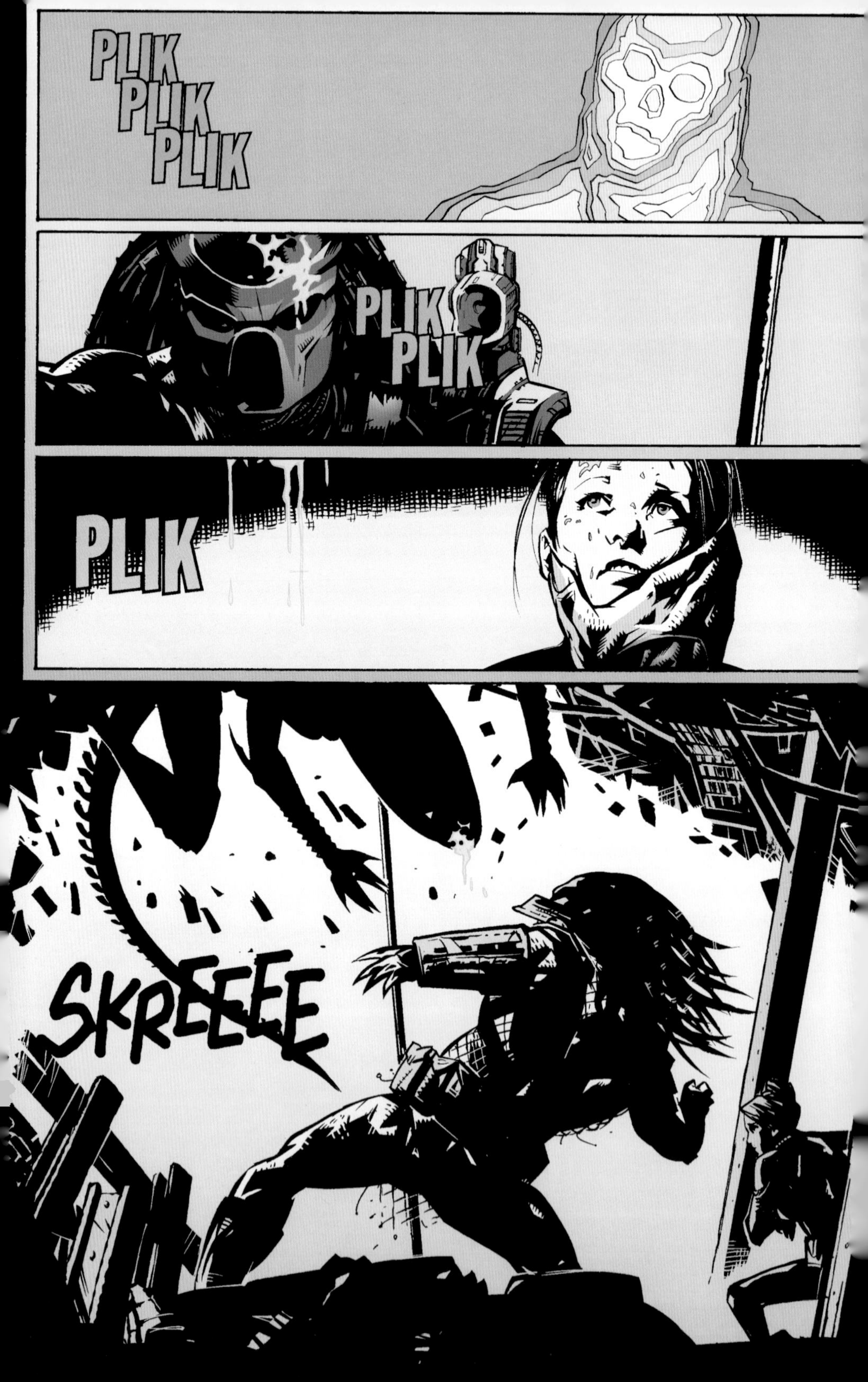
PLIK
PLIK
PLIK
PLIK
PLIK
PLIK
SKREEEE

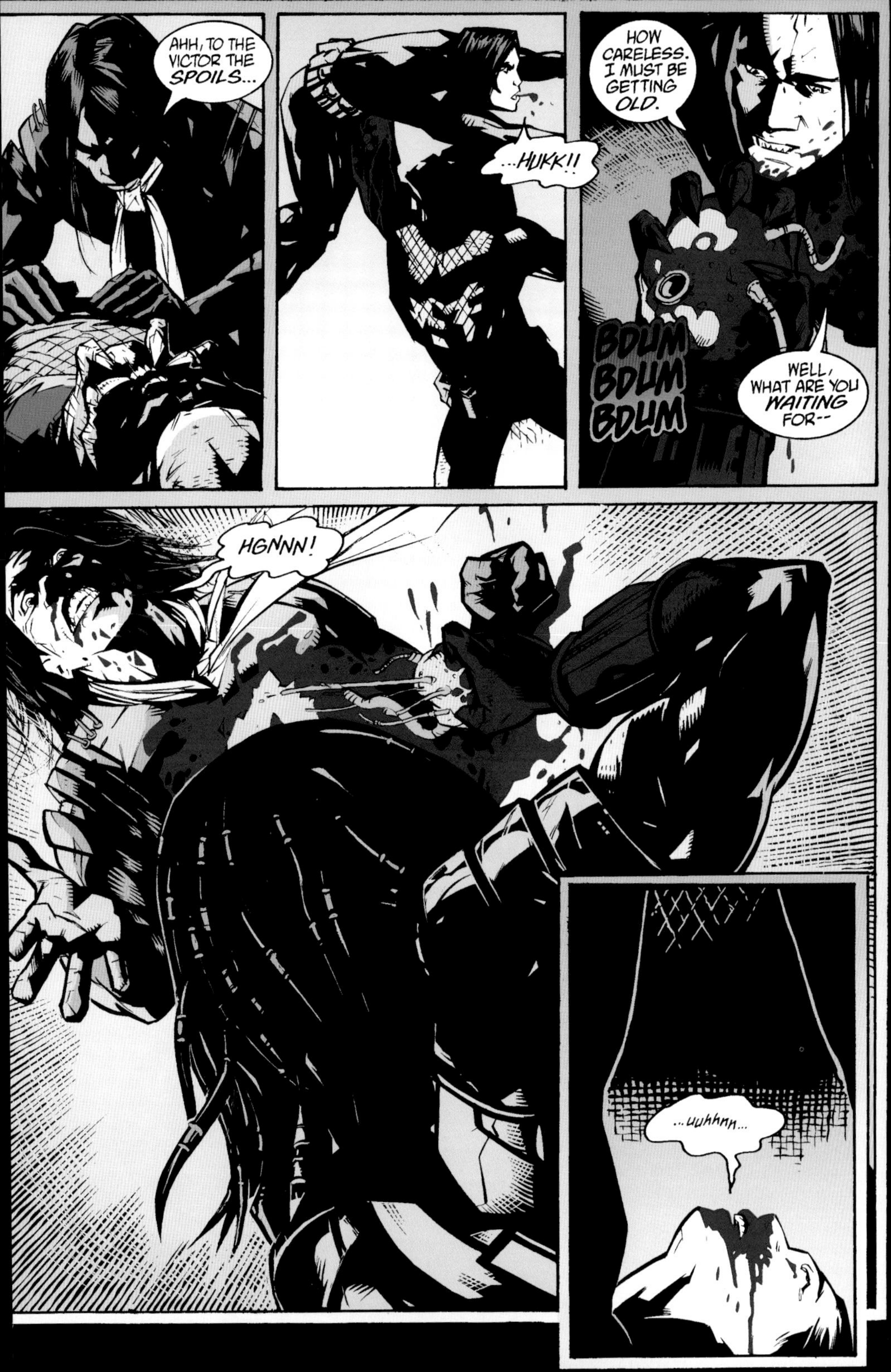
AHH, TO THE VICTOR THE SPOILS...
...HUKK!!
HOW CARELESS. I MUST BE GETTING OLD.
BDUM BDUM BDUM
WELL, WHAT ARE YOU WAITING FOR--
HGNNN!
...uuhhnn...

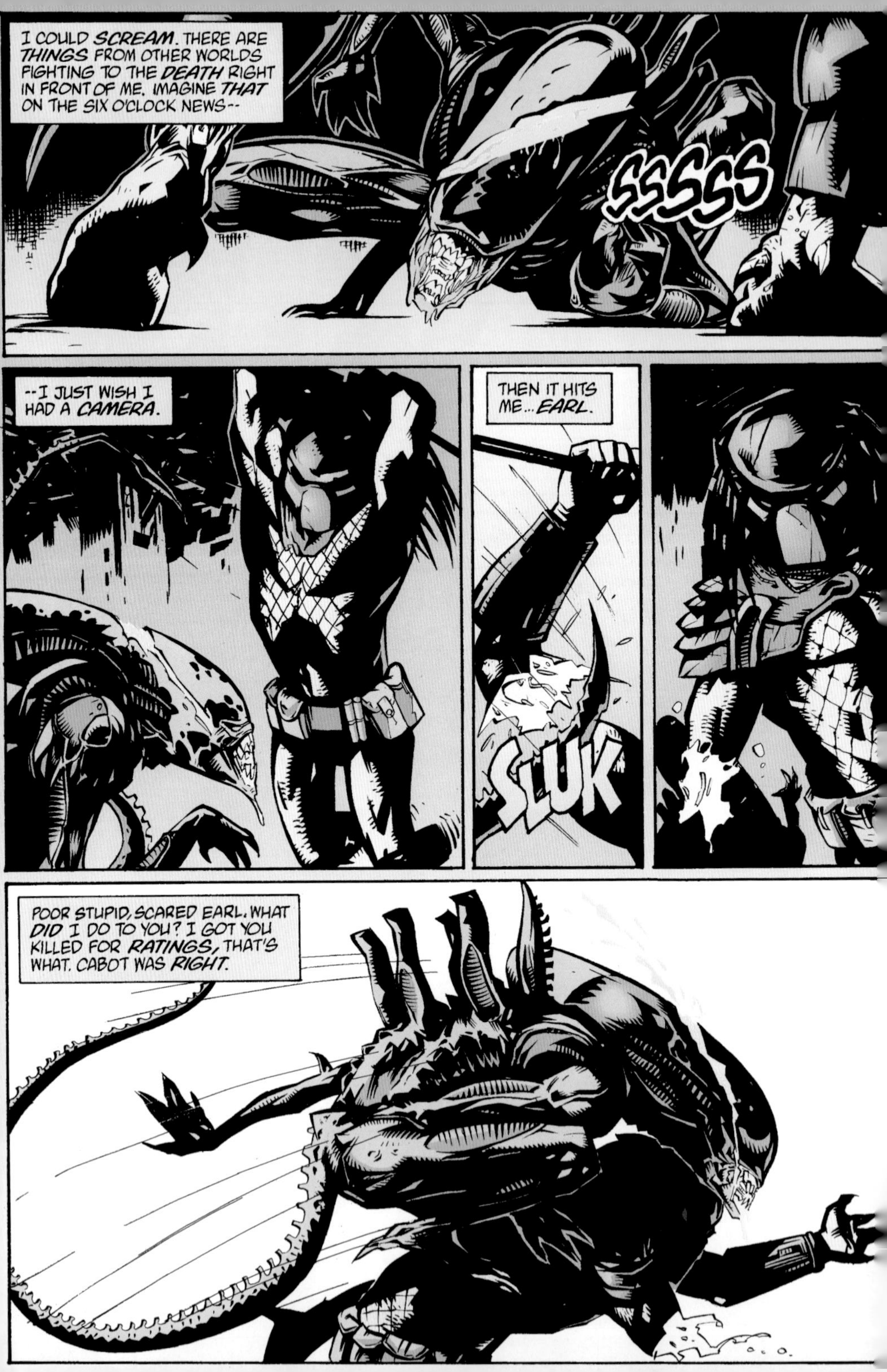
I COULD SCREAM. THERE ARE THINGS FROM OTHER WORLDS FIGHTING TO THE DEATH RIGHT IN FRONT OF ME. IMAGINE THAT ON THE SIX O'CLOCK NEWS--
SSSSS
--I JUST WISH I HAD A CAMERA.
THEN IT HITS ME... EARL.
SLUK
POOR STUPID, SCARED EARL. WHAT DID I DO TO YOU? I GOT YOU KILLED FOR RATINGS, THAT'S WHAT. CABOT WAS RIGHT.

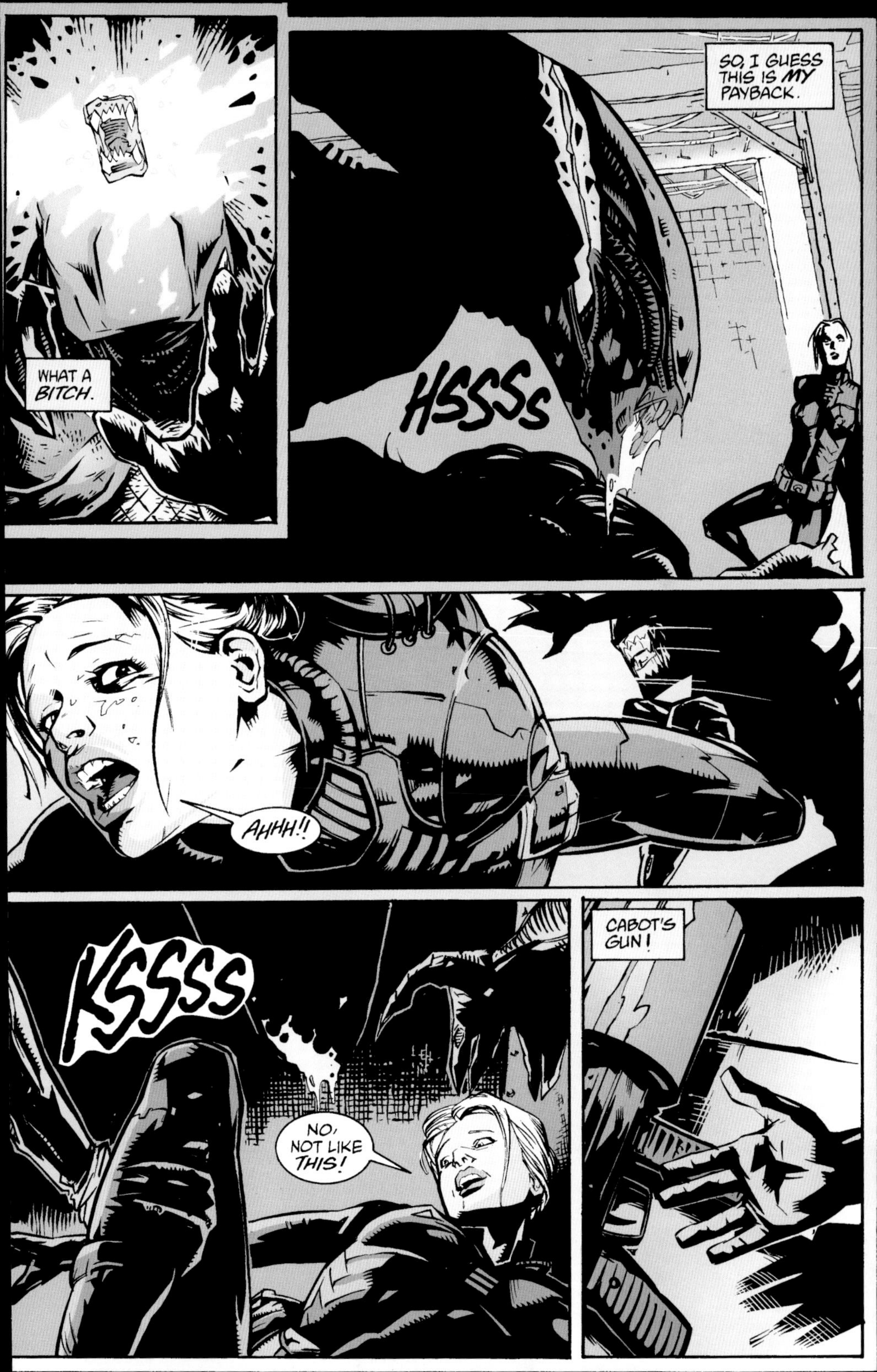
WHAT A *BITCH*.
SO, I GUESS THIS IS *MY* PAYBACK.
HSSSs
AHHH!!
KSSSS
NO, NOT LIKE *THIS*!
CABOT'S GUN!

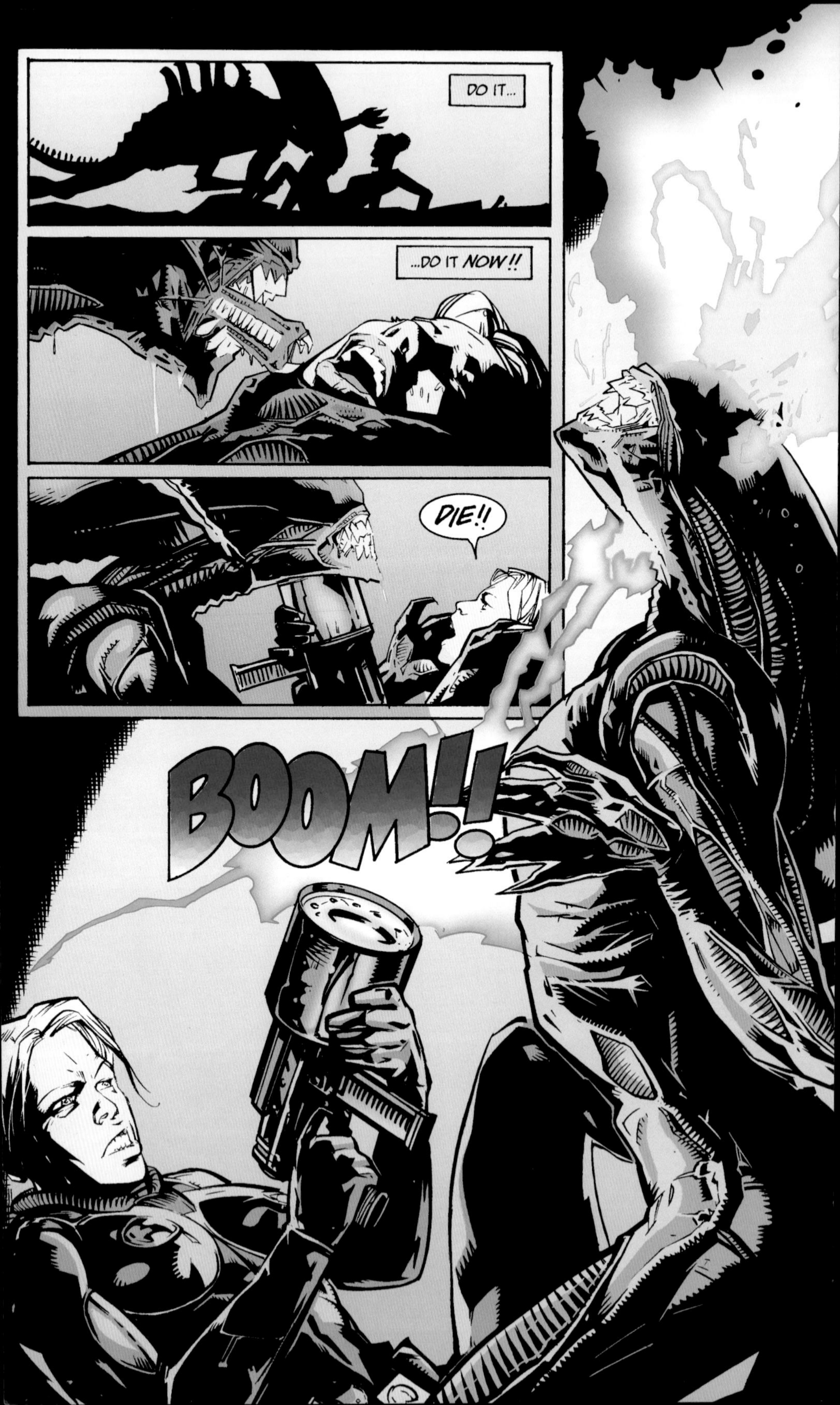
DO IT...
...DO IT NOW!!
DIE!!
BOOM!!

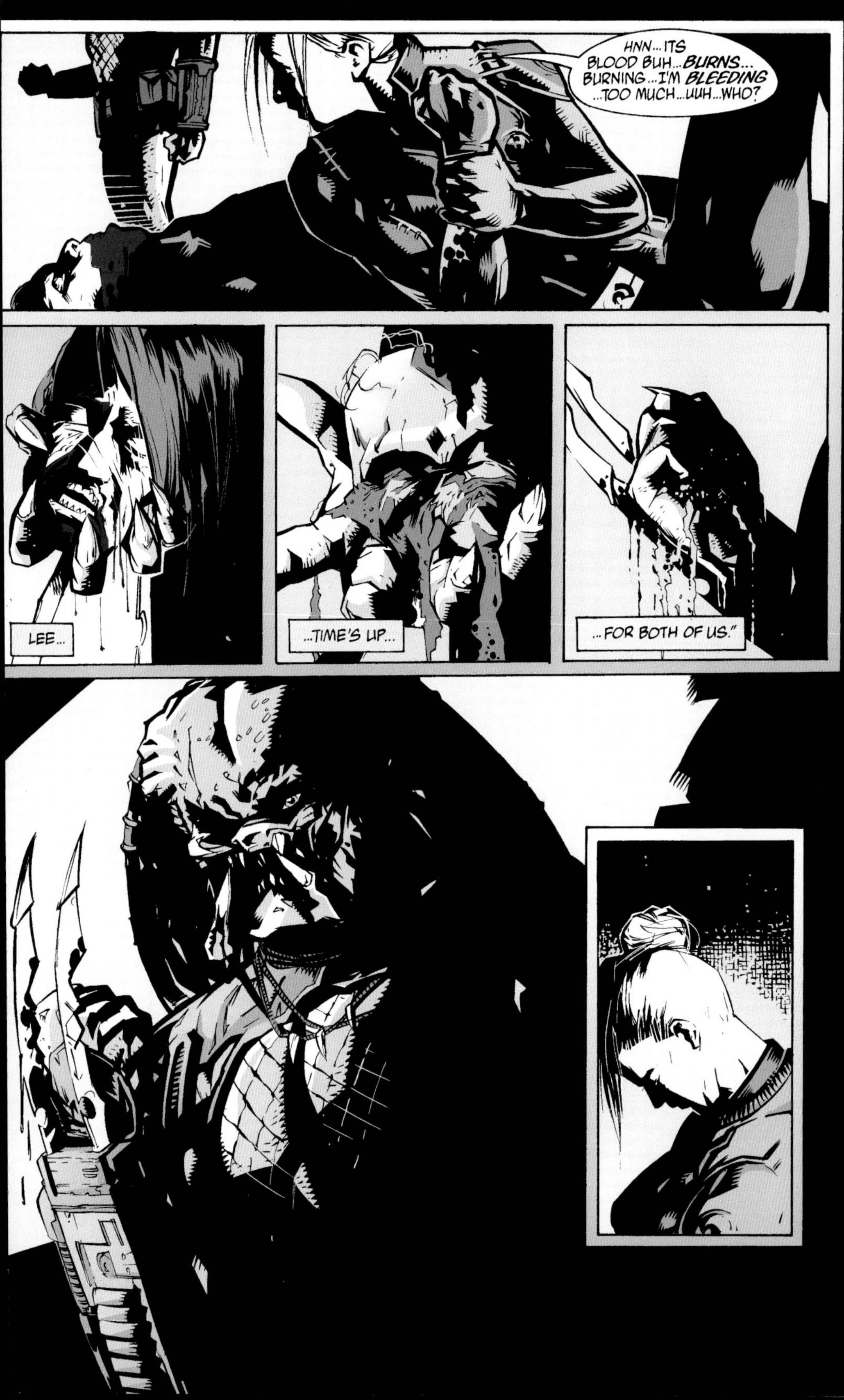
HNN...ITS BLOOD BUH...BURNS... BURNING...I'M BLEEDING ...TOO MUCH...UUH...WHO?
LEE...
...TIME'S UP...
...FOR BOTH OF US."

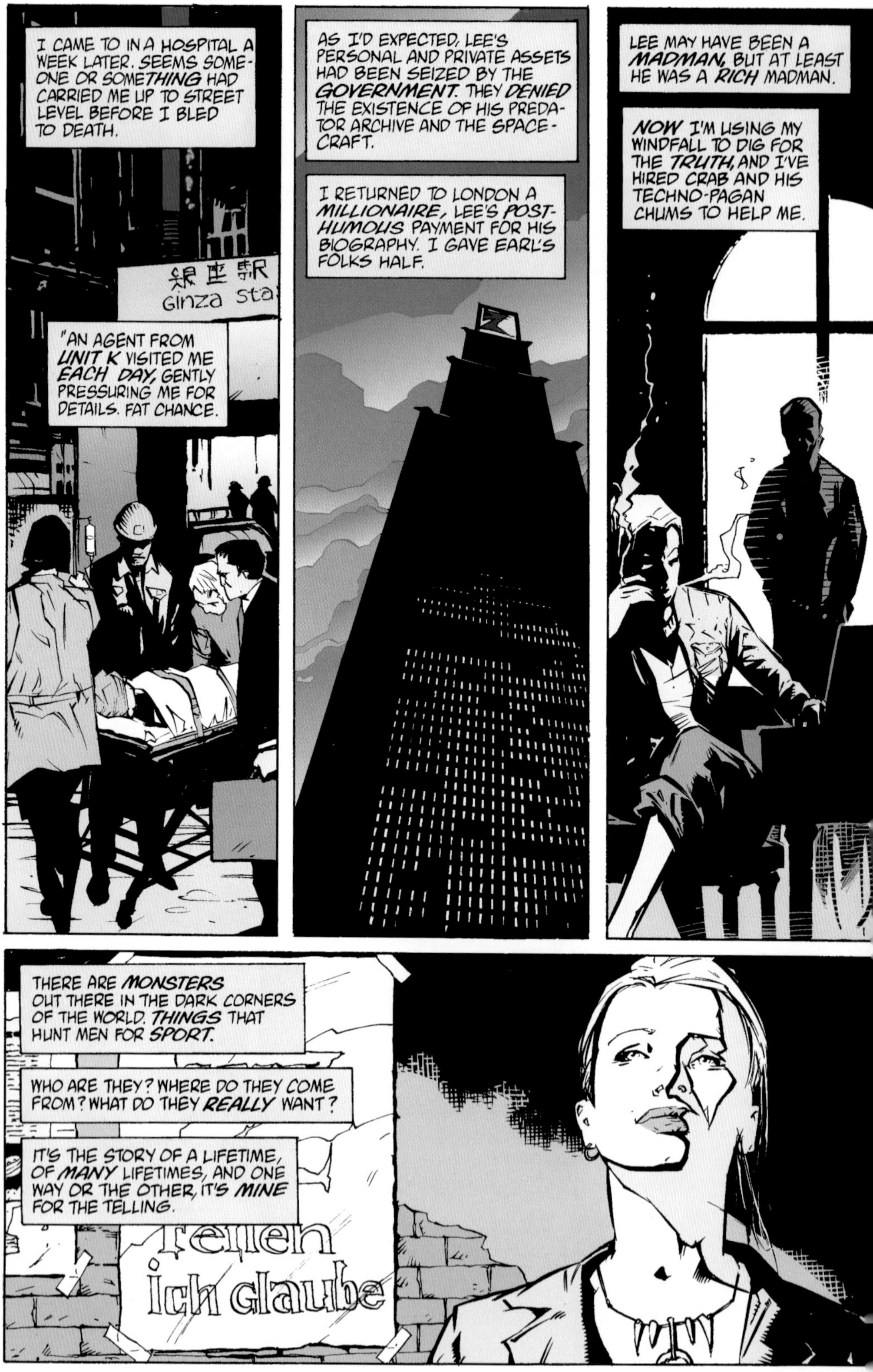
I CAME TO IN A HOSPITAL A WEEK LATER. SEEMS SOMEONE OR SOMETHING HAD CARRIED ME UP TO STREET LEVEL BEFORE I BLED TO DEATH.
銀座駅
Ginza Sta
"AN AGENT FROM UNIT K VISITED ME EACH DAY, GENTLY PRESSURING ME FOR DETAILS. FAT CHANCE.
AS I'D EXPECTED, LEE'S PERSONAL AND PRIVATE ASSETS HAD BEEN SEIZED BY THE GOVERNMENT. THEY DENIED THE EXISTENCE OF HIS PREDATOR ARCHIVE AND THE SPACECRAFT.
I RETURNED TO LONDON A MILLIONAIRE, LEE'S POSTHUMOUS PAYMENT FOR HIS BIOGRAPHY. I GAVE EARL'S FOLKS HALF.
LEE MAY HAVE BEEN A MADMAN, BUT AT LEAST HE WAS A RICH MADMAN.
NOW I'M USING MY WINDFALL TO DIG FOR THE TRUTH, AND I'VE HIRED CRAB AND HIS TECHNO-PAGAN CHUMS TO HELP ME.
THERE ARE MONSTERS OUT THERE IN THE DARK CORNERS OF THE WORLD. THINGS THAT HUNT MEN FOR SPORT.
WHO ARE THEY? WHERE DO THEY COME FROM? WHAT DO THEY REALLY WANT?
IT'S THE STORY OF A LIFETIME, OF MANY LIFETIMES, AND ONE WAY OR THE OTHER, IT'S MINE FOR THE TELLING.
Teilen
ich glaube

OLD SECRETS

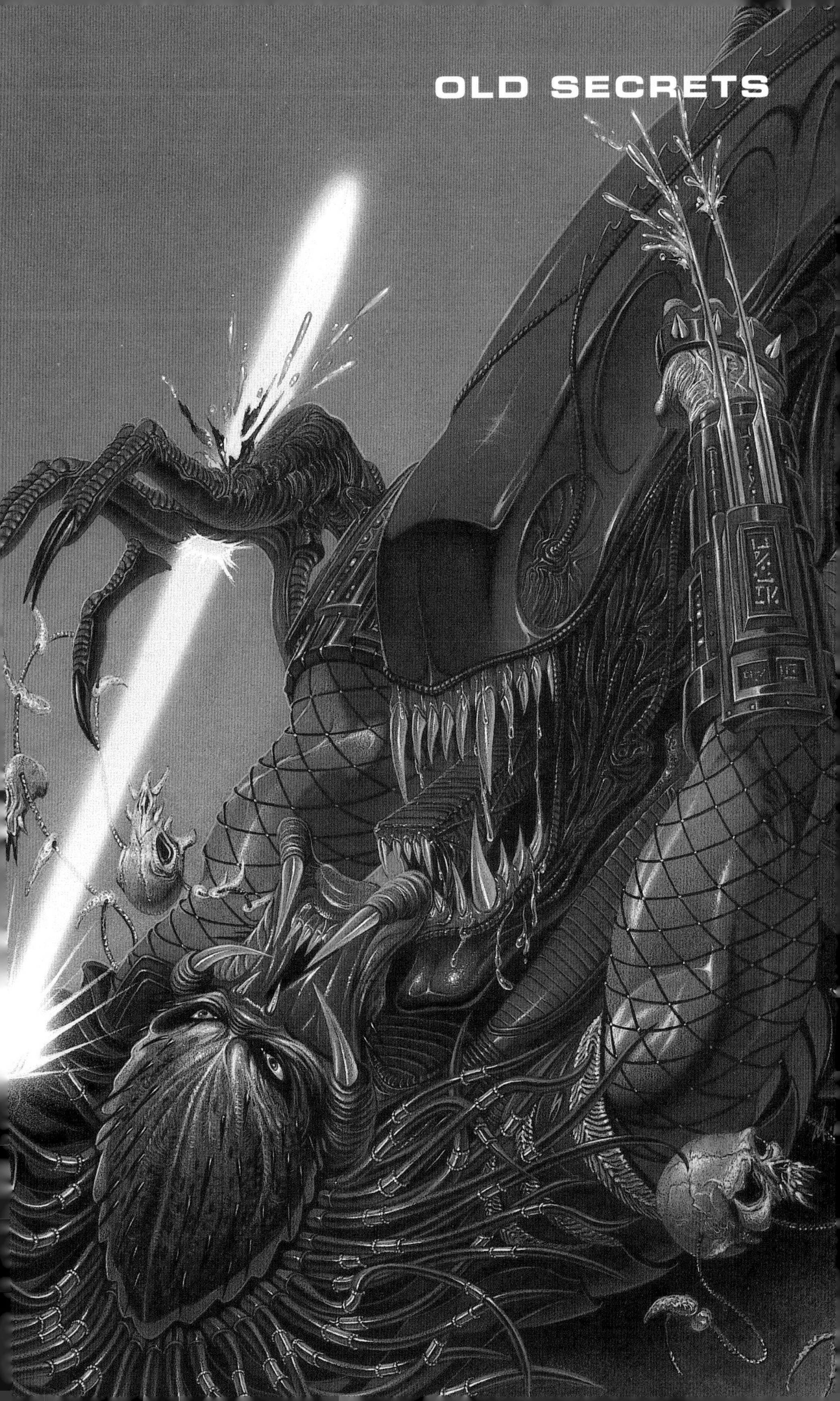

script and art
ALEX MALEEV

colors
STAISSI BRANDT

lettering
CLEM ROBINS

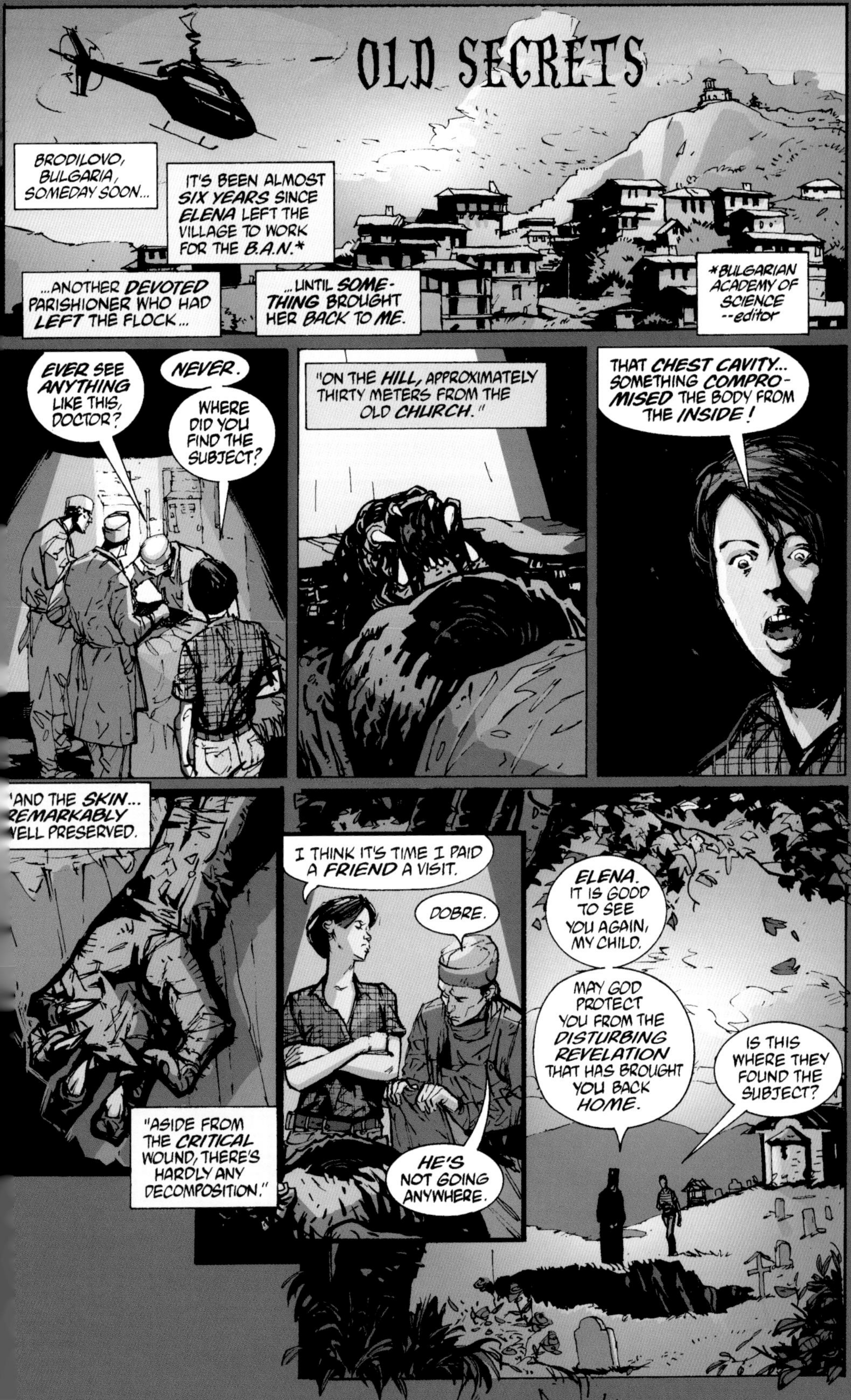
OLD SECRETS
BRODILOVO, BULGARIA, SOMEDAY SOON...
IT'S BEEN ALMOST SIX YEARS SINCE ELENA LEFT THE VILLAGE TO WORK FOR THE B.A.N.*
...ANOTHER DEVOTED PARISHIONER WHO HAD LEFT THE FLOCK...
...UNTIL SOMETHING BROUGHT HER BACK TO ME.
*BULGARIAN ACADEMY OF SCIENCE --editor
EVER SEE ANYTHING LIKE THIS, DOCTOR?
NEVER.
WHERE DID YOU FIND THE SUBJECT?
"ON THE HILL, APPROXIMATELY THIRTY METERS FROM THE OLD CHURCH."
THAT CHEST CAVITY... SOMETHING COMPROMISED THE BODY FROM THE INSIDE!
"AND THE SKIN... REMARKABLY WELL PRESERVED.
"ASIDE FROM THE CRITICAL WOUND, THERE'S HARDLY ANY DECOMPOSITION."
I THINK IT'S TIME I PAID A FRIEND A VISIT.
DOBRE.
HE'S NOT GOING ANYWHERE.
ELENA. IT IS GOOD TO SEE YOU AGAIN, MY CHILD.
MAY GOD PROTECT YOU FROM THE DISTURBING REVELATION THAT HAS BROUGHT YOU BACK HOME.
IS THIS WHERE THEY FOUND THE SUBJECT?

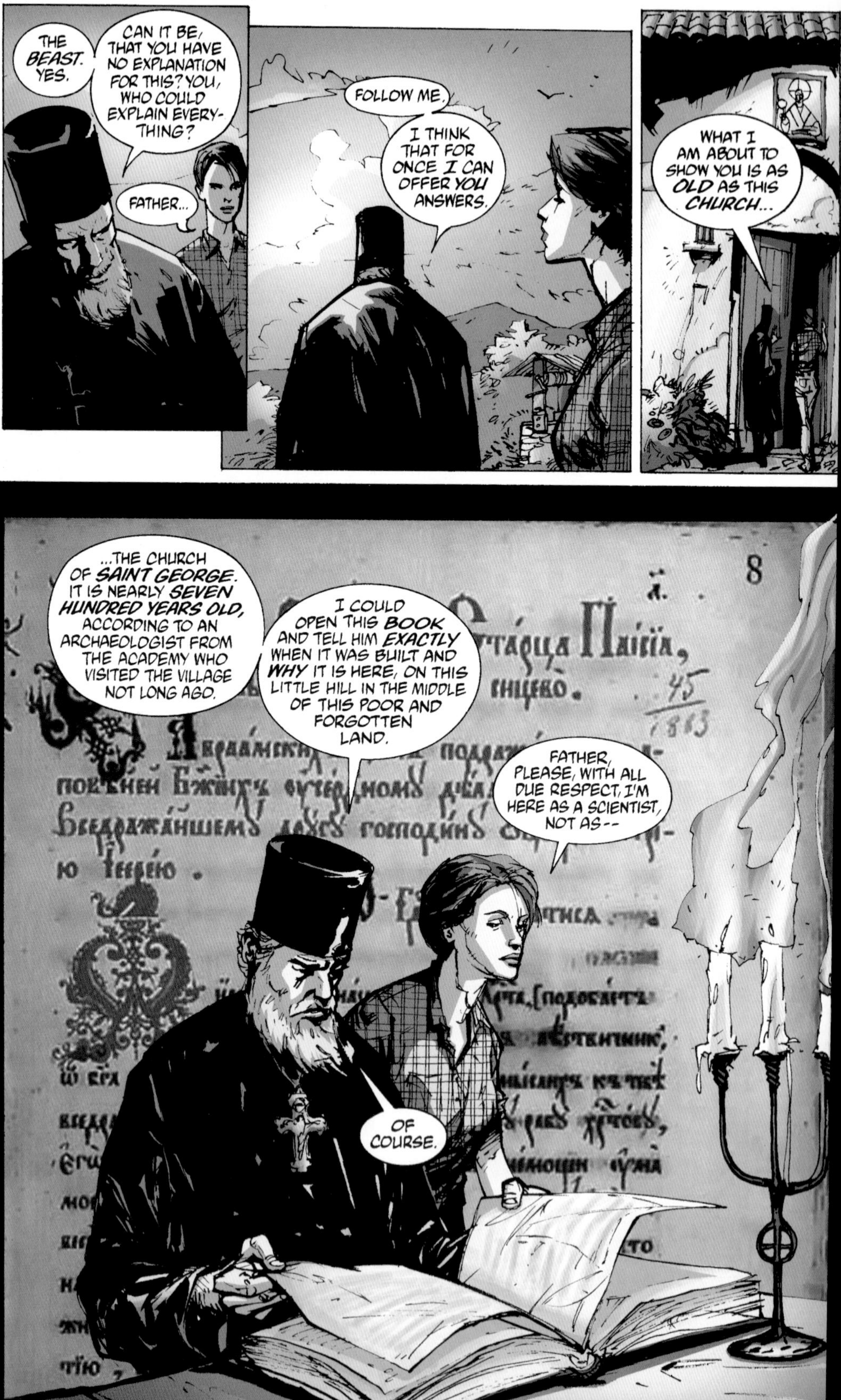
THE BEAST. YES.
CAN IT BE, THAT YOU HAVE NO EXPLANATION FOR THIS? YOU, WHO COULD EXPLAIN EVERY-THING?
FATHER...
FOLLOW ME.
I THINK THAT FOR ONCE I CAN OFFER YOU ANSWERS.
WHAT I AM ABOUT TO SHOW YOU IS AS OLD AS THIS CHURCH...
...THE CHURCH OF SAINT GEORGE. IT IS NEARLY SEVEN HUNDRED YEARS OLD, ACCORDING TO AN ARCHAEOLOGIST FROM THE ACADEMY WHO VISITED THE VILLAGE NOT LONG AGO.
I COULD OPEN THIS BOOK AND TELL HIM EXACTLY WHEN IT WAS BUILT AND WHY IT IS HERE, ON THIS LITTLE HILL IN THE MIDDLE OF THIS POOR AND FORGOTTEN LAND.
FATHER, PLEASE, WITH ALL DUE RESPECT, I'M HERE AS A SCIENTIST, NOT AS--
OF COURSE.

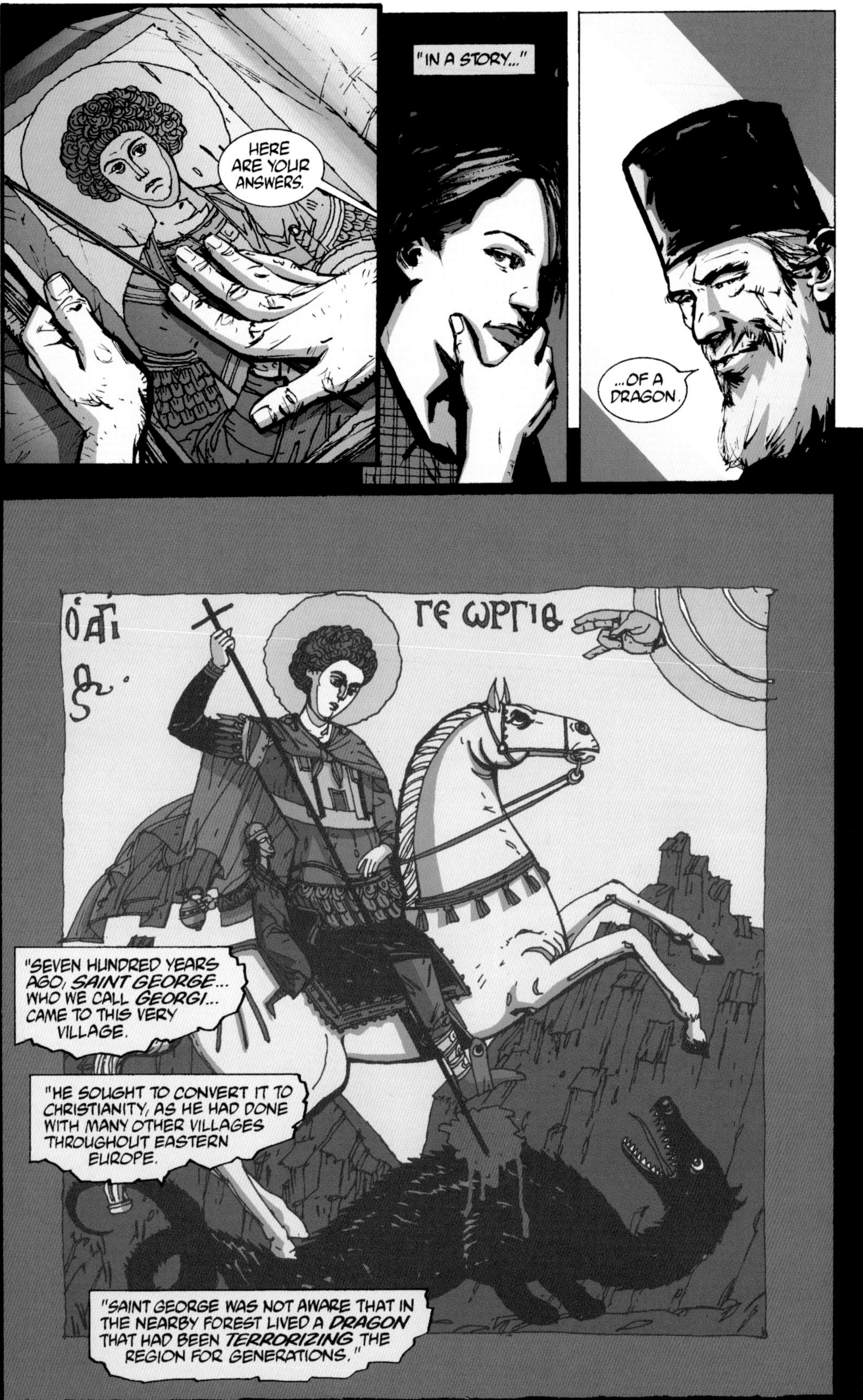
HERE ARE YOUR ANSWERS.
"IN A STORY..."
...OF A DRAGON.
"SEVEN HUNDRED YEARS AGO, SAINT GEORGE... WHO WE CALL GEORGI... CAME TO THIS VERY VILLAGE.
"HE SOUGHT TO CONVERT IT TO CHRISTIANITY, AS HE HAD DONE WITH MANY OTHER VILLAGES THROUGHOUT EASTERN EUROPE.
"SAINT GEORGE WAS NOT AWARE THAT IN THE NEARBY FOREST LIVED A DRAGON THAT HAD BEEN TERRORIZING THE REGION FOR GENERATIONS."

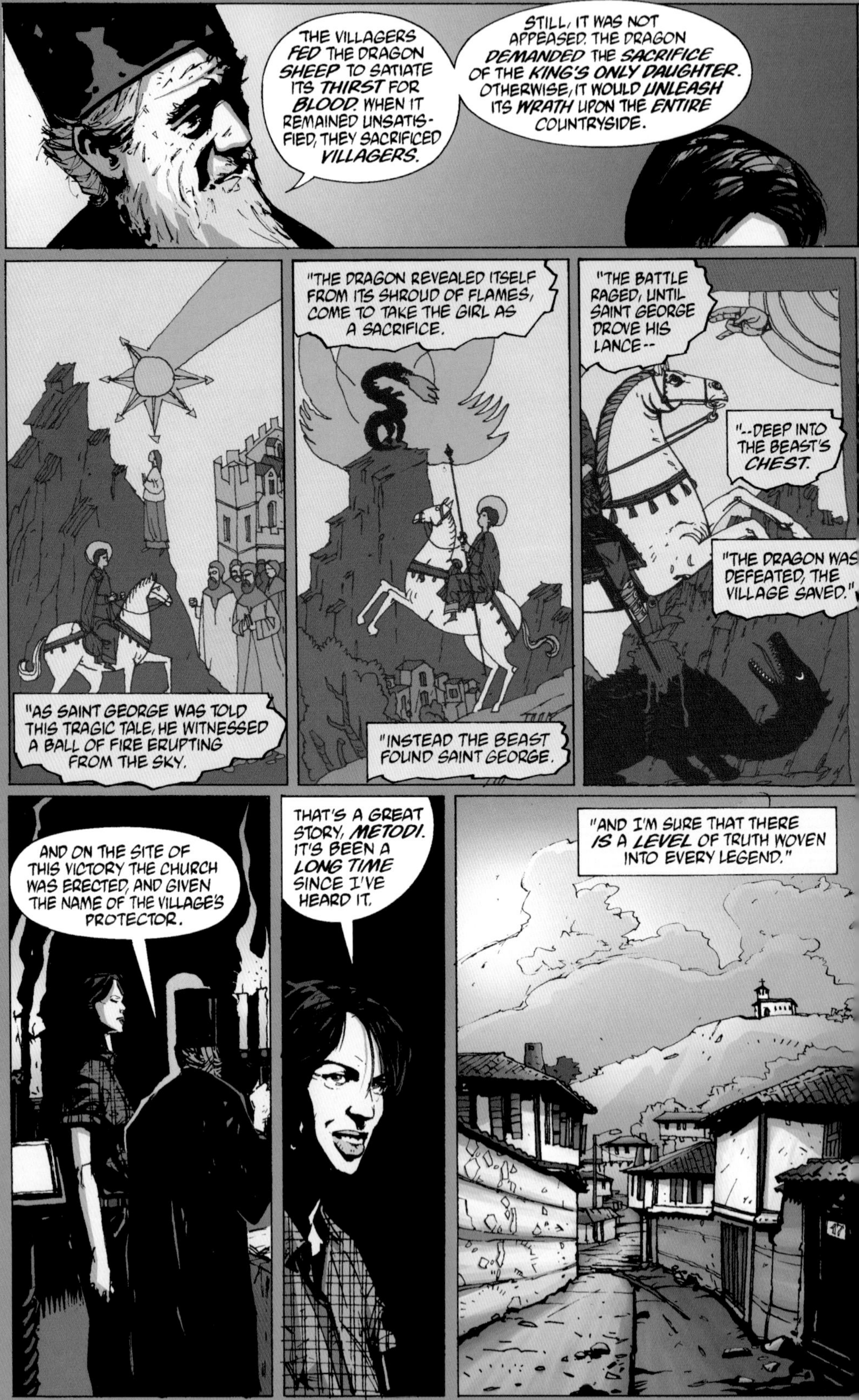
THE VILLAGERS FED THE DRAGON SHEEP TO SATIATE ITS THIRST FOR BLOOD. WHEN IT REMAINED UNSATIS-FIED, THEY SACRIFICED VILLAGERS.
STILL, IT WAS NOT APPEASED. THE DRAGON DEMANDED THE SACRIFICE OF THE KING'S ONLY DAUGHTER. OTHERWISE, IT WOULD UNLEASH ITS WRATH UPON THE ENTIRE COUNTRYSIDE.
"AS SAINT GEORGE WAS TOLD THIS TRAGIC TALE, HE WITNESSED A BALL OF FIRE ERUPTING FROM THE SKY.
"THE DRAGON REVEALED ITSELF FROM ITS SHROUD OF FLAMES, COME TO TAKE THE GIRL AS A SACRIFICE.
"INSTEAD THE BEAST FOUND SAINT GEORGE.
"THE BATTLE RAGED, UNTIL SAINT GEORGE DROVE HIS LANCE--
"--DEEP INTO THE BEAST'S CHEST.
"THE DRAGON WAS DEFEATED, THE VILLAGE SAVED."
AND ON THE SITE OF THIS VICTORY THE CHURCH WAS ERECTED, AND GIVEN THE NAME OF THE VILLAGE'S PROTECTOR.
THAT'S A GREAT STORY, METODI. IT'S BEEN A LONG TIME SINCE I'VE HEARD IT.
"AND I'M SURE THAT THERE IS A LEVEL OF TRUTH WOVEN INTO EVERY LEGEND."

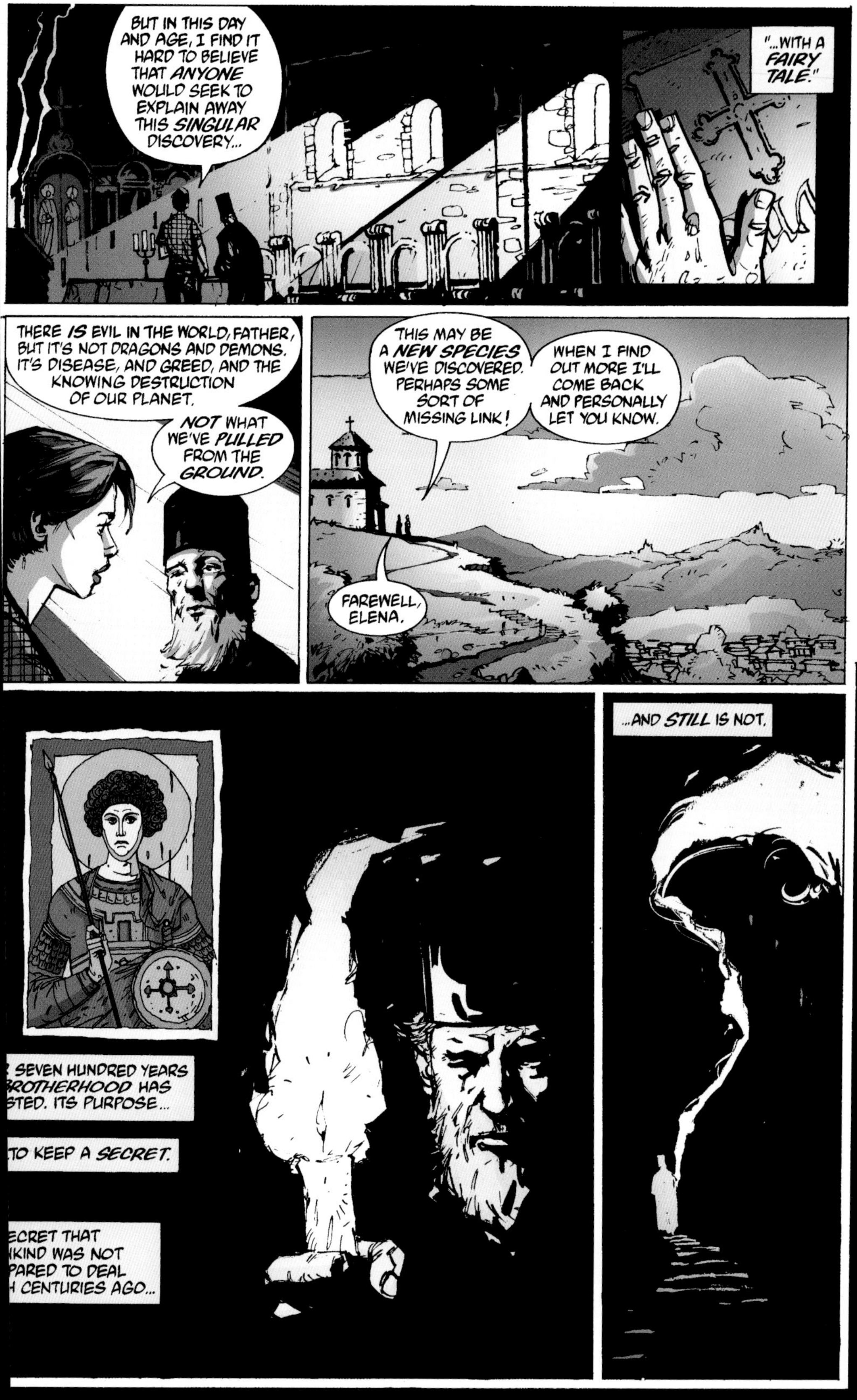
BUT IN THIS DAY AND AGE, I FIND IT HARD TO BELIEVE THAT ANYONE WOULD SEEK TO EXPLAIN AWAY THIS SINGULAR DISCOVERY...
"...WITH A FAIRY TALE."
THERE IS EVIL IN THE WORLD, FATHER, BUT IT'S NOT DRAGONS AND DEMONS. IT'S DISEASE, AND GREED, AND THE KNOWING DESTRUCTION OF OUR PLANET.
NOT WHAT WE'VE PULLED FROM THE GROUND.
THIS MAY BE A NEW SPECIES WE'VE DISCOVERED. PERHAPS SOME SORT OF MISSING LINK!
WHEN I FIND OUT MORE I'LL COME BACK AND PERSONALLY LET YOU KNOW.
FAREWELL, ELENA.
SEVEN HUNDRED YEARS BROTHERHOOD HAS STED. ITS PURPOSE...
TO KEEP A SECRET.
ECRET THAT KIND WAS NOT PARED TO DEAL H CENTURIES AGO...
...AND STILL IS NOT.

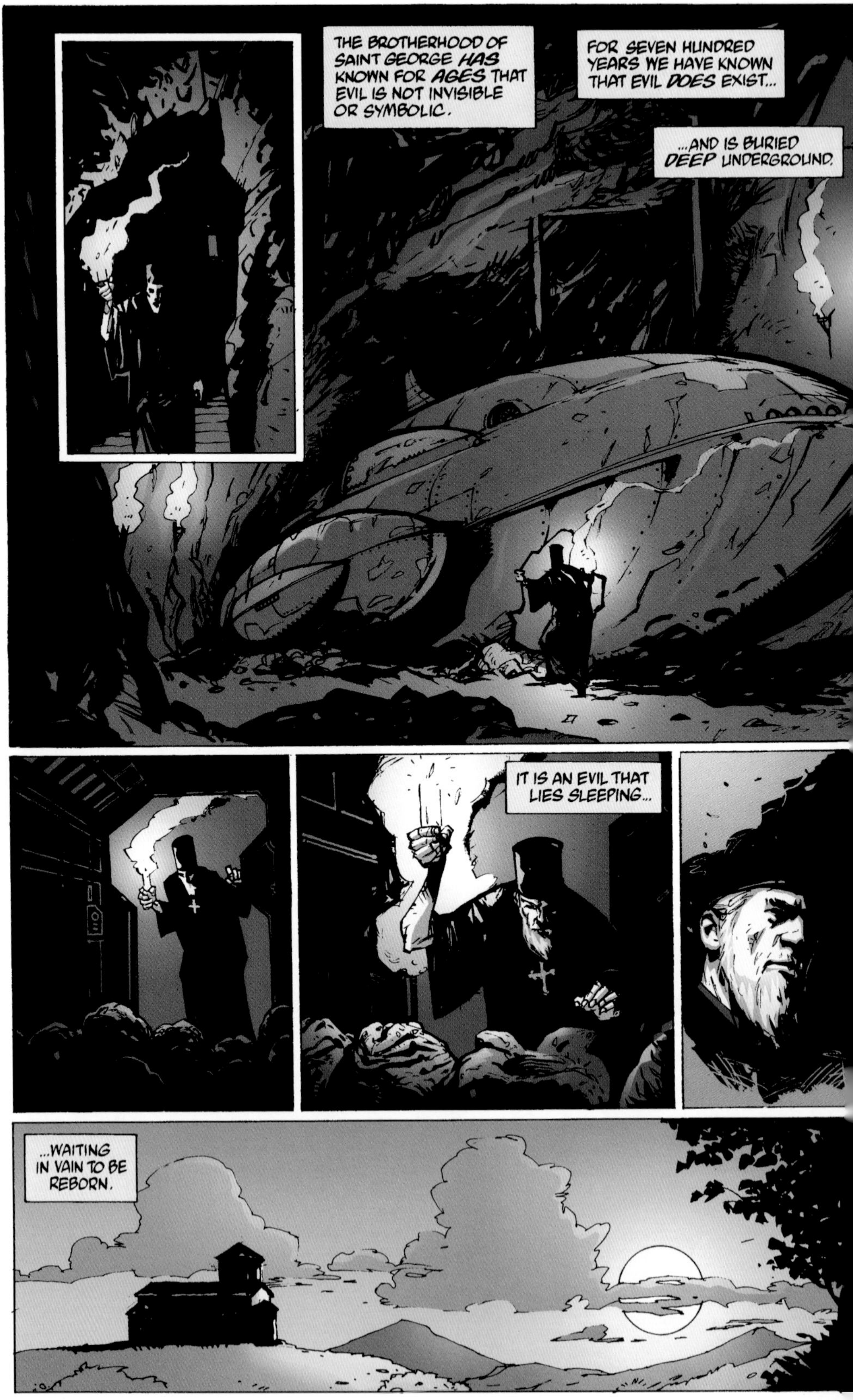
THE BROTHERHOOD OF SAINT GEORGE HAS KNOWN FOR AGES THAT EVIL IS NOT INVISIBLE OR SYMBOLIC.
FOR SEVEN HUNDRED YEARS WE HAVE KNOWN THAT EVIL DOES EXIST...
...AND IS BURIED DEEP UNDERGROUND.
IT IS AN EVIL THAT LIES SLEEPING...
...WAITING IN VAIN TO BE REBORN.

THE WEB

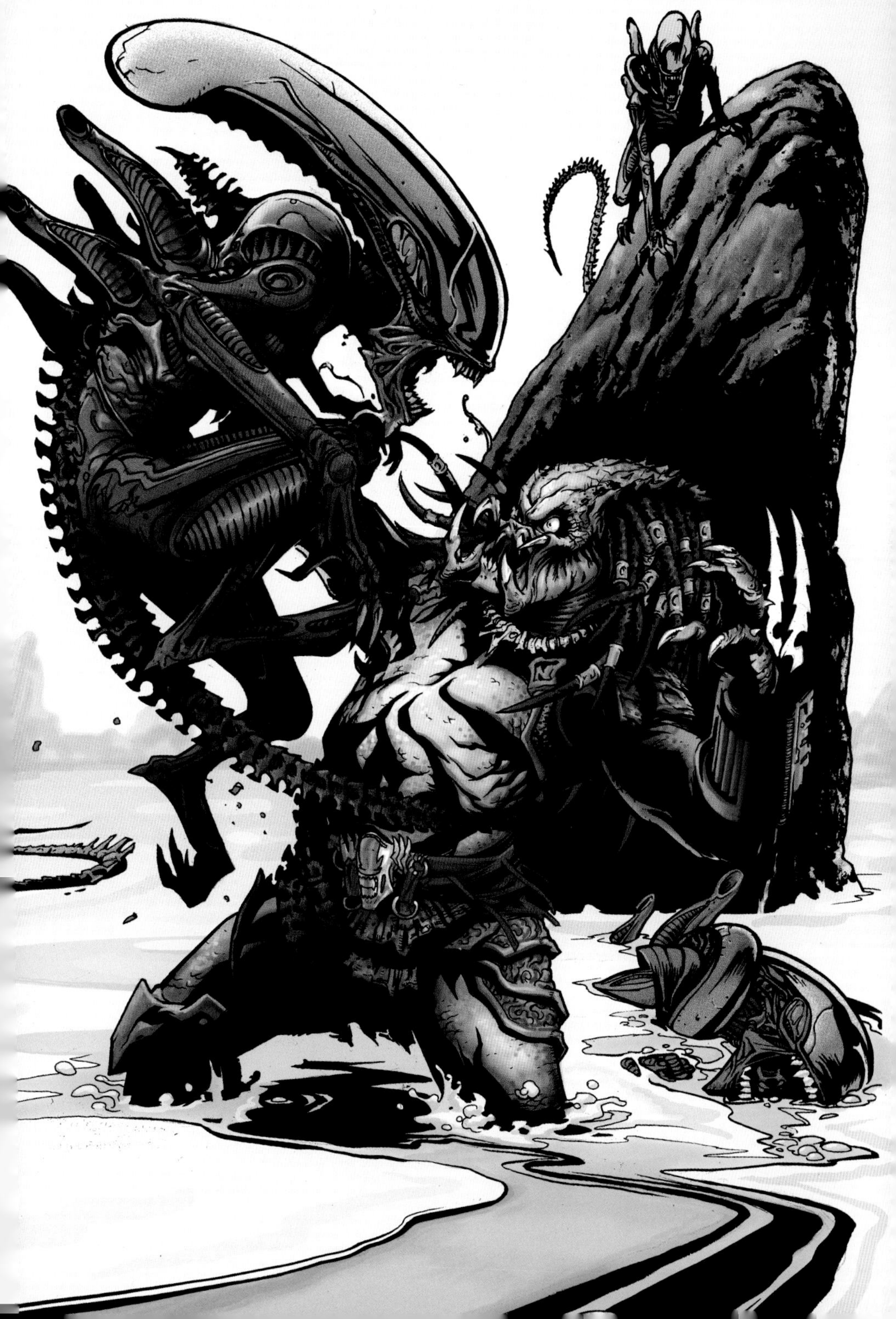

script
IAN EDGINTON

art
DEREK THOMPSON
BRIAN O'CONNELL

lettering
CLEM ROBINS

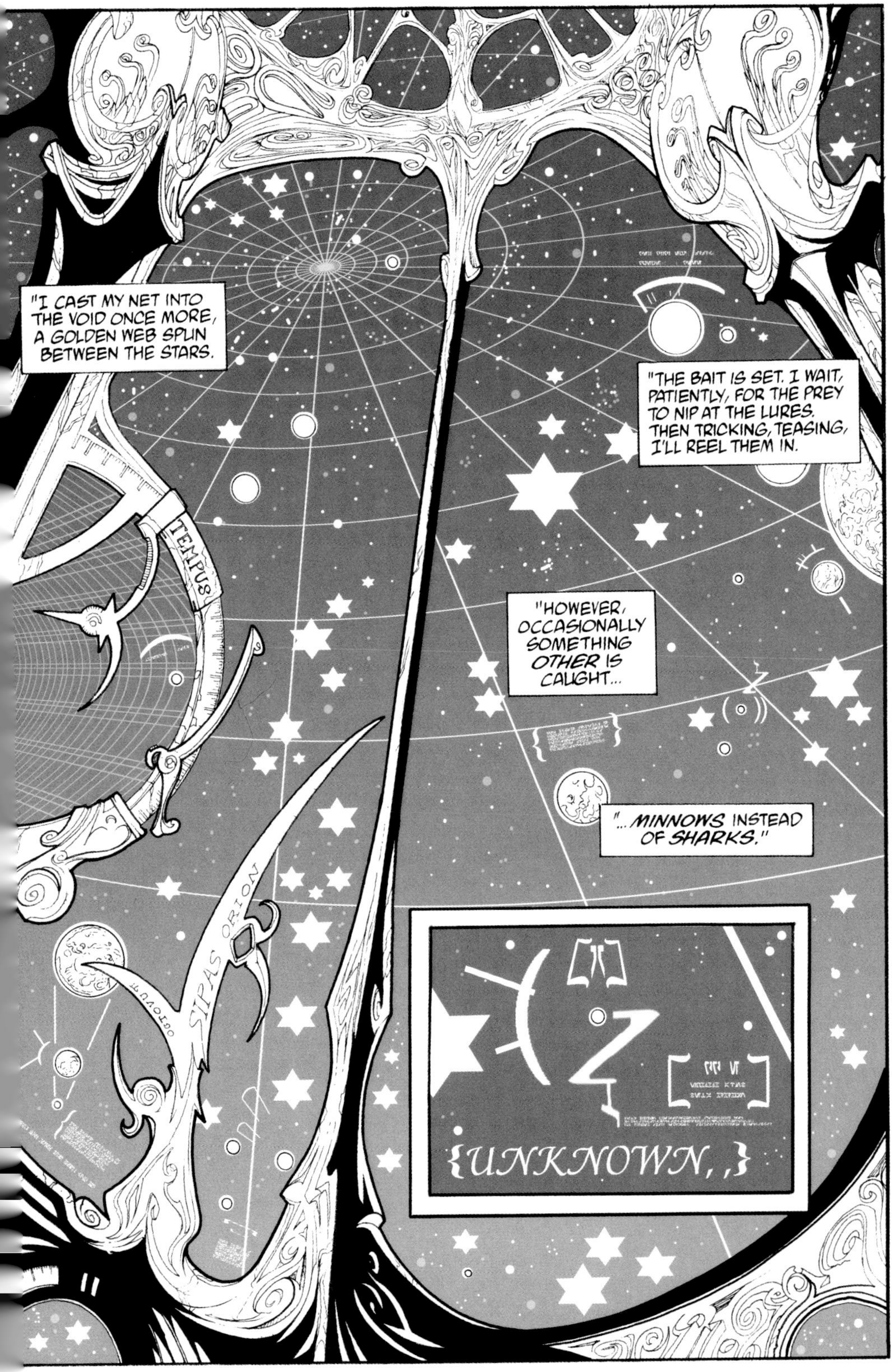
"I CAST MY NET INTO THE VOID ONCE MORE, A GOLDEN WEB SPUN BETWEEN THE STARS.
"THE BAIT IS SET. I WAIT, PATIENTLY, FOR THE PREY TO NIP AT THE LURES. THEN TRICKING, TEASING, I'LL REEL THEM IN.
TEMPUS
"HOWEVER, OCCASIONALLY SOMETHING *OTHER* IS CAUGHT...
"...*MINNOWS* INSTEAD OF *SHARKS*."
SIPAS ORION
{UNKNOWN, ,}

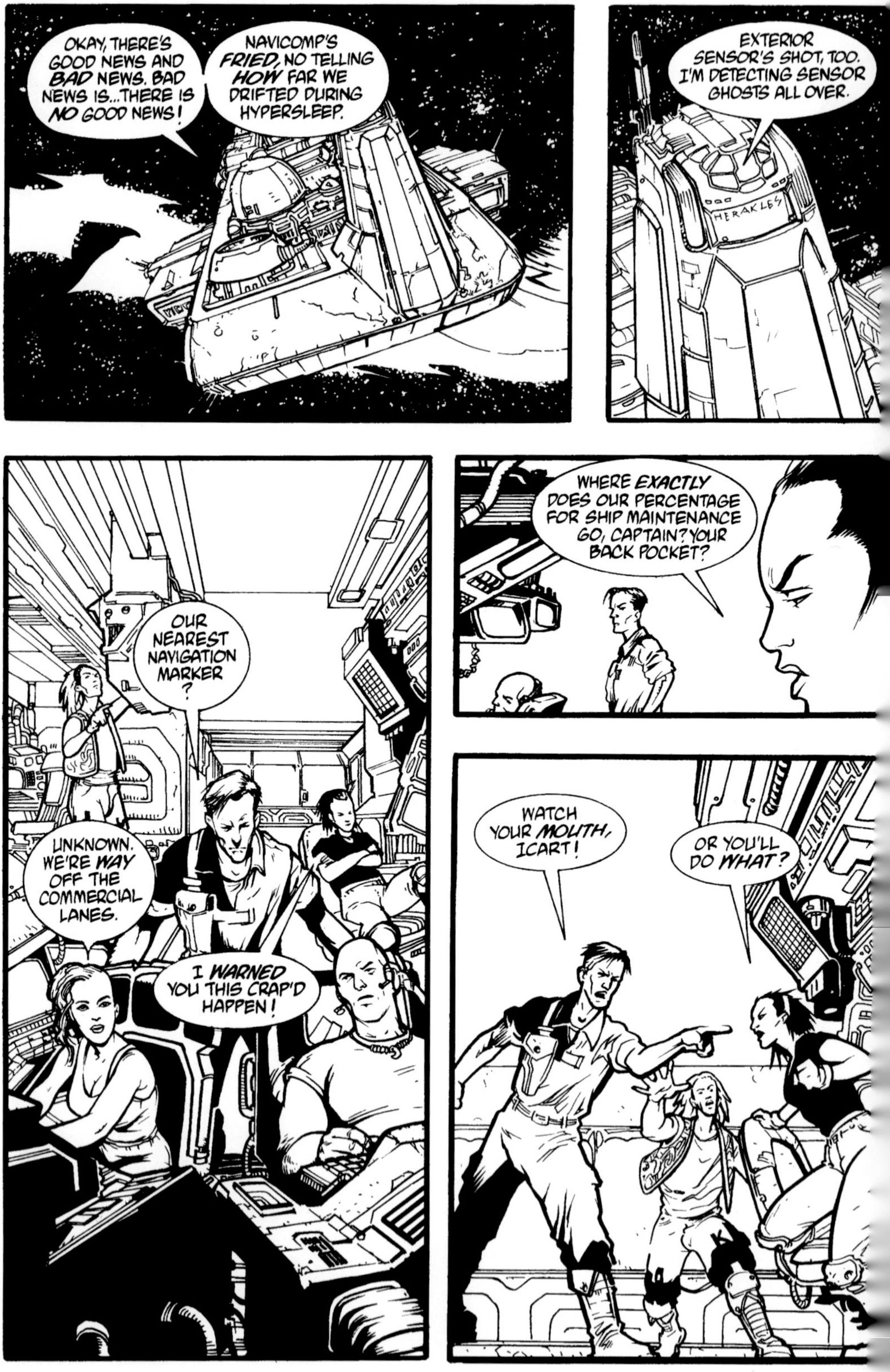
OKAY, THERE'S GOOD NEWS AND BAD NEWS. BAD NEWS IS...THERE IS NO GOOD NEWS!
NAVICOMP'S FRIED, NO TELLING HOW FAR WE DRIFTED DURING HYPERSLEEP.
EXTERIOR SENSOR'S SHOT, TOO. I'M DETECTING SENSOR GHOSTS ALL OVER.
HERAKLES
OUR NEAREST NAVIGATION MARKER?
UNKNOWN. WE'RE WAY OFF THE COMMERCIAL LANES.
I WARNED YOU THIS CRAP'D HAPPEN!
WHERE EXACTLY DOES OUR PERCENTAGE FOR SHIP MAINTENANCE GO, CAPTAIN? YOUR BACK POCKET?
WATCH YOUR MOUTH, ICART!
OR YOU'LL DO WHAT?

'EY, CHILDREN, HUSH IT UP NOW. WE BIN TOO LONG IN THIS CAN. IS CABIN FEVER, IS ALL.

CORD'S RIGHT. THIS'LL KEEP...FOR NOW.

CAPTAIN REBECK, A SIGNAL!

ON SPEAKERS.

CHKACHKA

A COMPUTER-ACTIVATED DISTRESS BEACON! LOCK ONTO IT.

BUT WE CAN'T 'ELP OURSELVES, LET ALONE ANOTHER.

WE'RE NOT HELPING ANYONE. I WANT THAT COMPUTER.

INSTALL IT IN THE NAVICOMP, WE'RE OUTTA HERE.

EXCELLENT.

JUDE, FIRE UP THE THRUSTERS...

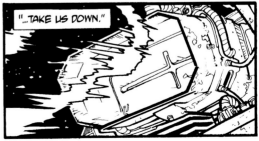

"...TAKE US DOWN."

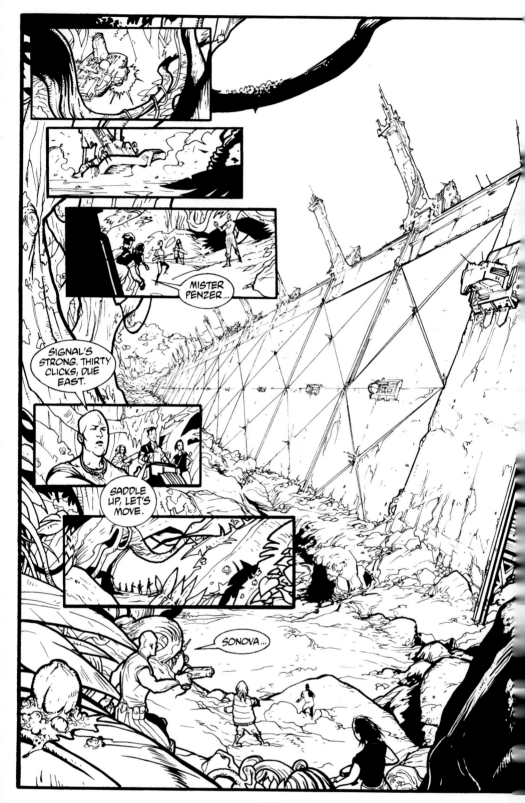

MISTER PENZER...

SIGNAL'S STRONG. THIRTY CLICKS, DUE EAST.

SADDLE UP, LET'S MOVE.

SONOVA...

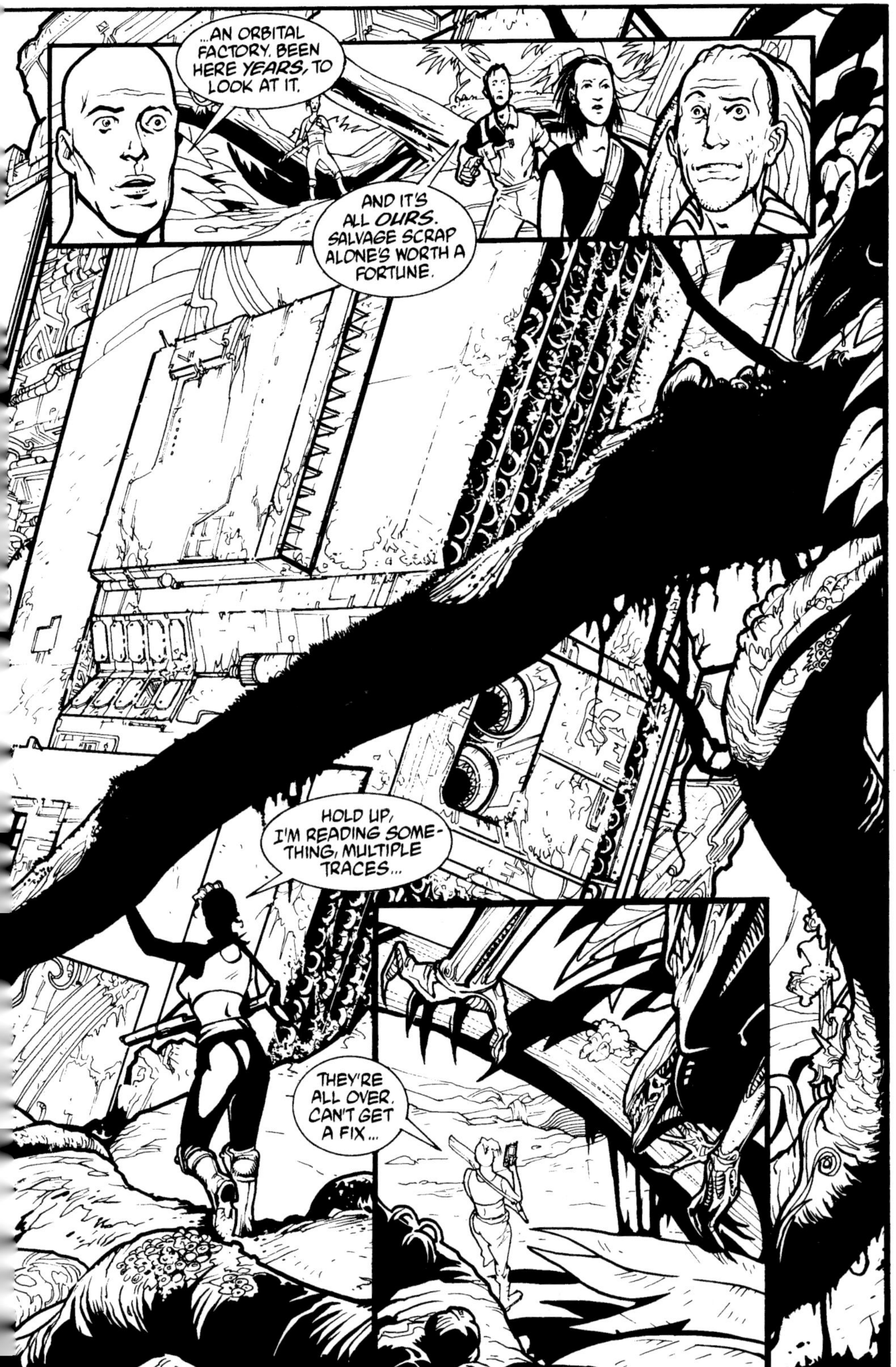
...AN ORBITAL FACTORY. BEEN HERE YEARS, TO LOOK AT IT.
AND IT'S ALL OURS. SALVAGE SCRAP ALONE'S WORTH A FORTUNE.
HOLD UP, I'M READING SOME-THING, MULTIPLE TRACES...
THEY'RE ALL OVER. CAN'T GET A FIX...

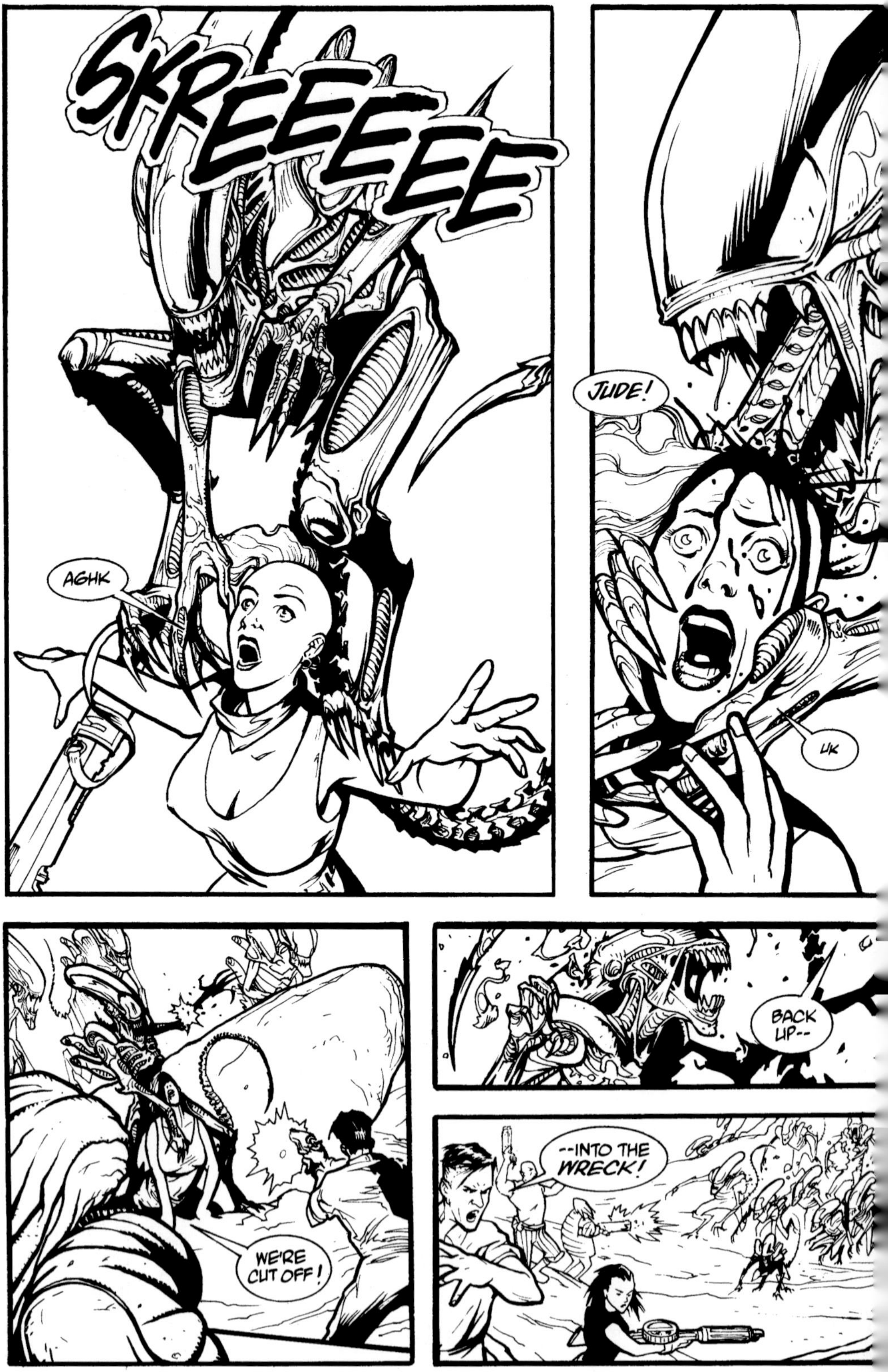
SKREEEEEE
AGHK
JUDE!
UK
WE'RE CUT OFF!
BACK UP--
--INTO THE WRECK!

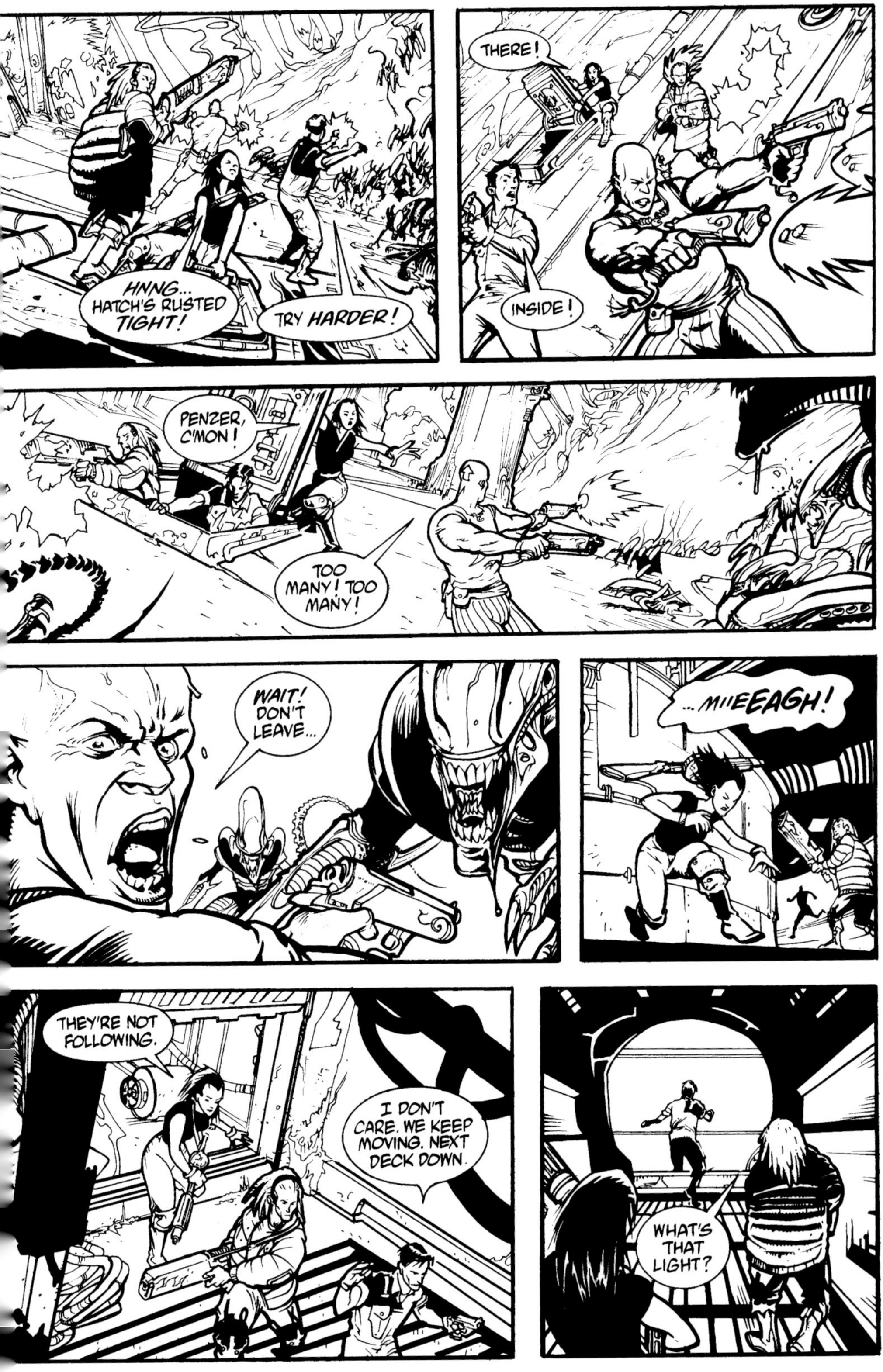
HNNG... HATCH'S RUSTED TIGHT!
TRY HARDER!
THERE!
INSIDE!
PENZER, C'MON!
TOO MANY! TOO MANY!
WAIT! DON'T LEAVE...
...MIIEEAGH!
THEY'RE NOT FOLLOWING.
I DON'T CARE. WE KEEP MOVING. NEXT DECK DOWN.
WHAT'S THAT LIGHT?

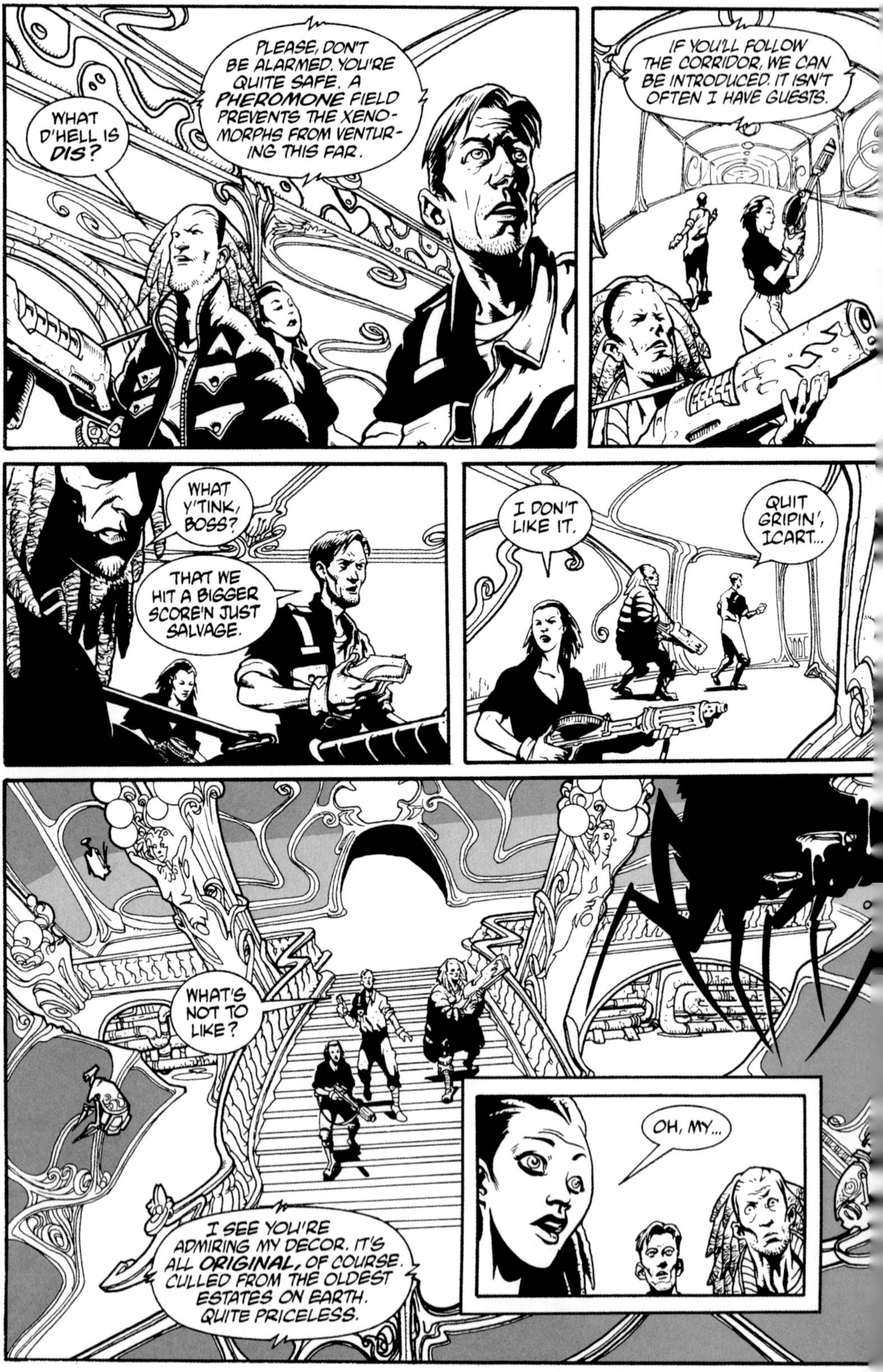
WHAT D'HELL IS DIS?
PLEASE, DON'T BE ALARMED. YOU'RE QUITE SAFE. A PHEROMONE FIELD PREVENTS THE XENO-MORPHS FROM VENTUR-ING THIS FAR.
IF YOU'LL FOLLOW THE CORRIDOR, WE CAN BE INTRODUCED. IT ISN'T OFTEN I HAVE GUESTS.
WHAT Y'TINK, BOSS?
THAT WE HIT A BIGGER SCORE'N JUST SALVAGE.
I DON'T LIKE IT.
QUIT GRIPIN', ICART...
WHAT'S NOT TO LIKE?
I SEE YOU'RE ADMIRING MY DECOR. IT'S ALL ORIGINAL, OF COURSE. CULLED FROM THE OLDEST ESTATES ON EARTH. QUITE PRICELESS.
OH, MY...

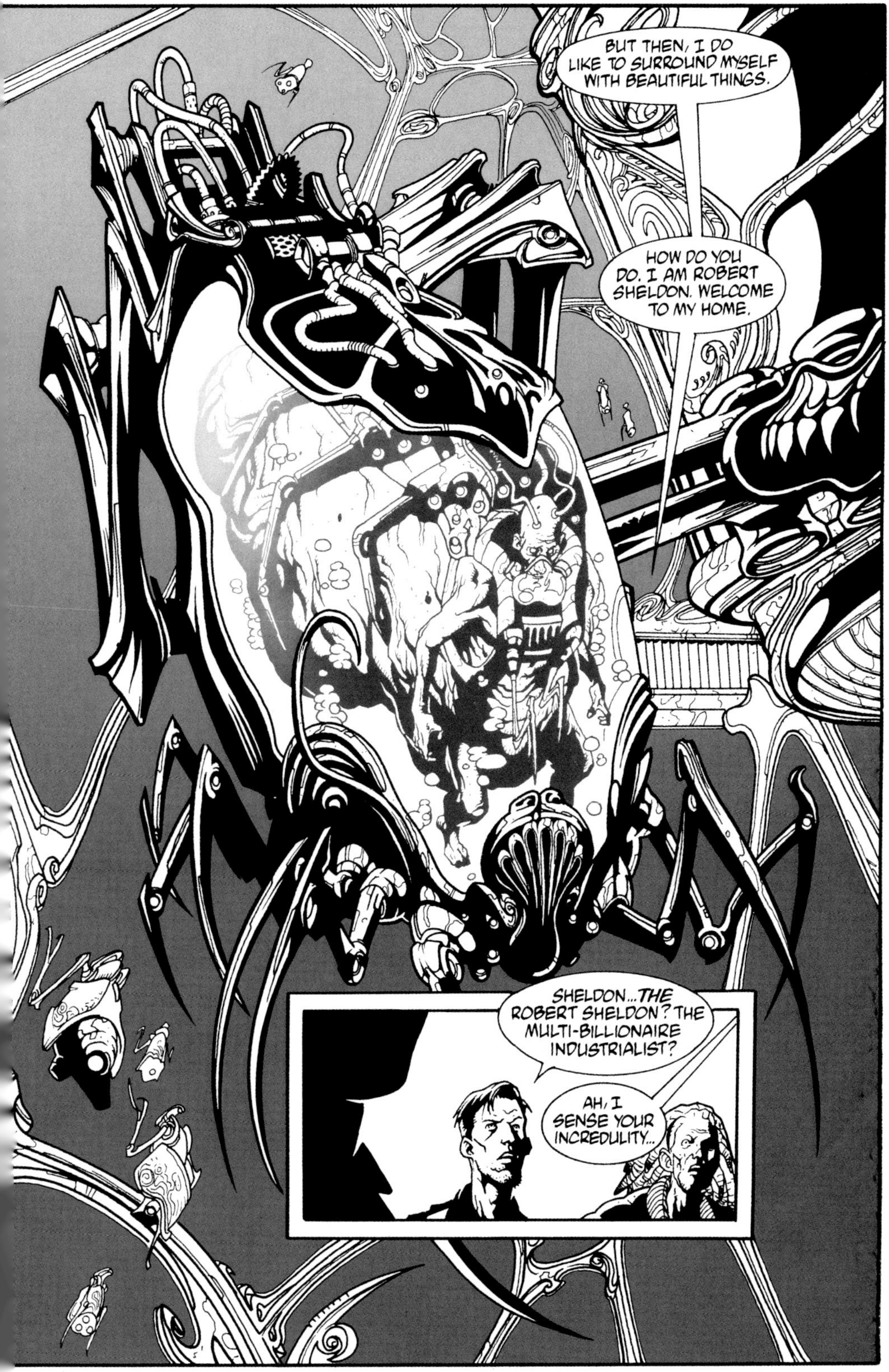
BUT THEN, I DO LIKE TO SURROUND MYSELF WITH BEAUTIFUL THINGS.
HOW DO YOU DO. I AM ROBERT SHELDON. WELCOME TO MY HOME.
SHELDON... *THE* ROBERT SHELDON? THE MULTI-BILLIONAIRE INDUSTRIALIST?
AH, I SENSE YOUR INCREDULITY...

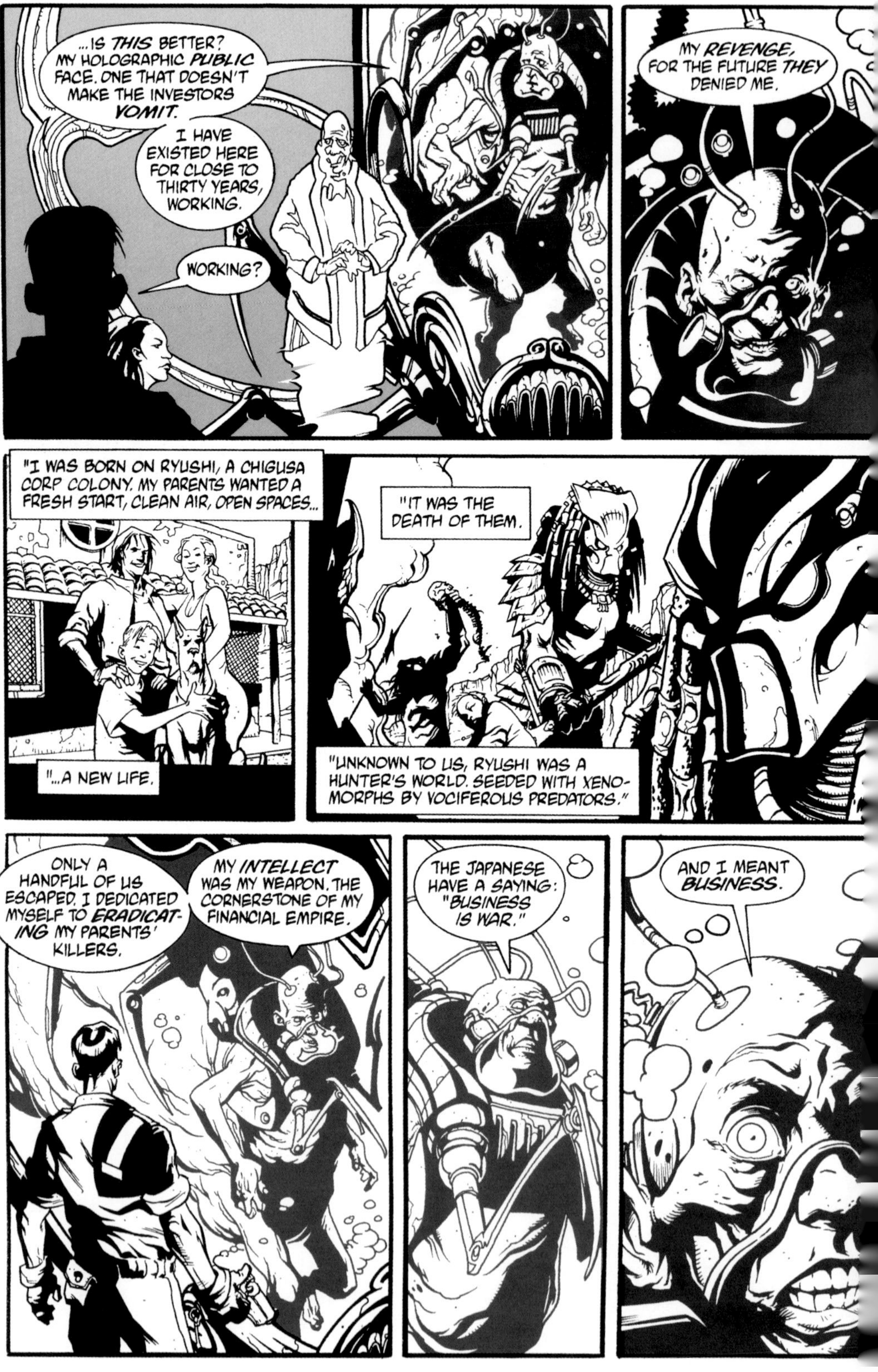
...IS THIS BETTER? MY HOLOGRAPHIC PUBLIC FACE. ONE THAT DOESN'T MAKE THE INVESTORS VOMIT.
I HAVE EXISTED HERE FOR CLOSE TO THIRTY YEARS, WORKING.
WORKING?
MY REVENGE, FOR THE FUTURE THEY DENIED ME.
"I WAS BORN ON RYUSHI, A CHIGUSA CORP COLONY. MY PARENTS WANTED A FRESH START, CLEAN AIR, OPEN SPACES...
"...A NEW LIFE.
"IT WAS THE DEATH OF THEM.
"UNKNOWN TO US, RYUSHI WAS A HUNTER'S WORLD. SEEDED WITH XENO-MORPHS BY VOCIFEROUS PREDATORS."
ONLY A HANDFUL OF US ESCAPED. I DEDICATED MYSELF TO ERADICAT-ING MY PARENTS' KILLERS.
MY INTELLECT WAS MY WEAPON. THE CORNERSTONE OF MY FINANCIAL EMPIRE.
THE JAPANESE HAVE A SAYING: "BUSINESS IS WAR."
AND I MEANT BUSINESS.

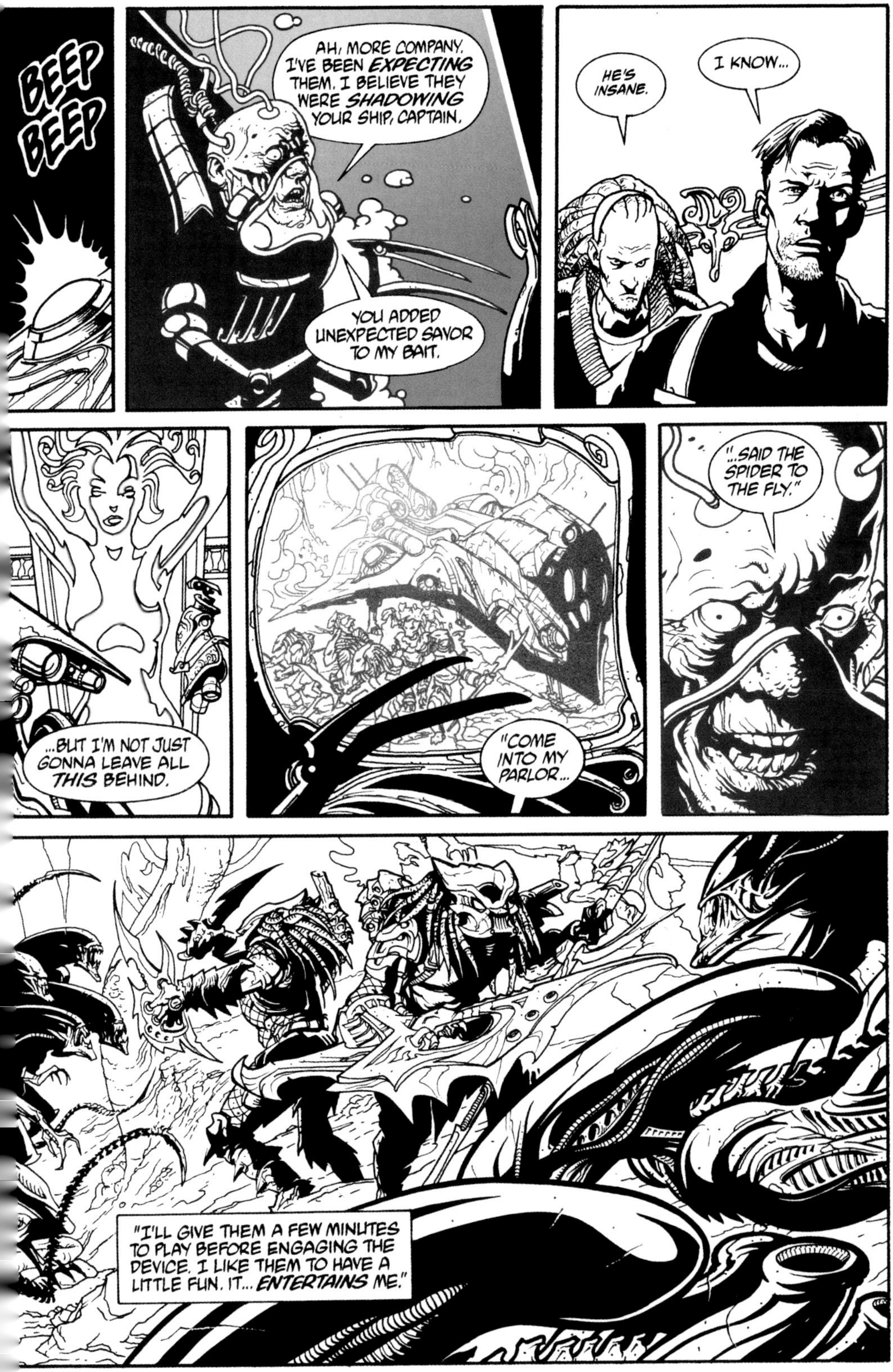
BEEP BEEP
AH, MORE COMPANY. I'VE BEEN *EXPECTING* THEM. I BELIEVE THEY WERE *SHADOWING* YOUR SHIP, CAPTAIN.
YOU ADDED UNEXPECTED SAVOR TO MY BAIT.
HE'S INSANE.
I KNOW...
...BUT I'M NOT JUST GONNA LEAVE ALL *THIS* BEHIND.
"COME INTO MY PARLOR...
"...SAID THE SPIDER TO THE FLY."
"I'LL GIVE THEM A FEW MINUTES TO PLAY BEFORE ENGAGING THE DEVICE. I LIKE THEM TO HAVE A LITTLE FUN. IT... *ENTERTAINS* ME."

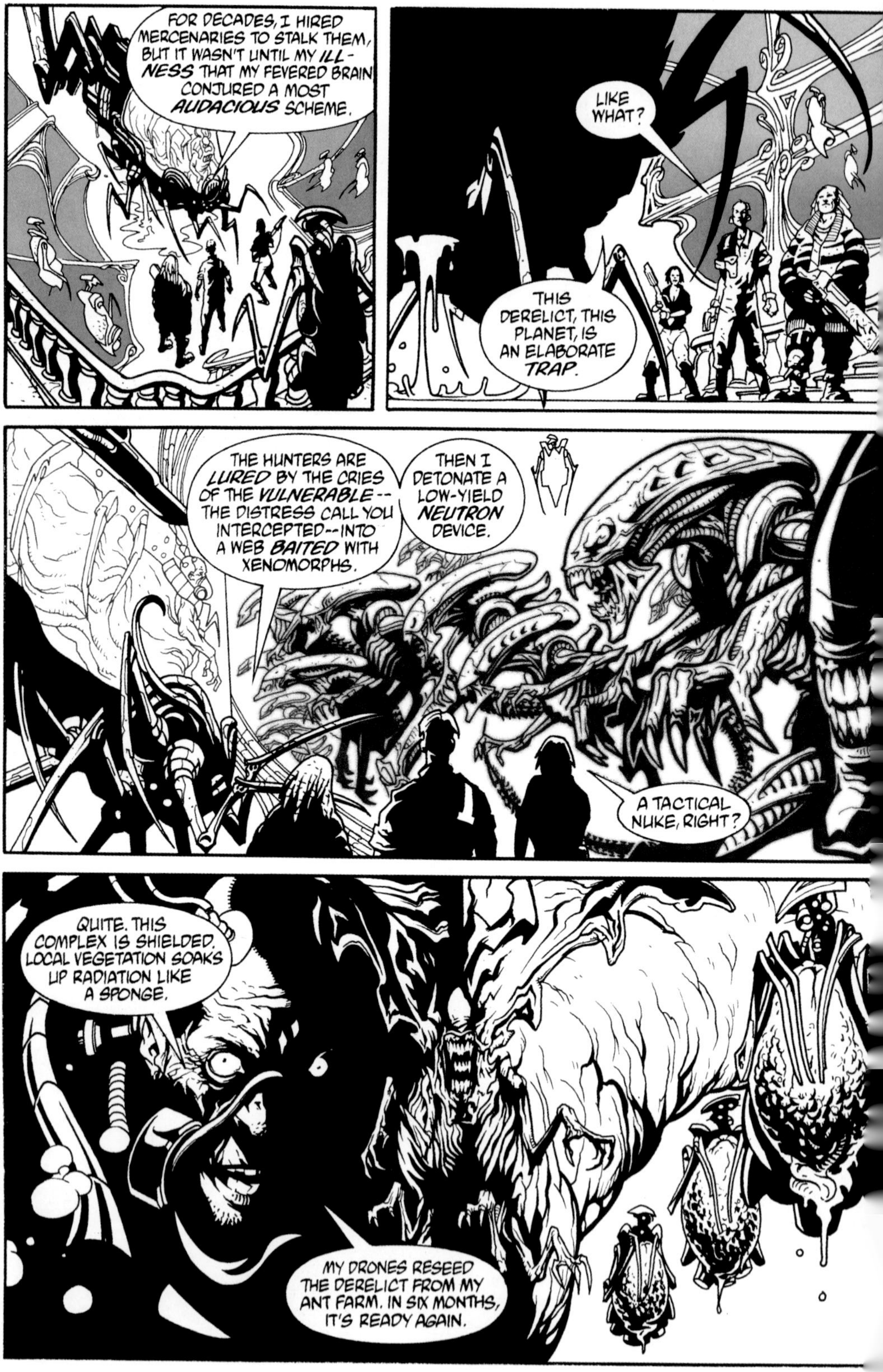
FOR DECADES, I HIRED MERCENARIES TO STALK THEM, BUT IT WASN'T UNTIL MY ILL-NESS THAT MY FEVERED BRAIN CONJURED A MOST AUDACIOUS SCHEME.
LIKE WHAT?
THIS DERELICT, THIS PLANET, IS AN ELABORATE TRAP.
THE HUNTERS ARE LURED BY THE CRIES OF THE VULNERABLE-- THE DISTRESS CALL YOU INTERCEPTED--INTO A WEB BAITED WITH XENOMORPHS.
THEN I DETONATE A LOW-YIELD NEUTRON DEVICE.
A TACTICAL NUKE, RIGHT?
QUITE. THIS COMPLEX IS SHIELDED. LOCAL VEGETATION SOAKS UP RADIATION LIKE A SPONGE.
MY DRONES RESEED THE DERELICT FROM MY ANT FARM. IN SIX MONTHS, IT'S READY AGAIN.

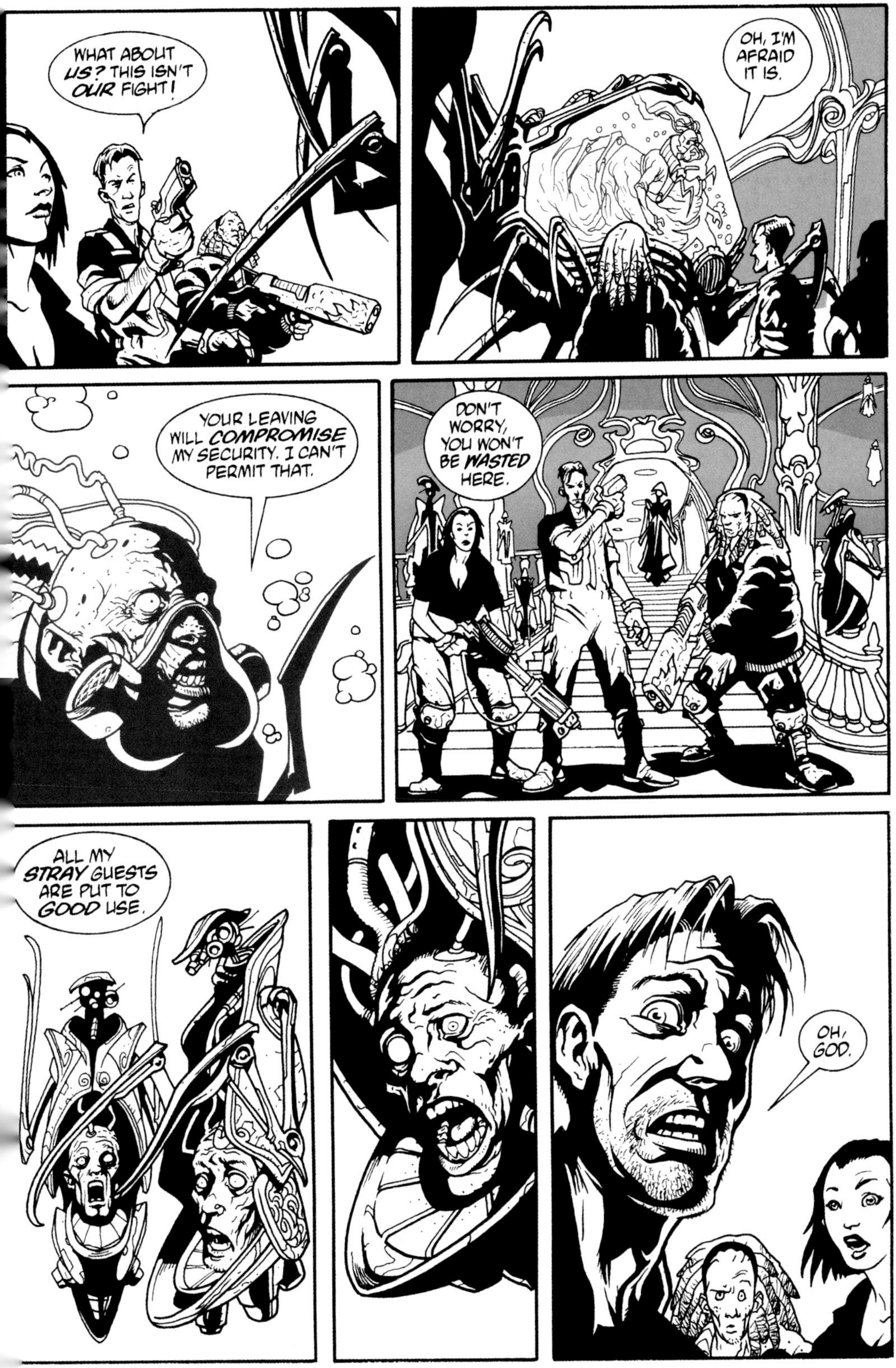
WHAT ABOUT US? THIS ISN'T OUR FIGHT!
OH, I'M AFRAID IT IS.
YOUR LEAVING WILL COMPROMISE MY SECURITY. I CAN'T PERMIT THAT.
DON'T WORRY, YOU WON'T BE WASTED HERE.
ALL MY STRAY GUESTS ARE PUT TO GOOD USE.
OH, GOD.

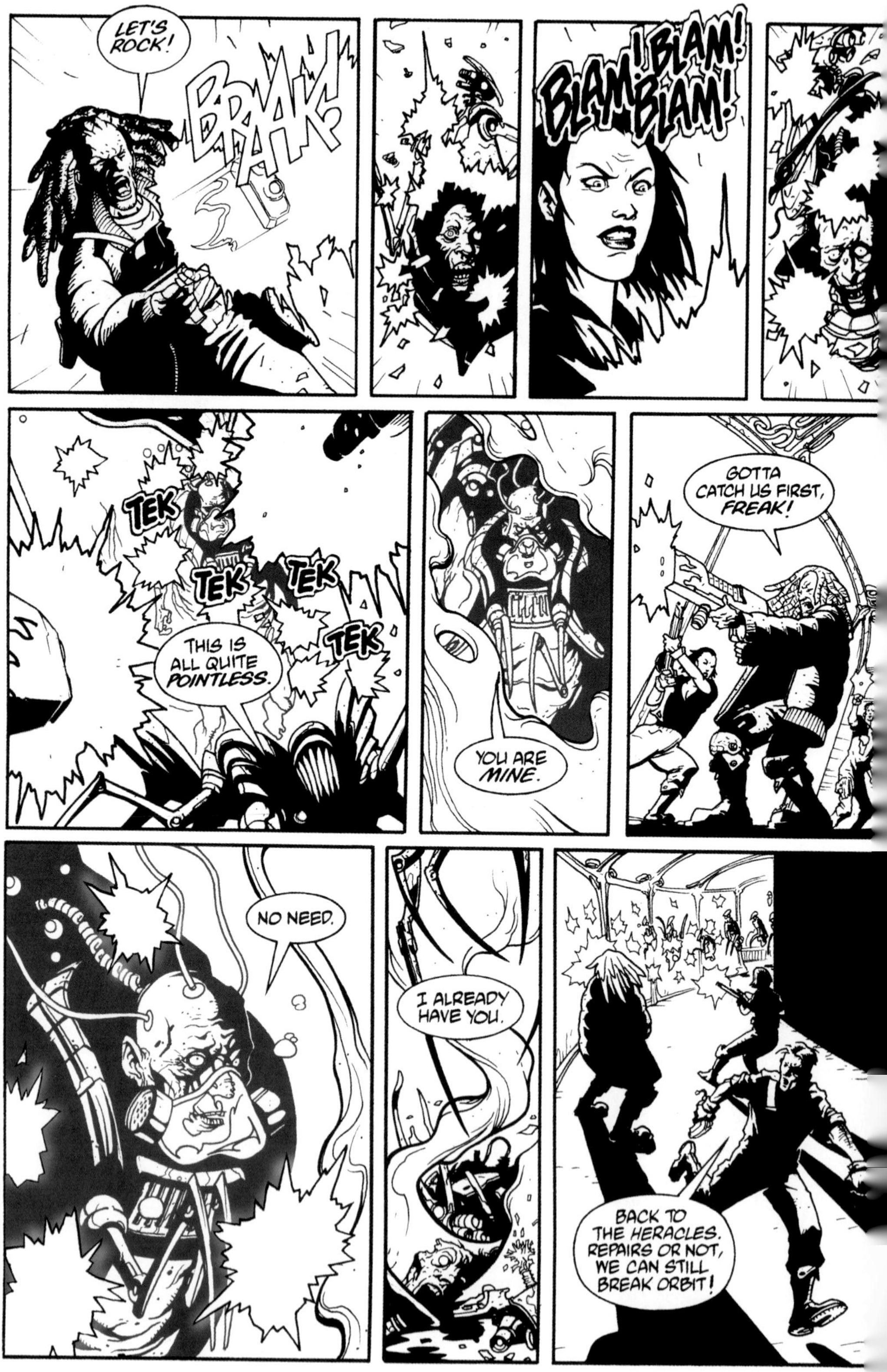
LET'S ROCK!
BRAAK!
BLAM! BLAM! BLAM! BLAM!
TEK
TEK
TEK
TEK
THIS IS ALL QUITE POINTLESS.
YOU ARE MINE.
GOTTA CATCH US FIRST, FREAK!
NO NEED.
I ALREADY HAVE YOU.
BACK TO THE HERACLES. REPAIRS OR NOT, WE CAN STILL BREAK ORBIT!

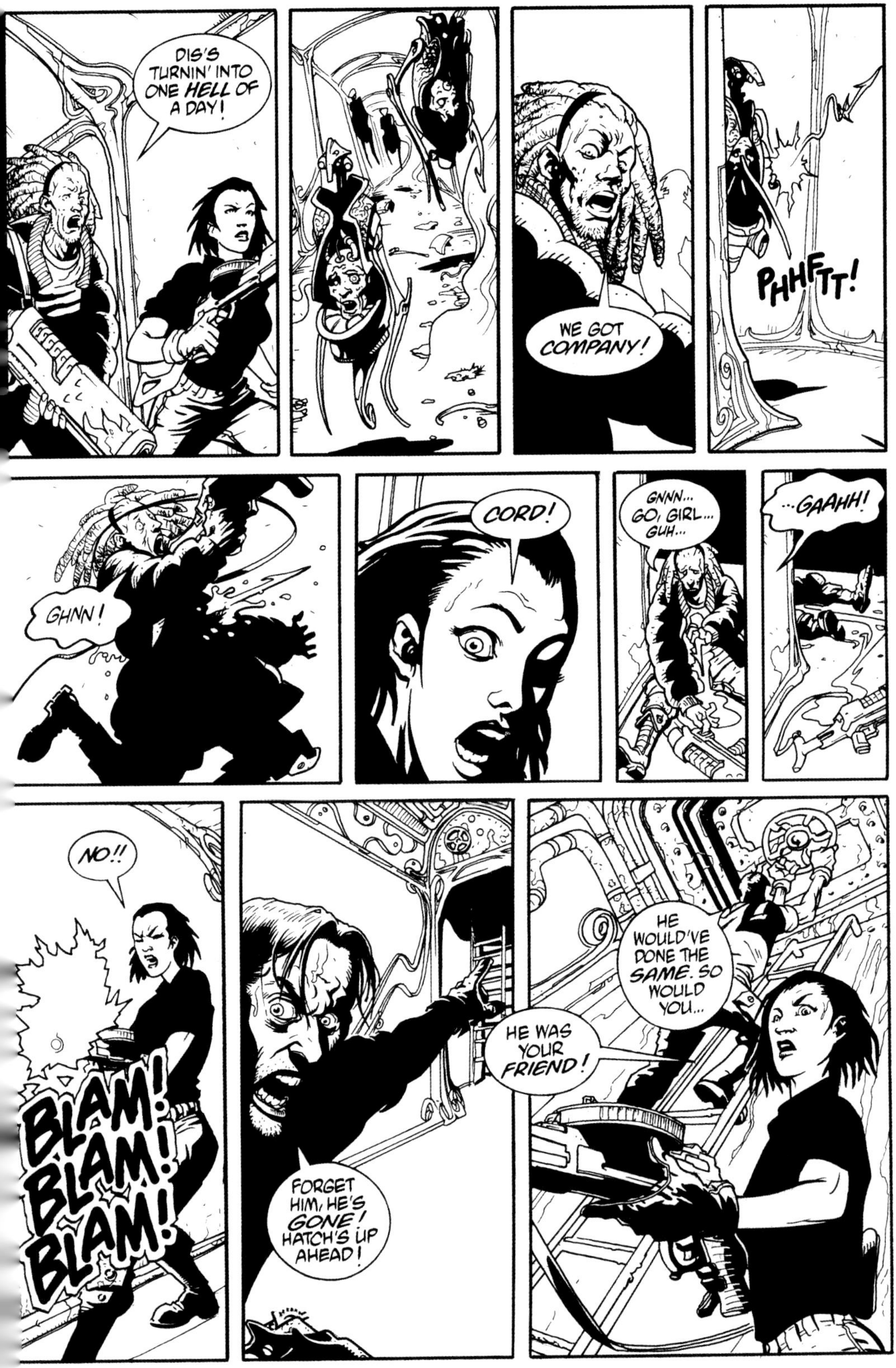
DIS'S TURNIN' INTO ONE HELL OF A DAY!
WE GOT COMPANY!
PHHFTT!
GHNN!
CORD!
GNNN... GO, GIRL... GUH...
...GAAHH!
NO!!
BLAM! BLAM! BLAM!
FORGET HIM, HE'S GONE! HATCH'S UP AHEAD!
HE WAS YOUR FRIEND!
HE WOULD'VE DONE THE SAME. SO WOULD YOU...

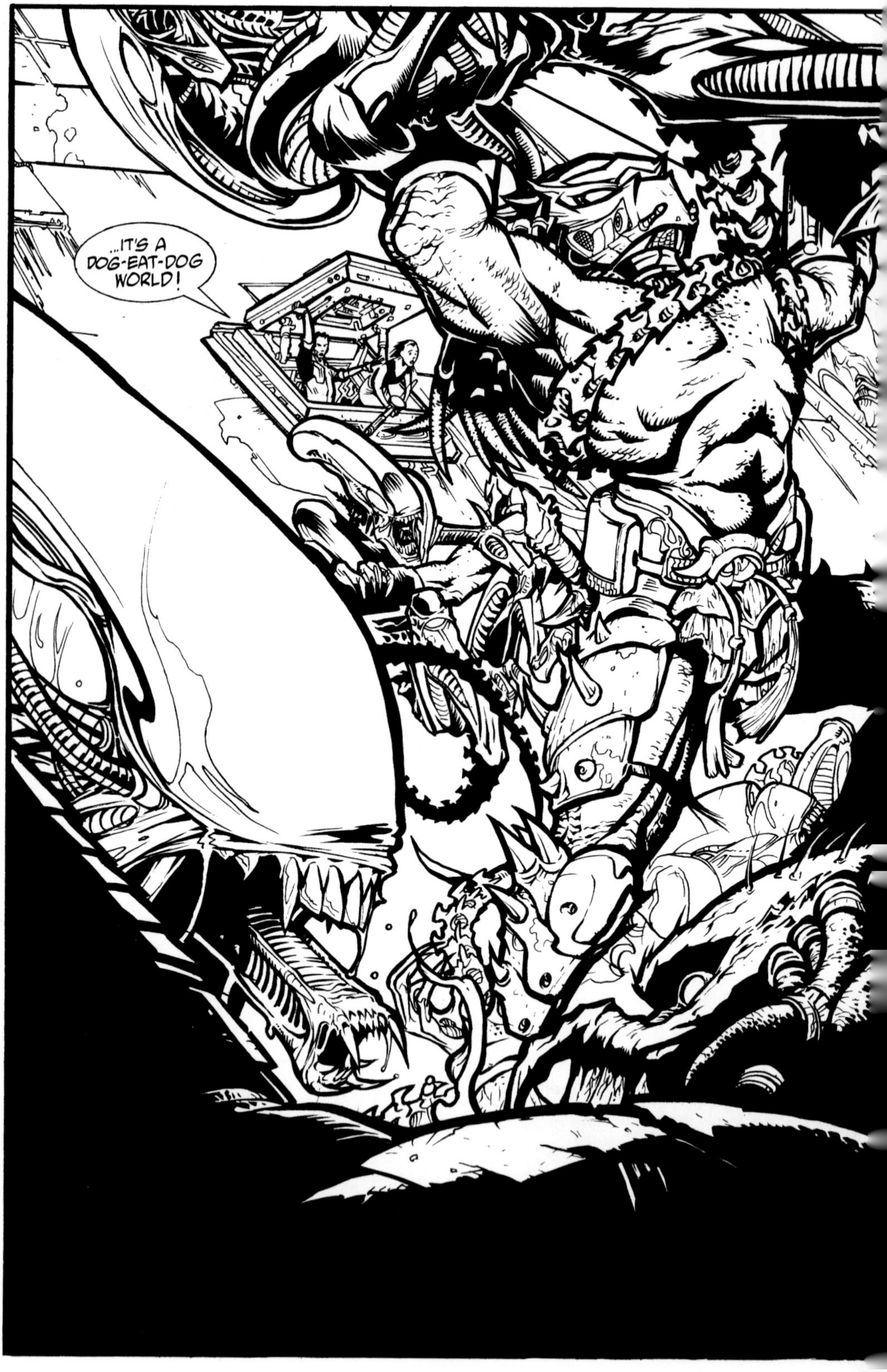
...IT'S A DOG-EAT-DOG WORLD!

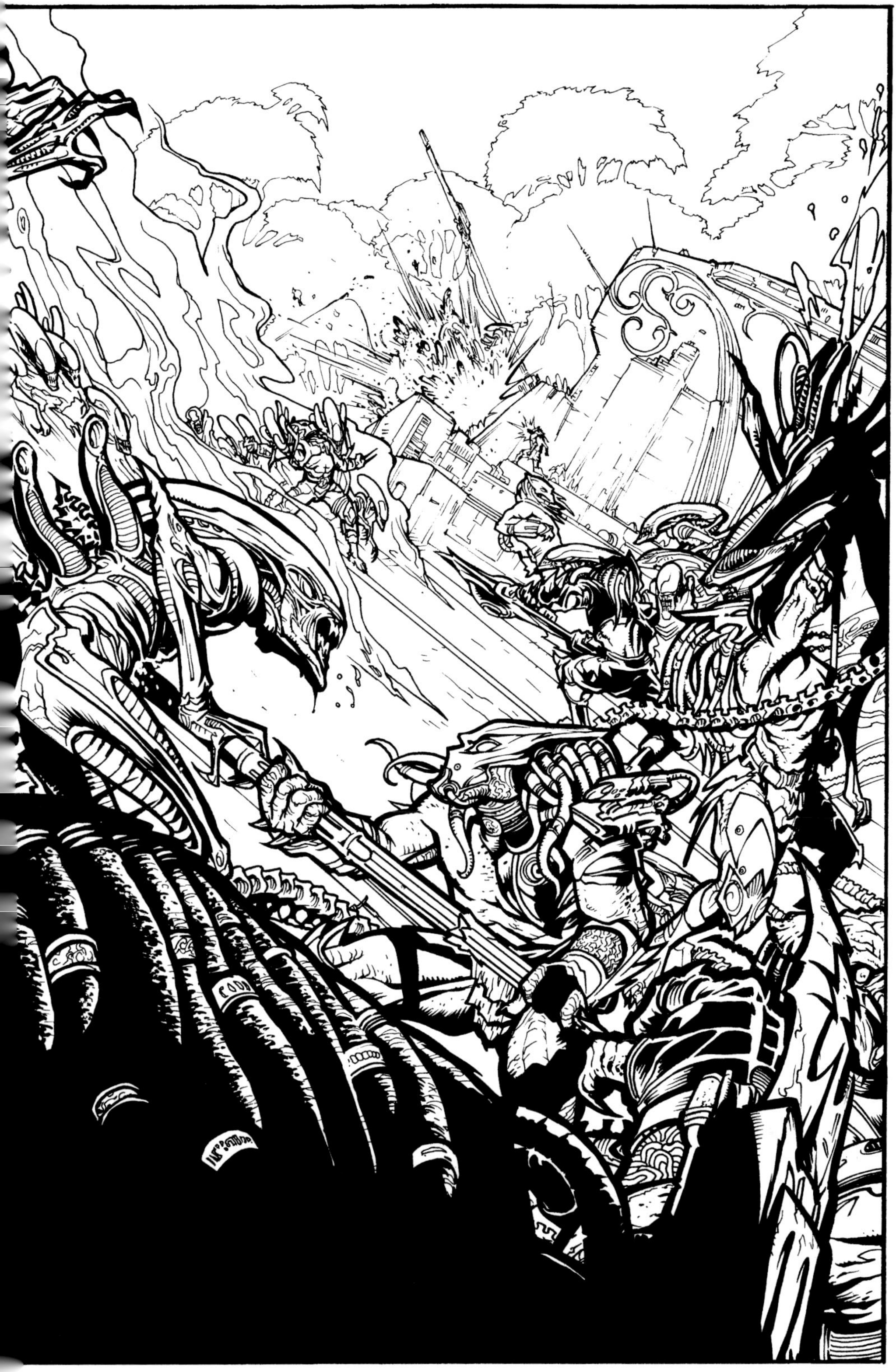

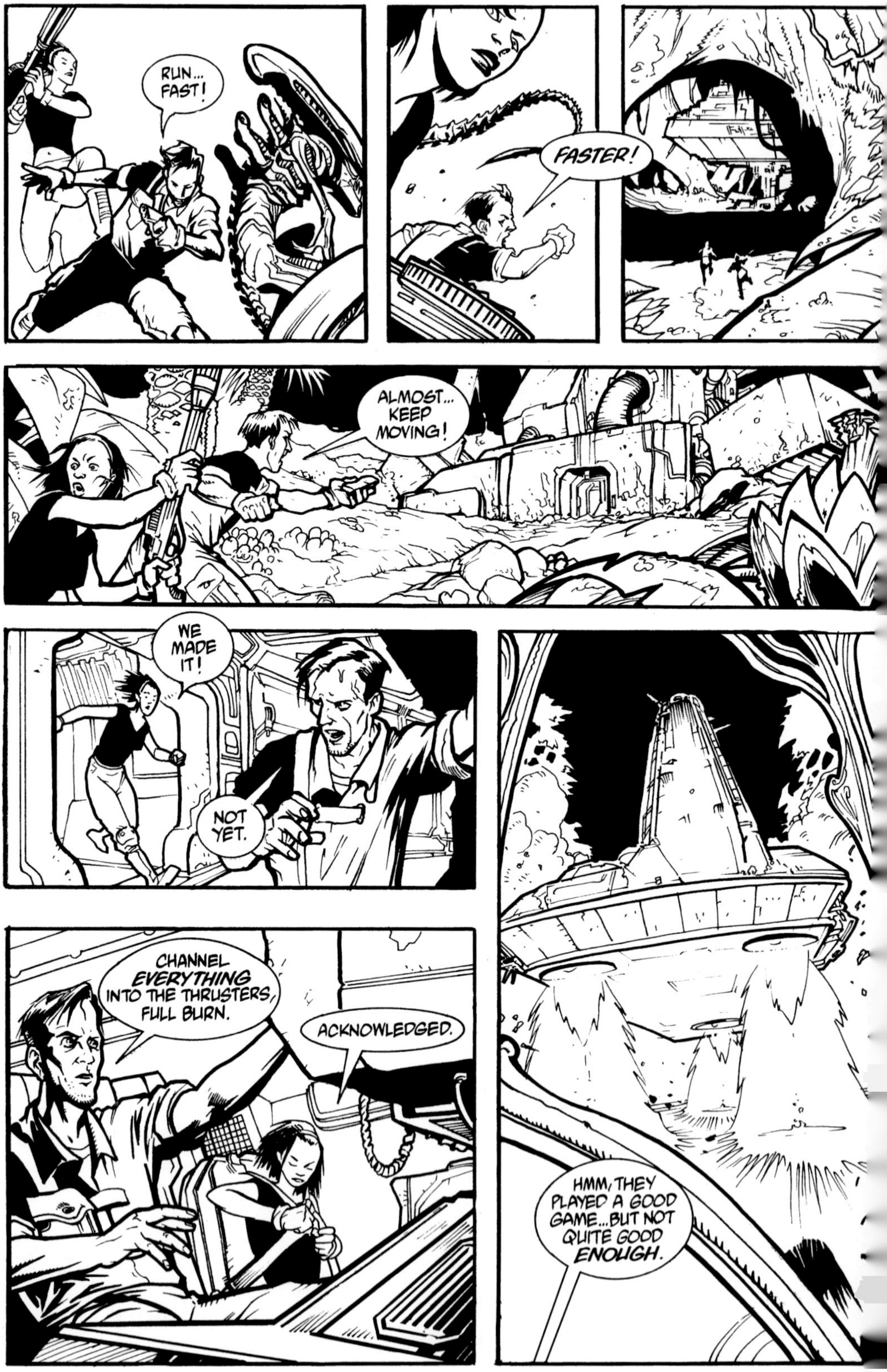
RUN... FAST!
FASTER!
ALMOST... KEEP MOVING!
WE MADE IT!
NOT YET.
CHANNEL EVERYTHING INTO THE THRUSTERS, FULL BURN.
ACKNOWLEDGED.
HMM, THEY PLAYED A GOOD GAME...BUT NOT QUITE GOOD ENOUGH.

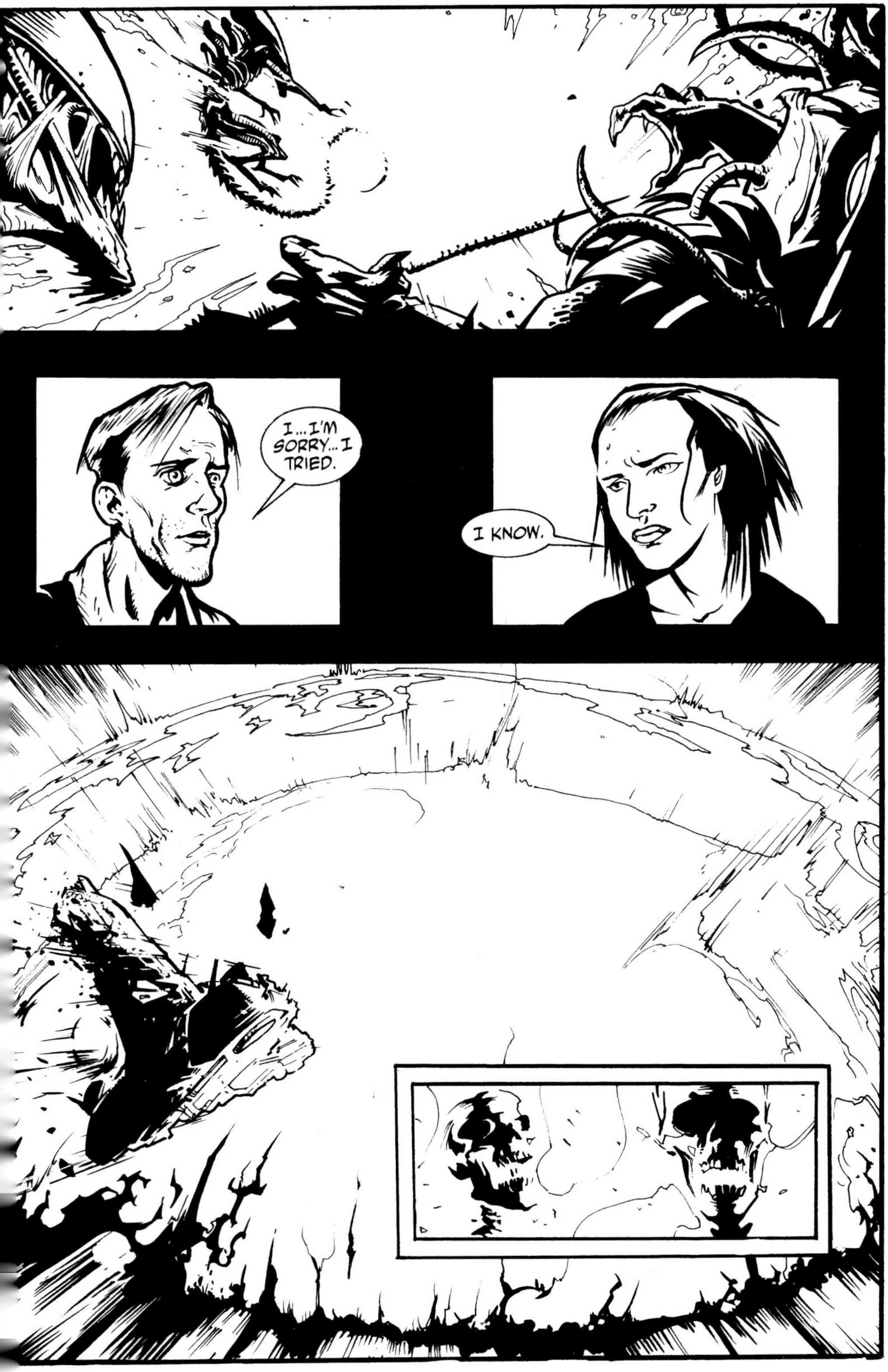
I...I'M SORRY...I TRIED.
I KNOW.

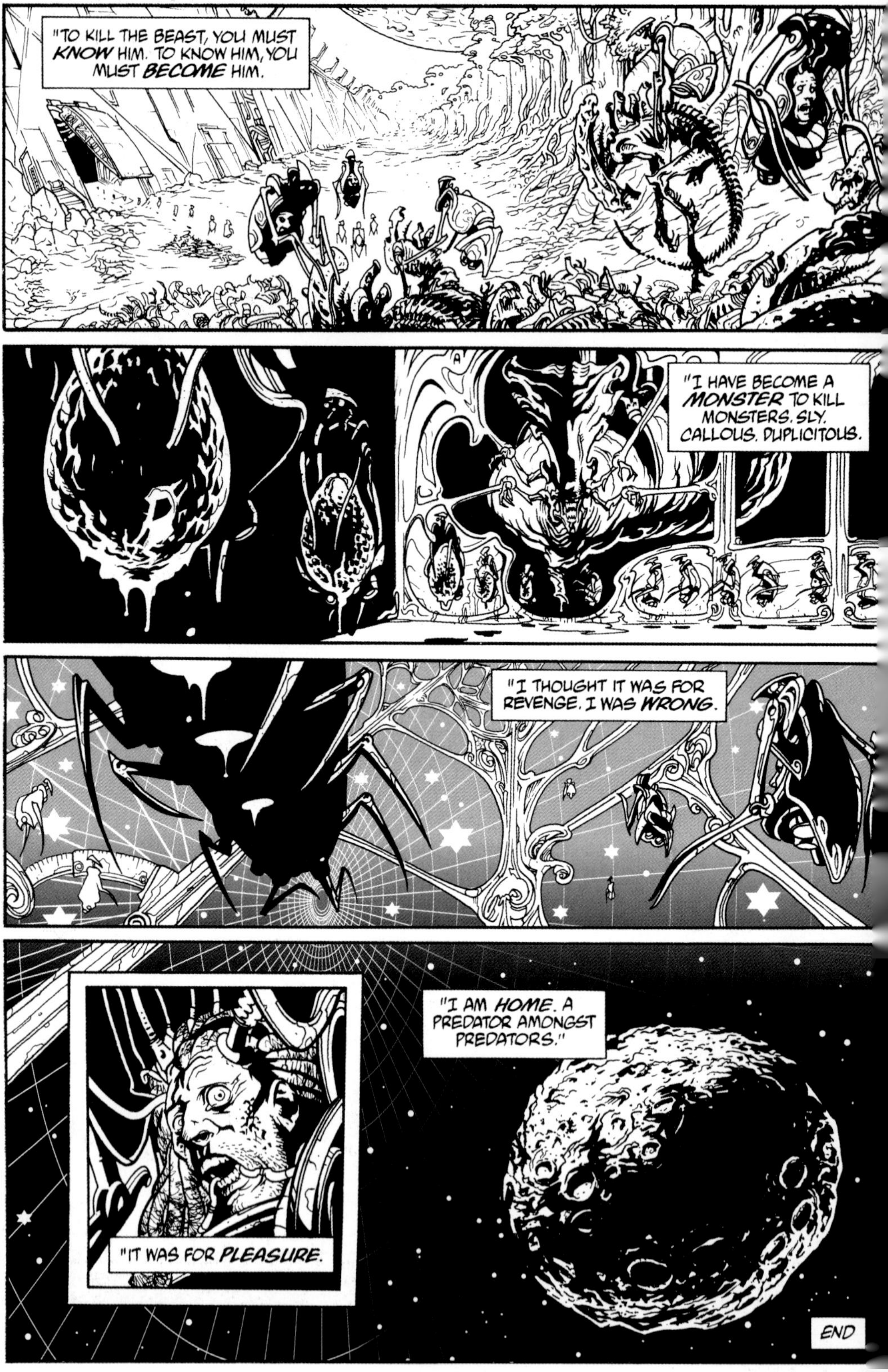
"TO KILL THE BEAST, YOU MUST KNOW HIM. TO KNOW HIM, YOU MUST BECOME HIM.
"I HAVE BECOME A MONSTER TO KILL MONSTERS. SLY. CALLOUS. DUPLICITOUS.
"I THOUGHT IT WAS FOR REVENGE. I WAS WRONG.
"IT WAS FOR PLEASURE.
"I AM HOME. A PREDATOR AMONGST PREDATORS."
END